MW01056185

MARK

Zondervan Exegetical Commentary on the New Testament

Editorial Board

General Editor

Clinton E. Arnold

Talbot School of Theology

Associate Editors

George H. Guthrie

Union University

Constantine R. Campbell

Trinity Evangelical Divinity School

Thomas R. Schreiner

Southern Baptist Theological Seminary

Mark L. Strauss

Bethel Seminary San Diego

Zondervan Editors

Editorial Advisor: Katya Covrett

Production Editor: Verlyn D. Verbrugge

Consulting Editors

Richard Bewes, Rector, All Souls Church, Langham Place, London, UK

Craig Blomberg, Professor of New Testament, Denver Seminary

Ajith Fernando, National Director of Youth for Christ, Sri Lanka

David E. Garland, Dean and William M. Hinson Professor of New Testament,
George W. Truett Theological Seminary

Paul Gardner, Archdeacon of Exeter, Exeter, UK

Carolyn Custis James, Author and Speaker, Orlando, FL

Karen Jobes, Gerald F. Hawthorne Professor of New Testament Greek & Exegesis,
Wheaton College and Graduate School

David W. Pao, Professor of New Testament and Chair of the New Testament Department,
Trinity Evangelical Divinity School

Frank Thielman, Presbyterian Professor of Divinity, Beeson Divinity School

Tite Tienou, Academic Dean and Professor of Theology of Mission, Trinity Evangelical Divinity School

MARK

ZONDERVAN
Exegetical
Commentary
ON THE
New Testament

MARK L. STRAUSS

CLINTON E. ARNOLD
General Editor

 ZONDERVAN®

To Roxanne, Daniel, Jamie, and Luke

ZONDERVAN

Mark
Copyright © 2014 by Mark L. Strauss

Requests for information should be addressed to:

Zondervan, 3900 *Sparks Drive SE, Grand Rapids, Michigan 49546*

Library of Congress Cataloging-in-Publication Data

Strauss, Mark L.
    Mark : Zondervan exegetical commentary on the New Testament / Mark L. Strauss ;
  Clinton E. Arnold, general editor.
     pages cm.
     Includes bibliographical references and index.
     ISBN: 978-0-310-24358-8 (hardcover)
     1. Bible. Mark — Commentaries. I. Title.
  BS2585.53.S77   2014
  226.3'077 — dc23   2013041202

Cover design: Tammy Johnson
Interior design: Beth Shagene

Printed in the United States of America

15 16 17 18 19 20 21 22 /DCI/ 25 24 23 22 21 20 19 18 17 16 15 14 13 12 11 10 9 8 7 6 5 4 3 2

Contents

Series Introduction

This generation has been blessed with an abundance of excellent commentaries. Some are technical and do a good job of addressing issues that the critics have raised; other commentaries are long and provide extensive information about word usage and catalogue nearly every opinion expressed on the various interpretive issues; still other commentaries focus on providing cultural and historical background information; and then there are those commentaries that endeavor to draw out many applicational insights.

The key question to ask is: What are you looking for in a commentary? This commentary series might be for you if

- you have taken Greek and would like a commentary that helps you apply what you have learned without assuming you are a well-trained scholar.
- you would find it useful to see a concise, one- or two-sentence statement of what the commentator thinks the main point of each passage is.
- you would like help interpreting the words of Scripture without getting bogged down in scholarly issues that seem irrelevant to the life of the church.
- you would like to see a visual representation (a graphical display) of the flow of thought in each passage.
- you would like expert guidance from solid evangelical scholars who set out to explain the meaning of the original text in the clearest way possible and to help you navigate through the main interpretive issues.
- you want to benefit from the results of the latest and best scholarly studies and historical information that help to illuminate the meaning of the text.
- you would find it useful to see a brief summary of the key theological insights that can be gleaned from each passage and some discussion of the relevance of these for Christians today.

These are just some of the features that characterize the new Zondervan Exegetical Commentary on the New Testament series. The idea for this series was refined over time by an editorial board who listened to pastors and teachers express what they wanted to see in a commentary series based on the Greek text. That board consisted of myself, George H. Guthrie, William D. Mounce, Thomas R. Schreiner, and Mark L. Strauss along with Zondervan senior editor at large Verlyn Verbrugge, and former Zondervan senior acquisitions editor Jack Kuhatschek. We also enlisted a board of consulting editors who are active pastors, ministry leaders, and seminary professors to help in the process of designing a commentary series that will be useful to the church. Zondervan senior acquisitions editor Katya Covrett has now been shepherding the process to completion, and Constantine R. Campbell is serving on the board.

We arrived at a design that includes seven components for the treatment of each biblical passage. What follows is a brief orientation to these primary components of the commentary.

Literary Context

In this section, you will find a concise discussion of how the passage functions in the broader literary context of the book. The commentator highlights connections with the preceding and following material in the book and makes observations on the key literary features of this text.

Main Idea

Many readers will find this to be an enormously helpful feature of this series. For each passage, the commentator carefully crafts a one- or two-sentence statement of the big idea or central thrust of the passage.

Translation and Graphical Layout

Another unique feature of this series is the presentation of each commentator's translation of the Greek text in a graphical layout. The purpose of this diagram is to help the reader visualize, and thus better understand, the flow of thought within the text. The translation itself reflects the interpretive decisions made by each commentator in the "Explanation" section of the commentary. Here are a few insights that will help you to understand the way these are put together:

1. On the far left side next to the verse numbers is a series of interpretive labels that indicate the function of each clause or phrase of the biblical text. The corresponding portion of the text is on the same line to the right of the label. We have not used technical linguistic jargon for these, so they should be easily understood.

2. In general, we place every clause (a group of words containing a subject and a predicate) on a separate line and identify how it is supporting the principal assertion of the text (namely, is it saying when the action occurred, how it took

place, or why it took place?). We sometimes place longer phrases or a series of items on separate lines as well.

3. Subordinate (or dependent) clauses and phrases are indented and placed directly under the words that they modify. This helps the reader to more easily see the nature of the relationship of clauses and phrases in the flow of the text.

4. Every main clause has been placed in bold print and pushed to the left margin for clear identification.

5. Sometimes when the level of subordination moves too far to the right — as often happens with some of Paul's long, involved sentences! — we reposition the flow to the left of the diagram, but use an arrow to indicate that this has happened.

6. The overall process we have followed has been deeply informed by principles of discourse analysis and narrative criticism (for the Gospels and Acts).

Structure

Immediately following the translation, the commentator describes the flow of thought in the passage and explains how certain interpretive decisions regarding the relationship of the clauses were made in the passage.

Exegetical Outline

The overall structure of the passage is described in a detailed exegetical outline. This will be particularly helpful for those who are looking for a way to concisely explain the flow of thought in the passage in a teaching or preaching setting.

Explanation of the Text

As an exegetical commentary, this work makes use of the Greek language to interpret the meaning of the text. If your Greek is rather rusty (or even somewhat limited), don't be too concerned. All of the Greek words are cited in parentheses following an English translation. We have made every effort to make this commentary as readable and useful as possible even for the nonspecialist.

Those who will benefit the most from this commentary will have had the equivalent of two years of Greek in college or seminary. This would include a semester or two of working through an intermediate grammar (such as Wallace, Porter, Brooks and Winbery, or Dana and Mantey). The authors use the grammatical language that is found in these kinds of grammars. The details of the grammar of the passage, however, are discussed only when it has a bearing on the interpretation of the text.

The emphasis in this section of the text is to convey the meaning. Commentators examine words and images, grammatical details, relevant OT and Jewish background to a particular concept, historical and cultural context, important text-critical issues, and various interpretational issues that surface.

Theology in Application

This, too, is a unique feature for an exegetical commentary series. We felt it was important for each author not only to describe what the text means in its various details, but also to take a moment and reflect on the theological contribution that it makes. In this section, the theological message of the passage is summarized. The authors discuss the theology of the text in terms of its place within the book and in a broader biblical-theological context. Finally, each commentator provides some suggestions on what the message of the passage is for the church today. At the conclusion of each volume in this series is a summary of the whole range of theological themes touched on by this book of the Bible.

Our sincere hope and prayer is that you find this series helpful not only for your own understanding of the text of the New Testament, but as you are actively engaged in teaching and preaching God's Word to people who are hungry to be fed on its truth.

Clinton E. Arnold, general editor

Author's Preface

My special interest in Mark's gospel began during my doctoral studies in Luke-Acts at the University of Aberdeen. Like most scholars, I came to believe that Luke had used Mark as one of his primary sources for the composition of his two-volume work. So as I wrote my thesis on Davidic messianism in Luke-Acts, I had a constant eye on the second gospel. I became fascinated by Mark's vivid and dramatic narrative, the sense of mystery and awe that pervades his story, and the power of his narrative theology. I hoped one day to turn my attentions more fully to this remarkable gospel. So I was excited when David Garland, New Testament editor of the revised *Expositor's Bible Commentary,* invited me to revise Walter Wessel's commentary on Mark. Walt had been a dear friend and my predecessor as professor of New Testament at Bethel Seminary San Diego, so it was a joy to bring his excellent volume up-to-date.

This revision, however, only whet my appetite to go further into Mark's narrative and theological world. So when Clint Arnold invited me to join the editorial team of the Zondervan Exegetical Commentary (as associate editor specializing in narrative literature), I was again thrilled to be able to choose Mark as the volume I would write. It has been a joy and pleasure to live and breathe Mark's narrative over the last decade.

Mark has sometimes been viewed as the most "coarse" and least literary of the Gospels — a string of traditions woven together into a rough and unsophisticated narrative. Yet the deeper I have dug into this gospel, the more I've been impressed by the author's literary design and theological skill. To be sure, Mark's narrative is energetic, forceful, unexpected — even shocking. Yet it is at the same time a well-structured, powerful theological drama that catches the reader up and carries them to a new destination. If Luke's narrative can be compared to a masterfully conducted orchestra performing in tuxedos in a formal concert hall, Mark's resembles a flash mob performing the Hallelujah Chorus at the local mall (Google it if you've never seen it). His story catches the reader off guard, surprising, enthralling, and then transforming them.

I am grateful to many people who have made this volume possible. Thanks go to general editor Clint Arnold for enlisting me for this project. He and my fellow associate editors, George Guthrie, Tom Schreiner, and Bill Mounce, have done great work in shaping the series and providing guidance along the way. I want to especially thank the students of Bethel Seminary San Diego (too many to name), who over the years have provided invaluable input in Gospel Survey classes and electives on Mark's gospel. Special thanks to Nathan Bruce, who read most of the volume with a keen editorial eye and gave many helpful suggestions. I am also most grateful to the whole Zondervan team, but especially Verlyn Verbrugge, senior editor at large for biblical and theological resources, who provided excellent feedback and made many corrections.

Finally, I want to dedicate this volume to my wonderful wife, Roxanne, for her constant support through the years, and to my three children, Daniel, Jamie, and Luke (two presently in college and one in high school). My joy in studying and proclaiming God's Word is exceeded only by my joy in them. As the apostle John says, "I have no greater joy than to hear that my children are walking in the truth" (3 John 4).

MARK L. STRAUSS

Abbreviations

Abbreviations for books of the Bible, pseudepigrapha, rabbinic works, papyri, classical works, and the like are readily available in sources such as *The SBL Handbook of Style* and are not included here.

AB	Anchor Bible
ABD	*Anchor Bible Dictionary*. Edited by D. N. Freedman, 6 vols. New York, 1992.
ABRL	Anchor Bible Reference Library
ACCS	Ancient Christian Commentary on the Scriptures
al	*alii* (manuscript notation: others)
AnBib	Analecta biblica
arm	Armenian (manuscripts)
b.	Babylonian Talmud
BAR	*Biblical Archaeology Review*
BBR	*Bulletin for Biblical Research*
BDAG	*A Greek-English Lexicon of the New Testament and Other Early Christian Literature*. W. Baur, F. W. Danker, W. F. Arndt, F. W. Gingrich, 4th edition. Chicago: University of Chicago Press, 2000.
BDF	*A Greek Grammar of the New Testament and Other Early Christian Literature*. F. Blass, A. Debrunner, R. W. Funk. Chicago: University of Chicago Press, 1961.
BETL	Bibliotheca ephemeridum theologicarum lovaniensium
BJRL	*Bulletin of the John Rylands University Library of Manchester*
BNTC	Black's New Testament Commentaries
boh	Bohairic (manuscripts)
BR	*Biblical Research*
BRev	*Bible Review*
BT	*The Bible Translator*
CBC	Cambridge Biblical Commentaries
CBQ	*Catholic Biblical Quarterly*
CEB	Common English Bible
CEV	Contemporary English Version

ConBNT	Coniectanea biblica: New Testament series
cop	Coptic (manuscripts)
DJG	*Dictionary of Jesus and the Gospels.* Edited by J. B. Green and S. McKnight. Downers Grove, IL: InterVarsity Press, 1992.
DSD	*Dead Sea Discoveries*
EBC	*Expositor's Bible Commentary*
EBC²	*Expositor's Bible Commentary*, revised edition
EKKNT	Evangelisch-katholischer Kommentar zum Neuen Testament
ESV	English Standard Version
ET	English Translation
eth	Ethiopic (manuscripts)
ExpTim	*Expository Times*
f^1	Family 1 (family of manuscripts)
f^{13}	Family 13 (family of manuscripts)
FRLANT	Forschungen zur Religion und Literatur des Alten und Neuen Testaments
FS	Festschrift
GNT	Good News Translation (formerly Today's English Version and Good News Bible)
GTJ	*Grace Theological Journal*
GW	God's Word Translation
HALOT	*The Hebrew and Aramaic Lexicon of the Old Testament.* Edited by L. Köhler, W. Baumgartner, et al. Leiden/New York: Brill, 1994 – 2000.
HCSB	Holman Christian Standard Bible
HDR	Harvard Dissertations in Religion
HNT	Handbuch zum Neuen Testament
HTKNT	Herders theologischer Kommentar zum Neuen Testament
HTR	*Harvard Theological Review*
HUCM	Hebrew Union College Monographs
IBS	*Irish Biblical Studies*
ICC	International Critical Commentary
IEJ	*Israel Exploration Journal*
Int	*Interpretation*
it	Old Italian (manuscript)
ITS	International Theological Studies
JBL	*Journal of Biblical Literature*
JETS	*Journal of the Evangelical Theological Society*
JJS	*Journal of Jewish Studies*
Jos.	Josephus
JR	*Journal of Religion*
JSNT	*Journal for the Study of the New Testament*

JSNTSup	Journal for the Study of the New Testament Supplement Series
JSP	*Journal for the Study of the Pseudepigrapha*
JTS	*Journal of Theological Studies*
KEK	Kritisch-exegetischer Kommentar über das Neue Testament
KJV	King James Version
Lat	Latin (manuscripts)
LD	Lectio divina
LNTS	Library of New Testament Studies
LXX	Septuagint
m.	Mishnah
𝔐	Majority text reading
MT	Masoretic Text
NA$^{27/28}$	*Novum Testamentum Graece* (27th/28th edition; edited by B. Aland et al.)
NAC	New American Commentary
NASB	New American Standard Bible
NASU	New American Standard Bible, 1995 Revision
NCB	New Century Bible
NET	New English Translation
NIBC	New International Biblical Commentary
NICNT	New International Commentary on the New Testament
NIGTC	New International Greek Testament Commentary
NIV	New International Version
NIVAC	NIV Application Commentary
NJB	New Jerusalem Bible
NKJV	New King James Version
NLT	New Living Translation (2nd edition)
NLT^1	New Living Translation (1st edition; 1996)
NovT	*Novum Testamentum*
NovTSup	Novum Testamentum Supplements
NRSV	New Revised Standard Version
NSBT	New Studies in Biblical Theology
NT	New Testament
NTG	New Testament Guides
NTL	New Testament Library
NTS	*New Testament Studies*
OT	Old Testament
OTP	*Old Testament Pseudepigrapha* (edited by James Charlesworth)
𝔓	Papyrus (manuscript)
pc	*pauca* (manuscript notation: a few)
PNTC	Pillar New Testament Commentary
Pss. Sol.	*Psalms of Solomon*

Q	*Quelle.* German for "source," designating the material common to Matthew and Luke not found in Mark
RB	*Revue biblique*
REB	Revised English Bible
RevExp	*Review and Expositor*
RNT	Regensburger Neues Testament
sah	Sahidic (manuscript)
SBLDS	Society of Biblical Literature Dissertation Series
SBLSS	Society of Biblical Literature Semeia Series
SBT	Studies in Biblical Theology
SE	*Studia evangelica*
SJLA	Studies in Judaism in Late Antiquity
SJT	*Scottish Journal of Theology*
SNTSMS	Society of New Testament Studies Monograph Series
SNTW	Studies in the New Testament and Its World
SP	Sacra pagina
Str-B	H. Strack and P. Billerbeck, *Kommentar zum Neuen Testament*, 6 vols.
SUNT	Studien zur Umwelt des Neuen Testament
syr	Syriac (manuscript)
TDNT	*Theological Dictionary of the New Testament.* Edited by G. Kittel and G. Friedrich; translated by G. W. Bromiley. 10 vols. Grand Rapids: Eerdmans, 1964–1976.
THKNT	Theologischer Handkommentar zum Neuen Testament
TJ	*Trinity Journal*
TNIV	Today's New International Version
trans.	translated by
TS	*Theological Studies*
TynBul	*Tyndale Bulletin*
TZ	*Theologische Zeitschrift*
UBS[4]	*The Greek New Testament.* Edited by B. Aland et al. 4th edition. Stuttgart: Deutsche Bibelgesellschaft and United Bible Societies, 1994.
VE	*Vox evangelica*
vg	Vulgate (manuscript)
vid	videtur (manuscript notation: reading uncertain)
WBC	Word Biblical Commentary
WTJ	*Westminster Theological Journal*
WUNT	Wissenschaftliche Untersuchungen zum Neuen Testament
ZNW	*Zeitschrift für die neutestamentliche Wissenschaft*

Introduction to Mark

Mark's Story of Jesus

Mark's gospel starts off with remarkable speed and energy. The author wastes no time with lengthy stories about Jesus' birth and childhood or genealogical lists tracing his legitimate messianic ancestry (as in Matthew and Luke). There is no exalted prologue identifying Jesus as the self-revelation of God and placing him within the scheme of salvation history (as in John). Within a few short paragraphs, Jesus is baptized by John, anointed by the Spirit, acclaimed by God as "my beloved Son," and tempted by Satan in the wilderness, and he embarks on a ministry of preaching the kingdom of God, calling disciples, healing, and exorcism. This is a gospel narrative on steroids!

The Mighty Messiah and Son of God

The first half of this energetic story is characterized by three main themes: *authority*, *awe*, and *opposition*. Mark begins by identifying Jesus as "the Messiah, the Son of God" (1:1), and this messianic authority is on display at every turn. Jesus' message is the arrival of God's eschatological reign through his own words and deeds. He calls disciples, who drop everything to follow him; he captivates his hearers with remarkable teaching; he commands demons to come out of people, and they obey. He heals the sick with a compassionate touch; he quiets a storm with a strong rebuke. The response to this is awe and wonder. The people are amazed at his authoritative teaching and his power over demons. They marvel when he heals the sick. The disciples stand in shock as he quiets the storm with a command. They wonder, "Who, then, is this, that the wind and the sea obey him!" (4:41).

Such audacious deeds attract not only acclaim but also opposition. The religious leaders of Israel are scandalized when Jesus claims to forgive sins, hangs out with sinners, and treats the revered Sabbath commands as apparently optional. They begin to plot against him, seeking a way to eliminate this upstart who challenges their influence with the people. Unable to deny his mastery over demons, they accuse him of being in league with the devil, casting out demons by Satan's power. Jesus responds by dismissing their authority and accusing them of standing in opposition to the work of God. By rejecting his authority they are blaspheming the Spirit of God, who is at work in him. Israel's "insiders" — the religious elite — have now become outsiders to the true people of God. In an implicit denial of their leadership, Jesus chooses and appoints twelve disciples, modeled after the twelve tribes of Israel and representing the restored people of God. His true family, the household of God in the kingdom age, is made up not of those who share physical descent from Abraham, but of those who do the will of God (3:34).

Everything Jesus says and does in the first half of the gospel confirms the author's initial claim: Jesus is indeed the mighty Messiah and Son of God (1:1). His popularity grows and grows, and he continues to amaze all who encounter the power of God through him. In a second wave of remarkable miracles, he casts out a "legion" of demons, heals incurable disease, raises a young girl from the dead, walks on water, and twice feeds massive crowds with a few loaves of bread and fishes. Yet he is also secretive and circumspect about his identity. He repeatedly silences demons and commands those he heals not to tell anyone about it. A sense of mystery and paradox surrounds his identity. The question, "Who is this person?" hangs in the air. It is as though the narrator is saying, "Yes, he is the Messiah, but there is much more to it than this."

This theme reaches a climax at the midpoint of the gospel. Jesus takes his disciples away for a retreat to Caesarea Philippi, north of Galilee, where he asks them a question, "Who do people say I am?" (8:27). Their response shows a variety of popular views: John the Baptist, Elijah, or one of the prophets. But when he asks them, "Who do *you* say I am?" Peter responds for the rest, "You are the Messiah" (8:28 – 29). The gospel narrative has been building to this climax: Jesus' words and deeds have confirmed the truth about his identity. He is indeed the Messiah and Son of God. Yet here the narrative takes a shocking and dramatic turn. Instead of affirming the traditional role of the conquering and ruling Messiah, Jesus predicts that he will be rejected by the religious leaders, arrested, and crucified, and that three days later he will rise from the dead. When Peter objects to this defeatist attitude and rebukes Jesus, Jesus rebukes him back, accusing him of acting as Satan's agent and pursuing a human rather than divine agenda. It is *God's* purpose for the Messiah to suffer and die!

The Suffering Servant of the Lord

If the first half of the gospel presents Jesus as the mighty Messiah and Son of God (1:1 – 8:30), the second half develops the theme of his suffering role (8:31 – 16:8). Three times Jesus predicts his death. Each time, the disciples miss the point and respond with some act of pride and self-interest. In response, Jesus repeatedly teaches that anyone who wants to be his disciple must take up their cross and follow him. Whoever wants to be first must be last, and the path to glory is through suffering.

This theme climaxes after Jesus predicts his death for a third time (10:33 – 34). Two of his disciples, James and John, approach him and ask for the seats of greatest honor beside the king when his kingdom is established in Jerusalem. The other disciples are indignant, and Jesus must gather them together again for a lesson on humility. He contrasts the world's model of leadership with his own:

> You know that those recognized as rulers of the Gentiles lord it over them, and their great ones exercise dominion over them. But it is not so among you. Rather, whoever wants to be great among you will be your servant, and whoever wants to be first will be slave of all. For even the Son of Man did not come to be served, but to serve, and to give his life as a ransom for many. (Mark 10:42 – 45)

Here we have the essence of Mark's story. Though Jesus is indeed the mighty Messiah and Son of God, his role is not to conquer the Romans. It is to suffer and die as a ransom payment for sins. This is a far greater achievement than physical conquest. He will provide victory over humanity's ultimate enemies: Satan, sin, and death. Those who would be his disciples must follow his path, taking up their own cross and following him in a life of self-sacrificial service — living for the kingdom and for others rather than for themselves.

The rest of the gospel plays out this theme. Jesus goes to Jerusalem, where he challenges the religious leaders and repeatedly thwarts their attempts to trap him in his words. Again we see his messianic wisdom and authority on full display. Yet the religious leaders plot against him, bribing one of Jesus' own, Judas, to betray him. They arrest Jesus, accuse him of blasphemy, and turn him over to the Roman authorities, who crucify him for sedition.

The crucifixion is a dark and isolated scene. Repeatedly the disciples have failed him. Not only have they acted with pride and self-interest, but they have failed to understand his teaching or his mission. They cannot stay awake in Gethsemane to watch and pray; they abandon him at his arrest; Peter follows the arresting party but then three times denies he knows Jesus. At his crucifixion Jesus is isolated and alone — apparently abandoned even by his Father in heaven. He dies after crying out from the cross, "My God, my God, why have you forsaken me?" (15:34; cf. Ps 22:1).

Yet even in apparent defeat, Jesus' messiahship is revealed. The gospel that began with heaven being "torn" open and the Father's proclaiming, "You are my beloved Son" (1:10 – 11), climaxes with the temple curtain "split" in two and the centurion at the foot of the cross crying out, "Truly this man was the Son of God!" (15:38 – 39). These hints at vindication are confirmed in the narrative that follows. On the third day after his burial, the women discover the empty tomb and hear the angel's announcement: "He has risen! He is not here" (16:6). Just as he predicted, Jesus has achieved victory over death, vindicating his messianic claims.

The Gospel ends, however, on a strange and puzzling note. Though Jesus has risen, the women are shell-shocked and afraid. They tell nothing to anyone (16:8).

This does not mean, of course, that the author has any doubts about the resurrection. In Mark's story, Jesus — an absolutely reliable character — has repeatedly predicted his own resurrection and said that his disciples will see him alive in Galilee after he rises from the dead (14:28; 16:7). For Mark and his readers, the resurrection is a historical reality, confirmed by the eyewitness testimony of the followers of Jesus. Yet the ending, like so much of this gospel, remains a paradox and a mystery.[1] It is as though the reader, like the women at the tomb, is being called to see with eyes of faith. Jesus is risen, but you do not yet see him. He has conquered sin and death, but evil, injustice, and suffering are still all around us. The kingdom of God has come, but the dominion of Satan still seems strong and pervasive.

Mark's gospel was almost certainly written to a suffering and persecuted church. It stands as a narrative call to discipleship for those facing trials, persecution, confusion, and suffering. Though in this world we still experience pain, evil, injustice, and oppression, Mark's story of Jesus reminds us that with the life, death, and resurrection of the Messiah, God's eschatological salvation has arrived. The power of death has been broken. The reign of God has been inaugurated for those who will enter it by faith. All who take up their cross to follow Jesus will share in this victory. In the midst of a world of bad news and suffering, this is the "good news" of Jesus the Messiah and Son of God.

Mark's Gospel in Historical Perspective

The Neglected Gospel

Though the most dramatic and fast-paced of the four Gospels, Mark's was also the most neglected in the early church. This was due primarily to the fact that it was the shortest, with approximately 90 percent of its stories appearing in either Matthew or Luke. Augustine of Hippo (AD 354–430), the first of the church fathers to comment on the relationship of the three Synoptic Gospels, viewed Mark as little more than an abbreviation of Matthew. He wrote, "Mark follows him [Matthew] closely, and looks like his attendant and epitomizer."[2] No commentary was written on Mark until the sixth century. At that time, Victor of Antioch, who could find no previous commentaries on Mark, resorted to gleaning comments on Mark from the expositions of the other gospels in the writings of Origen, Theodore of Mopsuestia, Chrysostom, and others.[3] Contrast this with the attention given to Matthew's gospel, the favorite of the early church. Between AD 650 and 1000, thirteen major

---

1. On the debate whether Mark intended to end his gospel with 16:8, or whether the original ending has been lost, see commentary on 16:1–8.

2. Augustine, *Cons.* 1.2.4. Cf. D. L. Dungan, "Mark: The Abridgement of Matthew and Luke," *Perspective* 11 (1970): 51–97.

3. H. Smith, "The Sources of Victor of Antioch's Commentary on Mark," *JTS* 19 (1918): 350–70; W. L. Lane, "From Historian to Theologian: Milestones in Markan Scholarship," *RevExp* 75 (Fall 1978): 601–17, esp. 611.

commentaries were written on Matthew, but only four on Mark.[4] In the manuscript tradition, Mark's gospel appears first in only one manuscript (codex Bobiensis), and sometimes it appears last.

Markan Priority and the Gospel's Rising Prominence

A dramatic change took place with the rise of historical criticism in the nineteenth century. In seeking to resolve the "Synoptic problem" (the question of the relationship between Matthew, Mark, and Luke), scholars came to view Mark's gospel as the earliest and one of the main sources for Matthew and Luke. For many, "Markan priority" meant not only that Matthew and Luke had utilized Mark, but also that Mark contained the earliest and least embellished narrative of the life of Jesus. The many books written during the nineteenth century "Life-of-Jesus movement" looked especially to Mark for the historical framework of Jesus' ministry.

The study of Mark took another major turn at the beginning of the twentieth century. Three works in particular prompted this change. First, Martin Kähler's *The So-Called Historical Jesus and the Historic, Biblical Christ* (1892)[5] argued that the quest for the historical Jesus was misguided, and that the only Jesus to be found in the Gospels was the Christ of faith, proclaimed by the apostles and worshiped in the church. This is because the *kerygma* (the proclamation of the gospel) is so much a part of the gospel narratives that it is impossible to extract from them a nonsupernatural "historical Jesus."[6]

Second, Albert Schweitzer's *The Quest of the Historical Jesus* (1901) inflicted a devastating blow on the Life-of-Jesus movement.[7] Schweitzer showed that the so-called "liberal Jesus" discovered by these scholars was in fact created in their own image and looked more like a nineteenth-century philanthropist than a first-century Jewish apocalyptic prophet.

Third, and most important, was the publication in 1901 of William Wrede's *The Messianic Secret in the Gospels.*[8] Wrede challenged the notion that Mark represented reliable history. The Evangelist's goals were not historical, but apologetic and theological. According to Wrede, although Mark's church confessed Jesus to be the Messiah, Mark could find little in the traditions he received to indicate that Jesus considered

---

4. Séan Kealy, *Mark's Gospel: A History of Its Interpretation from the Beginning until 1979* (New York: Paulist, 1982); Brenda D. Schildgen, *Power and Prejudice: The Reception of the Gospel of Mark* (Detroit: Wayne State University Press, 1999), 35–42; Francis J. Moloney, *Mark: Storyteller, Interpreter, Evangelist* (Peabody, MA: Hendrickson, 2004), 19.

5. Martin Kähler, *The So-Called Historical Jesus and the Historic, Biblical Christ* (trans. Carl E. Braaten; Philadelphia: Fortress, 1964).

6. For a similar contemporary perspective see Luke Timothy Johnson, *The Real Jesus: The Misguided Quest for the Historical Jesus and the Truth of the Traditional Gospels* (San Francisco: Harper, 1996).

7. Albert Schweitzer, *The Quest of the Historical Jesus: A Critical Study of Its Progress from Reimarus to Wrede* (trans. W. Montgomery; New York: Macmillan, 1954; first German edition in 1906 [*Von Reimarus zu Wrede*])

8. W. Wrede, *Das Messiasgeheimnis in den Evangelien* (Göttingen: Vandenhoeck & Ruprecht, 1901); ET: *The Messianic Secret* (trans. J. C. G. Greig; London: James Clarke, 1971). For further discussion see comments on 1:25; 1:45; and 8:30.

himself to be the Messiah or that he was recognized as such by others. Mark therefore took up and expanded on earlier traditions of a "messianic secret," whereby Jesus called for silence from those who saw his miracles or announced his messianic identity. Wrede concluded that "as a whole the Gospel no longer offers a historical view of the real life of Jesus. Only pale residues of a such a view have passed over into what is a suprahistorical view of faith. In this sense the Gospel of Mark belongs to the history of dogma."[9] Wrede's claim that Mark utilized the messianic secret to cover up an essentially unmessianic life has been largely rejected by scholars today, not least because the secret does not hold up even during Jesus' ministry (see 1:45; 7:36). Yet Wrede's perspective of the gospel as an essentially theological rather than historical work has had a profound impact on scholarship ever since.[10]

Form Criticism and the Gospel Tradition

Interest in the gospel as a literary and theological work waned in the early years of the twentieth century with the rise of form criticism. This methodology was already well developed in the OT, but was applied to the NT especially by German scholars K. L. Schmidt, Martin Dibelius, and R. Bultmann, and in Great Britain by Vincent Taylor.[11] Form critics sought to isolate and analyze the oral traditions that lay behind our written sources. They operated under the assumption that the Gospels arose from isolated units of tradition created, passed down, and modified in the preaching and teaching of the early church. In this environment, the Gospels came to be viewed as repositories for these traditions and the Evangelists as mere collectors and compilers rather than as authors and theologians in their own right. For most form critics, the early church so shaped these traditions in the transmission process that little of historical value could be discerned in the Gospels. They represent the theology of the early church more than the life of the historical Jesus.

Redaction Criticism: Mark as Theologian

The deficiencies of form criticism were remedied in part in the latter half of the twentieth century with the rise of redaction criticism (a "redactor" is an editor). Introduced first by G. Bornkamm[12] (Matthew), H. Conzelmann[13] (Luke), and W.

9. Wrede, *The Messianic Secret*, 131.

10. Significantly, Wrede apparently changed his view about Jesus' unmessianic life near the end of his career. In a private letter to Adolf von Harnack on January 2, 1905, almost two years before Wrede's death in November 1906 (at the age of 47), he wrote, "I am more inclined than before to believe that Jesus considered himself to be the chosen Messiah." (cited in Martin Hengel and Anna Maria Schwemer, *Der messianische Anspruch Jesu und die Anfänge der Christologie* [Tübingen: Mohr Siebeck, 2001], ix).

11. K. L. Schmidt, *Der Rahmen der Geschichte Jesu* (Berlin:

Trowitzsch, 1919); Martin Dibelius, *From Tradition to Gospel* (trans. B. H. Woolf; New York: Scribner's Sons, 1965; German original, 1919); R. Bultmann, *History of the Synoptic Tradition* (rev. ed.; Oxford: Blackwell, 1972); Vincent Taylor, *The Formation of the Gospel Tradition* (London: Macmillan, 1935).

12. G. Bornkamm, "Die Sturmstillung im Matthäusevangelium," *Wort und Dienst* 1 (1948): 49–54.

13. H. Conzelmann, *Die Mitte der Zeit* (Tübingen: Mohr [Siebeck], 1953); ET: *The Theology of St. Luke* (trans. G. Buswell; New York: Harper and Row, 1960).

Marxsen[14] (Mark), redaction criticism recognized the gospel writers as authors and evangelists in their own right. Redaction critics seek to show how the Evangelists edited, arranged, and shaped their sources to accomplish their theological purpose. In particular they examine the Evangelists' selection and arrangement of the material, modification of material, interpretive comments, summaries, introductions, and conclusions to sections, and seams or transitions. Redaction critics acknowledge three levels, or contexts, in which the tradition was developed and passed down: the context of the historical Jesus, the context of the earliest church communities, and each Evangelist's own church community.

Focusing primarily on this third level, the goal of redaction criticism is to discern: (1) how the gospel writers edited their sources, (2) what theological themes they emphasized, (3) what their purpose in writing was, and (4) the *Sitz im Leben* ("life setting") of the communities to which they wrote. Marxsen, for example, concluded that Mark wrote his gospel from Galilee in the early days of the Jewish War, about AD 67 – 69. Drawing especially from the narrative comment in 13:14, Marxsen claimed that Mark's purpose was to encourage the Jewish Christians of Jerusalem to flee the city and go to Galilee.[15] According to Marxsen, the prediction in 14:28 and 16:7 that Jesus would meet the disciples in Galilee was not a promise of a resurrection appearance, but of the coming parousia, which would take place in Galilee, not Jerusalem. Although Marxsen's idiosyncratic conclusions concerning the purpose of Mark have not been widely accepted, his and similar works paved the way for decades of redaction-critical studies of the Gospels.

New Approaches

The last thirty years have seen the rise of new methodologies in the study of the Gospels in general and Mark in particular.[16] These include a variety of literary approaches, including narrative criticism,[17] rhetorical criticism,[18] social-scientific approaches,[19] canon criticism,[20] reader-response criticism,[21] structuralism,[22] and

14. W. Marxsen, *Der Evangelist Markus: Studien zur Redaktionsgeschichte des Evangeliums* (Göttingen: Vandenhoeck & Ruprecht, 1956); ET: *Mark the Evangelist* (trans. James Boyce; Nashville: Abingdon, 1969).

15. Marxsen refers to the oracle, cited by Eusebius (*Hist. eccl.* 3.5.3), that called Christians to flee Jerusalem for the Decapolis city of Pella.

16. For an extensive bibliography on various methods see W. R. Telford, *Writing on the Gospel of Mark* (Dorsett: Deo, 2009), 255 – 327.

17. M. A. Powell, "Toward a Narrative-Critical Understanding of Mark," *Int* 47 (1993): 341 – 46; E. S. Malbon, "Narrative Criticism," in *Mark and Method: New Approaches in Biblical Studies* (ed. J. C. Anderson and S. D. Moore; 2nd ed.; Minneapolis: Fortress, 2008), 29 – 57.

18. J. Dewey, *Markan Public Debate: Literary Technique, Concentric Structure, and Theology in Mark 2:1 – 3:6* (SBLDS 48; Chico, CA: Scholars, 1980).

19. Bruce J. Malina and Richard L. Rohrbaugh, *Social-Science Commentary on the Synoptic Gospels* (Minneapolis: Fortress, 1992).

20. See B. S. Childs, *The New Testament as Canon: An Introduction* (London: SCM, 1984), esp. 86 – 90.

21. Robert M. Fowler, *Let the Reader Understand: Reader-Response Criticism and the Gospel of Mark* (Minneapolis: Fortress, 1991).

22. E. S. Malbon, "Galilee and Jerusalem: History and Literature in Marcan Interpretation," in W. R. Telford, ed., *The Interpretation of Mark* (Edinburgh: T&T Clark, 1995), 253 – 68 (reprint from *CBQ* 44 [1982]: 247 – 55).

deconstruction.[23] There have also been a variety of sociological and ideological approaches, including political and anti-imperialist readings,[24] and liberationist,[25] postcolonialist,[26] and feminist[27] approaches. These latter studies have been particularly helpful in reminding us that we all come to the Gospels with certain biases, with our own worldview and life experiences. We will inevitably read the text through the lens of these backgrounds. It can be enormously helpful to listen to the voices of others who come from different perspectives — some much closer to the NT world itself — and see the text through their eyes.

Narrative Criticism: The Gospel as Story

In terms of broad impact on studies of the Gospels, the most significant new methodology of the last few decades has been *narrative criticism,* which examines them as story. Groundbreaking work on Mark as narrative was done in 1982 in *Mark as Story* by David Rhoads and Donald Michie,[28] and many articles, monographs, and dissertations have followed.[29] While both redaction criticism and narrative criticism study the Gospels in their final form, redaction criticism is concerned with the history and transmission of the text — how authors edited and altered their sources to accomplish their purposes and address the needs of their communities. Narrative criticism, by contrast, has no interest in the history or sources of the text, but only in how each gospel functions as a unified story. Drawing categories from literary theory, narrative critics point to features common to narrative literature, such as point of view, narrators, plot, characters, and setting.

While redaction critics discuss authors and life settings, narrative critics speak of implied authors (the authorial perspective discerned through the narrative) and narrators (the voice telling the story). Such narrators can be first person ("I/we"),

23. S. D. Moore, "Turning Mark Inside Out," in *Mark and Method* (ed. Anderson and Moore), 95–110; idem, *Mark and Luke in Poststructuralist Perspectives: Jesus Begins to Write* (New Haven, CT: Yale University Press, 1992); G. Salyer, "Rhetoric, Purity, and Play," *Semeia* 64 (1993): 139–69.

24. C. Myers, *Binding the Strong Man: A Political Reading of Mark's Story of Jesus* (Maryknoll, NY: Orbis, 1988); R. A. Horsley, *Hearing the Whole Story: The Politics of Plot in Mark's Gospel* (Louisville: Westminster John Knox, 2001); Adam Winn, *The Purpose of Mark's Gospel: An Early Christian Response to Roman Imperial Propaganda* (WUNT 2/245; Tübingen: Mohr Siebeck, 2008).

25. R. R. Beck, *Nonviolent Story: Narrative Conflict Resolution in the Gospel of Mark* (Maryknoll, NY: Orbis, 1996); B. K. Blount, *Go Preach! Mark's Kingdom Message and the Black Church Today* (Bible & Liberation; Maryknoll, NY: Orbis, 1998).

26. T. B. Liew, "Tyranny, Boundary and Might: Colonial Mimicry in Mark's Gospel," *JSNT* 73 (1999): 7–31.

27. A.–J. Levine and M. Blickenstaff, eds., *A Feminist Companion to Mark* (Sheffield: Sheffield Academic, 2001); E. S. Fiorenza, *In Memory of Her: A Feminist Theological Reconstruction of Christian Origins* (New York: Crossroad, 1983).

28. David Rhoads and Donald Michie, *Mark as Story: An Introduction to the Narrative of a Gospel* (Philadelphia: Fortress, 1982). The 2nd and 3rd editions (1999, 2012) were coedited by Joanna Dewey.

29. For extensive bibliography see Telford, *Writing on the Gospel of Mark*, 290–97. Good summary introductions can be found in Mark Allen Powell, *What Is Narrative Criticism?* (Minneapolis: Fortress, 1990), and James L. Resseguie, *Narrative Criticism of the New Testament: An Introduction* (Grand Rapids: Baker, 2005). On Mark, see S. H. Smith, *A Lion with Wings: A Narrative-Critical Approach to Mark's Gospel* (Sheffield: Sheffield Academic, 1996); B. M. F. van Iersel, *Reading Mark* (Edinburgh: T&T Clark, 1989).

functioning as a character in the story, or third person, standing external to the story. All the Evangelists speak in the third person, except for Luke in certain places in Acts, where he uses the first person plural ("we"). Narrators can be limited in their knowledge or they can be omniscient, knowing the thoughts and intentions of characters. The gospel writers for the most part speak as omniscient narrators.

While redaction and form critics speak of pericopes, short vignettes arising from oral tradition, narrative critics speak of events (or scene parts), scenes (or episodes), and acts, which move the plot forward. Plot involves the progress of the story, from conflict to crisis to climax to resolution. Plots can move linearly, or back and forth through preview or flashback. Story time can move slowly, describing a scene and dialogue in detail, or it can move quickly, summarizing days, weeks, or even years in a single sentence.

Stories have not only plots, but also characters and settings. Characters can be positive (protagonists) or negative (antagonists), or ambivalent. They can be "round" (complex) or "flat" (simple and predictable). Jesus and God are, of course, the protagonists of the Gospels. Satan, demons, and the religious leaders (with a few exceptions) are the antagonists. The crowds function in various ways, sometimes positively and sometimes negatively. The disciples too are ambivalent. Though they are clearly on the side of Jesus, they waver and often serve as a negative example. This is especially true in Mark's gospel, where only Jesus serves as the ultimate model of discipleship.

Narratives also have settings, including local, temporal, and social settings. The Gospels are set in the context of first-century Judaism, during the Roman hegemony of Palestine. Mark's gospel, like the other Synoptics, links plot and setting, with a geographical progression from Galilee in the north to the story's climax in Jerusalem. The Sea of Galilee, and particularly journeys by boat, play an important narrative function in Mark's gospel. Whenever the disciples get in a boat, they exhibit some lack of faith or a failure to comprehend Jesus' words and mission. The manner in which Mark tells his story — the characters, setting, plot — reveals his key themes and theological perspectives. This is narrative theology.

The Approach of the Present Commentary

The present commentary is eclectic, drawing insights from historical-critical, social-scientific, and narrative methodologies. In line with redaction criticism, we assume a historical author and a narrative purpose arising from the author's life setting. We also recognize that this setting was part of the social and political world of the first century, more specifically Jewish Palestine under Roman hegemony.

With the majority of NT scholars, we also assume Markan priority,[30] a point that makes redactional analysis of Mark's sources necessarily more tentative. While

---

30. See Christopher M. Tuckett, "The Current State of the Synoptic Problem," in *New Studies in the Synoptic Problem* (ed. P. Foster et al.; BETL 239; Leuven/Paris/Walpole, MA: Peeters, 2011), 9–50.

redactional study on Matthew and Luke profits from examining how these authors edited Mark (and possibly Q and other sources), there is much greater uncertainty concerning the nature and scope of Mark's sources.[31] To be sure, Mark's editing can sometimes be detected through vocabulary and style, summaries, seams, and transitions. Yet without known sources, these conclusions are subjective and often speculative. Primary focus in this commentary will therefore be placed on a holistic narrative analysis of Mark's themes and theology.

Genre

There has been significant debate in recent decades concerning the genre, or literary form, of the Gospels.[32] Most scholars recognize that the Gospels arose in a particular literary environment and that the authors likely modeled their narratives after other literary works of their day. Identifying the genre of Mark should give us insight into how the author intended his gospel to be read and interpreted.

There are two inappropriate extremes concerning the genre of the Gospels. One is to treat them as without literary precedent, a sui generis, that arose through the kerygmatic (related to the proclamation of the gospel) activity of the early church. This perspective was commonly held by the form critics, who treated the Gospels as nonliterary works that arose as folk literature rather than as intentionally produced literary works.[33] Yet as noted above, it is widely acknowledged today that the Evangelists were more than merely compilers of traditions; they were authors and theologians in their own right. The other extreme is to identify the Gospels with a single literary category from the ancient world and to assume that the writers intentionally imitated this form. Scholars vigorously debate whether the Gospels are Greco-Roman biographies, aretalogies (accounts of miracle-working "divine men"), Hellenistic historiographies, foundational epics, Greek tragedies, Jewish novels, or something else. The problem is twofold. First, no single genre fits the Gospels well in terms of nature, purpose, or structure. Second, these genres themselves cannot be so strictly defined; individual works within a particular category (for example, historiography) exhibit significant variation among themselves.

A more balanced approach recognizes that the Gospels arose in the Greco-

31. Perhaps the best attempt to discern Markan redactional style is that of E. J. Pryke, *Redactional Style in the Marcan Gospel* (SNTSMS 33; Cambridge: Cambridge University Press, 1978).

32. Charles H. Talbert, *What Is a Gospel? The Genre of the Canonical Gospels* (Philadelphia: Fortress, 1977). For summaries of the debate, see L. Hurtado, "Gospel (Genre)," in *DJG*, 282; R. A. Guelich, "The Gospel Genre," in *The Gospel and the Gospels* (ed. P. Stuhlmacher; Grand Rapids: Eerdmans, 1991); 173–208; M. E. Vines, *The Problem of the Markan Genre: The*

Gospel of Mark and the Jewish Novel (Atlanta: Scholars, 2002). For bibliography, see Telford, *Writing on the Gospel of Mark,* 284–86. A good recent survey is Adela Yarbro Collins, *Mark* (Hermeneia; Minneapolis: Forress, 2007), 15–43, who identifies Mark as "Eschatological Historical Monograph."

33. The classic presentation of this may be seen in K. L. Schmidt, "Die Stellung der Evangelien in der allgemeinen Literaturgeschichte," in *Eucharisterion* (ed. H. Schmidt; FS H. Gunkel; Göttingen: Vandenhoeck & Ruprecht, 1923), 50–134.

Roman literary environment and the Evangelists were no doubt influenced by this environment and by various literary exemplars. Of the many suggestions, the most widely accepted is that the Gospels are closest to the broad category of writings known as "biographies" or "lives" (*bioi*) of famous people.[34] These *bioi* were generally written to preserve the memory and/or celebrate the exploits, virtues, or teachings of famous rulers, philosophers, or statesmen. Examples include Plutarch's *Parallel Lives,* Xenophon's *Memorabilia,* Suetonius's *Lives of the Caesars,* Philo's *Life of Moses*, and Philostratus's *Life of Apollonius of Tyana.* Like the Gospels, the *bioi* are selective and anecdotal accounts of exceptional individuals.

Yet while the Gospels contain some significant parallels with the *bioi* and can be profitably compared and contrasted with them, the Evangelists are not simply imitating this or any other genre. The Gospels are unique in both their origin and their content. First, as the form critics correctly asserted, a gospel arose out of the dynamic preaching and teaching of the early church. The gospel of Mark is not just a narrative. It is a written proclamation of the oral gospel. It is no accident that Mark uses the term "good news" (εὐαγγέλιον) to describe the Jesus event. This word has Old Testament roots related to Isaiah's announcement of eschatological salvation (Isa 52:7 LXX). The early Christians first adopted it with reference to the *oral proclamation* of the good news of Jesus' life, death, and resurrection (cf. 1 Thess 1:5; 2:2, 4, 8 – 9). Mark thus identifies his narrative as a *written version* of the *oral proclamation*. The Gospel writers are not just biographers and storytellers. They are preachers of the good news.

The content of the Gospels also bears this out. Mark's narrative is not just the story of Jesus of Nazareth. On a grander scale it represents the climax and center point of human history, the fulfillment of God's promise to Israel and the salvation of the world. Mark announces at the beginning that Isaiah's great prophecies of eschatological salvation are coming to fulfillment (1:1 – 2). Jesus' message is that "the kingdom of God is close at hand": the Creator is intervening in human history to claim back his creation. No Greco-Roman biography makes such audacious claims. This is much more than the remarkable exploits of an exceptional man. It is the arrival of God's end-time salvation.

While Mark's gospel thus represents the written version of the oral gospel, the author broke new ground by going beyond the oral proclamation of the gospel. Although the stories, anecdotes, and teaching of Jesus had been passed down in the preaching and teaching of the early church, Mark appears to have been the first to produce a *connected narrative* of the public ministry of Jesus.[35] His work goes beyond

---

34. See, e.g., Talbert, *What Is a Gospel?*; David E. Aune, *The New Testament in Its Literary Environment* (Philadelphia: Westminster, 1987), 17 – 76; Richard A. Burridge, *What Are the Gospels? A Comparison with Graeco-Roman Biography* (2nd ed.; SNTSMS 70; Grand Rapids: Eerdmans, 2004).

35. This is not to say that there was no narrative structure in the preaching of the early church. C. H. Dodd argued persuasively that the sermons in Acts represent the same basic narrative structure as Mark's gospel, showing that this structure predates his gospel (C. H. Dodd, "The Framework of the Gospel Narrative," *ExpTim* 43 [1932]: 396 – 400).

the announcement of salvation to the *story* of Jesus. His is the first (written) "gospel," setting it apart from anything yet produced by the early church.

Authorship

So who was the author of this innovative work? Strictly speaking, the four Gospels are all anonymous, since none of them names their authors. Luke and John come closest, the former with its first person introductory prologue (Luke 1:1 – 4) and the latter with its epilogue comments about "the disciple whom Jesus loved" (21:24; cf. 21:20). Neither Matthew nor Mark has any self-reference. Why this anonymity? Perhaps because these works are not the possession of any individual, but the common gospel proclaimed by the church — "the good news [gospel] about Jesus the Messiah" (Mark 1:1), not the gospel of *Mark*, *Matthew*, or *Luke*. This seems to be the point of the ancient titles, which appear in our manuscripts either as "The Gospel according to Mark"(εὐαγγέλιον κατὰ Μάρκον) or simply, "According to Mark" (κατὰ Μάρκον). These titles were probably not original, since such specificity would not have been necessary until the Gospels began to circulate together. Yet they appear in our oldest manuscripts as titles (*inscriptio*) and/or as postscripts (*subscriptio*), and so testify both to the antiquity of the traditional authorship and to the recognition that there is *one* gospel (εὐεαγγέλιον), being narrated by (κατά) four Evangelists.[36]

Despite this anonymity, there is strong and early tradition identifying the author of the Third Gospel as John Mark, part-time associate of both Paul and Peter. The earliest tradition is reported by the church historian Eusebius (c. AD 263 – 339), who quotes Papias, bishop of Hierapolis, in the latter's five-volume work known as *Interpretation of the Sayings of the Lord* (Λογίων κυριακῶν ἐξήγησις). Papias, likely writing around AD 95 – 110,[37] quotes John "the Elder" concerning the authorship of the Second Gospel:

> The Presbyter used to say this also: "Mark became Peter's interpreter and wrote down accurately, but not in order, all that he remembered of the things said and done by the Lord. For he had not heard the Lord or been one of his followers, but later, as I said, a follower of Peter. Peter used to teach as the occasion demanded, without giving systematic arrangement to the Lord's sayings, so that Mark did not err in writing down some things just as he recalled them. For he had one overriding purpose: to omit nothing that he had heard and to make no false statements in his account."[38]

Eusebius points out that though Papias did not himself know the apostles, he was

---

36. See Martin Hengel, "The Titles of the Gospels," in *Studies in the Gospel of Mark* (Philadelphia: Fortress, 1985), 64 – 84, esp. 65 – 66.

37. On this date, see R. Yarbrough, "The Date of Papias: A Reassessment," *JETS* 26 (1983): 181 – 91.

38. Eusebius, *Hist. eccl.* 3.39.15 (translation from P. Maier, *Eusebius: The Church History* (Grand Rapids: Kregel, 1999), 129 – 30.

in direct contact with those who had heard them, including John the Elder, Aristion, Polycarp, and the daughters of Philip the Evangelist (Eusebius, *Hist. eccl.* 3.39.1 – 9; cf. Acts 21:8 – 9).[39] We thus have a first-century tradition claiming that Mark accurately interpreted (or translated) Peter's eyewitness accounts, turning Peter's anecdotal stories into a connected narrative, though not necessarily in chronological order.[40]

Second-century sources make similar claims. The Anti-Marcionite Prologue to Mark (c. 160 – 180) identifies Mark as the author and links him to Peter: "Mark ... who was called 'stump-fingered' because for the size of the rest of his body he had fingers that were too short. He was Peter's interpreter. After the departure [or 'death'] of Peter himself, the same man wrote his Gospel in the regions of Italy."[41] The odd statement about Mark's disfigured fingers may point to a reliable tradition, since the church is unlikely to have invented such a disparaging remark.[42] We find here two additional pieces of information: that Mark wrote after Peter's death and that he wrote in Italy.

Irenaeus (c. 180), referring to Peter and Paul, similarly asserts, "Now Matthew published a written Gospel among the Hebrews in their own tongue, while Peter and Paul were evangelizing and founding the church in Rome. But after their departure [ἔξοδος; death?], Mark, the disciple and interpreter of Peter, himself also handed over to us, in writing, the things preached by Peter."[43] The implication is that Mark is writing from Rome after the deaths of Peter and Paul.

Clement of Alexandria (c. 180) specifically refers to Rome: "When, by the Spirit, Peter had publicly proclaimed the Gospel in Rome, his many hearers urged Mark, as one who had followed him for years and remembered what was said, to put it all in writing. This he did and gave copies to all who asked. When Peter learned of it, he neither objected nor promoted it."[44] Peter's apparent indifference to Mark's work suggests that this statement was not created as an apologetic defense of the Petrine tradition, since, if that were the case, one would expect a much more positive affirmation by Peter. Other early church writers, including Tertullian (*Marc.* 4.5), Origen (Eusebius, *Hist. eccl.* 6.25.5), and Jerome (*Comm. Matt.*, prologue 6), affirm Mark's role as author and that he was dependent on the eyewitness accounts of Peter.

---

39. "Papias thus admits that he learned the words of the apostles from their followers but says that he personally heard Aristion and John the presbyter. He often quotes them by name and includes their traditions in his writings" (Eusebius, *Hist. eccl.* 3.39.7; trans. Maier, *Eusebius*, 127).

40. The connection to Peter is also indirectly made by Justin Martyr (c. AD 150), who refers to Mark 3:16 – 17 (Jesus' naming of Simon as "Peter," and James and John as "Sons of Thunder") as coming from the memoirs of Peter (*Dial.* 106). For strong defenses of the authenticity of the Papias tradition, see Hengel, *Studies*, 47 – 53; Robert H. Gundry, *Mark: A Commentary on His*

Apology for the Cross (Grand Rapids: Eerdmans, 1993), 1026 – 45.

41. Cited by C. Black, *Mark: Images of an Apostolic Interpreter* (Columbia, SC: University of South Carolina Press, 1994), 119. The date of the Anti-Marcionite prologues is disputed, with some scholars placing them in the third century.

42. The same description is found in Hippolytus, *Haer.* 7.30.1 (see Black, *Mark*, 115 – 18).

43. Ireneaus, *Haer.* 3.1.1; translation from Black, *Mark*, 99 – 100.

44. Cited by Eusebius, *Hist. eccl.* 6.14.6 – 7 (trans. Maier, *Eusebius*, 218).

How many of these early witnesses are dependent on one another is not known. Yet their unanimity is impressive. No competing claims to authorship are found in the early church. Since John Mark was a relatively obscure figure, it seems unlikely that a gospel would have been attributed to him if he had not in fact written it. We could add to this the evidence of the titles to the Gospels, which, as noted above, appear in nearly all of our extant manuscripts.

Although internal evidence does not provide direct evidence for authorship, it can be used to help corroborate the external claims. (1) The author's many Aramaisms (Mark 3:17; 5:41; 7:11, 34; 10:45; 14:36) are compatible with a Palestinian Jew like John Mark (cf. Acts 12:12). (2) The large number of Latinisms would also fit a Roman provenance (place of origin; see Audience, below). (3) The identification of Rufus and Alexander as sons of Simon of Cyrene (15:21) is also significant, since it confirms that the author was known to his readers. It seems unlikely that the title "according to Mark" (κατὰ Μάρκον) could have been attached to the gospel so early if the original readers knew it came from someone else. Furthermore, if this Rufus is the same one mentioned in Rom 16:13, we have incidental confirmation of a Roman provenance.

At the same time, there are challenges to Markan authorship. The author's understanding of Jewish traditions is sometimes said to be deficient, rendering it unlikely that the gospel was composed by a Jerusalem Jew.[45] For example, Mark 7:3–4 says that "the Pharisees and all the Jews" practice ceremonial washing, when in fact this was a distinctly Pharisaic ritual, not practiced by all Jews. Similarly, Mark's geographical references at times seem confused, as when he says in 7:31 that Jesus left "the region of Tyre [and] went through Sidon to the Sea of Galilee." Since Sidon is twenty miles north of Tyre and Galilee thirty miles southeast, this is a circuitous route indeed.

Yet none of these alleged errors are decisive. Although Mark's statement about hand washing is certainly hyperbolic, ritual washings were widely practiced among the Jews and were viewed by Gentiles as one of their distinctive practices. Even a Jewish work like the *Letter of Aristeas* (305) uses language similar to Mark: "Following the custom of *all the Jews*, they washed their hands in the sea in the course of their prayers to God" (see further comments on 7:3). Similarly, Mark's geography in 7:31 is muddled only if we interpret this as a straight-line journey, rather than a general report of Gentile sites visited during this phase of his ministry. It is the fact *that* Jesus is foraying into Gentile lands rather than his precise itinerary that is Mark's concern. These and similar alleged discrepancies have plausible explanations, which will be discussed in the commentary.

Although the Papias tradition of Markan authorship is not a question of orthodoxy, nor does it affect the message of the gospel, there seems no good reason to

45. Joel Marcus, *Mark 1–8* (AB 27; New York: Doubleday, 2000), 19–21; K. Niederwinner, "Johannes Markus und die Frage nach dem Verfasser des zweiten Evangeliums," *ZNW* 58 (1967): 172–88.

doubt its veracity. But who was this Mark? Although the name (Latin: *Marcus;* Greek: Μάρκος) was a common name in antiquity, the most likely candidate is the John Mark of biblical tradition.[46] John Mark first appears in Acts 12, where we learn his mother, Mary, owned a house in Jerusalem used as a meeting place for the church. It was there that Peter returned after his late-night release from jail by an angel (12:12). According to Paul, Mark was Barnabas's cousin (Col 4:10). Luke reports that Mark accompanied Barnabas and Saul back to Antioch after the two had brought famine relief to Jerusalem (Acts 12:25). Mark then accompanied the two on their first missionary journey as a "helper" or "assistant" (ὑπηρέτης; 13:5), but then left them suddenly at Perga in Pamphylia and returned to Jerusalem (13:13). When the two later discussed returning to visit the churches started on their earlier journey, Barnabas wanted to take John Mark again, but Paul refused because of the latter's previous desertion. After what Luke calls a "sharp disagreement" (παροξυσμός), the two eventually parted ways, with Paul returning to Galatia and Barnabas taking John Mark with him to Cyprus (15:36 – 39).

Although this is the last we learn of Mark in Acts, the later Pauline letters suggest that the two eventually reconciled. In Col 4:10, Paul sends the Colossian church greetings from Mark and says, "You have received instructions about him; if he comes to you, welcome him." Philemon 24 also mentions similar greetings from Mark and other associates of Paul. Finally, Paul, languishing in prison shortly before his execution, tells Timothy, "Get Mark and bring him with you, because he is helpful to me in my ministry" (2 Tim 4:11). Mark's association with Peter appears not only in the Papias tradition, but also in 1 Pet 5:13, where the author writes, "She who is in Babylon, chosen together with you, sends you her greetings, and so does my son Mark." If "Babylon" is a cryptic reference to Rome, as seems likely, this would provide additional evidence both for the Petrine connection to Mark's gospel and its Roman provenance.

Some scholars, while acknowledging that the author of the Second Gospel was likely named Mark, deny he was the John Mark of the Pauline traditions.[47] Others accept that he was likely John Mark, but reject the Papias tradition and the association with Peter and with Rome.[48] Yet there seems no good reason to disregard either. First Peter 5:12 – 13, with its references to "Babylon" and Silvanus (Silas), another of Paul's companions, provides incidental confirmation to Mark's association with both Paul and Rome. When this is combined with Paul's own statements (likely from Rome)

46. For a comprehensive discussion of John Mark in biblical and postbiblical tradition (through the fourth century AD), see Black, *Mark*. Black's cautious investigation reaches mostly agnostic conclusions concerning whether John Mark was the author.

47. R. Pesch, *Das Markusevangelium* (HTKNT 2/1 – 2; Freiburg: Herder, 1977), 1:9 – 11, thinks that the gospel writer

was an unknown Mark, perhaps a Palestinian Jewish Christian in Rome, who later came to be associated with the John Mark of Acts.

48. Marcus, *Mark 1 – 8*, 24, concludes the author was likely named Mark, and perhaps the John Mark of Acts, but is unlikely to have had any connection with Peter.

in Col 4:10 and Phlm 24, the circumstantial case appears even stronger. While the possibility remains that an unknown person or a different Mark wrote the gospel, the traditional identification with John Mark remains the most likely conclusion.

Audience

A General or Specific Audience?

Since the rise of redaction criticism, it has been assumed that each of the Gospels was written within a specific first-century church community to address the specific needs and concerns of that community. Redaction critics sought to discern the *Sitz im Leben* in which each gospel arose. In this scenario, authors were generally considered to be leading members of these communities, so that the provenance and destination of each of the Gospels were the same. Mark, for example, has been widely viewed as written in Rome for the Roman church, Matthew in Syria for the church of Antioch, and John in Ephesus or more broadly Asia Minor for the churches there.

Although this view is still the majority one among NT scholars, it has been seriously challenged in recently years. In a collection of essays, *The Gospel for All Christians*, Richard Bauckham and others have argued that the Gospels were not written for specific church communities, but for the church at large.[49] Bauckham points out that first-century churches were not isolated enclaves, but part of a large network of interconnected communities. This is evident from the letters of Paul and other early Christian writings, which display much communication and travel within the early church.[50] The literary interdependence of the Synoptic Gospels also points in this direction. The fact that Matthew and Luke both independently used Mark confirms that the latter was widely circulated. Matthew and Luke likely intended their gospels to be circulated in the same way.[51] According to Bauckham, the Gospels have been wrongly compared to the Pauline letters, which *were* written to specific audiences to address specific concerns. Yet while the letters were meant to be a substitute for Paul's own presence while he was away, this is not the case for the Gospels, which (it is presumed) were written to and for the communities in which the authors lived. Bauckham concludes that it makes more sense that the Evangelists would have addressed specific concerns in their own communities through oral teaching rather than through a written gospel. He writes, "Indeed, why should [the Gospel writer] go to the considerable trouble of writing a Gospel for a community to which he was regularly preaching?"[52]

49. Richard Bauckham, ed., *The Gospels for All Christians: Rethinking the Gospel Audiences* (Grand Rapids: Eerdmans, 1998). Cf. Martin Hengel, *The Four Gospels and the One Gospel of Jesus Christ: An Investigation of the Collection and Origin of the Canonical Gospels* (trans. John Bowden; Harrisburg, PA: Trinity Press International, 1977), 106–15.

50. Bauckham, "For Whom Were Gospels Written?" in *The Gospels for All Christians*, 9–48.
51. Ibid., 12–13.
52. Ibid., 29.

While Bauckham and his colleagues have provided an important balance and corrective to those who claim the Gospels were written to isolated communities of idiosyncratic belief, their conclusions are probably overstated. There is good reason to suppose that, at least initially, Mark had a specific audience in mind.[53] There are a variety of reasons that an author would produce a written gospel for his own community, such as to provide an authoritative and legitimizing account of their history and beliefs. This would especially be the case if the community was under threat or if eyewitnesses were passing from the scene. Marcus points out that the Dead Sea Scrolls and other Second Temple literature provide examples of works produced within a community for that community itself.[54] The fact that Mark's gospel survived, despite the likelihood that both Matthew and Luke viewed their own as authoritative replacements, testifies to local support for each gospel and some distance between their communities.[55] The anonymity of the Gospels themselves may also point to a local address, suggesting that no byline was originally necessary.

There is also internal evidence for a specific destination. If Mark were writing to a general rather than a specific audience, why would he refer to Alexander and Rufus (15:21), the sons of Simon of Cyrene, as though his readers know them? The fact that both Matthew and Luke independently omit this reference suggests its irrelevancy for the church at large. It seems likely, therefore, that the gospel writers have specific audiences in mind and are writing primarily to address needs and concerns that would be relevant to those audiences. At the same time, the early and widespread circulation of the Gospels shows that these communities were not isolated islands, but were part of a larger network of churches and communities. It is not unlikely that the authors themselves expected their writings to be copied and disseminated to various churches, and that they wrote with this in mind.[56]

A Roman Origin and Destination?

As noted above, early tradition identifies Mark's gospel with Rome. The Anti-Marcionite Prologue says Mark wrote "in the regions of Italy," and Irenaeus and Clement of Alexandria both refer specifically to Rome. The close identification of Mark with Peter by all these writers (Papias, Justin Martyr, Irenaeus, Clement of Alexandria, Origen, Tertullian, etc.) also points to Rome, since strong church tradition places Peter in Rome later in his life. This, in turn, agrees with the biblical references

---

53. For responses to Bauckham, see P. F. Esler, "Community and Gospel in Early Christianity: A Response to Richard Bauckham's *Gospels for All Christians*," *SJT* 51 (1998): 235 – 48; D. C. Sim, "The Gospels for All Christians? A Response to Richard Bauckham," *JSNT* 24 (2001): 3 – 27; Marcus, *Mark 1 – 8*, 25 – 28.

54. Marcus, *Mark 1 – 8*, 27, also points to the *Letter of Aristeas* (Alexandria) and *Joseph and Aseneth* (Heliopolis) as examples of works likely produced within a community to address needs of that community.

55. Ibid., 26.

56. Cf. Edward Klink, ed., *The Audience of the Gospels: Further Conversation about the Origin and Function of the Gospels in Early Christianity* (LNTS 353; London/New York: T&T Clark, 2010).

to Mark being in Rome in association with both Paul (Col 4:10; Phlm 24; 2 Tim 4:11) and Peter (1 Pet 5:13; "Babylon" = Rome).

Internal evidence may help to corroborate this identification. Mark translates Aramaic words into Greek for his readers (3:17; 5:41; 7:11, 34; 15:22), which appears to rule out a Palestinian (or Syrian?) audience. More importantly, he uses a number of Latinisms or Latin loanwords. For example, in 12:42 he explains the value of a Greek coin, the *lepton* (λεπτόν) with a Roman one, a *quadrans* (κοδράντης), and identifies the "courtyard" or "palace" (αὐλή) as the *Praetorium* (πραιτώριον).[57] Hengel finds particularly significant the description of the woman who approaches Jesus in the region of Tyre in 7:24. She is called "a Greek, a Syrophoenician" (Ἑλληνίς, Συροφοινίκισσα). "Greek" identifies her language while "Syrophoenician" her ethnicity. Such an identification would be unusual and unnecessary in Syria (where "Phoenician" would do), but makes good sense in Rome, where it would be necessary to distinguish a Syrophoenician from a Libya-Phoenician (from Carthage).[58]

Others, however, have argued against a Roman context. Boring does so primarily on internal grounds, noting that, unlike other works emanating from Rome at the time, Mark's gospel shows no acquaintance with Paul's letter to the Romans or key terms of Pauline theology. Mark's negative portrait of Peter and the other disciples is also incompatible with the tradition of a gospel based on Petrine traditions. Neither 1 Peter nor *1 Clement*, which both come from Rome later in the first century, indicates awareness of Mark's gospel. Nor does the Old Roman Creed, ancestor of the Apostles' Creed, which jumps directly from Jesus' birth to "crucified under Pontius Pilate," with no place for the kind of narrative theology found in Mark.[59] Yet such arguments from silence are not strong, since narrative and epistolary literature have different purposes. In any case, Mark's strong narrative emphasis on the cross and the atonement language in 10:45 does have Pauline echoes. Furthermore, an allusion to Mark likely does occur in *1 Clem.* 15:2, where the citation of Isa 29:13 is closer to Mark 7:6 than to the Septuagintal reading.[60]

Marcus rejects a Roman origin more on external grounds, claiming that the per-

---

57. Other examples include *denarius, centurion, legion*. For fuller lists, see V. Taylor, *The Gospel according to Mark* (2nd ed.; London: Macmillan / New York: St. Martin's, 1966), 45; Robert H. Stein, *Mark* (BECNT; Grand Rapids: Baker, 2008), 11 – 12. Taylor points out that while some of these occur in the other Synoptics, a number are peculiar to Mark.

58. Hengel, *Studies*, 29. For Latinisms in the NT generally, see BDF, 4 – 6. Marcus, *Mark 1 – 8*, 32, and G. Theissen, *The Gospels in Context: Social and Political History in the Synoptic Tradition* (Minneapolis: Fortress, 1991), 245 – 49, counter that Mark is not substituting Western terms for Eastern ones, but explaining imprecise Greek terms with more precise Latin ones. This may be possible for "courtyard/Praetorium," but

seems less likely for the coins. Marcus also claims that the Syro-Phoenician woman may have married a Phoenician or (following Theissen) that she is being identified with the southern part of Syria (the Phoenician coast) rather than the northern part (Coele-Syria). Again, this explanation is possible, but less likely than the other. Hengel, *Studies*, 29, 137 – 38 n. 164, points to the commonness of the expression in the West but its rarity in the East.

59. Eugene Boring, *Mark: A Commentary* (NTL; Louisville: Westminster John Knox, 2006), 18 – 19.

60. Mark and *1 Clement* read οὗτος ὁ λαὸς τοῖς χείλεσίν με τιμᾷ, while Isa 29:13 LXX reads ὁ λαὸς οὗτος τοῖς χείλεσιν αὐτῶν τιμῶσίν με.

secution against believers described in Mark 13:9–13 looks more like sporadic persecution experienced by Christian missionaries throughout the Roman empire than the concerted actions of Nero against the church in Rome. He argues that if Mark were writing in response to the Neronian persecution, one would expect in Mark 13 the kind of language related to the "beasts" of Daniel 7 and Revelation 13. Nero is an unlikely candidate for the "abomination of desolation" since he never visited or planned to visit Palestine.[61] Yet these arguments hold water only if the Evangelist is composing the Olivet Discourse of Mark 13 intentionally to reflect the situation in Rome, rather than recounting Jesus' own prediction of the coming destruction of Jerusalem. Whether or not Mark wrote from Rome, there seems no reason to doubt that Jesus predicted both the empire-wide persecution of his followers and coming judgment against Jerusalem.

Other Proposals for Origin and Destination

The only contrary claim from the ancient world to the Roman origin comes from John Chrysostom, who claims Mark wrote from Egypt.[62] This, however, is likely a misunderstanding of the tradition from Eusebius that Mark first *preached his gospel* in Egypt: "And they say that this Mark was the first that was sent to Egypt, and that he proclaimed the Gospel which he had written and first established churches in Alexandria" (*Hist. eccl.* 2.16.1).

The two main alternatives to a Roman origin suggested by modern scholars are Galilee and Syria. The Galilean proposal draws primarily from the fact that so much of Mark's gospel occurs in Galilee and that Jesus promised to meet the disciples in Galilee after the resurrection (14:28; 16:7). Marxsen, as noted above, claimed that Mark wrote during the Jewish revolt of AD 66–70 to encourage Christians to flee Jerusalem and gather in Galilee, where the parousia would shortly occur.[63] W. H. Kelber also saw the destruction of Jerusalem as decisive for Mark's purpose, but claimed that Mark, who likely lived in Galilee, wrote shortly *after* the destruction of Jerusalem to address a crisis in the church. In the last days of the war, eschatological hopes had been high among the Jerusalem Christians that the parousia would shortly take place in Jerusalem. When this did not occur, discouragement set in. Mark wrote to affirm the Galilean Christian movement over against the Jerusalem church and to encourage the Judean Christians who had survived the destruction to join the Galilean community awaiting the kingdom of God.[64]

A recent significant defense of a Galilean provenance comes from H. N. Roskam, who claims (like Kelber) that the book was written to a Christian audience living in

---

61. Marcus, *Mark 1–8*, 32–33.

62. Chrysostom, *Hom. Matt.* 1:7: "Matthew … composed his Gospel in the language of the Hebrews. And Mark too, in Egypt, is said to have done this same thing at the entreaty of the disciples."

63. Marxsen, *Mark the Evangelist*, passim.

64. W. H. Kelber, *The Kingdom in Mark: A New Place and a New Time* (Philadelphia: Fortress, 1974).

Galilee some time after the destruction of Jerusalem.[65] Following this cataclysmic event, the Romans viewed any Jewish messianic movement with great suspicion and alarm. There was also concern among Jewish leaders in Galilee that such a movement would provoke retaliation by the Romans not only against the Christians, but against the larger Jewish community. According to Roskam, Mark's depiction of Jesus is meant to eliminate the political connotations associated with the title "Christ" and with Jesus' life and death. Mark seeks to show that Jesus was not an anti-Roman revolutionary and that the kingdom of God did not involve political rule over an earthly Israel. Rather, "Mark presents Jesus as God's final envoy, who proclaims the imminence of God's kingdom, and must die and rise again in order to return at the definitive break-through of God's reign to gather his faithful, to whom God will accord eternal life."[66] Mark therefore writes to call believers to resist pressure from the persecution and to persevere in their faith.

There are significant problems with the Galilean hypothesis, however. First, it is based on slim evidence. The Galilean focus of Jesus' early ministry and his choice of Galilean disciples are surely matters of historical tradition and cannot be attributed to Markan redaction. There is little therefore to suggest that this Galilean emphasis reflects the author's own community situation. Jesus' prediction of a Galilean resurrection appearance is hardly sufficient to posit an entire community's existence and concerns. Most decisive against this view, however, is the evidence in Mark of a predominantly Gentile and Greek-speaking audience. Mark's explanation of Jewish customs (7:3 – 4; 14:12; 15:42) and his interpretation of Aramaic words (3:17; 5:41; 7:11, 34; 15:22) would not fit a Galilean church, which — whether predominantly Jewish or mixed Jewish and Gentile — would speak Aramaic and be aware of Jewish customs.

A somewhat stronger case can be made for a Syrian provenance.[67] Marcus points out that the situation in Mark 13 mirrors closely the revolt in Palestine against the Romans in AD 66 – 73. Yet he rejects a Galilean origin for the reasons noted above. Galilee was overwhelmingly Jewish, whereas Mark's readers are most likely predominantly Gentile. Furthermore, Galilee would have been a war front at this time, and "a community living there would probably not have had the resources, time, or inclination to set about producing a Gospel."[68] By contrast, Syria was a predominantly Gentile region, but was close enough to feel the effects of the war. It was also an area of Pauline influence, where Mark's emphasis on Jesus' contact with non-Jews, freedom from the law, and his explanation of Jewish customs and Aramaic terms would have found a ready audience.[69]

While the theory of a Syrian origin of the gospel of Mark is certainly stronger

---

65. H. N. Roskam, *The Purpose of the Gospel of Mark in Its Historical and Social Context* (Leiden: Brill, 2004), passim.

66. Ibid., 238.

67. See H. C. Kee, *Community of the New Age: Studies in Mark's Gospel* (Philadelphia: Westminster, 1977), 100 – 105; Theissen, *Gospels in Context*; Marcus, *Mark 1 – 8*, 33 – 37.

68. Marcus, *Mark 1 – 8*, 35 – 36.

69. Ibid., 36.

than a Galilean one, it too is based on the thinnest of evidence. The only real support is the assumption that Mark is writing in direct response to the crisis in Jerusalem. Yet while Mark may indeed be writing with an awareness of storm clouds brewing over Palestine (see 13:14: "let the readers understand"), this observation could be made in the late 60s of the first century from almost anywhere in the Roman empire. There is no need to suppose that Mark is viewing events from Syria. Furthermore, as we will see in our discussion of Mark 13, the evidence is strong that the historical Jesus predicted the destruction of Jerusalem and that Mark 13 is based on dominical tradition. Mark's descriptions of the siege and destruction of Jerusalem are general enough that they are unlikely to have been composed after the fact or from firsthand knowledge of events in Palestine.[70]

In conclusion, while the provenance of Mark's gospel remains a debated question, the preponderance of internal and external evidence still points to the traditional identification of Rome. As with the question of authorship, this conclusion is tentative enough that, though it may inform our interpretation of the text, it should not control it.

Date

Like the origin and destination of Mark's gospel, the date is uncertain. There are three main possibilities: an early date (mid-50s to early 60s AD), a middle one (mid-60s), or a later one (late 60s to early 70s).

(1) *Mid-50s to early 60s, while Peter was preaching in Rome.* As noted earlier, Clement of Alexandria (according to Eusebius) claimed that Mark wrote while Peter was still ministering in Rome.[71] This would likely place the writing from the mid-50s to the early 60s of the first century. Eusebius reports that Peter came to Rome during the reign of the emperor Claudius (AD 41 – 54).[72] Since Peter was in Jerusalem for the council of Jerusalem in Acts 15 (around AD 49), he probably came to Rome sometime after this, perhaps in the mid-50s.[73] Peter appears to have visited Corinth or at least to have been known to the Corinthians when Paul wrote 1 Corinthians (c. AD 55; 1 Cor 1:12; 3:22; 9:5). Since church tradition places Peter's martyrdom during the persecutions of Nero (c. AD 64), the writing of Mark could have occurred sometime from the mid-50s to early 60s.

An early date may also be supported by Markan priority, with the likelihood that Luke used Mark in composing his gospel. If Acts were written while Paul was still

---

70. For other evidence against Marcus, see W. Wessel and M. L. Strauss, "Mark," *EBC²* (Grand Rapids: Zondervan, 2010), 9:684.

71. See Authorship above. Clement of Alexandria, *Hypotyposeis* 8 (cited by Eusebius, *Hist. eccl.* 2.15; 6.14.5 – 7).

72. Eusebius, *Hist. eccl.* 2.14.6.

73. It is possible, of course, that Peter went to Rome earlier, perhaps after he left Jerusalem in Acts 12:17, and that he later returned for the Jerusalem Council in AD 49. See John Wenham, "Did Peter Go to Rome in AD 42?" *TynBul* 23 (1972): 94 – 102; Rainer Riesner, *Paul's Early Period: Chronology, Mission Strategy, Theology* (Grand Rapids: Eerdmans, 1997), 119.

in prison in Rome (AD 60 – 62; Acts 28:30 – 31) and Luke used Mark as a source for his gospel, then Mark's gospel must be dated to the late 50s or early 60s. However, Luke may have had theological rather than historical reasons for ending the book of Acts with Paul in Rome, namely, to show that the gospel had reached "the ends of the earth" (Acts 1:8). Most scholars date Luke's gospel later, either shortly before or sometime after the destruction of Jerusalem in AD 70. Other possible support for an early date for Mark is Jesus' prediction in Mark 13:9 that his followers will be brought before local councils and synagogues. This looks more like the kind of sporadic persecution and opposition experienced by Paul and other believers in Acts than the concerted persecution of Nero or the crisis surrounding the siege and destruction of Jerusalem.

(2) *Mid-60s, related to the Neronian persecution.* A second suggested date and occasion for Mark's gospel is the mid-60s in association with the persecutions of Nero in Rome. As noted above, the Anti-Marcionite Prologue claims that Mark wrote *after* the death of Peter, and Irenaeus says it was after the "departure" of both Peter and Paul.[74] The Neronian persecutions were sparked by a devastating fire in Rome in AD 64, which burned for six days and destroyed over half the city. Only four of Rome's fourteen districts escaped the fire. Three were completely destroyed and seven others severely damaged. Rumors circulated that Nero himself had ordered the fire to make room for a new palace, and soldiers were supposedly seen fanning the flames. To quell the rumor, Nero accused the Christians, already a despised minority, of setting the fire. The Roman historian Tacitus describes the events:

> But all human efforts, all the lavish gifts of the emperor, and the propitiations of the gods, did not banish the sinister belief that the conflagration was the result of an order. Consequently, to get rid of the report, Nero fastened the guilt and inflicted the most exquisite tortures on a class hated for their abominations, called Christians by the populace. Christus, from whom the name had its origin, suffered the extreme penalty during the reign of Tiberius at the hands of one of our procurators, Pontius Pilatus, and a most mischievous superstition, thus checked for the moment, again broke out not only in Judea, the first source of the evil, but even in Rome, where all things hideous and shameful from every part of the world find their center and become popular. Accordingly, an arrest was first made of all who pleaded guilty; then, upon their information, an immense multitude was convicted, not so much of the crime of firing the city, as of hatred against mankind. Mockery of every sort was added to their deaths. Covered with the skins of beasts, they were torn by dogs and perished, or were nailed to crosses, or were doomed to the flames and burnt, to serve as a nightly illumination, when daylight had expired.[75]

If Peter was in fact martyred during this period, Mark may have written shortly

---

74. Irenaeus, *Haer.* 3.1.1.

75. Tacitus, *Ann.* 15.44, in *The Complete Works of Tacitus*   (trans. A. J. Church and W. J. Brodribb; ed. Moses Hadas; New York: Random House, 1942), 380 – 81.

afterward to encourage the church to hold firm to their faith in Jesus the Messiah and to persevere in the face of suffering and persecution.

(3) *Late 60s or early 70s, related to the destruction of Jerusalem.* The majority of scholars argue for a date for Mark in the late 60s or early 70s, closer to the destruction of Jerusalem. This might perhaps fit Irenaeus's claim that Mark wrote after the death of *both* Peter and Paul, if Paul was martyred during a second Roman imprisonment around AD 67.[76] The most compelling evidence for this date is Mark's cryptic narrative aside with reference to the abomination of desolation (13:14): "let the readers understand."[77] Mark seems to be pointing out to readers that Jerusalem's fate has been or is about to be decided.[78]

Scholars debate whether Mark is writing shortly before, during, or after the war. The first seems most likely, since, as noted above, the description of the siege is general and does not appear to have been written after the fact.[79] For example, no reference is made to the devastating fire that destroyed the city and temple. As noted above (see Audience), some scholars assume that a date related to Jerusalem's destruction indicates an origin in either Galilee or Syria because of their proximity to Jerusalem and to the war. This is unnecessary, however, since the church in Rome would have been aware of the revolt and the Roman legions preparing to quell it.[80] In conclusion, while the date of Mark's gospel remains an open question, in light of 13:14 a date in the late 60s shortly before the destruction of Jerusalem seems the most likely. This would take into account both the recent memory of the Neronian persecutions (view 2) and also the storm clouds brewing over Jerusalem (view 3).

Occasion and Purpose

As with the audience and date of Mark, no consensus has been reached on a specific occasion. As we have seen, the traditional view based on Papias is that the gospel is a recapitulation of Peter's preaching penned by Mark in the context of the

---

76. Cf. 2 Tim 4:11, where Paul asks Timothy, "Get Mark and bring him with you [to Rome], because he is helpful to me in my ministry." Could Mark's return to Rome be the occasion for the writing?

77. For the importance of the Olivet Discourse in dating Mark, see Collins, *Mark*, 11–14.

78. For other possible interpretations of this verse, see comments on 13:14.

79. For an opposing view, see the interesting proposal of Winn, *The Purpose of Mark's Gospel*, who claims that Mark is writing *in Rome after the Jewish war* in response to Vespasian's propaganda to establish his legitimacy as the new emperor of Rome. This propaganda included oracles and portents, divine healings, grand triumphs, and even the claim that Vespasian

himself fulfilled the Jewish messianic prophecies (Josephus, *J.W.* 6.5.4 §312–13; Tacitus, *Hist.* 5.13.1; and Suetonius, *Vesp.* 4.5). According to Winn, Mark writes to respond to the christological crisis this was causing in the church.

80. On the relevance of the temple's destruction for a Roman audience, see Brian J. Incigneri, *The Gospel to the Romans: The Setting and Rhetoric of Mark's Gospel* (Leiden: Brill, 2003), esp. 163–72; Timothy C. Gray, *The Temple in the Gospel of Mark: A Study of Its Narrative Role* (Grand Rapids: Baker, 2008), 154–55. Incigneri points out that the triumphal parade of Vespasian and Titus illustrates the vital relevance the suppression of the Jewish revolt and the destruction of the temple had for the city of Rome.

Neronian persecutions.[81] New proposals were introduced during the heyday of redaction criticism, when many scholars claimed that Mark was responding to a specific crisis or rising heresy in the church. We have already noted several of these. W. Marxsen proposed an eschatological crisis. Mark wrote his gospel from Galilee to encourage Jerusalem Christians to flee to Galilee, where the parousia would shortly take place. W. H. Kelber similarly saw Mark encouraging Jerusalem Christians after the war to join the Galilean community awaiting the kingdom of God.

Others saw a primarily christological purpose. W. Wrede proposed that Mark embellished the traditional messianic secret to confirm that, despite all appearances, Jesus truly was the Messiah. T. J. Weeden suggested that Mark wrote to combat a growing "divine-man" Christology, which had come to view Jesus as a kind of first-century magician and miracle worker. According to Weeden, Mark responded by emphasizing a "cross Christology," stressing Jesus as the suffering Messiah, who gives his life for others.[82] This view, though at one time popular, has been generally discredited in recent years. On the one hand, contrary to Weeden's claims, there is little evidence for a clearly definable category of "divine-man" in the first century.[83] On the other hand, Mark does not downplay or denigrate Jesus' remarkable acts of power, which he presents as *positive proof* of Jesus' messianic identity.

A different christological purpose was proposed by E. Schweizer (followed by R. P. Martin), who claimed that Mark wrote to combat a docetic tendency in post-Pauline Christianity. Docetism claims that Jesus only appeared to be human. According to Schweizer, Mark wrote at a time when some Christians were taking Paul's teaching about the cosmic Christ to an inappropriate extreme by emphasizing the believer's heavenly union with Christ to the exclusion of his authentic humanity. Mark sought to correct this by setting out the traditions of Jesus' earthly life (thus creating the literary-form "gospel") and making the passion central to the story, highlighting a theology of the cross.[84]

The main problem with these proposals is that, by focusing on one historical crisis (e.g., docetic teaching), Markan theme (e.g., messianic secret), or individual passage (e.g., the Olivet Discourse), so much of Mark's seemingly important material is overlooked or ignored. The diverse and often contradictory conclusions illustrate the challenge of viewing Mark's narrative as a window through which we can reconstruct

---

81. For recent defenses of the Petrine background to Mark's gospel, see Richard Bauckham, *Jesus and the Eyewitnesses* (Grand Rapids: Eerdmans, 2006), 155–239; James Dawsey, *Peter's Last Sermon: Identity and Discipleship in the Gospel of Mark* (Macon, GA: Mercer University Press, 2010). Dawsey treats the gospel as an oral sermon of the martyred Peter to the church.

82. T. J. Weeden, *Mark — Traditions in Conflict* (Philadelphia: Fortress, 1971); idem, "The Heresy That Necessitated Mark's Gospel," *ZNW* 59 (1968): 145–58. Weeden also argues that Mark's strong polemic against the disciples is because they

are seen as representing this divine-man Christology.

83. See especially C. H. Holladay, *"Theois Aner" in Hellenistic Judaism: A Critique of the Use of This Category in NT Christology* (Missoula, MT: Scholars, 1977).

84. See E. Schweizer, *The Good News according to Mark* (trans. D. H. Madvig; Richmond, VA: John Knox, 1970), 380–86; idem, "Mark's Theological Achievement," in *The Interpretation of Mark* (ed. Telford), 42–63; R. P. Martin, *Mark: Evangelist and Theologian* (Grand Rapids: Zondervan, 1972), 153–62.

a specific community situation.[85] Mark likely had a variety of purposes in writing, and it is more profitable to seek his general theological goals rather than a single or specific occasion or crisis in the church. There is a great deal of consensus that Mark's narrative is dominated by two broad theological themes: Christology and discipleship.

Confirmation of Jesus' Messianic Identity

Christology is on center stage throughout Mark's gospel and must be considered primary to his theological purpose. The book begins by identifying itself as "the good news about Jesus the Messiah, the Son of God" (1:1), and this identification is shortly confirmed by God's own voice from heaven: "You are my beloved Son; I am pleased with you" (1:11). Mark's narrative structure provides the key to his christological purpose. Throughout the first half of the gospel Jesus displays remarkable messianic authority by casting out demons, healing the sick, and raising the dead. By the midpoint in chapter 8 no honest enquirer could doubt this authority, and Peter (representing the disciples) confesses, "You are the Messiah." At this point the narrative takes its dramatic turn, as Jesus begins to predict that his messianic role is not what Peter and the disciples expected. He has not come to conquer Roman legions but to suffer and die as a ransom for sins. Mark's purpose is not to downplay or reject Jesus' authority and power, as in the "divine-man" hypothesis; it is to show that Jesus is the Son with divine authority who has come to defeat Satan, sin, and death by fulfilling the suffering role of the Messiah.

For anyone familiar with Christianity in the first century, the elephant in the room for both Jews and Gentiles was that this "Messiah" who Christians claimed was the Savior of the world had experienced the most horrific and shameful fate imaginable — Roman crucifixion. Mark's narrative is written to show that all along this was God's purpose and plan. It is through his *suffering and death* that Jesus has inaugurated the kingdom of God, bringing in God's eschatological salvation. Mark's purpose is to show that Jesus is indeed the mighty Messiah and Son of God, as confirmed through *both* his acts of power *and* his suffering and death.

There is much to commend Robert Gundry's claim that Mark's gospel is essentially "an apology for the cross."[86] Gundry turns the divine-man theory on its head, arguing that Mark does not seek to refute a theology of glory with a theology of the cross. Instead, Mark demonstrates that the theology of the cross *is* a theology of glory and shows that it is precisely *through* Jesus' passion that he achieves his glory. Where we would differ from Gundry is at two main points. First is his insistence that Mark is writing an apologetic for unbelievers rather than for believers.[87] While Mark may

---

85. For a good discussion of the difficulties in "mirror-reading" Mark's gospel to identify a specific occasion, see Dwight N. Peterson, *The Origins of Mark: The Markan Community in Current Debate* (Leiden: Brill, 2000).

86. Gundry, *Mark*, 3 – 4.

87. Ibid., 1026: "Mark writes apologetically not to keep Christians from apostatizing out of shame for the Cross ... but to convert non-Christians despite the shame of the Cross."

hope that his work fulfills an evangelistic purpose, together with most scholars we believe that Mark is writing primarily to Christians to encourage them and assure them in their faith. There is a great deal in Mark's gospel that implies an "insider's" view and familiarity with the story of Jesus.[88] Second, and as a corollary to this, Gundry downplays or dismisses the importance of discipleship in Mark's gospel.[89] Again, with the majority of scholars we believe that Mark's narrative purpose is not only christological, but also paraenetic, to call believers to follow the suffering path of the Son of Man.

A Call to Cross-Bearing Discipleship

This brings us to the second major purpose for Mark's writing, which is an exhortation to believers to follow the example of Jesus. This theme builds on Mark's Christology. The model for discipleship is not the Twelve, who repeatedly fail, but Jesus himself, who alone remains faithful to God's purpose. The disciples play an ambiguous and ambivalent role in Mark's gospel.[90] On the one hand, they are clearly on the side of Jesus. When he calls them from their occupations, they drop everything and follow him (1:16–20). They stand with Jesus as he disputes with the religious leaders (2:15–20, 23–28; 7:1–5). From among his many followers, he appoints twelve special "apostles," who represent a restored and reconstituted Israel (3:16–19). These are the "insiders," who receive the interpretation of his parables and with them the secrets of the kingdom of God. They are contrasted with the religious leaders, who oppose Jesus' kingdom proclamation and so become "outsiders," blinded to the parables and the message of the kingdom (4:10–12). Jesus sends the Twelve as his representatives and envoys to expand his ministry throughout Galilee, preaching, healing, and casting out demons (6:7–11). Peter, as representative of the Twelve, recognizes and confesses that Jesus is the Messiah (8:29). At the Last Supper, Peter and the others assert their willingness even to die for Jesus (14:29, 31).

On the other hand, despite the positive start and so much potential, the disciples repeatedly fall short of expectations. They fail to understand Jesus' parables (4:13); they have no faith in the face of a storm (4:40); they don't understand the significance of Jesus' miracles (6:52) or his teaching (7:18); their hearts are hardened (6:52); they are slow to learn (8:4) and cannot comprehend his messianic role (8:32; 9:32). They repeatedly act with self-interest and pride (9:38; 10:13, 37, 41). A key tipping point occurs in 8:14–18, when the disciples fail to understand Jesus' teaching about the

---

88. See Stein, *Mark*, 9–10.

89. Gundry, *Mark*, 1, seems to unduly limit the gospel's purpose when he says emphatically that Mark contains "No 'way'-symbolism for cross-bearing.... No boat-symbolism for the Church. No voyage-symbolism for Christian mission."

90. See Ernst Best, *Following Jesus: Discipleship in the Gospel*

of Mark (JSNTSup 4; Sheffield: University of Sheffield, 1981); idem, *Disciples and Discipleship: Studies in the Gospel of Mark* (Edinburgh: T&T Clark, 1986); R. C. Tannehill, "The Disciples in Mark: The Function of a Narrative Role," in *The Interpretation of Mark* (ed. W. R. Telford; 2nd ed.; Edinburgh: T&T Clark, 1955), 134–57.

"leaven of the Pharisees." He rebukes them and asks, "Are your hearts hardened? Do you have eyes but cannot see and ears but do not hear?" The statement sounds eerily close to the judgment against the religious leaders in 4:12, "so that they may look and look but not perceive, and hear and hear but not understand." The reader wonders, *Will the disciples go the way of the religious leaders?* In Gethsemane, Jesus' three closest disciples cannot even watch and pray, repeatedly falling asleep (14:32 – 42). All of his disciples desert him at the first sign of trouble (14:50). While Peter musters courage to follow the arresting party, three times he denies he knows Jesus (14:54, 66 – 72). Nor does Mark describe the restoration of the disciples. The gospel ends with the prediction that the disciples will see Jesus in Galilee (and by implication, be restored to him), but Mark does not describe these events. These are not idealized saints for Mark's readers to venerate. They are "anti-disciples" — examples *to avoid.*[91]

There are certainly positive examples of faith in Mark's gospel, especially in the so-called "minor characters":[92] the woman with a blood disease (5:34), Jairus, the synagogue ruler (6:36), the Syrophoenician woman (7:29), the father of a demon-possessed boy (9:24), blind Bartimaeus (10:47 – 48), the woman who anoints Jesus (14:3 – 9), Joseph of Arimathea (15:43), and the centurion at the cross (15:39). Yet for our author, there is only one ultimate model for discipleship, and that is Jesus himself. He is the one who pursues God's way and repeatedly affirms that all that is happening is according to God's plan (8:31; 9:12 – 13, 31; 10:33 – 34; 14:21, 27, 49). In Gethsemane he agonizes over his coming trial, but steadfastly affirms, "Not what I want, but what you want" (14:36).

The close connection between Jesus' three passion predictions and his teaching that follows confirms the importance of this discipleship theme for Mark. Each time Jesus predicts his coming death, the disciples follow with some act of pride or self-interest. Jesus then teaches about the necessity of humility, service, and self-sacrifice. After Peter's confession and the first passion prediction, Jesus says, "If anyone wants to follow after me, he must deny himself, take up his cross, and follow me" (8:34).

After the second passion prediction and the disciples' dispute over who is the greatest, Jesus teaches, "If anyone wants to be first, that person must be the very last and servant of all" (9:35); and after the third passion prediction and the request by James and John for the best seats in the kingdom, Jesus contrasts the world's leadership method of domination and oppression with that of his disciples: "Whoever wants to be great among you will be your servant, and whoever wants to be first will be slave of all. For even the Son of Man did not come to be served, but to serve, and to give his life a ransom for many" (10:43 – 45). There is no doubt from these passages that Mark's Christology serves this discipleship theme. As the suffering and

---

91. For this theme, see Mark L. Strauss, *Four Portraits, One Jesus: An Introduction to Jesus and the Gospels* (Grand Rapids: Zondervan, 2007), 197 – 98.

92. See Rhoads and Michie, *Mark as Story*, 130 – 36; Smith, *Lion with Wings*, 76 – 80.

self-sacrificial Son of God, Jesus is the model of discipleship for Mark's readers. All who aspire to be Jesus' disciples must deny themselves, take up their cross, and follow him. This is the path of true discipleship.

Literary Features

Mark's Structure

The structure of Mark's gospel is a matter of considerable debate, with most proposals focusing either on a theological movement or a geographical one.[93] We referred earlier to Mark's Christology developing in two stages, with the first part of the gospel illustrating Jesus' authority as Messiah and Son of God and the second revealing his suffering role. The key turning point is Peter's confession (8:27 – 30) and the first passion prediction (8:31 – 33). It is appropriate to structure Mark's gospel into two main parts, as Guelich does:[94]

> I. Introduction: "The Beginning" (1:1 – 13)
> II. Jesus' Public Ministry (1:14 – 8:26)
>   A. Jesus' Authority (1:14 – 3:12)
>   B. Jesus' Teaching (3:13 – 6:6)
>   C. Jesus and Mission (6:7 – 8:26)
> III. Jesus' Death (8:27 – 16:8)
>   A. Jesus' Instruction of the Disciples (8:27 – 10:52)
>   B. Jesus Confronts Jerusalem (11:1 – 13:37)
>   C. Jesus' Death and Resurrection (14:1 – 16:8)

Other scholars, while recognizing the important transition at 8:27 – 33, emphasize the geographical progression from Galilee to Jerusalem. Jesus' early ministry takes place in various stages in Galilee. He then travels to Jerusalem, where he fulfills his messianic mission. Lane provides a typical geographical outline:[95]

> I. Prologue to the Gospel (1:1 – 13)
> II. The Initial Phase of the Galilean Ministry (1:14 – 3:6)
> III. Later Phases of the Ministry in Galilee (3:7 – 6:13)
> IV. Withdrawal beyond Galilee (6:14 – 8:30)
> V. The Journey to Jerusalem (8:31 – 10:52)
> VI. Ministry in Jerusalem (11:1 – 13:37)
> VII. The Passion Narrative (14:1 – 15:47)
> VIII. The Resurrection of Jesus (16:1 – 8)

---

93. For a good survey of this issues, see Joel Williams, "Does Mark's Gospel Have an Outline?" *JETS* 49 (2006): 505 – 25.

94. Guelich, *Mark 1:1 – 8:26* (WBC 34A; Dallas: Word, 1989), xxxvii.

95. W. L. Lane, *The Gospel according to Mark* (NICNT; Grand Rapids: Eerdmans, 1974), 29 – 32.

Similar geographical outlines are followed by many commentators. France (following van Iersel) speaks of Mark's gospel as a "Drama in Three Acts," with the following structure:[96]

Heading and Prologue (1:1 – 13)
Act One: Galilee (1:14 – 8:21)
Act Two: On the Way to Jerusalem (8:22 – 10:52)
Act Three: Jerusalem (11:1 – 16:8)

While there is certainly a geographical progression from Galilee to Jerusalem in Mark, the geographical outline conflicts at various points with Mark's two-stage christological presentation. For example, long after Peter's confession in 8:27 – 30, Jesus is still "passing through Galilee" and visiting Capernaum (9:30, 33). He does not leave Galilee for Judea until 10:1, and Jerusalem is first mentioned as his destination in 10:32! So the "Journey to Jerusalem" is actually from 10:1 – 52 (see 10:1, 32), breaking up the apparently unified (and universally recognized) central section (8:22 – 10:52) structured around the three passion predictions (8:31; 9:31; 10:33 – 34). The narrative unity of this central section seems assured both because of the three-fold cycle of passion predictions and because this section is "framed" with two accounts of the healing of a blind man (8:22 – 26; 10:46 – 52).

Furthermore, the designation "Withdrawal beyond Galilee" in Lane's geographical outline (6:14 – 8:30) does not quite work, since much of this section takes place *in* Galilee (6:45, 53; 7:10, 13). The so-called "withdrawal" is only evident in Jesus' journey to Tyre, Sidon, Decapolis, and Caesarea Philippi (7:24, 31). In light of these incongruities, is seems best to follow a theological rather than a geographical structure, while at the same time recognizing the theological significance of Galilee and Jerusalem for Mark and the important transition in 10:1 – 52 from Jesus' ministry in Galilee to its climax in Jerusalem. The commentary will follow this structure, with a prologue and an epilogue:

I. Prologue: Introduction of the Messiah (1:1 – 13)
II. The Authority of the Messiah (1:14 – 8:21)
  A. The Kingdom Authority of the Messiah (1:14 – 3:6)
  B. The Disciple-Family of the Messiah and Those "Outside" (3:7 – 6:6a)
  C. The Expanding Mission of the Messiah (6:6b – 8:21)
III. The Way of Suffering of the Messiah (8:22 – 15:47)
  A. Revelation of the Messiah's Suffering (8:22 – 10:52)
  B. The Messiah Confronts Jerusalem (11:1 – 13:37)
  C. The Passion of the Messiah in Jerusalem (14:1 – 15:47)
IV. Epilogue: The Resurrection Announcement (16:1 – 8)

96. R. T. France, *The Gospel of Mark* (NIGTC; Grand Rapids: Eerdmans, 2002), 13 – 14; B. M. F. van Iersel, *Mark: A Reader-Response Commentary* (JSNTSup 164; Sheffield: Sheffield Academic, 1998), 75 – 86; idem, *Reading Mark*, 19 – 26.

Mark's Style

Mark writes with a fast-moving, dramatic style. Though he frequently refers to Jesus as a teacher, he focuses more on action than on extended teaching. There are only two lengthy teaching sections in Mark, the parables in ch. 4 and the Olivet Discourse in ch. 13, compared with at least five in Matthew. One of Mark's favorite terms is the adverb εὐθύς (*euthys*), often translated "immediately," which he uses forty-one times. Though the term does not always mean "just then," it carries the story forward at a rapid pace. Mark is also fond of the *historical present tense* (151 times), a Greek construction that uses present tense verbs in narrative to describe past actions. Though characteristic of a less refined Greek style, it also gives the narrative a vivid style, like an on-the-spot report.

Mark's Greek is generally rougher and less refined than the Greek of the other Synoptics, resulting primarily from its more Semitic style. The author likely spoke Aramaic as his mother tongue and Greek as a second language. We have already noted Mark's retention of a number of Aramaic words and phrases transliterated into Greek, like *talitha koum* (ταλιθα κουμ; 5:41), *corban* (κορβαν; 7:11), *ephphatha* (εφφαθα; 7:34), and *Abba* (αββα; 14:36). Especially characteristic of this Semitic style is Mark's use of *parataxis,* coordinate clauses connected by "and" (καί). More refined literary Greek prefers *hypotaxis,* a main clause with subordinate clauses and participial phrases (cf. Luke, Hebrews, James, etc.).[97]

Mark's style is also expansive, with lots of vivid and colorful detail, which Matthew (and to a lesser extent, Luke) tends to abbreviate.[98] Mark's account of the raising of Jairus's daughter, for example, is made up of 345 Greek words, while Matthew's is only 139 (Mark 5:21–43; cf. Matt 9:18–26). Mark's love for vivid detail is especially apparent in his description of the Gerasene demoniac, which Luke and Matthew greatly abbreviate:

MARK 5:2–5	LUKE 8:27	MATT 8:28
When he got out of the boat, immediately a man with a defiling spirit came out of the tombs and met him. He lived among the tombs and no one could restrain him anymore, not even with a chain, because he had often been bound with chains and shackles, but he tore apart the chains and broke the shackles. No one was strong enough to subdue him. Night and day among the tombs and in the hills he was constantly crying out and cutting himself with stones.	When Jesus stepped ashore, he was met by a demon-possessed man from the town. For a long time this man had not worn clothes or lived in a house, but had lived in the tombs.	When he arrived at the other side . . . two demon-possessed men coming from the tombs met him. They were so violent that no one was able to pass that way.

97. For other examples of Markan Semitisms, see Taylor, *Mark,* 55–66.

98. Ibid., 53, 135–39, attributes these details to the eyewitness traditions Mark received and so denies that they are part of the Evangelist's style. Yet whether they are traditional or not, the fact that Mark retains them means that they are part of his literary style.

This vivid style is enhanced by Mark's penchant for repetition and dual expressions.[99] This dualism appears at various levels, including phrases, sentences, and the structure of episodes. The dualism may simply reinforce, or may expand, clarify, or advance the thought. Consider the following redundant temporal expressions (lit. trans.):

- 1:32: "evening having come, when the sun set" (ὀψίας δὲ γενομένης, ὅτε ἔδυ ὁ ἥλιος)
- 1:35: "very early in the morning, while it was still dark" (πρωῒ ἔννυχα λίαν)
- 2:20: "then they will fast, in that day" (τότε νηστεύσουσιν ἐν ἐκείνῃ τῇ ἡμέρᾳ)
- 4:35: "on that day, evening having come" (ἐν ἐκείνῃ τῇ ἡμέρᾳ ὀψίας γενομένης)
- 10:30: "now, at this time" (νῦν ἐν τῷ καιρῷ τούτῳ)
- 13:29: "it is near, at the door" (ἐγγύς ἐστιν ἐπὶ θύραις)

Such repetition makes Mark especially appropriate for oral reading, since the repetition makes the narrative more vivid and memorable for the audience. There has been a great deal of research in recent years on Mark as oral performance.[100] We must remember that the gospel has been primarily *heard* rather than *read* for most of church history.

Intercalation

Perhaps Mark's most characteristic and important literary feature is his tendency to "sandwich" one episode in the middle of another, a device known as *intercalation*. Intercalation is similar but slightly different from *inclusio*. In the latter, two similar episodes appear at the beginning and end of an episode or a series of episodes, framing it with "bookends." For example, two similar accounts of the healing of blind men (8:22 – 26; 10:46 – 52) bracket the beginning and end of Mark's central section (8:22 – 10:52). This is inclusio. In intercalation, a single episode is interrupted by another and the two in some way mutually interpret or relate to one another.

For example, Mark sandwiches the account of Jesus' clearing of the temple between his cursing of the fig tree and its later discovery as withered (11:12 – 25). Both episodes relate symbolically to Israel's failure to produce fruit and her coming judgment. Similarly, the account of the raising of Jairus's daughter is interrupted by the healing of the woman with a blood disease (5:21 – 43). Both episodes concern

99. See F. Neirynck, *Duality in Mark: Contributions to the Study of Markan Redaction* (rev. ed.; BETL 31; Louvain: Leuven University Press, 1988); D. Rhoads, J. Dewey, and D. Michie, *Mark as Story* (3rd ed.; Minneapolios: Fortress, 2010), 49 – 51.

100. See E. Best, "Mark's Narrative Technique," *JSNT* 11 (1989): 43 – 58; W. H. Kelber, *The Oral and the Written Gospel: The Hermeneutics of Speaking and Writing in the Synoptic Tradition, Mark, Paul, and Q* (Bloomington: Indiana University Press, 1997); Whitney T. Shiner, *Proclaiming the Gospel: First-Century Performance of Mark* (Harrisburg, PA: Trinity Press International/Continuum, 2003); D. Rhoads, "Performing the Gospel of Mark," in *Reading Mark: Engaging the Gospel* (Minneapolis: Fortress, 2004), 176 – 201. The third edition of Rhoads, Dewey, and Michie, *Mark as Story*, emphasizes this aspect of performance, referring to ideal *hearers* and *audiences* rather than ideal *readers*.

ceremonial defilement and the need for faith. Mark intercalates the Beelzebul controversy in the middle of an episode in which Jesus' family comes to take charge (3:20 – 35). Both represent the rejection of Jesus by his own and the establishment of new family relationships based on spiritual allegiance rather than physical ancestry (see 3:34 – 35). The sordid account of the execution of John the Baptist by King Herod is sandwiched in the middle of the beginning and end of the mission of the Twelve (6:7 – 30). Mark is likely illustrating the ultimate cost of discipleship in the context of the disciples' mission in Galilee.

Some intercalations contrast one episode with another. The account of the woman of Bethany who anoints Jesus with perfume is intercalated between the plot against Jesus by the religious leaders and the fruition of that plot in the betrayal by Judas (14:1 – 11). Authentic devotion is contrasted with treachery and hypocrisy. Similarly, Peter's denial of Jesus is sandwiched in the middle of Jesus' trial before the Sanhedrin (14:53 – 72). While Jesus remains true to his calling, Peter fails in his test of faithfulness. The pause in the narrative produced by these intercalations not only emphasizes important Markan themes, but also provides dramatic suspense as the reader waits to learn the outcome.

Triads

Another common Markan pattern is the author's tendency to present events in triads, or groups of three.[101] Most of these are related in some way to the failure of the disciples or to Jesus' coming passion. There are three passion predictions (8:31 – 32; 9:31; 10:33 – 34) and three boat scenes in which the disciples fail to comprehend Jesus' mission (4:35 – 41; 6:45 – 52; 8:14 – 21). Three times the disciples fall asleep in Gethsemane (14:37, 40, 41), and three times Peter denies he knows Jesus (14:68, 70, 71). The crucifixion scene is also divided into three, three-hour segments (14:25, 33, 34).

Outline

I. Prologue: Introduction of the Messiah (1:1 – 13)
  A. John the Baptist Prepares the Way (1:1 – 8)
  B. The Baptism and Temptation of Jesus (1:9 – 13)
II. The Authority of the Messiah (1:14 – 8:21)
  A. The Kingdom Authority of the Messiah (1:14 – 3:6)
    1. Jesus Proclaims the Kingdom and Calls Disciples (1:14 – 20)
    2. Authority in Teaching, Healing, and Exorcism (1:21 – 45)
      a. Jesus Teaches and Drives Out an Evil Spirit (1:21 – 28)

---

101. Rhoads, Dewey, and Michie, *Mark as Story,* 54 – 55.

Select Bibliography

Commentaries

Anderson, Hugh. *The Gospel of Mark*. NCB. Greenwood, SC: Attic, 1976.

Boring, Eugene, *Mark: A Commentary*. NTL. Louisville/London: Westminster John Knox, 2006.

Branscomb, B. H. *The Gospel of Mark*. The Moffatt New Testament Commentary. London: Hodder & Stoughton, 1937.

Bratcher, R. G., and E. A. Nida. *Translator's Handbook on Mark*. Leiden: Brill, 1961.

Brooks, James A. *Mark*. NAC. Nashville: Broadman, 1991.

Collins, Adela Yarbro, *Mark*. Hermeneia. Minneapolis: Fortress, 2007.

Cranfield, C. E. B. *The Gospel according to Saint Mark*. Rev. ed. Cambridge: Cambridge University Press, 1977.

Donohue, J. R., and D. J. Harrington. *The Gospel of Mark*. SP 2. Collegeville, MN: Liturgical, 2002.

Edwards, James R. *The Gospel according to Mark*. PNTC. Grand Rapids: Eerdmans, 2002.

Ernst, J. *Das Evangelium nach Markus*. RNT. Regensburg: Pustet, 1981.

Evans, Craig A. *Mark 8:27 – 16:20*. WBC 34B. Nashville: Nelson, 2001.

France, R. T. *The Gospel of Mark*. NIGTC. Grand Rapids: Eerdmans, 2002.

Garland, David E. *Mark*. NIVAC. Grand Rapids: Zondervan, 1996.

Gnilka, J. *Das Evangelium nach Markus*. EKKNT 2/1 – 2. Zürich: Benzinger/Neukirchen-Vluyn: Neukirchener Verlag, 1978, 1979.

Gould, E. P. *A Critical and Exegetical Commentary on the Gospel according to Saint Mark*. ICC. New York: Scribner's, 1907.

Grundmann, W. *Das Evangelium nach Markus*. THKNT 2. Berlin: Evangelische Verlagsanstalt, 1977.

Guelich, R. A. *Mark 1:1 – 8:26*. WBC 34A. Dallas: Word, 1989.

Gundry, Robert H. *Mark: A Commentary on His Apology for the Cross*. Grand Rapids: Eerdmans, 1993.

Haenchen, E. *Der Weg Jesu: Eine Erklärung des Markus-Evangeliums und der kanonischen Parallelen*. Berlin: Töpelmann, 1966.

Hooker, Morna D. *The Gospel according to St. Mark*. BNTC. London: A. & C. Black, 1991.

Hurtado, L. W. *Mark*. NIBC. Peabody, MA: Hendrickson, 1989.

Klostermann, E. *Das Markusevangelium*. HNT 3. Tübingen: Mohr, 1950.

Lagrange, M.-J. *Evangile selon saint Marc*. Paris: Gabalda, 1929.

Lane, W. L. *The Gospel according to Mark*. NICNT. Grand Rapids: Eerdmans, 1974.

Levine, Amy-Jill, ed., with Marianne Blickenstaff. *A Feminist Companion to Mark*. Sheffield: Sheffield Academic, 2001.

Lohmeyer, E. *Das Evangelium Des Markus*. KEK 2. Göttingen: Vandenhoeck & Ruprecht, 1963.

Mann, C. S. *Mark*. AB 27. Garden City, NY: Doubleday, 1986.

Marcus, Joel. *Mark 1–8: A New Translation with Introduction and Commentary*. AB 27. New York: Doubleday, 2000.

———. *Mark 9–16: A New Translation with Introduction and Commentary*. AB 27A. New York: Doubleday, 2009.

Moloney, Francis J. *The Gospel of Mark: A Commentary*. Peabody, MA: Hendrickson, 2002.

Nineham, D. E. *The Gospel of St Mark*. Pelican New Testament Commentaries. Harmondsworth, UK / New York: Penguin, 1963.

Pesch, R. *Das Markusevangelium*. HTKNT 2/1–2. Freiburg: Herder, 1977.

Schweizer, E. *The Good News according to Mark*. Trans. D. H. Madvig. Richmond, VA: John Knox, 1970.

Stein, Robert H. *Mark*. BECNT, Grand Rapids: Baker, 2008.

Taylor, V. *The Gospel according to St Mark*. 2nd ed. London: Macmillan / New York: St. Martin's, 1966.

van Iersel, Bas M. F. *Mark: A Reader-Response Commentary*. JSNTSup 164. Sheffield: Sheffield Academic, 1998.

Wessel, W., and M. L. Strauss. "Mark," in *The Expositor's Bible Commentary*, vol. 9. Rev. ed. Grand Rapids: Zondervan, 2010.

Williamson, Lamar. *Mark*. Interpretation: A Commentary for Teaching and Preaching. Atlanta: John Knox, 1983.

Witherington, Ben, III. *The Gospel of Mark: A Socio-Rhetorical Commentary*. Grand Rapids: Eerdmans, 2001.

Other Works

Anderson, Janice Capel, and Stephen D. Moore, eds. *Mark and Method: New Approaches in Biblical Studies*. 2nd ed. Minneapolis: Fortress, 2008.

Bauckham, Richard, ed. *The Gospels for All Christians: Rethinking the Gospel Audiences*. Grand Rapids: Eerdmans, 1998.

Beasley-Murray, G. R. *Jesus and the Last Days: The Interpretation of the Olivet Discourse*. Peabody, MA: Hendrickson, 1993.

Best, Ernst. *Mark: The Gospel as Story*. Edinburgh: T&T Clark, 1983.

Black, C. *Mark: Images of an Apostolic Interpreter*. Columbia: University of South Carolina Press, 1994.

Blinzler, Josef. *The Trial of Jesus: The Jewish and Roman Proceedings against Jesus Christ Described and Assessed from the Oldest Accounts*. Trans. I. McHugh and F. McHugh. Westminster, MD: Newman, 1959.

Blomberg, Craig L. *Interpreting the Parables*. Downers Grove, IL: InterVarsity Press, 2012.

Bock, D. L. *Blasphemy and Exaltation in Judaism: The Charge against Jesus in Mark 14:53–65*. Grand Rapids: Baker, 1998.

Booth, R. P. *Jesus and the Laws of Purity: Tradition History and Legal History in Mark 7*. JSNTSup 13. Sheffield: JSOT Press, 1986.

Boring, M. Eugene, Klaus Berger, and Carsten Colpe, eds. *Hellenistic Commentary on the New Testament*. Nashville: Abingdon, 1995.

Brandon, S. G. F. *Jesus and the Zealots: A Study of the Political Factor in Primitive Christianity*. Manchester: Manchester University Press, 1967.

Brown, Raymond E. *The Death of the Messiah: From Gethsemane to the Grave. A Commentary on the Passion Narratives in the Four Gospels.* 2 vols. New York: Doubleday, 1994.

———. *The Gospel according to John.* AB 29, 29A (I–IX; X–XXI). Garden City, NY: Doubleday, 1966, 1970.

Bultmann, R. *History of the Synoptic Tradition.* Rev. ed. Oxford: Blackwell, 1972.

Burger, C. *Jesus als Davidssohn.* FRLANT 98. Göttingen: Vandenhoeck & Ruprecht, 1970.

Burridge, Richard A. *What Are the Gospels? A Comparison with Graeco-Roman Biography.* SNTSMS 70. 2nd ed. Grand Rapids: Eerdmans, 2004.

Casey, M. *Aramaic Sources of Mark's Gospel.* SNTSMS 102. Cambridge: Cambridge University Press, 1998.

Crossan, J. D. *In Parables.* New York: Harper and Row, 1973.

Crossley, James G. *The Date of Mark's Gospel: Insights from the Law in Earliest Christianity.* JSNTSup 299. London/New York: T&T Clark, 2004.

Croy, N. Clayton. *The Mutilation of Mark's Gospel.* Nashville: Abingdon, 2003.

Danove, P. L. *The End of Mark's Story: A Methodological Study.* Leiden: Brill, 1993.

Davies, W. D., and D. C. Allison. *A Critical and Exegetical Commentary on the Gospel according to Matthew.* 3 vols. ICC. Edinburgh: T&T Clark, 1988, 1991, 1997.

Deissmann, A. *Light from the Ancient East.* Trans. Lionel Strachan. Grand Rapids: Baker, 1965.

Dewey, J. *Markan Public Debate: Literary Technique, Concentric Structure, and Theology in Mark 2:1–3:6.* SBLDS 48. Chico, CA: Scholars, 1980.

Dibelius, M. *From Tradition to Gospel.* Trans. B. L. Woolf. New York: Scribner's Sons, 1965; German original, 1919.

Dodd, C. H. *The Parables of the Kingdom.* Rev. ed. New York: Charles Scribner's Sons, 1961.

Dwyer, T. *The Motif of Wonder in the Gospel of Mark.* JSNTSup 128. Sheffield: Sheffield Academic, 1996.

Elliott, James K., ed. *The Language and Style of the Gospel of Mark: An Edition of C. H. Turner's "Notes on Marcan Usage" Together with Other Comparable Studies.* NovTSup 71. Leiden: Brill, 1993.

Fitzmyer, J. A. *The Gospel according to Luke: A New Translation with Introduction and Commentary.* AB 28, 28A (I–IX, X–XXIV). New York: Doubleday, 1981, 1985.

Fowler, Robert M. *Loaves and Fishes: The Function of the Feeding Stories in the Gospel of Mark.* SBLDS 54. Chico, CA: Scholars, 1978.

France, R. T. *Jesus and the Old Testament.* London: Tyndale, 1971.

Geddert, T. J. *Watchwords: Mark 13 in Markan Eschatology.* JSNTSup 26. Sheffield: Sheffield Academic, 1989.

Gray, Timothy C. *The Temple in the Gospel of Mark: A Study of Its Narrative Role.* Grand Rapids: Baker, 2008.

Hahn, F. *The Titles of Jesus in Christology.* Trans. Harold Knight and George Ogg. New York: World, 1969.

Hengel, Martin. *The Charismatic Leader and His Followers.* New York: Crossroad, 1981.

———. *Crucifixion in the Ancient World and the Folly of the Cross.* Trans. John Bowden. Philadelphia: Fortress, 1977.

———. *The Four Gospels and the One Gospel of Jesus Christ: An Investigation of the Collection and Origin of the Canonical Gospels.* Trans. J. Bowden. Harrisburg, PA: Trinity Press International, 2000.

———. *The Son of God: The Origin of Christology and the History of Jewish-Hellenistic Religion.* Philadelphia: Fortress, 1976.

———. *Studies in the Gospel of Mark.* Philadelphia: Fortress, 1985.

Hoehner, Harold W. *Herod Antipas.* SNTSMS 17. Cambridge: Cambridge University Press, 1972.

Hooker, Morna D. *The Son of Man in Mark.* London: SPCK, 1967.

Horsley, R. A. *Hearing the Whole Story: The Politics of Plot in Mark's Gospel.* Louisville: Westminster John Knox, 2001.

Hull, J. M. *Hellenistic Magic and the Synoptic Tradition.* SBT 2/28. London: SCM, 1974.

Humphrey, Hugh M. *A Bibliography for the Gospel of Mark: 1854–1980.* New York: Mellen, 1982.

Incigneri, Brian J. *The Gospel to the Romans: The Setting and Rhetoric of Mark's Gospel.* Leiden: Brill, 2003.

Instone-Brewer, David. *Divorce and Remarriage in the Bible: The Social and Literary Context.* Grand Rapids: Eerdmans, 2002.

Jeremias, J. *The Eucharistic Words of Jesus.* Trans. N. Perrin. London: SCM, 1966.

———. *Jerusalem in the Time of Jesus.* Trans. F. H. Cave and C. H. Cave. Philadelphia: Fortress, 1969.

———. *New Testament Theology.* Vol. 1: *The Proclamation of Jesus.* New York: Scribner's, 1971.

———. *The Parables of Jesus.* Trans. S. H. Hooke. New York: Scribner's, 1963.

———. *The Prayers of Jesus.* Trans. J. Bowden. Philadelphia: Fortress, 1978.

Kealy, Séan P. *Mark's Gospel: A History of Its Interpretation from the Beginning until 1979.* New York: Paulist, 1982.

Kelber, W. H. *The Kingdom in Mark: A New Place and a New Time.* Philadephia: Fortress, 1974.

———. *The Oral and the Written Gospel: The Hermeneutics of Speaking and Writing in the Synoptic Tradition, Mark, Paul, and Q.* Bloomington: Indiana University Press, 1997.

Kingsbury, Jack Dean. *The Christology of Mark's Gospel.* Philadelphia: Fortress, 1983.

Klausner, J. *The Messianic Idea: From Its Beginning to the Completion of the Mishnah.* Trans. W. F. Stinespring. New York: Macmillan, 1955. German original, Cracow, 1903.

Kümmel, W. G. *Promise and Fulfillment: The Eschatological Message of Jesus.* London: SCM, 1957.

Lightfoot, R. H. *The Gospel Message of St Mark.* Oxford: Oxford University Press, 1962.

———. *Locality and Doctrine in the Gospels.* New York: Harper, 1938.

Louw, J. P., and E. A. Nida, eds. *Greek-English Lexicon of the New Testament: Based on Semantic Domains.* New York: United Bible Societies, 1989.

Magness, J. L. *Sense and Absence: Structure and Suspension in the Ending of Mark's Gospel.* Atlanta: Scholars, 1986.

Maier, P., trans. *Eusebius: The Church History: A New Translation with Commentary.* Grand Rapids: Kregel, 1999.

———. *Josephus: The Essential Works.* Grand Rapids: Kregel, 1994.

Malina, Bruce J., and Richard L. Rohrbaugh. *Social-Science Commentary on the Synoptic Gospels.* Minneapolis: Fortress, 1992.

Manson, T. W. *The Sayings of Jesus: As Recorded in the Gospels of St. Matthew and St. Mark.* Grand Rapids: Eerdmans, 1979.

———. *The Teaching of Jesus. Studies in Its Form and Content.* Cambridge: Cambridge University Press, 1963.

Marcus, Joel. *The Way of the Lord: Christological Exegesis of the Old Testament in the Gospel of Mark.* Louisville: Westminster John Knox, 1992.

Marshall, C. D. *Faith as a Theme in Mark's Narrative* SNTSMS 64. Cambridge: Cambridge University Press, 1989.

Marshall, I. H. *Last Supper and Lord's Supper.* Grand Rapids: Eerdmans, 1980.

Martin, R. P. *Mark: Evangelist and Theologian.* Grand Rapids: Zondervan, 1972.

Martínez, Florentino García, and Eibert J. C. Tigchelaar. *The Dead Sea Scrolls: Study Edition.* 2 vols. Grand Rapids: Eerdmans, 1997, 1998.

Marxsen, Willi. *Mark the Evangelist: Studies in the Redaction History of the Gospel.* Trans. James Boyce. Nashville: Abingdon, 1969.

Matera, F. J. *The Kingship of Jesus: Composition and Theology in Mark 15.* SBLDS 66; Chico, CA: Scholars, 1982.

Mauser, Ulrich W. *Christ in the Wilderness: The Wilderness Theme in the Second Gospel and Its Basis in the Biblical Tradition.* London: SCM, 1963.

McKnight, Scot. *Jesus and His Death: Historiography, the Historical Jesus, and Atonement Theory.* Waco, TX: Baylor University Press, 2005.

Meier, J. P. *A Marginal Jew: Rethinking the Historical Jesus.* ABRL. New York/London: Doubleday. Vol. 1: *The Roots of the Problem and the Person,* 1991. Vol. 2: *Mentor, Message and Miracle,* 1994. Vol. 3: *Companions and Competitors,* 2001.

Metzger, Bruce M. *A Textual Commentary on the Greek New Testament.* 2nd ed. New York/Stuttgart: United Bible Societies, 1994.

Moloney, Francis J. *Mark: Storyteller, Interpreter, Evangelist.* Peabody, MA: Hendrickson, 2004.

Morris, L. *The Gospel according to John.* NICNT. Grand Rapids: Eerdmans, 1971.

Myers, C. *Binding the Strong Man: A Political Reading of Mark's Story of Jesus.* Maryknoll, NY: Orbis, 1988.

Neirynck, F. *Duality in Mark: Contributions to the Study of Markan Redaction.* Rev. ed. BETL 31. Louvain: Leuven University Press, 1988.

Neusner, Jacob, W. S. Green, and E. S. Frerichs, eds. *Judaisms and Their Messiahs at the Turn of the Christian Era.* Cambridge: Cambridge University Press, 1987.

Peterson, Dwight N. *The Origins of Mark: The Markan Community in Current Debate.* Leiden: Brill, 2000.

Pryke, E. J. *Redactional Style in the Markan Gospel.* SNTSMS 33. Cambridge: Cambridge University Press, 1978.

Quesnell, Q. *The Mind of Mark: Interpretation and Method through the Exegesis of Mark 6.52.* AnBib 38. Rome: Biblical Institute Press, 1969.

Rhoads, D. *Reading Mark: Engaging the Gospel.* Minneapolis: Fortress, 2004.

Rhoads, D., J. Dewey, and D. Michie, *Mark as Story: An Introduction to the Narrative of a Gospel.* 3rd ed. Minneapolis: Fortress, 2012

Robbins, Vernon K. *Jesus the Teacher: A Socio-Rhetorical Interpretation of Mark.* Philadelphia: Fortress, 1984.

Roskam, H. N. *The Purpose of the Gospel of Mark in Its Historical and Social Context.* Leiden: Brill, 2004.

Sanders, E. P. *Jesus and Judaism.* Philadelphia: Fortress, 1985.

———. *Judaism: Practice and Belief 63 B.C.E. – 66 C.E.* Philadelphia: Trinity Press International, 1992.

Schildgen, Brenda D. *Power and Prejudice: The Reception of the Gospel of Mark.* Detroit: Wayne State University Press, 1999.

Schürer, Emil. *The History of the Jewish People in the Age of Jesus Christ (175 B.C. – A.D. 135).* Rev. and ed. Geza Vermes, Fergus Millar, and Matthew Black. Edinburgh: T&T Clark; vol. 1, 1973; vol. 2, 1979; vol. 3/1, 1986; vol. 3/2, 1987.

Sherwin-White, A. N. *Roman Society and Roman Law in the New Testament.* Oxford: Oxford University Press, 1963.

Shiner, Whitney T. *Proclaiming the Gospel: First-Century Performance of Mark.* Harrisburg, PA: Trinity Press International, 2003.

Smith, S. H. *A Lion with Wings: A Narrative-Critical Approach to Mark's Gospel*. Sheffield: Sheffield Academic, 1996.

Snodgrass, Klyne. *Stories with Intent: A Comprehensive Guide to the Parables of Jesus*. Grand Rapids: Eerdmans, 2008.

———. *The Parable of the Wicked Tenants: An Inquiry into Parable Interpretation*. Tübingen: Mohr (Siebeck), 1983.

Stock, A. *The Method and Message of Mark*. Wilmington, DE: Michael Glazier, 1989.

Strauss, Mark L. *The Davidic Messiah in Luke-Acts: The Promise and Its Fulfillment in Lukan Christology*. JSNTSup 110. Sheffield: Sheffield Academic, 1995.

———. *Four Portraits, One Jesus: An Introduction to Jesus and the Gospels*. Grand Rapids: Zondervan, 2007.

Stuhlmacher, Peter. *Jesus of Nazareth — Christ of Faith*. Peabody, MA: Hendrickson, 1993.

Sweat, Laura C. *The Theological Role of Paradox in the Gospel of Mark*. LNTS. Bloomsbury: T&T Clark, 2013.

Tannehill, Robert C. "The Disciples in Mark: The Function of a Narrative Role," *JR* 57 (1977): 386–405. Reprinted in *The Interpretation of Mark*. Ed. W. R. Telford. 2nd ed. Edinburgh: T&T Clark, 1995, pp. 134–57.

Taylor, Vincent. *The Formation of the Gospel Tradition*. London: Macmillan, 1935.

Telford, W. R. *The Barren Temple and the Withered Tree: A Redaction-Critical Analysis of the Cursing of the Fig-Tree Pericope in Mark's Gospel and Its Relation to the Cleansing of the Temple Tradition*. JSNTSup 1. Sheffield: JSOT Press, 1980.

———. *Writing on the Gospel of Mark*. Dorsett: Deo, 2009.

Telford, W. R., ed. *The Interpretation of Mark*. Philadelphia: Fortress, 1985.

Theissen, G. *The Gospels in Context: Social and Political History in the Synoptic Tradition*. Minneapolis: Fortress, 1991.

———. *The Miracle Stories of the Early Christian Tradition*. SNTW. Edinburgh: T&T Clark, 1983.

Tolbert, Mary A. *Sowing the Gospel: Mark's World in Literary-Historical Perspective*. Minneapolis: Fortress, 1989.

Tuckett, C. M., ed. *The Messianic Secret*. Philadelphia: Fortress, 1983.

Twelftree, Graham H. *Jesus the Exorcist: A Contribution to the Study of the Historical Jesus*. Peabody, MA: Hendrickson, 1993.

———. *Jesus the Miracle Worker*. Downers Grove, IL: InterVarsity Press, 1999.

van Iersel, B. M. F. *Reading Mark*. Edinburgh: T&T Clark, 1989.

Vermes, G. *Jesus the Jew: A Historian's Reading of the Gospels*. London: Collins, 1973.

Wallace, Daniel B. *Greek Grammar beyond the Basics: An Exegetical Syntax of the New Testament*. Grand Rapids: Zondervan, 1996.

Watts, Rikki E. *Isaiah's New Exodus in Mark*. Grand Rapids: Baker, 2000.

Weeden, T. J. *Mark — Traditions in Conflict*. Philadelphia: Fortress, 1971.

Winn, Adam, *The Purpose of Mark's Gospel: An Early Christian Response to Roman Imperial Propaganda*. WUNT 2/245. Tübingen: Mohr Siebeck, 2008.

Winter, Paul. *On the Trial of Jesus*. 2nd ed. Berlin: de Gruyter, 1974.

Wrede, William. *The Messianic Secret in the Gospels*. Trans. J. C. G. Greig. Cambridge: James Clarke, 1971.

Wright, N. T. *Jesus and the Victory of God*. Minneapolis: Fortress, 1996.

———. *The Resurrection of the Son of God*. Christian Origins and the Question of God 3. Minneapolis: Fortress, 2003.

CHAPTER 1

Mark 1:1 – 8

Literary Context

Mark begins his gospel with an introduction that sets the stage for the narrative that follows. The parameters of this prologue are debated. A few scholars include only vv. 1 – 8, the ministry of John the Baptist, as the fulfillment of Scripture and the forerunner of the Messiah.[1] Others continue through v. 13, the baptism and temptation, since all of these are preparatory events for Jesus' public ministry.[2] Still others continue through v. 15, treating the references to the "good news" (or "gospel"; εὐαγγέλιον) in vv. 1 and 15 as an *inclusio,* or "frame," around this introductory section.[3]

We will treat vv. 1 – 13 as the prologue, in four parts: (1) the beginning of the gospel as the fulfillment of Scripture (vv. 1 – 3); (2) the ministry of John the Baptist (vv. 4 – 8); (3) Jesus' baptism (vv. 9 – 11); and (4) Jesus' testing/temptation in the wilderness (vv. 12 – 13). Verses 14 – 15 may then be seen as the introduction of Jesus' ministry proper.

1. E. Haenchen, *Der Weg Jesu: Eine Erklärung des Markus-Evangeliums und der kanonischen Parallelen* (Berlin: Töpelmann, 1966), 38 – 39; cf. Gundry, *Mark,* 29.

2. C. E. B. Cranfield, *The Gospel according to Saint Mark* (rev. ed.; Cambridge: Cambridge University Press, 1977), 33;

Lane, *Mark,* 39 – 40; Morna D. Hooker, *The Gospel according to St. Mark* (BNTC; London: A. & C. Black, 1991), 31; Moloney, *Mark,* 27; France, *Mark,* 54 – 55.

3. Marcus, *Mark 1 – 8,* 137 – 38; R. A. Guelich, *Mark 1:1 – 8:26,* 3; Boring, *Mark,* 33; Collins, *Mark,* 134 – 35.

Main Idea

Mark introduces his narrative with the message and ministry of John the Baptist, whose role was to fulfill Scripture by preparing the way for the coming of Jesus, the Messiah and Son of God.

Translation

Mark 1:1–8

1	Intro./character description	**The beginning of the good news about Jesus the Messiah, the Son of God,**
2a	Assertion/comparison	**just as it is written in Isaiah the prophet:**
b	prophecy/Scripture quotation	"Look! I am sending my messenger ahead of you, [Exod 23:20a]
c	prophecy/Scripture quotation	who will prepare your way"— [Mal 3:1]
3a	prophecy/Scripture quotation	"a voice of one calling out in the wilderness,
b		*'Prepare the way for the Lord;*
c		*make straight paths for him!'"* [Isa 40:3]
4a	Character entrance	**John came,**
b	character description	baptizing in the desert region and
c	character description	preaching a baptism of repentance for the forgiveness of sins.
5a	Character entrance	**All the Judean countryside and all Jerusalem were going out to him.**
b	Action/Response to 3c	**They were being baptized by him in the Jordan River,**
c	condition	confessing their sins.
6a	Character description	**John was wearing camel's hair and a leather belt around his waist** and
	Character description	**eating locusts and wild honey.**
7a	Character description	**He was preaching this message:**
b	assertion/contrast	*"The one more powerful than I comes after me;*
c	assertion/contrast	*I am not worthy to stoop down and loosen the strap of his sandals.*
8a	assertion	*I baptize you with water,*
b	assertion/contrast	*but he will baptize you with the Holy Spirit."*

Structure

See Literary Context (above) for the structure of Mark's prologue. Here we discuss the first two parts: (1) the beginning of the gospel as the fulfillment of Scripture (vv. 2 – 3) and (2) the ministry of John the Baptist (vv. 4 – 8).

Exegetical Outline

→ **1. The Beginning of the Gospel as the Fulfillment of Scripture (1:1 – 3)**

2. The Ministry of John the Baptist (1:4 – 8)

    a. John's ministry (1:4 – 5a)

    b. The people's response: confession of sins and baptism (1:5b)

    c. John's appearance and lifestyle (1:6)

    d. The message of John (1:7 – 8)

        i. The coming Stronger One (1:7)

        ii. The superiority of the Coming One (1:8)

Explanation of the Text

1:1 The beginning of the good news about Jesus the Messiah, the Son of God (Ἀρχὴ τοῦ εὐαγγελίου Ἰησοῦ Χριστοῦ υἱοῦ θεοῦ). The first line of Mark's gospel can be understood either as (1) the title to the whole work,[4] or (2) the introduction to the first section of the gospel. If the former, the "beginning" refers to the whole ministry of Jesus, climaxing in his death and resurrection. If the latter, the "beginning" could refer to (a) the ministry of John the Baptist (vv. 4 – 8),[5] (b) the preparatory events including Jesus' baptism and temptation (vv. 4 – 13),[6] or (c) the whole series of introductory events, climaxing in Jesus' proclamation of the "good news" (vv. 4 – 15). Since this beginning is linked directly to the prophecy of Isaiah (vv. 2 – 3; "just as it is written …"), which in turn is connected to the coming of John the Baptist (vv. 4 – 8), the most likely answer is 2a. Mark identifies the appearance of John as the beginning of the gospel. This is congruent with the rest of the NT, where John's baptizing ministry is consistently presented as inaugurating the gospel (Matt 3:1 – 17; 11:12; Luke 3:1 – 20; 16:16; John 1:6 – 8, 19 – 36; Acts 1:22; 10:37; 13:24).

Although strictly speaking not a title, the first line still introduces the whole gospel, since it announces the "beginning" of its central theme: the good news about the life, death, and resurrection of Jesus the Messiah.[7] Mark may also be consciously echoing the opening phrase of the LXX (Gen 1:1 LXX: ἐν ἀρχή, "in the beginning"; cf. John 1:1; 1 John 1:1) and in this way marking the beginning of the new creation through the salvation available in Jesus Christ.

Some English versions render "gospel" (εὐαγγέλιον) as "good news" (NIV; NLT; NRSV), while others use "gospel" (NET; ESV; HCSB; REB). The English term comes from the old English *godspel*, which meant "glad tidings" or "good news." The term has an important Greco-Roman as well as a Jewish background. It was used in secular Greek of a celebratory announcement, such as a victory in battle or the enthronement of a king. The famous Priene inscription celebrating the birthday of the Roman emperor Augustus reads, "Good news [εὐαγγέλια] to the world!"[8] Even more important is the term's OT background, where it

---

4. Collins, *Mark*, 130; Boring, *Mark*, 29. Cf. M. Eugene Boring, "Mark 1:1 – 15 and the Beginning of the Gospel," *Semeia* 52 (1990): 43 – 80.

5. Hooker, *Mark*, 33.

6. Lane, *Mark*, 42; Cranfield, *Mark*, 34 – 35.

7. Stein, *Mark*, 39.

8. Friedrich, *TDNT*, 2:722, 724 – 25.

appears in contexts of eschatological restoration. Isaiah 52:7 reads:

> How beautiful on the mountains
>> are the feet of those who bring good news
>> [MT: *bāśar*; LXX: εὐαγγελίζω],
> who proclaim peace,
>> who bring good tidings,
>> who proclaim salvation,
> who say to Zion,
>> "Your God reigns!"

This and similar texts (cf. Ps 96:2; Isa 40:9; 61:1) celebrate the eschatological triumph of God and his sovereign reign over the cosmos. The term was therefore a fitting one for Jesus to draw on when proclaiming the nearness of the kingdom and the need for submission to God's reign: "The kingdom of God is close at hand; repent and believe in the good news [εὐαγγέλιον]" (1:14).

While this first line no doubt gave impetus to the early Christians to call this and similar accounts "gospels" (εὐαγγέλια), for Mark the "gospel" (εὐαγγέλιον) is not a literary genre but the proclamation of eschatological salvation that came to fulfillment in the life, death, and resurrection of Jesus the Messiah.

The genitive phrase "of Jesus Christ/Messiah" (Ἰησοῦ Χριστοῦ) could be taken either as an objective genitive ("about Jesus Christ") or as a subjective genitive ("proclaimed by Jesus Christ"). Both ideas are true, of course, since Jesus will begin proclaiming the good news in 1:14 – 15. But here Mark seems to have in mind the former, the whole

Jesus-event as the fulfillment of Scripture inaugurated by John.[9]

"Jesus" (Ἰησοῦς) is the Greek form of the Hebrew *yĕhôšua'* or *yēšua'*, translated in the OT as "Joshua" and meaning "Yahweh saves" or "Yahweh is salvation." Matthew and Luke identify the name as divinely appointed to Joseph (Matt 1:21) or Mary (Luke 1:31) before Jesus was born.

"Christ" (χριστός) was originally an adjective meaning "anointed"; it rendered the Hebrew *māšîaḥ*. Anointing with oil symbolized being set apart for God's service, and Israel's kings and priests were anointed. By the first century, the term had come to be used as a title for the promised eschatological king from the line of David (see 2 Sam 7:11 – 16; Pss 2; 89; 110; Isa 9:1 – 7; 11:1 – 16, Jer 23:1 – 6; Ezek 34:23 – 24; 37:24 – 25) — "the Messiah" — who would bring salvation to God's people. Although by Mark's day it was common to treat "Christ" as Jesus' second name, the term occurs only seven times in this gospel (1:1; 8:29; 9:41; 12:35; 13:21; 14:61; 15:32) and, with one possible exception (9:41), always functions as a title rather than a name. It would seem best, therefore, to translate the phrase as "Jesus the Messiah" (NIV 2011; NLT) rather than "Jesus Christ" (NIV 1984; NASU; ESV).

The concluding phrase "Son of God" (υἱοῦ θεοῦ) does not appear in some Greek manuscripts, including two important early uncials (ℵ Θ), and the decision to include or omit it is a difficult one.[10] Support for omission is strong. (1) In addition to

---

9. Cranfield, *Mark*, 35 – 36, takes it as a subjective genitive, though most commentators accept it as objective (Lane, *Mark*, 44 – 45; Pesch, *Markusevangelium*, 1:75; Schweizer, *Good News*, 30 – 31; Gundry, *Mark*, 31 – 32; David E. Garland, *Mark* [NIVAC; Grand Rapids: Zondervan, 1996], 21). Still others claim both nuances are present (Marcus, *Mark 1 – 8*, 147; Hugh Anderson, *The Gospel of Mark* [NCB; Greenwood, SC: Attic, 1976], 66 – 67); cf. Daniel B. Wallace, *Greek Grammar beyond the Basics: An Exegetical Syntax of the New Testament* [Grand Rapids: Zondervan, 1996], 119 – 21, who calls this a "plenary

genitive"). This is possible, although authors and speakers usually have one sense in mind when they use a word, unless they are making a pun or play on words.

10. For a fuller discussion, see J. Slomp, "Are the Words 'Son of God' in Mark 1:1 Original?" *BT* 28 (1977): 143 – 50; A. Y. Collins, "Establishing the Text: Mark 1:1," in T. Fornberg and D. Hellholm, eds., *Texts and Contexts: The Function of Biblical Texts in Their Situational and Situational Contexts* (Oslo: Scandinavian University Press, 1995), 111 – 27.

the early manuscript evidence, several quotations from early church leaders omit the phrase. Origen never cites it in the five times he quotes this passage. (2) It seems far more likely that a copyist added the title as a natural complement to "Jesus Christ" than that he intentionally removed it. Some have claimed the words were accidentally omitted through *homeoteleuton* ("same ending"), a technical term meaning a copyist passed over words because of their similar endings. The sentence in Greek has six identical genitive endings (ου), and a slip of the eye may have caused the copyist to pass over "Son of God" (υἱοῦ θεοῦ).[11] Yet accidental omission (caused by the copyist's fatigue?) seems unlikely in the first line of a book.[12]

Despite these arguments, there is good support for the phrase's inclusion. (1) The reading has strong textual support from a variety of manuscript families (B D L W 2427, etc.). (2) An early editor (א[1]) added the phrase to the margin of א, suggesting both readings were known at an early date. (3) The patristic evidence for omission is difficult to evaluate, since the church fathers sometimes paraphrased or abbreviated their Scripture quotations. Indeed, Irenaeus includes the phrase in two quotations and omits it in a third. (4) Accidental omission through homeoteleuton is not as unlikely as sometimes supposed, since the copyist may well have finished copying Matthew or other documents immediately before starting Mark. There is no certainty he was starting fresh at this point. (5) Finally, in terms of intrinsic internal evidence, the title fits well Mark's narrative, where Jesus as the Son of God is an important theme (1:11; 3:11; 5:7; 9:7; 12:6; 13:32; 14:36, 61; 15:39). Jesus' ministry

begins with the Father's announcement of Jesus' divine sonship (1:11) and climaxes with the centurion's words, "Truly this man was the Son of God!" (15:39). Of course, an answer to this could be that copyists would also have been aware of Mark's emphasis on divine sonship, and so could have added the title for that reason. In light of the balanced evidence, it seems safest to leave the phrase in the text (perhaps in brackets) with a footnote indicating its debatable authenticity.

The title "Son of God" could be understood in a variety of ways in the Greco-Roman world. Legendary heroes, kings, philosophers, and miracle workers were sometimes referred to as sons of God.[13] In Greek mythology Zeus was "the father of both men and gods."[14] Roman emperors at times claimed divine sonship. Caesar Augustus took the title *divi filius,* "son of the divinized," soon after the murder of Julius Caesar, and the title was translated in Greek inscriptions as "son of god" (υἱὸς θεοῦ). In Judaism, angelic beings are sometimes called "sons of God" (Gen 6:2, 4; Job 1:6; 38:7; Dan 3:25), and Israel as a nation is referred to as God's firstborn son (Exod 4:22 – 23; Hos 11:1).

Most important for Mark's usage, however, are the messianic (= royal) and divine implications of the title. The messianic implications go back to the Davidic covenant (2 Sam 7:11 – 16), the prophetic foundation for later messianic expectations. God promised David that his descendant would reign forever on his throne, and that "I will be his father, and he will be my son" (2 Sam 7:14; cf. Pss 2:7; 89:26). As God's representative before the people, Israel's king was meant to have a special father-son relationship with God. The ultimate Davidic

---

11. France, *Mark,* 49, points out this would have been especially likely if copied from manuscripts where divine titles were abbreviated in a conventional manner.

12. Collins, *Mark,* 130.

13. See W. v. Maritz, *TDNT,* 8:334 – 40; Martin Hengel, *The Son of God: The Origin of Christology and the History of Jewish-*

Hellenistic Religion (Philadelphia: Fortress, 1976), 21 – 30; A. Deissmann, *Light from the Ancient East* (trans. Lionel Strachan; Grand Rapids: Baker, 1965), 346 – 47.

14. Homer, *Il.* 1.544; 7.68; 5.426 – 30; *Od.* 1.28; 20.201; Hesiod, *Theog.* 542; Siculus, *Library of History* 4.9.1 – 1; Epictetus, *Diatr.* 2.16.44; etc.

king, the Messiah, would have a unique and unprecedented relationship with God.[15] Although this messianic sense of Son of God is predominant in the Synoptic Gospels (14:61; cf. Matt 16:16; 26:63; Luke 1:32), there are also implications of deity associated with the title. As the unique Son of God, the Messiah shares God's glory and power (1:11; 3:11; 5:7; 9:7; 13:32; cf. Matt 11:25 – 27; Luke 10:21 – 22).

1:2 Just as it is written in Isaiah the prophet: "Look! I am sending my messenger ahead of you, who will prepare your way." (καθὼς γέγραπται ἐν τῷ Ἠσαΐᾳ τῷ προφήτῃ· ἰδοὺ ἀποστέλλω τὸν ἄγγελόν μου πρὸ προσώπου σου, ὃς κατασκευάσει τὴν ὁδόν σου). Mark's opening sentence continues by affirming that this "beginning" of the good news was in fulfillment of Scripture, and so was part of God's sovereign purpose and plan. The comparative adverb "just as" (καθώς) commonly introduces fulfillment formulas.[16] The author affirms that "the beginning of the good news ... [happened/came to pass] just as it is written...."[17] The perfect passive verb, "it has been written" (γέγραπται), indicates completed action with continuing results, a common Jewish and early Christian way of quoting Scripture. In English we commonly say, "it is written" (NIV; NASB; NET; ESV; HCSB; etc.) to express the same sense. NLT has, "It began just as the prophet Isaiah had written" (cf. GNT; CEV).

The quotation that follows is a mixed one, combining Exod 23:20a; Mal 3:1; and Isa 40:3. The first phrase ("Look! I am sending my messenger ahead of you") agrees almost verbatim with the Exod 23:20a LXX, where God promises to send an angel ahead of the Israelites in the wilderness.[18] (The Greek and Hebrew words for "angel" and "messenger" are the same: Gk: ἄγγελος; Heb: *mal᾿āk*.) The present tense "I am sending" (ἀποστέλλω) is probably a futuristic present, meaning "I will send" or "I am about to send."[19] In Malachi this messenger (identified as Elijah in Mal 4:6) prepares for the eschatological coming of Yahweh to purge Israel and to judge the wicked. Jesus will identify John as this eschatological Elijah in Mark 9:13. The second phrase ("who will prepare your way") follows the Hebrew text of Mal 3:1, except that "my way" becomes "your way." With this change Mark allows for a messianic interpretation and also implies that Jesus is the embodiment of Yahweh himself.

Why does Mark attribute the mixed citation to Isaiah alone?[20] Some have claimed that Mark is simply in error, or that he is citing from a book of *testimonia,* collections of OT texts that the early Christians used in apologetic contexts to confirm

---

15. It is debated whether "Son of God" was a title used for the Messiah in first-century Judaism. Three texts from Qumran, however, suggest that this connection was being made: 4QFlor 1:11 [= 4Q174]; 1QSa 2:11:12 [= 1Q28a]; 4QpsDan Aᵃ [= 4Q246].

16. BDAG, 493. Cf. Matt 26:24; Mark 9:13; 14:21; Luke 2:23; Acts 15:15; Rom 1:17; 2:24; 3:4, 10; 4:17; 8:36; etc.

17. The punctuation here is debated. Collins, *Mark,* 130, claims that 1:1 is an independent sentence without a predicate and that v. 2 begins a new sentence (cf. UBS⁴; Nestle-Aland²⁸; NASB; REB; NRSV; ESV). Yet, as Guelich, *Mark 1:1 – 8:26,* 7, points out, καθώς never begins a sentence in Mark or elsewhere in the NT (except in the unrelated καθώς/οὕτως combination), and in a formula with γέγραπται it always refers to what precedes rather than to what follows. This indicates a close syntac-

tical relationship with 1:1 (cf. NIV; NLT; GNT; CEV).

18. It is difficult to determine if Mark is explicitly alluding to Exod 23:20a or if he is simply paraphrasing Mal 3:1, which reads (lit.), "Look, I am sending my messenger [or 'angel'], who will prepare the way ahead of me." The question becomes even more complex, since Malachi is likely already echoing Exodus. Later rabbis combined the two texts in a similar manner and linked the messenger with Elijah the prophet (Mal 4:6; *Exod. Rab.* 23.20; Guelich, *Mark 1:1 – 8:26,* 11).

19. See Wallace, *Greek Grammar,* 535 – 37, for this category.

20. Some Byzantine manuscripts read "in the prophets" (A W f¹³ 𝔐 vgᵐˢ syrʰ; Irenaeusᴸᵃᵗ; see KJV; NKJV) instead of "in Isaiah the prophet" (א B L Δ 33 565 892 1241 2427 syr cop; Origen). This is likely a scribal attempt to harmonize the text with the mixed citation that follows.

the fulfillment of Scripture. This latter option is possible, but a better solution is that Mark is affirming that the "beginning of the gospel" represents the fulfillment of Isaiah's broader vision of eschatological restoration and renewal. No OT prophet brings out this vision of redemption like Isaiah. Rikki Watts sees Isaiah's prophecies as the hermeneutical key to Mark's agenda. The introductory citation of Isaiah is programmatic for Mark and is the beginning of an Isaianic "new exodus" motif that runs throughout his narrative. Watts writes: "For Mark the long-awaited coming of Yahweh as King and Warrior has begun, and with it, the inauguration of Israel's eschatological comfort: her deliverance from the hands of the nations, the journey of her exiles to their home and their eventual arrival at Jerusalem, the place of Yahweh's presence."[21]

1:3 "A voice of one calling out in the wilderness, 'Prepare the way for the Lord; make straight paths for him!'" (φωνὴ βοῶντος ἐν τῇ ἐρήμῳ· ἑτοιμάσατε τὴν ὁδὸν κυρίου, εὐθείας ποιεῖτε τὰς τρίβους αὐτοῦ). This third quotation comes from Isa 40:3 LXX, except that the "the paths of our God" becomes "his paths," referring to Jesus. This identification would have come naturally for Mark and his community, where Jesus was worshiped and proclaimed as Lord (κύριος). In its original context, Isaiah 40 predicted a new exodus, when Yahweh would return and triumphantly lead his people out of their Babylonian exile and to the Promised Land. Whereas the Hebrew text refers to preparing a way "in the wilderness," Mark follows the LXX in speaking of *the voice* crying out in the wilderness. This connects the passage more

explicitly to John, whose ministry took place in the Judean desert.

Mark thus sets the ministry of John in the context of the fulfillment of Scripture and of eschatological renewal. John is God's messenger, a voice in the desert shouting out to God's people to prepare a path for the coming of the Messiah. The combination of fulfillment texts echoes not only the exodus from Egypt, God's greatest act of redemption in the OT, but Isaiah's prophetic vision for a new and more glorious exodus, when God will restore his people and dwell with them.

1:4 John came, baptizing in the wilderness and preaching a baptism of repentance for the forgiveness of sins (ἐγένετο Ἰωάννης βαπτίζων[22] ἐν τῇ ἐρήμῳ καὶ κηρύσσων βάπτισμα μετανοίας εἰς ἄφεσιν ἁμαρτιῶν). All four Gospels connect the public ministry of Jesus with that of John the Baptist (cf. Matt 3:1 – 17; Luke 3:1 – 2; John 1:6 – 8, 19 – 36). The same perspective appears in Acts, where John's ministry is viewed as the beginning of the gospel (Acts 1:22; 10:37; 13:24).

The precise location where John baptized is unknown. The term "desert" or "wilderness" (ἔρημος) could refer to any uninhabited place (see 1:35; 6:35). From verse 5 we know that it was somewhere along the Jordan River and that the inhabitants of Jerusalem and Judea were coming out to him. This suggests a southern location, perhaps just north of where the Jordan enters the Dead Sea.

It is not the specific place that interests Mark, but its desert location, since the wilderness plays an important role in Israel's history. It was the place of God's deliverance in the exodus, as well as a place of testing and failure for the nation. For Moses, the

---

21. Rikki E. Watts, *Isaiah's New Exodus in Mark* (Grand Rapids: Baker, 2000), 89. Cf. Joel Marcus, *The Way of the Lord: Christological Exegesis of the Old Testament in the Gospel of Mark* (Louisville: Westminster John Knox, 1992).

22. Some manuscripts include the article (ὁ) with the

participle, "baptizing" (βαπτίζων), making this a substantival participle, "John the Baptist came …," instead of an adverbial one, "John came baptizing." The article is likely a scribal assimilation to the familiar title found elsewhere (cf. Mark 6:14, 25; 8:28).

wilderness was a place of escape, solitude, and his first encounter with God (Exod 3). As noted above, prophetic predictions of a new exodus beginning in the wilderness excited the eschatological hopes and imaginations of the people. Josephus speaks of a number of messianic movements that began in the Judean desert (*J.W.* 2.13.4–5 §§259–263; 6.6.3 §351; cf. Matt 24:26; Acts 21:38). The Qumran community applied this imagery to themselves, and Isa 40:3 was interpreted to justify the establishment of their desert community. The Community Rule reads: "And when these have become a community in Israel … they are to be segregated from within the dwelling of the men of sin to walk to the desert in order to open there His path. As it is written, 'In the desert, prepare the way …'" (1QS 8.12–14).[23]

Scholars have debated the background to John's "baptism of repentance." Some point to ceremonial washings like those practiced at Qumran. Others suggest Jewish proselyte baptism, where a Gentile would undergo immersion as part of conversion to Judaism.[24] This latter would be particularly significant here, since it would mean John was treating the people of Israel as Gentiles and calling them to become once again members of the eschatological people of God (cf. Matt 3:9; Luke 3:8, where John questions the value of the religious leaders' Abrahamic ancestry).

Yet neither ceremonial washings nor proselyte immersion fits John's baptism exactly. Ceremonial washings were repeated regularly, whereas John's baptism appears to be a onetime act. The origin of

Jewish proselyte baptism is also debated, and we cannot be sure it was practiced in the first century. Furthermore, proselytes immersed themselves, while here the people were baptized by John (ὑπ' αὐτοῦ, v. 5). It seems best to conclude that John's baptism was a new practice that he initiated (no doubt drawing from Jewish precedents) and that its goal was to call the people of God to repentance and preparation for the eschatological coming of God.

The phrase "baptism of repentance" (βάπτισμα μετανοίας) is not easy to classify using traditional genitive categories.[25] It apparently means a baptism that symbolizes and so publicly announces the act of repentance. "Repentance" (μετάνοια) can mean to change one's mind, attitude, and/or actions. Behind John's use is probably the Hebrew *šûb* ("turn back, return"), which in the OT often carries the sense of returning to God, reorienting one's life in submission him (cf. Isa 55:7; Jer 18:11; Zech 1:4).[26] The result (εἰς, "for") of authentic repentance before God is his forgiveness of sins.

1:5 All the Judean countryside and all Jerusalem were going out to him. They were being baptized by him in the Jordan River, confessing their sins (καὶ ἐξεπορεύετο πρὸς αὐτὸν πᾶσα ἡ Ἰουδαία χώρα καὶ οἱ Ἱεροσολυμῖται πάντες, καὶ ἐβαπτίζοντο ὑπ' αὐτοῦ ἐν τῷ Ἰορδάνῃ ποταμῷ ἐξομολογούμενοι τὰς ἁμαρτίας αὐτῶν). The introductory "and" (καί; omitted in the translation) is common in Mark and is characteristic of a Semitic style of writing (imitating Heb. *waw*). In sentences like this it func-

---

23. Florentino García Martínez and Eibert J. C. Tigchelaar, *The Dead Sea Scrolls: Study Edition* (2 vols.; Grand Rapids: Eerdmans, 1997, 1998), 1:89.

24. See J. P. Meier, *A Marginal Jew: Rethinking the Historical Jesus* (3 vols.; ABRL; New York/London: Doubleday), 2:49–56, for further discussion.

25. Some might classify "of repentance" (μετανοίας) as a subjective genitive or a genitive of production (see Wallace, *Greek Grammar,* 104–6, 113–15). Yet repentance does not ac-

tually accomplish or produce the baptism. It is rather symbolized or represented by it. Genitives can describe an enormous variety of relationships between two nouns and between verbs and nouns. Though prescriptive grammarians try to simplify and limit these categories, the true number of genitive relationships is almost boundless. Even Wallace's thirty-six categories (*Greek Grammar,* 72) do not exhaust the genitive's potential.

26. Guelich, *Mark 1:1–8:26,* 18.

tions more like punctuation (a comma, period, or semicolon) than a conjunction. Repeatedly translating καί as "and" creates awkward and unnatural English style, so our translation will often replace it with punctuation. Mark uses hyperbole when he says "everyone" (πάντες) in Jerusalem and the Judean countryside went out to see John. The point is that John was creating quite a stir, as we would say, "Everyone is going to hear him!"

John's ministry is mentioned by the Jewish historian Josephus, the only extrabiblical reference to the Baptist (see comments on 6:14 – 29). Josephus notes that John's baptismal washing was "used not to gain pardon for whatever sins they committed, but as a purification of the body, implying that the soul was already thoroughly cleansed by righteous conduct" (*Ant.* 18.5.2 §§116 – 117).[27] This is similar to the portrait of John in the Gospels, where he baptizes as an outward sign of inward repentance. Josephus does not mention the more apocalyptic aspects of John's preaching or any connection to Jesus, but this is not surprising considering Josephus's general antipathy toward messianic movements.

1:6 John was wearing camel's hair and a leather belt around his waist and eating locusts and wild honey (καὶ ἦν ὁ Ἰωάννης ἐνδεδυμένος τρίχας καμήλου καὶ ζώνην δερματίνην περὶ τὴν ὀσφὺν αὐτοῦ καὶ ἐσθίων ἀκρίδας καὶ μέλι ἄγριον). John's clothing and diet portray him as an ascetic and a prophet (cf. Zech 13:4), living a rough outdoor existence without the niceties of city or palace life. The description is reminiscent of Elijah, who is described in 2 Kgs 1:8 as wearing "a garment of hair" (sometimes translated, "a hairy man") with "a leather belt around his waist." As noted above (v. 2), this link to Elijah is significant since the "messenger" of Mal 3:1 is identified in Mal 4:6 as the eschatological Elijah, whom Jesus will identify with John in Mark 9:13.

John's diet of locusts and honey sounds strange to us, but it is consistent in Israel with someone living off the land.[28] Josephus describes the ascetic Bannus as one who "used no other clothing than grew upon trees, and had no other food than what grew of its own accord" (*Life* 2 §11).[29] Locusts are listed in Lev 11:20 – 23 among clean foods that the Israelites could eat. The Dead Sea Scrolls even provide directions on how they must be prepared: "All species of locust must be put in fire or water while they are alive, because that befits their nature" (CD 12:14 – 15).

1:7 He was preaching this message: "The one more powerful than I comes after me; I am not worthy to stoop down and loosen the strap of his sandals." (καὶ ἐκήρυσσεν λέγων· ἔρχεται ὁ ἰσχυρότερός μου ὀπίσω μου, οὗ οὐκ εἰμὶ ἱκανὸς κύψας λῦσαι τὸν ἱμάντα τῶν ὑποδημάτων αὐτοῦ). As elsewhere in the gospel tradition, John identifies himself as the forerunner and herald of the Messiah.[30] The "more powerful [one]" (ὁ ἰσχυρότερός) who would follow him is much greater than he is. Removing a person's sandals was a lowly task appropriate only for a slave. The Talmud says that the disciple of a rabbi must do for him everything that a slave would do, except removing his shoes (*b. Ketub.* 96a). John places himself below the level of the Messiah's slave.

---

27. P. Maier, *Josephus: The Essential Works* (Grand Rapids: Kregel, 1994), 271.

28. There is no good lexical or cultural support for the traditional claim that these locusts were in fact carob pods, or locust-beans (BDAG, 39; J. P. Louw and E. A. Nida, *Greek-English Lexicon of the New Testament: Based on Semantic Domains* (New York: United Bible Societies, 1989), 45 – 46.

29. Locusts are distinguished from "flesh" in *m. Ḥul.* 8:1 ("If a man vowed to abstain from flesh, he is permitted the flesh of fish and locusts"), indicating they were acceptable for those who lived ascetic lifestyles, like Bannus and John (cf. Luke 1:15; 5:33; 7:33//Matt 11:18).

30. Matt 3:11 – 12; Luke 3:15 – 18; John 1:24 – 28; 3:23 – 36; cf. Acts 1:5; 10:37; 11:16; 13:24 – 25.

Some scholars have claimed that, historically, John's ministry had little to do with Jesus, but that John was expecting Yahweh himself to come and bring in the day of the Lord. It was the later Christians who transformed the apocalyptic prophet into the forerunner of the Messiah.[31] Evidence for this is John's self-identification as the herald of Isa 40:3 and the messenger of Mal 3:1, both of whom announce the coming of Yahweh himself. Against this proposal are John's own words. It would be a truism for a human prophet to assert that Yahweh was "more powerful" than himself. This, together with the reference to removing someone's sandals, suggests that John was expecting a human successor. John's later doubts about Jesus (Matt 11:2 – 19; Luke 7:18 – 35) would be inexplicable unless he already had some messianic expectations concerning him. The historicity of this latter episode seems assured, since it is unlikely the church would have invented a story in which John the Baptist expressed doubts about Jesus' identity.

1:8 I baptize you with water, but he will baptize you with the Holy Spirit (ἐγὼ ἐβάπτισα ὑμᾶς ὕδατι, αὐτὸς δὲ βαπτίσει ὑμᾶς ἐν πνεύματι ἁγίῳ). John contrasts his water baptism with the Spirit-baptism that the Messiah will accomplish. The pronoun "he" (αὐτός) is emphatic: "but *he* will baptize…." The preposition "in" (ἐν) could mean "in," "with," or "by means of." For Mark and his readers, this baptism would likely be interpreted in light of the eschatological outpouring of the Spirit on the day of Pentecost (Acts 2) and the subsequent manifestations of the Spirit in the life of the church.

But what about John's original hearers? While a "baptism" by the Spirit is not explicitly referred to in the OT, prophetic references to the eschatological outpouring of the Spirit abound (Isa 44:3; Ezek 36:26 – 27; Joel 2:28; cf. Jer 31:33 – 34). John's words would likely have been understood in this context, with "baptism" indicating a powerful eschatological deluge by the Spirit of God, which would purify the righteous and purge the wicked.

Both Matthew and Luke add "and [with] fire" to their baptism with the Holy Spirit (Matt 3:11; Luke 3:16). While this could refer to two separate baptisms, one for the righteous and one for the wicked, more likely it is synonymous with Mark's Spirit-baptism, referring to a single eschatological outpouring of the Spirit. Isaiah 4:4 speaks of the day when the Lord "will cleanse the bloodstains from Jerusalem by a spirit [or 'the Spirit'?] of judgment and a spirit ['the Spirit'] of fire."

Theology in Application

Mark's introduction lays the theological foundation for all that follows, identifying Jesus as the fulfillment of OT expectations and the center of God's redemptive purposes.

A New Beginning

Mark begins his narrative by announcing "the *beginning* of the gospel." The phrase not only echoes Gen 1:1 — the beginning of God's creative work (cf. John

---

31. For example, Boring, *Mark*, 42, writes, "Early on, the young Christian movement co-opted John into their understanding of salvation history as the one who prepares the way for the Messiah, namely Jesus."

1:1) — but signals two important things. First, God is initiating something new here. This is not just one more page in redemptive history, but the beginning of the long-awaited eschatological salvation. The "good news" promised by the prophets (Isa 52:7) is now coming to fulfillment in the life, death, and resurrection of Jesus the Messiah.

Second, the "beginning" of a narrative implies a middle and an end. There is an ongoing aspect to this story. The proclamation of good news that began with the appearance of John the Baptist and the coming of Jesus is continuing in Mark's community as he and his readers take this message of salvation to the ends of the earth. This good news also continues today, as we recognize that Mark's story is our story, identifying ourselves with the eschatological people of God.

Jesus the Messiah, the Content of the Good News

Mark leaves no doubt about the subject of his story. The gospel is about *Jesus the Messiah* and his role in God's redemptive plan. Jesus will assume center stage throughout. As the Messiah, Jesus is identified as God's vice-regent and agent of salvation. Furthermore, by taking OT passages that speak of the coming of Yahweh himself (Isa 40:3; Mal 3:1) and applying them to Jesus, the narrator confirms that Jesus represents God's presence on earth and fulfills his purpose. An implicit divine Christology runs throughout this gospel.

The centrality of Jesus in Mark's narrative is important for how we read and apply the gospel. This story is not first and foremost about the disciples (who mostly fail), or Israel's response to the gospel, or the defeat of Satan and his demons. It is about God's purposes through Jesus the Messiah. There is a tendency while reading biblical narratives to seek in every story moral lessons that can be immediately applied to our lives. For example, we might read Mark 1:16 – 20 and conclude that God is calling us to leave everything and follow Jesus, just as the disciples did. While such an application may be a legitimate one (see discussion on that passage), this episode is not primarily about the disciples' response or our own. It is about Jesus' authoritative presence, which results in immediate obedience to his call. The good news is about *Jesus the Messiah and God, who sent him.*

A Messenger Pointing to the Greater One

This focus on the centrality of Jesus brings up a third theological point: the role of John the Baptist. As the messenger preparing the way, John denies he is the Messiah and points to the "more powerful [one]" who is coming after him. John acts as a mirror, deflecting all the attention from himself and directing it to Jesus. His status in comparison to Jesus is lower even than the lowest slave. He is not worthy to do the most menial task for the Messiah. John's water baptism was merely an outward symbol of a person's repentance and confession of sins. Jesus' "Spirit-baptism" would accomplish true spiritual cleansing and an internal transformation, resulting in a right relationship with God.

The application for us is evident. Our lives and ministries should be focused not on our own promotion or self-importance, but on Jesus. We are his humble servants whose mission in life is to accomplish his will and follow his purpose.

CHAPTER 2

Mark 1:9 – 13

Literary Context

Unlike Matthew and Luke, who provide detailed accounts of Jesus' birth (Matt 1 – 2; Luke 1 – 2), Mark begins with Jesus' public ministry. Mark seems less interested than Matthew and Luke in establishing Jesus' messianic credentials as the divinely appointed descendant of David who was conceived by the Holy Spirit, and more intent on showing his exceptional power and authority as the Messiah and Son of God. Jesus suddenly appears on the scene as the "one more powerful" about whom John the Baptist has been preaching (1:7 – 8). While Matthew and Luke narrate three temptations by Satan (Matt 4:1 – 11; Luke 4:1 – 13), Mark gives a brief summary of the event. Most likely, he did not have available to him the source (Q?) for the more detailed account, or his omission may be related to his fast-paced, staccato style in this opening section.

I. Prologue: Introduction of the Messiah (1:1 – 13)
   A. John the Baptist Prepares the Way (1:1 – 8)
➡   **B. The Baptism and Temptation of Jesus (1:9 – 13)**
II. The Authority of the Messiah (1:14 – 8:21)

Main Idea

Mark's account of Jesus' baptism by John the Baptist and his temptation by Satan represents Jesus' preparation for ministry as Messiah and Son of God. At the baptism the Father affirms that Jesus is his dearly loved Son, who will fulfill the role of Davidic Son of God and Isaianic Servant of the Lord. Jesus' temptation or "testing" by Satan in the wilderness confirms that Jesus will succeed where Israel in the wilderness failed.

Translation

Mark 1:9 – 13

9a	setting (temporal)	In those days
b	Character entrance	**Jesus came from Nazareth in Galilee** and
c	action	**was baptized by John in the Jordan.**
10a	action/setting	As he was coming up out of the water,
b	Action/Theophany	**he saw the heavens splitting open** and
c	Action/Character entrance	**the Spirit descending like a dove upon him.**
11a	Theophany/character entrance	And **a voice came from heaven, saying,**
b	assertion/OT allusion	*"You are my beloved Son;* [Ps 2:7; Gen 22:2]
c	assertion/OT allusion	*I am pleased with you."* [Isa 42:1]
12	Action/setting (spatial)	And **immediately the Spirit compelled him into the wilderness.**
13a	Setting (spatial temporal)	And **he was in the wilderness forty days**
b	action	**being tested by Satan.**
c	Setting (circumstance)	**He was with the wild animals,**
d	Action	and **the angels were serving him.**

Structure

The protagonist enters the scene and prepares for the spiritual battle ahead. Two episodes comprise his preparation, the first about empowerment and divine affirmation and the second about testing and approval. For Mark, the greater emphasis is not on the baptism by John (which simply provides the context), but on the descent of the Spirit, which empowers Jesus for ministry, and the voice from heaven, which confirms his identity.

Exegetical Outline

→ **1. Jesus' Baptism by John and Affirmation by the Father (1:9 – 11)**

    a. Setting: Jesus comes from Galilee to the Jordan River (1:9a)

    b. The baptism (1:9b – 10a)

    c. The descent of the Spirit (1:10b)

    d. The divine announcement (1:11)

       i. The voice from heaven (1:11a)

       ii. Allusion to Psalm 2:7 (and Gen 22:2?) (1:11b)

       iii. Allusion to Isaiah 42:1 (1:11c)

2. Temptation/Testing in the Wilderness (1:12–13)

    a. The Spirit's compulsion (1:12)

    b. Tempted/tested by Satan for forty days (1:13a-b)

    c. Present with the wild animals; attended by angels (1:13c-d)

Explanation of the Text

1:9 In those days Jesus came from Nazareth in Galilee and was baptized by John in the Jordan (Καὶ ἐγένετο ἐν ἐκείναις ταῖς ἡμέραις ἦλθεν Ἰησοῦς ἀπὸ Ναζαρὲτ τῆς Γαλιλαίας καὶ ἐβαπτίσθη εἰς τὸν Ἰορδάνην ὑπὸ Ἰωάννου). Mark's introductory phrase (lit., "and it happened in those days") is a Semitic expression that means "at that time" (cf. Judg 19:1). By echoing the language of the OT, Mark recalls the story's OT background and reinforces his fulfillment theme (Mark 1:2).

Mark shows little interest in traditional biographical details, telling us nothing about Jesus' background or family except that he "came from Nazareth in Galilee." Nazareth was a small village in southwest Galilee. The village is not mentioned in the OT, the Talmud, or Josephus (see Nathanael's mocking disdain in John 1:46). Its obscurity contributes both to the lowliness of Jesus' origins and the mystery that pervades his identity.

Both Matthew and Luke record that, though he grew up in Nazareth, Jesus was born in Bethlehem in Judea (Matt 2:1, 23; Luke 2:4, 39). Herod the Great died in 4 BC, so Jesus must have been born shortly before this, around 6–4 BC. Luke identifies Jesus' age at the beginning of his public ministry as "about thirty years old" (Luke 3:23). These approximations result in uncertainties concerning the dates and length of Jesus' ministry. Luke says that John's ministry began in the fifteenth year of Tiberius Caesar (Luke 3:1), which could be either c. AD 27 or 30, depending on whether Luke is referring to Tiberius's coregency with Caesar Augustus (AD 11–12) or his sole reign after his father's

death (AD 14). The Synoptic Gospels mention only one Passover during Jesus' ministry, but John refers to three (John 2:13; 6:4; 11:55) and possibly four (5:1). This suggests a ministry of approximately three and a half years, perhaps either AD 27–30 or AD 30–33. The former seems slightly more likely in light of John 2:20, where we learn that Herod's temple construction had been going on for forty-six years (approx. 20 BC to AD 27).

Mark shows little interest in such details, however. He moves directly to Jesus' baptism and temptation, two key events that marked the beginning of his public ministry. Jesus will reveal his messianic credentials through his words and actions rather than through angelic visitations, miraculous conceptions, or Davidic ancestry (contrast Matt 1–2; Luke 1–3).

1:10 As he was coming up out of the water, he saw the heavens splitting open and the Spirit descending like a dove upon him (καὶ εὐθὺς ἀναβαίνων ἐκ τοῦ ὕδατος εἶδεν σχιζομένους τοὺς οὐρανοὺς καὶ τὸ πνεῦμα ὡς περιστερὰν καταβαῖνον εἰς αὐτόν). Mark begins with his characteristic "and immediately" (καὶ εὐθύς), left untranslated because it represents awkward English style and because the temporal rendering of the participle ("as he was coming") captures the sense of immediacy. As noted in the introduction, Mark uses "immediately" (εὐθύς) forty-two times in his gospel, twenty-five in the introductory phrase to a sentence, "and immediately" (καὶ εὐθύς). The adverb sometimes means "immediately" or "just then" (e.g., 1:10, 18, 20, 42; 14:43), but often serves as a simple connective, indicating the next thing that happened (1:12, 21, 29, 30). It can also mean "suddenly" (1:23 NLT). The overall effect is to propel Mark's narrative forward, giving it an urgent and on-the-spot feel.

The description of Jesus "coming up" out of the water suggests that John's baptism entailed full immersion of the recipient. Mark's forceful language of the "tearing" or "ripping open" (σχίζω) of the heavens indicates a theophany, or revelation of God.[1] Isaiah 64:1 reads, "Oh, that you would rend the heavens and come down, that the mountains would tremble before you!"[2] There may also be an inclusio ("bookends") between this passage and the centurion's cry at the climax of the Gospel (15:38–39), where the temple curtain is torn (σχίζω) in two and the centurion cries out, "Truly this man was the Son of God!" Acclamations of Jesus' divine sonship would therefore frame the Gospel narrative. If this inclusio is intentional, Mark is indicating that access to the Father is now available through Jesus the Son.

The Spirit's descent "like a dove" may mean that the Spirit looked like a dove, or that it descended in a birdlike manner. Whether there is any symbolism related to the dove has been a matter of much debate. Davies and Allison list sixteen possible interpretations![3] The most commonly cited are to the Spirit's hovering over the waters at creation (Gen 1:2) or Noah's dove as representing God's gracious deliverance after the flood (8:8–12).[4] We are on

more certain ground when considering the role of the Spirit. Isaiah predicted of the coming Davidic Messiah:

> The Spirit of the LORD will rest on him —
>   the Spirit of wisdom and of understanding,
>   the Spirit of counsel and of might,
>   the Spirit of the knowledge and fear of the
> LORD —
> and he will delight in the fear of the LORD.
> He will not judge by what he sees with his eyes,
>   or decide by what he hears with his ears;
> but with righteousness he will judge the needy,
>   with justice he will give decisions for the poor
>   of the earth. (Isa 11:2–4)

The Messiah is presented as one who will live in total dependence on God through the Spirit. Luke's gospel directly links the descent of the Spirit to Jesus' "anointing" by the Spirit (4:18; citing Isa 61:1–2; cf. Luke 3:22; 4:1, 14) and therefore to his identity as the Messiah (i.e., "Anointed One"). While Mark does not make this connection explicit, the descent of the Spirit clearly represents an affirmation of Jesus' identity and his empowerment for messianic service.

1:11 And a voice came from heaven, saying, "You are my beloved Son; I am pleased with you." (καὶ φωνὴ ἐγένετο ἐκ τῶν οὐρανῶν· σὺ εἶ ὁ υἱός μου ὁ ἀγαπητός, ἐν σοὶ εὐδόκησα). The voice from heaven[5] (clearly God's) contains two, possibly three, OT allusions.

1. Taylor, *Mark*, 160, writes, "The rending of the heavens is a common feature of apocalyptic thought, the underlying idea being that of a fixed separation of heaven from earth only to be broken in special circumstances." Cf. *2 Bar.* 22:1; *T. Levi* 2:6; 5:1; 18:6; *T. Jud.* 24:2; John 1:51; Acts 7:56; Rev 4:1; 11:19; 19:11.

2. Cf. *T. Levi* 18:6–7: "The heavens will be opened and from the temple of glory sanctification will come upon him, with a fatherly voice.... And the spirit of understanding and sanctification shall rest upon him" (alluding to Isa 11:2; *OTP*, 1:795).

3. W. D. Davies and D. C. Allison, *A Criticial and Exegetical Commentary on the Gospel according to Matther* (3 vols.; ICC;

Edinburgh: T&T Clark, 1988, 1991, 1997), 1:331–34.

4. Pesch, *Markusevangelium*, 1:91–92, thinks, perhaps rightly, that no symbolism is attached, but that a descent from heaven would naturally be explained as birdlike (what else descends from the sky?) and that the positive OT associations related to doves explain this choice of bird.

5. As in v. 10, "heaven" is plural in the Greek (τῶν οὐρανῶν), after the model of the Hebrew plural *šāmayim*. The sense remains the same as the singular — the presence of God. The Greek and Hebrew terms can mean various things: the skies/atmosphere, the planets and stars (outer space), or the presence of God.

1. "You are my Son" comes from Ps 2:7, an en-thronement psalm of the Davidic dynasty. In the psalm the kings of the earth conspire against Yahweh and against "his anointed" (2:2 – 3). Yet he laughs at their idle threats and responds that *he* has installed his king on Mount Zion (2:4 – 6) and has decreed his divine sonship: "You are my son; today I have become your father" (2:7).

2. The adjective "beloved" (ὁ ἀγαπητός) — idi-omatically translated in the NIV as "whom I love" — may be an allusion to Gen 22:2, where Abraham is commanded to offer Isaac, "your only son, whom you love," as a sacrifice.[6] The LXX renders Gen 22:2, "Take your beloved son, whom you love" (Λαβὲ τὸν υἱόν σου τὸν ἀγαπητόν, ὃν ἠγάπησας). This would suggest a Jesus/Isaac typology, where Abraham's willing-ness to sacrifice his beloved son is analogous to God's offering of his only Son.

3. The third phrase, "I am well pleased with you,"[7] echoes Isa 42:1, where the Spirit-endowed Ser-vant of the Lord is identified as God's chosen one. In the larger context of Isaiah's Servant Songs, this individual will give himself as an atoning sacrifice for the sins of his people (Isa 52:12 – 53:12).

If all three allusions are present, this remarkably concise acclamation presents Jesus as the Davidic Messiah and unique Son of God, who will offer himself as a sacrifice for sins.

How public this event was is unclear. Mark says that "he [Jesus] saw the heavens splitting open" (v. 10). In the Fourth Gospel, the Baptist, too, sees the descent of the Spirit (John 1:32 – 33). Although the reader of Mark's gospel is aware of

Jesus' identity (1:1), it is revealed only gradually to the characters in the drama. It is announced by the Father in 1:11 (cf. 9:7) and acknowledged by demons repeatedly (1:24, 34; 5:7). The first human recognition comes with Peter's confession in 8:29. The climax will come with the centurion's accla-mation in 15:38 – 39. This is significant for Mark's agenda since the full revelation of Jesus' identity as the Son of God comes in the context of suffering and sacrifice.

1:12 And immediately the Spirit compelled him into the wilderness (Καὶ εὐθὺς τὸ πνεῦμα αὐτὸν ἐκβάλλει εἰς τὴν ἔρημον). Mark connects Jesus' temptation directly to the baptism with his char-acteristic "and immediately" (καὶ εὐθύς; see v. 10). Mark's language that the Spirit "compelled" or even "drove" (ἐκβάλλω; a verb commonly used for cast-ing out demons) Jesus into the wilderness is stron-ger than the descriptions of Matthew or Luke, who both speak of the Spirit "leading" Jesus.[8] Mark does not mean the Spirit acted against Jesus' will, but that the Spirit was now in control of Jesus' messi-anic mission, impelling him forward in this urgent task.

1:13 And he was in the wilderness forty days being tested by Satan. He was with the wild ani-mals, and the angels were serving him (καὶ ἦν ἐν τῇ ἐρήμῳ τεσσεράκοντα ἡμέρας πειραζόμενος ὑπὸ τοῦ σατανᾶ, καὶ ἦν μετὰ τῶν θηρίων, καὶ οἱ ἄγγελοι διηκόνουν αὐτῷ). This is not merely "temptation," but a period of testing (πειράζω can mean either), where Jesus' messianic credentials are confirmed. While Matthew and Luke narrate three distinct

---

6. The adjective is in the second attributive position, which provides emphasis, almost in the sense of a second substantive in apposition: "my son, the beloved one." See Wallace, *Greek Grammar*, 306 – 7.

7. The aorist (εὐδόκησα) is usually translated as a present tense here, perhaps as a gnomic aorist (Wallace, *Greek Gram-mar*, 562). Marcus, *Mark 1 – 8*, 163, however, considers it to be

a true past tense (following the LXX of Isa 42:1, which uses an aorist), with the baptismal voice confirming God's past choice of the Messiah before creation (idem, *Way of the Lord*, 72 – 75).

8. Matthew uses ἀνάγω, while Luke uses ἄγω, suggesting that they have independently softened Mark's apparently harsh language.

temptations (Matt 4:1 – 11; Luke 4:1 – 13; "Q" material), Mark simply states that the temptation happened. Nor does Mark explicitly say that Jesus passed these tests, though this is evident from the successful ministry that follows, especially his authority over demons (1:26, 34). Mark's point is to emphasize that the struggle Jesus is engaged in is a spiritual one. Jesus' initial conflicts with Satan (1:12) and demons lay the framework for all that follows. Jesus is not here to conquer the Roman legions, but to take on the powers of evil, sin, and death.

The wilderness was a place of testing for Israel, and Jesus' forty days are analogous to Israel's forty years of wandering (Num 14:34).[9] Although Israel repeatedly failed through disobedience and unbelief (Ps 95:8 – 11), Jesus succeeds and receives God's approval.

"Satan" or "the Adversary" (ὁ σατανᾶς) comes from a Hebrew term meaning "adversary" or "accuser" (sāṭān). The Adversary appears in the OT as the tester or accuser of God's people (1 Chr 21:1; Job 1 – 2; Zech 3:1 – 2). While Mark always uses "Satan" (σατανᾶς; 1:13; 3:23, 26; 4:15; 8:33), elsewhere in the NT the Adversary is referred to as "Satan" (σατανᾶς, 36x) and as the "devil" (διάβολος,

34x). The latter is the Septuagint's rendering of the Hebrew sāṭān. In the NT Satan/the devil appears as a personal adversary, opposing God's purpose and his people.[10]

Only Mark among the Synoptics has the puzzling reference to Jesus being "with the wild animals" (μετὰ τῶν θηρίων). Some see here a positive allusion to the garden of Eden, where humans and animals communed together. Jesus' temptation would be analogous to that of Adam and Eve. He succeeds where they failed. While this is possible, more likely the animals indicate the severity and danger of the wilderness.[11] This would fit better the following statement about angelic assistance. The imperfect "were serving" (διηκόνουν, from διακονέω) commonly means table service, but it can refer to service of any kind. Since Ps 91:11 – 12 plays a role in the temptation accounts of Matthew (Matt 4:6) and Luke (Luke 4:10), it is not unlikely that Mark has this same psalm in view: "For he will command his angels concerning you to guard you in all your ways.... You will tread on the lion and the cobra.... I will protect him, for he acknowledges my name" (Ps 91:11 – 14).[12] Through his angels God provides for and protects his Anointed One.

Theology in Application

The Affirmation and Empowerment of the Messiah

The baptismal voice from heaven and Jesus' testing in the wilderness prepare the Messiah for the task on which he is about to embark. The baptism narrative is about

9. Forty days is a common period of time in the OT: forty days of rain during the flood (Gen 7:4), Moses twice on the mountain for forty days (Exod 24:18; 34:28), the spies in the Promised Land for forty days (Num 13:25), Goliath challenging Israel for forty days (1 Sam 17:16), and Elijah's forty-day journey to Mount Horeb (1 Kgs 19:8, 15).

10. Matt 4:1, 10; 13:39; John 8:44; 2 Cor 12:7; Eph 4:27; 1 Pet 5:8; Rev 12:9; 20:2.

11. Wild beasts are linked with Satan in *T. Iss.* 7:7 and *T.*

Naph. 8:4. If Mark is writing to a Roman audience during the Neronian persecution (see Introduction), when Christians were sometimes torn apart by wild animals, the reference may be meant to reassure them that Jesus has power even over these animals. This suggestion was made to me by Verlyn Verbrugge.

12. Ben Witherington III, *The Gospel of Mark: A Socio-Rhetorical Commentary* (Grand Rapids: Eerdmans, 2001), 76; S. Garrett, *The Temptations of Jesus in Mark's Gospel* (Grand Rapids: Eerdmans, 1988), 57.

empowerment and affirmation. Isaiah's portrait of eschatological salvation closely associates the coming Davidic Messiah (Isa 11:1 – 9) with the Suffering Servant (Isa 42:1; cf. Matt 12:18 – 21) and the prophetic herald of eschatological liberation (Isa 61:1 – 2; cf. Matt 11:5 par.; Luke 4:18 – 19; 7:22).[13] All three accomplish their mission in the Spirit's power. Having identified Jesus' mission in the context of Isaiah's prophecies (Mark 1:1 – 3), Mark now narrates the empowerment of the Spirit to accomplish this task. The heavens are torn open in a powerful theophany, and the Spirit descends like a dove. From this point on, everything Jesus will say and do is in the power of the Spirit (cf. John 5:30). Jesus' identity and mission are confirmed by the Father's voice of approval from heaven. God's words combine OT allusions to the Davidic Messiah (Ps 2:7) and Isaiah's Servant of the Lord (Isa 40:3), which suggests that the Messiah's role will involve suffering and sacrifice.

The baptism of Jesus by John was a problem for some in the early church, since one would expect the greater to baptize the lesser. Indeed, this episode has been used by some to argue that Jesus began as a disciple of John before launching his own ministry. Matthew's account reflects this tension as John tries to deter Jesus: "I need to be baptized by you, and do you come to me?" (Matt 3:14). Jesus responds that it is proper "to fulfill all righteousness" (3:15), which probably means to fulfill prophecy.[14] Mark shows no such unease with Jesus' baptism, having already affirmed his superiority to John as the "more powerful [one]" — the Messiah. For Mark, the baptism is merely the context in which the descent of the Spirit and the divine affirmation occur.

The Spirit's Empowering and Guiding Role

The Spirit's role in the life of Jesus provides an important model for believers. If Jesus, the Messiah and Son of God, did nothing apart from the power of the Spirit, how can we function successfully apart from the Spirit's guidance? In the Upper Room Discourse in John's gospel, Jesus tells his disciples that though he is leaving, they will do even greater works than he has done because of the Spirit he will give them (John 14:12). The Spirit will teach them, guide them into truth, remind them of what he taught them, and comfort them (14:16 – 20, 26 – 27; 15:26 – 27; 16:5 – 16). The same Spirit who filled and empowered Jesus at his baptism was poured out on the first disciples by the exalted Messiah on the day of Pentecost (Acts 2:1 – 4, 17, 33, 38). This same Spirit baptizes and empowers believers today (1 Cor 12:13). Christians can be successful only if they "abide" in Christ through the presence and power of the Holy Spirit (John 15:1 – 8).

13. See Mark L. Strauss, *The Davidic Messiah in Luke-Acts: The Promise and Its Fulfillment in Lukan Christology* (JSNTSup 110; Sheffield: Sheffield Academic, 1995), 239 – 43.

14. Davies and Allison, *Matthew*, 1:326 – 27.

Jesus' Testing and Ours

The testing/temptation of Jesus also has application for us. God's people often endure weakness, trials, and persecution that test their faith. Job was tested by Satan with great suffering, but he remained faithful to God (Job 1:20–22; 2:10). Peter says that such trials come "so that the proven genuineness of your faith … may result in praise, glory and honor when Jesus Christ is revealed" (1 Pet 1:7; cf. Heb 12:6–11; Jas 1:2–4). In the same way, at the beginning of his ministry, the Messiah endured testing/temptation at the hands of Satan. While in Matthew and Luke, three specific temptations challenge Jesus to act independently of the Father's will, Mark's brief summary sets the stage for the spiritual struggle that will follow.

While comparisons can be made between the testing of Jesus and our own trials,[15] care must be taken not to misread Mark's narrative. Mark's purpose in this passage is not primarily exemplary — to compare Jesus' temptation to our own or even to prepare us for testing — but christological, namely, to confirm that Jesus is indeed the Spirit-empowered Messiah who will defeat Satan and bring salvation to the people of God.

---

15. Analogies are sometimes drawn between the three temptations recorded in Matthew and Luke and the threefold "lust of the flesh," "lust of the eyes," and "pride of life" in 1 John 2:16 as well as Eve's temptation in the garden. Genesis 3:6 says the forbidden fruit was (1) "good for food," (2) "pleasing to the eye," and (3) "desirable for gaining wisdom."

Mark 1:14 – 20

Literary Context

In Mark's prologue he introduced John the Baptist as the "beginning of the good news" and described Jesus' baptism and testing in the wilderness as preparation for his mission. Now he moves on to the beginning of Jesus' public ministry in Galilee (1:14 – 3:6). The main theme of this section is *the authority of Jesus.* He demonstrates his authority by proclaiming the kingdom (1:14 – 15), calling disciples (1:16 – 20), casting out demons (1:21 – 28), healing the sick (1:29 – 34, 40 – 45; 2:8 – 12), and forgiving sins (2:5). This authority in turn provokes opposition from the religious leaders. They challenge his authority and accuse him of blasphemy (2:7), associating with sinners (2:16), and violating the Sabbath (2:24; 3:2). The section climaxes with a plot against Jesus' life (3:6).

  I. Prologue: Introduction of the Messiah (1:1 – 13)

→ **II. The Authority of the Messiah (1:14 – 8:21)**

     A. The Kingdom Authority of the Messiah (1:14 – 3:6)

        1. Jesus Proclaims the Kingdom and Calls Disciples (1:14 – 20)

        2. Authority in Teaching, Healing, and Exorcism (1:21 – 45)

Main Idea

Mark identifies Jesus' central message as the nearness of the kingdom of God and the need to respond with repentance and faith in the good news of God's message of salvation. At the beginning of his kingdom ministry, Jesus calls two pairs of fishermen brothers to follow him in discipleship and to learn to fish for people, which means to call others to obedience to God and his kingdom purposes.

Translation

Mark 1:14 – 20

Preaching the Kingdom of God
| | | |
14a | setting (temporal) | After John was arrested,
b | Action/Setting (spatial) | **Jesus went into Galilee**
c | Action/teaching | preaching God's good news.

15a | Teaching | **He was saying,**
b | assertion | *"The time is fulfilled,*
c | assertion | *the kingdom of God is close at hand;*
d | exhortation | *repent and believe in the good news."*

Calling Disciples
16a | setting (spatial) | As he walked beside the Sea of Galilee,
b | Action | **he saw Simon and   Andrew,**
c | | Simon's brother,
d | | casting a net into the sea,
e | explanation of 16d | because they were fishermen.

17a | Action | And **Jesus said to them,**
b | command/promise | *"Come, follow me, and I will teach you to fish for people."*

18a | manner of 18b | And   leaving their nets,
b | Response to 17 | **they immediately followed him.**

19a | setting (spatial) | And   going a little further,
b | Action | **he saw James the son of Zebedee and**
c | | **John his brother**
d | setting (spatial/ circumstantial) | in their boat preparing their nets.

20a | Action | **Immediately he called them;**

b | Response to 20a | leaving their father Zebedee in the boat with the hired men, **they followed him.**

Structure

This passage is comprised of a summary statement of the beginning of Jesus' kingdom ministry and message (vv. 14 – 15), followed by two call narratives (vv. 16 – 18 and 19 – 20). The three pieces follow a similar pattern, with a statement of setting (vv. 14, 16, 19), an authoritative statement or command by Jesus (v. 15b-c), and a response (vv. 18, 20b) or intended response (v. 15d: "repent and believe") by the hearers. This lays the foundation for the central theme of the first part of Mark's gospel: the *authority of Jesus* as announcer and inaugurator of the kingdom of God.

Exegetical Outline

➡ **1. The Context (1:14)**

    a. Temporal context: The arrest of John the Baptist (1:14a)

    b. Geographical context: The return to Galilee (1:14b)

  2. Jesus' Message (1:15)

    a. The nearness of the kingdom (1:15a-c)

    b. The need for repentance and faith (1:15d)

  3. The Call of the First Disciples (1:16 – 20)

    a. The call of Simon and Andrew (1:16 – 18)

      i. The setting (1:16)

      ii. The authoritative call to become fishers of people (1:17)

      iii. The immediate response (1:18)

    b. The call of James and John (1:19 – 20)

      i. The setting (1:19)

      ii. The authoritative call (1:20a)

      iii. The immediate response (1:20b)

Explanation of the Text

1:14 After John was arrested, Jesus went into Galilee preaching God's good news (Μετὰ δὲ τὸ παραδοθῆναι τὸν Ἰωάννην ἦλθεν ὁ Ἰησοῦς εἰς τὴν Γαλιλαίαν κηρύσσων τὸ εὐαγγέλιον τοῦ θεοῦ). Mark's purpose in this introductory summary (vv. 14 – 15) is threefold: (1) to provide a transition from the ministry of John to that of Jesus, (2) to establish Galilee as the setting for Jesus' early ministry, and (3) to summarize the content of Jesus' preaching: the need to repent and believe in the good news of the kingdom of God.

Mark refers in passing to John's arrest; later he will use a narrative flashback to describe John's imprisonment and execution (6:14 – 29). The verb translated "was arrested" (παραδοθῆναι; aorist passive) was often used as a technical term for "handing over into the custody of" (Latin: *trado;* BDAG) and so could be translated "arrested" (NASU) or "put in prison" (NIV; cf. NET). The active voice is used of Judas's betrayal of Jesus in 3:19 and 14:10 and of the future arrest and betrayal of believers during persecution (13:9, 11, 12). When the passive is used with reference to Jesus (9:31; 10:33; 14:21, 41), it is often interpreted by scholars as a divine passive, meaning "God delivered him over" — the emphasis being God's sovereign purpose in these events (see comments on 9:30 – 31).[1] This same divine passive could perhaps be intended here,[2] though it seems more likely that Mark has Herod Antipas in mind as the agent of John's arrest and imprisonment (see 6:17).

Although the Fourth Gospel describes a period of overlap between the ministries of Jesus and John (John 3:22 – 4:2), the Synoptics move John off the scene before Jesus' public ministry begins (cf. Matt 4:12; Luke 3:19 – 20). Their purpose is theological rather than chronological — to emphasize the transition from the old age of promise to the new age of fulfillment. John is the last and greatest of the OT prophets (Matt 11:9 – 11; Luke 7:26 – 28). In Luke's gospel, Jesus explains: "The Law and the Prophets were proclaimed until John. Since that time, the good news of the kingdom of God is being preached" (Luke 16:16). John is also a transitional figure, with one foot in each age. As the forerunner and herald of the Messiah, he passes the prophetic baton across the ages to Jesus. John announces the need to repent in light of the soon coming of escha-

tological judgment. Jesus will proclaim its arrival through his own words and deeds.

The genitive in "God's good news" (τὸ εὐαγγέλιον τοῦ θεοῦ) could be a subjective genitive (good news from God)[3] or an objective genitive (good news about God). As was noted in the comment on 1:1 ("the good news of Jesus Messiah"), the construction may be intentionally ambiguous, since God is both the source and content of the message. The good news from God is the message about God's kingdom (v. 15).

1:15   He was saying, "The time is fulfilled, the kingdom of God is close at hand; repent and believe in the good news" (καὶ λέγων ὅτι πεπλήρωται ὁ καιρὸς καὶ ἤγγικεν ἡ βασιλεία τοῦ θεοῦ· μετανοεῖτε καὶ πιστεύετε ἐν τῷ εὐαγγελίῳ). The "time" (καιρός) here is the eschatological time of salvation (Gal 4:4). The two phrases, "the time is fulfilled" and "the kingdom of God is close at hand" are parallel and coreferential, with both referring to this new age of salvation. The kingdom is shorthand for God's eschatological salvation, which is even now breaking into human history through Jesus' words and actions (see "In Depth: The Kingdom of God in Jesus' Preaching").

IN DEPTH: The Kingdom of God in Jesus' Preaching

There is nearly universal agreement that "the kingdom of God" was central to Jesus' message (cf. 4:11, 26, 30; 9:1, 47; 10:14 – 15, 23 – 25; 12:34; 14:25; 15:43). But what does this phrase mean? Though the exact expression does not appear in the OT, the concept of God's kingship and dominion is abundantly

---

1. Gundry, *Mark*, 63 – 64, argues against the divine passive here and elsewhere in Mark, since whenever an agent of Jesus' "delivering over" is stated, it is Judas (3:19; 10:33; 14:18, 21). Yet in 14:21, Judas is the one "through whom" (δι' οὗ) the Son of Man is betrayed, which suggests that Judas is the intermediary agent, with God being the ultimate one. See Wallace, *Greek Grammar*, 431 – 34, for διά indicating intermediary agency.

2. So Cranfield, *Mark*, 62; Pesch, *Markusevangelium*, 1:101; Guelich, *Mark 1:1 – 8:26*, 42; Marcus, *Mark 1 – 8*, 171; Stein, *Mark*, 71.

3. The subjective genitive is close to a genitive of source here, but the former category is to be preferred since εὐαγγέλιον is a verbal noun.

clear. Psalm 47:7 reads, "For God is the King of all the earth; sing to him a psalm of praise." Psalm 103:19 similarly says, "The LORD has established his throne in heaven, and his kingdom rules over all" (cf. Exod 15:18; Pss 29:10; 97:1; 99:1; Isa 43:15). The greatest emphasis is on the dynamic *reign* of God rather than a static *realm,* though the latter idea is not absent: "the LORD Almighty will reign on Mount Zion and in Jerusalem, and before its elders — with great glory" (Isa 24:23).

Though God reigns supreme over the cosmos, not everyone presently acknowledges his authority, and so sin and rebellion characterize the present age. The kingdom of God is therefore both a *present reality* and a *future hope.* The latter affirms that one day God will destroy (or reconcile) the last opposition and will be acknowledged by all as king. The apocalyptic Judaism of Jesus' day recognized the present reality of God's reign but placed greater emphasis on its consummation, when God would come to deliver his persecuted people, judge the wicked, and establish an eternal kingdom on earth. Note *1 En.* 1:3 – 9:

> The God of the universe, the Holy Great One, will come forth from his dwelling.... Mountains and high places will fall down and be frightened. And high hills shall be made low; and they shall melt like a honeycomb before the flame.... And to all the righteous he will grant peace. He will preserve the elect, and kindness shall be upon them. They shall all belong to God and they shall prosper and be blessed; and the light of God shall shine unto them. Behold, he will arrive with ten million of the holy ones in order to execute judgment upon all. He will destroy the wicked ones and censure all flesh on account of everything that they have done, that which the sinners and the wicked ones committed against him.[4]

Scholars have debated whether Jesus was announcing the presence or the future of the kingdom. Albert Schweitzer, following Johannes Weiss, drew on the apocalyptic expectations of Jesus' day to argue for a "consistent eschatology," claiming that Jesus was an apocalyptic prophet looking forward to the cataclysmic intervention by God in the near future to judge and to save. C. H. Dodd countered with a "realized eschatology," that Jesus was announcing the presence of the kingdom in his own words and deeds.[5] Both views have aspects of the truth, and Jesus' teaching in Mark includes both present and future dimensions. The parable of the growing seed speaks of the gradual growth of the

---

4. Translation from E. Isaac, "1 (Ethiopic Apocalypse of) Enoch," in *OTP,* 1:13 – 14.

5. See especially C. H. Dodd, *The Parables of the Kingdom* (rev. ed.; New York: Charles Scribner's Sons, 1961), 4 – 5. For discussion of this kingdom debate, see Guelich, *Mark 1:1 – 8:26,* 44. Classic summaries can be found in W. G. Kümmel, *Promise and Fulfillment: The Eschatological Message of Jesus* (London: SCM, 1957); G. E. Ladd, *Jesus and the Kingdom* (New York: Harper & Row, 1964); N. Perrin, *The Kingdom of God in the Teaching of Jesus* (Philadelphia: Westminster, 1963); idem, *Jesus and the Language of the Kingdom* (Philadelphia: Fortress, 1976).

kingdom until the day of harvest (4:26 – 29). The parable of the mustard seed similarly describes something tiny growing into something great (4:30 – 32).

In 10:15, Jesus says that "whoever does not receive the kingdom of God like a child will certainly not enter it.""Receiving" the kingdom in the present as a child is a prerequisite to "entering" it in the future. The kingdom will one day come with power for the disciples to see (9:1). At the Last Supper Jesus says he will not drink wine again until he does so in the (future) kingdom of God (14:25). The future coming of the kingdom is similarly implied in Jesus' teaching concerning the Son of Man who will come "with great power and glory … and he will gather his chosen ones" (13:26 – 27; cf. 8:38; 13:33 – 34; 14:62).

In light of this data, the kingdom of God in Mark must be seen as both a present reality and a future hope. It is "already" and "not yet."[6] People "enter" the kingdom by repenting and submitting to the kingdom. Yet Jesus did not simply call people to submit to God's sovereign reign. He called them to submit *in light of the dawn of eschatological salvation.* This is implicit in Jesus' assertion that "the time is fulfilled." Jesus will shortly identify himself as the bridegroom (2:19) — presumably presiding over the messianic banquet (cf. Isa 25:6 – 8) — and the present time as a new garment and new wine, incompatible with the old (2:21 – 22). All of this indicates that everything is changing. The age of promise is giving way to the age of fulfillment, and the age of fulfillment is inextricably linked to the kingdom of God, the submission of all things to the sovereign reign of God. Jesus clearly saw the kingdom as both a present reality and a future hope.

The verb translated "is close at hand" (ἤγγικεν; perfect tense of ἐγγίζω) could mean "has arrived," "has drawn near," or "is near," and is probably intentionally ambiguous.[7] This is because for Mark and his readers, the kingdom is directly related to Jesus himself. The king is present so the kingdom is near. It has drawn near *spatially* in Jesus' person and *temporally* in the actions of God to achieve eschatological salvation.

The appropriate response to this kingdom announcement is to "repent and believe in the good news." Repentance means turning away from sin (see comments on 1:4), and faith means acknowledging dependence on God. These are two sides of the same coin: repudiating a life focused on self and reorienting toward God and his purpose for the world.

1:16 As he walked beside the Sea of Galilee, he saw Simon and Andrew, Simon's brother, casting a net into the sea, because they were fishermen (Καὶ παράγων παρὰ τὴν θάλασσαν τῆς Γαλιλαίας εἶδεν Σίμωνα καὶ Ἀνδρέαν τὸν ἀδελφὸν Σίμωνος ἀμφιβάλλοντας ἐν τῇ θαλάσσῃ· ἦσαν γὰρ ἁλιεῖς).

---

6. See Hooker, *Mark*, 54; Kümmel, *Promise and Fulfillment*, 19 – 25; Stein, *Mark*, 73.

7. Guelich, *Mark 1:1 – 8:26*, 44.

Mark's description of Jesus' kingdom message is now individualized in his call of disciples, two pairs of fishermen brothers. Three of the four — Peter, James, and John — will become core disciples, sometimes called the "inner circle" (cf. 5:37; 9:2; 14:33; with Andrew in 13:3). Simon will not be called "Peter" (Πέτρος; meaning "rock" or "stone") until 3:16, where we learn Jesus gave him that nickname (cf. John 1:44). Peter is the most prominent of the Twelve. He is always named first in lists of the disciples (3:16 – 19) and "distinguishes himself by folly as well as insight"[8] (Mark 8:32 – 33; 9:5 – 6; 14:29 – 31, 66 – 72). According to the Fourth Gospel, Andrew was first a disciple of John the Baptist, and it was he who introduced his brother to Jesus (John 1:40 – 42).[9]

The "Sea of Galilee" is actually a large kidney-shaped inland lake, fourteen miles long and six miles wide and located 682 feet below sea level. The OT refers to it as (lit.) the "Sea of Kinnereth" (Num 34:11; Josh 13:27; perhaps from the Hebrew word for "harp," referring to its shape). Luke calls it the "Lake [λίμνη] of Gennesaret" (5:1), a Greek form of Kinnereth. It was also called the Sea of Tiberias (John 6:1; after the main city on the western shore, named after the Roman emperor Tiberias). Fishing was a major industry in Galilee. The brothers were "casting a net" (ἀμφιβάλλοντας), probably a round throw net, about fifteen feet across with weights on the edges. The net would sink to the bottom, trapping fish, which could then be gathered.

1:17 And Jesus said to them, "Come, follow me, and I will teach you to fish for people" (καὶ εἶπεν αὐτοῖς ὁ Ἰησοῦς· δεῦτε ὀπίσω μου, καὶ ποιήσω ὑμᾶς γενέσθαι ἁλιεῖς ἀνθρώπων). The Greek idiom (lit.)

"come after me" (δεῦτε ὀπίσω μου) is a call to discipleship, a relationship of learning from a master teacher. Discipleship was common among the rabbis of the first century, although Jesus' manner of calling was unusual. Normally a student would seek out a particular rabbi and ask to follow him. Jesus instead approaches disciples and calls them.[10] Mark's account emphasizes Jesus' authority, which demands an immediate response.[11] The image of fishing for people is found in the OT, though always in the context of impending judgment (Jer 16:16; Ezek 29:4 – 5; 38:4; Amos 4:2; Hab 1:14 – 17). Jesus reverses this image to one of salvation. To fish for people is to rescue them from sin and death by calling them into God's kingdom.[12]

The Greek clause (lit.) "I will make you to become fishers of people" (ποιήσω ὑμᾶς γενέσθαι ἁλιεῖς ἀνθρώπων) may mean either "I will send you out to fish for people" (NIV) or "I will teach you how to fish for people" (cf. GNT; GW; NLT), that is, to train them in the art of people-fishing.

1:18 And leaving their nets, they immediately followed him (καὶ εὐθὺς ἀφέντες τὰ δίκτυα ἠκολούθησαν αὐτῷ). While Mark's characteristic "immediately" (εὐθύς) often serves as a transitional word without temporal significance (see 1:10), here it certainly means "at once." The disciples drop what they are doing and follow him. If Mark is aware of any previous encounters between Jesus and the disciples (cf. John 1:35 – 42), he shows no interest in them. For him the important point is the authority of Jesus' words and the immediate response of the disciples. The kingdom of God is an urgent call and demands an absolute response.

8. Marcus, *Mark 1 – 8*, 180.

9. It is in this passage that Jesus nicknames Simon, *Kēphas* (or Cephas), the Aramaic original for the Greek Πέτρος; both mean "rock" or "stone."

10. See Martin Hengel, *The Charismatic Leader and His Fol-*

lowers (New York: Crossroad, 1981), 51 – 52.

11. The call has some parallels to Elijah's call of Elisha in 1 Kgs 19:19 – 21.

12. See W. H. Wuellner, *The Meaning of "Fishers of Men"* (Philadelphia: Westminster, 1967).

1:19 And going a little further, he saw James the son of Zebedee and John his brother in their boat preparing their nets (Καὶ προβὰς ὀλίγον εἶδεν Ἰάκωβον τὸν τοῦ Ζεβεδαίου καὶ Ἰωάννην τὸν ἀδελφὸν αὐτοῦ καὶ αὐτοὺς ἐν τῷ πλοίῳ καταρτίζοντας τὰ δίκτυα). The same scene is now repeated with two more fishermen brothers, James and John. The term "preparing" (καταρτίζοντας) can mean either "mending" (NET, HCSB) or "preparing [for a purpose]" (NIV, GNT). In either case they are getting the nets ready for more fishing. James was probably the older and firstborn son and so is named first and in relationship to his father. John is then named in relationship to James (cf. 3:17).

This James (Ἰάκωβος, from Heb. *yaʿăqōb*, "Jacob") is different from the lesser-known disciple, James the son of Alphaeus (3:18), as well as from James, the half brother of Jesus (Mark 6:3; Acts 1:14), who became a key leader in the Jerusalem church (Acts 12:17; 15:13; 21:18; Gal 2:9). This James will eventually be arrested and executed by Herod Agrippa I (Acts 12:1–2; AD 44), the first of the Twelve to suffer martyrdom. He and his brother John are nicknamed "sons of thunder" by Jesus (3:17), perhaps because of their volatile personalities (see 9:38; Luke 9:54). Later church tradition identifies John as the author of Fourth Gospel ("the disciple whom Jesus loved"), the Johannine Letters (1–3 John), and—in exile on Patmos—the book of Revelation. This identification is disputed, however, and some claim these books were authored by another John, known as "the Elder," who is referred to by Papias and other early church writers.[13]

1:20 Immediately he called them; leaving their father Zebedee in the boat with the hired men, they followed him (καὶ εὐθὺς ἐκάλεσεν αὐτούς. καὶ ἀφέντες τὸν πατέρα αὐτῶν Ζεβεδαῖον ἐν τῷ πλοίῳ μετὰ τῶν μισθωτῶν ἀπῆλθον ὀπίσω αὐτοῦ). Again, both the call and the response are immediate (cf. v. 18). The presence of hired servants suggests that Zebedee was a man of some wealth. Mark's purpose in naming these additional workers may be to show that James and John showed concern for their father's welfare and did not leave him without help. More likely, he is simply stating the fact that they were present, since Jesus never shies away from the radical commitment or sacrifice necessary for the kingdom of God (3:33–34; 8:34; 10:29–30).

Theology in Application

The Kingdom and God's Redemptive Purpose

Jesus' fundamental message, "the kingdom of God is close at hand" (v. 15), has profound implications for the biblical story and for human history. The Bible confirms that God reigns supreme (Exod 15:18). He is the sovereign Lord of the universe. Everything exists because of him and for his glory. Human beings represent the pinnacle of his creation and reflect his image (Gen 1:26–27; Ps 8). Yet the biblical story is also one of tragedy and alienation. Adam and Eve, tested by the Adversary, rejected God's sovereignty and defied his commands. Human nature entered a fallen

---

13. For details, see Daniel J. Harrington, *John the Son of Zebedee: The Life of a Legend* (Minneapolis: Fortress, 2000); Richard Bauckham, *The Testimony of the Beloved Disciple: Narrative, History, and Theology in the Gospel of John* (Grand Rapids: Baker, 2007), esp. 14–16, 33–91.

state and judgment followed. God's good creation was placed under a curse (Gen 3). Evil, sin, suffering, disease, decay, poverty, and death became the constants of human existence.

The message of the kingdom, however, is that human history is not an endless cycle of sin, suffering, and death. Redemptive history is not circular but linear, with a beginning, middle, and end. God started it and he will end it, because he is the sovereign Lord of the universe. And the end, the *eschaton*, is in fact a new beginning, the restoration of creation as it was intended to be. Jesus' announcement that "the kingdom of God is close at hand" means the endgame has begun. God's plan of redemption and restoration is entering its most important and decisive phase.

The Presence of the Kingdom

The kingdom is present not because God's authority is universally acknowledged, but because a right relationship with God is now available through God's agent of redemption. Jesus' message is an invitation to repent and believe in the kingdom, to submit to God's authority, and so to "enter" the kingdom. It is an invitation to reorient a life focused on self to a life focused on God. The kingdom is still future because Jesus is launching the plan that will bring about the final restoration of all things. His exorcisms reveal that the power of the Adversary is being neutralized; his healings demonstrate that fallen humanity is being restored (Isa 35:5, 6); his offer of forgiveness confirms that the power of sin is being broken; and his nature miracles show his divine authority to restore a fallen creation. All these are postcards from the kingdom, telling people that its power is really present and that its consummation is coming. Ultimately, Jesus' death on the cross will serve as a ransom for sins (Mark 10:45), breaking the endless cycle of sin and death and restoring humanity to eternal fellowship with God.

Jesus' Kingdom Authority and the Cost of Discipleship

Having announced the kingdom of God, Jesus sets out to establish a community of followers who will submit to God's reign. Two themes come through in the call narrative of the first four disciples. The first is the authority of Jesus, a theme that runs throughout the opening part of Mark's gospel. Using a harmonistic approach to the Gospels, one might conclude that Jesus has had previous encounters with these men (John 1:40 – 42). But this plays no part in Mark's story. For Mark, this is not a measured response to follow Jesus after seeing his miracles or weighing the cost. Rather, Jesus speaks and people obey. It is his overwhelming presence and authority that demand a response. Throughout this gospel, Jesus' words carry divine authority. When he speaks, demons are put to flight, diseases are healed, storm waves are calmed, and experts in debate are rendered speechless. Jesus speaks and acts with the authority of God.

The second theme is the willingness of the disciples to leave everything to follow Jesus. Discipleship has a cost. In the closest OT parallel to this narrative, the call of Elisha by Elijah, Elisha asks and is (apparently) given permission to go back and say good-bye to his parents (1 Kgs 19:19 – 21). In Mark's narrative, James and John simply leave their father in the boat to follow Jesus immediatly. This would have been shocking — even blasphemous — in a first-century context where honoring parents was among the greatest of values (Exod 20:12; Deut 5:16; Prov 23:22; Tob 51; Sir 3:1 – 16).[14]

Yet, as we will see throughout Mark's gospel, the demands of the kingdom are radical. They involve not only leaving wealth (10:21 – 24) and family (3:33 – 35; 10:29), but also denying yourself, taking up your cross (in death), and following him (8:34). This passage has profound implications for believers today. What does it mean — especially for those who possess wealth, position, and power — to leave everything and follow Jesus? This is the call of discipleship today, just as it was in Jesus' day.

14. Stein, *Mark*, 80.

Mark 1:21 – 28

Literary Context

Mark has set the stage for Jesus' messianic ministry with the preaching of John the Baptist and accounts of Jesus' baptism and testing in the wilderness (1:1 – 13). He then launches into Jesus' public ministry by describing Jesus' message — the proclamation of the kingdom of God and the need for repentance — and Jesus' call of his first disciples (1:14 – 20). Now he narrates a series of healings and exorcisms to demonstrate Jesus' authority over the forces of Satan and over disease. He describes four miracles: (1) an exorcism in the Capernaum synagogue (1:21 – 28), (2) the healing of Peter's mother-in-law and a summary of other healings (1:29 – 34), (3) the healing of a man with a skin disease (1:40 – 45), and (4) the healing of a paralyzed man (2:1 – 12). In these episodes, Mark emphasizes not only Jesus' power to heal, but also his growing popularity, his intimate prayer life with God, and the beginning of his conflict with the religious leaders.

In Mark's story the episodes described in 1:21 – 39 represent one long day of ministry in Capernaum (1:21 – 34) and the morning of the following day (1:35 – 38). Although many gospel pericopes appear without specific historical contexts and are arranged for theological and thematic rather than chronological reasons, there seems to be no reason to doubt that these events — teaching, an exorcism, the healing of Peter's mother-in-law, and other healings — occurred on a single day. If Peter was the source of much of Mark's material, as church tradition holds (see Introduction), such a series of events at the beginning of Peter's association with Jesus (especially one involving a family member!) is likely to have been recalled and passed down as a unified narrative.

II. The Authority of the Messiah (1:14 – 8:21)
   A. The Kingdom Authority of the Messiah (1:14 – 3:6)
      1. Jesus Proclaims the Kingdom and Calls Disciples (1:14 – 20)
→   **2. Authority in Teaching, Healing, and Exorcism (1:21 – 45)**
        a. Jesus Teaches and Drives Out an Evil Spirit (1:21 – 28)
        b. Jesus Heals Peter's Mother-in-Law and Others (1:29 – 34)
        c. Jesus' Prayer Life and Ministry Purpose (1:35 – 39)

Main Idea

At the beginning of his public ministry, Jesus amazes the people in the Capernaum synagogue and reveals his messianic authority by teaching with greater authority than the experts in the law and by casting out a demon, demonstrating his power over the forces of Satan.

Translation

(See next page.)

Structure

The episode is structured similarly to other gospel exorcisms: a statement of the problem (v. 23), the challenge to Jesus from the demon (v. 24), Jesus' authoritative command to silence and to come out (v. 25), the immediate obedience by the demon (v. 26) and the amazed response of the crowd (v. 27). What is unique is that Mark begins and ends by emphasizing Jesus' authoritative *teaching* rather than his powers as an exorcist. The people are first amazed that his teaching goes beyond the rote recital of the scribal traditions (v. 22). Even after the exorcism, they speak first about the "new teaching with authority" and only then about the exorcism (v. 27). Mark's point is that the exorcisms reveal Jesus' authority to accomplish his central mission and message: the proclamation and inauguration of the kingdom of God. Satan's realm is being beaten back at the advance of God's kingdom.

Mark 1:21 – 28

21a	Action/Setting (spatial)	**They went to Capernaum.**
b	Setting/character entrance	Entering the synagogue on the Sabbath,
c	Action	**he began teaching.**
22a	Reaction to 21c	**They were amazed at his teaching,**
b		because he was teaching them
c		as one who had authority, and
d	contrast to 22c	not like the experts in the law.
23a	Character entrance/Conflict	**Suddenly a man appeared in their synagogue**
b	character description	who was possessed by a defiling spirit.
24a	Action	**It cried out, saying,**
b	question/exclamation	*"What do you want with us, Jesus of Nazareth?*
c	rhetorical question	*Have you come to destroy us?*
d	assertion/challenge	*I know who you are: God's Holy One!"*
25a	Response to 24	But **Jesus rebuked him, saying,**
b	command	*"Silence! Come out of him!"*
26a	manner of 26c	Convulsing him and
b	manner of 26c	shrieking loudly,
c	Response to 25	**the defiling spirit came out of him.**
27a	Response to 26	**Everyone was astonished and asked each other,**
b	question	*"What is this?*
c	assertion	*A new teaching with authority!*
d	assertion	*He even commands the defiling spirits*
e	result of 27d	*and they obey him!"*
28a	Summary	**The news about him spread quickly**
b	setting of 28a (spatial)	throughout the whole region of Galilee.

Exegetical Outline

→ **1. The Context: The Capernaum Synagogue on the Sabbath (1:21a-b)**

2. Jesus Amazes the Crowds by Teaching with Authority (1:21c – 22)

3. Jesus Reveals His Authority by Casting Out a Demon (1:23 – 27)

a. The entrance of the man with the unclean spirit (1:23)

b. The challenge to Jesus by the demon (1:24)

c. Jesus' command to silence and to come out (1:25)

d. The immediate response by the demon (1:26)

e. The response of the people (1:27)

4. Jesus' Fame Spreads (1:28)

Explanation of the Text

1:21 They went to Capernaum. Entering the synagogue on the Sabbath, he began teaching (Καὶ εἰσπορεύονται εἰς Καφαρναούμ· καὶ εὐθὺς[1] τοῖς σάββασιν εἰσελθὼν εἰς τὴν συναγωγὴν ἐδίδασκεν). Jesus used Capernaum (from the Heb. *kēpar nāhûm,* meaning "village of Nahum") as a kind of base of operations for his Galilean ministry, returning there after itinerant preaching tours throughout Galilee (2:1; 9:33). The reason for this was likely his close association with Simon Peter and Andrew, who lived there (1:29). The Fourth Gospel says Peter and Andrew came from Bethsaida, a town on the northern shore of Galilee just east of where the Jordan River enters the Sea of Galilee (John 1:44). This can be easily harmonized if the brothers were raised in Bethsaida but moved to Capernaum for their fishing business. Capernaum is generally identified with *Tell Hûm,* which lies on the northwest shore of the lake. Today the white-stoned ruins of a fourth-century synagogue can be seen, below which lies a black basalt foundation — probably from the synagogue of Jesus' day.

Jesus enters the synagogue on the Sabbath, the day of Jewish communal worship. The Jewish day began in the evening, so the Sabbath ran from Friday sundown to Saturday sundown. The Greek word for "Sabbath" (σάββατον) frequently appears in a plural form in the LXX and the NT, even when it carries a singular meaning. The likely reason is that the Aramaic word for the Sabbath is *sabata,* which was transliterated into Greek as σάββατα. This form looks like a neuter plural form, so the word was either declined as a plural with a singular meaning (as in this verse: τοῖς σάββασιν = "on the Sabbath"), or it was changed into a neuter singular (σάββατον).

The earliest extant accounts of Jewish synagogue services actually appear in the NT: Jesus' preaching in the Nazareth synagogue (Luke 4:14 – 30) and Paul's in the synagogue of Pisidian Antioch (Acts 13:14 – 48).[2] The order of service described in these agrees in general with later rabbinic sources. The service likely included prayers and readings from the Law and the Prophets, followed by an oral Targum (an Aramaic translation of the Scripture reading), a homily on the text, and a closing benediction. Jewish custom allowed visiting teachers to speak by invitation of the synagogue leaders (see, e.g., Acts 13:15). Jesus' homily likely followed the reading from the Law and the Prophets (Luke 4:15 – 30). "Began teaching" (ἐδίδασκεν) is an inceptive or ingressive imperfect, emphasizing the beginning of the action.

Although Mark records far less of the content of Jesus' teaching than either Matthew or Luke, he frequently refers to Jesus as a teacher and notes times when he was teaching.[3] Though Jesus is clearly a man of action and miracles in Mark's gospel, these actions are in the service of the proclamation of the kingdom. It is the authority rather than the content that is important to Mark.[4]

1. On Mark's use of "immediately" (εὐθύς), see comments on 1:10. Here the word is left untranslated, since there is no sense of immediacy.

2. On the history of the synagogue, see D. D. Binder, *Into the Temple Courts: The Place of Synagogues in the Second Temple Period* (SBLDS 169; Atlanta: Scholars, 1999); Lee I. Levine, "The Nature and Origin of the Palestinian Synagogue Reconsidered," *JBL* 115 (1996): 425 – 48.

3. See Vernon K. Robbins, *Jesus the Teacher: A Socio-Rhetorical Interpretation of Mark* (Philadelphia: Fortress, 1984), passim; R. T. France, "Mark and the Teaching of Jesus," in *Gospel Perspectives 1* (ed R. T. France and D. Wenham; Sheffield: JSOT Press, 1980), 101 – 36. France points out that the lack of teaching in Mark can be overstated, and it is only in contrast to Matthew that it looks small. Roughly 50 percent of Mark's content is teaching.

4. Hooker, *Mark*, 61.

1:22 They were amazed at his teaching, because he was teaching them as one who had authority, and not like the experts in the law (καὶ ἐξεπλήσσοντο ἐπὶ τῇ διδαχῇ αὐτοῦ· ἦν γὰρ διδάσκων αὐτοὺς ὡς ἐξουσίαν ἔχων καὶ οὐχ ὡς οἱ γραμματεῖς). Mark does not tell us what Jesus preached, but it must have been the message of the kingdom of God (1:15). The people are "amazed" (ἐκπλήσσω; 6:2; 7:37; 10:26; 11:18) at Jesus' teaching. Words of amazement are common throughout Mark's gospel.[5] They were astonished because Jesus spoke with an authority (ἐξουσία), unlike the "experts in the law" (γραμματεῖς). Traditionally rendered "scribes" (KJV, NASB, etc.) or "teachers of the law" (NIV), these were experts in the interpretation and application of Jewish religious law. Luke occasionally refers to them as "law-teachers" (νομοδιδάσκαλοι; Luke 5:17; Acts 5:34) or "law-experts" (νομικοί; Luke 7:30; 10:25; 11:45; cf. Matt 22:35). The translation of the latter as "lawyers" is unfortunate (ESV, NASB, NKJV), since modern readers will inevitably think of today's secular lawyers.

While the Pharisees were a religious party (see 2:16), the office of scribe represented a professional skill or vocation. Many scribes were also Pharisees, since the Pharisees highly prized the Jewish oral traditions, and the two groups appear together frequently in the Gospels (Matt 5:20; 12:38; 15:1; Mark 7:1, 5). Mark refers in Mark 2:16 to "the experts in the law [scribes] who were Pharisees" (οἱ γραμματεῖς τῶν Φαρισαίων — a partitive genitive).[6] In Matthew 23 Jesus condemns both groups for their religious pride and hypocrisy. The scribes come in frequent conflict with Jesus in Mark's gospel (Mark 2:6, 16; 3:22; 7:1, 5) and will ally themselves with the elders and ruling priests of Je-

rusalem in the arrest and trial of Jesus (8:31; 10:33; 11:18; 14:1, 43, 53; 15:1).

Originality was not highly valued by the Jewish religious experts of Jesus' day. Rather, they would pass down the authoritative "traditions of the elders," the wisdom of the ages. This material was in oral form in Jesus' day but was eventually written down and codified in the Mishnah (c. AD 200) and later rabbinic works. The people are impressed by Jesus because he is not merely repeating traditions of others, but is speaking with the authority of God.

1:23 Suddenly a man appeared in their synagogue who was possessed by a defiling spirit (καὶ εὐθὺς ἦν ἐν τῇ συναγωγῇ αὐτῶν ἄνθρωπος ἐν πνεύματι ἀκαθάρτῳ). A "spirit" (πνεῦμα) here means a demon (δαιμόνιον; 1:34, 39; 3:15, 22; 6:13; 7:26, 29, 30; 9:38), an evil spiritual entity in opposition to God and in alliance with Satan. Mark uses "demon" (δαιμόνιον; 14x) and "defiling spirit" (πνεύματι ἀκαθάρτῳ; 11x) synonymously.

Though evil spirits are occasionally mentioned in the OT (1 Sam 16:14–23), discussions of their origin and nature do not appear until the Second Temple period (*Jub.* 2:2; *1 En.* 6:1–7:6; cf. *m. 'Abot* 5:6). *First Enoch* identifies the "sons of God" of Gen 6:1–4 as fallen angels who intermarried with the human beings, teaching them magical arts and producing giants as offspring. In Greek thought "demon" (δαιμόνιον) was used in a variety of ways, of personal and impersonal spiritual forces. A demon could be good, evil, or merely capricious. In the NT, by contrast, demons are always evil and aligned with Satan, "the ruler of demons" (Mark 3:22).

Finding a suitable translation for "defiling/unclean spirit" (πνεύματι ἀκαθάρτῳ) is difficult.

---

5. See 1:27; 2:12; 5:15, 20, 42; 6:51; 12:17; T. Dwyer, *The Motif of Wonder in the Gospel of Mark* (JSNTSup 128; Sheffield: Sheffield Academic, 1996), passim.

6. Wallace, *Greek Grammar*, 84–86.

The adjective "unclean" (ἀκάθαρτος) can mean "unclean, impure, defiled," or "defiling," and draws on the OT imagery of ritual defilement. Something "unclean" cannot be used for God's service and must be kept separate from God himself and from things that are "holy" (ἅγιος) or "clean, pure" (καθαρός). Here the sense may be that the spirit is itself "defiled" (which is true), or else that the presence of the spirit defiles the man, hence a "defiling spirit." The latter is most likely since exorcism is about purging an evil presence and restoring a person to a right relationship with God, family, and the religious community. Modern readers will likely hear "unclean spirit" as something related to hygiene; so contemporary versions often opt for "evil spirit" (NIV 1984, NLT, GNT, etc.) This is a good option for clarity, although it loses something of the sense of religious defilement. "Defiling" may be the best rendering.

The presence of the demon in the synagogue is shocking, since this is a place of prayer and devotion to God. But desperate circumstances call for drastic actions, and Satan's forces are intent on defeating the Son of God before his mission begins.

1:24 It cried out, saying, "What do you want with us, Jesus of Nazareth? Have you come to destroy us? I know who you are: God's Holy One!" (καὶ ἀνέκραξεν λέγων· τί ἡμῖν καὶ σοί, Ἰησοῦ Ναζαρηνέ; ἦλθες ἀπολέσαι ἡμᾶς; οἶδά σε τίς εἶ, ὁ ἅγιος τοῦ θεοῦ). Although Mark says simply "he/it cried out" (Greek verbs do not have gender), the demon is clearly speaking through the man. The question, "What do you want with us?" (τί ἡμῖν καὶ σοί; lit., "What to us and to you?") comes from a Hebrew idiom. It is a response to (perceived) inappropriate intervention and can mean, "What do

you have against me?" or "Why are you trying to involve me?" (*mah-lî wālāk*; cf. Judg 11:12; 2 Sam 16:10; 19:22; 1 Kgs 17:18; 2 Kgs 3:13; 2 Chr 35:21; cf. Matt 8:29; Mark 5:7; Luke 8:28; John 2:4). Here the question is rhetorical: "Mind your own business!" or "Get out of my face!"

The plural "us" could refer to the demon and the man, but this is unlikely since Jesus has no intention of destroying the man. Thus, it likely refers to fellow demons. The demonic hordes quake in fear at the thought of Jesus' arrival. This statement carries forward the eschatological theme of Mark's drama. The kingdom of God is invading the Adversary's domain, and his evil henchmen cower at the awesome authority of the Stronger One (1:7; 3:27).

The demon's claim that "I know who you are: God's Holy One!" is sometimes seen as an attempt to gain authority over Jesus.[7] In the ancient world, knowledge of a demon's name was thought to be a way to gain mastery over it. In the pseudepigraphic *Testament of Solomon,* a mixed Jewish and Christian document dating from the first to the third centuries AD, King Solomon uses a magic ring given to him by the archangel Michael to learn the names of various demons and coerce them to build the Jerusalem temple.[8] Yet for Mark, demonic recognition also serves to confirm Jesus' identity. If supernatural forces know (and fear) Jesus, he must be who they say he is (cf. 1:34; 3:11–12; 5:6–7).

"Holy One of God" (ὁ ἅγιος τοῦ θεοῦ) does not appear as a messianic title in the Jewish literature available to us, although it is an apt description for the Messiah. Similar terminology is used in the OT of Aaron (Ps 106:16) and Elisha (2 Kgs 4:9), who are referred to as set apart for God's service. Peter will later refer to Jesus as "the Holy and Righ-

7. J. M. Hull, *Hellenistic Magic and the Synoptic Tradition* (SBT 2/28; London: SCM, 1974), 67–69.

8. Though this work postdates the NT, many of its tradi-
tions come from earlier. The first-century Jewish historian Josephus describes Solomon's gifts of exorcism and the use of a ring in Solomon-like exorcisms (*Ant.* 8.2.5 §§42–49).

teous One" (τὸν ἅγιον καὶ δίκαιον) in Acts 3:14 (cf. 2:27; 13:35). Here the expression certainly carries this sense of God's instrument for service, but it also echoes the OT names for God, "the Holy One" (Job 6:10; Ps 22:3; Prov 9:10; Isa 40:25) and "the Holy One of Israel" (Ps 71:22; Isa 1:4; 32x in the OT). Jesus is acting with the power and authority of God.

1:25 But Jesus rebuked him, saying, "Silence! Come out of him!" (καὶ ἐπετίμησεν αὐτῷ ὁ Ἰησοῦς λέγων· φιμώθητι καὶ ἔξελθε ἐξ αὐτοῦ). This is the first example of what is called the "messianic secret" in Mark's gospel. Jesus (1) commands silence of demons (1:25, 34; 3:12), (2) orders those healed to keep quiet (1:44; 5:43; 7:36; 8:26), and (3) tells the disciples not to disclose his messianic identity (8:30; 9:9). William Wrede argued that the messianic secret was a literary device developed by the early church and by Mark to cover up Jesus' unmessianic life.[9] According to him, although Mark and his Christian community believed that Jesus was the Messiah, Mark found little evidence in the gospel tradition for this claim. To cover this up, Mark utilized the "messianic secret," whereby Jesus insists that others keep his identity a secret.

Wrede's thesis fails, however, because the secret is not kept even in Mark's gospel (see v. 28). Even though people are ordered to silence, they go around proclaiming Jesus' identity and his fame spreads (1:45; 7:36). Each of the three categories of commands to silence must be dealt with on its own terms. Jesus silences demons to demonstrate his messianic authority over them and to reveal himself in his own way and in his own time. The cries

of demons are a premature and distorted representation of Jesus' identity and mission. For Jesus' commands to those healed and to the disciples, see comments on 1:43 – 44 and 8:30, respectively.

1:26 Convulsing him and shrieking loudly, the defiling spirit came out of him (καὶ σπαράξαν αὐτὸν τὸ πνεῦμα τὸ ἀκάθαρτον καὶ φωνῆσαν φωνῇ μεγάλῃ ἐξῆλθεν ἐξ αὐτοῦ). Accounts of exorcisms, though not common, appear in both Jewish and non-Jewish sources.[10] Yet unlike other exorcists, Jesus does not use spells, rituals, or incantations to coerce demons into submission. His own authority is enough; he speaks and the demon obeys.

The convulsion and shriek are common features of exorcisms. They indicate both the last, futile attempt to injure the man as well as the visible confirmation that the demon has left. Jesus' authority is on display for all to see. The phrase "shouting with a great shout" (φωνῆσαν φωνῇ μεγάλῃ; translated idiomatically as "shrieking loudly") is a cognate dative,[11] where the verb and its modifying dative noun are from the same root. Redundant cognate expressions like this are common in Mark (cf. 4:41; 9:41; 10:38, 39; 13:7, 19, 20; 14:6).

1:27 Everyone was astonished and asked each other, "What is this? A new teaching with authority! He even commands the defiling spirits and they obey him!" (καὶ ἐθαμβήθησαν ἅπαντες ὥστε συζητεῖν πρὸς ἑαυτοὺς λέγοντας· τί ἐστιν τοῦτο; διδαχὴ καινὴ κατ' ἐξουσίαν· καὶ τοῖς πνεύμασι τοῖς ἀκαθάρτοις ἐπιτάσσει, καὶ ὑπακούουσιν αὐτῷ). For the second of many occasions (see v. 22), the people express amazement (θαμβέω; cf. 10:4, 32)

---

9. Wrede, *Messianic Secret*. For various perspectives through the years see the articles in C. M. Tuckett, ed., *The Messianic Secret* (Philadelphia: Fortress, 1983). For further discussion, see Mark's Gospel in Historical Perspective, in the introduction to Mark.

10. See G. Vermes, *Jesus the Jew: A Historian's Reading of the Gospels* (London: Collins, 1973), 61 – 69; Hull, *Hellenistic Magic*; G. H. Twelftree, *Jesus the Exorcist: A Contribution to the Study of the Historical Jesus* (Peabody, MA: Hendrickson, 1993), 13 – 47.

11. Wallace, *Greek Grammar*, 168 – 69.

at Jesus' authority. Notice that they refer *first* to Jesus' authority in teaching and only second to the exorcism.[12] Jesus' primary mission is to proclaim the good news of the kingdom. The exorcisms and healings are not showy displays of his power for self-aggrandizement, but evidence that the power of the kingdom of God is breaking into human history through the Messiah's words and deeds.

1:28 The news about him spread quickly throughout the whole region of Galilee (καὶ ἐξῆλθεν ἡ ἀκοὴ αὐτοῦ εὐθὺς πανταχοῦ εἰς ὅλην τὴν περίχωρον τῆς Γαλιλαίας). Already the so-called "messianic secret" is compromised (see v. 25), as Jesus' fame spreads throughout Galilee. Jesus' growing popularity is a common theme throughout this part of Mark's gospel (1:33, 37, 45; 2:1 – 2; 3:7 – 9).

Theology in Application

The Kingdom of God versus the Kingdom of Satan

Jesus' encounter with the demoniac in the Capernaum synagogue is the second conflict in Mark's gospel (the first was his temptation/testing by Satan in the wilderness, 1:13). By starting his gospel with two episodes involving the supernatural, Mark leaves no doubt about the nature of the Messiah's mission. This is no clash of empires, no mortal struggle between human authorities. It is a cosmic struggle between God and Satan, good and evil, light and darkness. The apostle Paul shares a similar worldview. The Christian life is about taking a stand against the devil's schemes: "For our struggle is not against flesh and blood, but against the rulers, against the authorities, against the powers of this dark world and against the spiritual forces of evil in the heavenly realms" (Eph 6:12). What is at stake is not territory or plunder, but the hearts and souls of human beings.

While Mark depicts Jesus' mission as a war between the kingdom of God and the kingdom of Satan, the outcome of this skirmish is not in doubt. The demon picks the fight, even challenging Jesus in the religious context of the Capernaum synagogue; but Jesus takes charge, commanding the demon's departure. Unlike the Hellenistic magicians of his day, he does not cast spells or recite incantations; he doesn't manipulate magical rings or mix potions. He merely speaks with authority and the demon obeys. This is a message the church today needs to hear. Satan's authority is no match for the awesome power and presence of the kingdom of God.

A Supernatural Worldview

Mark's perspective on spiritual warfare is in line with the biblical worldview. In the OT, Yahweh exercises supreme authority over all powers, whether physical or

---

12. The punctuation and attribution of authority is ambiguous in the Greek and the verse could be rendered, "A new teaching! With authority he even commands the defiling spirits and they obey him." The reference to Jesus' authoritative teaching in v. 22 as well as the position of the καί suggest that the text should be read as translated above and that the authority is specifically identified with Jesus' teaching.

spiritual. He created them, and they must do his bidding. The most powerful kings of the earth are mere pawns in his hands: "No sooner are they planted, no sooner are they sown, no sooner do they take root in the ground, than he blows on them and they wither" (Isa 40:24). Though spiritual forces may act in opposition to God, they are ultimately subject to his authority.

The Lord limits Satan's power over Job (1:12; 2:6) and sends a malevolent spirit to torment Saul (1 Sam 16:14 – 16). Leviathan and Rahab, the awesome creatures of the deep (Job 3:8 – 9; 41:12 – 39), are playthings of God that must do his bidding (Pss 74:14; 104:26). All such forces of chaos will be crushed in the end (Job 9:13; 26:12; Ps 89:9 – 10; Isa 27:1; 51:9). In the NT the victory of God over all spiritual forces is achieved through the inbreaking power of the kingdom and the atoning work of Christ on the cross. Jesus is the Stronger One, who through his exorcisms and healings is binding Satan and plundering his house (Mark 3:26 – 27). According to Paul, Jesus' death and resurrection disarmed the spiritual powers and authorities and made a public spectacle of them (Col 2:15). In the Apocalypse, John affirms that the victory of the Lamb who was slain results in the defeat and ultimate destruction of Satan, the great serpent of old (Rev 7:12; 12:9; 20:2, 10; cf. Rom 16:20).

While Mark and other biblical writers assume a supernatural worldview, many modern readers balk at the idea. During the eighteenth-century Enlightenment, rationalism became the philosophical order of the day, asserting that truth could be discerned only through empirical scientific investigation. The gospel miracle traditions were treated with skepticism and assumed to have arisen from the superstitious beliefs of primitive peoples. As a rationalist and a deist, Thomas Jefferson was so disturbed by the gospel miracle tradition that he edited his own Bible, removing the supernatural elements.[13]

Yet such a conclusion ignores both past history and present reality. For most of world history, the spiritual realm has been taken for granted. Even today most non-Western cultures assume a supernatural worldview, and spirit beings are viewed as a real presence in the world. Even in the Western world belief in God and the supernatural remains high. A recent survey on religious views in the U.S. conducted by Baylor University found that only 4.6 percent of Americans claimed they "did not believe in anything beyond the physical world."[14] Most people apparently have an innate awareness that there is more to reality than the physical universe. It is difficult to attribute all such beliefs to the delusions of primitive peoples.[15]

13. The volume was published posthumously. See *The Jefferson Bible* (ed. O. I. A. Roche; New York: Potter, 1964).

14. *American Piety in the 21st Century: New Insights to the Depth and Complexity of Religion in the US* (Waco, TX: Baylor University, 2006). Available at http://www.baylorisr.org/?s=American+Piety+in+the+21st+Century%3A+New+Insights+to+the+Depth+and+Complexity+of+Religion+in+the+US

(accessed September 6, 2013). For a summary of the survey's results, see www.thearda.com/Archive/Files/Codebooks/BRS2005_CB.asp (accessed September 6, 2013).

15. See Craig Keener, *Miracles: The Credibility of the New Testament Accounts* (2 vols.; Grand Rapids: Baker, 2011). See especially Keener's appendix on exorcisms.

So how should Christians respond to the reality of the demonic? Two extremes should be avoided. Some Christians become obsessed with the supernatural, seeing demons everywhere and blaming Satan for every disease or setback in life. This can become an unhealthy obsession, allowing individuals to deny responsibility for their actions and even opening them up to demonic influence. Others, though claiming to believe in God, live as practical atheists, never acknowledging the reality or influence of spiritual forces in their lives. A balanced approach recognizes that Satan and his forces are real and active in the world and that we must take up the spiritual "armor of God" to defend ourselves against his attacks (Eph 6:10 – 20). Yet Christ has achieved the decisive victory through his death and resurrection (Col 2:15), and those who confess his name can live victorious lives without fear of oppression.[16]

IN DEPTH: Jesus the Exorcist and Miracle Worker

The historical evidence that Jesus was renowned by his contemporaries as an exorcist and miracle worker is overwhelming. Exorcisms appear in various strata of the gospel tradition (Mark, Q, M, L) and in a variety of gospel genres, including miracle stories, pronouncement stories, controversy stories, sayings, parables, commissioning accounts, passion narratives, and summaries of Jesus' activities.[17] Although no exorcisms appear in John's gospel, this can be explained from his selective use of sources and his unique theological purpose.[18]

Sources outside the NT also refer to Jesus' miraculous activity. Josephus states that Jesus was "a doer of startling deeds" (*Ant.* 18.3.3 §63), a probable reference to his miracles. The Babylonian Talmud claims Jesus was executed because he practiced magic and led Israel astray (*b. Sanh.* 43a). While this passage is a strong polemic against Jesus and Christianity, it admits as reliable the tradition that Jesus performed supernatural acts. The early church leader Origen quotes his second-century pagan opponent Celsus as claiming that Jesus worked certain magical powers that he had learned in Egypt.[19] Even Jesus' opponents had to acknowledge that, whatever the source of his power, Jesus had extraordinary authority to perform miracles.

16. For a balanced perspective on the demonic realm, see Clinton E. Arnold, *Powers of Darkness: Principalities and Powers in Paul's Letters* (Downers Grove, IL: InterVarsity Press, 1992); idem, *Three Crucial Questions about Spiritual Warfare* (Grand Rapids: Baker, 1997).

17. Graham H. Twelftree, *Jesus the Miracle Worker* (Downers Grove, IL: InterVarsity Press, 1999), 256; Barry Blackburn, "Miracles and Miracle Stories," in *DJG*, 556.

18. See Graham H. Twelftree, *In the Name of Jesus: Exorcism among Early Christians* (Grand Rapids: Baker, 2007), 183 – 208.

19. Origen, *Cels.* 1:38.

Mark 1:29 – 34

Literary Context

The early Galilean ministry is characterized by Jesus' authority in teaching, healing, and exorcisms. After describing Jesus' kingdom preaching and the call of his first disciples (1:14 – 20), the narrator has moved on to a series of exorcisms and healings (1:21 – 2:12). Mark notes that the present episode occurred immediately after Jesus left the synagogue where he had taught and cast out a demon (1:21 – 28), and so it was part of the same long day of ministry in Capernaum (1:21 – 34). The episodes narrated here both personalize and generalize Jesus' healing ministry. The healing of Peter's mother-in-law illustrates his compassion and provides a personal touch to his healing ministry. The summary that follows shows the scope and diversity of his messianic authority over disease and demons. The "messianic secret" also appears here for a second time (cf. 1:25) as Jesus silences the demons he casts out (1:34).

Main Idea

Jesus demonstrates both compassion and messianic authority over disease and Satan as he heals Peter's mother-in-law and many others, and casts out many demons.

Translation

Mark 1:29–34

29a	setting of 29b (temporal/spatial)	After leaving the synagogue,
b	Action	**they went to Simon and Andrew's house,**
	setting of 29b (social)	together with James and John.
30a	Character entrance/Conflict	**Peter's mother-in-law was sick in bed with a fever,**
b	Request	and **at once they spoke with Jesus about her.**
31a	action/response to 30b	Going in to her and grasping her hand,
b	Action/Healing	**he raised her up.**
c	Result/Healing of 31a	**The fever left her**
d	Result of 31b	and **she began serving them.**
32a	setting (temporal)	When evening came, after sunset,
b	Action/Character entrance	**the people were bringing to him all those who were sick or demonized.**
33	Action	**The whole city was gathered at the door.**
34a	Response/Healings	And **he healed many who had various illnesses** and
b	Response/Exorcisms	**cast out many demons.**
c	Statement/Command	But **he would not allow the demons to speak,**
d	Reason for 34c	because they knew who he was.

Structure

The healing recorded here follows a typical pattern, with (1) a statement of the problem (v. 30a), (2) a plea for healing (v. 30b; implied), (3) healing through physical touch (v. 31a-b), and (4) the result of the healing (v. 31c-d). Missing is a statement of the amazed response of the onlookers. Instead, Mark comments that Peter's mother-in-law immediately began to serve Jesus and his disciples. The point is that the healing resulted in full restoration, such that she could resume her domestic duties. The incidental details and the unusual fact that the healing concerns a family member of a disciple (unique in the Gospels) has convinced most scholars that the account is authentic and may have been passed down by Peter himself.[1]

The healing is followed by a summary statement of an evening of healings and exorcisms (vv. 32–34). Such summaries highlight key Markan themes, provide narrative cohesion, and carry the plot forward.

---

1. Even the radical Jesus Seminar gave the episode a "pink" ("probably authentic") rating, noting that the story lacks most of the features that are characteristic of stereotyped healing stories and that there are no precedents for the account in the Hebrew Scripture. Robert Funk writes, "In sum, this simple tale appears to reflect the memory of a cure worked upon someone close to the inner circle of Jesus' followers; it does not appear to be fictive" (Robert Funk and the Jesus Seminar, *The Acts of Jesus: The Search for the Authentic Deeds of Jesus* [San Francisco: HarperSanFrancisco, 1998], 59).

Exegetical Outline

→ **1. The Healing of Peter's Mother-in-Law (1:29 – 31)**

    a. The setting: The home of Peter and Andrew (1:29)

    b. The dilemma: Peter's mother-in-law sick with a fever (1:30a)

    c. The (implied) request (1:30b)

    d. The healing (1:31a-b)

    e. The proof of the healing (1:31c-d)

2. Summary: Healings and Exorcisms (1:32 – 34)

    a. Setting (1:32a)

    b. The crowds bring their sick (1:32b – 33)

    c. Jesus heals the sick and exorcises demons (1:34a-b)

    d. Jesus silences the demons (1:34c-d)

Explanation of the Text

1:29 After leaving the synagogue, they went to Simon and Andrew's house, together with James and John (Καὶ εὐθὺς ἐκ τῆς συναγωγῆς ἐξελθόντες ἦλθον εἰς τὴν οἰκίαν Σίμωνος καὶ Ἀνδρέου μετὰ Ἰακώβου καὶ Ἰωάννου). Mark's introductory "and immediately" (καὶ εὐθύς) does not mean "at once," but serves as a connective meaning, "the next thing that happened" (see comments on 1:10). Since Simon Peter was married, the reference to the "Simon and Andrew's house" may seem odd to modern readers. Did Andrew (and his family?) live with Peter?

Yet in that culture it would be common for an extended family to live together under the same roof. Archaeologists have excavated a first-century house under the remains of a sixth-century octagonal church, just a few hundred feet from the Capernaum synagogue. Christian markings suggest that the home was used as a house church, and it is not unlikely that this was the actual location of Peter's home.[2] Though raised in Bethsaida

(John 1:44), Simon and Andrew probably moved to Capernaum as a base of operations for their fishing business (see comments on 1:21).

1:30 Peter's mother-in-law was sick in bed with a fever, and at once they spoke with Jesus about her (ἡ δὲ πενθερὰ Σίμωνος κατέκειτο πυρέσσουσα, καὶ εὐθὺς λέγουσιν αὐτῷ περὶ αὐτῆς). That Peter was married is attested independently by Paul (1 Cor 9:5). Nothing else is known about his wife or possible children. Ancient people sometimes considered a "fever" (πυρετός) to be a disease rather than a symptom, and this may be the case here.[3] "Immediately" (εὐθύς) may again function as a connective (cf. v. 29; both Matthew and Luke omit it in their parallels) or may give the request a sense of urgency, "at once." "They spoke" (λέγουσιν) is a historical present, a common form in Mark that gives the narrative a sense of vivid realism (see comments on Mark's style and literary features in the introduction). In light of Jesus' growing reputation

---

2. Stanislao Loffreda, *Recovering Capharnaum* (Jerusalem: Edizioni Custodia Terra Santa, 1984); James F. Strange and Hershel Shanks, "Has the House Where Jesus Stayed in Caper-

naum Been Found?" *BAR* 8/6 (November/December, 1982), 26 – 37; V. Cordo, "Capernaum," *ABD*, 1:867 – 68.

    3. K. Weiss, *TDNT*, 6:956 – 58.

as a healer, "they spoke with Jesus" is an indirect request for healing.

1:31 Going in to her and grasping her hand, he raised her up. The fever left her and she began serving them (καὶ προσελθὼν ἤγειρεν αὐτὴν κρατήσας τῆς χειρός· καὶ ἀφῆκεν αὐτὴν ὁ πυρετός, καὶ διηκόνει αὐτοῖς). In the previous episode, Jesus cast out a demon with a command. Here he heals with a touch, a common pattern in Mark's gospel (1:41; 5:41; 6:5; 7:32–33; 8:23–25). At times others touch Jesus and are healed (3:10; 5:27–28; 6:56). The touch reveals not only Jesus' authority to heal but also his compassion and empathy for the sufferer.

The verb "she began serving them" (διηκόνει) is an inceptive imperfect, emphasizing the initiation of an action.[4] "Serve" (διακονέω) commonly refers to waiting on tables, but can mean any kind of service. Here it is presumably meal preparation. The statement is not meant to be demeaning or to suggest her inferior role. The angels "served" Jesus in the wilderness (1:13), and Jesus teaches that a disciple's greatest role is to be a "servant" (9:35; 10:43; διάκονος), since even the Son of Man himself came not to be served but to "serve" (διακονέω; 10:45). Here the point is that the healing was both immediate and complete, so that Peter's mother-in-law could return to her full activities.

1:32 When evening came, after sunset, the people were bringing to him all those who were sick or demonized (Ὀψίας δὲ γενομένης, ὅτε ἔδυ ὁ ἥλιος, ἔφερον πρὸς αὐτὸν πάντας τοὺς κακῶς ἔχοντας καὶ τοὺς δαιμονιζομένους).[5] Mark follows the healing of Peter's mother-in-law with a summary of Jesus' activity that evening, a ministry of healing and exorcism (similar summaries appear in 3:10–12; 6:55–56). The narrator establishes the temporal setting with a redundant expression, "when evening came, after sunset." Such dual temporal phrases are characteristic of Markan style and provide emphasis and color to the narrative.[6] The Jewish day began at sunset, so the Sabbath is now over and the people can bring their sick to Jesus without violating the Sabbath command. The question of whether healing is prohibited on the Sabbath will arise shortly in Mark's narrative (3:1–6).

1:33–34 The whole city was gathered at the door. And he healed many who had various illnesses and cast out many demons. But he would not allow the demons to speak, because they knew who he was (καὶ ἦν ὅλη ἡ πόλις ἐπισυνηγμένη πρὸς τὴν θύραν. καὶ ἐθεράπευσεν πολλοὺς κακῶς ἔχοντας ποικίλαις νόσοις καὶ δαιμόνια πολλὰ ἐξέβαλεν καὶ οὐκ ἤφιεν λαλεῖν τὰ δαιμόνια, ὅτι ᾔδεισαν αὐτόν). "The whole city" is hyperbole and picks up the theme of popularity that will run throughout Jesus' Galilean ministry.[7] That Jesus healed "many" (πολλούς) does not necessarily mean that some were left unhealed (cf. 6:5). The term is used inclusively rather than exclusively (cf. 3:10; 10:45): many rather than just a few were healed. Jesus' healings and exorcisms were not isolated or sporadic events but pervasive features of his ministry. The reference to "various" (ποικίλαις) kinds of ill-

---

4. Wallace, *Greek Grammar*, 544–45.

5. The verb here translated "demonized" (δαιμονίζομαι) is commonly rendered "demon possessed," and there is significant debate as to the nature of this "possession" or "oppression." Does the verb indicate ownership (total control) or something less (influence)? Can Christians be possessed or only oppressed by demons? Since Mark does not address these issues, we have chosen the more neutral and ambiguous "demonized" over

either "possession" or "oppression." For in-depth discussion, see the sources cited in Theology in Application section on 1:21–28.

6. See 1:35; 2:20; 4:35; 10:30; 13:24; 14:12, 43; 15:42; see Neirynck, *Duality in Mark*.

7. See 2:2; 3:7–9, 20; 4:1; 5:21, 24; 6:14–15, 31–34; 7:24; 8:1–3; 9:14–15, 30.

nesses makes the same point. Jesus was not an itinerant Hellenistic magician with a few tricks up his sleeve, but the messianic Son of God inaugurating the kingdom of God — the restoration and renewal of a fallen creation (cf. Isa 35:5 – 6; Matt 11:4 – 6; 12:28; Luke 7:22 – 23; 11:20).

Jesus again silences the demons (cf. 1:25), "because they knew who he was." Luke is more specific: "because they knew he was the Messiah" (Luke 4:41). Elsewhere in Mark, demons identify Jesus as "God's Holy One" (1:24), "the Son of God" (3:11), and the "Son of the Most High God" (5:7). The awareness of Jesus' identity by the demons serves two important purposes in Mark's narrative. First, it testifies to Jesus' identity. The demons are privy to supernatural persons and events and so know his true identity.[8] Second, it confirms that Jesus' mission is not just a physical one being played out on the stage of human history, but also a cosmic one that concerns the spiritual forces of good and evil, the dominion of Satan versus the kingdom of God.

As in 1:25, the command to silence is not Mark's cover-up of an unmessianic life, but rather evidence of Jesus' authority over Satan's realm. He speaks and the demons must obey. It is also part of Jesus' resolve to define his mission on his own terms (see 1:25 and the discussion of the messianic secret in Mark's Gospel in Historical Perspective in the introduction).

Theology in Application

Jesus' Miracles and Eschatological Restoration

The central theological theme of these two episodes is the authority of Jesus in healings and exorcisms. Jesus' authority is displayed (1) by healing Peter's mother-in-law immediately and completely with a mere touch, so that she can fully resume her responsibilities; (2) by healing "many" with various diseases; and (3) by both casting out demons and silencing them. Yet this authority is not exercised for his own aggrandizement. Both the exorcisms and the healings demonstrate the power of the kingdom of God and the restoration of creation. Isaiah spoke of coming salvation, when God would right every wrong:

> "… your God will come,
>   he will come with vengeance;
> with divine retribution
>   he will come to save you."
> Then will the eyes of the blind be opened
>   and the ears of the deaf unstopped.
> Then will the lame leap like a deer,
>   and the mute tongue shout for joy. (Isa 35:4 – 6; cf. 29:18; 32:3; 42:7)

This is an eschatological picture of the new creation, when God will reclaim his fallen creation. Jesus' healings and exorcisms are a foretaste of this restoration. The miracles hold a secondary place to Jesus' proclamation of the kingdom (1:38), not

8. Stein, *Mark*, 97.

because they are unimportant but because they provide confirmation of this greater reality. Jesus is here on earth to do far more than heal the sick and free the demonized; he is here to reclaim this fallen creation and its broken people.

The Compassionate Healer

Although Jesus' kingdom authority is the central theme of the passage, his compassion is also on center stage. God has chosen to reclaim his creation because of his great love for those he created. Isaiah's promise of the coming of the Lord to bring restoration after exile — the model for John the Baptist's ministry (1:3; Isa 40:3) — begins, "Comfort, comfort my people, says your God" (Isa 40:1). God's passion, motivated by his compassion, is to bring comfort and healing to his people. The healing of Peter's mother-in-law demonstrates this personal touch as Jesus reaches out to take her hand. He is not healing for the acclaim of the crowds, but because of his deep love and compassion for people.

The difference between a compassionate shepherd and a mercenary is the shepherd's authentic concern for the sheep. In John's gospel, Jesus contrasts himself as the good shepherd with the thief, who comes to steal and kill and destroy, and with the hired hand, who abandons the sheep at the first threat of danger (John 10:1 – 16). Thieves and hired hands are motivated by self-interest. True shepherds are motivated by self-sacrificial love for the sheep.

Paul made a similar point when opponents at Thessalonica attacked the genuineness of his ministry. He responded that he and his fellow missionaries were delighted to share with the Thessalonian believers not only the gospel message, but their own lives as well. They were not motivated by greed, or power, or fame, but by their love for God and love for the Thessalonians (1 Thess 2:1 – 6). They cared for them like a mother cares for her children (2:7 – 8) and like a father, "encouraging, comforting and urging you to live lives worthy of God" (2:11 – 12). To be truly effective, pastoral leadership today must be motivated not by position and prestige but by love for God and compassion for his people.

A Balanced Perspective on Miracles Today

A third issue this passage raises for our contemporary context is what application should be drawn from Jesus' healing ministry. As with Jesus' exorcisms (see Theology in Application on 1:21 – 28), there are two wrong extremes with reference to healing. One is a lack of faith that God can or does heal today. It is sometimes argued that the period of Jesus and the apostolic church was a unique time and that God no longer heals today. But the same Spirit who healed then is with us today. Jesus told his disciples that they would do even greater works than he did because of the empowering presence of the Spirit (John 14:12). James explicitly calls on church leaders to pray for the sick and to expect their healing (James 5:13 – 18).

The opposite extreme is the insistence that God will always heal those who have enough faith.[9] While faith is sometimes stated as the prerequisite for healing (6:5 – 6), there is no evidence that God always provides physical healing in response to faith. Paul prayed repeatedly that his "thorn in my flesh" would be taken away, yet God responded, "My grace is sufficient for you, for my power is made perfect in weakness" (2 Cor 12:7 – 10). God often takes us *through* trials in order to produce greater dependence on him and a deeper level of spiritual maturity. Even the godliest of Christians will eventually die of disease or old age, since our ultimate healing won't take place until we see Christ face-to-face. This life is just a testing ground for eternity. While we should certainly pray for healing, our greater prayer should be, "your kingdom come, your will be done, on earth as it is in heaven" (Matt 6:10). Whether that is best accomplished through sickness or health, through our life or our death, is for God to decide (Phil 1:20 – 21).

---

9. Note that sometimes people are healed who do not request it, as in the case of the high priest's servant in Luke 22:51. There is no inevitable link between faith and healing.

6

Mark 1:35 – 39

Literary Context

Jesus' early Galilean ministry focuses on preaching about the kingdom of God and performing healings and exorcisms that demonstrate his authority to inaugurate the kingdom (1:14 – 2:12). The present episode, coming in the middle of four miracle stories, illustrates Jesus' complete dependence on God through prayer and his priority on proclaiming the message of the kingdom of God over receiving adulation from the crowds. The passage thus serves as a brief interlude, where Jesus affirms his kingdom priorities in the midst of Mark's fast-paced and action-packed narrative.

II. The Authority of the Messiah (1:14 – 8:21)
   A. The Kingdom Authority of the Messiah (1:14 – 3:6)
      1. Jesus Proclaims the Kingdom and Calls Disciples (1:14 – 20)
      2. Authority in Teaching, Healing, and Exorcism (1:21 – 45)
         a. Jesus Teaches and Drives Out an Evil Spirit (1:21 – 28)
         b. Jesus Heals Peter's Mother-in-Law and Others (1:29 – 34)
  ➡   **c. Jesus' Prayer Life and Ministry Purpose (1:35 – 39)**
         d. Jesus Heals a Man with a Skin Disease (1:40 – 45)
      3. Conflicts with the Religious Leaders (2:1 – 3:6)

Main Idea

Despite Jesus' ministry late into the night (1:32), he rises before dawn to spend time in prayer alone with God, his source of strength and guidance. When his disciples come looking for him, Jesus chooses to ignore the acclaim and move on to other villages of Galilee, since he has been sent to announce the coming of the kingdom of God.

Translation

Mark 1:35 – 39

35a	setting of 35b-c (temporal)	Very early the next morning, while it was still dark, rising,
b	Action	**he left there** and **went out to a deserted place.**
c	Action	And **he was praying there.**
36	Action	**Simon and those with him went out searching for him.**
37a	Action	**They found him and said to him,**
b	statement/request	*"Everyone is looking for you!"*
38a	Response to 37b	But **he said to them,**
b	command	*"Let's go elsewhere to the nearby towns,*
c	purpose for 38b	*so that I can preach there also,*
d	reason for 38c	*because this is why I came."*
39a	Action/Summary	And **he went**
b	action/detail of 39a	preaching in their synagogues throughout Galilee and
c	action/detail of 39a	casting out demons.

Structure

This episode is made up of three scene parts: Jesus' early morning prayer in soli-tude (v. 35), his discovery by Simon and the others (vv. 36 – 38), and a summary of his ongoing Galilean ministry (v. 39). The middle incident is a pronouncement story, climaxing in Jesus' claim that he has come to preach God's message throughout Gali-lee. In this way, Mark emphasizes the central place of the kingdom of God in Jesus' mission and message.

Exegetical Outline

→ **1. Jesus' Priority in Prayer (1:35)**

  2. Jesus' Priority in Proclaiming the Kingdom (1:36 – 38)

    a. The disciples search for and find Jesus (1:36 – 37a)

    b. The disciples' announcement: everyone is looking for you (1:37b)

    c. Jesus' response: The priority of preaching the good news (1:38)

  3. Summary of Jesus' Itinerant Galilean Ministry (1:39)

Explanation of the Text

1:35 Very early the next morning, while it was still dark, rising, he left there and went out to a deserted place. And he was praying there (Καὶ πρωῒ ἔννυχα λίαν ἀναστὰς ἐξῆλθεν καὶ ἀπῆλθεν εἰς ἔρημον τόπον κἀκεῖ προσηύχετο). Jesus made personal time with God a high priority, since this was his source of strength and guidance. As he frequently does throughout his gospel (see comments on 1:32), Mark begins with a redundant temporal expression: "very early in morning, while it was still night" (πρωῒ ἔννυχα λίαν). After a late, no doubt exhausting, night of teaching, healing, and exorcism, Jesus rises before sunrise to spend time alone with God.

We see Jesus at prayer three times in Mark's gospel: here at the beginning of his Galilean ministry, after the feeding of the five thousand (6:46), and in the garden of Gethsemane (14:32 – 39). He also repeatedly encouraged his disciples to pray (9:29; 11:24; 13:18; 14:38). The adjective "deserted" (ἔρημος) is the same term used for the "desert" or "wilderness" in 1:3, 4, 12, 13. While here the word simply means an unpopulated or isolated "place" (τόπος; there is no desert in the environs of Capernaum), Mark's readers would likely hear an echo of the wilderness motif introduced earlier (see comments on 1:4). Jesus escapes to a place where he can encounter God and prepare for the ministry ahead.

1:36 – 37 Simon and those with him went out searching for him. They found him and said to him, "Everyone is looking for you!" (καὶ κατεδίωξεν αὐτὸν Σίμων καὶ οἱ μετ᾽ αὐτοῦ, καὶ εὗρον αὐτὸν καὶ λέγουσιν αὐτῷ ὅτι πάντες ζητοῦσίν σε). Simon appears here as the spokesperson and representative of the disciples, a role he will perform throughout the gospel tradition (8:29; 9:5; 10:28; 11:21; etc.). "His companions" (οἱ μετ᾽ αὐτοῦ = "those with him") probably refers to

Andrew, James, and John (1:16 – 20, 29), since no other disciples have yet appeared in the narrative. Simon and the others are evidently awakened by the townspeople hoping to see Jesus perform more exorcisms and healings. The verb rendered "went out searching" (καταδιώκω) is a strong one that can mean to "pursue" or "persecute." Here the sense is urgent searching.

1:38 But he said to them, "Let's go elsewhere to the nearby towns, so that I can preach there also, because this is why I came." (καὶ λέγει αὐτοῖς· ἄγωμεν ἀλλαχοῦ εἰς τὰς ἐχομένας κωμοπόλεις, ἵνα καὶ ἐκεῖ κηρύξω· εἰς τοῦτο γὰρ ἐξῆλθον). The people of Capernaum want Jesus to stay because they are enamored by his teaching and his miracles. But Jesus has a greater purpose than fame or popularity: to announce and inaugurate the kingdom of God (cf. 1:14 – 15; 1:22). The healings and exorcisms serve merely to confirm the presence and power of the kingdom of God. This is why Jesus came. The aorist verb "came" (ἐξῆλθον) could refer to why he "came out" of Capernaum to pray, but more likely refers generally to his mission from God.

The compound noun translated "towns" (κωμόπολις) appears only here in the NT and apparently refers to a medium-sized municipality somewhere between a "village" (κώμη) and a "city" (πόλις), perhaps a "market-town" (BDAG). Yet these terms are imprecise, and "city" (πόλις) can be used of almost any municipality, from villages like Bethlehem (Luke 2:4) and Nazareth (Matt 2:23; Luke 1:26; 2:4), to medium-sized towns like Capernaum (Mark 1:33), to large walled cities like Jerusalem (Matt 21:10). In general, κώμη should be translated "village" or "town," while πόλις is usually rendered "town" or "city."

Mark's point here seems to be that Jesus is intentionally moving outward from Capernaum into the surrounding towns and villages throughout Galilee. Jesus apparently avoided the larger cities of Galilee, like Tiberias and Sepphoris, which are never mentioned in the Gospels. This may be because his popularity made it difficult to minister in larger population centers, or perhaps he was avoiding places where his religious opponents had the most influence.

1:39 And he went preaching in their synagogues throughout Galilee and casting out demons (καὶ ἦλθεν κηρύσσων εἰς τὰς συναγωγὰς αὐτῶν εἰς ὅλην τὴν Γαλιλαίαν καὶ τὰ δαιμόνια ἐκβάλλων). Mark concludes by summarizing Jesus' activity in Gali-

lee, described as "preaching" and "casting out demons." It is curious that healing is not mentioned (cf. 3:14), but this probably results from Mark's stylistic variety. The summaries in 1:32 – 34; 3:7 – 12; and 6:13 mention both healing and exorcism, while 6:53 – 56 refers only to healing. There may, however, be a slight hint of the priority of exorcism. The appointment of the Twelve mentions preaching and exorcism, but not healing, as the reason for appointing them (3:14); and when Jesus sends them on their mission, he gives them "authority over defiling spirits," without mentioning the authority to heal (6:7). The summary of what they actually did, however, includes all three: preaching, exorcism, and healing (6:12 – 13).

Theology in Application

Two key priorities are central to this episode: the priority of personal time with God and the priority of the kingdom of God.

The Priority of Personal Time with God

Mark stresses that in the midst of a hectic schedule, Jesus takes time to be alone with God. He realizes that the success of his mission depends on his trust and reliance on God. It is significant that Jesus' public ministry does not begin until he has been empowered by the Holy Spirit at his baptism (1:9 – 15). In John's gospel, Jesus repeatedly says that he does nothing on his own initiative but only what the Father tells him to do (John 5:30; 8:28, 42). Hebrews similarly notes that Jesus "offered up prayers and petitions with fervent cries and tears to the one who could save him from death," and that he "learned obedience from what he suffered" (Heb 5:7 – 8). Jesus realizes he can accomplish nothing apart from the empowerment and guidance that comes from the Father.

It is easy in our lives to get so busy with family, work, church, and recreation that we forget we have been created to be in relationship with God and that we will never find true fulfillment or real success apart from him. If Jesus, the Son of God, needed time alone with his Father in order to accomplish his life's purpose, how much more do we?

The Priority of the Kingdom of God

Though Jesus spent a great deal of time during his Galilean ministry healing and casting out demons, these activities were ultimately subordinate to the priority of proclaiming the kingdom of God. This is not to say that the healings and exorcisms were unimportant or insignificant. They demonstrated God's love and compassion for people, and hence the reason Jesus came (John 3:16). They also revealed the power and the presence of the kingdom and so confirmed the authority of Jesus' words. But Jesus' ultimate purpose was not to heal physical disease but to call people to repentance and submission to God's reign in their lives. Physical healing is temporary, but a right relationship with God is eternal, bringing physical and spiritual wholeness.

Jesus' parables of the hidden treasures and the pearl of great value (Matt 13:44 – 46) emphasize the incalculable value of the kingdom. Why would someone sell everything they have to buy a field or to buy one pearl? The answer is that the blessings of the kingdom of God are worth sacrificing all we have to obtain. Why would a young couple leave the conveniences and comfort of Western society to trek through snake-infested jungle, proclaiming the gospel to one more primitive tribe? Why would a talented executive leave a six-figure income and a nice home and cars to invest years of his life in a poverty-stricken country providing aid to the poor and developing clean water systems? Why would a gifted linguist turn down a tenured position at a prestigious university to spend decades painstakingly translating the Bible into one more tribal tongue? The answer for all is the eternal value of the kingdom of God.

For Jesus, the physical needs of the people in Capernaum were important, and he felt compassion for them. But he had a greater task to perform, which was to bring people the urgent message that God was taking back his creation — that the kingdom of God was at hand.

CHAPTER 7

Mark 1:40–45

Literary Context

This is the third in a series of four healings and exorcisms that illustrate Jesus' kingdom authority during his early Galilean ministry (1:14 – 3:6). We have seen his power to exorcise demons (1:21 – 28, 34) and to heal (1:29 – 31); now we see his ability to bring purity from defilement. "Unclean" (defiling) demons have been cast out; now defiling diseases are purged. Jesus has come to bring wholeness and holiness to a defiled people. By introducing the issue of leprosy and ceremonial purification, this episode also forms a transition to the next series of events, which concern conflicts with the religious leaders over authority and the OT law (2:1 – 3:6).

II. The Authority of the Messiah (1:14 – 8:21)

  A. The Kingdom Authority of the Messiah (1:14 – 3:6)

    1. Jesus Proclaims the Kingdom and Calls Disciples (1:14 – 20)

    2. Authority in Teaching, Healing, and Exorcism (1:21 – 45)

      a. Jesus Teaches and Drives Out an Evil Spirit (1:21 – 28)

      b. Jesus Heals Peter's Mother-in-Law and Others (1:29 – 34)

      c. Jesus' Prayer Life and Ministry Purpose (1:35 – 39)

➡   **d. Jesus Heals a Man with a Skin Disease (1:40 – 45)**

    3. Conflicts with the Religious Leaders (2:1 – 3:6)

Main Idea

Jesus continues to demonstrate his authority over disease, this time bringing physical healing and ceremonial purification to a man whose disease had isolated him from family relationships and from corporate worship with the people of God.

Translation

Mark 1:40 – 45

40a	Character entrance/ description	**A man with leprosy came to him,**
b	manner of 40a/request	begging him and falling to his knees, saying to him,
c	conditional clause/ Request	*"If you are willing,* *you can cleanse me."*
41a	char. descr./response to 40	Being indignant,
b	Action/Healing	**he reached out his hand, touched him, and said to him,**
c	assertion	*"I am willing.*
d	command	*Be cleansed!"*
42a	Result of 41	**Immediately,** **the leprosy left him**
b	Result of 41	and **he was cleansed.**
43a	manner of 43b	Warning him sternly,
b	Action/Command	**Jesus immediately sent him away, saying,**
44a	command	*"Do not say anything to anyone about this,*
b	command	*but go and show yourself to the priest*
c	command	*and offer the sacrifice for your cleansing*
d	description of 44c	*that Moses commanded*
e	purpose for 44c	*as a testimony to them."*
45a	Response to 44a	But going out,
b	Response to 44a	**he began to proclaim it greatly** and
c	Response to 44a	**to spread the story,**
d	result of 45a-bc	so that Jesus could no longer enter a town publicly, but
e	result of 45a-c	stayed out in remote areas.
f	Contradistinction to 45e-f	Yet **the people kept coming out to him from everywhere.**

Structure

The story is structured as a typical healing account, including a request for healing (v. 40), a positive response from Jesus and a command to heal (v. 41), the resultant cure (v. 42), and the response to the healing received (v. 45). Additional features include Jesus' command to silence (vv. 43 – 44a) and his command to the man to present himself to the priest (v. 44b-e). The former command is the first instance of the messianic secret with reference to a person who was healed. The latter is related to the nature of the disease, which required ceremonial purification for restoration to the community.

Exegetical Outline

→ **1. The Man's Request for Healing (1:40)**

2. Jesus' Response (1:41)

    a. Jesus' indignation (1:41a)

    b. Jesus' touch (1:41b)

    c. Jesus' words (1:41c-d)

3. The Result: Immediate Cleansing (1:42)

4. Jesus' Commands (1:43 – 44)

    a. Command to silence (1:43 – 44a)

    b. Command to obey the OT prescriptions (1:44b-e)

5. The Man's Response: Spreading the News (1:45a-c)

6. The Result: Overwhelming Popularity and Ministry Limitations (1:45d-f)

Explanation of the Text

1:40 A man with leprosy came to him, begging him and falling to his knees, saying to him, "If you are willing, you can cleanse me." (Καὶ ἔρχεται πρὸς αὐτὸν λεπρὸς παρακαλῶν αὐτὸν καὶ γονυπετῶν καὶ λέγων αὐτῷ ὅτι ἐὰν θέλῃς δύνασαί με καθαρίσαι). The Hebrew and Greek terms traditionally rendered "leprosy" (Heb., ṣāraʿat; Gk., λέπρα) refer to a variety of skin disorders, including, but not limited to, the flesh-rotting disease today known as "leprosy" (Hansen's disease). This is evident since the descriptions of the disease found in Lev 13 – 14 do not fit Hansen's disease alone.

The OT set out detailed steps for the diagnosis of the disease (Lev 13), which rendered the victim ceremonially unclean and required separation from family, friends, and the religious life of the community. Touching a leper, like touching a corpse, resulted in temporary ceremonial uncleanness. Only a priest could declare a person clean or unclean of the disease. Those judged unclean were required to live outside the community, wear torn clothing, leave their hair unkempt, cover the lower part of their face, and cry out, "Unclean! Unclean!"

(Lev 13:45 – 46; Num 5:2 – 4). This ostracism, together with the fear of contagion and a slow painful death, made leprosy one of the most dreaded diseases in the ancient world. Although the OT allows for the possibility that people could be cured (Lev 14), the disease was considered practically incurable, and all the biblical accounts of healing result from miraculous intervention (Exod 4:6 – 8; Num 12:9 – 15; 2 Kgs 5:1 – 27; Luke 17:11 – 19).

The man boldly approaches Jesus, ignoring the OT requirement to keep his distance. His statement, "If you are willing, you can cleanse me," confirms his faith in Jesus' healing power. Jesus' response, however, is surprising.

1:41 – 42 Being indignant, he reached out his hand, touched him, and said to him, "I am willing. Be cleansed!" Immediately, the leprosy left him and he was cleansed (καὶ ὀργισθεὶς ἐκτείνας τὴν χεῖρα αὐτοῦ ἥψατο καὶ λέγει αὐτῷ· θέλω, καθαρίσθητι· καὶ εὐθὺς ἀπῆλθεν ἀπ᾽ αὐτοῦ ἡ λέπρα, καὶ ἐκαθαρίσθη). There is a difficult textual issue here. Most manuscripts say Jesus "felt compassion" (σπλαγχνισθείς) for the man, but a few read that Jesus was "angry" or "indignant" (ὀργισθείς). The external evidence strongly favors the former, since "being indignant" (ὀργισθείς) appears in only a few Western manuscripts (D itᵃ ᵈ ff² r¹).

Yet the internal transcriptional evidence runs strongly in the other direction. (1) It is easy to understand why a copyist would have changed a potentially offensive reference to Jesus' anger to one of compassion, but almost impossible to explain the reverse. (2) In their parallels, neither Matthew nor Luke refers to Jesus' compassion or his anger. While their omission of a reference to anger is easily explained (both regularly alter Mark's potentially offensive remarks), their independent removal of a statement about Jesus' compassion seems inexplicable. Metzger, by contrast, defends the UBS⁴ decision for "feeling compassion" (σπλαγχνισθείς) by pointing out that copyists did not eliminate Markan references to Jesus' anger elsewhere (3:5; 10:14).[1] Yet in these other cases Jesus' anger is clearly justified; here it does not seem to be.[2] Though a firm decision is difficult, a reference to anger or indignation seems most likely. Among contemporary versions, only NIV (2011), REB, NEB, and CEB follow this reading (NIV: "Jesus was indignant"; REB: "Jesus was moved to anger"; CEB: "Incensed, Jesus ...").

If "being indignant" (ὀργισθείς) is the original text, what does it mean? It is unlikely that Jesus is angry with the man, since he is about to show compassion for him. Furthermore, since Jesus willingly touches him, he cannot be angry at him for violating the OT commands for quarantine (Lev 13:46). Most likely, Jesus is expressing anger and indignation at the ravaging effects of the disease and (especially) of the social and religious ostracism that it is causing. Mark's gospel portrays Jesus as God's authoritative agent of salvation, doing battle with disease, death, and the devil. It is not surprising that he would show the same disdain for disease, the result of a sinful and fallen world, that he does for Satan's evil forces.[3]

Jesus surprisingly reaches out and touches the man, an action that in Judaism would have rendered him ceremonially unclean. There are three possibilities as to what Jesus is doing: (1) James Crossley argues that Jesus simply accepted the ritual defilement that his action would cause.[4] Ritual defilement was not sin, but was a part of everyday life in Israel (cf. Lev 11–15; Num 19:11–26). Those who dealt with the bodies of animals (like tanners and butchers) regularly experienced ritual defilement (Lev 11:24, 39–40). Purity returned to a person after a period of waiting (e.g., "until evening") and/or through certain prescribed rituals. Evidence for this view is the fact that Jesus commands the man to go to the priest and offer the

---

1. Bruce M. Metzger, *A Textual Commentary on the Greek New Testament* (2nd ed.; New York/Stuttgart: United Bible Societies, 1994), 65. Metzger also claims that "being indignant" (ὀργισθείς) could have arisen in parallel with the strong language in v. 43 (ἐμβριμησάμενος, "speaking harshly") or from confusion between Aramaic words behind the text (compare Syriac *ethraham*, "he had pity," and *ethraʿem*, "he was enraged"). Yet confusion in an Aramaic source behind Mark does not explain the absence of Jesus' compassion in both Matthew and Luke (who are surely using a Greek version of Mark). For a recent defense of σπλαγχνισθείς based on its graphic similarity to ὀργισθείς, see Peter J. Williams, "An Examination of Ehrman's Case for ὀργισθείς in Mark 1,41," *NovT* 54 (2012): 1–12.

2. France, *Mark*, 115; Marcus, *Mark 1–8*, 206.

3. Both Hooker, *Mark*, 80, and Marcus, *Mark 1–8*, 209, claim Jesus' anger is directed against a demonic presence that is causing the leprosy. Marcus cites *b. Ketub.* 61b, where scale disease is ascribed to an evil spirit, and to a possible reference in the DSS (4Q272); cf. J. Baumgarten, "The 4Q Zadokite Fragments on Skin Disease," *JJS* 41 (1990): 153–65. The problem is that nothing in the context suggests a demonic presence. Marcus's reference to ἐκβάλλω ("cast out") in v. 43 doesn't work since Jesus "casts out" the man *after* he has been healed. We would have to assume that Mark has garbled an original source that said Jesus "cast out" the leprosy rather than the man.

4. James G. Crossley, *The Date of Mark's Gospel: Insights from the Law in Earliest Christianity* (JSNTSup 299; London/New York: T&T Clark, 2004), 90–91. This is part of Crossley's argument that Mark portrays Jesus as an entirely law-observant Jew.

prescribed sacrifice (Mark 1:44). The problem is that elsewhere in Mark, Jesus seems willing to abrogate the law, for example, when he "declared all foods clean" in apparent violation of the OT dietary laws (7:19).

(2) A second possibility is that by touching the man Jesus is intentionally challenging and rejecting the Jewish laws of purity and defilement. This is the view of those who identify Jesus as a Cynic-like sage, calling for an egalitarian society without social or religious hierarchy or divisions.[5] By touching the man, Jesus rejects the category of ritual defilement. The problem with this, as Crossley notes, is that Jesus immediately tells the man to offer the prescribed sacrifices that would restore him to the community. This is hardly a radical break with the hierarchical temple system.

(3) The third and most likely view is that Jesus is reversing the direction of impurity and cleansing the leper rather than being defiled by the disease. He is willing to touch the man because of the power and presence of the kingdom of God in his own words and deeds. The OT age of promise, with its ceremonial rules of purity, is giving way to the new age of fulfillment, where purity does not come through external ritual and ceremony but through the internal transformation and cleansing by the Holy Spirit. Just as John's water baptism was a symbolic precursor to the Messiah's true baptism with the Spirit (1:8), so the OT rituals were mere symbols and precursors to the eschatological cleansing that comes with the kingdom of God. Rather than being rendered unclean by touching the man, Jesus radically reverses the direction of purity and brings healing and cleansing from defilement. Jesus has not come to reaffirm the law (view 1) or to abolish it (view 2), but to fulfill it (Matt 5:17) — to bring it to its prophesied consummation in the kingdom of God.[6] (For more on this, see Theology in Application, below.)

The healing is "immediate" (εὐθύς) and complete. The man is not just healed of the disease, but "cleansed" (καθαρίζω) from defilement and so able to be restored to the community. As in the healing of Peter's mother-in-law, no rituals or incantations are necessary. Jesus heals through his own authority, with his word and his touch.

1:43 – 44 Warning him sternly, Jesus immediately sent him away, saying: "Do not say anything to anyone about this, but go and show yourself to the priest and offer the sacrifice for your cleansing that Moses commanded as a testimony to them." (καὶ ἐμβριμησάμενος αὐτῷ εὐθὺς ἐξέβαλεν αὐτὸν καὶ λέγει αὐτῷ· ὅρα μηδενὶ μηδὲν εἴπῃς, ἀλλὰ ὕπαγε σεαυτὸν δεῖξον τῷ ἱερεῖ καὶ προσένεγκε περὶ τοῦ καθαρισμοῦ σου ἃ προσέταξεν Μωϋσῆς, εἰς μαρτύριον αὐτοῖς). Jesus' command is surprisingly strong. The verb "warn sternly" (ἐμβριμάομαι) can mean to "bellow" or "snort" but is used metaphorically of deep feelings (John 11:33, 38) or a stern or angry rebuke (as here).[7] "Sent away" (ἐκβάλλω) is the same verb used for "casting out" demons but, as at 1:12, can also indicate strong compulsion. As the Spirit "compelled" Jesus into the desert, so Jesus now strongly insists that the man keep quiet about the miracle.

Here is Mark's first example of the "messianic secret" with reference to a healing (sometimes called

5. See, e.g., John D. Crossan, *Jesus: A Revolutionary Biography* (San Francisco: HarperSanFrancisco, 1994), 82: "I presume that Jesus, who did not and could not cure that disease or any other one, healed the poor man's illness by refusing to accept the disease's ritual uncleanness and social ostracization. Jesus thereby forced others either to reject him from this community or to accept the leper within it as well."

6. For a fuller discussion of this theme in the context of Jesus' meals, see Craig L. Blomberg, *Contagious Holiness: Jesus' Meals with Sinners* (NSBT; Downers Grove, IL: IVP Academic, 2005).

7. BDAG, 322.

the "miracle secret").[8] Previously Jesus has silenced demons (vv. 25, 34), but now he commands the former leper to keep the healing quiet. As with the silencing of demons, the command likely has to do with both the nature of Jesus' messianic identity and the timing of its revelation. The people are looking for a political Messiah who will free them from their Roman oppressors. While eventually acknowledging his messianic identity (8:30), Jesus will define his messianic role as the Son of Man who will suffer and die as a ransom for sin (8:31; 9:31; 10:45). As to its timing, rumors surrounding Jesus' identity risk inciting the crowds to messianic furor and so thwarting his plans to proclaim the kingdom of God throughout the towns and villages of Galilee (1:38). A premature and misinformed revelation of Jesus' identity will create a hindrance to his essential mission. This interpretation finds support in the following paragraph, where the crush of the crowds makes it impossible for Jesus to minister freely in the population centers (v. 45; cf. 2:2; 3:9 – 10, 20; 6:30 – 34, 53 – 36).

Jesus commands the man to go and show himself to the priest and to offer the prescribed sacrifices for his cleansing. The OT stipulated that a person must be declared clean by a priest, who must then perform an eight-day ritual that involved water cleansings, shaving of body hair, and sacrifices and offerings to the Lord (Lev 14). Mark's purpose in recording this command may be to show that Jesus did not oppose the law per se, but only the hypocritical way it was applied by the religious leaders. More likely, Jesus has social and societal concerns in mind, since these rituals were necessary for the man to be accepted back into his community and to participate in Israel's religious life.

The last phrase, "as a testimony to them" (εἰς μαρτύριον αὐτοῖς), is ambiguous, both with refer-

ence to the nature of the testimony and the identity of "them." It could mean (1) as evidence or proof of Jesus' faithfulness to the law, (2) as evidence or proof of Jesus' messianic identity, (3) as evidence or proof that the man was truly healed and so could be restored to society, or (4) as evidence *against* the religious leaders — who will reject Jesus despite the healing — to be presented on judgment day. In the first three, "to them" (αὐτοῖς) would be a dative of advantage ("for them") and could refer to the religious leaders or to all the people. For the fourth, αὐτοῖς would be a dative of disadvantage ("against them"), referring to the religious leaders. The same phrase is used in this sense at 6:11 and possibly at 13:9 (though this latter may be a dative of advantage).

The first view is unlikely, placing too much emphasis on legalistic questions. The second would directly contradict Jesus' command to silence and so is also doubtful. The fourth probably reads too much into the context, which suggests nothing about judgment. The most natural reading is the third, since the immediate context concerns the rituals that confirm the man's cleansing.

1:45 But going out, he began to proclaim it greatly and to spread the story, so that Jesus could no longer enter a town publicly, but stayed out in remote areas. Yet the people kept coming out to him from everywhere (ὁ δὲ ἐξελθὼν ἤρξατο κηρύσσειν πολλὰ καὶ διαφημίζειν τὸν λόγον, ὥστε μηκέτι αὐτὸν δύνασθαι φανερῶς εἰς πόλιν εἰσελθεῖν, ἀλλ' ἔξω ἐπ' ἐρήμοις τόποις ἦν· καὶ ἤρχοντο πρὸς αὐτὸν πάντοθεν). The man's excitement gets the best of him, and he breaks the silence that Jesus commanded (cf. 7:36). The implied reader would not condemn him for this, however, since the miracle was so stupendous that no human being could keep it quiet.

---

8. See F. Watson, "The Social Function of Mark's Secrecy Theme," *JSNT* 7 (1985): 49 – 69.

Rhetorically, the narrator uses the broken command to highlight the greatness of the miracle and the power of the miracle worker. The result for Jesus is such popularity that he cannot move about freely. Again, the result is negative, but the rhetorical point is positive. Jesus cannot preach in the towns as he would like (cf. v. 38), but his greatness is such that people will go anywhere to find him.

Theology in Application

Jesus' Messianic Authority

As throughout the early Galilean ministry, Jesus' authority is the central theme of this passage. The Messiah has authority in announcing the kingdom of God, in calling disciples, in teaching, over demons, over disease, and over ritual defilement. All of these confirm his role as God's agent in announcing and inaugurating the kingdom of God.

The Necessity of Faith

A secondary theme here is the importance of faith, as the man affirms Jesus' power to heal: "If you are willing, you can cleanse me." It is not the amount of faith that is important, but the object of faith (cf. Matt 17:20). The man's simple declaration that Jesus is able to heal stirs Jesus to respond.

Jesus' Compassion

A third theme is Jesus' compassion, which motivates the healing. Although v. 41 probably does not have an explicit reference to Jesus' compassion (see comments on vv. 41 – 42), Jesus' anger at the ravaging effects of the disease, his willingness to touch the man, and his words of healing all reveal his empathy. He also shows concern for the man's social restoration by insisting he perform the rituals necessary for purification. Those who minister effectively to people know that true healing concerns more than healing bodies or meeting physical needs. It involves emotional health, spiritual wholeness, and reconciliation with God and others.

The Sanctifying Power of the Kingdom of God

A fourth theme relates to the purifying touch of Jesus. Instead of becoming defiled by the man's leprosy, Jesus brings purity and healing. In the old covenant, Israel was called to be a people separated from the world around them and set apart to God. The whole ceremonial system confirmed the need to maintain separation from a world of sin and impurity. While believers today are also called to personal purity and sanctification, the kingdom has an outward rather than an inward focus, permeating the world and taking back territory for God. Jesus' parable of the strong man illustrates this (3:27). Jesus is not taking a defensive posture, but an offensive one, invading the domain of Satan and claiming back its captives. The people of God, Jesus says in Matthew, are to be salt and light (Matt 5:13 – 16), two substances that permeate and transform their environment (cf. 13:33).

The apostle Paul makes a similar point in 1 Cor 7:12 – 16. Some in the Corinthian church were evidently encouraging those married to unbelievers to divorce their spouses in order to avoid the defilement that an unbeliever brought to the marriage. This would be analogous to the situation in the OT book of Ezra, where the Israelites were called to divorce their pagan wives in order to maintain spiritual purity (Ezra 10:10 – 11; cf. Judg 3:6). Paul, however, encourages the Corinthians to remain with their spouses: "For the unbelieving husband has been sanctified through his wife, and the unbelieving wife has been sanctified through her believing husband. Otherwise your children would be unclean, but as it is, they are holy" (1 Cor 7:14).

It is significant that Paul uses the language of purity and defilement here. Paul is not saying that a person is saved by default because he or she is married to a believer, but rather that the children of the kingdom bring a purging and transforming influence wherever they go. In the new age of salvation, the old laws of ritual purity and defilement no longer apply because the kingdom is not an inward protective cocoon but an outward force of the Spirit with the power to transform the world and bring it once again into a right relationship with God.

The church today needs to claim back its authority as salt and light. We should not take a defensive stance, cringing back in fear at society's defiling encroachment on our values and beliefs. Instead we need to go on the offensive, transforming the world through the unconditional and self-sacrificial love of God. Rather than complaining about the world's defilement, we restore it to purity and wholeness by overcoming evil with good.

Mark 2:1 – 12

Literary Context

This episode is a mixed one (see Structure, below) that forms a transition from Mark's first series of healings and exorcisms (1:21 – 45) to a series of five controversies with the religious leaders (2:1 – 3:6). These five will climax with the first plot against Jesus' life (3:6). They are framed on either side with statements about Jesus' growing popularity (1:45; 3:7), no doubt a key reason for the increasing scrutiny and concern expressed by the religious leaders. As elsewhere in the early Galilean ministry, Jesus' authority is on center stage. Here he demonstrates his authority not only to heal disease, but also to forgive sins. The two are inextricably connected in Jesus' announcement of the kingdom of God and the restoration of creation that this entails.

> II. The Authority of the Messiah (1:14 – 8:21)
>   A. The Kingdom Authority of the Messiah (1:14 – 3:6)
>   1. Jesus Proclaims the Kingdom and Calls Disciples (1:14 – 20)
>   2. Authority in Teaching, Healing, and Exorcism (1:21 – 45)
> ➡   **3. Conflicts with the Religious Leaders (2:1 – 3:6)**
>   **a. Jesus Forgives and Heals a Paralyzed Man (2:1 – 12)**
>   b. Jesus Calls Levi and Eats with Sinners (2:13 – 17)

Main Idea

Jesus demonstrates his divine authority to forgive sins by healing a paralzyed man in front of a group of skeptical religious leaders. The episode confirms the close connection between the forgiveness of sins and the restoration of a fallen creation. The healing also confirms the importance of faith in Jesus' healing power.

Translation

Mark 2:1 – 12

1a	setting (temporal/spatial)	When he returned again to Capernaum several days later,
b	Setting (social)	**news quickly spread that he was home.**
2a	Setting (social)	**So many people gathered in the house that there was no more room, not ♫**
		even outside the door.
b	Action	And **he was preaching the word to them.**
c	Action	**Some people arrived,**
3a	manner of 2c	bringing to him a paralyzed man,
b	description of 3a	carried by four of them.
c		
4a	setting (social)/obstacle	When they weren't able to get to him because of the crowd,
b	Action/solution to 4a	**they uncovered the roof above where he was.**
c	means of 4d	Digging through,
d	Action	**they lowered the cot on which the paralyzed man was lying.**
5a	response to 4	Seeing their faith,
b	Action/response to 4	**Jesus said to the paralyzed man,**
c	pronouncement	*"Son, your sins are forgiven."*
6a	Setting (social)	But **some of the experts in the law were sitting there,**
b	Response to 5c	and **they began thinking in their hearts,**
7a	rhetorical question	*"How can this man talk like that?*
b	accusation	*He's blaspheming!*
c	rhetorical qu./accusation	*Who can forgive sins except God?"*
8a	Response to 6 – 7	**Right away Jesus knew in his spirit what they were thinking, and said to them,**
b	rhetorical qu./accusation	*"Why are you thinking these things in your hearts?*
9a	question/comparison	*Which is easier, to say to the paralyzed man,*
b		*'Your sins are forgiven,' or to say,*
c		*'Get up, pick up your cot, and walk'?*
10a	purpose of 11	*But so that you can know that the Son of Man has authority on earth to forgive sins"—*
b	Narrative aside	**he said to the paralyzed man—**
11	command	*"I say to you, get up, pick up your cot, and go home."*
12a	Response to 11	**He immediately got up,**
		picked up his cot, and
		walked right out in front of them all!
b	Response to 12a	**Everyone was stunned and**
		began praising God and saying,
c	Response to 12a	*"We've never seen anything like this!"*

Structure

The episode is a combination of forms: a healing account, a controversy story, and a pronouncement story.[1] The healing begins in a typical manner, with a statement of the problem: a paralyzed man is unable to reach Jesus because of the crush of the crowds (vv. 1 – 4). When the man's four friends improvise by tearing up the roof to lower him into the house, Jesus is impressed by their faith. We expect him to heal the man, but instead he shocks the onlookers by pronouncing that the man's sins are forgiven. The healing now turns to a controversy story, as the religious leaders secretly accuse Jesus of blasphemy for claiming the prerogative. Jesus bests his opponents by pronouncing his authority as the Son of Man to forgive sins on earth (v. 10) and then by healing the man as proof of this claim (vv. 11 – 12). The episode climaxes, as often in Mark, with the amazed reaction of the crowds, who praise God, saying, "We've never seen anything like this!"

Exegetical Outline

➡ **1. Setting (2:1 – 2)**

    a. Jesus returns to Capernaum (2:1a)

    b. The report goes out and crowds gather (2:1b – 2a)

    c. Jesus preaches the word (2:2b)

2. The Faith of Friends: The Problem and Its Solution (2:3 – 4)

    a. A paralyzed man cannot reach Jesus (2:3 – 4a)

    b. Friends dig through the roof and lower the man (2:4b-d)

3. Jesus' Authority to Heal and Forgive Sins (2:5 – 12a)

    a. Jesus' first pronouncement: forgiving sins (2:5)

    b. The charge of blasphemy by the religious leaders (2:6 – 7)

    c. Jesus' response and second pronouncement: the Son of Man's authority to heal and forgive (2:8 – 10)

    d. The healing (2:11 – 12a)

4. The Popular Response (2:12b-c)

---

1. Some have claimed that this mixed form argues against the story's integrity, and that a later editor or storyteller has added the debate about the forgiveness of sins (2:6 – 10) to a healing narrative (2:1 – 5, 11 – 12) (e.g., Taylor, *Mark*, 192 – 93). See Guelich, *Mark 1:1 – 8:26*, 82, for advocates and arguments pro and con. The form-critical claim that simple forms are more primitive and that mixed forms indicate secondary editing has been widely discredited.

Explanation of the Text

2:1 – 2 When he returned again to Capernaum several days later, news quickly spread that he was home. So many people gathered in the house that there was no more room, not even outside the door. And he was preaching the word to them (Καὶ εἰσελθὼν πάλιν εἰς Καφαρναοὺμ δι᾽ ἡμερῶν ἠκούσθη ὅτι ἐν οἴκῳ ἐστίν. καὶ συνήχθησαν πολλοὶ ὥστε μηκέτι χωρεῖν μηδὲ τὰ πρὸς τὴν θύραν, καὶ ἐλάλει αὐτοῖς τὸν λόγον). Although Jesus cannot "openly" enter towns because of his popularity (1:45), he is able to slip back into Capernaum after his preaching tour throughout Galilee (1:38). The Greek idiom "it was heard" (ἠκούσθη) means "word got around" or "news quickly spread." It is impossible to keep secrets in a small town. When this hometown prophet-made-good with a growing reputation for teaching and healing returns, Capernaum is quickly abuzz (cf. 1:45). The phrase translated "home" (ἐν οἴκῳ) could mean "in a/the house," perhaps the home of Peter and Andrew in Capernaum (cf. 1:29). Jesus apparently used their home as his base of operations while in the area.

Jesus' popularity is a recurring theme in the early chapters of Mark (1:37, 45; 3:7 – 10, 20; 4:1; 6:33). The neuter plural phrase translated "not even outside the door" (μηδὲ τὰ πρὸς τὴν θύραν) carries the sense of "places in proximity to" (τὰ πρός) and could mean "near" (NASB), "by" (NET), or "outside" (NIV, NLT, REB) the door. All access to Jesus has been blocked by the crowds, who stream to him for his teaching and especially his miracles (1:22, 27). Jesus' priority, however, is proclaiming the "word" (cf. 1:38), which here likely means the message of the kingdom of God (1:15).

2:3 – 4 Some people arrived, bringing to him a paralyzed man, carried by four of them. When they weren't able to get to him because of the crowd, they uncovered the roof above where he was. Digging through, they lowered the cot on which the paralyzed man was lying (καὶ ἔρχονται φέροντες πρὸς αὐτὸν παραλυτικὸν αἰρόμενον ὑπὸ τεσσάρων. καὶ μὴ δυνάμενοι προσενέγκαι αὐτῷ διὰ τὸν ὄχλον ἀπεστέγασαν τὴν στέγην ὅπου ἦν, καὶ ἐξορύξαντες χαλῶσι τὸν κράβαττον ὅπου ὁ παραλυτικὸς κατέκειτο). The actions of this man's friends show they are willing to do anything to get him to Jesus. Persistent faith in the face of opposition or obstacles is an important theme throughout Mark's gospel (5:23, 25 – 34, 36; 7:24 – 30, 32; 8:22; 9:24; 10:46 – 52).

Palestinian roofs were generally flat and made of wooden crossbeams covered with thatch and a layer of compact dirt. They were sturdy affairs and were used for work, storage, drying fruit, and sleeping on warm summer nights. An external staircase or ladder provided access. The four men go up to the roof by the external access and begin digging through[2] the dirt and pulling aside the thatch.[3] One can imagine the commotion below as dirt pours down on the heads of those trying to listen to Jesus. With the beams exposed, they lower the man between them to Jesus. The "cot" or "bed" (κράβαττος) may have been a "stretcher" (NET), or even a "mat" (NIV, NLT), held by the four corners. The reason for the man's condition — whether accident or disease — is not explained, only that he is lame or unable to walk.

---

2. ἀπεστέγασαν τὴν στέγην (lit., "unroofed the roof") is a cognate accusative (Wallace, *Greek Grammar,* 189), a common construction in Mark (4:41; 9:41; 10:38 – 39; 13:7; 14:6).

3. Luke says that the men lowered the man "through the tiles" (Luke 5:19). This may be his way of explaining the event to his Hellenistic readers more familiar with tile roofs, although it is possible the roof of this house was made of tiles.

2:5 Seeing their faith, Jesus said to the paralyzed man, "Son, your sins are forgiven." (καὶ ἰδὼν ὁ Ἰησοῦς τὴν πίστιν αὐτῶν λέγει τῷ παραλυτικῷ· τέκνον, ἀφίενταί σου αἱ ἁμαρτίαι). "Their faith" most naturally means the faith of the friends, though it could include the paralyzed man's faith. In Mark, healing and faith are often linked (1:40 – 45; 2:1 – 12; 5:21 – 24, 25 – 34, 35 – 43; 6:5 – 6; 7:31 – 34; 9:14 – 29; 10:46 – 52).[4] The friends and the crowd are expecting a healing, yet Jesus shocks them by pronouncing that the man's sins are forgiven.

Was the man's paralysis caused by sin? Possibly, but this is not a necessary implication in the story. While Scripture affirms that disease and physical death may be caused by individual sins (Deut 28:27; Ps 107:17 – 18; John 5:14; Acts 5:1 – 11; 1 Cor 11:30; 1 John 5:16),[5] this is certainly not always the case (Job 1:8; Luke 13:1 – 5; John 9:2 – 3). The fact that Jesus responds to the faith of the *friends* (rather than to the man's repentance) would argue against a direct link between the man's sin and his infirmity. Jesus' words are better understood as affirming the holistic nature of Jesus' healing ministry. The arrival of the kingdom of God will mean the full restoration of God's creation, both physically and spiritually. Dealing with the root cause of all disease and death — sinful rebellion against God — is essential for all true healing. Spiritual and physical healing are closely linked in Mark's gospel. When Jesus says, "Your faith has saved [σέσωκεν] you" (5:34; 10:52), he is referring to physical healing, but with the broader connotation of spiritual renewal.

How much authority is Jesus claiming here? "Your sins are forgiven" (ἀφίενταί σου αἱ ἁμαρτίαι)

could be a divine passive, meaning "God has forgiven your sins" (cf. 3:28; 4:12).[6] In this case Jesus would be functioning as God's spokesperson, announcing his forgiveness to others. The OT priests pronounced God's forgiveness on those who brought their offerings to the temple, and a prophet like Nathan could declare that God had forgiven David (2 Sam 12:13). Nevertheless, Mark makes it clear that Jesus is claiming his own authority to forgive sins, since the religious leaders immediately accuse Jesus of blasphemy (vv. 6 – 7). Jesus confirms this in v. 9 when he says that the Son of Man has authority on earth to forgive sins.

2:6 – 7 But some of the experts in the law were sitting there, and they began thinking in their hearts, "How can this man talk like that? He's blaspheming! Who can forgive sins except God?" (ἦσαν δέ τινες τῶν γραμματέων ἐκεῖ καθήμενοι καὶ διαλογιζόμενοι ἐν ταῖς καρδίαις αὐτῶν· τί οὗτος οὕτως λαλεῖ; βλασφημεῖ· τίς δύναται ἀφιέναι ἁμαρτίας εἰ μὴ εἷς ὁ θεός;). The experts in the law (γραμματεῖς; traditionally, "scribes") were mentioned already in 1:22 (see comments there), where their rote teaching was contrasted with Jesus' dynamic teaching "with authority." Mark does not say why they are present, but as the guardians of Israel's traditions, they are presumably checking out this upstart teacher and healer whose reputation has been spreading far and wide. Luke's parallel says that they came "from every village of Galilee and from Judea and Jerusalem" (Luke 5:17).

The Greek idiom "thinking in their hearts" (διαλογιζόμενοι ἐν ταῖς καρδίαις αὐτῶν) means "pondering/questioning to themselves" (cf. Luke

---

4. See C. D. Marshall, *Faith as a Theme in Mark's Narrative* (SNTSMS 64; Cambridge: Cambridge University Press, 1989), passim.

5. See Marcus, *Mark 1 – 8*, 221, for more on the scriptural connection between sin and disease; see also Theology in Application, below.

6. Guelich, *Mark 1:1 – 8:26*, 85 – 86; J. Jeremias, *New Testament Theology*; vol. 1: *The Proclamation of Jesus* (New York: Scribner's, 1971), 114; Schweizer, *Good News*, 61; Pesch, *Markusevangelium*, 1:156.

3:15), the heart being the center of intellect and emotion. The charge of blasphemy is a serious one, which, in Israel, carried the penalty of stoning (Lev 24:10 – 16). While the Mishnah defines blasphemy narrowly as the act of pronouncing the divine name (*m. Sanh.* 7:5), the term could also be used for a wider range of offenses.[7] To claim God's prerogative in forgiving sins would certainly qualify.[8] The somewhat awkward rhetorical question, "Who can forgive sins except one — God," using Greek "one" (εἷς) instead of "only, alone" (μόνος, as in Luke 5:21), may suggest an allusion to the Shema, the classic Jewish affirmation of monotheism from Deut 6:4: "Hear, O Israel: The LORD our God, the LORD is one." Jesus is accused of usurping God's unique position (cf. John 5:18; 10:33).

2:8 – 9 Right away Jesus knew in his spirit what they were thinking, and said to them, "Why are you thinking these things in your hearts? Which is easier, to say to the paralyzed man, 'Your sins are forgiven,' or to say, 'Get up, pick up your cot, and walk'?" (καὶ εὐθὺς ἐπιγνοὺς ὁ Ἰησοῦς τῷ πνεύματι αὐτοῦ ὅτι οὕτως διαλογίζονται ἐν ἑαυτοῖς λέγει αὐτοῖς· τί ταῦτα διαλογίζεσθε ἐν ταῖς καρδίαις ὑμῶν; τί ἐστιν εὐκοπώτερον, εἰπεῖν τῷ παραλυτικῷ· ἀφίενταί σου αἱ ἁμαρτίαι, ἢ εἰπεῖν· ἔγειρε καὶ ἆρον τὸν κράβαττόν σου καὶ περιπάτει;). There is heavy irony here. Even as the religious leaders are scoffing at Jesus' claim to divine authority, he is reading their minds — demonstrating a prerogative of God! Mark's characteristic "immediately" (εὐθύς) means "at the very time they were thinking it." That Jesus knew "in his spirit" (τῷ πνεύματι αὐτοῦ) means he supernaturally comprehends it. Mark does not

specify whether this supernatural insight comes from the Holy Spirit or Jesus' inherent deity.

Jesus challenges the leaders with a rabbinic style "lesser-to-greater" (*qal wahomer*) argument. It is easier to say, "Your sins are forgiven," than "Get up, pick up your cot, and walk," since the latter requires external proof. If Jesus can do the latter (the "harder"), then he can certainly do the former. Of course, Mark's readers might also detect a secondary ironic level of meaning, since what is easier *to say* ("Your sins are forgiven") is not necessarily easier *to do*. The informed reader knows that Jesus will ultimately do what is humanly impossible: he will "give his life as a ransom for many" (10:45) to bring true and complete forgiveness of sins. Healing a paralyzed man is a small thing compared to the cosmic significance of inaugurating the kingdom of God and restoring creation to a right relationship with him through a sacrificial death on the cross.

2:10 – 11 "But so that you can know that the Son of Man has authority on earth to forgive sins" — he said to the paralyzed man, "I say to you, get up, pick up your cot, and go home." (ἵνα δὲ εἰδῆτε ὅτι ἐξουσίαν ἔχει ὁ υἱὸς τοῦ ἀνθρώπου ἀφιέναι ἁμαρτίας ἐπὶ τῆς γῆς—λέγει τῷ παραλυτικῷ· σοὶ λέγω, ἔγειρε ἆρον τὸν κράβαττόν σου καὶ ὕπαγε εἰς τὸν οἶκόν σου). A number of commentators have argued that the first clause of v. 10 is not Jesus' words but a narrative aside by the author, who is telling his readers that Jesus has the authority to forgive sins.[9] This assertion is meant to preclude Jesus' own use of the Son of Man title until after his dramatic announcement in 8:31 that the Son of

7. D. L. Bock, *Blasphemy and Exaltation in Judaism: The Charge against Jesus in Mark 14:53 – 65* (Grand Rapids: Baker, 1998), ch. 2; France, *Mark*, 126.

8. Some have claimed that a fragmentary text from Qumran, *The Prayer of Nabonidus* (4Q242), presents a Jewish exorcist as claiming to forgive the sins of Nabonidus. Yet the text is fragmentary and its meaning is disputed. See J. A. Fitzmyer,

The Gospel according to Luke (AB 28 and 28A; New York: Doubleday, 1981, 1985), 1:585, and Marcus, *Mark 1 – 8*, 217, for details. Even if the text makes this claim, this would be one small exception to the rule.

9. G. H. Boobyer, "Mark II,10a and the Interpretation of the Healing of the Paralytic," *HTR* 48 (1954): 115 – 20; Lane, *Mark*, 96 – 98; Cranfield, *Mark*, 100.

Man must suffer and die. Primary evidence for this is that the Son of Man title (ὁ υἱὸς τοῦ ἀνθρώπου) occurs only twice before 8:31 (here and in 2:28, which is also disputed), but twelve times from 8:31 onward.[10] According to this view, Jesus first introduces the Son of Man title to disclose his suffering role to his disciples.

While intriguing, this conclusion is unlikely for a variety of reasons. (1) A sudden change of address directed to Mark's readers seems odd and out of place in the story. The "you" more naturally refers to the experts in the law. (2) Jesus' statement is critical to the narrative scene, since the religious leaders have challenged his *authority* to forgive sins. (3) Most significantly, apart from these two possible exceptions (2:10, 28), the Son of Man title in the Gospels always appears on the lips of Jesus,[11] never in the narrator's comments. For the meaning of the title for Jesus, see "In Depth: Jesus as the Son of Man."

IN DEPTH: Jesus as the Son of Man

The title "Son of Man" (ὁ υἱὸς τοῦ ἀνθρώπου) represents a somewhat awkward Greek rendering of the Hebrew phrase *ben-ʾādām* and the Aramaic *bar-ʾenaš*, both of which mean "a child of humanity" or "a human being." In the OT the phrase was used of humanity in general (cf. Ps 8:4), often with the sense of the weakness and frailty of people in contrast to the power and immortality of God. God addresses the prophet Ezekiel over ninety times with this designation (Ezek 2:1, etc.).

Jesus' use of the title certainly points to his humanity and solidarity with the human race. Yet his words go beyond this general sense. Scholars have categorized three types of Son of Man sayings in the Gospels: (1) those that confirm Jesus' messianic authority on earth (2:10, 28); (2) those that refer to his mission of service and suffering (8:31; 9:9, 12, 31; 10:33 – 34, 45; 14:21 [2x], 41); and (3) those that refer to his return in glory to save and judge (8:38; 13:26 – 27; 14:62). There is little doubt that the last ones allude to Dan 7:13 – 14, which describes an exalted messianic figure — "one like a son of man" (= in human form) — who comes with the clouds of heaven, receives authority, glory, and sovereign power from God, and establishes an eternal kingdom (cf. *1 En.* 37 – 71).[12] Yet passages about the suffering Son of Man (Mark 8:31; 9:9, 12, 31; 10:33 – 34) may also allude to Dan 7, where the "one like a son of man" is closely identified with the oppressed people of God, who are said to receive the sovereignty, power, and greatness of the kingdoms of the earth after a period of suffering (7:25 – 27).

The reason Jesus chose this unusual title, as well as its exact significance, is

---

10. See 8:31, 38; 9:9, 12, 31; 10:33, 45; 13:26; 14:21 [2x], 41, 62.

11. The one exception is John 12:34, where the crowds are referring to Jesus' words.

12. It has been greatly debated whether the *Similitudes of Enoch* (*1 En.* 37 – 71), with their description of the Danielic Son of Man as a heavenly redeemer figure, are pre- or post-Christian. See D. L. Bock and R. H. Charlesworth, eds., *Parables of Enoch: A Paradigm Shift* (London/New York: Bloomsbury T&T Clark, 2013).

hotly debated among scholars.[13] Most likely, for Jesus it expressed both his solidarity with the people of God and his messianic status, yet without the political and militaristic connotations of popular messianic titles like "Messiah" and "Son of David" (see Mark 10:47 – 48; 12:35).

The Son of Man has authority "on earth" (ἐπὶ τῆς γῆς) to forgive sins. "On earth" could be understood in various ways: (1) temporally, meaning "even now," during Jesus' time on earth and not just in the future in heaven;[14] (2) as a sphere of influence, on earth as opposed to the Father's authority in heaven;[15] or (3) qualitatively modifying "sins," "earthly sins," or the sins of human beings. The second interpretation is most likely, not in the sense of limiting Jesus' authority (on earth but not in heaven), but rather to show that the Son of Man's authority is equivalent to that which the Father exercises in heaven. Through the Son of Man, God's heavenly forgiveness has now come to earth.

The phrase "he said to the paralyzed man" (λέγει[16] τῷ παραλυτικῷ), is a parenthetic remark made by the narrator to indicate that Jesus has turned from addressing the religious leaders to speak to the paralyzed man.[17]

2:12 He immediately got up, picked up his cot, and walked right out in front of them all! Everyone was stunned and began praising God and saying, "We've never seen anything like this!" (καὶ ἠγέρθη καὶ εὐθὺς ἄρας τὸν κράβαττον ἐξῆλθεν ἔμπροσθεν πάντων, ὥστε ἐξίστασθαι πάντας καὶ

δοξάζειν τὸν θεὸν λέγοντας ὅτι οὕτως οὐδέποτε εἴδομεν). Mark's "immediately" (εὐθύς) here means just that (cf. 1:10, 18, 20, 42). The healing was instantaneous. The healing confirms Jesus' authority to forgive sins. "He did the miracle which they could see that they might know that he had done the other one that they could not see."[18]

In a cultural context where honor and shame are supreme values, there is also an element of humiliation here, as the religious leaders who have doubted Jesus' word lose face in front of the crowd. Mark notes that the man walked out "in front of them all" (ἔμπροσθεν πάντων), providing vivid testimony that Jesus was right and they were wrong.

The response of the crowd is again amazement (cf. 1:22, 27; 5:42; 6:51; 12:17) and praise to God. The participle "saying" (λέγοντας) could be modal. They praised God *by saying,* "We've never seen anything like this!" More likely it is circumstantial. They praised God *and said* to one another, "We've never seen anything like this!" The narrator uses this acclamation to show that God is doing something unique and unprecedented. Jesus will make the same point in 2:21 – 22, where he compares the kingdom of God to new wine that cannot be poured into old wineskins. A new day is dawning.

---

13. For surveys of the literature, see W. O. Walker, "The Son of Man: Some Recent Developments," *CBQ* 45 (1983): 584 – 607; J. R. Donahue, "Recent Studies on the Origin of 'Son of Man' in the Gospels," *CBQ* 48 (1986): 484 – 98.

14. Stein, *Mark*, 121.

15. France, *Mark*, 129.

16. λέγει is a historical present (see comments on 1:30).

17. This parenthetic remark appears in both Matthew and Luke, strong evidence for the literary interdependence of the Synoptics. What are the chances that all three would independently introduce a narrative aside at the same place in the episode?

18. A. M. Hunter, *The Gospel according to Mark* (Torch Bible Commentary; London: SCM, 1967), 38.

Theology in Application

The Authority of Jesus

Jesus' authority is on center stage throughout the early Galilean ministry, and this passage is no exception. Its central theme is the authority of Jesus as the Messiah both to heal disease and to forgive sins. Jesus' miracles confirm his message. The remarkable claim to forgive sins is verified in a profound and public manner as the man gets right up and walks out "in front of them all."

Forgiveness and Healing

The close connection between forgiveness and healing is also central to the story. Jesus' proclamation of the kingdom of God is not just about the salvation of souls. It is about God's reclamation of his creation. Since the sin of Adam and Eve, creation has been in a fallen state (Gen 3:17 – 18), resulting in disease, death, and decay. The OT prophets promised eschatological restoration and linked this with the forgiveness of sins and a reconciled relationship with God (Isa 40:2 – 3; Jer 31:34). For Paul, the peace with God achieved through Christ's sacrificial work on the cross (Rom 5:1) means not only forgiveness of sins, salvation of our souls, and eternal life (6:23), but also the restoration and renewal of creation (8:20 – 21), including the renewal of our bodies (1 Cor 15:42 – 44). At this time of eschatological renewal, "the eyes of the blind [will] be opened and the ears of the deaf unstopped. Then will the lame leap like a deer, and the mute tongue shout for joy" (Isa 35:5 – 6; cf. Matt 11:5; Luke 7:22). Jesus offers forgiveness of sins, and then restores this lame man as evidence of the presence and power of the kingdom of God.

Faith and Healing

While the authority of Jesus to heal and to forgive is central to the passage, there are important subsidiary points, including (1) the faith of the friends, (2) the blindness and hypocrisy of the religious leaders, and (3) the compassion of Jesus. The reader delights in the audacity of faith shown by the friends who are willing to demolish a roof and risk the ire of the homeowner to reach Jesus. Radical faith believes God can do anything and is willing to take a risk to see it happen.

Faith is closely linked to healing in Mark's gospel. Indeed, in 6:5 we are surprised to learn that Jesus "could not do any miracles" in Nazareth because of their lack of faith. This "failure" was not because of a lack of power on Jesus' part, but because he could do nothing for those who refused to acknowledge their need of him. While faith is not a magic formula that compels God to act (cf. 2 Cor 12:8; 2 Tim 4:20), it is a heartfelt expression of dependence on him and trust that he is able to save (Heb 11:6). The religious leaders, who here reject Jesus' messianic authority, will in the next episode refuse to acknowledge their need of him. They are the "healthy" who have no need of a doctor. Jesus has "not come to call righteous people, but sinners" (Mark 2:17) — those who recognize their need of him.

Sin and Disease

Finally, the passage raises the difficult question of the relationship between sin and disease. It was widely believed in Jesus' day that personal sin led to disease. In John 9:2, Jesus' disciples assume that a man's blindness was the result of sin: "Rabbi, who sinned, this man or his parents, that he was born blind?" But Jesus denies that either is the case. Paul, however, testifies that sin in the Corinthian congregation — especially disunity in the Lord's Supper — has resulted in sickness and even death (1 Cor 11:29 – 32). The Talmud reveals similar views in later Judaism: "No one gets up from his sick-bed until all his sins are forgiven" (*b. Ned.* 41a).

James encourages prayer and anointing with oil by the elders of the church for those who are sick and affirms that "the prayer offered in faith will make the sick person well.... If they have sinned, they will be forgiven" (James 5:15). This text confirms that infirmity *may or may not* be related to personal sin. In pastoral care, it is important to practice both compassion and discernment, allowing for the possibility that disease or misfortune may result from divine discipline, but never assuming this to be the case. Whatever the cause, the pastoral response should be the same: to pray for the person and to offer God's compassion, love, and forgiveness. Infirmity and hardship always provide opportunities for spiritual growth, calling us to a closer walk with God and a greater dependence on him.

Mark 2:13 – 17

Literary Context

Up to this point the narrator's primary concern has been to demonstrate Jesus' messianic status and authority, including his authority in proclaiming the kingdom of God (1:14 – 15), in calling disciples (1:16 – 20), over demonic forces (1:23 – 28, 34), in teaching (1:21 – 22), over disease (1:29 – 34, 40 – 45; 2:11 – 12), and in forgiving sins (2:1 – 12).

In the previous episode, the healing of the paralyzed man (2:1 – 12), Mark begins to narrate a series of five controversies between Jesus and the religious leaders — controversies that highlight authoritative pronouncements of Jesus. The call of Levi continues this theme in the context of another key Markan motif: *the humble recipients of God's salvation blessings.* Forgiveness of sins and healing come not to the self-righteous religious leaders, but to sinners and outcasts who respond with faith and repentance to Jesus' kingdom announcement.

II. The Authority of the Messiah (1:14 – 8:21)

   A. The Kingdom Authority of the Messiah (1:14 – 3:6)

      1. Jesus Proclaims the Kingdom and Calls Disciples (1:14 – 20)

      2. Authority in Teaching, Healing, and Exorcism (1:21 – 45)

      3. Conflicts with the Religious Leaders (2:1 – 3:6)

         a. Jesus Forgives and Heals a Paralyzed Man (2:1 – 12)

➡   **b. Jesus Calls Levi and Eats with Sinners (2:13 – 17)**

         c. Jesus Is Questioned about Fasting (2:18 – 22)

Main Idea

In the call of Levi, Mark epitomizes Jesus' kingdom ministry as a joyful invitation to outcasts and sinners who recognize their need of spiritual healing. It is not an identification with self-righteous people who claim to have earned a righteous status before God.

Translation

Mark 2:13–17

13a	Character entrance/Setting	**Jesus again went out beside the sea.**
b	Character entrance	**A large crowd gathered around him**
c	Action	and **he was teaching them.**
14a	setting	As he walked along,
b	Character entrance & description.	**he saw Levi son of Alphaeus sitting in the tax-collector's booth.**
c	Action	**He said to him,**
d		*"Follow me."*
e	Response to 14d	**Getting up, he followed him.**
15a	Setting (social & spatial)	**He went to a dinner party at his house,**
b	Character entrance	and **many tax collectors and sinners joined Jesus and his disciples at the table.**
c	Reason for 15b	For **many of them were now following him.**
16a	Reason for 16b	When the experts in the law who were Pharisees saw that Jesus was eating ☞ with sinners and tax collectors,
b	Action	**they said to his disciples,**
c	question/accusation	*"Why does he eat with tax collectors and sinners?"*
17a	Response	**Hearing this, Jesus responded,**
b	proverb	*"It is not healthy people who need a doctor, but sick people;*
c	application of proverb	*I did not come to call righteous people, but sinners."*

Structure and Literary Form

Two short incidents make up this scene. In both the stage is set with Jesus in a group, and then characters enter and interact with him. In the first, Jesus is teaching the crowds when Levi appears. In the second, Jesus is eating with sinners when the experts in the law appear. The first is a *call narrative*, where Jesus beckons the tax collector to come and follow him in discipleship (cf. 1:16–20). Levi's immediate response again highlights the authority of Jesus. The second incident is a *pronouncement story*, which climaxes in an authoritative statement by Jesus. The narrative is intended to "set up" this climactic pronouncement. When Jesus goes to dine with Levi and his friends — tax collectors and other sinners — the Pharisees question his association with such unscrupulous characters. Jesus responds by first quoting a proverb ("It is not healthy people who need a doctor, but sick people") and then applying this proverb to his ministry ("I did not come to call righteous people, but sinners"). Jesus' ministry is directed toward those who recognize their spiritual need of salvation.

Exegetical Outline

→ **1. The Call of Levi to Discipleship (2:13 – 14)**

    a. The setting: itinerant teaching by the lake (2:13)

    b. Jesus' call of Levi to discipleship (2:14a-d)

    c. Levi's immediate response (2:14e)

2. Dining with Sinners (2:15 – 17)

    a. The setting: dining with Levi and his associates (2:15)

    b. The accusation by the experts in the law (2:16)

    c. Jesus' response (the pronouncement) (2:17)

        i. A proverb (2:17a-b)

        ii. The application of the proverb to Jesus' ministry (2:17c)

Explanation of the Text

2:13 Jesus again went out beside the sea. A large crowd gathered around him and he was teaching them (Καὶ ἐξῆλθεν πάλιν παρὰ τὴν θάλασσαν· καὶ πᾶς ὁ ὄχλος ἤρχετο πρὸς αὐτόν, καὶ ἐδίδασκεν αὐτούς). As we have seen, much of Jesus' early ministry was spent in the towns and villages around the Sea of Galilee. Levi may have learned a great deal about Jesus' ministry even before this encounter. For Mark, however, the significance lies in Levi's immediate response to Jesus' authoritative call.

"All the crowd" (πᾶς ὁ ὄχλος) could be hyperbolic, as we might say, "Everyone was at the party." But Greek "all" (πᾶς) can also carry the sense of "a great deal" or "sufficient" (see 1 Cor 13:2, where "all faith" [πᾶς ἡ πίστις] means "sufficient faith"; cf. Rom 15:3; Phil 2:29). The imperfect "gathered" (ἤρχετο) suggests the gradual gathering of the crowd. Jesus' growing popularity is an important theme in these early chapters of Mark. The people are amazed at his teaching and miracles and so

they throng to him — another indication of his extraordinary authority. "He was teaching them" (ἐδίδασκεν αὐτούς) may be an inceptive (or ingressive) imperfect ("he began to teach them"; so NIV), emphasizing the beginning of the action; or it may be customary: whenever a crowd formed, Jesus took the opportunity to teach.[1]

2:14 As he walked along, he saw Levi son of Alphaeus sitting in the tax collector's booth. He said to him, "Follow me!" Getting up, he followed him (Καὶ παράγων εἶδεν Λευὶν τὸν τοῦ Ἀλφαίου καθήμενον ἐπὶ τὸ τελώνιον, καὶ λέγει αὐτῷ· ἀκολούθει μοι. καὶ ἀναστὰς ἠκολούθησεν αὐτῷ). "Of Alphaeus" (τοῦ Ἀλφαίου) is a genitive of relationship, meaning *"son* of Alphaeus." The parallel text in the First Gospel calls this individual "Matthew" (Matt 9:9) and identifies him as the disciple by that name (10:3). Although neither Mark nor Luke connects Levi with Matthew (Mark 3:18;

---

1. Wallace, *Greek Grammar*, 544, 548.

Luke 6:15), the most natural explanation is that the two are the same.[2] Some have suggested that Levi was Matthew's second name, or perhaps that Matthew was a Levite (most people named Levi in the first century were Levites).[3] If this latter were the case, Matthew would have been especially hated by his countrymen as one who should have pursued a religious vocation but chose a despised one instead.

There is also a textual question here, with some Western and Caesarean manuscripts reading, "James son of Alphaeus" (a name attributed to one of the Twelve, cf. Mark 3:18, pars.) instead of "Levi son of Alphaeus." This is likely a scribal harmonization under the assumption that Levi and James were the same individual, since they have the same father. James the son of Alphaeus may have been Levi's brother.[4]

The tax collector's booth (τὸ τελώνιον, 2:14) was probably not a tax office, but a tollbooth where customs would be collected on goods in transit.[5] Levi was presumably an official working for Herod Antipas, tetrarch of Galilee (see comments on 6:14 – 16), and the toll may be on fish caught in the Sea of Galilee or on goods in transit. Capernaum was the first major town through which travelers would pass as they came from the territories of Herod Philip northeast of Galilee.

Tax collectors were despised because of their reputation for dishonesty, their exorbitant surcharges, and their duplicity with oppressive rulers, both the Romans and their client kings like Herod Antipas. Since they made their living from the money they could collect over and above the taxes owed, extortion and corruption were rampant. The Mishnah prohibits even receiving alms from a tax collector at his office since the money was presumed to have been gained illegally (*m. B. Qam.* 10:1). If a tax collector entered a house, all that was in it became unclean (*m. Ṭehar.* 7:6). The rabbis went so far as to say it was permissible to lie to tax collectors to protect one's property (*m. Ned.* 3:4).

"Follow me" (ἀκολούθει μοι) is a present imperative, indicating continuous or linear action. Too much should not be made of this (it would be overtranslating to render "keep on following me"), since the verb "follow" always has an element of progression. But the similar call of the four fishermen in 1:16, 18 confirms that this is a call to discipleship.[6] Astonishingly, Jesus chooses a disciple from one of the most despised of all professions.

2:15 He went to a dinner party at his house, and many tax collectors and sinners joined Jesus and his disciples at the table. For many of them were now following him (Καὶ γίνεται κατακεῖσθαι αὐτὸν ἐν τῇ οἰκίᾳ αὐτοῦ, καὶ πολλοὶ τελῶναι καὶ ἁμαρτωλοὶ συνανέκειντο τῷ Ἰησοῦ καὶ τοῖς μαθηταῖς αὐτοῦ· ἦσαν γὰρ πολλοὶ καὶ ἠκολούθουν αὐτῷ). The Greek verb "recline" (κατάκειμαι) indicates attendance at a formal banquet or dinner party, where guests would recline on cushions around a low table.[7] The implication is that in grateful response to Jesus' call, Levi gave a banquet in Jesus' honor, inviting his tax-collecting colleagues together with Jesus and his disciples. While the Greek text refers ambiguously to "his house" (Jesus' or Levi's?), the context suggests that Levi's

2. M.-J. Lagrange, *Evangile selon saint Marc* (Paris: Gabalda, 1929), 42.

3. Marcus, *Mark 1 – 8*, 225.

4. Hooker, *Mark*, 94; Witherington, *Mark*, 119.

5. J. R. Donahue, "Tax Collectors and Sinners: An Attempt at Identification," *CBQ* 33 (1971): 39 – 61, esp. 42; Emil Schürer, *The History of the Jewish People in the Age of Jesus Christ (175 B.C. – A.D. 135)* (rev. and ed. Geza Vermes, Fergus Millar, and Matthew Black; Edinburgh: T&T Clark, 1973 – 1987), 1:373 – 74; Collins, *Mark*, 191.

6. Guelich, *Mark 1:1 – 8:26*, 100; Witherington, *Mark*, 120 – 21.

7. J. Jeremias, *The Eucharistic Words of Jesus* (trans. N. Perrin; London: SCM, 1966), 48 – 49.

is intended.[8] Luke explicitly says that Levi made a great feast at his house (Luke 5:29).

The "many tax collectors and sinners" were evidently Levi's friends and associates. The term "sinners" (ἁμαρτωλοί) could refer to (1) common Israelites, the *'am hā-'āreṣ* or "people of the land," who did not hold to the scrupulous standards of righteousness practiced by the Pharisees and so were despised by them.[9] In this case it would reflect the perspective of the scribes and Pharisees. (2) Or the term could refer more negatively to "the wicked," those of questionable moral behavior.[10] Since the sinners here are distinguished from Jesus' disciples (who would fit the former category but not the latter), the latter is probably intended. These were the unscrupulous riffraff, the scoundrels of first-century Jewish life. They found Jesus' iconoclastic teaching and ministry attractive and followed him. The Pharisees found such associations defiling and inappropriate for one who claimed to be a teacher and religious leader.

This is the first use of "disciples" (μαθηταί) in Mark's gospel. Mark can use the term with reference to the Twelve (who will not be appointed until 3:14), or to Jesus' followers in general (as here).[11] The last phrase (lit., "for there were many and they were following him") is a Semitism that means, "for there were many *who were following him*."[12] Grammatically, it could refer either to (1) the tax collectors and sinners or (2) the disciples.[13] The latter makes sense if Mark is trying to explain his reference to disciples. The former, however, fits the overall theme of the passage, which is Jesus' association with sinners.[14]

Some scholars believe that the passage should be punctuated with a period after "many" (πολλοί), so that "and they were following him" (καὶ ἠκολούθουν αὐτῷ) would be part of the next clause: "And the scribes of the Pharisees were also (καί) following him." But it seems highly unlikely that Mark would come so close to identifying the religious leaders as followers in the same sense as the disciples.

2:16 When the experts in the law who were Pharisees saw that Jesus was eating with sinners and tax collectors, they said to his disciples, "Why does he eat with tax collectors and sinners?" (καὶ οἱ γραμματεῖς τῶν Φαρισαίων ἰδόντες ὅτι ἐσθίει μετὰ τῶν ἁμαρτωλῶν καὶ τελωνῶν ἔλεγον τοῖς μαθηταῖς αὐτοῦ· ὅτι μετὰ τῶν τελωνῶν καὶ ἁμαρτωλῶν ἐσθίει;). The genitive phrase "scribes of the Pharisees" (οἱ γραμματεῖς τῶν Φαρισαίων) occurs only here in the NT (but see Acts 23:9). It is a partitive genitive,[15] referring to experts in the law (or "scribes") who were members of the sect of the Pharisees. While most scribes were aligned with the Pharisees, some were Sadducees; others were free from party affiliation. Some manuscripts read "the scribes and Pharisees," probably a copyist harmonization to the more common gospel phrase.

Though the scribes have been mentioned before (1:22; 2:6), this is Mark's first reference to the Pharisees. The Pharisees probably arose from the *Ḥasidim,* the pious Jews who fought with the Maccabees against the oppression by Antiochus IV Epiphanes (175 – 163 BC).[16] The word "Pharisee" is most likely derived from a Hebrew term meaning "separatists," which was applied to this group

---

8. For the view that it was Jesus', not Matthew's, house, see E. S. Malbon, "*Tē oikia autou:* Mark 2.15 in Context," *NTS* 31 (1985): 282 – 92.

9. Jeremias, *New Testament Theology,* 108 – 13.

10. E. P. Sanders, *Jesus and Judaism* (Philadelphia: Fortress, 1985), 174 – 211; Marcus, *Mark 1 – 8,* 226.

11. On the disciples in Mark, see Best, *Following Jesus,* passim.

12. Cranfield, *Mark,* 104; Taylor, *Mark,* 205.

13. Best, *Following Jesus,* 178 n. 2.

14. So most commentators.

15. Wallace, *Greek Grammar,* 84 – 86.

16. Some recent research has challenged traditional views of the Pharisees. See the bibliography and history of interpretation in A. J. Saldarini, "Pharisees," *ABD,* 5:303.

because of their obsession with holiness and the resultant separation from anything that would cause spiritual defilement.[17] The most distinctive characteristic of the Pharisees was their strict adherence to the law (Torah) — not only to the written law of the OT, but also the "oral law," a body of tradition that expanded and elaborated on the OT law. The goal of these traditions was to "build a fence" around the Torah so as to guard against any possible infringement that could cause defilement.[18] The modern identification of Pharisees as "hypocrites" would not have occurred to most first-century Israelites, who admired the Pharisees for their piety and scrupulous observance of the law.

Jesus had far more in common theologically with the Pharisees than the Sadducees (see 12:18 – 27). He did not criticize them for their goals of purity and obedience, but for the inconsistent and hypocritical ways they worked these goals out. They raised their arbitrary interpretations of the law (mere "traditions of men") to the level of God's commandments (7:8). They became obsessed with external things, neglecting the issues that mattered most to God: justice and mercy. In their concern for purity, they had lost God's heart for people.

Yet we must not paint the Pharisees with too broad a brush. As with most religious movements, there were surely different motivations among them, with many serving God in authenticity and integrity. The gospel writers have somewhat different views of them. In Luke's gospel Jesus ate and socialized with Pharisees on several occasions (Luke 7:36; 11:37), and on one occasion they even warned him about Herod's opposition (13:31). In Acts, the Pharisees are portrayed as more sympathetic to the Jesus movement than the priests and Sadducees, sharing many beliefs in common (Acts 23:6 – 8).

The imperfect "they were saying" (ἔλεγον) could be ingressive ("they began saying") or iterative ("they kept on saying"). But this verb sometimes has a simple past sense in narrative (an aoristic or instantaneous imperfect)[19] — hence, "they said." The Greek ὅτι may be recitative (introducing a quotation), in which case it is an exclamation and an accusation: "He eats with tax collectors and sinners!" Or, it could be interrogatory, in place of τί: "*Why* does he eat with tax collectors and sinners?" The latter fits the context better.

Meals were important social rituals in the ancient world, and one would normally eat only with those of similar social status. In Judaism a scrupulous Pharisee would never eat at the home of a common Israelite since he could not be sure that the food was ceremonially clean or that it had been properly tithed (*m. Demai* 2:2). He would especially not eat with a defiled and sinful tax collector. The Pharisees expect Jesus, a respected rabbi, to act in the same exclusive manner. The NLT translates evocatively, "Why does he eat with such scum?"

2:17 Hearing this, Jesus responded, "It is not healthy people who need a doctor, but sick people; I did not come to call righteous people, but sinners." (καὶ ἀκούσας ὁ Ἰησοῦς λέγει αὐτοῖς ὅτι οὐ χρείαν ἔχουσιν οἱ ἰσχύοντες ἰατροῦ ἀλλ᾽ οἱ κακῶς ἔχοντες· οὐκ ἦλθον καλέσαι δικαίους ἀλλὰ ἁμαρτωλούς). "Healthy people don't need a doctor" was a common proverb in both Jewish and non-Jewish circles.[20] Jesus takes the proverb and applies it to his ministry. He has not come to call the righteous but sinners.

The proverb and its application represent poetic

---

17. See A. I. Baumgarten, "The Name of the Pharisees," *JBL* 102 (1983): 411 – 28.

18. See *m. ʾAbot* 1:1; 3:14.

19. Wallace, *Greek Grammar*, 542.

20. *Mekilta* to Exod 15:26; Plutarch, *Apoph. Lac.* 230 – 31; Dio Chrysostom, *Orat.* 8.5. See Gundry, *Mark*, 129, for other references.

parallelism, with parallel contrasts ("but," ἀλλά) between "healthy people" and "sick people," and "righteous people" and "sinners." Jesus the Great Physician has come for the spiritually needy. While the implication is that the scribes are not righteous but self-righteous, the emphasis is not on this but on Jesus' positive call of sinners. The term "call" (καλέω) may indicate an invitation to a banquet. If so, Jesus the guest now functions as the host, inviting outcasts to dine with him.

Theology in Application

The central theme of the passage is God's heart for people and his offer of salvation for all who respond in faith. Jesus is no respecter of persons, but treats sinners and "saints" alike. The announcement of the kingdom of God means that *all* must repent and enter in humble submission. Ironically, it is often the despised members of society who recognize their sinful status and fall on God's grace for salvation. The self-righteous see no reason to repent and so reject God's salvation.

The Pharisaic scribes of the narrative view religion as strict separation from anything that would defile, whether objects or food or people. They despise sinners and expect Jesus to do the same. Yet Jesus has not come to gain prestige but to bring salvation to lost people. The key is not separation but transformation. Salt and light — images of the kingdom — do not provide defensive barriers, but permeate and transform their environment. The kingdom is not contaminated by sinners but brings restoration and healing, reconciling people to God. (See Theology in Application on 1:40 – 45, "The Sanctifying Power of the Kingdom of God.") Believers must not build walls of separation *from* the world. Rather, they are to carry the message of grace and transformation *into* the world. Doctors do no good for the sick if they hide in clinics behind locked doors.

A sermon or lesson on this passage could bring out various themes.

God Loves All People, Regardless of Social Status or Lot in Life

Our ministries, like Jesus', should focus especially on outsiders. This may include inner-city youth or financially deprived families, immigrant communities or ethnic minorities, documented and undocumented aliens, "down-and-out" street people and the mentally ill, the elderly and those in rest homes. When we include "sinners," this list can be expanded to include gang members, drug addicts and dealers, alcoholics, prostitutes, practicing homosexuals, pornographers, and those in prison or on parole. Jesus also associated with those of different religious traditions, like Samaritans and Gentiles, and so the list can be expanded to include Muslims, Buddhists, Hindus, Jews, and members of sects like Jehovah's Witnesses and Mormons.

We often cocoon ourselves in a Christian environment, separated from those who need to hear the gospel message. I remember on one occasion my wife and I attended a New Year's Eve party at the home of friends. I was surprised to notice that almost everyone present was an unbeliever, and I remember thinking, "I wonder if my friends are falling away from the faith?" When I came to my senses, I realized that perhaps it was *I* who was not living out the life of Christ. I was teaching at a Christian school, preaching at a Christian church, and socializing with Christian friends. By contrast, my friends were engaged with the world around them, modeling the love of God before their non-Christian friends. God calls us to be salt and light.

God's Salvation Is Offered Freely to All Who Respond in Faith

Salvation is not earned but is a free gift. The tax collectors and sinners did not need to demonstrate their righteousness in order to earn Jesus' fellowship. He accepted them where they were and offered them God's salvation. While a change in lifestyle inevitably follows authentic conversion, this transformation is the result rather than the condition of grace.

God Chooses the Lowly and Foolish Things of This World to Accomplish His Purposes

Fishermen and tax collectors are not the kinds of disciples we expect the Messiah to choose. I am reminded of a tongue-in-cheek memo from a pastoral search committee, noting candidates that the committee rejected because of serious inadequacies: Noah (no converts in 120 years), Moses (public-speaking problems; loses temper on occasion), Abraham (ran off to Egypt during hard times; lied to get out of trouble), David (adulterous affair), Hosea (family life in shambles), Jeremiah (too emotional and alarmist; a whiner), Amos (unsophisticated country bumpkin), Peter (bad temper; denied Christ), Paul (lacks tact; harsh; appearance is contemptible; preaches far too long), and even Jesus (challenges those in spiritual authority). The committee finally settled on Judas Iscariot, since "he seems to be very practical, cooperative, good with money, cares for the poor, and dresses well."

We must remember that God chooses the foolish things, the weak things, the lowly things to shame the wise and the strong, "so that no one may boast before [God]" (1 Cor 1:26 – 31). If Jesus had chosen the best and the brightest of his day, he would have chosen Pharisees and scribes! But God is more interested in a humble heart of dependence than pride in human abilities.

The Danger of Pride in Human Accomplishment

The religious leaders of Israel rejected Jesus' ministry because they believed they were in a different class from sinners. Their downfall was their pride and self-righteousness. This should remind us that we are all sinners saved by grace. Humility and compassion should characterize not only our salvation experience, but also our life of sanctification. Christian leaders seldom fall because of a shortage of gifts but rather because of sins of arrogance — deceiving ourselves that moral standards do not apply to us. Similarly, few churches split because of persecution from without or false teaching from within. Most problems arise from power struggles, whether board against pastor, pastor against pastor, or any number of other combinations. As servants of Jesus Christ we must constantly rehearse the attitude of our Lord, who was not thinking of himself when he took on the form of a servant and died for us. Like Jesus, we should "do nothing out of selfish ambition or vain conceit. Rather, in humility value others above yourselves" (Phil 2:3).

Mark 2:18 – 22

Literary Context

This is the third of five controversy stories Mark presents during Jesus' early Galilean ministry. While the first two concerned Jesus' claim to forgive sins (2:1 – 12) and his association with sinners (2:13 – 17), this one concerns fasting. The Pharisees and the disciples of John fasted regularly as a sign of devotion and piety. Some people wonder why Jesus and his disciples do not.

Main Idea

When Jesus is asked why his disciples do not fast like the disciples of John the Baptist and the Pharisees, he responds with a series of analogies that identify his presence as the arrival of God's eschatological salvation — a joyful celebration that is not just a reformation of Judaism, but is creating something radically new and transforming.

Translation

(See next page.)

Mark 2:18 – 22

18a	Setting (temporal & social)	Once when John's disciples and the Pharisees were fasting,
b	Character entrance/Action	**some people came to Jesus and asked,**
c	question	*"Why do John's disciples and*
		the disciples of the Pharisees fast,
d	contrast	*but your disciples don't fast?"*
19a	Action/response to 18	**Jesus replied,**
b	question	*"How can the wedding guests fast while the bridegroom is with them?*
c	assertion	*As long as they have the bridegroom with them, they cannot fast.*
20a	clarification	*But the days will come when the bridegroom will be taken away from them;*
b		*then they will fast in that day.*
21a	analogy	*No one sews a patch of unshrunk cloth on an old garment.*
b	condition of 21c	*If they do,*
c	result of 21b	*the patch shrinks and tears away from it—the new from the old—and the tear ↻*
		becomes worse.
22a	analogy	*And no one puts new wine into old wineskins.*
b	condition of 22c	*If they do,*
c	result of 22b	*the wine bursts the wineskins and both the wine and the wineskins are destroyed.*
d	assertion	*On the contrary, new wine is for new wineskins."*

Structure

This episode functions like a controversy/pronouncement story in that the narrative context (a question about fasting) sets up Jesus' authoritative teaching. The teaching in this case, however, is not a single pronouncement, but three analogies from everyday life that Jesus uses to illustrate the nature of his ministry. The first (a wedding celebration) illustrates the reason Jesus and his disciples are not fasting: the presence of Jesus is a time of celebration, not solemnity. The second and third (a new patch on old clothing and new wine in old wineskins) explain the nature and significance of this celebration. The kingdom of God is inaugurating a new age of salvation that is fundamentally incompatible with the old. Jesus is not here to put a patch on Judaism, but to inaugurate the new creation.

Exegetical Outline

→ **1. The Question about Fasting (2:18)**

   2. Jesus' Response (2:19 – 22)

      a. The bridegroom analogy (vv. 19 – 20)

      b. The incompatibility of the new with the old (vv. 21 – 22)

         i. A new patch on an old garment (v. 21)

         ii. New wine in old wineskins (v. 22)

Explanation of the Text

2:18 Once when John's disciples and the Pharisees were fasting, some people came to Jesus and asked, "Why do John's disciples and the disciples of the Pharisees fast, but your disciples don't fast?" (Καὶ ἦσαν οἱ μαθηταὶ Ἰωάννου καὶ οἱ Φαρισαῖοι νηστεύοντες. καὶ ἔρχονται καὶ λέγουσιν αὐτῷ· διὰ τί οἱ μαθηταὶ Ἰωάννου καὶ οἱ μαθηταὶ τῶν Φαρισαίων νηστεύουσιν, οἱ δὲ σοὶ μαθηταὶ οὐ νηστεύουσιν;). It was common in the Greco-Roman world for teachers of all sorts — rabbis, prophets, philosophers, etc. — to have disciples, or apprentices, and John the Baptist was no exception (cf. 6:29; Matt 11:2; 14:12; Luke 7:18; 11:1; John 3:25 – 26). The Fourth Gospel recounts that Andrew was a disciple of John before he followed Jesus and that he brought his brother, Cephas (Peter), to Jesus (John 1:35 – 42). A group of John's disciples appear later in Ephesus (Acts 19:1 – 7; cf. 18:25), which shows that they followed their master's teaching long after his death.

The reference to the "disciples of the Pharisees" is a bit puzzling since the Pharisees were a religio-political party and so did not have disciples. It would be like saying, "a follower of the Democrats" or "a follower of the Republicans," instead of simply "a Democrat" or "a Republican." Either you were a Pharisee or you were not. Yet many Pharisees were also scribes, or experts in the law (see 2:16), and so the reference is likely to younger Pharisees who had attached themselves to distinguished rabbis. The term may also be used in the nontechnical sense of "followers," referring to those sympathetic to Pharisaic beliefs.

Fasting could indicate a variety of things, including sorrow, grief, repentance, or devotion to God. It is often associated with prayer. The Mosaic

law established only one fast, on the Day of Atonement (Lev 16:29, 31; 23:27 – 32; Num 29:7; cf. Acts 27:9), but Zech 8:19 mentions four fasts during the postexilic period — in the fourth, fifth, seventh, and tenth months of the Jewish year (cf. Zech 7:5).[1] A fifth fast, associated with the festival of Purim, is established in Esth 9:31. Pious Pharisees of Jesus' day were even more scrupulous, fasting twice a week, on Monday and Thursday (Luke 18:12; *Did.* 8:1; *b. Taʿan.* 12a; cf. *m. Taʿan.* 2:9). The disciples of the Pharisees were probably observing one of these biweekly fasts.

John's somber message and ascetic lifestyle are mentioned elsewhere (Matt 11:18; Luke 7:33: "John … came neither eating nor drinking"), and his disciples probably joined their master in fasting in anticipation of the judgments associated with the kingdom of God (Matt 3:7 – 10; Luke 3:7 – 9). They would also likely be in prayer and fasting because of John's imprisonment (Mark 1:14). Though Mark does not indicate who asked the question, it clearly carries a critical tone. Pious people like the Pharisees fast; Jesus' disciples do not. What does this say about their devotion to God? While the question is directed against Jesus' disciples, their behavior is a reflection on him.

2:19 Jesus replied, "How can the wedding guests fast while the bridegroom is with them? As long as they have the bridegroom with them, they cannot fast." (καὶ εἶπεν αὐτοῖς ὁ Ἰησοῦς· μὴ δύνανται οἱ υἱοὶ τοῦ νυμφῶνος ἐν ᾧ ὁ νυμφίος μετ' αὐτῶν ἐστιν νηστεύειν; ὅσον χρόνον ἔχουσιν τὸν νυμφίον μετ' αὐτῶν οὐ δύνανται νηστεύειν). Jesus answers with an analogy, describing himself as a bridegroom and his disciples as groomsmen or

---

1. See Lane, *Mark*, 108 n. 57, for rabbinic commentary on these fasts.

wedding guests.[2] Jewish weddings of that day were festive and extravagant affairs. They were the largest social events of village life and lasted a week or more (Judg 14:17; Tob 8:20; 10:7).[3] To fast during such a time of celebration would be unthinkable.

Jesus' analogy also has eschatological significance, as the following analogies confirm (vv. 21 – 22). The OT sometimes depicts God's final salvation as a great banquet celebration, called by later rabbis the "messianic banquet" (Isa 25:6 – 8; 65:13 – 14; cf. Matt 8:11; Luke 13:29). In line with his proclamation of the coming of the kingdom of God, Jesus here presents himself as the host of the messianic banquet, the dawn of the kingdom of God. The passage parallels the Q passage (Matt 11:16 – 19//Luke 7:31 – 35), where John's somber message and ascetic lifestyle are compared to a funeral dirge, and Jesus' joyful announcement of the kingdom and celebratory lifestyle to a wedding song. Wedding imagery is also associated with the kingdom of God in Matt 22:1 – 14; 25:1 – 13; and Rev 19:7 – 9.

2:20 But the days will come when the bridegroom will be taken away from them; then they will fast in that day (ἐλεύσονται δὲ ἡμέραι ὅταν ἀπαρθῇ ἀπ' αὐτῶν ὁ νυμφίος, καὶ τότε νηστεύσουσιν ἐν ἐκείνῃ τῇ ἡμέρᾳ). Jesus makes it clear that he is not against fasting as a spiritual discipline. There is a time for rejoicing and a time for mourning (Eccl 3:4). When the bridegroom is taken away, then the disciples will fast.

The verb "taken away" (ἀπαίρω) occurs only here in the NT. The passive likely refers to Jesus' arrest and crucifixion (a violent removal), though possibly to his resurrection and ascension to the right hand of God (12:36; 14:62). The closest parallel may be Isa 53:8, where it is said of the Suffering Servant, "By oppression and judgment he was taken away [LXX: αἴρω]." So when will the disciples fast? Stein claims that "in that day" (ἐν ἐκείνῃ τῇ ἡμέρᾳ) refers to Jesus' arrest, death, and burial, rather than to the practice of fasting in the early church, arguing that there is little evidence of Christians fasting until the second century.[4]

This seems to be an overly narrow interpretation. While the disciples' sorrow on Good Friday may have been the model for the later practice of fasting on Fridays,[5] it seems excessively literal to take Jesus' "that day" as a single day and to limit the reference to fasting to this brief period.[6] Matthew 6:16 – 18, together with the references in the *Didache* (*Did.* 7:4; 8:1), suggests a pattern of fasting among Jesus' early followers.[7] More likely, Jesus is referring here to the time after his ascension, which for his disciples will be characterized by trials, testing, spiritual discipline, and preparation for his return (Mark 13:9 – 13, 33 – 37).

Jesus' apparent allusion to his own death has

---

2. The term νυμφών could mean either "bridal chamber" (where the bride and groom would spend their first night; cf. Tobit 6:14, 17 LXX) or "wedding hall" (where the wedding feast would be held; cf. Matt 22:10). The idiom "the children of the wedding hall/bridal chamber" (οἱ υἱοὶ τοῦ νυμφῶνος) meant either "wedding guests" (NLT, NET, HCSB, ESV) or "the attendants of the bridegroom" (NASB; cf. REB) — "that group of the wedding guests who stood closest to the groom and played an essential part in the wedding ceremony" (BDAG, 681; cf. Collins, *Mark*, 198).

3. See J. Jeremias, *The Parables of Jesus* (trans. S. H. Hooke; New York: Scribner's, 1963), 171 – 75.

4. Stein, *Mark*, 138 – 39, argues that Luke 2:27 is an example

of OT rather than NT piety and (correctly) notes that the references to fasting in Mark 9:29; Acts 10:31; 1 Cor 7:5 are all later scribal additions. Furthermore, the early church did not consider Jesus to be absent, but present (Heb 13:5). Cf. J. A. Ziesler, "The Removal of the Bridegroom: A Note on Mark II.18 – 22 and Parallels," *NTS* 19 (1972): 190 – 94.

5. H.-W. Kuhn, *Ältere Sammlungen in Markusevangelium* (SUNT; Göttingen: Vandenhoeck & Ruprecht, 1971), 63 – 71, among others.

6. Guelich, *Mark 1:1 – 8:26*, 112 – 13; France, *Mark*, 140.

7. *Didache* 8:1 calls on Christians to fast on Wednesdays and Fridays in contrast to the Pharisees ("the hypocrites"), who fasted on Tuesdays and Thursdays.

sometimes been treated as a later addition, read back into his life by the later church. This, of course, is unnecessary if we assume that Jesus had divine insight. Yet even from a merely human perspective, there is significant evidence that Jesus anticipated his own death. From the beginning, he faced opposition from the religious leaders, who viewed him as a threat to their influence and authority, a blasphemer (2:7), a Sabbath breaker (2:23 – 28; 3:1 – 6), in league with Satan (3:22 – 27), and a false prophet (14:65). He surely anticipated that this opposition could cost him his life. Jesus also spoke of the persecution and murder of the prophets before him and made it clear he expected a similar fate (6:4; 12:1 – 12; cf. Matt 5:12; 13:57; 23:29 – 39; Luke 4:24; 6:23, 26; 11:47 – 50; 13:33 – 35).

2:21 – 22 No one sews a patch of unshrunk cloth on an old garment. If they do, the patch shrinks and tears away from it — the new from the old — and the tear becomes worse. And no one puts new wine into old wineskins. If they do, the wine bursts the wineskins and both the wine and the wineskins are destroyed. On the contrary, new wine is for new wineskins (Οὐδεὶς ἐπίβλημα ῥάκους ἀγνάφου ἐπιράπτει ἐπὶ ἱμάτιον παλαιόν· εἰ δὲ μή, αἴρει τὸ πλήρωμα ἀπ᾽ αὐτοῦ τὸ καινὸν τοῦ παλαιοῦ καὶ χεῖρον σχίσμα γίνεται. καὶ οὐδεὶς βάλλει οἶνον νέον εἰς ἀσκοὺς παλαιούς· εἰ δὲ μή, ῥήξει ὁ οἶνος τοὺς ἀσκοὺς καὶ ὁ οἶνος ἀπόλλυται καὶ οἱ ἀσκοί· ἀλλὰ οἶνον νέον εἰς ἀσκοὺς καινούς). Jesus follows the wedding analogy with two further analogies. Though the transition seems abrupt, both pick up the theme of inappropriate actions in light of the coming of the Messiah and the dawn of eschatological salvation.

Just as no one mourns at a wedding, so no one should sew a new patch onto an old garment or put new wine into old wineskins. A new patch of cloth sewn onto an old already-shrunk garment would shrink when washed and tear the old garment, making it worse than before. Wine in the ancient world was stored in animal skins sewn together (Josh 9:13; Job 32:19; Jer 13:12; Hab 2:15). The new wine would ferment and stretch the wineskins. If new wine were poured into old (already stretched) wineskins, the skins would burst and the wine would be lost. The added dimension in both analogies is that the old is incompatible with the new. Jesus seems to be saying that the new wine of the kingdom of God cannot be poured into the old wineskins of Judaism.[8] His mission is not simply to reform, or "patch up," Israel's religion, but to inaugurate a new era of salvation — the kingdom of God.[9]

Theology in Application

The Celebration and Joy That Accompany the Coming of the Kingdom

Jesus does not reject fasting as a spiritual discipline (cf. Matt 6:6 – 18). Rather, he is giving an object lesson about the kingdom of God. A wedding celebration was the greatest celebratory event of Palestinian village life, and everyone anticipated the arrival of the bride and the groom with joy and excitement. In the same way, the coming of the Messiah — the bridegroom at the messianic banquet — was the most exciting and anticipated event in human history. Since the fall of Adam and Eve, all

8. See Jeremias, *Parables of Jesus,* 118 (citing John 2:11), and Marcus, *Mark 1 – 8,* 234, for identification of "new wine" with the coming age of salvation.

9. The last phrase in v. 22, "new wine in new wineskins," is a verbless clause in Greek and may have been a slogan in the wine industry.

creation had languished in sin, death, and decay. But God is now stepping in to begin restoring creation to its intended destiny. This is no time for gloom and doom; it is time to throw a party!

In the Gospels, especially Luke's, Jesus tells many parables containing banquet imagery, and he is frequently seen at celebratory meals.[10] The Pharisees were offended by this and accused him of being a glutton and a drunkard — a friend of tax collectors and sinners (Matt 11:19; Luke 7:34). Yet Jesus is intentionally illustrating both the *nature* and the *recipients* of the kingdom. This is a time of joy and celebration for those ready to acknowledge their need of God. The message of the kingdom is good news to the poor, the sick, the outcast, and sinners because they are the ones who need it most (cf. 2:17; Luke 4:18 – 19).

Christians ought to be the most joyful people in the world. We are the recipients and now the messengers for the greatest news the world has ever heard. At the same time we acknowledge that the kingdom has been inaugurated but not yet consummated, and that "we must go through many hardships to enter the kingdom of God" (Acts 14:22). In this interim period we seek to "consider it pure joy" when we face trials of many kinds, because the testing of our faith produces perseverance (Jas 1:2 – 3; cf. Matt 5:12; Col 1:24; 1 Pet 1:6; 4:13, 16). Spiritual disciplines like prayer and fasting help believers persevere through the time of Jesus' physical absence as we await his victorious return.

The Incompatibility of the New Age of Salvation with the Old Age of Promise

The second key theme in this passage is the incompatibility of the old with the new. Just as new wine cannot be put into old wineskins, so the message of the kingdom of God cannot simply be poured into the present institutions of Judaism. This statement must not be misconstrued. Jesus did not come to establish a new religion or to reject the Jewish foundation of his message. In Matt 13:52 he extols the virtues of a teacher of Torah who has been instructed in the kingdom of God and so can bring both old and new treasures from his storeroom (cf. Rom 15:4). The NT is in continuity with the OT, and believers in Jesus the Messiah receive the spiritual blessings promised to Abraham and his descendants. Jesus' point is that he is not here to launch a renewal movement within Judaism or to put a "patch" on the old. Unlike the OT prophets, he is not calling Israel to covenant renewal or to greater submission to the Torah. Rather, he is here to fulfill the Torah and to bring it to its consummation in the kingdom of God. The old covenant is giving way to the new (Jer 31), and the age of promise to the age of fulfillment — the kingdom of God.

---

10. See, e.g., Luke 6:21; 9:10 – 17; 12:35 – 40; 13:24 – 30; 14:7 – 11, 15 – 24; 15:23 – 25, 32; 22:30. Cf. John 2:1 – 12, where the choice wine Jesus creates at the wedding in Cana represents the messianic banquet and the dawning age of salvation. The feeding miracles (Mark 6:30 – 44 pars.; 8:1 – 13 pars.) are also anticipatory precursors for the messianic banquet.

Mark 2:23 – 3:6

Literary Context

These two pericopes represent the fourth and fifth in a series of five controversy stories that Mark presents in the context of Jesus' early Galilean ministry. The previous episode raised an issue of Jewish piety with a question about fasting. These two episodes concern questions about Jewish law, specifically the question of the sanctity of the Sabbath.

Main Idea

When the Pharisees accuse Jesus' disciples of picking grain (and so working) on the Sabbath, Jesus points to the example of David to show that the Sabbath was made for people and not vice versa. Another time Jesus openly heals a man on the Sabbath, even though the religious leaders were trying to trap him; Jesus' action demonstrates that the Sabbath is truly fulfilled by doing good rather than by doing evil.

Translation

(See next page.)

Mark 2:23 – 3:6

	Picking Grain on the Sabbath	
23a	Setting (temporal)	**It happened one Sabbath**
b	setting (spatial)	that he was passing through some grainfields,
c	setting (spatial)	and as his disciples made their way,
d	Action	**they began to pluck some heads of grain.**
24a	Response to 23d	But **the Pharisees began saying to him,**
b	accusation	*"Look! Why are they doing what is not allowed on the Sabbath?"*
25a	Response to 24	**He answered them,**
b	question	*"Have you never read what David did*
c	setting (social)	*when he was in need, and* *he and his companions were hungry:*
26a	action/setting	*how he came* *to the house of God* *during the time of Abiathar the high priest*
b	action	*and ate the consecrated loaves,*
c	clarification of 26b	*which only the priests are allowed to eat,*
d	action	*and gave some of it to those who were with him?"*
27a	Pronouncements	Then **he said to them,**
b	pronouncement/proverb	*"The Sabbath was made for mankind, not mankind for the Sabbath.*
28	pronouncement on authority	*So the Son of Man is Lord even of the Sabbath."*
	Healing on the Sabbath	
3:1a	Setting (temporal & spatial)	**On another occasion he came to the synagogue,**
b	Dilemma (prep. for healing)	and **a man was there who had a deformed hand.**
2a	Action	**They were watching him closely**
b	purpose of 2a	to see if he would heal him on the Sabbath,
c	result of 2b	so they could bring a charge against him.
3a	Action	**He said to the man with the deformed hand,**
b	command	*"Stand up in front of everyone."*
4a	Action	Then **he said to them,**
b	question	*"Which is allowed on the Sabbath,* *to do good or to do evil?*
c		*To save a life or to kill?"*
d	Response to 4a-c	But **they remained silent.**
5a	response to 4d	Looking around at them angrily, deeply grieved at the hardness of their hearts,
b	Action	**he said to the man,**
c	command	*"Stretch out your hand."*
d	Healing	**The man stretched it out and his hand was completely restored!**
6a	character exit	Leaving immediately,
b	Action	**the Pharisees began to plot against him with the Herodians,**
c	purpose	to see how they might destroy him.

Structure

Both episodes in this unit are controversy stories, but with mixed forms. The first (2:23 – 28) begins as a controversy with the Pharisees and concludes as a pronouncement story, with Jesus pronouncing his authority over the Sabbath. The second (3:1 – 6) is a combination of a controversy story and a healing. The healing, in turn, provokes a plot by the Pharisees and the Herodians against Jesus' life (3:6). This plot functions as the climax of the five controversy stories of 2:1 – 3:6 and the end of this first phase of Jesus' ministry.

Exegetical Outline

➡ 1. **Picking Grain on the Sabbath (2:23 – 28)**
   a. The setting: the disciples pick grain on the Sabbath (2:23)
   b. The challenge from the Pharisees (2:24)
   c. Jesus' first response: the example of David (2:25 – 26)
   d. Jesus' second response: Lord of the Sabbath (2:27 – 28)
2. **Healing on the Sabbath (3:1 – 6)**
   a. The setting: a synagogue on the Sabbath (3:1a)
   b. The problem: a man with a deformed hand (3:1b)
   c. The controversy: the religious leaders seek to trap Jeus (3:2)
   d. Jesus heals the man (3:3 – 5)
      i. Jesus' actions: bringing the man front and center (3:3)
      ii. Jesus' question: Which is lawful on the Sabbath? (3:4a-b)
      iii. The leaders' response: silence (3:4c)
      iv. Jesus' anger (3:5a)
      v. The healing (3:5b-d)
   e. The plot against Jesus (3:6)

Explanation of the Text

2:23 – 24 It happened one Sabbath that he was passing through some grainfields, and as his disciples made their way, they began to pluck some heads of grain. But the Pharisees began saying to him, "Look! Why are they doing what is not allowed on the Sabbath?" (Καὶ ἐγένετο αὐτὸν ἐν τοῖς σάββασιν παραπορεύεσθαι διὰ τῶν σπορίμων, καὶ οἱ μαθηταὶ αὐτοῦ ἤρξαντο ὁδὸν ποιεῖν τίλλοντες τοὺς στάχυας. καὶ οἱ Φαρισαῖοι ἔλεγον αὐτῷ· ἴδε τί ποιοῦσιν τοῖς σάββασιν ὃ οὐκ ἔξεστιν;). On the neuter plural form of "Sabbath," see comments on 1:21.

The time was likely early summer, since harvest time was near. The Pharisees are not objecting to the act of picking grain from someone else's field. This was allowed according to the law: "If you enter your neighbor's grainfield, you may pick kernels with your hands, but you must not put a sickle to their standing grain" (Deut 23:25). Rather, they are objecting that the disciples are violating the law by working on the Sabbath (Exod 20:8 – 11; Deut 5:14), a capital offense (Exod 31:14). The rabbis discussed activities that constituted Sabbath work, and the Mishnah forbids thirty-nine specific acts, one of which was reaping (*m. Šabb.* 7:2).

2:25 – 26 He answered them, "Have you never read what David did when he was in need, and he and his companions were hungry: how he came to the house of God during the time of Abiathar the high priest and ate the consecrated loaves, which only the priests are allowed to eat, and gave some of it to those who were with him?" (καὶ λέγει αὐτοῖς· οὐδέποτε ἀνέγνωτε τί ἐποίησεν Δαυὶδ ὅτε χρείαν ἔσχεν καὶ ἐπείνασεν αὐτὸς καὶ οἱ μετ᾽ αὐτοῦ, πῶς εἰσῆλθεν εἰς τὸν οἶκον τοῦ θεοῦ ἐπὶ Ἀβιαθὰρ ἀρχιερέως καὶ τοὺς ἄρτους τῆς προθέσεως ἔφαγεν, οὓς οὐκ ἔξεστιν φαγεῖν εἰ μὴ τοὺς ἱερεῖς, καὶ ἔδωκεν καὶ τοῖς σὺν αὐτῷ οὖσιν;).

As so often (cf. 2:8, 19, 25; 10:3, 18; 11:29 – 30; 12:15 – 16, 24), Jesus answers a question with a question, "Have you never read…?" The incident he refers to occurred in 1 Sam 21:1 – 6. David and his companions, hungry and on the run from Saul, came to the tabernacle at Nob[1] and requested food from Ahimelech the priest. Ahimelech gave them the only bread available, the consecrated bread or "bread of the Presence." These were twelve loaves baked of fine flour and set out before the Lord each Sabbath on the table in the Holy Place. When fresh loaves were brought in, the priests would eat the ones from the previous week (Lev 24:5 – 9; cf. Exod 25:30; 35:13; 39:36; cf. Jos. *Ant.* 3.10.7 §§255 – 56). Jesus acknowledges that David technically broke the law, since "only the priests are allowed to eat"

the consecrated bread (v. 26).[2] But he did not break the true spirit and purpose of the law, since human need supersedes mere ritual observance.

There may be an added dimension to this episode. In Mark 12:35 – 40, Jesus will quote Ps 110:1 – 2 to demonstrate that the Messiah is even greater than David himself, since David calls him "Lord." The present episode may therefore have messianic implications. If David, the Lord's anointed (1 Sam 16:1 – 13), and his companions could eat the consecrated bread, how much more could the Messiah, David's greater son, and his companions.[3] This interpretation gains further support from the fact that this whole section of Mark's gospel concerns the authority of Jesus in announcing and inaugurating the kingdom of God. As the Messiah, Jesus is establishing a new age of salvation, where the new wine of the kingdom is replacing the old wine of Judaism (2:22).

Mark's reference to Abiathar the high priest raises difficult historical questions, since, according to 1 Sam 21:1 – 6, Abiathar's father Ahimelech was the priest who gave David the consecrated bread.[4] The OT text itself reveals some confusion concerning these two men. While 1 Sam 22:20 calls Abiathar the son of Ahimelech, other passages reverse this, making Ahimelech the son of Abiathar (2 Sam 8:17; 1 Chr 18:16; 24:6). Mark may be following a different textual tradition in his account.

Another explanation lies in the meaning of Mark's elliptic Greek phrase (ἐπὶ Ἀβιαθὰρ ἀρχιερέως). While this may mean, "when Abiathar was high priest" (NET, NRSV; cf. NLT), it could refer more generally to "the time of Abiathar the high priest" (cf. NIV, NASB, ESV, REB, etc.) or

---

1. The tabernacle, originally set up at Shiloh (Josh 18:1; 1 Sam 1:9), had apparently been moved to Nob after the destruction of Shiloh (1 Sam 4:2 – 4; Jer 7:12).

2. There were some attempts in Judaism to justify David's actions. Josephus (*Ant.* 6.12.1 §§242 – 243) notes that David received provisions but does not mention the consecrated bread.

Later rabbinic sources suggest either that it was not really the consecrated bread or that the bread had already been removed from the holy table (Fitzmyer, *Luke*, 1:609; Str-B 1.618 – 19).

3. Cf. Collins, *Mark*, 205.

4. This difficulty may be why both Matthew (Matt 12:4) and Luke (Luke 6:4) omit the reference to Abiathar.

even "the account about Abiathar the high priest." The former ("the time of …") would be an example of eponymous dating (cf. Luke 3:2), since Abiathar was the high priest during David's reign.[5] The latter would be similar to Mark's use of the phrase in 12:26 with reference to Moses and the burning bush (ἐπὶ τοῦ βάτου; "in [the account of] the bush"). First Samuel 21 – 22 could be called "the account of Abiathar the high priest" since it is he who escaped Saul's murder of the priests of Nob and took refuge with David (22:20 – 23).[6]

2:27 – 28 Then he said to them, "The Sabbath was made for mankind, not mankind for the Sabbath. So the Son of Man is Lord even of the Sabbath." (καὶ ἔλεγεν αὐτοῖς· τὸ σάββατον διὰ τὸν ἄνθρωπον ἐγένετο καὶ οὐχ ὁ ἄνθρωπος διὰ τὸ σάββατον· ὥστε κύριός ἐστιν ὁ υἱὸς τοῦ ἀνθρώπου καὶ τοῦ σαββάτου). Jesus drives home his illustration about David with two pronouncements. The first is a proverb.[7] God created the Sabbath for the benefit of human beings (ἄνθρωπος = humanity) — the pinnacle of his creation; he did not create them as slaves to its ritual observance (Gen 1:26 – 2:3). The Sabbath was to be a day of renewal, rest for the body, and worship for the soul. In the next episode Jesus will illustrate this by healing a man on the Sabbath (3:1 – 6).

Some scholars understand the second pronouncement, "So the Son of Man is Lord even of the Sabbath," to be a narrative aside, with the narrator explaining to the reader that Jesus is here exercising his authority as Lord of the Sabbath.[8] This interpretation is part of the larger claim that Jesus himself first uses the Son of Man title in 8:31,

where it defines his suffering role. The title appears repeatedly after that (8:38; 9:9, 12, 31; 10:33; 13:26; 14:21, 41, 62). The title's use here (2:27) and in 2:10 would therefore be narrator comments. As discussed at 2:10 – 11, this interpetation is possible but unlikely, since in every other instance in the Gospels the title appears on the lips of Jesus.

A second question concerns the meaning of this second pronouncement. There is little doubt that for Mark and his readers the reference is to Jesus' own authority as the messianic Son of Man (see "In Depth: Jesus as the Son of Man" at 2:10 – 11). Yet since the Hebrew phrase "son of man" (*ben-'ādām*) means "human being" or "humanity," the clause could be interpreted to carry forward the thought of the previous proverb: "The Sabbath was made for mankind … so mankind ('the son of man') has authority (lordship) over the Sabbath."

Some scholars have argued that this was Jesus' original intent, but that Mark changed the meaning by applying the Son of Man title to Jesus.[9] Yet it seems unlikely that Jesus would have claimed that human beings in general have complete authority over a command instituted by God himself.[10] More likely, Jesus is making a play on words (cf. Ps 8:4), picking up the reference to humanity in the first proverb and then claiming even greater authority for himself as the epitome of that humanity.[11] Following the first pronouncement ("the Sabbath was made for mankind …"), Jesus affirms that as the messianic Son of Man — the consummate human being who came to inaugurate a new age of salvation and establish the kingdom of God (cf. Dan 7:13 – 14) — he has ultimate authority over the Sabbath.

---

5. Garland, *Mark*, 106 n. 10.

6. J. W. Wenham, "Mark 2,26," *JTS* 1 (1950): 156.

7. A similar proverb appears in the rabbinic literature. *Mekilta* 109b on Exod 31:13 – 14 reads, "The Sabbbath was delivered to you, not you to the Sabbath" (cf. *b. Yoma* 85b; 2 Esd 6:54; *2 Bar.* 14:18). For an example of setting aside the Sabbath

law in dire circumstances, see 1 Macc 2:38 – 41.

8. So Lane, *Mark*, 120.

9. Bultmann, *History*, 16.

10. France, *Mark*, 147; Guelich, *Mark 1:1 – 8:26*, 125; et al.

11. Guelich, *Mark 1:1 – 8:26*, 126.

3:1 On another occasion he came to the synagogue, and a man was there who had a deformed hand (Καὶ εἰσῆλθεν πάλιν εἰς τὴν συναγωγήν. καὶ ἦν ἐκεῖ ἄνθρωπος ἐξηραμμένην ἔχων τὴν χεῖρα). On Jesus' synagogue attendance and teaching, see comments on 1:21. The adjectival participle translated "deformed" (from ξηραίνω) can mean "dried" or "withered," and the deformity may have been a defect from birth or atrophy resulting from paralysis.

3:2 They were watching him closely to see if he would heal him on the Sabbath, so they could bring a charge against him (καὶ παρετήρουν αὐτὸν εἰ τοῖς σάββασιν θεραπεύσει αὐτόν, ἵνα κατηγορήσωσιν αὐτοῦ). Mark does not specify the identity of these individuals, but the assumption is that they are the Pharisees who opposed him in the previous episode (2:24) and will go out to plot his death at the end of this one (3:6). Luke explicitly identifies them as "the Pharisees and the teachers of the law" (Luke 6:7).

The rabbis debated the permissibility of medical attention on the Sabbath and generally concluded that it was allowed when life was threatened. The Mishnah says that "whenever there is doubt whether life is in danger this overrides the Sabbath" (*m. Yoma* 8:6; cf. CD 11:9 – 10; *m. Šabb.* 14:3 – 4). Midwives were allowed to work on the Sabbath since childbirth could not be delayed, and circumcision was allowed because it was a sacred act that did not profane the Sabbath (*m. Šabb.* 5:1 – 4). Since this man's life is not in danger, the Pharisees would consider any action by Jesus to help him a Sabbath violation (cf. Luke 13:10 – 17; John 7:23; 9:13 – 16).

Jesus has previously healed twice on the Sabbath in Mark's gospel without incident, casting out a demon in the Capernaum synagogue (1:21 – 28) and healing Peter's mother-in-law (1:29 – 31). The former occurred during a disruption to the syna-gogue service and so might have been seen as a necessary intervention; the latter occurred in a private home, away from public eyes. Reports of these incidents, however, may have prompted the Pharisees to try to catch Jesus in the act.

There is heavy irony here and throughout this passage. By seeking to trap Jesus in a healing, the religious leaders implicitly acknowledge that he performs miracles. But what should this tell them about his identity? Further irony is that they are scheming against Jesus — a malicious act — on their own holy day.

3:3 – 4 He said to the man with the deformed hand, "Stand up in front of everyone." Then he said to them, "Which is allowed on the Sabbath, to do good or to do evil? To save a life or to kill?" But they remained silent (καὶ λέγει τῷ ἀνθρώπῳ τῷ τὴν ξηρὰν χεῖρα ἔχοντι· ἔγειρε εἰς τὸ μέσον. καὶ λέγει αὐτοῖς· ἔξεστιν τοῖς σάββασιν ἀγαθὸν ποιῆσαι ἢ κακοποιῆσαι, ψυχὴν σῶσαι ἢ ἀποκτεῖναι; οἱ δὲ ἐσιώπων). As in 2:8, Jesus demonstrates divine authority by knowing their thoughts (cf. v. 5). Jesus could have responded by taking the man out back and healing him privately, avoiding a confrontation. Instead he directly challenges the Pharisees in their hypocrisy. "Arise in the middle" (ἔγειρε εἰς τὸ μέσον) means to stand up in front of the assembly where everyone could see him. This is the only place in Mark's gospel that Jesus initiates a healing without being asked or approached. This further confirms that Jesus is intentionally confronting the hypocrisy of the religious leaders.

Jesus' first question, whether it is permitted to do good or to do evil on the Sabbath, relates directly to the healing of the man. To heal him would obviously be a good deed. To leave him unhealed would show lack of compassion and so would be evil. Jesus' next question ("... to save a life or to kill?") is a "lesser-to-greater" argument. If it is right to do good and wrong to do evil on the Sabbath, then it is even more right to save a life and more wrong to kill. This question goes beyond the healing of the man, whose life is not in immediate danger, and alludes to the actions of the Pharisees that follow (v. 6). Again there is heavy irony here. While Jesus is preparing to do good, they are plotting his death! Which is the real Sabbath violation?

The religious leaders cannot answer Jesus's question and so fall silent. In Greco-Roman rhetoric, to silence an opponent was a way of shaming them and so winning the debate (cf. 11:33).

3:5 Looking around at them angrily, deeply grieved at the hardness of their hearts, he said to the man, "Stretch out your hand." The man stretched it out and his hand was completely restored! (καὶ περιβλεψάμενος αὐτοὺς μετ᾽ ὀργῆς, συλλυπούμενος ἐπὶ τῇ πωρώσει τῆς καρδίας αὐτῶν λέγει τῷ ἀνθρώπῳ· ἔκτεινον τὴν χεῖρα. καὶ ἐξέτεινεν καὶ ἀπεκατεστάθη ἡ χεὶρ αὐτοῦ). Mark is more willing than the other gospel writers to depict Jesus' human emotions. Yet Jesus' anger is rare even in Mark and appears elsewhere only in the disputed variant reading at 1:41. While the anger there is difficult to understand, here it is righteous anger at the hypocrisy of his enemies and their lack of compassion.

The religious leaders demonstrate "hardness/stubbornness of hearts" (πωρώσει τῆς καρδίας), a Hebrew idiom that can mean spiritual blindness or active resistance to God's purpose and will (cf. Exod 4:21; 7:3; 8:15; 2 Chr 36:13; Jer 3:17; 7:24; 13:10; Rom 11:25; 2 Cor 3:14). The "heart" in Hebrew thought was the seat of the mind as well as the emotions. In 6:52 and 8:17 Mark will attribute this same spiritual dullness to the disciples, who, at

that point in the narrative, are in danger of going the way of the religious leaders.

3:6 Leaving immediately, the Pharisees began to plot against him with the Herodians, to see how they might destroy him (καὶ ἐξελθόντες οἱ Φαρισαῖοι εὐθὺς μετὰ τῶν Ἡρῳδιανῶν συμβούλιον ἐδίδουν κατ᾽ αὐτοῦ ὅπως αὐτὸν ἀπολέσωσιν). Jesus' opponents are now explicitly named as the Pharisees, who leave the synagogue and begin to plot Jesus' death together with the Herodians. The Herodians appear only twice in the NT, here (par. Matt 22:16) and in Mark 12:13, where during Passion Week they again plot with the Pharisees to take Jesus' life. The Herodians were supporters of the Herodian dynasty, established by Herod the Great and now carried forward by his sons Herod Antipas, who ruled in Galilee and Perea, and Herod Philip, who ruled in Iturea and Traconitis (see comments on 6:14 – 16). Since this event occurs in Galilee, these are likely partisans of Antipas.

The Herodians' alliance with the Pharisees represents strange bedfellows. The Herodian dynasty was aristocratic and pro-Roman, since the Roman legions kept them in power. The Pharisees, by contrast, were anti-Roman (though not militantly so) and looking for a Messiah from David's line to overthrow the Romans and reestablish the Davidic dynasty (*Pss. Sol.* 17 – 18). Yet both view Jesus as a threat to their political and religious influence and so find common cause to eliminate him. The Greek idiom "give counsel" (συμβούλιον δίδωμι) here means to "plot together with" (cf. NIV, NET, NLT, HCSB, NKJV, NASB, etc.), not to "hold counsel" (ESV, RSV, KJV).

Theology in Application

Jesus' Messianic Authority

These two episodes form the climax to Jesus' early Galilean ministry and as such carry forward the dominant theme of this section: *the extraordinary authority of Jesus the Messiah.* The Messiah, who inaugurates God's kingdom, casts out demons, heals the sick, cleanses the leper, and forgives sins, now claims to be Lord over the Sabbath itself (2:28). This is an audacious claim, considering that the Sabbath principle was established by God at creation and arose directly from his rest on the seventh day (Gen 2:3). God alone is Creator and so Lord of the Sabbath; yet Jesus claims this prerogative for himself as the Son of Man.

Jesus' statement also indicates authority over the law, since the Sabbath command was the fourth commandment of the Decalogue (Exod 20:8 – 11; Deut 5:12 – 15) and had by Jesus' day become a cornerstone of Jewish identity. Jesus' comparison of his actions with those of David in 2 Sam 21 also points to his authority. If David, the Lord's anointed, had authority to eat the consecrated bread of the priests, how much more does his greater Son, the Messiah, have authority over the law.

The True Spirit of the Law

In addition to Jesus' authority, these two pericopes speak about the authentic spirit of the law. In the OT as well as the NT, God is not pleased with ritualistic observance of the letter of the law but wants joyful obedience to its spirit. When King Saul disregarded God's command to destroy all the plunder from the Amalekites, the prophet Samuel told him that the Lord does not delight in burnt offerings and sacrifices but in a heart of authentic obedience: "To obey is better than sacrifice, and to heed is better than the fat of rams" (1 Sam 15:22). Saul's arrogant disregard meant the kingdom would be taken from him and given to David — a man after God's own heart (13:13 – 14; 16:1 – 13).

The prophet Jeremiah similarly looks forward to God's new covenant with his people, when the law will be written on their hearts rather than on tablets of stone (Jer 31:33). The implication is that there will be no more need for written rules, because believers will be spiritually attuned to God's desires and purposes.

Jesus makes a similar point in the Sermon on the Mount when he pushes beyond external rules to God's true nature and purpose. Anger and hatred are equivalent to murder because the divine purpose behind the sixth commandment (Exod 20:13) is not just to curb violence, but to reveal God's love for human beings, who are created in his image (Gen 9:6). Lust is equivalent to adultery because the spirit of the law with regard to marriage requires faithfulness in heart and mind, not just in actions. In the present episode, Jesus condones the "work" performed by the disciples in the field and then heals the man in the synagogue because these capture the true spirit of the Sabbath, which is a joyful celebration of God's creation. Mark will make a similar point in chapter 7, where Jesus condemns the Pharisees and experts in the law ("scribes") for honoring God through external rituals while their hearts are far from him (7:6 – 23, citing Isa 29:13).

Christ's Fulfillment of the Sabbath

There is no doubt that these passages teach the true intent of the Sabbath command. But may they go even further to imply its eschatological fulfillment in Christ?[12] In a larger context, where Jesus has been speaking of himself as the bridegroom at the messianic banquet (2:19 – 20) and his ministry as new wine that cannot be placed in old wineskins (2:22), his self-identification as "Lord of the Sabbath" probably also carries eschatological implications. The Lord who created the Sabbath is now fulfilling it, bringing it to consummation in the kingdom of God. This interpretation fits the perspective of Hebrews, where the Sabbath rest for God's people becomes the eschatological salvation achieved through the once-for-all sacrifice of Christ (Heb 3:19 – 4:11). Paul also appears to assume that in the new age of salvation, the Sabbath has been fulfilled in Christ, so that one day no longer takes precedence over the others (Rom 14:5 – 6; Gal 4:10; Col 2:16). Every day is to be given wholly to the Lord.

This does not mean, of course, that the *principle* of the Sabbath has been abrogated. A sacred principle of rest is linked to God's rest after his work of creation (Gen 2:2), and so is part of his divine nature and purpose for his creation. Human beings created in his image should follow the model he has set. In our hectic, performance-driven lives, it is easy to forget this principle. Pastors and others in Christian ministry are particularly susceptible to this tendency and are prone toward workaholism. After a busy weekend of teaching and preaching, we often hit the ground running on Monday, trying to catch up on emails and other administrative duties. It is easy to forget that "the Sabbath was made for mankind" and that this rest is a gift from God to help us *be* all that God wants us to be, not just to *do* all that we want to get done. God created us first and foremost for relationship — to bask in his glory — and a Sabbath rest (whether in the form of a day off or time set aside throughout the week) allows us to stop, to rest, to reflect, and to simply enjoy communion with God and his creation.

---

12. For the ongoing debate related to the Sabbath command, see D. A. Carson, ed., *From Sabbath to Lord's Day: A Biblical, Historical and Theological Investigation* (Eugene, OR; Wipf & Stock, 2000); C. J. Donato, ed., *Perspectives on the Sabbath: 4 Views* (Nashville: B&H Academic, 2011).

Mark 3:7 – 12

Literary Context

The plot against Jesus that came as a climax to the first controversy with the religious leaders (3:6) together with this summary of Jesus' ministry in 3:7 – 12 indicates that a new phase of his ministry is beginning, sometimes identified as the "Later Galilean Ministry" (3:7 – 6:13). In one sense the events recounted here are more of the same: demonstrations of Jesus' messianic authority and growing opposition to him.

But there is an intensification of the conflict: Jesus not only heals the sick, but even calms an angry sea (3:35 – 41), defeats a "legion" of demons (5:1 – 20), and raises the dead (5:21 – 43). There is also an increased polarization of the forces for and against Jesus. On the one side are Jesus and his disciples. The section is framed on either side with the appointment of the Twelve (3:13 – 19) and their mission to preach and to heal (6:6b – 13). These twelve, the restored remnant of Israel, stand over against the religious leaders, who represent obstinate and apostate Israel.

In an important intercalation ("sandwich" structure; see Introduction: Literary Features), Jesus' own family considers him to be crazy and comes to take charge of him (3:20 – 21, 31 – 35; cf. 6:1 – 6a). Meanwhile, the religious leaders accuse Jesus of casting out demons by Satan's power and so blaspheme the Holy Spirit (3:22). Jesus follows this by teaching in parables. The purpose of these parables is to reveal the truth to the "insiders" — those who are responding in faith — but to blind those who have already rejected him. The battle lines have been drawn. The key questions of this section are "Who is this Jesus?" and "Are you for him or against him?"

Main Idea

Mark begins this second phase of Jesus' Galilean ministry by summarizing Jesus' activity, including his withdrawal to the Sea of Galilee, his ever-growing popularity, his healings and exorcisms, and his command to exorcised demons to keep silent about his identity.

Translation

Mark 3:7 – 12

7a	Setting (spatial)	**Jesus withdrew with his disciples to the sea,**
b	Character entrance/Action	and **great crowds followed him**
c		from Galilee.
8a	Action/Response	**Great crowds** **heard what he was doing**
b	Character entrance/Action	and **came to him**
	list item	from Judea, and
	list item	Jerusalem, and
	list item	Idumea, and
	list item	beyond the Jordan River, and
	list item	from the regions around Tyre and Sidon.
9a	Command	**He told his disciples to have a small boat ready for him,**
b	purpose of 9a	to keep the crowd from pressing him.
10a	Reason for 9/Cause of 10b	For **he had healed many people,**
b	reason for 9/result of 10a	so that all those with diseases were pushing forward to touch him.
11a	Action	**The defiling spirits, whenever they saw him, would fall down before him** ☞ **and cry out,**
b	recognition/acclamation	"You are the Son of God!"
12	Command	But **he strongly ordered them not to make him known.**

Structure

The passage summarizes Jesus' activity, with an emphasis on his broad and growing popularity resulting from his authoritative exorcisms and healings. The summary parallels the introduction in 1:14 – 15, where Jesus first comes into Galilee proclaiming the message of the kingdom of God. Both are similarly followed by accounts related to the disciples: the call of the four to be fishers of people in 1:14 – 20 and the appointment of the Twelve in 3:17 – 19.[1]

---

1. Lane, *Mark*, 127.

Exegetical Outline

→ **1. Setting: Jesus' Withdrawal to the Sea (3:7a)**

  2. Summary: Jesus' Ever-Growing Popularity (3:7b – 12)

    a. The crowds gather from all the locales (3:7b – 8)

    b. Jesus' response to the crush of the crowds: a boat at the ready (3:9)

    c. The reason for the crowds: Jesus' healings and exorcisms (3:10 – 12)

      i. The healing of many (3:10)

      ii. The response of the demons to his presence (3:11)

      iii. The command by Jesus for silence (3:12)

Explanation of the Text

3:7 – 8 Jesus withdrew with his disciples to the sea, and great crowds followed him from Galilee. Great crowds heard what he was doing and came to him from Judea, and Jerusalem, and Idumea, and beyond the Jordan River, and from the regions around Tyre and Sidon (Καὶ ὁ Ἰησοῦς μετὰ τῶν μαθητῶν αὐτοῦ ἀνεχώρησεν πρὸς τὴν θάλασσαν, καὶ πολὺ πλῆθος ἀπὸ τῆς Γαλιλαίας ἠκολούθησεν, καὶ ἀπὸ τῆς Ἰουδαίας καὶ ἀπὸ Ἱεροσολύμων καὶ ἀπὸ τῆς Ἰδουμαίας καὶ πέραν τοῦ Ἰορδάνου καὶ περὶ Τύρον καὶ Σιδῶνα πλῆθος πολὺ ἀκούοντες ὅσα ἐποίει ἦλθον πρὸς αὐτόν). In the face of growing opposition, Jesus "withdraws" to the Sea of Galilee. This is home turf for him, the place of his greatest success and his most loyal following.[2] The reference to "disciples" may mean the four Jesus called in 1:16 – 20 (and 2:14?) but more likely refers to a larger group of followers. It is from this larger group that Jesus will choose the Twelve in the episode that follows (3:13 – 19).

The Greek grammar of the second clause is awkward,[3] but the sense is clear: Jesus' growing reputation results in large crowds[4] streaming to him from throughout Israel and surrounding regions. Mark's geographical description begins with Galilee, the place of Jesus' home ministry, and then expands to the south, east, and northwest. Judea is the province to the south, named for, but somewhat larger than, the inheritance of the tribe Judah. Jerusalem is its chief city and the ultimate destination of Jesus' ministry.

Idumea (mentioned only here in the NT) is the Latinization of the name Edom, another name for Esau (Gen 25:30; 36:1), Jacob's twin brother. It refers to the region south of Judea (the Negev), settled by the Edomites. Judas Maccabeus repeatedly

---

2. Lane's claim (ibid., 128 – 29) that "the region of the sea is the sphere of the demonic" does not find support in Mark's narrative, where exorcisms are not directly associated with the sea. Only in the exorcism at Gerasa are demons connected with the sea (5:13).

3. Mark's redundant style — the repetition of πολὺ πλῆθος and two verbs used to describe their coming (ἠκολούθησεν, v. 7; ἦλθον, v. 8) — created confusion for copyists trying to figure out which verbs went with which geographical regions, resulting in a variety of textual variants. The most likely reading

has the singular ἠκολούθησεν associated with the great crowd from Galilee and the verb ἦλθον referring to the rest of the geographical regions (so NIV, NET, NRSV; see translation above). Others identify all the geographical regions with the verb ἠκολούθησεν and treat the final clause as a separate sentence: "When the great crowd heard all that he was doing, they came to him" (ESV; cf. NLT).

4. Only here and in v. 8 does Mark use πλῆθος instead of his more common ὄχλος (38 times). This may perhaps point to his use of a source.

defeated the Idumeans in battle, and they were forcibly converted to Judaism during the reign of the Hasmonean John Hyrcanus. Herod the Great, who ruled Israel at the time of Jesus' birth, was an Idumean.

"Beyond the Jordan" refers to the eastern side of the Jordan River, including Decapolis in the north and Perea in the south. Both of these, like Galilee, were under the rule of Herod Antipas (Luke 3:1), son of Herod the Great.

Tyre and Sidon were major Phoenician cities on the Mediterranean coast north of Israel (modern Lebanon). They are frequently identified together as a way of designating the region northwest of Israel.[5] Jesus will visit this region later in the gospel (7:24).

The reason for naming these particular places is unclear,[6] but the general sense is to show that people are coming from far and wide. The reference to Tyre and Sidon confirms that even Gentile regions are hearing of Jesus' ministry, foreshadowing the Gentile mission.

3:9 He told his disciples to have a small boat ready for him, to keep the crowd from pressing him (καὶ εἶπεν τοῖς μαθηταῖς αὐτοῦ ἵνα[7] πλοιάριον προσκαρτερῇ αὐτῷ διὰ τὸν ὄχλον ἵνα μὴ θλίβωσιν αὐτόν). The boat may have been for escape in case the crowd crushed forward, but more likely is meant for crowd control, a kind of platform or podium to keep from being jostled. Jesus will use a boat for this purpose in 4:1, sitting to teach while the people stand a few feet back on the shore.

Mark uses a diminutive form, "little boat"

(πλοιάριον). The force of the diminutive has decreased in Koine Greek, and Mark sometimes uses diminutives without any clear sense of smallness (cf. 6:9 and 14:47, where "sandals" and "ear" are diminutives). Here, however, the point seems to be a small dinghy suitable for a platform, instead of a larger fishing or transport vessel. The use of the present (continuous) tense for the subjunctives "make ready" (προσκαρτερῇ) and "press" or "crush" (θλίβωσιν) suggests that this is a pattern for teaching that Jesus is establishing (cf. 4:1).

3:10 For he had healed many people, so that all those with diseases were pushing forward to touch him (πολλοὺς γὰρ ἐθεράπευσεν, ὥστε[8] ἐπιπίπτειν αὐτῷ ἵνα αὐτοῦ ἅψωνται ὅσοι εἶχον μάστιγας). The reason ("for," γάρ) crowd control was needed is now made clear, as people are pressing forward to experience Jesus' healing touch. Both the verbs "press/crush" (θλίβω) in v. 9 and "push/fall upon" (ἐπιπίπτω) in v. 10 can carry negative senses ("oppress" and "attack," respectively), but in this context they are used positively.[9] It is excitement and enthusiasm for Jesus' healing power that is motivating the crowds. "Many" (πολλούς) does not carry an exclusive sense here (i.e., that some are not healed), but rather a superlative sense: many (not just a few) are healed (cf. 1:33; 10:45).

Jesus often heals with touch in Mark's gospel (1:41; 7:33; 8:22). The belief that touching a gifted healer's clothing could tap into that healer's power was common in the ancient world (cf. 5:25–34; 6:56; cf. 2 Kgs 13:21; Acts 5:15–16; 19:11–12). While the Gospels bear witness to such supersti-

---

5. Jer 25:22; 27:3; 47:4; Joel 3:4; Zech 9:2; Jdt 2:28; 1 Macc 5:15; 2 Esd 1:11; Matt 11:21; Luke 10:13.

6. Suggestions include: (1) areas where Jesus will visit in the gospel (Lane, *Mark*, 129), though Jesus never travels to Idumea; (2) the extent of Israel of old (Garland, *Mark*, 127), but it is strange that Samaria would be left out; (3) Jewish Palestine, areas with large Jewish populations (E. Klosterman, *Das Markusevangelium* [HNT 3; Tübingen: Mohr, 1950], 33), but

this would not apply well to Tyre or Sidon.

7. The ἵνα is epexegetical, indicating the content of the indirect command, "Jesus told them" (Stein, *Mark*, 163).

8. ὥστε with the infinitive (ἐπιπίπτειν) often indicates result: "with the result that …," "so that …."

9. Contra Marcus, *Mark 1–8*, 258–61, who sees an "undertone of threat."

tions, Jesus' healings are not based on an impersonal force residing within him, but rather on his active authority as Messiah and Son of God. Even in Mark 5:24, where a woman is healed by secretly touching him, Jesus makes it clear that it was her faith that resulted in the healing (5:34), not some impersonal force that she was able to tap into.

3:11 The defiling spirits, whenever they saw him, would fall down before him and cry out, "You are the Son of God!" (καὶ τὰ πνεύματα τὰ ἀκάθαρτα, ὅταν αὐτὸν ἐθεώρουν, προσέπιπτον αὐτῷ καὶ ἔκραζον λέγοντες ὅτι σὺ εἶ ὁ υἱὸς τοῦ θεοῦ). Mark now turns from healings to exorcisms, summarizing again Jesus' authority over demonic forces (for the significance of "defiling/unclean spirits" [τὰ πνεύματα τὰ ἀκάθαρτα], see comments on 1:23). The imperfect verb "were seeing" (ἐθεώρουν) is an iterative imperfect, indicating repeated action continuing over time, a point made clear in context by the temporal particle, "whenever" (ὅταν). The verb translated "fall down before" (προσπίπτω) can also mean to "move with force against" (BDAG, 884), but the context suggests the former is intended. As in 1:23–28, 34, the demons are no match for Jesus and immediately succumb to his overwhelming presence.

The demons acknowledge Jesus to be the "Son of God" (ὁ υἱὸς τοῦ θεοῦ). As noted at 1:24, this may be a futile attempt to gain mastery over Jesus, since some believed that you could manipulate spiritual forces by knowing their secret names. Elsewhere in Mark, demons identify him as "God's Holy One" (1:24) and the "Son of the Most High God" (5:7), and Jesus silences them "because they knew who he was" (1:34). The close connection Mark draws between Jesus' status as Messiah and Son of God indicates that the latter functions for Mark as a messianic title (1:1; 14:61; cf. 2 Sam 7:14; Pss 2:7; 89:26).[10] Jesus is the promised and anointed king who will reign forever on David's throne. Yet there are also strong implications of deity associated with the title. As the Son of God, Jesus shares the Father's glory, power, and authority (cf. comments on 1:1).

3:12 But he strongly ordered them not to make him known (καὶ πολλὰ ἐπετίμα αὐτοῖς ἵνα μὴ αὐτὸν φανερὸν ποιήσωσιν). As elsewhere, Jesus silences the demons (1:25, 34). His purpose for this command is likely twofold: first, to demonstrate his supreme authority over Satan's forces; second, because the demons are inappropriate heralds of his person and mission (cf. 1:25). Jesus will reveal his identity in his own time and through his own words and deeds.

Theology in Application

Acknowledging the Authority of the Messiah

Mark's summary in these verses continues to emphasize the central theme of Jesus' Galilean ministry: the authority of Jesus. This authority is seen in his acts of power over disease and demons, and in the popular acclaim of the crowds, who recognize him as a great teacher and healer. For the time being the crowds are protagonists, praising God for the miracles and extolling Jesus' mighty deeds (2:12). Their

---

10. In his parallel to 1:34, Luke says the demons shouted "'You are the Son of God!' ... because they knew he was the Messiah" (Luke 4:41).

vast numbers demonstrate his remarkable appeal. The sections that follow will reveal even more astounding miracles and a growing division between Jesus' true followers and those who doubt or oppose him. The lines will be drawn, as Jesus chooses and trains a select group of disciples and the religious leaders decisively reject him — committing blasphemy against the Holy Spirit.

Two implicit questions run throughout this section, and indeed through the whole first half of Mark's gospel: "Who is this Jesus?" and "Whose side are you on?" The reader knows Jesus' identity, since Mark has introduced his work as "the good news about Jesus the Messiah." The demons know and repeatedly shout it out, but Jesus is not interested in such acclaim from his enemies and authoritatively silences them.

Obedience to God's Kingdom Purposes

This passage reminds us that recognition of Jesus' identity and authority is not enough. The crowds who clamor to him for healing will eventually become indifferent and then hostile to his ministry. The demons who acknowledge his divine status as Son of God still oppose and reject him. Throughout Scripture it is not enough to recognize God's greatness. One must also submit to his authority. Pharaoh was forced to concede defeat to the God of Israel after ten plagues (Exod 12:31), yet he still defiantly sent his troops to destroy the Israelites at the Red Sea (Exod 14). The Israelites, who marveled at God's miracles in parting the Red Sea and feeding them in the wilderness, subsequently worshiped false gods and refused to trust God to enter the Promised Land.

Sometimes we worship and praise God in church on Sunday but then live our lives by a different standard the rest of the week. Jesus repeatedly confronts this, pointing out that not everyone who says "Lord, Lord" will enter the kingdom of God (Matt 7:21 – 22) and chastising those who claim him as Lord but do not do what he says (Luke 6:46). Simply acknowledging God's greatness or paying lip service to him is not the same as truly loving and serving him. An authentic relationship with God requires both faith and obedience.

CHAPTER 13

Mark 3:13 – 19

Literary Context

The summary of 3:7 – 12 concluded the first part of Jesus' Galilean ministry (characterized by Jesus' authority to preach and to heal as well as growing opposition to him by the religious leaders) as well as introduced a second phase of ministry in Galilee (3:7 – 6:13). This section is framed with accounts concerning the disciples: their appointment as apostles (3:13 – 19) and the mission on which Jesus sends them out to preach and to heal (6:6 – 13). The main theme of this section is the increasing division between two sides, those for Jesus and those against him. The disciples whom Jesus appoints in this passage become "insiders" to Jesus' authoritative teaching. By contrast, those whom one would expect to be closest to Jesus — the religious leaders of Israel, his own family, and the people of his hometown — in fact reject his authority and become "outsiders" to the message of the kingdom.

Main Idea

From among his many followers, Jesus appoints twelve special disciples, or "apostles," to represent the restored remnant of Israel and to expand Jesus' ministry of preaching and healing throughout Israel.

Translation

Mark 3:13 – 19

13a	Action/Setting (spatial	**He went up onto the mountain and summoned those he wanted,**
b	Action/Response	and **they came to him.**
14a	Action/clarification	And **he appointed twelve** [calling them "apostles"]
b	purpose of 14a	to accompany him and
c	purpose of 14a	so that he could send them out to preach and
15	manner of 14a	with authority
		to cast out demons.
16a	Assertion/List	**He appointed twelve:**
b	list item/character description	To Simon, he gave the name Peter;
17a	list item/character description	James the son of Zebedee and John the brother of James,
b	character description	to whom he gave the name Boanerges, meaning ⟐
		"sons of thunder," and
18a	list item	Andrew,
b	list item	Philip,
c	list item	Bartholomew,
d	list item	Matthew,
e	list item	Thomas,
f	list item/character description	James the son of Alphaeus,
g	list item	Thaddaeus,
h	list item/character description	Simon the Zealot, and
19	list item/character description	Judas Iscariot, who betrayed him.

Structure

The structure is a call and appointment narrative, followed by a list. Since most of the Twelve will play no role in the subsequent narrative (seven of the twelve are mentioned only here), Mark's purpose is to emphasize the constitution of the body rather than their individual roles. The authoritative Messiah and Son of God is reconstituting a faithful remnant within Israel.

Exegetical Outline

➡ **1. The Setting: Withdrawal to the Galilean Hills (3:13a)**

2. The Call and Appointment of the Twelve (3:13b – 19)

　　a. The gathering of the disciples (3:13b)

　　b. The appointment of the Twelve (3:14a)

　　c. The roles of the Twelve (3:14b – 15)

　　d. The names of the Twelve (3:16 – 19)

Explanation of the Text

3:13 He went up onto the mountain and summoned those he wanted, and they came to him (Καὶ ἀναβαίνει εἰς τὸ ὄρος καὶ προσκαλεῖται οὓς ἤθελεν αὐτός, καὶ ἀπῆλθον πρὸς αὐτόν). The Greek "onto the mountain" (εἰς τὸ ὄρος) was also an idiomatic way of saying "into the hills" (BDAG, 725; Tob 5:6). Since no specific mountain is identified, the hills around the Sea of Galilee are likely meant (cf. REB: "into the hill-country"). Some see theological significance in the reference, since mountains — especially Mount Sinai — were places of solitude and revelation in Israel's history.[1] Matthew in particular stresses such mountaintop experiences (5:1; 14:23; 15:29; 17:1; 28:16), portraying Jesus as a kind of new Moses. While the same could be true of Mark, he makes much less of such mountains, and his references to mountaintop experiences appear to come from the traditions he received.[2] "Those he wanted" (οὓς ἤθελεν αὐτός) may refer to the Twelve he is about to appoint, but it more likely refers to a larger group of his followers from among whom he chooses the Twelve.

3:14 – 15 And he appointed twelve [calling them "apostles"] to accompany him and so that he could send them out to preach and with authority to cast out demons (καὶ ἐποίησεν δώδεκα [οὓς καὶ ἀποστόλους ὠνόμασεν][3] ἵνα ὦσιν μετ' αὐτοῦ καὶ ἵνα ἀποστέλλῃ αὐτοὺς κηρύσσειν καὶ ἔχειν ἐξουσίαν ἐκβάλλειν τὰ δαιμόνια). Jesus calls his followers together and selects twelve to be his closest disciples. The verb commonly translated "make" or "do" (ποιέω) has a large semantic range, and it here

means to appoint or commission. From this point on, the term "disciples" (μαθηταί) refers almost exclusively to the Twelve.

The number twelve is surely significant, recalling the twelve tribes of Israel and indicating that Jesus viewed himself, in some sense at least, as restoring, reforming, or reconstituting the remnant of Israel. The role of the Twelve as leaders and representatives of eschatological Israel is made explicit by Jesus in Matt 19:28 and Luke 22:30. The choice of twelve has profound significance concerning the messianic self-consciousness of the historical Jesus, confirming that he viewed himself as God's agent for covenant renewal and the eschatological restoration of Israel.[4] Furthermore, by not identifying himself as one of the Twelve (and so part of eschatological Israel), Jesus apparently presents himself in the position of Yahweh, who created and elected Israel as his covenant people.

If the phrase "calling them 'apostles'" (οὓς καὶ ἀποστόλους ὠνόμασεν) is authentic (see textual note), this would be Mark's first use of the term. "Apostle" means a "messenger" or one sent with a task or commission. While Luke commonly refers to the Twelve as apostles (6:13; 9:10; 11:49; 17:5; 22:14; 24:10; and 28x in Acts), Mark does so only here and at 6:30 (see comments there).

As in the earlier call narratives (1:14 – 20; 2:14 – 17), Jesus' authority is on center stage. He seeks out, chooses, and appoints his own disciples. The role he assigns to them is an extension of his own. First, they are simply to "accompany him" or

---

1. Lane, *Mark*, 132; Marcus, *Mark 1 – 8*, 206.
2. Guelich, *Mark 1:1 – 8:26*, 156 – 57.
3. The phrase οὓς καὶ ἀποστόλους ὠνόμασεν (lit., "whom he also called apostles") is textually questionable. Its external evidence is strong, appearing in a number of early and important manuscripts (א B Θ *f*[13] 28 *pc* sy[h,mg] cop), but the internal

evidence is weak, since the phrase appears to be a scribal harmonization to Luke's parallel (6:13; cf. Matt 10:2).
4. See Scot McKnight, "Jesus and the Twelve," in *Key Events in the Life of the Historical Jesus* (ed. D. L. Bock and R. L. Webb; Grand Rapids: Eerdmans, 2010), 181 – 214.

"be with him" (ἵνα ὦσιν μετ᾽ αὐτοῦ; the ἵνα + subjunctive indicates purpose). The best way to learn is to be with the Master, watching him and modeling his behavior (see Theology in Application, below). Second, they are to do what he does: to preach and cast out demons. The preaching would be the proclamation of the coming of the kingdom of God (1:14 – 15; see comments there). Casting out demons demonstrates the authority of the kingdom of God, which invades and overwhelms the kingdom of Satan — a point Jesus will make in the next passage (3:23 – 27).

It is surprising that healing the sick is not mentioned, but this may be due to Mark's stylistic variety (see comments on 1:39). Or perhaps slight priority is given to exorcisms, since these represent direct confrontation with the kingdom of Satan. When Jesus sends the Twelve on their first mission, he similarly gives them "authority over defiling spirits" with no mention of the authority to heal (6:7). At their return, however, Mark summarizes that they participated in all three activities: preaching, exorcism, and healing (6:12 – 13).

3:16 – 17 He appointed twelve: To Simon, he gave the name Peter; James the son of Zebedee and John the brother of James, to whom he gave the name Boanerges, meaning "sons of thunder" ([καὶ ἐποίησεν τοὺς δώδεκα,][5] καὶ ἐπέθηκεν ὄνομα τῷ Σίμωνι Πέτρον, καὶ Ἰάκωβον τὸν τοῦ Ζεβεδαίου καὶ Ἰωάννην τὸν ἀδελφὸν τοῦ Ἰακώβου καὶ ἐπέθηκεν αὐτοῖς ὀνόμα[τα] βοανηργές, ὅ ἐστιν υἱοὶ βροντῆς). Similar lists of the apostles appear in Matt 10:2 – 4; Luke 6:14 – 16; and Acts 1:13, with minor variations.

Simon Peter is always named first in these lists, and throughout the gospel tradition he serves as the representative and spokesperson for the others. Mark notes that Jesus nicknamed Simon "Peter" (Πέτρος), meaning a "rock" or "stone."[6] According to John 1:42, Jesus originally used the Aramaic *Kephā᾽* ("Cephas," meaning "rock" or "stone"), which was subsequently translated into Greek as "Peter" (Πέτρος). Mark gives no explanation for the nickname, and indeed Peter appears impetuous and wavering throughout the gospel tradition, even denying that he knows Jesus (Mark 14:66 – 72). But he is the first to confess Jesus as the Messiah (Mark 8:29), and Jesus clearly sees great potential in him. According to Matthew, at Peter's confession Jesus entrusts to him the "keys of the kingdom" and predicts he will be a foundation stone for the apostolic church (Matt 16:13 – 20).[7] Sure enough, after the resurrection, Jesus restores Peter to a position of leadership (John 21:15 – 19; cf. Luke 4:34), and in the early chapters of Acts Peter takes the lead among the apostles (Acts 1:15 – 26; 5:3 – 9), preaching the inaugural sermon of the early church in Acts (Acts 2:14 – 41), boldly standing firm in the face of opposition (3:11 – 26; 4:8 – 12), and opening the door of the gospel to Jews, Samaritans, and Gentiles alike (8:14 – 17; 10:1 – 11:18; 15:7 – 11).

Matthew (Matt 10:2) and Luke (Luke 6:14) place Peter's brother Andrew next in the list, but Mark first names the fishermen brothers, James and John. The likely reason is that Peter, James, and John form a kind of "inner circle" of disciples, accompanying Jesus on special occasions: the raising of Jairus's daughter (Mark 5:37), the transfiguration (9:2), and in the garden of Gethsemane

---

5. καὶ ἐποίησεν τοὺς δώδεκα is absent in some manuscripts (A C² D L Ė *f*[1.33] 2427 𝔐 lat syr boh). It was likely omitted by copyists seeking to avoid repetition with the same phrase in v. 14.

6. It is unclear when Jesus first gave Simon his nickname, whether at their first meeting (John 1:42), at the appointment

of the Twelve (Mark 3:16), or following Peter's confession (Matt 16:18).

7. For evidence that Peter is here identified as the "rock" (πέτρα), see Davies and Allison, *Matthew*, 2:627, who call other options (the confession itself, Jesus' teaching, Jesus himself, etc.) "special pleading."

(14:33). James and John were called together with Peter and Andrew from their fishing business to follow Jesus (1:6–20).

Mark says that Jesus gave James and John the nickname Boanerges (βοανηργές), which he interprets to mean "sons of thunder" (υἱοὶ βροντῆς; 3:17).[8] No explanation for the name is given, but it may have been because of their volatile personalities, evidenced at various points in the gospel tradition (e.g., 10:35–39; Luke 9:49, 54). In Acts, James becomes the first apostolic martyr, arrested and executed by Herod Agrippa I (Acts 12:1–2). John too appears in several scenes in Acts as a leading apostle beside Peter (3:1; 4:1; 8:14, 25). He is traditionally identified as the Beloved Disciple, the author of the Fourth Gospel (13:23; 20:2; 21:7, 20–24), the letters of 1–3 John, and the book of Revelation.

3:18–19 And Andrew, Philip, Bartholomew, Matthew, Thomas, James the son of Alphaeus, Thaddaeus, Simon the Zealot, and Judas Iscariot, who betrayed him (καὶ Ἀνδρέαν καὶ Φίλιππον καὶ Βαρθολομαῖον καὶ Μαθθαῖον καὶ Θωμᾶν καὶ Ἰάκωβον τὸν τοῦ Ἀλφαίου καὶ Θαδδαῖον καὶ Σίμωνα τὸν Καναναῖον καὶ Ἰούδαν Ἰσκαριώθ, ὃς καὶ παρέδωκεν αὐτόν). Andrew, named fourth, was called by Jesus together with his brother Simon (1:16–18). He and Peter were from Bethsaida (John 1:44), but operated their fishing business out of Capernaum (Mark 1:29).

The Fourth Gospel relates a different call narrative, identifying Andrew as originally a disciple of John the Baptist, who followed Jesus when the Baptist pointed him out as the "Lamb of God." An-

drew then brought his brother Simon to meet Jesus (John 1:40–44) and subsequently appears in John as the disciple who brings others to Jesus: the boy with the loaves and fishes (6:8–9) and, together with Philip, a group of Greeks who wanted to meet Jesus (12:20–22). Although Andrew was not one of the so-called "inner circle" (Peter, James, and John), Mark gives him a measure of prominence as he appears with these other three at the healing of Peter's mother-in-law and on the Mount of Olives (Mark 1:29; 13:3).

Philip is named only here in Mark's gospel. According to the Fourth Gospel, he, like Peter and Andrew, is from Bethsaida and subsequently introduces Nathanael to Jesus (John 1:44–45). Outside of the lists of disciples, he appears only in a few scenes in John's gospel (6:5–7; 12:21–22; 14:8–9). Bartholomew means (in Aramaic) "son of Tolmai" and is a patronymic rather than a personal name. It may be assumed, therefore, that he had another name. Some have identified him with Nathanael (John 1:45).

The gospel of Matthew identifies the disciple Matthew as the tax collector referred to as "Levi" by Mark and Luke (Matt 9:9; Mark 2:14; Luke 5:27). Some dispute this, since Mark nowhere identifies Levi with Matthew. Yet this remains the simplest solution, especially since the call of Levi parallels the call of other disciples (1:16–20; 2:14).

Thomas, also known as Didymus (meaning "the twin"), is best known as the disciple who doubted Jesus' resurrection until he saw and touched Jesus himself (John 20:24–29). Mark mentions him only here, though he plays a more prominent role in John's gospel (11:16; 14:5; 20:24–28; 21:2). Church

---

8. The etymology of βοανηργές is unclear, since it does not obviously mean "sons of thunder" in either Aramaic or Hebrew (one would expect the Hebrew *bĕnê ra'am*). Many suggestions have been made (see the summary in Guelich, *Mark 1:1–8:26*, 162), perhaps the most likely being an unusual (dialectic?) transliteration of the Hebrew *bĕnê regeš*, meaning "sons

of commotion/crowd" (cf. Ps 2:1). An Arabic word related to *regeš* means "thunder," so this may have been one sense of the word in Mark's day. For details and other possibilities, see R. Buth, "Mark 3:17 ΒΟΗΕΡΓΕΣ and Popular Etymology," *JSNT* 4 (1981): 29–33; J. T. Rook, "'Boanerges, Sons of Thunder,' (Mark 3:17)," *JBL* 100 (1981): 94–95; France, *Mark*, 161–62.

tradition claims Thomas later evangelized eastward into India.

"James the son of Alphaeus" is sometimes identified with "James the younger" of Mark 15:40. It is possible he was the brother of Matthew/Levi since the fathers of both are named Alphaeus (2:14). Thaddaeus is the most disputed name among the Twelve. Matthew and Mark refer to him by this name (though some Western manuscripts read "Lebbaeus" [Λεββαῖος]),[9] while Luke instead has "Judas the son of James." These could be two names for the same person.

Mark and Matthew identify Simon as the "Cananaean" (Καναναῖον), from an Aramaic term meaning "zealous one" (qan'ānā'). The KJV mistranslated this as "Canaanite" and other versions transliterate "Cananaean" (RSV, NRSV). Since many readers will misread this as a Canaanite, it seems better to translate the Aramaic term as "the Zealot" (NIV, NASB, NET, HCSB, NLT, REB, etc.). Luke himself does this, translating the Aramaic term into Greek: "Simon, called the Zealot" (Σίμωνα τὸν καλούμενον ζηλωτή; 6:15; cf. Acts 1:13). The term may refer either to religious zeal (cf. Acts 21:20; 22:3; Gal 1:14) or to patriotic fervor, as it came to be used during the Jewish war of AD 66 – 73. Of course, in Judaism the two often went hand-in-hand.[10]

Last in the list comes Judas Iscariot, "who betrayed him." Mark's readers are already well aware of the role Judas will play in the story (cf. 14:10 – 11, 43 – 45). The significance of "Iscariot" (Ἰσκαριώθ) is debated, but it probably means "man from Kerioth" (îš qĕrîyōt), a town of uncertain location in Judea. If this identification is correct, Judas was the only Judean of Jesus' disciples. Other less likely etymologies include: (1) sicarius, meaning "dagger," and used for the freedom fighters or "assassins" who killed Roman officials and Jewish collaborators; (2) the Hebrew root šqr, meaning "liar," and so a name given after the fact to Judas; (3) "man of Sychar," making Judas a Samaritan. According to John 6:71, Iscariot was a family name, since Judas is "the son of Simon Iscariot." The Fourth Gospel asserts that Judas, as treasurer, used to pilfer the group's money even before he betrayed Jesus (John 12:6).

Theology in Application

Jesus and the Twelve

The appointment of the Twelve represents an important narrative marker in the gospel. From this point on these disciples will constantly be at Jesus' side, learning from him and sharing in his ministry. They will be the "insiders" who gain special insight from Jesus' teaching and are set in contrast to the "outsiders" — Israel's religious leaders, the people of Jesus' hometown, and even his own family members — who respond negatively to Jesus' ministry. Yet while the disciples are clearly on the side of Jesus, they will play a primarily negative role in Mark's narrative, failing to comprehend Jesus' message and mission (4:13, 40; 6:37, 52; 7:18; 8:4, 17 – 21, 32 – 33;

---

9. See B. Lindars, "Matthew, Levi, Lebbaeus and the Value of the Western Text," NTS 4 (1957 – 1958): 220 – 22. Lindars suggests that Λεββαῖος was a scribal attempt to get Levi (2:14) into the list, if he was not to be identified with Matthew.

10. See Martin Hengel, The Zealots: Investigations into the Jewish Freedom Movement in the Period from Herod until 70 A.D. (Edinburgh: T&T Clark, 1989). Although Collins, Mark, 222, correctly notes that the party of "the Zealots" did not arise until the Jewish War, there were certainly political "zealots" prior to this.

9:18 – 19, 31 – 32, 38 – 39; 10:13 – 14, 35 – 45). They are not the heroes of the story; Jesus is, and this call narrative is more about Jesus and his mission than the stellar qualifications of these men. The number twelve, especially when seen in conjunction with Jesus' proclamation of the kingdom of God, indicates his reconstitution and restoration of eschatological Israel. Jesus is gathering to himself the end-time people of God.

The fact that Jesus is not one of the Twelve is also significant. He plays a role similar to that of Yahweh in the OT, who called out his chosen people from among the nations. Just as Israel was meant to be a light of revelation to the Gentiles, so these twelve will take Jesus' message to all nations (13:10; cf. Matt 28:18 – 20; Acts 1:8).

Modeling Discipleship

Jesus' purpose for the Twelve may also be seen as a model for discipleship training. Jesus appoints them, first of all, "to accompany him," that is, "to be with him." They are to watch and learn from him. Then he will send them out to preach and to cast out demons, that is, to broaden the scope of his own ministry. Jesus knew that the best way to train disciples was, first, to model his life before them, and second, to send them out to do it for themselves. People learn best not by reading manuals or hearing lectures, but by watching someone do something and then practicing it themselves. Hands-on training is key.

The apostle Paul followed this same discipleship method. He frequently encouraged his disciples and churches to learn by watching him: "Follow my example, as I follow the example of Christ" (1 Cor 11:1; cf. 4:16; Phil 3:17; 4:9; 1 Thess 1:6; 2 Thess 3:7 – 9; 2 Tim 2:2). His disciples watched him work and were then sent out to do the work of the ministry (Titus 1:5). In his little classic, *The Master Plan of Evangelism*, Robert Coleman describes Jesus' method of training the Twelve: "Jesus had no formal school, no seminaries, no outlined course of study, no periodic membership classes in which he enrolled his followers. . . . Amazing as it may seem, all Jesus did to teach these men his way was to draw them close to himself. He was his own school and curriculum."[11]

Jesus' model is a great example for us. Everyone in Christian ministry should be training their replacements, encouraging others to carry on the ministry after them. Too often pastors jealously guard their pulpits for fear of losing status or because of their own insecurities. Associates and others with teaching or leadership gifts can be viewed as competition rather than as partners in ministry to be encouraged and lifted up. Yet the ministry is not about personal achievement or influence, but about the kingdom of God. By appointing the Twelve, Jesus is beginning to implement a strategy that will take the message of salvation to the ends of the earth.

---

11. Robert Coleman, *The Master Plan of Evangelism* (Westwood, NJ: Revell, 1964), 38.

14

Mark 3:20 – 35

Literary Context

Jesus' appointment of the Twelve (3:13 – 19) — the beginning of the second phase of his Galilean ministry — sets the stage for a larger narrative complex in Mark where lines are drawn between those who support Jesus and those who reject him. The five controversies with the religious leaders (2:1 – 3:6) that occurred in the first phase of Jesus' Galilean ministry now reach a climax in the Beelzebul controversy, an explicit and decisive rejection of Jesus' person and authority (3:20 – 35). In this extended episode, Jesus' own family reveals skepticism and doubt about Jesus (3:20 – 21, 31 – 35), and Israel's religious leaders accuse him of being in league with Satan (3:22 – 30). Those who should be his greatest supporters are, in fact, rejecting him.

This, in turn, will lead to Jesus' teaching in parables (ch. 4), where the parable of the sower illustrates the various negative and positive responses to the preaching of the word (Jesus' kingdom proclamation). When his disciples ask him about the parable, Jesus explains why he teaches in parables: to those on the "inside" — to those with ears to hear, who have submitted to kingdom authority — the "secrets of the kingdom" have been revealed. But to those on the "outside" (the religious leaders rejecting his proclamation of the kingdom), the parables conceal the message. The present episode sets the contrast between these two groups.

Main Idea

The skepticism from his own family and the outright rejection by the Jewish religious leaders result in Jesus' accusation that the religious leaders have committed blasphemy against the Holy Spirit. Jesus subsequently teaches that true spiritual relationships come not through physical ancestry but through identifying with God's will and purpose in the world.

Translation

Mark 3:20–35

20a	Setting/Character entrance	Then **he went home and again the crowd gathered,**
b	result of 20a	so that they were not even able to eat.
21a	reason for 21b	When his family heard this,
b	Action	**they came to take charge of him,**
c	reason for 21b/assertion	because they said, "He's out of his mind."
22a	Character entrance/Action	And **the experts in the law who had come down from Jerusalem were saying,**
b	accusation/assertion	*"He is possessed by Beelzebul! By the ruler of demons he is casting out demons."*
23a	Action	**Calling them over, he began speaking to them in parables:**
b	rhetorical question/assertion	*"How can Satan cast out Satan?*
24a	condition	*If a kingdom is divided against itself,*
b	result	*that kingdom cannot stand.*
25a	condition	*And if a house is divided against itself,*
b	result	*that house cannot stand.*
26a	condition	*And if Satan has risen in revolt against himself and is divided,*
b	result	*he is not able to stand; his end has come.*
27a	result	*On the other hand, no one can enter a strong man's house to plunder his possessions*
b	condition	*unless he first ties up the strong man.*
c	result	*Then he can plunder his house.*
28a	Veracity statement	*Truly I say to you,*
b		*the children of humanity will be forgiven all their sins and all the blasphemies they utter.*
29a		*But whoever blasphemes against the Holy Spirit will never be forgiven,*
b		*but is guilty of an eternal sin."*
30a	Explanation for 28–29	**He said this because they were saying,**
b		*"He has a defiling spirit."*

Continued on next page.

Continued from previous page.

31a	Character entrance	Then **his mother and his brothers and sisters arrived.**
b	setting	Standing outside,
c	Action	**they sent word to him,**
d	purpose of 31c	summoning him.
32a	Setting/Response to 31c-d	**A crowd was sitting around him, and they told him,**
b	assertion	*"Jesus, your mother and brothers and sisters are outside asking for you."*
33a	Response	**He answered them,**
b	rhetorical question	*"Who are my mother and my brothers and sisters?"*
34a	action	Looking around at those seated around him in a circle,
b	Action	**he said,**
c	Assertion	*"Here are my mother and brothers and sisters.*
35	Pronouncement/Explanation	*For whoever does God's will is my brother and sister and mother."*

Structure

This is the first of Mark's famous "intercalations," a literary device where one episode is interrupted by another, each playing off the other with interrelated themes (cf. 5:21 – 43; 6:7 – 30; 11:12 – 25; 14:1 – 11; see Introduction: Literary Features). In this case, the story of Jesus' family coming to take charge of him because they think he's crazy (3:20 – 21, 31 – 35) is interrupted by the Beelzebul controversy, where the experts in the law accuse him of casting out demons by the power of Satan (3:22 – 30). The skepticism and false conclusions about Jesus made by his family are parallel to the rejection and false claims about him made by the religious leaders of Israel. In both cases, Jesus' own people reject him. Jesus then goes on to teach that true spiritual relationships do not come through ancestry or ethnic identity, but through a willingness to follow God's purpose in the world. His true mother and brothers are those who do God's will (v. 35). This, in turn, is part of Mark's larger narrative complex, where those who should be insiders become outsiders and lose out on the blessings of the kingdom.

In terms of form-critical categories, the two episodes are controversy stories climaxing with authoritative teaching or pronouncements by Jesus. The Beelzebul controversy climaxes with Jesus' teaching refuting their accusation and warning against the blasphemy of the Holy Spirit (3:22 – 30). The controversy with his family (3:20 – 21, 31 – 35) climaxes with Jesus' pronouncement that whoever does God's will is his brother and sister and mother (vv. 34 – 35).

Exegetical Outline

→ **1. Setting (3:20)**

    a. Jesus returns home and a crowd gathers (3:20a)

    b. No time to even eat (3:20b)

2. Jesus' Family, Part 1 (3:21)

    a. The report to Jesus' family (3:21a)

    b. The family goes to get Jesus (3:21b)

    c. The accusation: he is crazy (3:21c)

3. The Beelzebul Controversy (3:22 – 30)

    a. The accusation by the experts in the law (3:22)

    b. Jesus' refutation: Satan would not cast out Satan (3:23 – 26)

    c. Jesus' clarification: Satan *is* being defeated (3:27)

    d. Warning against blasphemy against the Holy Spirit (3:28 – 30)

4. Jesus' Family, Part 2 (3:31 – 35)

    a. The report about the family (3:31 – 32)

    b. Jesus' response: his true family (3:33 – 35)

Explanation of the Text

3:20 Then he went home and again the crowd gathered, so that they were not even able to eat (Καὶ ἔρχεται εἰς οἶκον· καὶ συνέρχεται πάλιν ὁ ὄχλος, ὥστε μὴ δύνασθαι αὐτοὺς μηδὲ ἄρτον φαγεῖν). Jesus returns to Capernaum, his base of operations in Galilee. The Greek phrase "to a house" (εἰς οἶκον) can also mean "home," and this is probably what is meant here (cf. 2:1). The home where he is ministering is likely Peter and Andrew's, where Peter's mother-in-law was healed (1:29) and perhaps where the four men lowered their paralyzed friend through the roof (cf. 2:1). Jesus' extraordinary popularity, a key theme of the Galilean ministry,[1] is again evident as a large crowd gathers. So great are their needs that Jesus and his disciples don't even have time to eat. "To eat bread" (ἄρτον φαγεῖν) often refers to sustenance of any kind (BDAG, 136). Mark's use of the his-torical present tense (ἔρχεται … συνέρχεται; "Jesus comes … the crowd gathers") provides a vivid and dramatic picture of the growing crowd.

3:21 When his family heard this, they came to take charge of him, because they said, "He's out of his mind." (καὶ ἀκούσαντες οἱ παρ᾽ αὐτοῦ ἐξῆλθον κρατῆσαι αὐτόν· ἔλεγον γὰρ ὅτι ἐξέστη). The phrase translated "his family" (οἱ παρ᾽ αὐτοῦ, "the ones alongside him") is a Greek idiom that can mean family, friends, or associates. The continuation of the scene in v. 31 suggests that Jesus' family is meant. This is the first reference to Jesus' family in Mark's gospel. They will be described more fully in 6:3 as consisting of his mother Mary, four brothers (James, Joseph, Judas, and Simon), and at least two sisters (see discussion there). The omission of his father may imply that Joseph was deceased by this time.

---

1. See 1:33 – 34; 2:2; 3:7 – 9; 4:1; 5:21, 24; 6:14 – 15, 31 – 34; 7:24; 8:1 – 3; 9:14 – 15, 30.

The family is presumably in Nazareth when they receive reports that the intensity of Jesus' ministry is taking its toll, so they set out toward Capernaum to "take charge" (κρατέω) of him. The verb often means to "arrest, seize, take possession of," indicating an attempt to forcibly remove him for his own good. They assume that he must be "out of his mind" (ἐξίστημι) from stress and overwork. In a Middle Eastern culture where honor and shame were among the highest of values, their purpose would also be to remove Jesus from a situation that could reflect badly on the family.

The journey of Jesus' family to Capernaum provides a pause in the narrative. Mark uses this pause to introduce a change in scene, as Jesus is approached by a delegation of religious leaders from Jerusalem. Mark's narrative and theological purpose is to link the skepticism and concern from his own family with the opposition from the leaders of his own people.

3:22 And the experts in the law who had come down from Jerusalem were saying, "He is possessed by Beelzebul! By the ruler of demons he is casting out demons." (καὶ οἱ γραμματεῖς οἱ ἀπὸ Ἱεροσολύμων καταβάντες ἔλεγον ὅτι Βεελζεβοὺλ ἔχει καὶ ὅτι ἐν τῷ ἄρχοντι τῶν δαιμονίων ἐκβάλλει τὰ δαιμόνια). The "scribes" (οἱ γραμματεῖς; see comments on 1:22) or experts in the law have already appeared repeatedly as Jesus' opponents, accusing him of blasphemy (2:6 – 7) and associating with sinners (2:16). They are also closely associated with the Pharisees, who began plotting against Jesus in 3:6 because of his apparent Sabbath violations (2:18, 24). That they have "come down"[2] from Jerusalem (cf. 7:1) suggests some kind of official

delegation sent by the Jerusalem leadership. The implication is that Jesus' unorthodox behavior has resulted in a decision to accuse and discredit him.

The accusation they make is that Jesus is possessed by "Beelzebul ... the ruler of demons" (ὁ ἄρχων τῶν δαιμονίων), and that by Satan's power he casts out demons. To "have [ἔχω] a demon" is a common collocation for demonization or demonic possession. "By the ruler" (ἐν τῷ ἄρχοντι) is a dative of agency, hence "by the power of" (cf. NLT, TEV) or "with the help of" (GW). In the other two Synoptics, this accusation is prompted by the account of the healing of the blind and mute demoniac (cf. Matt 12:22; Luke 11:14). Mark relates it more generally to Jesus' previous exorcisms (1:21 – 28, 34, 39; 2:11 – 12, 15).

The name "Beelzebul" is of uncertain origin. It was originally a title of the Canaanite god Baal, meaning either "Baal the Prince" or "Baal of the Exalted Dwelling."[3] The Israelites evidently mocked this name, changing Baal-Zebul to Baal-Zebub, "Lord of the Flies" (see Judg 10:6; 2 Kgs 1:2, 3, 6).[4] The Vulgate and Syriac versions use Beelzebub here in Mark (cf. KJV, NIV 1984), no doubt under the influence of 2 Kgs 1:2. But there is no evidence for this reading in the Greek manuscripts. How the name became associated with Satan is not known. The pseudepigraphic *Testament of Solomon* (1st to 3rd AD?) refers to Beelzebul as the "ruler of demons" (3:1 – 6; 4:2; 6:1 – 8), but its date is uncertain and it may have been dependent on the present account.

Whatever the name's origin, Jesus' response ("How can Satan cast out Satan?" v. 23) confirms that Mark viewed Beelzebul as another name for Satan, the ruler of the demonic realm. A similar

---

2. One always goes up to, and descends (καταβαίνω) from, Jerusalem, both because of its geographical elevation and because it is the Holy City of God.

3. For the background to Beelzebul, see L. Gaston, "Beelzebul," *TZ* 18 (1962): 247 – 55.

4. The LXX translates the Hebrew *ba'al zĕbûb 'ĕlōhê 'eqrôn* ("Baal-Zebub, god of Ekron") as Βααλ μυριαν θεον Ακκαρων ("Baal fly god of Ekron"; 2 Kgs 1:2, 3, 6; cf. Josephus, *Ant.* 9.2.1 §19).

accusation of demon-possession is made against Jesus in John 10:20 ("He is demon-possessed and raving mad"). Insanity and demon-possession were often linked in the ancient world, as they are today. This provides another narrative link to the previous scene, where Jesus' family questioned his sanity (v. 21).

The accusation is also significant from a historical perspective, confirming that Jesus' contemporaries considered him to be an exorcist.[5] The early church is unlikely to have invented a story where Jesus was accused of being demon-possessed. The best explanation, therefore, is that Jesus' opponents reluctantly admitted that he performed exorcisms, but sought a malevolent explanation. Further evidence of this accusation is the later Jewish polemic that Jesus practiced sorcery and led Israel astray.[6]

3:23 – 26 Calling them over, he began speaking to them in parables: "How can Satan cast out Satan? If a kingdom is divided against itself, that kingdom cannot stand. And if a house is divided against itself, that house cannot stand. And if Satan has risen in revolt against himself and is divided, he is not able to stand; his end has come." (Καὶ προσκαλεσάμενος αὐτοὺς ἐν παραβολαῖς ἔλεγεν αὐτοῖς· πῶς δύναται σατανᾶς σατανᾶν ἐκβάλλειν; καὶ ἐὰν βασιλεία ἐφ᾽ ἑαυτὴν μερισθῇ, οὐ δύναται σταθῆναι ἡ βασιλεία ἐκείνη· καὶ ἐὰν οἰκία ἐφ᾽ ἑαυτὴν μερισθῇ, οὐ δυνήσεται ἡ οἰκία ἐκείνη σταθῆναι. καὶ εἰ ὁ σατανᾶς ἀνέστη ἐφ᾽ ἑαυτὸν καὶ ἐμερίσθη, οὐ δύναται στῆναι ἀλλὰ τέλος ἔχει). Jesus summons his accusers and speaks to them "in parables" (ἐν παραβολαῖς). The semantic range of this Greek word is much broader than that of the English "parables," referring to a variety of literary forms, including proverbs, metaphors, similes, similitudes, parables, analogies, riddles, illustrations,

and the like. The meaning here is illustration, analogy, or even riddle. The imperfect verb "was saying" (ἔλεγεν) is probably an inceptive imperfect, meaning, "He began speaking."[7] Jesus first refutes the accusation by pointing out its absurdity. Why would Satan cast out his own demons? This would result in his sure destruction.

The poetic parallelism between a kingdom divided and a house divided suggests that "house" here refers to a royal dynasty (cf. 2 Sam 7:16: "Your house and your kingdom will endure forever"). The ancient world was full of examples of internal weakness and civil war resulting from dynastic rivalries. The division of Israel into the northern (Israel) and southern (Judah) kingdoms after the death of Solomon resulted from civil war between Jeroboam and Solomon's son Rehoboam (1 Kgs 12). The rivalry of two Hasmonean claimants to the throne, Aristobolus II and Hyrcanus II, allowed the Roman general Pompey to take Palestine in 63 BC with hardly a fight (Josephus, *Ant.* 14.3 – 4 §34 – 77).

Jesus concludes the first part of his refutation by applying his analogies to Satan: if Satan "has risen" (in revolt; ἀνέστη, a consummative aorist) against himself, his kingdom will not stand; it has come to an end. The present activity of demons is proof that Satan is not yet defeated and that his kingdom has yet to collapse.

3:27 On the other hand, no one can enter a strong man's house to plunder his possessions unless he first ties up the strong man. Then he can plunder his house (ἀλλ᾽ οὐ δύναται οὐδεὶς[8] εἰς τὴν οἰκίαν τοῦ ἰσχυροῦ εἰσελθὼν τὰ σκεύη αὐτοῦ διαρπάσαι, ἐὰν μὴ πρῶτον τὸν ἰσχυρὸν δήσῃ, καὶ τότε τὴν οἰκίαν αὐτοῦ διαρπάσει). Jesus follows his refutation with a clarification about the true

---

5. See Twelftree, *Jesus the Exorcist*, passim.
6. See *b. Sanh.* 43a; cf. Justin, *Dial.* 69; Origen, *Cels.* 1.6.
7. Wallace, *Greek Grammar*, 544 – 45.

8. The double negative in Greek (οὐ δύναται οὐδείς; lit., "no one is not able") is an emphatic negation, not a positive.

nature of his exorcisms. It is certainly true that Satan would never destroy his own kingdom by casting out his own demons. But that doesn't mean that Satan's kingdom is safe and secure. It is under siege by Jesus himself, who is storming Satan's ramparts and taking back Satan's captives through his exorcisms. The strong adversative "but," or "on the other hand" (ἀλλά), serves to clarify Jesus' previous statement. Although Satan would never fight against himself (vv. 23–26), he is indeed being destroyed (v. 27). The parable envisions a home invasion, where the stronger man (Jesus) ties up the strong man (Satan) and seizes his property (the people Jesus is freeing by his exorcisms).

Jesus' point in the context of Mark's narrative is clear. Through his healings and exorcisms, the power of the kingdom of God is invading and overwhelming the domain of Satan. This connection to Jesus' fundamental message of the kingdom of God is made explicit in the Q saying that precedes this one in Matthew and Luke: "But if I drive out demons by the finger [Matthew: 'Spirit'] of God, then the kingdom of God has come upon you" (Luke 11:20; cf. Matt 12:28).[9]

3:28–30 "Truly I say to you, the children of humanity will be forgiven all their sins and all the blasphemies they utter. But whoever blasphemes against the Holy Spirit will never be forgiven, but is guilty of an eternal sin." He said this because they were saying, "He has a defiling spirit." (Ἀμὴν λέγω ὑμῖν ὅτι πάντα ἀφεθήσεται τοῖς υἱοῖς τῶν ἀνθρώπων τὰ ἁμαρτήματα καὶ αἱ βλασφημίαι ὅσα ἐὰν βλασφημήσωσιν· ὃς δ' ἂν βλασφημήσῃ εἰς τὸ πνεῦμα τὸ ἅγιον, οὐκ ἔχει ἄφεσιν εἰς τὸν αἰῶνα, ἀλλὰ ἔνοχός ἐστιν αἰωνίου ἁμαρτήματος. ὅτι

ἔλεγον· πνεῦμα ἀκάθαρτον ἔχει). After defending himself against the accusation that he is acting with Satan's authority, Jesus goes on the offensive. He implies that his opponents have blasphemed the Holy Spirit, an unforgivable and eternal sin.

This is the first example of Jesus' solemn formula, "Truly I say to you" (ἀμὴν λέγω ὑμῖν), which occurs thirteen times in Mark (cf. 8:12; 9:1, 41; 10:15, 29; 11:23; 12:43; 13:30; 14:9, 18, 25, 30) and fifty-one times in the Synoptics. In John (25x) the term is doubled for emphasis: "Truly, truly I say to you" (ἀμὴν ἀμὴν λέγω ὑμῖν). The Greek term *amēn* (ἀμήν) is a transliteration of the Hebrew word *ʾāmēn*, from a root meaning "confirmed" or "verified." In the OT it always appears at the end of a saying to confirm its validity (Deut 27:15; Ps 41:13; etc.). Jesus' use at the *beginning* of his sayings is unprecedented, emphasizing his unique authority.[10] The Jewish teachers of Jesus' day tended to appeal to the wisdom of their predecessors ("Rabbi so-and-so said …"). Jesus speaks with his own authority, "Truly I say to you." The closest OT parallel may be the solemn declaration of the prophets, "Thus says the LORD." Jesus claims to speak for God.

Following this affirmation, Jesus begins with a statement expressing the broad scope of forgiveness. The words "all things will be forgiven" (πάντα ἀφεθήσεται) are placed first for emphasis. The traditional "sons of men" (υἱοῖς τῶν ἀνθρώπων) is a Semitic expression often found in poetry (Gen 11:5; 2 Sam 7:14; 1 Kgs 8:39; Pss 4:2; 11:4; 12:1, 8, etc.). It might better be rendered as "children of humanity," since the phrase indicates common descent from human ancestry. In English we would simply say "people."

The redundancy of the expression "whatever

---

9. Matthew and Luke (Q) also include a further refutation of the accusation. If Jesus is casting out demons by Satan's power, then by whom do the "sons" (= disciples) of the teachers of the law cast them out (Matt 12:27; Luke 11:19)? How can the Jewish leaders claim Jesus' exorcisms are the work of

Satan, but their own are the work of God?

10. See J. Jeremias, *The Prayers of Jesus* (trans. J. Bowden; Philadelphia: Fortress, 1978), 108–115; J. D. G. Dunn, *Jesus and the Spirit* (Philadelphia: Westminster, 1975), 79.

blasphemies they may blaspheme" (lit. trans. of αἱ βλασφημίαι ὅσα ἐὰν βλασφημήσωσιν) provides additional emphasis, strengthening the contrast with the one unforgivable sin. Redundancy again adds emphasis with the use of αἰών and αἰώνιος: whoever blasphemes against the Holy Spirit will "never" (εἰς τὸν αἰῶνα; "to the age") be forgiven; that person is guilty of an "eternal" (αἰώνιος) sin.

This passage is one of the more difficult ones in the NT, suggesting as it does that there is an unforgivable sin (see Theology in Application). Yet Mark clarifies Jesus' statement, adding, "He said this because they were saying, 'He has a defiling spirit.' " In short, the blasphemy of the Spirit (in the present context at least) entails attributing the work of the Holy Spirit to Satan and his demons. In the full face of the light, the religious leaders turn to darkness.

3:31 – 32 Then his mother and his brothers and sisters arrived. Standing outside, they sent word to him, summoning him. A crowd was sitting around him, and they told him, "Jesus,[11] your mother and brothers and sisters are outside asking for you." (Καὶ ἔρχεται ἡ μήτηρ αὐτοῦ καὶ οἱ ἀδελφοὶ αὐτοῦ καὶ ἔξω στήκοντες ἀπέστειλαν πρὸς αὐτὸν καλοῦντες αὐτόν. καὶ ἐκάθητο περὶ αὐτὸν ὄχλος, καὶ λέγουσιν αὐτῷ· ἰδοὺ ἡ μήτηρ σου καὶ οἱ ἀδελφοί σου καὶ αἱ ἀδελφαί σου ἔξω ζητοῦσίν σε). The scene changes again, as Jesus' family arrives from Nazareth.

The Greek term "brothers" (ἀδελφοί) often means "siblings" (= "brothers and sisters"). Although most English versions here render the term

"brothers," the more likely meaning is "brothers and sisters." We know that Jesus had sisters (6:3), and the presence of Jesus' mother suggests this is a family affair. Furthermore, when Jesus switches to singulars in v. 35 to describe spiritual kinship, he explicitly says, "this is my mother and brother and sister" (οὗτος ἀδελφός μου καὶ ἀδελφὴ καὶ μήτηρ ἐστίν), implying that the generic sense has been the point all along.[12]

By interrupting (intercalating) the two family scenes (vv. 20 – 22, 31 – 35) with the Beelzebul controversy (vv. 23 – 30), Mark links the two incidents and emphasizes the opposition that Jesus is receiving from his own people. Jesus' family arrives, but they stay outside — presumably because of the crowds — and send a message to him in the house. The contrast between Jesus' physical family who are "outside" (ἔξω, vv. 31, 32) and his spiritual family who are "sitting around him" inside is striking and will be taken up in the next chapter. Jesus will soon tell his disciples that the secrets of the kingdom of God have been given to them, but those on the "outside" get the message only in parables, "so that they may look and look but not perceive" (4:11 – 12). In the changing relationships of the kingdom of God, the insiders (the religious leaders and the physical heirs of Abraham's promise) become outsiders, and outsiders (sinners, tax collectors, Gentiles, etc.) will become insiders and the recipients of God's salvation.

3:33 – 35 He answered them, "Who are my mother and my brothers and sisters?" Looking

---

11. The report to Jesus that his family is outside is introduced with the Greek particle ἰδού. Originally the aorist imperative of εἶδον, ἰδού came to be used as a particle drawing attention to what follows (BDAG, 468). In many contexts there is no good English equivalent, since "look" or "behold" is too strong, functioning in English more as a command than a request for attention. In English, we would simply touch a person's shoulder or say "excuse me," or address the person by name — hence the translation, "Jesus, your mother and broth-

ers and sisters are outside." In some contexts the interjection "hey" may be the closest English equivalent, though that would not be deferential enough for a disciple to a master.

12. See comments on 6:3 for more on the brothers of Jesus and the debate over whether these siblings were (1) born to Mary after Jesus was born, (2) Joseph's children by a previous marriage, or (3) cousins rather than brothers (the traditional Roman Catholic view).

around at those seated around him in a circle, he said, "Here are my mother and brothers and sisters. For whoever does God's will is my brother and sister and mother." (καὶ ἀποκριθεὶς αὐτοῖς λέγει· τίς ἐστιν ἡ μήτηρ μου καὶ οἱ ἀδελφοί μου; καὶ περιβλεψάμενος τοὺς περὶ αὐτὸν κύκλῳ καθημένους λέγει· ἴδε ἡ μήτηρ μου καὶ οἱ ἀδελφοί μου. ὃς γὰρ ἂν ποιήσῃ τὸ θέλημα τοῦ θεοῦ, οὗτος ἀδελφός μου καὶ ἀδελφὴ καὶ μήτηρ ἐστίν). In response to the request from his family, Jesus asks a rhetorical question, "Who are my mother and brothers and sisters?" (for this meaning of ἀδελφοί see v. 32, above). Those seated around him would include the Twelve (3:14) and perhaps others from his larger body of followers.

As in v. 32, the Greek particle (ἴδε) does not function as a command ("look"), but as a gesture marker. Jesus waves toward those around him and says, "Here are [ἴδε][13] my mother and brothers and sisters." He then clarifies that, "Whoever does God's will is my brother and sister and mother." In the context of Mark's narrative, following God's will means responding in repentance and faith to Jesus' proclamation of the kingdom (1:15). In the kingdom age, true family relationships are based on obedience to God and faithfulness to his Word rather than on national or ethnic identity. In the context of Mark's gospel, Jesus is the model disciple who fully "does God's will." While the disciples repeatedly fail to comprehend Jesus' mission and will desert him at his moment of greatest trial, Jesus stays faithful to the plan of God. Even in his agony in the garden of Gethsemane he prays, "Not what I want, but what you want" (14:36).

Jesus' words about his family would be shocking in the group-oriented culture of the Middle East, where loyalty to one's own family, clan, and nation was among the highest of cultural values. Jesus is not rejecting his own family. He is establishing a new society in which family is defined not by ethnic or national identity but by common allegiance to the kingdom of God and his purpose in the world. Jesus' words here would have great significance for the church of Mark's day, where allegiance to Jesus Christ often resulted in rejection by one's own family. Jews who accepted Jesus as the Messiah were often disowned and treated as apostate; Gentile converts were viewed as abandoning the gods of their ancestors. Both suffered social and cultural ostracism.

This episode has a strong claim to historicity. Jesus' brothers James and Jude became prominent leaders in the early Christian movement, making it unlikely that the church would have invented a story that put Jesus' own family in such a poor light.

Theology in Application

Blaspheming the Holy Spirit

This passage and its Synoptic parallels are the only biblical references to the blasphemy of the Holy Spirit or to an "eternal sin." The closest OT parallel is the distinction between intentional and unintentional sins. Atonement was allowed only in the latter case (Lev 4–5; Num 15); willful, intentional, or defiant sins could not be atoned for and carried severe punishment, including capital punishment and being

---

13. Like ἰδού, ἴδε was originally the imperative of εἶδον, but has come to be used stereotypically as a particle. It is used when more than one person is addressed and when that which is to be observed is in the nominative (BDAG, 466).

"cut off from the people" (Num 15:30; cf. Deut 17:12; Lev 20). The closest NT parallel is what John calls a "sin that leads to death" (1 John 5:16). In contrast to other sins, John does not encourage his readers to pray for those who have committed this sin.

In its Markan context, the "blasphemy of the Holy Spirit" occurs when the religious leaders witness the work of the Holy Spirit in Jesus' exorcisms but attribute it to Satan or an evil spirit. In other words, they look directly at the light but then turn to darkness. This raises the difficult question of whether this sin can be committed today. Many professing Christians, mired down in repeated sins, have agonized over whether they have blasphemed the Holy Spirit and so lost hope of salvation. In response, some interpreters claim that the sin is unique to Jesus' ministry and involves the rejection of the gospel by Israel's leaders. Yet Jesus' words seem more encompassing than this, since in the same context he refers to "all sins" of the "children of humanity." Although the immediate referents are the religious leaders, the statement likely relates to the broader work of the Holy Spirit.

So what does it mean? Since the Holy Spirit is the one who draws people to God and reveals the truth to them, those who reject this testimony have no other opportunity for salvation. We could therefore define the blasphemy of the Holy Spirit as defiant, willful, and final rejection of the Spirit's work in a person's life. If that person intentionally turns to darkness at the moment of greatest light, by definition no greater opportunity for salvation will ever take place. There is no greater source of revelation than the Holy Spirit and no other means through which people respond to God. It would also be true, then, that those who anguish over whether they have blasphemed the Spirit certainly have not, since such fears reveal a conscience still wrestling with God. Furthermore, since only God knows the entire course of a person's life, the only sure proof that someone has blasphemed the Holy Spirit will come on judgment day, when the hearts of all people will be revealed.

Jesus' True Family

Another aspect in the present episode that is disturbing for some readers is Jesus' apparent disrespect for his own family. In light of the fourth commandment (to honor one's parents, Exod 20:12), should Jesus have acted differently toward his mother and siblings? Related to this, how could Jesus' mother have doubted Jesus' sanity (v. 21), since she was aware of his messianic identity (cf. Luke 1:31 – 35)? Concerning the second question, it is necessary to point out that Mark does not include a birth narrative and so has not told us anything about Mary to this point. Yet he is also careful not to directly connect Mary or Jesus' brothers to the charge of insanity, referring opaquely to the family as those "associated with" Jesus (οἱ παρ᾽ αὐτοῦ; see comments on v. 21). Mark's readers would almost certainly be aware that Mary and Jesus' brothers became active members of the early church. At the present point in the story, however, they are experiencing confusion and concern over Jesus' actions.

Nor should we read Jesus' words as communicating disrespect for his family. Rather, he is using forceful rhetoric to drive his point home: the radical values of the kingdom of God demand new allegiances and a new orientation in human relationships. Mark's narrative and theological purpose is twofold: (1) to show that even Jesus' own people do not understand him or his mission (a prelude to his rejection by Israel), and (2) to reveal the ultimate priority of spiritual relationships over physical ones (a prelude to the Gentile mission that will follow his resurrection).

Jesus' teaching about the priority of spiritual relationships has profound significance for all forms of tribalism and nationalism in the world today. Paul points out that in Christ "there is neither Jew nor Gentile, neither slave nor free, nor is there male and female, for [we] are all one in Christ Jesus" (Gal 3:28). Yet tragically, those claiming to be Christians have sometimes promoted ethnic or tribal superiority and prejudice. The most notorious examples — the enslavement of Africans in North America, apartheid in South Africa, the Holocaust by Nazi Germany, tribal genocide in Rwanda — reveal the horrific consequences when professing Christians place ethnic identity above their loyalty to Christ and his teaching of love and servanthood. Even today American patriotism and nationalism are sometimes treated as benchmarks of Christian commitment. Yet loyalty to one's identity as an American should take a distant second to loyalty to Christian brothers and sisters around the world, whether in Sudan, China, Pakistan, or Palestine. Jesus came to create a new people, whose allegiance is first and foremost to Jesus Christ and the kingdom of God.

Jesus' teaching should also have profound practical implications for the way the church functions as a family. Jesus acknowledged that his gospel would divide families, pitting brother against brother and children against their parents (Mark 13:12 – 13; Luke 12:51 – 53). The church of Jesus Christ is full of refugees, those separated from or rejected by their own families, friends, or people group. Whether it is widows or widowers, single parents, children or spouses of unbelievers, those who've never married, ostracized converts from other religions, recovering addicts, or those with special needs — the church is the family of God. As adopted children of God, we are "brothers and sisters" (ἀδελφοί) in Christ who share a bond far stronger than any genetic or ethnic ties. The church needs to cultivate actively a family environment for meeting emotional, physical, and spiritual needs, such as through soup kitchens, pregnancy crisis centers, visitation programs for shut-ins, nursing home worship services, addiction recovery groups, men's and women's accountability groups, one-on-one discipleship, youth mentoring programs, young mothers' support groups, and so on. This is what it means to be a family.

Mark 4:1 – 20

Literary Context

The opposition building against Jesus from the religious leaders in 2:1 – 3:6 came to a head in the Beelzebul controversy, where they accused him of casting out demons by Satan's power. Jesus responded by accusing them of blaspheming the Holy Spirit, an eternal sin. The battle lines have been drawn. Mark now presents Jesus' teaching in parables, which illustrates the various responses of rejection and reception to the gospel proclamation. This is the second longest-teaching section by Jesus in Mark's gospel; only the Olivet Discourse (ch. 13) is longer. While Mark frequently refers to Jesus as a "teacher"[1] or as teaching,[2] he gives far less of the content of Jesus' teaching than the other three gospels.

II. The Authority of the Messiah (1:14 – 8:21)

    B. The Disciple-Family of the Messiah and Those "Outside" (3:7 – 6:6a)

        1. Summary of Jesus' Ministry (3:7 – 12)

        2. Choosing the Twelve (3:13 – 19)

        3. Jesus' True Family and the Beelzebul Controversy (3:20 – 35)

→   **4. Parables about the Kingdom of God (4:1 – 34)**

          a. Parable of the Sower and Its Intepretation (4:1 – 20)

          b. More Parables (4:21 – 34)

Main Idea

The central theme of the parable of the sower is the need to "hear" and respond to the good news of the kingdom of God (vv. 3, 9, 15, 16, 18, 20, 23, 24). The purpose of the parables is *both to reveal and to conceal*: to those open to the kingdom proclamation, the parables reveal the truth; but for the hard-hearted, the parables blind

---

1. Mark 4:38; 5:35; 9:17, 38; 10:17, 20, 35; 11:17 – 18; 12:14, 19, 32; 13:1; 14:14.   2. Mark 1:21 – 22, 27; 2:13; 4:1 – 2; 6:2, 6, 34; 8:31; 10:1; 12:35, 38; 14:49.

them further. In this way God accomplishes his sovereign purposes even through the opposition and hard-heartedness of sinful people.

Translation

Mark 4:1 – 20

1a	Setting	**Again he began to teach by the sea.**
b	Character entrance/Action	**A great crowd gathered around him,**
c	response	so he got into a boat on the sea and sat down,
d	character description	while the whole crowd remained on the shore by the sea.
2a	Action	**He was teaching them many things with parables.**
b	Parable	**This is what he taught them:**
3		*"Listen! A sower went out to sow seed.*
4a		*And it so happened*
		while he was sowing,
b	location of seed (1)	*(1) some of the seed fell along the path,*
c	fate of seed (1)	*and the birds came and gobbled it up.*
5a	location of seed (2)	*(2) Other seed fell upon the rocky ground,*
		where it did not have much soil.
b	fate of seed (2)	*It sprouted quickly because of the shallow soil;*
6a		*but when the sun rose it was scorched,*
b	reason (for 6c)	*and because it did not have deep roots,*
c	fate of the seed (2)	*it withered.*
7a	location of seed (3)	*(3) Other seed fell among the thorns,*
b	fate of seed (3)	*and the thorns grew up and choked it,*
c		*and it produced no grain.*
8a	location of seed (4)	*(4) Still other seed fell onto good soil,*
b	fate of seed (4)	*and it produced grain,*
c		*sprouting,*
		growing up, and
d		*some yielding thirtyfold,*
		some sixtyfold, and
		some a hundredfold."
9a	Action	And **he was saying,**
b	command/exhortation	*"Whoever has ears to hear, let them hear."*
10a	setting (social)	When he was alone,
b	Question	**the Twelve and others around him were asking him about the parables.**
11a	Action	**He was saying to them,**
b	assertion	*"The secret of the kingdom of God has been given*
		to you.
c	contrast	*But to those on the outside,*
		everything comes in parables,

12a	OT citation/purpose	so that *"they may look and look but not perceive,*
b		*and hear and hear but not understand;*
c		*otherwise, they might return and be forgiven."* [Isaiah 6:9 – 10]
13a	Action	Then **he said to them,**
b	question	*"Don't you understand this parable?*
c	rhetorical question	*How then will you understand any of the parables?*
14	Interpretation of parable	*The sower sows the message.*
15a	interpretation of seed (1)	*(1) These are the ones*
		who *are along the path where the message was sown.*
b		*When they hear the message,*
c		*Satan quickly comes and snatches away the message* ☙
		that was sown in them.
16a	interpretation of seed (2)	*(2) These are the ones sown on rocky ground,*
b		*who,* *when they hear the message,*
c		*immediately*
d		*receive it joyfully, but*
17a		*they do not have strong roots and so are short-lived.*
b		*When trouble or persecution comes along*
c		*because of the message,*
d		*they quickly fall away.*
18a	interpretation of seed (3)	*(3) Still others are those sown among the thorns;*
b		*these are the ones who hear the message,*
19a		*but the cares of this age and*
		the deceitfulness of wealth and
		the desires for other things come in
		and *choke out the message,*
b		*and it produces no crop.*
20a	interpretation of seed (4)	*(4) Then there are those that are sown in good ground,*
b		*who hear the message and accept it, and*
c		*produce a crop,*
		some thirtyfold,
		some sixtyfold, and
		some a hundredfold."

Structure

The parable of the sower and its interpretation (4:1 – 9, 13 – 20) take up the bulk of the material and are followed by three shorter parables (or analogies): the parable of the lamp with additional teaching (4:21 – 25), the parable of the secretly growing seed (4:26 – 29), and the parable of the mustard seed (4:30 – 32). Mark frequently uses groups of three in his narrative (see Introduction: Literary Features), and the parable of the sower is structured around two sets of three. Three groups of seed fail to produce a crop because they fall (1) along the path, (2) on rocky ground, or (3) among thorns. Other seed falls on good ground and produces a crop multiplying (1) thirty,

(2) sixty, and (3) one hundred times. This pattern of two threes is clearer in Greek than English since the words translated "some … some … other …" (ὃ μὲν … ἄλλο … ἄλλο; vv. 4, 5, 7) are singular, while the word translated "other" (ἄλλα) in v. 8 is plural. (The parable's interpretation in vv. 13 – 20 uses plurals throughout.) Between the parable and its interpretation, Jesus explains to his disciples why he teaches in parables (vv. 11 – 13).

Exegetical Outline

→ **1. Introduction and Setting (4:1 – 2)**

2. The Parable of the Sower 4:3 – 9)

    a. Three examples of failed seed on poor soil (4:3 – 7)

        i. Seed along the path (4:3 – 4)

        ii. Seed on rocky ground (4:5 – 6)

        iii. Seed among the thorns (4:7)

    b. Three examples of seed on good soil: thirty, sixty, and a hundredfold (4:8)

    c. Those who have hears to hear (4:9)

3. The Secret of the Kingdom of God (4:10 – 12)

    a. The question from the Twelve (4:10)

    b. Jesus' response (4:11 – 12)

4. Interpretation of the Parable of the Sower (4:13 – 20)

    a. Opening rebuke (4:13)

    b. The seed is the message of the kingdom (4:14)

    c. The interpretation of the failed seeds (4:15 – 19)

        i. Along the path: Satan snatches away (4:15)

        ii. On rocky ground: trouble and persecution (4:16 – 17)

        iii. Among the thorns: cares of the world (4:18 – 19)

    d. The interpretation of the receptive soil (4:20)

Explanation of the Text

4:1 Again he began to teach by the sea. A great crowd gathered around him, so he got into a boat on the sea and sat down, while the whole crowd remained on the shore by the sea (Καὶ πάλιν ἤρξατο διδάσκειν παρὰ τὴν θάλασσαν· καὶ συνάγεται πρὸς αὐτὸν ὄχλος πλεῖστος, ὥστε αὐτὸν εἰς πλοῖον ἐμβάντα καθῆσθαι ἐν τῇ θαλάσσῃ, καὶ πᾶς ὁ ὄχλος πρὸς τὴν θάλασσαν ἐπὶ τῆς γῆς ἦσαν). The episode begins with two themes pervasive throughout Jesus' Galilean ministry: (1) the priority of teaching and (2) his growing popularity with the crowds. Jesus has made his teaching ministry — the proclamation of the kingdom of God — his highest priority, because, as he affirms, "this is why I came" (1:38; cf. 1:22, 27; 2:2, 13). The healings and exorcisms confirm the message by revealing the presence and the power of the kingdom.

From a narrative perspective, Jesus' popularity

with the crowds and the awe that he inspires result from the authority of his words and actions. The Greek superlative πλεῖστος (trans. here "very large") could mean the largest yet in Jesus' ministry, but a Greek superlative is also an idiomatic way of saying "great" or "very large." The boat from which Jesus teaches provides crowd control (cf. 3:9: "to keep the crowd from pressing him"), serving as a natural podium and allowing him to teach without being jostled. Sitting was a common position for teaching (9:35; 13:3; cf. Matt 5:1; 15:29; Luke 4:20).

4:2 He was teaching them many things with parables. This is what he taught them (καὶ ἐδίδασκεν αὐτοὺς ἐν παραβολαῖς πολλὰ καὶ ἔλεγεν αὐτοῖς ἐν τῇ διδαχῇ αὐτοῦ). This is the second time Mark has referred to Jesus' teaching "in parables" (ἐν παραβολαῖς; see comments on 3:23 – 26). The Greek term can refer to various kinds of figurative and analogical language. In 3:23 – 28 it is used for a series of sayings and analogies. Here it refers to a true parable (4:3 – 8), followed by other sayings, proverbs, parables, and analogies (4:21 – 32).

IN DEPTH: Parables about the Kingdom of God

Parables are the most distinctive feature of Jesus' teaching and the method he utilized most to explain the kingdom of God, to illustrate the character of God, and to demonstrate God's expectations for his people.[3] Although he was not the first to use parables (they are found in the OT, the rabbinic writings, and Greek literature), Jesus utilized them more often and more effectively than anyone in history. He raised parable telling to an art form. Both the Hebrew and Greek for parables (*māšāl*; παραβολή) have a wider semantic range than the English "parable" and can refer to a variety of literary forms, including proverbs, riddles, analogies, metaphors, and the like (see comments on 3:23 – 26). By contrast, the English term normally refers to stories from everyday life that illustrate spiritual truths. We will utilize this simple definition here, while acknowledging that Jesus' parables are themselves varied, ranging from short similitudes to longer and more complex allegories.

Since the time of Adolf Jülicher, there has been considerable debate about the nature and function of Jesus' parables. In a two-volume work published in 1888 – 1889, Jülicher challenged the common notion that parables were allegories, with each element carrying spiritual meaning.[4] Allegorization had certainly been abused by interpreters of the past. The most often cited example of this is Augustine's interpretation of the parable of the good Samaritan, which allegorized nearly every element of the story, including the wounded

3. Klyne Snodgrass, "Parable," in *DJG*, 591. Good surveys of the nature and purpose of parables can be found in Craig L. Blomberg, *Interpreting the Parables* (Downers Grove, IL: InterVarsity Press, 2012); Klyne Snodgrass, *Stories with Intent: A Comprehensive Guide to the Parables of Jesus* (Grand Rapids:

Eerdmans, 2008); J. D. Crossan, *In Parables* (New York: Harper and Row, 1973); and Robert H. Stein, *An Introduction to the Parables of Jesus* (Philadelphia: Westminster, 1981).

4. A. Jülicher, *Die Gleichnisreden Jesu* (2 vols.; Tübingen: J. C. B. Mohr [Paul Siebeck], 1888 – 89).

man (Adam), the robbers (the devil and his angels), the binding of the man's wounds (restraint of sin), the oil and wine (comfort of hope and encouragement to work), the Samaritan's animal (the incarnation of Christ), the inn (the church), the innkeeper (the apostle Paul), and the two denarii (the twin commandments of love).[5] This is truly allegorization gone off-kilter. Jülicher went to the opposite extreme, however, arguing that Jesus' parables were not allegories but similitudes, simple analogies carrying only one point of comparison and so only one message. He went so far as to claim that any allegorical elements in the parables were not part of Jesus' original story, but were later additions by the evangelists or the early church.

Jülicher's approach has been criticized as going too far, and today most interpreters take a more balanced view, recognizing that Jesus' parables often had allegorical elements and could make more than one point. For example, while the central message of the parable of the great banquet in Luke (Luke 14:15 – 24) is God's free offer of salvation to all people regardless of their social status, allegorical elements related to Jesus' own ministry are also present. The invited guests who make excuses no doubt represent the religious leaders rejecting Jesus' invitation to the kingdom. Similarly, the outsiders who are subsequently invited to the banquet represent the poor, the sinners, and the tax collectors, who are responding favorably to Jesus' preaching. Yet it is going too far to identify the servant who takes the invitation with a specific historical person (such as the apostle Paul), since this would take the meaning outside the context of Jesus' ministry.

Two key principles should be kept in mind when interpreting the parables: (1) Jesus' parables must be understood first and foremost in the context of his own ministry and, in particular, his proclamation of the kingdom of God. Most parables illuminate the nature of the kingdom and the appropriate response to Jesus' announcement of it. (2) Allegorical elements should relate directly to this context, rather than to a later church context or to the church of today. Accurate exegesis of the parables must come first and serve as the foundation for appropriate application. While the parable of the sower may eventually be *applied* to the contemporary preaching of the Word of God, it must first be understood within the context of Jesus' proclamation of the kingdom of God to the people of Israel in the first century.

---

5. Augustine, *Quaest ev.* 2:19; Dodd, *Parables of the Kingdom*, 1 – 2.

4:3 "Listen! A sower went out to sow seed." (Ἀκούετε. ἰδοὺ ἐξῆλθεν ὁ σπείρων σπεῖραι). The parable of the sower begins with a call to attention, "Listen!" (ἀκούετε), a theme that permeates this teaching section (vv. 9, 15, 16, 18, 20, 23, 24). The present imperative indicates the need for continual spiritual attentiveness. Marcus makes much of the doubling of the verbs of perception (ἀκούετε and ἰδού), translating them "Listen! Look!" and claiming they call readers to bring all their senses to bear because of the supreme importance of the parable.[6] This seems to be overtranslating. More likely, the repetition confirms just how weak the force of "behold" (ἰδού) had become in Hellenistic Greek. It functions more as a literary marker and a mild call for attention than as an imperative. Most versions — even the more literal ones — leave it untranslated (NIV, RSV, ESV, NRSV; but see NKJV: "Listen! Behold …"). HCSB offers a mediating solution: "Listen! Consider the sower who went out to sow."

4:4 And it so happened while he was sowing,[7] some of the seed fell along the path, and the birds came and gobbled it up (καὶ ἐγένετο ἐν τῷ σπείρειν ὃ μὲν ἔπεσεν παρὰ τὴν ὁδόν, καὶ ἦλθεν τὰ πετεινὰ καὶ κατέφαγεν αὐτό). The first seed is sown παρὰ τὴν ὁδόν, which could mean either "along [= on] the path" or "beside the path."[8] In either case, the point seems to be that the ground is hard-packed and so the seed is left exposed to hungry birds.

Commentators have debated the nature of plowing and sowing in first-century Palestine. In his classic study of the parables, J. Jeremias cited rabbinic evidence to argue that plowing followed sowing, so that a farmer would scatter seed across his field and then go back to plow it into the soil.[9] This would explain the seemingly careless way the farmer scatters seed: on the path, on rocky ground, and among the thorns. He expects to return to plow all of it into the soil. Others have challenged Jeremias, arguing that plowing normally preceded sowing, or that there were multiple plowings before and after sowing.[10] In this case, the parable describes seed that has accidentally fallen outside the prepared soil. In either case, the essential message of the parable remains the same. External conditions render the seed either productive or not.

4:5 – 6 Other seed fell upon the rocky ground, where it did not have much soil. It sprouted quickly because of the shallow soil; but when the sun rose it was scorched, and because it did not have deep roots, it withered (καὶ ἄλλο ἔπεσεν ἐπὶ τὸ πετρῶδες ὅπου οὐκ εἶχεν γῆν πολλήν, καὶ εὐθὺς ἐξανέτειλεν διὰ τὸ μὴ ἔχειν βάθος γῆς· καὶ ὅτε ἀνέτειλεν ὁ ἥλιος ἐκαυματίσθη καὶ διὰ τὸ μὴ ἔχειν ῥίζαν ἐξηράνθη). The "rocky ground" (τὸ πετρῶδες) is probably a thin layer of topsoil on bedrock. This soil allows the seed to germinate quickly, but the rock prevents it from establishing deep roots. Without such roots it cannot draw sufficient moisture from the ground, and the sun scorches it so that it withers (cf. Luke 8:6: "the plants withered because they had no moisture").

4:7 Other seed fell among the thorns, and the thorns grew up and choked it, and it produced

---

6. Marcus, *Mark 1 – 8*, 292; cf. Stein, *Mark*, 196 – 97.

7. ἐν τῷ plus the infinitive (σπείρειν) is a common way to express a temporal relationship in Greek: "while he was…."

8. Luke appears to take the former view, since he adds that it was "trampled on" (Luke 8:5).

9. *Jubilees* speaks of crows stealing the grain "before they plowed in the seed" (*Jub.* 11:11; cf. *m. Šabb.* 7:2; *b. Šabb.* 73b; *y. Šabb.* 7.2).

10. K. D. White, "The Parable of the Sower," *JTS* 15 (1964): 300 – 307; P. B. Payne, "The Order of Sowing and Ploughing in the Parable of the Sower," *NTS* 25 (1978 – 1979): 123 – 29. Cf. Isa 28:24 and Jer 4:3, where plowing appears to precede sowing (Stein, *Mark*, 198).

no grain (καὶ ἄλλο ἔπεσεν εἰς τὰς ἀκάνθας, καὶ ἀνέβησαν αἱ ἄκανθαι καὶ συνέπνιξαν αὐτό, καὶ καρπὸν οὐκ ἔδωκεν). Thorns appear commonly in Scripture as impediments to good crops (Gen 3:18; Jer 12:13) or evidence of agricultural neglect (Isa 5:6; 7:24; 32:13; 34:13). Jeremiah 4:3 speaks metaphorically of the danger of sowing among thorns. There appears to be a natural progression in terms of the point of failure. The first seed is eaten by birds before it can germinate; the second germinates, but withers shortly after it sprouts; the third sprouts and grows but is eventually choked out. The good seed similarly represents a progression in terms of yield: from thirty, to sixty, to a hundredfold (4:8).

4:8 "Still other seed fell onto good soil, and it produced grain, sprouting, growing up, and some yielding thirtyfold, some sixtyfold, and some a hundredfold." (καὶ ἄλλα ἔπεσεν εἰς τὴν γῆν τὴν καλὴν καὶ ἐδίδου καρπὸν ἀναβαίνοντα καὶ αὐξανόμενα καὶ ἔφερεν ἐν τριάκοντα καὶ ἐν ἑξήκοντα καὶ ἐν ἑκατόν). The three verbs used to describe the successful growth of the good seed may be intended to contrast with the failed seed: it "sprouts" (ἀναβαίνοντα — in contrast to that which the birds eat), "grows up" (αὐξανόμενα — in contrast to that which sprouts but then withers), and "yields" (ἔφερεν — in contrast to that which grows up, but is choked out by thorns).

Scholars debate the significance of the yield. Some argue that a typical Palestinian yield would be on the order of five or tenfold at most, so that the references to thirty, sixty, and one hundred are

remarkable and even miraculous, symbolizing the eschatological harvest at the end of time.[11] Others argue that these yields indicate an abundant, but not unrealistic, harvest. A conclusion here depends, in part, on how the grain is counted. If the harvest represents the number of stalks produced per seed, then these numbers would be truly over the top. More likely, however, the reference is to the number of kernels per stalk, in which case a yield of 30 to 100 is excellent, but not miraculous.[12]

This is more in line with ancient computations. In Gen 26:12, Isaac is blessed by the Lord with a bountiful harvest of a hundredfold (cf. *Sib. Or.* 3:261–64), and yields of a fifty or hundredfold are reported by other ancient writers.[13] Contrast these with the staggering numbers cited in eschatological contexts that describe miraculous harvests in the messianic age. Papias, for example, claimed that in the eschaton, "a grain of wheat shall bring forth ten thousand ears, and every ear shall have ten thousand grains."[14] If Jesus were using extreme hyperbole, we might expect numbers closer to these.

4:9 And he was saying, "Whoever has ears to hear, let them hear." (καὶ ἔλεγεν· ὃς ἔχει ὦτα ἀκούειν ἀκουέτω). Jesus concludes the parable with an exhortation to spiritual discernment, thus "framing" (inclusio) the parable in calls to hear and respond (vv. 3, 9). The statement recalls Jer 5:21 and Ezek 12:2, where the people of Israel have eyes, but cannot see, and ears, but cannot hear. Similar refrains are common elsewhere with reference to parabolic teaching (4:23; Matt 11:15; 13:43; Luke 14:35; Rev 2:7, 11, 17, 29; cf. *Gos. Thom.* 8, 21,

---

11. Jeremias, *Parables*, 150; Witherington, *Mark*, 165–66; Marcus, *Mark 1–8*, 293.

12. So Guelich, *Mark 1:1–8:26*, 195; France, *Mark*, 192–93; Davies and Allison, *Matthew*, 1:385; White, "The Parable of the Sower," 301–2.

13. Varro, *On Agriculture* 2.44.2; Strabo, *Geogr.* 15.3.11; Pliny the Elder, *Nat.* 18.21.95. Contra Marcus, *Mark 1–8*, 293, who calls these "tall tales told by foreigners returning from ex-

otic locations (citing R. McIver, "One Hundred-fold Yield— Miraculous or Mundane? Matthew 13.8, 23; Mark 4.8, 20; Luke 8.8," *NTS* 40 [1993]: 606–8).

14. Papias, cited by Irenaeus, *Haer.* 5.33.3–4; cf. *1 En.* 10:19 (a thousandfold); *2 Bar.* 29:5 (ten thousandfold); *b. Ketub.* 111b–112a (it will take an entire ship to carry one grape); Davies and Allison, *Matthew*, 1:385.

24, 63, 65, 96). The meaning could be either (1) anyone who has ears (i.e., everyone) should hear and respond to Jesus' message; or (2) those given "ears" (i.e., special spiritual insight) by God ought to listen.[15] The latter fits the following context well, where Jesus says the disciples have been given the secrets of the kingdom of God, but that others are blind and deaf to the message (Mark 4:11 – 12). Furthermore, in Matt 13:43 the saying appears in a context of private instruction to the disciples (cf. 13:36).

However, the saying more often occurs in contexts addressed to the crowds (Matt 11:7, 15; Luke 14:25, 35), where the "them" (i.e., the crowds) is contrasted with the disciples, who receive the parable's explanation.[16] Furthermore, the saying generally *follows* rather than precedes parabolic teaching, which in this case is directed to the people in general (4:1). The best solution is probably the first, that the saying is a general proverb directed to everyone — all who have ears to hear — with the implication that some will not heed the call for spiritual discernment. This also fits the background texts of Jer 5:21 and Ezek 12:2, where the people *have* eyes and ears but still fail to respond to the message.

4:10 When he was alone, the Twelve and others around him were asking him about the parables (Καὶ ὅτε ἐγένετο κατὰ μόνας, ἠρώτων αὐτὸν οἱ περὶ αὐτὸν σὺν τοῖς δώδεκα τὰς παραβολάς). Private instruction for the disciples is a common theme in Mark (4:34; 7:17 – 23; 9:28 – 29, 35; 10:10 – 12, 32 – 34; 12:43 – 44; 13:3 – 37). The phrase "others around him" (οἱ περὶ αὐτόν) shows that Mark envisions a larger group of disciples than the Twelve. This was implied already when Jesus chose the

Twelve from among a larger band of followers (3:13). John's gospel similarly speaks of followers in addition to the Twelve, some of whom desert Jesus when his teaching becomes too difficult (John 6:60 – 71). At the beginning of Acts, Luke refers to a core group of about 120 disciples present after the resurrection (Acts 1:15).

How many were present here Mark does not say, but it is clearly a much smaller group than the masses flocking to see Jesus (Jesus is now "alone" [κατὰ μόνας] = away from the crowds). The plural "parables" (παραβολάς) shows that the disciples have more than the parable of the sower in mind. This may be Mark's way of saying that Jesus taught much more than he is reporting (cf. the plural "parables" in v. 2). Or, it may indicate that Mark has moved this scene forward, and that it originally followed the parables given in v. 21 – 32. Mark's purpose in this case would be to bring the interpretation of the parable of the sower closer to the parable itself (vv. 3 – 8, 13 – 20) and also to highlight the purpose of parables (vv. 10 – 12) with reference to the parable of the sower, which itself concerns the various responses to the message.

4:11 – 12 He was saying to them, "The secret of the kingdom of God has been given to you. But to those on the outside, everything comes in parables, 'so that they may look and look but not perceive, and hear and hear but not understand; otherwise, they might return and be forgiven." (καὶ ἔλεγεν αὐτοῖς· ὑμῖν τὸ μυστήριον δέδοται τῆς βασιλείας τοῦ θεοῦ· ἐκείνοις δὲ τοῖς ἔξω ἐν παραβολαῖς τὰ πάντα γίνεται, ἵνα βλέποντες βλέπωσιν καὶ μὴ ἴδωσιν, καὶ ἀκούοντες ἀκούωσιν καὶ μὴ συνιῶσιν, μήποτε ἐπιστρέψωσιν καὶ ἀφεθῇ αὐτοῖς). Jesus responds to the disciples

15. Guelich, *Mark 1:1 – 8:26*, 201. Marcus, *Mark 1 – 8*, 297, points to a similar idea from the Qumran Hymns scroll, where the author praises God for having "uncovered my ears to marvelous mysteries" (1QH 1:21; cf. 1QM 10:11).

16. Stein, *Mark*, 201. It is debated whether Mark 4:23 is directed to the crowds or the disciples. See comments on 4:21.

by first discussing the reason he teaches in parables (vv. 11 – 12) and then by interpreting the parable of the sower (vv. 14 – 20).

The word "secret" or "mystery" (μυστήριον) appears in the Gospels only here and in the Synoptic parallels (Matt 13:11; Luke 8:10), but it is common throughout Paul (21x). Its primary sense in the NT is not something strange or mysterious, but rather something formerly secret that God has now revealed to his people. In the context of Jesus' ministry in Mark, the secret to which the disciples are privy is that the power and presence of the kingdom of God are breaking into human history through the words and deeds of Jesus the Messiah. Jesus' healings, exorcisms, and offer of forgiveness to sinners are all sure signs of the kingdom of God.

Here, however, Jesus' point is not about the nature of the secret but its recipients. While the secret of the kingdom "has been given" (δέδοται, a divine passive, meaning "God has given") to the disciples, "those on the outside" receive everything in parables. The reference to outsiders alludes back to the Beelzebul controversy and the episode related to Jesus' family (3:20 – 35), where Jesus contrasts the religious leaders and his physical relatives — who are standing "outside" (3:31 – 32) — with those who do the will of his Father, his true spiritual family (3:34 – 35).

To support his statement Jesus quotes from Isa 6:9 – 10. The text in Mark differs from both the MT and the LXX and is closest to the Aramaic Targum.[17] Like Mark, the Targum uses third person constructions ("they will look …") instead of the second person ("you will look …," MT, LXX) and ends with a reference to forgiveness instead of healing (MT, LXX). This may indicate an Aramaic

source behind Mark's account, or perhaps Jesus himself quoted from the Targum. Mark also differs from both the LXX and MT by omitting the first three lines of Isa 6:10 ("Make the heart of this people calloused; make their ears dull and close their eyes") and by introducing the quote with "so that" (ἵνα).

This ἵνα clause makes this passage one of the most difficult in the NT, since Jesus appears to be saying that he teaches in parables in order to blind the eyes of his listeners (taking the ἵνα clause in its most common sense of purpose). Both Matthew and Luke soften Mark's language. Matthew changes the ἵνα clause ("so that") to a ὅτι clause ("because" or "so that"), suggesting that Jesus speaks in parables either *because* of their refusal to believe (causal clause) or *resulting* in their unbelief (result clause). Luke retains Mark's ἵνα but omits the clause "otherwise [μήποτε], they might return and be forgiven."

Interpreters have offered a variety of creative alternatives to explain Jesus' words in Mark, some appealing to the meaning of an underlying Aramaic term.[18] (1) Some have argued that an original Aramaic *de* ("who") in the Targum has been mistranslated as "in order that" (ἵνα). The text should have read, "But to those on the outside … who look and look but do not perceive."[19]

(2) Another Aramaic explanation claims that the Greek term usually translated "lest" or "otherwise" (μήποτε) has behind it the Aramaic *dilēmâ*, meaning "unless." In this case the text would be saying that they will remain blind and deaf "unless" they turn and repent.[20] The problem with both these suggestions is that, while offering intriguing possibilities for Jesus' original meaning, they

17. Guelich, *Mark 1:1 – 8:26*, 210; T. W. Manson, *The Teaching of Jesus: Studies in Its Form and Content* (Cambridge: Cambridge University Press, 1979), 77 – 78; Jeremias, *Parables of Jesus*, 15.

18. See C. A. Evans, *To See and Not Perceive: Isaiah 6:9 – 10*

in *Early Jewish and Christian Interpretation* (JSOTSup 64; Sheffield: JSOT Press, 1989), 91 – 99. See Wallace, *Greek Grammar*, 471 – 76; BDAG, 475 – 77, for the various functions of ἵνα.

19. Manson, *Teaching of Jesus*, 76 – 80.

20. Jeremias, *Parables of Jesus*, 17.

do not explain Mark's Greek words, which strongly suggest purpose.

Other explanations appeal to less common meanings of ἵνα. (3) Some claim ἵνα here has a causal sense (similar to ὅτι): "I speak in parables *because* they look and look and do not perceive";[21] or as result clause (similar to ὥστε): "I speak in parables *with the result that* they look and look. . . ."[22] But there are no clear examples of either of these senses elsewhere in Mark.

(4) Jeremias, followed by Lane, argues that ἵνα represents a citation formula, which is an abbreviated version of "in order that it might be fulfilled" (ἵνα πληρωθῇ).[23] The problem, again, is that ἵνα never functions this way elsewhere in Mark.

(5) Another possibility is that ἵνα is being used epexegetically, qualifying or interpreting Jesus' teaching in parables: "I speak in parables, *which means* they look and look. . . ."[24] Guelich goes on to interpret μήποτε as an indirect question meaning not "lest," but "if they had," leaving open the possibility of forgiveness.[25]

(6) B. Hollenbach offers a different explanation from the perspective of a Bible translator. He proposes that the quotation is meant to be ironic (both in Isaiah and Mark), and that Jesus means the opposite of what he says. The text could be translated, "so that they may indeed see but not perceive ... because the last thing they want is to turn and have their sins forgiven!"[26] While this interpretation is possible, irony is notoriously difficult to identify on the printed page, and as France points out, "irony must therefore always be a slippery tool

for the exegete, and can too easily be invoked as a counsel of despair."[27]

(7) The most natural sense is to take ἵνα as a purpose clause, in which case Jesus would be saying that his purpose for teaching in parables is to blind the eyes and make deaf the ears of those who are "outside." Yet this negative function of the parable must be understood within the narrative contexts of both Isaiah and Mark. In Isa 5 – 6, the context is a judicial and final pronouncement of coming judgment. In the allegory of the vineyard (5:1 – 7), God is portrayed as the owner who cared for and loved his vineyard (Israel). Because Israel failed to produce fruit (covenant faithfulness), God says he will remove her wall of protection and allow the Assyrians to act as his agents of judgment. Isaiah's words of warning will now fall on deaf ears, first because of Israel's unfaithfulness, and now because God has pronounced judgment and has determined what he will do. He will *use their rejection* to accomplish his sovereign purpose.

This pattern occurs repeatedly in Scripture. When God sent Moses to Pharaoh, Pharaoh first hardened his own heart by rejecting God's command. God then hardened Pharaoh's heart to accomplish his purpose in the glorious exodus from Egypt (Exod 8:15, 32; 9:12; 10:1; cf. Rom 11:25 – 32). It is the same pattern in Mark's gospel. As discussed in 3:22 – 30, the "scribes," or experts in the law, have committed the blasphemy against the Spirit by attributing the work of the Spirit in Jesus' exorcisms to the power of Satan. This "eternal sin" (3:29) means their fate is sealed. God will

21. E. Lohmeyer, *Das Evangelium des Markus* (KEK 2; Göttingen: Vandenhoeck & Ruprecht, 1963), 84. This causal sense is rare if present at all, occurring only in idiomatic expressions with certain verbs (e.g., ποιέω ... ἵνα = "make/cause to ..."; John 11:37; Col 4:16; Rev 3:9; 13:16). These could all be treated as epexegetical.

22. C. F. D. Moule, *An Idiom-Book of New Testament Greek* (Cambridge: Cambridge University Press, 1953), 142 – 46.

23. Jeremias, *Parables of Jesus*, 17; Lane, *Mark*, 159.

24. Guelich, *Mark 1:1 – 8:26*, 211 – 12, citing P. Lampe.

25. Guelich, *Mark 1:1 – 8:26*, 212; Manson, *Teaching of Jesus*, 78.

26. B. Hollenbach, "Lest They Should Turn and Be Forgiven: Irony," *BT* 34 (1983): 312 – 21.

27. France, *Mark*, 201.

now accomplish his sovereign purpose of salvation not just *despite* their rejection, but *by means of* it. To do this, he will blind their eyes and shut their ears. Jesus' words, like Isaiah's, are a judicial pronouncement of coming judgment that will accomplish God's sovereign purpose.

Understood in this manner, Jesus' words may be seen as indicating both purpose and result. The judicial pronouncement (teaching in parables to hide the truth) *results* from the rejection by Israel's leaders in Mark 3. Its *purpose* now will be to blind them to the truth so they will inadvertently fulfill God's plan of redemption in the death of Jesus. (See more on this in Theology in Application, below.)

The parable should not be assumed to teach a permanent hardening of Israel. It concerns these leaders and this generation who are rejecting Jesus and will suffer the consequences. The last part of Isa 6 suggests that Israel's hardening is not permanent and that there will be restoration after judgment.

4:13 Then he said to them, "Don't you understand this parable? How then will you understand any of the parables?" (Καὶ λέγει αὐτοῖς· οὐκ οἴδατε τὴν παραβολὴν ταύτην, καὶ πῶς πάσας τὰς παραβολὰς γνώσεσθε;). Having explained why he speaks in parables, Jesus now interprets the parable of the sower for the disciples. There is a mild rebuke in the rhetorical question, "Don't you understand this parable?" The spiritual dullness of the disciples is an important theme in Mark's gospel and grows in intensity throughout the narrative (4:40; 6:52; 7:18; 8:17 – 18; 8:32; 9:19, 32). At one point Jesus will even say, "Do you have eyes but cannot see, and ears but do not hear?" (8:18). This is language drawn from Jer 5:21 and Ezek 12:2, but clearly echoes Isa 6:9 – 10 and the present passage. The tension created by the fact that the disciples

are Jesus' chosen followers, yet still struggle and fail, is important for Mark's theology of discipleship. Jesus is the only true model of discipleship in the gospel. Those who wish to be his disciples must *deny themselves, take up their cross, and follow him* (8:34).

Jesus' second rhetorical question, that if the disciples do not understand this parable, "How will you understand any of the parables?" helps to explain the special prominence given to the parable of the sower. It concerns receptivity to the message and so is "the parable about parables."[28] Those who comprehend the message about good soil producing good fruit will be receptive to the "word" sown in the other parables.

4:14 – 15 The sower sows the message. These are the ones who are along the path where the message was sown. When they hear the message, Satan quickly comes and snatches away the message that was sown in them (ὁ σπείρων τὸν λόγον σπείρει. οὗτοι δέ εἰσιν οἱ παρὰ τὴν ὁδὸν ὅπου σπείρεται ὁ λόγος· καὶ ὅταν ἀκούσωσιν, εὐθὺς ἔρχεται ὁ σατανᾶς καὶ αἴρει τὸν λόγον τὸν ἐσπαρμένον εἰς αὐτούς). Jesus' interprets the parable with reference to its three elements: the farmer, the seed, and the soil. Though the story is traditionally called the "parable of the sower," the farmer appears only at the beginning and plays a relatively small role. It is really the parable of the seed and the soils.

In the context of Jesus' ministry, the farmer represents Jesus himself, who is sowing the seed of the "message" (ὁ λόγος, v. 14) — the message of the kingdom of God. Yet by extension it could also refer to his disciples, who will shortly be sent out to preach (6:6 – 13, 30). Like many of Jesus' parables, this one is not an allegory per se, but it contains allegorical elements.

The meaning of the seed and the soils is more

complicated. Jesus identifies the seed as the "message," i.e., the message of the kingdom (v. 14), and in v. 15 the soil appears to be those who receive the message. The Greek reads something like, "But these are the ones beside the path where the word was sown" (οὗτοι δέ εἰσιν οἱ παρὰ τὴν ὁδόν ὅπου σπείρεται ὁ λόγος). Yet the imagery is fluid, and the verses that follow appear to identify the hearers not as the soil, but as the seed ("those who are sown"; οἱ … σπειρόμενοι), which either bears fruit or does not (vv. 16, 17, 18, 20).

The NASB makes the imagery consistent by referring to soils throughout (v. 16: "these are the ones on whom seed was sown"; cf. vv. 18, 20).[29] Most other versions retain the more natural reading of the Greek, shifting from soil imagery in v. 14 to seed imagery in vv. 15, 16, 18, and 20.[30] The difficulty arises from the nature of the agricultural metaphor, where the seed sown (not the soil!) becomes the plant that produces a crop. It might be best to say that the recipients of the message are portrayed as the dynamic interplay between seed and soil, which together produce a crop.

The first seed does not take root because of the hard-packed soil of the path, representing those who are unresponsive to the message. In the context of Mark's narrative, we think of the Pharisees and experts in the law (i.e., scribes), who are hostile to Jesus' kingdom preaching from the start. Jesus identifies the birds that gobble up the seed with Satan, who snatches away the word before it takes root (on Satan, see comments on 1:13). Birds, as predators, seed-snatchers, and scavengers, are

sometimes associated with Satan and the forces of evil in Jewish literature.[31] In Mark's narrative, the mention of Satan reminds the reader that Jesus is engaged in a spiritual struggle pitting the kingdom of God against that of Satan, and light against darkness (1:13, 23 – 24, 14; 2:22 – 27).

4:16 – 17   These are the ones sown on rocky ground, who, when they hear the message, immediately receive it joyfully, but they do not have strong roots and so are short-lived. When trouble or persecution comes along because of the message, they quickly fall away (καὶ οὗτοί εἰσιν οἱ ἐπὶ τὰ πετρώδη σπειρόμενοι, οἳ ὅταν ἀκούσωσιν τὸν λόγον εὐθὺς μετὰ χαρᾶς λαμβάνουσιν αὐτόν, καὶ οὐκ ἔχουσιν ῥίζαν ἐν ἑαυτοῖς ἀλλὰ πρόσκαιροί εἰσιν, εἶτα γενομένης θλίψεως ἢ διωγμοῦ διὰ τὸν λόγον εὐθὺς σκανδαλίζονται). A second category of hearers responds favorably to the message, but they fall away when trials and persecution come.

In the context of Mark's narrative, we think of the popular masses, which throng to Jesus for healing, exorcism, and free bread, but quickly disappear when Jesus calls for cross-bearing discipleship. John's gospel speaks of many disciples who stopped following Jesus when his teaching became too difficult (John 6:66). The verb "fall away" (σκανδαλίζομαι) can mean "cause to sin" (9:42 – 47), but here means desertion from the faith. Jesus uses the same verb when he predicts that all of his disciples will "fall away from," or "desert," him at his arrest (14:27 – 30).

As with the first seed, the failure has two causes:

---

29. Stein, *Mark*, 217 – 18, adopts this solution, suggesting that σπειρόμενοι is not a substantival participle ("those who are sown"), but an attributive one, modifying οἱ ἐπὶ τὰ πετρώδη and so meaning "those upon the rocky-soil, *where the seed was sown.*" While this keeps the imagery the same throughout, it is a less natural reading of the Greek.

30. Oddly, NLT[1] (1996) also mixes the metaphors, but does so in the reverse order, identifying the recipients as the seed in v. 14 ("the seed … represents"), but as the soils in v. 16 ("the

rocky soil represents …") and v. 18 ("the thorny ground represents …").

31. See *Jub.* 11:11; *Apoc. Abr.* 13:3 – 7; *1 En.* 90:8 – 13; *b. Sanh.* 107a (Marcus, *Mark 1 – 8*, 309). The closest parallel is *Jub.* 11:11, where "Prince Mastema" [= Satan] causes famine in the days of Terah, Abraham's father, by sending birds to pick the grain off the ground "before they plowed in the seed." These, however, are literal birds sent to cause physical destruction, rather than an allegorical portrayal of Satan's work.

inadequate soil and an external threat. In the first, the soil was hard, preventing the seed from germinating, so the birds devoured it. Here the soil is rocky, resulting in weak or shallow roots, and so the sun withers it. The Greek idiom, they do not have "a root in themselves" (οὐκ ἔχουσιν ῥίζαν ἐν ἑαυτοῖς), means "adequate roots," that is, enough to draw sufficient moisture from the ground. The (implied) heat of the sun that withers the plant is interpreted as "trouble," "trials," or "tribulation" (θλίψις) and "persecution" (διωγμός). The first word is more general, referring to trials of various kinds. Jesus will use it in the Olivet Discourse to describe a period of intense tribulation associated with the destruction of Jerusalem and the coming of the Son of Man (13:19, 24). "Persecution" (διωγμός) means harassment or mistreatment by one's enemies.

"Because of the word" (διὰ τὸν λόγον) is shorthand for "because of their allegiance to Jesus and the gospel message." There is an assumption here that trials and persecution will be part of the Christian life — something Jesus teaches elsewhere in Mark (8:34 – 38; 10:30, 39; 13:9 – 13) and a theme that occurs throughout the NT (Rom 5:3; 12:12; 2 Cor 4:17; 1 Thess 3:3; 2 Tim 3:12; Jas 1:2 – 3; 1 Pet 1:3 – 6). When such trials come, only deep spiritual roots will prevent failure. If Mark's gospel was written to Roman Christians during the Neronian persecution (see Introduction), this text would have sounded a strong warning to those considering abandoning the faith.

4:18 – 19 Still others are those sown among the thorns; these are the ones who hear the message, but the cares of this age and the deceitfulness of wealth and the desires for other things come in and choke out the message, and it produces no crop (καὶ ἄλλοι εἰσὶν οἱ εἰς τὰς ἀκάνθας σπειρόμενοι·

οὗτοί εἰσιν οἱ τὸν λόγον ἀκούσαντες καὶ αἱ μέριμναι τοῦ αἰῶνος καὶ ἡ ἀπάτη τοῦ πλούτου καὶ αἱ περὶ τὰ λοιπὰ ἐπιθυμίαι εἰσπορευόμεναι συμπνίγουσιν τὸν λόγον καὶ ἄκαρπος γίνεται). The third seed has initial success, but then is choked out. While the second seed succumbed to external attack — trials and persecution — this third falls victim to the distractions of the world.

"Cares" (μέριμναι) refers to the stressful concerns and anxiety that life's challenges can bring (2 Cor 11:28; 1 Pet 5:7). The cares "of this age" or "the (present) age" (τοῦ αἰῶνος) carries the sense of this present evil age that is passing away (cf. 1 John 2:17: "The world and its desires pass away, but whoever does the will of God lives forever"). Wealth is deceitful (ἀπάτη)[32] because it provides the illusion of security but has no eternal value. Money can be a means to accomplish great good, but love of it can also be "a root of all kinds of evil" (1 Tim 6:10), producing greed, envy, and selfishness. In the context of Mark's gospel, we think of the rich young man, who deeply desires eternal life but cannot bring himself to leave his riches and follow Jesus (Mark 10:17 – 27). The desire for "other things" (τὰ λοιπά, "the rest") is a catchall description for anything that draws one away from God's priorities (REB: "desires of all kinds").

4:20 Then there are those that are sown in good ground, who hear the message and accept it, and produce a crop, some thirtyfold, some sixtyfold, and some a hundredfold (καὶ ἐκεῖνοί εἰσιν οἱ ἐπὶ τὴν γῆν τὴν καλὴν σπαρέντες, οἵτινες ἀκούουσιν τὸν λόγον καὶ παραδέχονται καὶ καρποφοροῦσιν ἐν τριάκοντα καὶ ἐν ἑξήκοντα καὶ ἐν ἑκατόν). While all the seeds "hear" the word, only this fourth group accepts the message and produces a crop. We have previously concluded that these numbers represent an abundant, but not unrealistic, harvest (see com-

---

32. The word can mean "pleasure" or "delight" in Hellenistic Greek (BDAG, 99) and could perhaps have that meaning

here; cf. NET: "seductiveness [of wealth]" (HCSB: "seduction"; NLT: "lure").

ments on v. 8). There is no emphasis in the parable on the difference in yield (30, 60, 100), but rather in the contrast between the seeds that were successful and those that failed.

Luke speaks of the reason for their responsiveness: they had "a noble and good heart" (καρδία καλή καὶ ἀγαθή, Luke 8:15). Mark simply states that they responded positively to the message. In the context of Mark's gospel, this means they repented and believed the good news of the kingdom of God (Mark 1:15). The nature of the fruit is not specified, though continued allegiance to Jesus and participation in his mission would surely be intended. Jesus' disciples will soon bear fruit as Jesus sends them out to preach the good news, heal the sick, and drive out demons (6:12).

Theology in Application

Hearing and Heeding the Message of the Kingdom

The pervasive theme throughout the parable of the sower is the need not only to hear the message of the kingdom, but to respond to it with faith and so produce fruit. Jesus punctuates the parables with the refrain, "Whoever has ears to hear, let them hear" (4:9, 23). The religious leaders heard Jesus' message, but they rejected it, blaspheming the Holy Spirit by accusing him of complicity with Satan (3:22 – 29). They are unfruitful, like the barren fig tree that Jesus will symbolically curse in the last week of his ministry (11:12 – 14, 19 – 26).

Many interpreters have noted the relationship between two key parables at the beginning and end of Jesus' ministry, the parable of the sower (4:1 – 20) and the parable of the wicked tenant farmers (12:1 – 12). Both use agricultural metaphors to portray the unfruitfulness of Israel's leaders and their rejection of Jesus. The parable of the sower immediately follows the accusation by the religious leaders that Jesus is in league with Satan. Jesus responds by accusing them of blasphemy against the Spirit and then teaches in parables designed to *blind* them to the truth (4:11 – 12). The parable of the wicked tenant farmers comes in the last week of Jesus' ministry and also allegorically depicts the unfruitfulness of these leaders. Ironically, its purpose is just the opposite. While the parables previously blinded them, here they clearly recognize that Jesus is speaking the parable against them and so seek to arrest him (12:12). In this way they inadvertently (and ironically) carry forward God's purpose and plan for the suffering of the Messiah (cf. Acts 2:23; 3:18; 4:28).

The Necessity of Bearing Fruit

The need to "bear fruit" for God and the dangerous consequences of barrenness are common themes in the OT and Judaism. Most significantly, barrenness appears in Isaiah's song of the vineyard (Isa 5:1 – 7), which Jesus allegorically adapts in the parable of the wicked tenant farmers (12:1 – 12). As noted above, this Markan parable has important parallels with the present one and serves as an important climax in

Mark's narrative. It is also significant that in the present passage (4:12) Jesus quotes Isa 6:9 – 10, which is closely related to Isaiah's song of the vineyard. In both cases it is Israel's unfruitfulness that will bring spiritual blindness, leading to judgment.

In Rom 9 – 11 Paul uses another agricultural metaphor to describe Israel's rejection of the gospel. Apostate Israel is described as branches broken off of an olive tree (probably representing the patriarchs and the remnant of God's people), to which wild branches (the Gentiles) are grafted in (11:17 – 21). God sovereignly accomplishes his purpose despite the rejection of many in Israel.

Hearing the Parable Today

Though Jesus told this parable with special reference to the rejection of his message by Israel's leaders, it has great significance for today. The same message that Jesus proclaimed — the coming of the kingdom of God and the need to repent and believe — is the message his church proclaims today, and people respond to it in a variety of ways. For some it never gets through and is snatched away by Satan's lies — such as there is no God, or that personal pleasure, fame, or wealth is the ultimate goal of life, or that success comes through personal effort and self-reliance.

For others, the message sounds good and is welcomed with joy, but it never penetrates beyond a superficial level of faith. It is based on emotionalism or is inherited from family, but it has no roots of its own. For these, church is a nice social club to meet and develop friendships. The essence of Christianity is being a good person and helping others, or supporting patriotic American values or a conservative social agenda. The idea of radical commitment to the kingdom and its mission remains an alien concept.

Still others hear the message and are even assimilated into the community of faith, but the distractions of the world — its worries and wealth — mean that faith never results in transformation.

But others respond to the message and persevere until they bear fruit. Bearing fruit could mean bringing others to Christ, but it is much broader than this. It is a life change that results in transformation until we share God's values for the world and develop the mind of Christ (Rom 12:2; 1 Cor 2:16; 2 Cor 4:16 – 17).

Sometimes the question is raised as to which, if any, of the first three seeds and soils are in fact "saved." But this question misses the point of the parable. All three are unfruitful and so all three have failed. It is not a matter of whether any "escape through the flames" (1 Cor 3:15). Rather, in Jesus' ministry there are two kinds of people, those who accept the kingdom and those who reject it. The three failed seeds represent the latter. True faith produces fruit (Eph 2:8 – 10; Phil 2:12 – 13; Jas 2:14 – 26).

Mark 4:21 – 34

Literary Context

This passage continues Jesus' teaching that began with the parable of the sower, the seed, and the soils (4:1 – 9). These sayings continue the themes of that parable (revelation and response) and expand on it, describing the nature and growth of the kingdom of God.

Main Idea

Jesus continues his parabolic teaching with two groups of sayings and two parables. The sayings (vv. 21 – 25) continue the theme of the parable of the sower: the revelation of the message, the need to respond, and the consequences of rejection. The two parables that follow (vv. 26 – 32) move from the responses to the kingdom of God to the nature of that kingdom.

Translation

(See next page.)

Mark 4:21 – 34

21a	Introduction	And **he was saying to them,**
b	rhetorical question	*"Do you bring in a lamp to put it under a bowl or under a bed?*
c	contrast	*Don't you put it on a lampstand?*
22a	aphorism	*For nothing is hidden*
b	contrast	*except to be revealed,*
c	aphorism	*and nothing is concealed*
d	contrast	*except to be brought out into full view.*
23	exhortation to hear	*If anyone has ears to hear, let them hear."*
24a	Introduction	And **he was saying to them,**
b	exhortation to hear	*"Pay attention to what you hear.*
c	aphorism	*By the measure you measure, you will be measured,*
d		*and even more will be added.*
25a	aphorism	*For the one who has will be given more;*
b	aphorism/contrast to 25a	*and the one who does not have, even what he has will be taken from him."*
26a	Introduction	**He continued saying,**
b	analogy	*"This is what the kingdom of God is like:*
c	action	*It is like a person who scatters seed on the ground and goes to sleep and gets up,*
27a	result	*night and day, and the seed sprouts and grows,*
b		*though he doesn't know how.*
28a	result	*The soil produces grain all by itself,*
b		*first the blade, then the head, then the full kernel in the head.*
29a	response	*Then when the grain is ripe,*
b		*he sends in the sickle,*
c		*because the harvest has arrived."*
30a	Introduction	**He continued saying,**
b	parable introduction	*"To what shall we compare the kingdom of God,*
c		*or what parable shall we use to describe it?*
31a	analogy	*It is like a mustard seed, which is planted in the earth.*
b		*Although it is the smallest of all the seeds of the earth,*
32a		*when planted it grows up and becomes the largest of all the garden plants.*
b		*It puts out large branches so that the birds can nest in its shade."*
33a	summary	**With many parables like this he was speaking the message to them,**
b		as much as they could understand.
34a		**He did not speak to them without using parables,**
b		but **privately he explained everything to his own disciples.**

Structure

Mark's structure includes two collections of sayings (vv. 21 – 23 and vv. 24 – 25), followed by two short parables or similitudes (vv. 26 – 29 and vv. 30 – 32) and a conclusion about Jesus' teaching in parables (vv. 33 – 34). The sayings occur in the same basic order in Luke following the parable of the sower (Luke 8:16 – 18), but in various contexts in Matthew (Matt 5:15; 7:2; 10:26; 13:12; 25:29). Similar sayings also appear elsewhere in Luke (Luke 11:33; 12:2; 19:26). Verses 21, 22, and 25 also have parallels in the Gnostic *Gospel of Thomas*.[1] The parable of the secretly growing seed (vv. 26 – 29) is unique to Mark. The parable of the mustard seed (vv. 30 – 32) appears in the same collection of parables in Matthew (Matt 13:31 – 32), but in a later context in Luke (Luke 13:18 – 19).

The sayings of vv. 21 – 25 are structured into two groups, each introduced by the clause, "and he was saying to them" (καὶ ἔλεγεν αὐτοῖς; vv. 21a, 24a). In each saying, a concrete analogy is expressed (a lamp on a stand; a measure in the marketplace), followed by a proverbial saying explaining the analogy. The first saying is explained in synonymous parallelism and the second in antithetical parallelism. The first group ends with an exhortation to listen (v. 23), while the second group begins with one (v. 24b).

"And he was saying to them …" (v. 21a)	
"Do you bring in a lamp …" (v. 21b)	Analogy
"For nothing is hidden…." (v. 22a)	Proverbial explanations in
"And nothing is concealed …" (v. 22c)	synonymous parallelism
"If anyone has ears to hear …" (v. 23)	Exhortation to listen
"And he was saying to them …" (v. 24a)	
"Pay attention …" (v. 24b)	Exhortation to listen
"By the measure you measure …" (v. 24c)	Analogy
"For the one who has …" (v. 25a)	Proverbial explanations in
"And the one who does not have …" (v. 25b)	antithetical parallelism

The two short parables that follow are also introduced similarly: "He continued saying" (καὶ ἔλεγεν; vv. 26a, 30a), followed by an analogy drawn to the kingdom of God. The first analogy is a direct comparison: "This is what the kingdom of God is like" (v. 26), while the second is a pair of rhetorical questions: "To what shall we compare the kingdom of God, or what parable shall we use to describe it?" (v. 30). The meaning is the same. The two parables also follow a similar pattern: planting, nature of growth, and result (see Exegetical Outline, below). The passage concludes with a statement of Jesus' consistent parabolic teaching to the crowds and his private interpretation for the disciples (vv. 33 – 34).

---

1. *Gos. Thom.* 5 – 6, 33, 41, 108b.

Exegetical Outline

→ **1. Analogy of the Lamp on a Stand (4:21 – 23)**

    a. The analogy (4:21)

    b. The proverbial application (4:22)

    c. Call to hear (4:23)

2. Analogy of the Measure (4:24 – 25)

    a. Call to hear (4:24a-b)

    b. The analogy (4:24c)

    c. The proverbial application (4:25)

3. The Parable of the Growing Seed (4:26 – 29)

    a. Comparison to the kingdom of God (4:26a-b)

    b. The sowing (4:26c)

    c. The growing seed (4:27 – 28)

    d. The result (4:29)

4. The Parable of the Mustard Seed (4:30 – 32)

    a. Comparison to the kingdom of God (4:30)

    b. The planting (4:31)

    c. The growth (4:32a)

    d. The result (4:32b)

5. Summary of Parabolic Teaching (4:33 – 34)

Explanation of the Text

4:21 – 22 And he was saying to them, "Do you bring in a lamp to put it under a bowl or under a bed? Don't you put it on a lampstand? For nothing is hidden except to be revealed, and nothing is concealed except to be brought out into full view." (Καὶ ἔλεγεν αὐτοῖς· μήτι ἔρχεται ὁ λύχνος ἵνα ὑπὸ τὸν μόδιον τεθῇ ἢ ὑπὸ τὴν κλίνην; οὐχ ἵνα ἐπὶ τὴν λυχνίαν τεθῇ; οὐ γάρ ἐστιν κρυπτὸν ἐὰν μὴ ἵνα φανερωθῇ, οὐδὲ ἐγένετο ἀπόκρυφον ἀλλ᾽ ἵνα ἔλθῃ εἰς φανερόν). Mark does not specify the "them" to whom these sayings are given. It could be the crowd (4:1 – 2) or the disciples (4:10 – 12). The nearest antecedent would suggest the latter, since no change in audience is noted. Verses 33 – 34, however, indicate that Jesus is teaching the crowds, since after addressing "them" in parables, Jesus explains everything privately to his disciples.

If Mark has a particular audience in mind, it seems best to see vv. 21 – 25 as directed to the disciples, while the parables of vv. 26 – 32 are assumed to have a more general audience. This would fit the twin themes of consistently teaching the crowds in parables (vv. 11, 34) while interpreting their meaning and the secrets of the kingdom for the disciples privately (vv. 11, 22, 24 – 25). Mark has a tendency to present material thematically, so there is no reason to assume that all the material in this chapter was given on a particular occasion.

The first rhetorical question (with μήτι) expects a negative answer (BDAG, 649); the second (with οὐχ) a positive one. The Greek of the first question is unusual, reading something like, "Does not the lamp come …?" (μήτι ἔρχεται ὁ λύχνος). Some commentators have argued that the use of the verb "come" (ἔρχεται) indicates that Mark is referring to a personal agent, and that Jesus himself is the lamp (cf. John 1:4; 8:12; 9:5, Jesus as the light of the world).[2] This is possible, but more likely this is simply Mark's more literal rendering of an Aramaic original.[3] In context, the lamp more likely represents either (1) the message of the kingdom of God or (2) the kingdom itself, the coming of which Jesus has been announcing (1:15).[4] Either of these fits the context, since the other parables concern especially either the message of the kingdom (parable of the sower, 4:10–20) or the nature of the kingdom itself (parables of the secretly growing seed [4:26–29] and the mustard seed [4:30–32]).

The lamp (λύχνος) here is a clay lamp filled with olive oil, used to light rooms at night. The "bowl" (NIV; μόδιος) refers to a measure of grain a little over two gallons (8.75 liters), and so by metonymy the container that holds it: "bushel basket" (NRSV), "measuring bowl" (REB), "clay pot" (CEV). The "bed" (κλίνη) may be a sleeping bed or a dining couch (BDAG, 549). In Matt 5:15, the saying appears in the Sermon on the Mount and refers to good deeds Jesus' followers ought to shine for others to see. Here the point is that the (message of the) kingdom of God is not meant to be hidden, but to be fully revealed.

Verse 22 continues the thought but takes it further. In Luke's version of this saying, the point is that what is presently hidden will one day come into the open: "For there is nothing hidden that will not be disclosed, and nothing concealed that will not be known or brought out into the open"

(Luke 8:17; cf. 12:2).[5] This may also be the point in Mark: the kingdom of God, though presently veiled, will one day be revealed.

When this revelation will take place is not specified. It could refer to the disciples' preaching of the gospel following the resurrection (cf. 9:9) or the revelation of the Son of Man at the consummation of the kingdom (13:26–27). The statement would thus serve to clarify the secrecy motif that runs through the gospel (1:25, 34; 3:11–12; 1:44; 5:43; 7:36; 8:26; 8:30; 9:9). Though Jesus presently commands silence from others concerning his words and actions and privately explains the meaning of the parables to his disciples, the day will come when all will be revealed.

Yet Mark's language in v. 22 is somewhat different from Luke's and may carry unique connotations. In Mark, Jesus says that the present hiddenness is *for the purpose of* revelation — lit., "in order that it might be revealed" (ἵνα φανερωθῇ). The second clause then says that the present concealment is (lit.) "in order that it might come into view" (ἵνα ἔλθῃ εἰς φανερόν). Paradoxically, the present hiddenness of the kingdom serves the purpose of revelation. While this might seem contradictory, it fits perfectly Jesus' teaching earlier in this chapter about the purpose of the parables. To those open to the kingdom of God, the parables reveal the truth. But to those who reject Jesus' kingdom message, the parables conceal the truth (4:11–12). This blindness and rejection, however, is all part of God's plan and is the means by which

---

2. Lane, *Mark*, 165–66; Cranfield, *Mark*, 164; Hooker, *Mark*, 133; Boring, *Mark*, 135. Boring, *Mark*, 133, suggests the unusual Greek may indicate an Aramaic idiom. Some scribes changed ερχεται to απτεται ("is lit"; D W *f*[13] it sah[mss] boh[pt]).

3. Both Matthew (Matt 5:15) and Luke (Luke 8:16) modify Mark's original and speak of someone lighting a lamp. Apparently they do this independently of one another, since they use two different Greek words for lighting. Both Matthew and Luke

also omit the article from ὁ λύχνος, indicating that they are thinking less of a specific referent (Jesus or the kingdom) and more of a general proverb.

4. France, *Mark*, 208.

5. Matthew has a similar saying in Matt 10:26, where believers are encouraged not to fear persecution, since they will be vindicated in the end when all truth is revealed (cf. Luke 12:2–3).

he will accomplish his salvation purposes (8:31; 9:31; 10:33 – 34).[6]

If this is the correct interpretation, then Mark's use of the aorist tense "was" (ἐγένετο) in the second clause is probably also intentional. While most interpreters consider the two clauses to be synonymous, meaning "what is concealed will one day be revealed," the use of the aorist suggests the meaning of the second is, "whatever *was* concealed...."[7] If this is the case, it is referring to the *present* manifestation of the kingdom, which the disciples are now receiving through the parables and their explanation by Jesus (4:10 – 11, 33 – 34). The kingdom is presently being revealed to those open to God's salvation purposes.

4:23 "If anyone has ears to hear, let them hear." (εἴ τις ἔχει ὦτα ἀκούειν ἀκουέτω). This kind of teaching demands spiritual discernment, so the command of 4:9 is repeated (see discussion there). As in 4:9, it is uncertain whether the phrase means (1) everyone should hear and respond to Jesus' message; or (2) those given "ears" (= special spiritual insight) by God ought to listen. If vv. 21 – 25 are directed to the disciples, as suggested above (v. 21), the latter is most likely.

4:24 And he was saying to them, "Pay attention to what you hear. By the measure you measure, you will be measured, and even more will be added." (Καὶ ἔλεγεν αὐτοῖς· βλέπετε τί ἀκούετε. ἐν ᾧ μέτρῳ μετρεῖτε μετρηθήσεται ὑμῖν καὶ προστεθήσεται ὑμῖν). The second group of sayings begins with another call to attention. The combination of visual and aural senses is striking: lit., "See what you hear!" (βλέπετε τί ἀκούετε).

The proverb that follows reflects the grain market,[8] where a person's integrity was evident from

the accuracy of their scales and measuring vessels (cf. Luke 6:38). It essentially means, "You get back what you give."[9] The saying occurs in both Matthew and Luke, but in different contexts and with different applications. Matthew 7:2 refers to the danger of judging others hypocritically: "In the same way you judge others, you will be judged, and with the measure you use, it will be measured to you." Luke 6:37 – 38 refers more generally to receiving back in equal measure, whether in judgment, forgiveness, or giving. In rabbinic literature the proverb often relates to divine judgment mediated justly (*m. Soṭah* 1:7; *b. Sanh.* 100a).[10]

Here in Mark the proverb takes on a different nuance appropriate to the present context. Those who take the time and energy to hear and respond to Jesus' kingdom teaching will receive back their investment, and even more. The last phrase, "and even more will be added," is unique to Mark and prepares for the following sentence about the "insiders" who receive even greater revelation. "Will be measured" (μετρηθήσεται) and "will be added" (προστεθήσεται) are divine passives, meaning *God* will measure and *God* will add.

4:25 "For the one who has will be given more; and the one who does not have, even what he has will be taken from him." (ὃς γὰρ ἔχει, δοθήσεται αὐτῷ· καὶ ὃς οὐκ ἔχει, καὶ ὃ ἔχει ἀρθήσεται ἀπ᾽ αὐτοῦ). As in v. 24, a common proverb is applied to the present topic: hearing and receiving the kingdom message. The twin antithetical proverbs ("the one who has ... the one who does not have") occur in different contexts in Matthew and Luke. In Matthew's parable of the talents (Matt 25:29) and Luke's parable of the minas (Luke 19:26), similar sayings refer to good or bad stewardship of God's resources. Those

---

6. For this interpretation, see Marcus, *Mark 1 – 8*, 318 – 19; Stein, *Mark*, 225 – 26.

7. Marcus, *Mark 1 – 8*, 314, 319; Stein, *Mark*, 225.

8. France, *Mark*, 210, citing B. Couroyer, "De la mesure

dont vous mesurez il vous sera mesuré," *RB* 77 (1970): 366 – 70.

9. A negative version is, "Those who live by the sword, die by the sword" (cf. Matt 26:52).

10. France, *Mark*, 211.

who utilize well the resources God has given them will be given even more responsibility, while those who squander such resources will lose even what little they have.

Here in Mark (cf. Matt 13:12), the proverb refers to the reception of divine revelation.[11] Those who hear and respond to the message of the kingdom of God will receive even greater revelation, while those who reject what they have heard will be blinded even further. The sayings thus parallel Jesus' explanation for why he teaches in parables in 4:11 – 12. To those who are responsive to Jesus' kingdom teaching, the parables provide even greater spiritual insight. But for the hard-hearted "outsiders" who reject the message, they will "look and look but not perceive, and hear and hear but not understand" (4:12). Their spiritual blindness will only increase. Again we have divine passives (cf. v. 24), "it will be given" (δοθήσεται) and "it will be taken" (ἀρθήσεται), which mean "God will give" and "God will take," respectively.

4:26 – 28 He continued saying, "This is what the kingdom of God is like: It is like a person who scatters seed on the ground and goes to sleep and gets up, night and day, and the seed sprouts and grows, though he doesn't know how. The soil produces grain all by itself, first the blade, then the head, then the full kernel in the head." (Καὶ ἔλεγεν· οὕτως ἐστὶν ἡ βασιλεία τοῦ θεοῦ ὡς ἄνθρωπος βάλῃ τὸν σπόρον ἐπὶ τῆς γῆς καὶ καθεύδῃ καὶ ἐγείρηται νύκτα καὶ ἡμέραν, καὶ ὁ σπόρος βλαστᾷ καὶ μηκύνηται ὡς οὐκ οἶδεν αὐτός. αὐτομάτη ἡ γῆ καρποφορεῖ, πρῶτον χόρτον εἶτα στάχυν εἶτα πλήρη[ς] σῖτον ἐν τῷ στάχυϊ). The two analogies of the lamp (vv. 21 – 23) and the measure (vv. 24 – 25) concerned the positive and negative

responses to the message of the kingdom of God. Now Jesus tells two parables (or similitudes) concerning the nature and growth of the kingdom: the secretly growing seed (vv. 26 – 29) and the mustard seed (vv. 30 – 32).

Both parables are introduced with similar formulas identifying them as analogies describing the kingdom. Like the parable of the sower, both concern seeds growing into plants. While the parable of the sower (4:1 – 8) concerned the success or failure of the seed (= the word of God) to produce, the parable of the secretly growing seed concerns the mysterious power of the seed to grow apart from human intervention, and the parable of the mustard seed concerns the phenomenal growth that will characterize the kingdom of God.

While the teaching in vv. 21 – 25 appears to have been directed to the disciples, the audience here, like the parable of the sower, is apparently the crowds in general (see vv. 33 – 34, and comments on vv. 21 – 22). The address in both parables is general. Our translation, "He continued saying" (καὶ ἔλεγεν; vv. 26, 30), picks up the sense of the imperfect tense that this was part of Jesus' ongoing teaching ministry. Though no change of location or audience is explicitly made, the gospel writers often order Jesus' teaching topically rather than chronologically, and Mark likely introduced these parables here for thematic reasons.

The parable of the secretly growing seed is unique to Mark, one of the few episodes (and the only parable) that do not appear in either Matthew or Luke. Its main point is the mysterious power of the seed to grow and produce a crop without human intervention or understanding. A farmer (ἄνθρωπος = "person") scatters seed and then goes about his daily life. He sleeps and rises, night

---

11. Hooker, *Mark*, 134, cites some interesting rabbinic parallels, where the proverb is used in a similar manner to what is here in Mark; *b. Ber.* 40a says that God "puts more into a full vessel, but not into an empty one; for it says 'If hearkening you will hearken' (Exod 15:26), implying, if you hearken you will go on hearkening, and if not you will not hearken" (cf. *b. Sukkah* 46a-b).

and day, while the seed sprouts and grows by it-self into a plant. The order "night and day" (νύκτα καὶ ἡμέραν) probably reflects the Hebrew way of conceiving a day as beginning in the evening (see Gen 1:5). The tense of the five verbs illustrates well the nature of Greek verbal aspect. The scattering (βάλῃ) of seed is an aorist subjunctive (simple or undefined action),[12] while sleeping (καθεύδῃ), rising (ἐγείρηται), sprouting (βλαστᾷ), and growing (μηκύνηται) are all present subjunctives, indicating continuous or ongoing action.

The parable teaches that the kingdom of God is ultimately the work of God and that he will sover-eignly bring it to pass. The point is not that humans play no role in the work of God or the advance of the kingdom. Like most parables, this one teaches one key truth about the kingdom. It does not tell the whole story. Indeed, a real farmer might in-tervene in a variety of ways — watering, weeding, fertilizing, removing pests; but this is to miss the point. Here the point is God's sovereign purpose.

Not only does the farmer not cause the growth, but he also doesn't know *how* it happens (ὡς οὐκ οἶδεν αὐτός). The nature of the kingdom's growth is a mystery. This would seem to rule out an al-legorical identification of the farmer with Jesus (in contrast to the parable of the sower). The parable is not an allegory of Jesus' ministry but a simili-tude making one theological point — the secret and mysterious growth of the kingdom. This probably also rules out the suggestion by Marcus that the stages of growth (blade, head, full kernel, v. 28b) are intended to represent periods of salvation his-tory (Jesus, the church, the eschaton).[13] While the kingdom's growth can certainly be seen in these general stages, it is unlikely that Mark intends his

readers to catch so nuanced an interpretation. The progress from blade to head to full kernel is simply the way grain grows.

The seed produces grain "by itself" (αὐτομάτη; v. 28), which in context must mean by the provi-dence and divine work of God. There is no sug-gestion here of a deistic worldview where nature functions independently of divine intervention. Rather, Mark assumes the biblical worldview that it is God who makes the sun rise, the rains fall, the seed sprout, and the grass grow (Job 38 – 42; Isa 40; Matt 5:45). God is in charge of human history, and he will bring the kingdom of God to its destined consummation. No human action or opposition can change that.

4:29 "Then when the grain is ripe, he sends in the sickle, because the harvest has arrived." (ὅταν δὲ παραδοῖ ὁ καρπός, εὐθὺς ἀποστέλλει τὸ δρέπανον, ὅτι παρέστηκεν ὁ θερισμός). To "send in the sickle" (ἀποστέλλει τὸ δρέπανον) is a Hebraism (Joel 4:13 MT and LXX) that may mean to swing with a sickle; or the sickle may be a metonymy for the harvesters, in which case the owner is "sending" the harvesters into the field. Harvest is a common metaphor for the final judgment in both Judaism and early Christianity.[14] Although the parable as a whole is not allegorical, it is not unlikely that Mark and his readers would have understood the har-vest in this way. The closest biblical parallel is Joel 3:13: "Swing [or, 'send out'; LXX: ἐξαποστείλατε] the sickle, for the harvest is ripe. Come, trample the grapes, for the winepress is full and the vats overflow — so great is their wickedness!" Mark's persecuted readers could rest in the assurance that whatever trials or suffering they were experienc-

---

12. The aorist does not necessarily mean "point-in-time" or "once-for-all" action. It is rather the default, simple, or "un-defined" Greek tense. Yet the use of the aorist by an author is a deliberate choice *not* to stress linear, progressive, or continu-ous action (a present or imperfect), and this can be significant.

See Wallace, *Greek Grammar,* 554 – 57.

13. Marcus, *Mark 1 – 8,* 328 – 29.

14. Isa 17:5 – 6; 18:5; Mic 4:12; 2 Esd 4:28 – 39; *2 Bar.* 70:2; Matt 3:12; Rev 14:15.

ing, the consummation of the kingdom will bring salvation and vindication for God's people and judgment against his enemies.

4:30 He continued saying, "To what shall we compare the kingdom of God, or what parable shall we use to describe it?" (Καὶ ἔλεγεν· πῶς ὁμοιώσωμεν τὴν βασιλείαν τοῦ θεοῦ ἢ ἐν τίνι αὐτὴν παραβολῇ θῶμεν;). The parable of the mustard seed is the third and last of Mark's parables about seed sown (4:1 – 9, 26 – 29, 30 – 32). While the previous parable was unique to Mark, this one has parallels in Matthew (Matt 13:31 – 32), Luke (Luke 13:18 – 19), and the *Gospel of Thomas* (*Gos. Thom.* 20).

The parable begins exactly as the previous one, "He continued saying" (Καὶ ἔλεγεν), without specifying the audience. The crowds in general are probably in view (see vv. 33 – 34, and comments on v. 21). Both parables draw an explicit comparison to the kingdom of God — the previous one with a statement, this one with two rhetorical questions ("To what shall we compare ... or what parable shall we use...?").

4:31 – 32 It is like a mustard seed, which is planted in the earth. Although it is the smallest of all the seeds of the earth, when planted it grows up and becomes the largest of all the garden plants. It puts out large branches so that the birds can nest in its shade." (ὡς κόκκῳ σινάπεως, ὃς ὅταν σπαρῇ ἐπὶ τῆς γῆς, μικρότερον ὂν πάντων τῶν σπερμάτων τῶν ἐπὶ τῆς γῆς, καὶ ὅταν σπαρῇ, ἀναβαίνει καὶ γίνεται μεῖζον πάντων τῶν λαχάνων καὶ ποιεῖ κλάδους μεγάλους, ὥστε δύνασθαι ὑπὸ τὴν σκιὰν αὐτοῦ τὰ πετεινὰ τοῦ οὐρανοῦ κατασκηνοῦν).

The mustard seed — about the size of a grain of sand — was proverbial in Judaism for its smallness.[15] Jesus says elsewhere that with faith the size of a mustard seed his disciples could move mountains (Matt 17:20; Luke 17:6). Some have challenged the precision of Jesus' words, since the mustard seed is not in fact "the smallest of all seeds of the earth."[16] The seeds of some epiphytic orchids (family Orchidaceae) that grow in tropical rainforests are much smaller. Some are as small as 1/300th of an inch long, a mere speck of dust, and cannot be seen without magnification.[17] Jesus, however, is not giving a lesson in botany but is speaking proverbially in language his audience would understand. From the perspective of a first-century Palestinian audience, the mustard seed is the smallest seed in the world.

The mustard seed would grow into a large, tree-like shrub, sometimes ten or more feet high, and so became the "largest of all the garden plants." The parallels in Matthew and Luke refer to it as a "tree" (δένδρον; Matt 13:32; Luke 13:19). It is certainly large enough for birds to find shelter in its branches. The idiom "birds of the sky/heaven" (τὰ πετεινὰ τοῦ οὐρανοῦ) means wild, as opposed to tame, birds.[18] In normal English, we would simply say "birds." The verb "nest" (κατασκηνόω) could mean to find protection or to find a home (= build a nest). The latter seems more likely.

The point of the parable is that the kingdom of God will have small and insignficant beginnings, but will grow into something great. The significance of the birds is debated. Some see them as simply illustrating the size of the plant.[19] Though

---

15. See *m. Nid.* 5:2; *m. Ṭehar* 8:8; *m. Naz.* 1:5; Str-B 1:669.
16. We have translated the comparative "smaller" (μικρότερον) here as a superlative, "smallest," and the comparative "greater" (μεῖζον) in v. 32 as "greatest." Though the comparative can be used in a superlative sense in Greek (Wallace, *Greek Grammar,* 299 – 300), here we have true comparatives. But since the comparison is between the mustard seed and "all" the other seeds and between the mustard plant and "all" the

other garden plants, the sense is identical to the superlative. See Wallace, *Greek Grammar,* 300 – 301 for the possibility of an elative sense here.
17. See http://diogenesii.wordpress.com/2007/06/22/what-is-the-smallest-seed-in-the-world/ (accessed Sept. 17, 2013).
18. BDAG, 809.
19. Stein, *Mark,* 236.

once a tiny seed, it is now large enough for birds to nest in it. Others see allegorical significance, with the birds representing the Gentiles who will find a place in the kingdom of God.[20] Ancient Near Eastern imagery often depicted empires as great trees, and Ezekiel's two parables of cedar trees (Ezek 17:1 – 24; 31:1 – 14) and Nebuchadnezzar's dream in Daniel 4:10 – 12, 14, 21 depict the Assyrian and Babylonian empires as trees under which birds and animals find protection. It is not unlikely, therefore, that Mark's readers would have understood the image to represent the Gentile nations finding rest in the kingdom of God.

While the tiny size of a mustard seed may be sufficient to account for Jesus' choice of this imagery, some commentators have noted how strange it is to use this plant as an image of the kingdom of God.[21] One might expect the kingdom of God to be compared to a mighty oak or a stately cedar of Lebanon. But a mustard bush? Mustard was invasive and even dangerous to gardens. Pliny the Elder wrote that the plant "grows entirely wild, though it is improved by being transplanted; but on the other hand when it has once been sown it is scarcely possible to get the place free of it, as the seed when it falls germinates at once" (*Nat.* 19.170 – 71). Witherington suggests that in addition to describing the amazing growth of the kingdom, the parable may indicate that the spreading kingdom "was a threat to the existing garden or field of early Judaism. If Jesus' proclamation took root, it stood in danger of subverting existing kingdom visions and power structures in Israel."[22]

4:33 – 34 With many parables like this he was speaking the message to them, as much as they could understand. He did not speak to them without using parables, but privately he explained everything to his own disciples (Καὶ τοιαύταις παραβολαῖς πολλαῖς ἐλάλει αὐτοῖς τὸν λόγον καθὼς ἠδύναντο ἀκούειν· χωρὶς δὲ παραβολῆς οὐκ ἐλάλει αὐτοῖς, κατ᾽ ἰδίαν δὲ τοῖς ἰδίοις μαθηταῖς ἐπέλυεν πάντα). The section ends with Mark's summary of Jesus' parabolic teaching. The phrase "with many parables like this" suggests that this is only a sampling of the kinds of parables Jesus told (cf. John 20:30 – 31). Nor should we assume that these parables were necessarily all given on a single day or to the same audience (see comments on 4:21 – 22). The "message" (λόγος) is the message of the kingdom of God (1:15; 4:14). The audience here ("to them") is assumed to be the people in general, since Jesus "privately … explained everything to his own disciples."

The clause "as much as they could understand" (καθὼς ἠδύναντο ἀκούειν) could mean that Jesus gave them teaching appropriate to their level of knowledge, simplifying the message so they could easily understand it. This is unlikely, however, in light of Jesus' earlier teaching concerning the purpose of parables (see comments on 4:11 – 12). Rather, the point is that the people's comprehension depended on whether they had "eyes to see" and "ears to hear," that is, whether they were the insiders, "able to hear" (ἠδύναντο ἀκούειν) Jesus' message of the kingdom of God, or "outsiders," with hard hearts and closed minds.

This meaning is supported by the following sentence, where Mark notes that Jesus spoke to the crowds exclusively in "parables" (here having the broad meaning of analogies, similitudes, parables, etc.), but then explained everything privately to his own disciples. As in 4:11 – 12, the purpose of the parables is both to reveal and to conceal. To those

---

20. Marcus, *Mark 1 – 8*, 331; Hooker, *Mark*, 136; France, *Mark*, 216 – 17.

21. Witherington, *Mark*, 172; J. D. Crossan, *The Historical Jesus: The Life of a Mediterranean Jewish Peasant* (San Francisco: Harper, 1991), 277 – 79.

22. Witherington, *Mark*, 172.

open and responsive to the word, the parables illuminate the truth. But for those who refuse to respond, the parables conceal it. We should add that although the parables are a word of judgment against those rejecting the kingdom message (4:11 – 12; cf. Isa 6:9 – 10), the boundary between "insiders" and "outsiders" is not yet sealed (the disciples themselves will waver; see 8:17 – 18), and the kingdom is open to all who will respond in faith and repentance.

That Jesus "did not speak to them without using parables" (χωρὶς δὲ παραβολῆς οὐκ ἐλάλει αὐτοῖς) may be Markan hyperbole. Mark does not record a great deal of Jesus' actual teaching compared with Matthew and Luke, and most (if not all)[23] of it is in short epigrams, analogies, and parables. Mark's primary point, however, is to emphasize Jesus' private instruction of the disciples, a common Markan theme (7:17 – 23; 9:28 – 29, 35; 10:10 – 12, 32 – 34; 12:43 – 44; 13:3 – 37). The "disciples" here certainly means the Twelve, but that term may also include the larger body of followers mentioned in 4:10 with reference to the interpretation of the parable of the sower (οἱ περὶ αὐτόν, "others around him").

Theology in Application

The sayings and parables of this section elaborate on the nature and significance of the kingdom of God, reflecting important themes for Mark and for biblical theology.

A Light to Shine Forth for the World to See

Just as the purpose of a lamp is to provide light to a room, so the message of the kingdom is light for a dark world. Light and darkness are common images throughout Scripture to symbolize good and evil, the forces of God versus the forces of evil. In the beginning God creates the present universe by calling forth light from darkness and pronouncing the light "good" (Gen 1:3 – 4). Paul picks up this creation imagery when he says that "God, who said, 'Let light shine out of darkness,' made his light shine in our hearts to give us the light of the knowledge of God's glory displayed in the face of Christ" (2 Cor 4:6). Isaiah predicts that the coming of the Messiah will represent a light shining on those in darkness, a new dawn for those who live in the land of the shadow of death (Isa 9:2). Though Mark does not use light and darkness imagery elsewhere in his gospel (cf. Matt 4:16; 5:14 – 16; 6:22 – 23), the metaphors of blindness and sight function in much the same way. Knowledge of God's kingdom and purpose in the world comes through having eyes to see and ears to hear.

The Present Hiddenness of the Kingdom

The present hiddenness of the kingdom is only temporary and part of God's purpose and plan. While in Matthew the lamp imagery is part of a command to let

---

23. See France, *Mark*, 218 – 19, who notes that the only *public* teaching of Jesus that is not in epigrammatic sayings is in chapter 12, which may not be classified as "teaching" or "speaking the word."

your good deeds "shine" before others in order to bring glory to God (Matt 5:16), in Mark the primary point is the present hiddenness of the kingdom and its eventual full disclosure (Mark 4:21 – 22). While the Jews of Jesus' day would have expected the kingdom to come with the destruction of the Roman legions and the reestablishment of the Davidic monarchy, Jesus inaugurates the kingdom in a surprising way by healing the sick, casting out demons, and announcing the "good news" of God.

It is not certain what Jesus means by the disclosure of what is presently concealed (4:22). It could refer to the revelation of Jesus' glory at his transfiguration (9:3 – 7), at his entrance into Jerusalem (11:9 – 10), at the resurrection (16:6 – 7), or at his return in glory to consummate the kingdom (13:26 – 27, 35 – 37). This last is most likely. In any case, the present hiddenness of the kingdom and the rejection of the Messiah are part of God's purpose and plan, and they will be used by God to accomplish his salvation purposes (8:31 – 32; 9:31; 10:32 – 34, 45). Though the kingdom will begin in a lowly and insignificant way, like a tiny mustard seed (4:30 – 32), it will eventually become the greatest transforming power in the world.

Responding Positively to the Kingdom Message Results in Greater Light

Although the kingdom is hidden to many, those who respond positively to the message of God's reign receive eyes to see and ears to hear. "The one who has will be given more" (v. 25) does not mean that "the rich get richer," but rather that those who are open to the truth will receive even greater revelation and more discernment into the mysteries of God. This is an irrefutable principle of spiritual growth. Those who express faith and trust in God find him faithful and so gain greater confidence and trust in him.

The Sovereign Work of God

The growth and success of the kingdom is the sovereign work of God, not the result of human actions or ambition. The parable of the secretly growing seed teaches that the growth and expansion of the kingdom is the work of God rather than any human accomplishment. This is a biblical pinciple. Proverbs 16:9 says that "in their hearts humans plan their course, but the LORD establishes their steps." Proverbs 19:21 similarly asserts that "many are the plans in a person's heart, but it is the LORD's purpose that prevails" (cf. 16:33). God is the sovereign Lord of history.

The message of the OT prophets is that God is the creator and sustainer of all things. The nations are a drop in the bucket, mere dust on the scales compared to him (Isa 40:15). The book of Revelation identifies him as the Alpha and the Omega, the beginning and the end (Rev 1:8; 21:6; 22:13). He began human history and will bring it to its ultimate consummation. In light of his sovereign control over all things, we can surely trust him in even the smallest areas of our lives.

The Kingdom Will Grow into Great Success

Despite its small and insignificant beginnings, the kingdom will grow into great success, since it is the work of God. The parable of the mustard seed reminds us that what is viewed as small and insignificant in human terms can be used by God to accomplish great things. Throughout Scripture God uses the small and insignificant to accomplish his purposes. Gideon's tiny army of three hundred men defeated the mighty army of the Midianites (Judg 7). David, a mere shepherd boy and the youngest son of Jesse, defeated the giant Goliath and eventually became Israel's greatest king (1 Sam 16 – 17), the model and prototype of the coming Messiah (2 Sam 7). As Paul would later tell the Corinthian church:

> God chose the foolish things of the world to shame the wise; God chose the weak things of the world to shame the strong. God chose the lowly things of this world and the despised things — and the things that are not — to nullify the things that are. (1 Cor 1:27 – 28)

From small beginnings God accomplishes great things. When Jesus left this earth, he had little more than a hundred followers. Yet that mustard seed of a movement swept across the Mediterranean region and throughout the world, transforming the lives of millions and changing the course of human history.

CHAPTER 17

Mark 4:35 – 41

Literary Context

Having illustrated Jesus' teaching in parables, Mark returns to the theme of his messianic authority. In an earlier series of episodes, Jesus demonstrated extraordinary authority in teaching, healing, exorcisms, and forgiving sins (1:21 – 3:6), with growing opposition from the religious leaders (2:1 – 3:6). Mark now returns to this theme of messianic authority with four more miracles. These go beyond the earlier ones as Jesus demonstrates his authority over the forces of nature (4:35 – 41), massive demonic oppression (5:1 – 20), long-term chronic disease (5:25 – 34), and even death itself (5:21 – 24, 35 – 43).

Main Idea

By calming the storm, Jesus demonstrates his divine authority over the forces of nature, calls the disciples to greater faith in him, and provokes their awe as they wonder in amazement, "Who, then, is this, that the wind and the sea obey him!" (v. 41).

Translation

Mark 4:35 – 41

35	Setting (temporal)	When evening had come on that day,
		he said to them,
	command	*"Let's go to the other side of the sea."*
36		Leaving the crowd,
	Action	**they took him along in the boat, just as he was,**
	setting	and **some other boats were with him.**
37	Crisis	Then **a great windstorm came up,**
	circumstances	and **waves were breaking over the boat,**
	result	so that the boat was about to be swamped.
38	Setting (social)	But **he was in the stern,**
		sleeping on the cushion!
	Action	**They awoke him and said to him,**
	entreaty	*"Teacher, don't you care that we're perishing?"*
39	Action	**Getting up, he rebuked the wind**
		and **said to the sea,**
	command	*"Silence! Be still!"*
	Result/nature miracle	And **the wind stopped and it became completely calm.**
40	Response	**He said to them,**
	rhetorical question/rebuke	*"Why are you so afraid? Do you not yet have faith?"*
41	Response	**They were terrified and were saying to one another,**
	response/exclamation	*"Who, then, is this, that the wind and the sea obey him!"*

Structure

This is the first of Jesus' "nature miracles" in Mark, a type of miracle distinguished from healings, exorcisms, and raising the dead, where Jesus demonstrates authority over the forces of the natural world. Other nature miracles in Mark include multiplying loaves and fishes (6:30 – 44; 8:1 – 13), walking on water (6:45 – 52), and withering a fig tree with a command (11:12 – 14, 20 – 21). In John's gospel, Jesus turns water to wine (2:1 – 12). This is also the first of three boat scenes in Mark (4:35 – 41; 6:45 – 52; 8:14 – 21), each of which in some way illustrates the disciples' lack of faith or failure to comprehend Jesus' mission or identity. Mark is fond of triads, frequently arranging material in patterns of three (see Introduction to Mark: Literary Features).

This episode has some interesting parallels with the OT story of Jonah. Like Jesus, Jonah is sleeping through a storm at sea (Jonah 1:5). Jonah is awakened by sailors in fear for their lives (1:6), and after he is thrown into the sea, it immediately grows calm (1:15); this provokes fear and awe among the observers (1:16).[1] Of course, there are also many differences, since it is Jonah's disobedience that causes the storm, and God's discipline against Jonah stills it. While the captain tells Jonah to pray to his god, Jesus himself commands the wind and the waves; and the sailors' fear and awe are directed toward Jonah's god, not toward Jonah himself. If the parallels are intentional on Mark's part, they serve to confirm that "something greater than Jonah is here" (Matt 12:41; Luke 11:32).

Exegetical Outline

➡ **1. The Setting (4:35 – 36)**
   2. The Storm on the Lake (4:37 – 38)
   3. The Miracle (4:39)
   4. The Response (4:40 – 41)
     a. Jesus' rebuke (4:40)
     b. The disciples' awe (4:41)

Explanation of the Text

4:35 When evening had come on that day, he said to them, "Let's go to the other side of the sea." (Καὶ λέγει αὐτοῖς ἐν ἐκείνῃ τῇ ἡμέρᾳ ὀψίας γενομένης· διέλθωμεν εἰς τὸ πέραν). Mark's reference to evening "on that day" (ἐν ἐκείνῃ τῇ ἡμέρᾳ) indicates that the boat episode occurs at the end of a day of teaching in parables (4:1 – 34). While such temporal transitions may simply be part of Mark's narrative style rather than marking a strict chronology, there is no reason to doubt the historicity of this remark. Such details were likely part of the tradition Mark received.

Of course, as noted in the previous episode, we need not insist that *all* of the teaching in chapter 4 took place on any single occasion. Mark's more topical organization elsewhere, together with the changes in audience implied in 4:1, 10, 26, 33 – 34 (see comments there), indicates that the author felt free to organize material thematically as well as chronologically.

The "them" refers to Jesus' disciples, for whom he has been interpreting the miracles (4:34). "He said" (λέγει) is a historical present tense, a common feature throughout Mark's gospel (150x), where a past episode is described with a present tense verb (see Introduction to Mark: Literary Features). While characteristic of less refined Greek, it gives the narrative a sense of vivid realism. The beginning of the story mixes present and imperfect tenses, reading something like, "he *says* to them … they *are taking* him … some other boats *were* with them … a great storm *is coming up* … the waves *were breaking* … the boat *is already being filled* … he *was sleeping* … they *are waking him and are saying*…." Though a grammatical monstrosity in English, this works well in Greek and provides the story with a dramatic, on-the-spot style.

"Let's go" is a hortatory subjunctive, functioning here as a command.[2] "The other side" (τὸ πέραν) of the lake refers to the southeastern shore (see 5:1), a

---

1. For parallel vocabulary, see Boring, *Mark*, 143.

2. Wallace, *Greek Grammar*, 464.

predominantly Gentile region. No reason is stated for the journey, though in light of Mark's narrative comments concerning Jesus' intense popularity (3:7 – 12, 20 – 21; 4:1), Jesus may have been seeking a time of respite from the crush of the crowds.

4:36 Leaving the crowd, they took him along in the boat, just as he was, and some other boats were with him (καὶ ἀφέντες τὸν ὄχλον παραλαμβάνουσιν αὐτὸν ὡς ἦν ἐν τῷ πλοίῳ, καὶ ἄλλα πλοῖα ἦν μετ' αὐτοῦ). The boat (τὸ πλοῖον) is likely the boat that Jesus asked to have ready in 3:9 and from which he taught in 4:1. No indication is given here of the size of the boat, but the discovery in 1986 of a remarkably well-preserved first-century fishing boat near Kibbutz Ginosar provides a likely model. The boat measured 8.2 meters (27 feet) long, 2.3 meters (7.5 feet) wide, was made of cedar planks and an oak frame, and could hold about fifteen people.[3] Jesus and the Twelve could have fit in such a boat.

The meaning of the phrase "just as he was" (αὐτὸν ὡς ἦν) is uncertain, but it probably means that Jesus embarked without going back to shore[4] (cf. HCSB: "since He was already in the boat"; REB: "in the boat in which he had been sitting"). They shoved off directly from his teaching platform. The "other boats" that accompanied them probably contained other followers of Jesus, part of the larger group mentioned in 4:10. These boats are not mentioned again and play no role in the story. This and other incidental details (e.g., the cushion on which Jesus is sleeping) may indicate a historical recollection, perhaps drawn from Peter's eyewitness testimony.[5] Attempts to explain what

happened to these boats in the storm (returned to shore? destroyed? arrived with Jesus in Gerasa?) are pure speculation and of no concern to Mark.

4:37 Then a great windstorm came up, and waves were breaking over the boat, so that the boat was about to be swamped (καὶ γίνεται λαῖλαψ μεγάλη ἀνέμου καὶ τὰ κύματα ἐπέβαλλεν εἰς τὸ πλοῖον, ὥστε ἤδη γεμίζεσθαι τὸ πλοῖον). The geography of the Sea of Galilee, located as it is in the Jordan Rift with steep hills on all sides, makes it susceptible to sudden storms. Cooler air from the hills can rush down and collide with warm air in the lake's basin, creating sudden squalls.[6] Mark's (lit.) "great windstorm of wind" (λαῖλαψ μεγάλη ἀνέμου) could refer simply to a violent wind, but in context it suggests a full-blown storm. The description of waves crashing over the boat threatening to swamp it is typical of Mark's vivid narrative style. In a culture where swimming was not a recreational activity, sinking in rough seas in the middle of the lake would likely result in loss of life (cf. Matt 14:30).

4:38 But he was in the stern, sleeping on the cushion! They awoke him and said to him, "Teacher, don't you care that we're perishing?" (καὶ αὐτὸς ἦν ἐν τῇ πρύμνῃ ἐπὶ τὸ προσκεφάλαιον καθεύδων. καὶ ἐγείρουσιν αὐτὸν καὶ λέγουσιν αὐτῷ· διδάσκαλε, οὐ μέλει σοι ὅτι ἀπολλύμεθα;). Jesus' sleep during the storm recalls Jonah 1:5, but for Jonah the implication is that he is oblivious to the needs of those around him. Why was Jesus asleep? Restful sleep despite danger can indicate trust in God (Pss 3:5; 4:8; Prov 3:24), and this idea is likely present here.[7] But equally significant is that Jesus is exhausted after a long day of ministry. Although,

3. See Shelley Wachsmann, "The Galilee Boat: 2,000-Year-Old Hull Recovered Intact," *BAR* 14/5 (1988): 18 – 33; idem, *The Sea of Galilee Boat* (Ed Rachal Foundation Nautical Archaeology Series; College Station, TX: Texas A&M University Press, 2009).

4. Hooker, *Mark*, 139.

5. Taylor, *Mark*, 271; Cranfield, *Mark*, 172; Lane, *Mark*, 175.

6. G. A. Smith, *The Historical Geography of the Holy Land* (New York: Armstrong and Son, 1909), 441 – 42.

7. Marcus, *Mark 1 – 8*, 334; D. E. Nineham, *The Gospel of St Mark* (Pelican New Testament Commentaries; Harmondsworth, UK/New York: Penguin, 1963), 146.

for Mark, Jesus is the mighty and authoritative Son of God, he is also fully human, with the limitations and weaknesses characteristic of human nature.

The disciples address Jesus as "Teacher" (διδάσκαλε), probably a translation for the Hebrew "Rabbi" (9:5; 11:21; 14:45) or Aramaic "Rabboni" (10:51). Matthew's parallel has "Lord" (κύριε), and Luke has "Master, Master" (ἐπιστάτα, ἐπιστάτα). In Mark's narrative, the address represents a more striking contrast, as the Jewish rabbi is about to be revealed as Lord of the wind and the waves.

The rhetorical question of the disciples, "Don't you care that we are perishing?" (οὐ μέλει σοι ὅτι ἀπολλύμεθα;), is certainly a cry for help, but also carries an accusatory tone. Can't the one who heals the sick and casts out demons save his own disciples? Stein claims this interpretation is unlikely, since Mark's post-Easter church would not have envisioned the disciples rebuking Jesus.[8] But this misses the fact that the disciples are here failing, revealing a lack of faith (v. 40) and an inability to fully comprehend Jesus' identity (v. 41). In the episodes that follow, the disciples will repeatedly demonstrate pride, ignorance, and a lack of understanding (4:40; 6:52; 7:18; 8:17 – 18; 9:5 – 6, 19, 32). In 8:32, after the first passion prediction, Peter will (again) rebuke Jesus. As elsewhere in Mark's gospel, the disciples function here as foils for Jesus' spiritual insight and trust in God.

4:39 Getting up, he rebuked the wind and said to the sea, "Silence! Be still!" And the wind stopped and it became completely calm (καὶ διεγερθεὶς ἐπετίμησεν τῷ ἀνέμῳ καὶ εἶπεν τῇ θαλάσσῃ· σιώπα, πεφίμωσο. καὶ ἐκόπασεν ὁ ἄνεμος καὶ ἐγένετο γαλήνη μεγάλη). Demonstrating his divine authority over nature, Jesus rebukes the wind and silences the sea. The OT describes God as the Lord of creation, who speaks and the seas obey. Psalm 104:7

reads, "at your rebuke the waters fled, at the sound of your thunder they took to flight" (cf. Pss 18:15; 106:9; Isa 50:2; Nah 1:4). At his command, they are silenced: "You rule over the surging sea; when its waves mount up, you still them" (Ps 89:9: cf. Ps 65:5 – 7). Psalm 107:23 – 29 sounds almost like a poetic paraphrase of the present episode:

> Some went out on the sea in ships;
>   they were merchants on the mighty waters....
> They reeled and staggered like drunkards;
>   they were at their wits' end.
> Then they cried out to the LORD in their trouble,
>   and he brought them out of their distress.
> He stilled the storm to a whisper;
>   the waves of the sea were hushed.

Only God commands the wind and the waves (see Theology in Application, below). Yet Jesus speaks and nature obeys. At his command the "great" (μεγάλη) storm (v. 37) is replaced by a "great" (μεγάλη) calm (v. 39).

Various commentators have noted that Jesus' language of rebuking (ἐπιτιμάω) and silencing (φιμόω) the storm parallels the exorcism language of 1:25 (cf. 3:12; 9:25) and have argued that the sea is here portrayed as a demonic force in opposition to God.[9] This would fit with ancient Near Eastern mythology, where the sea was often a symbol of chaos and evil. However, the language of rebuke is not exclusive to exorcisms and appears in a variety of contexts in Mark's gospel (8:30 – 33; 10:13, 48). So also Jesus' commands to silence extend beyond demons (1:44; 5:43; 7:36; 8:30; 9:9). A more likely background is found in the OT texts cited above, where God's sovereignty over nature is described in anthropomorphic terms, as he "stills" the sea with a "rebuke" (Pss 89:9; 104:4; etc.). Creation is the servant responding immediately to its master's command.

---

8. Stein, *Mark*, 243; cf. Gundry, *Mark*, 239.
9. Hooker, *Mark*, 139; Marcus, *Mark 1 – 8*, 333, 339; Bor-ing, *Mark*, 146 – 47; Lamar Williamson, *Mark* (Interpretation; Atlanta: John Knox, 1983), 101 – 2; Collins, *Mark*, 261.

4:40 He said to them, "Why are you so afraid? Do you not yet have faith?" (καὶ εἶπεν αὐτοῖς· τί δειλοί ἐστε; οὔπω ἔχετε πίστιν;). Having rebuked the sea, Jesus now rebukes the disciples. Two rhetorical questions are asked, one about their fear (or cowardice; δειλοί) and one about their lack of faith. The two go hand in hand. Followers of Jesus need boldness in the face of life's challenges and trust in God's ability to bring them through. This is the beginning of a series of failures of the disciples that will continue throughout the gospel (6:52; 7:18; 8:17 – 18, 32; 9:5 – 6, 19, 33 – 37; 10:35 – 45), climaxing in the events surrounding Jesus' arrest and trial (14:37, 50, 60 – 72). There is a clear narrative tension introduced here. The disciples have just been presented as the "insiders," the recipients of the secrets of the kingdom of God (4:11). Yet they will repeatedly waiver and fail. Mark's gospel is not a call to emulate the disciples, but to follow Jesus and to align one's life with God's kingdom purposes.

4:41 They were terrified and were saying to one another, "Who, then, is this, that the wind and the sea obey him!" (καὶ ἐφοβήθησαν φόβον μέγαν καὶ ἔλεγον πρὸς ἀλλήλους· τίς ἄρα οὗτός ἐστιν ὅτι καὶ ὁ ἄνεμος καὶ ἡ θάλασσα ὑπακούει αὐτῷ;). The verb "to fear" (φοβέομαι) followed by a cognate accusative, "fear" (φόβον), provides emphasis: "They feared a great fear," or, in real English, "They were terrified." Their fear of the storm — rebuked by Jesus because of their cowardice and lack of faith — now becomes a healthy fear of the Divine, as they experience the awesome power of God. The answer to their question, "Who is this?" is already known to the reader (1:1, 11), but it will only gradually unfold throughout the gospel until it climaxes with the centurion's cry at the foot of the cross, "Truly this man was the Son of God."

Theology in Application

Two important theological themes are present in this episode, the first related to the identity of Jesus, the second to the faith of the disciples. The former, however, is the more important. Mark's purpose is first and foremost christological, demonstrating Jesus' extraordinary authority over the forces of nature.

Jesus, Lord of the Wind and the Waves

The central theme of Mark's gospel up to this point has been Jesus' authority as Messiah and Son of God. This episode takes this theme to a new level as Jesus effectively commands the forces of nature. The climactic question of the disciples, "Who is this...?" will be repeated in various forms in the narrative that follows. The people wonder about Jesus' identity, whether he is John the Baptist, Elijah, or one of the prophets (6:14 – 15). Herod too wonders whether Jesus might be John back from the dead (6:16). Jesus then raises the question of his identity with his own disciples (8:27 – 30): "Who do people say that I am?" They respond with the same answers given in 6:14 – 15, to which he responds, "But what about *you*?... Who do *you* say I am?" Peter answers by affirming that "You are the Messiah."

While in Matthew's gospel Peter's knowledge comes through divine revelation from the Father (Matt 16:17), Mark's narrative implies that it is through the miracles that Jesus has been performing: healing the sick, casting out demons, commanding nature, and raising the dead. The present narrative is therefore part of the larger picture that Jesus has divine authority to announce and inaugurate the kingdom of God — the restoration of God's reign over his fallen creation.

In our exegesis above, we have noted OT parallels to this passage. In OT theology, the fallenness of creation is symbolized by the powerful forces of the sea, the primeval "deep" characterized by chaos. The promise of restoration is found in the reminder that God has never relinquished his sovereign lordship over these forces. He created the ocean depths; he speaks and the surging waves are stilled; he commands the monsters of the deep. Leviathan, the great Canaanite serpent of chaos, is a mere pawn in God's hands. He puts a fishhook in its mouth and it does his will (Job 41:1 – 34; cf. Pss 74:13 – 17; 104:26; Isa 27:1). In his wisdom, he cuts Rahab to pieces (Job 26:12; cf. Isa 51:9). Psalm 89:9 – 11 brings these themes together:

> You rule over the surging sea;
>> when its waves mount up, you still them.
> You crushed Rahab like one of the slain;
>> with your strong arm you scattered your enemies.
> The heavens are yours, and yours also the earth;
>> you founded the world and all that is in it.

By stilling the storm, Jesus declares his lordship over heaven and earth.

Paul picks up the theme of the coming restoration of creation in Rom 8. Though creation was subjected to frustration through the fall, it is now longing for its liberation from bondage to decay, to be brought into the freedom and glory of the children of God (8:20 – 21). This glorious restoration is possible because God "did not spare his own Son, but gave him up for us all" (8:32). The ransom payment for sin that the Markan Jesus is soon to achieve (Mark 10:45) will bring about the establishment of the kingdom and the restoration of fallen creation. Jesus' lordship over the wind and the waves is a preview of that restoration.

The Need for Faith in the Face of Life's Storms

Beside this christological theme is a secondary one concerning the response of the disciples and their failure to trust in Jesus through the storm. As early as Tertullian (c. AD 160 – 220), the boat in our story has been seen to symbolize the church facing the storms of persecution,[10] a view developed more recently by Ernst Best.[11] While it is unlikely that Mark understood the episode in so allegorical a manner, throughout his gospel the disciples are models (primarily negative ones) for discipleship. When Jesus says, "Do you not yet have faith?" he is referring back to the

---

10. Tertullian, *Bapt.* 12; Clement of Alexandria, *Quis div.* 34.3; Boring, *Mark*, 145.

11. Ernst Best, "The Church as Ship," in idem, *Following Jesus*, 230 – 34.

healings and exorcisms that they have already seen. If they have already witnessed the inbreaking of the kingdom of God, should they not have trusted him in the midst of the present storm?

As noted earlier, this is the beginning of a pattern of failure that will run throughout the second half of Mark's gospel, where Jesus alone functions as the faithful model of discipleship. The disciples fail repeatedly through a combination of pride (8:32; 9:33 – 34; 10:13, 35 – 45), lack of faith (9:19), and an inability to comprehend the work of God (6:52; 7:18; 8:17 – 18, 32; 9:5 – 6). These three go hand in hand. Success in the Christian life comes from a humble heart of service, faith in God's power to sustain us through trials, and sensitivity to God's purpose in the world. Instead of pursuing one's own ambitions, believers are called to "seek first the kingdom of God" (Matt 6:33), and they will receive all they need to prosper spiritually.

The NT epistles teach these same fundamental truths. Paul says that he can delight in weaknesses, insults, hardships, and persecution, because when he is weak — and fully dependent on God — that is when he is strong (2 Cor 12:10). He has learned how to be content in any and every circumstance, because he can do all things through the one who strengthens him (Phil 4:12 – 14). Trials are opportunities *for growth* because suffering produces perseverance, which produces character, which produces hope — and hope in Christ never fails (Rom 5:3 – 5). James encourages believers to be joyful in various trials because the testing of our faith produces perseverance, and perseverance produces Christian maturity (Jas 1:2 – 4). Peter says that such trials come so that "the proven genuineness of your faith — of greater worth than gold, which perishes even though refined by fire — may result in praise, glory and honor when Jesus Christ is revealed" (1 Pet 1:7). We need to look at life's storms not as disasters, but as opportunities to see God's transforming power at work in our lives.

18

Mark 5:1 – 20

Literary Context

The healing of the Gerasene demoniac represents the second in a series of four powerful miracles demonstrating Jesus' messianic authority — including authority over nature (4:35 – 41), demons (5:1 – 20), chronic disease (5:25 – 34), and death (5:21 – 24, 35 – 43). Earlier exorcisms confirmed the authority of the kingdom of God over individual agents of Satan's realm (1:21 – 28, 34; 3:10 – 12, 23 – 27). This one goes even further, as Jesus confronts and easily overcomes a "Legion" of demons in a hostile environment.

The episode is linked to the previous one as the disciples now arrive on the eastern shore of the Sea of Galilee on the boat that passed through the storm (4:35 – 41). The chronology is difficult, since the storm happened at night and yet they (apparently) arrive at Gerasa during the day, after a journey that should have taken only a few hours. Perhaps Mark envisions the storm to have occurred late in the night with an early morning arrival.

II. The Authority of the Messiah (1:14 – 8:21)

  B. The Disciple-Family of the Messiah and Those "Outside" (3:7 – 6:6a)

    3. Jesus' True Family and the Beelzebul Controversy (3:20 – 35)

    4. Parables about the Kingdom of God (4:1 – 34)

    5. Jesus' Authority over Natural and Supernatural Powers (4:35 – 5:43)

      a. Authority over Nature: Calming the Storm (4:35 – 41)

→   **b. Authority over Demons: The Gerasene Demoniac (5:1 – 20)**

      c. Authority over Disease and Death (5:21 – 43)

Main Idea

By casting out multiple demons from the Gerasene demoniac, Jesus demonstrates his authority over Satan's forces of darkness. The episode concludes with two very different responses to the miracle: fear and rejection by the townspeople, but gratitude and a desire to be Jesus' disciple from the man who was healed.

Translation

Mark 5:1 – 20

1a	Setting (spatial)	So **they came to the other side of the sea,**
b		to the region of the Gerasenes.
2a	setting (spatial)	When he got out of the boat,
b	Character entrance/Crisis	**immediately a man with a defiling spirit came out of the tombs and met him.**
3a	Character description	**He lived among the tombs**
b	Character description	and **no one could restrain him anymore, not even with a chain,**
4a		because he had often been bound with chains and shackles,
b		but he tore apart the chains and broke the shackles.
c	Character description	**No one was strong enough to subdue him.**
5a		Night and day among the tombs and in the hills
b	Character description	**he was constantly crying out and cutting himself with stones.**
6		When he saw Jesus at a distance,
7a	Action	**he ran and fell on his face before him,**
b	Entreaty	shrieking loudly,
c		*"What do you want with me, Jesus, Son of the Most High God?*
d		*I swear to you by God, don't torment me!"*
8a	Command/Flashback	For **Jesus had already said to him,**
b		*"Come out of this man, you defiling spirit."*
9a	Question	**Then Jesus asked him,**
b		*"What is your name?"*
c	Response	**He replied,**
d		*"My name is Legion, for we are many."*
10	Entreaty	And **he repeatedly begged Jesus not to send them out of the region.**
11	Setting	**A large herd of pigs was feeding on the hillside nearby.**
12a	Entreaty	And **they begged him,** saying,
b		*"Send us into the pigs, so that we can enter them."*
13a	Response/Exorcism	**Jesus permitted them,**
b	Action	and **the defiling spirits came out and entered the pigs,**
c	Action	and **the herd rushed down the steep bank into the sea**—about ♫ two thousand of them—
d	Action	and **they drowned in the sea.**
14a	Action/Response to 13	**Those tending them fled and reported this in the town and the countryside,**
b	Character entrance	and **the people came to see what had happened**.
15a	Response	**They came to Jesus and saw the demonized man sitting there,**
b		clothed and
c		in his right mind (the one who had the "Legion"!),
d	Response	and **they were afraid.**

Continued on next page.

Continued from previous page.

16	Report	Those who had seen what happened to the demonized man and to the pigs ✍ reported it to the people,
17	Response	*and* they began to beg him to leave their region.
18a	Character departure	*While Jesus was getting in the boat,*
b	Entreaty	the man who had been demonized began begging Jesus to let him go with him.
19a	Response to 18b	He would not let him, *but instead* said to him,
b		*"Go home to your people and tell them* *what the Lord has done for you and*
c		*how he has shown you mercy."*
20a	Response to 19	So he left and began to proclaim in the Decapolis what Jesus had done for him,
b		*and* everyone was amazed.

Structure

The episode has features typical of other exorcisms (cf. 1:23 – 24, 34; 3:11 – 12): a challenge to Jesus by a demon-possessed man (v. 2; cf. 1:23; 3:11), recognition of Jesus' identity by the demon (v. 7; cf. 1:24, 34; 3:11), a command to the demon to come out (v. 8; cf. 1:25, 34), and an amazed reaction by others (v. 20; cf. 1:27). The episode is unique, however, in the level of detail given to the description of the man's condition (vv. 3 – 5) and in the riposte that takes place between Jesus and the demon (vv. 6 – 13). While Jesus stays in complete control of the situation, he is willing to negotiate with the demons concerning their fate. It is an ironic negotiation, however, since the request Jesus grants leads to their destruction. The episode is also unique in that the healed man is not commanded to silence (1:25, 34; 3:11 – 12), but is rather told to tell others what God has done for him (v. 19). The reason is likely that the location is in Gentile territory, where the messianic secret is unnecessary (see comments on v. 19).

Exegetical Outline

➡ **1. The Setting (5:1 – 5)**

    a. Arrival in Gerasa (5:1)

    b. Encounter with the demoniac (5:2)

    c. Description of the man's condition (5:3 – 5)

2. The Confrontation and Exorcism (5:6 – 13)

    a. The demon's challenge (5:6 – 8)

    b. Jesus' question (5:9a-b)

    c. The demon's response and request (5:9c – 12)

    d. Jesus' response and the destruction of the pigs (5:13)

3. The Response of the Townspeople (5:14 – 17)

    a. The herders' report (5:14)

    b. The people witness the scene (5:15 – 16)

    c. The people beg Jesus to leave (5:17)

4. The Response of the Man Healed (5:18 – 20)

    a. The man's desire to go with Jesus (5:18)

    b. Jesus' response (5:19)

    c. The man's testimony and the amazement of the people (5:20)

Explanation of the Text

5:1 So they came to the other side of the sea, to the region of the Gerasenes (Καὶ ἦλθον εἰς τὸ πέραν τῆς θαλάσσης εἰς τὴν χώραν τῶν Γερασηνῶν). This statement connects the present narrative to the previous one about the storm at sea. The "other side" (τὸ πέραν) is the southeastern shore, in the region of the Decapolis (see comments on v. 20), a predominantly Gentile region. The presence of pigs confirms the Gentile nature of this place. Mark may be hinting in this episode that the gospel will eventually go to the Gentiles.

The name of the place is disputed. While the earliest manuscripts speak of the region "of the Gerasenes" (Γερασηνῶν), others read "of the Gadarenes" (Γαδαρηνῶν), and still others "of the Gergesenes" (Γεργεσηνῶν).[1] The problem evidently arose because Gerasa (modern Jerash) is located thirty-five miles southeast of the lake, too far away for this episode. Gadara, the most likely reading in Matthew's parallel (8:28), was another city in the Decapolis, located about five miles southeast the lake. This also seems too distant for the pig herders to have returned quickly with the townspeople (v. 14). The third reading, Gergesa (the preferred reading in Luke 8:26, 37), is an otherwise unknown

place, but was identified as the location by the third-century church father Origen (c. 185 – 254).[2] It may perhaps be identified with Khursi, or Kersa, a location with steep banks on the eastern side of the lake.

While this last one makes the most sense geographically, it has the weakest textual evidence. A decision is difficult here. If copyists were aware of the geographical problems with Gerasa, they may have tried to find a closer location, opting for either Gadara or Gergesa. Conversely, the original may have had Gergesa, and copyists unaware of this location substituted the more well-known places Gerasa or Gadara. In light of the strong external evidence, the former seems most likely. If so, the geographical problem may be mitigated by putting the emphasis on the word "region" (χώρα) of Gerasa, meaning the general territory of the Decapolis on the eastern side of the lake.

5:2 When he got out of the boat, immediately a man with a defiling spirit came out of the tombs and met him (καὶ ἐξελθόντος αὐτοῦ ἐκ τοῦ πλοίου εὐθὺς ὑπήντησεν αὐτῷ ἐκ τῶν μνημείων ἄνθρωπος ἐν πνεύματι ἀκαθάρτῳ). As Jesus disembarks,[3] he

---

1. (1) Γερασηνῶν: ℵ B D it cop[sa] 2427[vid]; (2) Γαδαρηνῶν: A C K *f*[13] 𝔐 syr[p.h]; (3) Γεργεσηνῶν: L Δ Θ *f*[1] 28 33 565 579 700 892 1241 1424 2542 *al* syr[s] boh.

2. Origen, *Comm. Jo.* 27; cited in T. C. Oden and C. A. Hall,

eds., *Mark* (ACCS 2; Downers Grove, IL: InterVarsity Press, 1998), 67.

3. ἐξελθόντος αὐτοῦ is a genitive absolute, used when the participial phrase has a different subject than the main clause.

is confronted by a demon-possessed man.[4] For Mark's interchangeable use of "demon" (δαιμόνιον) and "defiling spirit," see comments on 1:23. While "immediately" (εὐθύς) is often a general connective in Mark without a sense of immediacy, here it apparently means "just then" (see comments on 1:10).

The man is said to have a "defiling" or "impure" (ἀκάθαρτος) spirit. Traditionally translated "unclean," the term has nothing to do with hygiene or cleanliness but rather ceremonial defilement (see comments on 1:23). In the OT, things that were ceremonially impure could not enter the tabernacle/ temple or stand in God's presence. We have translated with the active term "defiling," rather than the passive "defiled," because the primary point seems to be not that demons were impure (though that is true), but that the demonic presence renders a *person* ceremonially defiled and so unable to relate properly to God. The present account is full of terms of ceremonial defilement.

Tombs are unclean because touching a corpse rendered a person ceremonially defiled (Num 19:11, 16). Pigs are unclean animals according to the OT law (Lev 11:1–8; Deut 14:8). Isaiah 65:4 describes apostate Israel as a people "who sit among the graves and spend their nights keeping secret vigil; who eat the flesh of pigs, and whose pots hold broth of impure meat." The theme of impurity will carry over into the next episode, where Jesus will encounter a woman with a menstrual disorder and the body of a girl who has died. In each case, Jesus is not rendered impure by such contact, but rather he turns defilement into purity and wholeness.

5:3–4 He lived among the tombs and no one could restrain him anymore, not even with a chain, because he had often been bound with **chains and shackles, but he tore apart the chains and broke the shackles. No one was strong enough to subdue him** (ὃς τὴν κατοίκησιν εἶχεν ἐν τοῖς μνήμασιν, καὶ οὐδὲ ἁλύσει οὐκέτι οὐδεὶς ἐδύνατο αὐτὸν δῆσαι διὰ τὸ αὐτὸν πολλάκις πέδαις καὶ ἁλύσεσιν δεδέσθαι καὶ διεσπάσθαι ὑπ᾽ αὐτοῦ τὰς ἁλύσεις καὶ τὰς πέδας συντετρῖφθαι, καὶ οὐδεὶς ἴσχυεν αὐτὸν δαμάσαι). The phrase "among the tombs" could mean either "in" or "among." Since caves were often used for tombs, the former is certainly possible. In rabbinic literature, demons are sometimes said to inhabit tombs (*b. Sanh.* 65b).[5]

Mark's detailed description of the attempts to subdue the man is typical of his dramatic and colorful style. Compare Matt 8:28, which mentions only that the (two) demoniacs were so fierce that no one could pass that way. The word "shackles" (πέδαι) is related to the word "foot" (πούς) and probably refers to leg irons. "Chains" (ἁλύσεις) is a more general term for chain restraints, though they may perhaps be handcuffs (cf. Acts 28:20). The detailed description emphasizes the hopelessness of the man's situation. He is beyond human help and so in need of divine intervention. Similarly, Mark's comment that "no one was strong enough to subdue him" magnifies Jesus' incomparable power to deliver.

5:5 Night and day among the tombs and in the hills he was constantly crying out and cutting himself with stones (καὶ διὰ παντὸς νυκτὸς καὶ ἡμέρας ἐν τοῖς μνήμασιν καὶ ἐν τοῖς ὄρεσιν ἦν κράζων καὶ κατακόπτων ἑαυτὸν λίθοις). If the previous statement described the violent danger that the demons posed to others, this one points to the man's own desperate and pitiable condition. The term "hills" (τά ὄρη) can mean any raised eleva-

---

4. Matt 8:28 mentions two men (cf. 20:30, where Matthew refers to two blind men, while Mark 10:46 mentions only one, Bartimaeus).

5. The Talmud describes characteristics of the demon-possessed as going out alone at night, sleeping in a graveyard, ripping their clothes, and losing what is given to them (*y. Ter.* 1:1 [40b]; cited in M. Eugene Boring, Klaus Berger, and Carsten Colpe, eds., *Hellenistic Commentary on the New Testament* [Nashville: Abingdon, 1995], 72; cf. Str-B 1:491).

tion (hills, foothills, mountains); here it likely refers to the "hills" (NIV, NLT) or "hillsides" (REB) around the lake and its villages rather than "in the mountains" (HCSB, ESV). Self-destructive behavior is often associated with demonic oppression (cf. 9:22, 26).

5:6 – 7 When he saw Jesus at a distance, he ran and fell on his face before him, shrieking loudly, "What do you want with me, Jesus, Son of the Most High God? I swear to you by God, don't torment me!" (καὶ ἰδὼν τὸν Ἰησοῦν ἀπὸ μακρόθεν ἔδραμεν καὶ προσεκύνησεν αὐτῷ καὶ κράξας φωνῇ μεγάλῃ λέγει· τί ἐμοὶ καὶ σοί, Ἰησοῦ υἱὲ τοῦ θεοῦ τοῦ ὑψίστου; ὁρκίζω σε τὸν θεόν, μή με βασανίσῃς). Is the man's approach to Jesus an attack or a cry for help? That is, is the demon fully in control and its purpose is to drive Jesus away, or does the man have enough willpower and presence of mind to seek help from the one place he could still find it? The fact that the man "fell prostrate" (προσεκύνησεν) might suggest the latter, but since the words that follow clearly come from the demon, the former seems more likely.[6]

The verb used here (προσκυνέω) does not always mean "worship" (contra KJV, NKJV) but can also mean "bow down, do obeisance to, fall prostrate before."[7] Since Jesus demonstrates complete mastery over the demons throughout this scene, the sense here seems to be "fell on his face." Though rushing out to challenge Jesus, the demoniac instead collapses in a heap of submission before him.

See comments on 1:24 for the Hebrew rhetorical question, "What to me and to you?" (τί ἐμοὶ καὶ σοί). Here the idiom means something like, "Why

are you interfering with me?" (NLT) or "Stay out of my affairs!" As elsewhere in Mark's gospel, the demon recognizes Jesus' identity (1:24, 34; 3:11, 12), here calling him "Son of the Most High God."[8] Some commentators relate this to the exorcist's trick of gaining mastery over a spiritual entity by learning its secret names. But there is little evidence for this here or in contemporary sources.[9] More likely, it is part of Mark's revelation of Jesus' messianic identity. Although human characters in the narrative struggle to comprehend who Jesus is (4:41), the reader knows through God's own testimony (1:11; 9:7) and the terrified response of demons (1:24, 34; 3:11). Undeniable proof that Jesus is the Son of God and inaugurator of the kingdom of God comes from those whose evil empire is under assault.

Strangely, in appealing to Jesus not to torment him, the demon swears "by God" (ὁρκίζω σε τὸν θεόν). Similar formulas are sometimes used by exorcists against demons, but the reverse is strange indeed.[10] Twelftree suggests this is a vain attempt to bind Jesus or put a curse on him.[11] But this does not explain why the demon would appeal *to God*, his adversary. Surely God would side with Jesus! More likely, Mark presupposes the eschatological interpretation of Matthew's parallel (8:29), where the demons call on Jesus not to torment them "before the time" (πρὸ καιροῦ), that is, before the eschatological judgment. The demon knows its ultimate fate, which God has decreed. In the face of *immediate* expulsion by Jesus, it seeks to delay by appealing to God's decree of *future* judgment. The demon accuses Jesus of jumping the gun. This

---

6. It is possible, of course, that both are involved and that the scene displays a conflict raging within the man.

7. BDAG, 882.

8. Various commentators have noted that the title "Most High God" (τοῦ θεοῦ τοῦ ὑψίστου) commonly occurs in the OT in Gentile contexts (Gen 14:18 – 20; Num 24:16; Isa 14:14; Dan 3:26, 42), making it particularly relevant here as Jesus en

ters Gentile territory (so Lane, *Mark*, 279; Hooker, *Mark*, 143; Hurtado, *Mark*, 82, etc.)

9. For references, see comments on 1:24; 3:11; cf. Guelich, *Mark 1:1 – 8:26*, 279.

10. H. C. Kee, "The Terminology of Mark's Exorcism Stories," *NTS* 14 (1967 – 1968): 232 – 46, 246.

11. G. H. Twelftree, "Demon, Devil, Satan," in *DJG*, 166.

would also explain why Jesus seems willing to negotiate the demon's fate (5:10 – 14).

5:8 For Jesus had already said to him, "Come out of this man, you defiling spirit." (ἔλεγεν γὰρ αὐτῷ· ἔξελθε τὸ πνεῦμα τὸ ἀκάθαρτον ἐκ τοῦ ἀνθρώπου). Mark now explains the reason for the demon's panic. Jesus had already commanded it to come out of the man. The imperfect "he was saying" (ἔλεγεν) is functioning in a pluperfective sense, "to indicate a time prior to the action occurring in the narrative."[12] This is a brief parenthetic flashback.[13]

5:9 Then Jesus asked him, "What is your name?" He replied, "My name is Legion, for we are many." (καὶ ἐπηρώτα αὐτόν· τί ὄνομά σοι; καὶ λέγει αὐτῷ· λεγιὼν ὄνομά μοι, ὅτι πολλοί ἐσμεν). Story time slows, as Jesus carries on a conversation with the demon. The question, "What is your name?" is unlikely to be Jesus' attempt to gain mastery over the demon by learning its secret name (see vv. 6 – 7, above). Jesus is already in total control. Rather, from a narrative perspective the revelation of the name demonstrates the massive nature of the demonic oppression and so emphasizes the greatness of the miracle.

Although the demon has been referred to in the singular up to this point (vv. 2, 8), a multiple possession is now revealed. A legion (λεγιών) was a Roman military unit made up of approximately six thousand troops. This doesn't mean there were six thousand demons, but only (as the demon says) that "we are many" (πολλοί ἐσμεν). Multiple possessions appear elsewhere in the gospel tradition (Matt 12:45//Luke 11:26). Luke 8:2 says Mary Magdalene was freed from seven evil spirits.

Some see the "Legion" reference as an allusion to the Roman occupation, with Mark presenting a political allegory of Jesus' mission to liberate Palestine from the Romans.[14] This seems unlikely. First, Jesus elsewhere shows no signs of political ambitions or Zealot tendencies (12:17; cf. John 18:36). Furthermore, the episode takes place in Gentile rather than Jewish territory and so is unlikely to be a symbol of Jewish insurrection. Third, there is no theme of opposition to Rome in Mark's gospel, which will climax with the Roman centurian's cry, "Truly this man was the Son of God!" (15:39).[15] However, the militaristic connotations of "Legion" do fit well with Mark's emphasis on the reality of spiritual warfare. Jesus has already described his ministry as a clash of kingdoms, with the kingdom of God attacking and overwhelming the "strong man's house" — the kingdom of Satan (3:23 – 27).

5:10 – 12 And he repeatedly begged Jesus not to send them out of the region. A large herd of pigs was feeding on the hillside nearby. And they begged him, saying, "Send us into the pigs, so that we can enter them." (καὶ παρεκάλει αὐτὸν πολλὰ ἵνα μὴ αὐτὰ ἀποστείλῃ ἔξω τῆς χώρας. ἦν δὲ ἐκεῖ πρὸς τῷ ὄρει ἀγέλη χοίρων μεγάλη βοσκομένη· καὶ παρεκάλεσαν αὐτὸν λέγοντες· πέμψον ἡμᾶς εἰς τοὺς χοίρους, ἵνα εἰς αὐτοὺς εἰσέλθωμεν). "Repeatedly" (πολλά) could mean "many times" or "much" (= intensely). Here they are essentially the same: with desperate insistence.

"Out of the region" (ἔξω τῆς χώρας) likely means out of the region of Gerasa (v. 1), though the reason for this request is uncertain.[16] The implication seems to be that evil spirits are territorial beings, who seek to retain control over certain locales

---

12. Wallace, *Greek Grammar*, 549.

13. Some have attributed this disjointed chronology to Mark's use of two sources, but it could just as easily have resulted from the author's desire to give a full description of the demoniac before describing Jesus' response.

14. Myers, *Binding the Strong Man*, 190 – 94; G. Theissen,

The Miracle Stories of the Early Christian Tradition (SNTW; Edinburgh: T&T Clark, 1983), 255 – 56.

15. Collins, *Mark*, 269.

16. In Luke 8:31, the demons request not to be sent into the Abyss, evidently the place of confinement where they await final judgment (2 Pet 2:4; Jude 6; Rev 20:1 – 3).

(Dan 10:13; Tob 8:3). This also helps to explain the strange request to enter the pigs. If they could not remain in the man, they hope at least to be allowed to stay in the region.[17] The presence of the pigs confirms that we are in Gentile territory, since Jews were forbidden to raise or eat pigs (Lev 11:7; Deut 14:8; cf. Isa 65:4; 66:17; *m. B. Qam.* 7:7).

5:13 Jesus permitted them, and the defiling spirits came out and entered the pigs, and the herd rushed down the steep bank into the sea — about two thousand of them — and they drowned in the sea (καὶ ἐπέτρεψεν αὐτοῖς. καὶ ἐξελθόντα τὰ πνεύματα τὰ ἀκάθαρτα εἰσῆλθον εἰς τοὺς χοίρους, καὶ ὥρμησεν ἡ ἀγέλη κατὰ τοῦ κρημνοῦ εἰς τὴν θάλασσαν, ὡς δισχίλιοι, καὶ ἐπνίγοντο ἐν τῇ θαλάσσῃ). A herd of two thousand pigs was huge at that time and would have been worth a fortune. The size confirms the magnitude of the miracle and the power of Jesus to cast out so many demons.

The tangible manifestation of the demons through the pigs also confirms the reality of the exorcism[18] and the fact that Jesus is not simply dealing with a man who has a severe psychological disorder. Some commentators have suggested that the miracle represented a purging or purification of the land, as both "defiling spirits" and "defiling pigs" were removed.[19] But there is no indication of this in the passage, and Mark's mostly Gentile readers are unlikely to have considered the pigs to be a defiling presence.

Modern readers are often bothered by Jesus' apparent disregard for the welfare of the pigs or for the financial loss to the herders. Mark does not address such ethical concerns. The losses must be seen as casualties in the war being waged between the kingdom of God and the kingdom of Satan. While God is out to save, Satan is bent on destruction. In this battle scene, Jesus delivers the man from oppression, while the demons destroy the pigs. The relative value of human and animal life must also be considered. People, Jesus says in Matt 12:12, are more valuable than sheep.[20] In the end, the financial loss is also irrelevant. Disciples of Jesus must be willing to give up all for the kingdom, including homes, land, and family (10:17 – 31; cf. 8:34 – 37).

Another puzzling question is what happened to the demons after the destruction of the pigs? Were they destroyed? Were they banished to wander aimlessly (cf. Matt 12:43 – 45)? The irony of the narrative would suggest that their desperate attempt to stay in the region has failed, and their worst fears are realized. Since the depths of the sea are often associated with the netherworld, perhaps Mark envisions them as now banished to "hell [*tartaros*] … in chains of darkness" (2 Pet 2:4; cf. Jude 6), awaiting their final judgment (Rev 20:1 – 3). This would seem to agree with the parallels in Matthew and Luke (the earliest commentaries on Mark),[21] where the greatest fear of the demons is to be tormented and banished to the Abyss before the eschatological judgment (Matt 8:29; Luke 8:31).

5:14 – 15 Those tending them fled and reported this in the town and the countryside, and the people came to see what had happened. They came to Jesus and saw the demonized man

---

17. On animals as demonic hosts, see Hull, *Hellenistic Magic*, 40 – 41, and Boring et al., eds., *Hellenistic Commentary*, 72 – 73, where examples are provided of the banishment of disease into wild goats and of a demon into the head of a bull.

18. For the use of visible proof to confirm an exorcism, see Josephus, *Ant.* 8.2.5 §48; Philostratus, *Vit. Apoll.* 4.20. In these cases, however, the physical manifestation results from an agreement between the demon and the exorcist (France, *Mark*, 231).

19. So Guelich, *Mark 1:1 – 8:26*, 283: "the destruction of the herd of swine extends the expulsion of the unclean spirits to signify Jesus' authoritative deliverance in the land of Gentiles."

20. France, *Mark*, 230.

21. This is assuming Markan priority and the use of Mark by Matthew and Luke. See Introduction to Mark: Mark's Gospel in Historical Perspective.

sitting there, clothed and in his right mind (the one who had the "Legion"!), and they were afraid (καὶ οἱ βόσκοντες αὐτοὺς ἔφυγον καὶ ἀπήγγειλαν εἰς τὴν πόλιν καὶ εἰς τοὺς ἀγρούς· καὶ ἦλθον ἰδεῖν τί ἐστιν τὸ γεγονὸς καὶ ἔρχονται πρὸς τὸν Ἰησοῦν καὶ θεωροῦσιν τὸν δαιμονιζόμενον καθήμενον ἱματισμένον καὶ σωφρονοῦντα, τὸν ἐσχηκότα τὸν λεγιῶνα, καὶ ἐφοβήθησαν).

The narrative now shifts to the response to the miracle, as the herdsmen report in the town and countryside what has occurred. The "city" (πόλις) here is probably not Gerasa (see v. 1), since the distance is too great, but rather the town or village where the pig herders lived. "Town" (πόλις) can refer to any municipality, even a small village (see Luke 2:4, where the term is used of little Bethlehem).

The description of the man as sitting calmly, "clothed and in his right mind," stands in stark contrast to the detailed description of the demoniac's uncontrollable violence in vv. 3 – 5.[22] Mark surprisingly calls him "the demonized one" (ὁ δαιμονιζόμενος), a present participle, where we might expect a perfect participle ("the one who *had been* demonized"). The point is that this is how townspeople knew the man. Compare the present participle in Luke 1:36, where the angel tells Mary that Elizabeth, "the one called barren" (τῇ καλουμένῃ στείρᾳ; present participle), is in her sixth month of pregnancy. From a human perspective the situation is hopeless, but by the power of God, "the barren one" is pregnant and "the demonized one" sits calmly and in his right mind. Further emphasis is added with the unnecessary and redundant, "the one who had the 'Legion'!" (τὸν ἐσχηκότα τὸν λεγιῶνα; this time a perfect parti-

ciple), as if to poke the reader again and say, "Can you believe it? The one with a legion of demons!"

The reaction of the townspeople is fear, the same response the disciples had in the previous episode when Jesus calmed the sea (4:41). This is a normal response when witnessing the awesome power of God. The only question is what will they do with that fear: fall down before God to worship him and offer their service to him (cf. Isa 6:5), or seek to escape his presence? While the disciples stay with Jesus (perhaps because they were stuck in the boat!), the townspeople beg him to leave (v. 17).

5:16 – 17 Those who had seen what happened to the demonized man and to the pigs reported it to the people, and they began to beg him to leave their region (καὶ διηγήσαντο αὐτοῖς οἱ ἰδόντες πῶς ἐγένετο τῷ δαιμονιζομένῳ καὶ περὶ τῶν χοίρων. καὶ ἤρξαντο παρακαλεῖν αὐτὸν ἀπελθεῖν ἀπὸ τῶν ὁρίων αὐτῶν). Two opposite reactions to the miracle are reported by Mark, a negative one by the townspeople and a positive one by the man. Just as the demons "begged" Jesus not to send them out of the area (v. 10) and to send them into the pigs (v. 12), so now the townspeople "beg" (παρακαλέω) him to leave (cf. v. 18). The reason is fear (v. 15), but fear of what? Some have said they are afraid of greater financial loss. They cared more for the pigs than for the welfare of the man.[23] This is possible, though Mark does not say so. More likely, Jesus is seen as a dangerous disruption to their peaceful lives. The inbreaking power of the kingdom of God does not bring a comfortable life and the status quo but rather a radical transformation of individuals and societies.

5:18 While Jesus was getting in the boat,[24] the man who had been demonized began begging

---

22. Luke 8:27 reports that the demoniac was naked prior to the exorcism.

23. Boring, *Mark*, 152 – 53, argues against this view, claiming that it is more a concern of a modern capitalist society than

of such villagers, who do not complain about the financial loss or ask for compensation.

24. Another genitive absolute (see v. 2).

Jesus to let him go with him (καὶ ἐμβαίνοντος αὐτοῦ εἰς τὸ πλοῖον παρεκάλει αὐτὸν ὁ δαιμονισθεὶς ἵνα μετ᾽ αὐτοῦ ᾖ). In striking contrast to the negative reaction of the townspeople is the positive response of the man. Again Mark uses the same word for "beg" (παρακαλέω; vv. 10, 12, 17). The townspeople beg Jesus to leave, fearful of his amazing power and what it might do to their peaceful lives. But the man begs to be *with Jesus*.[25] He has experienced the healing and wholeness brought by the kingdom of God.

5:19 He would not let him, but instead said to him, "Go home to your people and tell them what the Lord has done for you and how he has shown you mercy." (καὶ οὐκ ἀφῆκεν αὐτόν, ἀλλὰ λέγει αὐτῷ· ὕπαγε εἰς τὸν οἶκόν σου πρὸς τοὺς σοὺς καὶ ἀπάγγειλον αὐτοῖς ὅσα ὁ κύριός σοι πεποίηκεν καὶ ἠλέησέν σε). Why does Jesus not allow the man to go with him? Mark does not say. Perhaps it is because he is a Gentile, or because the Twelve had already been appointed (3:13 – 18), or because Jesus always took the initiative in choosing his disciples. Or maybe there is no room in the boat! In any case, Jesus provides a positive reason for the man to stay: to announce to others what the Lord has done for him. "The Lord" (ὁ κύριος) here is probably a reference to God the Father, who is at work through Jesus. The title almost never refers to Jesus in this gospel (only in 11:3, which is also disputed).

The command is surprising, since elsewhere Jesus commands those healed to silence (1:44; 5:43; 7:36; 8:26). The likely reason is that Jesus is in Gentile rather than Jewish territory. This would confirm our earlier conclusion (see comments on 1:43 – 44) that Jesus wants to define his messiah-

ship on his own terms, not on the basis of traditional messianic expectations. He is also concerned to quell overzealous messianic ambitions among the crowds. Neither of these would be a concern in a Gentile region.

5:20 So he left and began to proclaim in the Decapolis what Jesus had done for him, and everyone was amazed (καὶ ἀπῆλθεν καὶ ἤρξατο κηρύσσειν ἐν τῇ Δεκαπόλει ὅσα ἐποίησεν αὐτῷ ὁ Ἰησοῦς, καὶ πάντες ἐθαύμαζον). While the herders had "announced" (ἀπαγγέλλω) to the townspeople about what had happened (v. 14), this man now "proclaims" (κηρύσσω) to everyone what Jesus had done for him. Though the terms can be synonymous, the latter is more commonly used of the proclamation of the message of salvation.[26] The content of the proclamation is "what Jesus had done for him" (ὅσα ἐποίησεν αὐτῷ ὁ Ἰησοῦς). The close parallel in v. 19, "what the Lord has done for you," shows how closely Jesus is identified with God in Mark's gospel. The work of Jesus is the work of God.

The Decapolis (meaning "Ten Cities") was a region to the east and southeast of the Sea of Galilee made up of a confederation of cities with defense and trade ties. Of the cities, only Scythopolis (Beth Shean) lay west of the Jordan River. The name "Ten Cities" may have come from the original alliance, since the number varied over time; as many as eighteen cities are named in some lists.[27] The Decapolis refers more to a region than to the cities themselves. The inhabitants were primarily Gentile. Jesus will return to the Decapolis in 7:31 – 8:10, where he will heal a deaf man and feed the four thousand. Mark likely intends the present episode to represent a foreshadowing and preview of the

---

25. A similar expression, "in order that he might be with him" (ἵνα μετ᾽ αὐτοῦ ᾖ), is used in 3:14 of Jesus' appointment of the Twelve (Stein, *Mark*, 258; Boring, *Mark*, 153).

26. John the Baptist (1:4, 7); Jesus (1:14, 38, 39); the disciples (3:14; 6:12; 13:10); those healed (1:45; 5:20).

27. The earliest list we have is that of Pliny the Elder, who names the following ten: Damascus, Philadelphia, Rhaphana, Scythopolis, Gadara, Hippo, Dion, Pella, Galasa, and Canatha (*Nat.* 5.16). Other lists include Gerasa, Al Husn, Capitolias, and Arabella. Ptolemy lists eighteen cities.

proclamation of the gospel to the Gentiles (cf. 13:10; 14:9), a mission in full swing in Mark's day.

The response to the man's message is amazement, a common response throughout Mark's gospel (1:22, 27; 2:12; 5:15, 20; 42; 6:51; 12:17; see comments on 1:22). Hurtado downplays the amazed response, claiming that "this does not connote full understanding or acceptance of Jesus," since even those who reject Jesus are amazed (the

people of his hometown, 6:2 – 4; Pilate, 15:5, 44). The amazement of the disciples merely likens their failure to the failure of the crowds.[28] While it is true that amazement doesn't necessarily mean full belief, this is too negative a spin. The theme in Mark does not emphasize a lack of faith, but rather that everyone who comes in contact with Jesus — whether friend or foe — cannot help but be amazed at the power of God evident in his words and deeds.

Theology in Application

The Authority of the Son of God

As elsewhere throughout the first half of Mark's gospel, the primary theme of this episode is the authority of Jesus as God's agent inaugurating the kingdom of God. While the previous episode demonstrated his authority over the forces of nature, this one reveals that same authority over the demonic realm. Jesus has cast out demons before, but this is a "legion" of demons — a major battle in the spiritual war. Yet despite the magnitude of the opposition, Jesus shows no strain or fear of failure in this fight. He has complete mastery of the situation. He simply speaks and the demons obey.

The reality of spiritual warfare is an important theme elsewhere in the NT. Peter affirms that Satan is alive and well on planet earth, prowling like a lion, seeking someone to devour (1 Pet 5:8). Paul likewise asserts that "our struggle is not against flesh and blood, but against the rulers, against the authorities, against the powers of this dark world and against the spiritual forces of evil in the heavenly realms" (Eph 6:12). Yet we need not fear, since Christ has achieved complete victory over spiritual forces through his death and resurrection. He has "disarmed the spiritual rulers and authorities. He shamed them publicly by his victory over them on the cross" (Col 2:15 NLT).

Believers today need to find a healthy balance on the issue of spiritual warfare, recognizing its reality but not living in fear of its destructive power. There are two negative extremes. Some Christians function as practical atheists, with little or no awareness of the supernatural struggle raging in their world. Others see a demon behind every bush, attributing every challenge, setback, or illness to the work of Satan. The former do not recognize how much Satan's purposes are impacting society's values, and so they are oblivious to its effect on their thought and behavior. The latter often live in fear and depression, unable to experience the freedom found in

28. L. W. Hurtado, *Mark* (NIBC; Peabody, MA: Hendrickson, 1989), 85.

Christ. The balanced solution is to acknowledge both the reality of the war and the certainty of its outcome and to claim the victory available through Jesus Christ (see also Theology in Application on 1:21 – 28).

Responding to Jesus

An important secondary theme concerns the contrasting responses to the miracle by the townspeople and the man who was healed. As in the parable of the sower, we see various responses to the gospel message. Some respond positively and bear fruit; others are distracted or deceived. The seed sown among thorns, Jesus says, was choked out by "the cares of this age and the deceitfulness of wealth and the desires for other things" (4:19). Whether the townspeople were concerned about greater financial loss or a disruption to their peaceful lives, they allow such distractions to blind them to their own desperate position and the solution found in Jesus' proclamation of the good news. Radical evil and complete brokenness — as epitomized by the man's condition — demand a radical solution, the awesome transforming power of the kingdom of God.

In contrast to the townspeople is the healed man, who has experienced this transforming power and so begs to join Jesus in the work of the kingdom. As Paul says in Rom 1:16, "I am not ashamed of the gospel, because it is the power of God that brings salvation to everyone who believes: first to the Jew, then to the Gentile." Paul (a Jew) experienced that transforming power on the Damascus road. The man in Mark 5 (a Gentile) experiences it on the shores of Galilee. To those who have never had this transforming encounter with God, the message of the gospel is a stumbling block and foolishness, "but to those whom God has called, both Jews and Greeks, Christ the power of God and the wisdom of God" (1 Cor 1:24).

The man in his desperate situation may also be seen to epitomize fallen humanity, dead in its "transgressions and sins" and enslaved to the power of Satan (Eph 2:1). He is as good as dead (living in tombs!) and beyond human help. Yet through Christ, he is made alive and whole, raised up with Christ to a state of true humanity (Eph 2:4 – 5). His task now was simply to proclaim to others "what Jesus had done for him" (Mark 5:20), that is, to bear testimony to the grace of God and the transforming power of his kingdom. This is the essence of what it means to be a Christian witness. It is not about learning the right words or developing the most persuasive method. It is bearing simple testimony to what God has done for you. As John Newton so simply and profoundly wrote,

> Amazing grace, how sweet the sound,
> That saved a wretch like me.
> I once was lost, but now am found,
> Was blind, but now I see.

CHAPTER 19

Mark 5:21 – 43

Literary Context

This is the third and fourth in a series of four powerful miracles that go beyond anything Jesus had done before during his Galilean ministry. In the previous two episodes Jesus commanded the forces of nature (4:35 – 41) and overcame massive demonic possession (5:1 – 20). Now, in this double episode, he heals a long-term chronic disease that has baffled physicians (5:25 – 34) and defeats the greatest enemy of all — death itself (5:21 – 24, 35 – 43).

The four passages are also linked literarily by boat journeys. After calming the storm at sea (4:35 – 41), Jesus arrives on the eastern shore of the lake, where he exorcises the Gerasene demoniac (5:1 – 20). Now he returns to the western shore (5:21).

Another possible connection between the three healings in Mark 5 is the issue of ceremonial impurity, a topic Jesus will address in chapter 7 (7:1 – 23). The demoniac was possessed by a "defiling spirit" and lived in tombs, whose corpses rendered him unclean (Isa 65:4). The demons were cast into pigs, which were ceremonially unclean (Lev 11:7 – 8). The woman in the present episode has a blood disease that renders her ceremonially impure (Lev 15:19 – 31; Ezek 36:17). Similarly, the little girl's dead body would have passed on ceremonial impurity to anyone who touched it (Num 19:11 – 13, 22; Hag 2:13). In each case Jesus' healing touch brings restoration and wholeness, reversing the results of defilement and ostracism. It must be added that Mark does not explicitly refer to the question of impurity in the texts, so it is unclear how important the theme was to him.

Main Idea

The healings of Jesus, which have played such a prominent role in revealing Jesus' messianic authority, now reach a climax in Mark's gospel as Jesus heals a long-term chronic disease and then raises a girl from the dead. The miracles demonstrate that the arrival of the kingdom of God brings hope of restoration and renewal to a fallen creation. Jesus' special concern for women also illustrates the countercultural values of the kingdom.

Translation

Mark 5:21 – 43

21a	Setting (spatial)	When Jesus had crossed over again in the boat to the other side,
b	Setting (spatial)	**a large crowd gathered around him**
c		while he was beside the sea.
22a	Character entrance	**One of the synagogue leaders, a man named Jairus, approached him.**
b		When he saw Jesus,
23a	Entreaty	**he fell at his feet and urgently pleaded with him**,
b		*"My little girl is dying.*
c		*Please come and lay your hands on her so that her life may be saved."*
24a	Response to 23	So **he went with him,**
b	Setting (social)	and **a large crowd was accompanying him and pressing against him.**
25a	Character entrance	**A woman was there**
b	Character description	who had been sick with a bleeding disorder for twelve years.
26a	Character description	**She had suffered a great deal under the care of many doctors and**
b		**had spent everything she had, but**
c		instead of getting better,
d		**she had only gotten worse.**
27a	Action	Having heard about Jesus,
b		**she came up behind him in the crowd and touched his robe.**
28a	Reason for 27	For **she was saying to herself,**
b		*"If I can just touch his clothes, I will be healed."*
29a	Healing	**Immediately her bleeding stopped,**
b		and **she felt in her body that she was healed of her affliction.**
30a	Response to 27b	**Jesus realized at once that power had gone out of him.**
b		Turning to the crowd,
c		**he said,**
d		*"Who touched my clothes?"*

Continued on next page.

Continued from previous page.

31a	Response to 30	**His disciples said to him,**
b		*"You see the crowd pressing against you, and yet you ask,*
c		*'Who touched me?'"*
32		**But he kept looking to see the woman who had done this.**
33a	Response to 30, 32	Then **the woman,**
b		fearful and trembling
c		because she knew what had happened to her,
d	Action/Confession	**came and fell down in front of him and told him the** ✍
		whole truth.
34a	Response	But **he said to her,**
b	Healing announcement	*"Daughter, your faith has saved you.*
c		*Go in peace and be healed of your affliction."*
35a	Action/Character entrance	While he was speaking,
b		**some people came from the house of the synagogue leader and said,**
c		*"Your daughter has died. Why bother the teacher any more?"*
36a	Response to 35	But **Jesus,**
b		overhearing what they said,
c		**said to the synagogue leader,**
d		*"Don't be afraid; just believe."*
37a	Action	**He did not let anyone accompany them,**
b		except Peter, James, and John, the brother of James.
38a	Action	**They came to the house of the synagogue leader,**
b	Setting (social)	and **he saw a commotion,**
c	character description	people weeping and wailing loudly.
39a	action	Going inside,
b	Response to 38b	**he said to them,**
c	rhetorical question	*"Why are you making a commotion and weeping?*
d	announcement	*The child has not died, but is sleeping."*
40a	Response to 39d	**They began laughing at him.**
b	response to 40a	But putting them all outside,
c	Action	**he took the child's father and mother and those who were with him**
d		and **went in where the child was.**
41a	action	Taking the hand of the child,
b	Command for healing	**he said to her,**
c		*"Talitha koum!"*
	parenthetic remark	*(which means, "Little girl, I say to you, get up!")*
42a	Healing/parenthetic remark	**Immediately the little girl stood up and began to walk** (for she was twelve ✍
		years old).
b	Response to 42a	**They were completely astounded.**
43a	Command	**He gave them strict orders not to let anyone know about this,**
b	Command	and **told them to give her something to eat.**

Structure

This is the second of Mark's intercalations, where one episode is "sandwiched" in the middle of another (cf. 3:20 – 35; 6:7 – 30; 11:12 – 25; 14:1 – 11, 53 – 72; see Introduction to Mark: Literary Features). Sometimes the two stories share a common theme; in others, one part interprets the other. The intercalation can also provide dramatic effect, slowing the narrative and creating a temporal delay. Here the temporal delay is important, since the death of the little girl takes place during this period. The common theme of the two scenes is faith. Jesus announces to the woman that her faith has healed her and calls Jairus to greater faith in the face of apparent hopelessness at the death of his daughter.

There are both contrasts and similarities between the two accounts. The main contrast is in the social status of the two supplicants.[1] Jairus is a Jewish male and a leader in his community at the top of the social ladder. The woman is poor and helpless, and is an outcast on the lower rungs of society. She remains chronically ill, despite having spent all she had on doctors. Her bleeding disorder renders her ceremonially impure and so separated from Israel's religious life.

Equally striking are the parallels between the two episodes: both concern females who are in hopeless situations (chronic disease and death); both situations relate to ceremonial impurity (the woman's condition and the little girl's dead body); both are identified as "daughters," and a period of twelve years is significant for each (the onset of the woman's disease; the age of the girl); the healing in both involves Jesus' touch and is linked to faith. Jesus tells the woman that "your faith has healed you" and encourages Jairus not to fear, but to persevere in faith. These lessons in faith will stand in stark contrast to the episode that follows, where Jesus' hometown suffers from a complete "lack of faith" (6:6).

Exegetical Outline

→ **1. The Setting: Back in Jewish Territory (5:21)**

2. A Synagogue Leader Pleads with Jesus to Heal His Daughter (5:22 – 24)
  a. Jairus's identity and approach (5:22a)
  b. Jairus's request (5:22b – 23)
  c. Jesus' response (5:24a)
  d. The presence of the crowd (5:24b)

3. Healing the Woman with a Bleeding Disorder (Intercalation) (5:25 – 34)
  a. The woman's condition (5:25 – 26)
  b. The woman's approach (5:27 – 28)

---

1. See Boring, *Mark*, 157.

    c. The healing (5:29)

    d. Jesus' response (5:30)

    e. The disciples' answer (5:31)

    f. Jesus and the woman (5:32 – 34)

4. Jesus Raises Jairus's Daughter (5:35 – 43)

    a. The report arrives from Jairus's home (5:35)

    b. Jesus' reply: Don't fear; just believe (5:36)

    c. Encounter with the mourners (5:37 – 40a)

    d. The healing of the girl (5:40b – 42a)

    e. The response and orders by Jesus (5:42b – 43)

Explanation of the Text

5:21 When Jesus had crossed over again in the boat to the other side, a large crowd gathered around him while he was beside the sea (Καὶ διαπεράσαντος τοῦ Ἰησοῦ ἐν τῷ πλοίῳ[2] πάλιν εἰς τὸ πέραν συνήχθη ὄχλος πολὺς ἐπ᾽ αὐτόν, καὶ ἦν παρὰ τὴν θάλασσαν). Jesus now returns by boat to the western side of the lake. He is back in Jewish territory. This is evident from the presence of the synagogue leader and Jesus' Aramaic words in v. 41. The appearance of a large crowd (ὄχλος πολύς) renews the theme of Jesus' popularity during his Galilean ministry (1:33 – 34; 2:2; 3:7 – 9, 20; 4:1).

Mark's rather redundant "and he was by the lake" (καὶ ἦν παρὰ τὴν θάλασσαν) may be meant to show that the crowd was waiting for him when he arrived, emphasizing his popularity. Or the clause may go with the next one to show that Jairus met Jesus before he came into town (REB), indicating Jairus's desperate urgency. Both themes are present in what follows.

5:22 – 23 One of the synagogue leaders, a man named Jairus, approached him. When he saw Jesus, he fell at his feet and urgently pleaded with him, "My little girl is dying. Please come and lay your hands on her so that her life may be saved." (Καὶ ἔρχεται εἷς τῶν ἀρχισυναγώγων, ὀνόματι Ἰάϊρος, καὶ ἰδὼν αὐτὸν πίπτει πρὸς τοὺς πόδας αὐτοῦ καὶ παρακαλεῖ αὐτὸν πολλὰ λέγων ὅτι τὸ θυγάτριόν μου ἐσχάτως ἔχει, ἵνα ἐλθὼν ἐπιθῇς τὰς χεῖρας αὐτῇ ἵνα σωθῇ καὶ ζήσῃ). A "synagogue leader" (ἀρχισυνάγωγος) was an administrator of the synagogue, maintaining the facilities and organizing worship services.[3] The phrase "one of the synagogue leaders" (εἷς τῶν ἀρχισυναγώγων) may identify Jairus as one of a committee of ruling elders. Acts 13:15 speaks of "the leaders of the synagogue" in the plural at Pisidian Antioch. Other texts, however, refer to the office in the singular (Luke 13:14; Acts 18:8, 17), and the phrase could mean either "a certain synagogue leader" (εἷς as a Semitism for τις)[4] or "a leader of one of the synagogues (of Galilee)."[5] The first option remains the most likely and is followed by most versions (NIV, NET, HCSB, etc.).

It is unusual to have an individual named in a

---

2. The phrase "in the boat" (ἐν τῷ πλοίῳ) is absent in some early manuscripts ($\mathfrak{P}^{45vid}$ D Θ f^1 28 565 700 2542), but appears in many others (א A (B) C L 0132 f^{13} 33 𝔐). Its omission was likely accidental or an assimilation to Luke 8:40 (Metzger, *Textual Commentary*, 73).

3. W. Schrage, *TDNT*, 7:847; BDAG, 139; cf. Luke 13:14; Acts 13:15; 18:8, 17.

4. See Taylor, *Mark*, 287.

5. So Boring, *Mark*, 156.

miracle story; that feature occurs in Mark only here and in the case of Bartimaeus (10:46). While some suggest the name is a later addition,[6] it could just as easily be explained as a historical recollection in light of the enormity of the miracle (see comments on v. 41). Jairus "fell at his feet," an action that can indicate entreaty (7:25) or submission (3:11; 5:6). While both are present here, the former is most prominent (cf. v. 33).

Jairus is helpless in the face of his daughter's illness and begs Jesus for help. Mark uses the historical present to good effect here (ἔρχεται … πίπτει … παρακαλεῖ; "he comes … he falls … he begs"), adding stylistically to the vivid urgency of the scene.[7] Jairus's approach to Jesus reminds the reader that not all of Israel's leaders oppose Jesus (cf. 12:34; 15:43; John 19:38 – 39). Israel does not stand uniformly against Jesus, but is divided in its response.

The term "little girl" (lit., "little daughter," θυγάτριόν) is a diminutive form. Although the force of the diminutive was declining in Koine Greek (see comments on 3:9), the sense of "little" seems appropriate here. The reader will learn in v. 42 that the girl is twelve. Our translation as "my little girl" captures the sense well in contemporary English. A father's heart is breaking as he sees his little girl dying. Only Luke (8:42) notes that this was Jairus's only daughter, making the potential loss even more profound.[8]

Jairus requests that Jesus come and "lay hands on her," a common means of healing both in Mark's gospel (1:31, 41; 5:41; 6:5; 7:32; 8:23, 25) and in the

ancient world.[9] The apparently redundant expression "might be saved and live" (σωθῇ καὶ ζήσῃ) is likely hendiadys (two words expressing a single idea), meaning that "her life might be saved" (REB).

5:24 So he went with him, and a large crowd was accompanying him and pressing against him (καὶ ἀπῆλθεν μετ᾽ αὐτοῦ. καὶ ἠκολούθει αὐτῷ ὄχλος πολὺς καὶ συνέθλιβον αὐτόν). As Jesus heads off to Jairus's home, the crowd appears again as a character. Crowds in Mark are both indicators of popularity[10] and impediments to those trying to reach Jesus (2:2 – 4). The latter is most prominent here. The mobbing crowds prepare the reader for Jesus' compassion and his sensitivity to the woman's desperate touch.

5:25 – 26 A woman was there who had been sick with a bleeding disorder for twelve years. She had suffered a great deal under the care of many doctors and had spent everything she had, but instead of getting better she had only gotten worse (Καὶ γυνὴ οὖσα ἐν ῥύσει αἵματος δώδεκα ἔτη καὶ πολλὰ παθοῦσα ὑπὸ πολλῶν ἰατρῶν καὶ δαπανήσασα τὰ παρ᾽ αὐτῆς πάντα καὶ μηδὲν ὠφεληθεῖσα ἀλλὰ μᾶλλον εἰς τὸ χεῖρον ἐλθοῦσα). Mark's intercalation begins here as the narrative shifts from Jairus to the actions of the woman (see Structure, above).

Mark describes the woman's troubles and her attempt to get to Jesus in one long sentence in Greek (vv. 25 – 28) with a main verb ("she touched";

---

6. A few Western manuscripts omit the name here (D it), prompting speculation that scribes took it from Luke 8:41. But the external evidence is overwhelmingly in support of its retention. Some form critics (e.g., Bultmann) claimed the name was a later addition, part of the tendency to embellish stories. But this is an oversimplification, since the tradition sometimes goes in the opposite direction. Matthew, for example, drops the name here, and neither Matthew (Matt 20:30) nor Luke (Luke 18:35) names Bartimaeus.

7. ἵνα … ἐπιθῇς may be an imperatival use of ἵνα plus the subjunctive ("Please come and lay hands on …"), or it may be elliptical, with a verb like "I ask you …" implied.

8. Matthew presents the girl as already dead (9:18), part of his tendency to abbreviate accounts. The result, however, is to present Jairus as having even greater faith in Jesus to raise the dead.

9. Theissen, *Miracle Stories,* 92.

10. See 1:33 – 34; 2:2; 3:7 – 9, 20; 4:1; 5:21, 24; 6:14 – 15, 31 – 34; 7:24; 8:1 – 3; 9:14 – 15, 30.

ἥψατο) and seven subordinate participles. Though elaborate descriptions are characteristic of Mark (e.g., the demoniac in 5:3–5), the use of subordinate participial phrases (hypotaxis) instead of parallel indicative verbs connected by "and" (parataxis) is unusual for Mark and serves to highlight the woman's troubles and her desperation.[11]

For twelve years this woman has had a "flow of blood" (ῥύσει αἵματος), a chronic bleeding disorder of some kind, probably menstrual in nature. She has suffered much under the care of many doctors, spending "everything she had," getting no better (μηδὲν ὠφεληθεῖσα; "gaining nothing"), but only worse. Like the Gerasene demoniac (5:3–5), she is portrayed as beyond human help. Commentators have noted, not without some amusement, that Luke states only that "no one could heal her" (8:43), dropping Mark's reference to the woman's suffering at the hands of many doctors. Was Luke protecting his profession?

The woman's condition would not only have been detrimental to her health, but it also would have rendered her ceremonially unclean, limiting her participation in Israel's religious life.[12] Such impurity was a significant concern in the OT law (Lev 15:19–31; Ezek 36:17), and an entire tractate in the Mishnah is devoted to it (m. Niddah; cf. m. Zabim). Mark does not explicitly refer to this issue. However, the woman's reticence in approaching Jesus, the issues of ceremonial defilement present in the previous narrative (5:2, 3, 11), and Jesus' teaching that follows in 7:1–22 may indicate Mark's awareness of it.

5:27–28 Having heard about Jesus, she came up behind him in the crowd and touched his robe. For she was saying to herself, "If I can just touch

his clothes, I will be healed." (ἀκούσασα περὶ τοῦ Ἰησοῦ, ἐλθοῦσα ἐν τῷ ὄχλῳ ὄπισθεν ἥψατο τοῦ ἱματίου αὐτοῦ· ἔλεγεν γὰρ ὅτι ἐὰν ἅψωμαι κἂν τῶν ἱματίων αὐτοῦ σωθήσομαι). Verse 27 continues the long sentence in Greek that began in v. 25. Jesus' reputation as a healer has spread throughout Galilee, and the woman finally sees a ray of hope. Why she approached Jesus secretly is not stated. She may have felt ashamed because of her condition or perhaps feared rebuke by the crowds or the disciples for touching the rabbi in her impurity. In either case, she approaches Jesus as an outcast, desperate for healing but unworthy of his time or attention.

The woman's desire to touch Jesus reflects a common belief in the ancient world that a person's power could be transmitted through their clothing. We have already seen this in Mark 3:10; and in 6:56 Mark states that "all who touched him were healed." Similar beliefs and results are reported in Acts by those trying touch Peter's shadow (Acts 5:15) and Paul's handkerchiefs and work aprons (19:12). These accounts are sometimes disturbing to modern Christians because they appear to reflect a magical view of healing. Mark has no such concerns, but will clarify that the healing resulted from faith, not through some magical ritual. "Your faith has saved [healed] you" (v. 34) is a shorthand way of saying that God has healed you in response to your faith.

5:29–30 Immediately her bleeding stopped, and she felt in her body that she was healed of her affliction. Jesus realized at once that power had gone out of him. Turning to the crowd, he said, "Who touched my clothes?" (καὶ εὐθὺς ἐξηράνθη ἡ πηγὴ τοῦ αἵματος αὐτῆς καὶ ἔγνω τῷ σώματι ὅτι ἴαται ἀπὸ τῆς μάστιγος. καὶ εὐθὺς ὁ

---

11. France, Mark, 236; C. D. Marshall, Faith as a Theme, 104.

12. So most commentators. Some, however, claim ritual impurity is not an issue here. See Collins, Mark, 283–84; Shaye

J. D. Cohen, "Menstruants and the Sacred in Judaism and Christianity," in Women's History and Ancient History (ed. S. B. Pomeroy; Chapel Hill/London: University of North Carolina Press, 1991), 273–99, esp. 278–79.

Ἰησοῦς ἐπιγνοὺς ἐν ἑαυτῷ τὴν ἐξ αὐτοῦ δύναμιν ἐξελθοῦσαν ἐπιστραφεὶς ἐν τῷ ὄχλῳ ἔλεγεν· τίς μου ἥψατο τῶν ἱματίων;). The woman's faith in Jesus' authority to heal pays off, and she "immediately" (εὐθύς) realizes that she has been healed. Jesus too immediately feels the effect, as "power had gone out of him."

This scene reveals the convergence of the human and divine in Jesus' person. A woman is healed because of the supernatural power residing within Jesus. Furthermore, through supernatural insight and sensitivity, Jesus is aware of a single desperate touch in the midst of a pressing crowd (cf. other examples of divine insight in 2:8; 3:5; 8:17; 12:15). At the same time, he is unsure of who touched him and must look around and ask. Yet this latter is less about the limitations of Jesus' humanity and more about Jesus' desire to provoke faith. From a narrative perspective, Jesus' searching provides the woman with an opportunity to come forward and bear witness to what has happened to her.

5:31 – 32 His disciples said to him, "You see the crowd pressing against you, and yet you ask, 'Who touched me?'" But he kept looking to see the woman who had done this (καὶ ἔλεγον αὐτῷ οἱ μαθηταὶ αὐτοῦ· βλέπεις τὸν ὄχλον συνθλίβοντά σε καὶ λέγεις· τίς μου ἥψατο; καὶ περιεβλέπετο ἰδεῖν τὴν τοῦτο ποιήσασαν). In contrast to Jesus' sensitivity, the disciples are clueless to the events that have just transpired. From a rationalistic perspective, their question is perfectly normal: "Who touched you? Everyone!" There is a crowd mobbing around Jesus. Yet the reader perceives a spiritual insensitivity on their part, one that will grow as the narrative progresses (see comments on 4:40; cf. 6:52; 7:18; 8:17 – 18, 21; 9:6, 19, 32). Jesus will not be deterred, however, and he "kept looking"

(περιεβλέπετο; imperfect, indicating continuous action) around to identify the person.[13]

5:33 Then the woman, fearful and trembling because she knew what had happened to her, came and fell down in front of him and told him the whole truth (ἡ δὲ γυνὴ φοβηθεῖσα καὶ τρέμουσα, εἰδυῖα ὃ γέγονεν αὐτῇ, ἦλθεν καὶ προσέπεσεν αὐτῷ καὶ εἶπεν αὐτῷ πᾶσαν τὴν ἀλήθειαν). "Fear and trembling" (φοβηθεῖσα καὶ τρέμουσα) can result from a perceived threat (Gen 9:2; Exod 15:16; Deut 2:25 LXX) or, as previously in Mark, from awe in the presence of divine power and authority (4:41; 5:15). It is certainly possible that the woman feared retribution for drawing Jesus' attention away or for rendering the rabbi unclean by touching him in her impurity. Yet this is at best secondary, since Mark attributes the fear to knowing "what has happened to her." She is overwhelmed with awe by the power of God to heal and restore.

As Jairus fell down before Jesus in supplication (v. 22), so now the healed woman falls down before him in awe and worship. She tells him "the whole truth," meaning her attempt to be healed secretly. Of course, by telling the whole truth she is also proclaiming the good news, that is, bearing testimony to the power of Jesus to heal.

5:34 But he said to her, "Daughter, your faith has saved you. Go in peace and be healed of your affliction." (ὁ δὲ εἶπεν αὐτῇ· θυγάτηρ, ἡ πίστις σου σέσωκέν σε· ὕπαγε εἰς εἰρήνην καὶ ἴσθι ὑγιὴς ἀπὸ τῆς μάστιγός σου). Jesus responds by praising the woman's faith and sending her off restored. This is the only place in the Gospels where Jesus addresses someone as "daughter" (θυγάτηρ). It recalls Jesus' address to the paralyzed man in 2:5 ("son": τέκνον; cf. 10:24) and is a term of familial affection and

---

13. Stein, *Mark*, 270, insists that Jesus knows it is a woman who touched him, since a singular feminine article is used of her in v. 32: τὴν τοῦτο ποιήσασαν ("the one [=woman] who did

this"). But this is surely an overreading of the Greek. These are the words of the narrator, not of Jesus, and the narrator would naturally continue to refer to the woman with feminine forms.

acceptance, essentially welcoming her back to the community of God.

Jesus attributes the healing to the woman's faith: "Your faith has saved [healed] you" (ἡ πίστις σου σέσωκέν σε). It was not the magical power of Jesus' robe or some spiritual force residing within him. Rather, it was God's gracious response to her faith in Jesus' messianic authority and power to heal. Jesus says the same thing when he restores Bartimaeus's sight (10:52).

The Greek verb "to save" (σῴζω) has a wide semantic range and can refer to spiritual salvation (8:35; 10:26; 13:13), physical rescue (13:20; 15:30, 31), preservation of life (3:4; 8:35), or physical healing/restoration (5:23, 28, 34; 6:56; 10:52). It is sometimes said that these senses play off each other, so that spiritual and physical restoration are seen as one and the same. It is certainly true that in the Gospels the two go hand in hand *theologically*, and the arrival of the kingdom of God brings both physical restoration and spiritual forgiveness (see 2:5, 10). But this is not the same as saying that, in any particular context, the lexeme σῴζω means *both* spiritual and physical restoration. Neither Jairus (5:23) nor the woman (5:28) is seeking spiritual salvation from Jesus. They are seeking physical healing. Yet when Jesus says, "your faith has saved [healed] [σῴζω] you" (v. 34; 10:52), the two senses certainly shade together, since faith is the prerequisite for both spiritual and physical restoration.

The traditional Hebrew farewell, "Go in peace" (ὕπαγε εἰς εἰρήνην = *lēk lĕšālôm*; cf. Judg 18:6; 1 Sam 1:17; 20:42; James 2:16), here means more than just "good-bye." It is an affirmation of not only the woman's healing, but also her restoration to wholeness (*šālôm*) in the community of God.

5:35 While he was speaking, some people came from the house of the synagogue leader and said,

"Your daughter has died. Why bother the teacher any more?" (Ἔτι αὐτοῦ λαλοῦντος ἔρχονται ἀπὸ τοῦ ἀρχισυναγώγου λέγοντες ὅτι ἡ θυγάτηρ σου ἀπέθανεν· τί ἔτι σκύλλεις τὸν διδάσκαλον;). One person's joy is another's agony, as word reaches Jairus that his daughter has now died. The restoration of one "daughter" (v. 34) has resulted in the death of another. Yet even this tragedy is not outside of God's sovereign purpose, and the delay caused by the interruption (vv. 25–34) will result in an even greater miracle. A similar situation occurs in John's gospel. Jesus' delay in coming to Lazarus results in his death; but his subsequent raising results in greater glory for God (John 11:4, 14, 40, 42, 45).

"From the ... synagogue leader" (ἀπὸ τοῦ ἀρχισυναγώγου) is elliptical, meaning "From *the house of*...." "Has died" is a consummative aorist, indicating the completed nature of the action.[14] The rhetorical question from the messengers, "Why bother the teacher any more?" indicates the hopelessness of the situation. Even a great teacher and healer like Jesus surely cannot cheat death itself.

5:36 But Jesus, overhearing what they said, said to the synagogue leader, "Don't be afraid; just believe." (ὁ δὲ Ἰησοῦς παρακούσας τὸν λόγον λαλούμενον λέγει τῷ ἀρχισυναγώγῳ· μὴ φοβοῦ, μόνον πίστευε). "Overhearing" (παρακούω) can also mean "ignore" or "pay no attention" (NET, GNT; cf. NAB: "disregard"). Both senses fit the context well, since Jesus first hears and then ignores (or, disregards) the message about the girl's death. Whichever sense was intended by Mark, the other is necessarily implied.

Jesus calls on Jairus not to fear, but to believe. Both "fear" (φοβοῦ) and "believe" (πίστευε) are present imperatives. It has often been asserted that

---

14. Wallace, *Greek Grammar*, 559.

in Greek a negative prohibition in the present tense means to "stop doing" an action, while the aorist tense means not to start. This is not accurate. It is rather the *context* together with the tense/aspect that determines whether the action is already in progress.[15] In the present context, of course, Jairus is already afraid and so Jesus tells him to put away that fear. The present tense is appropriate here because both fear and faith are *ongoing* actions. Jairus came to Jesus out of fear for his daughter's life and faith in Jesus' healing power. Now Jesus calls him to put aside the greater fear caused by the girl's death and to progress to even greater faith.

5:37 He did not let anyone accompany them, except Peter, James, and John, the brother of James (καὶ οὐκ ἀφῆκεν οὐδένα μετ᾽ αὐτοῦ συνακολουθῆσαι εἰ μὴ τὸν Πέτρον καὶ Ἰάκωβον καὶ Ἰωάννην τὸν ἀδελφὸν Ἰακώβου). This is the first reference to these three as part of an "inner circle" of disciples who will accompany Jesus at several key points in his ministry: here, at the transfiguration (9:2), and in Gethsemane (14:33). Andrew appears with them at the Olivet Discourse (13:3). The four (with Andrew) were first called by Jesus from their fishing occupation (1:16 – 20) and then appointed together with the Twelve (3:13 – 19) and will soon be sent to preach and heal (6:6 – 31). Why these three are singled out here is not stated. It may have been the limited space in the home or perhaps the others were left to keep the crowd at bay. In any case, the three will serve as key witnesses to this remarkable miracle.

5:38 – 39 They came to the house of the synagogue leader, and he saw a commotion, people weeping and wailing loudly. Going inside, he said to them, "Why are you making a commotion and weeping? The child has not died, but is sleeping." (καὶ ἔρχονται εἰς τὸν οἶκον τοῦ ἀρχισυναγώγου, καὶ θεωρεῖ θόρυβον καὶ κλαίοντας καὶ ἀλαλάζοντας πολλά, καὶ εἰσελθὼν λέγει αὐτοῖς· τί θορυβεῖσθε καὶ κλαίετε; τὸ παιδίον οὐκ ἀπέθανεν ἀλλὰ καθεύδει). The weeping and wailing of the people is evidence that the child has died. The crowd likely included paid mourners, playing flutes and singing dirges, a common practice in the ancient Near East (Matt 9:23; 11:17; Luke 7:23). The volume and intensity of the mourning was viewed as an indicator of the great love for the deceased. The Mishnah says, "Even the poorest in Israel do not hire less than two flute players and one wailing woman" (*m. Ketub.* 4:4).[16] A "commotion" may be any kind of noisy tumult, such as a riot (Mark 14:2; Acts 17:5; 20:10; 24:18), but in this case it means the noise and confusion as mourners arrive and news of the girl's death spreads.

Jesus, however, always in control, calls for a halt to the noise and tumult, rhetorically asking, "Why are you making a commotion and weeping?" and assuring the crowd that the girl is only sleeping. Some commentators have taken Jesus' words literally and tried to explain the healing as a resuscitation from a coma. But this is certainly not how the gospel writers understood it. The entire flow

---

15. See K. L. McKay, "Aspect in Imperatival Constructions in New Testament Greek," *NovT* 23 (1985): 201 – 26; J. P. Louw, "On Greek Prohibitions," *Acta Classica* 2 (1959): 43 – 57, who challenge the earlier view of Henry Jackson, "Prohibitions in Greek," *Classical Review* 18 (1904): 262 – 63. McKay concluded that "in the imperative the *essential* difference between the aorist and the imperfective is that the former urges an activity *as whole action* and the latter urges it as *ongoing process*" (pp. 206 – 7). For examples, see Wallace, *Greek Grammar*, 714 – 15; J. L. Boyer, "The Classification of Imperatives: A Statistical Study," *GTJ* 8 (1987): 35 – 54.

16. Jeremiah assumes this practice when he says, "Call for the wailing women to come; send for the most skillful of them. Let them come quickly and wail over us till our eyes overflow with tears and water streams from our eyelids" (Jer 9:17 – 18). Josephus similarly describes the great lamentation and "a great many hired mourners" playing pipes and singing dirges for the inhabitants of Jotapata. Josephus, never one for modesty, points out the mourning was especially profound, all of Jerusalem was in great sorrow, because they thought Josephus himself had been killed! (*J.W.* 3.9.5 §437).

of the story, including the report of the death and the derision of the mourners, confirms that the girl had died. Matthew explicitly states this (Matt 9:24). "Sleep" is a common euphemism for death in the NT, pointing to its temporary nature for believers (John 11:11 – 14; 1 Cor 15:51; 1 Thess 4:13 – 14). While in these passages, believers will awake to resurrection life, Jesus has in view "sleep" as a temporary pause in the girl's mortal life.

5:40 They began laughing at him. But putting them all outside, he took the child's father and mother and those who were with him and went in where the child was (καὶ κατεγέλων αὐτοῦ. αὐτὸς δὲ ἐκβαλὼν πάντας παραλαμβάνει τὸν πατέρα τοῦ παιδίου καὶ τὴν μητέρα καὶ τοὺς μετ᾽ αὐτοῦ καὶ εἰσπορεύεται ὅπου ἦν τὸ παιδίον). The mourners, who know the child is dead, react with scorn at Jesus' suggestion. Their immediate change from mourning to laughing indicates the superficiality of their grief. The mocking also prepares us for the miracle, contrasting the confident assurance of Jesus with the derision of those insensitive to God's work. These are the ones who have eyes but cannot see and ears but cannot hear (4:12). Fools mock, while the Son of God prepares to do the impossible. The scene also "anticipates the mocking of Jesus in 14:65 and 15:16 – 20, which will be refuted by Jesus' rising from the dead."[17]

Jesus takes charge of the situation and puts the noisy crowd out. The term "put them out" (ἐκβάλλω) carries a sense of strong compulsion. It is used throughout Mark of exorcisms (1:12) and also of the Spirit's compulsion in sending Jesus into the wilderness (1:12; cf. 1:43). Jesus allows entry only to the parents and "those who were with him," that is, the three disciples mentioned in v. 37.

5:41 Taking the hand of the child, he said to her, "Talitha koum!" (which means, "Little girl, I say to you, get up!") (καὶ κρατήσας τῆς χειρὸς τοῦ παιδίου λέγει αὐτῇ· ταλιθα κουμ, ὅ ἐστιν μεθερμηνευόμενον· τὸ κοράσιον, σοὶ λέγω, ἔγειρε). As elsewhere, Jesus heals with a simple touch (1:31, 41; 6:5; 7:32; 8:23, 25) and a command (1:41; 2:11; 10:52). He uses no prayers, incantations, or rituals, but rather speaks with his own messianic authority. Contrast this with the prayers and rituals performed by Elijah and Elisha in the two closest OT parallels (1 Kgs 17:19 – 22; 2 Kgs 4:29 – 35).[18] Significantly, the laws of impurity are reversed. Jesus' touch does not render him ceremonially unclean, but rather brings restoration and healing to the afflicted (cf. 1:41; 5:27 – 29).

The Aramaic *Talitha* means "lamb" and was used as a pet name for children, hence Mark's translation of the Aramaic into Greek as "little girl" (τὸ κοράσιον, a diminutive).[19] Why did Mark record the Aramaic phrase (cf. 3:17; 7:11, 34; 10:46; 14:36)? Some have claimed it is treated as a magical formula, but this fits neither its nature as a simple command nor the fact that Mark translates the Aramaic into Greek. This is not an incantation, but an act of divine authority, as Jesus commands death itself. The more likely reason for retaining the Aramaic is the profound impact the event had on the onlookers. Jesus' actual words, *Talitha koum*, were no doubt ringing in their ears as they witnessed the impossible — the restoration of life — and these words would have been repeated again and again as the story was told and retold in the church.[20]

5:42 Immediately the little girl stood up and began to walk (for she was twelve years old). They were completely astounded (καὶ εὐθὺς ἀνέστη τὸ

---

18. France, *Mark*, 240.

19. Commentators have noted the similarity in sound to Peter's words in Acts 9:40, "Tabitha, get up." Is this merely coincidental?

20. For other Aramaic expressions in Mark, see 3:17; 7:11, 34; 14:36; 15:34; cf. Matt 5:22; 6:24.

κοράσιον καὶ περιεπάτει· ἦν γὰρ ἐτῶν δώδεκα. καὶ ἐξέστησαν εὐθὺς[21] ἐκστάσει μεγάλῃ). The girl gets up "immediately" (εὐθύς), which here has its full temporal force (contrast 1:10), and begins to walk around. These actions confirm the reality of the miracle.

Mark probably mentions the girl's age to explain how she could walk about: she was not an infant, but a grown child. Boring claims that revealing the age means that this is a young woman, "ready to launch on a meaningful and fulfilled life." Just as the woman with the menstrual disorder is now healed and can bear children, so this young woman "now stands on the threshold of puberty, marriage, and family."[22] Whether Mark read so much into the girl's age is uncertain. What is clear is that Jesus brings life from death and turns the parents' grief into joy.

The clause (lit.) "they were amazed with a great amazement" (ἐξέστησαν ἐκστάσει μεγάλῃ) is a cognate dative,[23] which, like a cognate accusative, adds emphasis. The "they" no doubt refers to both the parents and the disciples. On the theme of amazement in Mark, see comments on 1:22 (cf. 1:27; 2:12; 5:15, 20; 6:51; 12:17).

5:43 He gave them strict orders not to let anyone know about this, and told them to give her something to eat (καὶ διεστείλατο αὐτοῖς πολλὰ ἵνα μηδεὶς γνοῖ τοῦτο, καὶ εἶπεν δοθῆναι αὐτῇ φαγεῖν). Jesus is back in Jewish territory and so the command to silence returns (1:44; 7:36; 8:26; cf. 1:25, 34; 3:11 – 12; 8:30; 9:9).[24] Of course, it will be impossible to keep, since the whole village certainly knew that the girl was dead. The point, however, is that Jesus again seeks to dampen messianic expectations and to shape his ministry on his own timetable (see comments on 1:43 – 44).

The command to give the girl something to eat is probably intended to be proof of her full recovery. It also reveals Jesus as a compassionate healer who is personally concerned about the girl's welfare.

Theology in Application

The Authority of Jesus to Bring Restoration and New Life

Throughout the first half of Mark's gospel, Jesus' *authority* as the announcer and inaugurator of the kingdom of God is on center stage. The miracles serve as "snapshots" of the coming kingdom, the restoration of creation, and the reconciliation of God and humanity. In the first cycle of miracle stories in chapters 1 – 3, the exorcisms symbolize the victory of God's kingdom over Satan's realm; the healings provide a glimpse of the future restoration of fallen humanity; and the forgiveness of sins previews the reconciliation between God and his people.

In this second cycle of miracles in 4:30 – 5:43, this restoration theme intensifies. The calming of the storm shows that the Messiah has authority over the forces of nature. He is the one who will restore a broken world. The exorcism of the Gerasene

---

21. The manuscript evidence for εὐθύς is well divided. It is omitted in 𝔓[45] A W È *f*[1.13] lat syr[p.h] boh[mss] but included in ℵ B C L Δ 33 579 892 2427 *pc* sah[mss] boh. It was likely omitted by copyists because of its awkwardness.

22. Boring, *Mark*, 158, 162.

23. Wallace, *Greek Grammar*, 168.

24. The ἵνα subjunctive clause (ἵνα μηδεὶς γνοῖ τοῦτο) is a substantival clause functioning as the direct object or content of the verb of commanding (διεστείλατο).

demoniac teaches that even the most powerful of Satan's forces stand helpless before the authority of the Son of God. Now, in the intercalated episode of Jairus's daughter and a sick woman, Jesus demonstrates his authority over the most persistent of diseases and even death itself. By raising this little girl, Jesus provides a preview of the coming victory that will be achieved through his sacrifice for sins (10:45) and resurrection from the dead.

The theme of conquest over death has deep roots in the OT. When God placed Adam and Eve in the garden of Eden, he warned them that if they ate from the tree of knowledge of good and evil, they would surely die (Gen 2:17). Their decision to disobey God resulted in immediate spiritual death and eventually physical death. From a biblical worldview, human death is not a natural part of an endless "cycle of life." It is a tragic intrusion into God's created intention for humanity, an aberration resulting from a fallen creation (Rom 5:12). Death is the consequence and penalty of human sin: "the wages of sin is death" (Rom 6:23).

Yet from the moment of humanity's fall, God launched a rescue plan to restore true life to his wayward people. The OT prophets predicted the day when God would "destroy the shroud that enfolds all peoples, the sheet that covers all nations; he will swallow up death forever" (Isa 25:7 – 8; cf. 26:19; Dan 12:2, 13). For the NT writers, that day has been inaugurated through the life, death, and resurrection of Jesus Christ. Jesus' death paid the penalty for sin, and his resurrection is the beginning of the end-time resurrection of the dead. By virtue of identification with him in his life, death, and burial, believers are spiritually raised with him into the new age of salvation and seated with him at the right hand of God (Rom 6:3 – 6; Eph 2:1 – 10; Col 2:12; 3:1 – 4). This is the victory Paul celebrates in 1 Corinthians 15. By virtue of Christ's resurrection, "death has been swallowed up in victory"(1 Cor 15:54).

Like all such resuscitations in the OT and NT,[25] the raising of Jairus's daughter is not a true "resurrection." True resurrection means the renewal to immortal, imperishable life (1 Cor 15:53 – 54). Jesus himself is the "firstborn from among the dead" (Col 1:18; cf. Rev 1:5). Jairus's daughter, like these others, is raised to mortal, perishable life. These resuscitations are therefore a preview and foreshadowing of Jesus' coming death and resurrection, and the immortal, eternal life believers receive through their identification with him. Like the other miracles in Jesus' ministry, they are "snapshots" of the coming kingdom of God.

The Need for Faith

The second major theme of the passage is the faith that Jesus expects from those who follow him. Faith is recognizing that there is nothing we can do to save ourselves

---

25. 1 Kgs 17:19 – 22 (the widow of Zarephath's son); 2 Kgs 4:29 – 35 (the Shunammite's son); Luke 7:11 – 16 (the widow's son); John 11 (Lazarus); Acts 9:36 – 43 (Dorcas); 20:7 – 12 (Eutychus).

and expressing our full dependence on God's saving power. Jairus demonstrates faith by coming to Jesus, despite the fact that to do so could mean ostracism from the religious establishment of Galilee. The woman's faith is demonstrated through her approach to Jesus, despite her shame in her condition and fear of rejection by others. Both believe Jesus has the power to save. Faith is not a single act, but means enduring in faith. When Jairus's daughter dies, Jairus faces an even greater challenge. Jesus calls him away from his fear to even greater faith in his power to raise the dead.

These two episodes on the need for faith stand in contrast to episodes that frame it on either side. Jesus rebukes the disciples for their failure to believe in the face of the angry storm (Mark 4:40), and the townspeople in Gerasa respond to Jesus' amazing exorcism with rejection instead of faith (5:18). In the next episode, Jesus will face rejection from his own people in his hometown of Nazareth. While everyone is amazed at Jesus' miraculous power throughout his Galilean ministry, in that episode Jesus himself will be "amazed" at their lack of faith (6:6).

For Mark's readers (as for us), these lessons on faith remind us that the Christian life is not always a comfortable walk in the park. It entails trials, suffering, and persecution. When the pressure comes — whether through persecution, illness, accidents, loss of job, betrayal by a friend, a broken relationship, or the death of a loved one — God calls us to turn to him in hope and faith, recognizing that he has a purpose and that, in the end, nothing can separate us from the love of God that is in Christ Jesus our Lord (Rom 8:39).

Jesus' Concern for Women

A third important theme in this episode is Jesus' care for those of low social status. Jesus turns away from Jairus, a religious male of high social status, to meet the needs of a woman whose gender and illness render her of little value by society's standards. As both a female and a child, Jairus's daughter would also be low on the social pecking order. Through Jesus' willingness to touch and heal these two women, he challenges both social norms and purity laws and demonstrates the restorative power and inclusivity of the kingdom of God. As followers of Jesus Christ, we are called to treat all people, whatever their position or status, with respect and compassion and to break down barriers that divide and alienate.

Mark 6:1 – 6a

Literary Context

In the episodes leading up to this one, Jesus has performed a series of powerful miracles, demonstrating his authority over natural and supernatural powers: calming the storm, exorcising a "legion" of demons, healing a woman with a chronic disease, and raising a dead girl back to life (4:35 – 5:43). Jesus is riding a wave of powerful deeds and popular acclaim. Mark now brings the reader back to earth as Jesus returns to his hometown of Nazareth and faces rejection by his own people. Those whom one might expect to be the most receptive turn out to be most opposed.

This episode recalls Mark's earlier collection of controversy stories (2:1 – 3:6), which were followed by a visit to Jesus from his family (3:20 – 21, 31 – 35), the Beelzebul episode (3:22 – 30), and Jesus' teaching in parables (4:1 – 32). While Jesus' family thought he was crazy and came to take charge of him, Jesus identifies his true family as "whoever does God's will" (3:35). These are those who understand the parables because they have eyes to see and ears to hear (4:9 – 12).

This episode concludes the second phase in Jesus' Galilean ministry. Just as the series of miracles and controversy stories in Jesus' early Galilean ministry climaxed in a statement of opposition and a plot against Jesus (3:1 – 6), so the later Galilean ministry (3:7 – 6:13) climaxes with a similar episode of opposition and rejection (6:1 – 6a).

Main Idea

Despite his extraordinary teaching and healing ministry, Jesus faces rejection by the people of his own hometown. The lack of faith of the Nazarenes stands in contrast to the faith of Jairus (5:36) and the woman with the bleeding disorder (5:34). The episode also serves to foreshadow the rejection from his own people that Jesus will face when he goes to Jerusalem.

Translation

Mark 6:1 – 6a

1a	Character entrance/Setting	**He left there and went to his hometown,**
b	Setting (social)	and **his disciples were accompanying him.**
2a	setting (temporal)	When the Sabbath arrived,
b	Action	**he began to teach in the synagogue.**
c	Response to 2b	**Many who heard him were amazed and said,**
d	rhetorical question	*"Where did this man get these abilities?*
e	rhetorical question	*And what is this wisdom that has been given to him?*
f	rhetorical question	*What are these powerful miracles being performed by his hands?*
3a	rhetorical question	*Isn't this the carpenter,*
b		*the son of Mary and*
c		*the brother of James, Joseph, Judah, and Simon?*
d	rhetorical question	*Aren't his sisters here with us?"*
e	Response to 2b	And **they took offense at him.**
4a	Response	**Jesus said to them,**
b	proverb/pronouncement	*"A prophet is shown honor everywhere*
c		*except in his own hometown and among his relatives and his own family."*
5a	Result	**He could not do any miracles there,**
	exception to 5a	except,
b		laying his hands on a few sick people,
c		he healed them.
6a	Response	And **he was amazed at their lack of faith.**

Structure

From a form-critical perspective, this is a pronouncement story, climaxing in an authoritative pronouncement by Jesus (cf. 1:36 – 38; 2:13 – 17, 18 – 22, 23 – 28; 3:31 – 35). Using categories of Hellenistic rhetoric, Witherington identifies it as a classic example of a *chreia,* "a short narrative about an historical figure climaxing with a memorable saying (6:4)."[1] Jesus' teaching, as usual, produces amazement (v. 2), but amazement soon turns to offense, as Jesus' neighbors and relatives are scandalized by his authoritative words and deeds. Jesus responds with amazement of his own, resulting from their lack of faith.

This is almost certainly the same historical event as Luke's Nazareth sermon in Luke 4:14 – 30. Luke's version, however, is much longer and plays a more prominent role in his narrative, serving as a programmatic introduction and preview of Jesus' whole ministry. Luke moves the episode forward to the beginning of Jesus' ministry,[2] provides the content of Jesus' teaching, and includes the violent response of the townspeople.[3] He also introduces the theme of Jesus' rejection as well as his ministry of liberation to the poor and the oppressed and God's love for the Gentiles. For Mark, the episode serves as one more reminder that Israel is divided between those receptive to Jesus' kingdom announcement and those rejecting it.

Exegetical Outline

→ **1. Setting: Jesus Returns to his Hometown (6:1)**

  2. Jesus Teaches on the Sabbath (6:2a-b)

  3. The Response of the Townspeople (6:2c – 3)

  4. Jesus' Pronouncement: A Prophet's Rejection in His Hometown (6:4)

  5. The Result (6:5 – 6a)

    a. He could not do many miracles there (6:5)

    b. He was amazed at their lack of faith (6:6a)

Explanation of the Text

6:1 He left there and went to his hometown, and his disciples were accompanying him (Καὶ ἐξῆλθεν ἐκεῖθεν καὶ ἔρχεται εἰς τὴν πατρίδα αὐτοῦ, καὶ ἀκολουθοῦσιν αὐτῷ οἱ μαθηταὶ αὐτοῦ). Mark had not identified where Jairus lived, though it was clearly on the western shore of Galilee (5:21 – 22), perhaps in Capernaum. Jesus leaves Jairus's home and travels to his "hometown" (πατρίς) of Nazareth, about twenty-five miles to the south. Though

Mark does not specifically name the town, the reader knows from 1:9 that Jesus came from Nazareth, and in 1:24 he is referred to as "Jesus of Nazareth."

Nazareth was a small village in Jesus' day and is not mentioned in the OT, the Talmud, or Josephus. Its obscurity is reflected in the Fourth Gospel in Nathanael's disdainful, "Can anything good come from [Nazareth]?" (John 1:46). Both

---

1. Witherington, *Mark*, 191; cf. his discussion of Mark's literary use of *chreia* on p. 9.

2. Luke's chronological reordering is evident from the fact that Jesus refers in Luke 4:23 to his ministry in Capernaum, even though he has not yet been there in Luke's narrative (4:31).

3. See Strauss, *Davidic Messiah*, 219 – 60; C. J. Schreck, "The Nazareth Pericope, Luke 4,16 – 30 in Recent Study," in *L'Évangile de Luc – The Gospel of Luke* (BETL 32; Leuven: Leuven University Press, 1989), 399 – 471.

Matthew and Luke identify Bethlehem as Jesus' birthplace but Nazareth as the place he was raised (Matt 2:1, 23; Luke 2:4, 39). Mark shows no interest in Jesus' birthplace or his Davidic descent (but see 12:35 – 37) and refers only to Nazareth as his hometown.

Almost as an afterthought Mark mentions that the disciples are with Jesus. He likely does so because, though incidental to this episode, they are integral to Jesus' ministry. In contrast to his relatives and neighbors in Nazareth, they are his true family who do the will of God (3:35) — the "insiders" with eyes to see and ears to hear the message of the kingdom of God (4:11 – 12).

6:2 When the Sabbath arrived, he began to teach in the synagogue. Many who heard him were amazed and said, "Where did this man get these abilities? And what is this wisdom that has been given to him? What are these powerful miracles being performed by his hands?" (καὶ γενομένου σαββάτου ἤρξατο διδάσκειν ἐν τῇ συναγωγῇ, καὶ πολλοὶ ἀκούοντες ἐξεπλήσσοντο λέγοντες· πόθεν τούτῳ ταῦτα, καὶ τίς ἡ σοφία ἡ δοθεῖσα τούτῳ, καὶ αἱ δυνάμεις τοιαῦται διὰ τῶν χειρῶν αὐτοῦ γινόμεναι;). Jesus had gained a reputation throughout Galilee as an authoritative teacher and healer (1:21 – 22, 27, 39; 3:1), and his return to Nazareth creates a stir. Jewish custom allowed any qualified male to speak in the synagogue by invitation of the synagogue leaders (cf. 1:21, 39; Acts 13:15), but Jesus' status as a "hometown boy" would have made this a particularly special occasion.

As throughout Jesus' Galilean ministry, his teaching produces "amazement" in the hearers (1:22, 27; 2:12).[4] The people respond with a series of five rhetorical questions, the first three related to Jesus' ministry and the last two concerning his local origins. While the final result is negative ("they took offense at him"; v. 3e), it is not clear whether the initial response is positive or negative.

Some commentators see an initial positive response followed by a negative one.[5] Others consider the response to be negative throughout.[6] The people express wonder at Jesus "abilities" (ταῦτα = "these things"), his "wisdom" (σοφία), and his "powers" (δυνάμεις) — that is, the miracles he is performing. The repeated demonstrative pronouns "this person" (τούτῳ) may be contemptuous in tone ("Who is *this guy?*"; cf. 2:7; 14:69),[7] but this is not certain, since the demonstrative is commonly used in Greek in place of the personal pronoun (cf. 3:35; 4:41). It seems best to conclude that the initial response is neither positive nor negative, but surprise and amazement. They are deeply impressed, but don't know what to make of Jesus and cannot explain the source of his authority, his depth of wisdom, or his miraculous powers.

6:3 "Isn't this the carpenter, the son of Mary and the brother of James, Joseph, Judah, and Simon? Aren't his sisters here with us?" And they took offense at him (οὐχ οὗτός ἐστιν ὁ τέκτων, ὁ υἱὸς τῆς Μαρίας καὶ ἀδελφὸς Ἰακώβου καὶ Ἰωσῆτος καὶ Ἰούδα καὶ Σίμωνος; καὶ οὐκ εἰσὶν αἱ ἀδελφαὶ αὐτοῦ ὧδε πρὸς ἡμᾶς; καὶ ἐσκανδαλίζοντο ἐν αὐτῷ). Two more rhetorical questions, related to Jesus' humble local origins, follow the first three.

The term "carpenter " (τέκτων) is a general one and could refer to a worker in wood, metal, or stone. Possible translations include "carpenter," "builder," "craftsman," "stonemason," or "construc-

---

4. ἐκπλήσσω does not mean that they were "knocked down" (contra Witherington, *Mark*, 192; Gundry, *Mark*, 189), an etymological fallacy. It means they were "amazed," "astounded," or "overwhelmed" (BDAG, 308).

5. Stein, *Mark*, 280 – 81; Marcus, *Mark 1 – 8*, 377 – 79.

6. Boring, *Mark*, 165; Gundry, *Mark*, 290; J. R. Donahue and D. J. Harrington, *The Gospel of Mark* (SP 2; Collegeville, MN: Liturgical, 2002), 184; Cranfield, *Mark*, 193; Collins, *Mark*, 290.

7. So Boring, *Mark*, 164; Gundry, *Mark*, 290; France, *Mark*, 242.

tion worker." The major Hellenistic-Jewish city of Sepphoris was only a few miles from Nazareth and was being rebuilt during Jesus' youth. It is possible that Joseph and his sons found work there. Matthew refers to Jesus as "the carpenter's son" (13:55) rather than "the carpenter," and some manuscripts of Mark's gospel follow this reading. This is likely an assimilation to Matthew's gospel, perhaps by copyists who could not envision the Son of God as a lowly craftsman.[8] While manual labor was viewed as degrading by most Greeks,[9] Jews considered working with their hands to be a noble profession, and a "carpenter" would have been an essential and respected profession in village life (though not as noble as a scribe who studied the law).[10] The people are not saying, "He's nothing but a common laborer," but rather, "He's no better than *anyone of us.*"

The description of Jesus as "the son of Mary" (ὁ υἱὸς τῆς Μαρίας) is unusual, since a man would normally be identified with his father. Indeed, Jesus is called the "son of Joseph" in Luke's parallel (4:22) and in John 1:45; 6:42. Some have seen here hints of illegitimacy (cf. John 4:41; 9:29); that is, Jesus is called "the son of Mary" because Joseph was not his real father.[11] This is speculative, however, since Mark does not recount the virgin birth and never mentions Joseph, either in 3:31 – 35 or here, where the entire family is described. The more likely explanation is that Joseph is now dead and so Jesus is identified as part of Mary's family. While it would still be unusual to refer to a son as his mother's child (a father may die, but would not be forgot-

ten!), if Joseph had died many years earlier, during Jesus' childhood or youth, he would be a distant memory in the minds of the townspeople. Perhaps Jesus had long been "Mary's son."

Jesus' brothers are named James (or Jacob; Ἰάκωβος), Joseph (or Joses; Ἰωσῆς), Judah (or Jude, or Judas; Ἰούδας), and Simon (or Simeon; Σίμων).[12] All these names were drawn from the Hebrew Scriptures and were common in first-century Israel. According to John 7:5, Jesus' brothers did not believe in him during his earthly ministry. They became believers in the post-resurrection church. They are mentioned, together with Mary, as present with the disciples in Jerusalem after the resurrection (Acts 1:14) and are later identified by Paul as traveling missionaries in the church (1 Cor 9:5).

James, or "Jacob," was likely the oldest of the four since he is always named first. He is the most prominent of Jesus' brothers in the NT. Paul refers to a resurrection appearance to him (1 Cor 15:7) and identifies him as a prominent leader in the Jerusalem church (Gal 1:19; 2:9, 12). He appears in Acts as the senior leader of the church and renders the decision at the council of Jerusalem (Acts 12:17; 15:13 – 21; 21:18). He is also traditionally identified as the author of the NT letter that bears his name. Both the Jewish historian Josephus (*Ant.* 20.9.1 §200) and the early church historian Eusebius (*Hist. eccl.* 2.33) record James's martyrdom at the instigation of the high priest Ananus.

Jude is identified as the author of the epistle of Jude, where he identifies himself as a "brother of James" (Jude 1). We know nothing else about Jo-

8. When the antagonist Celsus mocked Christianity for being founded by a lowly carpenter, the early church father Origen claimed that none of the manuscripts available to him identified Jesus as a "carpenter" (*Cels.* 6.34, 36). Metzger responds, "Either Origen did not recall Mk 6:3, or the text of this verse in copies known to him had already been assimilated to the Matthean parallel" (Metzger, *Textual Commentary*, 75 n. 1).

9. Cf. Origen, *Cels.* 6.34, 36.

10. See Sir 38:24 – 39:11, where the vocation of scribe is celebrated and contrasted with that of craftsmen and laborers.

11. Str-B 1:39 – 43; Origen, *Cels.* 1.28.

12. The various spellings arise, in part, from the movement from Hebrew to Greek to English and in part from textual variations. Matthew's parallel reads "Joseph" (Ἰωσήφ) in the best manuscripts, with some manuscripts reading either Joses (Ιωσης) or John (Ιωαννης).

seph and Simon, nor about Jesus' sisters. The fact that the sisters are identified as "here with us" (ὧδε πρὸς ἡμᾶς) may mean that they had married local men and so were living in Nazareth.[13]

There are three main views concerning the relationship of these siblings to Jesus. (1) The view of Epiphanius was that these were Jesus' stepbrothers and stepsisters, Joseph's children by a previous marriage.[14] One problem with this view is that there is no mention of these children in the birth narratives of Matthew or Luke. (2) Jerome's view was that these were not actually brothers, but cousins. The strongest argument for this view is John 19:26 – 27, where Jesus entrusts the care of his mother to the Beloved Disciple rather than to his own brothers (or stepbrothers). The greatest problem with the view is that Greek has a distinct word for cousin (ἀνεψιός; cf. Col 4:10). Why would Mark use "brother" (ἀδελφός) here if he meant "cousin"? (3) The view of Helvidius remains the simplest and the most likely: these were brothers and sisters born to Joseph and Mary after the birth of Jesus. Matthew 1:25 suggests that Joseph and Mary had normal marital relations after the birth of Jesus.

The Nazareth townspeople are said to be offended or "scandalized" (imperfect passive of σκανδαλίζω) by Jesus. The verb can mean to cause to sin, to stumble, or to be shocked, angered, or offended. The idea here is that they rejected Jesus' message and his authority. Mark does not explicitly state the reason for this offense, but the implication is that they refused to believe that one from such humble and familiar origins could be God's

agent for inaugurating the kingdom of God. They are offended (and perhaps jealous) that this young upstart is acting with greater authority than his family background and social status warrant (see Theology in Application. below).

6:4 Jesus said to them, "A prophet is shown honor everywhere except in his own hometown and among his relatives and his own family." (καὶ ἔλεγεν αὐτοῖς ὁ Ἰησοῦς ὅτι οὐκ ἔστιν προφήτης ἄτιμος εἰ μὴ ἐν τῇ πατρίδι αὐτοῦ καὶ ἐν τοῖς συγγενεῦσιν αὐτοῦ καὶ ἐν τῇ οἰκίᾳ αὐτοῦ). In response to the townspeople's rejection, Jesus cites a proverb about a prophet's rejection among his own people. The Greek says that "a prophet is not dishonored except …" (οὐκ ἔστιν προφήτης ἄτιμος εἰ μή), but since the double negative sounds more convoluted in English than in Greek, we have translated it positively.[15]

Secular parallels speak of philosophers, physicians, and other great men who are not honored in their own country. Apollonius of Tyana said, "Until now my own country [πατρίς] alone ignores me," and Dio Chrysostom said that "all the philosophers held life to be difficult in their homeland (πατρίδι)."[16] A similar English proverb is "familiarity breeds contempt."

The identification of Jesus as a "prophet" is unusual for Mark, occurring only here in his gospel. For Mark, Jesus is more than a prophet; he is the Messiah and Son of God (8:28 – 29; cf. 6:14 – 15). Yet Jesus will suffer the fate of the prophets. The theme of the rejection and suffering of the prophets is common in the OT[17] as well as throughout

13. See France, *Mark*, 165 n. 31; G. D. Kilpatrick, "Jesus, His Family and His Disciples," *JSNT* 5 (1982): 3 – 19.

14. For a recent defense of this view, see Richard J. Bauckham, *Jude and the Relatives of Jesus in the Early Church* (Edinburgh: T&T Clark, 1990); idem, "The Brothers and Sisters of Jesus: An Epiphanian Response to John P. Meier," *CBQ* 56 (1994): 698 – 700.

15. Parallels appear in Luke 4:24; John 4:44; *Gos. Thom.* 31;

P.Oxyr. 1.6. Luke's version reads, "No prophet is accepted in his hometown," and John has that Jesus "had pointed out that a prophet has no honor in his own country." The versions in the *Gospel of Thomas* and *P.Oxyr.* 1 appear to be dependent on Luke.

16. Apollonius of Tyana, *Ep.* 44; Dio Chrysostom 47.6; both cited by Davies and Allison, *Matthew*, 2:460.

17. 1 Kgs 13:4; 18:13; 19:2; 22:26 – 27; 2 Kgs 1:9; 6:31; 2 Chr 24:21; Jer 18:18, 23; 26:11, 20 – 23; 36:1 – 38:13.

Luke's gospel with reference to Jesus' suffering role (Luke 4:24; 7:16, 39; 11:47 – 51; 13:33 – 34; 24:19; cf. Acts 3:22; 7:37). The three relationships — hometown (πατρίς), relatives (συγγενεῖς), family (or "household"; οἰκία) — appear to be narrowing from more general to more intimate relationships: from community to clan to immediate family.

6:5 – 6a He could not do any miracles there, except, laying his hands on a few sick people, he healed them. And he was amazed at their lack of faith (καὶ οὐκ ἐδύνατο ἐκεῖ ποιῆσαι οὐδεμίαν δύναμιν, εἰ μὴ ὀλίγοις ἀρρώστοις ἐπιθεὶς τὰς χεῖρας ἐθεράπευσεν. καὶ ἐθαύμαζεν διὰ τὴν ἀπιστίαν αὐτῶν). This statement apparently limiting Jesus' power is shocking, especially in the context of a gospel where Jesus' amazing authority over demons, disease, storms, and death has been on center stage. It was evidently too much for Matthew, who modifies it to say simply that Jesus "did not do many miracles there" (Matt 13:58).

Yet Mark's statement makes good sense in a context where Jesus has been performing miracles in response to faith (2:5; 4:40; 5:34, 36; 9:23 – 24; 10:52; 11:22 – 24). When faith is the prerequisite for spiritual blessings, there can be no miracles without it. The unbelief in Nazareth stands in stark contrast to the previous episode, where the faith of the sick woman (5:34) and of Jairus (5:36) resulted in healing and new life.

Despite this rejection, the kingdom advances, and some are healed (6:6). Mark's qualification, "except, laying his hands on a few sick people, he healed them" (6:5), is ironic and even comical. In most any context, ancient or modern, the miraculous healing of "a few" would be a momentous event, hardly classified as "doing no miracle" (ποιῆσαι οὐδεμίαν δύναμιν). Yet in contrast to Jesus' remarkable ministry up to this point, it is considered a failure. Jesus could have done so much more if the people of Nazareth would have only believed.

Amazement has been a major theme throughout the Galilean ministry (1:22, 27; 2:12; 5:15, 20; 5:42; 6:51; cf. 12:17), but always as a response to Jesus' words and deeds. Now it is *Jesus* who is amazed (only here in Mark). Was he truly surprised? Mark elsewhere shows the true humanity of Jesus, revealing a range of human emotions (1:41; 3:5; 6:34; 10:21; 14:33 – 34) and limits of knowledge and power (13:32; 14:33 – 34; cf. 8:23 – 24). His primary point here, however, is not that Jesus is taken off guard, but that those who should be most responsive to Jesus' kingdom proclamation are in fact the most resistant to it. The implied reader is as shocked as Jesus is by their lack of faith.

Theology in Application

The Rejection of Jesus by His Own People

Mark here returns to the theme of opposition to Jesus that began in 2:1 – 3:6. There, Jesus faced rejection from Israel's religious leaders for claiming to forgive sins, associating with sinners, ignoring fasting traditions, and supposed violations of the Sabbath. The result was a plot by the Pharisees and the Herodians to kill Jesus (3:6). These controversy stories were followed by the Beelzebul episode (3:22 – 30), "sandwiched" (intercalated) between two episodes concerning Jesus' family (3:20 – 21, 31 – 35). Jesus faced opposition from his own family and from the religious leaders of his own nation. The present passage thus renews the Markan theme that Jesus' own people reject him and foreshadows his coming rejection in Jerusalem. From the perspective of biblical theology, it can be seen as a narrative commentary on John 1:11: "He came to that which was his own, but his own did not receive him."

This passage would have been important for Mark's readers, who were suffering rejection and persecution from their countrymen, perhaps even relatives and neighbors (cf. 13:12 – 13). To become a Christ follower means that our citizenship is in heaven (Phil 3:20), and in this life we live as foreigners and exiles in an alien land (1 Pet 1:1, 17; 2:11). It means a willingness to give up all — family, friends, and even life itself — to follow him (Mark 8:34 – 36; 10:29).

The Lowly Origins of the Messiah

In Western culture, the possibility of upward mobility is taken for granted. The "American dream" is to move, through hard work and ingenuity, from poverty to wealth, from obscurity to fame, and from powerlessness to a position of influence. We celebrate entrepreneurs, athletes, celebrities, and politicians who have pulled themselves up by their own bootstraps to become something great. The ancient world had different values. One's family identity and social status were considered to be established at birth, and people were expected to respect the social boundaries that the gods had ordained. Those with noble roots were to rule, while the lowly and poor were to be content in their humble positions and roles. This helps to explain the scandal felt by the Nazareth townspeople at Jesus' authoritative claims. They cannot believe that one of their own, a lowly carpenter from the backwater village of Nazareth, could be God's agent of salvation.

Mark does nothing to "correct" this image of Jesus' humble origins. Unlike Matthew and Luke, he tells us nothing about Jesus' royal ancestry through David or his Bethlehem birthplace. No magi from the east come searching for "the king of the Jews" (Matt 2:1 – 2). Jesus appears as a humble servant, who gives himself for others. The path to greatness, Jesus teaches his disciples, is through service and sacrifice. Whoever wants to be great must become a servant, and whoever wants to be first must be a slave of all, "for even the Son of Man did not come to be served, but to serve, and to give his life as a ransom for many" (10:45).

The Suffering Role of God's Messengers

By citing the proverb in v. 4, Jesus identifies his rejection at Nazareth with the suffering role of the prophets in the past. The rejection of God's messengers is a common theme in the biblical tradition. Queen Jezebel killed the prophets of the Lord (1 Kgs 18:4, 13) and sought to kill Elijah for his defeat of the prophets of Baal (19:2); Micaiah was imprisoned for prophesying defeat for King Ahab (22:27); Zechariah was stoned to death (2 Chr 24:20 – 22); Jeremiah was threatened with death (Jer 26:8), imprisoned (37:16), thrown in a well (38:6), and deported to Egypt (42:1 – 43:7); his prophecies were burned (36:20 – 26).

This theme appears frequently in the NT. Just before suffering martyrdom himself, Stephen accuses Israel's leaders of persecuting the prophets, murdering those who predicted the coming Messiah, and finally killing the Righteous One himself (Acts 7:51 – 52). The writer to the Hebrews describes those faithful witnesses of the past who were stoned, sawn in two, and put to death by the sword, and went about destitute, persecuted, and mistreated (Heb 11:37).

Jesus' identification as a suffering prophet is a major theme in Luke's gospel and serves as one of Luke's key explanations for the rejection of Jesus. Jesus must go to Jerusalem, since "no prophet can die outside of Jerusalem" (Luke 13:33 – 34; cf. 4:24; 11:47 – 51; cf. Acts 3:22; 7:37, 51 – 52). As God's agent of salvation, Jesus suffers the fate of all God's messengers. Though this theme appears only here in Mark, the connection between Jesus and the prophets will come to expression again in Mark's parable of the wicked tenant farmers (12:1 – 12). The farmers (symbolizing Israel's religious leaders) beat, humiliate, and kill the servants (the prophets) sent by the vineyard owner (God) to collect the crop. Finally, they reject and kill his own son (Jesus). For Mark's readers, the rejection of the Messiah and his messengers is a reminder that all who desire to live godly lives will suffer persecution (2 Tim 3:12). But in the end, suffering and persecution will give way to vindication and salvation: "For whoever wants to save their life will lose it, but whoever loses their life for me and for the gospel will save it" (Mark 8:35).

Mark 6:6b – 13

Literary Context

Here begins the third major phase of Jesus' public ministry, as Jesus expands his ministry through the mission of the Twelve and expands his reach beyond Galilee (6:6b – 8:21; see Outline, below). This unit includes the mission of the Twelve (6:6b – 13), an account of the death of John the Baptist (6:14 – 29), two feeding miracles (6:30 – 44; 8:1 – 10), and additional healings (6:53 – 56; 7:24 – 30, 31 – 37) and controversy stories (7:1 – 23; 8:11 – 13, 14 – 21). The miracle of Jesus' walking on water (6:45 – 52) parallels his earlier calming of the storm (4:35 – 41). The central theme continues to be the authority of Jesus as inaugurator of the kingdom of God. Secondary themes include increasing conflict with the religious leaders and the growing spiritual dullness of the disciples.[1] There is a decided tension here as, on the one hand, the disciples fulfill the crucial role of spiritual "insiders" and Jesus' key representatives (6:12 – 13), while on the other hand, they are unresponsive and slow to understand (6:51 – 52; 8:14 – 21).

Mark earlier recorded the *call* of Jesus' first disciples (1:16 – 19) and the *appointment* of the Twelve (3:13 – 19). Now Jesus *sends them out* to replicate his ministry throughout Galilee (6:6b – 13). Structurally, then, we have a key episode concerning the role of the disciples at the beginning of each of the three phases of Jesus' ministry in and around Galilee (1:14 – 3:6; 3:7 – 6:6a; 6:6b – 8:21), confirming the disciples' role as critical to his mission. Furthermore, just as the opposition to Jesus and the plot against him in 3:1 – 6 served as the climax to Jesus' early Galilean ministry (1:14 – 3:6), so the opposition and rejection of Jesus by the people of Nazareth (6:1 – 6a) functioned as the climax to the later Galilean ministry (3:7 – 6:6a). This juxtaposition of episodes concerning the rejection of Jesus by his opponents on the one hand and the role of the disciples on the other will become significant at the end

---

1. Stein, *Mark*, 287 – 88, points to the unusual number of episodes here that concern food: the two feeding miracles (6:30 – 44; 8:1 – 10), Jesus' teaching about clean and unclean foods (7:1 – 23), the discussion about the leaven of the Pharisees and the disciples' failure to bring bread (8:14 – 21), the Gentile woman's request for the "crumbs" that the children drop (7:27 – 28), and the banquet setting that leads to the death of John the Baptist (6:14 – 29). This, however, seems more coincidental than an intentional theme by Mark.

of the present section (8:14 – 21), where the disciples seem in danger of going the way of those who "have eyes but cannot see and ears but do not hear" (8:18; cf. 4:11 – 12).

Some commentators treat the present passage as the end of the previous section (3:7 – 6:13)[2] rather than as the beginning of the next (6:6b – 8:21). In fact, it is transitional, serving both as a sequel to the appointment of the Twelve in 3:13 – 19 and as the beginning of the expansion of Jesus' ministry beyond Galilee. Its connection to the material that follows is evident in that the beginning (6:6b – 13) and end of the journey (6:30) "sandwiches" (intercalates) the account of the death of John the Baptist (6:14 – 29; see Structure, below). For this reason we have treated it in our outline as the introduction to phase 3 of Jesus' public ministry.

In 3:14 – 15 Jesus appointed the Twelve (1) to be with him, and (2) to send them out (a) to preach and (b) to drive out demons. While the Twelve have fulfilled the first part of this commission — being with Jesus and observing and learning from him — now for the first time Jesus sends them out to expand his ministry: preaching, healing, and casting out demons.

II. The Authority of the Messiah (1:14 – 8:21)
   A. The Kingdom Authority of the Messiah (1:14 – 3:6)
   B. The Disciple-Family of the Messiah and Those "Outside" (3:7 – 6:6a)
→ **C. The Expanding Mission of the Messiah (6:6b – 8:21)**
      1. Sending out the Twelve (6:6b – 13)
      2. Flashback to the Death of John the Baptist (6:14 – 29)

Main Idea

Jesus commissions the Twelve and sends them out to replicate his ministry: casting out demons, healing the sick, and calling people to repentance in light of the inbreaking power of the kingdom of God. Jesus' instructions to the Twelve call for a life of simple dependence on God and on the generous hospitality of those who welcome them and their message.

---

2. E.g., Lane, *Mark*, 126, 210.

Translation

Mark 6:6b – 13

6b	Summary	Then **he went around teaching in their villages.**
7a	Action/Commissioning	**He summoned the Twelve** and
b		**began to send them out two by two,** and
c		**gave them authority over defiling spirits.**
8a	Instructions	**He instructed them to take nothing for their journey**
b	exception to 8a	except only a staff
c	clarification of 8a	— no bread, no bag, no money in their belts.
9a	clarification of 8a	While they could wear sandals,
b	Clarification of 8a	**they could not take an extra tunic.**
10a	Instructions	**He continued saying to them,**
b	setting/condition	*"Whenever you enter a home,*
c	command/result	*stay there until you leave that place.*
11a b	condition (protasis)	*If any place does not welcome you or listen to you,*
		as you leave there
c	Result (apodosis)	*shake the dust off your feet*
d	purpose of 11c	*as a testimony against them."*
12a	Response to instruction	Going out,
b	Action/Preaching	**they preached that people should repent.**
13a	Action/Exorcism	**They drove out many demons**
b	Action/Healing	and **anointed many sick people with oil and healed them.**

Structure

The account of the sending of the Twelve is a commissioning narrative, as Jesus instructs and sends out his disciples to expand his ministry. The episode is framed by two summaries, the first concerning the continuation of Jesus' teaching ministry (6:6b) and the second concerning the preaching and healing ministry of the disciples as they go out at Jesus' command (6:12 – 13). The framing structure of the episode itself illustrates its function: to narrate the expansion of Jesus' ministry through his disciples.

The other important structural feature of the passage is its intercalation ("sandwiching") with the martyrdom of John the Baptist. The disciples depart in vv. 12 – 13 and then return in v. 30, after the long interlude about the account of the death of John the Baptist (6:14 – 29). This is the third of Mark's intercalations (cf. 3:20 – 35; 5:21 – 43; see Introduction to Mark: Literary Features), though its function is less clear than others. While typically the episodes interpret, explain, or illustrate one another, the relationship between these is more uncertain. Perhaps the theme is discipleship. Jesus commissions his disciples to fulfill the role he has entrusted to them, and the martyrdom of John the Baptist serves as a vivid illustration of the ultimate cost of discipleship.

Exegetical Outline

→ **1. Summary: Jesus' Teaching from Village to Village (6:6b)**

2. Commissioning the Twelve (6:7)
   a. Sending out two by two (6:7a-b)
   b. Authority to cast out demons (6:7c)

3. Instructions for the Twelve (6:8 – 11)
   a. Take a staff, but no provisions (6:8)
   b. Wear sandals, but no extra tunic (6:9)
   c. Acceptance of hospitality (6:10)
   d. Judgment for rejection (6:11)

4. The Mission of the Twelve (6:12 – 13)
   a. Their departure (6:12a)
   b. Their preaching (6:12b)
   c. Their exorcism (6:13a)
   d. Their healing (6:13b)

Explanation of the Text

6:6b Then he went around teaching in their villages (Καὶ περιῆγεν τὰς κώμας κύκλῳ διδάσκων). Despite the rejection by his own people of Nazareth (6:1 – 6a), Jesus is undeterred in his goal to proclaim the gospel to all the towns and villages of Galilee (cf. 1:38: "this is why I came"). Jesus' mission is to proclaim the message to all Israel so that Israel can be a "light for the Gentiles" to bring God's salvation "to the ends of the earth" (Isa 49:6; cf. 42:6; 60:3; Mark 13:10; 14:9). This is consistent with Paul's vision that the gospel is "first to the Jew, then to the Gentile" (Rom 1:16).

6:7 He summoned the Twelve and began to send them out two by two, and gave them authority over defiling spirits (καὶ προσκαλεῖται τοὺς δώδεκα καὶ ἤρξατο αὐτοὺς ἀποστέλλειν δύο δύο καὶ ἐδίδου αὐτοῖς ἐξουσίαν τῶν πνευμάτων τῶν ἀκαθάρτων). "The Twelve" (τοὺς δώδεκα) recalls 3:14, where their appointment likely indicates Jesus' reconstitution of a "restored Israel" (see comments at 3:14). Jesus appointed them "to preach and with authority to cast out demons" (3:14 – 15), but this is the first time we see them actually doing this. Sending them out "two by two" (δύο δύο) is no doubt for support, protection, and fellowship, but it also may reflect the OT injunction for the need of two witnesses to confirm a testimony in court (Deut 17:6; 19:15; cf. Num 35:30). Jesus follows this same procedure in Luke's mission of the seventy (Luke 10:1), and in Acts the apostles regularly travel in pairs (3:1 – 11; 8:14; 11:30; 13:1 – 2; 15:22, 39 – 40; cf. 2 Cor 12:18).

It is somewhat surprising that only exorcism is mentioned as their task. But this is probably just

Mark's shorthand summary since, in the description of their actual work, they preach, heal, and cast out demons (vv. 12 – 13; cf. v. 30). Exorcism is likely highlighted to emphasize the spiritual war that is raging with the coming of the kingdom of God — a major Markan theme early in his gospel (cf. 1:13, 23 – 24, 34; 3:22 – 27).

Jesus here demonstrates remarkable authority. Not only does he have divine authority to preach, heal, and cast out demons, but he can pass that authority on to others. It is more than just delegated; it is his own authority to give.

6:8 – 9 He instructed them to take nothing for their journey except only a staff — no bread, no bag, no money in their belts. While they could wear sandals, they could not take an extra tunic (καὶ παρήγγειλεν αὐτοῖς ἵνα μηδὲν αἴρωσιν εἰς ὁδὸν εἰ μὴ ῥάβδον μόνον, μὴ ἄρτον, μὴ πήραν, μὴ εἰς τὴν ζώνην χαλκόν, ἀλλὰ ὑποδεδεμένους σανδάλια, καὶ μὴ ἐνδύσησθε δύο χιτῶνας). Jesus provides detailed instructions concerning what they can and cannot take on their journey. The ἵνα clause after "instructed" indicates the content of the instruction. The central message is clear: they must travel light, unencumbered by the things of the world, trusting in God and depending on the hospitality of others.

They should carry only the clothes on their back, sandals on their feet, and a walking stick.[3] They must not carry provisions ("bread") or extra clothing, nor even the money to purchase such things.

The "bag" (πήρα) is likely a knapsack or traveler's bag, although the word could have a more specialized sense of the "beggar's bag" carried by Cynic philosophers.[4] In this case Jesus may be saying not to act like the Cynics, who claimed to be detached from the world but begged from others for food and money.[5] However, the influence of such philosophers in Jesus' contexts is uncertain. Closer to the Palestinian context are the descriptions of prophets like Elijah and John the Baptist, who traveled about with staff, sandals, and simple clothing.[6]

The word translated "money" (χαλκός) can refer to various metals — copper, brass, or bronze — or things made of such metals. Here, the sense is "coins," or perhaps "small change."[7] The phrase translated "take an extra tunic" is, literally, "wear two tunics" (ἐνδύσησθε δύο χιτῶνας). A tunic was a long, shirtlike undergarment that would be worn next to the skin. Wearing two seems unnecessary, so this may be an idiomatic way of saying not to "take an extra one." Or perhaps the second was for

---

3. The specifics in Mark differ somewhat from those in Matthew and Luke (Matt 10:11 – 14; Luke 10:1 – 12; Q?). While Mark allows a "staff" or "walking stick" (ῥάβδος), these are forbidden in Matthew (Matt 10:10) and Luke (Luke 9:3). Similarly, sandals are allowed in Mark, but not in Matthew (Luke does not mention them). Various solutions have been proposed for the apparent contradiction. Some have claimed that Matthew and Luke are referring to taking or acquiring an *extra* staff. This may perhaps be implied by Matthew's imperative not to "get" or acquire (κτήσησθε) these things (Matt 10:9 – 10). Luke, however, speaks of "taking" or "carrying" (αἴρετε) a staff (Luke 9:3), so this solution seems stretched. In any case, why would anyone travel with more than one staff? Another suggestion is that Mark means a walking stick, while Matthew and Luke are referring to a shepherd's staff or club. Again, this is possible, but it is unlikely, since the same word is used in all three gos-

pels. Matthew and Mark use different words for the footwear (Matt: ὑποδήματα; Mark: σανδάλια), so perhaps "sandals" are allowed but not "shoes." But this again seems far-fetched. No other footwear than sandals was common among Palestinian men. Furthermore, Mark uses a cognate verb "wear/shod in" (ὑποδεδεμένους), which is related to Matthew's term for sandals (ὑποδήματα). We may, of course, have an early scribal corruption, but the evidence for this is also lacking. It seems best to acknowledge that we simply don't know the answer.

4. BDAG, 811; Hengel, *Charismatic Leader*, 28; Guelich, *Mark 1:1 – 8:26*, 322; Boring, *Mark*, 175; Boring et al., eds., *Hellenistic Commentary*, §§78 – 81, pp. 80 – 81.

5. See Collins, *Mark*, 299 – 300, for similarities and differences from the Cynics.

6. France, *Mark*, 248 – 49.

7. BDAG, 1076.

added warmth against the chill of the night.[8] In either case, any surplus clothing is forbidden (cf. Luke 3:11).

Some have seen further symbolism in Jesus' words, echoing the command given to the Israelites in preparation for the exodus. They had to be ready to leave, "with your cloak tucked into your belt, your sandals on your feet and your staff in your hand" (Exod 12:11).[9] Marcus suggests that Mark here envisions the missionaries as participating with Jesus in a new exodus.[10] While possible, such an allusion seems too nuanced and remote to have been Mark's intention. Items like staffs and sandals were so much a part of everyday life that their mere mention is unlikely to have recalled exodus imagery. It would be different if Jesus had said something like, "Be ready to leave, with sandals on and staff in hand."[11]

6:10 – 11 He continued saying to them, "Whenever you enter a home, stay there until you leave that place. If any place does not welcome you or listen to you, as you leave there shake the dust off your feet as a testimony against them." (καὶ ἔλεγεν αὐτοῖς· ὅπου ἐὰν εἰσέλθητε εἰς οἰκίαν, ἐκεῖ μένετε ἕως ἂν ἐξέλθητε ἐκεῖθεν. καὶ ὃς ἂν τόπος μὴ δέξηται ὑμᾶς μηδὲ ἀκούσωσιν ὑμῶν, ἐκπορευόμενοι ἐκεῖθεν ἐκτινάξατε τὸν χοῦν τὸν ὑποκάτω τῶν ποδῶν ὑμῶν εἰς μαρτύριον αὐτοῖς). As the disciples travel, they are to depend on the hospitality of others.

Hospitality was among the highest of values in the Middle East, both ancient and modern, and the early Christian missionaries depended on it

as they traveled from place to place (see Theology in Application). An interesting Jewish parallel comes from Josephus, who describes the bond of hospitality that existed among members of the Essene community. They would travel throughout the country unencumbered by provisions or extra clothing (except weapons to protect themselves from bandits), receiving hospitality from fellow Essenes (Josephus, *J. W.* 2.8.4 §124).

Jesus envisions two responses the disciples will face, one positive and one negative. If they are welcomed into a home, Jesus says, they must stay there until they leave (cf. Matt 10:11; Luke 9:4; 10:10). This command reflects concern both for the motives of the missionaries and the unity of the messianic community. The natural human tendency for the travelers would be to move up the social ladder, accepting better and better accommodations from wealthier people. Such favoritism is not only sinful (Jas 2:1 – 13), but could produce jealousy and disunity. For the missionaries themselves it would foster a culture of greed and lack of dependence on God, running counter to the very reasons for accepting the hospitality of others.

While some would welcome the disciples, others would reject them (as they had just rejected Jesus in his hometown of Nazareth; 6:1 – 6). Such rejection entails both a failure to "welcome you" (δέξηται ὑμᾶς; i.e., lack of hospitality) and an unwillingness to "listen to you" (ἀκούσωσιν ὑμῶν; i.e., a rejection of the message of the kingdom). When this happens, Jesus tells them to "shake the dust off your feet." This action may be related to the rab-

---

8. Lane, *Mark*, 208. The reference sometimes cited from Josephus to a man wearing two tunics is not relevant here, since in that case the messenger is wearing a second shirt to conceal a letter sewn into its lining (*Ant.* 17.5.7 §136).

9. Ulrich W. Mauser, *Christ in the Wilderness: The Wilderness Theme in the Second Gospel and Its Basis in the Biblical Tradition* (London: SCM, 1963), 133 – 34; Lane, *Mark*, 207 – 8 n. 31.

10. Marcus, *Mark 1 – 8*, 389 – 90.

11. Others have pointed to the command in the Mishnah forbidding entrance into the temple with staff, sandals, wallet, or dust on one's feet (*m. Ber.* 9:5). T. W. Manson, *The Sayings of Jesus: As Recorded in the Gospels of St. Matthew and St. Mark* (Grand Rapids: Eerdmans, 1979), 181, says the forbidding of these things (in Luke and Matthew) demonstrates the sacredness of the mission. This, of course, would not apply to Mark, who allows them. Yet even for Matthew and Luke, such nuance seems far beyond the Evangelists' intention.

binic tradition of shaking the dust of foreign lands off one's garments when returning to the Holy Land.[12] The missionaries would thus be declaring the place of rejection to be pagan or "defiled."

Whether this is the background or not, the gesture is clearly one of disassociation, leaving that place to suffer the consequences of its rejection. Paul and Barnabas do this on their first missionary journey when they are driven out of Pisidian Antioch (Acts 13:51; cf. 18:6). The phrase "as a testimony to/against them" (εἰς μαρτύριον αὐτοῖς) could be viewed positively or negatively, either (1) as a witness *to* them, or (2) as a judicial pronouncement *against* them (cf. comments on 1:44). The latter is more likely and finds support in Luke 10:12, where a similar statement is followed by the pronouncement that "it will be more bearable on that day for Sodom than for that town."

6:12 – 13 Going out, they preached that people should repent. They drove out many demons and anointed many sick people with oil and healed them (Καὶ ἐξελθόντες ἐκήρυξαν ἵνα μετανοῶσιν, καὶ δαιμόνια πολλὰ ἐξέβαλλον, καὶ ἤλειφον ἐλαίῳ πολλοὺς ἀρρώστους καὶ ἐθεράπευον). While the statement of commissioning in v. 7 mentioned only

casting out demons,[13] it now becomes clear that the disciples' mission involved preaching, exorcism, and healing — the same activities Jesus had been performing. The content of the preaching is "that people should repent" (ἵνα μετανοῶσιν).[14] Hooker points out that this message is closer to that of John the Baptist in 1:4 than to Jesus' in 1:15 and so may indicate that the disciples, like John, were meant to prepare the way for Jesus.[15] More likely, however, as in v. 7, Mark is abbreviating, so that this is his shorthand way of summarizing Jesus' full proclamation: "The time is fulfilled, the kingdom of God is close at hand; repent and believe in the good news" (1:15). This is evident from the fact that the disciples are replicating the key features of Jesus' ministry: preaching, healing, and casting out demons.

The reference to being "anointed … with oil" in conjunction with healing occurs only here in the Gospels, and elsewhere in the NT only at Jas 5:14 – 15. Oil was used medicinally in biblical times (Isa 1:6; Luke 10:34), but the oil here is more likely being used to represent the healing presence of the Spirit of God. The disciples are not functioning as physicians, but as agents of the reconciling power of the kingdom of God.

Theology in Application

The Role of the Disciples as Jesus' Representatives

We have already discussed the important narrative and theological connection between this episode and the call and appointment of the disciples in 1:16 – 19 and 3:13 – 19 (see Literary Context, above). Jesus chooses, appoints, and then sends out his "apostles" ("messengers, sent ones") to represent the restored Israel and to take his message to Israel and beyond. We have also noted the ambivalent role of the

---

12. See *m. 'Ohal* 2:3; *m. Ṭehar* 4:5; *b. Šabb.* 15b.

13. The fact that v. 7 refers to "defiling spirits" (πνεύματα ἀκάθαρτα) and v. 13 to "demons" (δαιμόνια) shows that these two designations are synonymous for Mark.

14. ἵνα plus the subjunctive here indicates the content of the preaching; cf. v. 8.

15. Hooker, *Mark*, 157. She qualifies this, however, by noting that the summaries in 1:34 and 3:10 – 11 suggest that Mark sees them as participating in Jesus' ministry.

disciples throughout Mark's gospel. These are the "insiders" who are privy to the secrets of the kingdom of God. They are Jesus' representatives, who will expand his ministry now and eventually take the message of the kingdom of God to the ends of the earth (13:10; 14:9). Yet they also appear in Mark almost as "anti-disciples," acting with pride and selfishness and failing to comprehend Jesus' message and mission (6:52; 7:18; 8:17 – 18, 32; 9:5 – 6, 19, 33 – 37; 10:35 – 45).

Jesus uses even the most flawed instruments to accomplish his purposes. As Paul reminds the Corinthians, not many of them were wise or influential or of noble birth when God called them. God chose the weak, the foolish, and the despised things of the world to shame the wise and the strong (1 Cor 1:27 – 29).

The disciples will become a powerful force to change the world because they are not acting in their authority, but in the power and authority of Jesus and the kingdom of God. This has an important application for us today. Though the church today is far from perfect, as heirs of the commission given to the disciples (Matt 28:18 – 20), we are the "body" of Christ, his hands and feet in the world (1 Cor 12:27; Eph 1:22 – 23; Col 1:24). We are "jars of clay" who have been filled with treasure, "to show that this all-surpassing power is from God and not from us" (2 Cor 4:7). Our task is simply to proclaim the message of salvation: that God takes sinners and transforms them into saints and that he has rescued us from the dominion of darkness and brought us to the kingdom of his beloved Son (Col 1:13).

Instructions for Missions

The commands given to the disciples in this passage provide us with a lesson in contextualization (the application of the text in new and changing circumstances). It should be obvious that the specific commands given here do not apply *directly* to all Christian workers or missionaries everywhere. We have already noted differences among the Synoptics, with Mark's version allowing a staff and sandals, but Matthew (and Luke for the staff) forbidding them. These differences may be due in part to the Evangelists' editing in light of later missionary activity. In Luke's gospel, Jesus himself modifies his instructions at the end of his ministry, encouraging his disciples to now take a purse, a bag, and even a sword (Luke 22:35 – 36).

No doubt the missionaries in Acts traveled at times with additional clothing and provisions, and certainly missionaries today cannot follow Jesus' instructions to the letter. While most would have no trouble leaving their walking stick at home, imagine being told you can't bring a suitcase, a change of clothes, or even footwear to a distant land! Jesus' commands are obviously *for these individuals in this particular mission,* not for the church of all time.

So what aspects of these commands represent the heart of God? Can we draw principles from these commands that do apply to Christians involved in missions work today? Here are three that I believe can be legitimately gleaned from Jesus' instructions:

(1) Cultivate a simple lifestyle to avoid becoming enamored by the fleeting things of this world. The Bible is full of warnings about the danger of wealth and the accumulation of possessions, which distract us from God's purpose in the world (Prov 23:5; Matt 6:19; Mark 4:19; Luke 6:24 – 25; 16:13 – 15, 19 – 31; 18:18 – 25; 1 Tim 6:10, 17; Heb 13:5; Jas 5:1 – 6; 1 Pet 1:18). The adoption of a lifestyle that focuses only on basic needs is among the greatest of challenges for Christians in the West, where there is a constant temptation to acquire more and more possessions and to be distracted from things that truly count for eternity.

(2) We should depend on God rather than on our own talents or resources. The command for the missionaries not to bring provisions required constant trust in God for their next meal and place of lodging. Paul similarly speaks to the Philippians about the contentment he has learned in any and all circumstances, knowing that "I can do all this through him who gives me strength" and that "my God will meet all your needs according to the riches of his glory in Christ Jesus" (Phil 4:13, 19). We experience the presence and power of God most fully in times of need, when we are forced to trust in him. The testing of our faith produces spiritual maturity (Rom 5:3 – 5; Jas 1:2 – 4), and when we are weak in our own power, that is when we are strong in God's power (1 Cor 12:10). This does not mean, of course, that missionaries today should not plan carefully, work out a budget, and raise financial support to meet their needs. Elsewhere Jesus encourages his followers to plan ahead, weigh the cost, and act prudently with their resources (Matt 25:14 – 30; Luke 14:28 – 33; 16:1 – 12; 19:12 – 27). Yet in doing so, they should always place their trust and confidence in God.

(3) The command to stay in one home in each town is a reminder that we are not to show partiality in Christian ministry. Rather, we are to treat others equally, regardless of their social status, ethnic identity, wealth, or influence. We live in a celebrity culture, and there is a strong tendency among Christians to give special favor and attention to the wealthy, professional athletes, celebrities, and those with political influence. James warns against such favoritism (Jas 2:1 – 7), since all people are equal in the body of Christ. Jesus' own pattern of sensitivity and attention given to outcasts (Mark 5:30; 7:24 – 30), to children (10:13 – 16), and to the poor (10:46; 12:42) provides a model for us to follow.

The Church as a Community of Sharing

A third theological theme in this passage may be found in the disciples' dependence on the hospitality of others, reminding us that the church is a family, a place of support, provision, and protection for its members. We see this clearly in the early chapters of Acts, where the church takes care of its own, with individuals even selling property to meet financial needs of the new believers (Acts 2:44 – 45; 4:32 – 37). Sharing food and lodging also became an essential part of the expansion of the gospel.

Christians throughout the Roman empire would open their homes to traveling missionaries and preachers (Acts 16:15; Rom 15:24, 28; 1 Cor 4:17; 16:10; Phil 2:25; 4:14; Phlm 22). The little letters of 2 and 3 John deal with issues of hospitality for traveling missionaries, praising those who welcome them (3 John 5 – 10), but warning against false teachers (2 John 11 – 12). The *Didache* (late first century) similarly provides instructions concerning hospitality for traveling teachers and cautions against those who would abuse this privilege:

> Let every apostle who comes to you be welcomed as if he were the Lord. But he is not to stay for more than one day, unless there is need, in which case he may stay another. But if he stays three days, he is a false prophet. And when the apostle leaves, he is to take nothing except bread until he finds his next night's lodging. But if he asks for money, he is a false prophet. (*Did.* 11:4 – 6)[16]

The church is to be both a place of caring and of generosity and a place that encourages responsible stewardship. While feeding the hungry is an essential part of Christian benevolence, the church must not allow manipulative or deceptive people to squander its resources. This means being discerning about the people and causes the church supports as well as being responsible in the ways it cares for the poor and needy in the community. Sometimes, simply giving away money or goods is not the best way to help people rise above the poverty level to become responsible citizens. Things like job training, work opportunities, and the establishment of long-term relationships must go hand in hand with generous giving if the church is going to be a force for social change in the world.

---

16. Michael Holmes, ed. and trans., *The Apostolic Fathers* (3rd ed.; Grand Rapids: Baker, 2007), 363.

Mark 6:14 – 29

Literary Context

As the twelve disciples head out on their mission (6:12 – 13), Mark's narrative enters an interlude. Two scenes, the concerns of Herod Antipas about Jesus (6:14 – 16) and a flashback related to the death of John the Baptist (6:17 – 29), are intercalated ("sandwiched") between the beginning (vv. 6b – 13) and end (v. 30) of the mission of the Twelve. This is the third major intercalation in Mark's gospel (cf. 3:20 – 35; 5:21 – 43; see Introduction to Mark: Literary Features). While the interlude provides a helpful narrative pause (during which the mission of the Twelve takes place), the thematic and theological relationship between the two episodes is less clear than in Mark's other intercalations. The most likely relationship is that both episodes illustrate the nature and cost of true discipleship. The Twelve are commissioned to set aside their possessions, comfort, and personal ambitions to proclaim the good news of the kingdom. John the Baptist, meanwhile, pays the ultimate cost of discipleship — giving his life in faithfulness to his calling.

The martyrdom of John is the only episode in Mark's gospel that does not directly concern Jesus. It does, however, pick up the important Markan theme of the suffering role of the followers of Christ, who must take up their crosses and follow him (8:34). As a model disciple, John the Baptist gives his life for the gospel (cf. 9:10 – 13).

Main Idea

The account of the martyrdom of John the Baptist illustrates the true cost of discipleship, as John gives up his life for his faithful testimony (6:17–29) — a preview and prefigurement of the death of Jesus. The episode also provides a stark contrast between Jesus, the true servant King, and Herod, the sham king, whose corrupt behavior results in the martyrdom of one of God's greatest servants. Finally, the introduction to the passage continues to highlight the enigmatic question of the first half of Mark's gospel: "Who is this Jesus?" (6:14–16).

Translation

Mark 6:14–29

14a	Setting (social)	**King Herod heard about this,**
b		because Jesus' name had become well known.
c	Assertion	**Some people were saying,**
d		*"John the Baptist has been raised from the dead;*
e		*that is why miraculous powers are at work in him."*
15a	Assertion	**Others were saying,**
b		*"He is Elijah,"*
c	Assertion	and **still others,**
d		*"He is a prophet like one of the prophets of old."*
16a	Response	Hearing these things,
b		**Herod said,**
c		*"John, whom I beheaded, has been raised!"*
17a	Explanation/Flashback	**For Herod himself had sent men to arrest John and lock him up in prison**
b	reason for 17a	because of Herodias,
c	character description	his brother Philip's wife,
d		whom ↵
		Herod had married.
18a	Action/Rebuke	**John had been telling Herod,**
b		*"It is against God's law for you to have your brother's wife."*
19a	Response to 18a	So **Herodias nursed a grudge against John and wanted to kill him.**
b	Obstacle	But **she could not,**
20a		because Herod feared John,
b		knowing that he was a righteous and holy man, and
c		protected him.
d	Action	When Herod listened to John,
e		**he would become greatly perplexed,**
f		but **he liked listening to him.**

21a	Setting (temporal)	**Eventually an opportunity arose,**
b	setting (social)	when Herod gave a banquet on his birthday for his ↵ high officials and
c		military commanders and
d		the leading men of Galilee.
22a	action	When Herodias's daughter came in and danced,
b	Response	**she pleased Herod and his dinner guests.**
c	Grant vow	**The king said to the girl,**
d		*"Ask me for whatever you want and I will give it to you."*
23a	Grant vow	And **he vowed to her,**
b		*"Whatever you ask I will give you, up to half my kingdom."*
24a	Response to 23	Going out,
b		**she said to her mother,**
c		*"What should I ask for?"*
d	Response to 24	**Her mother said,**
e		*"The head of John the Baptist."*
25a	response to 24d-e	So immediately hurrying back in to the king,
b	Request	**she made her request, saying,**
c		*"I want you to give me right now the head of John the Baptist on a platter."*
26a	concession	Although the king was greatly distressed
b	cause	because of the oaths he had made in front of his dinner guests,
c	Result	**he didn't want to refuse her.**
27a	Result	So **the king sent an executioner immediately with orders to bring his head.**
b	action	Going out,
c	Action	**the man beheaded John in prison,**
28a	Action	and **brought his head on a platter**
b	Action	and **gave it to the girl,**
c	Action	and **the girl gave it to her mother.**
29a	setting (temporal)	When John's disciples heard about this,
b	Action	**they came and took his body and laid it in a tomb.**

Structure

This section is made up of two episodes: Herod's concerns related to the identity of Jesus (6:14 – 16), and a flashback to the arrest and execution of John the Baptist (6:17 – 29). The former sets the stage for the latter, which serves as a detailed explanation of and follow-up to the earlier brief mention of John's imprisonment (1:14). The passage has parallels to Elijah's conflict with Ahab and Jezebel in the OT (1 Kgs 16:29 – 19:3; 21:1 – 29). Both stories concern an angry queen bent on destroying God's prophet. Both involve inappropriate marriages: Ahab to Jezebel, which led Israel into Baal worship (16:30 – 31), and Herod's remarriage to his brother Philip's wife, Herodias, which was in violation of the OT law. In both, the king is weak and vacillating, fearing the prophet but prepared to listen to him. While Jezebel was unsuccessful in her attempts to kill Elijah, Herodias is successful in eliminating John.[1]

From a form-critical perspective, John's execution may be called a martyrology, a heroic account of a faithful servant's martyrdom. But apart from the brief mention of the reason Herod imprisoned John (v. 18), there is little in the story typical of martyr tales, such as the testimony of the martyr, his courage and boldness in the face of the threat, or his heroic last words. Instead, all the emphasis is on the petty and diabolical machinations of Herod and Herodias.

Exegetical Outline

→ 1. **Herod Antipas's Concerns about Jesus (6:14 – 16)**

    a. Herod hears about Jesus' activity (6:14a)

    b. The people's opinions about Jesus (6:14b – 15)

    c. Herod's conclusion: John has been raised! (6:16)

2. **Flashback to the Arrest and Execution of John (6:17 – 29)**

    a. John's arrest resulting from his criticism of Herod and Herodias (6:17 – 20)

    b. The banquet opportunity (6:21)

    c. A daughter's dance and a king's vow (6:22 – 23)

    d. Herodias's scheme: request for the head of John (6:24 – 25)

    e. The execution of John (6:26 – 28)

    f. The burial of John by his disciples (6:29)

Explanation of the Text

6:14 – 16 King Herod heard about this, because Jesus' name had become well known. Some people were saying, "John the Baptist has been raised from the dead; that is why miraculous powers are at work in him." Others were saying, "He is Elijah," and still others, "He is a prophet like one of the prophets of old." Hearing these things, Herod said, "John, whom I beheaded, has been raised!" (Καὶ ἤκουσεν ὁ βασιλεὺς Ἡρῴδης, φανερὸν γὰρ ἐγένετο τὸ ὄνομα αὐτοῦ, καὶ ἔλεγον ὅτι Ἰωάννης ὁ βαπτίζων ἐγήγερται ἐκ νεκρῶν καὶ διὰ τοῦτο ἐνεργοῦσιν αἱ δυνάμεις ἐν αὐτῷ. ἄλλοι δὲ ἔλεγον ὅτι Ἡλίας ἐστίν· ἄλλοι δὲ ἔλεγον ὅτι προφήτης ὡς εἷς τῶν προφητῶν. ἀκούσας δὲ ὁ Ἡρῴδης ἔλεγεν· ὃν ἐγὼ ἀπεκεφάλισα Ἰωάννην, οὗτος ἠγέρθη).

The mission of the Twelve served to expand the breadth and scope of Jesus' ministry, resulting in greater public exposure and bringing Jesus' activity to the attention of Herod Antipas. The Greek simply says that Herod "heard," without specifying the object or content of the reports. While the closest antecedent is the mission of the Twelve (vv. 12 – 13), the following clause makes it clear

---

1. Hooker, *Mark*, 160.

that Herod has been hearing about Jesus. As Jesus' representatives, the disciples are expanding his ministry and increasing his reputation.

The Herod referred to here is Herod Antipas, son of Herod the Great and tetrarch of Galilee and Perea from 4 BC to AD 39.[2] His mother was Malthace, a Samaritan, one of Herod the Great's ten wives. Antipas's actual title was "tetrarch" (cf. Matt 14:1; Luke 3:1, 19; 9:7; Acts 13:1), which originally meant "ruler of a fourth part," but came to mean a lower-level ruler below the status of a king. Mark refers to him as "king" (βασιλεύς), but this is probably a popular designation rather than an official title.[3] Herod did, in fact, aspire to be king of the Jews, like his father before him, and it was his attempt to gain that title that eventually led to his banishment by the emperor Caligula in AD 39.[4] The "Herodians" (Ἡρῳδιανοί) referred to in 3:6 and 12:13 were probably Herod's political followers in Galilee, who supported his aspirations for a greater share of his father's kingdom. Antipas is also the Herod before whom Jesus stood at his trial (Luke 23:7 – 12).

The three claims about Jesus' identity are presented as popular speculation ("they were saying," ἔλεγον; iterative or customary imperfect). The same three answers are given by the disciples in 8:27 – 28. It is not clear what is meant by John "raised from the dead." It cannot mean that the end-time resurrection had begun. Most likely, it is the superstitious belief that John's ghost had come back to haunt his murderer. The term "miraculous powers" (δυνάμεις) is commonly used of miracles in Mark (6:2, 5; 9:39) and elsewhere in the NT (Matt 7:22;

11:20 – 23; 13:54; Luke 10:13; 19:37; Acts 2:22; 8:13; 1 Cor 12:28; Heb 2:4; etc.). Although the angel Gabriel predicted John would come "in the spirit and power of Elijah" (ἐν πνεύματι καὶ δυνάμει Ἠλίου; Luke 1:17), there is no record of John's performing miracles, and John 10:41 explicitly says he did not. The likely meaning here is not that Jesus' miracles are similar to John's, but that such miracles were proof that John's *ghost* was back, since a ghost might be presumed to have greater powers than a man.[5]

The second speculation by "others" (ἄλλοι) is that Jesus is the prophet Elijah (v. 15a-b). Many Jews expected Elijah to return before judgment day, a tradition arising from Elijah's unusual departure to heaven (2 Kgs 2:11 – 12) and from the prophecies of Malachi 3:1; 4:5 – 6 (cf. Mark 9:10 – 13; 15:35 – 36; John 1:21 – 25).

The third speculation is that, if not Elijah, Jesus is another prophet. The redundancy of "a prophet like one of the prophets" (προφήτης ὡς εἷς τῶν προφητῶν) means one from the classic line of OT prophets. Though Mark does not emphasize Jesus' prophetic role, Jesus alludes to himself as a prophet in 6:4, and some of his miracles are similar to Elijah's (cf. 5:21 – 43; 1 Kgs 17:17 – 24). Elsewhere in the gospel tradition, especially in Luke, Jesus identifies himself as a prophet (Luke 4:24; 11:47 – 51; 13:33 – 34) and is heralded by others as a great prophet (Luke 7:16, 39; 9:8; 24:19; Acts 3:33; 7:37; cf. Matt 21:46).

Herod considers the popular speculation and pessimistically chooses the most threatening one: "John ... has been raised [ἠγέρθη]!" The verb is a

---

2. See Harold W. Hoehner, *Herod Antipas* (SNTSMS 17; Cambridge: Cambridge University Press, 1972). At the death of Herod the Great, his kingdom was divided among three of his sons, Archelaus, Antipas, and Philip. Because of misrule, Archelaus was eventually replaced by Roman governors (prefects and procurators).

3. Some claim that, by referring to Herod as "king," Mark

is mocking his aspirations to that office (Lane, *Mark*, 211; Hurtado, *Mark*, 97; Marcus, *Mark 1 – 8*, 398). But that seems too subtle in this context.

4. Josephus, *Ant.* 18.7.1 – 2 §§240 – 256; *J.W.* 2.9.0 §§181 – 188.

5. See 6:49, where a "ghost" (φάντασμα) is presumed to be capable of walking on water. Cf. Wisd 17:15 (LXX 17:14); Josephus, *Ant.* 1.20.2 §331.

divine passive, meaning "God has raised him" (also v. 14; cf. 1:41; 4:11 – 12, 24).[6] Herod doesn't just fear retribution from John; his conscience is telling him he has done a great evil and will answer to God. Instead of repenting, however, he responds with fear.

6:17 – 18 For Herod himself had sent men to arrest John and lock him up in prison because of Herodias, his brother Philip's wife, whom Herod had married. John had been telling Herod, "It is against God's law for you to have your brother's

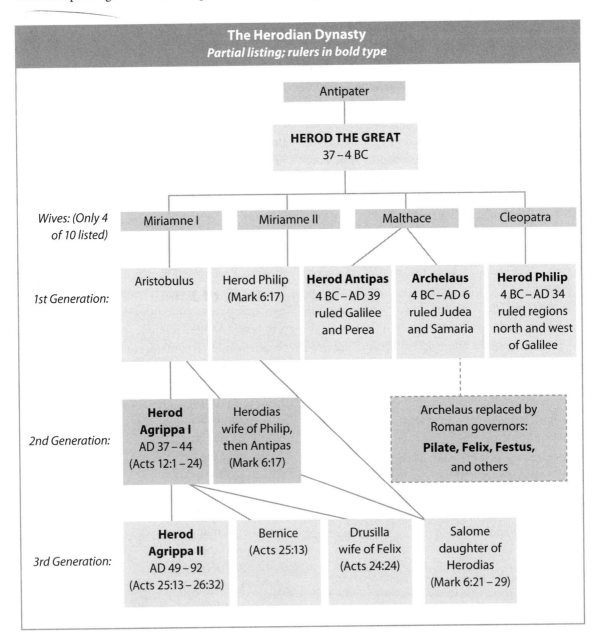

The Herodian Dynasty			
Partial listing; rulers in bold type			

Antipater

HEROD THE GREAT
37 – 4 BC

| *Wives: (Only 4 of 10 listed)* | Miriamne I | Miriamne II | Malthace | Cleopatra |

| *1st Generation:* | Aristobulus | Herod Philip (Mark 6:17) | **Herod Antipas** 4 BC – AD 39 ruled Galilee and Perea | **Archelaus** 4 BC – AD 6 ruled Judea and Samaria | **Herod Philip** 4 BC – AD 34 ruled regions north and west of Galilee |

| *2nd Generation:* | **Herod Agrippa I** AD 37 – 44 (Acts 12:1 – 24) | Herodias wife of Philip, then Antipas (Mark 6:17) | | Archelaus replaced by Roman governors: **Pilate, Felix, Festus,** and others |

| *3rd Generation:* | **Herod Agrippa II** AD 49 – 92 (Acts 25:13 – 26:32) | Bernice (Acts 25:13) | Drusilla wife of Felix (Acts 24:24) | Salome daughter of Herodias (Mark 6:21 – 29) |

6. Marcus, *Mark 1 – 8,* 393.

wife." (Αὐτὸς γὰρ ὁ Ἡρῴδης ἀποστείλας ἐκράτησεν τὸν Ἰωάννην καὶ ἔδησεν αὐτὸν ἐν φυλακῇ διὰ Ἡρῳδιάδα τὴν γυναῖκα Φιλίππου τοῦ ἀδελφοῦ αὐτοῦ, ὅτι αὐτὴν ἐγάμησεν· ἔλεγεν γὰρ ὁ Ἰωάννης τῷ Ἡρῴδῃ ὅτι οὐκ ἔξεστίν σοι ἔχειν τὴν γυναῖκα τοῦ ἀδελφοῦ σου). The Greek idiom "sending, he arrested" (ἀποστείλας ἐκράτησεν) may mean "he gave orders to arrest," or "he sent men to arrest." In either case, the result is the same and John lands in prison.

The Jewish historian Josephus also provides an account of the arrest and execution of John the Baptist. Significantly, his discussion arises in the context of the same issue Mark introduces here: Antipas's divorce of his first wife and remarriage to Herodias. According to Josephus, Antipas's first wife was the daughter of King Aretas IV of Nabatea. When Antipas divorced her and mar-

ried Herodias, Aretas went to war with Herod, defeating his army in battle. According to Josephus, many believed Herod's defeat was punishment from God for Herod's execution of John the Baptist (*Ant.* 18.5.1 §§109–115). As in Mark, the death of John is presented by Josephus as a flashback (*Ant.* 18.5.2 §§116–119).

John's objection to Herod's marriage is because he married his brother's wife (v. 18), a union forbidden in the OT (Lev 18:6; 20:21; cf. Josephus, *Ant.* 18.5.4 §136). Marriage to a husband's brother was allowed only in the case of levirate marriage, when the brother had died without offspring (Deut 25:5–10). Herodias's divorce of Herod Philip would also have raised eyebrows in Jewish society, since Jewish law did not allow a woman to divorce her husband. Roman law did, however, and this was likely the loophole that Herodias used.[7]

IN DEPTH: Josephus and Mark on the Death of John

Josephus's account of John's death differs somewhat from Mark's, causing some to question the latter's historicity. (1) While Mark says Herod arrested John because of his preaching against Herod's divorce and remarriage to Herodias, Josephus attributes the arrest and execution to Herod's fear of John's power and influence among the people. (2) Josephus refers to Herodias's first husband simply as "Herod," while Mark calls him "Philip." According to Josephus, Salome, not Herodias, was the wife of Philip. (3) While Josephus says John was imprisoned and executed at Machaerus, a fortress in southern Perea east of the Dead Sea, the banquet Mark describes would likely have taken place at Tiberias, Herod's capital city in Galilee.

All of these apparent differences have plausible explanations. (1) Concerning the reason for John's arrest, Herod Antipas no doubt had many reasons to arrest the Baptist, including his bold ethical preaching and the influence he had among the people. Luke says that Herod arrested John both for his preaching against the marriage and for "all the other evil things [Herod] had done" (Luke 3:19). Mark refers to the moral concerns John addressed, while

7. Hooker, *Mark*, 160; France, *Mark*, 256–57.

Josephus refers to the popular unrest and political problems this created for Herod.[8]

(2) On the identity of Herodias's first husband, we must first acknowledge that the Herod family tree is enormously complex with a great deal of (sometimes incestuous) intermarriage. This, together with the names we don't know, makes relationships difficult to untangle. Salome, for example, Herodias's daughter by her first marriage, was at the same time Herod Antipas's niece (the daughter of his half brother Philip), his grandniece (since Herodias, his wife, was also his half brother Aristobolus's daughter), and his stepdaughter (his new wife Herodias's daughter).[9] We must add to this the fact that all of the Herods (Antipas, Aristobolus, Philip, Archelaus, etc.) can be referred to simply as "Herod." Finally, there are many people in this tangled genealogy with the same name. The simplest solution is that there were two Herod Philips. Herodias's first husband—referred to simply as "Herod" by Josephus (*Ant.* 18.5.1 §109; 18.5.4 §136)—was actually named Herod Philip, as Mark asserts (6:17).[10] He was a different son of Herod the Great than Philip the Tetrarch (Luke 3:1), who later married Salome, Herodias's daughter (*Ant.* 18.5.4 §137).

(3) There are various possible solutions concerning the place of John's execution. (a) Herod may have moved John to Galilee prior to his banquet. (b) The banquet may have been at Machaerus, rather than in Galilee. Though it would have been quite a distance for the Galilean nobles to travel, Machaerus was a palace fortress and would surely have had banquet accommodations.[11] (c) There may have been a time gap between the order to execute John (v. 27) and the presentation of his head to Herodias (v. 28). This last, though not impossible, is a less natural reading of the text.

6:19–20 So Herodias nursed a grudge against John and wanted to kill him. But she could not, because Herod feared John, knowing that he was a righteous and holy man, and protected him. When Herod listened to John, he would become greatly perplexed, but he liked listening to him (ἡ δὲ Ἡρῳδιὰς ἐνεῖχεν αὐτῷ καὶ ἤθελεν αὐτὸν ἀποκτεῖναι, καὶ οὐκ ἠδύνατο· ὁ γὰρ Ἡρῴδης ἐφοβεῖτο τὸν Ἰωάννην, εἰδὼς αὐτὸν ἄνδρα δίκαιον καὶ ἅγιον, καὶ συνετήρει αὐτόν, καὶ ἀκούσας αὐτοῦ πολλὰ ἠπόρει, καὶ ἡδέως αὐτοῦ ἤκουεν). As noted above (see Structure), Herodias's grudge against

8. Marcus, *Mark 1–8*, 400, argues that the motives are entirely different, since in Mark, Antipas is protecting John, while in Josephus he wants to kill him (cf. Matt 14:5). But this ignores the complexity of human nature and our fascination with charismatic individuals. People may loathe a serial killer, for example, but listen in fascination for hours to an interview with him. Herod at the same time feared John but was fascinated by him.

9. Marcus, *Mark 1–8*, 395.
10. So Hoehner, *Herod Antipas*, 131–36.
11. Gundry, *Mark*, 313–14, cites archaeological evidence for a palace, a prison, and a large and small dining room at Machaerus (the smaller for the women). For a description of Machaerus, see Josephus, *J.W.* 7.6.2 §§171–177.

John and her desire to kill him echoes the OT story of Jezebel's hatred of Elijah for killing the prophets of Baal (1 Kgs 19:2). So too Herod's combination of fear and respect for John recalls King Ahab's complex relationship with Elijah (see 21:20 – 29).

Although Herodias wanted to kill John, Herod knew he was a "righteous [or 'innocent'] and holy man" and "was protecting him" (συνετήρει αὐτόν; imperfect, indicating continuous action). The verb here could mean simply "kept in custody," but in context it clearly means "kept safe," that is, protected from Herodias's schemes. A parallel between the deaths of Jesus and John is evident here. Pilate will know Jesus is innocent and will resist putting him to death, but he eventually concedes to pressure from others (15:1 – 15; see Theology in Application).

Instead of "he was greatly perplexed" (πολλὰ ἠπόρει), some manuscripts read that "he did many things" (πολλὰ ἐποίει; cf. KJV, NKJV),[12] which may be an Aramaic idiom meaning "he visited John often" to listen to him.[13] The former, however, is the harder reading (the verb ἀπορέω occurs only here in Mark) and is supported by somewhat better manuscripts.[14] Herod "liked listening to him" (ἡδέως αὐτοῦ ἤκουεν, "heard him gladly"; cf. 15:37) but was baffled by John's prophetic and apocalyptic message.

6:21 Eventually an opportunity arose, when Herod gave a banquet on his birthday for his high officials and military commanders and the leading men of Galilee (Καὶ γενομένης ἡμέρας εὐκαίρου ὅτε Ἡρῴδης τοῖς γενεσίοις αὐτοῦ δεῖπνον ἐποίησεν τοῖς μεγιστᾶσιν αὐτοῦ καὶ τοῖς χιλιάρχοις καὶ τοῖς πρώτοις τῆς Γαλιλαίας). An "opportunity" (ἡμέρας εὐκαίρου = "suitable day") for Herodias ar-

rived when Herod threw a birthday party for himself, inviting the most influential leaders in Galilee. The three categories of guests appear to be government officials (μεγισταί; "nobles"), military leaders (χιλιάρχοι; "tribunes" = "leaders of a thousand"), and the local aristocracy (πρῶτοι τῆς Γαλιλαίας; "leading men of Galilee"), though the sense of the first and third of these may be reversed. In any case, it is "everyone who is anyone" — the political, military, and social elite.

Such birthday celebrations were common among the aristocracy, but were considered pagan celebrations by pious Jews.[15] As noted in the sidebar, there is a potential discrepancy here, since Josephus says that John was imprisoned in Machaerus, in Perea, about a two days' journey from Galilee. It is possible that the nobles journeyed to Machaerus for the party (the extravagance of which would justify the journey),[16] or perhaps Herod had already brought John to Tiberias, his headquarters in Galilee.

6:22 – 23 When Herodias's daughter came in and danced, she pleased Herod and his dinner guests. The king said to the girl, "Ask me for whatever you want and I will give it to you." And he vowed to her, "Whatever you ask I will give you, up to half my kingdom." (καὶ εἰσελθούσης τῆς θυγατρὸς αὐτῆς τῆς Ἡρῳδιάδος καὶ ὀρχησαμένης ἤρεσεν τῷ Ἡρῴδῃ καὶ τοῖς συνανακειμένοις, εἶπεν ὁ βασιλεὺς τῷ κορασίῳ· αἴτησόν με ὃ ἐὰν θέλῃς, καὶ δώσω σοι· καὶ ὤμοσεν αὐτῇ πολλὰ ὅ τι ἐάν με αἰτήσῃς δώσω σοι ἕως ἡμίσους τῆς βασιλείας μου).

There is a textual problem here. (1) Some manuscripts read "his daughter, Herodias" (τῆς θυγατρὸς αὐτοῦ Ἡρῳδιάδος),[17] suggesting that the girl is

12. A C D f¹ f¹³ 33 𝔐 lat syr.

13. BDF §4145. ; C. C. Torrey, *Our Translated Gospels* (New York: Harper, 1936), cited by Metzger, *Textual Commentary*, 76. Those who support this reading suggest that the other reading arose under the influence of the similar statement in Luke 9:7.

14. ℵ B L [W] Θ 2427 cop; Metzger, *Textual Commentary*, 76.

15. m. ʿAbod. Zar. 1:3.

16. For a similar extravagant party given by Herod Antipas, see Josephus, *Ant.* 18.4.5 §102.

17. ℵ B D L Δ 565 pc.

identified as *Herod's* daughter (or stepdaughter) and that her name is Herodias, the same as her mother's. Yet Josephus identifies Herodias's daughter as "Salome" (*Ant.* 18.5.4 §136–137). (2) Other manuscripts read "her daughter, the [daughter] of Herodias" (τῆς θυγατρὸς αὐτῆς τῆς Ἡρῳδιάδος).[18] This somewhat awkward expression, perhaps meaning "the daughter of Herodias herself," leaves the daughter unnamed. While this latter makes better sense historically (since Josephus calls the girl Salome), it has somewhat weaker manuscript support. In its favor, Matthew's gospel (14:6) reads "the daughter of Herodias," perhaps indicating that his copy of Mark read "her daughter."[19] This latter reading seems to have a slight advantage and so is adopted here.

The girl's age is not stated, and it is unclear whether the dance is a child's performance or a young woman's erotic dance.[20] The latter is the traditional understanding and makes the best sense of the scene that follows. It seems unlikely — even in Herod's debauched court — that a severed head would be given to a little girl (v. 28). Furthermore, the daughter seems well aware of the court intrigue going on here, since she embellishes her mother's request by asking for John's head "on a platter" (v. 25). While some have objected that an erotic dance is unlikely to have been performed by a member of the royal family, the scene fits well the infamous decadence of the Herodians.

The dance so pleases Herod and his guests that he makes the girl an extravagant offer: she can have anything she wants, up to half his kingdom. The offer is similar to that of King Ahasuerus to Esther (Esth 5:3, 6; 7:2) and is certainly hyperbolic, a stereotypical way of saying, "Ask for anything at all! I'm the king, so I can grant it" (cf. 1 Kgs 13:8).

6:24–25 **Going out, she said to her mother, "What should I ask for?" Her mother said, "The head of John the Baptist." So immediately hurrying back in to the king, she made her request, saying, "I want you to give me right now the head of John the Baptist on a platter."** (καὶ ἐξελθοῦσα εἶπεν τῇ μητρὶ αὐτῆς· τί αἰτήσωμαι; ἡ δὲ εἶπεν· τὴν κεφαλὴν Ἰωάννου τοῦ βαπτίζοντος. καὶ εἰσελθοῦσα εὐθὺς μετὰ σπουδῆς πρὸς τὸν βασιλέα ᾐτήσατο λέγουσα· θέλω ἵνα ἐξαυτῆς δῷς μοι ἐπὶ πίνακι τὴν κεφαλὴν Ἰωάννου τοῦ βαπτιστοῦ).

The fact that the girl consults with her mother suggests that the "opportunity" (v. 21) arose spontaneously from Herod's foolish offer, rather than through Herodias's prior planning. The girl's complicity (or at least desire to please her mother) is indicated in the narrative by the haste (μετὰ σπουδῆς) with which she returns to the party and the embellishment of her mother's request: she wants John's head "on a platter" (ἐπὶ πίνακι) and she wants it "right now" (ἐξαυτῆς). The immediate demand ensures that Herod will not be able to withdraw his offer after his guests have left.

6:26–28 **Although the king was greatly distressed because of the oaths he had made in front of his dinner guests, he didn't want to refuse her. So the king sent an executioner immediately with orders to bring his head. Going out, the man beheaded John in prison, and brought his head on a platter and gave it to the girl, and the girl gave it to her mother** (καὶ περίλυπος γενόμενος ὁ βασιλεὺς διὰ τοὺς ὅρκους καὶ τοὺς ἀνακειμένους οὐκ ἠθέλησεν ἀθετῆσαι αὐτήν· καὶ εὐθὺς ἀποστείλας ὁ βασιλεὺς σπεκουλάτορα ἐπέταξεν ἐνέγκαι τὴν κεφαλὴν αὐτοῦ. καὶ ἀπελθὼν ἀπεκεφάλισεν αὐτὸν ἐν τῇ φυλακῇ καὶ ἤνεγκεν τὴν κεφαλὴν αὐτοῦ ἐπὶ πίνακι καὶ ἔδωκεν αὐτὴν τῷ κορασίῳ, καὶ τὸ κοράσιον ἔδωκεν αὐτὴν τῇ μητρὶ αὐτῆς).

18. A C Θ f[13] 33 2427 𝔐 syr[h].
19. Stein, *Mark*, 305.
20. For an insightful feminist reading of the episode, see Janice Capel Anderson, "Feminist Criticism: The Dancing Daughter," in *Mark and Method* (ed. Anderson and Moore), 111–43, esp. 123–40.

If Herod was drunk when he made his offer — as seems likely — he quickly sobers up when he realizes what he has done. It would be a horrific loss of face to back down now, so, "because of the oaths he had made in front of his dinner guests,"[21] he concedes to the girl's request. Herod is revealed to be an immoral, vacillating, and pathetic ruler, who takes the easy way out to save face rather than standing up for what is right. He is the antithesis of John, who spoke truth even at the risk of his life.

The term translated "executioner" (σπεκουλάτωρ) is of Latin derivation and originally meant a spy or scout. It came to refer to a king's elite bodyguards or henchmen, who would do his dirty work.[22] While it is possible that the executioner was dispatched from Tiberias to Machaerus, delaying the execution by several days, the more natural reading is that the execution took place that night, and that the banquet was at the same location as John's imprisonment, either in Tiberias or Machaerus (see "In Depth: Josephus and Mark on the Death of John"). The final note about the presentation of the head to Herodias serves as verification that the dark deed has been done.

6:29 When John's disciples heard about this, they came and took his body and laid it in a tomb (καὶ ἀκούσαντες οἱ μαθηταὶ αὐτοῦ ἦλθον καὶ ἦραν τὸ πτῶμα αὐτοῦ καὶ ἔθηκαν αὐτὸ ἐν μνημείῳ). In stark contrast to the debauchery of the preceding scene, John's loyal disciples now come and give him an honorable burial. The scene parallels and foreshadows the burial of Jesus by Joseph of Arimathea (15:42 – 47) after his equally ignoble execution performed by another unethical and vacillating tyrant.

Theology in Application

The Cost of Discipleship

The martyrdom of John illustrates the ultimate cost of discipleship, an important Markan theme in the chapters that follow. Jesus will teach that anyone who wants to be his disciple must deny themselves, take up their cross, and follow him (8:34). Whoever saves their "life" (ψυχή) will lose their "soul" (ψυχή), but whoever gives up their life for the gospel will save their soul (8:35). By giving up his life, John shows himself to be a model disciple. Herod, by contrast, loses his soul by caving to the pressure of others in pride and cowardice. By "sandwiching" the death of John between the beginning and end of the mission of the Twelve, Mark shows that the path of true discipleship is one of self-denial and self-sacrifice.

Jesus and John Parallels

John is not just a model "follower" of Jesus, he is also the forerunner of the Messiah, and his death serves as a foreshadowing and preview of Jesus' arrest and

---

21. The Greek, "because of the oaths and the ones dining" (διὰ τοὺς ὅρκους καὶ τοὺς ἀνακειμένους) is likely hendiadys, two words functioning as a single idea (Gundry, *Mark*, 321). So NLT: "because of the vows he had made in front of his guests." Antipas would have no qualms about breaking an oath (like a marriage covenant!), but he did not want to lose face in front of his guests.

22. See Hoehner, *Herod Antipas*, 119 – 20 n. 3; Marcus, *Mark 1 – 8*, 397.

crucifixion. Both Jesus and John are arrested for challenging the powers that be. Both are put to death by self-seeking rulers who know their victims are innocent but vacillate under pressure and choose expediency over justice. The bodies of both are taken and buried by sympathetic followers. After John's death, rumors arise that he has risen from the dead. But Jesus actually does rise from the dead![23]

These implicit parallels between John and Jesus in Mark find similar expression in the other gospels. In Luke, for example, the births of Jesus and John are paralleled, heralded by angelic announcements and miraculous conceptions (Luke 1). Yet in this parallelism, Jesus is shown to be the superior. While John is "*prophet* of the Most High" (Luke 1:76; cf. 1:17), Jesus is the "*Son* of the Most High" (1:32). John's birth to a *barren woman* is a miracle (like similar births in the OT), but Jesus' birth to a *virgin* is unprecedented. John's role is to *prepare the way for the Lord* (1:17, 76); Jesus *is that Lord* — the Savior, who is Messiah and Lord (2:11; cf. 1:43).

This theme is carried forward in John's public ministry. John says that the one who will come after him is so much greater than he that John is not worthy to unlatch his sandals. While John baptizes with water, Jesus will baptize with the Holy Spirit (1:7–8). Jesus must increase, while John must decrease (John 3:3). Here we find the true essence of discipleship. It is following Christ's model, but always in service to him. It is a willingness to give up one's life, not for our own glory, but for the glory of Christ. As Christian leaders, this is one of the most difficult principles to apply. So much of our self-worth is tied to our position, prestige, and influence. To live a life of self-sacrificial giving, promoting the cause of others over ourselves, goes against our natural human tendency to self-promote. Yet it is the epitome of authentic Christian leadership.

---

23. See Hooker, *Mark*, 158–59.

Mark 6:30 – 44

Literary Context

The miracle of the feeding of the five thousand — the only miracle to appear in all four Gospels — begins with the return of the Twelve from their mission of preaching and healing (6:30 – 31). Some commentators link these verses with what follows, while others with what precedes. In fact, they are transitional, concluding the episode running from 6:6a – 30 — comprised of the martyrdom of John (6:14 – 29) sandwiched (intercalated) between the beginning (6:6a – 12) and end (6:30) of the mission of the Twelve — and introducing the account of the miraculous feeding of five thousand (vv. 30 – 44). After sending the disciples out to preach and to heal, Jesus calls them away for a private time of rest and rejuvenation (v. 31). The crowds follow, however, and Jesus ends up ministering to their spiritual and physical needs.

Various commentators have noted the irony of this episode in relation to the incident that precedes.[1] In contrast to the debauched banquet of the corrupt king Herod Antipas, which ended in the tragic murder of John the Baptist, Jesus, the great shepherd of Israel, compassionately meets the needs of God's people in a prefigurement of God's end-time messianic banquet (Isa 25:6 – 9). While Galilee's aristocrats feast sumptuously in Herod's ornate palace, Jesus feeds the poor and humble — the true heirs of the kingdom — in the open fields on the shores of Galilee.

In terms of what follows, the feeding miracle begins a series of two parallel cycles of events. Each begins with a feeding miracle (6:31 – 44; 8:1 – 10) followed by a trip across the lake (6:45 – 52; 8:10 – 21), and each ends with a miracle of healing — a deaf and mute man (7:31 – 37) and a blind man (8:22 – 26), respectively. Both also include a dispute with the Pharisees (7:1 – 13; 8:11 – 13) and a discussion about bread (7:27 – 29; 8:14 – 21).[2]

---

1. See, e.g., Donahue and Harrington, *Mark*, 209.

2. Hooker, *Mark*, 163. P. J. Achtemeier and others have suggested that Mark has incorporated a pre-Markan cycle of miracles made up to two catenae ("Toward the Isolation of Pre-Marcan Miracle Catenae," *JBL* 89 [1970]: 265 – 91). Further evidence for this are the parallels with John's gospel. John follows the feeding with an account of walking on water (John

6:16 – 21) similar to Mark's, followed by a discourse and disputation with the Jews (6:22 – 65), and an acclamation of Jesus by Peter (6:66 – 71), which is John's parallel to the confession of Peter (Mark 8:27 – 30). See Raymond Brown, *The Gospel according to John* (AB 29, 29A; Garden City, NY: Doubleday, 1966, 1970), 1:238 and further comments on Structure below.

Main Idea

Through his account of Jesus feeding over five thousand people in a "wilderness" location, Mark continues to answer the question that dominates the first half of his gospel: "Who is this man?" Jesus reveals himself to be Israel's good shepherd who cares for his sheep, a new and greater Moses who feeds God's people in the wilderness, and the end-time messianic King hosting the messianic banquet. Since God alone causes the earth to produce food, Jesus also reveals his divine authority over the forces of nature (cf. 4:35 – 41).

Translation

Mark 6:30 – 44

30a	Character entrance	**The apostles rejoined Jesus**
b	Action	and **reported to him all that they had done and taught.**
31a	Response/Action	**He said to them,**
b	command	*"Come away by yourselves to a remote place and rest awhile."*
c	Reason for 31a-b	**This was because so many people were coming and going**
d	Result of 31c	and **they didn't even have a chance to eat.**
32a	Action/Setting	So **they went away**
		by themselves
b		in a boat
c		to a remote place.
33a	Response/Character entrance	But **many people saw them leaving and recognized them.**
b	Action	**They ran on foot from all the towns**
c	Action	and **arrived there ahead of them.**
34a	setting (temporal/spatial)	When he came ashore,
b	Action	**he saw the great crowd and had compassion on them,**
c	reason for 34b	because they were like sheep without a shepherd.
d	Result of 34b	**So he began teaching them many things.**

35a	setting (temporal)	Late in the day,
b	Action/Request	**his disciples came to him and said,**
c		*"This is a remote place, and it is already late in the day.*
36a		*Send the people away*
b		*so they can go into the surrounding countryside and villages and*
c		*buy themselves something to eat."*
37a	Response/Command	But **he answered,**
b		*"You give them something to eat."*
c	Response/Excuse	**They said to him,**
d		*"It would cost two hundred denarii worth of bread to feed them!*
e		*Are we to go and spend that much to give them something to eat?"*
38a	Response	**He said to them,**
b	question	*"How much bread do you have?*
c	command	*Go and see."*
d	Response	**They checked and said,**
e		*"Five loaves and two fish."*
39	Command	**He ordered them all to sit down in dining groups on the green grass.**
40	Response	So **they sat down in groups of hundreds and fifties.**
41a	action	Taking the five loaves and the two fish and looking up to heaven,
b	Action	he **said a blessing,**
c	Action	**broke the bread,**
	Action	and **gave it to his disciples to set before the people.**
d	Action	Then **he divided the fish among them all.**
42	Miracle	**They all ate and were satisfied.**
43	Result	Then **they picked up twelve baskets full of broken pieces of bread and fish.**
44	Summary	**The number of men who ate the loaves was five thousand!**

Structure

The episode is structured as a typical miracle story, with a description of the setting (vv. 30 – 34), the problem (vv. 35 – 37), the miracle (vv. 38 – 41), and the result (vv. 42 – 44). It is also the second "nature miracle" in Mark's gospel, where Jesus demonstrates his authority over the natural world (cf. 4:35 – 41). In terms of OT parallels, the scene has some conceptual similarities to Elisha's feeding of a group of one hundred prophets with twenty barley loaves (2 Kgs 4:42 – 44). If there is an intentional comparison between the two, however, Jesus' miracle far exceeds that of Elisha; he feeds thousands with even less bread.

The primary purpose of this commentary is not to defend the historicity of individual episodes or to trace their tradition history, but because of the striking similarities between this miracle and the feeding of the four thousand in 8:1 – 10 (par. Matt 15:32 – 39), a few comments are in order. Many commentators consider the two accounts to be a "doublet," meaning two stories that arose from a single tradition (for another example, see the healing of two blind men in Matt 9:27 – 31 and 20:29 – 34).

Because of the number of non-Markan terms in both episodes, most argue that the two accounts arose in the pre-Markan tradition, perhaps as part of a larger doublet comprised of 6:30 – 7:37 and 8:1 – 26, respectively.[3] Others, however, claim that Mark himself created one or the other of the feeding miracles. R. Fowler argues that Mark composed the feeding of the five thousand (6:30 – 44) from the feeding of the four thousand (8:1 – 9).[4] K. P. Donfried argues for the reverse.[5]

In response, we can only point to the difficulty and subjectivity of proving or disproving such hypotheses. What is clear is that the two stories differ considerably from one another, including the number of loaves, fish, people, and leftover baskets of food. Matthew and Mark both treat them as two separate incidents and even have Jesus referring back to them as two independent events (Matt 16:9 – 10; Mark 8:19 – 20).[6] Mark certainly believed there were two feedings, and as France points out, "it is not easy to envisage a situation within the mid-first-century church which would allow Mark to remain unaware that only one such incident had in fact occurred."[7] France further asserts that the nature of the two stories runs counter to the normal pattern of oral transmission. The normal tendency is "to preserve specific details like numbers unchanged while varying the 'scenery.'" The two feeding accounts in Mark show precisely the opposite phenomenon, a similar story line but with all the numbers changed. "Since the numbers are emphasized in each account, it is hard to believe that tradition would have treated them with such negligence."[8]

Exegetical Outline

→ 1. **The Return of the Apostles (6:30)**
   2. **The Attempt at a Retreat (6:31 – 32)**
   3. **The Pursuit of the Crowds (6:33)**
   4. **Jesus' Compassionate Response (6:34)**
   5. **The Problem of a Hungry Crowd (6:35 – 37)**
   6. **The Miracle of the Loaves and Fish (6:38 – 41)**
   7. **The Aftermath of the Miracle (6:42 – 44)**

3. Klosterman, *Markusevangelium*, 74 – 75; L. H. Jenkins, "A Marcan Doublet," in *Studies in History and Religion* (FS H. W. Robinson; ed. E. A. Payne; London: Lutterworh, 1942), 87 – 111; Q. Quesnell, *The Mind of Mark: Interpretation and Method through the Exegesis of Mark 6.52* (AnBib 39; Rome: Biblical Institute Press, 1969), 28 – 32. For doubts about the unity of this larger complex, see Taylor, *Mark*, 628 – 32; Guelich, *Mark 1:1 – 8:26*, 402.

4. Robert M. Fowler, *Loaves and Fishes: The Function of the Feeding Stories in the Gospel of Mark* (SBLDS 54; Chico, CA: Scholars, 1978), 43 – 90. Against the view of a Markan creation

of 6:30 – 44, see S. Masuda, "The Good News of the Miracle of the Bread: The Tradition and Its Markan Redaction," *NTS* 28 (982): 191 – 219.

5. K. P. Donfried, "The Feeding Narratives and the Marcan Community: Mark 6,30 – 45 and 8,1 – 10," in *Kirche: Festschrift für Günther Bormkamm zum 75. Geburtstag* (ed. D. Lührmann and G. Strecker; Tübingen: Mohr [Siebeck], 1980), 95 – 103.

6. See Gundry, *Mark*, 398 – 401, for a detailed discussion and defense of two separate miracles.

7. France, *Mark*, 306.

8. Ibid.

Explanation of the Text

6:30 The apostles rejoined Jesus and reported to him all that they had done and taught (Καὶ συνάγονται οἱ ἀπόστολοι πρὸς τὸν Ἰησοῦν καὶ ἀπήγγειλαν αὐτῷ πάντα ὅσα ἐποίησαν καὶ ὅσα ἐδίδαξαν). The return of the Twelve completes their mission introduced in 6:6a – 13 and closes off the intercalation (sandwich) around the martyrdom of John (6:14 – 29). The apostles' report echoes 6:12 – 13 and forms an inclusio (bookend) with it. "All that they had done" (ὅσα ἐποίησαν) refers to the healings and exorcisms (v. 13) and "[all that they had] taught" to the preaching that people should repent (v. 12).

The term "apostles" (ἀπόστολοι) is used only here in Mark's gospel, with the possible exception of 3:13 (see comments there). The term can carry a nontechnical sense of "those who were sent," and this fits well the present context, where the disciples had been sent out as Jesus' authorized representatives. Yet Mark's readers would surely know the later technical sense referring to the Twelve (Luke 6:13; 22:14; Acts 1:26, etc.) and others like Paul (Acts 14:14; Rom 1:1, etc.), who were foundational leaders in the early church.

6:31 – 32 He said to them, "Come away by yourselves to a remote place and rest awhile." This was because so many people were coming and going and they didn't even have a chance to eat. So they went away by themselves in a boat to a remote place (καὶ λέγει αὐτοῖς· δεῦτε ὑμεῖς αὐτοὶ κατ᾽ ἰδίαν εἰς ἔρημον τόπον καὶ ἀναπαύσασθε ὀλίγον. ἦσαν γὰρ οἱ ἐρχόμενοι καὶ οἱ ὑπάγοντες πολλοί, καὶ οὐδὲ φαγεῖν εὐκαίρουν. Καὶ ἀπῆλθον ἐν τῷ πλοίῳ εἰς ἔρημον τόπον κατ᾽ ἰδίαν). After the rigors of their mission, Jesus calls the disciples to a time of rest and recuperation.[9]

The adjective translated "remote" (ἔρημος) is commonly used in the LXX with reference to Israel's "wilderness" wanderings. Although Mark does not identify the place as a true desert or wilderness (Jesus is in Galilee near towns and villages; vv. 33, 36), his repeated use of the term here (vv. 31, 32, 35) is probably meant to echo the experience of Israel in the wilderness. Just as God supplied manna to the Israelites in the desert, so Jesus will feed Israel in a "desert" place.

The withdrawal is necessary because of Jesus' intense popularity and the press of the crowds (v. 31c), themes that have appeared throughout Jesus' Galilean ministry.[10] As in 3:20, there is no time even to eat. As shepherd and guide for his disciples, Jesus recognizes their need for physical and spiritual renewal (cf. 1:35; 6:46; 7:24; 9:2; 14:35). Jesus has used a boat for crowd control (3:9; 4:1) — presumably one of the disciple's fishing boats (1:19 – 20) — and now uses it for escape. This is the third boat trip described by Mark (cf. 4:35 – 5:1; 5:21 – 22).

6:33 But many people saw them leaving and recognized them. They ran on foot from all the towns and arrived there ahead of them (καὶ εἶδον αὐτοὺς ὑπάγοντας καὶ ἐπέγνωσαν πολλοὶ καὶ πεζῇ ἀπὸ πασῶν τῶν πόλεων συνέδραμον ἐκεῖ καὶ προῆλθον αὐτούς). The attempt to escape the crowds is unsuccessful. Seeing Jesus and the disciples leave, and perhaps guessing where they are going, the crowd runs ahead and gets there first. The implication is that Jesus and the disciples are

---

9. Characteristic of Mark's style, the expression is redundant and emphatic in the Greek: an imperative ("come"; δεῦτε), an emphatic personal pronoun ("you"; ὑμεῖς), and an adjectival intensive ("yourselves"; αὐτοί).

10. See 2:4, 13; 3:9, 32; 4:1, 36; 5:21, 24, 30 – 32.

not traversing the entire sea, but traveling from one point on the northern shore to another.

On Mark's use of "town" (πόλις) for any municipality (whether village, town, or city), see comments on 1:38. Mark does not identify the place where Jesus lands, but Luke says it was near Bethsaida (9:10), presumably Bethsaida Julias, just east of where the Jordan enters Galilee. The traditional site of the feeding miracle is further west at Tabgha, on the northwestern shore of the lake near Capernaum.[11] A small chapel was built there in the fourth century, where today stands the Church of the Multiplication.

6:34 When he came ashore, he saw the great crowd and had compassion on them, because they were like sheep without a shepherd. So he began teaching them many things (Καὶ ἐξελθὼν εἶδεν πολὺν ὄχλον καὶ ἐσπλαγχνίσθη ἐπ᾽ αὐτούς, ὅτι ἦσαν ὡς πρόβατα μὴ ἔχοντα ποιμένα, καὶ ἤρξατο διδάσκειν αὐτοὺς πολλά). Jesus sees the crowd and feels compassion for them, an emotion he will demonstrate in the second feeding miracle as well (cf. the variant at 1:41).[12] Images of shepherds and sheep are pervasive throughout the OT and Judaism, and Israel's leaders are often compared to shepherds. In Num 27:17 Moses encourages the appointment of Joshua as his successor "so the LORD's people will not be like sheep without a shepherd" (cf. 1 Kgs 22:1; 2 Chr 18:16). Without a shepherd, the people will be scattered and devoured by wild animals (Ezek 34:5).

David was a successful king because he "shepherded [Israel] with integrity of heart" (Ps 78:72;

cf. 1 Kgs 9:4), and the coming Messiah from David's line was predicted to be a shepherd over God's flock (Jer 23:1 – 6; Ezek 34:22 – 23; Mic 5:2 – 4; Zech 13:7; *Pss. Sol.* 17:40 – 41). Of course, the Lord is the ultimate shepherd over his people (Pss 23; 80:1; Isa 40:11). The reference here that the people of Israel are "like sheep without a shepherd" (ὡς πρόβατα μὴ ἔχοντα ποιμένα) is an indictment on the present leadership of Israel, who are neglecting and exploiting the sheep rather than caring for them. Similar indictments of Israel's leaders as false shepherds are common in the OT (Isa 56:11; Jer 10:21; Ezek 34:2 – 6; Zech 10:2 – 3; 11:17).

Jesus' compassion is expressed through his teaching. Although Mark provides less actual teaching material than the other gospels, he frequently refers to Jesus' teaching (1:21 – 22, 27; 2:13; 4:1 – 2; 6:2, 6, 34; 8:31; 10:1; 12:35, 38; 14:49). The content of that teaching undoubtedly relates to the kingdom of God (1:15; 4:26, 30). Jesus feeds the people first on the word of God, since "man shall not live on bread alone" (Matt 4:4; Luke 4:4).[13] The miracle in John's gospel is followed by Jesus' extended teaching that he is the true manna, life-giving bread from heaven (John 6:25 – 58).

6:35 – 37b Late in the day, his disciples came to him and said, "This is a remote place, and it is already late in the day. Send the people away so they can go into the surrounding countryside and villages and buy themselves something to eat." But he answered, "You give them something to eat." (Καὶ ἤδη ὥρας πολλῆς γενομένης προσελθόντες αὐτῷ οἱ μαθηταὶ αὐτοῦ ἔλεγον ὅτι ἔρημός ἐστιν

---

11. On the historical problem of the location of the feeding and the direction of the boat trip afterward, see comments on 6:45.

12. Mark often expresses Jesus' emotions (1:41; 3:5; 10:21; 14:33 – 34).

13. Wisdom is often compared to food in Jewish Wisdom literature (Prov 9:5; Sir 15:3; 24:19 – 21; 2 Bar. 77:13 – 15). Sirach says, "She [Wisdom] will feed him with the bread of learn-

ing, and give him the water of wisdom to drink" (15:3 NRSV). *Second (Syriac Apocalypse of) Baruch* (early second century AD) similarly compares Israel's leaders to shepherds who impart wisdom from the law. But "the shepherds of Israel have perished, and the lamps which gave light are extinguished, and the fountains from which we used to drink have withheld their streams" (2 Bar. 78:13 – 16; trans. A. F. J. Klijn, in OTP, 1:647).

ὁ τόπος καὶ ἤδη ὥρα πολλή· ἀπόλυσον αὐτούς, ἵνα ἀπελθόντες εἰς τοὺς κύκλῳ ἀγροὺς καὶ κώμας ἀγοράσωσιν ἑαυτοῖς τί φάγωσιν. ὁ δὲ ἀποκριθεὶς εἶπεν αὐτοῖς· δότε αὐτοῖς ὑμεῖς φαγεῖν). The temporal genitive absolute, (lit.) "already the hour becoming great" (ἤδη ὥρας πολλῆς γενομένης), probably means it was already late afternoon, since evening will not arrive for some time (v. 47). For a third time, the place is referred to as a "remote" or "desert" (ἔρημός) place (cf. vv. 31, 32).

On the surface, the disciples' statement in v. 36 seems reasonable and even compassionate, since they are concerned about the people's need for food. It is Jesus' response that seems unreasonable (v. 37a): "You give them something to eat." Where could they possibly come up with food to feed five thousand people? But in the context of the story, the disciples have just returned from a mission in which they have exhibited the authority of Jesus to teach, heal, and cast out demons (vv. 12–13). They went without money or bag or food (v. 8), yet God provided. Here Jesus is challenging them to even greater faith and greater action. As in v. 31, the "you" (ὑμεῖς) is grammatically unnecessary and so emphatic: *You* feed them.

6:37c-e They said to him, "It would cost two hundred denarii worth of bread to feed them! Are we to go and spend that much to give them something to eat?" (καὶ λέγουσιν αὐτῷ· ἀπελθόντες ἀγοράσωμεν δηναρίων διακοσίων ἄρτους καὶ δώσομεν αὐτοῖς φαγεῖν;). Again the disciples answer with an apparently reasonable and practical response. To translate the Greek of v. 37b literally would make it sound like the disciples are asking Jesus' permission to go buy bread ("Shall we go …?" cf. ESV, HCSB, NASB). But this is surely not the sense. Rather, they

are saying, "Surely you don't mean we should go…!" The price is prohibitive.

A denarius was worth about a day's wage for a laborer (Matt 20:2). While economic equivalents between ancient and modern times (and between industrial and peasant societies) are always precarious to propose, we might think of a figure of about $10,000 as the equivalent of two hundred denarii.[14] This is certainly not pocket change for a group of unemployed fishermen and other commoners traveling with an itinerant rabbi. But Jesus is trying to get them to think of kingdom values rather than human economics.

6:38 He said to them, "How much bread do you have? Go and see." They checked and said, "Five loaves and two fish." (ὁ δὲ λέγει αὐτοῖς· πόσους ἄρτους ἔχετε; ὑπάγετε ἴδετε. καὶ γνόντες λέγουσιν· πέντε, καὶ δύο ἰχθύας). Now it is Jesus who gets practical. He takes an inventory of the resources and finds that — by kingdom values — it is more than enough for the crowd. In John's gospel, the five loaves and two fish come from a young boy (παιδάριον) brought to Jesus by Andrew (John 6:9). The five loaves would likely have been pita-sized flatbread about eight inches across and one inch thick, and the fish either of the dried or smoked variety.[15] These are two staples of the Galilee region. Many have attempted to allegorize the numbers, suggesting, for example, that the bread represents the five books of Moses and the two fish as the tablets of the Decalogue. Such proposals are both unlikely and unnecessary.[16]

6:39–40 He ordered them all to sit down in dining groups on the green grass. So they sat down in groups of hundreds and fifties (καὶ ἐπέταξεν αὐτοῖς ἀνακλῖναι πάντας συμπόσια συμπόσια ἐπὶ

---

14. At approximately $50 per day for a field worker's wage, and providing $2 worth of bread for each of 5,000 family units.

15. John 6:9 refers to the fish as ὀψάριον, which usually meant cooked or preserved fish (BDAG, 746).

16. Contra Boring, *Mark*, 185; Marcus, *Mark 1–8*, 407.

τῷ χλωρῷ χόρτῳ. καὶ ἀνέπεσαν πρασιαὶ πρασιαὶ κατὰ ἑκατὸν καὶ κατὰ πεντήκοντα). The description of seating arrangements is unusual. In language reminiscent of a banquet, Jesus orders them to "recline" (ἀνακλῖναι) in "dining groups" or "party by party" (συμπόσια συμπόσια; a distributive sense). The term συμπόσια originally referred to a drinking party, but it came to mean a dinner party or banquet. This may indicate an allusion to the "messianic banquet," God's end-time salvation symbolized as a great feast, with the finest of meats and the best of wines (Isa 25:6 – 9; see Theology in Application).

Also puzzling is the reference to the "green grass" (χλωρὸς χόρτος). This could simply be an historical reminiscence, in which case it would confirm that the miracle occurred in the springtime.[17] If the reference has symbolic value, in light of the shepherd imagery earlier (v. 34), it could echo Ps 23:2, "He makes me lie down in green pastures." Or, if we use the messianic banquet imagery and the location of the miracle in a remote (ἔρημός) place, it could point to the eschatological restoration, when the "wilderness" (ἔρημός) will bloom again (Isa 35:1 LXX).[18]

The people sit down "group by group" (πρασιαὶ πρασιαί; another distributive use). The term here originally meant a "bed of leeks" and so a "garden plot," but it came to mean an orderly arrangement. It could be used of military organization (cf. HCSB, "ranks"), and some have suggested military implications here. Possible evidence for this is the fact that only "men" (ἄνδρες) are mentioned in the final count (6:44; Matt 14:21; Luke 9:14; John 6:10), and that, in John's account, the people attempt to make Jesus king by force (6:15). Yet Mark makes nothing

of this, and it seems best to take the groupings as necessary for an orderly distribution of food.

If any allusions are present, it would likely be to continue the messianic banquet imagery. In Exod 18:21 (cf. Deut 1:15), Israel is organized in companies of thousands, hundreds, fifties, and tens, and the sectarians at Qumran took these groupings as the model for their organization.[19] The Rule of the Congregation (1QSa [1Q28a]) says that the Messiah of Israel will enter the congregation and preside over the messianic banquet, distributing bread and wine to the "head of the thousands of Israel" (1QSa 2:11 – 22).

6:41 – 42 Taking the five loaves and the two fish and looking up to heaven, he said a blessing, broke the bread, and gave it to his disciples to set before the people. Then he divided the fish among them all. They all ate and were satisfied (καὶ λαβὼν τοὺς πέντε ἄρτους καὶ τοὺς δύο ἰχθύας ἀναβλέψας εἰς τὸν οὐρανὸν εὐλόγησεν καὶ κατέκλασεν τοὺς ἄρτους καὶ ἐδίδου τοῖς μαθηταῖς [αὐτοῦ] ἵνα παρατιθῶσιν αὐτοῖς, καὶ τοὺς δύο ἰχθύας ἐμέρισεν πᾶσιν. καὶ ἔφαγον πάντες καὶ ἐχορτάσθησαν).

Although the meal is not identified as a eucharistic celebration (it is bread and fish, not bread and wine), the language used here would certainly recall for Mark's readers Jesus' later institution of the Lord's Supper (14:22 – 25).[20] That meal thus becomes part of the constellation of ideas that come together to provide a picture of eschatological salvation, including the provision of manna in the wilderness, the messianic banquet, and Israel's Passover celebration. John's narrative explicitly brings these images together as Jesus identifies himself as the "bread that came down from heaven"

---

17. Taylor, *Mark*, 321; Witherington, *Mark*, 219; Marcus, *Mark 1 – 8*, 408. Cf. John 6:4, which says the Passover was near. Passover occurred on the 14th of Nisan (=March/April).

18. Hooker, *Mark*, 166.

19. 1QS 2:21 – 22; CD 13:1; 1QM 4:1 – 5:17; 1 QSa 1:14 – 15, 28 – 29; Guelich, *Mark 1:1 – 8:26*, 341.

20. For the eucharistic language of "breaking bread," see Acts 2:42, 46; 20:7, 11; 1 Cor 10:16 – 17; 11:23.

(John 6:41) and calls on the people to eat his flesh and drink his blood (6:53–58).

Looking up to heaven is the posture of prayer (cf. 7:34; John 11:41). Since no object for the verb "blessed" (εὐλόγησεν) is expressed, the Greek could mean either, "He blessed [God] and broke the bread" or "He blessed and broke the bread." The former seems more likely, especially in light of the ancient Jewish blessings over meals: "Blessed art thou, O Lord our God, King of the universe, who bringest forth bread from the earth."[21] Gundry points out that the substitution of "giving thanks" (εὐχαριστήσας) in 8:6 as well as the parallel between thanksgiving and blessing in 8:6–7; 14:22–23 favors this interpretation.[22]

The miracle is described simply and without fanfare. Despite the meager provisions, "all ate and were satisfied." The abundance of food again has eschatological implications, since the time of God's final salvation will be one of peace, prosperity, and abundance (Isa 25:6; 35:1–10; 51:3; 55:1–2; 60:5–6).

6:43–44 Then they picked up twelve baskets full of broken pieces of bread and fish. The number of men who ate the loaves was five thousand! (καὶ ἦραν κλάσματα δώδεκα κοφίνων πληρώματα καὶ ἀπὸ τῶν ἰχθύων. καὶ ἦσαν οἱ φαγόντες τοὺς ἄρτους πεντακισχίλιοι ἄνδρες). The surplus of food recalls the statement made following Elisha's feeding of one hundred men with twenty barley loaves: "they ate and had some left over" (2 Kgs 4:44). Is there symbolism in the twelve baskets collected? Some see here an allusion to the restoration of twelve tribes of Israel. While possible, Mark makes nothing of this, and the more likely (and mundane) explanation is that the twelve disciples each carried a basket, so that twelve baskets were collected.[23]

Mark identifies the number of "men" (ἄνδρες) who ate as five thousand. The Greek term usually means males, but it can refer to people in general (cf. Matt 12:41; 14:35; Rom 4:8; Eph 4:13; Jas 1:12, 20; 3:2). Matthew's account specifies the former by adding, "besides women and children" (Matt 14:21). This would make the total number fed much greater than five thousand. As noted above, the reference to men has suggested to some commentators that the gathering has militaristic and revolutionary implications—an attempt to make Jesus king (cf. John 6:15). Mark, however, does not emphasize this point and probably uses "men" to mean family units.

No response of the people to the miracle is recorded. This is especially surprising considering how pervasive the theme of amazement is throughout Mark's gospel (1:22, 27; 2:12; 5:15, 20; 5:42; 6:51; 12:17).[24] The implication is that most of the crowd was unaware of where the food had come from, though the disciples certainly knew (cf. 8:19).[25]

21. *The Standard Prayer Book* (trans. Simeon Singer; New York: Block, 1915), 424; cf. *m. Ber.* 6:1; *b. Ber.* 37a, 38a, 42a, etc.

22. Gundry, *Mark*, 325–26. Stein, *Mark*, 317, however, counters that Jesus "blesses" the fish in 8:7.

23. The term "basket" (κοφίνος) is a Latin loanword. The Roman satirist Juvenal mocks the Jews of Rome for carrying such baskets wherever they went (*Sat.* 3:14; 6.542). Their size is debated. BDAG (563) speaks of "a large, heavy basket, probably of var. sizes, for carrying things," while Lane (*Mark*, 231 n. 109) identifies them as "small wicker baskets ... used to hold such things as a light lunch and general odds and ends."

24. Hooker, *Mark*, 468.

25. How do we harmonize this with the attempt in John to make Jesus king? This action may have been taken by the relative few who recognized the miracle.

Theology in Application

Jesus, the Good Shepherd Who Cares for His Sheep

The passage begins with Jesus' concern for the welfare of his disciples and his call for them to get away to a "quiet" (NIV) or "remote" (ἔρημος) place to get some rest (v. 31). Ministry, like that conducted by the disciples in their mission, is exhausting, and Jesus recognizes the need for a time of retreat and rejuvenation. Tension arises, however, when Jesus sees the greater needs of the people, who are "sheep without a shepherd," and is drawn to meet those needs. As the good shepherd, he will ultimately lay down his life for the sheep (John 10:11). Here he sets aside his own personal needs and ministers to others. Significantly, Jesus meets both spiritual needs and physical ones, first teaching and then feeding the people. This is a good model for us today, where a "social gospel" that meets the physical needs of people should not be isolated from the message, but should be an essential and indispensable part of the proclamation of the saving work of Christ.

As undershepherds over the flock of God, Christian leaders are called to give up their lives for Christ and for the gospel (Rom 12:1 – 2). This, however, does not mean becoming a "workaholic-for-Christ" or ministering to the breaking point. Jesus repeatedly insists on the need for times of spiritual retreat, prayer, solitude, and rest. There is great irony in the fact that the day of worship for Christians is often a time of exhausting work for ministers of the gospel. While there is great joy and refreshment in meeting the spiritual needs of others, there is also the need to keep one's own battery charged.

When Paul addresses the Ephesian elders in Acts 20, he uses shepherd imagery to describe their task as spiritual leaders: "Keep watch over yourselves and all the flock of which the Holy Spirit has made you overseers" (Acts 20:28). Paul first tells these leaders to keep watch over *themselves* so that they can successfully keep watch over the flock of God. Christian leaders will be of no benefit to the people of God if they do not first take care of their own physical health, their own personal purity, their own spouse and family, and other pressing personal needs.

I often tell my students who are headed for full-time ministry to beware of the "seduction" of Christian ministry. There is a tendency among pastors and other Christian leaders to immerse themselves in ministry, where their congregants honor, esteem, and value them, and to neglect their family life. At church they are viewed as "the Lord's anointed," but at home they are the absentee spouse (or father, or mother) who seems constantly distracted or too busy to help out around the house or to share in the child raising. Our natural tendency in such situations is to pull away from the place of criticism (the home) and toward the environment in which we are esteemed — hence the seduction of ministry. This is a dangerous direction, often resulting in broken homes and broken ministries. It is essential to heed Paul's counsel to "keep watch over ourselves" first, then to shepherd the flock of God.

Manna in the Wilderness, the Eucharist, and the Messianic Banquet

As we have seen, this passage also has strong eschatological implications. Just as God fed Israel in the wilderness with manna through Moses, so now Jesus feeds the people of God in a "desert" place. This miracle, in turn, points forward to God's future eschatological banquet and its present preview in the celebration of the Lord's Supper. While these themes are alluded to in Mark, they become explicit in John's account of the miracle. When the people remind Jesus that "our ancestors ate manna in the wilderness" (John 6:31), Jesus informs them that he is the "true bread from heaven" that "gives life to the world" (6:32 – 33; cf. vv. 41 – 51). This life is received by eating his flesh and drinking his blood (vv. 53 – 58), that is, by appropriating the atoning death of Christ (symbolized in the Eucharist) and thereby receiving his resurrection life.

The Eucharist is not just a remembrance of things past, but an anticipation of the consummation of salvation when Christ returns, as we "proclaim the Lord's death until he comes" (1 Cor 11:26). Jesus' feeding miracle thus points forward to the eschatological banquet that symbolizes God's final salvation (Isa 25:6 – 9). In the affluent West, where few go to bed hungry and grocery stores are stocked from floor to ceiling, it is hard to comprehend the impact these words would have had on first-century readers: "They all ate and were satisfied" (v. 42). For people who lived daily at the level of subsistence, this was "good news" indeed, an anticipation of the eschatological feast in the presence of God.

Even more significantly, the metaphor of the banquet points forward to the restoration of creation and eternal fellowship with our Creator God, when "he will destroy the shroud that enfolds all peoples … he will swallow up death forever" (Isa 25:7 – 8). The same theme appears in Jesus' discourse following the feeding miracle in John: "Whoever eats this bread will live forever" (John 6:51).

The Failure of the Disciples

In the context of Mark's larger narrative, the bread imagery also has a more foreboding side. In the present passage, the failure of the disciples is muted. They first encourage Jesus to send the crowd away to find food (6:35) — an apparently legitimate request — and then express dismay at Jesus' suggestion that *they* feed the people (v. 37). For those with eyes of faith, these are failures, but any pragmatist would forgive the disciples for failing to anticipate such a miracle.

Yet this lapse is the beginning of a series of events that will increase in severity, highlighting the disciples' lack of faith. When Jesus walks on water in the following episode, the disciples are baffled, Mark says, "because they had not understood about the loaves; their hearts were hardened" (6:52). Hard hearts are far more serious than a failure to anticipate a miracle. Then, before the second feeding miracle (8:1 – 13), they respond in the same way as the first, asking how they could possibly feed so many in a "desolate place" (8:4). What appeared here to be a realistic assessment of the situation now looks like spiritual blindness. Did they not remember the first feeding?

The drama intensifies when Jesus warns the disciples about the "leaven of the Pharisees" (8:15). They misinterpret this as a reference to physical bread, so Jesus must remind them of the two feeding miracles and warns them against having eyes that fail to see and ears that fail to hear (8:14 – 21). This shocking indictment recalls Jesus' reason for teaching in parables and puts the disciples in danger of becoming like the religious leaders — "outsiders" who are blind and deaf to the mysteries of the kingdom of God (4:10 – 11). The disciples seem on the brink of disaster. Will their lack of faith grow into outright rejection? Stay tuned.

The feeding miracle reminds us that spiritual success does not come through human effort or resources, but through trust and dependence on the One who "brings forth bread from the earth." When we face difficulties and challenges, we should look beyond our own circumstances and ask, "What could the Creator God accomplish here?" While God does not call us to be naïve or reckless in our Christian life, he does call us to live by faith, believing that his will and purpose will be done, "on earth as it is in heaven."

Mark 6:45–52

Literary Context

In this second miracle at sea (cf. 4:35–41), Mark continues to provide the answer to the key question of the first half of Mark's gospel: *Who is this man?* (4:41; 6:14–16). Mark links the miracle of walking on water closely to the previous episode of the feeding of the five thousand. They are linked as a continuous narrative, since Jesus sends the disciples off by boat while he dismisses the crowd; and they are linked theologically in that the narrator notes that the disciples are amazed at this second miracle, "because they had not understood about the loaves; their hearts were hardened" (vv. 51–52).

Both miracles exhibit the failure of the disciples to recognize the significance of Jesus' divine authority over the forces of nature. Both may also indicate a "greater than Moses" theme, where the disciples fail to recognize that Jesus is much more than a prophet. As the feeding miracle recalled the manna in the wilderness, so Jesus' walking on the sea may perhaps reenact the Israelites' passing through the Red Sea (cf. Pss 77:19–20; 78:13–25; Isa 43:16; 51:10).[1]

In Mark's larger narrative, the miracle is part of two cycles, each of which includes a feeding miracle (6:32–44; 8:1–10), a trip across the lake (6:45–52; 8:11–21), a dispute with the Pharisees (7:1–13; 8:11–13), a discussion about bread (7:27–29; 8:14–21), and a healing miracle (7:31–37; 8:22–26). In turn, the two cycles lead up to the climax of the first half of Mark's gospel: the confession by Peter and Jesus' first passion prediction (8:27–9:1).

---

1. Hooker, *Mark*, 169.

Main Idea

Since only God "treads on the waves of the sea" (Job 9:8), Jesus demonstrates his divine authority by walking on the water. Yet even such a self-revelation demands eyes of faith, and the disciples remain perplexed and undiscerning, because "their hearts were hardened" (Mark 6:52).

Translation

Mark 6:45 – 52

45a	Action	**Immediately he made his disciples get into the boat** and
b	Action	**go across ahead of him to Bethsaida,**
c	setting (temporal & social)	while he dismissed the crowd.
46a	setting (temporal & social)	After sending them on their way,
b	Action	**he went up to the mountain to pray.**
47a	setting (temporal)	When evening came,
b	Setting/Statement of fact	**the boat was in the middle of the sea,**
	Setting/Statement of fact	and **he was alone on the land.**
48a	observation/setting	Seeing them straining at the oars,
b	reason for 48a	because the wind was against them,
c	setting (temporal)	in the very early morning hours,
d	Action/Epiphany	**he came to them,**
e	manner of 48d	walking on the sea,
f	Action/Intention	and **intended to pass by them.**
49a	reason for 49b	When they saw him walking on the sea,
b	Result of 49a	**they thought he was a ghost.**
c	Action/Exclamation	**They cried out,**
50a	reason for 49c	because they all saw him and were terrified.
b	Response to 49	But **he spoke to them at once and said,**
c	exhortation	*"Have courage!*
	assertion	*It is I.*
	encouragement	*Don't be afraid."*
51a	Action	Then **he climbed into the boat with them**
b	Response/Miracle	and **the wind stopped.**
c	Summary/Response to 48 – 51	**They were totally amazed,**
52a	reason for 51c	because they had not understood about the loaves;
b	Statement of fact/ indictment	**their hearts were hardened.**

Structure

The episode exhibits a certain tension in terms of its genre. Is this a rescue episode, as in the storm at sea of 4:35 – 41? Or is it a theophany, where Jesus manifests the divine presence?[2] Or is it a combination of both? The former is indicated by the struggle of the disciples as they "strain at the oars" but make little headway (v. 48) and by the climax in v. 51, where the wind dies down immediately when Jesus enters the boat. A theophany is evident in Jesus' treading on the seas and perhaps by his intention to "pass by" the boat (see comments on v. 48). Whatever its pre-Markan form,[3] the episode is certainly meant to recall the earlier storm scene and so functions both to demonstrate Jesus' mastery over nature and his provision for and protection of the disciples. Mark also uses it to show the regression of the disciples. Despite the stupendous nature of the two miracles, their hearts remain hard (v. 52).

Exegetical Outline

➡ **1. The Setting (6:45 – 46)**
    a. Jesus sends the disciples away and dismisses the crowd (6:45)
    b. Jesus prays on the mountainside (6:46)
2. The Miracle on the Waves (6:47 – 51b)
    a. The disciples' struggle (6:47 – 48b)
    b. Jesus walks on water (6:48c-f)
    c. The disciples' terror (6:49 – 50a)
    d. Jesus' reassuring response (6:50b-c)
    e. Jesus enters the boat and the wind dies down (6:51a-b)
3. The Response (6:51c – 52)
    a. Amazement (6:51c)
    b. Spiritual dullness (6:52)

2. Gundry, *Mark*, 342, denies the episode is a rescue story, since "the narrative carries not a hint of mortal danger." Cf. Hooker, *Mark*, 169, who links it to the "more than Moses" theme: "Jesus does not come to rescue the disciples from a storm; they are there to witness his epiphany."

3. Bultmann, *History*, 216, claimed that a pre-Markan redactor had turned a theophany into a rescue story.

Explanation of the Text

6:45 – 46 Immediately he made his disciples get into the boat and go across ahead of him to Bethsaida, while he dismissed the crowd. After sending them on their way, he went up to the mountain to pray (Καὶ εὐθὺς ἠνάγκασεν τοὺς μαθητὰς αὐτοῦ ἐμβῆναι εἰς τὸ πλοῖον καὶ προάγειν εἰς τὸ πέραν⁴ πρὸς Βηθσαϊδάν, ἕως αὐτὸς ἀπολύει τὸν ὄχλον. καὶ ἀποταξάμενος αὐτοῖς ἀπῆλθεν εἰς τὸ ὄρος προσεύξασθαι). Immediately after the feeding miracle, Jesus sends the disciples away by boat and goes into the hills to pray.

The sense of urgency ("immediately"; εὐθύς) in sending the disciples away and the strong verb "made" or "compelled" (ἠνάγκασεν) have suggested to some that the reason for Jesus' actions is to be found in John's parallel, where the people try to make Jesus king by force (John 6:14 – 15). Jesus heads off these messianic intentions by sending the disciples away quickly to keep them from revealing to the crowds the miraculous nature of the meal. In this view, Jesus' withdrawal for prayer is to overcome the temptation to be this kind of conquering Messiah.⁵ Though this motivation is possible, Mark makes nothing of it. The feeding miracle certainly has messianic overtones (cf. Isa 25:6 – 8), but Mark presents it as an act of compassionate shepherding and nothing about the crowd's behavior indicates messianic ambitions or expectations.

There is a historical question here, related both to the place of the feeding miracle and the direction of the boat trip. Mark says that Jesus sent the disciples (eastward?) toward Bethsaida, presumably Julias Bethsaida, just east of the Jordan River (v. 45). This makes sense if the feeding miracle

took place at Tabgha, the traditional site. Yet they end up in the opposite direction, at Gennesaret, on the western shore of Galilee (6:53). This apparently agrees with John's account (6:17), which says the boat headed (westward) toward Capernaum after the miracle. Is Mark's geography confused?

Several solutions have been proposed. (1) The reference to Bethsaida in Mark 6:45 could be a scribal error, in which case the feeding miracle occurred near Bethsaida, as Luke says (9:10), and was followed by a westward trip towards Capernaum. The problem is that there is no manuscript evidence for such an omission.

(2) Others propose that there were two Bethsaidas. The miracle occurred near Bethsaida Julias east of the Jordan, after which the disciples returned to a small village of the same name near Capernaum and Chorazin (cf. Matt 11:21, 23; John 12:21).

(3) A third view also proposes two Bethsaidas, but has the miracle occurring in the west near Tabgha and the village of Bethsaida. The disciples then head east by boat toward Bethsaida Julias (6:45), but are blown back and arrive instead at Gennesaret (Mark 6:53; John 6:17). The problem with these last two views is that there is no firm evidence that such a village existed.

(4) A fourth, and perhaps most likely, solution reads the text differently. Jesus sent his disciples ahead of him to nearby Bethsaida, "while he dismissed the crowd" (ἕως αὐτὸς ἀπολύει τὸν ὄχλον). He planned to meet them there, but if he was delayed, they were to embark westward toward Capernaum and Gennesaret. This solution finds

---

4. Some mss omit εἰς τὸ πέραν ("to the other side"; 𝔓⁴⁵ᵛⁱᵈ W *f*¹ syrˢ). This was probably a scribal attempt to avoid the problem of heading "across the lake" to Bethsaida, since Luke said the feeding miracle took place there (Luke 9:10).

5. James Edwards, *Mark* (PNTC; Grand Rapids: Eerdmans,

2002), 197; Hurtado, *Mark*, 106; Lane, *Mark*, 234 – 35. Lane cites R. H. Lightfoot, "A Consideration of Three Passages in St. Mark's Gospel," in *In Memoriam E. Lohmeyer* (Stuttgart: Evangelisches Verlagswerk, 1951), 110 – 15.

some support from Matthew's account, which says they were to go ahead of him "while [ἕως οὗ] he dismissed the crowd" (Matt 14:22). It would also explain why the disciples were still in the middle of the lake hours later (v. 48), i.e., they first went to Bethsaida and waited several hours for Jesus. Only later, when Jesus was delayed on the mountain, did they embark toward Gennesaret.[6]

After sending off the disciples and "saying farewell" (ἀποταξάμενος)[7] to the crowds, Jesus goes up to the mountain to pray. In light of the Moses/exodus allusions in the near context (the feeding miracle; passing through the sea), there may be an echo here of Moses' ascent to Mount Sinai (Exod 19).[8] The other two references to Jesus' prayer in Mark have him similarly praying at night and in solitude (1:35; 14:35).

6:47 When evening came, the boat was in the middle of the sea, and he was alone on the land

(καὶ ὀψίας γενομένης ἦν τὸ πλοῖον ἐν μέσῳ τῆς θαλάσσης, καὶ αὐτὸς μόνος ἐπὶ τῆς γῆς). The chronology is difficult here. When the feeding miracle began, it was already "late in the day" (v. 35). Yet the entire feeding miracle, the dismissal of the crowds, and the disciples reaching the middle of the sea takes place by "evening" (6:47). But then Jesus doesn't walk on the water until early morning (3 – 6 a.m.; "the fourth watch of the night"). Perhaps by "evening" Mark means late at night. Or, if the sequence set out in view 4 above is correct (see vv. 45 – 46), the disciples may have reached Bethsaida in the evening but did not embark for Capernaum until much later during the night.

6:48 Seeing them straining at the oars, because the wind was against them, in the very early morning hours, he came to them, walking on the sea, and intended to pass by them

(καὶ ἰδὼν αὐτοὺς βασανιζομένους ἐν τῷ ἐλαύνειν, ἦν γὰρ ὁ ἄνεμος ἐναντίος αὐτοῖς, περὶ τετάρτην φυλακὴν τῆς νυκτὸς ἔρχεται πρὸς αὐτοὺς περιπατῶν ἐπὶ τῆς θαλάσσης καὶ ἤθελεν παρελθεῖν αὐτούς). Mark reckons here by Roman time, which divided the night into four watches. The "fourth watch" (τετάρτη φυλακή) was 3 – 6 a.m. — hence our translation, "in the very early morning hours."

Mark does not tell his readers how Jesus could see the plight of the disciples in the dark and at such a distance, whether in the moonlight,[9] in the predawn light,[10] or through supernatural insight.[11] What is important for him is how Jesus comes to them — walking on the water! This action clearly carries theophanic significance, since God alone "treads on the waves of the sea" (Job 9:8). In the exodus God "made a way through the sea, a path through the mighty waters" (Isa 43:16; cf. 51:10; Ps 77:19; Sir 24:5 – 6). Jesus is acting with divine authority, doing what only God can do.[12]

The Greek here is one sentence, with the subordinate participial phrase, "seeing them straining" (ἰδὼν αὐτοὺς βασανιζομένους), modifying the main verb, "he came to them" (ἔρχεται πρὸς αὐτούς; historical present tense). The point is that Jesus comes in response to their struggle. It is strange, then, that the next clause says, "and [he] intended to pass by them" (καὶ ἤθελεν παρελθεῖν αὐτούς). If he was coming to help, why would he pass them?

---

6. For this view, see D. A. Carson, "Matthew," in *EBC*[2] , 392 – 93; L. Morris, *The Gospel according to John* (NICNT; Grand Rapids: Eerdmans, 1971), 349.

7. BDAG, 123.

8. So Marcus, *Mark 1 – 8*, 422 – 23; Hooker, *Mark*, 170.

9. Cranfield, *Mark*, 225.

10. France, *Mark*, 271.

11. Garland, *Mark*, 261.

12. There have been many attempts to explain Jesus' actions in a nonsupernatural manner. H. E. G. Paulus, for example, claimed Jesus was walking on the shore but that a mist covered his feet (see Schweitzer, *Quest of the Historical Jesus*, 52). This is certainly not Mark's perspective, since he unambiguously says Jesus was "walking on the sea" (περιπατῶν ἐπὶ τῆς θαλάσσης) and says that Jesus was passing the boat, which was "in the middle of the sea" (ἐν μέσῳ τῆς θαλάσσης, v. 47).

Various suggestions have been made. (1) The verb "wished" (θέλω) could mean "was about to" (functioning like μέλλω), as the NIV translates it. In this case it is the disciples' perspective, rather than Jesus' intention, that is being described. It "seemed as though" he was going to pass them by.[13]

(2) Another possibility is that Jesus is passing in front of them "to make himself visible to the disciples to relieve their fear and to reveal his power to them."[14] Of course in this view, his plans are frustrated since they are terrorized instead of relieved.

(3) Still others interpet the phrase as a Hebrew idiom meaning to "spare from catastrophe" (cf. Amos 7:8), so that Jesus is coming to help them.[15]

(4) The most likely explanation, and one increasingly adopted by interpreters, is that this is an intentional echo of OT language of theophany, where God reveals himself to his people by "passing by" them.[16] In Exod 33:18 – 23 Moses asks God to show him his glory. The Lord responds, "I will cause all my goodness to pass in front of you." Although no one can see God's face and live, God "passes by" and shows Moses his back. Similarly, in 1 Kings 19:10 – 12, when Elijah expresses frustration that he is the only faithful person left in Israel, God tells him to "stand on the mountain in the presence of the LORD, for the LORD is about to pass by." God then reveals himself, not in a powerful wind or a mighty earthquake, but in a tiny whisper. By "passing by" the disciples, Jesus is revealing his divine glory.

6:49 – 50 When they saw him walking on the sea, they thought he was a ghost. They cried out, because they all saw him and were terrified. But he spoke to them at once and said, "Have courage!

It is I. Don't be afraid." (οἱ δὲ ἰδόντες αὐτὸν ἐπὶ τῆς θαλάσσης περιπατοῦντα ἔδοξαν ὅτι φάντασμά ἐστιν, καὶ ἀνέκραξαν· πάντες γὰρ αὐτὸν εἶδον καὶ ἐταράχθησαν. ὁ δὲ εὐθὺς ἐλάλησεν μετ᾽ αὐτῶν, καὶ λέγει αὐτοῖς· θαρσεῖτε, ἐγώ εἰμι· μὴ φοβεῖσθε). The disciples are terrified and think they are seeing a "ghost" (φάντασμα). The word is used in the NT only here and in the parallel at Matt 14:26. It carries the sense of a disembodied spirit or apparition.[17] As France points out, they are not thinking of *Jesus'* ghost; there is no reason to suppose he is dead. They simply do not yet recognize him and assume this is an apparition.[18]

Jesus assures them by calling them to courage and by identifying himself, "It is I" (ἐγώ εἰμι). In light of the theophany in the immediate context, it is tempting to see here an allusion to God's self revelation in the OT as the "I AM." In the account in Exod 3:14, God reveals his name to the Israelites through Moses as "I AM WHO I AM" ('*ehyeh 'ăšer 'ehyeh*; cf. Deut 32:39), and in Isaiah, God repeatedly identifies himself as the one true God with the designation, "I am he" ('*ănî-hû'*; Isa 41:4; 43:10, 13, 25; 46:4; 48:12; 51:12). In John's gospel, Jesus no doubt alludes to this divine title when referring to himself (John 8:58; 18:5 – 6).

But is it present here in Mark? The phrase "I am [he]" (ἐγώ εἰμι) is a normal way of self-identification in Greek and so would not by necessity recall these OT allusions. In the present context, Jesus' purpose is to assure the disciples that it is he and not a ghost. Furthermore, an explicit divine claim would be unusual in Mark's gospel, where Jesus reveals his divine authority through his *actions,* but never directly through his words (but cf. 14:62, where the same phrase

---

13. Cranfield, *Mark*, 226; France, *Mark*, 272.

14. Hurtado, *Mark*, 103.

15. H. Fleddermann, " 'And He Wanted to Pass by Them' (Mark 6:48c)," *CBQ* 45 (1983): 389 – 95.

16. Lane, *Mark*, 236; Guelich, *Mark 1:1 – 8:26*, 350; Garland,

Mark, 263 – 64; Marcus, *Mark 1 – 8*, 426; Stein, *Mark*, 325; Collins, *Mark*, 334.

17. BDAG, 1049. The word is common in the Greek magical papyri.

18. France, *Mark*, 272.

is used). It seems unlikely, therefore, that Mark understands Jesus to be saying emphatically, "I am Yahweh!" Whether Mark's readers in the post-resurrection church would have picked up such an allusion is a more difficult question.

6:51 – 52 Then he climbed into the boat with them and the wind stopped. They were totally amazed, because they had not understood about the loaves; their hearts were hardened (καὶ ἀνέβη πρὸς αὐτοὺς εἰς τὸ πλοῖον καὶ ἐκόπασεν ὁ ἄνεμος, καὶ λίαν ἐκ περισσοῦ[19] ἐν ἑαυτοῖς ἐξίσταντο· οὐ γὰρ συνῆκαν ἐπὶ τοῖς ἄρτοις, ἀλλ᾽ ἦν αὐτῶν ἡ καρδία πεπωρωμένη). The immediate cessation of the wind represents a second miracle, recalling the calming of the storm in 4:35 – 41 and again demonstating Jesus' authority over nature. Though secondary to the theophany, this makes the episode a deliverance story as well. In v. 48 the wind was the enemy, which had prevented the disciples from making headway. Now they can finish their course.

The disciples express amazement, a common theme throughout Mark's gospel (1:22, 27; 2:12; 5:20, 42; 12:17). Yet there is a surprising twist. While amazement in this gospel has typically been a positive response to the power of God, here it

is negative, indicating perplexity and unbelief. Mark connects the amazment to the previous episode: "because they had not understood about the loaves" (οὐ γὰρ συνῆκαν ἐπὶ τοῖς ἄρτοις). This begs the question *what* had they not understood and why Mark singles out this miracle among the many others Jesus did in Galilee. The reason may be the miracle's proximity, having occurred just prior. Or perhaps, as Hooker suggests, the two miracles carry forward an exodus theme.[20] The disciples fail to recognize that one greater than Moses is here and that an event greater than the exodus is unfolding before their eyes.

Mark adds that the disciples' failure to comprehend was related to their hard heart[21] (ἀλλ᾽ ἦν αὐτῶν ἡ καρδία πεπωρωμένη). Here we have another possible exodus allusion, since it was Pharaoh's hardened heart that led to the exodus (Exod 7:3, 13, 22; 8:15, 32; 9:12; 10:1). This is a serious condition indeed. It was a characteristic of Jesus' opponents in 3:5 when they sought to trap Jesus (cf. 10:5), and it signals the beginning of an increasingly negative portrayal of the disciples in Mark's narrative.[22] Will they go the way of those "outsiders" who have eyes but do not see?

Theology in Application

The Divine Authority of Jesus

As in most of the passages throughout the first half of Mark's gospel, the primary emphasis here is christological. Jesus' divine authority is on center stage as he once again exhibits mastery over nature (cf. 4:35 – 41; 6:30 – 44). Just as God treads on the mighty seas (Job 9:8) and made a way through the sea at the exodus (Exod 13), so Jesus walks on water toward the disciples. Similarly, just as Yahweh "passed before"

---

19. On the reading ἐκ περισσοῦ, Metzger points out that while the double superlative (λίαν ἐκ περισσοῦ) is characteristic of Markan style and is included in a variety of diverse witnesses, its omission from important manuscripts (א B L Δ 892 *al*) renders it questionable (Metzger, *Textual Commentary*, 79).

20. Hooker, *Mark*, 169.

21. The singular "heart" is curious and probably is intended to view the disciples collectively as a single character in Mark's gospel. They rise or fall together.

22. See Quesnell, *The Mind of Mark*, passim.

Moses (Exod 33:18 – 23) and Elijah (1 Kgs 19:10 – 12) to reveal his glory, so Jesus reveals his divine authority by passing in front of the disciples in the boat.

Edwards points to the irony of attempts to explain away the miracle on rationalistic grounds, since Job 9:10 — in the same context that speaks of God treading on the waters (9:8) — says, "He performs wonders that cannot be fathomed, miracles that cannot be counted."[23] If God is truly unfathomable, then his works are unexplainable as natural phenomena.

Jesus' Care for His Disciples

When the disciples struggle in their boat against a headwind, Jesus comes to their aid. Although apparently passing them by, he hears their cries and turns to meet them, expressing first words of assurance and then calming the wind that is preventing their progress. Though divine care and rescue are not the primary point of the episode, it is an important secondary one.

Throughout church history, this passage, like 4:35 – 41, has been understood as Christ's rescue through the storms of life. While we must be cautious against overallegorizing passages such as this, the challenges the disciples face are certainly analogous to the spiritual and physical challenges in our lives. Just as the disciples rowed hour after hour but made little progress, so we sometimes seem to be going nowhere in the headwinds of life. It is at times like these that Jesus comes to us with words of encouragement. Notice too that Jesus does not deliver the disciples to land (as in John 6:21), but enables them to continue their journey. God doesn't always remove our obstacles, but calms the wind and gives us strength to push toward our goal.

The Disciples' Astonishment and Lack of Faith

In stark contrast to Jesus' mastery over nature and divine self-revelation stands the disciples' failure to respond. First stymied by the wind, they then react in terror at Jesus' numinous presence. From a human perspective, this might seem like a natural response. Yet these are the disciples who have seen Jesus heal the sick, cast out demons, and raise the dead. They have just witnessed Jesus' divine authority to feed multitudes with a few loaves and fish. By now their faith should be strong, yet they react with fear and disbelief.

At the end of Matthew's version of the story, the disciples cry out, "Truly you are the Son of God," and they worship him (14:33). Mark has a different slant.[24] This is the beginning of a downward spiral that will bring the disciples to a dangerous turning point. In 8:14 – 21 (an episode again involving a boat, bread, and "hard hearts"),

---

23. Edwards, *Mark*, 199.

24. The two accounts may perhaps be harmonized by assuming that Matthew is stressing the positive side of their amazement, while Mark emphasizes its insufficient and fleeting nature. Or perhaps among themselves the disciples were at different levels of understanding.

Jesus will warn the disciples against having eyes that cannot see and ears that cannot hear. Their faith is in the balance.

The disciples' problem is not that they are unable to make headway against the wind or that they are not rowing hard enough. It is that they have not learned the lesson of the loaves — that God is at work through Jesus to accomplish his saving purpose. Disciples of Jesus are not expected to be fearless in every circumstance, but they are expected to learn from God's faithfulness in the past and to grow in their faith for the future.

25

Mark 6:53 – 56

Literary Context

This short summary is literarily connected to the previous episode with the arrival of the boat at Gennesaret, on the western shore of the Sea of Galilee. In the broader context of Mark's gospel, it is the third summary of Jesus' ministry (1:32 – 34; 3:7 – 12). In all three, Jesus' popularity is emphasized. While the first two mention both healings and exorcisms, this one focuses exclusively on the healings. This is probably not an intentional theological movement away from Jesus' role as an exorcist (see 9:14 – 28), but simply an example of Markan variety (cf. 6:7, where only exorcisms are mentioned).

Jesus' arrival in Gennesaret and the summary that follows represent the end of a series of boat narratives (4:35 – 5:2; 5:21; 6:32 – 34; 6:45 – 54) and a transition to a new emphasis in Jesus' ministry. What follows is a teaching section on ritually clean and unclean things, which leads to Jesus' ministry in Gentile regions, that is, among ritually "unclean" people. Thus we have a summary of Jesus' ministry among the Jews in western Galilee before his ministry to Gentiles in Phoenicia and the Decapolis.

Main Idea

This third summary highlights key themes of Jesus' public ministry around Galilee, including his travel by boat, his intense popularity, and his healing the sick.

Translation

Mark 6:53 – 56

53a	setting (temporal & spatial)	After they had crossed over,
b	Action	**they landed at Gennesaret and anchored the boat there.**
54a	setting (temporal & spatial)	When they got out of the boat,
b	Response/Action	**the people immediately recognized Jesus.**
55a	Response/Action	**They ran throughout that whole region**
b		and **began to bring the sick on cots to wherever he was reported to be.**
56a	setting (spatial)	Wherever he went — into villages, towns, or countryside —
b	Action/Response	**they would place the sick in the marketplaces**
c	Entreaty	and **would beg him to let them touch even the** tassels of his cloak.
d	Healing	And **all who touched him were healed.**

Structure

In terms of its genre, the episode is a summary, highlighting Jesus' healing ministry and the popular enthusiasm that it generated.

Exegetical Outline

➡ **1. Setting: Arrival in Gennesaret (6:53)**
  2. Jesus' Popularity and Healing Ministry (6:54 – 56)

Explanation of the Text

6:53 After they had crossed over, they landed at Gennesaret and anchored the boat there (Καὶ διαπεράσαντες ἐπὶ τὴν γῆν ἦλθον εἰς Γεννησαρὲτ καὶ προσωρμίσθησαν). For historical questions related to the direction and destination of this boat trip, see comments on 6:45 – 46. Gennesaret was a fertile plain on the northwest shore of the Sea of Galilee between Capernaum on the north and Magdala on the south. Josephus describes the beauty of the region, with its temperate climate and fertile soil ideal for fruit trees and other agricultural products (*J.W.* 3.10.8 §516).

Gennesaret was not just the name of the plain, but also a town, sometimes called "Kinneroth" (Josh 11:2; 19:35). The Sea of Galilee is also called the "Lake of Gennesaret" both by Luke and Josephus (λίμνη Γεννησαρέτ; Luke 5:1; Josephus, *Ant.* 18.2.1 §28). Jesus is back in the region of his greatest popularity, near his homebase of Capernaum (1:21; 2:1; 9:33). The term "anchored" (προσορμίζω) can mean to harbor, anchor, or bring to shore a boat, depending on the type of anchorage.

6:54 – 55 When they got out of the boat, the people immediately recognized Jesus. They ran throughout that whole region and began to bring the sick on cots to wherever he was reported to be (καὶ ἐξελθόντων αὐτῶν ἐκ τοῦ πλοίου εὐθὺς ἐπιγνόντες αὐτὸν περιέδραμον ὅλην τὴν χώραν ἐκείνην καὶ ἤρξαντο ἐπὶ τοῖς κραβάττοις τοὺς κακῶς ἔχοντας περιφέρειν ὅπου ἤκουον ὅτι ἐστίν). As so often during his Galilean ministry, reports of Jesus' arrival produce large crowds eager for healing.[1] The passage is similar to other summaries (1:32 – 34; 3:7 – 12), except that here there is no mention of Jesus' authoritative teaching or his exorcisms. Not surprisingly, Jesus' healings brought him the greatest renown, and crowds would gather whenever he was rumored to be nearby.

6:56 Wherever he went — into villages, towns, or countryside — they would place the sick in the marketplaces and would beg him to let them touch even the tassels of his cloak. And all who touched him were healed (καὶ ὅπου ἂν εἰσεπορεύετο εἰς κώμας ἢ εἰς πόλεις ἢ εἰς ἀγρούς, ἐν ταῖς ἀγοραῖς ἐτίθεσαν τοὺς ἀσθενοῦντας καὶ παρεκάλουν αὐτὸν ἵνα κἂν τοῦ κρασπέδου τοῦ ἱματίου αὐτοῦ ἅψωνται· καὶ ὅσοι ἂν ἥψαντο αὐτοῦ ἐσῴζοντο). Jesus' popularity reached to every mu-

nicipality — villages, towns, and countryside.[2] The marketplace (ἀγορά) was the social, economic, and political hub of every village and town, and so this is where the sick are brought.

The passage recalls 3:10, where people are "pushing forward" to touch Jesus, as well as the sick woman in 5:28, who seeks to touch Jesus' clothes. The term "tassels" (κρασπέδον) could mean simply the "edge" of his robe, but likely here refers to the four blue tassels that Jewish men wore on their robes as a sign of piety (Num 15:38 – 39; Deut 22:12; cf. Matt 9:20; 23:5; Luke 8:44). The implication is that Jesus is an observant Jew.

The people "were begging" (παρεκάλουν; iterative imperfect) Jesus to let them touch him, a common request in Mark (1:40; 5:10, 12, 17, 18, 23), and Mark reports that "all who touched him were healed." We can assume that — as with the woman in 5:34 — it is not magic but faith that results in healing. Mark's primary emphasis, however, is not on faith but on Jesus' amazing power to heal. Some commentators claim the summary has a negative tone, so that the absence of reference to Jesus' teaching means the people are interested only in Jesus' miracles rather than in the proclamation of the word.[3] Yet Mark does not make this point; instead, he stresses Jesus' immense popularity and remarkable power.

Theology in Application

In this summary Mark stresses both the continuing popularity and the immense power of Jesus. He is treated like a rock star wherever he goes, with the masses clamoring to touch him for healing. While the needs are great, Jesus' power is greater, and "all who touched him were healed." It is tempting to contrast the faith of the people

---

1. Mark 1:33 – 34; 2:2, 4, 13; 3:7 – 9, 20; 4:1, 36; 5:21, 24, 30 – 32; 6:14 – 15, 31 – 34; 7:24; 8:1 – 3; 9:14 – 15, 30.

2. Though πόλεις is often translated "cities," the term can refer to any size municipality. Since there were no large cities

in this part of Galilee, πόλεις probably here means "towns" and κώμαι "villages."

3. So Lane, *Mark*, 241.

who are healed with the fear and spiritual dullness of the disciples in the previous episode (6:52). Yet Mark says nothing about the people's faith. Conversely, some stress the fickleness of the people, who are interested only in their needs and not in the kingdom of God. But again, this goes beyond Mark's narrative purpose. Rather, all the emphasis is on Jesus' amazing presence and the enthusiasm and awe this generates among the population. Jesus is indeed the Messiah and Son of God, whose authoritative actions confirm his authoritative message of the kingdom of God.

26

Mark 7:1 – 23

Literary Context

Mark returns to the theme of opposition to Jesus' ministry by the religious leaders, which had characterized the early Galilean ministry (2:1 – 3:6; 3:20 – 30). This episode, which includes a controversy story and teaching by Jesus, is introduced without chronological or geographical connection to what precedes. Though there are no narrative links, there are thematic ones, including the reference to bread (ἄρτους; 7:2) and the growing theme of the spiritual dullness of the disciples (7:18; cf. 6:52; 8:17).

Mark probably introduces Jesus' teaching on "clean" and "unclean" (defiled) things here in order to prepare for the episodes that follow, where Jesus will travel into Gentile territory and interact with "unclean" Gentiles. Jesus will heal the daughter of a Syrophoenician woman (7:24 – 30), give hearing and speech to a deaf and mute man in the Decapolis (7:31 – 37), and feed an (apparently) Gentile crowd of four thousand (8:1 – 10).

Main Idea

When the Pharisees and the experts in the law criticize Jesus' disciples for not ceremonially washing their hands before a meal, Jesus responds by accusing them of elevating their human traditions above God's law and violating the higher principles that characterize the heart of God. It is not external things like food and drink that make a person "clean" or "unclean," but thoughts and actions that come from an evil and hard heart.

Translation

Mark 7:1 – 23

1a	Character entrance	**The Pharisees and some of the experts in the law… gathered around Jesus**
b		who came from Jerusalem
2a	Setting (social)	and **saw some of his disciples eating food with hands that were defiled,** that is,
b		unwashed.
3a	Narrative aside/Explanation	**(The Pharisees and all the Jews do not eat**
b		unless they have washed their hands,
c		holding to the
		traditions of the elders.
4a		When they come from the marketplace,
b		**they do not eat unless they wash themselves.**
c		And **they observe many other traditions,**
d		such as washing cups, pitchers, and copper utensils [and dining couches].)
5a	Question	So **the Pharisees and the experts in the law asked him,**
b		*"Why don't your disciples follow the tradition of the elders,*
c		*instead of eating their food with defiled hands?"*
6a	Response	**He replied to them,**
b	Scripture quotation/rebuke	*"Isaiah prophesied correctly about you hypocrites, as it is written,*
7a		*'This people honors me with their lips, but their heart is far from me.*
b		*They worship me in vain,*
c		*their teaching is merely man-made rules.'* [Isaiah 29:13]
8a	conclusion/rebuke	*You have abandoned the commandment of God and*
b		*are holding on to human traditions."*
9a	Rebuke	**He continued,**
b	assertion	*"You are very good at rejecting the commandment of God*
c	purpose of 9c	*in order to observe your own tradition!*
10a	Scripture quotation	*For example, Moses said,*
b		*'Honor your father and your mother,'* [Exod 20:12; Deut 5:16]
c		*and 'Whoever speaks evil about their father or mother must be put to death.'*
		[Exod 21:17; Lev 20:9]
11a	example/illustration	*But you say that if a person tells his father or mother,*
b		*'Whatever help you might have received from me is Corban' (that is, a gift for God)*
12	result of 11ab	*— you no longer permit him to do anything for his father or mother.*
13a	result of 12	*In this way you nullify the word of God*
b	means of 13a	*by your own tradition that you have handed down.*
	summary	*And you do many things like this."*

Continued on next page.

Continued from previous page.

14a	Character entrance	**Then he summoned the crowd again and said to them,**
b	command to listen	*"Listen to me, all of you, and understand:*
15a	assertion	*Nothing that enters a person from the outside can defile them.*
b	contrast	*Rather, it is what comes out of a person that defiles them."*

17a	Character departure/Setting	When he had left the crowd and entered the house,
b	Question	**his disciples were asking him about this parable.**
18a	Response	**He said to them,**
b	rebuke	*"Are you so ignorant?*
c	assertion	*Don't you see that nothing that enters a person can defile them,*
19a	cause of 18c	*because it doesn't enter 𒄑*
		their heart but
		their stomach,
b		
c		*and then it goes out into 𒄑*
		the latrine?"
d	Narrative Aside/Summary	**(He thus declared all foods clean.)**
20	Assertion	**He continued,**
		"What comes out of a person, that is what defiles that person.
21	list	*For from within, from the human heart, come evil thoughts, resulting in*
	list item	*sexual sins,*
	list item	*acts of theft,*
	list item	*murders,*
22	list item	*adulterous acts,*
	list item	*acts of greed,*
	list item	*wicked deeds,*
	list item	*deceit,*
	list item	*debauchery,*
	list item	*envy,*
	list item	*slander,*
	list item	*pride,*
	list item	*foolishness.*
23	summary	*All these evil things come from within and defile a person."*

Structure

The passage is comprised of a controversy story (vv. 1 – 13) followed by teaching from Jesus (vv. 14 – 23). The controversy story is similar to those in 2:1 – 3:6 and includes a challenge to Jesus from the religious leaders (7:1 – 5), followed by a twofold response (vv. 6 – 8, 9 – 13). The first response (vv. 6 – 8) sets out the theme — they have elevated human traditions at the expense of God's command (v. 8) — supported with a quotation from Isa 29:13. The second response (vv. 9 – 13) illustrates the theme with the issue of Corban, supported by more OT quotations (Exod 20:12; 21:17; Lev 20:9; Deut 5:6). This illustration is "framed" (an inclusio) on either side with a restatement of the theme (vv. 9, 13).

The teaching that follows (vv. 14 – 23) is also comprised of two parts, public teaching to the crowds (vv. 14 – 15) and private teaching for the disciples (vv. 17 – 23). The public teaching introduces a "parable" about defilement, which does not come from outside a person but from within. Jesus then interprets this privately for his disciples with reference to food taken into the body and a person's evil thoughts and actions that proceed outward.

In his response to the religious leaders, Jesus does not actually address the issue of ritual purity. Instead, he attacks the source of their authority, the "traditions of the elders" (v. 3), and then deals with the question of ritual purity when speaking publicly to the crowds and privately to the disciples.

Exegetical Outline

➡ **1. The Controversy with the Scribes and Pharisees (7:1 – 13)**

    a. The challenge (7:1 – 5)

    b. The response (7:6 – 13)

        i. First response: the principle supported by Isa 29:13 (7:6 – 8)

        ii. Second response: the illustration using the practice of Corban (7:9 – 13)

2. The Result of the Controversy: Teaching on Clean and Unclean Things (7:14 – 23)

    a. Public teaching for the crowds: the parable (7:14 – 15)

    b. Private teaching for the disciples: explaining the parable (7:17 – 23)

Explanation of the Text

7:1 – 2 The Pharisees and some of the experts in the law who came from Jerusalem gathered around Jesus and saw some of his disciples eating food with hands that were defiled, that is, unwashed (Καὶ συνάγονται πρὸς αὐτὸν οἱ Φαρισαῖοι καί τινες τῶν γραμματέων ἐλθόντες ἀπὸ Ἱεροσολύμων[1] καὶ ἰδόντες τινὰς τῶν μαθητῶν αὐτοῦ ὅτι κοιναῖς χερσίν, τοῦτ᾽ ἔστιν ἀνίπτοις, ἐσθίουσιν τοὺς ἄρτους). The last conflict with the religious leaders came in the Beelzebul episode in 3:22 – 30 at the end of a series of controversies (2:1 – 3:6). In that case too it concerned the experts in the law

(or "scribes"; γραμματέις; see comments on 1:22) who had come down from Jerusalem, perhaps as an official delegation. The Pharisees first appeared in 2:16 (see comments there), where they criticized Jesus for dining with sinners, another episode concerning ritual purity (cf. 2:18, 24; 3:6). It is unclear from the grammar whether both the scribes and Pharisees had come from Jerusalem or only the scribes. In either case, Jerusalem is established as the center of opposition to Jesus. It is there the showdown will take eventually place.

The accusation against the disciples is not one

---

1. We have punctuated this text differently from the UBS text, which introduces a full stop after the first sentence (ending in "Jesus" in English; Ἱεροσολύμων in Greek) and begins a new sentence with "and seeing some of his disciples...." The UBS text thus makes "and seeing ..." the beginning of a new (and incomplete) sentence, which is broken by the parenthetic remark in vv. 3 – 4.

of hygiene but of ceremonial impurity. The word translated "defiled" (κοινός) can mean simply "common," but it came to be used in Judaism of anything that was ritually impure or unworthy of God's presence. Mark explains for his Gentile readers that this means "unwashed" (ἀνίπτοις) hands. The OT law did not require washing of hands before meals, though priests were required to wash their hands before entering the Tent of Meeting and offering sacrifices (Exod 30:20–21; 40:12, 30–32). The scribes and Pharisees apparently understood these priestly ordinances to be applicable to all Israel, since all God's people were meant to be holy. Whether or not this was their motivation,[2] by Jesus' time hand washing was widely, though not universally, practiced by the Jews.[3]

Some have seen in the reference to "some" (τινάς) of Jesus' disciples hints of an ongoing debate in Mark's community between those who observed the purity laws and those who did not.[4] This seems unlikely in light of vv. 3–4, where Mark explains the nature of ritual purity for his (presumably Gentile) readers. If such a debate were raging in his community, Mark would hardly have to explain the Jewish practice.[5] More likely, Mark uses the episode as a whole to defend the church's claim that the purity laws of the OT are no longer bind-

ing on believers, since they have been fulfilled in Christ (see Theology in Application).

Gundry sees in the anaphoric definite article[6] and the plural "the loaves" (τοὺς ἄρτους; translated "food" above) as referring to the loaves left over from the feeding miracle in 6:38–44.[7] Yet while bread is a recurring theme throughout this section (6:37, 38, 41, 44, 52; 7:2, 5, 27; 8:4–6, 14–17, 19), there is little indication in the context that Mark is thinking of the same bread. The noun, both singular and plural, can mean food in general.

7:3–4 (The Pharisees and all the Jews do not eat unless they have washed their hands, holding to the traditions of the elders. When they come from the marketplace, they do not eat unless they wash themselves. And they observe many other traditions, such as washing cups, pitchers, and copper utensils [and dining couches].)[8] (οἱ γὰρ Φαρισαῖοι καὶ πάντες οἱ Ἰουδαῖοι ἐὰν μὴ πυγμῇ νίψωνται τὰς χεῖρας οὐκ ἐσθίουσιν, κρατοῦντες τὴν παράδοσιν τῶν πρεσβυτέρων, καὶ ἀπ᾽ ἀγορᾶς ἐὰν μὴ βαπτίσωνται οὐκ ἐσθίουσιν, καὶ ἄλλα πολλά ἐστιν ἃ παρέλαβον κρατεῖν, βαπτισμοὺς ποτηρίων καὶ ξεστῶν καὶ χαλκίων [καὶ κλινῶν]).

As Mark qualified that "common" or "defiled" hands meant "unwashed" (v. 2), so now he explains for his Gentile readers the issue of ceremo-

---

2. On the debate whether the Pharisees were imitating priestly regulations, see the different views of J. Neusner, *From Politics to Piety: The Emergence of Pharisaic Judaism* (Englewood Cliffs, NJ: Prentice Hall, 1973), and E. P. Sanders, *Judaism: Practice and Belief 763 B.C.E. – 66 C.E.* (Philadelphia: Trinity Press International, 1992). A mediating position is found in Martin Hengel and Roland Deines, "E. P. Sanders' 'Common Judaism,' Jesus and Pharisees," *JTS* 46 (1995): 170.

3. See R. P. Booth, *Jesus and the Laws of Purity: Tradition History and Legal History in Mark 7* (JSNTSup 13: Sheffield: JSOT Press, 1986), 117–87.

4. Marcus, *Mark 1–8*, 440; Donahue and Harrington, *Mark*, 219; A. Hultgren, *Jesus and His Adversaries: The Form and Function of the Conflict Stories in the Synoptic Tradition* (Minneapolis: Augsburg, 1979), 118.

5. Stein, *Mark*, 338; Gundry, *Mark*, 348.

6. Wallace, *Greek Grammar*, 217–18; anaphoric means "previous reference."

7. Gundry, *Mark*, 348–49.

8. The phrase "and beds" (or perhaps "and dining couches," καὶ κλινῶν) is omitted from a number of important early witnesses (𝔓45vid B L Δ 28), though it has the support of many others (A D W Θ f1,13 33). It is difficult to tell whether a copyist added it under the influence of the purity regulations of Lev 15:4–6, 19–30 (where touching a bed occupied by a man with a discharge or a menstruating woman causes uncleanness), or whether it was dropped by scribes because of the strangeness of the image of purifying furniture (Metzger, *Textual Commentary*, 80). The former seems slightly more likely because of the strong external evidence.

nial washing. The statement represents a narrative aside, or parenthesis. The reference to "all the Jews" (πάντες οἱ Ἰουδαῖοι) is not strictly correct, since many Jews did not practice ritual washing. But Mark's point is a general one: it is not just the scribes and Pharisees, but Jews in general who practiced hand washing.

A similar statement is made in the *Letter of Aristeas,* a second-century BC document that recounts the (legendary) events surrounding the translation of the Septuagint, the Greek OT. The letter says that the translators washed their hands in the course of their prayers, "as is the custom of all the Jews" (*Let. Aris,* 305; cf. *Sib. Or.* 3.591 – 593; John 2:6). Such washing was part of the "tradition(s) of the elders" (τὴν παράδοσιν τῶν πρεσβυτέρων; vv. 3, 5; cf. "human traditions," v. 8; "your own tradition," v. 13), which means the oral body of tradition related to the interpretation of the law that had arisen already in Jesus' day and would eventually be codified in the Mishnah (c. AD 200). The Pharisees considered these traditions to be fully authoritative, even claiming that they had been received and passed down by Moses at Mount Sinai (*m. 'Abot* 1:1 – 2; cf. Josephus, *Ant.* 13.10.6 §297). The rabbis believed they were putting a "fence around the Torah" (*m. 'Abot* 1:1; 3:14) to protect God's law from violations. Ceremonial cleanness was such an important issue that the last twelve tractates of the Mishnah (*Ṭeharot,* "cleannesses") are dedicated to it.[9]

The dative noun (πυγμῇ) Mark uses to describe the washing is an unusual one and could mean "with a fist," "by a fist," or even "to [the end of] the fist." The phrase may refer to washing (1) with a handful of water, (2) up to the wrist or elbow, or (3) with cupped hands.[10] The first view may be supported by *m. Yad.* 1:1, which specifies that a "quarter-log" of water, about the bulk of an egg and a half, must be used. The second view has some support from *m. Yad.* 2:3, which says that hands are rendered clean by pouring water over them up to the wrist.[11]

Another difficult question arises in the illustration that follows. The phrase translated "When they come from the marketplace" in Greek is simply, "from the marketplace" (ἀπ᾽ ἀγορᾶς) and could refer to washing themselves or washing things purchased in the marketplace. The latter would fit the following sentence, which refers to purifying utensils (though not food) with water. The former, however, is most likely: (1) It finds support in the aorist middle voice of the verb "wash" or "immerse" (βαπτίσωνται), which probably means wash themselves.[12] (2) It is smoother Greek since it retains the same subject as eating: "they do not eat unless they wash."[13] The reference here may be to full immersion in a *mikveh* (a Jewish ritual pool) before eating, support for which appears in Tobit 7:9, where the pious Jews "bathe and wash" before dining. The implication is that in the push and shove of the marketplace, contact with persons and things could cause ritual defilement.

Mark concludes by summarizing that this is just the tip of the iceberg. The Pharisees ritually wash

---

9. See J. Neusner, *The Idea of Purity in Ancient Israel* (SJLA 1; Leiden: Brill, 1973).

10. The difficulty prompted some copyists to omit the phrase completely (Δ syr^s cop^sa Diatessaron^p) and others to substitute another word that to them made better sense, such as πυκνά ("often" or "thoroughly"; ℵ W syr^{p.h} boh). Cf. Metzger, *Textual Commentary,* 80.

11. Marcus, *Mark 1 – 8,* 441.

12. There are three textual variants here, (1) the aorist middle βαπτίσωνται (A D W Θ *f*^{1.13} 33 𝔐 latt; Or); (2) the present middle or passive βαπτίζωνται (L Δ pc); and (3) the aorist middle ῥαντίσωνται, "sprinkle" (ℵ B pc sa). The second has little manuscript support and the third was likely introduced by a scribe who wished to preserve βαπτίζω for Christian baptism. But βαπτίζω is a perfectly acceptable way to refer to washing or immersion.

13. Stein, *Mark,* 340.

many other things, including cups, pitchers, and copper utensils.

7:5 So the Pharisees and the experts in the law asked him, "Why don't your disciples follow the tradition of the elders, instead of eating their food with defiled hands?" (καὶ ἐπερωτῶσιν αὐτὸν οἱ Φαρισαῖοι καὶ οἱ γραμματεῖς· διὰ τί οὐ περιπατοῦσιν οἱ μαθηταί σου κατὰ τὴν παράδοσιν τῶν πρεσβυτέρων, ἀλλὰ κοιναῖς χερσὶν ἐσθίουσιν τὸν ἄρτον;). Having briefly explained ritual purity, Mark now moves to the accusation made by the religious leaders. They do not accuse the disciples of breaking the OT law, but of failing to "walk in" (περιπατοῦσιν) the tradition passed down by the elders. The metaphoric use of "walk" means to live by a particular standard or to observe certain rules. The term *halakhah* ("walking") came to be used of the legal portions of Jewish oral law, while *haggadah* ("telling") was used for nonlegal illustrative and homiletic material.

Why do the religious leaders attack Jesus' disciples instead of Jesus himself? Are we to assume that Jesus observed the ceremonial washings? While this is possible, it seems unlikely in light of Jesus' disregard for such rituals in the teaching that follows. The simplest explanation comes from v. 2, where we learn that the religious leaders had observed the disciples (not Jesus) eating with unwashed hands. They approach Jesus with their complaint because a rabbi was considered responsible for his disciples' actions.[14]

7:6–8 He replied to them, "Isaiah prophesied correctly about you hypocrites, as it is written, 'This people honors me with their lips, but their heart is far from me. They worship me in vain, their teaching is merely man-made rules.' You have abandoned the commandment of God and are holding on to human traditions." (Ὁ δὲ εἶπεν αὐτοῖς· καλῶς ἐπροφήτευσεν Ἠσαΐας περὶ ὑμῶν τῶν ὑποκριτῶν, ὡς γέγραπται ὅτι οὗτος ὁ λαὸς τοῖς χείλεσίν με τιμᾷ, ἡ δὲ καρδία αὐτῶν πόρρω ἀπέχει ἀπ' ἐμοῦ· μάτην δὲ σέβονταί με διδάσκοντες διδασκαλίας ἐντάλματα ἀνθρώπων. ἀφέντες τὴν ἐντολὴν τοῦ θεοῦ κρατεῖτε τὴν παράδοσιν τῶν ἀνθρώπων).

Jesus offers two responses (vv. 6–8 and 9–13). For this first one, he quotes from Isa 29:13. The adverb "correctly" (καλῶς) does not mean Isaiah prophesied "well" (ESV), but that he did so "rightly" (NASB) or "correctly" (HCSB, NET). The word "hypocrite" (ὑποκριτής) originally meant a play-actor[15] but later came to mean a pretender, someone who claimed to be one thing but was actually another. Matthew, with his strong denunciations against the religious leaders, uses the term thirteen times, but it occurs only here in Mark. "Prophesied" does not mean Isaiah predicted the coming of these particular leaders, but rather that the prophet "preached against" actions such as theirs. Biblical prophecy is more often "forthtelling" than "foretelling."

Two main points are made in the Isaiah quote. First, the people were merely giving God lip service rather than a true dedication of their heart;[16] second, this has resulted in the elevation of their own traditions above the authentic commands of God. Both points will be developed in the illustration that follows in vv. 9–13.

The quotation from Isa 29:13 is closer to the

---

14. Marcus, *Mark 1–8*, 443; D. Daube, "Responsibilities of Master and Disciples in the Gospels," *NTS* 19 (1972–1973): 1–15.

15. BDAG, 845.

16. The singular "heart" appears in both the Hebrew (MT:

lēb) and Greek (LXX: ἡ καρδία) texts of Isa 29:13, referring back to the singular antecedent ('*ām* in MT; ὁ λαός in LXX) and emphasizing the corporate nature of their actions. The leaders are representing Israel as a whole and their actions will have consequences for the whole nation.

LXX than the MT, particularly in the last sentence. The MT reads, "their fear [or 'worship'] of me is a human commandment that has been taught [or perhaps, 'learned by rote']." The LXX has, "vainly they worship me, teaching human commandments and teachings" (μάτην δὲ σέβονταί με διδάσκοντες ἐντάλματα ἀνθρώπων καὶ διδασκαλίας). The two, however, make essentially the same point, summarized in v. 8: "You have abandoned the commandment of God and are holding on to human traditions."

7:9 He continued, "You are very good at rejecting the commandment of God in order to observe your own tradition!" (καὶ ἔλεγεν αὐτοῖς· καλῶς ἀθετεῖτε τὴν ἐντολὴν τοῦ θεοῦ, ἵνα τὴν παράδοσιν ὑμῶν τηρήσητε).[17] Mark introduces Jesus' second response (vv. 9 – 13) with an introduction similar to the first (v. 6). In standard English we can say, "He continued ..." In this case Jesus starts with the statement of principle and then moves to an illustration.

Jesus' words are probably meant to be ironic sarcasm. While the Pharisees prided themselves in meticulously keeping the law, Jesus congratulates them for become experts at "rejecting" or "nullifying" (ἀθετέω) God's commands. The NAB captures the sense nicely: "How well you have set aside the commandment of God!"[18] For the fifth time in the passage the word "tradition" (παράδοσις) is used (vv. 3, 4, 5, 8, 9), with the last two (cf. v. 13) contrasting "*God's* commandments" with mere "*human* traditions." There is also a play on words with v. 6. Just as Isaiah prophesied "well" (= "correctly"; καλῶς) about their hypocrisy (v. 6), so they have done very "well" (καλῶς) at practicing that hypocrisy (v. 9).

7:10 "For example, Moses said, 'Honor your father and your mother,' and 'Whoever speaks evil about their father or mother must be put to death.'" (Μωϋσῆς γὰρ εἶπεν· τίμα τὸν πατέρα σου καὶ τὴν μητέρα σου, καί· ὁ κακολογῶν πατέρα ἢ μητέρα θανάτῳ τελευτάτω). Jesus next provides an illustration of rejecting or nullifying God's commands in favor of human tradition. He quotes from two passages; the first is the fifth commandment of the Decalogue concerning honoring parents (Exod 20:12; cf. Deut 5:16), and the second concerns the penalty of death for disobedience (Exod 21:17; cf. Lev 20:9). Honoring parents was among the highest of values in biblical times, as in Middle Eastern cultures today. In Jewish tradition, as in the present passage (vv. 11 – 12), honor especially meant caring for the physical needs of ones' parents in their old age (Sir 3:3, 8, 12 – 16; Philo, *Decal.* 116 – 118). To "speak evil" (κακολογέω) can mean to slander, revile, or curse. Marcus points out that this could be an example of the kind of eschatological sharpening that appears elsewhere in the Synoptic tradition.[19] Just as anger is equivalent to murder (cf. Matt 5:21 – 22), so withholding support for parents is equivalent to cursing them.

7:11 – 12 "But you say that if a person tells his father or mother, 'Whatever help you might have received from me is Corban' (that is, a gift for God) — you no longer permit him to do anything for his father or mother." (ὑμεῖς δὲ λέγετε· ἐὰν εἴπῃ ἄνθρωπος τῷ πατρὶ ἢ τῇ μητρί· κορβᾶν, ὅ ἐστιν δῶρον, ὃ ἐὰν ἐξ ἐμοῦ ὠφεληθῇς—οὐκέτι ἀφίετε αὐτὸν οὐδὲν ποιῆσαι τῷ πατρὶ ἢ τῇ μητρί). God commanded honor for parents, Jesus says, "but *you* say...." The "you" is emphatic, both because of its

---

17. While some manuscripts read "keep" or "observe" (τηρήσητε; ℵ A [B 2427: τήρητε] L *f*¹³ 33 𝔐 aur vg syrʰ cop), others read "establish" (στήσητε; D W Θ *f*¹ 28 565 2542 it syrˢ·ᵖ). We have chosen the former (against the UBS text), since it is the harder reading and also has slightly better manuscript attestation.

18. Another possibility is that καλῶς here means "well" in the sense of "cleverly" or "skillfully" (so NLT, REB), which would make it less sarcasm and more accusatory.

19. Marcus, *Mark 1 – 8*, 444.

placement at the beginning of the sentence and because it is redundant (the Greek verb already containing person and number). With their traditions the religious leaders found ways to negate God's command.

Jesus cites the example of "Corban," whereby a son could withhold support for his parents by declaring his property to be dedicated to God and thus off limits to them. "Corban" (κορβᾶν) is a Greek transliteration of a Hebrew term (*qorbān*) meaning "offering" or "vow" (Lev 2:1, 4, 12, 14). Mark explains it to his Gentile readers as "a gift [for God]" (δῶρον). In rabbinic literature, *qorbān* is often used of something dedicated to God and so unavailable for human use.[20] The OT commanded that vows must not be broken (Num 30:2; Deut 23:21–23), and vows were taken seriously in Judaism. An entire tractate of the Mishnah is dedicated to them (*Nedarim*). It is unclear in the present example whether the gift was already given to the temple or was merely dedicated to it, remaining under the control of the owner. The latter seems to be the case, since the goal here was to protect one's property.[21]

We must not assume the rabbis were unaware of these issues. The rabbinic literature discusses whether a *qorbān* oath could be broken if it conflicted with other commandments or caused hardship for others. With reference to the fifth commandment, the Mishnah favors release of the vow for the sake of the parents (*m. Ned.* 8:1–9:1). While some have said this contradicts Jesus' illustration, the Mishnaic ruling merely shows that this was an issue of rabbinic debate, and that some rabbis argued that the oath was inviolable.[22] It is this

view that Jesus presupposes when he concludes, "you no longer permit him to do anything" (οὐκέτι ἀφίετε αὐτὸν οὐδὲν ποιῆσαι). While the motives of the person making such a vow were probably not pure, the religious leaders made it even worse by refusing him the right to rescind the oath.

7:13 "In this way you nullify the word of God by your own tradition that you have handed down. And you do many things like this." (ἀκυροῦντες τὸν λόγον τοῦ θεοῦ τῇ παραδόσει ὑμῶν ᾗ παρεδώκατε· καὶ παρόμοια τοιαῦτα πολλὰ ποιεῖτε). Jesus sums up the essential problem: by following their human traditions, they have nullified God's law. Jesus condemns this use of *qorbān*, not just because honor for parents supersedes vow-taking, but because the selfish motives behind such traditions are contrary to the heart of God and the true spirit of the law. The statement repeats in a different form the similar ones in vv. 8 and 9 (each contrasting the "commandment/word of God" with mere human "tradition") and forms an inclusio with the latter, framing the illustration about *qorbān* (vv. 10–12):

v. 8 "abandoned the commandment of God … holding on to human traditions"
v. 9 "rejecting the commandment of God … to observe your own tradition"
v. 13 "nullify the word of God by your own tradition"

To drive home the point that this is just one example among many such abuses, Jesus adds, "And you do many things like this."

7:14–15 Then he summoned the crowd again and said to them, "Listen to me, all of you, and

20. *m. Ned.*; Josephus, *Ant.* 4.4.4 §§72–73; *Ag Ap.* 1.22 §167. Fitzmyer cites an ossuary inscription of the early first century AD that reads: "All that a man may find to his profit in this ossuary is *qorbān* to God from him who is within it" (J. A. Fitzmyer, "The Aramaic Qorban Inscription from Jebel Hallet Et-turi and Mk 7:11/Mt 15:5," *JBL* 78 [1959]: 60–66).

21. See the interesting example cited by France, *Mark*, 287, from *m. Ned.* 5:6, which shows both that the *qorbān* was considered unalterable and that the property remained at the disposal of the original owner.

22. Guelich, *Mark 1:1–8:26*, 370.

understand: **Nothing that enters a person from the outside can defile them. Rather, it is what comes out of a person that defiles them." [16]**[23] (Καὶ προσκαλεσάμενος πάλιν τὸν ὄχλον ἔλεγεν αὐτοῖς· ἀκούσατέ μου πάντες καὶ σύνετε. οὐδέν ἐστιν ἔξωθεν τοῦ ἀνθρώπου εἰσπορευόμενον εἰς αὐτὸν ὃ δύναται κοινῶσαι αὐτόν, ἀλλὰ τὰ ἐκ τοῦ ἀνθρώπου ἐκπορευόμενά ἐστιν τὰ κοινοῦντα τὸν ἄνθρωπον). Jesus' response to the scribes and Pharisees (vv. 6 – 13) did not address the issue of eating with "unclean" hands, but rather attacked their source of authority, the traditions of the elders. Now, however, he turns to the crowd to address the question of ceremonial impurity. Jesus often summons (προσκαλέω) his disciples for teaching (3:13; 6:7; 8:1, 34; 10:42; 12:43), but only here and in 8:34 does he summon the crowd.

The call to "listen" (ἀκούω) and "understand" (σύνιημι) recalls Jesus' repeated injunction to listen to his parables (4:3, 9, 23, 24) and especially his warning in the same context against the religious leaders who "hear and hear but [do] not understand" (ἀκούοντες ἀκούωσιν καὶ μὴ συνιῶσιν; 4:12, quoting Isa 6:9 – 10). In this part of Mark's gospel, the disciples are repeatedly said to lack understanding (6:52; 7:18; 8:17, 21) and are in danger of going the way of the religious leaders.

The point that must be understood, Jesus says, is that it is not what enters a person that defiles them, but what comes out of them.[24] The saying is a difficult one, since it appears to contradict the OT law, where eating unclean food was in fact defiling (Lev 11; 17; etc.). Matthew mutes this force somewhat by relating it back to the tradition of hand washing rather than eating food (Matt 15:10, 20).

The saying could be understood in line with the prophets' insistence that God had no desire for Israel's sacrifices and offerings when her heart was far from him. "I desire mercy, not sacrifice," the Lord says in Hos 6:6 (cf. Isa 11:11 – 17; Jer 7:22 – 23; Amos 5:21 – 27). The point is not that the Lord is abrogating the sacrificial system, but that Israel's failure to obey God renders their sacrifices meaningless. In the present case Jesus could be saying something like, "What a person eats is not nearly as defiling as what a person says and does." Yet this is clearly not how Mark understood Jesus' words since, in v. 19d, he interprets it as a declaration that all foods are now clean.

So is Jesus being inconsistent, accusing the scribes of elevating their tradition above God's law and then ignoring that law himself? The answer must be found in the larger context of Mark's gospel and the Synoptic tradition, where Jesus is inaugurating the kingdom of God and so fulfilling the OT purity laws (cf. Matt 5:17). We will take up this question further in Theology in Application, below.

7:17 When he had left the crowd and entered the house, his disciples were asking him about this parable (Καὶ ὅτε εἰσῆλθεν εἰς οἶκον ἀπὸ τοῦ ὄχλου, ἐπηρώτων αὐτὸν οἱ μαθηταὶ αὐτοῦ τὴν παραβολήν). The scene changes again as Jesus leaves the crowd and privately teaches the disciples. Such private instruction is common in Mark[25] and here parallels Jesus' parabolic teaching in Mark 4, where the disciples are the "insiders" who get both the parable and its interpretation (4:11, 34). The present passage is strikingly similar to 4:10 – 14,

---

23. Verse 16, which reads: "If anyone has ears to hear, let them hear" (εἴ τις ἔχει ὦτα ἀκούειν ἀκουέτω), is absent from early Alexandrian manuscripts (א B L Δ* 0274 28 2427 sah^mss boh^pt) and was likely "a scribal gloss (derived perhaps from 4.9 and 4.23), introduced as an appropriate sequel to ver. 14" (Metzger, *Textual Commentary*, 81).

24. In addition to Matthew and Mark, the *Gospel of Thomas* (sec. 14) has the same saying, which is widely recognized as an authentic saying of Jesus.

25. See 4:34; 7:17 – 23; 9:28 – 29, 35; 10:10 – 12, 32 – 34; 12:43 – 44; 13:33 – 34; cf. 6:31 – 32.

since it follows a call to hear (4:9), involves private instruction to the disciples (4:10), is prompted by a request from the disciples to explain the "parable" (4:10), and is introduced with a statement accusing the disciples of a lack of understanding (4:13). On the variety of meanings of "parable" (παραβολή), see 3:26–29. While here the word could mean a "saying," "proverb," or even "riddle," it is best to translate it "parable," since the parables in Mark relate especially to the secrets of the kingdom of God (4:11), and Jesus' teaching here is closely related to the radical transformation coming with the arrival of the kingdom of God.

7:18–19 He said to them, "Are you so ignorant? Don't you see that nothing that enters a person can defile them, because it doesn't enter their heart but their stomach, and then it goes out into the latrine?" (He thus declared all foods clean.) (καὶ λέγει αὐτοῖς· οὕτως καὶ ὑμεῖς ἀσύνετοί ἐστε; οὐ νοεῖτε ὅτι πᾶν τὸ ἔξωθεν εἰσπορευόμενον εἰς τὸν ἄνθρωπον οὐ δύναται αὐτὸν κοινῶσαι ὅτι οὐκ εἰσπορεύεται αὐτοῦ εἰς τὴν καρδίαν ἀλλ' εἰς τὴν κοιλίαν, καὶ εἰς τὸν ἀφεδρῶνα ἐκπορεύεται, καθαρίζων πάντα τὰ βρώματα;).

The accusation of ignorance picks up the theme introduced by the narrator following Jesus' walking on water (6:52) and will recur in 8:17, 21.[26] In the context of the interpretation of this "parable" (v. 17) it also recalls 4:13, where, before explaining the parable of the sower, Jesus says, "Don't you understand this parable? How then will you understand any of the parables?" The disciples are persistently dull in their spiritual understanding and unable to discern Jesus' teaching.

Jesus interprets the first line of v. 15 in vv. 18–19 and the second line in vv. 20–23. Food cannot defile a person because it never comes in contact with the "heart" (καρδία), the inner life of a person. It merely enters the physical body, passing through the stomach and being eliminated (lit., "it goes out into the latrine"). Mark then adds a parenthetic comment, "cleansing all foods" (καθαρίζων πάντα τὰ βρώματα). Though clipped, the participial phrase has Jesus as its subject and so means that Jesus "thus declared all foods clean [= undefiled]."[27] Though the early church struggled over the question of the applicability of Jewish dietary laws for its Gentile members (Acts 10:12–15; 15:5, 19–20; Rom 14:13–23; Gal 2:11–14; Col 2:21–23), they would find powerful support for Gentile freedom in Jesus' words here. Mark's comment does not necessarily mean that his community was divided over the issue of purity laws (see v. 2). What it does show is that Mark felt the need to justify the church's interpretation of the OT dietary laws as no longer applicable to the messianic community of faith.

7:20–23 He continued, "What comes out of a person, that is what defiles that person. For from within, from the human heart, come evil thoughts, resulting in sexual sins, acts of theft, murders, adulterous acts, acts of greed, wicked

---

26. The "you" (ὑμεῖς) is again emphatic (see v. 11) and the καί could mean either "also" (= ignorant like the crowds; NLT, ESV, HCSB), or more likely, "indeed" or "so," adding emphasis.

27. Some interpreters deny that Jesus here abrogates the dietary laws. (1) Some claim that the phrase was a later marginal gloss and not part of Mark's original. But there is no manuscript evidence to support this. (2) Others claim that the participle refers not to Jesus but to the latrine, which itself "cleanses" food by eliminating it. Sometimes this is said to be the pre-Markan meaning, which the Evangelist altered to make Jesus the subject (M. Black, *An Aramaic Approach to the Gospels and Acts* (3rd ed.; Oxford: Clarendon, 1967), 217–18; Vermes, *Jesus the Jew*, 29). The problem, at least for the Markan text, is that "latrine" (ἀφεδρῶνα) is in the accusative case, while the participle is nominative and so must refer to Jesus. See Gundry, *Mark*, 367; Guelich, *Mark 1:1–8:26*, 378; Lohmeyer, *Markus*, 142; Marcus, *Mark 1–8*, 455; France, *Mark*, 291–92; Stein, *Mark*, 345–46; Collins, *Mark*, 356.

deeds, deceit, debauchery, envy, slander, pride, foolishness. All these evil things come from within and defile a person." (ἔλεγεν δὲ ὅτι τὸ ἐκ τοῦ ἀνθρώπου ἐκπορευόμενον, ἐκεῖνο κοινοῖ τὸν ἄνθρωπον. ἔσωθεν γὰρ ἐκ τῆς καρδίας τῶν ἀνθρώπων οἱ διαλογισμοὶ οἱ κακοὶ ἐκπορεύονται, πορνεῖαι, κλοπαί, φόνοι, μοιχεῖαι, πλεονεξίαι, πονηρίαι, δόλος, ἀσέλγεια, ὀφθαλμὸς πονηρός, βλασφημία, ὑπερηφανία, ἀφροσύνη· πάντα ταῦτα τὰ πονηρὰ ἔσωθεν ἐκπορεύεται καὶ κοινοῖ τὸν ἄνθρωπον). Here Jesus interprets the second part of the saying in v. 15, that true defilement comes from within the human heart. Vice lists like this appear elsewhere in the NT[28] and in Judaism.[29]

The Greek word order suggests that "evil thoughts" (οἱ διαλογισμοὶ οἱ κακοί) at the head of the list is an overarching category and that the twelve vices that follow are the result of these thoughts (hence our translation, "resulting in …").[30] What follows are six terms in the plural, which in-

dicate evil actions, and six terms in the singular, which indicate attitudes or character traits.

The list begins with "sexual immoralities" (πορνεῖαι), a term that can mean any kind of sexual impurity, including prostitution, fornication, or adultery. The next four — acts of theft, murders, adulterous acts, and acts of greed — are all violations of the Decalogue (Exod 20:13 – 15, 17; Deut 5:17 – 19, 21).[31] The term translated "envy" is, literally, "evil eye" (ὀφθαλμὸς πονηρός; cf. Matt 20:15; Deut 15:9). "Slander" (βλασφημία) could also mean "blasphemy," if it is directed against God. The last term in the list, "foolishness" (ἀφροσύνη), does not mean stupidity or ignorance, but rather "arrogant rejection of God."[32] The biblical picture of the fool is the one who says in his heart, "there is no God" (Pss 14:1; 53:1). Jesus ends the list by restating the proposition: "All these evil things that come from within and defile a person."

Theology in Application

This passage carries forward several themes important to Mark's gospel, including Jesus' continuing controversy with the religious leaders and the spiritual dullness of the disciples (7:18; cf. 4:13, 40; 6:52; 8:17 – 18, 21, 32; 9:5 – 6, 19, 32). Jesus had clashed with the religious leaders repeatedly in 2:1 – 3:6, climaxing in the plot to kill him in 3:7. Shortly thereafter, Jesus was accused of casting out demons by Satan's power and responded by accusing the religious leaders of blaspheming the Holy Spirit (3:22, 29). Now, in chapter 7, the controversies begin again, this time over the question of ritual purity. Previous controversies had been related to the OT law and tradition (fasting and the Sabbath; 2:18 – 3:4) and contact with "unclean" people (tax collectors and sinners; 2:14 – 17). But this is the first time the specific question of ritual purity has been raised. We will discuss three key themes raised here.

---

28. Rom 1:29 – 31; 1 Cor 5:10 – 11; 6:9 – 10; 2 Cor 12:20 – 21; Gal 5:19 – 21; Col 3:5 – 8; 1 Tim 1:9 – 10; 3:2 – 5; Titus 3:3; 1 Pet 4:3.

29. Wisd 14:25 – 26; *1 En.* 91:6 – 7; 4 Macc 1:2 – 8; 1QS 4.9 – 11; Philo, *Sacrfices* 32.

30. Collins, *Mark*, 357.

31. This is even clearer in Matthew's version, which lists only six items, five of which follow the order of the last five of the Ten Commandments.

32. Boring, *Mark*, 205.

The Dangers of Traditionalism

A distinction must first be drawn between "tradition" and "traditionalism." *Tradition* is a good thing and a necessary part of life. We would have no laws to govern our society if not for traditions related to order and governance. We are particularly hard on the Pharisees (as Jesus was) with reference to their many traditions, but their motivation was a noble one. The OT law could not cover every area of life, nor could it account for new and changing circumstances. The Jewish religious leaders therefore sought to "put a fence around the Torah" (*m. ʾAbot* 1:1; 3:14), both to guard against its violation and to define its specific limitations.

For example, the OT law forbade work on the Sabbath (under penalty of death! Exod 31:14–15; 35:2). But what constituted work? This was a critical question for daily life. Debates and judicial conclusions on issues like this constituted the "traditions of the elders" — the oral body of tradition eventually written down in the Mishnah and later rabbinic documents (e.g., Tosephta, Gemara, Talmud, etc.).

Christians too had traditions. Paul encourages his churches to hold fast to the "traditions" he passed on to them (1 Cor 11:2; 2 Thess 2:15; 3:6), referring to great truths like the liturgy of the Lord's Supper (11:2) and the resurrection narratives (15:3). The great creeds of the church, formulated through centuries of debate and controversy, provide us with clarification of biblical truth. While each generation needs to return to Scripture to confirm its spiritual heritage, we would be much the poorer without the wisdom of the ages — the traditions of our elders.

Tradition, however, can become *traditionalism.* Two great dangers are common with traditionalism — legalism and hypocrisy. Both are addressed in this passage. *Legalism* means elevating human traditions to the level of God's law. The religious leaders had made ritual washings mandatory and criticized Jesus' disciples for not practicing them. Jesus rejects their rules. What they call the "tradition of the elders" (v. 3), he calls "*human* traditions" (v. 8) and "*your* own tradition" (vv. 9, 13), to be contrasted with "the commandment of God" (vv. 8–9) and "the word of God" (v. 13).

Such legalism has been common throughout history. In American Christianity righteousness has sometimes been gauged by abstention from practices like attending movies, playing cards, dancing, certain types of music, long hair on men, drinking alcohol, and even women wearing pants. While almost anything in life can be abused, practices like these are not inherently wrong and so become matters of personal conscience. This, of course, does not mean that Christians should not have high standards. Some people consider any Christian who abstains from certain practices to be legalistic. But high standards are not legalism. Legalism is claiming that such things are standards of righteousness, or worse yet, are necessary for salvation.

The other great danger of traditionalism is *hypocrisy*. When religion becomes a series of dos and don'ts, there is a tendency to simply follow the rules and miss the heart of God. Jesus accuses the Pharisees of being hypocrites not because they had high standards, but because they emphasized nonessential things like ritual hand washing and then ignored the weightier matters of the law, such as love and justice. This leads to our second important theme in this passage: the true spirit of the law.

The True Spirit of the Law

Jesus' example of Corban illustrates the danger of hypocrisy resulting from traditionalism. The Pharisees were using the OT laws related to oaths to negate the fifth commandment, honoring one's parents. In this way they played one part of the law against another and so missed its true meaning. No oath should be taken or enforced that harms another person. The prophets castigated Israel for keeping the letter of the law — going through the formal show of religion with their offerings and sacrifices — but failing to love and obey God with their hearts (Isa 11:11 – 17; Jer 7:22 – 23; Hos 6:6; Amos 5:21 – 27).

Jesus addressed this same issue of the true spirit of the law in his Sermon on the Mount. The command against murder has behind it the greater purpose of respect for human life created in the image of God. Anger and hatred are equivalent to "murder in the heart" because they violate this greater principle. The greater purpose behind the command against adultery relates to sexual purity. To lust is therefore equivalent to "adultery of the heart" since it violates the greater principle (Matt 5:12 – 48). James is referring to the same higher law when he speaks of the perfect law of liberty (Jas 1:25) and the "royal law" to "love your neighbor as yourself" (2:8).

Jesus illustrated the true spirit of the law in his care for outcasts. He defies purity laws by reaching out and touching a man with leprosy (1:41), allowing a menstruating woman to touch him (5:27 – 28), and taking the hand of a dead girl (5:41). In each case he demonstrates that these purity laws were never intended to forbid acts of love and compassion. Reaching out in love actually *fulfills* the purity laws, since it reflects God's character and so his holiness.

Of course, there is something else going on here as well. When Jesus touches these impure things, he is not defiled, but rather brings cleansing and purification. This is the transformative power of the kingdom of God, which leads us to our third point.

The Coming of the Kingdom of God and the Fulfillment of the Law

Although Jesus' response to ritual hand washing is understandable as opposition to merely human traditions, how do we explain his apparent abrogation of the OT dietary laws? The OT declared certain foods to be defiling, yet Jesus says that nothing that enters a person's body can render them unclean. Is Jesus not doing the very thing he accuses the religious leaders of doing — elevating himself above the law of God? The answer is, yes and no. Jesus is indeed elevating himself above the OT law, but contrary to the religious leaders, he has the authority to do so. Jesus' authority over the food laws is related to *who he is* and *what he is accomplishing.* As Jesus declared earlier in another controversy, "the Son of Man is Lord even of the Sabbath" (2:28). As the divine Son of Man and Son of God, Jesus alone exercises the prerogative of God with reference to the OT law. Since God instituted it, he has the authority to modify it.

Furthermore, that Jesus is inaugurating the new age of salvation means that everything is changing. The law is coming to fulfillment through his words and deeds (Matt 5:17). With the coming of the kingdom of God, the law will no longer be written on tablets of stone but on the hearts of God's people (Jer 31:33). They will be filled, empowered, and led by his Spirit (Isa 44:3; Ezek 11:19; 36:26; 39:29; Joel 2:28). This transition from the age of promise to the age of fulfillment is the key to Jesus' words. The gospel is new wine (Mark 2:22). It is something radically new and transformative that cannot simply be poured into the old wineskins of Judaism and the OT law.

This perspective of the old age giving way to the new is evident throughout the NT. Paul can say with reference to the Sabbath that "one person considers one day more sacred than another; another considers every day alike. Each of them should be fully convinced in their own mind" (Rom 14:5; cf. Col 2:16). Similarly, concerning OT dietary laws, he says that "nothing is unclean in itself" (Rom 14:14; cf. 14:20; Col 2:16 – 17). Such external regulations are no longer applicable to Christians since "the kingdom of God is not a matter of eating and drinking, but of righteousness, peace and joy in the Holy Spirit" (Rom 14:17). This fulfillment of the law is not a license to sin. The greater principle behind the law is to love God with heart, soul, mind, and strength and to love others as yourself (Mark 12:30 – 31). Our liberty must be used to build others up, never to break them down or cause them to sin (Rom 14:20 – 21; Gal 5:13).

Mark 7:24 – 30

Literary Context

For the second time in Mark's gospel, Jesus' itinerant ministry takes him into Gentile territory (cf. 5:1 – 20). The journey immediately follows Jesus' teaching on clean and unclean things (7:1 – 23). Jesus' pronouncement of all foods being clean (vv. 18 – 19) not only fulfills the OT dietary laws, but symbolically prepares the reader for Jesus' ministry to "unclean" Gentiles here (7:24 – 30) and in the next two episodes (7:31 – 37; 8:1 – 10). A parallel may thus be drawn to Peter's vision of clean and unclean animals in Acts, which introduces the Cornelius episode and metaphorically prepares for the entrance of Gentiles into the church (Acts 10 – 11).

II. The Authority of the Messiah (1:14 – 8:21)

   C. The Expanding Mission of the Messiah (6:6b – 8:21)

      4. Walking on the Water (6:45 – 52)

      5. Healings near Gennesaret (6:53 – 56)

      6. Commandments of God and Human Traditions (7:1 – 23)

➡   **7. The Faith of the Syrophoenician Woman (7:24 – 30)**

      8. Healing a Deaf and Mute Man (7:31 – 37)

Main Idea

The account of the persistent faith of the Syrophoenician woman powerfully illustrates both the priority of Israel in salvation history and the full inclusion of the Gentiles in the blessings of that salvation.

Translation

Mark 7:24 – 30

24a		Rising from there,
b	Setting (spatial)	**he went to the region of Tyre.**
c	setting	Entering a house,
d	Purpose of 24c	**he did not want anyone to know about it;**
e	Result of 24b	but **he could not escape notice.**
25a	Character entrance	But **a woman ... soon heard about him.**
b	character description	whose daughter was possessed by a defiling spirit
c		
d		Coming,
e	Action	**she fell at his feet.**
26a	Character description	**The woman was** a Greek,
b		a Syrophoenician by birth.
c	Entreaty	**She begged him to cast the demon out of her daughter.**
27a	Response	**He said to her,**
b		"First let the children eat their fill,
c		for it is not good to take the bread from the children and throw it to the dogs."
28a	Counterresponse	But **she responded to him,**
b		"Yes, Lord, but even the dogs under the table eat the children's crumbs."
29a	Healing announcement	**He said to her,**
b		"Because of this answer, go, the demon has left your daughter."
30a	character departure	Going home,
b	Result of healing	**she found the child lying in bed and the demon gone.**

Structure

The episode has features typical of a healing narrative, including an approach with a request for healing (vv. 25 – 26), an obstacle to be overcome (v. 27), a response of faith (v. 28), Jesus' pronouncement of healing (v. 29), and confirmation of the healing (v. 30). Yet the account may also be treated as a controversy/pronouncement story, since Jesus' initial rejection is challenged by the woman, after which he makes an authoritative pronouncement. What is highly unusual here, and indeed unique in the Gospels, is that Jesus is apparently bested in debate, conceding to the woman's argument and her request. Ironically, Jesus' rhetorical "defeat" turns out to be a victory for the kingdom of God, making clear that God's salvation is available to all who believe, apart from ethnic identity or social status.

Exegetical Outline

→ **1. Setting: The Region of Tyre — Gentile Territory (7:24)**

2. The Encounter with the Syrophoenician Woman (7:25 – 29)

    a. Her approach (7:25 – 26)

    b. Jesus' initial rebuff (7:27)

    c. The woman's wise and witty response (7:28)

    d. Jesus' commendation and the healing pronouncement (7:29)

3. The Result: The Girl Is Healed (7:30)

Explanation of the Text

7:24 Rising from there, he went to the region of Tyre.[1] Entering a house, he did not want anyone to know about it; but he could not escape notice (Ἐκεῖθεν δὲ ἀναστὰς ἀπῆλθεν εἰς τὰ ὅρια Τύρου. Καὶ εἰσελθὼν εἰς οἰκίαν οὐδένα ἤθελεν γνῶναι, καὶ οὐκ ἠδυνήθη λαθεῖν). Jesus leaves Galilee and heads northwest to the region around the city of Tyre in Phoenicia (modern Lebanon). Tyre was located about thirty-five miles northwest of Galilee along the Mediterranean coast. The city is often paired in the literature with Sidon, twenty-two miles to the north, since both were powerful city-states and centers for trade and commerce.

Although both David and Solomon had trade alliances with the king of Tyre, the two cities came to symbolize idolatry and paganism. King Ahab of Israel married the Sidonian princess Jezebel, who promoted Baal worship in Israel, and the prophets repeatedly pronounced judgment against Tyre for her arrogance and greed (Isa 23; Ezek 26 – 28; Amos 1:9 – 10; Zech 9:2 – 3). This animosity continued into the NT period, and Josephus refers to Tyre as one of Israel's bitterest enemies (*Ag. Ap.*

1.13 §70). Jesus, however, finds here a woman of faith.

Mark does not say why Jesus left Galilee for this region. It could have been to escape Herod's jurisdiction (in light of the growing concerns in Herod's court about his ministry; 6:16) or to remove himself from the increasing hostility of the religious leaders. Or perhaps Jesus is seeking to avoid the crowds to spend more time with his disciples. This last may be implied in Jesus' desire to keep his whereabouts unknown. In any case, Mark's narrative purpose is to illustrate the faith of a Gentile woman and so provide a foreshadowing of the Gentile mission.

Although Jesus wishes to be anonymous, his reputation as a healer and exorcist precedes him, and he cannot remain hidden. Several Markan themes reappear here: Jesus' withdrawal from the crowds,[2] the setting of a house as a place of privacy, teaching, and/or healing,[3] and the overwhelming popularity that makes it impossible to keep Jesus' location a secret.[4]

---

1. A number of important manuscripts add "and Sidon" (καὶ Σιδῶνος; ℵ A B *f*[1,13] 33 2427 𝔐 lat syr[p.h] cop), but this is likely a later copyist's addition of a natural complement and an assimilation to Matt 15:21 and Mark 7:31.

2. See 1:35; 3:7, 20; 4:36; 6:31 – 32; 7:24; 9:30.

3. See 1:29; 2:1; 3:20; 7:17; 9:28; 10:10.

4. See 1:33 – 34; 2:2, 4, 13; 3:7 – 9, 20; 4:1, 36; 5:21, 24, 30 – 32; 6:14 – 15, 31 – 34; 7:24; 8:1 – 3; 9:14 – 15, 30.

7:25 – 26 But a woman whose daughter was possessed by a defiling spirit soon heard about him. Coming, she fell at his feet. The woman was a Greek, a Syrophoenician by birth. She begged him to cast the demon out of her daughter (ἀλλ᾽ εὐθὺς ἀκούσασα γυνὴ περὶ αὐτοῦ, ἧς εἶχεν τὸ θυγάτριον αὐτῆς πνεῦμα ἀκάθαρτον, ἐλθοῦσα προσέπεσεν πρὸς τοὺς πόδας αὐτοῦ· ἡ δὲ γυνὴ ἦν Ἑλληνίς, Συροφοινίκισσα τῷ γένει· καὶ ἠρώτα αὐτὸν ἵνα τὸ δαιμόνιον ἐκβάλῃ ἐκ τῆς θυγατρὸς αὐτῆς). Despite Jesus' attempt at privacy, a woman in desperate need hears of his reputation as a healer and seeks him out.[5]

This woman is identified as a "Greek, a Syrophoenician by birth." "Greek" (Ἑλληνίς) does not mean an ethnic Greek, but rather a (Greek-speaking) Gentile, a common sense of the term in Paul (cf. Rom 1:16; 2:9 – 10; 3:9; 10:12; 1 Cor 12:13; Gal 3:28). Ethnically (τῷ γένει; "by race/family/birth"), she is Phoenician. Since Phoenicia was under the administration of Syria, Mark probably uses the term "Syrophoenician" to distinguish her from the Libyophoenicians of North Africa.[6] Matthew refers to the woman as a "Canaanite" (15:22), recalling the ancient pagan residents of the land of Israel.

The woman's daughter is described as having an "unclean" or "defiling spirit" (πνεῦμα ἀκάθαρτον) in v. 25 and a "demon" (δαιμόνιον) in v. 26. Mark uses the terms synonymously and with about the same frequency (see comments on 1:23).

7:27 He said to her, "First let the children eat their fill, for it is not good to take the bread from the children and throw it to the dogs." (καὶ ἔλεγεν αὐτῇ· ἄφες πρῶτον χορτασθῆναι τὰ τέκνα, οὐ γάρ ἐστιν καλὸν λαβεῖν τὸν ἄρτον τῶν τέκνων καὶ τοῖς κυναρίοις βαλεῖν). Jesus responds with an analogy that, at first sight, seems offensive and shocking. The "children" clearly refers the people of Israel and the "dogs" to Gentiles. In the OT, Israel is often referred to as God's children.[7] The Jews did not view dogs as lovable pets, but as wild animals and scavengers (1 Kgs 14:11; 21:19 – 24; Ps 22:16; *m. Kelim* 8:6). To call someone a dog was a grave insult (1 Sam 17:43; Isa 56:10 – 11); heretics and false teachers are often given this epithet (Phil 3:2; 2 Pet 2:22; Rev 22:15; Ignatius, *Eph* 7:1).[8]

Two points may mitigate the harshness of Jesus' words. First he uses the diminutive form of "dog" (κυνάριον) rather than the more common one (κύων; Phil 3:2; 2 Pet 2:22; Rev 22:15). Some commentators claim that this means "little puppies" or household pets.[9] While this is possible, the force of the diminutive had weakened considerably in Hellenistic Greek and diminutives are often used with no sense of smallness.[10] Nevertheless, Jesus' word choice does soften his statement somewhat, and

---

5. The Greek translates awkwardly into English since the adversative "but" (ἀλλά) does not contrast with its nearest antecedent ("he could not escape notice") but with the previous clause ("he … did not want anyone to know about it"). The woman finds him *despite* his attempt at privacy.

6. See Hengel, *Studies*, 29, 137 – 38 n. 164, who uses this to defend a Roman provenance for Mark's gospel. For a different view, see Theissen, *Gospels in Context*, 245 – 47, who claims the designation is to distinguish Syrians from the Phoenician coast and those from the north (Syria Coele). Cf. Collins, *Mark*, 366; Marcus *1 – 8*, 32.

7. Exod 4:22 – 23; Deut 14:1; 32:20; Ps 82:6; Isa 1:1 – 2; 17:9; 63:8; Jer 3:19; Hos 11:1; cf. Rom 9:4; *m. 'Abot* 3:15.

8. On the more positive portrayal of dogs in other ancient cultures, see J. Botterweck, "*Keleb*," *TDOT*, 7:147 – 52; Edwards, *Mark*, 219 n. 10.

9. To varying degrees, see Taylor, *Mark*, 350; Cranfield, *Mark*, 248; Lane, *Mark*, 262; D. Rhoads, "Jesus and the Syrophoenician Woman," in Rhoads, *Reading Mark*, 78.

10. This is evident even in this passage, where "daughter" appears in both diminutive (θυγάτριον, v. 25) and nondiminutive (θυγατρός, v. 26) forms. Two different terms for children are also used, one diminutive (παιδία, vv. 28, 30) and one nondiminutive (τέκνα, v. 27; cf. the diminutive ψιχία, in v. 28). For Mark's style in this regard, see C. H. Turner, "Marcan Usage: Notes, Critical and Exegetical, on the Second Gospel," in James K. Elliott, *The Language and Style of the Gospel of Mark* (NovTSup 71; Leiden: Brill, 1993), 123 – 26; Collins, *Mark*, 364, 367.

this is picked up by the woman, who introduces the image of domestic dogs present under the table (v. 28). This is a more Gentile image, since dogs were rarely pets in Jewish culture.[11]

A second mitigating factor is that Jesus does not deny that the "dogs" will eat, but only that the "children" (Israel) must eat *first* (πρῶτον). Matthew's parallel for Jesus' words is stronger, where he explicitly says he was sent only to the lost sheep of Israel (Matt 15:24, 26).[12] This is no contradiction, however, since both Matthew and Mark see an order to God's salvation, to the Jew *first* (cf. Matt 28:18 – 20). Salvation comes first to the people of Israel, who are meant to be a light of revelation to the nations (Isa 42:6; 49:6). This is also Paul's perspective. Salvation is for the Jews first, then for the Gentiles (Rom 1:16 – 17). As the people of God, Israel is meant to be a kingdom of priests, mediating God's salvation to the world (see Theology in Application).

There are two ways to view Jesus' response. The first is that he is simply stating his ministry as he sees it. It is for the Jews first. In this case the woman's clever response catches him off guard and impresses him so much he grants her wish. The second way to view the episode is that Jesus is being intentionally provocative, seeking to draw out a response of persistent faith from the woman. He wants her to claim what is rightfully hers — the opportunity to participate in the eschatological salvation available through Jesus the Messiah. While Jesus "loses" the debate, he is delighted to do so, since his purpose is to provoke even greater faith.

This latter one seems the most likely interpretation, since Jesus is always in charge in the gospel and never caught off guard. Furthermore, the kingdom of God is both "already" and "not yet" in Jesus' preaching; the presence and power of the kingdom is *already available* to all who respond in faith — whether Jew or Gentile. While the orderly progress of the gospel remains intact (from Jews to Gentiles), at all times salvation comes by grace through faith for all who believe, not through membership in ethnic Israel (Rom 9:6 – 8). Jesus' choice of the verb "eat their fill" or "be satisfied" (χορτάζω) may also be significant here. The only other times Mark uses this word is in the two feeding miracles (Mark 6:42; 8:4, 8). While the first of these represents Israel's presence at the messianic banquet, the second likely previews the presence of the Gentiles.

7:28 But she responded to him, "Yes,[13] Lord, but even the dogs under the table eat the children's crumbs." (ἡ δὲ ἀπεκρίθη καὶ λέγει αὐτῷ· ναί, κύριε· καὶ τὰ κυνάρια ὑποκάτω τῆς τραπέζης ἐσθίουσιν ἀπὸ τῶν ψιχίων τῶν παιδίων). Despite Jesus' negative response, the woman will not be put off. Her response is at the same time respectful and profound. She begins by addressing Jesus with the

---

11. Occasional statements in Judaism may refer to dogs as household pets, such as Tob 6:1; 11:1 (some mss); *b. 'Abod. Zar.* 54b; *b. Šabb.* 155b; *Midr. Ps.* 4.11 (Marcus, *Mark 1 – 8*, 464). But these are exceptional. A distinction is made in *Jos. Asen.* 10:14 between Asenath's household pets and wild ("strange") dogs, but this is in an Egyptian setting.

12. Marcus, *Mark 1 – 8*, 464, points to some later Jewish evidence that domestic dogs could symbolize righteous Gentiles, who will be present at the messianic banquet but will not dine as sumptuously as the invited guests or the family (= the Jews; *Midr. Ps.* 4:11). He suggests that "dogs at the banquet" may have been a fixed image for the participation of the Gentiles at the

messianic banquets. Though intriguing, this is speculative.

13. The inclusion of "yes" (ναί) in the majority of manuscripts, either as ναί, κύριε, καί ("yes, Lord, but …"; ℵ B Δ 28 33 579 892 1241 2427 syrᵖ) or as ναί, κύριε, καὶ γάρ ("yes, Lord, for also"; A L *f*¹ 𝔐 lat syr), is sometimes said to be an assimilation to Matt 15:27 (Metzger, *Textual Commentary*, 82). More likely, as France, *Mark*, 295, points out, its strong textual attestation suggests that it was intentionally omitted in a particular tradition (𝔓⁴⁵ W Θ *f*¹³ 565 700 syrˢ) "because it was misunderstood as turning the woman's reply into a meek acceptance of Jesus' words … rather than, as it should be, a firm repudiation of his οὐκ ἐστιν καλόν."

vocative "Lord" (κύριε), the only place this address is used in Mark's gospel. While the Greek term can simply mean "sir," Mark's readers would likely see more to it than this — a woman who "gets it" in terms of Jesus' identity.

Furthermore, rather than being offended, she willingly accepts the epithet "dogs" and thus the priority of the Jews in God's order of salvation. But she then turns the image to her advantage: even the dogs get the crumbs that the children drop. Two points are important here. First, the woman recognizes that the salvation of the Jews means blessings for the Gentiles (Gen 12:3). The dogs will be fed, meaning the Gentiles will receive a share in God's salvation. There is a strong stream of OT theology indicating that God's final salvation will extend to the nations (Isa 2:2 – 3; 19:25; 25:6 – 8; Mic 4:1 – 2; Dan 7:14; Amos 9:12; Zech 9:10).[14]

Second, she asserts that the dogs don't have to wait until the children are finished, but can even now eat the bread that falls from the table. Ironically, while Jesus expresses a traditional Jewish perspective that God's salvation is *first* for the Jews and eventually for the Gentiles, the woman affirms the "already/not yet" nature of the kingdom that Jesus has been proclaiming. Even now God's final salvation is breaking into human history and is available to all who humbly respond in faith.

7:29 He said to her, "Because of this answer, go, the demon has left your daughter." (καὶ εἶπεν αὐτῇ· διὰ τοῦτον τὸν λόγον ὕπαγε, ἐξελήλυθεν ἐκ τῆς θυγατρός σου τὸ δαιμόνιον). Impressed by the woman's answer, Jesus grants her request. In Matthew, Jesus explicitly refers to her "great faith"

(15:28). This is implied in Mark, but more important here is her spiritual insight into the ways of God and the availability of salvation to all people everywhere. As noted above, there are two ways Jesus' answer could be understood: either "because of this answer I have changed my mind" or "because of this answer you have passed the test of faith." Our conclusion on v. 27 has suggested the latter is intended.

Jesus not only heals from a distance, but he pronounces it already done — the demon "has left" (ἐξελήλυθεν; perfect tense). This is the only time Jesus heals from a distance in Mark, but Matthew and Luke record the healing of a centurion's servant (Matt 8:5 – 13; par. Luke 7:1 – 10), and John has a similar episode involving the healing of the son of a royal official (John 4:46 – 54).[15] The healing at a distance is unlikely to be because the house of a Gentile would be "unclean," as some have suggested, since Jesus shows a lack of concern for such purity issues elsewhere (1:41; 2:14 – 17; 5:25 – 34, 40 – 42; 7:1 – 23).[16] The point, rather, is to demonstrate once again Jesus' extraordinary authority.

7:30 Going home, she found the child lying in bed and the demon gone (καὶ ἀπελθοῦσα εἰς τὸν οἶκον αὐτῆς εὗρεν τὸ παιδίον βεβλημένον ἐπὶ τὴν κλίνην καὶ τὸ δαιμόνιον ἐξεληλυθός). The story ends with a statement of the evidence of the cure. Since the verb translated "lying" (βεβλημένον; perfect participle of βάλλω) often means to "cast" or "throw" (v. 27), some commentators suggest that the girl was "thrown down" in a final convulsion by the demon (cf. 1:26; 9:26).[17] This strained interpretation results from an overly literal reading of the

---

14. Cf. *Sib. Or.* 3.716 – 27, 772 – 75; *T. Benj.* 9:2; *1 En.* 10:21; 48:5; 90:33; *2 Bar.* 68:5; Str-B, 3:150 – 52; Boring, *Mark*, 213.

15. Healings at a distance occur occasionally in ancient literature, including the healing of Rabbi Gamaliel's son by Hanina ben Dosa (*b. Ber.* 34b) and a healing from afar by Apol-

lonius of Tyana (Philostratus, *Vit. Apoll.* 3.38).

16. Stein, *Mark*, 354.

17. Gundry, *Mark*, 375; Marcus, *Mark 1 – 8*, 470; Lane, *Mark*, 263.

verb. The verb "cast" (βάλλω) has a large semantic range and can mean to "put," "place," or "lay" something, such as a person, on a bed.[18] In Matt 9:2 a paralyzed man is brought to Jesus "lying on a mat" (ἐπὶ κλίνης βεβλημένον). Surely his friends didn't throw him there![19] The point is that the girl has been "put to bed" and is now resting peacefully, free from the demon's power.

Theology in Application

As noted in our comments above, this is a remarkable episode that is unique in the Gospels, since Jesus, normally the master debater who confounds his opponents at every turn, here concedes that his interlocutor is right and he is wrong. It is doubly surprising that he is defeated *not* by a learned rabbi, but by a Gentile and a woman, two strikes that in rabbinic Judaism would disqualify her from having any spiritual insight.

Mark's message to his readers is profound. The temporal priority of Israel in salvation is reaching its culmination in the final salvation inaugurated through the coming of Jesus the Messiah. While the guest list for the messianic banquet includes only Abraham's descendants, these are now seen to include all those who have Abraham's faith in God's provision for a Savior (cf. Rom 4; Gal 3:6 – 9). The doors of the banquet hall have swung open, and all are welcome who will come in humility and faith. Three key theological points may be seen in the episode.

To the Jew First: Israel's Priority in Salvation-History

God chose Israel as his chosen people, and Jesus here emphasizes the nation's priority in salvation history. Paul, the great advocate of Gentile salvation, also makes this same point. "What advantage, then, is there in being a Jew?" he asks. "Much in every way! First of all, the Jews have been entrusted with the very words of God" (Rom 3:1 – 2). Israel was set apart by God as his special people and his special possession. This privilege, however, came with a responsibility. They were to be holy, as he is holy; and they were to mediate his presence to the nations and to establish the line through which the Messiah would come (cf. Rom 9:4 – 5).

Jesus clearly saw his ministry to Israel as his primary concern. He chose twelve disciples, representing the twelve tribes of Israel, and commissioned them for a mission to their fellow Jews (6:7 – 11). Matthew's gospel bring this out more strongly than Mark's. In the commissioning of the Twelve, Jesus explicitly says, "Do not go

---

18. BDAG, 163.

19. Stein, *Mark*, 354, offers another suggestion, that this is a play on words between the "casting" of bread to the dogs in 7:27 and this "casting," so that the girl's healing is an example of giving bread to the Gentiles. This seems overly subtle. Again,

by overanalyzing Greek words, interpreters tend to see connections that would never have occurred to a native Greek speaker. βάλλειν ... ἐπὶ τὴν κλίνην is simply a collocation for being placed on a bed.

among the Gentiles or enter any town of the Samaritans" (Matt 10:5), and in Matthew's parallel to the present account Jesus says, "I was sent only to the lost sheep of Israel" (15:24). Yet this exclusive mission was not because of the exclusivity of salvation. Rather, Israel must be restored and a faithful remnant called out so that they could be the mediators of God's salvation, "a light for the Gentiles" (Isa 42:6; 49:6). This pattern is seen in the missionary journeys of Paul, whose philosophy and methodology was "first to the Jew, then to the Gentile" (Rom 1:16). In every town where Paul went, he would go first to the synagogue, where he would proclaim the message to Jews and Gentile God-fearers. With the faithful remnant of Israel called out, he would then turn his full attention to the Gentiles (Acts 13:46; 18:6; 28:28).

Also for the Gentiles: The Universal Scope of God's Salvation

While Israel's priority in salvation is well established in biblical theology, so too are the blessings that overflow to the nations. The promise to Abraham was that through his descendants (Israel) all nations of the earth would be blessed (Gen 12:3; 18:18; 22:18; 26:4; 28:14). There are two theological streams in Judaism with reference to the nations. One stream that occurs frequently is God's righteous judgment against the nations for their evil, idolatry, pride, and cruelty to God's people. Oracles against the Assyrians, Babylonians, Egyptians, Syrians, Philistines, Moabites, Edomites, and others appear throughout the prophets. Yet beside this tradition is the promise of salvation for the nations. Isaiah envisioned a day when all nations would stream to the mountain of the Lord to learn his ways and to worship him (Isa 2:2 – 3; cf. Mic 4:1 – 2). The messianic banquet is similarly presented as a great feast that the Lord Almighty will prepare "for all peoples" (Isa 25:6).

Jesus' preaching clearly emphasizes this latter. He warns the religious leaders that they will have no place at the messianic banquet, but that "people will come from east and west and north and south, and will take their places at the feast in the kingdom of God" (Luke 13:29). Matthew's version of this saying appears in the context of the healing of the centurion's servant, an episode with close parallels to the present one (Matt 8:11).

Yet there is something more here. In Judaism, the inclusion of the Gentiles occurs at God's final salvation. For Jesus, the kingdom of God is at hand. The already/not yet message of the kingdom means that even now God's salvation is breaking into human history and the Gentiles are able to receive the same salvation blessings experienced by the Jews.

The Reward of Faith, Humility, and Spiritual Discernment

This Gentile woman is a remarkable model of faith. Although a true outsider to Israel's elite by virtue of her gender and ethnicity, she demonstrates the attributes that God is seeking in his people. The first is faith. Although only Matthew's account explicitly refers to this faith, it is implicit in her behavior and actions. She approaches Jesus because she believes that he is able to cast the demon out of her daughter. This is also persistent faith that will not fail because of Jesus' initial reluctance. God calls us to persevere in faith, not because he is a reluctant Father who is slow to meet the needs of his people, but because he wants us to step out in greater dependence and deeper trust in his ability to accomplish far more than we can ask or imagine "according to his power that is at work within us" (Eph 3:20).

In addition to faith, the woman demonstrates humility. Instead of being offended or put off by Jesus' initial rebuff, she humbly accepts the epithet "dog," but then turns it to her advantage. She acknowledges that she is undeserving, with no rightful place at the table, but then falls at Jesus' feet (literally) and asks for mercy. This is our only appropriate approach to God, as humble sinners in need of his grace. We bring nothing to the table except our emptiness and the promise of a loving and merciful God.

Though humble, the woman also demonstrates remarkable spiritual discernment. Ironically, this Gentile woman is the first character in Mark's gospel to comprehend the nature and scope of God's salvation. It is a salvation that begins with the Jews but is meant for all people everywhere. It is a salvation available not just for the religious elite, but for all those who respond in repentance and faith. For Mark's readers, the woman becomes a model disciple, who is willing to be last instead of first and who discerns the inclusive nature of the gospel message. It is this inclusive gospel of grace through faith that is so essential to Mark's church and to the progress of the mission of the early church.

CHAPTER

28

Mark 7:31 – 37

Literary Context

This is the second of three miracles performed by Jesus in Gentile territory (7:24 – 8:10) introduced by Mark after Jesus' teaching on clean and unclean things (7:1 – 23). Geographically, Jesus continues a circuitous journey, first traveling north from the region of Tyre toward Sidon, then southeast to the eastern shores of Galilee in the Decapolis (see v. 31). Theologically, the passage builds on the previous account of the Syrophoenician woman to show that God's salvation will go to all people everywhere, even "unclean" Gentiles. The passage also forms a pair with the healing of the blind man in 8:22 – 26, both pointing to the eschatological renewal of Isa 35:5 – 6. These episodes, in turn, frame Jesus' rebuke of the disciples in 8:17 – 18 and so draw an implicit contrast between the spiritual dullness of the disciples (cf. 6:52; 7:18; 8:15) and those with eyes to see and ears to hear.

This miracle is unique to Mark's gospel (cf. 8:22 – 26). Some have suggested that Matthew and Luke omitted the story because of the unusual way Jesus performs the miracle, which might suggest the use of magic (vv. 33 – 34). While this might be the case for Matthew, the episode is part of a much larger omission in Luke, which includes everything from Mark 6:45 – 8:26 (Luke's so-called "great omission"). Matthew replaces the episode with a summary of Jesus' healing, which similarly alludes to Isa 35:5 – 6 and the eschatological restoration of strength to the lame, sight to the blind, and speech to the mute (Matt 15:29 – 31).

Main Idea

Jesus continues to demonstrate his messianic authority in Gentile territories by healing a deaf and mute man in the Decapolis; this illustrates the fulfillment of the eschatological promise of Isa 35:5 – 6.

Translation

Mark 7:31 – 37

31a	character departure	Then,
b	Setting (spatial)	leaving the region of Tyre,
		he went through Sidon to the Sea of Galilee in the region of Decapolis.
32a	Character entrance	**Some people brought to him a man**
b	character description	who was deaf and could not speak well,
c	Entreaty	and **they were begging him to place his hands on him.**
33a	Response: withdrawal	After taking him away from the crowd privately,
b	Action	**Jesus put his fingers into the man's ears;**
c	Action	spitting,
		he touched the man's tongue.
34a	action	Looking up to heaven,
b	Command	**he sighed and said to him,**
c		*"Ephphatha,"*
d	interpretation	which means, "Be opened!"
35a	Healing	**Immediately, his hearing was restored**
b		and **his tongue was set loose**
c		and **he spoke clearly.**
36a	Command to silence	**He commanded them not to tell anyone.**
b	Response to 36a	But **the more he commanded them,**
c		**the more they were proclaiming it.**
37a	Response to 35	**They were utterly astonished and said,**
b		*"He has done all things well.*
c		*He even makes the deaf hear and the mute speak."*

Structure

The story follows a common pattern for a healing story, with an approach and request, a healing, and an amazed response by the crowds. As in 1:44; 5:43; and 8:26, there is also a command to silence (7:36), which is broken because of the stunning nature of the miracle. Many commentators have noted the striking parallels between this episode and the healing of a blind man at Bethsaida (8:22 – 26): (1) the location of each is specified as predominantly Gentile territory; (2) an unnamed group brings a person in need of healing to Jesus; (3) they "plead" (παρακαλέω) with Jesus (4) to lay hands on him; (5) Jesus takes the person away privately and heals him (6) by touching him (7) on the afflicted part of his body (8) using saliva; (9) Jesus commands silence (v. 36) or tells the healed person to return home without going into the village square (8:26).[1]

Exegetical Outline

→ **1. Setting: Journey from Tyre to Decapolis (7:31)**

2. The Healing of a Deaf Man (7:32 – 35)
   a. The approach by the friends (7:32)
   b. Jesus' withdrawal with the man (7:33a)
   c. Jesus' unusual actions (7:33b – 34)
   d. The healing (7:35)

3. The Aftermath (7:36 – 37)
   a. The command to silence (7:36a)
   b. The response of the people (7:36b – 37)

Explanation of the Text

7:31 Then, leaving the region of Tyre, he went through Sidon to the Sea of Galilee in the region of Decapolis (Καὶ πάλιν ἐξελθὼν ἐκ τῶν ὁρίων Τύρου ἦλθεν διὰ Σιδῶνος εἰς τὴν θάλασσαν τῆς Γαλιλαίας ἀνὰ μέσον τῶν ὁρίων Δεκαπόλεως). Mark picks up geographically where the previous episode, the healing of the daughter of a Syrophoenician woman near Tyre, left off. Sidon was about twenty-two miles north of Tyre, and the two are frequently identified together in the literature as key Phoenician cities of trade and commerce (see comments on 7:24).[2]

The route taken represents a circuitous journey, as Jesus first heads north toward Sidon and then returns southeast, apparently to the eastern shores of the Sea of Galilee, in the Decapolis.[3] Some have accused Mark of geographical confusion, since Jesus apparently starts off in the wrong direction. But this assumes that Mark is giving an account of a particular journey. More likely, he is simply describing the general direction and destinations of Jesus during this phase of his ministry. Jesus may be staying clear of Capernaum and the western side of Galilee, his previous base of operations, to avoid

---

1. Boring, *Mark*, 215.
2. Marcus, *Mark 1 – 8*, 472, points out that Tyre and Sidon are in Lebanon, and that Isa 35:5 – 6 and 29:17 – 19 (two key background passages for this healing) both mention Lebanon. Yet it seems a stretch to claim that the references to Tyre and Sidon are an intentional allusion to these OT passages. This

miracle doesn't actually take place in Lebanon, but far to the south in the Decapolis.

3. An alternate manuscript tradition says that Jesus, "departing from the regions of Tyre and Sidon, went to the Sea of Galilee" ($\mathfrak{P}^{45}$ A W 0131 $f^{1.13}$ 𝔐). This is apparently an attempt by a later scribe to smooth out Mark's awkward geographical note.

threats from Herod or controversy with the religious leaders (see comments on 7:24).

The Decapolis refers to the region to the east and southeast of Galilee, made up of a confederacy of cities with defense and trade ties. The alliance was originally "ten cities" (= "Decapolis"), but the number varied over time (see comments on 5:20). Jesus visited this area earlier when he exorcised the the legion of demons from the Gerasene demoniac (5:1 – 20). The phrase "in the midst of the borders" (ἀνὰ μέσον τῶν ὁρίων) is an idiom meaning "within the region of."[4] This area had a predominantly Gentile population and so Mark's readers would likely assume that Jesus' interactions here were with Gentiles.

7:32 Some people brought to him a man who was deaf and could not speak well, and they were begging him to place his hands on him (καὶ φέρουσιν αὐτῷ κωφὸν καὶ μογιλάλον καὶ παρακαλοῦσιν αὐτὸν ἵνα ἐπιθῇ αὐτῷ τὴν χεῖρα). Those who brought the man are not specified (φέρουσιν; "they are bringing"), but they must have been friends of the man since they beg or implore (παρακαλέω) Jesus to heal him. Mark uses the historical present tense for both verbs, giving the scene a sense of vivid realism, then switches to aorists in v. 33.

The request to "lay hands on" the afflicted is common in Mark's gospel (5:23; 6:5; 8:22, 25) and in healing stories generally. The man is described as "deaf" (κωφός), a term that can mean deaf, mute, or both.[5] Here deafness is intended, since Mark adds "and could not speak well" (καὶ μογιλάλος). This word is a *hapax legomenon* (occurring only once) in the NT and appears in the LXX only at Isa 35:6. Mark is no doubt intentionally echoing that passage in order to connect Jesus' healing with the

eschatological signs of salvation.[6] Etymologically, the word means "to speak with difficulty" (μόγις, "scarcely, with difficulty" + λαλέω, "speak"), but it was also used of the inability to speak at all, i.e., "mute." Most of the ancient versions translate it this way.[7] The end of the story, however, suggests the former sense, since the man now is able to speak "clearly" or "correctly" (ὀρθῶς). Apparently, the speech impediment resulted from the deafness, a common symptom for those who cannot hear.

7:33 – 34 After taking him away from the crowd privately, Jesus put his fingers into the man's ears; spitting, he touched the man's tongue. Looking up to heaven, he sighed and said to him, "Ephphatha," which means, "Be opened!" (καὶ ἀπολαβόμενος αὐτὸν ἀπὸ τοῦ ὄχλου κατ' ἰδίαν ἔβαλεν τοὺς δακτύλους αὐτοῦ εἰς τὰ ὦτα αὐτοῦ καὶ πτύσας ἥψατο τῆς γλώσσης αὐτοῦ, καὶ ἀναβλέψας εἰς τὸν οὐρανὸν ἐστέναξεν καὶ λέγει αὐτῷ· εφφαθα, ὅ ἐστιν διανοίχθητι). As in the healing of Jairus's daughter (5:40), Jesus withdraws from the crowd to perform the miracle "in private" (κατ' ἰδίαν). He will withdraw in a similar manner with the blind man at Bethsaida (8:22 – 23). The reason is not stated, but is consistent with the messianic secret that occurs throughout Mark's gospel (1:44; 5:43; 7:36; 8:2).

The healing is described in great detail. After withdrawing with the man, Jesus performs six actions: (1) putting his fingers in the man's ears; (2) spitting; (3) touching the man's tongue; (4) looking up to heaven; (5) sighing; (6) and saying "Ephphatha," meaning, "Be opened!" Jesus often heals by touch in Mark's gospel (1:31, 41; 5:23; 6:5; 8:25), but only here and in 8:23, 25 does he touch the affected organ. Hull suggests that Jesus puts his

---

4. τό ὅριον means a boundary or border, but is always used in our literature in the plural, with the sense of "the region of" (BDAG, 723).

5. BDAG, 580.

6. The rabbis interpreted Isa 35:5 – 6 as fulfilled in the messianic age (*Gen. Rab.* 95; *Midr. Ps.* 146.8).

7. BDAG, 656.

fingers in the man's ear to create a passage for a demon to escape.[8] But there is no mention of demonic possession in the context. It seems more likely that Jesus is using touch as a sign of compassion and to symbolically open the ears.

Jesus uses spittle in three healings in the gospel tradition: here, 8:23, and in John 9:6. The text does not say why Jesus spit or whether he spit into his hands before touching the man's tongue (cf. 8:23, where he spits into the man's eyes). Spittle was commonly viewed in the ancient world as having medicinal and/or magical powers,[9] and the saliva of an important person was considered to be particularly powerful. Both Tacitus and Suetonius relate an account of a blind man who approached the emperor Vespasian in Alexandria, Egypt, and begged to be healed by his saliva.[10] While the use of spittle was rejected by some rabbis as magical, others accepted its medicinal value.[11] Touching the tongue, like touching the ears, is probably meant both to demonstrate compassion and to transfer Jesus' healing power.

"Looking up to heaven" (ἀναβλέψας εἰς τὸν οὐρανόν) indicates an attitude of prayer (Ps 123:1; Luke 18:13; John 11:41; 17:1; Acts 7:55). Jesus does the same thing before blessing the loaves in the feeding miracle (6:41). The sigh or groan (ἐστέναξεν) is puzzling and has been variously interpreted as: (1) a part of a magical procedure or incantation;[12] (2) the exhalation of breath, which carries life force and so the power to heal;[13] (3) an expression of deep compassion for the sufferer or heartache at the ravages of disease;[14] (4) an indication of strain or emotional involvement in the healing;[15] (5) an expression of heartfelt prayer.[16] This last seems most likely, since it immediately follows the look heavenward. Compare Rom 8:26, where Paul uses the noun form of the same root to describe the Spirit interceding for us "with sighs [στεναγμοῖς] too deep for words" (NRSV).

Jesus' unusual actions with their apparently magical connotations have disturbed many modern readers. Did Jesus consider these actions efficacious, either medicinally or magically? Was he merely condescending to the expectations of his contemporaries? We simply do not know. Yet we should be cautious in attributing magical technique to Jesus in light of the paucity of such material elsewhere in the gospel tradition (only 8:23; John 9:6). Whatever the significance of these actions, the healing itself does not come through any technique but through the authoritative command of Jesus: "Be opened!" It is Jesus' messianic authority rather than magic that accomplishes the healing.

Scholars have debated whether Jesus' expression, "Ephphatha" (εφφαθα), is Hebrew or Aramaic, though the consensus favors the latter.[17] As else-

---

8. Hull, *Hellenistic Magic*, 83.

9. See the list in Gundry, *Mark*, 389; Hull, *Hellenistic Magic*, 76–78; Str-B 2:17. Medicinal uses of saliva are described in Galen, *On Natural Faculties* 3.7.

10. Tacitus, *Hist.* 4:81; Suetonius, *Vesp.* 7.

11. Contrast Rabbi Akiba's opposition to it as magical in *t. Sanh.* 12:10 with the account of Rabbi Hanina sending people to be healed by his son's saliva (*b. B. Bat.* 126b).

12. Marcus, *Mark 1–8*, 474; Collins, *Mark*, 371–72; Hull, *Hellenistic Magic*, 84. Hull thinks Jesus is imitating the restoration of speech and also the rejection of the demon. C. Bonner, "Traces of Thaumaturgic Technique in the Miracles," *HTR* 20 (1927): 171–81, cites a charm from the Paris Magical Papyrus

that reads, "After reciting this, throw incense on the fire, sigh and descend [from the roof]" (p. 172).

13. Gundry, *Mark*, 383–84.

14. Taylor, *Mark*, 355.

15. France, *Mark*, 303–4.

16. Witherington, *Mark*, 234.

17. The argument for Hebrew is made by I. Rabinowitz, "'Be Opened' = Ἐφφαθά (Mark 7,34): Did Jesus Speak Hebrew?" *ZNW* 53 (1962): 229–38; idem, "ΕΦΦΑΘΑ (Mark VII.34): Certainly Hebrew, Not Aramaic," *JSS* 16 (1971): 151–56. Cf. the response by S. Morag, "Ἐφφαθά (Mark vii.34): Certainly Hebrew, Not Aramaic?" *JSS* 17 (1971): 198–202.

where, Mark provides a translation for his Greek-speaking readers: "Be opened!" (διανοίχθητι; cf. 3:17; 5:41; 7:11; 10:46; 14:36). Jesus' use of Aramaic is not unusual here, since a dialect of Aramaic would have been widely spoken in the Decapolis (together with Greek). Some have suggested the word functions as a magical formula, but this is unlikely since this was Jesus' normal language of discourse and since, as elsewhere, Mark provides a translation for his Greek readers. More likely, as in 5:41, the powerful healing left such an impression on the disciples that the actual words of Jesus were remembered and passed down as the story was told and retold within the church.

7:35 Immediately, his hearing was restored and his tongue was set loose and he spoke clearly (καὶ εὐθέως ἠνοίγησαν αὐτοῦ αἱ ἀκοαί, καὶ ἐλύθη ὁ δεσμὸς τῆς γλώσσης αὐτοῦ καὶ ἐλάλει ὀρθῶς). The healing takes place instantaneously (εὐθέως).[18] The Greek phrase "the bond/chain of his tongue was loosed" (ἐλύθη ὁ δεσμὸς τῆς γλώσσης αὐτοῦ) is an idiom indicating the restoration of speech and does not necessarily imply freedom from demonization. As noted earlier, the fact that he spoke "correctly" or "clearly" (ὀρθῶς) probably indicates that he had a speech impediment caused by the deafness, rather than that he was completely mute.

In addition to Isa 35:5 – 6 (the main background passage), the healing also recalls Exod 4:10, where Moses complains to God that he cannot be God's mouthpiece to Pharaoh since he is not eloquent and is "slow of speech and tongue." The Lord responds, "Who gave human beings their mouths? Who makes them deaf or mute? Who gives them sight or makes them blind? Is it not I, the LORD?" (4:11). By giving the man hearing and voice, Jesus acts with the authority of God.

7:36 – 37 He commanded them not to tell anyone. But the more he commanded them, the more they were proclaiming it. They were utterly astonished and said, "He has done all things well. He even makes the deaf hear and the mute speak." (καὶ διεστείλατο αὐτοῖς ἵνα μηδενὶ λέγωσιν· ὅσον δὲ αὐτοῖς διεστέλλετο, αὐτοὶ μᾶλλον περισσότερον ἐκήρυσσον. καὶ ὑπερπερισσῶς ἐξεπλήσσοντο λέγοντες· καλῶς πάντα πεποίηκεν, καὶ τοὺς κωφοὺς ποιεῖ ἀκούειν καὶ τοὺς ἀλάλους λαλεῖν). Four times in Mark Jesus commands silence after a healing (1:44; 5:43; 7:36; 8:26). The "them" here could be the friends who brought him to Jesus or the crowd more generally.

The command is surprising in this context since in Jesus' previous visit to the Decapolis (5:1 – 20) he encouraged the man freed of multiple demons to announce "what the Lord has done for [him]" (5:19). Perhaps Jesus' reputation had become so well known by this time that even in the Decapolis the command was necessary to cool messianic fervor or to allow greater privacy for training the Twelve.

In any case, as in 1:45, the command is broken. The phrase "rather more" (μᾶλλον περισσότερον) is typical Markan redundancy. While the total disregard of Jesus' command would seem to be a negative response, "proclaim" (κηρύσσω) always has the positive sense in Mark of the announcement of the good news of salvation (1:4, 7, 14, 38, 39; 3:14; 6:12; 7:36; 13:10; 14:9) or of healing (1:45; 5:20; 7:36). Mark's point is that the good news is so good that it overwhelms those who experience it and cannot be kept a secret.

The reason for the proclamation is that they were "utterly astonished" (ὑπερπερισσῶς ἐξεπλήσσοντο) at the miracle. The term "utterly" (ὑπερπερισσῶς)

---

18. The manuscripts are well divided between those that include εὐθέως (𝔓[45] A W Θ *f*[1.13] 𝔐) and those that omit it (א

B D L Δ). We have retained it in light of Mark's fondness for the term elsewhere.

is another *hapax legomenon* (see v. 32) and is doubly emphatic (ὑπερ ["beyond"] + περισσῶς ["exceptionally"]), meaning over-the-top amazement. Their words, "He has done all things well" (καλῶς πάντα πεποίηκεν), may echo the creation account in Genesis 1:31 LXX, where God sees "all things" he has "made" and pronounces it "very good." It is also verbally similar to Eccl 3:11 LXX: "He has made everthing beautiful in its time" (τὰ πάντα ἐποίησεν καλὰ ἐν καιρῷ αὐτοῦ). If these allusions are present, they reinforce the theme of the restoration of creation found in Isa 35:5 – 6. The passage ends with this same theme: "He even makes the deaf hear and the mute speak."

Theology in Application

Spiritually Seeing and Hearing

As noted above, this episode forms an interesting pair with the healing of the blind man in 8:22 – 26. The two not only have structural features in common, but together they pick up the theme of spiritual sight and hearing that are so important for Mark's narrative. While teaching in parables, Jesus repeatedly called for spiritual discernment, hearing, and heeding the word: "Whoever has ears to hear, let them hear" (4:9, 23); "Listen!" (4:3). The seed sown on good soil hears and accepts the word and so bears fruit (4:20; cf. 4:15, 16, 18). The religious leaders who are rejecting Jesus' kingdom preaching get the message only in parables, "so that they may look and look but not perceive, and hear and hear but not understand" (4:12, citing Isa 6:9 – 10). These two healing miracles connect to this earlier theme by framing the episode of the "leaven of the Pharisees and Herod," where Jesus warns the disciples that they are in danger of having eyes but failing to see and ears but failing to hear (8:17 – 18). Responding to the kingdom means a heart receptive to God's purpose in the world.

We are reminded by this analogy that deafness is not just a physical condition; it can be a spiritual one. In our modern world it is easy to become deafened by all the "noise" around us and fail to hear God's voice. For some people the distraction comes from the constant quest for human relationships that will bring physical comfort and emotional security. We fail to recognize that only a relationship with our Creator God can bring true peace and fulfillment. For others it is the constant quest for material things that bring temporary thrills but will soon pass away. For others, the spiritual deafness comes from addiction to drugs, alcohol, gambling, or sex, things that dull our spiritual sensitivity to God's purpose in our lives. As a cure for these deafening distractions, we need to move away from the crowds and humble ourselves before God, being still and knowing that he is God (Ps 46:10).

The Renewal of All Creation

Another theme implicit but clearly present in this episode is the coming restoration of creation. Passages like Isa 35:5 – 6 (cf. 29:18; 32:3; 42:7) form the backdrop to Jesus' healings here and throughout the gospel tradition:

> Then will the eyes of the blind be opened
> > and the ears of the deaf unstopped.
> Then will the lame leap like a deer,
> > and the mute tongue shout for joy.
> Water will gush forth in the wilderness
> > and streams in the desert. (Isa 35:5 – 6)

The immediate context of this OT passage is the promise of Israel's return from exile. But like so many similar promises, it points forward to the ultimate restoration of all things, marked by the judgment of the wicked, salvation for the righteous, and eternal joy and peace for God's people (Isa 35:4, 10).

Healing episodes like this are therefore "snapshots" of the coming kingdom. They serve as "coming attractions," a glimpse and preview of the restoration that has been inaugurated through the first coming of Jesus the Messiah and will be consummated at his return in glory. Healings and exorcisms may be spectacular for those who observe them and life-changing for those who experience them. Yet they are both temporary and temporal. Those healed of their physical infirmities eventually died, and the world continued as a place of sin, suffering, and fallenness. Yet the brief snapshot before us points to the future reality, when the salvation achieved through Jesus' life, death, and resurrection will be consummated with the restoration of all creation. At that time, "they will enter Zion with singing; everlasting joy will crown their heads. Gladness and joy will overtake them, and sorrow and sighing will flee away" (Isa 35:10).

As we live in this interim period "between the ages," when God's great salvation has been inaugurated but not yet consummated, we need to follow Jesus' example. He fed the hungry and healed the sick, reaching out to those with physical needs. Yet he always did so with an eye on eternity, calling people to repentance and submission to the kingdom of God and a right relationship with their Creator God.

29

Mark 8:1 – 10

Literary Context

As noted in the two previous episodes, the feeding of the four thousand is part of a sequence of events involving Jesus' activities among Gentiles in Gentile regions. After teaching on "clean" and "unclean" things (7:1 – 23), Jesus casts a demon out of the daughter of a Syrophoenician woman (7:24 – 30), heals a deaf and mute man in the Decapolis (7:31 – 37), and now feeds a second (Gentile?) multitude starting with a few loaves and fishes. Immediately following this episode, the Pharisees — representing Israel's leadership — demand a sign from Jesus (8:11 – 13), and Jesus warns his disciples about the "leaven of the Pharisees and the leaven of Herod" (8:15). Mark seems to be contrasting Gentile openness to the gospel with Jewish resistance to it.

As noted in the Literary Context discussion on 6:30 – 44, many scholars have noted parallels in the sequence of events of 6:31 – 7:37 and 8:1 – 30:[1]

6:31 – 44	Feeding the multitude	8:1 – 9
6:45 – 56	Crossing the sea and landing	8:10
7:1 – 23	Conflict with the Pharisees	8:11 – 13
7:24 – 30	Conversation about bread	8:14 – 21
7:31 – 36	Healing	8:22 – 26
7:37	Confession of faith	8:27 – 30

Though these parallels are not exact, the pattern seems to be intentional and related to the spiritual (mis-)understanding of the disciples. Jesus calls for spiritual discernment in 7:14 – 18, but the disciples fail to comprehend the significance of either of the feeding miracles (6:52; 8:14 – 21). The two healing accounts — first of a deaf and mute man (7:31 – 36) and then of a blind man (8:22 – 26) — illustrate the spiritual deafness and blindness of Israel's leadership, maladies that threaten to afflict the disciples as well (8:18).

---

1. Lane, *Mark*, 269. This pattern is often said to be a pre-Markan doublet, also reflected in the series of events recorded in John 6:1 – 69.

Yet through Jesus' healings and other miracles, enough light begins to dawn that, in 8:29, Peter will acknowledge that Jesus is the Messiah. Though this is an important first step, Peter's understanding is far from perfect (like the partial sight of the blind man in 8:24). While correctly recognizing Jesus' identity as the Messiah, Peter (representing the disciples as a whole) still fails to comprehend his messianic mission (8:32) and the nature of authentic discipleship. This theme will be on center stage throughout chapters 8 – 10.

II. The Authority of the Messiah (1:14 – 8:21)
   C. The Expanding Mission of the Messiah (6:6b – 8:21)
      6. Commandments of God and Human Traditions (7:1 – 23)
      7. The Faith of the Syrophoenician Woman (7:24 – 30)
      8. Healing a Deaf and Mute Man (7:31 – 37)
      9. Feeding the Four Thousand (8:1 – 10)
      10. Requesting a Sign from Heaven (8:11 – 13)

Main Idea

This second feeding miracle, like the first, portrays Jesus as the authoritative Messiah and a compassionate shepherd feeding his people in a "wilderness" place — a preview of the messianic banquet. By narrating this second miracle in the Decapolis and placing it in the context of Jesus' interaction with Gentiles, Mark implicitly affirms that the invitation to the messianic banquet is not for Israelites alone, but for all people everywhere.

Translation

Mark 8:1 – 10

1a	Setting	**In those days a large crowd was again present.**
b	reason	Since they had nothing to eat,
c	Result/Command	**he summoned his disciples and said to them,**
2a	assertion	*"I feel compassion for the crowd,*
b	reason	*because they have already been with me three days and have nothing to eat.*
3a	condition	*If I send them to their homes hungry,*
b	result	*they will collapse on the way.*
c	explanation	*And some of them have come from far away."*

Continued on next page.

Continued from previous page.

4a	Response	**His disciples answered him,**
b	question	*"Where in this desolate place can anyone get enough bread to satisfy them?"*
5a	Response	**He asked them,**
b	question	*"How many loaves do you have?"*
c	Response	**They said,**
d	answer	*"Seven."*
6a	Command	**He directed the crowd to sit down on the ground.**
b	Action	Taking the seven loaves and giving thanks,
c		**he broke them and began to give them to his disciples to distribute,**
d	Action	and **they distributed them to the crowd.**
7a	Elaboration	**They also had a few fish.**
b		Blessing these,
c	Command	**he told them to distribute these as well.**
8a	Action/Miracle	**They ate and were satisfied,**
b	Result	and **they picked up seven baskets of leftover pieces.**
9a	Summary	**There were about four thousand present.**
b	Character departure	Then **he dismissed them.**
10a	Character departure	And at once getting into the boat with his disciples,
b		**he went to the region of Dalmanutha.**

Structure

Like the first feeding miracle (6:30 – 44), this one has features typical of a miracle story, with a description of the setting (v. 1), the problem (vv. 2 – 4), the miracle (vv. 5 – 7), and the result (vv. 8 – 10). The significant parallels between the two have raised questions concerning whether they represent a "doublet," that is, two episodes arising from a single event. This question has been discussed above (see Structure on 6:30 – 44), where we noted that the non-Markan vocabulary suggests that Mark himself did not create either episode. Furthermore, the differences in numbers argue against a common antecedent, since the normal pattern of tradition is "to preserve specific details like numbers unchanged while varying the 'scenery.'"[2] The following chart summarizes the similarities and differences between the two episodes.

FEEDING FIVE THOUSAND (6:30 – 44)	FEEDING FOUR THOUSAND (8:1 – 10)
A "great crowd" (πολὺς ὄχλος) arrives ahead of the boat (6:34).	A "large crowd" (πολὺς ὄχλος) gathers "in those days" (8:1).
The crowd runs to the site from the "towns" (πόλεις) of northwestern Galilee (6:33).	The miracle apparently occurs in the Decapolis; some are from "far away" (μακρόθεν) (8:3).
Jesus "had compassion" (σπλαγχνίζομαι), because they are sheep without a shepherd (6:34).	Jesus "had compassion" (σπλαγχνίζομαι) because they have been with him three days without food (8:2).
Jesus teaches them (6:34).	No teaching mentioned.
Food is necessary because it is "late" on the same day (6:35).	Food is necessary because the crowd has been there for three days (8:2).
The disciples initiate, asking Jesus to send the crowd away to buy food, since it is late and "this is a remote/desert/wilderness place" (ἔρημός ἐστιν ὁ τόπος) (6:35 – 36).	Jesus initiates, not wanting to send the crowd away hungry, lest they collapse on the way (8:3).
Jesus says, "You give them something to eat," and the disciples respond with concern for the exorbitant cost (6:37).	The disciples wonder where they will get bread to feed so many since they are in a "remote/desert/ wilderness place" (ἐρημία) (8:4).
Jesus asks how many loaves they have; the answer is five loaves and two fish (6:38).	Jesus asks how many loaves they have; the answer is seven loaves (8:5); a "few fish" are mentioned at the distribution (8:7).
Jesus directs (ἐπιτάσσω) them to recline (ἀνακλίνω) in groups on the green grass (6:39); groups of hundreds and fifties (6:40).	Jesus commands (παραγγέλλω) the crowd to recline (ἀναπίπτω) on the ground (8:6).
Jesus looks to heaven, blesses (εὐλογέω) and breaks (κατακλάω) the bread, and gives it to the disciples to distribute (παρατίθημι) (6:41).	Jesus gives thanks (εὐχαριστέω) and breaks (κλάω) the bread, and gives it to the disciples to distribute (παρατίθημι) (8:6).
Jesus "divides" (μερίζω) the two "fish" (ἰχθύς) among them (6:41).	Jesus "blesses" (εὐλογέω) the few "small fish" (ἰχθύδιον) and orders their distribution (8:7).
All eat and are "satisfied" (χορτάζω) (6:42).	They eat and are "satisfied" (χορτάζω) (8:8).
Twelve baskets (κοφίνος) of fragments (κλασμάτα) are picked up (6:43).	Seven baskets (σπυρίς) of fragments (κλασμάτα) are picked up (8:8).
Five thousand "men" (ἄνδρες) ate, presumably not including women and children (6:44).	Four thousand are present (8:9).
No response to the miracle is recorded.	No response to the miracle is recorded.
Jesus sends the disciples ahead of him to Bethsaida by boat (6:45).	Jesus embarks with the disciples by boat for Dalmanutha (8:10).

Exegetical Outline

Explanation of the Text

8:1a In those days a large crowd was again present (Ἐν ἐκείναις ταῖς ἡμέραις πάλιν πολλοῦ ὄχλου ὄντος). The general time reference, "in those days" (ἐν ἐκείναις ταῖς ἡμέραις), links the episode loosely to the previous one and thus probably to the region of the Decapolis (7:31).[3] The reference to a "large crowd" (πολὺς ὄχλος) last occurred in the previous feeding miracle (6:34), so that "again" (πάλιν) points back to that event.

The most important question here with reference to Mark's narrative theology is whether he envisions the context as predominantly Gentile, thus being a complement to the (Jewish) feeding of the five thousand. While a few scholars have rejected this,[4] the majority affirm it[5] based on a number of considerations.

1. The broader context in Mark's gospel is Jesus' excursion into Gentile territories and healings involving Gentiles, including the faith of the Syrophoenician woman (7:24 – 30) and the healing of a deaf and mute man in the Decapolis (7:31 – 37).

2. Without further contextual or geographical indicators, we may assume the event occurred in the Decapolis (7:31; 8:1), a predominantly Gentile region.

3. Mark says some of the people had come from "afar" (μακρόθεν), an expression commonly referring to Gentile lands (Isa 60:4, 9; Jer 46:27 LXX; see comments on 8:1b – 3).

4. Mark's inclusion of a second, nearly identical feeding miracle begs for an explanation; Jewish

3. The claim that "in those days" has eschatological connotations (in light of 1:9; 13:17, 24; etc.) seems far-fetched (contra Marcus, *Mark 1 – 8*, 487; Boring, *Mark*, 219). The phrase is too general for such a connotation to be present without further contextual indicators.

4. Hooker, *Mark*, 187 – 88; Stein, *Mark*, 367 – 68; Fowler, *Loaves and Fishes*, 60 – 61.

5. E.g., Cranfield, *Mark*, 255; Guelich, *Mark 1:1 – 8:26*, 408 – 9; Marcus, *Mark 1 – 8*, 487; Hurtado, *Mark*, 121 – 23; Boring, *Mark*, 219; Donahue and Harrington, *Mark*, 246; France, *Mark*, 305; F. W. Danker, "Mark 8:5," *JBL* 82 (1963): 215 – 16.

and Gentile feedings provide a logical one and fit well with Mark's narrative theology concerning the expansion of the gospel beyond Israel.

5. While the term for "basket" used in the first feeding is commonly associated with the Jews (6:43, κοφίνος; Juvenal, *Sat.* 3:14; 6.542), the one used here is a more general one and fits a broader Gentile audience (σπυρίς, 8:8).

6. The number "twelve" in the baskets of leftovers in the first feeding naturally recalls Israel. Whether the number "seven" can be identified with Gentiles is more debated. Some suggested allusions include the seven Hellenistic "deacons" of Acts 6:1 – 6,[6] the traditional seventy nations of the world in rabbinic Judaism (cf. Luke 10:1),[7] the seven Noachide commandments for all nations (Gen 9:4 – 7),[8] and the seven nations of Canaan (Deut 7:1; Acts 13:19). None of these is convincing. The seven men chosen in Acts 6 were Hellenistic Jews, not Gentiles, and the number seven is not the same as seventy. Seven is a common number in Scripture, often indicating completeness, without any Gentile connotations. While these last two arguments are far from convincing, the cumulative case for a Gentile context is strong.

8:1b – 3 Since they had nothing to eat, he summoned his disciples and said to them, "I feel compassion for the crowd, because they have already been with me three days and have nothing to eat. If I send them to their homes hungry, they will collapse on the way. And some of them have come from far away (καὶ μὴ ἐχόντων τί φάγωσιν, προσκαλεσάμενος τοὺς μαθητὰς λέγει αὐτοῖς· σπλαγχνίζομαι ἐπὶ τὸν ὄχλον, ὅτι ἤδη ἡμέραι τρεῖς προσμένουσίν μοι καὶ οὐκ ἔχουσιν τί φάγωσιν· καὶ ἐὰν ἀπολύσω αὐτοὺς νήστεις εἰς οἶκον αὐτῶν, ἐκλυθήσονται ἐν τῇ ὁδῷ· καί τινες αὐτῶν ἀπὸ μακρόθεν ἥκασιν).

There are both similarities and differences with the feeding of the five thousand. There the disciples initiated the discussion (6:35 – 36); here it is Jesus (8:3). There the crowd had been present for the whole day (6:35); here it has been three days (8:2). In both Jesus feels compassion for the crowds (σπλαγχνίζομαι),[9] though in the first miracle it was because the people were like sheep without a shepherd (6:34); here it is because they had been with him "three days" with nothing to eat and would collapse on the journey home (8:2). This, of course, does not mean that no one had eaten anything for three days, but rather that there was no organized food distribution and that any personal provisions would have been exhausted.

The reference to three days is intended to show the severity of the problem and the pressing need for food. It is overly subtle to find an allusion to biblical journeys of three days,[10] three-day fasts before a significant event,[11] or even the resurrection of Jesus.[12] Sometimes a time reference is simply a time reference, without symbolic significance; such seems to be the case here.

Jesus does not want to send the people home hungry, since some have come "from afar" (μακρόθεν).

6. Klosterman, *Markusevangelium*, 75; W. Grundmann, *Das Evangelium nach Markus* (THKNT 2; Berlin: Evangelische Verlagsanstalt, 1977), 284.

7. Pesch, *Markusevangelium*, 1:404. In addition to the "table of nations" in Gen 11, there is the Animal Apocalypse in *1 En.* 83 – 90; L. Ginzberg, *The Legends of the Jews* (7 vols.; Philadelphia: Jewish Publication Society, 1909 – 38), 5:194 – 95 n. 72; Marcus, *Mark 1 – 8*, 489.

8. Marcus, *Mark 1 – 8*, 489.

9. Jesus is said to act out of compassion twice in Mark's gospel, here and in 6:34, though there is also the textually disputed reference in 1:41, the healing of the man with leprosy.

10. Gen 30:36; Exod 3:18; 5:3; 8:27; Num 10:33; Josh 1:11; so Donahue and Harrington, *Mark*, 244.

11. 1 Sam 30:12; Esth 4:16; Donahue and Harrington, *Mark*, 244.

12. Boring, *Mark*, 219; Marcus, *Mark 1 – 8*, 492. Boring also sees eschatological overtones in the introduction, "in those days."

As noted above, this may hint at a predominantly Gentile crowd. The LXX commonly uses this word with reference to Gentile lands (Deut 28:49; 29:22; Josh 9:6; 60:4; cf. 1 Kgs 8:41 [ἐκ γῆς πόρρωθε]), and similar language appears in the NT. Peter tells the Jews of Jerusalem that "the promise is for you and your children and for all who are far off [πᾶσιν τοῖς εἰς μακράν] — for all whom the Lord our God will call" (Acts 2:39; cf. 22:21). Paul, too, says Christ "came and preached peace to you who were far away [ὑμῖν τοῖς μακρὰν] and peace to those who were near" (Eph 2:17) — again a reference to the Gentiles (cf. vv. 11–13).

8:4 His disciples answered him, "Where in this wilderness can anyone get enough bread to satisfy them?" (καὶ ἀπεκρίθησαν αὐτῷ οἱ μαθηταὶ αὐτοῦ ὅτι πόθεν τούτους δυνήσεταί τις ὧδε χορτάσαι ἄρτων ἐπ᾽ ἐρημίας;). The disciples' question, which was understandable in the context of the first feeding miracle (6:37), seems inexplicable now. How could they have forgotten so quickly what Jesus did before?[13] Cranfield offers various suggestions, including the possibility that considerable time has passed since the first feeding miracle, or that the disciples did not want to presume that Jesus would respond to every human need with a miracle.[14]

Gundry offers a different solution, claiming that the disciples' question does not present them in a negative light but rather reflects their more dire circumstances. This time they are in a true wilderness (ἐρημία; 8:4) rather than simply a "remote place" (ἔρημος τόπος; 6:31, 32, 35) in an otherwise populated territory. Their plight is also more desperate since three days have passed without food

(8:2), rather than merely an afternoon of teaching (6:35).[15] The disciples are therefore responding appropriately under the circumstances. But this explanation seems stretched in light of close parallels between the two accounts and the negative portrayal of the disciples in the near context (8:17–18). Furthermore, there is little evidence that Mark is drawing a distinction between a "wilderness" (ἐρημία; 8:4) and a "remote place" (ἔρημός τόπος; 6:31, 32, 35).

The disciples' question is better understood in the context of Mark's narrative theology, where it serves two purposes: first, to emphasize the authority of Jesus, and second, to contrast this with the spiritual dullness of the disciples. As with the first feeding miracle, Jesus provides bread in the wilderness in the same way God provided manna to the Israelites. The disciples' question, "Who could provide food for this crowd…?" is resoundingly answered in the narrative with, "Jesus the Messiah can!"

Second, the question develops the theme of the spiritual insensitivity of the disciples. Throughout this part of the gospel, Mark presents the disciples in an increasingly negative light. In 6:52, after Jesus walks on water, Mark points out that their hearts were hard so that they could not understand the (first) miracle of the loaves. In an episode that follows, Jesus will warn them against the leaven of the Pharisees and the leaven of Herod (8:15). Throughout chapters 8–10 they will repeatedly misunderstand Jesus' suffering role and repeatedly demonstrate pride and self-centeredness. The question here fits this pattern of spiritual insensitivity to God's purpose.

---

13. Some have claimed that the disciples' question is evidence for a doublet (so Boring, *Mark*, 220). But Mark would not have been so clumsy of editor as to retain the question, unless it were part of his narrative presentation. And if it fits well with his narrative intention, there is no need to attribute it

to a doublet. We would also have to attribute the same editorial blunder to Matthew, since he too retains the question in his version (Matt 15:33).
14. Cranfield, *Mark*, 205.
15. Gundry, *Mark*, 393–94.

8:5 – 7 He asked them, "How many loaves do you have?" They said, "Seven." He directed the crowd to sit down on the ground. Taking the seven loaves and giving thanks, he broke them and began to give them to his disciples to distribute, and they distributed them to the crowd. They also had a few fish. Blessing these, he told them to distribute these as well (καὶ ἠρώτα αὐτούς· πόσους ἔχετε ἄρτους; οἱ δὲ εἶπαν· ἑπτά. καὶ παραγγέλλει τῷ ὄχλῳ ἀναπεσεῖν ἐπὶ τῆς γῆς· καὶ λαβὼν τοὺς ἑπτὰ ἄρτους εὐχαριστήσας ἔκλασεν καὶ ἐδίδου τοῖς μαθηταῖς αὐτοῦ ἵνα παρατιθῶσιν, καὶ παρέθηκαν τῷ ὄχλῳ. καὶ εἶχον ἰχθύδια ὀλίγα· καὶ εὐλογήσας αὐτὰ εἶπεν καὶ ταῦτα παρατιθέναι).

The story plays out in much the same way as the first feeding miracle, though with less detail. As noted above (v. 1a), though the twelve basketfuls of the first feeding may symbolize Israel, there is no clear symbolism related to the number seven. None of the proposed "sevens" makes much sense. It seems best to avoid allegorization and accept the number at face value. This conclusion is reinforced by the general reference to "a few fish" in v. 7.

As in the first miracle, Jesus tells the people to "recline" (here ἀναπίπτω rather than ἀνακλίνω), but there is no reference to "green grass" or to the militaristic-sounding groupings of hundreds and fifties (6:39 – 40). The distribution of the bread has eucharistic connotations similar to those as in the first feeding. Instead of "blessing" (εὐλογέω) and "breaking" (κατακλάω) the bread (6:41), Jesus here "gives thanks" (εὐχαριστέω) and "breaks" (κλάω) the bread, but then "blesses" (εὐλογήσας) the fish. The fish are presented almost as an afterthought, perhaps to give priority to the eucharistic imagery associated with the bread. Mark's account of the Last Supper uses similar language, but reverses the order of "blessing" (εὐλογέω) and "thanking" (εὐχαριστέω; 14:22 – 23). The differences are stylistic, since "thanking" and "blessing" are practically synonymous.

8:8 – 9a They ate and were satisfied, and they picked up seven baskets of leftover pieces. There were about four thousand present (καὶ ἔφαγον καὶ ἐχορτάσθησαν, καὶ ἦραν περισσεύματα κλασμάτων ἑπτὰ σπυρίδας. ἦσαν δὲ ὡς τετρακισχίλιοι). As in the first feeding, the disciples both distribute the food and pick up the leftovers. While the first miracle concluded with "*All ate* and were satisfied" (6:42), this one simply says, "*They ate* and were satisfied." Again the emphasis is on the superabundance of food, reminiscent of the messianic banquet (Isa 25:6 – 8). In the first feeding, the number of baskets of leftovers corresponded to the number of disciples who gathered them; here the number corresponds to the loaves distributed.[16] The number has no obvious symbolic sense (completeness?) and probably simply indicates an abundance that overflows into surplus. While the first miracle apparently fed five thousand "men" (ἄνδρες), not counting the women and children, this one refers simply to "four thousand," presumably the total number of people present.

8:9b – 10 Then he dismissed them. And at once getting into the boat with his disciples, he went to the region of Dalmanutha (καὶ ἀπέλυσεν αὐτούς. Καὶ εὐθὺς ἐμβὰς εἰς τὸ πλοῖον μετὰ τῶν μαθητῶν αὐτοῦ ἦλθεν εἰς τὰ μέρη Δαλμανουθά). The UBS text punctuates v. 9b as a separate sentence (as in our translation; cf. KJV, NASB, ESV, NET), but it is closely connected to the departure and could be seen as an introductory clause to v. 10 ("After dismissing them …"; cf. NIV, HCSB, REB).

---

16. As noted earlier, the present account uses a more general term for "basket" (σπυρίς), which appears in Acts 9:25 for a basket large enough to lower the apostle Paul over the wall of Damascus. The first feeding miracle had κοφίνος, evidently a small wicker basket used by Jews to carry possessions or food.

The sentence functions both as the conclusion to the present episode and the introduction to the next (which is "framed" by boat trips; vv. 10, 13). Both feeding miracles end with Jesus dismissing the crowds (6:45; 8:9b) and a boat journey (6:45; 8:10). After the first, Jesus sent the disciples away and then came to them walking on the water (6:45, 48). In this second, Jesus departs with them by boat to the environs of "Dalmanutha."

No location with the name Dalmanutha (Δαλμανουθά) is known from ancient sources, but it was apparently located on the western (Jewish) shore of the lake, since Jesus is met there by Pharisees (8:11). The unknown location accounts for a variety of textual variants, including "Magadan" (Μαγαδάν) — also an unknown location — and "Magdala," a village located about five kilometers north of Tiberias on the northwestern shore of Galilee (the likely hometown of Mary Magdalene).[17] These readings appear to be assimilations to Matthew's text (15:39), which has both variants. "Magadan" (Μαγαδάν) has the better attestation in Matthew (א B D) and was likely his original reading, though the two may be alternate spellings of the same place. Our best guess is that Dalmanutha was an anchorage or village in the environs of Magdala/Magadan, a fishing village north of Tiberias.[18]

Theology in Application

Mark's second feeding miracle repeats the main themes found in the first (6:30 – 44).

Jesus' Messianic Authority

He is the good shepherd who has compassion on the sheep and the spiritual and physical resources to meet their needs. God's people can rest assured that in times of need he will provide for them.

Symbolizing God's Salvation — Past, Present, and Future

The feeding also has salvation-historical and eschatological significance, pointing to God's actions in the past, present, and future. It looks back to Israel's provision of manna in the wilderness, where God demonstrated his power to provide for his people when they were without resources in a "desert" region. Its eucharistic imagery (cf. 14:22 – 24) reminds readers in the present of the bread and cup as remembrance of the gift of salvation provided through Christ's life, death, and resurrection. The miracle also points forward to the messianic banquet (Isa 25:6 – 7), symbolic of God's final salvation and eternal provision for his people. That the people eat until they are satisfied, with abundant leftovers, is a picture of the new creation, when there will be no more famine or shortage.

---

17. τα μερη Μαγδαλα: Θ *f*¹ ¹³ 565 2542 pc it; τα ορια Μαγαδα: D aur c.

18. See J. F. Strange, "Dalmanutha," *ABD*, 2:4.

The Spiritual Failure of the Disciples

While in the first miracle the disciples' failure to anticipate Jesus' miraculous provision was understandable, here it seems inexcusable. Although there is no explicit rebuke from Jesus or from the narrator, the larger context makes this point. The narrator's comments in 6:52 that "they had not understood about the loaves" and Jesus' strong rebuke that will follow in 8:17 – 21 make it clear that the disciples are on the verge of spiritual blindness and deafness.

Salvation for the Gentiles

A new application, not present in the first feeding, is the expansion of the salvation blessings to the Gentiles. Some scholars, as we have seen, deny the presence of this theme here, since there is no explicit reference to Gentiles or to Gentile lands. Yet there is sufficient evidence in the near context to affirm it, including Jesus' ministry to Gentiles (7:24 – 30) and his presence in the Decapolis (7:31). The inclusion of the nations is not surprising in a passage with such strong eschatological implication. Mark's favorite prophet, Isaiah, envisioned the day when the nations would stream to the mountain of the Lord to learn his ways and to worship him (Isa 2:2 – 3; cf. Mic 4:1 – 2); the messianic banquet is not for Israel alone, but "for all peoples" everywhere (Isa 25:6). God's salvation is destined to go forth to the ends of the earth (49:6; Acts 1:8), to those who are near as well as those who are "far off" (Acts 2:39).

30

Mark 8:11 – 13

Literary Context

The request for a sign by the Pharisees serves several purposes in the literary context of Mark's gospel. As noted previously (see table in Literary Context on 8:1 – 10), the sequence of episodes in 6:31 – 7:37 parallels those of 8:1 – 30, so that the conflict with the Pharisees in 7:1 – 23 has its counterpart here (8:10 – 13). The passage also serves as the last in a series of conflicts with the religious leaders during Jesus' Galilean ministry (2:16, 18, 24; 3:6; 7:1, 5), which sets the stage for the showdown in Jerusalem. Finally, the conflict with the Pharisees forms a pair with the next episode, where the disciples are warned about the "leaven of the Pharisees" and are in danger of succumbing to the same failure of faith (8:14 – 21).

Main Idea

When the Pharisees — representing the present generation of unrepentant Israel — test Jesus by asking for a sign from heaven, Jesus expresses deep frustration and refuses to give them a sign.

Translation

Mark 8:11 – 13

11a	Character entrance	Then **the Pharisees came and began to question him,**
b		asking him for a sign from heaven in order to ☞
		test him.
12a		Sighing deeply in his spirit,
b	Response	**he said,**
c	question	*"Why does this generation ask for a sign?*
d	veracity statement	*Truly I say to you, no sign will be given to this generation."*
13a	Character departure	Then leaving them and
b		getting into the boat again,
		he crossed to the other side.

Structure

The passage is a combination of a controversy and a pronouncement story and has a chiastic structure:

A Jesus crosses the Sea of Galilee to Dalmanutha (v. 10).

   B The Pharisees request a sign (v. 11).

   B′ Jesus responds (v. 12).

A′ Jesus travels back across the sea (v. 13).

The challenge by the Pharisees is met with Jesus' authoritative pronouncement, "Truly I say to you, no sign will be given to this generation" (v. 12).

Exegetical Outline

➡ **1. The Request of the Pharisees: A Sign from Heaven (8:11)**

  2. Jesus' Response: No Sign Will Be Given (8:12)

  3. Return to the "Other Side" (8:13)

Explanation of the Text

8:11 Then the Pharisees came and began to question him, asking him for a sign from heaven in order to test him (Καὶ ἐξῆλθον οἱ Φαρισαῖοι καὶ ἤρξαντο συζητεῖν αὐτῷ, ζητοῦντες παρ᾿ αὐτοῦ σημεῖον ἀπὸ τοῦ οὐρανοῦ, πειράζοντες αὐτόν). The boat trip to Dalmanutha in 8:10 both concludes the feeding miracle and introduces the present story, which is framed on either side by a boat trip. The whole episode is oddly abrupt: Jesus crosses the sea (v. 10), has a brief conversation with the Pharisees (vv. 11 – 12), then immediately crosses back (v. 13).[1] Mark uses it to remind readers of the Pharisaic opposition to Jesus and to prepare for the passage on the "leaven of the Pharisees" that follows (8:14 – 21).

The verb translated "question" (συζητέω) can mean "discuss, dispute, debate, argue." Mark sometimes uses it in a neutral sense of discussion (1:27; 9:10), but more often in contexts of hostile challenge or argumentation (8:11; 9:14, 16; 12:28). The goal of the Pharisees here is "to test" (πειράζοντες) him, an adverbial participle indicating purpose. The same verb is used of Jesus' testing/temptation by Satan in the wilderness (1:13) and will appear again in 10:2 and 12:15 in further attempts by the Pharisees to trap Jesus in his words.

Here they request "a sign from heaven." Although "sign" (σημεῖον) is commonly used in John's gospel with reference to Jesus' miracles (2:11, 23; 3:2; 4:48, 54, etc.), here it means something more general like "proof" or "authentication." Mark generally uses "power/miracle" (δύναμις) for individual miracles, such as healings and exorcisms (6:2, 5; 9:39).[2] A sign "from heaven" (ἀπὸ τοῦ οὐρανοῦ) may mean a cosmic or apocalyptic sign in the sky (Matt 24:30; Luke 11:16; 21:11, 25; Acts 2:19; Rev 12:3; 13:13; 15:1),[3] but more likely it is used here as a circumlocution for "from God."[4] It is unlikely that the Pharisees denied that Jesus performed miracles, especially in light of his remarkable reputation as a healer and exorcist. In 3:22 the Pharisees acknowledge Jesus' exorcisms, but attribute them to Satan. So they are not just asking for a miracle. They are demanding evidence that his authority indeed comes from God.

Authenticating signs are common in the OT and Judaism, especially with reference to the Exodus (Exod 4:8 – 9, 17, 28; 10:1 – 2; Deut 4:34). Yet they are not ultimate tests of divine authority, since false prophets can also perform them (Deut 13:1 – 2; cf. Mark 13:22; 2 Thess 2:9; Rev 13:11 – 15). While God sometimes provides signs to those who request them (Judg 6:36 – 40; 2 Kgs 20:8 – 11) and even demands that Ahaz ask for a sign (Isa 7:10 – 12), in general such requests are considered dangerously presumptive, an example of "testing" the Lord God (Matt 4:7; Luke 4:12; cf. Deut 6:16). In the Gospels, those who ask for signs have refused to believe the evidence already given to them (Matt 12:39; 16:4; Luke 11:16, 29; John 2:18 – 19; 6:30).[5] The passage

---

1. Marcus, *Mark 1 – 8*, 502.

2. The same is true of the other Synoptics, although in Acts, Luke frequently uses "sign" (σημεῖον) in the sense of authenticating miracles.

3. J. Gibson, "Jesus' Refusal to Produce a 'Sign' (MK 8.11 – 13)," *JSNT* 11 (1989): 37 – 66.

4. Guelich, *Mark 1:1 – 8:26*, 413 – 14; Pesch, *Markusevangelium*, 1:407; J. Gnilka, *Das Evangelium nach Markus* (EKKNT 2/1 – 2; Zürich: Benzinger/Neukirchen-Vluyn: Neukirchener Verlag, 1978), 1:306 – 7.

5. The request for a sign in John 6:30 has striking parallels with this one, since it occurs after a feeding miracle (6:1 – 15) and a journey across the lake (6:16 – 21) and is followed by a discussion about bread (6:31 – 58). This is sometimes used as evidence that the second feeding miracle is a doublet, since it has these features in common with John's account of the feeding of the five thousand. The discussion about bread, however, is very different in the two gospels. With all the boat journeys in Mark, the parallels are likely to be coincidental.

recalls Paul's statement in 1 Cor 1:22 that, while Greeks seek wisdom, "Jews demand signs."

8:12 Sighing deeply in his spirit, he said, "Why does this generation ask for a sign? Truly I say to you, no sign will be given to this generation." (καὶ ἀναστενάξας τῷ πνεύματι αὐτοῦ λέγει· τί ἡ γενεὰ αὕτη ζητεῖ σημεῖον; ἀμὴν λέγω ὑμῖν, εἰ δοθήσεται τῇ γενεᾷ ταύτῃ σημεῖον). Jesus' "deep sighing" has been interpreted in a variety of ways. Marcus considers it to be evidence of a demonic struggle.[6] This is unlikely, since there is no mention of the demonic in the context. Many others view it as grief and deep frustration at the hardness of hearts evident in Israel's religious leaders.[7] Still others find here a summoning of deep inner strength in preparation for a prophetic action or pronouncement (cf. John 13:21; Ezek 21:11 – 12 LXX).[8]

Although the verb "sigh deeply" (ἀναστενάζω) is a *hapax legomenon* (occurring only once) in the NT, its cognate "to sigh" (στενάζω) appears in 7:34 with reference to Jesus' healing of the deaf and mute man. In that case, Jesus appears to be responding with intense prayer in preparation for the healing. Here he could be drawing on inner strength to make his authoritative pronouncement ("Truly I say to you …"). In light of the context, however, a sigh of grief and frustration at the obstinacy of the religious leaders seems more likely.

Jesus begins with a rhetorical question that already reveals the hypocrisy of the Pharisees' request.[9] The request for a sign is unnecessary since they have already been blessed with the power and presence of the kingdom of God in Jesus' words and deeds! The phrase "this generation" (ἡ γενεὰ αὕτη) can be used neutrally in the Bible, but often it carries a pejorative sense, as when recalling the sinful generation of the flood (Gen 7:1) or the grumbling generation of Israelites in the wilderness (Deut 1:35; 32:5, 20; Ps 95:10 – 11).[10] This latter is particularly significant in light of the "desert/wilderness" context of both feeding miracles and their allusions to the provision of manna in the wilderness. Mark's readers would surely think of the sinful wilderness generation and the punishment they received for their disobedience. Jesus will speak again of "this adulterous and sinful generation" in 8:38 and "O unbelieving generation" in 9:19.

This is the second occurrence of Jesus' solemn introductory formula, "Truly I say to you" (ἀμὴν λέγω ὑμῖν), which appears thirteen times in Mark (see comments at 3:28). What follows is a Semitic oath formula. The oath is commonly translated in English versions as something like, "No sign will be given to this generation!"[11] But a literal rendering of the Greek is, "If a sign will be given to this generation" (εἰ δοθήσεται τῇ γενεᾷ ταύτῃ σημεῖον). This is the protasis (the "if" part) of a conditional sentence. The apodosis ("May God …") is implied and has dropped through ellipsis. The oath is self-imprecatory and means something like, "May God judge me severely if a sign will be given to this generation" — hence the idiomatic translation: "No

6. Marcus, *Mark 1 – 8*, 474, 504; cf. Bonner, "Thaumaturgic Technique in the Miracles," 171 – 81.

7. Taylor, *Mark*, 362; Lane, *Mark*, 277; Hooker, *Mark*, 192; France, *Mark*, 312; Jeffrey B. Gibson, "Mark 8.12a: Why Does Jesus 'Sigh Deeply'?" *BT* 38 (1987): 122 – 25.

8. Pesch, *Markusevangelium*, 1:408; Guelich, *Mark 1:1 – 8:26*, 414; Gundry, *Mark*, 404; Stein, *Mark*, 376.

9. Guelich, *Mark 1:1 – 8:26*, 414.

10. E. Lövestam, *Jesus and "This Generation": A New Testament Study* (ConBNT 25; Stockholm: Almqvist & Wiuksell, 1995), 24 – 26; Marcus, *Mark 1 – 8*, 501; Moloney, *Mark*, 158.

The rabbis spoke of these generations being unworthy of sharing in the world to come (*m. Sanh.* 10:3).

11. While in Mark Jesus refuses to give any more signs, in the "Q" parallels in Matthew and Luke he offers the "sign of the prophet Jonah" (Matt 12:39; 16:4; Luke 11:29). For Matthew this is the resurrection: as Jonah was in the belly of the great fish three days and nights, so will the Son of Man be in the heart of the earth (Matt 12:40). For Luke, the sign appears to be the preaching of Jonah to the Ninevites, which resulted in their repentance.

sign will be given to this generation." Similar oath formulas appear in the OT. Psalm 94:11 LXX (English: 95:11) reads, "So I swore in my anger, if they will enter into my rest" (ὡς ὤμοσα ἐν τῇ ὀργῇ μου εἰ εἰσελεύσονται εἰς τὴν κατάπαυσίν μου), meaning, "They will surely *not* enter my rest" (cf. Gen 14:23; Num 32:11; Deut 1:35; 1 Kgs 3:14).

8:13 Then leaving them and getting into the boat again, he crossed to the other side (καὶ ἀφεὶς αὐτοὺς πάλιν ἐμβὰς ἀπῆλθεν εἰς τὸ πέραν). Jesus' authoritative pronouncement in v. 12 has a sense of finality about it, and he now turns and leaves as abruptly as he came. The finality recalls Jesus'

words in 4:11 – 12, where he declared that the religious leaders would be ever seeing but never perceiving, ever hearing but never understanding (Isa 6:9 – 10). It is significant, then, that the next episode with the disciples will echo these very words (Mark 8:18).

The "other side" of the lake is the northeastern shore, since the boat will arrive at Bethsaida in 8:22. This departure appears to close a major chapter in Jesus' ministry. Although he will have brief contact with the Pharisees again in 10:2, this is the last real opposition he will face from them before Jerusalem. For the next three chapters Jesus will be working primarily with his disciples.

Theology in Application

The Pharisees as Opponents of Jesus and the Kingdom of God

This short passage brings the Pharisees back into the narrative and reminds the reader of their intractable opposition to Jesus and his mission (2:16, 24; 3:6; 7:1, 5; cf. 2:6; 3:22). The episode is both ironic and climactic. It is ironic since in the feeding of the four thousand Jesus has just given a remarkable sign, which parallels the "bread from heaven" that God gave Israel in the wilderness. It is climactic in that it serves as the last in a series of controversies with the Pharisees that occur during Jesus' Galilean ministry. Though Jesus has been performing remarkable signs, the Pharisees seem blind to their significance and demand further confirmation. Jesus, in turn, rebukes them sternly and announces that no sign will be given to "this generation."

Like the wilderness generation of Moses' day, who put God to the test, the religious leaders test Jesus out of their unbelief and stubborn hearts. The consequence is that no sign will be given. Jesus "departs" across the lake and leaves them to their fate. The passage recalls 3:22 – 30, where, in the face of similar rejection, Jesus accuses the Pharisees of blaspheming the Holy Spirit and then begins teaching them in parables, so that they will keep on seeing but not perceive, and keep on hearing but not comprehend (4:11; citing Isa 6:9 – 10). Though the disciples are also stubborn and spiritually dull, they remain (tenuously) on the side of Jesus and he remains faithful to them. In the chapters that follow, Jesus will model for them the humble path of service and suffering that leads to glory.

The Dangers of Pride and Spiritual Blindness

Like the Pharisees, we are sometimes blind to the spiritual realities around us and the "signs" that are manifestations of God's presence and power. How could the Pharisees not have recognized the hand of God in Jesus' miracles? The likely answer is that they were obsessed with their own authority and position and viewed Jesus as a threat. All of us need to take care lest the things of this world — position, power, money — blind us to the greater purposes of the kingdom of God.

31

Mark 8:14 – 21

Literary Context

This episode fits structurally into Mark's gospel in at least three ways. (1) It is connected to the previous one both in its narrative context (it takes place during the boat journey begun in v. 13) and its theme. The Pharisees' decisive rejection of Jesus in vv. 11 – 13 forms the backdrop to his conversation with the disciples, who are dangerously close to going the way of the Pharisees. (2) It is also part of the sequence of episodes in 8:1 – 30 that parallels those of 6:31 – 7:37 (see chart in Literary Context on 8:1 – 10). Jesus' discussion about bread with the Syrophoenician woman (7:24 – 30) parallels the discussion about bread with the disciples (8:14 – 21). Her remarkable spiritual insight that God's plan of salvation involves even the Gentiles stands in stark contrast to the disciples' dullness when it comes to spiritual truth. (3) Finally, this is the third of three boat scenes in Mark (4:35 – 41; 6:45 – 52; 8:13 – 21), each of which, in some way, illustrates the disciples' lack of faith or failure to comprehend Jesus' mission or identity.

II. The Authority of the Messiah (1:14 – 8:21)

    II. The Authority of the Messiah (1:14 – 8:21)
        C. The Expanding Mission of the Messiah (6:6b – 8:21)
            8. Healing a Deaf and Mute Man (7:31 – 37)
            9. Feeding the Four Thousand (8:1 – 10)
            10. Requesting a Sign from Heaven (8:11 – 13)
    →   **11. Warning against the Leaven of the Pharisees and of Herod (8:14 – 21)**
    III. The Suffering Way of the Messiah (8:22 – 15:47)

Main Idea

Jesus cautions the disciples against the "leaven" of the Pharisees and of Herod and warns them against spiritual blindness and deafness. Though they are in danger of going the way of the religious leaders (cf. 4:12), Jesus seeks to stir up their faith by reminding them of the two feeding miracles and the overflowing blessings of the kingdom of God.

Translation

Mark 8:14 – 21

14a	Statement of fact	**They had forgotten to bring bread,**
b	exception	except for one loaf they had with them in the boat.
15a	Instruction/Warning	**He warned them, saying,**
b		*"Watch out! Beware the leaven of the Pharisees and the leaven of Herod."*
16	Response to 15a	**They began arguing with one another about not having bread.**
17a		Aware of their discussion,
b	Response to 16/Warning	Jesus said to them,
c	rhetorical question	*"Why are you arguing about not having bread?*
d	rhetorical question	*Do you not yet comprehend or understand?*
e	rhetorical question	*Are your hearts hardened?*
18a	rhetorical question	*Do you have eyes but cannot see and*
b		*ears but do not hear?*
c	rhetorical question	*And don't you remember?*
19a	question	*When I broke the five loaves for the five thousand,*
b		*how many baskets full of pieces did you pick up?"*
c	Response to 19a	**They answered him**
d		*"Twelve."*
20a	question	*"And when I broke the seven loaves for the four ☙ thousand,*
b		*how many baskets full of fragments did you pick up?"*
c	Response to 20b	**They said,**
d		*"Seven."*
21a	Rhetorical question	**He was saying to them,**
b		*"Do you not yet understand?"*

Structure

The episode is a controversy story involving the disciples (8:14 – 17a) and teaching provided by Jesus (8:17b – 21). The first half concerns a conversation about bread, highlighting the misunderstanding of the disciples. Jesus then rebukes them for their misunderstanding and teaches them through a series of five rhetorical questions (vv. 17 – 18), two Socratic-style questions (vv. 19 – 20), and a final rhetorical question (v. 21) — all meant to lead them into greater spiritual understanding. The eight questions are framed on either side by the most important one, repeated for emphasis: "Do you not yet … understand?" (vv. 17, 21). Though emphasizing their lack of spiritual insight, the "not yet" (οὔπω) indicates there is still opportunity to respond.

Exegetical Outline

→ **1. Confusion about Leaven and Bread (8:14 – 16)**

    a. The disciples' failure to bring bread (8:14)

    b. Jesus' warning against the leaven of the Pharisees and of Herod (8:15)

    c. The misunderstanding of the disciples (8:16)

2. Jesus' Response (8:17 – 21)

    a. Warning against spiritual blindness and deafness (8:17 – 18)

    b. Reminder of the abundance of the feeding miracles (8:19 – 20)

    c. Final warning (8:21)

Explanation of the Text

8:14 They had forgotten to bring bread, except for one loaf they had with them in the boat (Καὶ ἐπελάθοντο λαβεῖν ἄρτους καὶ εἰ μὴ ἕνα ἄρτον οὐκ εἶχον μεθ᾽ ἑαυτῶν ἐν τῷ πλοίῳ). The subject, though unexpressed, is clearly the disciples. The plural "breads" (ἄρτους) means small loaves of bread, so the singular is appropriately translated "loaf." These would have been small, pita-sized loaves suitable for one person's lunch.

The referent of the "one loaf" has been debated. Some consider it to be Jesus himself.[1] Evidence for this, it is said, is the christological focus of the present pericope and Jesus' identification of himself as the bread in the eucharistic words of the Last Supper (14:22). First Corinthians 10:17 uses the term "one loaf" with reference to the Eucharist. Marcus writes, "For Mark's readers, then, our passage would be reminiscent of 4:35 – 41: the anxiety of the disciples is needless; they have Jesus with them 'in the boat,' which may be a symbol of the church."[2]

Mark, however, tends not to use such allegorical

symbols, and there are few indicators in the context of such a symbolic meaning.[3] It would also seem to be disjunctive with the "leaven" of the Pharisees and Herod, which is the primary point of the story.[4] More likely, the point is that the one loaf is inadequate in the disciples' thinking to feed the twelve disciples, just as the five and seven loaves were inadequate to feed the multitudes.

8:15 He warned them, saying, "Watch out! Beware the leaven of the Pharisees and the leaven of Herod." (καὶ διεστέλλετο αὐτοῖς λέγων· ὁρᾶτε, βλέπετε ἀπὸ τῆς ζύμης τῶν Φαρισαίων καὶ τῆς ζύμης Ἡρῴδου). Jesus' warning is emphatic. The verb "warn" (διαστέλλω) elsewhere refers to strong orders that must be obeyed (5:43; 7:36; 9:9). This is followed by two present imperatives that are near synonyms (ὁρᾶτε, βλέπετε; cf. 1:44; 4:24; 13:5, 9, 23, 33), both meaning "watch out," "beware," or "be careful to avoid."

"Leaven" (ζύμη) refers to a small amount of dough left over from the previous week's batch that

---

1. Boring, *Mark*, 226 – 27; Pesch, *Markusevangelium*, 1:414 – 15; Marcus, *Mark 1 – 8*, 509 – 10; Garland, *Mark*, 310; Quesnell, *The Mind of Mark*, 231 – 32; N. A. Beck, "Reclaiming a Biblical Text: The Mark 8:14 – 21 Discussion about Bread in the Boat," *CBQ* 43 (1981): 49 – 56; E. LaVerdiere, "'Who Do You Say That I Am?'" *Emmanuel* 96 (1990): 454 – 63; J. Manek,

"Mark viii. 14 – 21," *NovT* 7 (1964): 10 – 14.

2. Marcus, *Mark 1 – 8*, 510.

3. Opposing this view are Guelich, *Mark 1:1 – 8:26*, 421; Gundry, *Mark*, 410 – 11; France, *Mark*, 315 n. 19.

4. Edwards, *Mark*, 237 n. 12.

was mixed in with the new to make the bread rise.[5] Though leaven can be used biblically in a positive or neutral sense (Matt 13:33; par. Luke 13:21), it more commonly serves as a symbol of unholiness, sin, or evil (cf. Matt 16: 6–8; 1 Cor 5:6; Gal 5:9).[6] The OT background is God's command related to the exodus and the Feast of Unleavened Bread, when leaven was to be removed from the home and the penalty of eating bread with leaven was to be cut off from the congregation of Israel (Exod 12:14–20). In Exod 12:39 this command is associated with the haste with which the Israelites left Egypt and their inability to prepare food (no time for bread to rise); but leaven came to be associated with the permeating power of sin. As Paul says in 1 Cor 5:6, "a little [leaven] leavens the whole batch of dough."

Mark does not say what this "leaven" is. Matthew, who refers to the leaven of the Pharisees *and the Sadducees*, identifies it as their "teaching" (Matt 16:11–12), and Luke, who refers only to the Pharisees, calls it their "hypocrisy" (Luke 12:1). The reference to Herod is indeed odd (which explains its omission from Matthew and Luke), since the Pharisees and Herod had little in common.[7] Some identify the leaven with the desire for a sign,[8] which fits the Pharisees in the near context (8:12) but is less obvious for Herod (though 6:14 shows him wondering about Jesus' identity, and in Luke's gospel [Luke 23:8] he hopes to see a sign from Jesus). Others see the leaven as the dangers of nationalism or

violent political ambitions.[9] For this, however, one would have expected the pro-Roman Herod to be contrasted with the Zealots or other anti-Roman groups. The Pharisees, though certainly not apolitical, did not advocate violent revolution.

The most likely identification for the leaven is blindness to Jesus' identity and opposition to the kingdom of God.[10] These are equally true of both Herod and the Pharisees. We should reiterate, however, that Mark himself leaves the leaven unexplained, perhaps to mark Jesus' statement as a "parable," requiring eyes to see and ears to hear (cf. 4:11–13; 7:17; cf. Isa 6:9–10).[11] This fits the narrative that follows, where the disciples are in danger of the same blindness to the mysteries of the kingdom of God that afflicted the Pharisees in 4:11–12.

8:16 They began arguing with one another about not having bread (καὶ διελογίζοντο πρὸς ἀλλήλους ὅτι ἄρτους οὐκ ἔχουσιν). The verb "argue" (διαλογίζομαι) can mean to discuss, debate, or argue. Mark uses the verb seven times, generally with negative connotations, meaning either arguing (8:16, 17; 9:33) or conspiring (2:6–8; 11:31). The former is the sense here. The imperfect tense may be durative ("they *continued* arguing") or inceptive ("they *began* to argue"). If the former, the disciples are already arguing about the bread (perhaps implied in v. 14) and ignore Jesus when he introduces the spiritual metaphor about leaven.[12] The latter, however, seems more likely, since Jesus' criticism in v. 17 appears to be in response to their

5. Most modern versions translate ζύμη as "yeast" (NIV, NLT, GNT, HCSB, NET), which is functionally correct as a symbol of permeating power, but not historically precise. "Yeast" in English refers either to the fungus present in the leaven that causes the bread to rise (*Saccharomyces*), or to a commercial product made with this fungus used for baking and brewing and as a source of vitamins and protein.

6. Str-B 1:728–29; H. Windisch, *TDNT*, 2:905–6. In the rabbinical writings leaven is often a symbol for "the evil influence" (*yēṣer haraʿ*) or the wicked ways and human dispositions (Str-B 1:728–29; Marcus, *Mark 1–8*, 510–11).

7. Some manuscripts replace "Herod" with "Herodians" (𝔓[45] W Θ *f*[1,13] 28 565 2542), likely an assimilation to Mark 3:6 and 12:13, where the two groups appear together.

8. Donahue and Harrington, *Mark*, 252; Gundry, *Mark*, 408; Collins, *Mark*, 386.

9. Lohmeyer, *Markus*, 157; Pesch, *Markusevangelium*, 1:413.

10. Cf. Edwards, *Mark*, 239; Guelich, *Mark 1:1–8:26*, 423–24.

11. France, *Mark*, 316.

12. Taylor, *Mark*, 366; Grundmann, *Markus*, 208; France, *Mark*, 317.

misunderstanding.[13] The disciples take Jesus' statement about leaven as criticism of their failure to bring bread and begin arguing about whose fault it is (cf. Matt 16:12).[14] Ironically, their failure to comprehend Jesus' metaphor itself illustrates their susceptibility to the leaven of the Pharisees and of Herod (i.e., blindness to things of the kingdom of God).

8:17 – 18 Aware of their discussion, Jesus said to them, "Why are you arguing about not having bread? Do you not yet comprehend or understand? Are your hearts hardened? Do you have eyes but cannot see and ears but do not hear? And don't you remember?" (καὶ γνοὺς λέγει αὐτοῖς· τί διαλογίζεσθε ὅτι ἄρτους οὐκ ἔχετε; οὔπω νοεῖτε οὐδὲ συνίετε; πεπωρωμένην ἔχετε τὴν καρδίαν ὑμῶν; ὀφθαλμοὺς ἔχοντες οὐ βλέπετε καὶ ὦτα ἔχοντες οὐκ ἀκούετε; καὶ οὐ μνημονεύετε). Since he is with them in the boat, we might expect Jesus to have "heard" instead of "known" (γνούς) what they said. The latter need not imply supernatural knowledge, however, and simply means he became aware of their conversation.[15]

Jesus begins with a series of five rhetorical questions, all pointing to the disciples' lack of spiritual insight. In the first Jesus isn't criticizing them for arguing, but for missing the spiritual significance of the "leaven." The second emphasizes this lack of spiritual insight: "Do you not yet comprehend or understand?" (οὔπω νοεῖτε οὐδὲ συνίετε).[16] Jesus asked a similar double question in 7:18 concerning the disciples' failure to understand his "par-

able": "Are you so ignorant? Don't you see?" (ὑμεῖς ἀσύνετοί ἐστε; οὐ νοεῖτε;).

The third rhetorical question goes even further. While failure to understand may be attributed to ignorance, hardening one's heart entails turning away from revealed truth (cf. Pharaoh in Exod 7:3; 13, 22; 8:15, 32; 9:12; 10:1). As Edwards points out, "An ignorant heart cannot harden itself. Only a knowing heart can harden itself, and that is why those closest to Jesus — the Pharisees (3:5 – 6) and the disciples (6:52; 8:17) — stand in gravest danger."[17] In 3:5 – 6 Jesus was distressed at the hardness of the Pharisees' hearts when they sought to use a healing miracle to accuse him of healing on the Sabbath. Healings such as this demonstrate the power of the kingdom of God; yet the Pharisees see only an opportunity for evil. In 6:52 the disciples witness Jesus' walking on water — clear evidence of his divine authority — yet they respond with hard hearts. These parallels indicate that the danger here is grave indeed.

The fourth rhetorical question, "Do you have eyes but cannot see and ears by cannot hear?" continues this theme. The language is close to Jer 5:21 and Ezek 12:2 (cf. Ps 115:5 – 6; Ezek 3:7) but is conceptually similar to Isa 6:9, recalling again Jesus' words in Mark 4:11 – 12. The disciples appear ominously close to becoming like those "outsiders" (the religious leaders) who cannot understand the parables because their eyes are blinded to the secrets of the kingdom.

While the situation is grave, it is by no means hopeless. The fact that Jesus addresses the disciples

13. Pesch, *Markusevangelium*, 1:414; Guelich, *Mark 1:1 – 8:26*, 424; Lane, *Mark*, 281.

14. The grammar here is difficult and is complicated by a textual issue. While the majority of Greek manuscripts read ἔχομεν ("we have"; ℵ A C L Θ *f*[13] 33 𝔐 aur vg; cf. KJV, NIV, NJB), a significant minority read ἔχουσιν ("they have"; 𝔓[45] B W *f*[1] 28 565 700 2427). The former appears to be an assimilation to Matt 16:7. Assuming the latter reading, the ὅτι could

be taken as indirect discourse, "They were discussing with one another that they had no bread" (cf. NASB, ESV, HCSB); as causal, "because they had no bread" (cf. NLT, NAB); or as an indirect interrogative, "why they had no bread" (see Taylor, *Mark*, 366, for support of this last one).

15. Cf. Gundry, *Mark*, 409; contra Marcus, *Mark 1 – 8*, 508.

16. Guelich, *Mark 1:1 – 8:26*, 424.

17. Edwards, *Mark*, 240.

with questions rather than pronouncements (as he did with the Pharisees in 8:12) confirms that their future is still open.[18] From a narrative context, the disciples remain on the side of Jesus.

The fifth rhetorical question ("Don't you remember?") brings this out, pointing forward to the next two questions, where Jesus spurs them to faith by reminding them of the two feeding miracles and the bountiful provisions available through the kingdom of God.

8:19–20 "When I broke the five loaves for the five thousand, how many basketfuls of pieces did you pick up?" They answered him, "Twelve." "And when I broke the seven loaves for the four thousand, how many baskets full of fragments did you pick up?" They said, "Seven." (ὅτε τοὺς πέντε ἄρτους ἔκλασα εἰς τοὺς πεντακισχιλίους, πόσους κοφίνους κλασμάτων πλήρεις ἤρατε; λέγουσιν αὐτῷ· δώδεκα. ὅτε τοὺς ἑπτὰ εἰς τοὺς τετρακισχιλίους, πόσων σπυρίδων πληρώματα κλασμάτων ἤρατε; καὶ λέγουσιν [αὐτῷ]· ἑπτά). Jesus follows his five rhetorical questions with two real questions, that is, ones expecting answers. The questions repeat the specifics of the two feeding miracles, not only in the number of loaves available, the numbers fed, and the amount of leftovers, but even in the specific Greek words for "basket" from each story (κόφινος and σπυρίς, respectively).[19]

Ironically, Jesus returns to the topic of literal bread to reinforce for his disciples that the leaven he spoke of was not about literal bread. But what is the purpose of this reminder? While Jesus' questions recall for the disciples the enormous numbers

fed with meager provisions, the answers he seeks relate particularly to the abundance of leftovers. Some see symbolic significance in the number of baskets. Yet as we have seen (see comments on 6:43–44; 8:8–9a), while "twelve" could point to Israel, "seven" is not so easily associated with the Gentiles. Others see significance in the diminishing numbers fed between the first and second feedings, indicating either the decline of miraculous powers resulting from increasing rejection of Jesus[20] or as an indication that time is running out for people to respond to the kingdom of God.[21]

Whether these factors are present or not, Mark's primary emphasis is in Jesus' call for greater faith and understanding. If he is capable of superabundantly providing for so many, why are the disciples worried about having enough bread? More importantly, why are they obsessed with mundane issues when Jesus has been revealing to them the presence and power of the kingdom of God? Jesus' question thus has both christological and eschatological implications. Through his miracles Jesus has been revealing his authority as the Messiah and Son of God, a point that will shortly come to light in Peter's confession (8:27–30). By recalling the superabundance of bread in the wilderness, he points to his mission as host of the messianic banquet and inaugurator of the kingdom of God.

8:21 He was saying to them, "Do you not yet understand?" (καὶ ἔλεγεν αὐτοῖς· οὔπω συνίετε;). This last rhetorical question repeats almost verbatim the one in v. 17, "Do you not yet comprehend or understand?" which frames the series of

---

18. Boring, *Mark*, 227.

19. There is a great deal of consistency here; κόφινος is always used with reference to the feeding of the five thousand (Matt 14:20; 16:9; Mark 6:43; 8:19; Luke 9:17; John 6:13), and σπυρίς with the four thousand (Matt 15:37; 16:10; Mark 8:8, 20).

20. Mary A. Tolbert, *Sowing the Gospel: Mark's World in Literary-Historical Perspective* (Minneapolis: Fortress, 1989), 183.

21. J. Sergeant, *Lion Let Loose: The Structure and Meaning of St. Mark's Gospel* (Exeter: Paternoster, 1988), 56–57; cited by France, *Mark*, 319 n. 27. L. W. Countryman more broadly sees the decline in the ease and efficacy of miracles over the course of Mark's narrative as his way of showing that miracles alone are an inadequate basis for faith ("How Many Baskets Full? Mark 8:14–21 and the Value of the Miracles in Mark," *CBQ* 47 [1985]: 643–55).

questions. Although the pericope ends on a solemn note, all is not yet lost. As noted above, the fact that these are questions rather than pronouncements, together with the repeated use of "not yet" (οὔπω; vv. 17 and 21), opens the possibility that they *will* one day understand. Mark's readers are certainly aware that the apostles went on to suc-cess as leaders of the early church (cf. 9:9; 13:9 – 13; 16:7). Yet we must not gloss over the severity of Jesus' rebuke. The disciples are presented as teetering on the brink of Pharisaic blindness. There are dark days ahead, and in the episodes to come the disciples will continue to demonstrate pride, self-centeredness, and lack of spiritual insight.

Theology in Application

Throughout Mark's gospel the Pharisees have been the persistent opponents of Jesus (2:16, 24; 3:6; 7:1, 5; 8:11 – 13; cf. 2:6; 3:22). In the previous episode (8:11 – 13) they demanded a sign, prompting Jesus to decisively turn away. Signs are of no value for those who have turned to the darkness in the face of the light. Now Jesus warns his own disciples — who have shown a similar lack of spiritual insight (4:13, 40; 6:52; 7:18) — of this same hard-heartedness and persistent unbelief.

Warning of Spiritual Blindness

For Mark the "leaven of the Pharisees and the leaven of Herod" likely refers to their blindness to Jesus' identity and their opposition to the kingdom of God (see comments on 8:15). This theme will play out in the chapters ahead. The two-stage healing of the blind man in the next passage (8:22 – 26) symbolizes the partial sight of the disciples. Though Peter, after witnessing all the miracles, recognizes and confesses that Jesus is the Messiah (8:29), his view of the Messiah's mission is still fuzzy. The kingdom of God will be inaugurated not through physical power or conquest, but through suffering and servanthood (8:31 – 9:1; 9:33 – 37; 10:35 – 45).

Warning of the Permeating Power of Sin

Sin is like leaven in that it spreads and permeates all that it comes in contact with. In 1 Corinthians 5, Paul calls on the Corinthian church to expel a member involved in unrepentant sexual sin, since "a little yeast leavens the whole batch of dough" (5:6). Examples of sin begetting sin are everywhere in our world, whether it is an endless cycle of violence between nations and ethnic groups, the damaging effects of addictions that persist from generation to generation, or the tendency to repeat patterns of dysfunctional relationships from our past. These destructive cycles can only be broken by the power of the Spirit and by adopting a "kingdom mind-set," which means loving instead of hating and giving instead of taking. This is the model of self-sacrificial service that Jesus will demonstrate in the chapters to come, as the Servant Messiah heads to Jerusalem "to give his life as a ransom for many" (10:45)

In Luke's gospel, the leaven of the Pharisees is identified as hypocrisy, a common permeating sin among those in religious leadership. Leaders often feel the need to cover up their personal failures while demanding high standards in others. The Pharisees, Jesus said, "strain out a gnat but swallow a camel" (Matt 23:24). They place heavy burdens on others that they are unwilling to carry themselves (23:4; Luke 11:46). Hypocrisy is a real danger in any religious context, and like a disease, it spreads easily. Its antidote is nurturing a culture of authenticity, accountability, openness, and honesty about our sins and failings.

Warning of Distraction by the Things of This World

The disciples are embarrassed when they fail to bring bread and begin to argue with one another. Pride and self-interest distracts them from hearing and responding to Jesus' words. Jesus responds by calling them to remember the miracles of the loaves and fishes, which reveal his identity as God's Messiah and the agent of eschatological salvation. It is time to get their focus off themselves and onto God's kingdom purposes.

There is a similar tendency in all of us to miss out on God's work because of worldly distractions and selfish ambition. In Christian ministry, where value is often measured by the size of your church, the acclaim you receive, the books you have written, or the size of your paycheck, it is easy to forget that Christian leadership is not about power, prestige, or position, but about submitting to the lordship of Christ and following his path of service and sacrifice.

32

Mark 8:22 – 26

Literary Context

This episode is linked chronologically to the previously one as the boat journey that began in 8:13 comes to an end at Bethsaida. Even more important is its role in Mark's narrative structure as a critical transition to the second major section of Mark's gospel (8:22 – 10:52). While the first major section of the gospel (1:14 – 8:21) emphasized Jesus' ministry in and around Galilee and his role as the mighty wonder-working Messiah, this second part will stress the suffering role of the Servant Messiah.

Being transitional, this passage has important links both to what precedes and what follows. In terms of the former, it is the penultimate episode in the series that runs from 8:1 – 30, which parallels the series from 6:31 – 7:37 (see chart in Literary Context on 8:1 – 10). In this sequence, the healing of the blind man has its counterpart in the healing of the deaf-mute man in 7:31 – 37 (see Structure, below, for the close parallels). Both episodes illustrate the spiritual deafness and blindness of the religious leaders (7:1 – 23; 8:11 – 13) and the danger the disciples face of this same malady (6:52; 8:14 – 21). In terms of what follows, the healing of this blind man forms an inclusio with the healing of blind Bartimaeus in 10:46 – 52. The two episodes frame Mark's central section (8:22 – 10:52), during which Jesus seeks to open the blind eyes of the disciples by predicting his death three times and teaching them about the suffering path to the cross.

So does this passage go with what precedes or with what follows? The commentators are divided,[1] but Mark was probably not concerned with a definitive "outline" of the book. This passage, together with the two that follow (8:27 – 33; 8:34 – 9:1), forms a transitional bridge as Jesus' ministry turns decisively toward his suffering fate.

---

1. Judging from their outlines, the former is held by Cranfield, *Mark*, 14; Guelich, *Mark 1:1 – 8:26*, 430; Lane, *Mark*, 30; Hurtado, *Mark*, 12; the latter by France, *Mark*, 320ff.; Williamson, *Mark*, 147; Stein, *Mark*, 386; Marcus, *Mark 1 – 8*, 573; Garland, *Mark*, 33; Boring, *Mark*, 229. Many of these note the transitional nature of the passage.

Main Idea

The healing of the blind man at Bethsaida, like other healing miracles of Jesus' Galilean ministry, confirms that Jesus is fulfilling the signs of eschatological salvation (Isa 35:5 – 6). The miracle also serves for Mark as an enacted parable. The failure of Israel's religious leaders to "see" and "hear" the message of the kingdom of God is contrasted with the man's restoration of sight, and the two-stage healing represents the disciples' gradual progression toward spiritual understanding.

Translation

Mark 8:22 – 26

22a	Setting	**They came to Bethsaida,**
b	Character entrance/ Entreaty	and **some people brought a blind man to him and begged him to touch him.**
23a	Action	Taking the blind man's hand,
b		**he led him out of the town.**
c	Action	Spitting on his eyes and placing his hands on him,
d	Question	**Jesus asked him,**
e		*"Can you see anything?"*
24a		Looking up,
b	Response to 23d-e	**he said,**
c	healing (partial)	*"I see people; they look like trees walking around."*
25a	Action	Then **he again placed his hands on his eyes**
b	Healing	and **he saw clearly;**
c		**his sight was restored and he could see everything clearly.**
26a	Response to 25/Command	**He sent him to his home, saying,**
b		*"Don't even go into the town."*

Structure

The episode represents a typical healing miracle, but with a surprising two-stage process. There is a statement of the problem, withdrawal from the city, the healing by Jesus (in two steps), and an implied command to silence. No response to the miracle is noted, probably because of its private nature. Structurally, there are a number of striking features in common with the healing of the deaf and mute man in 7:31 – 37; and, as noted above (Literary Context), the two function in similar ways to illustrate the restoration of spiritual sight and hearing.[2] The parallels include: (1) in both cases a group of unnamed people bring the man to Jesus and (2) "beg" (παρακαλέω) Jesus to heal him with his touch. (3) Jesus takes the man away privately, (4) touches the organs affected, (5) and uses spittle for the healing. (6) After the miracle he enjoins silence (implied in 8:26).

These are the only two miracles unique to Mark's gospel. Matthew may have omitted them because of the unusual healing method using spittle and, in the present case, the apparent failure of Jesus' first attempt to fully heal the man. Luke's reasons for omission are less clear, since he does not include any material from Mark 6:45 – 8:26 (his so-called "great omission").

Exegetical Outline

→ **1. Arrival in Bethsaida (8:22a)**

   2. Request for Healing (8:22b)

   3. The Two-Stage Healing (8:23 – 25)

      a. First attempt (8:23)

      b. The result (8:24)

      c. Second attempt (8:25a)

      d. The result (8:25b-c)

   4. Command to Avoid Town (8:26)

---

2. The similarities in the two accounts have caused some to claim that they are a doublet (two episodes arising from a single story; so Bultmann, *History,* 213). Most commentators, however, attribute the parallels to Mark's editing of two different stories. For details, see Guelich, *Mark 1:1 – 8:26,* 429; Edwards, *Mark,* 241 n. 22.

Explanation of the Text

8:22 They came to Bethsaida, and some people brought a blind man to him and begged him to touch him (Καὶ ἔρχονται εἰς Βηθσαϊδάν. καὶ φέρουσιν αὐτῷ τυφλὸν καὶ παρακαλοῦσιν αὐτὸν ἵνα αὐτοῦ ἅψηται). The boat lands at "Bethsaida" (Βηθσαϊδάν), on the northeastern shore of the lake, east of the Jordan River. The town, whose name means "house of fishing," was in Lower Gaulanitis, part of the tetrarchy of Philip. It was mentioned once before in Mark, at 6:45, where it was the intended destination of the boat after the feeding of the five thousand (though they end up at Gennesaret after the storm; 6:53).[3] The town was also the hometown of three of Jesus' disciples, Peter, Andrew, and Philip (John 1:44; 12:21). Jesus pronounces "woes" against Chorazin and Bethsaida (Matt 11:21; par. Luke 10:13) for failing to repent in spite of the many miracles performed there.

Mark's identification of the place as a "village" or "town" (κώμη; vv. 23, 26) is surprising, since it appears to have been a fairly large municipality. Josephus says that Philip enlarged the "village" (κώμη) to a "city" (πόλις) and renamed it Bethsaida-Julias, after the daughter of Caesar Augustus.[4] Matthew and John similarly refer to it as a "city" (πόλις). Too much should not be made of this language, however, since these terms have wide semantic ranges. Even the small village of Bethlehem could be called a "city" (πόλις; Luke 2:4, 11). We should probably think of Bethsaida as an intermediary "town" somewhere between a village and a city.[5]

When Jesus comes ashore, some people approach him, "begging" (παρακαλέω) him to touch and heal a blind man. Pleading for healing is common in Mark (1:40; 5:23; 6:56; 7:32; cf. 5:18), which indicates both the desperation of people and Jesus' renown as a healer. As in the case of the paralyzed man (2:3) and the deaf-mute (7:32), it is the man's friends who make the request. Jesus often heals with touch in Mark's gospel (1:31, 41; 5:23, 41; 6:5; 7:32; 8:23, 25; 9:27), and the crowds are portrayed as seeking to touch him for healing (3:10; 5:28; 6:56).

8:23 Taking the blind man's hand, he led him out of the town. Spitting on his eyes and placing his hands on him, Jesus asked him, "Can you see anything?" (καὶ ἐπιλαβόμενος τῆς χειρὸς τοῦ τυφλοῦ ἐξήνεγκεν αὐτὸν ἔξω τῆς κώμης καὶ πτύσας εἰς τὰ ὄμματα αὐτοῦ, ἐπιθεὶς τὰς χεῖρας αὐτῷ ἐπηρώτα αὐτόν· εἴ τι βλέπεις;). As in 7:33, the healing is done away from the crowds. Mark does not say why Jesus takes the man outside the town, but the most likely reason is to avoid the publicity that the miracle would cause. This is consistent with the messianic secret throughout Mark's gospel (1:34, 44; 3:12; 5:43, 7:36; 8:30) and also fits the end of the story, where Jesus tells the man to go home without reentering the town (v. 26).

The puzzling use of saliva to heal appears only here, in 7:33, and in John 9:6 (see comments on 7:33 – 34 for its background). Jesus' question, "Can you see anything?" (εἴ τι βλέπεις;) is unique in the

---

3. Luke, however, places the feeding miracle itself near Bethsaida (9:10). See comments on 6:45 – 46 for the geographical difficulties and possible solutions.

4. Josephus, *Ant.* 18.2.1 §28. F. Strickert ("The Coins of Philip," in *Bethsaida: A City by the North Shore of the Sea of Galilee* [ed. R. Arav and R. A. Freund; Kirksville, MO: Truman State University Press, 1995], 1:165 – 89) asserts that Bethsaida was not named for Augustus's biological daughter, Julia, but for Augustus's wife, Livia, who was adopted as the emperor's

daughter into the Julian family and given the name Julia after her husband's death. Note that Josephus says that Betharanphtha was also named "Julias, from the name of the emperor's wife" (Josephus, *Ant.* 18.2.1 §27).

5. Guelich, *Mark 1:1 – 8:26*, 432, further notes that despite its size and new name, Bethsaida remained organizationally a "village" under Herod Philip, citing A. H. M. Jones, *The Cities of the Eastern Roman Provinces* (2nd ed.; Oxford: Clarendon, 1971), 282.

Gospels — the only time Jesus inquires about the success of a healing. This prepares the reader for the partial healing that follows. Though "if" (εἰ) is commonly used to introduce indirect questions (3:2; 10:2; 15:36, 44), its use for a direct question appears only here in Mark. This use is likely a Semitism, appearing in the LXX and elsewhere in the NT (cf. Matt 12:10; 19:3; Luke 13:23; Acts 1:6; 7:1).[6]

8:24 Looking up, he said, "I see people; they look like trees walking around." (καὶ ἀναβλέψας ἔλεγεν· βλέπω τοὺς ἀνθρώπους ὅτι ὡς δένδρα ὁρῶ περιπατοῦντας). The verb translated "looking up" (ἀναβλέπω) can also mean "seeing again," and this may be its meaning here (cf. REB: "The man's sight began to come back").[7] The Greek is awkward, with a "that" (ὅτι) clause and the repetition of verbs of seeing: "I see [βλέπω] people that I see [ὁρῶ] walking as trees." While some have proposed a mistranslation of an original Aramaic, which should have read *whom* I see as trees walking,"[8] more likely we simply have a vivid reporting of the man's staccato speech.

Whatever the reason for the unusual Greek, the sense is perfectly clear. The man's vision is still so blurred he can only see vertical objects moving about. Since Jesus has led the man outside the town, the people he sees are probably the friends who brought him to Jesus, or perhaps the disciples, who are nowhere else mentioned in the episode. Some claim that the man had not been born blind, since he knows what a tree looks like.[9] But this is unnecessary, since the man would surely know what trees were by having touched them in the past.

8:25 Then he again placed his hands on his eyes and he saw clearly; his sight was restored and he could see everything clearly (εἶτα πάλιν ἐπέθηκεν τὰς χεῖρας ἐπὶ τοὺς ὀφθαλμοὺς αὐτοῦ, καὶ διέβλεψεν καὶ ἀπεκατέστη καὶ ἐνέβλεπεν τηλαυγῶς ἅπαντα). The completeness of the cure is emphasized with three parallel clauses: "he saw clearly" (διέβλεψεν), "his sight was restored" (ἀπεκατέστη), and "he saw everything clearly" (ἐνέβλεπεν τηλαυγῶς ἅπαντα). Indeed, the piling up of terms for seeing is a remarkable feature of the whole passage. In vv. 23–25, there are two words for "eyes" (ὄμματα; ὀφθαλμοί), five verbs of seeing (βλέπω [2x]; ὁρῶ; διαβλέπω; ἐμβλέπω), and two verbs related to "restoration of sight" (ἀναβλέπω; ἀποκαθίστημι).

So why the two-stage healing? From a historical perspective, the apparent difficulty is evidence of the historicity of the event, since the church is unlikely to have invented a story in which Jesus' has only limited success. In this regard the passage is similar to the difficulty in 6:5, where Jesus is unable to do miracles in Nazareth.

But what is its purpose in Mark's gospel? Some have suggested that it is to show the power of Jesus, that he can overcome even the most difficult cases. But it is not clear why this cure should be any more challenging than others. A better explanation is that Mark includes the story to illustrate the gradual illumination of the identity of Jesus. If so, the partial sight of the man could refer to (1) the inadequate view of the people, which is contrasted with Peter's full recognition that Jesus is the Messiah, or (2) Peter's myopic understanding of Jesus' messiahship, which will only be fully comprehended by the disciples after the resurrection. This latter interpretation is much more likely since, in the episodes that follow, Jesus will repeatedly predict his death and the disciples will respond with pride and lack of spiritual insight. Only after the resurrection do they truly "see."

---

6. France, *Mark*, 324.

7. E. S. Johnson, "Mark viii.22–26: The Blind Man from Bethsaida," *NTS* 25 (1978–79): 370–83, esp. 376–77; Collins, *Mark*, 394.

8. See Taylor, *Mark*, 371; Guelich, *Mark 1:1–8:26*, 433.

9. Johnson, "Mark viii.22–26," 376–77; Lane, *Mark*, 285; Hurtado, *Mark*, 134.

**8:26 He sent him to his home, saying, "Don't
even go into the town."** (καὶ ἀπέστειλεν αὐτὸν εἰς
οἶκον αὐτοῦ λέγων· μηδὲ εἰς τὴν κώμην εἰσέλθῃς).
The man must have lived either on the outskirts
of the city or in the countryside since Jesus tells
him to go home but to avoid the city. The reason
is almost certainly part of Mark's messianic secret
(1:44; 5:43; 7:36; see Introduction: Mark's Gospel in Historical Perspective; and comments on
1:25; 1:43 – 44).[10] Jesus is seeking to avoid excessive publicity and a presumptive attempt to make
him king.[11] As the next passage will make clear, his
messianic role is not to quash the Romans, but to
journey to Jerusalem to suffer and die.

Theology in Application

The passage plays an important role in Mark's gospel. First, it continues to illustrate the eschatological signs of the new age, evidence of the coming restoration
of creation (Isa 35:5 – 6; cf. 29:18; 32:3; 42:7). Jesus confirms the inauguration of the
kingdom of God through his words and deeds. Second, the passage symbolically illustrates the disciples' progress of faith. They have experienced Jesus' authority from
the beginning: responding to his authoritative call (1:16 – 20), being appointed as
his apostles (3:16 – 19), hearing his proclamation of the kingdom, and witnessing his
healings, exorcisms, and nature miracles.

From a spiritual perspective they certainly "see" — as Peter's confession of Jesus'
messiahship in the next passage will illustrate. But like the blind man after Jesus'
first touch, they see only dimly. They do not fully understand Jesus' identity or his
mission. They are still hard-hearted, prideful, and weak in faith, in danger of succumbing to the "leaven of the Pharisees" (8:15). Though threatening, these obstacles
to faith are not insurmountable, and in the passages to come Jesus will reveal to them
the suffering way of the cross. These disciples, like all Jesus' followers, must decide
whether they will follow the authentic path of God, which entails suffering and sacrifice, or their own human plans (cf. 8:33). The following two themes are particularly
important in biblical theology.

Sight and Light as Symbols of God's Truth

All of Jesus' miracles symbolize the presence and power of the kingdom of God
and the coming restoration of creation. Yet his healing of sight is a particularly rich
biblical metaphor. In the beginning the Creator God spoke and brought light from

---

10. This is how later copyists understood the statement,
since many variants add "not even to say anything in the town"
(μηδὲ εἴπῃς τινὶ ἐν τῇ κώμῃ; A C 33[vid] 𝔐) or similar phrases to
clarify Jesus' command.

11. Contra Gundry, *Mark*, 419 – 20, who says Jesus' command is in fact intended to publicize the miracle. Going home
alone shows that the man does not need assistance any longer

from his friends and not entering the town means he no longer
needs to resume his begging. Similar commands to go home in
Mark, he claims, are for the purpose of confirming the miracle
(2:11 – 12; 5:19; 7:29 – 30; cf. the command to go to the priest,
1:44). A typical reader, however, is unlikely to have understood
it this way in light of Jesus' many other commands to silence
related to demons, the disciples, and others who are healed.

darkness (Gen 1:3). Paul picks up this creation of light imagery to illustrate the restoration available through Jesus: "For God, who said, 'Let light shine out of darkness,' made his light shine in our hearts to give us the light of the knowledge of God's glory displayed in the face of Christ" (2 Cor 4:6). In the prologue to the Fourth Gospel, the author similarly describes Jesus as the life who is the "light of all mankind," which the darkness could not overcome/comprehend (John 1:4 – 5; cf. v. 9). Jesus is "the light of world," who provides the light of life to those who formerly walked in darkness (John 8:12; cf. Isa 9:1 – 2; Matt 4:16). Though, as fallen humanity, we were once in darkness, now, Paul says, "You are light in the Lord. Live as children of light" (Eph 5:8; cf. 1 Thess 5:5).

Dozens of passages could be added to this list. Light signifies God's purity and holiness available to his holy people. In Rev 21:23 the eternal city is described as having no sun or moon, "for the glory of God gives it light, and the Lamb is its lamp." God, who lives in unapproachable light (1 Tim 1:16), has given his children an inheritance in "the kingdom of light" (Col 1:12). Light signifies knowledge over ignorance and truth over falsehood (John 3:21). Though Satan masquerades as an angel of light (2 Cor 11:14), he is in fact the prince of darkness and the father of lies (John 8:44; Acts 26:18). Believers are called to shine their light by living lives of purity, goodness, righteousness, and truth, all to the glory of God (Matt 5:14 – 16).

Faith as a Process

The gradual healing of the blind man illustrates the gradual progress of faith in the life of the disciples. Though they have begun their journey by choosing to follow Jesus, they have much to learn. There is a long and challenging road ahead, and it will be full of fits and starts.

It is the same for us today. The kingdom of God was inaugurated through the life, death, and resurrection of Jesus, but it has yet to be consummated. Before that time, creation groans "as in the pains of childbirth," and "we ourselves, who have the firstfruits of the Spirit, groan inwardly as we wait eagerly for our adoption to sonship, the redemption of our bodies" (Rom 8:22 – 23). Though in our flesh we still struggle and fall, the key is to get up, brush off, and keep moving forward in the power of the Spirit. Paul says it well: "No, dear brothers and sisters, I have not achieved it, but I focus on this one thing: Forgetting the past and looking forward to what lies ahead, I press on to reach the end of the race and receive the heavenly prize for which God, through Christ Jesus, is calling us" (Phil 3:13 – 14 NLT).

Mark 8:27 – 33

Literary Context

Although the confession of Peter (vv. 27 – 29) and Jesus' passion prediction (vv. 31 – 33) are sometimes treated as two distinct episodes, we will deal with them together since they represent the key hinge on which the gospel of Mark turns. During his ministry in and around Galilee (1:14 – 8:21), Jesus has been proclaiming the kingdom of God and performing the signs of eschatological salvation: casting out demons, healing the sick, raising the dead, and in the previous episode, healing a blind man (cf. Isa 35:5 – 6; cf. 26:19). Peter's confession and Jesus' first passion prediction will turn the narrative in a new direction, as Jesus begins to teach his disciples about his suffering role. This will be the main theme of the following chapters, as Jesus three times predicts his death and teaches the disciples concerning the suffering way of the cross (8:31 – 10:45). This will climax in Jesus' arrival in Jerusalem, where he will "give his life as a ransom for many" (10:45).

The healing of the blind man in the previous episode (see Structure on 8:22 – 26), as we saw, functioned as an enacted parable for the disciples' gradual growth in spiritual comprehension. At the same time, the partial restoration of the man's sight (8:23 – 24) paralleled their inadequate understanding of Jesus and the kingdom of God. Peter and the disciples' inadequate view of Jesus' messiahship (vv. 29, 32) is contrasted with Jesus' true understanding of the suffering role of the Messiah (v. 31). Although Jesus repeatedly predicts his suffering and death, the disciples respond with pride and misunderstanding each time. Peter and the other disciples do not "see clearly" during this phase of Jesus' ministry. Only after the resurrection will they truly have "eyes that see and ears that hear."

Main Idea

The first half of Mark's gospel reaches a decisive climax as Peter confesses that Jesus is the Messiah. The Markan narrative now takes a decisive turn, as Jesus defines his messianic role as one of suffering and sacrifice.

Translation

Mark 8:27 – 33

27a	Setting (spatial)	**Jesus and his disciples went on to the villages of Caesarea Philippi.**
b	Setting (spatial & temporal)	**On the way, he was asking his disciples,**
c	Question	*"Who do people say I am?"*
28	Response to 27b-c	**They said,**
		"Some say John the Baptist; others, Elijah; still others, one of the prophets."
29a	Question	**He asked them,**
b		*"But what about you? Who do you say I am?"*
c	Response to 29a	**Peter said to him,**
d		*"You are the Messiah."*
30	Response/Warning	**He strongly warned them not to tell anyone about him.**
31a	Instruction/Prophecy	Then **he began to teach them that it was necessary for the Son of Man** ☞
		to suffer many things and
		to be rejected
b		by the elders and
		the ruling priests and
		the experts in the law, and
c		**to be killed,** and
		after three days
d		**to rise again.**
32a	Clarification	**He was speaking this message plainly.**
b		Pulling him aside,
c	Response to 31 – 32	**Peter began to rebuke him.**
33a		Turning and looking at his disciples,
b	Response to 32c	**he rebuked Peter and said,**
c	command	*"Get behind me, Satan,*
d	reason for 33c	*because you are not thinking about God's concerns, but*
		about merely human ones!"

Structure

This dual account includes a dialogue between Jesus and his disciples and teaching by Jesus. It also functions as a conflict story, with Peter rebuking Jesus for speaking about his death and Jesus counterrebuking Peter for failing to comprehend the suffering role of the Messiah.

Exegetical Outline

→ **1. Peter's Confession (8:27 – 30)**

    a. The context (8:27a)

    b. Jesus' first question: Who do people say I am? (8:27b-c)

    c. The disciples' response: John the Baptist, Elijah, or one of the prophets (8:28)

    d. Jesus' second question: Who do *you* say I am? (8:29a-b)

    e. Peter's response: You are the Messiah (8:29c-d)

    f. Command to silence (8:30)

2. First Passion Prediction (8:31 – 33)

    a. The prediction (8:31)

    b. Peter's rebuke (8:32)

    c. Jesus' counterrebuke (8:33)

Explanation of the Text

8:27 Jesus and his disciples went on to the villages of Caesarea Philippi. On the way, he was asking his disciples, "Who do people say I am?" (Καὶ ἐξῆλθεν ὁ Ἰησοῦς καὶ οἱ μαθηταὶ αὐτοῦ εἰς τὰς κώμας Καισαρείας τῆς Φιλίππου· καὶ ἐν τῇ ὁδῷ ἐπηρώτα τοὺς μαθητὰς αὐτοῦ λέγων αὐτοῖς· τίνα με λέγουσιν οἱ ἄνθρωποι εἶναι;). Jesus takes his disciples twenty-five miles north of Bethsaida, where the healing of the blind man took place (8:22), to the region of Caesarea Philippi.[1] This city, located in the southwestern foothills of Mount Hermon, was previously called Paneas or Panion, after Pan, the Greek god of nature and the woodlands. The name is preserved in the modern name Banias. Herod Philip expanded the city after his appointment as tetrarch, and in AD 14 named it Caesarea in honor of Caesar Augustus.[2] It is to be distinguished from Caesarea Maritima, the Roman administrative capital of Judea built by Herod the Great along the Mediterranean coast.

Some commentators have stressed the pagan and idolatrous nature of the place, suggesting that Jesus intentionally took his disciples into the heart of paganism to declare his messiahship. Yet Mark says the journey was to "the villages of Caesarea Philippi" (τὰς κώμας Καισαρείας τῆς Φιλίππου), meaning the surrounding region, not the city itself, and that Jesus asked the question about his identity "on the way." Mark does not state the reason for heading north, but it was more likely for retreat and escape from the crowds than for entering a pagan environment. Some have seen allusions in Mark's reference to "the way" to the self-description of the early church as "the Way" (Acts 9:2; 19:9, 23; 22:4; 24:22) or to "the way" to Jerusalem, upon which Jesus will shortly embark (cf. 10:32, 52).[3] Neither of these is likely since the expression is commonplace for any journey and since Jesus has not yet taken the decisive turn toward Jerusalem.

Jesus first asks about popular opinion: "Who do

---

1. The unusual location is often cited as evidence for the historicity of the event, since there seems to be no symbolic or theological associations with it (so Hooker, *Mark*, 202; Gundry, *Mark*, 425 – 26; Craig A. Evans, *Mark 8:27 – 16:20* [WBC 34B;

Nashville: Nelson, 2001], 10, 13; Stein, *Mark*, 398).

2. Josephus, *Ant.* 18.2.1 §28; *J.W.* 2.9.1 §168.

3. Hooker, *Mark*, 202.

people say I am?" The question of Jesus' identity has been a central theme of Mark's gospel, from the narrator's introduction (1:1), to the Father's acclamation (1:11), to demonic recognition (1:24, 34; 3:11 – 12; 5:6 – 7). The people are amazed at his miraculous power and wonder what this is all about (1:27; 2:12; 6:2, 14 – 16; 7:37), and Herod Antipas wonders if Jesus might be John the Baptist risen from the dead (6:14 – 16). After Jesus calms the storm, the disciples explicitly ask, "Who, then, is this, that the wind and the sea obey him!" (4:41). The narrative has been leading up to this initial climax.

8:28 They said, "Some say John the Baptist; others, Elijah; still others, one of the prophets." (οἱ δὲ εἶπαν αὐτῷ λέγοντες ὅτι Ἰωάννην τὸν βαπτιστήν, καὶ ἄλλοι Ἠλίαν, ἄλλοι δὲ ὅτι εἷς τῶν προφητῶν). The language of popular speculation about Jesus is an abbreviated version of 6:14 – 16. Herod had superstitiously feared that John the Baptist had risen from the dead to avenge his murder (6:17 – 29), and the people had evidently taken up (or perhaps started) these rumors. Since the ministries of Jesus and John overlapped, such rumors seem illogical, but those who started them may not have heard of Jesus before John's arrest and execution.

There was much speculation in Judaism concerning the return of Elijah, drawn especially from Mal 3:1; 4:5 – 6 and spurred on by Elijah's unusual departure from the earth (2 Kgs 2:11). That these hopes were alive in the first century is evident from Sir 48:1 – 14, where it is said of Elijah, "You were taken up by a whirlwind of fire, in a chariot with horses of fire. At the appointed time, it is written, you are destined to calm the wrath of God before it breaks out in fury, to turn the hearts of parents to their children [Mal. 4:5 – 6], and to restore the tribes of Jacob" (Sir 48:9 – 10 NRSV). Jewish expectation for the return of Elijah also appears in the Gospels (cf. Matt 11:14; 17:10 – 12; 27:49; Mark

9:11 – 12; 15:36; John 1:21, 25) and at Qumran (4Q558 [4QVision]). In the next chapter Jesus will point out that Elijah is indeed coming, but that he has already come in the person of John the Baptist (9:11 – 13).

"One of the prophets" means one of the OT prophets, perhaps with hints of the eschatological "prophet like Moses" of Deut 18:15 (cf. Acts 3:22; 7:37; John 1:21, 25; 6:14; 7:40). In Mark 6:4 Jesus identified himself implicitly as a prophet, a christological theme that is even more prominent in Luke-Acts (Luke 4:24; 7:16; 13:33; 24:19; Acts 3:22; 7:37). As God's spokesperson, Jesus is indeed a prophet, but he is much more than that.

It is perhaps surprising that there is no speculation that Jesus is the Messiah. In light of the many messianic figures who had arisen in Judaism during the first century, one might expect this question to have been raised about Jesus. In Mark's narrative presentation the purpose is clear: Peter is to be the first human character to proclaim that Jesus is the Messiah. Though the disciples have a long way to go, they are on the right path of understanding.

8:29 He asked them, "But what about you? Who do you say I am?" Peter said to him, "You are the Messiah." (καὶ αὐτὸς ἐπηρώτα αὐτούς· ὑμεῖς δὲ τίνα με λέγετε εἶναι; ἀποκριθεὶς ὁ Πέτρος λέγει αὐτῷ· σὺ εἶ ὁ χριστός). The "you" (ὑμεῖς) is doubly emphatic, both because it is unnecessary in Greek (the verb carries person) and because of its position at the head of the sentence. What have they learned, Jesus wants to know, from their position as "insiders" in the kingdom of God (4:11)?

Peter responds as representative of the disciples, a role he often plays in Mark (9:5; 10:28; 11:21; 14:37) and elsewhere in the gospel tradition (Matt 14:28; 15:15; 18:21; 19:27). "You are the Messiah" (σὺ εἶ ὁ χριστός) stresses Jesus' most fundamental identity as God's end-time agent of salvation (see comments on 1:1). Although Jesus does not use the title for himself, probably because of its nationalistic and militaristic connotations (see "In Depth: Jewish Expectations for the 'Messiah,'" below), this does not mean it is not true.[4] From Mark's perspective Jesus is indeed the Messiah (1:1), the promised Savior from the line of David, who will accomplish God's end-time salvation and establish God's eternal kingdom in justice and righteousness (2 Sam 7:11 – 16; Isa 9:1 – 5; 11:1 – 10). Yet Jesus will define this messiahship on his own terms.

IN DEPTH: Jewish Expectations for the "Messiah"

"Christ" (χριστός) is a Greek translation of the Hebrew *māšîaḥ*, originally an adjective meaning "anointed" or (substantivally) "anointed one." Anointing with oil in the OT signified setting apart for service to God. The term could be used of priests (Lev 4:3, 5, 16; 6:22), prophets (1 Kgs 19:16), and even the Persian king Cyrus as God's agent for the return from exile (Isa 45:1). Its most important application, however, was to Israel's king, the "LORD's anointed" (1 Sam 16:6; 24:6), who served as God's vice-regent. With the possible exception of Dan 9:25 – 26, the title is never used in the OT in the absolute sense of "the Messiah." Yet the "messianic idea" was alive and well in Israel.[5] It arose especially from the Davidic covenant, in which God promised king David the perpetuity of his royal line and that his "seed" (= descendant[s]) would reign forever on his throne (2 Sam 7:11 – 16).

With the division of the kingdom and the decline and eventual collapse of the Davidic dynasty, the OT prophets began to predict that one day God would fulfill his promise to David by restoring the Davidic line and raising up a king who would reign forever in justice and righteousness (Pss 2; 89; 110; Isa 9:1 – 5; 11:1 – 10; Jer 23:5 – 6; 33:15 – 16; Ezek 34:23 – 24, 37:24 – 25; Mic 5:1 – 5). Though this coming Davidic king is never called "the Messiah" in the OT, during the Second Temple period the titular use of the term began to be employed. This expectation for the Messiah and "son of David" is most clearly expressed in the pseudepigraphic *Psalms of Solomon*, composed in the first century BC:

> See, Lord, and raise up for them their king, the son of David,
> to rule over your servant Israel....

---

4. F. Hahn, *The Titles of Jesus in Christology* (trans. Harold Knight and George Off; New York: World, 1969), 223 – 28, famously argued that the historical Jesus in fact rejected Peter's acclamation of Jesus' messiahship, and the rebuke in v. 33 was originally a response to Peter's confession instead of to Peter's subsequent rebuke. This seems unlikely. How could the church have come to believe so firmly in Jesus' messiahship if he had explicitly rejected it? In any case, Mark himself certainly views Peter's confession as true (cf. 1:1), even if it is not the whole story.

5. See J. Klausner, *The Messianic Idea: From Its Beginning to the Completion of the Mishnah* (trans. W. F. Stinespring; New York: Macmillan, 1955). J. Coppens, *Le messianisme royal. Ses origines, son développement, son accomplissement* (LD 54; Paris: Cerf, 1968); S. Mowinckel, *He That Cometh: The Messiah Concept in the Old Testament and Later Judaism* (Grand Rapids: Eerdmans, 2005); J. A. Fitzmyer, *The One Who Is to Come* (Grand Rapids: Eerdmans, 2007); Strauss, *Davidic Messiah*, 35 – 57.

> Undergird him with the strength to destroy the unrighteous rulers,
> to purge Jerusalem from Gentiles who trample her to destruction;
> in wisdom and in righteousness to drive out the sinners from the inheritance;
> to smash the arrogance of sinners like a potter's jar;
> to shatter all their substance with an iron rod;
> to destroy unlawful nations with the word of his mouth;
> at his warning the nations will flee from his presence;
> and he will condemn sinners by the thoughts of their hearts.[6]
>
> (*Pss. Sol.* 17:21–25)

The diverse communities of first-century Judaism had a variety of messianic expectations and hopes.[7] The priestly led community at Qumran, for example, anticipated two anointed figures, a royal messiah from the line of David and a priestly one from the line of Aaron (1QS 9:11). Other groups, like the Sadducees, had little interest in a coming messiah, content as they were with the political status quo and their own (priestly) leadership. Despite this diversity, there is good evidence for a strong and persistent expectation for the coming of a king from the line of David, who would free the nation, crush Israel's enemies, and establish a kingdom of righteousness and justice centered in Jerusalem. When Peter says, "You are the Messiah," it is likely that he has this expectation in mind.

How did Peter come to believe Jesus was the Messiah? In Matthew's account Jesus attributes it to divine revelation ("This was not revealed to you by flesh and blood, but by my Father in heaven"; Matt 16:17). While Mark would certainly not deny that Peter's insight came from God, in the progress of his narrative it is Jesus' self-revelation through his words and actions that has brought Peter to this point: proclaiming the kingdom, healing the sick, casting out demons, feeding the multitudes, and raising the dead.[8]

8:30 He strongly warned them not to tell anyone about him (καὶ ἐπετίμησεν αὐτοῖς ἵνα μηδενὶ λέγωσιν περὶ αὐτοῦ). The word for "warn"

(ἐπιτιμάω) is a strong one. It is used of rebuking demons (1:25), rebuking the storm (4:39), and sternly warning others to silence (3:12). It will be used of Peter and Jesus in the exchange that follows (vv. 32–33). The warning here relates to Mark's "messianic secret," Jesus' intentional suppression of publicity concerning his true identity (see Introduction: Mark's Gospel in Historical Perspective; and comments on 1:25; 1:43–44).

In the past, Jesus had silenced the demons to avoid the "bad press" that would result if they announced his identity (1:25, 34; 3:11–12). He also silenced those he had healed, probably to avoid publicity that could spark a messianic revolt (1:44;

---

6. R. B. Wright, "Psalms of Solomon," in *OTP*, 2:667.

7. Jacob Neusner, W. C. Green, and E. S. Frerichs, eds., *Judaisms and Their Messiahs at the Turn of the Christian Era* (Cambridge: Cambridge University Press, 1987); James H. Charlesworth et al., *The Messiah: Developments in Earliest Ju-*

daism and Christianity (Minneapolis: Fortress, 1992).

8. Contra Boring, *Mark*, 238, who claims Peter's inference has nothing to do with having observed or participated in the miracles.

5:43; 7:36; 8:26). Finally, he now commands the disciples to keep his messiahship a secret until he has defined its true nature (cf. 9:9). This purpose becomes clear in the following verses, as Jesus begins to define his suffering role as the Son of Man.

8:31 Then he began to teach them that it was necessary for the Son of Man to suffer many things and to be rejected by the elders and the ruling priests and the experts in the law, to be killed, and after three days to rise again (Καὶ ἤρξατο διδάσκειν αὐτοὺς ὅτι δεῖ τὸν υἱὸν τοῦ ἀνθρώπου πολλὰ παθεῖν καὶ ἀποδοκιμασθῆναι ὑπὸ τῶν πρεσβυτέρων καὶ τῶν ἀρχιερέων καὶ τῶν γραμματέων καὶ ἀποκτανθῆναι καὶ μετὰ τρεῖς ἡμέρας ἀναστῆναι). As noted above, Mark's "began to teach them" marks a key turn in the narrative, as Jesus for the first time explicitly predicts his coming suffering in Jerusalem. Matthew similarly recognizes the significance of this transition and marks it off even more clearly: "From that time on Jesus began to explain to his disciples …" (Matt 16:21). This so-called "passion prediction" is repeated two more times in the chapters leading up to Jesus' entrance into Jerusalem (9:31; 10:33 – 34).

On the background and significance of the "Son of Man" title, see "In Depth: Jesus as the Son of Man" at 2:10 – 11. Jesus teaches the "necessity" (δεῖ) of the suffering of the Son of Man. It is necessary both because Scripture predicted the Messiah's suffering (cf. Isa 52:13 – 53:12) and because it has been divinely ordained by God.[9] Jesus will suffer "many things" (πολλά), meaning the whole complex of events of the passion: arrest and trial, humiliation, beatings, mocking, and the agony of crucifixion. "To be rejected" (ἀποδοκιμασθῆναι) may allude to Ps 118:22 ("The stone the builders rejected [LXX: ἀπεδοκίμασαν] …"). This verse will be quoted by

Jesus at the climactic end of the parable of the tenant farmers (12:10 – 11).[10]

The three groups Jesus mentions constituted the Sanhedrin, the Jewish high court. The "elders" (πρεσβύτεροι) were lay leaders, the "aristocratic leaders of the Jewish patrician families."[11] The "ruling priests" (ἀρχιερεῖς), traditionally called "chief priests," were the priestly aristocracy of Jerusalem, made up of leading members of the high priest's family and other influential priests (cf. Acts 4:6). This is the first time these two groups have been named in Mark's gospel. It is only when Jesus goes to Jerusalem that he encounters and is challenged by the Jerusalem hierarchy. The "experts in the law," or "scribes" (γραμματεῖς), were authoritative experts in the interpretation and application of the Jewish law (see comments on 1:22). While there were many scribes throughout Israel, the most influential ones served on the Sanhedrin.

Jesus says he will be raised "after three days" (μετὰ τρεῖς ἡμέρας). This expression, also used in the other two Markan passion predictions (9:31; 10:33 – 34; cf. Matt 27:63), seems at first sight problematic, since Jesus was crucified on Friday and raised on Sunday morning. Matthew and Luke both use the phrase "on the third day" (τῇ τρίτῃ ἡμέρᾳ) in their parallels (Matt 16:21; 17:23; 20:19; Luke 9:22; 18:33; cf. 24:7, 46), perhaps to alleviate the chronological problem.

Some see here an allusion to Hosea 6:2, "After two days he will revive us; on the third day he will restore us." In context this is a prediction of Israel's restoration, and "on the third day" refers to a short period of time. Some commentators take this as Jesus' original meaning — that he would be vindicated by God in a short time — thus eliminating the chronological problem. The disciples then

---

9. Stein, *Mark*, 401.

10. The psalm will be also cited by the onlookers at Jesus' entrance to Jerusalem (11:9 – 10, with Ps 118:25 – 26 cited).

11. Grant Osborne, "Elders," in *DJG*, 201.

interpreted Jesus' words literally after discovering the empty tomb.[12] While this is possible, it seems more likely that the disciples discovered Hos 6:2 *after* the resurrection. Indeed the Matthean and Lukan modification of the saying is closer to Hosea's wording than Mark's. A better solution is that "after three days" reflects the Jewish custom of treating any part of a day as a full day, so that "after three days" is the same as "on the third day."[13]

8:32 He was speaking this message plainly. Pulling him aside, Peter began to rebuke him (καὶ παρρησίᾳ τὸν λόγον ἐλάλει. καὶ προσλαβόμενος ὁ Πέτρος αὐτὸν ἤρξατο ἐπιτιμᾶν αὐτῷ). That Jesus spoke "plainly" or "with boldness" (παρρησίᾳ) can be contrasted with his parabolic teaching in the past. There is no doubt about Jesus' meaning, and it produces an immediate response from Peter. He will not stand for this kind of defeatist talk and so pulls Jesus aside and begins to rebuke him (ἐπιτιμάω; see v. 30). The reason for Peter's rebuke is clear: "he is committed to the expectation of a Davidic Messiah who would defeat the Romans and their Jewish collaborators and reestablish an autonomous kingdom of Israel."[14] Though Peter has shown insight by acknowledging Jesus' messiahship, he cannot comprehend his suffering role.

Whether there were any expectations for a suffering Messiah in the Judaism of Jesus' day is debated among scholars.[15] Some claim that such expectations existed, but that they were later suppressed in Jewish sources in opposition to Christian claims.[16] Others insist that "there is no serious evidence … of the bringing together of the concepts of the suffering servant and the Davidic Messiah before the Christian era."[17] The Targum of Isaiah, for example, identifies the sufferings associated with the "servant" of Isa 52:13 – 53:12 as referring to the people of Israel, not the Messiah.[18] Whether such expectations existed in any circles within Judaism, the weight of evidence from both the NT and Second Temple Jewish literature confirms that popular expectations centered on a conquering Messiah, not a suffering one. In this context, Peter's response is not surprising (see Theology in Application, below).

8:33 Turning and looking at his disciples, he rebuked Peter and said, "Get behind me, Satan, because you are not thinking about God's concerns, but about merely human ones!" (ὁ δὲ ἐπιστραφεὶς καὶ ἰδὼν τοὺς μαθητὰς αὐτοῦ ἐπετίμησεν Πέτρῳ καὶ λέγει· ὕπαγε ὀπίσω μου, σατανᾶ, ὅτι οὐ φρονεῖς τὰ τοῦ θεοῦ ἀλλὰ τὰ τῶν ἀνθρώπων). Peter's rebuke cannot go unanswered, and Mark uses the same strong term of rebuke (ἐπιτιμάω) for Jesus' reply. That Jesus turned and looked at all the disciples suggests that Peter's comment reflected their view as well, and Jesus' responds to them all. Another possible interpretation, however, is that the phrase means "turning and *seeing* his disciples" (NJB, NASB, ESV); that is, Jesus realized that they had

---

12. So Evans, *Mark 8:27 – 16:20*, 17. Evans cites the Targum on Hos 6:2 ("on the day of the resurrection of the dead he will raise us up") as evidence for the eschatological interpretation of the verse.

13. Taylor, *Mark*, 378; France, *Mark*, 336 – 37; Stein, *Mark*, 402. At least twice Josephus refers to events that occurred "after three days" as the same as "on the third day" (*Ant.* 7.11.6 §§280 – 281; 8.8.1 §§214, 218).

14. Collins, *Mark*, 407.

15. A balanced perspective can be found in S. H. T. Page, "The Suffering Servant between the Testaments," *NTS* 31 (1985): 481 – 97. The later rabbinic tradition of two messiahs,

one who suffers and one who is victorious, almost certainly arose after failure of the Bar Kokhba revolt of AD 132 – 35. See Klausner, *Messianic Idea*, 483 – 501; S. H. Levey, *The Messiah: An Aramaic Interpretation: The Messianic Exegesis of the Targum* (HUCM 2; Cincinnati: Hebrew Union College, 1974), 15 – 17, 127 – 28; Str-B 2:292 – 99; A. S. van der Woude, *TDNT*, 9:526 – 27.

16. J. Jeremias, *TDNT*, 5:677 – 717; Cranfield, *Mark*, 277.

17. H. H. Rowley, "The Suffering Servant and the Davidic Messiah," in *The Servant of the Lord and Other Essays on the Old Testament* (London: Lutterworth, 1952), 90.

18. Schürer, *History of the Jewish People*, 2:547 – 49.

overheard Peter's remark. In this case, Jesus has to respond so that they will not be led astray by Peter's misapprehension of the role of the Messiah.

The severity of Jesus' response is shocking, identifying Peter with Satan, the archenemy of God. Evans seeks to soften this, suggesting that since the word "Satan" (σατανᾶς; Heb. *sāṭān*) means "opponent," Jesus' original comment may have been adjectival, meaning, "Get behind me, you who oppose me!" Evidence for this is the fact that Jesus associates Peter's rebuke with "human concerns" (v. 33), not satanic ones.[19]

While this is possible, it cannot have been Mark's intent, since Satan has been repeatedly identified as the personal opponent of Jesus (1:13; 3:23, 26; 4:15), who snatches the seed of the word away (4:15) and tests/tempts Jesus to depart from God's purpose (1:13). To avoid the cross — the goal and centerpiece of Mark's gospel — would be diabolical to the extreme. It would also be a "human" concern, since human weakness and depravity desire the path of least resistance and greatest power. Peter's challenge to Jesus may be compared to the temptation account in Matthew and Luke (Q), where Satan offers Jesus the kingdoms of the world in exchange for his worship, without the need to embark on his suffering path (Matt 4:8–10; Luke 4:5–8).

"Get behind me" (ὕπαγε ὀπίσω μου) may mean either "Fall back in line," calling Peter to renounce his insubordination and fall in line with the rest of the disciples,[20] or, "Get away from me!" similar to Jesus' words in Matt 4:10: "Away from me, Satan" (ὕπαγε, σατανᾶ).[21] This latter is most likely, in light of the severity of the rebuke, the same verb (ὑπάγω) being used, and the use of the term "Satan." If Peter is expressing satanic intentions, these must be banished.

Theology in Application

The question of Jesus' identity and mission have been in the forefront of Mark's gospel since the opening line: "The beginning of the good news about Jesus the Messiah." Up till now the answer to the question "Who is this?" has been implicitly answered through Jesus' words and actions. He is the one who teaches with authority, casts out demons, heals the sick, raises the dead, calms the sea, walks on water, and feeds the multitudes. Most importantly, he is the one who announces and inaugurates the kingdom of God. Three themes related to Jesus' identity run through this passage.

Human Perceptions about Jesus

When Jesus asked his disciples, "Who do people say that I am?" he was raising the question of the ages, one that has been asked and answered in a multitude of ways throughout the centuries. Perceptions of Jesus have varied enormously over time and place. Some say he was a great teacher of wisdom; others a proclaimer

19. Evans, *Mark 8:27–16:20*, 19.

20. Gundry, *Mark*, 433; Evans, *Mark 8:27–16:20*, 19; Boring, *Mark*, 242.

21. Cranfield, *Mark*, 280; France, *Mark*, 338; Hooker, *Mark*, 206; B. A. E. Osborne, "Peter: Stumbling-Block and Satan," *NovT* 15 (1973): 187–90.

of social justice and care for the poor; still others a wild-eyed apocalyptic prophet announcing God's cataclysmic judgement and the end of the world. Members of the infamous Jesus Seminar viewed him as a Cynic-like philosopher promoting an egalitarian society without hierarchy or social distinctions. Others claim he was a political revolutionary, advocating the violent overthrow of the government, or a social revolutionary, calling for a "bottom-up" peasant revolution.

Other world religions have their own take on Jesus. To Muslims he is a great prophet of Allah, who is second only to Mohammed in importance but whose true mission was obscured when he was deified by his Christian followers. To ancient Gnostics and their modern counterparts in Hinduism and New Age religions, he is an enlightened mystic whose spiritual knowledge can bring about a higher consciousness and union with the Divine. To pseudo-Christian cults he is the brother of Satan, the physical son of a union between Jehovah God and Mary (Mormons), or an exalted created being, otherwise known as Michael the Archangel (Jehovah's Witnesses).[22]

In the midst of the cacophony of voices comes the answer of Peter. It is the answer the gospel has been building to since its first sentence: *"You are the Messiah."* Is this answer right or wrong? The answer, of course, is both. It is certainly right that Jesus is the promised Messiah foretold by the OT prophets. He is the longed-for king who will accomplish God's end-time salvation and bring in his eternal kingdom. Yet Peter's answer is also wrong, in that he misunderstands the Messiah's role. He cannot conceive of a Messiah who will suffer and die.

The tendency to create Jesus in our own image is a danger still with us. Our perceptions of Jesus are inevitably shaped by our felt needs. The wealth and prosperity gospel claims that Jesus is there to make us personally happy and financially successful. There is a proclivity to ignore or pass over those passages that call for a renunciation of wealth or sacrifice for the kingdom. Those who despise others out of racial prejudice or nationalistic pride tend to pick up on biblical passages about the judgment of the wicked but ignore Jesus' calls to love our enemies and to pray for those who persecute us. Like Peter, all of us need to hear Jesus' rebuke of our self-promoting perceptions of the Messiah and submit ourselves to his authority and lordship.

Jesus' Messianic Identity and Authority

There is a lively scholarly debate concerning expectations for the "Messiah" in first-century Judaism. On one extreme are those who claim there was no such thing as a "messianic hope" in Judaism. The Christians, it is argued, created this supposed Jewish expectation to explain the identity of the enigmatic figure of Jesus. W. S.

---

22. On the accusatory claims about Jesus' identity during his ministry, see Scot McKnight and Joseph B. Modica, eds., *Who Do My Opponents Say That I Am? An Investigation of the Charges against Jesus* (London: T&T Clark, 2008).

Green, for example, claims that the term Messiah "is all signifier with no signified … notable primarily for its indeterminacy."[23] "By naming Jesus *christos* and depicting him as foretold and expected … early Christian writers gave the figure of the messiah a diachronic dimension. They situated the messiah's origin not in the present but in Israelite antiquity and thus established the Hebrew scriptures as a sequence of auguries."[24]

On the other extreme are those who consider the "Messiah" to be a universally recognized and precisely defined figure, fully recognizable to all Jews of Jesus' day. The truth is somewhere in the middle, though certainly leaning toward the latter perspective. While there was certainly diversity within first-century Judaism concerning the nature and function of the Messiah, there is much evidence that most Jews of the first century were anticipating the coming of the Messiah, God's end-time agent of salvation.[25] In this historical context Peter's confession becomes entirely feasible.

It is also true that expectations for this coming one revolved primarily around a military and political figure, a warrior king from the line of David who would defeat Israel's enemies and reign in Jerusalem over a reunited and restored Israelite kingdom. Though Mark does not tell us the reason for Peter's rebuke, it seems clear that Peter could not accept that the Messiah could suffer and die at the hands of the religious leaders. Yet for Jesus, this was central to his messianic identity. There could be no salvation without the one who would die "as a ransom for many" (10:45).

The Suffering Role of the Messiah

We have touched on the question whether any Jews of the first century might have expected a Messiah who would suffer and die. While the evidence is inconclusive, it seems certain that any such expectation would be a minority view. Israel had suffered under a series of devastating conquests and had been subjugated by one empire after another. The brief period of Jewish independence under the Hasmoneans (164–63 BC) only whetted the appetite of the people for a sovereign state under the Messiah, when Israel could worship God freely and without hindrance from pagan nations.

From a human perspective, such freedom could never be achieved except through military victory. As Jesus will say to his disciples in 10:42, "You know that those recognized as rulers of the Gentiles lord it over them, and their great ones exercise dominion over them." The way of the world is conquest and subjugation. Yet the way of Jesus is radically different: "But it is not so among you. Rather, whoever

---

23. W. S. Green, "Messiah in Judaism: Rethinking the Question," in *Judaisms and Their Messiahs* (eds. Neusner, Green, and Frerichs), 2–4.

24. Ibid., 5.

25. *Pss. Sol.* 17–18; 4QFlor (= 4Q174); 4QPBless (4Q252); 4QpIsaᵃ (= 4Q161); 1QS 9:11; *1 En.* 49:3; 2 Esd 7:28–29; 12:34, 32. For a detailed survey of the literature, see Strauss, *Davidic Messiah*, 38–57.

wants to be great among you will be your servant, and whoever wants to be first will be slave of all" (10:43 – 44). Jesus teaches service instead of domination, and sacrifice instead of conquest. This is how true salvation will be achieved and how the kingdom of God will be inaugurated. Though Peter has correctly discerned Jesus' messianic identity, he has yet to learn the suffering role of the cross.

This passage has enormous application for Christian leaders today. In American Christianity, the leaders with the greatest following are often those who are the most influential, persuasive, charismatic, or appealing. Service and sacrifice are not typically the path to the pastorate of a megachurch or to the senior leadership of a ministry agency. Yet the great paradox of the Christian faith is that by serving we lead, and by sacrificing our lives we gain the kingdom. As Jesus will teach in the next passage and in the chapters to come, true leaders are those who lift up and empower others rather than exalt themselves.

IN DEPTH: Did Jesus Predict His Own Death?

Much debate has centered on the question of whether Jesus predicted his own death and, more specifically, whether the gospel passion predictions represent authentic dominical sayings. On the former question, the majority of scholars today acknowledge that the volatile religious and political climate of first-century Judaism renders it likely that Jesus would have foreseen the possibility, and even the likelihood, that he would die a martyr's death. (1) The execution of John the Baptist by Herod Antipas must have been a warning to Jesus that he could face the same fate from the political or religious authorities. The rumors that Jesus might be John back from the dead show that their two ministries were linked in the popular imagination. (2) There is no doubt historically that Jesus faced strong opposition from the Jewish religious establishment and that they viewed him as a threat. This tradition appears at all levels of gospel sources and stratum (Mark; Q; M; L; John). (3) Jesus repeatedly identified himself with the OT prophets and their suffering fate (6:4 pars; 12:1 – 11 pars.; Matt 5:12; 23:29 – 39; Luke 6:23, 26; 11:47 – 50; 13:33 – 35). It is unlikely that the church created these "prophet" sayings since the early believers preferred more exalted titles for Jesus, like Messiah, Lord, and Son of God.

But what about the passion predictions themselves? Some scholars have claimed that their specificity renders it unlikely that Jesus could have uttered them in this form. Yet certain features point to their historicity.[26]

1. None of the passion predictions speak of crucifixion as the means of execution, a point that is surprising if the church invented them after the fact.

26. See Witherington, *Mark*, 242 – 43.

2. The title "Son of Man" is used in all three Markan passion predictions, a title characteristic of Jesus himself but not used by the church in its confessions.

3. It is unlikely that the church invented the phrase "after three days," which occurs in the Markan (and earliest) version of these sayings, because of the chronological difficulties of a Friday crucifixion and a Sunday resurrection. If these sayings were placed in the mouth of Jesus after the resurrection, one would expect "on the third day."

4. Finally, the passion predictions display little atonement theology. Since "Christ died for our sins" was an early creedal formula (1 Cor 15:3), one would expect something similar to be said in any passion prediction invented by the church. In their present form, the sayings could be taken as no more than the death of a martyr. Only in passages like Mark 10:45 and 14:24 do we hear Jesus using atonement language.

Together, these points provide strong evidence for the general historicity of the passion predictions.[27]

27. See Hans Bayer, *Jesus' Predictions of Vindication and Resurrection: The Provenance, Meaning and Correlation of the Synoptic Predictions* (WUNT 2/20; Tübingen: Mohr [Siebeck], 1986).

CHAPTER 34

Mark 8:34 – 9:1

Literary Context

From the beginning of his ministry, Jesus has been performing remarkable miracles that demonstrate his messianic authority as the Son of God. The narrative has reached an initial climax in the previous episode when, for the first time, one of Jesus' disciples openly acknowledges that Jesus is the Messiah (8:29). This confession by Peter results in a dramatic turn in the narrative, as Jesus now predicts his coming death — the first of three "passion predictions."

Mark, who is so fond of triads (groups of three), will present three "cyles" of events during this phase of Jesus' ministry. In each cycle, Jesus will first predict his death (8:31; 9:30 – 31; 10:32 – 34), followed by some demonstration of pride, ignorance, and/or self-interest by the disciples (8:32; 9:33 – 34; 10:35 – 41), followed by teaching from Jesus about humility, self-sacrifice, and the suffering way of the cross (8:34 – 38; 9:35 – 37; 10:42 – 45). The present passage is in the midst of the first cycle. Following Jesus' passion prediction (8:31), Peter rebuked him (8:32); now Jesus teaches about cross-bearing discipleship (8:34 – 38).

Main Idea

This collection of sayings picks up the theme of Jesus' passion prediction and applies it to the disciples and all who follow Jesus. Whoever wishes to be his disciple must renounce their own ambitions and follow Jesus wholly, even to the point of death. Paradoxically, to lose one's life for Jesus and for the gospel means to gain true life.

Translation

Mark 8:34–9:1

34a	summons	Calling the crowd together with his disciples,
b	Instruction	**he said to them,**
c	condition of 34d	*"If anyone wants to follow after me,*
d	result of 34c	*he must deny himself, take up his cross, and follow me.*
35a	condition of 35b	*For whoever wants to save their life*
b	result of 35a	*will lose it,*
c	condition of 35d	*but whoever loses their life for me and for the gospel*
d	result of 35c	*will save it.*
36	teaching	*For what does it benefit a person to gain the whole world and lose their soul?*
37	teaching//parallelism with 36	*For what can a person give in exchange for their soul?*
38a	condition of 38c	*For whoever is ashamed of me and my words*
b	context	*in this adulterous and sinful generation,*
c	result of 38a	*the Son of Man will be ashamed of him*
d	setting of 38c	*when he comes in his Father's glory with the holy angels."*
9:1a	Instruction/Prophecy	And **he was saying to them,**
b	veracity statement	*"Truly I say to you,*
c	prophecy	*some who are standing here will certainly not taste death*
d	condition of 9c	*until they see the kingdom of ☙* *God come in power."*

Structure

This passage is comprised of five sayings of Jesus dealing with the cost and consequences of discipleship (vv. 34 – 38), followed by an enigmatic saying that some of the apostles will not die before they see the kingdom of God come with power (9:1). Since three of the sayings have parallels not only at this point in Matthew and Luke (Matt 16:24 – 48; Luke 9:23 – 27), but also elsewhere in the Synoptics,[1] these may have been independent sayings that Mark has gathered together around the common theme of the cost of discipleship (see comments on 8:34). The sayings begin with the condition of discipleship (8:34c) and then follow with the consequences of true or false discipleship (8:35 – 9:1). The sacrifice of one's life for Jesus and the gospel results in the infinite blessings of the kingdom of God. It is this theme that links the first five sayings to the last one (9:1). "Seeing the kingdom" signifies the vindication of those who have remained faithful to Jesus and the gospel message.

---

1. 8:34 = Matt 10:38; Luke 14:27; *Gos. Thom.* 55b; 8:35 = Matt 10:39; Luke 17:33; cf. John 12:25; 8:38 = Matt 10:33; Luke 12:9.

Exegetical Outline

→ **1. Introduction (8:34a-b)**

   2. Conditions of Discipleship (8:34c-d)

   3. Consequences of True or False Discipleship (8:35 – 9:1)

      a. Gaining or losing one's life/soul (8:35 – 37)

      b. Being unashamed or ashamed at the Son of Man's coming (8:38)

      c. Promise of vindication for the faithful: to see the kingdom of God (9:1)

Explanation of the Text

8:34 Calling the crowd together with his disciples, he said to them, "If anyone wants to follow after me, he must deny himself, take up his cross, and follow me." (Καὶ προσκαλεσάμενος τὸν ὄχλον σὺν τοῖς μαθηταῖς αὐτοῦ εἶπεν αὐτοῖς· εἴ τις θέλει ὀπίσω μου ἀκολουθεῖν, ἀπαρνησάσθω ἑαυτὸν καὶ ἀράτω τὸν σταυρὸν αὐτοῦ καὶ ἀκολουθείτω μοι). The first passion prediction was given to his disciples, but now Jesus calls together the "crowd." This is surprising since the previous scene was apparently on a private retreat with the disciples to the region of Caesarea Philippi. Was this crowd present all along? Or were they from the surrounding villages and heard about Jesus' presence in the region? While either is possible, most likely Mark has taken these sayings from elsewhere in the tradition (where they were addressed to the crowds) and has introduced them here as a complement to Jesus' passion prediction. Mark retains the traditional address to expand Jesus' call to all his followers, not just the Twelve.

A conditional clause ("If anyone wants to follow after me ...") is followed by three third-person imperatives:[2] (1) he must deny himself, (2) take up his cross, and (3) follow me. It seems odd that Jesus says, "if anyone wants to follow after me, he must ... follow me." The point is that the one who would be counted as a "follower" (i.e., a disciple) must actually take action.

To follow Jesus means more than just identifying yourself as a Christ-follower. It means renouncing self and journeying with him even to death. To "deny oneself" does not mean to live a life of self-denial or self-discipline. It is to renounce your claim to yourself — desires, ambitions, personal goals — and to submit to Christ as his slave. It is a denial of autonomy and self-sufficiency.[3] Similarly, to "take up your cross" does not mean to accept a life of hardship, as the idiom is sometimes used today. It means to subject oneself to excruciating and shameful execution by crucifixion. Of course, this will not mean actual martyrdom for all, but a willingness to renounce all for Christ. Luke explicitly introduces this metaphorical sense by adding "daily" (καθ' ἡμέραν; 9:23) to Mark's "take up his cross."

This is the first mention of the cross in Mark's

---

2. "Deny oneself" (ἀπαρνησάσθω) and "take up" (ἀράτω) are aorist imperatives, while "follow" (ἀκολουθείτω) is a present imperative, which may indicate that "the 'act' of denying oneself and taking up one's cross is followed by the process of following Jesus" (Stein, *Mark*, 407; following Best, *Following Jesus*, 32). Too much should not be made of this, however, since the aorist indicates undefined rather than "point-in-time" ac-

tion. Indeed, Luke speaks of taking up your cross "daily," but still uses the aorist imperative (ἀράτω; 9:23).

3. The verb ἀπαρνέομαι is used in the NT eleven times, eight of which are related to Peter's denial (14:30, 31, 72; etc.). In these contexts it means the renunciation of any association with a person (cf. Luke 12:9).

gospel. Crucifixion will not be mentioned again until the events leading up to Jesus' death (15:13 – 32). The term "cross" (σταυρός) originally meant a "stake" set in an upright position. Prior to the Romans, the Persians, Greeks, and others practiced crucifixion as a means of exposing an executed corpse to shame and humiliation. The Romans perfected the method, and it became for them a favorite method of execution for the worst of criminals and the greatest of enemies.[4] The goal was to produce both maximum torture and humiliation.

Crucifixion was also meant as a weapon of terror, to warn any would-be revolutionaries of the consequences of opposing Rome. Most crucifixion sites were near major roads to make them visible to the populace and passing travelers. Generally, the upright stake (the *pallus*) was left at the place of execution while the crossbeam (the *patibulum*) was carried by the victim (see 15:20 – 21). The victim would then be tied or nailed (cf. John 20:25; Col 2:14) to the cross and allowed to slowly die from exposure, festering wounds, and asphyxiation.[5] Death on a cross could take many days. The body would often be left as carrion for birds or dogs, which increased the shame, since an honorable death required burial in one's ancestral tomb.

8:35 For whoever wants to save their life will lose it, but whoever loses their life for me and for the gospel will save it (ὃς γὰρ ἐὰν θέλῃ τὴν ψυχὴν αὐτοῦ σῶσαι ἀπολέσει αὐτήν· ὃς δ᾽ ἂν ἀπολέσει τὴν ψυχὴν αὐτοῦ ἕνεκεν ἐμοῦ καὶ τοῦ εὐαγγελίου σώσει αὐτήν). The "for" (γάρ) introduces the consequences or results of taking up one's cross and following Jesus. There is a chiastic structure and a play on words based on the various senses of the words "preserve/save" (σῴζω), "life/soul" (ψυχή), and "lose/sacrifice" (ἀπόλλυμι). Those who choose to "preserve" (σῴζω) their physical "life" (ψυχή) (by avoiding martyrdom) will "lose" (ἀπόλλυμι) their "soul" (ψυχή); but those who "sacrifice" (ἀπόλλυμι) their physical "life" (ψυχή) for the sake of Jesus and the gospel will "save" (σῴζω) their "soul" (ψυχή).

"For [ἕνεκεν] me and for the gospel" could mean "on account of" or "for the sake of."[6] The latter active sense is much more likely and is the sense of the almost identical phrase in 10:29, where people leave homes and family "for my sake and for the sake of the gospel" (ἕνεκεν ἐμοῦ καὶ ἕνεκεν τοῦ εὐαγγελίου). "For me" refers to loyalty to Jesus as Lord and "for the gospel" means in submission and obedience to the message of the kingdom of God (1:14 – 15).[7]

8:36 – 37 For what does it benefit a person to gain the whole world and lose their soul? For what can a person give in exchange for their soul? (τί γὰρ ὠφελεῖ ἄνθρωπον κερδῆσαι τὸν κόσμον ὅλον καὶ ζημιωθῆναι τὴν ψυχὴν αὐτοῦ; τί γὰρ δοῖ ἄνθρωπος

---

4. On crucifixion, see esp. Martin Hengel, *Crucifixion in the Ancient World and the Folly of the Cross* (trans. John Bowden; Philadelphia: Fortress, 1977), passim.

5. The bones of a crucified man named Jehohanan (*Yĕhôḥānān*) were discovered in an ossuary in 1968 at Giv'at ha-Mivtar in the Kidron Valley northeast of the Old City. Archaeologists have dated the remains between AD 7 and 70. He was probably a victim of one of the various insurrectionist movements of the first century. A nail was still embedded in his heal, left there because it was bent after hitting a knot in the wood and so could not be removed. On the original excavation findings see N. Haas, "Anthropological Observations on the Skeletal Remains from Giv'at ha-Mivtar," *IEJ* 20 (1970):

38 – 59. On a reassessment of the evidence, see J. Zias and E. Sekeles, "The Crucified Man from Giv'at ha-Mivtar — A Reappraisal," *IEJ* 35 (1985): 22 – 27; J. Zias and J. H. Charlesworth, "Crucifixion: Archaeology, Jesus, and the Dead Sea Scrolls," in *Jesus and the Dead Sea Scrolls* (ed. J. H. Charlesworth; New York: Doubleday, 1992), 273 – 89.

6. BDAG, 334.

7. The parallels in Matthew and Luke (Matt 16:25; Luke 9:24) omit the phrase "for the gospel" both here and in 10:29 (Matt 19:29; Luke 18:29), one of the unusual agreements of Matthew and Luke against Mark (and a challenge to Markan priority).

ἀντάλλαγμα τῆς ψυχῆς αὐτοῦ;). Verses 36 – 37 include two rhetorical questions that tease out the implications of v. 35. In v. 36 the idea of saving one's physical life is taken to its ultimate end. What if one does not just survive in the world but rises to rule it, gaining all its power, prestige, and wealth (cf. Satan's offer in Matt 4:8 – 9; Luke 4:5 – 6)? What profit is it to "gain the whole world" yet forfeit your soul, that is, to lose your relationship with the creator God? One would be left with nothing, since the present world is passing away (1 Cor 7:31).

If v. 36 looks at the emptiness of preserving one's physical life, v. 37 speaks of the inestimable value of saving one's soul. The verse can be understood in one of two ways: (1) as emphasizing the great value of gaining immortal life, or (2) as stressing the impossibility of buying back a life/soul once it has been lost. If the former, the question means, "What would be worth sacrificing in this temporal, transitory world to gain eternal life?" The answer is, "Everything and more!" One thinks of Jesus' parable of the pearl of great price, where a man is willing to sell everything to buy the most precious of pearls — the kingdom of God (Matt 13:45 – 46).

In the second interpretation, the phrase serves as an implication of v. 36. Once you have lost your life/soul, what could you pay to buy it back? In this case, the answer to the rhetorical question is "Nothing at all."[8] This latter interpretation, which seems more likely, recalls Ps 49:7 – 9, which speaks of the impossible ransom price for a human life: "the ransom for a life is costly, no payment is ever enough — so that they should live on forever and not see decay."

8:38 **"For whoever is ashamed of me and my words in this adulterous and sinful generation, the Son of Man will be ashamed of them when he comes in his Father's glory with the holy angels."** (ὃς γὰρ ἐὰν ἐπαισχυνθῇ με καὶ τοὺς ἐμοὺς λόγους ἐν τῇ γενεᾷ ταύτῃ τῇ μοιχαλίδι καὶ ἁμαρτωλῷ, καὶ ὁ υἱὸς τοῦ ἀνθρώπου ἐπαισχυνθήσεται αὐτόν, ὅταν ἔλθῃ ἐν τῇ δόξῃ τοῦ πατρὸς αὐτοῦ μετὰ τῶν ἀγγέλων τῶν ἁγίων). Verse 38 provides another consequence of true or false discipleship, now couched in the Middle Eastern values of honor and shame.

To be "ashamed of [ἐπαισχύνομαι] me and my words" is parallel to "saving one's life" by repudiating Jesus and the gospel (v. 35). Those who refuse to identify with Jesus in his shameful death in the present earthly realm will experience the same rejection by the Son of Man when he comes to consummate his reign.[9] The phrase "adulterous and sinful generation" appears only here in Mark, but Jesus spoke of the Pharisees disdainfully as "this generation" in 8:12, and Matthew, in his parallel, speaks of "a wicked and adulterous generation" (γενεὰ πονηρὰ καὶ μοιχαλίς; 12:39; 16:4; cf. 12:45; 17:17). A "generation" in this sense is a group of people exhibiting "common characteristics or interests" (BDAG, 191), referring here to those in Israel who refuse to respond to Jesus' proclamation of the kingdom of God. Their description as "adulterous" (μοιχαλίς) recalls the prophets' description of the nation Israel as an unfaithful wife to God, her husband (Isa 1:4, 21; Ezek 16:32; Hos 2:3).

The "coming" of the Son of Man is usually interpreted as the parousia, the final return of the

---

8. Stein, *Mark*, 409.

9. H. E. Tödt (*The Son of Man in the Synoptic Tradition* [trans. D. M. Barton; London: SCM, 1965], passim), Bultmann (*History,* 112, 151 – 52), and others have argued that in this passage and others like it, Jesus was not referring to himself, but to the messianic Son of Man (of Dan 7:13 – 14) who would come after him. There is little evidence in the gospel tradition, however, that Jesus expected a successor. As Evans, *Mark 8:27 – 16:20,* 27, notes, "If Jesus had in mind some other figure, then it is difficult to explain the disappearance of such an important eschatological element in his teaching." The gospel writers certainly understand the Son of Man title to be self-referential.

Messiah to judge and to save (cf. 13:26; 14:62). Some, however, understand it to refer to the Son of Man's entrance into his heavenly glory at his ascension.[10] This, it is argued, is in line with Dan 7:13 – 14, where "one like a son of man" approaches the Ancient of Days in his heavenly court and is given authority, glory, and sovereign power. This interpretation seems unlikely, since the context is one of judgment, when those who have repudiated Jesus will themselves be rejected. This will occur at the parousia, not the ascension.

The Son of Man is said to come in "his Father's glory." Though the divine voice from heaven (1:11; cf. 9:7) identified Jesus as "my beloved Son" and demons announced he was the Son of God (3:11; 5:7), this is Jesus' first self-identification of his father-son relationship with God in Mark's gospel. Jesus will refer to himself as "the Son" in 13:32 and will address God in prayer as "Abba, Father" in 14:36. Such an identification is not surprising in its first-century context, since the Messiah was predicted to have a unique father-son relationship with God (2 Sam 7:14; Pss 2:7; 89:26; 4QFlor 1:11 [= 4Q174]; see comments on 1:1). The connection between Jesus' divine sonship and his role as the Son of Man will appear again in the trial scene at 14:61 – 62.

9:1 And he was saying to them, "Truly I say to you, some who are standing here will certainly not taste death until they see the kingdom of God come in power." (Καὶ ἔλεγεν αὐτοῖς· ἀμὴν λέγω ὑμῖν ὅτι εἰσίν τινες ὧδε τῶν ἑστηκότων οἵτινες οὐ μὴ γεύσωνται θανάτου ἕως ἂν ἴδωσιν τὴν βασιλείαν τοῦ θεοῦ ἐληλυθυῖαν ἐν δυνάμει). Jesus' last saying in this series represents one of the most difficult in Gospels, since it seems to indicate that Jesus will return before the death of his disciples. Similar difficulties arise with 13:26, where in the Olivet Discourse Jesus seems to connect the return of the Son of Man with the destruction of Jerusalem in AD 70, and 14:61 – 62, where he tells the high priest that "you will see the Son of Man … coming with the clouds of heaven."[11]

The saying is strongly emphatic, beginning with Jesus' solemn introductory formula, "Truly I say to you" (ἀμὴν λέγω ὑμῖν; 13 times in Mark; see comments on 3:28 – 30) and with the the emphatic negation, "certainly not" (οὐ μή). To "taste death" (γεύομαι θανάτου) is an idiom that means simply to die.

There have been many interpretations for what it means that some of the disciples will not die "until they see the kingdom of God come in power":[12] (1) the present manifestation of the kingdom in Jesus' words and actions, which the disciples must see with eyes of faith;[13] (2) a preview of the glory of the kingdom revealed in the transfiguration of Jesus that follows;[14] (3) the crucifixion of Jesus,[15] or both his death and resurrection as the inauguration of the kingdom;[16] (4) the coming of Spirit at Pentecost in the beginning of the kingdom age;[17] (5) the

---

10. So France, *Mark*, 342 – 43; Myers, *Binding the Strong Man*, 248 – 49.

11. Paul too seems to expect the return of Christ within his lifetime (1 Cor 15:51; Phil 4:5; 1 Thess 4:15 – 17). But these do not create quite the same problem, since Paul never makes an authoritative prediction, but works from his assumption that the eschatological "end is near."

12. See K. E. Brower, "Mark 9:1: Seeing the Kingdom in Power," *JSNT* 3 (1980): 17 – 41.

13. Evans, *Mark 8:27 – 16:20*, 29; Dodd, *Parables of the Kingdom*, 53 – 54.

14. Taylor, *Mark*, 385 – 86; Cranfield, *Mark*, 287 – 88; Lane, *Mark*, 313; Pesch, *Markusevangelium*, 2:67; Gnilka, *Markus*, 2:2; Witherington, *Mark*, 262; Stein, *Mark*, 411. Taylor thinks that this was the meaning for Mark, but that Jesus himself viewed it as "a visible manifestation of the Rule of God displayed in the life of an Elect Community."

15. M. Bird, "The Crucifixion of Jesus as the Fulfillment of Mark 9:1," *TJ* 24 (2003): 23 – 36.

16. Garland, *Mark*, 330; Edwards, *Mark*, 259 – 61.

17. H. B. Swete, *The Gospel according to St Mark* (London: Macmillan, 1913; repr., Grand Rapids: Eerdmans, 1952), 186.

destruction of Jerusalem in AD 70 as a preview of the final judgment;[18] or (6) the coming of the Son of Man and the consummation of the kingdom.[19] According to this last one, Jesus must have been mistaken since he thought the kingdom would be consummated within the present generation.

While this last view might seem at first sight the most natural reading, it has its own problems. Elsewhere Jesus denies knowledge of the time of the end (13:32), so why would he predict it here? The most widely held and most likely interpretation is the second, where the transfiguration functions as a preview and guarantee of the coming parousia. This seems to be Mark's intention, since he follows the saying immediately with the transfiguration account and connects the two with the specific time reference, "After six days …" (9:2).

The greatest problem with this view is the oddity that Jesus would say that *some* of the disciples would not die before witnessing this event. Why would anyone expect *any* of the disciples to die within the next few days? Cranfield offers a plausible explanation, suggesting that the "some … who will not die" is meant to contrast the three disciples who would experience the glory of the kingdom *in this life* (i.e., at the transfiguration) with the others who would not experience that glory until the final resurrection.[20] This also helps to explain Jesus' reference to the kingdom coming "in power" (ἐν δυνάμει). While all the disciples were presently experiencing the presence and the power of the kingdom in Jesus' words and deeds, Peter, James, and John would have a unique experience of its glory ("in power") on the mountain.

Theology in Application

Jesus has just defined his messiahship, not as conquest but as suffering and death. Now he turns to the crowds and calls all who would be his disciples to take up their own crosses and follow him. The paradox of the Christian faith is that by dying to ourselves and following God's way, we inherit true life.

The Cost of Discipleship

The paradox of salvation is that it costs us nothing, yet it costs us everything. Salvation comes through faith alone, apart from any works that we can do (Eph 2:8 – 9). Yet to depend on Christ for salvation means giving up your old life, with its pride, conceit, and ambition. Jesus says if you want to be his disciple, you must "deny yourself," that is, renounce any claim to your own life and live wholly for God.

Paul uses a slave-market analogy to make the same point. Though we were once slaves to sin, we now have a new master. We are slaves to God, a new ownership that

18. N. T. Wright, *Jesus and the Victory of God* (Minneapolis: Fortress, 1996), 365.

19. Manson, *Teaching of Jesus*, 277 – 84; Nineham, *Mark*, 231 – 32; Collins, *Mark*, 412 – 13. Manson, *Teaching of Jesus*, 282, concludes that "Jesus expected the consummation of the Kingdom to take place at some time in the immediate future,

and that this expectation was not realized." Collins, *Mark*, 413, affirms that "the claim that some who heard Jesus … would live until the coming of the Son of Man is evidence of the imminent expectation of that event on the part of the author of Mark."

20. Cranfield, *Mark*, 500; cf. France, *Mark*, 345; Stein, *Mark*, 411.

leads to obedience and righteousness (Rom 6:16 – 18). This slavery, however, is in fact true freedom, freedom to be the people we were created to be: "But now that you have been set free from sin and have becomes slaves of God, the benefit you reap leads to holiness, and the result is eternal life" (Rom 6:22). Such "slavery" is true "sonship," since through it we become "heirs of God and co-heirs with Christ, if indeed we share in his suffering in order that we may also share in his glory" (8:17).

This partnership in suffering and in glory is Jesus' point in the present passage. To gain true freedom and to share in Christ's glory we must first take up our cross and follow him (8:34). Dietrich Bonhoeffer wrote, "The cross is laid on every Christian. The first Christ suffering which every man must experience is the call to abandon the attachments of this world."[21] Freedom *from* the things of this world means freedom to become all that God wants us to be.

The Great Paradox: By Dying We Live

The result of the decision to renounce all and follow Christ is the great paradox of the Christian life. By giving up our physical lives for Jesus and for the gospel, we gain true spiritual life. Those who strive to protect all they have — wealth, power, prestige — in the end lose it, since this world is passing away (1 Cor 7:31).

This is a constant refrain throughout the NT. James tells the rich to "take pride in their humiliation — since they will pass away like a wild flower" (Jas 1:10). Peter quotes Isa 40:6, 8: "All people are like grass, and all their glory is like the flowers of the field; the grass withers and the flowers fall, but the word of the Lord endures forever" (1 Pet 1:24 – 25). John reminds his readers that "the world and its desires pass away, but whoever does the will of God lives forever" (1 John 2:17). From a human perspective, it sometimes seems as if the wicked prosper and the powerful succeed. But in the end there will be a great reversal, as God brings low the proud and exalts the humble.

The Great Reversal: The Humble Inherit the Earth

This theme of reversal appears throughout the NT, but it is especially prominent in Luke's gospel. Jesus preaches "good news to the poor" (Luke 4:18), and his beatitudes for the poor (6:20 – 21) are balanced with woes against the rich (6:24). He tells parables of radical reversals of fortune like the rich fool (12:13 – 21) and the rich man and Lazarus (16:19 – 31), and he recounts stories of reversal like the salvation of the hated tax collector Zacchaeus (19:1 – 10) and the repentant criminal on the cross (23:39 – 43). Reversal is also a prominent theme in the parables of the Pharisee and

---

21. Dietrich Bonhoeffer, *The Cost of Discipleship* (New York: Simon & Schuster, 1995), 89.

the tax collector (18:9 – 14) and the good Samaritan (10:30 – 37), where those considered to be "righteous" turn out to be only self-righteous, and those who demonstrate humility and servanthood become models for kingdom living.

The Reward for Faithfulness

Though believers are called to humility, service, sacrifice, and even martyrdom, there is also the promise of vindication and reward. Those who give up their lives for Jesus and for the gospel will inherit true life (v. 35). They will become "heirs of God and co-heirs with Christ" (Rom 8:17). The promise of reward is also implicit in Jesus' statement, "whoever is ashamed of me and my words ... the Son of Man will be ashamed of him" (Mark 8:38). The reverse must also be true and is explicitly affirmed in both Matthew and Luke: "Whoever acknowledges me before others, I will also acknowledge before my Father in heaven" (Matt 10:32; cf. Luke 12:8). The promise of the transfiguration is a glimpse of this coming glory.

The reward of glory for those who persevere is another theme throughout the biblical narrative. Paul speaks of the "crown of righteousness," which the Lord will give not only to him but to all those who long for his appearing (2 Tim 4:8), and James of the "crown of life" that the Lord has promised to those who love him (Jas 1:12). For Peter it is the "crown of glory" that will never fade away (1 Pet 5:4). At the end of Revelation the glorified Christ makes the promise, "Look, I am coming soon! My reward is with me" (Rev 22:12; cf. 2:10; 3:11). Just as the Son of Man will be vindicated at the right hand of the Father after suffering, so his followers who persevere will also be glorified.

Mark 9:2 – 13

CHAPTER 35

Literary Context

Coming shortly after Jesus' first passion prediction and his teaching concerning the suffering path of true discipleship (8:27 – 9:1), the transfiguration provides confirmation and reassurance for Jesus' disciples that he is indeed the Messiah and Son of God, God's agent of salvation, and that he will be vindicated and glorified after his suffering. The event also sets the stage for the climax of Jesus' ministry in Jerusalem. Jesus consults with Elijah and Moses, two great OT prophets and leaders, as he prepares to head toward Jerusalem to accomplish his messianic task.

III. The Suffering Way of the Messiah (8:22 – 15:47)

    A. Revelation of the Messiah's Suffering (8:22 – 10:52)

        2. Peter's Confession and First Passion Prediction (8:27 – 33)

        3. Requirements of Discipleship (8:34 – 9:1)

➡   **4. The Transfiguration and the Question about Elijah (9:2 – 13)**

        5. Healing a Boy with an Evil Spirit (9:14 – 29)

Main Idea

At the transfiguration the veil over Jesus' divine glory is lifted and the "inner circle" of disciples — Peter, James, and John — are given a glimpse of his true glory, glory that will be revealed after his resurrection and even more fully when he returns to judge and to save.

Translation

Mark 9:2 – 13

2a	setting (temporal)	After six days
b	Action	**Jesus took Peter, James, and John**
c	Action	and **led them to a high mountain to be alone.**
d	Theophany/Character descr.	**And he was transfigured before them.**
3a	Theophany/Character descr.	**His clothing became dazzling, brilliantly white,**
b	explanation	whiter than any clothing specialist on earth could bleach ⤷ them.
4a	Character entrance	Then **Elijah appeared to them with Moses,**
b	Action	and **they were talking with Jesus.**
5a	Response	**Peter responded,** saying to Jesus,
b	assertion	*"Rabbi, it is good for us to be here.*
c	request/suggestion	*Let us make three shelters, one for you and one for Moses and one for Elijah."*
6a	Narrative aside	For **he did not know how to respond,**
b	reason	since they were so frightened.
7a	Setting	Then **a cloud appeared,** overshadowing them,
b	Theophany	and **a voice came from the cloud,**
c	affirmation	*"This is my beloved Son, listen to him."* [Isa 42:1; Deut 18:15]
8a		Suddenly, when they looked around,
b	Character departure	**they no longer saw anyone with them except Jesus alone.**
9a	setting (temporal)	As they were descending from the mountain,
b	Command	**he commanded them not to tell anyone what they had seen**
c	exception/qualification	until the Son of Man arose from the dead.
10a	Response	So **they kept the matter to themselves,**
b		discussing what it meant to rise from the dead.
11a	Question	**Then they asked him,**
b		*"Why do the experts in the law say that Elijah must come first?"*
12a	Response to 11	**He said to them,**
b	prophecy	*"Coming first, Elijah indeed restores all things.*
c	question/riddle	*So how then is it written about the Son of Man that he must suffer many things ⤷ and be treated shamefully?*
13a	clarification/assertion	*But I tell you, Elijah has indeed come,*
b	assertion	*and they did to him whatever they wanted,*
c	comparison	*just as it was written about him."*

Structure

In terms of its genre, the transfiguration is a theophany, a manifestation of the divine. Many history-of-religions parallels have been suggested, including pagan accounts of the epiphanies of gods, goddesses, or angels, and the deification of human beings.[1] The closest parallel, however, is to traditions related to Moses and his ascent to Mount Sinai to receive the law. Garland summarizes these parallels:[2]

JESUS	MOSES
Jesus takes three disciples up the mountain (Mark 9:2).	Moses goes with three named persons plus seventy of the elders up the mountain (Exod 24:1, 9).
Jesus is transfigured and his clothes become radiantly white (Mark 9:2 – 3).	Moses' skin shines when he descends from the mountain after talking with God (Exod 34:29).
God appears in veiled form in an overshadowing cloud (Mark 9:7).	God appears in veiled form in an overshadowing cloud (Exod 24:15 – 16, 18).
A voice speaks from the cloud (Mark 9:7).	A voice speaks from the cloud (Exod 24:16).
The people are astonished when they see Jesus after he descends from the mountain (Mark 9:15).	The people are afraid to come near Moses after he descends from the mountain (Exod 35:30).

Some scholars have claimed that the transfiguration was originally a resurrection appearance that the early church projected back into the ministry of Jesus.[3] Evidence for this are various features in common with resurrection narratives: a mountaintop context (v. 3; cf. Matt 28:16), the presence of a cloud (v. 7; cf. Acts 1:9), the identification of Jesus as the Son of God (9:7; cf. Rom 1:4), and the use of the verb "appear" (v. 4; cf. Luke 24:34; 1 Cor 15:5 – 8).

Yet there are even greater differences.[4] Jesus is silent in the transfiguration account, whereas he always speaks in the resurrection narratives. A voice comes from heaven here, but not in the gospel resurrection scenes. Resurrection appearances always begin with Jesus absent and then he "appears" to his disciples. Here Jesus is with his disciples from the beginning, and Moses and Elijah "appear." While brightness and glory appear in some of the later apocryphal resurrection narratives (cf. *Gospel of Peter*), the glory seen in the transfiguration is not present in the earlier resurrection accounts of the canonical Gospels. Finally, a confirmatory voice from heaven would

---

1. See the appendix "History-of-Religions Backgrounds to the Transfiguration," in Joel Marcus, *Mark 9 – 16* (AB 27A; New York: Doubleday, 2009), 1108 – 20. Marcus concludes that "the most important background for the Markan transfiguration are traditions about Moses, the Feast of Tabernacles, and royal epiphanies."

2. Garland, *Mark*, 342.

3. Bultmann, *History*, 259 – 61; Weeden, *Mark — Traditions in Conflict*, 118 – 26; Watson, "The Social Function of Mark's Secrecy Theme," 55; J. M. Robinson, "Jesus: From Easter to Valentinus (or the Apostles' Creed)," *JBL* 101 (1982): 5 – 37, esp. 8 – 9.

4. See C. H. Dodd, "The Appearances of the Risen Christ: An Essay in Form Criticism of the Gospels," in *Studies in the Gospels* (ed. D. E. Nineham; Oxford: Blackwell, 1967), 9 – 35, esp. 25; R. H. Stein, "Is the Transfiguration Account (Mark 9:2 – 8) a Misplaced Resurrection Account?" *JBL* 95 (1976): 79 – 96; Gundry, *Mark*, 471 – 73.

hardly seem necessary in a resurrection narrative, for the very presence of the resurrected Lord is confirmation enough.[5] It seems more likely that the transfiguration from the beginning was considered part of the public ministry of Jesus, and that it occurred in close proximity to the confession of Peter and Jesus' first passion prediction ("after six days ..."; v. 2).

Exegetical Outline

→ **1. The Context (9:2a-c)**

  2. The Transfiguration (9:2d – 8)

    a. The transformation of Jesus' appearance (9:2d   3)

    b. The appearance of Elijah and Moses (9:4)

    c. Peter's inappropriate response (9:5 – 6)

    d. The voice from heaven (9:7)

    e. The conclusion of the vision (9:8)

  3. Descending the Mountain (9:9 – 13)

    a. The command to silence (9:9)

    b. The disciples discuss the meaning of the resurrection (9:10)

    c. The question about Elijah (9:11)

    d. Jesus' response to the question (9:12 – 13)

Explanation of the Text

9:2 After six days Jesus took Peter, James, and John and led them to a high mountain to be alone. And he was transfigured before them (Καὶ μετὰ ἡμέρας ἓξ παραλαμβάνει ὁ Ἰησοῦς τὸν Πέτρον καὶ τὸν Ἰάκωβον καὶ τὸν Ἰωάννην καὶ ἀναφέρει αὐτοὺς εἰς ὄρος ὑψηλὸν κατ᾽ ἰδίαν μόνους. καὶ μετεμορφώθη ἔμπροσθεν αὐτῶν). Specific time references are unusual for Mark, occurring only here and at 14:1.[6] From a narrative perspective, "after six days" (μετὰ ἡμέρας ἓξ) connects the transfiguration to the preceding narrative. The number also recalls the exodus account, where the cloud settled

on Mount Sinai for six days before God spoke to Moses from the mountain (Exod 24:15 – 16).

Jesus takes with him his inner circle of disciples — Peter, James, and John — who are similarly distinguished from the other disciples at the raising of Jairus's daughter (5:37 – 43) and Jesus' prayer in Gethsemane (14:33).[7] No reason is stated for this choice, although it may be seen to fulfill the prediction of 9:1 that "some" of the disciples will experience the kingdom of God in this life.

The traditional site of the transfiguration is Mount Tabor, located at the eastern end of the

5. John Dominic Crossan's claim for the antiquity of the highly embellished resurrection narrative of the *Gospel of Peter* is unconvincing (*The Cross That Spoke: The Origins of the Passion Narrative* [San Francisco: Harper & Row, 1988]). See Evans, *Mark 8:27 – 16:20*, 34.

6. Hooker, *Mark*, 214.

7. The three also appear together with Peter's brother Andrew at the Olivet Discourse (13:3), but in that case they come to Jesus with a question rather than being chosen by him.

Jezreel Valley in lower Galilee, about eleven miles southwest of the Sea of Galilee. This identification seems unlikely, however, since Tabor is only 1,886 ft (557 m) above sea level, not really a "high mountain."[8] Other suggested sites include Mount Carmel, a coastal range in northern Israel (1,724 ft/525.4 m); Mount Meron, northwest of the Sea of Galilee (3,926 ft/1197 m);[9] and Mount Hermon, part of the Anti-Lebanon range on the border of Lebanon and Syria (9,234 ft/2,814 m). This last is perhaps the most likely, both because of its height and because it is located near Caesarea Philippi, the place of Peter's confession (8:27). One strike against it is the presence of a crowd when Jesus descends the mountain, including scribes and a man seeking exorcism for his son. Would the scribes have pursued Jesus this far north? In any case, Mark's interest is not in the name of the mountain, but in the mountaintop experience. Throughout Scripture mountains are places of divine revelation.[10]

Jesus "was transfigured" (μετεμορφώθη) in front of the disciples. This verb (μεταμορφόω) means to change in form, though this transformation could be physical or spiritual, external or internal.[11] The verb is used four times in the NT: here, in the Matthean parallel (Matt 17:2), and twice in Paul, where it refers to the believer's spiritual transformation into the likeness of Christ (Rom 12:2; 2 Cor 3:18). Mark 9:3 defines it more precisely as a glorification: "His clothing became dazzling, brilliantly white." Luke's parallel elaborates, "the appearance of his face changed" (Luke 9:29), and Matthew says, "his face shone like the sun" (Matt 17:2). The verb's passive voice in Mark is significant. This is not Jesus' self-revelation, but a revelation of the Son by the Father.[12] The voice from heaven that follows (Mark 9:7) confirms that this is God's declaration of Jesus' true identity.

9:3 His clothing became dazzling, brilliantly white, whiter than any clothing specialist on earth could bleach them (καὶ τὰ ἱμάτια αὐτοῦ ἐγένετο στίλβοντα λευκὰ λίαν, οἷα γναφεὺς ἐπὶ τῆς γῆς οὐ δύναται οὕτως λευκᾶναι). With typical Markan redundancy, Jesus' transformation is described as "dazzling" or "shining brightly" (στίλβοντα) and as "brilliantly white" (λευκὰ λίαν). Heavenly beings are frequently described in apocalyptic Judaism and in the NT as having white and shining garments.[13]

Only Mark of the Synoptics adds the comment that this brightness exceeded anything achievable on earth. A "clothing specialist" (γναφεύς) is an expert in one or more aspects of the treatment of clothing, including fulling, carding, cleaning, and bleaching.[14] As noted above, Matthew and Luke both (in different ways) refer to Jesus' face being "changed" (Luke 9:29) or "shining like the sun" (Matt 17:2). These may be attempts on their part to connect the scene even closer to Exod 34:29 and the description of Moses' shining face.[15]

8. There may also have been a Roman garrison on Mount Tabor at the time, though this is uncertain. Josephus speaks of fortifying the mountain himself when he served as a general in Galilee during the early years of the Jewish War (AD 66–74) and notes that Vespasian subdued the Jewish rebels who had seized the mountain (*J.W.* 2.20.6 §§572–73; 4.1.8 §§54–61).

9. W. Liefeld, "The Transfiguration Narrative," in *New Dimensions in New Testament Study* (ed. R. N. Longenecker and M. C. Tenney; Grand Rapids: Zondervan, 1974), 167.

10. See Gen 22:2; Exod 24:15; Deut 34:1; 1 Kgs 18:20; 19:11; Ezek 40:2; Matt 5:1; 14:23; 28:16; Mark 6:46; John 4:20; 6:3,

15; Acts 1:12; Rev 14:1; 21:10; H. Riesenfeld, *Jésus Transfiguré* (Acta Seminarii Neotestamentici Upsaliensis 17; Copenhagen: Munksgaard, 1947), 243–45; Edwards, *Mark*, 262 n. 64.

11. See J. Behm, *TDNT*, 4:755–59; BDAG, 639; BDF, §159 (4).

12. This insight came from my student Nathan Bruce.

13. Matt 28:3; Mark 16:5; Luke 24:4; John 20:12; Act 1:10; Dan 7:9; *1 En.* 14:20; *2 En.* 22:8–9; *T. Job* 46:7–9; France, *Mark*, 351.

14. BDAG, 202.

15. Marcus, *Mark 9–16*, 631.

Scholars debate the significance of the transfiguration. Is this a revelation of Jesus' (1) preincarnate glory, (2) resurrection/exaltation glory,[16] or (3) the glory of the parousia?[17] The latter two are more likely than the first since Mark, unlike John, does not refer elsewhere to Jesus' preincarnate state (cf. John 1:1 – 2, 14; 17:5). Hooker is likely right that Mark himself would not wish to distinguish resurrection glory from parousia glory, since both demonstrate Jesus' vindication.[18]

Indeed, the immediate context refers to both. In the previous passage Jesus has just referred to the coming of the kingdom (9:1) and the return of the Son of Man (8:38), indicating a parousia allusion. Yet after the vision, Jesus tells his disciples not to reveal the event until after his resurrection (9:9). If a choice must be made, the second coming has a slight advantage, since Mark elsewhere refers to the "glory" ($\delta\acute{o}\xi\alpha$) of the Son of Man at the parousia (8:38; 13:26) but does not use light or glory language for the resurrection.[19] But this does not negate the likelihood that Mark views this event also as an unveiling of divine glory that Jesus presently possesses. The glory to be manifested at the parousia must be viewed as a revelation of Jesus' true identity as the Son of God.

9:4 Then Elijah appeared to them with Moses, and they were talking with Jesus (καὶ ὤφθη αὐτοῖς Ἡλίας σὺν Μωϋσεῖ καὶ ἦσαν συλλαλοῦντες τῷ Ἰησοῦ). Appearing with Jesus are two important OT figures, Elijah and Moses. Mark says little about the nature of this appearance. We can be assured it is not necromancy, communication with the dead through rituals or mediums (as in the case of Saul summoning Samuel through the witch of Endor in 1 Sam 28). It is best understood as a proleptic eschatological vision, with Elijah and Moses appearing in their resurrection glory.

The chronological order with Elijah first is surprising and is reversed by both Matthew (Matt 17:3) and Luke (Luke 9:30). When Peter speaks in v. 5 he will revert to "Moses and Elijah." The reason for this order may be Elijah's greater prominence in eschatological contexts, or perhaps Mark is simply setting the stage for the conversation that takes place while descending the mountain (v. 11).

Why these two OT men? Some have suggested that they represent the Law and the Prophets, the two main divisions of the Hebrew Scriptures. But if this were the case, one might expect one of the great writing prophets, like Isaiah or Jeremiah, rather than Elijah. Others note the mysterious circumstances related to each of their deaths. Elijah was caught up to heaven in a fiery chariot (2 Kgs 2:11) and, though Moses is said to have died in Deut 34:5 – 6, later Jewish traditions said he was taken directly to heaven.[20] But if this were the key factor here, one would expect Enoch instead of Moses (Gen 5:24).

There is also the eschatological role the two were expected to play in Judaism. For Elijah, speculation arose especially around Mal 4:5 (cf. vv. 11 – 12 below), and for Moses, around traditions related to the "prophet like Moses" passage in Deut 18:15 (Acts 3:22; 7:37). In a few Jewish traditions Moses and Elijah appear together in an eschatological context (*Deut. Rab.* 3:17 [on 10.1]; cf. 2 Esd 6:25 – 26; Rev 11:3 – 12).

Most importantly, these two represent heroic

---

16. Garland, *Mark*, 343 – 44.

17. So most commentators: Cranfield, *Mark*, 287 – 88; Lane, *Mark*, 313 – 14; Pesch, *Markusevangelium*, 2:67; Evans, *Mark 8:27 – 16:20*, 36; G. H. Boobyer, *St Mark and the Transfiguration Story* (Edinburgh: T&T Clark, 1942), passim.

18. Hooker, *Mark*, 215.

19. Cf. Jesus' "glory" referred to by James and John in 10:37, though they are thinking of an earthly reign in Jerusalem.

20. Josephus, *Ant.* 4.8.48 §326; Philo, *QG* 1.86; C. Begg, "Josephus's Portrayal of the Disappearance of Enoch, Elijah, and Moses: Some Observations," *JBL* 109 (1990): 691 – 93.

figures in Israel's history who did God's will and accomplished his purpose. As Garland points out, "both Elijah and Moses witnessed theophanies on mountains. Both were faithful servants who suffered because of their obedience, were rejected by the people of God, and were vindicated by God."[21] In this way they provide continuity with the OT and serve as confirmatory witnesses of Jesus' messianic authority and mission. The end of the vision will bring out an additional point: as the two fade away, Jesus is left alone, confirming that he is the climax of salvation history and the fulfillment of what Moses and Elijah came to accomplish. God's self-revelation reaches its climax in Jesus, the Messiah and Son of God.

While Luke identifies the topic of conversation as the "departure" (ἔξοδος) Jesus was about to fulfill in Jerusalem (Luke 9:31), Mark says only that Moses and Elijah were talking with Jesus. He is more interested in their confirmatory presence than the specifics of their conversation. Nor does Mark tell us how Moses and Elijah were identified by the disciples (divine revelation? identification by Jesus? name tags?), another point irrelevant to the story.

9:5 – 6 Peter responded, saying to Jesus, "Rabbi, it is good for us to be here. Let us make three shelters, one for you and one for Moses and one for Elijah." For he did not know how to respond, since they were so frightened (καὶ ἀποκριθεὶς ὁ Πέτρος λέγει τῷ Ἰησοῦ· ῥαββί, καλόν ἐστιν ἡμᾶς ὧδε εἶναι, καὶ ποιήσωμεν τρεῖς σκηνάς, σοὶ μίαν καὶ Μωϋσεῖ μίαν καὶ Ἠλίᾳ μίαν. οὐ γὰρ ᾔδει τί ἀποκριθῇ, ἔκφοβοι γὰρ ἐγένοντο). Peter fulfills the role seen

so often in the gospel tradition as an eager but impulsive representative of the disciples.

The verb translated "responded" (ἀποκρίνομαι) often means to "answer" someone, but it can indicate any response that carries forward a scene.[22] Peter's enthusiasm is expressed in his affirmation, "Rabbi, it is good for us to be here." Too much should not be made of Peter's address to Jesus as "Rabbi" (ῥαββί), as though this indicates Peter's inadequate view of him.[23] If anything, it points to the verisimilitude of the scene, since the Hebrew term is how the disciples addressed Jesus and is unlikely to have been created by the church.[24]

Peter's odd statement about building three "shelters" or "booths" (σκηναί) has been interpreted in a variety of ways. Some suggest that Peter is trying to provide a shrine or place of honor for these esteemed guests[25] or to prolong the experience with them.[26] Others see some kind of connection to the Jewish Feast of Tabernacles (Lev 23; Deut 16; Neh 8:14 – 17), perhaps viewing the event as the beginning of the new exodus deliverance and the erection of a new tabernacle in the wilderness.[27] Whatever Peter's intention, Mark dismisses it as irrelevant. Out of fear and awe (cf. 4:41; 6:50), all three disciples ("they") are at a loss concerning what to say. But impetuous Peter speaks anyway!

9:7 Then a cloud appeared, overshadowing them, and a voice came from the cloud, "This is my beloved Son, listen to him." (καὶ ἐγένετο νεφέλη ἐπισκιάζουσα αὐτοῖς, καὶ ἐγένετο φωνὴ ἐκ τῆς νεφέλης· οὗτός ἐστιν ὁ υἱός μου ὁ ἀγαπητός, ἀκούετε αὐτοῦ). Clouds commonly symbolize God's presence in Scripture.[28] Most significant for

21. Garland, *Mark*, 344 n. 6.

22. BDAG, 113: "speak up."

23. Contra Hooker, *Mark*, 217; France, *Mark*, 353 – 54; Stein, *Mark*, 417 – 18, and esp. M. E. Thrall, "Elijah and Moses in Mark's Account of the Transfiguration," *NTS* 16 (1970): 305 – 17, esp. 308 – 9.

24. Evans, *Mark 8:27 – 16:20*, 37.

25. Stein, *Mark*, 418 n. 11; Moloney, *Mark*, 179 – 80; Collins, *Mark*, 424.

26. Cranfield, *Mark*, 291.

27. Lane, *Mark*, 319; Hooker, *Mark*, 217; Witherington, *Mark*, 263; Evans, *Mark 8:27 – 16:20*, 37.

28. Exod 13:21 – 22; 16:10; 19:9; 33:9; 40:34 – 38; Lev 16:2; Num 11:25; 1 Kgs 8:10 – 13; Isa 4:5.

the present episode is the cloud at Mount Sinai, which descended on the mountain for six days and then, "on the seventh day the LORD called to Moses from within the cloud" (Exod 24:16; cf. 19:9, 16; 34:5). It is unclear whether the "them" covered by the cloud included the disciples or just Jesus and the two OT saints. That the voice came to the disciples "from the cloud" may imply the latter.

The first part of the voice from the cloud echoes the baptismal voice, "You are my beloved Son" (1:11), except that in this case the address is in the third person and directed to the disciples ("This is …"). Whereas the baptism was divine approval and commissioning for Jesus himself, this is for the benefit of his disciples, who need courage and assurance to take up their cross and follow him. As at the baptism, "This is my Son" likely alludes to Ps 2:7, the royal Davidic psalm, where Yahweh affirms his chosen king and warns the nations against revolt (see comments on 1:11).

The voice thus confirms Peter's confession that Jesus is the Messiah (8:29). As at 1:11, the substantival adjective "the beloved" (ὁ ἀγαπητός), may allude to Gen 22:2 and a Jesus/Isaac typology, where Abraham's willingness to sacrifice his beloved son is analogous to God's offering of his own Son. This would fit the present scene, since Jesus has just been speaking of his suffering and death (Mark 8:31).

Whereas at Jesus' baptism, the third phrase of the divine voice alluded to Isa 42:1 ("I am pleased with you"; 1:11), here the disciples are told to "listen to him" (ἀκούετε αὐτοῦ). This is likely an allusion to Deut 18:15, where Moses tells the Israelites that God will raise up a "prophet like me" from among their fellow Israelites and that "you must listen to him" (LXX: αὐτοῦ ἀκούσεσθε). "Listen to him" means far more than simply hearing Jesus'

words. It means hearing with understanding and then acting on them.

The command to listen applies to all of Jesus' teaching. This is in line with the prophet-like-Moses allusion, which means to accept him as God's spokesperson. More specifically, the command to hear refers in the immediate context to the revelation of the suffering of the Messiah (8:31 – 32a) and its implication for discipleship (8:34 – 38). It is this that Peter and the disciples, with their skewed view of Jesus' messiahship (8:32b-c), must hear and heed.

9:8 Suddenly, when they looked around, they no longer saw anyone with them except Jesus alone (καὶ ἐξάπινα περιβλεψάμενοι οὐκέτι οὐδένα εἶδον ἀλλὰ τὸν Ἰησοῦν μόνον μεθ᾽ ἑαυτῶν). The sudden disappearance of Moses and Elijah has several implications. First, it confirms the miraculous nature of the event, as those two disappear as quickly as they arrived. Second, it confirms the preeminence of Jesus. The vision is about him, not these other two. He is the Son of God to whom they must listen. Third and by implication, the prior revelation through Moses, Elijah, and the prophets is being superseded by the new revelation given through Jesus. It is *to him* they must listen. The kingdom of God is at hand, and the new wine of the kingdom cannot be placed in the old wineskins of the old covenant (2:22). God is doing something new.

9:9 As they were descending from the mountain, he commanded them not to tell anyone what they had seen until the Son of Man arose from the dead (Καὶ καταβαινόντων αὐτῶν ἐκ τοῦ ὄρους διεστείλατο αὐτοῖς ἵνα μηδενὶ ἃ εἶδον διηγήσωνται, εἰ μὴ ὅταν ὁ υἱὸς τοῦ ἀνθρώπου ἐκ νεκρῶν ἀναστῇ). This is the only time Jesus sets out the terminus of the messianic secret.[29] The disciples may reveal Jesus' identity only after he has risen from the

29. See 1:25, 34, 43 – 44; 3:11 – 12; 5:43; 7:36; 8:26, 30; 9:9.

dead. It is this passage in particular that W. Wrede pointed to when formulating his theory of the messianic secret in Mark, namely, that the Evangelist created this motif to explain away Jesus' apparently unmessianic life (see Introduction to Mark: The Gospel in Historical Perspective; see also comments on 1:25; 1:43 – 44). As noted at 1:25, Wrede's thesis fails since the secret is broken numerous times throughout Jesus' life, as people proclaim his miracles far and wide (1:28, 45; 7:36, etc.). If Mark's purpose was to show why Jesus' messiahship was unrecognized during his earthly life, he did a poor job of it.

A better explanation relates to popular expectations concerning a political Messiah. Jesus wants to prevent premature proclamation of his messiahship until he has fulfilled the messianic task. The glory of his messianic reign — proleptically seen in the transfiguration — will *not* be realized at his first entrance into Jerusalem, but after his suffering, death, and resurrection, and, ultimately, at his return to judge and to save.

9:10 So they kept the matter to themselves, discussing what it meant to rise from the dead (καὶ τὸν λόγον ἐκράτησαν πρὸς ἑαυτοὺς συζητοῦντες τί ἐστιν τὸ ἐκ νεκρῶν ἀναστῆναι). In this case the disciples heed Jesus' words and keep the events of the transfiguration a secret until after the resurrection. Yet Jesus' statement about the resurrection confuses them, and they discuss what "to rise from the dead" means. The confusion likely arose because Jews conceived of the resurrection of the dead as taking place at the end of the age, when graves would be opened and the dead would rise for the final judgment (Dan 12:2 – 3).[30] Jesus' discussion of the resurrection of the Son of Man within history was inconceivable to them.

The adverbial prepositional phrase "to themselves" (πρὸς ἑαυτούς) may be taken either with the verb "keep/seize" (κρατέω) or "discuss/argue" (συζητέω). Most versions follow the former (NIV, NLT, NET, HCSB, ESV), though the REB (cf. NASB) follows the latter: "They seized upon those words, and discussed among themselves what this 'rising from the dead' could mean."

9:11 Then they asked him, "Why do the experts in the law say that Elijah must come first?" (καὶ ἐπηρώτων αὐτὸν λέγοντες· ὅτι λέγουσιν οἱ γραμματεῖς ὅτι Ἠλίαν δεῖ ἐλθεῖν πρῶτον;). On the "experts in the law" or "scribes" (οἱ γραμματεῖς), see comments on 1:22. What sparked this question from the disciples? Several factors may have contributed to it, including the presence of Elijah on the mountain (9:4 – 5), the eschatological discussion of the return of the Son of Man (8:38), and the earlier speculation by the people that Jesus was Elijah (8:28).

Evidently, Jesus' mention of resurrection in 9:10 (an end-time event in the minds of the disciples) and the presence of Elijah on the mountain caused them to ask about the prophecies concerning the eschatological coming of Elijah. If Jesus was in the process of inaugurating the kingdom of God, where do the prophecies about Elijah's coming fit in? As noted at 8:28, end-time speculation related to Elijah was common in Judaism[31] and arose both from his unusual departure from earth (2 Kgs 2:11) and from Malachi's prophecies that he would return before the great and dreadful day of the Lord (Mal 4:5 – 6; cf. 3:1).

9:12 – 13 He said to them, "Coming first, Elijah indeed restores all things. So how then is it written about the Son of Man that he must

---

30. On the Jewish conception of the resurrection, see, N. T. Wright, *The Resurrection of the Son of God* (Minneapolis: Fortress, 2003), 85 – 206.

31. Sir 48:9 – 10; 4Q558 (4QVision); cf. Matt 11:14; 17:10 – 12; 27:49; Mark 15:36; John 1:21, 25.

suffer many things and be treated shamefully? But I tell you, Elijah has indeed come, and they did to him whatever they wanted, just as it was written about him." (ὁ δὲ ἔφη αὐτοῖς· Ἠλίας μὲν ἐλθὼν[32] πρῶτον ἀποκαθιστάνει πάντα· καὶ πῶς γέγραπται ἐπὶ τὸν υἱὸν τοῦ ἀνθρώπου ἵνα πολλὰ πάθη καὶ ἐξουδενηθῇ; ἀλλὰ λέγω ὑμῖν ὅτι καὶ Ἠλίας ἐλήλυθεν, καὶ ἐποίησαν αὐτῷ ὅσα ἤθελον, καθὼς γέγραπται ἐπ' αὐτόν).

The logic of these verses is difficult. Jesus first says that the experts in the law are right: Elijah indeed comes first to restore everything (v. 12b). (The particle μέν as used here may be emphatic ["indeed"] or could have the sense "on the one hand …," preparing for Jesus' two qualifications.) We would expect v. 13 to follow at this point, clarifying that in fact Elijah has already come in the person of John the Baptist. Instead we get a statement about the suffering of the Son of Man (v. 12b). Matthew evidently saw this difficulty, since he reverses the order of vv. 12c and 13 (Matt 17:11 – 12). For him the suffering of the Son of Man becomes an example of suffering like that of John the Baptist.

Several attempts have been made to explain the difficulty. C. C. Torrey argues that in Aramaic, v. 12b was originally a question, "Does Elijah come first to restore all things? How then is it written…?"[33] Marcus adopts this view, arguing that the suffering Son of Man saying is intended to refute traditional Jewish expectations about Elijah and the Messiah. Verse 13 then clarifies that Elijah has indeed come as John the Baptist, but he prepared

for the Son of Man not by restoring everything, but by suffering like him.[34] While imaginative, this interpretation seems unlikely (no versions follow it). Mark's emphatic use of the particle μέν fits a declaration better than a question, and Matthew certainly understood it this way.[35]

Another way to resolve the logical difficulty is proposed by Casey, who suggests that since the Hebrew/Aramaic idiom "son of man" simply means "a human being," the Son of Man saying in v. 13 was not originally about Jesus, but about John the Baptist.[36] This would resolve the difficulty by making all three verses about John. While this interpretation might work with reference to the pre-Markan tradition, it is impossible to believe that Mark or his readers could have taken Son of Man as a reference to anyone but Jesus.

A better explanation of the logic of these verses is to see vv. 12c and 13 as two clarifications of v. 12b, the first explaining the relationship of the eschatological coming of Elijah to the suffering of the Son of Man (v. 12c) and the second related to *how* Elijah has come (v. 13). The first comes in the form of a rhetorical question: If Elijah's role is to restore everything, how then can Scripture predict the *suffering* of the Messiah? Jesus' purpose here is similar to that of his first passion prediction, where he sharply qualifies Peter's traditional understanding of the Messiah by pointing to the suffering of the Son of Man (8:31 – 32). In the same way v. 12c sharply qualifies Elijah's eschatological restoration of all things by defining it with reference to the

---

32. The aorist participle ἐλθών could be circumstantial ("comes and restores"), temporal ("when he comes and restores"), or instrumental ("by coming restores").

33. C. C. Torrey, *Our Translated Gospels* (London: Hodder and Stoughton; New York: Harper & Brothers, 1936), 56 – 58.

34. So Marcus, *Mark 9 – 16*, 649 – 50; idem, *Way of the Lord*, 97 – 107; cf. Garland, *Mark*, 347 – 48. Garland points out that this interpretation fits the context of Mal 4:5 – 6, where, if the people do not respond to Elijah's call for reconciliation, God will "strike the land with total destruction." In Mark 13 Jesus

will predict that in the days ahead "brother will hand over brother to death and a father his child" (13:12), and the temple will be destroyed. The rejection of John (and Jesus) brings destruction, not restoration, to the nation.

35. See Stein, *Mark*, 425; Evans, *Mark 8:27 – 16:20*, 43.

36. M. Casey, *Aramaic Sources of Mark's Gospel* (SNTSMS 102; Cambridge: Cambridge University Press, 1998), 124; cf. W. Wink, *John the Baptist in the Gospel Tradition* (SNTSMS 7; Cambridge: Cambridge University Press, 1968), 14; Evans, *Mark 8:27 – 16:20*, 43 – 44.

suffering of the Son of Man.[37] The restoration predicted from Elijah will be accomplished through Christ's suffering and death.

The second clarification (v. 13) qualifies *how* Elijah has come, which is in the person of John the Baptist. Unlike Matthew (Matt 17:13), Mark does not explicitly say that John the Baptist fulfills the role of eschatological Elijah, but the meaning is clear from the perfect tense in the phrase, "Elijah has come" (Ἠλίας ἐλήλυθεν). "They did to him whatever they wanted" refers to the execution of John by Herod Antipas (Mark 6:14 – 29).

The identification of John with Elijah is a common one throughout the gospel tradition. Though John is not literally Elijah risen from the dead (John 1:21), he has come in the spirit and power of Elijah to fulfill Mal 4:5 – 6 and Isa 40:3 (Luke 1:17; 3:4). Jesus says in Matt 11:14, "if you are willing to accept it, he is the Elijah who was to come" — i.e.,

the eschatological Elijah. How John's death fulfills Scripture is not altogether clear. This could refer to the parallels between Jezebel's actions against Elijah (1 Kgs 19:1 – 3) and Herodias's schemes against John (6:19, 22),[38] or perhaps to general OT statements about the persecution of the prophets.[39]

Did Jesus consider John to be the complete fulfillment of the eschatological coming of Elijah, or did he envision a still future coming before the parousia? Verse 12b could be read either as a past or still-future coming. If the latter, the strong adversative in v. 13 ("but"; ἀλλά) would introduce the paradox that although Elijah is coming, in fact *an Elijah* has already come in the person of John the Baptist. Possible support for this view is the fact that the restoration of all things, like the kingdom of God, awaits a still-future consummation. Whether Rev 11:1 – 14 reflects such a tradition is unclear, since the two witnesses there are not named.

Theology in Application

Confirmation of Jesus as the Messiah and Son of God

This passage contains several important Markan themes. The first is christological — the second announcement from heaven in Mark's gospel confirming Jesus' identity. The first was for Jesus' benefit, assuring Jesus at his baptism of his identity and the Father's love and confidence in him (1:11). This one confirms for the disciples what they have come to believe — that Jesus is indeed God's Anointed, the agent of salvation. While the testimony of demons about Jesus was true, since they have access to spiritual realities (1:24; 3:11; 5:17), their purpose was sinister, for they wished to defame and destroy him. Peter's confession was accurate as far as it went (8:29), but it represented an inadequate understanding of the messianic task (8:31). The

---

37. Jesus does not specify where it is written that the Son of Man must suffer many things and be treated shamefully. Several possibilities include Isa 53:3, where the Suffering Servant is "despised and rejected by mankind," or Ps 118:22, where "the stone the builders rejected has become the cornerstone [capstone]." Jesus will cite this passage in Mark 12:10. Though the verb for rejected (ἐξουδενέομαι) is different from that used in Ps 118:22 LXX and in Mark 12:10 (ἀποδοκιμάζομαι), the for-

mer verb appears in the quote from Psalm 118:22 in Acts 4:11. A third possibility is Ps 22:6 (LXX: 21:7), where the LXX uses a cognate noun of the verb "treated shamefully" (ἐξουδενέομαι): "But I am a worm and not a man, scorned by everyone and despised [ἐξουδένημα] by the people."

38. Hooker, *Mark*, 220 – 21.

39. See 1 Kgs 13:4; 18:13; 19:2; 22:26 – 27; 2 Kgs 1:9; 6:31; 2 Chr 24:21; Jer 18:18, 23; 26:11, 20 – 23; 36:1 – 38:28.

Father's announcement is profound and indisputable. God himself speaks, proclaiming that Jesus is his Son and that what he says must be heeded.

Son of God is a title for the Messiah as God's vice-regent and agent of redemption (2 Sam 7:14; Pss 2:7; 89:26). Yet in this context it is certainly more, expressing a unique Father-Son relationship shared by no one else. Peter would later recall this incident, stating that "we were eyewitnesses of his majesty. He received honor and glory from God the Father when the voice came to him from the Majestic Glory" (2 Pet 1:16 – 17). The writer to the Hebrews similarly calls Jesus "the radiance [ἀπαύγασμα] of God's glory and the exact representation of his being" (Heb 1:3). As the Son, he is far more than an angel or agent: "For to which of the angels did God ever say, 'You are my Son; today I have become your Father' [Ps 2:7]? Or again, 'I will be his Father, and he will be my Son' [2 Sam 7:14]" (Heb 1:5). The angels themselves worship him (Heb 1:6). On the mountain Jesus is revealed as the divine Son of God, worthy of all glory, honor, and praise (Rev 5:12 – 13; 7:12).

Jesus as the Fulfillment of the Old Testament

The presence of Moses and Elijah on the mountain signifies all that has come before in Israel's history. Jesus is the fulfillment of the OT and the climax of salvation history. By identifying the topic of their conversation as Jesus' Jerusalem denouement, Luke 9:31 makes explicit what is implicit in Mark: Jesus is about to accomplish all that Moses and prophets predicted. The episode that follows further confirms this, as Jesus speaks of his suffering and death as that which was written about, and the suffering of "Elijah" (= John the Baptist) as predicted in Scripture (Mark 9:12 – 13). The opposition to Jesus and his death on the cross is not a surprise to God or a setback in his plan. All along it was his purpose for redemption.

Jesus as Greater Than Moses and Elijah

As the vision on the mountain fades, Moses and Elijah disappear and Jesus is left alone. The fate of the world rests on his shoulders. Everything that has come before was mere preparation for his coming and the salvation he would accomplish. The superiority of the new to the old is the central theme of the letter to the Hebrews. The writer begins with the thematic statement that everything God spoke through the prophets in the past was partial and preparatory, but "in these last days he has spoken to us by his Son" (Heb 1:2). Jesus is far greater than any who have come before — the creator and sustainer of all things, the heir of the universe, who provided purification for sins (Heb 1:2 – 4). History has its culmination in him.

This is also a central theme of the book of Revelation. Jesus is the Alpha and the Omega, the First and the Last, the Beginning and the End (Rev 22:13). As the Lamb who was slain, he restores all creation to a right relationship with God. Though Mark's gospel does not use such exalted language, the glimpse of Jesus' glory here is a preview of the vision of the Son of Man that John will experience on the island of Patmos — the glory of his exaltation and second coming (Rev 1:12 – 16; 19:11 – 16).

Confirmation of Vindication after Suffering

Coming on the heels of the first passion prediction, the transfiguration functions both as confirmation of Jesus' identity and assurance of his vindication. The command to "listen to him" likely refers to what Jesus has just taught — his own suffering and death and the call for all true disciples to take up their crosses and follow him. The path of discipleship is not easy, entailing suffering and even death. The conversation coming down the mountain is also dominated by this theme. When the disciples ask about the restoration of all things through Elijah, Jesus redirects them to the suffering of the Son of Man (v. 12) and John the Baptist (v. 13).

The promise of the transfiguration is that this suffering and sacrifice are not in vain. The vision of the glorified Christ is confirmation that after his humiliation, suffering, and death will come his vindication and glorification. This is a message not just about Jesus, but about all who follow him in authentic discipleship. Whatever the difficulties we face in this life, God is the sovereign Lord of history, who will restore and reward all who remain faithful to him (Rom 8:31 – 39; Rev 2:7, 10, 17, 26; 3:5, 12, 21).

36

Mark 9:14 – 29

Literary Context

This episode takes place as Jesus is returning with Peter, James, and John from his transfiguration on the mountain. From a narrative and theological perspective, this exorcism seems a bit out of place in Mark's narrative. The first part of Mark's gospel highlighted Jesus' messianic authority in healing the sick, casting out demons, and performing other miracles. With Peter's confession and Jesus' first passion prediction (8:29 – 31), the narrative has taken a decisive turn, focusing now on the suffering role of the Messiah and the call for cross-bearing discipleship. Only two healing miracles occur after Peter's confession, this one and the healing of Blind Bartimaeus (which forms a "bookend" with the healing of the blind man at Bethsaida; see Literary Context on 8:22 – 26).

Yet Mark clearly has a purpose in the present episode, using it to highlight the present faithless generation that is unable to believe in the transforming power of the kingdom of God (v. 19) and the necessity of faith in the challenging days ahead (v. 23). In this way Mark develops two themes that are prominent in his central section (8:22 – 10:52): Jesus' coming rejection and the training of the Twelve on his way to the cross.

Main Idea

Jesus' healing of a demonized boy with epileptic-like symptoms illustrates once again the authority of Jesus as the Messiah and Son of God. An equally important theme is the primacy of faith and dependence on God, as Jesus castigates the "present generation" for its unbelief, calls the child's father to greater faith, and tells his disciples of the need for prayer in the face of the power of evil in the world.

Translation

Mark 9:14 – 29

14a	setting (social)	When they came to the disciples,
b	Action/Setting	**they saw a large crowd around them** and
c	Setting/Conflict	**the experts in the law arguing with them.**
15a		When the whole crowd saw him,
b	Action/Response to 15a	**they were greatly amazed and ran to greet him.**
16a	Question	**He asked them,**
b		*"What are you arguing with them about?"*
17a	Response to 16	**One from the crowd answered him,**
b	explanation	*"Teacher, I brought my son to you;*
c	character description	*he has a spirit that makes him mute.*
18a	character description	*Whenever it seizes him,*
b		*it throws him down, he foams at the mouth, grinds his teeth, and becomes rigid.*
c	explanation	*I asked your disciples to drive the demon out, but they could not."*
19a	Response to 17 – 18	**Jesus responded,**
b	address	*"O unbelieving generation,*
c	rhetorical question	*how long will I be with you?*
d	rhetorical question	*How long must I endure you?*
e	command	*Bring him to me."*
20a	Response to 19e	So **they brought the boy to Jesus.**
b		When the spirit saw him,
c	Response to 20a/Action	**immediately he threw the boy into convulsions.**
d		Falling to the ground,
e		**he rolled around,**
f		foaming at the mouth.
21a	Question	**He asked his father,**
b		*"How long has this been happening to him?"*
c	Response	**He answered,**
d	answer	*"From childhood.*

Continued on next page.

Continued from previous page.

22a	character description	*Often it throws him into the fire or into bodies of water to destroy him.*
b	condition	*But if you can do anything,*
c	Entreaty	*have pity on us and help us."*
23a	Response to 22c	**Jesus said to him,**
b	challenge to condition 22b	*"If you can?*
c	assertion	*Everything is possible for the one who believes."*
24a	Response to 23	Immediately crying out,
b		**the boy's father said,**
c	affirmation	*"I believe!*
d	entreaty	*Help my unbelief!"*
25a	setting (social)	Seeing that a crowd was quickly gathering,
b	Command/Exorcism	**Jesus rebuked the defiling spirit, saying to it,**
c	address	*"You spirit of deafness and muteness,*
d	command	*I command you: Come out of him and never enter him again."*
26a	action/character descr.	After crying out loudly and convulsing the boy violently,
b	Action/Exorcism	**it came out,**
c	result	leaving him like a dead person.
d	Result	**As a result, many said,**
e		*"He's dead."*
27a	Action	But **Jesus,** grasping his hand, **raised him up,**
b	Action	and **he got up.**
28a		When he went inside,
b	Question	**his disciples were asking him privately,**
c		*"Why could we not cast it out?"*
29a	Response	**He said to them,**
b		*"This kind cannot be cast out except by prayer."*

Structure

This episode begins as a controversy story with the religious leaders and then develops as an exorcism followed by teaching from Jesus. The narrative is typical of Mark's expansive style, full of repetition and colorful detail. The story told in 272 words by Mark is abbreviated to 144 words in Luke 9:37 – 43a and a mere 110 in Matt 17:14 – 20.[1] The demon's dramatic effect on the boy is mentioned four times: by the father (vv. 17 – 18), in the actions of the demon itself (v. 20), in the discussion between Jesus and the father (vv. 21 – 22), and again as the demon convulses the boy before coming out (v. 26). Faith or faithlessness is mentioned four times: by Jesus concerning the present generation (v. 19), in Jesus' exhortation to the man (v. 23), in the man's response (v. 24), and implicitly in Jesus' call for more prayer (v. 29).

---

1. France, *Mark*, 362.

Exegetical Outline

→ **1. The Context (9:14 – 16)**

    a. The return to the disciples and their conflict with the scribes (9:14)

    b. The response of the people to Jesus' return (9:15)

    c. Jesus' question about the conflict (9:16)

2. Dialogue between Jesus and the Boy's Father (9:17 – 24)

    a. The description of the demonization (9:17 – 18)

    b. Jesus' response to an unbelieving generation (9:19)

    c. The demon's destructive actions (9:20)

    d. Jesus' question and the father's response (9:21 – 22)

    e. Jesus' call for faith and the father's response (9:23 – 24)

3. The Exorcism (9:25 – 27)

    a. Jesus' command (9:25)

    b. The demon's last convulsion (9:26)

    c. Jesus raises the boy up (9:27)

4. The Aftermath in the House (9:28 – 29)

    a. The disciples' question (9:28)

    b. Jesus' response: the need for prayer (9:29)

Explanation of the Text

9:14 When they came to the disciples, they saw a large crowd around them and the experts in the law arguing with them (Καὶ ἐλθόντες πρὸς τοὺς μαθητὰς εἶδον ὄχλον πολὺν περὶ αὐτοὺς καὶ γραμματεῖς συζητοῦντας πρὸς αὐτούς). Jesus returns with the three disciples (cf. 9:2) to find a crowd gathered and the other nine disciples involved in a dispute with the Jewish scribes (γραμματεῖς; see comments on 1:22). These experts in the Mosaic law have been Jesus' intractable opponents throughout Mark's gospel (2:6 – 7, 16; 3:22; 7:1 – 5).

The verb translated "arguing" (συζητέω) can mean simply discussing or questioning (1:27; 9:27) but often carries connotations of dispute or debate (8:11; 12:28). Perhaps the scribes accompanied the man in his quest for Jesus in order to test Jesus and challenge his authority. When the disciples tried and failed to cast out the demon, an argument over spiritual authority ensued. After this initial confrontation the experts in the law disappear from the scene and play no further role. What begins as a controversy story becomes a healing and teaching narrative.

9:15 When the whole crowd saw him, they were greatly amazed and ran to greet him (καὶ εὐθὺς πᾶς ὁ ὄχλος ἰδόντες αὐτὸν ἐξεθαμβήθησαν καὶ προστρέχοντες ἠσπάζοντο αὐτόν). Why were the people so amazed when Jesus approached? Amazement is a common theme throughout Mark's gospel, but elsewhere always in response to either a miracle (1:27; 2:12; 5:15, 20, 42; 6:2, 51; 7:37; 12:17; cf. 4:41) or Jesus' authoritative teaching (1:22; 6:2; 11:18; 12:17). The most likely explanation is that Jesus exhibited the lingering affects of the transfiguration.[2] Though Mark does not say this, the preceding narrative is the only clue in the wider context.[3] The emphatic compound form of the verb suggests strong emotional distress or alarm (ἐκθαμβέω: 14:33; 16:5–6), something more than just excitement over Jesus' sudden appearance or his celebrity status. Additional support for this suggestion is the parallel with Moses' return from Mount Sinai with a radiant face, provoking fear in the gathered Israelites (Exod 34:29–30; cf. 2 Cor 3:12–13).

9:16–18 He asked them, "What are you arguing with them about?" One from the crowd answered him, "Teacher, I brought my son to you; he has a spirit that makes him mute. Whenever it seizes him, it throws him down, he foams at the mouth, grinds his teeth, and becomes rigid. I asked your disciples to drive the demon out, but they could not." (καὶ ἐπηρώτησεν αὐτούς· τί συζητεῖτε πρὸς αὐτούς; καὶ ἀπεκρίθη αὐτῷ εἷς ἐκ τοῦ ὄχλου· διδάσκαλε, ἤνεγκα τὸν υἱόν μου πρὸς σέ, ἔχοντα πνεῦμα ἄλαλον· καὶ ὅπου ἐὰν αὐτὸν καταλάβῃ ῥήσσει αὐτόν, καὶ ἀφρίζει καὶ τρίζει τοὺς ὀδόντας καὶ ξηραίνεται· καὶ εἶπα τοῖς μαθηταῖς σου ἵνα αὐτὸ ἐκβάλωσιν, καὶ οὐκ ἴσχυσαν).

Mark does not specify to whom Jesus addresses his question. The "you" could be the disciples, the scribes, or the crowd. Though the crowd is the closest antecedent (v. 15), the disciples and the scribes are the ones arguing, so it is likely one or both of them. In any case, someone from the crowd steps forward and answers. He had brought his son to Jesus (πρὸς σέ; "to you [sing.]") to be healed; in Jesus' absence, his disciples had tried to cast out the demon but had failed. Jesus had given the disciples authority to cast out demons (3:15; 6:7), and they had done so successfully in the past (6:13). In 9:29 Jesus will attribute this failure to a particularly challenging demonic presence and the need for prayer.

The boy is described as having a "mute spirit," presumably a demon that rendered him unable to speak. In v. 25 Jesus apparently also speaks of deafness (see comments there). The symptoms, however, have little to do with lack of speech and are remarkably similar to epilepsy — collapse, foaming at the mouth, grinding teeth, and paralysis.[4] In Matthew's parallel he uses a term often associated with epilepsy (σεληνιάζομαι: "have seizures"; Matt 17:15).[5] Yet Mark and the other Synoptics repeatedly identify this as a case of demon possession (vv. 17–18, 25–26; Matt 17:18; Luke 9:39–40, 42).

This cannot simply be ancient naïveté about the cause of disease, since the Gospels and other ancient literature often distinguish between disease and demonization.[6] At the same time, demons are

2. Gundry, *Mark*, 487–88; Hooker, *Mark*, 222–23; Witherington, *Mark*, 205; Evans, *Mark 8:27–16:20*, 50. Contra Boring, *Mark*, 273; Cranfield, *Mark*, 301. Collins, *Mark*, 437, calls it "a literary device to highlight the significance and authority of Jesus."

3. The claim that Jesus' command to silence in 9:9 renders this unlikely (so Lane, *Mark*, 330 n. 48) is not a convincing argument, since Jesus' intention with reference to the disciples has little to do with his own appearance. Indeed the argument could be turned on its head to say that the reason Jesus commanded silence was that his appearance might provoke curiosity about what happened on the mountain.

4. For a discussion of the text from a medical perspective, see J. Wilkinson, "The Case of the Epileptic Boy," *ExpTim* 79 (1967/68): 39–42.

5. Because of its strange symptoms, epilepsy was sometimes referred to in the ancient world as the "sacred disease" (Donahue and Harrington, *Mark*, 281). The verb "to have seizures" (σεληνιάζομαι) is related to the Greek word for "moon" (σελήνη), reflecting ancient belief that such seizures were caused by the moon (Galen 9.903). Lucian, *Philops.* 16, refers to demon-possessed people who "fall down in the light of the moon, and roll their eyes and fill their mouths with foam." This etymology is evident in English words like "lunatic" and "moonstruck." For the Jewish perspective on seizures and epilepsy, see Str-B 1:758.

6. See Edwin Yamauchi, "Magic or Miracles? Diseases, Demons and Exorcisms," in *Gospel Perspectives*, vol. 6, *The Miracles of Jesus* (ed. David Wenham and Craig Blomberg; Sheffield: JSOT Press, 1986), 89–184.

often said to cause physical symptoms, including muteness (Matt 9:32), blindness (12:22), deformity (Luke 13:11), and violent behavior (Mark 5:1 – 20). If we accept the possibility that demons exist, as the Evangelists certainly believed, we should speak of epileptic-like symptoms rather than epilepsy per se.[7]

The father concludes by pointing to the inability of the disciples to drive out the demon. Jesus' indictment that follows (v. 19), his discussion with the father about faith (vv. 22 – 24), and his private teaching of the disciples (vv. 28 – 29) all show that the failure of the disciples and the need for greater faith is a major theme of the episode.[8]

9:19 Jesus responded, "O unbelieving generation, how long will I be with you? How long must I endure you? Bring him to me." (ὁ δὲ ἀποκριθεὶς αὐτοῖς λέγει· ὦ γενεὰ ἄπιστος, ἕως πότε πρὸς ὑμᾶς ἔσομαι; ἕως πότε ἀνέξομαι ὑμῶν; φέρετε αὐτὸν πρός με). Jesus responds with a prophetic lament against this "unbelieving" or "faithless" (ἄπιστος) "generation" (γενεά; cf. Deut 1:35; 32:5, 20; Ps 78:8; Jer 7:29; Phil 2:5).[9] The interjection "O" (ὦ) is often left untranslated or rendered as "You," since it represents awkward and archaic English (so NIV, HCSB, NLT, NRSV, REB, NJB). Here it functions as an emotional personal address (BDAG, 1101).

But whom does Jesus call a faithless generation? In context it could be the scribes, the crowd, the father, the disciples, or any combination of these. While some limit the address to the crowd (including the scribes) and the father,[10] others say it is directed only toward the disciples.[11] It is best, however, to see the address as to all who are present.[12]

The disciples are unlikely to be excluded, since their failure is on center stage in the immediate context (v. 18), at the end of the episode (vv. 28 – 29), and throughout this section of Mark's gospel. Yet a sweeping term like "generation" (γενεά) is unlikely to be limited to the nine disciples. In 8:12 Jesus used it of the religious leaders and in 8:38 of all his contemporaries.

There is a high implicit Christology here, as Jesus speaks from a "God-ward perspective ... he differentiates himself not only from unbelieving scribes, crowds, and disciples, but from unbelieving humanity as such."[13] He is not part of this present generation, but speaks to it from above (cf. Deut 32:20).

The two rhetorical questions, "How long will I be with you?" and "How long must I endure you?" are expressions of frustration at stubborn and persistent unbelief. Yet this frustration does not result in rejection but in action, as Jesus calls for the boy to be brought to him. Despite the pervasive unbelief around him, Jesus remains faithful to his messianic calling.

9:20 – 22 So they brought the boy to Jesus. When the spirit saw him, immediately he threw the boy into convulsions. Falling to the ground, he rolled around, foaming at the mouth. He asked his father, "How long has this been happening to him?" He answered, "From childhood. Often it throws him into the fire or into bodies of water to destroy him. But if you can do anything, have pity on us and help us." (καὶ ἤνεγκαν αὐτὸν πρὸς αὐτόν. καὶ ἰδὼν αὐτὸν τὸ πνεῦμα εὐθὺς

---

7. For arguments against identifying this as epilepsy, see P. J. Achtemeier, "Miracles and the Historical Jesus: A Study of Mark 9:14 – 29," *CBQ 37* (1975): 471 – 91, 481 n. 35.

8. Contra Stein, *Mark*, 433, who claims discipleship is a minor theme compared to Mark's christological concerns.

9. Some manuscripts include "perverse" (διεστραμμένη; 𝔓45vid *f*13 2542 pc) but this is almost certainly an assimilation to Matt 17:17 and Luke 9:41.

10. Gundry, *Mark*, 489; Edwards, *Mark*, 278.

11. Cranfield, *Mark*, 301.

12. Hooker, *Mark*, 223; Witherington, *Mark*, 267; Stein, *Mark*, 433.

13. Boring, *Mark*, 274. Cf. Lane, *Mark*, 332.

συνεσπάραξεν αὐτόν, καὶ πεσὼν ἐπὶ τῆς γῆς ἐκυλίετο ἀφρίζων. καὶ ἐπηρώτησεν τὸν πατέρα αὐτοῦ· πόσος χρόνος ἐστὶν ὡς τοῦτο γέγονεν αὐτῷ; ὁ δὲ εἶπεν· ἐκ παιδιόθεν· καὶ πολλάκις καὶ εἰς πῦρ αὐτὸν ἔβαλεν καὶ εἰς ὕδατα ἵνα ἀπολέσῃ αὐτόν· ἀλλ᾽ εἴ τι δύνῃ, βοήθησον ἡμῖν σπλαγχνισθεὶς ἐφ᾽ ἡμᾶς).

The repetition here not only illustrates Mark's colorful storytelling style, but also emphasizes the seriousness of the demonization. The spirit sees Jesus, but it does not cry out as in other exorcisms (1:24; 3:11, 12; 5:6 – 7), confirming its identity as a mute-causing spirit (v. 17). What was described in v. 18 by the father is now vividly illustrated as the demon throws the boy to the ground and sends him into convulsions. The same basic symptoms are described using different terminology (only "foaming" [ἀφρίζω] is repeated). Grinding the teeth is not mentioned again, nor is rigidity. This latter will occur in the demon's final convulsion in v. 26.

Jesus' question, "How long has this been happening to him?" sounds almost like a detached physician performing an interview before providing treatment. From a narrative perspective the purpose of the question and its answer — "from childhood" — is to illustrate Jesus' compassion and especially to reiterate the seriousness of the situation and the apparent hopelessness for a cure (cf. 5:25; Luke 13:11, 16; John 5:5; 9:1).

The father's continuing description underlines this seriousness. The demonic presence not only torments the boy but seeks to destroy him, throwing him in the fire and the water.[14] As in the case of the drowning of the pigs in 5:13, it is unclear why killing the boy would be to the demon's advantage, since it would lose its host. But demons are

portrayed as evil and destructive creatures, whose actions are fundamentally malicious rather than rational. The ever-present danger of death for the boy adds urgency to the situation.

The apparent hopelessness of the situation and the disciples' failure to exorcize the demon has caused the father's faith to waver, and his request is couched in uncertainty: "if you are able to do anything [εἴ τι δύνῃ] …" The man pleads for Jesus to have compassion (σπλαγχνίζομαι) and help (βοηθέω). Both are necessary. Someone may feel great compassion for those in need but have no power or resources to help. Conversely, someone may have plenty of resources, but not care enough to do anything. Jesus has both the compassion and the authority to heal the boy.

9:23 – 24 Jesus said to him, "If you can? Everything is possible for the one who believes." Immediately crying out, the boy's father said, "I believe! Help my unbelief!" (ὁ δὲ Ἰησοῦς εἶπεν αὐτῷ· τὸ εἰ δύνῃ, πάντα δυνατὰ τῷ πιστεύοντι. εὐθὺς κράξας ὁ πατὴρ τοῦ παιδίου ἔλεγεν· πιστεύω· βοήθει μου τῇ ἀπιστίᾳ). This exchange between Jesus and the man is one of the most poignant and powerful in Scripture. Jesus first challenges the man's assumption that his power may be insufficient for the task: "What do you mean, 'If I can?'" (NLT).[15]

The issue is not Jesus' ability but a willingness to respond in faith, since "everything is possible for the one who believes." The point is *not*, of course, that with enough faith you can do anything. It is rather that *God* has the power to do anything. It is not the amount of faith that is important, but it is the object of that faith. With the faith of a mustard

---

14. The plural "waters" (ὕδατα) probably means bodies of water (as our translation has indicated), meaning lakes and streams.

15. The neuter article τό in the phrase τὸ εἰ δύνῃ is probably intended to make the whole phrase substantive : "now

concerning this 'If you can?'" Its cumbersome nature resulted in several textual variants, some turning the phrase into Jesus' encouragement to the man, "If you are able to believe" (εἰ δύνῃ πιστεῦσαι).

seed you can move mountains (Matt 17:20; cf. Luke 17:6), because that faith is in the sovereign Lord of the universe. In the same way, the absence of faith is a critical hindrance to success. In Nazareth, Jesus "could not do any miracles there" because of their unbelief (6:5). God takes over when people let go and put their trust in him.

The man realizes his own faith is wavering and so cries out, "I believe! Help my unbelief!" The dual statement reflects two sides of the same coin. "I believe" is a conscious decision — despite his wavering feelings — to step out in faith. "Help my unbelief" is a recognition that his humanity is still weak and that only in the power of God will he have sufficient faith. Ironically, this second cry is an act of faith, since calling on God for greater faith is trusting in him rather than in ourselves — the essence of true faith.

9:25 Seeing that a crowd was quickly gathering, Jesus rebuked the defiling spirit, saying to it, "You spirit of deafness and muteness, I command you: Come out of him and never enter him again." (ἰδὼν δὲ ὁ Ἰησοῦς ὅτι ἐπισυντρέχει ὄχλος, ἐπετίμησεν τῷ πνεύματι τῷ ἀκαθάρτῳ λέγων αὐτῷ· τὸ ἄλαλον καὶ κωφὸν πνεῦμα, ἐγὼ ἐπιτάσσω σοι, ἔξελθε ἐξ αὐτοῦ καὶ μηκέτι εἰσέλθῃς εἰς αὐτόν). The statement of a gathering crowd is odd, since a "large crowd" (ὄχλος πολύς) has been present from the beginning (v. 14). Perhaps Jesus had stepped aside from the crowd to gain some privacy (cf. 5:40; 7:33; 8:23). More likely, Mark means the crowd has continued to grow as more and more people hear of Jesus' presence and rush to join him.[16] Jesus wants to perform the miracle quickly to avoid undue messianic acclaim (cf. 1:44; 5:43; 7:36; 8:26).

As at 1:25, Jesus "rebukes" (ἐπιτιμάω) the "defiling" (ἀκάθαρτος) spirit. The demon is truly a defiling presence for the boy that must be purged by Jesus (see comments at 1:23). Jesus refers to the spirit here as both "mute and deaf" (ἄλαλον καὶ κωφόν; cf. 7:32). Though the term translated "deaf" (κωφός) can mean either unable to hear or unable to speak,[17] by combining the words Mark suggests that the boy can neither speak nor hear. The translation "mute and deaf spirit" (ESV, NET, HCSB; cf. NIV, REB) is not quite right, since the spirit was causing these maladies rather than being afflicted by them (see v. 26). The NRSV gets it right: "You spirit that keeps this boy from speaking and hearing." The command to "never enter him again" (μηκέτι εἰσέλθῃς εἰς αὐτόν) is unique in the gospel exorcism accounts but not surprising, since it was believed that demonization could recur in a person if proper defenses were not put in place.[18]

9:26 – 27 After crying out loudly and convulsing the boy violently, it came out, leaving him like a dead person. As a result, many said, "He's dead." But Jesus, grasping his hand, raised him up, and he got up (καὶ κράξας καὶ πολλὰ σπαράξας ἐξῆλθεν· καὶ ἐγένετο ὡσεὶ νεκρός, ὥστε τοὺς πολλοὺς λέγειν ὅτι ἀπέθανεν. ὁ δὲ Ἰησοῦς κρατήσας τῆς χειρὸς αὐτοῦ ἤγειρεν αὐτόν, καὶ ἀνέστη). As in 1:25 – 26, the exorcism is marked by screams and violent convulsions. The fact that the demon cries out shows that it was not itself mute, but rather it was afflicting the boy with these symptoms. Its violent departure demonstrates the virulence of this particular demon. So also does the result: the demon seems to have killed the boy. The adjective "dead"

---

16. ἐπισυντρέχω is a *hapax legomenon* that means to "run together" or "gather quickly" (BDAG, 382).

17. See BDAG, 580, for examples.

18. Cf. Matt 12:43 – 45//Luke 11:24 – 26. Josephus refers to Solomon's superior exorcizing abilities, by which he would

drive out demons "so that they never returned" (Josephus, *Ant.* 8.2.5 §§45, 47). Similarly, Philostratus records how Apollonius commanded a demon to "leave the young boy and never possess anyone else" (*Vit. Apoll.* 4.20).

(νεκρός) is functioning substantivally: "He became like a dead body" (i.e., a corpse).

Jesus, however, takes the boy's hand and lifts him up. The language here recalls the raising of Jairus's daughter, and the same three verbs are used: "grasping," "raising," and "getting up" (κρατέω, ἐγείρω, ἀνίστημι; 5:41 – 42). Some commentators see here a resurrection allusion. Lane writes that "the accumulation of the vocabulary of death and resurrection in vv. 25 – 27, and the parallelism with the narrative of the raising of Jairus's daughter, suggest that Mark wished to allude to a death and resurrection. The dethroning of Satan is always a reversal of death and an affirmation of life."[19] Boring similarly claims that "Mark's miracle stories point to the Christ event as a whole and communicate resurrection faith."[20] This may be reading too much into what is common language for taking a hand and lifting a person from the ground. Still, the echoes of 5:41 – 42 certainly emphasize Jesus' authority to renew and restore the boy's life.

9:28 – 29 When he went inside, his disciples were asking him privately, "Why could we not cast it out?" He said to them, "This kind cannot be cast out except by prayer." (Καὶ εἰσελθόντος αὐτοῦ εἰς οἶκον οἱ μαθηταὶ αὐτοῦ κατ' ἰδίαν ἐπηρώτων αὐτόν· ὅτι ἡμεῖς οὐκ ἠδυνήθημεν ἐκβαλεῖν αὐτό; καὶ εἶπεν αὐτοῖς· τοῦτο τὸ γένος ἐν οὐδενὶ δύναται ἐξελθεῖν εἰ μὴ ἐν προσευχῇ). The episode concludes with a discussion between Jesus and his disciples "privately" (κατ' ἰδίαν) inside ("in a/the house"; εἰς οἶκον). In Mark's gospel Jesus often instructs the disciples privately (4:10, 34; 6:31; 7:17; 9:35; 10:10, 32; 12:43; 13:3).[21] This is part of the theme established in 4:10 – 12 that the disciples are "insiders" to the secrets of the kingdom of God. The disciples, however, are now baffled. Jesus had given them authority to cast out demons (6:7), authority they had exercised in the past (6:13). Why were they now failing?

Jesus' response is that this "kind" (γένος) can only come out with prayer.[22] The statement is puzzling in various respects. First, does Jesus mean this kind of demon, as if some demons were more powerful than others? Or does he mean this kind of challenge, that is, one involving spiritual warfare? The former is certainly the more natural reading, since the language of "casting out" would more naturally apply to exorcism than to miracles in general.[23] Certainly the graphic descriptions of demonic power in episodes like this one (vv. 18, 20, 22, 26) and the Gerasene demoniac (5:3 – 5, 9, 13) suggest degrees of demonic oppression.

The other puzzling part of Jesus' response is his reference to prayer, since prayer has not been mentioned up to this point in the story. Mark does not even refer to Jesus praying before the exorcism. Yet *faith* has been a central theme of the episode, and there is an intimate connection between faith and prayer. Faith is the issue both in Jesus' indictment of the "present generation" and in his discussion with the boy's father.[24] Prayer is more than just communicating with God. It is acknowledging one's dependence on him for all of our needs.

Jesus' disciples were evidently beginning to

---

19. Lane, *Mark*, 334.

20. Boring, *Mark*, 275.

21. For "house" as a teaching venue, see 2:1 – 2; 3:20; 7:17; 9:28; 10:10.

22. The great majority of manuscripts add "and fasting" (και νηστεια 𝔓⁴⁵vid ℵ² A C D L W Θ Ψ 𝑓¹·¹³ 33 𝔐 lat syrʰ cop). Although this is an impressive array of manuscripts, the phrase's absence in early Alexandrian manuscripts (ℵ* B), the scribal tendency to add natural complements (1 Cor 7:5 and Acts 10:30 have similar additions in the mss tradition), and an increasing emphasis on fasting in the early church all suggest that these words were an early scribal gloss. See Metzger, *Textual Commentary*, 85. Cf. 2:19, where Jesus rules out fasting for his disciples while he is with them.

23. So Marcus, *Mark 9 – 16*, 655; contra France, *Mark*, 370.

24. See Marshall, *Faith as a Theme*, 222 – 23.

think that their authority came from their own status as Jesus' disciples or the techniques they learned from him. Jesus reminds them that they have no power on their own; it is only by faith through prayer that can they tap the infinite power of God. Even the most dangerous and destructive demon is no match for the Son of God, who is in a relationship of intimate fellowship with the Father.

Theology in Application

The Supremacy of Jesus

The supremacy of Jesus, announced at the transfiguration (9:7), is now revealed through exorcism. While the disciples try and fail to exorcize the demon, Jesus casts it out with a single command. Jesus is no Hellenistic magician who uses potions, rituals, and incantations to coax spiritual forces to act on his behalf. He is the Son of God, who acts with divine power and authority. Jesus' supremacy is seen throughout the episode. When he arrives, the crowd is amazed and rushes to greet him; while the disciples are powerless against the demon, he easily casts it out. Moreover, he forbids it from returning. This is power over time and place. When the demon leaves the boy comatose after its violent departure, Jesus takes his hand, lifts him up, and restores him. This is power over life and death.

The Struggle for Faith to Accomplish God's Purposes

A second theme beside Jesus' authority is the need for greater faith. This is illustrated both in the failure of the disciples to cast out the demon, noted at the beginning and end of the episode (vv. 17, 28 – 29), and in the father's struggle for greater faith in the middle (vv. 22 – 24). The father's cry, "I believe! Help my unbelief!" is one Christians have resonated with through the ages. Our genuine faith in God is challenged by difficult circumstances. We want to believe, and we *do* believe, but that faith wavers when the storms of life arrive.

Like Peter, who has faith to get out of the boat but then is distracted by the wind and the waves (Matt 14:25 – 33), we have initial faith but then slip into the waters of doubt and despair. It is at this point we need to claim Jesus' promise, "Everything is possible for the one who believes." When our faith wavers, it is not because we are not striving hard enough to succeed or are not confident enough in our own abilities. It is because we have gotten our eyes off Jesus. Jesus' words here echo those of Paul: "I can do all this *through him who gives me strength*" (Phil 4:13, italics added). We can accomplish *anything* when we acknowledge that we can accomplish *nothing* on our own. Mustard-seed faith is a little bit of faith in a very big God.

The disciples are right to come to Jesus after the episode. They want to know why they failed in order to avoid such a fiasco in the future. But Jesus' answer does not focus on procedure. Their failure was not because they said the wrong words or followed the wrong ritual. Their problem was that their past successes had given them confidence in their own abilities. Jesus calls them to more prayer, that is, greater dependence on God, who alone has authority over the forces of evil. The disciples' authority to cast out demons was always *mediated* authority; they are Jesus' representatives acting in his power.

The same is true for us today. The most powerful servant of God is the one who recognizes that "when I am weak, then I am strong" (2 Cor 12:10). Doing great things for God means seeking his guidance, being led by his Spirit, and allowing his power to work through us.

The Reality of Spiritual Warfare

Like other exorcisms in Mark's gospel, this one reminds us of the reality of spiritual warfare and the demonic realm. Though we may not always experience it existentially or acknowledge it openly, this conflict is real. The disciples' failure and Jesus' response teaches those involved in deliverance ministries that the most important weapon we bring to this battle is not the right rituals or incantations. It is prayer — our complete dependence on the one who has "disarmed the powers and authorities ... triumphing over them by the cross" (Col 2:15).

Mark 9:30 – 50

Literary Context

This is the second of three "cycles" that appear in this section of Mark (8:22 – 10:52). In each cycle Jesus first predicts his death. This is followed by some act of pride or self-interest on the part of the disciples, and then by Jesus' teaching on the humble and self-sacrificial role of true disciples. The first passion prediction (8:31) was followed by Peter's rebuke (8:32) and Jesus' teaching on cross-bearing disciple-ship (8:33 – 38). This second passion prediction (9:31) is followed by the disciples' argument about who is the greatest (vv. 33 – 34) and then Jesus' teaching on true greatness (vv. 35 – 37) and further teaching on discipleship (vv. 38 – 50). The third passion prediction (10:32 – 34) will be followed by the request of James and John for chief seats in the kingdom (10:35 – 37) and Jesus' teaching on servant leadership (10:38 – 45). All of these illustrate Mark's christological transition from the first to the second part of his gospel. Jesus is the mighty Messiah and Son of God (1:1 – 8:30), but his role is that of the Suffering Servant of the Lord, who offers himself as a ransom for sins (8:31 – 15:47).

Main Idea

When Jesus predicts for a second time his coming suffering and death in Jerusa-lem, his disciples respond with incomprehension, pride, and jealousy. Jesus answers by teaching about true greatness, which means setting aside personal ambition and welcoming the least of God's people. He also teaches about the high cost of disciple-ship, which calls for radical self-denial in light of the eternal consequences of sin.

Translation

Mark 9:30 – 50

30a	character departure	Leaving that place,
b	Setting (spatial)	**they were passing through Galilee.**
c	Explanation	**He did not want anyone to know**
31a	reason for 30c	because he was teaching his disciples and telling them,
b	Instruction/Prophecy	*"The Son of Man will be delivered into human hands,*
c		*and they will kill him.*
d		*But three days after being killed,*
e		*he will rise again."*
32a	Response to 31	But **they did not understand this statement**
b		and **were afraid to ask him.**
33a	Setting (spatial)	**They came to Capernaum.**
b	setting (spatial)	When he was in the house,
c	Question	**he asked them,**
d		*"What were you arguing about on the way?"*
34a	Response to 33c-d	**But they were silent,**
b	reason for 34a	because on the way they had been arguing with one another ☞
		about who was the greatest.
35a	setting (social)	Sitting down,
b	Summons/Instruction	**he called the Twelve and said to them,**
c	aphorism	*"If anyone wants to be first,*
d		*that person must be the very last and*
		servant of all."
36a	Object lesson/Illustration	Taking a child,
b		**he placed it in front of them.**
c		Taking the child into his arms,
d	Instruction	**he said to them,**
37a		*"Whoever welcomes one of these little children in my name*
b		*welcomes me,*
c		*and whoever welcomes me*
d		*does not welcome me but*
e		*the one who sent me."*
38a	Report	**John said to him,**
b		*"Teacher, we saw someone casting out demons in your name*
c		*and we tried to stop him,*
d		*because he was not following us."*

39a	Response to 38/Instruction	**But Jesus said,**
b	command	"Don't stop him,
c	reason fo 39b	because no one who does a miracle in my name can quickly speak evil against me.
40	aphorism	*For* whoever is not against us is for us.
41a	aphorism	*For* whoever gives you a cup of water
b		because you belong to the Messiah,
c	veracity statement	truly I say to you,
d	aphorism	that person will certainly not lose their reward.
42a	aphorism	*And* whoever causes one of these little ones who believe in me to stumble,
b		it would be better for them to have a large millstone hung around their neck and ⳑ be thrown into the sea.
43a	aphorism	If your hand causes you to stumble,
b		cut it off.
c		It is better for you to enter life maimed
d		than with two hands
		to go to Gehenna,
e		to the unquenchable fire.
45a	aphorism	*And* if your foot causes you to stumble,
b		cut it off.
c		It is better for you to enter life crippled
d		than with two feet
		to be thrown into Gehenna.
47a	aphorism	*And* if your eye causes you to stumble,
b		tear it out.
c		It is better for you to enter the kingdom of God one-eyed
d		than with two eyes
		to be thrown into Gehenna,
48a	Scripture quotation	'Where their worm does not die
b		and the fire is not quenched.' [Isa 66:24]
49	aphorism	*For* everyone will be salted with fire.
50a	aphorism	Salt is good.
b		*But* if salt becomes unsalty,
c		with what will you make it salty?
d	aphorism	Have salt among yourselves
e		*and* live in peace with one another."

Structure

The passage may be broken down into four episodes. We treat these together because of the related theme of authentic discipleship. The second passion prediction (vv. 33 – 32) is followed by the disciples' argument concerning who is the greatest and Jesus' response on the first being last (vv. 33 – 37). Mark then recounts a short pronouncement story concerning John and the unknown exorcist (vv. 38 – 40), followed by more sayings loosely connected to the theme of discipleship (vv. 41 – 50).[1] Mark links these sayings with a series of catchwords: "if" (vv. 35, 43, 45, 47, 50), "whoever" (vv. 37, 39, 40, 41, 42), "(one of these) … child/children/little ones" (vv. 36, 37, 42), "in (my) name" (vv. 37, 38, 39), "cause to stumble" (vv. 42, 43, 45, 47), "(it is) better" (vv. 42, 43, 45, 47), "be thrown into" (vv. 42, 45, 47), "Gehenna" (vv. 43, 45, 47), "fire" (vv. 43, 48, 49), "salt/salted" (vv. 49, 50).[2]

Exegetical Outline

➡ **1. Second Passion Prediction (9:30 – 32)**

2. Debate about Who Is the Greatest (9:33 – 37)

    a. Jesus' question in the house (9:33)

    b. The disciples' silence (9:34)

    c. Jesus' teaching on the first being last (9:35)

    d. Illustration with a child (9:36 – 37)

3. The Unknown Exorcist (9:38 – 40)

    a. John's statement (9:38)

    b. Jesus' dual pronouncement (9:39 – 40)

4. Teaching on Discipleship (9:41 – 50)

    a. Giving a cup of water in Jesus' name (9:41)

    b. The severe price of causing a little one to stumble (9:42)

    c. Radical measures against stumbling (9:43 – 48)

    d. Sayings about salt (9:49 – 50)

Explanation of the Text

9:30a-b Leaving that place, they were passing through Galilee (Κἀκεῖθεν ἐξελθόντες παρεπορεύοντο διὰ τῆς Γαλιλαίας). The participial phrase, (lit.) "Having gone out from there," could mean from the house mentioned in 9:28 or from that region. If the transfiguration (9:2) took place at Mount Hermon near Caesarea Philippi (8:27), Jesus would be moving southwest "passing through Galilee" toward Capernaum on the northwest shore of the lake, his next destination (v. 33).

9:30c – 31 He did not want anyone to know because he was teaching his disciples and telling them, "The Son of Man will be delivered into human hands, and they will kill him. But three days after being killed, he will rise again." (καὶ οὐκ ἤθελεν ἵνα τις γνοῖ· ἐδίδασκεν γὰρ τοὺς

---

1. Some of these sayings appear together in Matt 18:1 – 9 and Luke 9:46 – 50, while others have different contexts in the other Synoptics. In Matthew, the saying about salt losing its saltiness is found in the Sermon on the Mount (Matt 5:13) and the reward for giving a cup of cold water to a disciple in 10:42. In Luke, the millstone saying is found in Luke 17:1 – 2 and the saying about salt in 14:34 – 35.

2. See Boring, *Mark*, 279; Stein, *Mark*, 441, etc. Cf. J. I. H. McDonald, "Mark 9:33 – 50: Catechetics in Mark's Gospel," in *Studia Biblica*, vol. 2: *Papers on the Gospels* (ed. E. A. Livingstone; JSNTSup 2; Sheffield: JSOT Press, 1980), 171 – 77.

μαθητὰς αὐτοῦ καὶ ἔλεγεν αὐτοῖς ὅτι ὁ υἱὸς τοῦ ἀνθρώπου παραδίδοται εἰς χεῖρας ἀνθρώπων, καὶ ἀποκτενοῦσιν αὐτόν, καὶ ἀποκτανθεὶς μετὰ τρεῖς ἡμέρας ἀναστήσεται). Jesus' attempt at privacy is certainly part of Mark's messianic secret (Jesus' attempt to keep a lid on the messianic ambitions of the crowds),[3] but is specified here as for the purpose of private instruction for the Twelve. As Jesus begins to set his sights on Jerusalem, he prepares his disciples for the traumatic events that will occur there. Since Peter's confession (8:29 – 30), Jesus' ministry focus has shifted from public teaching and miracles — demonstrating the authority of the kingdom of God — to private instruction for the Twelve. "He was teaching" (ἐδίδασκεν) is an iterative imperfect,[4] meaning this was a repeated theme (cf. 8:31; 10:32 – 34).

Of the three passion predictions, this one is the briefest, and some scholars consider it to be the earliest of the three and the most likely to go back to the historical Jesus (see the chart in Structure at 10:32 – 35, comparing the three).[5] The present tense "is delivered" (παραδίδοται) is a futuristic present ("will be delivered"), confirming the certainty of the events foretold.[6] The verb could mean "betrayed," referring to the actions of Judas (cf. 3:19; 14:18, 21, 42, 44; cf. 13:9), or "handed over,"

referring either to the actions of the religious leaders in turning Jesus over to Pilate (15:1, 10) or to Pilate "delivering" Jesus to be crucified (15:15). In 1:14 the same verb is used for the arrest of John the Baptist. More likely, however, this is a divine passive, referring to God's purpose in "delivering up" Jesus as a sacrifice for sins (cf. 10:33).[7]

Support for this is reference to "human hands" (χεῖρας ἀνθρώπων), which may suggest a divine-to-human transfer. Paul uses the verb in this sense to speak of God's "delivering" his own Son (Rom 4:25; 8:32; 1 Cor 11:23; cf. Gal 2:20, where Jesus "gave [delivered] himself" for us). In Acts Peter similarly reports (though using a different word) that Jesus was "handed over" [ἔκδοτον; an adjective] to you by God's deliberate plan and foreknowledge (Acts 2:23; cf. 3:18). The same verb (παραδίδωμι) is also used in the Suffering Servant passages in the LXX (Isa 53:6, 12 LXX) of God's actions in delivering over his servant to suffering and death.[8]

9:32 But they did not understand this statement and were afraid to ask him (οἱ δὲ ἠγνόουν τὸ ῥῆμα, καὶ ἐφοβοῦντο αὐτὸν ἐπερωτῆσαι). The disciples' spiritual dullness has been a consistent theme since Jesus began to teach in parables.[9] Two things about his statement would have been incomprehensible to the disciples. First, the Messiah would suffer and

---

3. Contra Gundry, *Mark*, 503, who claims that since Mark is writing to Gentiles, who had no nationalistic messianic expectations, this cannot be his purpose. But even Gentile Christianity arose first in the synagogue among Jews and God-fearers, where such messianic expectations were well known. The question of why Jesus did not establish a physical kingdom in Jerusalem would surely have been a live issue for both Jewish and Gentile Christians.

4. Wallace, *Greek Grammar*, 546 – 47.

5. Evans, *Mark 8:27 – 16:20*, 56; Jeremias, *New Testament Theology*, 281 – 82; Pesch, *Markusevangelium*, 2:100. For evidence that Jesus foresaw and predicted his own death, see "In Depth: Did Jesus Predict His Own Death?" at 8:27 – 33.

6. Stein, *Mark*, 439; Taylor, *Mark*, 403; Wallace, *Greek Grammar*, 535 – 37.

7. So most commentators: Hooker, *Mark*, 226; Evans, *Mark 8:27 – 16:20*, 57; Witherington, *Mark*, 268 – 69; Edwards, *Mark*, 284; Stein, *Mark*, 439; Boring, *Mark*, 277; Collins, *Mark*, 441.

8. Boring, *Mark*, 277. If Jesus' "Son of Man" language comes from Dan 7:13, there are significant verbal connections between the Danielic "son of man" and the "holy people of the Most High" who are "delivered into the hands" (7:25) of the "horn" for a time and then are given an everlasting kingdom (7:27). Jesus may therefore be drawing from Dan 7, both for the Son of Man title as well as for the suffering language of the passion predictions. See J. Schaberg, "Daniel 7, 12 and the New Testament Passion-Resurrection Predictions," *NTS* 31 (1985): 208 – 22; cf. Scot McKnight, *Jesus and His Death: Historiography, the Historical Jesus, and Atonement Theory* (Waco, TX: Baylor University Press, 2005), 239.

9. See 4:13, 40; 6:52; 7:18; 8:17 – 18, 21; 8:32; 9:5 – 6, 19.

die. He was the one who was destined to establish an eternal kingdom of justice and righteousness (2 Sam 7:16; Isa 9:7). Second, the Messiah would rise from the dead. The resurrection was viewed in Judaism as occurring at the end of time, when all the dead would rise and be judged by God (Dan 12:2 – 3). The resurrection of an individual within history was outside their worldview.

Why were the disciples afraid to ask Jesus? Some commentators have suggested that they were afraid that the answer might include their own suffering.[10] But nothing in the context suggests this. Others point to Mark's use of fear and awe elsewhere in the gospel and see this as "holy fear" inspired by Jesus' awesome presence.[11] This is possible, since incomprehension and fear have appeared together elsewhere (see the boat scene at 6:51 – 52). But Jesus has done nothing in the present context to inspire such awe. The simplest solution is that the disciples are intimidated and afraid to ask because Jesus has been accusing them of spiritual dullness (4:13; 7:18; 8:18, 21). How could they now admit that they still don't understand?

9:33 – 34 They came to Capernaum. When he was in the house, he asked them, "What were you arguing about on the way?" But they were silent, because on the way they had been arguing with one another about who was the greatest (Καὶ ἦλθον εἰς Καφαρναούμ. Καὶ ἐν τῇ οἰκίᾳ γενόμενος ἐπηρώτα αὐτούς· τί ἐν τῇ ὁδῷ διελογίζεσθε; οἱ δὲ ἐσιώπων· πρὸς ἀλλήλους γὰρ διελέχθησαν ἐν τῇ ὁδῷ τίς μείζων). Capernaum was Jesus' base of operations during his Galilean ministry (1:21; 2:1), so it is not surprising that he returns here. The home is not identified, but it could be Peter's (1:29). More

important is the Markan theme that this is private instruction for the disciples.[12]

The spiritual ignorance noted in v. 32 is illustrated through the disciples' actions as they argue about who is the greatest. As the first passion prediction was followed by a spiritual failure (Peter's rebuke of Jesus; 8:32), so this one is similarly followed by acts of pride. Jesus' question is almost rhetorical, "What were you arguing about on the way?" He clearly knows, either through overhearing their conversation or through divine insight. The verb "argue" (διαλογίζομαι) can mean simply to discuss something (2:6, 8; 8:16 – 17; 11:31), but the present context indicates a dispute.

While this debate about greatness may sound inappropriate and egotistical to Western ears, it would seem less so in the honor/shame culture of the first century, where boasting was considered necessary to confirm one's social status in the community (see Paul's reluctant boasting in 2 Cor 11:16 – 12:19). The same issues of position and greatness will arise in 10:35 – 37, when James and John ask Jesus for the best seats in the kingdom. Jesus' messiahship had come onto center stage since Peter's confession in 8:29, and now the disciples are vying for the best positions in his kingdom.

Yet as Jesus has been teaching them, this is not the way of the kingdom of God. The disciples' silence betrays their guilt. Had they heard Jesus' teaching about his coming suffering and were unwilling to process it? Or did they know from Jesus' earlier teaching that he would disapprove of such pride talk (8:34 – 36)?

9:35 Sitting down, he called the Twelve and said to them, "If anyone wants to be first, that person must be the very last and servant of all." (καὶ

10. Best, *Following Jesus*, 73; Evans, *Mark 8:27 – 16:20*, 57 – 58.

11. Stein, *Mark*, 440; Dwyer, *Motif of Wonder*, 150; Gundry, *Mark*, 504; cf. 4:41; 5:15, 33; 6:50; 11:18.

12. Mark 4:10, 34; 7:17; 9:28 – 29, 30; 10:10 – 12, 32 – 34; 12:43 – 44; 13:3 – 4.

καθίσας ἐφώνησεν τοὺς δώδεκα καὶ λέγει αὐτοῖς· εἴ τις θέλει πρῶτος εἶναι, ἔσται πάντων ἔσχατος καὶ πάντων διάκονος). As he will do throughout this section, Jesus responds with instruction (8:34 – 38; 10:42 – 45). Sitting is the position of a teacher (4:1 – 2; 13:3; Matt 5:1; 13:1 – 3; 26:55; Luke 4:20; 5:3; John 8:2); school is now in session. Jesus begins with an aphorism: those who want to be first must be last. This "last" position is defined as "servant of all." The word "servant" (διάκονος) could mean a table waiter, but the term was used more generally of anyone who served as the agent of or at the behest of a superior.[13]

Jesus will respond similarly to the request by James and John in 10:43 – 44: "Whoever wants to become great among you will be your servant [διάκονος], and whoever wants to be first will be slave [δοῦλος] of all."[14] The ultimate model is the Son of Man, who came not to be served but to serve and "to give his life as a ransom for many" (10:45). In a cultural context of strict social distinctions and hierarchy, this statement would sound shockingly countercultural.

9:36 – 37 Taking a child, he placed it in front of them. Taking the child into his arms, he said to them, "Whoever welcomes one of these little children in my name welcomes me, and whoever welcomes me does not welcome me but the one who sent me." (καὶ λαβὼν παιδίον ἔστησεν αὐτὸ ἐν μέσῳ αὐτῶν καὶ ἐναγκαλισάμενος αὐτὸ εἶπεν αὐτοῖς· ὃς ἂν ἓν τῶν τοιούτων παιδίων δέξηται ἐπὶ τῷ ὀνόματί μου, ἐμὲ δέχεται· καὶ ὃς ἂν ἐμὲ δέχηται, οὐκ ἐμὲ δέχεται ἀλλὰ τὸν ἀποστείλαντά με). Jesus follows his statement about the first becoming last (v. 35) with an illustration of what it means to be a servant leader. The presence of a child is not sur-

prising since the context is a home (v. 33). Was this one of Peter's children? Perhaps.

Hooker argues that the saying that follows does not really fit here and actually works better at 10:15 in the context of the story about people bringing their children to Jesus. She further notes that the saying in 10:15 ("Whoever does not receive the kingdom of God like a child will certainly not enter it") fits better here and that the two sayings may have been accidently switched during their oral transmission. Possible evidence for this is the fact that Matthew introduces a saying similar to Mark 10:15 in his parallel to the present passage (Matt 18:1 – 4) and then omits that saying in his parallel to Mark 10:15 (Matt 19:13 – 15).[15]

Yet whatever the tradition history of these sayings, Hooker is wrong that the saying does not fit well here. While in Western culture we tend to view children as innocent, vulnerable, gentle, even pure, in first-century culture they were viewed as insignificant and having no social status. Welcoming a "little child" (παιδίον; diminutive of παῖς) means breaking social norms, lowering oneself to accept another of lower status and thereby risking one's own position of power and prestige.[16]

The question arises, however, who the child here represents. Is Jesus referring to welcoming (1) actual children, (2) lowly members of society, or (3) believers? In context these three cannot be so neatly distinguished. Verse 37 says that receiving one of these is the same as receiving Jesus. Since those who represent Jesus are his followers, the child must represent a follower of Jesus. Similarly, in v. 41 Jesus will say that anyone who gives "you" (i.e., the disciples) a cup of water "will certainly not lose their reward" (cf. Matt 10:40 – 42; Luke

---

13. BDAG, 230.

14. Cf. Matt 20:26 – 27; 23:11; Luke 9:48; 22:26.

15. Hooker, *Mark*, 228.

16. Collins, *Mark*, 445 – 46, suggests that the saying may

have originally been an encouragement to parents not to kill or expose their infants, a common practice among the poor in the Greco-Roman world. See Suzanne Dixon, *The Roman Family* (Baltimore/London: Johns Hopkins University Press, 1992).

10:16), and in v. 42 Jesus will speak of the danger of causing one of "these little ones who believe in me to stumble," which again indicates that the child represents a follower of Jesus, and more specifically, a vulnerable and lowly one. Jesus' point, therefore, is that true servant leadership means welcoming those of his followers who are deemed irrelevant and unworthy of such recognition. True servant leadership flips social hierarchy on its head, lifting up and serving those of lower status in the eyes of the world.

Since a "name" represents the person, to welcome someone "in my name" (ἐπὶ τῷ ὀνόματί μου) could mean "for my sake," "as my representative," or "with my authority." Gundry, however, argues that the phrase means "on the ground of my name," that is, because the child bears Jesus' name and has been received by him.[17] This fits the following clause, where welcoming that child is the same as welcoming Jesus. The image here is that of an emissary sent by a king. To "receive" that person is to offer one's service to the king himself. Those who serve the weakest and least significant of Jesus' followers are serving Jesus and in turn the one who sent him.[18]

9:38 John said to him, "Teacher, we saw someone casting out demons in your name and we tried to stop him, because he was not following us." (Ἔφη αὐτῷ ὁ Ἰωάννης· διδάσκαλε, εἴδομέν τινα ἐν τῷ ὀνόματί σου ἐκβάλλοντα δαιμόνια καὶ ἐκωλύομεν αὐτόν, ὅτι οὐκ ἠκολούθει ἡμῖν). The phrase "in your name" (ἐν τῷ ὀνόματί σου) is the catchword that links this episode to the previous one (v. 37). Conceptually, it is loosely connected around the themes of service and discipleship. Just as authentic servants welcome those of low social status

(vv. 36 – 37), so also they don't jealously guard their own personal authority, for they recognize that the advancement of the kingdom of God is more important than personal ambition (vv. 38 – 40).

This is the only episode in Mark's gospel where the disciple John appears on his own, though the scene fits John's personality as depicted elsewhere in the Gospels. In Mark 10:35 – 45 John and his brother James seek self-promotion by requesting the chief seats in Jesus' kingdom. Similarly, in Luke 9:51 – 55 they wish to call down fire on a Samaritan village that rejects Jesus and are rebuked by him. Perhaps "sons of thunder" (Boanerges), the nickname Jesus gave the two brothers (3:17), was intended to describe their fiery personalities. Many commentators have pointed out the irony of the episode, since the disciples themselves were unable to cast out a demon in 9:14 – 29.[19] Yet, curiously, it is John who makes the remark, and he was on the mountain with Jesus (9:2) rather than with the nine who failed in that exorcism.

To drive out demons "in your name" means "by your power," since a person's name was believed to evoke their authority. So who was this exorcist? Was he a nondisciple, like the seven sons of Sceva in Acts 19:13 – 17, who was using Jesus' name as a magical formula to exorcize demons? This is unlikely. Mark does not treat Jesus' authority as a magical power that can be manipulated (note the fate of the sons of Sceva in Acts 19:16). More likely, this was a true believer outside the circle of the Twelve.

Jesus had many followers in addition to the Twelve, including the seventy-two he sent out in Luke 10:1 – 17 to preach, heal, and cast out demons (Luke 10:9, 17). John's words betray his self-interest. He says they opposed the man "because he was not

---

17. Gundry, *Mark*, 510.

18. While Jesus as the one sent from God is a common theme throughout John's gospel, it is less common in the Synoptics, occurring in Mark only here and in the parable of the

tenant farmers (12:6). Cf. Matt 10:40; 15:24; 21:37; Luke 4:18, 43; 9:48; 10:16.

19. So Lane, *Mark*, 344; Evans, *Mark 8:27 – 16:20*, 65; Stein, *Mark*, 446; Boring, *Mark*, 282; etc.

following *us*" (ὅτι οὐκ ἠκολούθει ἡμῖν). He does not say, "following *you*." Though the idiom means, "he was not one of our group," the language echoes that of discipleship (1:18; 2:14; 6:1; 8:34; 10:21), where loyalty belongs to Jesus alone.

9:39 – 40 But Jesus said, "Don't stop him, because no one who does a miracle in my name can quickly speak evil against me. For whoever is not against us is for us." (ὁ δὲ Ἰησοῦς εἶπεν· μὴ κωλύετε αὐτόν. οὐδεὶς γάρ ἐστιν ὃς ποιήσει δύναμιν ἐπὶ τῷ ὀνόματί μου καὶ δυνήσεται ταχὺ κακολογῆσαί με· ὃς γὰρ οὐκ ἔστιν καθ᾿ ἡμῶν, ὑπὲρ ἡμῶν ἐστιν). Jesus instructs all the disciples (second person plural, "do not hinder" [μὴ κωλύετε]) not to oppose the man and offers two closely related reasons. First, those who perform miracles in Jesus' name will not soon speak evil of him. The qualification "soon," or "quickly," indicates that this is a general rather than an absolute truth. In general, those who evoke the name of Christ are his authentic followers. Exceptions no doubt occur, as when Jesus speaks of those who will prophesy, perform miracles, and cast out demons in his name, yet he will say to them, "I never knew you" (Matt 7:21 – 23).

Jesus' second response is proverbial, "For whoever is not against us is for us."[20] Jesus states the same proverb in Luke 9:50, but its reverse in Matt 12:30 (par. Luke 11:23): "Whoever is not with me is against me, and whoever does not gather with me scatters." The two are not contradictory, evidenced by the fact that Luke includes them both in his gospel. Proverbs are general rather than absolute truths, appropriate to specific contexts and occasions (cf. Prov 26:4 – 5). Here Jesus is opposing partisanship and cliques, those who are so focused on their own personal agendas and authority that they neglect God's greater kingdom purposes. The op-

posite proverb would apply to other circumstances, such as when people are sitting on the fence, unwilling to commit to Jesus. In that case, not to be *for him* is to be against him, since those who reject the kingdom are ultimately God's enemies.

This episode recalls Num 11:26 – 30, where Joshua complains to Moses that Eldad and Medad are prophesying outside the camp, even though they are not among the seventy select elders. Moses replies, "Are you jealous for my sake? I wish that all the LORD's people were prophets and that the LORD would put his Spirit on them!" It is the divine message, not the messenger, that is important. Similarly, in the present case it is the spiritual victory over demons that is important, not the identity of the exorcist.

9:41 For whoever gives you a cup of water because you belong to the Messiah, truly I say to you, that person will certainly not lose their reward (Ὃς γὰρ ἂν ποτίσῃ ὑμᾶς ποτήριον ὕδατος ἐν ὀνόματι ὅτι Χριστοῦ ἐστε, ἀμὴν λέγω ὑμῖν ὅτι οὐ μὴ ἀπολέσῃ τὸν μισθὸν αὐτοῦ). This statement is linked to the previous one by the catchwords "for" (γάρ) "who(ever)" (ὅς) and "in (my) name" (ἐν ὀνόματι). Conceptually, it picks up themes from both v. 37 and vv. 39 – 40. Verse 37 speaks of welcoming the least significant of Jesus' followers "in my name," illustrated now as offering a cup of water to them. Verse 40 speaks of those who are "for us," that is, those working for the kingdom of God. Offering a cup of water to the Messiah's followers illustrates what it means to be "for us." The Greek idiom (lit.) "in name because" (ἐν ὀνόματι ὅτι) means "on the basis that" or "on account of,"[21] so that the whole phrase means "because you belong to the Messiah." A parallel saying in Matthew speaks of giving a cup of cold water (lit.) "in the

---

20. A similar proverb appears in Cicero, *Lig.* 11, where the philosopher pleads with Caesar on behalf of a client: "We have often heard you say that, while we considered all who were

not with us as our enemies, you considered all who were not against you as your friends."

21. BDF 397(3); France, *Mark*, 378.

name of a disciple" (εἰς ὄνομα μαθητοῦ), i.e., "because they are my disciple" (Matt 10:42).

This saying, then, does not mean "charity will be rewarded." Rather, it emphasizes that those who provide love and support for Jesus' lowly and persecuted disciples are working for the kingdom and will be rewarded. For emphasis, Jesus introduces the statement about reward with his solemn affirmation formula, "Truly I say to you," (ἀμὴν λέγω ὑμῖν; 13x in Mark; see comments on 3:28 – 30). This saying parallels not only Matt 10:40 – 47, but also Jesus' parable of the sheep and goats in 25:31 – 46. When the Son of Man returns as king to judge and to save, eternal reward will be granted to those who showed care and compassion for "the least of these brothers and sisters of mine" (25:34 – 40), and eternal punishment to those who neglected them (25:41 – 46).

Jesus' identification of himself as the "Messiah" (Χριστός) has been seen as problematic by some, since nowhere else in Mark does Jesus use the title in a self-referential sense.[22] Yet this is not impossible, since Peter has acknowledged Jesus to be the Messiah in 8:29. Though Jesus has commanded his disciples to silence about his messiahship, the present passage is private instruction for them, not public teaching.

9:42 And whoever causes one of these little ones who believe in me to stumble, it would be better for them to have a large millstone hung around their neck and be thrown into the sea (Καὶ ὃς ἂν σκανδαλίσῃ ἕνα τῶν μικρῶν τούτων τῶν πιστευόντων εἰς ἐμέ, καλόν ἐστιν αὐτῷ μᾶλλον εἰ περίκειται μύλος ὀνικὸς περὶ τὸν τράχηλον αὐτοῦ καὶ βέβληται εἰς τὴν θάλασσαν). Scholars debate whether this statement is better connected with what precedes or what follows. It is linked to

what follows by the catchword "cause to stumble" (σκανδαλίζω; vv. 43, 45, 47). It is linked to what precedes by the relative clause beginning with "whoever" (ὃς ἄν). Conceptually, it forms the antithesis to v. 41. Verse 41 speaks of the reward for those who aid the followers of Jesus, while v. 42 speaks of the punishment for those who oppose them.

The term "cause to stumble" (σκανδαλίζω) may mean to "cause to sin" (ESV), "fall into sin" (NLT), or "lose faith" (GW). But it is perhaps better left ambiguous as "stumble" (NIV) or "downfall" (HCSB, REB), since in context it could mean any kind of spiritual downfall. That the failure is spiritual rather than merely physical is implied by the following paragraph, where "stumbling" results in the spiritual judgment of Gehenna.

Who are the "little ones" (οἱ μικροί) referred to here? Matthew's parallel apparently identifies them as children who believe in Jesus (Matt 18:5 – 6). The same sense is possible here. However, in light of the previous verse (where the disciples are in view), as well as our conclusions on vv. 37 – 38, it is best to see them as any of Jesus' lowly and insignificant followers, including children, who are vulnerable to spiritual failure. Jesus says it would be better to drown in the sea with a large millstone around one's neck than to cause one of these little ones to stumble. "Large millstone" is literally "millstone of a donkey" (μύλος ὀνικός), meaning one that required a large animal to turn rather than one turned by human hands. Jesus does not say specifically what being drowned would be better than, but divine judgment is clearly in view. The following verses speak of the unquenchable fire of Gehenna (vv. 43 – 48).

9:43 – 48 If your hand causes you to stumble, cut it off. It is better for you to enter life maimed

---

22. A number of manuscripts read μου ("of me") instead of Χριστοῦ ("of the Messiah"; אּ* C³ D Θ W *f*¹³ 𝔐). Taylor, *Mark*, 408, suggests that the original reading was μοι ("to me") and the phrase meant, "because you are mine."

than with two hands to go to Gehenna, to the unquenchable fire. And if your foot causes you to stumble, cut it off. It is better for you to enter life crippled than with two feet to be thrown into Gehenna. And if your eye causes you to stumble, tear it out. It is better for you to enter the kingdom of God one-eyed than with two eyes to be thrown into Gehenna, "Where their worm does not die and the fire is not quenched." (Καὶ ἐὰν σκανδαλίζῃ σε ἡ χείρ σου, ἀπόκοψον αὐτήν· καλόν ἐστίν σε κυλλὸν εἰσελθεῖν εἰς τὴν ζωὴν ἢ τὰς δύο χεῖρας ἔχοντα ἀπελθεῖν εἰς τὴν γέενναν, εἰς τὸ πῦρ τὸ ἄσβεστον. καὶ ἐὰν ὁ πούς σου σκανδαλίζῃ σε, ἀπόκοψον αὐτόν· καλόν ἐστίν σε εἰσελθεῖν εἰς τὴν ζωὴν χωλὸν ἢ τοὺς δύο πόδας ἔχοντα βληθῆναι εἰς τὴν γέενναν. καὶ ἐὰν ὁ ὀφθαλμός σου σκανδαλίζῃ σε, ἔκβαλε αὐτόν· καλόν σέ ἐστιν μονόφθαλμον εἰσελθεῖν εἰς τὴν βασιλείαν τοῦ θεοῦ ἢ δύο ὀφθαλμοὺς ἔχοντα βληθῆναι εἰς τὴν γέενναν, ὅπου ὁ σκώληξ αὐτῶν οὐ τελευτᾷ καὶ τὸ πῦρ οὐ σβέννυται).

Jesus now gives three parallel sayings, linked to the previous context with the catchword "cause to stumble" (σκανδαλίζω).[23] Here, however, it is temptations from within rather than pressure from others that result in such failure. Each of the three sayings contains a conditional clause with a protasis in the subjunctive mood ("if your hand/foot/ eye causes you to stumble …") and an apodosis ("… then cut it off/tear it out"),[24] followed by a comparative statement describing that it would be better to enter "life" (ζωή) maimed than to be thrown into Gehenna, or hell's fire, with a complete

body. "Life" here is clearly eternal life in God's presence. The third statement uses "the kingdom of God" (ἡ βασιλεία τοῦ θεοῦ) instead of "life," showing that the two are coreferential.

Gehenna is further defined in the first saying as "unquenchable fire" and in the third as a place where "their worm does not die and the fire is not quenched." Both of these phrases are allusions to Isa 66:24, which describes the eternal fate of the wicked who have rebelled against God. The term Gehenna (γέεννα), often translated "hell," comes from the Hebrew *gê [ben] hinnōm*, meaning the "valley of [the son of] Hinnom" (Josh 15:8; 18:16; Neh 11:30). This was the valley on the southern side of the city of Jerusalem, used in OT times for human sacrifices to the Canaanite gods Molech and Baal (2 Chr 28:3; 33:6; Jer 7:31; 19:5 – 6; 32:35). King Josiah desecrated the valley to stop the practice (2 Kgs 23:10), and the place came to be used for dumping and burning garbage. In the intertestamental period the name began to be used symbolically of the place of divine punishment — the fires of hell.[25] According to Matt 25:41, such hellfire was prepared for the devil and his angels (cf. Rev 20:10).

The three body parts may be metonymy, with the hand signifying what is done, the foot where one goes, and the eyes what one sees with. Another possibility is that they allude to sexual sins. Will Deming, noting parallels to Matt 5:27 – 32 and rabbinic literature, sees sexual euphemisms throughout this section: causing a little child to "stumble" in v. 42 refers to sexual molestation; a hand causing

---

23. These sayings appear twice in Matthew, in this context (Matt 18:9) and in the Sermon on the Mount (5:29 – 30).

24. These are third class conditions. Though in Classical Greek, this usage generally indicated a "future more probable" condition, by the time of the Koine it functioned in a variety of ways, including "what is likely to occur in the future, what could possibly occur, or even what is only hypothetical and will not occur" (Wallace, *Greek Grammar*, 469 – 71).

25. In *1 En.* 26 – 27, Enoch is given a vision of Jerusalem by the angel Uriel, and the valley that runs beside it: "This accursed valley is for those accursed forever; here will gather together all those accursed ones, those who speak with their mouth unbecoming words against the Lord and utter hard words concerning his glory. Here they shall be gathered together, and here shall be their judgment, in the last days" (27:2; cf. 90:26; 2 Esd 7:36; *2 Bar.* 59:5 – 11; Str-B 4/2.1,016 – 165; J. Jeremias, *TDNT*, 1:657 – 58).

to stumble (v. 43) refers to masturbation;[26] and a "foot" (a common euphemism for the male sexual organ[27]) that causes stumbling (v. 45) refers to adultery.[28] It is doubtful Mark's readers would have recognized such subtle euphemisms from late rabbinic literature.[29] More often in Scripture, the hand stands for "the basic corporeal instrument for accomplishing one's purposes" (cf. Exod 19:13; Deut 28:12; Eccl 2:11; 9:10; Pss 28:4; 90:17, etc.) and "the feet are the means of transport to the place where sins are committed" (cf. Job 31:1 – 12; 1QS 1:6).[30]

In any case, Jesus' statements are clearly hyperbolic and are not meant to encourage self-mutilation. This is obvious from the fact, first, that self-mutilation was forbidden in Judaism,[31] and second, that even such mutilation would not prevent sin.[32] Jesus' point is to challenge his hearers to take seriously their actions in life, since these actions have eternal consequences.[33] The hyperbole, the threefold repetition, and the graphic description of hellfire all drive home the urgency of Jesus' commands and the reality of divine judgment.

Verses 44 and 46, found in the KJV, are absent from contemporary versions because they do not appear in the earliest and best Greek manuscripts.[34] These sentences repeat verse 48 and were no doubt added by a later scribe attempting to bring greater symmetry to the three sayings (verse numbers, of course, are a later addition).[35]

9:49 For everyone will be salted with fire (Πᾶς γὰρ πυρὶ ἁλισθήσεται). This saying is linked to the previous ones with the catchword "fire" (πῦρ; vv. 43, 48) and then connects to the following two sayings with the common theme of salt (v. 50). Its meaning, however, is elusive, which is perhaps why Matthew and Luke omitted it. Commentators have proposed a range of interpretations. Perhaps the most likely gets its clue from a variant reading, where a scribe introduced the phrase, "Every sacrifice will be salted with salt."[36] This alludes to Lev 2:13, where salt appears as a purifying agent in the OT sacrificial system (cf. Ezek 16:4; 43:24). The combination of salt and fire may indicate the purification that takes place through the fires of persecution and trials, as believers offer themselves as living sacrifices before God (Rom 12:1 – 2). Fire can symbolize both persecution and purification (1 Cor 3:13 – 15; 1 Pet 1:7; 4:12; Rev 3:18). This would connect well to the theme of self-sacrificial discipleship throughout this section.

9:50 "Salt is good. But if salt becomes unsalty, with what will you make it salty? Have salt among yourselves and live in peace with one another." (καλὸν τὸ ἅλας· ἐὰν δὲ τὸ ἅλας ἄναλον γένηται, ἐν τίνι αὐτὸ ἀρτύσετε; ἔχετε ἐν ἑαυτοῖς ἅλα καὶ εἰρηνεύετε ἐν ἀλλήλοις). Salt in these two sayings has a different connotation from the previous

26. Cf. *m. Nid.* 2:1 and its interpretation in *b. Nid.* 13a, which prescribes cutting off the hand of a masturbater.

27. Cf. Exod 4:25; Judg 3:24; Ruth 3:7; Isa 7:20.

28. Will Deming, "Mark 9:42 – 10:12; Matthew 5:27 – 32 and B. Nid. 13b: A First-Century Discussion of Male Sexuality," *NTS* 36 (1990): 130 – 41; cf. Gundry, *Mark*, 524; Collins, *Mark*, 450 – 53.

29. Stein, *Mark*, 448.

30. Marcus, *Mark 9 – 16*, 689, 691. As Marcus muses, "to paraphrase Freud, sometimes a hand is just a hand, and in the Bible the term is usually taken literally."

31. Garland, *Mark*, 369, citing Deut 14:1; 1 Kgs 18:28; Zech 13:6.

32. Stein, *Mark*, 449.

33. Cutting off a hand or foot was sometimes seen as more merciful than execution, and so one way to save a life. Josephus describes how he cut off the hand of a young man named Clitus, who was guilty of sedition, because Josephus did not want to execute one of his own people (Josephus, *Life* 34 §§169 – 173; *J.W.* 2.21.10 §§642 – 646).

34. These verses appear in A D Θ *f*[13] 𝔐 lat syr[p.h]. They are absent from ℵ B C L W Ä Ψ 0274 *f*[1] 28 565 892 2427 syr[s] cop.

35. See Metzger, *Textual Commentary*, 86 – 87.

36. Some manuscripts substitute this reading for the present text (πασα γαρ θυσια αλι αλισθησεται; D it); others combine the two readings (πᾶς γὰρ πυρὶ ἁλισθήσεται και πασα θυσια αλι αλισθησεται; A C Θ Ψ 𝔐 lat syr[p.h] boh[pt]).

verse. Here it likely carries a more common domestic sense. Salt was used for many purposes in the ancient world, for flavoring, preservation, fertilizer, and cleansing. The saying about salt losing its saltiness appears in different contexts in Matthew (Matt 5:13) and Luke (Luke 14:34 – 35).

This is a surprising statement, since sodium chloride is a stable compound and cannot lose it saltiness. Two interpretations have been proposed. One is that Jesus is speaking hypothetically: "If salt were to lose its saltiness, what good would it be?" Another is that Jesus is referring to the kind of salt found near the Dead Sea, which includes various compounds. When water evaporates, the sodium chloride crystallizes first and can be removed, leaving gypsum and other impurities. What remains is "salt" that has lost its saltiness.[37] Jesus is encouraging his followers not to lose the characteristics that bring preservation and life to the world.

The second saying, like v. 49, begins with an enigmatic statement, "Have salt among yourselves." In this case, however, it is explained by its second part, which stands in synonymous parallelism: "and live in peace with one another."[38] Sharing salt probably refers to having meals together, a symbol of fellowship and peace between friends and family.[39] This kind of harmony is antithetical to the self-serving approach seen in the disciples' argument about who was greatest (v. 34), in their jealous protection of their own authority (v. 38), and in the actions of those who cause "one of these little ones" to stumble (v. 42). It is in line, however, with being the servant of all (v. 35), welcoming the insignificant and humble (v. 37), and offering a cup of water to those in need (v. 41). These things characterize a true servant leader and produce peace and authentic fellowship among believers.

Theology in Application

This passage continues the key themes of the second part of Mark's gospel: the suffering role of the Messiah and the call for his disciples to follow him in self-sacrificial service. After the second passion prediction, Jesus' disciples argue about who is the greatest, and Jesus responds with a collection of loosely related teachings around the theme of discipleship and service. This is a crucial theme throughout the NT. Believers are called to live lives of giving instead of taking and to think first about the needs of others. In Phil 2:1 – 11, Paul points to the incarnation of Jesus Christ as the ultimate example of the servant leader.

The Danger of Pride

The disciples' argument about who was the greatest must be understood in the context of the honor/shame culture of the Greco-Roman world and the ancient Near East, where status within the community was among the highest of values and where servants and slaves had low status and few personal rights. In this context the disciples arrogantly argue over which of them deserves the greatest honor in Jesus'

---

37. France, *Mark*, 385.
38. Gundry, *Mark*, 528.

39. Garland, *Mark*, 370. Cf. Acts 1:4, where the verb translated "gather together" (συναλίζω) is a compound whose root indicates "[sharing] salt with" (σύν + ἁλίζω).

coming kingdom (cf. 10:37). While Christian leaders today may not normally seek praise so openly or publicly, we all have subtle ways of asserting ourselves and seeking to increase our status in the eyes of others. Whether it is the athlete or actor who is given celebrity status or Christian leaders who are treated with deference everywhere they go, we as humans love the praise of others.

Jesus responds by defining the true nature of Christian leadership. It is not about being first, but about being last and the servant of all. The essence of leadership is servanthood. While this has become something of a cliché in Christian circles, what is the essence of servant leadership? The role of the slave or servant in the first century was to meet the needs of the master, to do whatever was necessary to help that person succeed. It is the same in the church. Christian leadership is not about personal accolades or accomplishments, but about equipping God's people to do the work of the ministry (Eph 4:12). It is about enabling others to be all that God has called them to be. Every pastor, teacher, ministry leader, and Christian parent is first and foremost a discipler, training others to live as servants and givers in a world of takers (2 Tim 2:2).

Welcoming the Smallest and Least Significant

Jesus illustrates what it means to be a servant leader with a child, telling his disciples that to "welcome" a child is the same as welcoming him, and welcoming him is the same as welcoming God the Father. As noted in the commentary, children were not viewed as sweet or innocent or gentle in the ancient world, but as irrelevant and without social status. To welcome a child, then, is to show love and concern for even the least significant, refusing to show favoritism or prejudice toward others. This applies especially to "these little ones who believe in me" (v. 42), that is, the most vulnerable of Jesus' followers.

There is a natural human tendency to give deference to those of position, power, and influence because they, in turn, can advance our social status and position. I remember attending an academic conference where all participants wear name tags. It was interesting to watch as people walked by one another and glanced at people's name tags. If the person was a "nobody," the eyes quickly averted and moved on to the next person. But if the person was a "celebrity," a well-known academic, they would establish eye contact, smile, and greet that person. The response depended on the status.

The apostle James had harsh words for those who show such partiality in the context of the Christian community. He illustrates this with the example of a rich and powerful visitor who enters your congregation and you give him a position of great honor, while a poor man is relegated to a position on the fringe: "You stand there" or "Sit on the floor by my feet" (Jas 2:2–3). Such discrimination, James says, is evil, since "God [has] chosen those who are poor in the eyes of the world to be rich in faith and to inherit the kingdom he promised those who love him" (2:5).

Years ago my wife, Roxanne, was involved in a ministry at our church of signing for the deaf during services. The signers had a music stand where they would place their notes while signing. Often after the service the ushers would take the stand and put it into storage, making it difficult for the signers to find it the next time. So they began putting a note on the stand, saying, "Please leave this stand here for the deaf ministry." The note was repeatedly ignored and the stand was put away again and again. Evidently the deaf ministry did not have sufficient clout or influence. One Sunday, however, she signed the note "R. Strauss." The stand never moved an inch after that. The reason, we realized, was the senior pastor of the church was named Richard Strauss (my father), and the ushers must have assumed the note was from him! While the person doing the deaf ministry could be ignored, this was now someone with position and respect. Such partiality, James says, is wrong and contrary to the gospel of Jesus Christ.

Those Who Are Not against Us Are for Us

Competition for power and attention can be as much a part of the Christian world as it is of the secular world. John and the other disciples are jealous of their own position and power and so try to silence an unknown exorcist. But Jesus rebukes them because ministry is not about *their* authority and power; it is about the influence and advance of the kingdom of God. The proverb Jesus states that "whoever is not against us is for us" (v. 40) illustrates that God's purpose in the world is larger than our individual church, community, or denomination. (The inverse of the parable, "Whoever is not with me is against me" [Matt 12:30; Luke 11:23], is equally true for other contexts, since those who seek to remain neutral are ultimately opponents of the kingdom of God.) Jesus here addresses the kind of partisanship and competition that is so often part of the Christian community. People rally around human leaders instead of the higher values of the kingdom of God.

It is easy in the Christian world to be jealous of the success of others. One pastor has a stagnant church experiencing little growth while another's church is thriving because of the pastor's dynamic speaking or charismatic personality. It is a common human tendency to be jealous of the gifts and accolades given to others. Yet Jesus reminds us that our ministries are not about us; they are about the business of the kingdom of God. Paul again illustrates this well in his letters. In Phil 1:15 – 18, he is languishing under house arrest in Rome, and some of his ministry rivals are taking the opportunity to cause trouble for him; yet he rejoices even in their success. Paul was less concerned about his own influence or success than about the progress of the gospel.

Causing Others to Stumble

Jesus warns about the severe judgment that will come on those who cause others — Jesus' "little ones" — to fall spiritually. His use of hyperbole is characteristic of the historical Jesus (e.g., a camel passing through the eye of a needle [10:25]; a plank protruding from one's eye [Matt 7:3 – 5], etc.). Here the hyperbole relates to the preference of cutting off one's own body parts to prevent spiritual stumbling, since it is better to enter eternal life maimed than to end up "whole" in Gehenna. The statements are obviously hyperbole: no one will enter eternal life maimed, and self-mutilation is never condoned in Scripture (though some church leaders took these commands literally; e.g., Origen castrated himself). The point, rather, is to warn of the severe consequences of practices that could cause spiritual catastrophe for oneself or for others and that drastic measures are in order to avoid this.

The apostle Paul also has much to say in this regard. Both in 1 Cor 9 and in Rom 14, he speaks of his willingness to sacrifice anything in his life for the spiritual benefit of others. He will gladly give up his rights to hospitality, to remuneration, even to marriage in order to win others to Christ. To the Jews Paul would become a Jew, to win the Jews. To the Gentiles he became a Gentile in order to win them. "I have become all things to all people so that by all possible means I might save some" (1 Cor 9:22).

Enduring Persecution and the Need for Christian Unity

Such warnings against spiritual catastrophe are necessary, Jesus says, since "everyone will be salted with fire" (v. 49). This likely means that all believers will face trials and persecution (2 Tim 3:12). It is in such contexts that there is a tendency to give in to trials, to compromise our spiritual values. Yet trials, when seen as opportunities for growth, can produce endurance in our lives, and endurance can produce spiritual maturity (Rom 5:3 – 4; Jas 1:2 – 4).

One of the best ways to stay strong in the face of persecution is through the support and fellowship of other believers, and Jesus' last saying in this collection points to this. "Share salt" likely means to experience true Christian fellowship and unity. The unity of the body of Christ is a major theme throughout the NT. Paul repeatedly calls his churches to unity around the things they share in Christ (1 Cor 1:19; Eph 4:3; Phil 2:1 – 4), and in the Upper Room Discourse in John, Jesus prays that his disciples "may be one ... just as you are in me and I am in you" (John 17:21). When racked by division and dissension, the church turns inward upon itself and loses its effectiveness in the world. Yet when believers strive together for a common purpose, by the power of the Spirit they can be the potent force in the world.

Mark 10:1 – 12

Literary Context

This passage may at first sight seem out of place in the narrative, since it returns to the earlier theme of conflict with the religious leaders. Jesus' primary focus since 8:31 has been preparing the disciples for his passion in Jerusalem and for their role as servant leaders in his church.

In fact, however, the passage fits well this narrative theme since it contains additional private instruction for the disciples (vv. 10 – 12) and carries forward the theme of the challenge of discipleship.[1] Most of Mark 10 can be read as Jesus' teaching about the radical demands of the kingdom with reference to marriage (10:1 – 12), children (10:13 – 16), and finances (10:17 – 31). With regard to marriage, Jesus' followers must not abandon difficult marriage relationships simply because they are not meeting their personal needs. Authentic discipleship is not about self-gratification, but about giving oneself in sacrificial service for the kingdom of God. The powerful message of reconciliation between God and human beings is exemplified in believers through their commitment to the marriage relationship.

The passage also connects to the passages before and after with the theme of God's love and concern for the lowest members of society, since in the ancient world women (10:5 – 9) and children (9:36 – 37, 42; 10:14 – 16) were among the most vulnerable to exploitation and abuse.

III. The Suffering Way of the Messiah (8:22 – 15:47)

    A. Revelation of the Messiah's Suffering (8:22 – 10:52)

        5. Healing a Boy with an Evil Spirit (9:14 – 29)

        6. Second Passion Prediction and Teaching on Discipleship (9:30 – 50)

        ➡ **7. Teaching on Divorce (10:1 – 12)**

        8. Blessing the Children (10:13 – 16)

---

1. Hooker, *Mark*, 234.

Main Idea

Jesus answers a question about divorce by returning to first principles. Marriage is a sacred institution established by God at creation and entails a lifelong commitment between a man and a woman. Breaking this sacred covenant and marrying another is tantamount to adultery.

Translation

Mark 10:1 – 12

1a	character departure	Leaving there,
b	Setting (spatial)	**he went into the region of Judea and across the Jordan.**
c	Setting (social)	**Crowds again gathered to him,**
d	Action/Instruction	and **again as usual he began teaching them.**
2a	character entrance	Coming to him,
b	Question/Challenge	**some Pharisees were asking him,**
c		*"Is it lawful for a man to divorce his wife?"*
d	narrative aside	**— they were testing him.**
3a	Response to 2/Question	Answering, **he said to them,**
b		*"What did Moses command you?"*
4a	Response to 3	**They said**,
b		*"Moses permitted a man to write a certificate of divorce and send her away."*
		[Deut 24:1 – 4]
5a	Response to 4	**Jesus said to them,**
b	explanation	*"It was because of your hard-heartedness that he wrote this command to you."*
6	assertion/Scripture quotation	*But from the beginning of creation he*
		'made them male and female.' [Gen 1:27]
7a	Scripture quotation	*'For this reason a man will leave his father and mother*
b		*and be united to his wife.*
8a		*And the two will become one flesh.'* [Gen 2:24]
b	conclusion	*So they are no longer two but one flesh.*
9a	command	*Therefore,* *what God has joined together,*
b		*let no person separate."*
10a	setting	When they were in the house again,
b	Question	**the disciples were asking him about this.**
11a	Response to 10/Instruction	**He said to them,**
b	condition	*"Whoever divorces his wife and*
		marries another
c	result	*commits adultery against her.*
12a	condition	*And if after divorcing her husband she marries another,*
b	result	*she commits adultery."*

Structure

The passage begins as a controversy story (vv. 2 – 4), followed by public teaching (vv. 5 – 9), and then private teaching for the disciples (vv. 10 – 12). The question from the Pharisees reflects a typical rabbinic debate over halakhah (= legal issues), similar to the question of hand washing in 7:1 – 15.[2] As in that case, Jesus here emphasizes the spirit of the law over its letter and the goal of pursuing God's character and purpose instead of legalistic minutia.

Jesus' teaching on divorce in v. 11 has particularly strong claims to historicity since it appears independently in multiple early sources: Mark (par. Matt 19:9), Q (Matt 5:32; Luke 16:18), and Paul (1 Cor 7:10).

Exegetical Outline

➡ **1. Departure for Judea (10:1)**

2. Discussion about Divorce (10:2 – 9)

   a. The Pharisees' first question (10:2)

   b. Jesus' first response (10:3)

   c. The Pharisees' response (10:4)

   d. Jesus' teaching on divorce (10:5 – 9)

      i. The hardness of human hearts (10:5)

      ii. God's will from the beginning: Gen 1:27; 2:24 (10:6 – 8)

      iii. The conclusion: What God has joined, let no one separate (10:9)

3. Private Instruction for the Disciples (10:10 – 12)

   a. The disciples' question (10:10)

   b. Jesus' response: Divorce and remarriage is tantamount to adultery (10:11 – 12)

---

2. France, *Mark*, 387.

Explanation of the Text

10:1 Leaving there, he went into the region of Judea and across the Jordan. Crowds again gathered to him, and again as usual he began teaching them (Καὶ ἐκεῖθεν ἀναστὰς ἔρχεται εἰς τὰ ὅρια τῆς Ἰουδαίας καὶ πέραν τοῦ Ἰορδάνου, καὶ συμπορεύονται πάλιν ὄχλοι πρὸς αὐτόν, καὶ ὡς εἰώθει πάλιν ἐδίδασκεν αὐτούς). "From there" (ἐκεῖθεν) probably means from Capernaum (9:33). Mark's description of the journey is puzzling since one might expect the reverse order, crossing the Jordan into Perea first (in order to avoid Samaria), and then crossing back into Judea. Early copyists saw this as problematic and attempted to correct it.[3] While some commentators have accused the author of "an inexact knowledge of geography,"[4] Mark's geography is only strange if one assumes that Jesus is trying to avoid Samaria. There is nothing unusual about first moving south through Samaria into Judea and then crossing the Jordan into Perea.[5] If this is the case, the Pharisees may have chosen Perea for this encounter to try to provoke political opposition to Jesus from Herod Antipas (see comments on v. 2).

Jesus encounters "crowds" (ὄχλοι; plural only here in Mark) and resumes his teaching ministry (cf. 1:21–22, 27; 2:13; 4:1–2; 6:2, 6, 34; 11:18). The presence of the crowds, even far from Jesus' Galilean homeland, is Mark's way of showing that his popularity has not diminished, despite his attempts for more private instruction time with his disciples. "Began teaching" (ἐδίδασκεν) is an ingressive imperfect. Though Mark records less of Jesus' actual teaching than the other Synoptics, he often refers to Jesus as a teacher or as teaching.[6] This is one more sign of his messianic authority (cf. 1:27).

10:2 Coming to him, some Pharisees were asking him, "Is it lawful for a man to divorce his wife?" — they were testing him (Καὶ προσελθόντες Φαρισαῖοι ἐπηρώτων αὐτὸν εἰ ἔξεστιν ἀνδρὶ γυναῖκα ἀπολῦσαι, πειράζοντες αὐτόν). The Pharisees last appeared in the narrative in 8:11 (cf. 8:15), where they similarly tested Jesus by asking for a sign from heaven (cf. 12:15). Their question about whether divorce is lawful is unusual, since the right to divorce was generally assumed within Judaism (based on Deut 24:1–4).[7] What was debated by the rabbis was the legitimate grounds for divorce.[8]

---

3. There are three main readings. (1) The majority of later Byzantine manuscripts (A 𝔐 syr^h) have Jesus going "through" (διά) the far side of the Jordan, that is, the traditional route of bypassing Samaria by traveling down the eastern side of the Jordan. (2) Early Alexandrian texts (ℵ B C* L Ψ 0274 892 2427) have Jesus journeying into Judea "and" (καί) across the Jordan. (3) A third reading, appearing in some Western and Caesarean manuscripts (D W Δ Θ f^1.13 28 565 579 1241 1424 2542), omits the "and" (καί) before "across" (πέραν), so that the verse reads "into the region of Judea across the Jordan." This is the hardest reading since it seems to assume Perea is part of Judea. It may, however, merely use "Judea" in a general sense of the southern part of the country, including Perea. It seems best to go with the second reading in light of its superior external evidence and the likelihood that the third reading was an assimilation to the parallel in Matt 19:1. See Metzger, *Textual Commentary*, 87–88.

4. Boring, *Mark*, 286.

5. Another possibility is that Mark names Judea first because it is Jesus' ultimate goal, but he means that Jesus went to Judea via the eastern side of the Jordan. In this case, the copyist who added "through" (διά) correctly discerned Mark's intent (Gundry, *Mark*, 529).

6. See 1:21–22, 27; 2:13; 4:1–2, 38; 5:35; 6:2, 6, 34; 8:31; 9:17, 31, 38; 10:1, 17, 35; 11:17–18; 12:14, 19, 32, 35, 38; 13:1; 14:14, 49; Robbins, *Jesus the Teacher*, passim.

7. See David Instone-Brewer, *Divorce and Remarriage in the Bible: The Social and Literary Context* (Grand Rapids: Eerdmans, 2002), ch. 5.

8. For OT and Jewish background on divorce and remarriage see ibid.; also esp. Craig S. Keener, ... *And Marries Another: Divorce and Remarriage in the Teaching of the New Testament* (Peabody, MA: Hendrickson, 1991); W. A. Heth and G. J. Wenham, *Jesus and Divorce: Towards an Evangelical Understanding of New Testament Teaching* (3rd ed.; Carlisle: Paternoster, 2002).

The stricter school of Shammai allowed divorce only in the case of adultery, while the more liberal school of Hillel allowed it for almost any reason (even burning a meal!). Rabbi Akiba went so far as to say divorce was allowed even if a man "found another fairer than she" (*m. Giṭ* 9:10).[9] In Judaism only the man could initiate divorce, though powerful upper-class women sometimes did (Josephus, *Ant.* 15.7.10 §259). The right to remarry was assumed and was an integral part of the divorce formula: "You are free to marry whomever you wish" (*m. Giṭ* 9:3).

Matthew's parallel seems to reflect this rabbinic debate over legitimate grounds, since the question there is whether divorce is allowed "for any and every reason" (Matt 19:3). The question here in Mark may simply be shorthand for the same thing, "Under what circumstances is it lawful...?" Or it may reflect a more rigid position among some Jews, who ruled out divorce for any reason.[10] Such a perspective may perhaps be found in Mal 2:13 – 16 ("'For I hate divorce!' says the LORD"; NLT) and at Qumran, where marrying more than one wife is condemned (CD 4:21; 11QTemple [=11Q19] 57:17 – 19).

Yet the Malachi reference is obscure in the Hebrew, and many scholars claim that it should be translated, "The man who hates and divorces his wife..." (NIV; cf. ESV), and the Qumran references probably condemn polygamy rather than divorce.[11] It is not clear, therefore, whether any rabbi in Jesus' day would have condemned divorce outright. A casual attitude towards divorce seems to have been the order of the day. Sirach counsels a man that if his wife does not follow his direction, "separate her from yourself" (Sir 25:26), and Josephus describes how he divorced his first wife because he "was not pleased with her behavior" (*Life* 76 §426). Summarizing the OT law on divorce (Deut 24:1 – 4), Josephus writes:

> He that desires to be divorced from his wife for any cause whatsoever (and many such causes happen among men), let him in writing give assurance that he will never use her as his wife any more; for by this means she may be at liberty to marry another husband, although before this bill of divorce be given, she is not to be permitted so to do. (Josephus, *Ant.* 4.8.23 §253)

It is possible that the Pharisees are aware of Jesus' strong stand against divorce and raise the question here to entrap him. John the Baptist had been arrested and eventually executed by Herod Antipas for criticizing his divorce and remarriage to Herodias (see 6:17 – 18). If Jesus is in Herod's territory, across the Jordan in Perea, he would be vulnerable to a similar fate.[12]

10:3 Answering, he said to them, "What did Moses command you?" (ὁ δὲ ἀποκριθεὶς εἶπεν αὐτοῖς· τί ὑμῖν ἐνετείλατο Μωϋσῆς;).

In Deut 24:1 – 4 Moses did not command divorce; rather, he assumed its reality and provided stipulations to protect both parties. Why, then, did Jesus say "command"?[13] (1) He may be intentionally drawing a contrast between the ultimate will of God and what he permits. By referring to what "Moses permitted" (v. 4) the Pharisees are looking for loopholes, what they can do and still stay within the legal limits of

---

9. All three based their interpretation on Deut 24:1, but read it differently. Shammai interpreted "something indecent" (*'erwat dābār*) as marital unfaithfulness, while Hillel interpreted it as anything that displeased the husband. Akiba picked up on the previous clause of Deut 24:1, "if she finds no favor in his eyes" (*'im-lō' timṣā'-ḥēn bĕ'ênāyw*), to justify remarriage to a more beautiful woman (*m. Giṭ* 9:10; cf. *b. Giṭ* 90a-b).

10. Hooker, *Mark*, 235; Evans, *Mark 8:27 – 16:20*, 81.

11. Instone-Brewer, *Divorce and Remarriage*, 61 – 72. Contra Evans, *Mark 8:27 – 16:20*, 81; J. A. Fitzmyer, "The Matthean Divorce Texts and Some New Palestinian Evidence," *TS* 37 (1976): 197 – 226.

12. Evans, *Mark 8:27 – 16:20*, 81.

13. In Matt 19:7 it is the Pharisees who call it a "command."

the law. Jesus redirects them from what God permits to what he commands — his ultimate will for human relationships. What God "commanded" was lifelong commitment to the marriage covenant (v. 6). What he "permitted" was divorce because of the hardness of human hearts.

(2) Or Jesus' statement may be an invitation to the Pharisees to "correct" him by acknowledging what Scripture actually said. By asking, "What did Moses *command*?" he invites the Pharisees to acknowledge that Moses never commanded divorce but only permitted it for less than ideal conditions. They were treating Moses' teaching on divorce as a command; in fact, it was a concession by God in light of human depravity.

10:4 They said, "Moses permitted a man to write a certificate of divorce and send her away." (οἱ δὲ εἶπαν· ἐπέτρεψεν Μωϋσῆς βιβλίον ἀποστασίου γράψαι καὶ ἀπολῦσαι). The Pharisees quote from Deut 24:1–4, a text that neither mandates divorce nor sets out legitimate grounds for divorce. Its purpose, rather, is to forbid a husband from remarrying his wife after he has divorced her and she remarries. If her second husband divorces her or dies, the first husband may not remarry her. The reason for this is unclear, but may have been to emphasize the finality of the divorce and so protect the woman from accusations of adultery or from the first husband's attempts to ruin her second marriage. Or it may have prevented the first husband from exploiting her for financial gain by remarrying her to reclaim the dowry or to get the inheritance from her second husband. In any case, the rabbis found in this text the justification and legitimation for divorce. A whole tractate in the Mishnah discusses rules related to divorce (*m. Giṭṭin*).

10:5 Jesus said to them, "It was because of your hard-heartedness that he wrote this command to you." (ὁ δὲ Ἰησοῦς εἶπεν αὐτοῖς· πρὸς τὴν σκληροκαρδίαν ὑμῶν ἔγραψεν ὑμῖν τὴν ἐντολὴν ταύτην). While the Pharisees saw in Deut 24:1–4 law, Jesus saw it as concession because of the hardness of human hearts. Although the term "hardheartedness" (σκληροκαρδία) appears only here in Mark's gospel (but cf. 16:14), similar expressions are used with regard to the disciples (6:52; 8:17) and the religious leaders (3:5; 4:12; 7:6).

This term appears five times in the LXX (Deut 10:16; Prov 17:20; Jer 4:4; Ezek 3:7; Sir 16:10), always in the context of stubborn resistance to God. Here the term indicates insensitivity to God's kingdom purposes, resulting in disobedience or even outright rejection. God did not sanction divorce; it is never good or right. But it is sometimes necessary because of the human fallenness and for preventing even greater harm. Yet it was never God's intention for marriage. To demonstrate this, Jesus goes back to the nature and purpose of marriage in God's created order.

10:6–8 But from the beginning of creation he "made them male and female." "For this reason a man will leave his father and mother and be united to his wife. And the two will become one flesh." So they are no longer two but one flesh (ἀπὸ δὲ ἀρχῆς κτίσεως ἄρσεν καὶ θῆλυ ἐποίησεν αὐτούς· ἕνεκεν τούτου καταλείψει ἄνθρωπος τὸν πατέρα αὐτοῦ καὶ τὴν μητέρα καὶ προσκολληθήσεται πρὸς τὴν γυναῖκα αὐτοῦ, καὶ ἔσονται οἱ δύο εἰς σάρκα μίαν· ὥστε οὐκέτι εἰσὶν δύο ἀλλὰ μία σάρξ). To prove his point, Jesus quotes from two texts, Gen 1:27 and 2:24.

"From the beginning of creation" (ἀπὸ δὲ ἀρχῆς κτίσεως) means in mankind's prefallen state. According to Jesus, the creation account establishes heterosexual ("male and female"; ἄρσεν καὶ θῆλυ) lifelong monogamy as God's created order for marital relationships. Any other sexual union is outside God's purpose and will for human sexuality. Genesis 1:27 is similarly quoted at Qumran (CD

4:21) in defense of monogamy over polygamy (and possibly divorce). Becoming "one flesh" (μία σάρξ) is a powerful and evocative image. In a mysterious way, two distinct individuals now become united as a single entity — a couple. This new entity takes priority over previous allegiance both to parents ("leave his father and mother") and to individual rights.[14] The two are now responsible for the needs of the other (cf. 1 Cor 7:3 – 4). The one-flesh union probably refers both to the sacred covenant established by God and the consummation of that covenant through the sexual union of a husband and wife (cf. 6:16).

10:9 "Therefore, what God has joined together, let no person separate." (ὃ οὖν ὁ θεὸς συνέζευξεν ἄνθρωπος μὴ χωριζέτω). Jesus concludes with an imperative. Since marriage is a sacred union accomplished by God himself, no human being has the right to rip that union apart. "Separate" (χωρίζω) is a word commonly used of divorce. The "one" (ἄνθρωπος) in this case likely refers to the husband, since in Judaism it was only the husband who could initiate divorce. According to rabbinic tradition, a divorce could be accomplished by the husband simply sending his wife away with a statement of her right to remarry (see comments on v. 4). Jesus attacks this casual attitude toward divorce and calls his hearers to honor the sacred marriage covenant.

10:10 When they were in the house again, the disciples were asking him about this (Καὶ εἰς τὴν οἰκίαν πάλιν οἱ μαθηταὶ περὶ τούτου ἐπηρώτων αὐτόν). As is common in Mark, Jesus provides further instruction for the disciples in private.[15] For a "house" (οἶκος/οἰκία) as the place of this instruction, see 7:17; 9:28, 33. In light of the generally casual attitude toward divorce in Judaism, Jesus' strong statement surprises the disciples and provokes further questions.

Some have seen behind Jesus' "private" teaching evidence of controversy within the Markan community. Hooker suggests that "the picture of private coaching is perhaps Mark's way of spelling out what he believes to be the implications of Jesus' words for the Christian community. The saying takes the form of a 'community rule' and may represent a maxim familiar to the Church (represented by the disciples)."[16] While this is possible, it seems a stretch to treat all private instruction in Mark as community rules and maxims. Yet it clearly represents for Mark the high standards of Christian discipleship.

10:11 He said to them, "Whoever divorces his wife and marries another commits adultery against her." (καὶ λέγει αὐτοῖς· ὃς ἂν ἀπολύσῃ τὴν γυναῖκα αὐτοῦ καὶ γαμήσῃ ἄλλην μοιχᾶται ἐπ' αὐτήν). If Jesus' words in v. 9 were surprising to the disciples, this additional instruction is even more shocking.[17] Not only is divorce contrary to God's purpose, Jesus says, but it results in adultery when the divorced spouse remarries.[18] The logic here draws from Jesus' teaching in vv. 6 – 9. If the first marriage is permanent in God's eyes, then

---

14. The phrase "and be united to his wife" (καὶ προσκολληθήσεται πρὸς τὴν γυναῖκα αὐτοῦ) is absent from some important early manuscripts (א B Ψ 892* 2427 syrˢ), yet seems necessary for the sense (otherwise "the two" could refer back to the parents!). It was probably accidently omitted when a copyist's eye jumped from one καί to the other. See Metzger, *Textual Commentary*, 88 – 89.

15. See 4:10, 34; 7:17 – 23; 9:28 – 29, 30, 35; 10:10 – 12, 32 – 34; 12:43 – 44; 13:3 – 4.

16. Hooker, *Mark*, 236.

17. This shock is evident in the parallel in Matt 19:10, where the disciples respond that if this is the case, perhaps "it is better not to marry."

18. While Matthew's parallels (Matt 5:32; 19:9) introduce an exception clause, "except for sexual immorality" (μὴ ἐπὶ πορνείᾳ), neither Mark nor Luke (Luke 16:18) includes this phrase. See Theology in Application.

remarriage after divorce is equivalent to adultery against the former wife.

Some commentators have argued that the phrase "against her" (ἐπ᾽ αὐτήν) should be translated "with her," referring to the second wife. This is because in Judaism adultery was always assumed to be against a husband rather than a wife.[19] Yet in light of Jesus' countercultural teaching throughout this passage and his positive stance toward women generally, there seems no reason to reject the more natural reading "against her" (cf. 3:24 – 26; 13:8, 12).[20] Like Paul in 1 Cor 7:4, Jesus assumes that a wife has authority over her husband's sexual behavior just as he has authority over hers. This was radical teaching indeed in the patriarchal context of first-century Judaism.

Some have claimed that Jesus here allows divorce (v. 5) but rules out remarriage (vv. 11 – 12). This, however, misses the point of the passage in two ways. First, divorce without the right to remarriage was inconceivable in first-century Judaism. By its very definition, divorce meant the right to remarriage (see comments on v. 2). Second, while Jesus acknowledges the reality of divorce (v. 5), he

in no way condones it, viewing it as contrary to God's will. Verses 11 – 12 do not therefore introduce teaching different from vv. 5 – 9, but rather explain its implications.[21] Divorce is contrary to God's purpose for marriage, arises from hard human hearts, and produces spiritual adultery. See Theology in Application for further discussion on the question of "grounds" for divorce and remarriage.

10:12 "And if after divorcing her husband she marries another, she commits adultery." (καὶ ἐὰν αὐτὴ ἀπολύσασα τὸν ἄνδρα αὐτῆς γαμήσῃ ἄλλον μοιχᾶται). This last sentence is often considered Mark's own explanation of Jesus' previous saying for his audience. Although Jewish women could not initiate divorce,[22] Roman women could, so Mark may be contextualizing for his own day by pointing out that what applies to the husband also applies to the wife. Nevertheless, it is not unlikely that Jesus said these words, since Jewish women sometimes did initiate divorce.[23] If so, Jesus may be alluding to the divorce and remarriage of Herodias and Herod Antipas (6:17).[24] That he was not averse to commenting on the politics and politicians of his day is evident from Luke 13:21 – 32.

Theology in Application

This passage has great significance for the contemporary church. We start with a general hermeneutical issue and move to more specific questions related to divorce and remarriage.

19. N. Turner, "The Translation of Μοιχαται επ αυτην in Mark 10.11," *BT* 7 (1956): 151 – 52; B. Schaller, " 'Commits Adultery with Her' Not 'against Her,' Mk. 10.11," *ExpTim* 83 (1972): 107 – 8.

20. France, *Mark*, 394; Gundry, *Mark*, 533, 541 – 42; Witherington, *Mark*, 277 – 78; Collins, *Mark*, 469.

21. France, *Mark*, 393; contra Hooker, *Mark*, 256.

22. Josephus states this when describing the case of Salome, who sent a bill of divorce to her husband, "though this was not according to the Jewish laws; for with us it is lawful for a

husband to do so; but a wife, if she departs from her husband, cannot of herself be married to another, unless her former husband put her away" (*Ant.* 15.7.10 §259).

23. As in the high profile cases of Herodias and Salome (Josephus, *Ant.* 15.7.10 §259; 18.5.4 §136). See Edwards, *Markus*, 304, for additional evidence.

24. E. Bammel, "Markus 10.11f. und das judische Eherech," *ZNW* 61 (1970): 95 – 101; F. C. Burkitt, *The Gospel History and Its Transmission* (Edinburgh: T&T Clark, 1906), 99 – 101; Hooker, *Mark*, 237; Witherington, *Mark*, 278.

The Heart of God and the True Significance of the Law

Jesus' teaching here parallels much of his teaching elsewhere in the gospel tradition, where he pushes beyond the external regulations of the law to the nature and purpose of God (cf. Matt 5:21 – 48; 23:1 – 32). The Pharisees want a legal ruling from Jesus on the legitimacy of divorce. Whether this is a test of Jesus' legal knowledge or an attempt to trick him into provoking the ire of Herod Antipas, Jesus refuses to play their game. Instead of ruling on legitimate "grounds" for divorce, he turns them to more fundamental issues: the true nature and purpose of marriage and the hardness of human hearts that leads to divorce.

Marriage is a sacred covenant between God, a husband, and a wife, whereby the man and woman commit themselves to a lifelong, one-flesh union — to love one another, to sacrifice themselves for the good of the other, and to work constantly toward reconciliation. This relationship reflects the nature of God, who is all-loving, all-giving, and working constantly toward reconciliation with his wayward children. Divorce should be inconceivable in a situation where both parties are committed to promoting the best for the other person.

The Pharisees come seeking legitimate grounds, that is, *God's will* regarding divorce. Jesus responds that God's will was clearly set out *for marriage* in Gen 1 – 2 long before regulations for divorce were given. Marriage is a lifelong, one-flesh union between a husband and a wife. Divorce is therefore always outside of God's perfect will. While Jesus acknowledges that divorce happens (and so is regulated in the OT law), it was always a condescension to human fallenness.

It is not surprising, then, that divorce is one of the examples Jesus' uses in the Sermon on the Mount to illustrate the true spirit of the law. While the law expressly condemns murder, its true spirit also condemns anger and hate, since these are the heart attitudes that lead to murder (Matt 5:21 – 22). While the law expressly forbids adultery, lusting after a woman is adultery of the heart (5:27 – 28). In the same way, remarriage after divorce constitutes adultery, since it breaks the one-flesh union established by God (5:31 – 32).

Redefining Marriage and Divorce

While responding to the Pharisees' question about the legitimate grounds for divorce, Jesus implicitly redefines both marriage and divorce. Marriage is not simply a contract between two families that can be dissolved on a whim. It is a sacred *covenant* made before God, which is meant to last a lifetime. Nor is marriage a man taking a wife into his household as his possession. Jesus refers back to the Genesis account and points out that the wife is not property, but a partner. The one-flesh union means that she is "bone of my bones and flesh of my flesh" (Gen 2:23). Together the two make up one new person.

Paul says something similar in 1 Cor 7:2 – 4, where he expresses what would be viewed as a radical sexual ethic for Judaism. While acknowledging that a wife does not have authority over her body but yields it to her husband (something assumed in Judaism and the Greco-Roman world), he then astonishingly says the reverse, that a husband does not have authority over his own body but yields it to his wife (1 Cor 7:4). The purpose of marriage is not just to meet one's own needs, but to meet the needs of the other person (cf. Eph 5:28 – 31).

Jesus also implicitly redefines divorce in this passage. Judaism defined it as a husband's "right," and then debated under what circumstances he could exercise this right. Jesus points out that divorce is neither a right nor a privilege, but rather a condescension to human sinfulness. It is always contrary to God's will, even though it is "permitted" in certain circumstances. These points have important implications for how the church deals with divorce.

The Church's Attitude toward Divorce

There are three main views concerning divorce and remarriage in the church today. (1) Some say divorce is never allowed and that any divorce is viewed as illegitimate in God's eyes. (2) Others say divorce is allowed, but remarriage is not. (3) Still others allow for remarriage, but only if legitimate "grounds" have been established. The most common grounds defended are adultery or desertion. Those defending adultery point to the exception clause in Matthew's two accounts of Jesus' teaching on divorce: "But I tell you that anyone who divorces his wife, *except for sexual immorality* [πορνεία], makes her the victim of adultery" (Matt 5:32, italics added; cf. 19:9). Desertion is defended from Paul's statement in 1 Cor 7:15, where he says that if an unbelieving spouse leaves, the believing spouse is not "bound" to him or her. This "binding" language, it is argued, is Jewish legal terminology for the right to remarry.[25] Those who reject remarriage for any reason counter that Matthew's exception does not legitimate remarriage, but only qualifies the adultery clause: if a wife has already been unfaithful, her husband can hardly be said to have "[made] her the victim of adultery" (Matt 5:32). Nor does Paul's statement in 1 Cor 7:15 legitimate remarriage. It only confirms that a believer cannot make their unbelieving spouse stay.

Dealing in detail with these complex questions is beyond the scope of this commentary.[26] Certain conclusions, however, may be made concerning Jesus' teaching here. First, divorce is always tragic, a failure of a sacred covenant. Jesus responds to the cavalier attitude of his contemporaries with the shocking claim that, in light of the one-flesh union, remarriage after divorce constitutes adultery. While this statement is likely hyperbolic, it points to the true nature of marriage as a one-flesh union and the great tragedy that is divorce.

25. See Instone-Brewer, *Divorce and Remarriage*, chapter 2.

26. For various views on remarriage after divorce, see *Three Views on Remarriage after Divorce* (ed. Mark L. Strauss; Grand Rapids: Zondervan, 2006). See also the works cited above.

Second, though sometimes necessary, divorce is always a result of human sinfulness. Though God allowed divorce, he never sanctioned it. This makes the goal of
seeking "grounds" an inappropriate one. Ironically, we often turn to these passages to
discern the legitimate grounds for divorce; yet Jesus explicitly rejects the Pharisees'
question! Anyone seeking "grounds" is implicitly asking under what conditions they
can dissolve their marriage without sinning. Yet there is no such thing as an innocent
party in any relationship, let alone in a broken marriage.

We come to God every day as sinners in need of his grace. Those contemplating
divorce or considering remarriage must approach this decision with prayer, repentance, humility, caution, and godly counsel from friends and pastors. Even if one
party were primarily responsible for the failure, marriage is always a two-way street.
Refusing to acknowledge and assess one's own role in the decision to marry and the
failure that resulted, and then rushing into a new marriage, can have tragic results.
At the same time, there is no sin that Christ did not pay for on the cross and no
emotional damage that the Spirit of God cannot eventually heal. To say that remarriage after a divorce is never an option (or is an option only if "grounds" have been
established) seems to limit the power of the gospel to bring renewal and restoration
to broken people.

Another problem with seeking grounds for divorce is the fact that none of the
passages about divorce in the Bible was written to identify such grounds. Jesus' teaching was a response to the easy-divorce approach of many rabbis, and Paul is dealing
with the desertion of an unbelieving spouse. What if the question of physical abuse
had arisen in another of Paul's letters? Would he have allowed separation or divorce?
We cannot say for sure, but I suspect he would. A husband who is physically abusing
his wife is clearly violating the command to love his wife as Christ loved the church
(Eph 5:25). Unfortunately, we simply don't know how Paul would respond in such a
case, whether by allowing for separation or divorce, calling for strong church intervention, or in some other way.

All this to say that church leaders must take care before establishing absolute
rules concerning divorce and remarriage, since each situation is unique and the
Bible does not deal comprehensively with this topic. Church leaders need to affirm
strongly the true significance of marriage, the tragedy of divorce, *and* the redemptive
power of the gospel.

With these points in mind, the church needs to take greater steps to ensure the
success of marriages. This means providing premarital counseling and classes, hosting seminars and classes for maintaining healthy marriage relationships, and preaching regularly on how to maintain God-centered and self-sacrificial relationships. It
also means providing divorce recovery groups and classes for those who have experienced the tragedy of divorce. The church needs to be proactive both in preventing
divorce in the first place and in preventing its recurrence.

CHAPTER 39

Mark 10:13 – 16

Literary Context

This short episode continues the theme of the nature and cost of discipleship developed throughout the second part of Mark's gospel (8:31 – 10:52). Following the second passion prediction (9:30 – 32), Jesus taught about the humility and sacrifice necessary for authentic discipleship by using a child as an illustration (9:33 – 37). Here he returns to this theme by pointing to the childlike faith necessary to enter the kingdom of God.

Other connections to the surrounding context are also present. The discussion related to children follows naturally on the discussion of marriage and divorce (10:1 – 12). Women and children were often victims of exploitation and abuse in the ancient world (as today), and Jesus' concern for them in these two passages is in line with his teaching elsewhere about defending the cause of the lowly and outcast. This passage also introduces requirements for entrance into the kingdom of God, a key theme in the episode of the rich man that follows (10:17 – 31). The kingdom belongs to those who come to God empty and with childlike faith (10:14 – 15), but power and riches represent nearly insurmountable obstacles to those wanting to enter it (10:23 – 25).

Main Idea

When the disciples rebuke people for bringing their children to be blessed by Jesus, he responds with indignation and insists that the children be allowed to come.

The kingdom of God is made up of people like this — meaning those who are lowly and dependent on God.

Translation

Mark 10:13 – 16

13a	Setting (social)/Action	**They were bringing children for him to touch them,**
b	Response to 13a	but **the disciples rebuked them.**
14a	Response to 13b	When Jesus saw this,
b		**he was indignant and said to them,**
c	instruction	*"Let the children come to me and do not prevent them.*
15a	reason for 14b	*For the kingdom of God belongs to ones like this.*
b	veracity statement	*Truly I say to you,*
c	condition	*whoever does not receive the kingdom of God like a child*
d	result	*will certainly not enter it."*
16a	action	And taking them in his arms and placing his hands on them,
b	Action/Blessing	**he blessed them.**

Structure

The episode is a conflict and pronouncement story, introduced by the setting of parents bringing their children to Jesus (v. 13a). Jesus responds to the disciples' rebuke with indignation (v. 14b) and two pronouncements. The first (v. 14c – 15a) asserts that children are to be welcomed because the kingdom of God belongs to such as these. The second (v. 15b-d) explains the reason: entering the kingdom demands a childlike response — faith and dependence on God. The episode closes with Jesus illustrating his own injunction by welcoming and blessing the children (v. 16).

Exegetical Outline

➡ 1. **Setting: Bringing Children to Jesus (10:13a)**

   2. **The Disciples' Rebuke (10:13b)**

   3. **Jesus' Indignation and Response (10:14 – 15)**

      a. Jesus' indignation (10:14a-b)

      b. Permission for the children to come (10:14c)

      c. Childlikeness and the kingdom of God (10:15)

   4. **Jesus' Application of His Teaching: Blessing the Children (10:16)**

Explanation of the Text

10:13 They were bringing children for him to touch them, but the disciples rebuked them (Καὶ προσέφερον αὐτῷ παιδία ἵνα αὐτῶν ἅψηται· οἱ δὲ μαθηταὶ ἐπετίμησαν αὐτοῖς). The text does not state who brought the children, but it was presumably their parents. "They were bringing" (προσέφερον) is a conative imperfect (also called voluntative or tendential), which "portrays the action as something that was desired (voluntative), attempted (conative), or at the point of almost happening (tendential)."[1] Jesus often heals with touch in Mark's Gospel (1:31, 41; 5:41; 6:5, 56; 7:33; 8:23 – 25), and people press forward to touch him (3:10; 5:23, 27; 6:56; 7:32). Here, however, the parents are seeking a blessing (v. 16) from this great teacher, a common practice in Judaism.[2]

The age of the "children" (παιδία) is not specified. The term is a general one and was used of Jairus's twelve-year old daughter (5:41 – 42) and an eight-day-old infant (Gen 17:12 LXX). Babies or small children are likely intended since Luke's parallel calls them "babies" (βρέφη; Luke 18:15; cf. *Gos. Thom.* 22) and since Jesus takes them in his arms (v. 16).

Why do the disciples rebuke them? Children were generally viewed as without social status and so the disciples do not consider them worthy of the Master's time.[3] The disciples have also repeatedly demonstrated pride (9:34) and an exclusive right to Jesus' authority (9:38). Their response here should be surprising in light of Jesus' previous teaching about welcoming children (9:36 – 37) and not caus-

ing "one of these little ones" to fall (9:42). But it is not surprising in light of Mark's consistent presentation of the disciples as prideful, spiritually insensitive, and slow to learn.[4]

10:14 – 15a When Jesus saw this, he was indignant and said to them, "Let the children come to me and do not prevent them. For the kingdom of God belongs to ones like this." (ἰδὼν δὲ ὁ Ἰησοῦς ἠγανάκτησεν καὶ εἶπεν αὐτοῖς· ἄφετε τὰ παιδία ἔρχεσθαι πρός με, μὴ κωλύετε αὐτά, τῶν γὰρ τοιούτων ἐστὶν ἡ βασιλεία τοῦ θεοῦ). Jesus responds to the disciples' action with anger or indignation (ἠγανάκτησεν). Mark more than the other Synoptics reveals Jesus' human emotions, including negative ones like anger and frustration (1:41, 43; 3:5; 8:12, 17 – 21; 9:19). A different word for indignation is used in a variant reading in 1:41 (ἐμβριμάομαι).

Some see in the statement "do not prevent them" (μὴ κωλύετε αὐτά) a defense of infant baptism, since "prevent" is used elsewhere in the baptismal contexts.[5] The Ethiopian eunuch asks Philip, "What can stand in the way [κωλύει] of my being baptized?" (Acts 8:36; cf. 10:47; 11:17). Yet Mark gives no hint here that baptism is his concern. It is the disciples' pride, exclusivity, and lack of spiritual discernment that is at issue. The closer parallel is to 9:38 – 39, where the disciples seek to "prevent" an unknown exorcist from casting out demons, "because he was not following us."

The genitive "of such ones" (τῶν τοιούτων) means, as we have translated it, "ones like this."

---

1. Wallace, *Greek Grammar,* 550; cf. 9:38.

2. Cf. Gen 48:14; Str-B 1:807 – 8; Grundmann, *Markus,* 206.

3. On the status of children in the Greco-Roman world, see T. Wiedemann, *Adults and Children in the Roman Empire* (London: Routledge, 1989); B. Rawson, ed., *The Family in Ancient Rome* (Ithaca, NY: Cornell University Press, 1986).

4. See 4:13, 40; 6:52; 7:18; 8:17 – 18, 21, 32; 9:5 – 6, 19, 32; 10:35 – 45.

5. See, e.g., Oscar Cullmann, *Baptism in the New Testament* (SBT 1; trans. J. K. S. Reid; Naperville, IL: Allenson, 1958); J. Jeremias, *Infant Baptism in the First Four Centuries* (trans. David Cairns; Philadelphia: Westminster, 1960), 48 – 55.

The kingdom of God belongs to those who are childlike in their faith. As noted in 9:37 – 38, this almost certainly does not mean innocent, gentle, or pure. Children were not viewed this way in the ancient world. It means small, insignificant, needy, and without social status — those who come in complete dependence on God. The next sentence makes this clear. Jesus' teaching here parallels the Beatitudes in Matt 5:3, 5, where the poor are those to whom the kingdom of heaven belongs — a close parallel to the phrase here — and the meek are those who will inherit the earth.

10:15b-d "Truly I say to you, whoever does not receive the kingdom of God like a child will certainly not enter it." (ἀμὴν λέγω ὑμῖν, ὃς ἂν μὴ δέξηται τὴν βασιλείαν τοῦ θεοῦ ὡς παιδίον, οὐ μὴ εἰσέλθῃ εἰς αὐτήν). Jesus now explains why the kingdom of God belongs to those who are childlike. The statement is doubly emphatic. Jesus begins with his solemn introduction, "Truly I say to you" (ἀμὴν λέγω ὑμῖν; see comments on 3:28 – 30), and ends with an emphatic negation. Whoever does not receive the kingdom like a child will "certainly not" (οὐ μή + subjunctive) enter it. The strength of the assertion may be because the statement is so counterintuitive and shocking in its cultural context.[6] More important, it encapsulates the essence of salvation and of the gospel. To receive the kingdom like a child means by faith and in complete dependence on God.

Some interpreters read the sentence differently, with "child" (παιδίον) functioning as the object instead of the subject of the comparative clause.[7] In-

stead of receiving the kingdom "as a child receives it," this would mean, "as they receive a child."[8] Though grammatically possible and exegetically defensible (Jesus spoke of welcoming a child in 9:37), this interpretation is more awkward and less appropriate to the present context. Jesus has just said that the kingdom of God belongs "to ones like this," i.e., those with childlike faith, not to those who welcome them. Though Jesus will himself welcome children in the next verse, he does so not to illustrate that he himself is worthy of the kingdom, rather, that these children are equal participants in it. The Matthean parallel to 9:36 – 37 makes this interpretation explicit, when Jesus says you must "become like little children" to enter the kingdom of God (Matt 18:3).

Commentators often point to this statement as evidence of both the present and future dimensions of the kingdom of God. Those who "receive" the kingdom in the present will "enter" it in the future. The kingdom of God is both already and not yet, inaugurated in Jesus' proclamation (1:15) but consummated in the future (see Theology in Application).

10:16 And taking them in his arms and placing his hands on them, he blessed them (καὶ ἐναγκαλισάμενος αὐτὰ κατευλόγει τιθεὶς τὰς χεῖρας ἐπ᾽ αὐτά). The reason the parents were bringing their children to Jesus is now made explicit as he "blesses" (κατευλογέω)[9] them. Jesus illustrates his teaching by welcoming those whom the world does not consider worthy of its time and attention. The children are to be welcomed into the kingdom

---

6. Witherington, *Mark*, 280.

7. Since παιδίον is neuter it could be a nominative or an accusative.

8. See F. A. Schilling, "What Means the Saying about Receiving the Kingdom of God as a Little Child (τὴν βασιλείαν τοῦ θεοῦ ὡς παιδίον, Mk. x.15; Lk. xviii.17), *ExpTim* 77 (1965): 56 – 58. Schilling claims that the kingdom of God is here de-

picted as a child, meaning at the beginning of life and in need of affection. People must embrace it as they do a child.

9. The compound verb for blessing (κατά + εὐλογέω) occurs only here in the NT and may have an emphatic force. In strong contrast to the disciples' exclusion, Jesus warmly welcomes the children.

because they epitomize trust and dependence on God. As in 9:36, Jesus' "embracing" or "hugging" (ἐναγκαλίζομαι) the children shows authentic care and affection. "Laying on of hands" (τιθεὶς τὰς χεῖρας) expresses the manner in which he blessed them. This not a formal liturgical ritual, but a symbol of identification[10] and a traditional manner of bestowing a blessing (Gen 48:14 – 18).[11]

Theology in Application

This passage is not about the innocence or purity of children, nor is it a defense of infant baptism (see comments on v. 14). Its primary point is the need to be like a child, that is, fully dependent on God, in order to enter the kingdom of God. The same issue drives the next pericope, where the rich man must give up his love for and dependence on earthly possessions in order to inherit the kingdom of God.

Faith and Dependence Necessary to Enter the Kingdom of God

This theme has appeared earlier in Mark's gospel. Jesus' initial announcement of the kingdom is to "repent and believe in the good news" (1:15). Repentance means recognizing one's unworthiness, acknowledging sin, and turning from it. Believing the good news means trusting in God's provision for salvation, not in our own good works. At the home of Levi, Jesus tells the religious leaders that he has not come to call righteous people but sinners, that is, those ready to acknowledge their sinfulness and express their need of the Great Physician (2:17).

This theme is common throughout Scripture, where it is those who are lowly, broken, and contrite who receive God's grace (Ps 147:6; Prov 3:34; Zeph 2:3; Luke 1:51 – 52; 5:8; 14:11; Phil 2:3; 1 Pet 5:5). I was recently in the downtown district of a major city, and there were street people and beggars on almost every street corner. I found myself pitying them but also looking down on them, thankful I was not like them. Yet this passage reminds us that, in reality, we are like that. We come to God empty and hopeless, having no wealth, power, or position through which to succeed. We are completely in need of God's grace.

The Pride and Failure of the Disciples

This passage continues to develop the theme of discipleship in Mark's gospel, where the disciples demonstrate pride and fail to comprehend Jesus' mission and purpose (6:52; 7:18; 8:17 – 18, 32; 9:5 – 6, 19, 33 – 37; 10:35 – 45). In contrast to the children, who come to Jesus in humble dependence on others, the disciples act with pride and superiority. They have obviously not learned the lesson Jesus taught in

10. See Matt 19:13, 15; Acts 6:6; 8:17, 19; 9:17; 13:3; 19:6; 1 Tim 5:22.

11. France, *Mark*, 398.

9:36 – 37, that to welcome a child means to welcome him, and to welcome him is to welcome God, who sent him. The irony is that they see themselves as protecting Jesus, preventing distracting "nobodies" from monopolizing their time. Yet by rejecting children they are in fact rejecting him and failing to comprehend the nature and power of the gospel. Jesus will continue to instruct them that if they want to be first, they must become last and the servant of all (9:33; cf. 8:34 – 37; 10:43 – 44). Jesus himself is the model, the Son of Man who came not to be served but to serve, and to give himself as a ransom for many (10:45).

The Presence and Future of the Kingdom of God

Though a subordinate point, the passage also provides insight into the nature of the kingdom of God, especially its present and future dimensions. Jesus speaks of those who "receive" the kingdom in the present, yet will "enter" it in the future. This present and future nature of the kingdom is common throughout Mark's gospel and the rest of the NT. In Mark, Jesus speaks of a future time when the disciples will see the kingdom of God come with power (9:1) and longs for the day he will drink again from the fruit of the vine in the (future) kingdom (14:25). Joseph of Arimathea is longing for the kingdom of God (15:43), and Jesus speaks of the coming of the Son of Man "with great power and glory" (13:26; cf. 8:38; 13:33 – 34; 14:62).

Yet in other passages the kingdom is clearly present already. Jesus uses parables to describe the kingdom as the slow growth from seed to plant until the day of harvest (4:26 – 29) and as a tiny mustard seed that is growing into a great plant (4:30 – 32). In both parables, the kingdom is something that begins with Jesus' ministry and is consummated at his return. Salvation for the believer is both a present possession and a future hope (2 Cor 1:22; 5:5; 6:2; Eph 1:14; 1 Pet 1:3 – 8)

40

Mark 10:17 – 31

Literary Context

This episode continues the theme of discipleship that is so prominent in the second part of Mark's gospel (8:22 – 10:53). More specifically, it relates to the second passion prediction and the collection of teaching related to discipleship that followed (9:30 – 50). In its immediate context, the passage picks up the theme of entrance into the kingdom of God, introduced in the previous episode. On the positive side, childlike faith and dependence on God are necessary for entrance into the kingdom (10:13 – 16). On the negative side, love of riches and trust in them represent an insurmountable obstacle to the trust in God necessary to inherit eternal life (vv. 23 – 27).

Main Idea

In one of the most powerful episodes in the gospel of Mark, Jesus tells a rich man that if he wishes to enter the kingdom of God, he must sell all he has, give the proceeds to the poor, and follow Jesus. The point is that no one can enter the kingdom on their own merit; all must enter with childlike faith and in complete dependence on God.

Translation

Mark 10:17 – 31

17a	setting	As he was setting off on his way,
b	Action/Question	**a man** ran up to him, knelt down before him and **asked,**
c		*"Good teacher, what must I do to inherit eternal life?"*
18a	Response to 17	**Jesus said to him,**
b	rhetorical question	*"Why do you call me good?*
c	assertion	*No one is good except God alone.*
19a	answer/list	*You know the commandments:*
b	list item	*'Do not murder;*
c	list item	*do not commit adultery;*
d	list item	*do not steal;*
e	list item	*do not give false testimony;*
f	list item	*do not defraud;*
g	list item	*honor your father and mother.'"*
		[Exod 20:12 – 16; Deut 5:16 – 20]
20a	Response to 18 – 19	**He said to him,**
b	assertion	*"Teacher, all these I have kept since my youth."*
21a	Response to 20	But **Jesus,** looking at him, **loved him, and said to him,**
b	assertion	*"One thing you lack.*
c	command/condition	*Go,*
d	(series/progression)	*sell everything you have*
e		*and give to poor,*
f	result	*and you will have treasure in heaven.*
g	command	*Then come, follow me."*
22a	response	Stunned at this statement,
b	Action/Result	**he went away sad,**
c	reason	for he had many possessions.
23a	Response/Action	Then **Jesus,** looking around, **said to his disciples,**
b	instruction/assertion	*"How difficult it is for those with wealth to enter the kingdom of God."*
24a	Response to 23	**The disciples were amazed at his words.**
b	Response to 24a	**But Jesus again said to them,**
c	assertion	*"Children, how difficult it is to enter the kingdom of God!"*
25a	analogy/assertion	*"It is easier for a camel to pass through the eye of a needle*
b	comparison	*than for a rich person to enter the kingdom of God."*
26a	Response to 24 – 25	**They were even more shocked and said to one another,**
b	question	*"Then who can be saved?"*
27a	Answer to 26	Looking at them, **Jesus said,**
b	assertion	*"For people, it is impossible, but not for God,*
c	reason for 27b	*because all things are possible for God."*
28a	Response to 21	**Peter then spoke to him,**
b	assertion	*"See, we have left everything and followed you."*

Continued on next page.

Continued from previous page.

29a	Response to 28	**Jesus said,**
b	veracity statement	*"Truly I say to you,*
c	condition	*anyone who has left* home or
		brothers or sisters or
		mother or father or
		children or fields
d		for my sake and
		for the sake of the gospel
30a	result	will receive a hundred times as much
		in the present age:
		homes and
b		brothers and sisters and
		mothers and children and
		fields
		— together with persecutions — and
c		in the age to come,
		eternal life.
31a	aphorism	*But many who are first will be last and*
b		the last first."

Structure

The passage is made up of the dialogue with the rich man (vv. 17 – 22), Jesus' teaching about the danger of riches (vv. 23 – 27), Peter's comment (v. 28), and the promised reward for those who give up all for the kingdom (vv. 29 – 31). The same sequence appears in all three Synoptics (Matt 19:16 – 30; Luke 18:18 – 30), except that after Peter's question, Matthew introduces the Q saying about the Son of Man sitting on his throne and the twelve disciples judging the twelve tribes of Israel (19:28; cf. Luke 22:28 – 30).

Exegetical Outline

→ **1. Dialogue with the Rich Man (10:17 – 22)**

    a. The man's question (10:17)

    b. Jesus' initial answer: Keep the commandments (10:18 – 19)

    c. The man's affirmation (10:20)

    d. Jesus' final requirement (10:21)

    e. The man's dejected departure (10:22)

2. Jesus' Teaching on Riches and the Kingdom of God (10:23 – 27)

    a. Jesus' pronouncement: the difficulty of entering the kingdom of God (10:23)

b. The disciples' amazed response (10:24a)

c. Jesus' second pronouncement and "the eye of the needle" saying (10:24b – 25)

d. The disciples' shock and second question (10:26)

e. Jesus' conclusion: all things are possible with God (10:27)

3. Peter's Response and Jesus' Promise of Reward (10:28 – 31)

a. Peter's response: we have left all (10:28)

b. Jesus' promise of reward in this life and the future life (10:29 – 30)

c. Jesus' final proverb: the first will be last (10:31)

Explanation of the Text

10:17 As he was setting off on his way, a man ran up to him, knelt down before him, and asked, "Good teacher, what must I do to inherit eternal life?" (Καὶ ἐκπορευομένου αὐτοῦ εἰς ὁδὸν προσδραμὼν εἷς καὶ γονυπετήσας αὐτὸν ἐπηρώτα αὐτόν· διδάσκαλε ἀγαθέ, τί ποιήσω ἵνα ζωὴν αἰώνιον κληρονομήσω;). The genitive absolute, "as he set off on his way," reminds the reader that Jesus is heading toward Judea (10:1) and Jerusalem (10:32). This is the "way" (ὁδός) of the cross. The man is identified only as "one" or "someone" (εἷς). The fact that he is rich is not mentioned until v. 22. The episode is often called the story of the "rich young ruler," but only Matthew says he was young (Matt 19:20, 22) and Luke refers to him as a "ruler" (ἄρχων; Luke 18:18). Mark focuses only on the man's wealth, and his delay in even mentioning this produces a dramatic climax.

"Running" and "kneeling" are actions typical of a servant or slave, indicating the man's deference for Jesus and perhaps the urgency of his request. There is no suggestion of false motives, as confirmed by Mark's comment in v. 21, where Jesus, "looking at him, loved him."[1] The man's question is a sincere one. The address to Jesus as "good teacher" (διδάσκαλε ἀγαθέ) is unusual, and the

phrase is not attested elsewhere in Judaism.[2] From a narrative perspective, it prepares the reader for Jesus' challenge in v. 18 about the nature of true goodness.

The man's question concerns inheriting "eternal life" (ζωὴν αἰώνιον), which means ultimate salvation in God's presence (Dan 12:2).[3] In context it is synonymous with being "saved" (v. 26) and "entering the kingdom of God" (vv. 23, 25). The idea of eternal life as an "inheritance" fits the OT concept of Israel as God's children (Exod 4:22; Deut 14:1; Isa 43:6; Jer 3:4, 19; 31:9, 20; Hos 11:1), who are heirs of God's blessings. In the LXX "inherit" is commonly used for possessing the Promised Land (Lev 20:24; Num 34:13; Ps 37:9) and came to be used in later Judaism for the reception of eschatological blessings (*Pss. Sol.* 14:10; *1 En.* 40:9).[4]

Yet the man recognizes that such an inheritance is not merely a given, so he asks, "What must I do...?" (τί ποιήσω). The man's question has sometimes been seen as wholly negative, seeking to be saved by "doing," that is, earning or meriting his own salvation through works instead of through faith in God. But Jesus also responds with what the man must do: first, keep the commandments; then, sell all he has and give to the poor. So the

1. Contra Nineham, *Mark*, 270, who says, "The stranger was altogether too obsequious and effusive in his approach."
2. France, *Mark*, 400; Evans, *Mark 8:27 – 16:20*, 95.
3. Though the topic is not developed in detail in the OT

(except in Dan 12:2), Second Temple Judaism illustrates hope for the afterlife in the presence of God (*Pss. Sol.* 9:5; 13:11; 14:4 – 7, 10; *1 En.* 37:4; 40:9; 58:3).
4. Boring, *Mark*, 294.

point is not "faith versus works" in a Pauline sense. It is rather the man's love for riches over his love for God, and his *trust* in those riches instead of his humble dependence on God.

10:18 Jesus said to him, "Why do you call me good? No one is good except God alone." (ὁ δὲ Ἰησοῦς εἶπεν αὐτῷ· τί με λέγεις ἀγαθόν; οὐδεὶς ἀγαθὸς εἰ μὴ εἷς ὁ θεός). Jesus does not at first answer the question, but instead responds to the man's address to him as a "good teacher." Jesus' answer has caused great consternation in the history of the church. Is he claiming that he is not good (and so denying his own sinlessness)? Is he claiming he is not God (and so denying his deity)? Matthew apparently modified the saying because of these concerns, so that Jesus says, "Why do you ask me about what is good?" (Matt 19:17). Yet neither Mark nor Luke saw any reason to change it.

The reason, it would seem, is that it was not intended to be a christological statement, but rather a rhetorical one, setting the stage for Jesus' teaching that follows.[5] The man is about to claim that he has fully kept God's commandments, presumably qualifying him to inherit eternal life (v. 20). Jesus preemptively challenges this notion of goodness. In comparison to God's perfection, no one is good and worthy of eternal life. Jesus is not denying his own deity, but is rather adopting the man's perspective, that Jesus is a good teacher. Jesus responds, "How can you address any human teacher as 'good'? Only God is truly good (= perfect)." Jesus nullifies the man's assertion about his own goodness before he has made it and sets up the conclusion that no one can merit God's salvation (v. 27). As in the case

of the Syrophoenician woman, Jesus' apparently naïve answer (7:27) is intended to provoke deeper thought and response.

The phrase "No one is good except God alone" (οὐδεὶς ἀγαθὸς εἰ μὴ εἷς ὁ θεός) may also be translated, "No one is good except one — God," and may be intended to echo the Shema: "Hear, O Israel: The Lord our God, the Lord is one" (Deut 6:4; cf. Mark 12:29).

10:19 "You know the commandments: 'Do not murder; do not commit adultery; do not steal; do not give false testimony; do not defraud; honor your father and mother.' " (τὰς ἐντολὰς οἶδας· μὴ φονεύσῃς, μὴ μοιχεύσῃς, μὴ κλέψῃς, μὴ ψευδομαρτυρήσῃς, μὴ ἀποστερήσῃς, τίμα τὸν πατέρα σου καὶ τὴν μητέρα). Jesus responds by citing the second table of the Ten Commandments, those associated with a person's relationship with others (Exod 20:12 – 17; Deut 5:16 – 21). They are recited in Hebrew order,[6] except that the fifth (honoring parents) is moved to last, and the tenth, "do not covet" (οὐκ ἐπιθυμήσεις; LXX), is replaced with "do not defraud" (μὴ ἀποστερήσῃς).[7]

This latter substitution may be intended to apply the command more directly to the rich, whose wealth means they are less likely to covet what others have, but more likely to have gained their riches through fraud or corruption.[8] Other interpreters suggest that since the other commands are all concrete actions (murder, adultery, stealing, false testimony), perhaps defrauding is viewed as the concrete action that follows the internal sin of coveting.[9]

Jesus' answer should not be seen as merely rhe-

---

5. Contra Collins, *Mark*, 477, who claims, "Jesus shows his modesty and piety by not claiming for himself qualities or prerogatives that belong to God alone."

6. The majority of LXX manuscripts have a different order, though some follow the Hebrew order.

7. Some manuscripts omit μὴ ἀποστερήσῃς (B* K W Δ Ψ *f*[1.13] 28 579 700 2542 al vg[ms] syr[s]; Clement) either because it is

different from the term used in the LXX or by assimilation to Matthew and Luke, who also omit it.

8. Evans, *Mark 8:27 – 16:20*, 96.

9. The form of Mark's commandments also differs from the LXX, since he uses μή + aorist subjunctive instead of the LXX's οὐ + future indicative (which is closer to the Hebrew *lōʾ* + imperfect).

torical, as though he were simply setting up the man for failure. The purpose of the law is not only negative, as some have claimed, meant to reveal sin and bring people to despair. Rather, the commandments are holy, righteous, and good (Rom 7:12), and are intended to provide the foundation for fellowship with God. Obedience, however, is more than external compliance. It is a heart of love toward God that produces an internal transformation. In Deut 30:15 – 16 God promised Israel life and blessings in the land if they would love him and obey his commandments. True obedience arises from a heart oriented toward God, and Jesus' subsequent teaching will demonstrate that the man's heart is divided.

10:20 He said to him, "Teacher, all these I have kept since my youth." (ὁ δὲ ἔφη αὐτῷ· διδάσκαλε, ταῦτα πάντα ἐφυλαξάμην ἐκ νεότητός μου). "From my youth" may mean thirteen years old, the Jewish age of accountability (cf. *m. Nid.* 5:6; Luke 2:42), though the formal *bar mitzvah* ceremony is not attested at this early date. The man's response is not meant to be arrogant, as Jesus' response in v. 21 will show, but expresses confidence that he has lived a righteous life before God. He is no doubt thinking of outward compliance to the law, keeping its letter, rather than the true heart righteousness Jesus speaks about in the Sermon on the Mount (Matt 5:21 – 28). Paul expressed similar confidence in his ability to keep the law before coming to Christ (Phil 3:6; cf. Acts 26:4). Yet the man must sense that something is still lacking, since he implicitly pursues the issue with Jesus.

10:21 But Jesus, looking at him, loved him, and said to him, "One thing you lack. Go, sell everything you have and give to the poor, and you will have treasure in heaven. Then come, follow me." (ὁ δὲ Ἰησοῦς ἐμβλέψας αὐτῷ ἠγάπησεν αὐτὸν

καὶ εἶπεν αὐτῷ· ἕν σε ὑστερεῖ· ὕπαγε, ὅσα ἔχεις πώλησον καὶ δὸς [τοῖς] πτωχοῖς, καὶ ἕξεις θησαυρὸν ἐν οὐρανῷ, καὶ δεῦρο ἀκολούθει μοι). Only Mark mentions Jesus' prolonged gaze (ἐμβλέψας) and love for the man, both of which dramatize the moment and confirm the man's positive motives. This is no trap set by the religious leaders. It is rather the earnest desire of a true seeker. Some have claimed that the aorist verb "loved" (ἠγάπησεν) indicates a tangible action, like an embrace.[10] This is possible, but not necessary. The narrator is more likely confirming Jesus' disposition, his sensitivity to the man's plight and his authentic desire to see change.

Jesus then drops the bombshell. He says that the man lacks "one thing," but goes on to give four imperatives: go, sell everything, give to the poor, and follow Jesus. The four in fact form one imperative: to give up one's own life to live wholly for God. Though shocking in context, this is nothing new. Jesus has already taught that discipleship entails denying yourself, taking up your cross, and following him (8:34; cf. 1:17 – 18, 20; 2:14). The implication is that the man's wealth was his first love and was keeping him from fulfilling the greatest commandment — to love God with heart, soul, mind, and strength. He loved his riches more than he loved God and was trusting in them instead of in God.

At the beginning of his ministry, Jesus points to the two things necessary to receive the kingdom of God: "repent and believe" (1:15). Jesus' command here recalls these. This man must repent of his love for riches and put his faith in Jesus instead. His problem is he is trusting in himself, his righteous deeds, and his personal resources. As the previous passage has affirmed, to inherit eternal life one must become like a child, empty and without status (10:14 – 15).

The promise of "treasure in heaven" (θησαυρὸν

---

10. Nineham, *Mark*, 274 – 75; Anderson, *Mark*, 249.

ἐν οὐρανῷ) appears also in the Q saying in Matt 6:19–21 (par. Luke 12:33–34), where Jesus affirms the incorruptibility of heavenly rewards in contrast to the transitory nature of earthly things (cf. 1 Tim 6:17–20). The idea of future spiritual reward for present sacrifice appears elsewhere in Judaism, especially with reference to almsgiving. Tobit 4:8–9 reads, "If you have many possessions, make your gift from them in proportion; if few, do not be afraid to give according to the little you have. So you will be laying up a good treasure for yourself against the day of necessity" (NRSV; cf. Sir 29:10–12).[11] Such riches are not about mansions or wealth in heaven, but represent eternal life in relationship with God (cf. *Pss. Sol.* 9:5: "The one who does what is right saves up life for himself with the Lord").

10:22 Stunned at this statement, he went away sad, for he had many possessions (ὁ δὲ στυγνάσας ἐπὶ τῷ λόγῳ ἀπῆλθεν λυπούμενος· ἦν γὰρ ἔχων κτήματα πολλά). The man's sincerity is evident as he leaves, sad and grieving. Yet he leaves without salvation because the power of riches has such a firm grip on him. The blessing of riches becomes a curse when they become an obstacle to a right relationship with God.

The verb translated "stunned" (στυγνάζω) carries the sense of shocked dismay.[12] The verb appears only once elsewhere in the NT, where it indicates a gloomy, threatening sky before a storm (Matt 16:3). In the LXX it refers to those appalled and terrified by devastation that has befallen others (Ezek 27:35; 28:19; 32:10). Here now we learn that the man was "very rich," providing a dramatic climax. The clause (lit.) "he was having many pos-

sessions" (ἦν ἔχων κτήματα πολλά) is a periphrastic construction and idiom meaning "he was very rich" or "he had great wealth."

10:23–24 Then Jesus, looking around, said to his disciples, "How difficult it is for those with wealth to enter the kingdom of God." The disciples were amazed at his words. But Jesus again said to them, "Children, how difficult it is to enter the kingdom of God!" (Καὶ περιβλεψάμενος ὁ Ἰησοῦς λέγει τοῖς μαθηταῖς αὐτοῦ· πῶς δυσκόλως οἱ τὰ χρήματα ἔχοντες εἰς τὴν βασιλείαν τοῦ θεοῦ εἰσελεύσονται. οἱ δὲ μαθηταὶ ἐθαμβοῦντο ἐπὶ τοῖς λόγοις αὐτοῦ. ὁ δὲ Ἰησοῦς πάλιν ἀποκριθεὶς λέγει αὐτοῖς· τέκνα, πῶς δύσκολόν ἐστιν εἰς τὴν βασιλείαν τοῦ θεοῦ εἰσελθεῖν). Jesus now turns to the disciples and provides commentary on the scene that has played out before them.

Private instruction for the disciples is common throughout Mark.[13] The verb "look around" (περιβλέπω) occurs six times in Mark's gospel (3:5, 34; 5:32; 9:8; 10:23; 11:11; elsewhere in the NT only in Luke 6:10). Here it signifies "a commanding survey of the situation, as though Jesus looks to see whether the disciples will follow the rich man's example."[14] Jesus first states the difficulty the rich have in entering the kingdom of God (v. 23); after the disciples express shock (v. 24a), he repeats the statement (v. 24b-c) and drives the point home with a shocking analogy (v. 25). Jesus' use of a different word for possessions in v. 23 (χρήματα; v. 22: κτήματα) is likely stylistic, providing variety and emphasis.[15] Verse 25 will introduce a third term (πλούσιος; "a rich person").

The amazement of the disciples (v. 24a) probably

---

11. At the same time, Jewish tradition warned against giving away too much (more than one fifth), lest one become destitute and dependent on others (*m. ʿArak.* 8:4; *b. Ketub.* 50a; Martin Hengel, *Property and Riches in the Early Church: Aspects of a Social History of Early Christianity* [Philadelphia: Fortress, 1974], 20–21).

12. BDAG, 949.

13. See 4:10, 34; 7:17–23; 9:28–29, 30, 35; 10:10–12, 32–34; 12:43–44; 13:3–4.

14. Edwards, *Mark*, 313.

15. Contra Edwards, *Mark*, 313–14, who claims the first term indicates real estate and the second wealth in general.

arose because of the common Jewish perspective that riches were a sign of divine favor and blessing (Deut 28:1 – 14; Job 1:10; 42:10; Ps 128:1 – 2; Isa 3:10; Sir 11:17). Proverbs 10:22 says, "The blessing of the LORD brings wealth." At the same time the OT warns against the danger of riches and criticizes the rich who exploit the poor.[16] Both perspectives appear together in the intertestamental book Sirach, where on the one hand, "One who loves gold will not be justified," and yet, "Blessed is the rich person who is found blameless" (Sir 31:5 – 10 NRSV). Jesus' teaching certainly emphasizes the former. He frequently speaks of the destructive power of riches (Mark 4:19; Matt 6:19 – 21, 24; Luke 12:13 – 34) and the great reversal that the kingdom of God will bring (Luke 1:53; 6:24 – 25; 16:19 – 31).

When Jesus repeats the statement in v. 24c, he does not mention the rich.[17] This is probably stylistic ellipsis rather than generalization, since the statements both before and after refer to the rich.[18] Jesus' address to the disciples as "children" (τέκνα) occurs only here in Mark (cf. 2:5) and provides an affectionate tone. It may also be meant to recall the wisdom of Proverbs, where wise counsel for living is passed from father to son (Prov 1:8, 10; 2:1; etc.).[19] Jesus may also be alluding back to those who must become like "children" to enter the kingdom of God (10:15 – 16; cf. 9:36 – 37), but this is less likely, since in those passages Mark consistently uses a different word for children (παιδία).

10:25 "It is easier for a camel to pass through the eye of a needle than for a rich person to enter the kingdom of God." (εὐκοπώτερόν ἐστιν κάμηλον διὰ τῆς τρυμαλιᾶς τῆς ῥαφίδος διελθεῖν ἢ πλούσιον εἰς τὴν βασιλείαν τοῦ θεοῦ εἰσελθεῖν). If Jesus' previous statement was shocking, the analogy he now draws is even more so. Its difficulty has resulted in various attempts to soften it. Perhaps the most famous is the claim that there was a small gate leading into Jerusalem known as the "Needle's-Eye Gate." A camel could pass through only by having its baggage removed and then crawling on its knees. In this case Jesus would be teaching that the rich can enter the kingdom only by unburdening themselves of their love of riches and coming humbly to God. The problem with this interpretation is that there is no reliable evidence for the existence of such a gate in Jerusalem. It was apparently first suggested by Theophylact, an eleventh-century Byzantine commentator.[20]

Another proposal follows a few late manuscripts that read "rope" or "towline" (κάμιλος) instead of "camel" (κάμηλος).[21] Of course, this does not help much, since (though a less absurd image) a rope still cannot pass through the eye of a needle. As evidence that Jesus meant what he said are several rabbinic parallels that draw the equally absurd analogy of an elephant passing through the eye of a needle.[22] While the elephant was the largest land animal of Mesopotamia (where the Babylonian

---

16. Pss 10:2 – 11; 12:5; 37:12 – 22; Prov 11:28; 16:8; 19:1, 10; 22:1; 28:11; Isa 10:1 – 4; 53:9; Amos 2:6 – 8; Mic 2:1 – 5; Marcus, *Mark 9 – 16*, 735.

17. The variant τους πεποιθοτας επι [τοις] χρημασιν ("for those who trust in riches"; A C D Θ *f*[1.13] 2427 𝔐 lat syr boh[pt] Clement), is almost certainly a scribal attempt to soften Jesus' shocking statement of v. 23.

18. Contra Marcus, *Mark 9 – 16*, 736, who says Jesus now expands to include all people in his statement. Marcus points to parallels in the Q saying about the narrow gate (Matt 7:13 – 14// Luke 13:23 – 24) and apocalyptic literature that restricts salva-

tion to the few (4 Ezra 7:59 – 61; *T. Abr.* A 11:11).

19. The LXX generally uses υἱέ ("son") in these contexts, though τέκνον in Prov 31:2, 28.

20. Gundry, *Mark*, 565; Paul Minear, "The Needle's Eye: A Study in Form Criticism," *JBL* 61 (1942): 157 – 69. Garland, *Mark*, 401 n. 14, points out that Mark 10:25 and Luke 18:25 use two different words for "needle" (ῥαφίς and βελόνη, respectively) something that would be unlikely if the name of a gate were intended.

21. *f*[13] 28 579 geo.

22. *b. Ber.* 55b; *b. B. Maṣ* 38b; *b. Erub.* 53a.

Talmud was compiled), the camel was the largest in Israel. The eye of a needle was the smallest opening imaginable. The image of a camel trying to squeeze through one is delightfully absurd and impossible.

In one sense Jesus' statement is certainly hyperbolic. It is an intentional exaggeration meant to shock the disciples. In another sense, however, it is not hyperbole, since the point Jesus will make in v. 27 is that it is indeed *impossible* to enter the kingdom of God without divine intervention. What is impossible for human beings has been made possible by God. No rich person can enter the kingdom of God *while trusting in their riches.*

10:26–27 They were even more shocked and said to one another, "Then who can be saved?" Looking at them, Jesus said, "For people, it is impossible, but not for God, because all things are possible for God." (οἱ δὲ περισσῶς ἐξεπλήσσοντο λέγοντες πρὸς ἑαυτούς· καὶ τίς δύναται σωθῆναι; ἐμβλέψας αὐτοῖς ὁ Ἰησοῦς λέγει· παρὰ ἀνθρώποις ἀδύνατον, ἀλλ᾽ οὐ παρὰ θεῷ· πάντα γὰρ δυνατὰ παρὰ τῷ θεῷ). The disciples are now "even more shocked" (περισσῶς ἐξεπλήσσοντο) and discuss among themselves,[23] "Then who can be saved?" If this man — who has apparently kept the commandments his whole life and who has been blessed by God with great riches — cannot be saved, then who can?[24] Unusual for Mark, the verb "saved" (σῴζω) here carries the sense of spiritual salvation (cf. 13:13) rather than the restoration of physical health; it is synonymous with "inherit[ing] eternal life" (v. 17) and "enter[ing] the kingdom of God" (vv. 23, 24, 25)

Jesus' gaze ("looking at them"; ἐμβλέψας αὐτοῖς, the same verb as in v. 21) creates a narrative pause and adds gravity to the saying that follows. Jesus' answer is the climax to which the episode has been building: *What is impossible for human beings is possible for God.*[25] Though no one can be saved by their own efforts, God has provided a way. That way, though not stated here, is the gift of salvation available through Jesus Christ, the Son of Man, who will give his life as a ransom for many (10:45).

10:28 Peter then spoke[26] to him, "See, we have left everything and followed you." (Ἤρξατο λέγειν ὁ Πέτρος αὐτῷ· ἰδοὺ ἡμεῖς ἀφήκαμεν πάντα καὶ ἠκολουθήκαμέν σοι). In contrast to the rich man's failure to repent (give up all) and believe (follow Jesus), Peter asserts that the disciples have done just that. For once in Mark the disciples serve as a positive example. Though the disciples have many shortcomings, they are on the side of Jesus and so heirs of the kingdom of God.

It is curious that Peter says, "We have left everything," since it seems he still possessed a home and a fishing boat (1:29; 3:9; 4:1, 36; cf. John 21:3). This suggests, at least, that Jesus does not call on everyone to divest of everything they own to follow him. Since Jesus does not deny Peter's claim, it seems that "giving up all" means sacrificing those things that represent a roadblock to authentic faith and trust in God (see Theology in Application). If there is any inappropriate pride in Peter's remark, Mark does not highlight it, and Jesus' response affirms that Peter and the disciples represent the antithesis of the rich man's failure.

---

23. The phrase "among themselves" or "to one another" (πρὸς ἑαυτούς) could be translated "to themselves," but the former makes better sense in context (cf. 8:16). The ambiguity likely led to the variants: προς αυτον ("to him"; ℵ B C Δ Ψ 892 2427 cop) and προς αλληλους ("to one another"; M* k syr).

24. Stein, *Mark*, 472; Evans, *Mark 8:27–16:20*, 101; Donahue and Harrington, *Mark*, 304–5.

25. The closest OT parallel to Jesus' saying occurs in Gen 18:14 LXX, where, in response to Sarah's disbelief that she will have a son, the angel says, "Nothing is impossible with God" (cf. Job 10:13 LXX; Zech 8:6 LXX; Marcus, *Mark 9–16*, 732).

26. The idiom "began to speak" (ἤρξατο λέγειν) here apparently means that Peter spoke up in response to Jesus' words.

10:29 – 30 Jesus said, "Truly I say to you, anyone who has left home or brothers or sisters or mother or father or children or fields for my sake and for the sake of the gospel will receive a hundred times as much in the present age: homes and brothers and sisters and mothers and children and fields — together with persecutions — and in the age to come, eternal life." (ἔφη ὁ Ἰησοῦς· ἀμὴν λέγω ὑμῖν, οὐδείς ἐστιν ὃς ἀφῆκεν οἰκίαν ἢ ἀδελφοὺς ἢ ἀδελφὰς ἢ μητέρα ἢ πατέρα ἢ τέκνα ἢ ἀγροὺς ἕνεκεν ἐμοῦ καὶ ἕνεκεν τοῦ εὐαγγελίου, ἐὰν μὴ λάβῃ ἑκατονταπλασίονα νῦν ἐν τῷ καιρῷ τούτῳ οἰκίας καὶ ἀδελφοὺς καὶ ἀδελφὰς καὶ μητέρας καὶ τέκνα καὶ ἀγροὺς μετὰ διωγμῶν, καὶ ἐν τῷ αἰῶνι τῷ ἐρχομένῳ ζωὴν αἰώνιον).

Jesus begins with his solemn assertion, "Truly I say to you" (ἀμὴν λέγω ὑμῖν; 13x in Mark; see comments on 3:28 – 30). Several of these *amen* statements, like this one, concern the question of ultimate rewards (cf. 3:28; 9:1, 41; 10:15). The double negative in Greek, lit., "there is no one who has left … will not receive" (οὐδείς ἐστιν ὃς ἀφῆκεν … ἐὰν μὴ λάβῃ) makes awkward English and so has been translated in the positive, "anyone who has left … will receive." The things "left" or "forsaken" (ἀφῆκεν), including home, family, and property ("fields"), parallel those things gained, except that "father" is not mentioned in the latter. This is perhaps because believers have one Father in heaven (cf. Matt 23:9). Curiously, while parents, siblings, and children are mentioned, spouses are not (contrast Luke 18:29), perhaps because Jesus has just taught about the indissolubility of marriage (10:1 – 12). It is significant, as well, that in 1 Cor 9:5 Paul notes that Peter and the other apostles traveled and ministered with their wives.

The believer's commitment is "for my sake" (ἕνεκεν ἐμοῦ) and "for the sake of the gospel" (ἕνεκεν τοῦ εὐαγγελίου), confirming the close identification of Jesus with the "good news" of the kingdom of God (1:15). The kingdom arrives through his life, death, and resurrection. The things lost are connected by "or" (ἤ), while the things gained are connected by "and" (καί). While this distinction may be primarily stylistic, together with the "hundredfold" increase it emphasizes the fact of receiving so much more than what is lost. The gains are in both epochs of salvation history, "this present age" (νῦν ἐν τῷ καιρῷ τούτῳ) and "the age to come" (ἐν τῷ αἰῶνι τῷ ἐρχομένῳ).

Eternal life in the age to come is clear enough. But in what sense does the believer gain homes and family and fields in the present age? The likely answer is that all believers stand together as one family — as brothers and sisters in Christ — whose possessions are ultimately God's and so shared by all (cf. Acts 2:42; 4:32). Any Christian who has experienced the fellowship and hospitality of fellow believers in some remote corner of the world understands Jesus' words. It is significant that early in Mark's gospel Jesus identifies his followers as his true mother and brothers and sisters (3:33 – 34).

The qualification "together with persecutions" (μετὰ διωγμῶν) may well reflect the realities of the Markan community and perhaps the Neronian persecution in Rome (see Introduction to Mark: Occasion and Purpose). However, this does not necessarily mean that this phrase was added by Mark. Jesus repeatedly predicted not only his own suffering, but the suffering of his followers (8:34 – 38; 9:49; 10:38 – 39; 13:9 – 13), and these passages suggest a more general context of persecution beyond that of Nero and Rome.

In the present age, though the blessings of salvation are already present, they are also "not yet," and Jesus' followers must be prepared to suffer as he did. Yet the certainty of ultimate reward — eternal life in the age to come — should provide comfort and consolation. The phrase "eternal life" (ζωὴν αἰώνιον) provides a kind of inclusio with v. 17. What the rich man came seeking is the certain inheritance of those who forsake all to follow Jesus.

10:31 But many who are first will be last and the last first (πολλοὶ δὲ ἔσονται πρῶτοι ἔσχατοι καὶ οἱ ἔσχατοι πρῶτοι). A similar saying, but in reverse order, appears in both Matt 20:16 and Luke 13:30. In Matthew it appears after the parable of the laborers in the vineyard and refers to the workers who were hired last but received equal pay. In Luke it follows Jesus' teaching about the exclusion of many "insiders" from the messianic banquet and the inclusion of those from the east, west, north, and south. The common thread is the great eschatological reversal that is characteristic of the present and the future appearance of the kingdom of God. In contrast to the rich and powerful, who appear to be first in the present age, stand the persecuted disciples, who have forsaken all to follow Jesus. In terms of spiritual realities, they are receiving far more in the present age and eternal life in the age to come.

Theology in Application

To the affluent Western church, this is one of the most challenging and difficult passages in the Bible. Jesus' teaching stands in stark contrast to those who advocate a "prosperity gospel," in which wealth is seen as a sure sign of God's blessings. Even those who recognize the errors of a prosperity approach find the rich man's plight uncomfortably close to home. As we have seen, a variety of exegetical attempts have been made to avoid the plain meaning of the text, including the invention of a "Needle's Eye Gate" in Jerusalem or the emendation of the text to read "rope" instead of "camel" (see v. 25). Others explain away the passage by assuming that there are two levels of discipleship and that Jesus' radical call is for those who would attain a higher level. But this completely misses the point of the passage, which concerns the most fundamental issue for every believer, whether it be called eternal life (vv. 17, 30), entrance into the kingdom (vv. 23, 24, 25), or salvation (v. 26).

Still others seek to dodge the text's explosive impact by watering it down, as some copyists did, so that only "those who trust in their riches" fall under Jesus' indictment. It is true, of course, that Jesus did not command all his followers to sell their possessions and give to the poor. Some of his disciples evidently retained both homes and tools of their livelihood (1:29; 3:9; 4:1, 36; cf. John 21:3). Joseph of Arimathea was a man of means and a follower of Jesus (Mark 15:42 – 46). Luke refers to prominent women who supported Jesus' ministry from their own means, something impossible to do had they sold it all (Luke 8:1 – 3). After Zacchaeus announces that he is giving half (not all) of his possessions to the poor and repaying fourfold anyone he has defrauded, Jesus announces that "salvation has come to this house" (Luke 19:9). The early church too had wealthy members who gave generously but also retained a portion of their wealth (Acts 4:34 – 37; 5:1 – 4). These passages show that the early church (unlike, for example, the Qumran sect)[27] was neither communist nor communal, and did not require the selling or pooling of all resources.

---

27. 1QS 1.11: "All those who submit freely to his [God's] truth will convey all their energies and their riches to the Community of God" (cf. 1QS 6.13 – 23). On the communal living of the Essenes, see Josephus, *J. W.* 2.8.3 §122.

Yet those who might breathe a sigh of relief at such exceptions are precisely the ones to whom Jesus is speaking. In other words, all of us! Before we dismiss this passage as "for others," we need to read the whole of Scripture, which consistently teaches (1) the seductive and destructive power of riches, (2) the need to reach out generously to those in need, and (3) that nothing we do for ourselves can merit eternal life. It is only through faith in God's gift of grace — coming like a child — that we can be saved. We will develop these three points below.

The Dangerous Seduction of Riches

In the present episode the man's great wealth is the one thing keeping him from the greatest of all rewards, eternal life. The danger of wealth is a leading theme in Jesus' teaching, especially in Luke's gospel. In addition to beatitudes for the poor, he pronounces woes against the rich and powerful (Luke 6:20 – 26). The parable of the rich man and Lazarus illustrates the great reversal that will come to the rich who ignore the needs of the poor (16:19 – 31), and the parable of the rich fool relates the fate of those who store up things for themselves but are not rich toward God (12:16 – 21). Riches are dangerous because they bring superficial happiness rather than true joy and distract us from what is truly important and of eternal value. You cannot serve both God and mammon (Matt 6:24; Luke 16:13). They also tend to breed sins of selfishness, like pride and greed and coveting. In the Pastorals, Paul points both to the fleeting nature of riches and to their destructive power:

> For we brought nothing into the world, and we can take nothing out of it. But if we have food and clothing, we will be content with that. Those who want to get rich fall into temptation and a trap and into many foolish and harmful desires that plunge people into ruin and destruction. For the love of money is a root of all kinds of evil. Some people, eager for money, have wandered from the faith and pierced themselves with many griefs. (1 Tim 6:7 – 10; cf. 6:17 – 19)

The story is told of a rich man who stood up in church to recount how God had blessed him in remarkable ways. He told how, as a young man, he was sitting in church after he had received his first small paycheck from his first job. As the offering plate was passed, a small voice inside him said, "Give it all to God." At first he resisted, but the voice persisted until he signed the check over to the church and dropped it in the offering place. He explained to the congregation that from that point on, God had blessed him immeasurably and that he had become a wealthy man. After he sat down a dear old lady sitting behind him leaned forward and whispered in his ear, "I dare you to do it again!" How hard it is for a rich man, who has been given so much, to relinquish it all for the kingdom of God!

Stewardship of Wealth: Resources for God's Kingdom

If riches are not meant to bring us personal happiness, what are they for? They are *God's resources* entrusted to us to accomplish his purposes. These purposes include caring for the poor and reaching out to those in need. Jesus proclaimed the gospel as good news to the poor and freedom for the oppressed (Luke 4:18). He fed the multitudes and cared for the sick. He pronounced beatitudes on the poor because they are recipients of God's grace and his kingdom (Luke 6:20 – 23). The early church consistently met the needs of its own, reaching out to widows (Acts 6:1 – 6; cf. Jas 1:27) and sharing resources (Acts 2:42; 4:32). The church in Antioch provided famine relief to Jerusalem through Paul and Barnabas (11:27 – 30), and Paul collected funds from the diaspora churches of Galatia, Greece, and Asia Minor to meet the needs of the famine-ravaged Jerusalem church (Rom 15:25 – 27; 1 Cor 16:1 – 4; 2 Cor 8 – 9).

Essential for all believers is the principle of good stewardship, that all we have is God's and should be used for his purposes. Luke's parable of the minas (Luke 19:11 – 27) and Matthew's parable of the talents (Matt 25:14 – 30) teach the need for good stewardship, treating everything we have as a sacred trust from God. Before making purchases believers need to ask: How will this help to accomplish *God's purpose* on earth? With this investment am I seeking God's kingdom (Matt 6:33) or my own selfish desires?

The Secret to Eternal Life

While the danger of riches and the importance of good stewardship are important in the application of this passage, it begins and ends with the fundamental question of eternal life (vv. 17, 31). On the surface, this rich man appears to have everything going for him. He is both a good man and a gifted one. No better candidate for church membership could have stepped forward. But Jesus makes it clear that this is not enough. Jesus does not speak here out of anger at the man's ill-gained wealth, greed, or inadequate service toward God. He speaks rather out of deep love and desperate concern for the man's eternal destiny (v. 21). He sees that this man has made wealth and personal success his god.

Only radical surgery will cure this cancer and allow God's grace to transform him. He must give up everything — his whole life — and follow Jesus. The command to sell everything is equivalent to Jesus' earlier command to his disciples to "deny themselves and take up their cross and follow me" (8:34). Salvation comes not through human effort or meritorious work, but rather through the renunciation of self and dependence of God — becoming like a child. Salvation, though it costs us nothing, costs everything, our very lives. To follow Jesus truly means to follow him fully.

Mark 10:32 – 45

Literary Context

This is the third passion prediction and the third cycle of events during which Jesus predicts his death, the disciples exhibit pride and self-interest, and Jesus teaches about the sacrificial and self-giving role of true discipleship (8:31 – 38; 9:31 – 50; 10:32 – 45). The parallels between the latter two are especially close. Both have the disciples competing for positions of authority (9:34; 10:32), and in both Jesus speaks of those wishing to be first becoming last and becoming the servant of all (9:35; 10:43 – 44). This third cycle functions as the climax to the three cycles and prepares the way for Jesus' entrance into Jerusalem (11:1 – 11) and the last week of his life, when he will "give his life as a ransom for many" (10:45).

Main Idea

The third passion prediction and the request by James and John for the best seats in the kingdom serve as the climax of Mark's central section (8:22 – 10:52) and summarize the sacrificial mission of the Servant Messiah. While the disciples vie for positions of power and prestige in the glorious kingdom to come, Jesus identifies the true model of Christian leadership as the sacrificial service of the Son of Man, who will give his life as a ransom for many.

Translation

Mark 10:32 – 45

32a	Setting	**They were on the way,**
b		going up to Jerusalem,
c	Action	and **Jesus was going before them.**
d	Response to 32c	**They were amazed,**
e	Response to 32c	but **those who followed were afraid.**
f		Again taking the Twelve aside,
g	Instruction/Passion prediction	**he began to tell them what was going to happen to him.**
33a	action (Sequence)	*"Look! We are going up to Jerusalem,*
b	action	*and the Son of Man will be delivered to the ruling priests and the experts in the law.*
c	action	*They will condemn him to death and will hand him over to the Gentiles.*
34a	action	*They will mock him and spit on him, and flog and kill him.*
b	contrast with 34a	*But after three days he will arise."*
35a	Character entrance	Then **James and John, the sons of Zebedee, came to him.**
b	Request	**They said to him,**
c		*"Teacher, we want you to do for us whatever we ask."*
36a	Response to 35	**He asked,**
b		*"What do you want me to do for you?"*
37a	Response to 36/Request	**They said to him,**
b		*"Grant us to sit one on your right and one on your left in your glory."*
38a	Response to 37	**Jesus said to them,**
b	rebuke	*"You don't know what you are asking.*
c	question	*Are you able to drink the cup that I drink, or*
d		*to be baptized with the baptism I am baptized with?"*
39a	Response to 38	**They answered,**
b		*"We are able!"*
c	Response to 39	**Jesus said to them,**
d		*"The cup that I drink you will drink,*
e		*and the baptism I am baptized with you will be baptized with.*
40a		*But to sit at my right or my left is not for me to grant;*
b		*rather, it is for those for whom it has been prepared."*
41a	Response to 37	When the ten heard this,
b		**they became indignant toward James and John.**
42a		After calling them together,
b	Response to 41/Instruction	**Jesus said to them,**
c	statement of fact	*"You know that those recognized as rulers of the Gentiles lord it over them,*
d	parallel statement of fact	*and their great ones exercise dominion over them.*
43a	contrast	*But it is not so among you.*
b	exhortation	*Rather, whoever wants to be great among you will be your servant,*
44	parallel exhortation	*and whoever wants to be first will be slave of all.*
45a	reason for 43 – 44	*For even the Son of Man did not come to be served, but*
b	contrast with 45a	*to serve, and*
c		*to give his life as a ransom for many."*

Structure

This third passion prediction is the most detailed of the three:

8:31	9:31	10:32 – 34
Then he began to teach them that it was necessary for the Son of Man to suffer many things and to be rejected by the elders and the ruling priests and the experts in the law, and to be killed, and after three days rise again.	… because he was teaching his disciples and telling them, "The Son of Man will be delivered into human hands, and they will kill him. But three days after being killed, he will rise again."	Again taking the Twelve aside, he began to tell them what was going to happen to him. "Look! We are going up to Jerusalem, and the Son of Man will be delivered to the ruling priests and the experts in the law. They will condemn him to death and will hand him over to the Gentiles. They will mock him and spit on him, and flog and kill him. But after three days he will arise."

All three passion predictions identify Jesus as the "Son of Man" (see comments on 2:10 – 11; 8:31), describe his being "killed" (ἀποκτείνω), and speak of the resurrection "after three days" (μετὰ τρεῖς ἡμέρας). The first identifies his rejection (ἀποδοκιμασθῆναι) by three groups: the elders, the ruling priests, and the experts in the law. The second and third speak of him being "delivered over" (παραδίδοται), respectively, to "human hands" (9:31) and to "the ruling priests and the experts in the law" (10:34). Only the third speaks of the religious leaders delivering him to the Gentiles and his being mocked, spit on, and flogged.

Since these latter details closely parallel the events themselves, many interpreters claim the prediction was composed after the fact (*vaticinium ex eventu*). It is certainly possible that Mark, or the tradition before him, added these details,[1] but this is not likely: (1) the order of the events is not identical to Mark's actual narrative (but see comments on vv. 33 – 34); (2) the word for "flog" (μαστιγόω; v. 34) is different from 15:15 (φραγελλόω); (3) the lack of reference to crucifixion as the means of death argues against an invention *ex eventu*; (4) the expression "after three days" is problematic for a Sunday morning resurrection and so is unlikely to have been introduced after the fact. The larger question, of course, is whether Jesus predicted his own death; on this see "In Depth: Did Jesus Predict his Own Death?" in Theology in Application on 8:27 – 33.

The request by James and John may be divided into two parts, the dialogue with the two disciples (10:35 – 40) and Jesus' teaching on servant leadership (10:42 – 45), with the indignant response of the other disciples forming a transition between the two (v. 41). Although Luke omits the episode from his account of Jesus' journey to Jerusalem, Jesus' teaching in vv. 42 – 45 (cf. Matt 20:25 – 27) appears in a modified form in Luke's Last Supper narrative (Luke 22:24 – 27).

1. Evans, *Mark 8:27 – 16:20*, 106.

Exegetical Outline

→ **1. The Third Passion Prediction (10:32 – 34)**

2. The Request of James and John (10:35 – 40)

    a. The request for chief seats in the kingdom (10:35 – 37)

    b. The dialogue about Jesus'"cup" and "baptism" (10:38 – 40)

3. The Indignation of the Ten (10:41)

4. Jesus' Response: Teaching on Servant Leadership (10:42 – 45)

    a. The leadership methods of pagan rulers (10:42)

    b. The leadership model for the disciples (10:43 – 44)

    c. The ultimate example of the Son of Man (10:45)

Explanation of the Text

10:32 They were on the way, going up to Jerusalem, and Jesus was going before them. They were amazed, but those who followed were afraid. Again taking the Twelve aside, he began to tell them what was going to happen to him (Ἦσαν δὲ ἐν τῇ ὁδῷ ἀναβαίνοντες εἰς Ἱεροσόλυμα, καὶ ἦν προάγων αὐτοὺς ὁ Ἰησοῦς, καὶ ἐθαμβοῦντο, οἱ δὲ ἀκολουθοῦντες ἐφοβοῦντο. καὶ παραλαβὼν πάλιν τοὺς δώδεκα ἤρξατο αὐτοῖς λέγειν τὰ μέλλοντα αὐτῷ συμβαίνειν). For the first time Mark explicitly identifies Jesus' Jerusalem goal. Pilgrims always "go up" (ἀναβαίνω) to Jerusalem, both because of its altitude and because it is the Holy City.

The subjects of the three third person plural verbs are not altogether clear. (1) The "they" who are going up to Jerusalem are Jesus, the disciples, and probably other followers and pilgrims from Galilee heading to Jerusalem for the Passover festival. (2) Those "amazed" (ἐθαμβοῦντο)[2] would include the Twelve, and perhaps others.

They recognize a change in Jesus. He has a new intensity and is out in front of the group instead of in his usual position as a rabbi walking beside them (cf. Luke 9:51, where "Jesus resolutely set out for Jerusalem"). (3) The response is amazement by all, but fear by "those who were following" (οἱ ἀκολουθοῦντες).

Who is this third group, and why are they afraid? The answer almost certainly relates to Peter's messianic acclamation in 8:29 and Jesus' (tacit) acceptance of it. If Jesus is the Messiah and is heading for Jerusalem, this can only mean one thing — messianic war with the Romans. It also potentially meant civil war, since the priestly leadership would be unsympathetic to a peasant revolt that would threaten its position and power. Jesus' new intensity therefore produces amazement by all of his followers, but fear among some, who begin to fall back.[3] This interpretation also helps to explain the request of James and John (vv. 35 – 40),

---

2. Some commentators interpret θαμβέω to mean "distressed," pointing to the cognate ἐκθαμβέω used of Jesus' distress in Gethsemane (14:33), and refer the distress to both Jesus and the disciples (Hooker, *Mark*, 245). This is unlikely. The verb means "astonishment" in its other two uses in Mark (1:27; 10:24), and there is no indication here that Jesus and the disciples are experiencing the same emotions.

3. Contra Evans, *Mark 8:27 – 16:20*, 108, who sees this "fear" in the OT sense of awe in the presence of the divine (cf. 4:41; 5:33; 9:32; 16:8), and so essentially the same as the amazement. Yet Mark also uses the verb in the sense of fear for one's safety or security (5:15, 36; 6:20, 50; 11:18, 32; 12:12), and the adversative use of δέ suggests a different emotion from those who are astonished.

who see Jesus' messianic aspirations in Jerusalem as an opportunity for advancement and positions of prestige in the coming kingdom.

In this context Jesus again seeks to set the record straight about the nature of his messiahship (8:31; 9:31). As often in Mark, we have private instruction for the disciples.[4] "Taking the Twelve aside" (παραλαβὼν πάλιν τοὺς δώδεκα) implies the presence of a larger group of followers and pilgrims accompanying Jesus to the festival. The passion prediction that follows confirms that the coming events are neither tragic nor unexpected. They are part of God's purpose and plan for the Messiah and the salvation he will accomplish.

10:33 – 34 "Look! We are going up to Jerusalem, and the Son of Man will be delivered to the ruling priests and the experts in the law. They will condemn him to death and will hand him over to the Gentiles. They will mock him and spit on him, and flog and kill him. But after three days he will arise (ὅτι ἰδοὺ ἀναβαίνομεν εἰς Ἱεροσόλυμα, καὶ ὁ υἱὸς τοῦ ἀνθρώπου παραδοθήσεται τοῖς ἀρχιερεῦσιν καὶ τοῖς γραμματεῦσιν, καὶ κατακρινοῦσιν αὐτὸν θανάτῳ καὶ παραδώσουσιν αὐτὸν τοῖς ἔθνεσιν καὶ ἐμπαίξουσιν αὐτῷ καὶ ἐμπτύσουσιν αὐτῷ καὶ μαστιγώσουσιν αὐτὸν καὶ ἀποκτενοῦσιν, καὶ μετὰ τρεῖς ἡμέρας ἀναστήσεται). See chart above for a comparison to the other two passion predictions. While the passive "will be delivered to" (παραδοθήσεται) could refer to the actions of Judas (14:10, 43), more likely it is a divine passive, referring to God's actions (see comments on 1:14; 9:31).

Only this passion prediction describes the two-step nature of Jesus' trial. He will first be "condemned to death" by the Jewish leaders and will then be handed over to the Gentiles (= the Roman authorities) for execution. This fits what we know about the authority of Jewish leadership of the

time, who could pronounce guilt but could not carry out capital punishment (John 18:31; *y. Sanh.* 1:1; 7:2). The "ruling priests" (ἀρχιερεῖς) are the aristocratic members of the high priest's family and other influential priests (see comments on 8:31; cf. Acts 4:6). They will be allied with the "scribes" or "experts in the law" (γραμματεῖς; see comments on 1:22). In 8:31 Jesus had mentioned three groups, adding the "elders" (πρεσβύτεροι), who were the lay leadership of the Sanhedrin. The reason for their omission here is not clear; perhaps it is simple abbreviation.

The events described here occur rapidly in the narrative that follows. At the climax of his Jewish trial, Jesus will be "condemned" (κατακρίνω) as worthy of death by the Sanhedrin (14:64) and the next morning be "handed over" (παραδίδωμι) to Pilate for trial (15:1). Grammatically, the actions described here — mocking, spitting, flogging, and killing — could refer to the Gentiles alone, or to both the Jewish leaders and the Gentiles. In Mark's trial and crucifixion narrative, Jesus will be mocked by both Roman soldiers (15:17 – 20) and Jewish leaders (15:31 – 32), spit on by both (14:65; 15:19), beaten by Jewish temple guards (14:65) and flogged by Pilate's soldiers (15:15; cf. John 19:1),[5] and crucified under Pilate's orders (15:24).

Mark's description of the resurrection "after three days" (μετὰ τρεῖς ἡμέρας) is the same in all three passion predictions and means essentially the same thing as Matthew and Luke's "on the third day" (τῇ τρίτῃ ἡμέρᾳ; Matt 16:21; 17:23; 20:19; Luke 9:22; 18:33; see comments and notes on Mark 8:31).

10:35 – 36 Then James and John, the sons of Zebedee, came to him. They said to him, "Teacher, we want you to do for us whatever we ask." He asked, "What do you want me to do for you?"

---

4. See 4:10, 34; 7:17 – 23; 9:28 – 29, 30, 35; 10:10 – 12; 12:43 – 44; 13:3 – 4.

5. Flogging was often done in preparation for crucifixion. See Josephus, *J. W.* 2.14.9 §306.

(Καὶ προσπορεύονται αὐτῷ Ἰάκωβος καὶ Ἰωάννης οἱ υἱοὶ Ζεβεδαίου λέγοντες αὐτῷ·ν διδάσκαλε, θέλομεν ἵνα ὃ ἐὰν αἰτήσωμέν σε ποιήσῃς ἡμῖν. ὁ δὲ εἶπεν αὐτοῖς· τί θέλετε ποιήσω ὑμῖν;). Only here and at their original call (1:16–20) are James and John named apart from Peter in Mark's gospel (though John appears alone in 9:38). It is perhaps not surprising that they would make this play for authoritative roles in the kingdom since Jesus had already singled them out (together with Peter) for special leadership roles as his "inner circle" of disciples (5:37; 9:2; cf. 14:33). The nickname Jesus gave them, "sons of thunder" (3:17), may indicate volatile or aggressive personalities, and it is perhaps this disposition that prompts them to act.

Jesus is nearing Jerusalem amid expectations that he is the Messiah. But who will be his chief advisors when he assumes the messianic throne? James and John seize the opportunity to make their request.[6] By asking Jesus to grant "whatever we ask," they are evidently hoping to receive carte blanche approval from Jesus before he hears the nature of their request. Jesus is too smart to fall for this and pursues the matter further, asking what they want.[7]

10:37 They said to him, "Grant us to sit one on your right and one on your left in your glory."

(οἱ δὲ εἶπαν αὐτῷ· δὸς ἡμῖν ἵνα εἷς σου ἐκ δεξιῶν καὶ εἷς ἐξ ἀριστερῶν καθίσωμεν ἐν τῇ δόξῃ σου). The requested seats of honor may be at the messianic banquet (Isa 25:6–8; cf. Luke 13:29; Matt 8:11) or thrones adjacent to the Messiah's in his throne room (Mark 14:62; Ps 110:1; Matt 19:28; 25:31–46). For both images together, see Luke 22:30. The latter is more likely here, since one might expect a verb for "recline"[8] instead of "sit" (καθίζω) if a banquet scene were in view. The right hand indicates the place of greatest honor, often the position of the son and heir, or a chief advisor.[9] Though the left side could have negative connotations in the ancient Near East,[10] in this context it clearly means the next best place in the kingdom after the right side.[11] As France points out, "there are of course only two such places, leaving no room for Peter."[12]

"In your glory" (ἐν τῇ δόξῃ σου) does not mean heavenly glory or the glory of the parousia. The disciples are thinking of the glory of an earthly messianic kingdom in Jerusalem. Jesus has told the disciples that some of them would "not taste death until they see the kingdom of God come in power" (9:1), and Peter, James, and John had been given a glimpse of Jesus' glory at his transfiguration (9:3). Matthew's parallel reads "in your king-

---

6. In Matthew's parallel, their mother makes the request (Matt 20:20–21). Many commentators conclude that Matthew has modified the story to present the disciples in a better light. This is possible, but it is just as likely that Mark is summarizing to show that the request ultimately came from the brothers. (Something similar occurs in Luke 7:1–9, the healing of the centurion's son. In Matthew the request for healing comes directly from the centurion [Matt 8:5–13], while in Luke it comes through the Jewish elders.) Evidence that the brothers are the source of the request is Mark's consistently negative critique of the disciples and the fact that in Matthew's account, Jesus speaks as though the request came from the brothers ("You [pl.] don't know what you [pl.] are asking. Can you [pl.] ...?"; Matt 20:22).

7. The manuscripts are divided between the subjunctive (ποιήσω) and infinitive (ποιήσαι) here. The original expression

was probably the subjunctive, τί θέλετε ποιήσω ὑμῖν; ("What do you wish I might do for you?" C Θ f1.13 565), with an understood ἵνα (omitted through ellipsis). The awkward ellipsis was smoothed out by copyists with an infinitive, τί θέλετε ποιήσαι με ὑμῖν ("What do you want me to do for you?" A 𝔐), and then the two readings were conflated in the "syntactically impossible reading," τί θέλετέ με ποιήσω (א1 B Ψ 2427; France, Mark, 414).

8. Mark 6:26; 14:18; 16:14 (ἀνακείμαι); 6:40; 8:6 (ἀναπεσεῖν); cf. Luke 7:36; 9:14–15; 14:8; 24:30 (κατακλίνω).

9. Ps 110:1; Sir 12:12; 1 Esd 4:29.

10. Taylor, Mark, 440; France, Mark, 415 n. 42.

11. Josephus describes Saul's placement of his son Jonathan on his right side and Abner, the captain of his army, "on the other hand" (Ant. 6.11.9 §235). Cf. 1 Kgs 22:19; Neh 8:4.

12. France, Mark, 415.

dom" (20:21), correctly reflecting the disciples' expectations.

In one sense, the request of James and John is commendable, reflecting their belief that Jesus is the Messiah and that he will prove victorious in his messianic role. In this way the passage parallels Peter's confession in 8:27–30. At the same time, the request is appalling. First, Jesus has been repeatedly teaching the disciples the humble servant role of true disciples and that to be first they must become last (9:33–36). James and John have obviously not learned this lesson. Second, he has just predicted his own suffering and death for the third time. The two must not have been listening! Or perhaps, like Peter in 8:32, they are seeking to combat Jesus' defeatist attitude. For Mark the request is further confirmation that the disciples are spiritually dull and do not comprehend Jesus' messianic role (4:13, 40; 6:52; 7:18; 8:17–18, 21, 32; 9:5–6, 19, 32).

10:38 Jesus said to them, "You don't know what you are asking. Are you able to drink the cup that I drink, or to be baptized with the baptism I am baptized with?" (ὁ δὲ Ἰησοῦς εἶπεν αὐτοῖς· οὐκ οἴδατε τί αἰτεῖσθε. δύνασθε πιεῖν τὸ ποτήριον ὃ ἐγὼ πίνω ἢ τὸ βάπτισμα ὃ ἐγὼ βαπτίζομαι βαπτισθῆναι;). Jesus first responds that the request itself is misguided. They do not understand either the nature or the gravity of Jesus' messianic role. "Are you able to drink...?" is a rhetorical question, meaning, "You cannot drink ...," though the two will take it as a real question and will answer in v. 39.

Jesus compares his suffering to two parallel images, a cup (ποτήριον) and a baptism or immersion (βάπτισμα). Both are metaphors for his suffering and death.[13] Jesus will use the cup metaphor again in Gethsemane (14:36; cf. John 18:11). "The cup" is something you drink and so, metaphorically, something experienced. It is occasionally used of blessings received (Pss 16:5; 23:5; 116:13), but more often of suffering, especially in the context of divine judgment (Ps 75:8; Isa 51:17–23; Jer 25:15–29; 49:12; Lam 4:21; Ezek 23:31–34; Hab 2:16; *Pss. Sol.* 8:14; Rev 14:10; 16:19). As applied to Jesus, the metaphor may imply that he will experience the wrath of God as a vicarious sacrifice for sins. This is not certain, however, since the image can mean suffering in general, as the nonvicarious application to James and John in the next verse shows.

The use of "baptism" (βάπτισμα) in the sense of suffering is more obscure.[14] Suffering is sometimes described as an overwhelming deluge of water (Pss 42:7; 69:1–2; Isa 43:2), and the verb "baptize" (βαπτίζω) can carry this sense of being overwhelmed or deluged.[15] Here it refers to Jesus being swept away in death by the events that will shortly unfold in Jerusalem.[16] Jesus uses the same metaphor in Luke 12:50 as he contemplates his Jerusalem suffering. For Mark's readers, of course, Jesus' words would bring to mind Christian baptism and their own identification with Christ in his death, burial, and resurrection (Rom 6:3–4). It is tempting, in light of the close parallel between the baptism and cup sayings, to see here sacramental

---

13. For background to both images, see A. Feuillet, "La coupe et le baptême de la passion (*Mc*, x,35–40; cf. *Mt*, xx,20–23; *Lc*, xii,50)," *RB* 74 (1967): 356–91.

14. See G. Delling, "βάπτισμα βαπτισθῆναι," *NovT* 2 (1957–58): 92–115.

15. Josephus speaks of the rabble who "overwhelmed the city [Jerusalem] with misery" (ἐβάπτισεν τὴν πόλιν πλήθει; *J.W.* 4.3.3 §137. Cf. Isa 21:4 LXX: "lawlessness overwhelms me"

(ἡ ἀνομία με βαπτίζει). See BDAG, 165.

16. The expression "the baptism I am baptized with" (τὸ βάπτισμα ὃ ἐγὼ βαπτίζομαι) is a cognate accusative (cf. 4:41; 9:41; 10:38, 39; 13:7; 14:6), where the accusative object is etymologically related to its verb (cf. Luke 12:50: βάπτισμα ... βαπτισθῆναι). See Wallace, *Greek Grammar*, 189–90; BDF, 153(2).

imagery related to baptism and the Lord's Supper, both of which symbolize Christ's sacrificial death.

10:39–40 They answered, "We are able!" Jesus said to them, "The cup that I drink you will drink, and the baptism I am baptized with you will be baptized with. But to sit at my right or my left is not for me to grant; rather, it is for those for whom it has been prepared." (οἱ δὲ εἶπαν αὐτῷ· δυνάμεθα. ὁ δὲ Ἰησοῦς εἶπεν αὐτοῖς· τὸ ποτήριον ὃ ἐγὼ πίνω πίεσθε καὶ τὸ βάπτισμα ὃ ἐγὼ βαπτίζομαι βαπτισθήσεσθε, τὸ δὲ καθίσαι ἐκ δεξιῶν μου ἢ ἐξ εὐωνύμων οὐκ ἔστιν ἐμὸν δοῦναι, ἀλλ᾽ οἷς ἡτοίμασται). James and John hear Jesus' words as a call to greater commitment and so express their willingness to suffer and die for him: "We are able!" They are likely thinking of the potential of martyrdom in the messianic war that is coming. Though their request for the best seats was misguided, they show some courage (and overzealous pride?) in their willingness to answer Jesus' call to give up their lives for him and his cause (9:34–35).

Jesus responds by affirming the cost of their commitment. Though they cannot drink Jesus' cup, they will indeed suffer and so in their own way experience Jesus' "cup" and "baptism." Many commentators have claimed that this prediction was invented after the fact (*vaticinium ex eventu*) in light of the martyrdom of James by Herod Agrippa I in the early 40s (Acts 12:2).[17] If so, one would expect greater details and a reference to James alone. Though some later traditions claim John was martyred with his brother (probably arising to harmonize with this passage),[18] the earlier and more

reliable traditions have him outliving the other apostles and continuing a ministry in Asia Minor late into the first century.[19] It is unlikely that the church would invent a saying that contradicted the tradition as they knew it.[20]

Remarkably, Jesus then states that granting such places of honor is not his prerogative, but "[It is granted] for those for whom it has been prepared" (οἷς ἡτοίμασται; v. 40). "It has been prepared" is a divine passive, indicating that the prerogative belongs to God alone.[21] Again we have evidence of authenticity, since the church is unlikely to have invented a saying in which Jesus speaks of the limitation of his own authority (cf. 13:32).

So who are those "for whom it has been prepared"? The text does not say and perhaps that is the point: only God determines such things.[22] Or perhaps the key is in the larger context, where Jesus says that the first will be last (9:35), the lowliest receive the kingdom (10:15), and servants and slaves are made first and greatest (10:44). It is not by merit but by humble submission to God that rank is determined in the kingdom. Various commentators have pointed to the irony that in Mark's narrative the only characters to assume positions on the right and left of Jesus are the two rebels crucified beside him, "one on his right and one on his left" (ἕνα ἐκ δεξιῶν καὶ ἕνα ἐξ εὐωνύμων αὐτοῦ; 15:27).[23]

10:41 When the ten heard this, they became indignant toward James and John (Καὶ ἀκούσαντες οἱ δέκα ἤρξαντο ἀγανακτεῖν περὶ Ἰακώβου καὶ Ἰωάννου). The scheme of James and John has not gone unnoticed by the other disciples, who now

---

17. So Bultmann, *History,* 24; Klosterman, *Markusevangelium,* 107; B. H. Branscomb, *The Gospel of Mark* (MNTC; London: Hodder & Stoughton, 1937), 60; Lohmeyer, *Markus,* 223.

18. The tradition comes from Philip of Side (c. AD 430) and two martyrologies from Edessa and Carthage (5th–6th centuries). See Brown, *John,* 1:lxxxix.

19. Irenaeus, *Haer.* 3.1.1–2; 3.3.4; cf. Rev 1:9–11.

20. Those defending the historicity include Hooker, *Mark,*

247; Schweizer, *Good News,* 218; Gundry, *Mark,* 584–85; France, *Mark,* 417; Evans, *Mark 8:27–16:20,* 117–18; Stein, *Mark,* 486.

21. Matthew makes this explicit by adding, "prepared *by my Father*" (20:23).

22. Boring, *Mark,* 301.

23. Hooker, *Mark,* 247; Evans, *Mark 8:27–16:20,* 118; France, *Mark,* 418.

become indignant (ἀγανακτέω) toward them.[24] Though this verb can mean righteous indignation, as in Jesus' response to the disciples' rebuke of the children (10:14; cf. 2 Cor 7:11; 4 Macc 4:21; Wis 5:2), here it must mean selfish anger or indignation (cf. 14:4; Matt 21:15; 26:8; Luke 13:14; Wis 12:27). They are angry not because of the two brothers' callous insensitivity to Jesus' teaching, but because James and John have beaten them to the punch. They want the best seats in the kingdom! This interpretation fits the Markan portrayal of the disciples, who have not only demonstrated spiritual insensitivity, but have argued over who is the greatest (9:34) and have sought to guard Jesus' authority for themselves (9:38) and to keep "insignificant" children away from him (10:13).

10:42 – 44 After calling them together, Jesus said to them, "You know that those recognized as rulers of the Gentiles lord it over them, and their great ones exercise dominion over them. But it is not so among you. Rather, whoever wants to be great among you will be your servant, and whoever wants to be first will be slave of all." (καὶ προσκαλεσάμενος αὐτοὺς ὁ Ἰησοῦς λέγει αὐτοῖς· οἴδατε ὅτι οἱ δοκοῦντες ἄρχειν τῶν ἐθνῶν κατακυριεύουσιν αὐτῶν καὶ οἱ μεγάλοι αὐτῶν κατεξουσιάζουσιν αὐτῶν. οὐχ οὕτως δέ ἐστιν ἐν ὑμῖν, ἀλλ' ὃς ἂν θέλῃ μέγας γενέσθαι ἐν ὑμῖν ἔσται ὑμῶν διάκονος, καὶ ὃς ἂν θέλῃ ἐν ὑμῖν εἶναι πρῶτος ἔσται πάντων δοῦλος). Again Jesus calls the disciples together for private instruction.[25] They have consistently failed to respond to Jesus' teaching, and there is a ponderous sense of redundancy as Jesus summons them again for another lesson on servant leadership. This will serve as the climax of

his teaching on the suffering role of the Messiah and cross-bearing discipleship (8:31 – 38; 9:31 – 50; 10:32 – 45).

Jesus begins by contrasting leadership in the world with leadership in God's kingdom with two pairs of sayings, each in synonymous parallelism:

1. The World's Way ("You know that . . .")	
a. [the] rulers of the Gentiles	lord it over them
b. their great ones	exercise dominion over them
2. The Kingdom Way ("But it is not so with you . . .")	
a. whoever wants to be great	will be your servant
b. whoever wants to be first	will be slave of all.

"You know" (οἴδατε) introduces what is common knowledge through everyday experience. One did not need to look far in first-century Palestine to see the heavy-handed rule of the Romans and the Herodian dynasty. The world's rulers, Jesus says, rule by power and coercion. The two emphatic (κατα-) forms, "lord over" (κατακυριεύω; cf. 1 Pet 5:3) and "exercise dominion" (κατεξουσιάζω), emphasize a negative sense of power and oppression. The unusual expression "those seeming to rule" (οἱ δοκοῦντες ἄρχειν) may simply be an idiomatic way of saying, "those recognized as rulers";[26] or it may carry the more striking sense, "those who appear to rule." If the latter, Jesus is claiming that human power and dominion are merely illusory, since God is the only sovereign Lord.[27]

While this is the world's way of leadership, Jesus' followers are to operate under a different set of values. Using the present tense, Jesus does not so much command what they must do, but rather states the way things are: "It is not so among you" (οὐχ οὕτως . . . ἐστιν ἐν ὑμῖν).[28] As Edwards points

---

24. The Greek for "began to be indignant" (ἤρξαντο ἀγανακτεῖν) indicates the entrance into this state, hence our translation "became indignant."

25. For summoning the disciples, see 3:13; 6:7; 8:1, 34; 12:43. For private instruction, see 4:10, 34; 7:17 – 23; 9:28 – 29, 30, 35; 10:10 – 12, 32 – 34; 12:43 – 44; 13:3 – 4.

26. BDAG, 254.

27. Boring, *Mark*, 298.

28. The variant reading of the future tense (ἔσται, A C[3] f[1.13] 𝔐 boh[m]) is an assimilation either to the following future tense verbs or to the Matthean parallel, which has the future.

out: "Verse 43a is thus not an admonition to behave in a certain way as much as a description of the way things actually are in the kingdom of God."[29]

In two more lines of synonymous parallelism, the self-sacrificial nature of servant leadership is set out (vv. 43b – 44). The saying repeats and drives home what Jesus has already said in 9:35. Whoever wants to become great must be a servant and whoever wants to become first must be a slave. Though "servant" (διάκονος) and "slave" (δοῦλος) can be used synonymously, the latter is the more lowly term, indicating complete ownership and subjugation.[30]

This is further emphasized with the qualification that one must be slave "of all" (πάντων; cf. 9:35: "servant of all" [πάντων διάκονος]). So there is both repetition and intensification. To be first is better than being great, and to be "slave of all" is lower than a mere servant. The indication is of leadership that is radically other-centered, focused on meeting the needs of others rather than controlling others to meet one's own ends. The values of the kingdom turn the world's system upside down.

10:45 **"For even the Son of Man did not come to be served, but to serve, and to give his life as a ransom for many."** (καὶ γὰρ ὁ υἱὸς τοῦ ἀνθρώπου οὐκ ἦλθεν διακονηθῆναι ἀλλὰ διακονῆσαι καὶ δοῦναι τὴν ψυχὴν αὐτοῦ λύτρον ἀντὶ πολλῶν). The climax of Jesus' teaching comes as he applies this paradox to himself. The ultimate act of servant leadership is the Son of Man's sacrificial death as a ransom payment for the sins of the world.

As noted previously (see comments on 2:10 – 11), the primary background to Jesus' favorite self-designation ("Son of Man") is Dan 7:13 – 14,

where one like "a son of man" (Aramaic: *bar-'enāš* = a human being) comes with the clouds of heaven before the Ancient of Days (God himself). He is given authority, glory, and sovereign power, is worshiped by all nations and peoples, and receives an eternal reign and kingdom that will never be destroyed. This glorious and exalted picture of the Messiah explains why Jesus says *"even* [καί] the Son of Man did not come to be served, but to serve." No one would expect the One destined to receive eternal glory, worship, honor, and rule to come as a lowly servant. Still less would they expect him to "give his life as a ransom for many" (δοῦναι τὴν ψυχὴν αὐτοῦ λύτρον ἀντὶ πολλῶν).

The Greek for "ransom" (λύτρον) means "the price of release" and was especially used in Hellenistic Greek of the price paid for the manumission of slaves.[31] In the LXX the term is used of various types of payments, such as compensation for crimes (Exod 21:30; Num 35:31 – 32) and buying back inheritance land that has been sold due to poverty (Lev 25:26, 51 – 52). Since Israel's firstborn, whether human or animal, belonged to the Lord, a price was paid to redeem the firstborn son (Num 8:15).

The verb form, "redeem" (λυτρόω), could mean to free by paying a ransom, but was also used in the more general sense, "to liberate from an oppressive situation, set free, rescue, redeem."[32] It is commonly used in the LXX of God's deliverance of the nation Israel from slavery in Egypt (Exod 6:6; 15:13; Deut 7:8; 9:26, 13:6; etc.). Though the noun "ransom" (λύτρον) appears in the NT only here and in the Matthean parallel (20:28), the verb (λυτρόω) and its cognate nouns (ἀπολύτρωσις, "re-

---

29. Edwards, *Mark*, 325.

30. A διάκονος can be a "servant," "helper," "assistant," "agent," "courier," "deacon," "minister," and a range of other service roles and functions. While a δοῦλος could occupy any number of social positions, from a lowly galley slave to a

wealthy household manager, the primary connotation is that of ownership by another, for whom total allegiance is given.

31. BDAG, 606.

32. Ibid.

demption"; ἀντίλυτρον, "ransom") are common in the NT to describe the redemption accomplished through the sacrificial death of Christ.[33] Ephesians 1:7 says that in Christ "we have redemption through his blood, the forgiveness of sins." The sense here in Mark is that the Son of Man's death will pay the necessary price to set his people free.

Though the preposition "for" (ἀντί) can mean simply "on behalf of" or "for," its more common sense is that of substitution, "in place of" or "instead of."[34] In Matt 2:22 Archelaus is reigning "in place of" (ἀντί) his father Herod, and in Matt 5:38 Jesus cites the OT law, "Eye for [ἀντί] eye, and tooth for [ἀντί] tooth" (cf. Exod 21:24). In collocational relationship with "ransom" (λύτρον), the two senses of the preposition are essentially the same, since a ransom payment is both "on behalf of" and "in place of" the person who is freed. The ransom payment in this case is "his life" (τὴν ψυχὴν αὐτοῦ); the Son of Man gives his own life to provide redemption or release.[35]

The qualification "for many" (ἀντὶ πολλῶν) does not mean "for some, but not all," but instead contrasts the *one* who died with the *many* who are redeemed. A single life is given for the ransom of others.[36] Evidence for this is found in Romans 5, where the "one" and the "many" (5:15, 19) are parallel and equivalent to the "one" and the "all" (5:18), and in 1 Tim 2:6, where Jesus' death provides "a ransom *for all*" (ἀντίλυτρον ὑπὲρ πάντων).[37] The phrase almost certainly has as its background Isa 53:11 – 12, where the suffering Servant will "justify many" and "bear their iniquities" (see "In Depth: The Ransom Saying of Mark 10:45").

IN DEPTH: The Ransom Saying of Mark 10:45

Mark 10:45, which may be seen as a theme verse for the whole of Mark's gospel, has been a storm of controversy in two key areas: its conceptual background and its authenticity.

Background. The earlier consensus that the background of the ransom saying is to be found in the fourth of Isaiah's Servant Songs (Isa 52:13 – 53:12)[38] has been seriously challenged in recent years by a variety of scholars, including C. K. Barrett, M. D. Hooker, M. Casey, S. McKnight, and others.[39] Most assert that a more likely background is to be found in Dan 7 and/or in the experience of the

---

33. λυτρόω: Luke 24:21; Titus 2:14; 1 Pet 1:18; Heb 9:12; ἀπολύτρωσις: Rom 3:24; 8:23; 1 Cor 1:30; Eph 1:7; Col 1:14; ἀντίλυτρον: 1 Tim 2:6. For similar "purchase" imagery, but without the λυτρ- word group, see 1 Cor 6:20; 7:23.

34. BDAG, 87.

35. The church through the centuries has puzzled over and debated the nature of this "ransom." To whom was it paid? Some have claimed the ransom was paid to Satan (so Origen, *Comm. Matt.* 16:8; Gregory of Nyssa, *Great Catechism* 21 – 23); others, that it was paid to God (Gregory of Nazianzus, *Or. Bas.* 45.22; John Damascene, *Concerning the Orthodox Faith* 3.27; cited by Marcus, *Mark 9 – 16*, 757).

36. R. G. Bratcher and E. A. Nida, *Translator's Handbook*

on *Mark* (Leiden: Brill, 1961), 337.

37. Gnilka, *Markus*, 104; Stein, *Mark*, 489.

38. On this consensus, see I. Engnell, "The 'Ebed-Jahweh Songs and the Suffering Messiah in 'Deutero-Isaiah,'" *BJRL* 31 (1948): 54 – 64.

39. C. K. Barrett, "The Background of Mark 10:45," in *New Testament Essays* (ed. A. J. B. Higgins; Manchester: Manchester University Press, 1959), 1 – 18; Hooker, *Mark*, 129 – 31; idem, *Jesus and the Servant: The Influence of the Servant Concept of Deutero-Isaiah in the New Testament* (London: SPCK, 1959), 74 – 79; idem, *The Son of Man in Mark* (London: SPCK, 1967); Casey, *Aramaic Sources*, 209 – 17; McKnight, *Jesus and His Death*, 159 – 339.

Maccabean martyrs (2 Macc 7:37 – 38; 4 Macc 6:28 – 29; 17:21 – 22) than in the Isaianic Servant of the Lord.

Yet despite these challenges, the preponderance of evidence still points to an Isaianic background.

1. Critics point out that the verb for "serve" (διακονέω) in Mark 10:45 does not appear in the LXX and that Isa 52:13 LXX uses another word for "servant" (παῖς), not the ones used in Mark 10:43 – 44 ("servant" [διάκονος]; "slave" [δοῦλος]). Yet the terms are conceptually similar and the cognate verb "to serve" (δουλεύω) does appear with reference to the Servant in Isa 53:11 LXX. The language of service that permeates Mark 10:43 – 45 conceptually parallels the role of the Servant, who sacrificially gives himself for others.

2. Despite Hooker's claim to the contrary, the phrase "to give his life" (δοῦναι τὴν ψυχὴν αὐτοῦ) in Mark 10:45 is close to Isa 53:12, where the servant "poured out his life unto death" (LXX: παρεδόθη εἰς θάνατον ἡ ψυχὴ αὐτοῦ; cf. 53:10b).

3. In Isa 53:10 the Lord makes the Servant's life a "an offering for sin," that is, a sacrifice for the sins of others. Similar language appears throughout the fourth Servant Song: he "took up our pain and bore our suffering" (Isa 53:4); he was "pierced for our transgressions" and "crushed for our iniquities" (53:5a); "the punishment that brought us peace was on him, and by his wounds we are healed" (53:5b); "the Lᴏʀᴅ has laid on him the iniquity of us all" (53:6); he "bore the sin of many, and made intercession for the transgressors" (53:12). Barrett and Hooker reject these allusions, since the LXX does not use the ransom/redemption (λύτρ-) word group. Yet as Evans asserts, "Mark 10:45 is not a translation of any portion of Isa 52:13 – 53:12 … it is a summary of the task of the Servant." And the conceptual similarities are striking.

4. Most important, the striking image of the *one* suffering for the *many* is common to Isa 53:11 – 12 and Mark 10:45 (cf. 14:24).

Though individually, none of these allusions is conclusive, together they make a compelling case that behind Jesus' words lies Isaiah's image of the Suffering Servant, who offers himself as a sacrifice for others.[40]

This does not mean that allusions to Daniel are absent. The title "Son of Man" certainly comes from Dan 7:13 – 14. The Messiah's role to serve rather than "be served" (διακονηθῆναι) may at first sight seem to contradict that of the Danielic

---

40. Recent defenders of an Isaianic background include Watts, *Isaiah's New Exodus in Mark*, 349 – 65; R. T. France, *Jesus and the Old Testament* (London: Tyndale, 1971), 116 – 21; W. J. Moulder, "The Old Testament Background and Interpretation of Mark x. 45," *NTS* 24 (1977 – 78): 120 – 27; Martin Hengel, *The Atonement: The Origins of the Doctrine in the New Testament* (Philadelphia: Fortress, 1981), 49 – 65; Pesch, *Markusevangelium*, 2:163 – 64; Peter Stuhlmacher, *Jesus of Nazareth: Christ of Faith* (Peabody, MA: Hendrickson, 1993), 49 – 57; J. Painter, *Mark's Gospel* (New Testament Readings; London: Routledge, 1997), 150; Evans, *Mark 8:27 – 16:20*, 120 – 24; and others.

son of man, who will be given glory, honor, and worship (Dan 7:14). Yet in the broader context of Daniel 7, the son of man is identified in some sense with the corporate people of God, who themselves suffer at the hands of an evil ruler (the "horn") before being vindicated and receiving sovereignty, power, and an eternal kingdom (7:21 – 22, 26 – 27). The two portraits may therefore be seen to complement rather than contradict one another. Evans concludes:

> The Danielic elements do not necessarily compete with or contradict the underlying elements from Isaiah. The two scriptural traditions complement each other, with the Suffering Servant of Isa 53 redefining the mission and destiny of the "son of man" of Dan 7. Indeed, the "son of man" will someday "be served," but he first must serve, even suffer and die, as the Servant of the Lord.[41]

Authenticity. The question of the historicity of Mark 10:45 is a more difficult (and subjective) one. Did Jesus attribute atoning significance to his own death? One's answer to this question depends to a large extent on one's view of the gospel tradition as a whole. Opponents of historicity point especially to the paucity of additional evidence in Mark that Jesus understood his death as a sacrifice of atonement and the parallel in Luke 22:25 – 28, which replaces Jesus' ransom saying with a simple statement of servanthood: "But I am among you as one who serves" (22:27).[42] They argue that this latter is the original form and Mark has added the ransom saying under the influence of Pauline theology.[43] Yet sacrificial language does appear in the eucharistic words of Jesus, which have a strong claim to authenticity (see comments on 14:22 – 25).

A good number of commentators have come out in defense of authenticity.[44] Though a detailed defense is beyond our scope, the following points should be noted. (1) The claim that the saying was created under the influence of Pauline atonement theology is rendered less likely since Paul never uses "ransom" (λύτρον) for the redemption available through Christ.[45] (2) The saying has a strong Semitic flavor and so is likely to have arisen with Jesus or the early Palestinian church rather than in a later Hellenistic context.[46] (3) The concept of the suffering or death of one person providing atonement or benefit

41. Evans, *Mark 8:27 – 16:20*, 123.

42. Klosterman, *Markusevangelium*, 108 – 9; Bultmann, *History*, 14; Pesch, *Markusevangelium*, 2:162 – 64; S. K. Williams, *Jesus' Death as Saving Event: The Background and Origin of a Concept* (HDR 2; Missoula, MT: Scholars, 1975), 211 – 12.

43. Branscomb, *Mark*, 190 – 91; Nineham, *Mark*, 280 – 81.

44. See, e.g., Taylor, *Mark*, 119; idem, "The Origin of the Markan Passion-Sayings," *New Testament Essays* (London: Epworth, 1970), 60 – 71; Cranfield, *Mark*, 343 – 44; Hooker, *The Son of Man in Mark*, 140 – 47; Barrett, "Background of Mark 10:45," 1 – 18; J. Jeremias, *TDNT*, 5:706 – 15; Gundry, *Mark*, 587 – 93; France, *Jesus and the Old Testament*, 116 – 21; Evans, *Mark 8:27 – 16:20*, 124 – 25; Stein, *Mark*, 288 – 89.

45. Cranfield, *Mark*, 344.

46. S. Kim, *The Son of Man as the Son of God* (Grand Rapids: Eerdmans, 1985), 39; Witherington, *Mark*, 289.

for others was not alien to Jesus' world, for it appears in Maccabean and other Jewish sources.[47] (4) The use of "son of man" itself points to the authenticity of the saying, since the Semitic phrase (which is natural Hebrew and Aramaic, but awkward Greek and Latin) certainly has its origin in the ministry of Jesus rather than in the later Hellenistic church. (5) Similarly, the description of Jesus as "servant" "would be open to serious misunderstanding, even ridicule," in the Greco-Roman world. As the gospel moved out of its Jewish and Palestinian contexts, titles like "Lord," "Son of God," and "Savior" became preferred titles for Jesus. In short, both the Son of Man traditions arising from Daniel 7 and the Servant traditions of Isaiah "are better explained as originating in the teaching of Jesus than in the early church."[48]

Theology in Application

This passage represents the climax of the central section of Mark's gospel (8:22 – 10:52) and is thematic for the entire gospel, concluding with what may be seen as the "theme verse" of the gospel (10:45). Three themes are prominent.

The Sovereign Purpose of God

The third passion prediction (9:32 – 34), like the previous two (8:31; 9:31), points to God's sovereignty in Jesus' life, death, and resurrection. The Messiah will suffer and die, but after suffering comes vindication. These events are no accident or catastrophe, but were all along part of God's purpose and plan. The additional details provided here, that Jesus will be handed over to the Gentiles and will be mocked, spit on, and flogged, drive home the point that the path ahead has been mapped out by God, who is in control of the details.

Jesus' authority is once again on center stage. He is out in front, leading the way, and understands fully the events that await him in Jerusalem. The sense of divine necessity here (cf. 8:31) comes out even more strongly in Luke's writings, which repeatedly emphasize the necessity ($\delta\epsilon\hat{\iota}$) and paradox of the passion. Though wicked people put Jesus to death, this was part of the plan of God, who vindicated Jesus through the resurrection (Luke 13:33; 17:25; 24:7, 26, 44; Acts 1:16; 2:23 – 24; 3:13 – 15; 4:10 – 12, 27 – 28; 10:39 – 40; 13:27 – 31; 17:3).

The Messiah's passion reminds God's people that the path to glory is through

47. 2 Macc 7:37 – 38; 4 Macc 6:27 – 29; 17:22; 18:4; 1QS 5:6; 11QtgJob 38:2 – 3; Pr Azar 3:38 – 40; *L.A.E.* 3:1; cf. Evans, *Mark 8:27 – 16:20*, 122; McKnight, *Jesus and His Death*, 168 – 71; Witherington, *Mark*, 289.

48. Evans, *Mark 8:27 – 16:20*, 124.

suffering. Jesus cannot promise James and John the chief seats in the kingdom, but he can assure them that they will share in his sufferings. For Paul, sharing in Christ's suffering is an essential part of his calling, as he fills up in his flesh "what is still lacking in regard to Christ's afflictions" (Col 1:24) and comes to know Christ by "participation in his sufferings" and "becoming like him in his death" (Phil 3:10). Peter too assures the Christians of Asia Minor that their suffering is a part of their calling "in Christ" and that Christ has left an example that they should follow (1 Pet 2:21; 4:12 – 13).

Yet the reality of suffering always comes with the promise of vindication. The resurrection of the Messiah is confirmation that his followers will also be vindicated. Throughout the NT believers are called to persevere in light of the certainty of their redemption, which is both a present reality and a future hope. The writer to the Hebrews calls on his readers to persevere in the race of faith with their eyes set on Jesus, who "for the joy set before him … endured the cross, scorning its shame, and sat down at the right hand of the throne of God" (Heb 12:2). Paul reminds the persecuted Thessalonian believers that their hope is in Christ, whom God raised from the dead and "who rescues us from the coming wrath" (1 Thess 1:10). The exhortation and promise to believers in the book of Revelation is to persevere, because Christ is the Resurrected One: "I was dead, and now look, I am alive for ever and ever!" (Rev 1:18). And with vindication comes reward: "I am coming soon! My reward is with me" (22:12; cf. 3:11; 22:7, 20).

The Upside-Down Values of the Kingdom of God

By approaching Jesus for the best seats in the kingdom, James and John exhibit the natural human tendency for power and self-promotion. History is full of examples of leaders who achieved their position by coercion and manipulation. The church tends to emulate the world's leadership style. We hold up as models those in positions of power and influence — celebrities, athletes, musicians, politicians, business leaders — rather than those who have devoted themselves to "lowly" service to others: the custodian with thirty years of faithful service, the aid worker in a Third World country, the volunteer gardener who keeps the church grounds in top shape, the caregiver who selflessly meets the needs of an Alzheimer's-stricken spouse or parent.

We tend to judge leaders by their number of followers, the loyalty of their fans, and the influence they can wield. Potential Christian leaders often enter the ministry because they love to be up front or because of the recognition they receive. A student once told me his goal after college was to earn a doctoral degree so that he could write books and go on a speaking tour. While I'd like to believe this just reflected his passion for the cause of Christ, I suspect he was craving the recognition he saw other Christian leaders receiving.

Jesus says this attitude reflects the world's value system: "Not so among you." To be first, you have to be last. To lead, you have to serve. True Christian leaders shun honor and recognition. When praised, they respond, "We have only done our duty" (Luke 17:10). While James and John are talking about *getting* front-row seats, Jesus is talking about *giving up* his life for others. The corollary to this is that true discipleship is radically other-centered. Paul says it best in Philippians 2:3 – 4: "Do nothing out of selfish ambition or vain conceit. Rather, in humility value others above yourselves, not looking to your own interests but each of you to the interests of the others." This is a ministry that focuses not on self-aggrandizing *power,* but on self-sacrificial *empowerment,* encouraging and helping others to be all God has called them to be.

Christ's Death as a Redeeming Sacrifice

In addition to its message on leadership and discipleship, this passage also has important soteriological significance. Jesus' death is presented as a ransom payment that delivers God's people. The seeds are certainly here for the atonement theology developed in greater detail in the NT letters. Paul identifies Jesus' death on the cross as a sacrifice of atonement (ἱλαστήριον) that accomplishes our redemption, the forgiveness of our sins (Rom 3:24 – 25; 5:9; Eph 1:7, 14; Col 1:14). For the writer to the Hebrews, Jesus' death represents his once-for-all entrance into the Most Holy Place to achieve eternal redemption (Heb 7:27; 9:11 – 12, 28; 10:11 – 14). For John, Jesus is "the atoning sacrifice [ἱλασμός] for our sins, and not only for ours but also for the sins of the whole world" (1 John 2:2; cf. 4:10). Peter says we were not redeemed with perishable things like silver and gold, but "with the precious blood of Christ, a lamb without blemish or defect" (1 Pet 1:18 – 19). And in Revelation, Jesus is the Lamb who was slain, who deserves all glory, honor, and power because with his blood he purchased people from every tribe, language, people, and nation (Rev 5:9 – 11; 7:14; 12:11; 13:8).

Mark 10:46 – 52

Literary Context

This is the last healing miracle in Mark's gospel and the final episode before Jesus' entrance into Jerusalem. At first sight the miracle seems a bit out of place, since most of Mark's miracles appear in the first third of his gospel, where Jesus' messianic authority is revealed through healings, exorcisms, and nature miracles. One likely reason the miracle appears here is because of its traditional association with Jericho (v. 46), which is near Jerusalem. Mark may have introduced it at this point for geographical and chronological reasons.

At the same time the miracle serves well Mark's literary and theological interests. The healing of the blind man forms an inclusio with the similar healing in 8:22 – 26, framing this section of the gospel (8:22 – 10:45). The two blind men who received their sight stand in contrast to the spiritual blindness of the religious leaders and the blurred vision of the disciples. This passage also relates to what follows. The "Son of David" cry of the blind man prepares for Jesus' entrance into Jerusalem (11:1 – 11), where the pilgrims cry out, "Blessed is the coming kingdom of our father David!" (11:10). The episode reminds readers that Jesus is indeed the Davidic Messiah, who has come to Jerusalem to fulfill the messianic task.

Main Idea

The healing of Bartimaeus forms a fitting conclusion to Jesus' journey to Jerusalem and brings together a number of important Markan themes: (1) the identification of Jesus as the Davidic Messiah and Son of God; (2) his compassion for the poor and the outcast, recipients of God's grace; (3) the contrast between the spiritual *insight* of the blind man and the spiritual *blindness* of the disciples; and (4) the renewal of sight as symbolic of the promised restoration of creation in the new age of salvation (Isa 35:5 – 6).

Translation

Mark 10:46 – 52

46a	Setting	**They came to Jericho.**
b	setting (spatial)	And as he was leaving Jericho
c	setting (social)	with his disciples and a significant crowd,
d	Character entrance	**the son of Timaeus (Bartimaeus), a blind beggar, was sitting beside the road.**
47a		When he heard that it was Jesus of Nazareth,
b	Entreaty	**he began to cry out and say,**
c		*"Son of David, Jesus, have mercy on me!"*
48a	Response to 47	**Many rebuked him, telling him to be quiet,**
b	Entreaty	but **he cried out all the more,**
c		*"Son of David, have mercy on me!"*
49a	Response to 47, 48b-c	Stopping, **Jesus said,**
b		*"Call him over."*
c	Response	So **they called to the blind man, saying,**
d		*"It's alright. Get up! He's calling you."*
50a		Throwing off his cloak and jumping up,
b	Action	**he came to Jesus.**
51a	Response	Responding,
b		**Jesus said to him,**
c	Question	*"What do you want me to do for you?"*
d	Answer/Entreaty	**The blind man said to him,**
e		*"Rabbi, I want to see."*
52a	Response	**Jesus said to him,**
b	healing command	*"Go, your faith has saved you."*
c	Healing	**Immediately he could see!**
d	Response to 52c	And **he began following him on the road.**

Structure

The episode is a healing miracle and an implicit call narrative. It includes a statement of the context and the problem (v. 46a), a cry for help and an obstacle introduced (vv. 46 – 48), Jesus' response and dialogue with the man (vv. 49 – 51), and the healing and its result (v. 52). The result in this case is not an amazed response by the onlookers, but the man's following of Jesus along the way, signifying his obedience to the call of discipleship.

Exegetical Outline

➡ **1. The Context (10:46a-c)**

2. The Request of the Blind Man (10:46d – 48)

    a. Bartimaeus's situation (10:46d)

    b. Bartimaeus's cry (10:47)

    c. The people's rebuke (10:48a)

    d. Bartimaeus's persistence (10:48b-c)

3. Jesus Heals the Blind Man (10:49 – 52)

    a. Jesus calls for Bartimaeus (10:49 – 50)

    b. Jesus' dialogue with Bartimaeus (10:51)

    c. The healing and response (10:52)

Explanation of the Text

10:46 They came to Jericho. And as he was leaving Jericho with his disciples and a significant crowd, the son of Timaeus (Bartimaeus), a blind beggar, was sitting beside the road (Καὶ ἔρχονται εἰς Ἰεριχώ. Καὶ ἐκπορευομένου αὐτοῦ ἀπὸ Ἰεριχὼ καὶ τῶν μαθητῶν αὐτοῦ καὶ ὄχλου ἱκανοῦ ὁ υἱὸς Τιμαίου Βαρτιμαῖος, τυφλὸς προσαίτης, ἐκάθητο παρὰ τὴν ὁδόν). Jericho is located in an oasis in the Judean desert about seventeen miles northeast of Jerusalem and ten miles north of the Dead Sea.[1] It is among the oldest cities in the world, with settlements dating back to 9,000 BC. It is also perhaps the lowest, lying 825 feet below sea level.

A winding seventeen-mile road, made famous in Luke's parable of the good Samaritan, rises 3,500 feet to Jerusalem (10:30). There were two Jerichos in Jesus' day. The old city, which was now either uninhabited or sparsely settled, was the first city conquered by Joshua and the Israelites when they entered the Promised Land (Josh 5). The new city, located a mile to the south, had been built by the Hasmoneans and expanded by Herod the Great.

Luke says this event occurred as Jesus approached Jerusalem (Luke 18:35), while Mark locates it "as he was leaving" (ἐκπορευομένου αὐτοῦ). Luke may have reordered the account to place the healing before Jesus encounters Zacchaeus (19:1 – 10).[2] Or perhaps Luke's idiom (ἐν τῷ ἐγγίζειν

---

1. See Josephus, *J.W.* 4.8.3 §§459 – 475.

2. So Evans, *Mark 8:27 – 16:20*, 131; Fitzmyer, *Luke*, 2:1213.

αὐτὸν εἰς Ἰεριχὼ) actually means "in the vicinity of Jericho."[3] The large crowd may represent pilgrims heading to Jerusalem for the Passover (Ps 42:4),[4] but throughout Mark's narrative the crowds demonstrate Jesus' enormous popularity because of his authoritative teaching and healing.[5]

Beggars were a common sight in the ancient Near East (cf. John 9:8). Without a social welfare system, begging was the only means of support for those who could not work or did not have family to care for them. A location on a major thoroughfare was a prime spot, particularly when religious-minded crowds were heading to Jerusalem for Passover (cf. the beggar at the temple gates in Acts 3:1 – 2).

Only Mark among the Synoptics names the man, and this is the only time he identifies a recipient of Jesus' healing by name (but cf. Jairus, the father of a raised girl; 5:22).[6] Perhaps Bartimaeus was known to Mark's readers because of his later role in the church. Mark provides his readers with a Greek translation, "the son of Timaeus" (ὁ υἱὸς Τιμαίου), followed by the Aramaic name, "Bartimaeus" (Βαρτιμαῖος). The order is unusual, since Mark normally provides the Aramaic name first, followed by "which means ..." (ὅ ἐστιν; 3:17; 7:11, 34; ὅ ἐστιν μεθερμηνευόμενον; 5:41). Perhaps the order is because his father, Timaeus, was also known to the church. The name itself is also unusual because *bar* ("son of") is Aramaic, but "Ti-maeus" is a common Greek name (Τιμαῖος). The latter, however, may be derived from a Hebrew name like *Ṭim'ay*.[7]

10:47 When he heard that it was Jesus of Nazareth, he began to cry out and say, "Son of David, Jesus, have mercy on me!" (καὶ ἀκούσας ὅτι Ἰησοῦς ὁ Ναζαρηνός ἐστιν ἤρξατο κράζειν καὶ λέγειν· υἱὲ Δαυὶδ Ἰησοῦ, ἐλέησόν με). "Jesus" (Ἰησοῦς = Joshua; Yeshua) was a common first-century name, so "of Nazareth" or "the Nazarene" (ὁ Ναζαρηνός)[8] was used to distinguish him from others. The blind man cries to Jesus as "Son of David," a title that appears to have just been coming into common use in Jesus' day as a designation for the Messiah (see "In Depth: The Messiah as 'Son of David'" at 10:47).

This title is particularly surprising in the context of Mark's narrative. While Matthew and Luke both have birth narratives that emphasize Jesus' Davidic ancestry (Matt 1:1, 6, 17, 20; Luke 1:27, 32, 69; 2:4, 11), and "Son of David" is Matthew's favorite messianic title for Jesus (1:1; 9:27; 12:23; 15:22, 20:30 – 31; 21:15; 22:42), nowhere else in Mark is Jesus' Davidic ancestry mentioned. The only other reference to Davidic ancestry is in 12:35, where Jesus raises the enigmatic question from Ps 110:1 – 2 of how the Messiah can be both David's "son" and David's "Lord." While some commentators have argued that Jesus here rejects the

---

3. S. E. Porter, "'In the Vicinity of Jericho': Luke 18:35 in the Light of Its Synoptic Parallels," *BBR* 2 (1992): 91 – 104. Much less likely is the proposal of P. Keller ("Zur Lokalisierung der Blindenheilung bei Jericho," *Bib* 15 [1934]: 411 – 18) that Jesus was between the two cities, leaving old Jericho (Mark) and entering new (Luke).

4. Lane, *Mark*, 386 – 87.

5. Mark 1:33 – 34, 37; 2:2, 4, 13; 3:7 – 9, 20; 4:1, 36; 5:21, 24, 30 – 32; 6:14 – 15, 31 – 34; 7:24; 8:1 – 3; 9:14 – 15, 30.

6. Matthew refers to two blind men, both in his parallel to this episode (Matt 20:30) and in the possible doublet of 9:27 – 31 (cf. 8:28 – 34, where Matthew has two demoniacs to Mark's one). Many commentators attribute this to Matthean redaction, perhaps as further verification of the miracle since the

law required two witnesses (cf. 9:27 – 31). Other (harmonizing) solutions are that Matthew is drawing from another tradition that recalled two blind men, or that Mark intentionally focuses on the one because only he remained a disciple of Jesus.

7. Cranfield, *Mark*, 344; France, *Mark*, 423. See Collins, *Mark*, 508 – 9, for various proposals about the etymology and significance of the name.

8. Jesus is variously referred to with the adjectives Ναζαρηνός (6x) or Ναζωραῖος (13x) in the Gospels and Acts, both meaning "the Nazarene" or "the one from Nazareth." Occasionally he is called "Jesus from Nazareth" (Ἰησοῦς ὁ ἀπὸ Ναζαρὲθ, Matt 21:11; John 1:45; Acts 10:38). Mark always uses Ναζαρηνός (1:24; 10:47; 14:67; 16:6), though, not surprisingly, there are many textual variants.

title,[9] Mark gives no indication of this. Indeed, the triumphal entry that follows shows that Mark affirms traditional Davidic expectations for the Messiah, even as he affirms that the Messiah's surprising role is to suffer and die as a ransom for sins (10:45).

From a narrative perspective, the present passage thus prepares the reader for Jesus' approach to Jerusalem, where the crowds will herald "the coming kingdom of our father David" (11:10).[10] Up to this point, Peter is the only human character openly to acknowledge Jesus as the Messiah (8:29). Now, as Jesus is about to enter Jerusalem, a blind beggar shows remarkable spiritual insight by recognizing him as the coming Davidic king.

IN DEPTH: The Messiah as "Son of David"

The promise of a king from David's line arose from the OT Davidic promise tradition (2 Sam 7:11 – 16; Ps 89), and Davidic ancestry became a key component of messianic hope in the prophets (Isa 9:1 – 5; 11:1 – 10; Jer 23:5 – 6; Ezek 34:23 – 24, 37:24 – 25; Mic 5:1 – 5; see "In Depth: Jewish Expectations for the 'Messiah'" at 8:29). The first use of the title "Son of David" in extant Jewish literature is in *Pss. Sol.* 17:21, a work composed in the middle of the first century BC.[11] After describing God's choice of David as king and the "despoiling" of the Davidic throne by arrogant usurpers (the Hasmonean priest-kings), the psalmist cries out to God: "See, Lord, and raise up for them their king, the son of David, to rule over your servant Israel.... Undergird him with strength to destroy the unrighteous rulers, to purge Jerusalem from Gentiles ... to drive out sinners from the inheritance" (*Pss. Sol.* 17:21 – 22). The "unrighteous rulers" are the Hasmoneans, and the Gentiles are the Romans.[12]

In light of Jewish expectations for the Son of David as a conquering king and a righteous judge (*Pss. Sol.* 17), scholars have puzzled over Bartimaeus's use of the title in a request for healing. There seems to have been little expectation that the Davidic Messiah would be healer or miracle worker.[13] Some interpreters point to traditions related to David's son Solomon, whose great wisdom, according to Jewish tradition, included esoteric knowledge for healings and exorcisms.[14] Josephus claims that the wisdom God gave Solomon "enabled him to learn that skill which expels demons" and that "he composed such incantations also by which distempers are alleviated."[15] These traditions relate

---

9. Kelber, *The Kingdom in Mark*, 95; E. S. Johnson, "Mark 10:46 – 52: Blind Bartimaeus," *CBQ* 40 (1978): 191 – 204, 197.

10. C. Burger, *Jesus als Davidssohn* (FRLANT 98; Göttingen: Vandenhoeck & Ruprecht, 1970), 42 – 46, 49 – 63; Vernon K. Robbins, "The Healing of Blind Bartimaeus (10:46 – 52) in the Marcan Theology," *JBL* 92 (1973): 224 – 43; Jack D. Kingsbury, *The Christology of Mark's Gospel* (Philadelphia: Fortress, 1983), 102 – 8; Strauss, *Davidic Messiah*, 68 – 69.

11. Strauss, *Davidic Messiah*, 38 – 57.

12. The conquest of Jerusalem by the Roman general Pompey is alluded to in *Pss. Sol.* 2:1 – 2; 8:15 – 22; 17:11 – 18.

13. Hahn, *Titles*, 253 – 54; cf. 189 – 90; Klausner, *Messianic Idea*, 506: "the Messiah ... is never mentioned anywhere in the Tannaitic literature as a wonder-worker *per se.*"

14. D. C. Duling, "Solomon, Exorcism and the Son of David," *HTR* 68 (1975): 235 – 52.

15. Josephus, *Ant.* 8.2.5 §§46 – 49; cf. *T. Sol.* 20.

primarily to exorcism, however, and concern Solomon, not David's greater son, the Messiah.

A more likely background to the present passage are traditions related to the Messiah as righteous judge, who will champion the cause of the lowly, poor, and oppressed. Isaiah 11:4 says of the coming Davidic king that "with righteousness he will judge the needy, with justice he will give decisions for the poor of the earth." Psalm 72:12 similarly says the ideal Davidic king will "deliver the needy who cry out, the afflicted who have no one to help"—a striking parallel to Bartimaeus's circumstances and cry for help (cf. *Pss. Sol.* 17:40–41; *T. Jud.* 24.6; 2 Esd 12:34). These traditions, together with the Isaianic expectations for healing and restoration in the messianic age, when "the eyes of the blind [will] be opened, and the ears of the deaf unstopped" (Isa 35:5–6; cf. 29:18–19; 61:1), provide sufficient background to explain the passage. Of course, an even simpler explanation relates to the historical circumstances surrounding Jesus himself, who was both renowned as a mighty healer and rumored to be the Messiah. Putting these two together, Bartimaeus cries out for mercy and healing from the one he hopes will bring healing and deliverance to Israel.

How did Bartimaeus know of Jesus' Davidic ancestry? While he may have simply assumed it on the basis of messianic claims made about Jesus, it is likely that Jesus' family had an awareness of their Davidic ancestry. It is a question of significant scholarly debate whether Jesus was actually a descendant of David or whether this claim was a later invention by the church to provide him with legitimate messianic credentials.[16] In support of Jesus' Davidic descent is its independent attestation in the early pre-Pauline hymn of Rom 1:3–4 (cf. 2 Tim 2:8), the birth narratives and genealogies of Matthew (Matt 1:1, 6, 17, 20) and Luke (Luke 1:27, 32, 69; 2:4, 11; 3:31), the titles used of Jesus in Revelation (Rev 5:5; 22:16), the ironic affirmation in John 7:42, and implicitly in Heb 7:14 (Jesus' descent from Judah). Some argue that first-century Jews were unaware of their tribal ancestry, but this is refuted in the cases of Paul (Phil 3:5; a Benjamite), Hannah (Luke 2:36; from Asher), and Josephus, who provides his genealogy at the beginning of his autobiography (*Life* 1 §3). Awareness of Davidic ancestry even after the destruction of Jerusalem is attested by the early church chronicler Hegesippus (c. AD 110–180), who reports that several Roman emperors sought out Davidic descendants to eliminate potential claimants to Israel's throne.[17]

16. For arguments in support of Jesus' Davidic descent, see O. Cullmann, *The Christology of the New Testament* (NTL; trans. S. Guthrie and C. Hall; Philadelphia: Westminster, 1963), 127–33; W. Michaelis, "Die Davidssohnschaft Jesu als historisches und dogmatisches Problem," in *Der historische Jesus und der kerygmatische Christus: Beiträge zum Christusverständnis in Forschung und Verkündigung* (eds. H. Ristow and K.

Matthiae; Berlin: Evangelische Verlagsanstalt, 1963), 317–30; Hahn, *Titles*, 240ff.; Raymond E. Brown, *The Birth of the Messiah: A Commentary on the Infancy Narratives in Matthew and Luke* (New York: Doubleday, 1977), 505–12.

17. Cited by Eusebius, *Hist. eccl.* 3.12 (Vespasian); 3.19–20 (Domitian); 3.32 (Trajan).

10:48 Many rebuked him, telling him to be quiet, but he cried out all the more, "Son of David, have mercy on me!" (καὶ ἐπετίμων αὐτῷ πολλοὶ ἵνα σιωπήσῃ· ὁ δὲ πολλῷ μᾶλλον ἔκραζεν· υἱὲ Δαυίδ, ἐλέησόν με). The "many" (πολλοί) who rebuke the man are not identified, but one assumes they are the larger group of followers and pilgrims accompanying Jesus to Jerusalem, perhaps including the disciples. The reason for the rebuke is not given. Most likely a blind beggar was viewed as too socially insignificant to bother an important rabbi like Jesus. This fits the near context, where the disciples had rebuked those bringing (insignificant) children to Jesus (10:13–16).

The man will not be silenced, however, and he cries out all the more. Persistence is an important sign of faith in Mark's gospel and is frequently rewarded by Jesus (2:5; 5:23, 34; 7:27–29, 32; 8:22; 9:24). That Jesus does not rebuke or correct the man shows that he accepts for himself the Son of David title, even if he will qualify it in 12:35–37. From a narrative perspective, the repetition of the man's cry emphasizes Jesus' status as the Davidic Messiah.

10:49–50 Stopping, Jesus said, "Call him over." So they called to the blind man, saying, "It's alright. Get up! He's calling you." Throwing off his cloak and jumping up, he came to Jesus (καὶ στὰς ὁ Ἰησοῦς εἶπεν· φωνήσατε αὐτόν. καὶ φωνοῦσιν τὸν τυφλὸν λέγοντες αὐτῷ· θάρσει, ἔγειρε, φωνεῖ σε. ὁ δὲ ἀποβαλὼν τὸ ἱμάτιον αὐτοῦ ἀναπηδήσας ἦλθεν πρὸς τὸν Ἰησοῦν). The participle "standing" (στάς) does not mean that Jesus had been sitting and teaching,[18] but indicates stopping short or "standing still." As in the case of the sick woman in 5:30,

Jesus responds to a desperate plea for help amid the bustling crowd. The verb "call" (φωνέω) appears three times in the verse and here means to summon or call over (BDAG, 1071; cf. 9:35; 15:35; Tob 5:9).

The people then respond to Jesus' authority and change from obstacles to advocates. "It's alright" (θάρσει) is the present imperative of θαρσέω, which means "to be firm or resolute in the face of danger or adverse circumstances."[19] The verb appears seven times in the NT and always, except here, on the lips of Jesus.[20] It is translated variously as "cheer up" (NIV, NLT, GW), "take heart" (REB, ESV), "have courage" (NET, HCSB), or "don't be afraid" (CEV). In contemporary English we would probably say, "It's alright" or "It's okay."

The man responds immediately. His "garment" (τὸ ἱμάτιον) was likely an outer cloak, which may have been wrapped around his shoulders or laid on the ground to collect the alms. The emphasis seems to be on the man's exuberant joy rather than a symbolic sense of leaving his old life behind.[21] The suggestions that the man was only partially blind since he made his own way to Jesus[22] or that others guided him[23] both read too much into the narrative. Mark's only point is that Jesus calls and the man responds.

10:51 Responding, Jesus said to him, "What do you want me to do for you?" The blind man said to him, "Rabbi, I want to see." (καὶ ἀποκριθεὶς αὐτῷ ὁ Ἰησοῦς εἶπεν· τί σοι θέλεις ποιήσω; ὁ δὲ τυφλὸς εἶπεν αὐτῷ· ῥαββουνί, ἵνα ἀναβλέψω). As in the case of the Syrophoenician woman (7:24–30) and the man with the demon-possessed boy (9:14–29), Jesus does not immediately heal the

18. Contra Evans, *Mark 8:27–16:20*, 133.
19. BDAG, 444; Matt 9:2, 22; 14:27; Mark 6:50; 10:49; John 16:33; Act 23:11.
20. Matt 9:2, 22; 14:27; Mark 6:50; 10:49; John 16:33; Act 23:11.
21. France, *Mark*, 424; Stein, *Mark*, 496; contra Marshall, *Faith as a Theme*, 141–44.
22. Taylor, *Mark*, 449.
23. Evans, *Mark 8:27–16:20*, 133.

man, but instead carries on a dialogue intended to provoke faith. The question he asks is the same one he asked James and John in the previous episode (10:36), but the intention is different. There it was to expose their pride and manipulation; here it is to discern the nature of the request and to provoke greater faith. Does the man just want money, or can he trust Jesus to do the impossible?

The blind man addresses Jesus as "Rabbouni" (ῥαββουνί), a heightened form of "Rabbi" ("my lord/master"; 9:5; 11:21; 14:45), which appears only here and in John 20:16 (BDAG, 902). The reason Mark retains the Aramaic is not clear, though it may be intended "to crown Jesus with a numinous quality."[24] The man expresses his desire to see. The Greek, "in order that I might see" (ἵνα ἀναβλέψω), is ellipsis, with "I want" (θέλω) implied.

10:52 Jesus said to him, "Go, your faith has saved you." Immediately he could see! And he began following him on the road (καὶ ὁ Ἰησοῦς εἶπεν αὐτῷ· ὕπαγε, ἡ πίστις σου σέσωκέν σε. καὶ εὐθὺς ἀνέβλεψεν καὶ ἠκολούθει αὐτῷ ἐν τῇ ὁδῷ). Jesus often tells those healed to "go" (ὕπαγε). The reasons are varied: to gain priestly confirmation of the healing (1:44), to return to home or family (2:11; 5:19 [to bear testimony]), to reunite with the loved

ones (7:29). In all these the departure is also Jesus' dismissal, confirmation that the healing is complete (cf. 5:34).

The clause "your faith has healed/saved you" (ἡ πίστις σου σέσωκέν σε) also appears in 5:34. "Saved" can refer to physical rescue (13:20; 15:30, 31), preservation of life (3:4; 8:35), bodily healing/restoration (5:23, 28, 34; 6:56; 10:52), or spiritual salvation (8:35; 10:26; 13:13). For the interrelationship of these, see comments on 5:34. Both physical and spiritual restoration seem to be in view here, since the man apparently follows Jesus in discipleship.

Unlike in similar healings, Jesus does not touch the man (1:31, 41; 5:27, 41; 7:33–34; 8:22–26) or make an authoritative pronouncement (2:11; 3:5); he simply announces that the healing has taken place. Bartimaeus's sight is immediately restored (εὐθύς; contrast 8:24). The appropriate response is discipleship. The verb "he began following" (ἠκολούθει) is an ingressive (or inceptive) imperfect, stressing "the beginning of an action, with the implication that it continued for some time."[25] Though the verb in context means he accompanied Jesus along the road, it echoes previous calls to discipleship and implies a faith commitment (1:18; 2:14; 8:34; 10:21, 28).

Theology in Application

This episode sets the stage for the climax of Mark's story. Jesus prepares to enter Jerusalem as the Son of David, the messianic king predicted in Scripture. It is there that the next act in the drama of redemption will unfold. The faith and restoration of sight of the blind man stands in sharp contrast to the stubborn spiritual blindness of the religious leaders, who will oppose Jesus and plot his death. Three themes are particularly prominent in this passage.

---

24. Gundry, *Mark*, 595.   25. Wallace, *Greek Grammar*, 544.

The Humble Recipients of God's Grace

As the Messiah, God's agent of salvation, Jesus came not to be served but to serve, and to give his life as a ransom for many (10:45). Though unwavering in his commitment to reach his Jerusalem goal (10:32), Jesus still hears the cry of a blind beggar and turns aside to help. Bartimaeus is among the lowest of the low in Israel's society, a blind beggar with little more than a cloak to his name. Yet he is in a better position to receive God's blessings than the rich man Jesus encountered along the way (10:17 – 31). While the latter lists the good deeds he hopes will earn him eternal life, Bartimaeus cries out for mercy. He comes empty and so receives the gift of physical healing and spiritual sight. The rich man comes with his life full of riches and so has no room left for God's grace, the only thing that will provide entrance into the kingdom of God.

The poor, the sick, the blind, the oppressed, and the outcast — these are the recipients of God's grace. This theme began in Mark's gospel with the call of Levi. Jesus did not come to call the (self-)righteous but sinners, those who recognize their need of him (2:14 – 17). The prideful and self-righteous religious leaders reject the kingdom proclaimed and so receive blind eyes and deaf ears (4:11 – 12), while blind Bartimaeus regains his sight by crying out to God for mercy.

This theme of God's love for the lowly and the outcast is even more prominent in Luke's gospel. Mary, the humble servant of the Lord, magnifies her God, who humbles the proud and exalts the lowly (Luke 1:52). The repentant prodigal's return is celebrated with a great feast, while the self-righteous older brother refuses to attend (15:11 – 32). The poor beggar Lazarus, who suffered so much in life, now sits at the messianic banquet beside father Abraham, while the rich man languishes in Hades (16:19 – 31). The humble and repentant tax collector leaves the temple justified, while the self-righteous Pharisee receives no forgiveness — "For all those who exalt themselves will be humbled, and those who humble themselves will be exalted" (18:14).

This theme has two main applications for contemporary Christians. The first is to recognize our own status as sinners saved by God's grace alone. This should create both gratitude to God and humility toward one another. Second, God's love for the lost should prompt us, his people, to show the same love and concern for those on the margins of society, whether the poor, the disabled, or those weighed down by the burdens of life.

Jesus the Davidic Messiah

Beside Bartimaeus's cry for mercy lies his equally important acclamation that Jesus is the "Son of David." While at first sight the political and militaristic connotations associated with that title may seem out of place beside Mark's Servant Christology (cf. *Pss. Sol.* 17), in fact they are essential to it. Mark begins his gospel by announcing that Jesus is the "Messiah." This title, like Son of David, expresses the fundamental continuity between Israel's hopes for a Savior and the suffering role of the Messiah. Jesus is indeed Israel's king, the promised Messiah who will reign forever in power and righteousness on David's throne. In the book of Revelation, the climax of the biblical story, Jesus is the "Root and Offspring of David" (Rev 22:16), who comes in judgment riding on a white horse and with a sharp sword of judgment coming from his mouth (19:15). He will rule the nations with an iron rod (2:27; 5:5; 19:15; cf. Ps 2:9; Isa 11:4). Yet at his first coming, the Lion of the tribe of Judah is the Lamb who was slain (Rev 5:6 – 10), whose conquest is not over the legions of Rome, but over the powers of sin, Satan, and death. He is here to give his life as a ransom for sins and to break the powers of darkness.

Mark's Christology throughout his gospel is structured around this dual focus. In the first eight chapters Jesus comes on the scene as the mighty Messiah and Son of God with divine authority over disease, demons, and forces of nature (1:1 – 8:30). Yet beginning with Peter's confession, he reveals that the path to glory is through the cross (8:31 – 15:47). Now he beckons his disciples to take up their crosses and follow him through suffering to glory.

True Discipleship: Persistent Faith in the Face of Obstacles

In this episode Bartimaeus serves as a model disciple. Not only does he come humbly, asking for mercy, but when the crowd tries to silence him, he persists in his cry. The theme of faith despite obstacles is prominent in Mark's gospel. The friends of the paralyzed man must dig through a roof to reach Jesus (2:1 – 12); the woman with a blood disease has to overcome her fear in order to experience Jesus' healing touch (5:28); Jairus must continue to believe despite the news of his daughter's death (5:35 – 36); the Syrophoenician woman needs to persist in her request despite Jesus' initial rebuff that his mission is only to the Jews (7:27 – 28); and the father of the demonized boy must summon even greater faith in Jesus' ability to heal (9:24).

True discipleship involves not only a persevering faith, but also a willingness to leave all and follow Jesus. After being given his sight, Bartimaeus "follows Jesus on the way." The healing he has been given is an opportunity to follow the way of Jesus. Discipleship means giving up pride and self-interest and seeking God's kingdom first. It is significant that while James and John seek the best seats in the kingdom, Bartimaeus asks only for mercy. Curiously, Jesus asks both the same question: *What do you want me to do for you?* Yet their motives are very different. James and John seek power and glory; the blind man wants only to see. True discipleship means seeing the world God's way and submitting our life to his purpose and will.

Mark 11:1 – 11

Literary Context

Chapter 11 begins the last third of Mark's gospel (chs. 11 – 16), comprising Jesus' final ministry in Jerusalem (chs. 11 – 13), the Passion Narrative (chs. 14 – 15), and the resurrection (16:1 – 8). In Mark's gospel this is Jesus' first visit to Jerusalem. John, by contrast, has Jesus visiting Jerusalem on several occasions (2:13; 5:1; 10:22). This latter chronology makes sense historically, since Jewish males would regularly visit Jerusalem for the major festivals. Yet Mark (and the other Synoptics) moves Jesus' ministry in a relatively straight line from Galilee to its climax in Jerusalem.

Mark's gospel has sometimes been called a Passion Narrative with an introduction because so much emphasis is placed on this final week of Jesus' life. Although this period is known as Passion "Week," Mark himself does not specify that these events took place over the span of a single week.[1] The traditional chronology is derived instead from John's gospel, where Jesus arrives in Bethany at the home of Lazarus six days before Passover, and the triumphal entry takes place the next day (John 12:1, 12 – 15). Harmonizing with this Johannine sequence, we can arrive at the following chronology for Mark's Passion Narrative:

DAY	EVENTS IN MARK	PARALLELS
Sunday	Entrance into Jerusalem, return to Bethany (11:1 – 11)	Matt 21:1 – 11; Luke 19:28 – 44; John 12:12 – 19
Monday	Cursing the fig tree (11:12 – 14) Cleansing the temple, return to Bethany (11:15 – 19)	Matt 21:10 – 17; Luke 19:45 – 48
Tuesday (and Wednesday?)[2]	Discovery of the withered fig tree (11:20 – 25) Controversies with religious leaders (11:27 – 44) Olivet Discourse (13:1 – 37)	Matt 21:23 – 24:51; Luke 20:1 – 21:36

Continued on next page.

---

1. Edwards, *Mark*, 332 – 33, suggests that Mark has telescoped a much longer period, perhaps several months, into a single week for catechetical and liturgical purposes.

2. It is unknown which, if any, of these events occurred on Wednesday.

DAY	EVENTS IN MARK	PARALLELS
Thursday[3]	Anointing at Bethany, betrayal by Judas (14:1 – 11) Passover and Last Supper (14:12 – 31) Gethsemane (14:32 – 42) Arrest and Jewish trial (14:43 – 72)	Matt 26:1 – 75; Luke 22:1 – 65; John 13:1 – 18:27
Friday	Roman trial (15:1 – 15) Crucifixion (15:16 – 32) Burial (15:42 – 47)	Matt 27:1 – 66; Luke 23:1 – 56; John 18:28 – 19:42
Saturday	In the grave	Matt 27:62 – 66
Sunday	Resurrection (16:1 – 8)	Matt 28:1 – 20; Luke 24:1 – 49; John 20:1 – 29

More important for Mark than the chronology is the climactic significance of these events. Jesus' entrance into Jerusalem as the Davidic Messiah is followed by symbolic acts of judgment against the nation of Israel: first in cursing an unfruitful fig tree (11:12 – 14, 20 – 21), then in clearing the temple of money-changers and sellers (11:15 – 17). With these actions Jesus is laying down the gauntlet, challenging the legitimacy of Israel's spiritual leaders. They respond by questioning the source of his authority (11:27 – 28), engaging him in a series of controversies (11:27 – 12:33), and plotting against his life (11:18; 12:12). Jesus responds with great wisdom, repeatedly defeating the leaders in debate (11:27 – 33; 12:13 – 34) and portraying them as wicked tenant farmers over God's vineyard (12:1 – 12).

During this final week Jesus also teaches his disciples about the coming destruction of Jerusalem, which Israel's rejection of the Messiah will provoke (ch. 13), and at the Last Supper he speaks of his coming death and its significance as a new Passover, an atonement for sins that will establish the new covenant (14:17 – 25). All this sets the stage for the final denouement of the gospel in Jesus' arrest, trial, crucifixion, and resurrection (14:43 – 16:8).

III. The Suffering Way of the Messiah (8:22 – 15:47)
    A. Revelation of the Messiah's Suffering (8:22 – 10:52)
        10. Third Passion Prediction and the Request of James and John (10:32 – 45)
        11. Restoring Blind Bartimaeus's Sight (10:46 – 52)
→   **B. The Messiah Confronts Jerusalem (11:1 – 13:37)**
      1. The Triumphal Entry (11:1 – 11)
      2. Prophetic Action in the Temple and Cursing a Fig Tree (11:12 – 25)

3. Since the Jewish day begins in the evening, the Last Supper, arrest, and Jewish trial of Jesus would have occurred, by Jewish reckoning, on Friday (Thursday evening).

Main Idea

Jesus' approach to Jerusalem, traditionally called the "triumphal entry," is his first public declaration that he is indeed the Messiah. Though Jesus makes no explicit claim, his acquisition of the colt of a donkey to ride into Jerusalem is no doubt an intentional fulfillment of Zech 9:9, which predicts the coming of Israel's Messiah to Jerusalem.

Translation

Mark 11:1 – 11

1a	setting (temporal & spatial)	As they approached Jerusalem,
b	setting (spatial)	toward Bethphage (and Bethany) near the Mount of Olives,
c	Action	**he sent two of his disciples**
2a	Instruction/Command	and **said to them,**
b		*"Go to the village ahead of you.*
c		*As soon as you enter it,*
d		*you will find a colt tied there,*
e		*which no one has ever ridden.*
f		*Untie it and bring it here.*
3a	condition of 3c-d	*If anyone says to you,*
b		*'Why are you doing this?'*
c	result of 3a-b	*say,*
d		*'The Lord needs it and will send it back here again shortly.'"*
4a	Action	**They went and found a colt tied up at a doorway outside in the street,**
b	Action	and **they untied it.**
5a	Response to 4	**Some of the people standing there said to them,**
b		*"What are you doing untying the colt?"*
6a	Response to 5	**They answered them just as Jesus told them to,**
b	Response to 6a	and **they let them go.**
7a	Action (sequence)	**They brought the colt to Jesus and**
b	Action	**placed their garments on it,**
c	Action	and **he sat on it.**
8a	Response/Action	**Many people spread their garments on the road,**
b		while others spread branches they had cut in the field.
9a	Action	**Those who led the way and those who followed were shouting,**
b	acclamation	*"Hosanna! Blessed is the one who comes in the name of the Lord!*
		[Ps 118:25 – 26]
10a		*Blessed is the coming kingdom of our father David!*
b		*Hosanna in the highest!"*
11a	Action	**He entered Jerusalem and went into the temple courts.**
b	Action	**He looked around at everything,**
c	condition of 11d	but since it was already late,
d	Result of 11c	**he returned to Bethany with the Twelve.**

Structure

The passage has three parts: a description of the acquisition of the colt (vv. 1 – 6), Jesus' approach to Jerusalem and the joyful proclamation of the crowd (vv. 7 – 10), followed by Jesus' brief entrance into the temple courts and return to Bethany for the night (v. 11). Some have argued that the episode was created after the fact by the church to provide a fulfillment of Zech 9:9.[4] This is unlikely, however, since Mark's unadorned account does not quote the OT passage or refer specifically to its fulfillment. It is Matthew (Matt 21:5) and John (John 12:15) who introduce the OT passage to confirm the theological significance of the event.

The episode's odd and anticlimactic ending — that Jesus finds little going on in the temple because of the lateness of the hour and so returns to Bethany — also argues in favor of its authenticity. A story created by the church would likely end with an immediate temple clearing and a challenge by the religious leaders. (Both Matthew and Luke edit the story in this direction.) Mark records a historical reminiscence that nothing happened on Jesus' first entrance to the temple.

Exegetical Outline

➡ **1. Preparation for the Entrance to Jerusalem (11:1 – 6)**

    a. The approach to Jerusalem via the Mount of Olives (11:1a-b)

    b. Instructions for two disciples to bring a colt (11:1c – 3)

    c. The disciples acquire the colt (11:4 – 6)

2. The Approach to Jerusalem as Messianic King (11:7 – 10)

    a. Jesus mounted on the colt (11:7)

    b. Cloaks and branches for the path of the King (11:8)

    c. The shouts of the pilgrims (Ps 118:25 – 26) (11:9 – 10)

3. Entrance into the Temple Courts and Return to Bethany (11:11)

Explanation of the Text

11:1a-b As they approached Jerusalem, toward Bethphage (and Bethany) near the Mount of Olives (Καὶ ὅτε ἐγγίζουσιν εἰς Ἱεροσόλυμα εἰς Βηθφαγὴ καὶ Βηθανίαν πρὸς τὸ ὄρος τῶν ἐλαιῶν). Jesus is traveling west from Jericho (10:46) to Jerusalem. The village of Bethany was located about two miles from Jerusalem (John 11:18) on the eastern slopes

of the Mount of Olives. It was the hometown of Lazarus and his sisters, Mary and Martha (John 11:1; cf. Luke 10:38). Though Mark does not mention it, Jesus likely stayed with them while visiting Jerusalem, coming into Jerusalem from Bethany each morning (11:11 – 12; 14:3).

The precise location of Bethphage (which means

"house of figs") is unknown, though rabbinic references place it within the environs of Jerusalem, closer to Jerusalem than Bethany.[5] Mark's order therefore seems backward. Cranfield and others suggest he mentions Bethphage first since it is closer to Jesus' Jerusalem goal.[6] Edwards more plausibly points out that the old Roman road lay north of Bethany, running directly up to the summit of the Mount of Olives near Bethphage. Mark's meaning, then, would be, "And on their way to Jerusalem they came to Bethphage (near Bethany) on the Mount of Olives." Bethany is mentioned only because it is where Jesus will be spending nights while he stays in Jerusalem.[7]

The Mount of Olives lies directly east of Jerusalem, rising to 2,600 feet above sea level and overlooking the Temple Mount. The hill played an important eschatological role in Judaism and early Christianity. Zechariah 14:4 identifies it as the place where the Lord will stand on the day of judgment (cf. Ezek 11:23; 43:2). This is significant since Jesus will approach Jerusalem fulfilling another eschatological passage in Zechariah (Zech 9:9). In Acts, Jesus ascends to heaven from the Mount of Olives, and the angels will announce his return in the same manner (Acts 1:11 – 12).[8]

11:1c – 2 He sent two of his disciples and said to them, "Go to the village ahead of you. As soon as you enter it, you will find a colt tied there, which no one has ever ridden. Untie it and bring it here." (ἀποστέλλει δύο τῶν μαθητῶν αὐτοῦ καὶ λέγει αὐτοῖς· ὑπάγετε εἰς τὴν κώμην τὴν κατέναντι ὑμῶν, καὶ εὐθὺς εἰσπορευόμενοι εἰς αὐτὴν εὑρήσετε πῶλον δεδεμένον ἐφ᾽ ὃν οὐδεὶς οὔπω ἀνθρώπων ἐκάθισεν· λύσατε αὐτὸν καὶ φέρετε). From the Mount of Olives Jesus sends two (unnamed) disciples to procure the animal that he will ride into Jerusalem (cf. 14:13 – 15, where similar instructions are given). The "village" (κώμη) is not identified and could be Bethany, Bethphage, or another village on the outskirts of Jerusalem. The term "colt" (πῶλος) could refer to the young of various animals, but without qualification normally referred to a horse.[9] The allusion to Zech 9:9 and the parallels in Matthew and John (Matt 21:2, 5, 7; John 12:15) confirm that a young donkey is intended here (cf. Gen 32:15; Judg 10:4).

A second OT allusion to the messianic prophecy of Gen 49:9 – 11 may also be present. There the future king from the tribe of Judah will "tether his donkey to a vine, his colt to the choicest branch."[10] The colt is described as one on which "no one has ever sat." The idea seems to be one of purity. In the OT animals that had never been yoked were used in sacrifices (Num 19:2; Deut 21:3) and for pulling the ark of the covenant (1 Sam 6:7). The Mishnah says that the king's horse cannot be ridden by anyone except the king.[11]

Jesus' instructions may reflect the ancient practice of *angaria*, or impressment, where a king or government official could claim temporary rights to an item or person for immediate service (cf. 15:21; 1 Sam 8:16).[12] Again we see royal implications in the scene.

---

5. See Lane, *Mark*, 394 n. 10.

6. So Cranfield, *Mark*, 348; Lane, *Mark*, 394; Stein, *Mark*, 503; Evans, *Mark 8:27 – 16:20*, 141.

7. Edwards, *Mark*, 334, citing R. Beuvery, "La route romaine de Jérusalem a Jéricho," *RB* 66 (1957): 72 – 101.

8. Josephus speaks of a particular false prophet, who called people to the Mount of Olives, claiming that from there he would command the walls of Jerusalem to fall down (*Ant.* 20.8.6 §169).

9. BDAG, 900.

10. The LXX of Gen 49:11 uses the same word for "colt" (πῶλος) and a cognate of Mark's "bind" (δέω) for "tether" (δεσμεύω).

11. *m. Sanh.* 2:5: "No one may ride his horse, and no one may sit in his throne, and no one may use his scepter." Cf. Homer, *Il.* 6.94; Horace, *Epod.* 9.22 (Evans, *Mark 8:27 – 16:20*, 142).

12. J. D. M. Derrett, "Law in the New Testament: The Palm Sunday Colt," *NovT* 13 (1971): 243 – 49; Witherington, *Mark*, 309; Hooker, *Mark*, 258; Pesch, *Markusevangelium*, 2:180; Evans, *Mark 8:27 – 16:20*, 142.

11:3 **"If anyone says to you, 'Why are you doing this?' say, 'The Lord needs it and will send it back here again shortly.' "** (καὶ ἐάν τις ὑμῖν εἴπῃ· τί ποιεῖτε τοῦτο; εἴπατε· ὁ κύριος αὐτοῦ χρείαν ἔχει, καὶ εὐθὺς αὐτὸν ἀποστέλλει πάλιν ὧδε). Jesus gives the disciples instructions on how to respond if they are challenged. The referent to the "Lord" (κύριος) is debated. It could refer to Jesus (cf. 1:3; 2:28; 5:19; 7:28; 12:36, 37),[13] God (the animal is needed for God's service; cf. 11:19; 12:11, 29–30, 36; 13:20),[14] or to the "owner" of the colt (κύριος can mean "master" or "owner"; cf. 12:9; 13:35).[15]

This third option would indicate that Jesus has prearranged with the owner to take the animal. Most English translations rule out this option by capitalizing the word "Lord," indicating it was either Jesus or God who needed it (NIV, NLT, NET, HCSB, NASB). Luke's account also rules it out, since he says the colt's owners (οἱ κύριοι αὐτοῦ) raised the objection to taking it (Luke 19:33). The most natural referent in context is Jesus himself, which agrees with Mark's consistent emphasis on his messianic authority.

Mark does not say whether Jesus had prearranged to take the colt (cf. 14:12–16)[16] or whether he is here demonstrating divine insight.[17] Most commentators favor the former. Otherwise, it is hard to explain why those present so quickly concede to the request by apparent strangers to take the animal. Yet Mark's emphasis elsewhere on Jesus' remarkable authority and insight (1:18, 20;

2:8, 10–12, etc.) might tip the balance in favor of the latter.

The subject of the last clause is ambiguous (καὶ εὐθὺς αὐτὸν ἀποστέλλει πάλιν ὧδε); it could mean either "and he [Jesus] will send it back here to you shortly" — a continuation of the instructions on what to say (NIV, NET, HCSB, NLT, ESV), or "and he [the owner of the colt] will send it here to us immediately" — a prediction of the result of the request (NASB, NKJV). If God is the referent of κύριος, the latter must be intended, and Matthew appears to have taken it this way (Matt 21:3). Since we have taken the "Lord" as a reference to Jesus, the former works well, picking up Jesus as the immediate antecedent. In either case the present tense of "sends" (ἀποστέλλει) is functioning as a futuristic present (cf. 9:12, 31).[18]

11:4–6 **They went and found a colt tied up at a doorway outside in the street, and they untied it. Some of the people standing there said to them, "What are you doing untying the colt?" They answered them just as Jesus told them to, and they let them go** (καὶ ἀπῆλθον καὶ εὗρον πῶλον δεδεμένον πρὸς θύραν ἔξω ἐπὶ τοῦ ἀμφόδου καὶ λύουσιν αὐτόν. καί τινες τῶν ἐκεῖ ἑστηκότων ἔλεγον αὐτοῖς· τί ποιεῖτε λύοντες τὸν πῶλον; οἱ δὲ εἶπαν αὐτοῖς καθὼς εἶπεν ὁ Ἰησοῦς, καὶ ἀφῆκαν αὐτούς). The events unfold exactly as Jesus has described them. Even if the procurement of the colt were by prior arrangement, the scene suggests that every-

---

13. Gundry, *Mark*, 624, 628; Nineham, *Mark*, 295; Gnilka, *Markus*, 2:117; Edwards, *Mark*, 335; Timothy C. Gray, *The Temple in the Gospel of Mark: A Study of Its Narrative Role* (Grand Rapids: Baker, 2008), 11–13. Gray goes further in claiming that Mark intentionally avoids using "Lord" for Jesus until this point in his narrative in order to make it climactic. By using the title here, Mark points the reader back to the title's use in 1:2–3 in the quotation from Isa 40:3 and Mal 3:1. In this way, Jesus is presented in the narrative that follows as the Lord who comes to the temple in judgment.

14. France, *Mark*, 432; Evans, *Mark 8:27–16:20*, 143.

15. Taylor, *Mark*, 455; Cranfield, *Mark*, 350; Lane, *Mark*, 395. Lane suggests that the owner may have been with Jesus at the time.

16. So Lane, *Mark*, 395; France, *Mark*, 432; Evans, *Mark 8:27–16:20*, 142–43; Edwards, *Mark*, 335; Stein, *Mark*, 503.

17. So Hooker, *Mark*, 258; Gundry, *Mark*, 624; Garland, *Mark*, 427.

18. Some manuscripts (G W Ψ f^1 700) alter the present to the more natural reading, future.

thing is proceeding as planned and Jesus is fully in charge of the circumstances.

11:7 – 8 They brought the colt to Jesus and placed their garments on it, and he sat on it. Many people spread their garments on the road, while others spread branches they had cut in the field (καὶ φέρουσιν τὸν πῶλον πρὸς τὸν Ἰησοῦν καὶ ἐπιβάλλουσιν αὐτῷ τὰ ἱμάτια αὐτῶν, καὶ ἐκάθισεν ἐπ᾽ αὐτόν. καὶ πολλοὶ τὰ ἱμάτια αὐτῶν ἔστρωσαν εἰς τὴν ὁδόν, ἄλλοι δὲ στιβάδας κόψαντες ἐκ τῶν ἀγρῶν). Since the colt has never been ridden, there is no saddle, so the disciples prepare a makeshift one with their cloaks. Significantly, nowhere else in the Gospels is Jesus seen riding on an animal. Jewish pilgrims ascended to Jerusalem walking, not riding on horseback. This confirms again that this event is special and performed by Jesus to fulfill the messianic implications of Zech 9:9.

Jesus' approach is reminiscent of several OT and Jewish texts, all of which have royal significance: (1) the anointing and coronation of Solomon, when he enters Jerusalem on David's mule to music and rejoicing (1 Kgs 1:32 – 48); (2) the anointing of Jehu as king of Israel at Elisha's command, when the people spread their garments under his feet (2 Kgs 9:1 – 13); (3) the entrance of the Davidic Messiah in Zech 9:9 – 10, which itself is reminiscent of Solomon's coronation; and (4) the entrance of Simon Maccabeus into Jerusalem, accompanied by the waving of palm branches, music, and praise (1 Macc 13:50 – 51).

Both the garments and branches spread on the ground are meant to prepare a road for Jesus, a kind of "red carpet" treatment. The term rendered "branches" (στιβάδες) is a general one for vegetation and could refer to leaves, branches, or tall grass. These were likely cut from nearby fields. Only John's gospel refers specifically to "palm

branches" (τὰ βαΐα τῶν φοινίκων; John 12:13), the inspiration for the title "Palm Sunday." Some commentators suggest that this detail indicates that, historically, this approach to Jerusalem by Jesus occurred at the Feast of Tabernacles rather than at Passover, since the waving of branches of palm, willow, myrtle, or citron and shouting "Hosanna" were characteristic of Tabernacles (2 Macc 10:7; *m. Sukkah* 3:1 – 9).[19] Yet it would take more than one detail to overturn the strong tradition that this event was associated with Jesus' last Passover visit to Jerusalem. Songs and rejoicing characterize all the pilgrim festivals, and the branches set in Jesus' path appear to be a spontaneous act to honor him, not necessarily a traditional part of the festival.

11:9 – 10 Those who led the way and those who followed were shouting, "Hosanna! Blessed is the one who comes in the name of the Lord! Blessed is the coming kingdom of our father David! Hosanna in the highest!" (καὶ οἱ προάγοντες καὶ οἱ ἀκολουθοῦντες ἔκραζον· ὡσαννά· εὐλογημένος ὁ ἐρχόμενος ἐν ὀνόματι κυρίου· εὐλογημένη ἡ ἐρχομένη βασιλεία τοῦ πατρὸς ἡμῶν Δαυίδ· ὡσαννὰ ἐν τοῖς ὑψίστοις). Those who led the way and those who followed are not two separate groups, one coming and one going (as in John 12:12 – 13), but describe the throngs around Jesus.

The shouts of the crowd have a chiastic structure (ABBA), with "Hosanna" at the beginning and end, and two statements of blessing in the center. The first two lines are from Ps 118:26, one of the Hallel psalms (Pss 113 – 118) used liturgically at the Feasts of Tabernacles and Passover. In its original context, the blessing was on festival pilgrims coming to the temple "in the name of the Lord," that is, to worship him and celebrate his goodness. The original readers of Mark's gospel are likely to have understood this "one who comes" (ὁ ἐρχόμενος) to

19. Edwards, *Mark*, 332.

be Jesus, who is coming to Jerusalem "in the name of the Lord" (with God's affirmation) as Messiah and Savior. Whether, historically, this is how those shouting understood the words is uncertain.[20] In Luke's gospel, it is the "crowd of disciples" (τὸ πλῆθος τῶν μαθητῶν) who cry out (19:37).

"Hosanna" (ὡσαννά) is from the Hebrew *hôšî'â-nā'*, which originally meant "Save now!" but had come to be used as a general shout of praise (cf. Matt 21:9, 15; *m. Sukkah* 4:5).[21] It is repeated in v. 10 with "in the highest" (ἐν τοῖς ὑψίστοις), a circumlocution meaning "in heaven" or "in God's presence" (cf. Luke 2:14).

The second blessing, for "the coming kingdom of our father David"[22] (which is not part of Ps 118), is also ambiguous and could be a cry of hope and expectation for the messianic kingdom by any Jewish pilgrims entering Jerusalem for the festival. Yet in the context of Mark's narrative, where Jesus has just been acclaimed by Bartimaeus as "Son of David" (10:47 – 48)[23] and where he is presently fulfilling the prediction of the messianic king in Zech 9:9, it points unmistakably to Jesus as the one who will reestablish the throne of David (2 Sam 7:14 – 16; Isa 9:1 – 7; 11:1 – 16; Jer 23:5 – 6; 33:14 – 16; Mic 5:2). Whether anyone in the crowd is thinking this way is unclear, but Mark's readers are no doubt intended to see this connection.[24] The cries in the other gospels are even more explicit, with Matthew's "Hosanna to the Son of David!" (Matt 21:9), Luke's "Blessed is the king who comes …" (Luke 19:38), and John's "Blessed is the king of Israel" (John 12:13).

Although Mark does not explicitly quote Zech 9:9 – 10 (unlike Matt 21:5 and John 12:15), this passage is no doubt in the background:

> Rejoice greatly, Daughter Zion!
>> Shout, Daughter Jerusalem!
> See, your king comes to you,
>> righteous and victorious,
> lowly and riding on a donkey,
>> on a colt, the foal of a donkey.
> I will take away the chariots from Ephraim
>> and the warhorses from Jerusalem,
>> and the battle bow will be broken.
> He will proclaim peace to the nations.
>> His rule will extend from sea to sea
>> and from the River to the ends of the earth.

The Messiah is here portrayed as both humble and conquering. This fits Mark's portrait of Jesus as the one who first came to serve (10:45), but will return one day in triumph to judge and to rule (13:26 – 27; 14:62). Of course, Jesus has already been victorious — over Satan, demons, disease, and the forces of nature — but his final triumph awaits the future, after his suffering.

11:11 He entered Jerusalem and went into the temple courts. He looked around at everything, but since it was already late, he returned to Bethany with the Twelve (Καὶ εἰσῆλθεν εἰς Ἱεροσόλυμα

---

20. The Targum of Ps 118 interprets the psalm messianically, identifying David as the rejected stone and the "builders" as priests who eventually come to accept him as the legitimate king (Evans, *Mark 8:27 – 16:20*, 146; France, *Mark*, 434 n. 18).

21. See J. A. Fitzmyer, "Aramaic Evidence Affecting the Interpretation of *Hosanna* in the New Testament," in *Tradition and Interpretation in the New Testament* (ed. G. F. Hawthorne and O. Betz; Grand Rapids: Eerdmans, 1987), 110 – 18.

22. For "our father David," see Acts 4:25 (cf. 2:29; Luke 1:32; Sir 44:1). For its historicity, see Evans, *Mark 8:27 – 16:20*, 145 – 46, and Pesch, *Markusevangelium*, 2:185, who argue

against claims that only Abraham, Isaac, and Jacob were called "fathers."

23. Although Jesus will soon challenge the *adequacy* of the Son of David in 12:35 – 37 (since the Messiah is also David's "Lord"), he appears to accept it in 10:47 – 48 as a legitimate title for himself.

24. Contra Moloney, *Mark*, 220, who claims that the cry of the crowds and the disciples represents a "false messianic expectation" — a nationalistic misunderstanding of Jesus' true mission and identity.

εἰς τὸ ἱερὸν καὶ περιβλεψάμενος πάντα, ὀψίας ἤδη οὔσης τῆς ὥρας, ἐξῆλθεν εἰς Βηθανίαν μετὰ τῶν δώδεκα). The "temple courts" (ἱερόν) here refers not to the temple building proper (ναός), but to the whole complex of buildings that filled the Temple Mount. The scene seems anticlimactic when compared to the other Synoptics, where the whole city is stirred up (Matt 21:1), the religious leaders challenge Jesus (Luke 19:39 – 40), and he enters the temple to clear it. Jesus merely looks around and then leaves the city.[25] Mark explains the reason: evening had arrived and the hour was late.

The implication is that most people had left and so Jesus holds off on any action until the next morning. As Garland observes, Jesus' arrival in Jerusalem is not that of a gawking tourist, marveling at the magnificent temple, nor of a pious worshiper offering prayer or sacrifice.[26] He comes as Lord and King inspecting his domain. On the next day, he will render his judgment (11:12 – 17). Again, the implication is that he has a purpose and plan. As France points out, "What happens in the morning will not be a spontaneous act of outrage, but a planned demonstration."[27]

Jesus and the disciples return to Bethany, where they will spend the night, perhaps at the home of Lazarus (see v. 1; Luke 10:38; John 11:1) or Simon the Leper (Mark 14:3). At Passover Jerusalem swelled with so many visitors that most were forced to stay in neighborhoods around the city. It was only the Passover meal itself that needed to be eaten within the city walls.[28]

Theology in Application

Jesus, the Messiah and King

Central to this passage is its christological significance. The messianic secret is ending. Throughout Mark's gospel Jesus has taken steps to silence the acclamations of others, whether those healed (1:44; 5:43; 7:36; 8:26), disciples (8:30; 9:9), or demons (1:25, 34; 3:11 – 12). Now, however, he takes intentional steps that reveal his status as the messianic King of the Jews. The procurement of the colt and Jesus' approach to Jerusalem riding it represent an intentional fulfillment of Zech 9:9 with its promise of the coming of Israel's King.

Unlike Matthew and Luke, Mark has had little in his gospel that is explicitly messianic. Matthew and Luke both include birth stories that strongly stress Jesus' royal Davidic credentials (Matt 1:1, 6, 17, 20; 2:1, 5 – 6; Luke 1:27, 32, 69; 2:4, 11), and both provide genealogies tracing Jesus' ancestry through the line of David (Matt

---

25. P. B. Duff, "The March of the Divine Warrior and the Advent of the Greco-Roman King: Mark's Account of Jesus' Entry into Jerusalem," *JBL* 111 (1992): 55 – 71, claims that Mark intentionally combines imagery of the Divine Warrior of Zech 14 with elements of the Greco-Roman triumphal procession to present Jesus as a conquering ruler. Yet the procession ends abruptly and anticlimactically in v. 11. According to Duff, this is part of Mark's means of provoking his readers to reconsider their presuppositions about messiahship, discipleship, and the kingdom of God.

26. Garland, *Mark*, 428 – 29. Garland points to the parallel in Mal 3:1 – 2, a passage Mark quoted at the beginning of his gospel (Mark 1:2), where the Lord is predicted to come "suddenly … to his temple" on the day of judgment.

27. France, *Mark*, 442.

28. See J. Jeremias, *Jerusalem in the Time of Jesus* (trans. F. H. Cave and C. H. Cave; Philadelphia: Fortress, 1969), 60 – 62.

1:1 – 17; Luke 3:23 – 38). Matthew repeatedly uses the title "Son of David" (Matt 1:1, 20; 9:27; 12:23; 15:22; 20:30 – 31; 21:9, 15; 22:42), and Luke highlights this royal Davidic theme both in the birth narrative and repeatedly in the speeches of Acts (Acts 2:29 – 36; 13:32 – 37; 15:16 – 18).

Yet while Mark's presentation is more subtle, he has left no doubt about Jesus' identity. In his first line he identifies Jesus as the "Messiah" (χριστός; 1:1), and the Father's voice from heaven identifies him as "my beloved Son" (ὁ υἱός μου ὁ ἀγαπητός; 1:11), an allusion to the royal Davidic psalm (Ps 2:7). Demons, who are cognizant of spiritual realities, repeatedly acknowledge Jesus' messianic status (Mark 1:24 – 25, 34; 3:11 – 12), and Peter finally acclaims it before the disciples (8:29). Jesus' reluctance to make this known is not a _denial_, but a _delay_, as he has sought to define his messiahship on his own terms.

Now, however, the time has come to act. The "Son of David" cry of Bartimaeus (10:47 – 48) and Jesus' approach to Jerusalem on a donkey set the stage for the joyful acclamation of the crowds for the "coming kingdom of our father David" (11:10). This will be followed by Jesus' act of messianic judgment in clearing the temple (11:15 – 17, 28) and challenging Israel's religious leaders (12:1 – 40). At Jesus' trial he will acknowledge before Caiaphas that he is "the Messiah, the Son of the Blessed One" (14:61), and will be executed as "the king of the Jews" (15:2, 9, 12, 18, 26; cf. 15:32). Mark's readers know that though Jesus did not assume his earthly throne at his entrance to Jerusalem, his messiahship was vindicated through his resurrection, and he will one day return to judge and to reign (13:26 – 27; 14:62).

The implications for Jesus' messiahship today are profound. If Jesus is King, then his followers owe him total allegiance. For many people today, the Christian faith is a self-help program. If I put my faith in Jesus, what will he do for me? Christianity is fine if it meets my needs. Yet Jesus' kingship reminds us that our lives are not our own, but belong completely to the one who "rescued us from the dominion of darkness and brought us into the kingdom of the Son" (Col 1:13). As mere servants in the kingdom of the Son, we live to serve him.

The Messiah Who Brings Peace

While the approach to Jerusalem confirms that Jesus is indeed the Davidic Messiah, it also points to the surprising way the promises will be fulfilled. The humble king of Zech 9:9 comes bringing peace. Peace, of course, is a relative thing. With the establishment of Caesar Augustus as emperor, the vast Roman empire entered an unprecedented period of stability known as the _Pax Romana_ ("Roman peace"). Yet that "peace" was enforced through ruthless oppression at the slightest sign of dissent or rebellion. The Scottish ruler Calgacus, on the eve of a battle with the Roman legions, is reported to have spoken sarcastically of this Roman "peace": "Robbery, butchery and rapine they call government; they create a desert and call it peace."[29] One person's peace is another's oppression and devastation.

True peace cannot be achieved by crushing one's enemies; it can only be found through reconciliation and restoration. Jesus, the Servant Messiah, came not to be served but to serve. His death will bring about true peace, a reconciliation between God and human beings. The apostle Paul says in Rom 5:1 that "since we have been justified through faith, we have peace with God through our Lord Jesus Christ" (cf. Eph 2:14 – 15, 17; Col 1:20). True peace means a relationship with God and access to his presence. This is what Jesus came to bring.

The Appropriate Response to King Jesus

The self-revelation of Jesus as the Messiah demands a response. The shouts of the crowd confirm that they are on the right track, longing for "the coming kingdom of our father David." There is a measure of faith here as they rightly claim the OT promises of God for the kingdom of God. Yet the days ahead in Jerusalem will reveal at least two kinds of inadequate faith. The first is a self-centered and misdirected faith. Like Peter, who confessed Jesus as the Messiah (8:29), and James and John, who sought the kingdom's best seats (10:37), the crowds are longing for a kingdom that will exalt Israel as a political and military power over Rome. The same kind of misdirected faith can happen today, as people embrace Christianity because it will raise their status in the community or for business or political gain. Yet in contrast to the nationalistic and political ambitions of the disciples and the crowds, Jesus calls for repentance, humility, and servanthood as true kingdom values.

The second inadequate faith is a wavering and fickle one. The same crowds who rejoice at Jesus' approach to Jerusalem will quickly turn on him at his arrest and trial (15:11 – 15). The disciples will flee at the first sign of trouble (14:50), and Peter will three times deny he even knows Jesus (14:68, 70, 71). Authentic faith is persevering faith. It's easy to proclaim faith in Jesus when times are good. Yet authentic Christianity is a willingness to stay faithful during the most difficult times, to take up our cross and follow him, no matter the cost.

---

29. Cited by Tacitus, *Agr.* 30.

44

Mark 11:12 – 25

Literary Context

Having approached Jerusalem as the messianic King in fulfillment of Zech 9:9 (Mark 11:1 – 11), Jesus offers two symbolic actions in this episode: cursing an unfruitful fig tree and clearing the Jerusalem temple of sellers become his first authoritative actions as Messiah in Jerusalem. This episode is linked to the previous one with the references to Bethany (12:11, 12), Jerusalem (11:11, 15), and the temple (11:11, 15). The evening before, Jesus entered the temple courts and "looked around at everything," but he took no action, returning to Bethany for the night (11:11).

This reconnaissance now gives way to action, as Jesus clears the temple of its merchants, challenging the authority of Israel's religious hierarchy. In the following episodes, Jesus' authority will be questioned because of his actions in the temple (11:27 – 33), he will portray the religious leaders as wicked tenant farmers over God's vineyard Israel (12:1 – 12), and he will engage in a series of controversies with them (12:13 – 40). The present episode thus sets the stage for this Jerusalem showdown.

III. The Suffering Way of the Messiah (8:22 – 15:47)
    A. Revelation of the Messiah's Suffering (8:22 – 10:52)
    B. The Messiah Confronts Jerusalem (11:1 – 13:37)
        1. The Triumphal Entry (11:1 – 11)
➡   **2. Prophetic Action in the Temple and Cursing a Fig Tree (11:12 – 25)**
        3. Controversies in the Temple (11:27 – 12:44)

Main Idea

By "sandwiching" the clearing of the temple between the beginning and end of the fig tree episode, Mark suggests that both events have symbolic meaning, representing God's judgment against Jerusalem and the temple because Israel has failed to bear spiritual fruit.[1]

Translation

Mark 11:12–25

12a	setting (temporal & spatial)	The next day as they were leaving Bethany,
b	Statement of fact	**he was hungry.**
13a	setting	Seeing in the distance a fig tree with leaves,
b	Action	**he went to find out if there was anything on it.**
c	action	When he came to it,
d	Result of 13a-b	**he found nothing but leaves,**
e	reason for 13d	because it was not the season for figs.
14a	Response to 13d	**In response he said,**
b		*"May no one ever eat fruit from you again!"*
c	Response	And **his disciples heard what he said.**
15a	Action (sequence)	**They arrived in Jerusalem.**
b		Entering the temple courts,
c	Action	**he began to throw out those selling and**
		buying in the temple courts.
d	Action	**He turned over the tables of money changers and**
		the chairs of those selling doves,
16	Action	and **would not allow anyone to carry merchandise through the temple** ⟳
		courts.
17a	Instruction	**He began to teach them with these words,**
b	Scripture quotation	*"Is it not written,*
c		*'My house will be called a house of prayer for all the nations'?* [Isa 56:7]
d	accusation	*But you have made it 'a den of robbers.'"* [Jer 7:11]
18a	Response	**The ruling priests and**
		the experts in the law heard this and
b		**began looking for a way to destroy him,**
c	reason for 18b	for **they** **feared** him
d	reason for 18c	because the whole crowd was amazed at his teaching.

Continued on next page.

---

1. For a broad-ranging discussion of the significant of these events historically and theologically, see W. R. Telford, *The Barren Temple and the Withered Tree* (JSNTSup 1; Sheffield: JSOT Press, 1980); idem, "More Fruit from the Withered Fig Tree," in *Templum Amicitiae* (ed. W. Horbury; JSNTSup 48; Sheffield: JSOT, 1991), 264–304.

Continued from previous page.

19a	setting	When evening came,
b	Action/Character departure	**they went out of the city.**
20a	setting	Early the next morning as they passed by,
b	Action/Observation	**they saw the fig tree withered away from the roots.**
21a		Remembering,
b	Response to 20	**Peter said to him,**
c		*"Rabbi, look! The fig tree you cursed has withered."*
22a	Response/Instruction	Jesus replied to them,
b	exhortation	*"Have faith in God.*
23a	veracity statement	*Truly I say to you,*
b	instruction/promise	*if anyone says to this mountain, 'Be lifted up and thrown into the sea,' and*
c	condition	*does not doubt in his heart, but*
d		*believes that what he says will happen,*
e	result	*it will be done for him.*
24a		*Therefore I tell you,*
b	instruction/promise	*whatever you pray and ask for,*
c	condition	*believe that you have received it,*
d	result	*and it will be yours.*
25a	exhortation	*And*
		whenever you stand praying,
b	condition	*if you have anything against anyone,*
c		*forgive them,*
d	result	*so that your Father in heaven will forgive you your sins."*

Structure

This section consists of four parts: Jesus' cursing of an unfruitful fig tree (vv. 12 – 14), his clearing of the temple (vv. 15 – 19), the discovery of the withered fig tree (vv. 20 – 21), and Jesus' resulting teaching about faith, prayer, and forgiveness (vv. 22 – 25). As noted above (see Main Idea), the first three scenes form one of Mark's characteristic intercalations, or "sandwiches," in which one episode is interrupted by another (ABA) and the two mutually interpret each another (see Introduction to Mark: Literary Features). France, however, sees a broader (ABABA) structure related to the temple, which begins with Jesus' first entrance into Jerusalem in 11:11 and concludes in 11:27 with Jesus' third entrance:

A First visit to the *temple* (11:11)
 B Cursing of the *fig tree* (11:12 – 14)
A′ Jesus takes action in the *temple* (11:15 – 19)
 B′ The *fig tree* is found to be dead (11:20 – 25)
A″ Jesus returns to the *temple* (11:27)[2]

---

2. France, *Mark*, 436, 442.

This makes sense, he says, because now the whole complex focuses on the temple, which is the context for the controversies and teaching that follow (11:27 – 13:37). It also helps to explain Jesus' brief entrance into Jerusalem in 11:11, which otherwise seems to be an anticlimactic end to Jesus' triumphal approach to Jerusalem.[3] Against this proposal, however, is the fact that it breaks Mark's typical three-part pattern of intercalation, where one episode interrupts another. Furthermore, Jesus' apparently unrelated teaching in vv. 22 – 24 seems to break the continuity between temple references. A more logical structure is to keep v. 11 with the triumphal entry (11:1 – 11), so that the three episodes recount three arrivals in Jerusalem on consecutive days (11:11, 15, 27).

In terms of its literary form, the cursing of the fig tree is a nature miracle (cf. 4:35 – 41; 6:30 – 44, 45 – 52; 8:1 – 13; John 2:1 – 12),[4] though it might more specifically be called a "curse" or "judgment" miracle or a prophetic oracle that is quickly fulfilled.[5] This is the only miracle of destruction in the Gospels. Miracles of judgment and destruction do appear in the OT, especially in the story of the exodus (Exod 7 – 14) and the Elijah and Elisha narratives (2 Kgs 1:4, 10 – 14; 2:23 – 24; 5:27; cf. 1 Kgs 13:1 – 5; 15:5; 2 Chr 26:16 – 21). Similarly, in Acts, Peter pronounces judgment against Ananias and Sapphira (5:1 – 11), and Paul strikes blind the sorcerer Elymas Bar-Jesus (13:6 – 12). Yet all these concern judgments against people, not objects of nature.[6] (For a discussion of the problem of Jesus' apparently capricious action against an "innocent" tree, see comments on 11:13c – 14.)

Matthew's version omits the intercalation and the fig tree withers "immediately" (παραχρῆμα) following Jesus' curse (Matt 21:18 – 19).[7] The whole episode occurs in the morning after the clearing of the temple, which itself occurs immediately after Jesus enters Jerusalem (21:10 – 17). Luke omits the fig tree episode completely, perhaps because of embarrassment over Jesus' apparent capriciousness or because Luke wants to avoid duplication, having already introduced the parable of the barren fig tree (Luke 13:6 – 9).[8]

All three Synoptics place the temple clearing near the end of Jesus' ministry, during Passion Week (cf. Matt 21:12 – 13; Luke 19:45 – 46). John's gospel, however, places it at the beginning of Jesus' ministry, as one of his first public acts (John 2:14 – 22). Most commentators consider the Synoptic account to be more accurate chronologically and discount the possibility of two separate events.[9] Surely the temple authorities would have been ready for Jesus the second time!

---

3. Gundry also sees 11:11 as the introduction to this episode, "since Mark likes to start pericopes with indications of topographical movement" (*Mark*, 634).

4. Bultmann, *History*, 227 – 31.

5. Evans, *Mark 8:27 – 16:20*, 150; Pesch, *Markusevangelium*, 2:291.

6. There is also the apocryphal story in the *Infancy Gospel of Thomas* 3:1 – 3 — likely arising from Matthew's parallel (Matt

21:19 – 20) — where the boy Jesus turns out to be a capricious and dangerous playmate, cursing a child who is pestering him so that the boy withers like a barren tree!

7. This is in line with Matthew's tendency to abbreviate and condense episodes (Matt 8:5 – 13; 9:18 – 26).

8. Evans, *Mark 8:27 – 16:20*, 348.

9. For details, see Brown, *John*, 1:116 – 20.

This argument, however, is not decisive. The fact that no immediate action is taken against Jesus by the Jewish temple police or by the Roman authorities — either in John or the Synoptics — suggests that the episode is a brief and relatively minor affair. Such an event would surely have been forgotten in the intervening years, and Jesus could easily have caught the temple authorities off-guard after entering Jerusalem with the large Passover crowds. While it is possible (and perhaps most likely) that John moved the episode forward for theological reasons,[10] it is not impossible that Jesus acted in a similar manner twice.[11]

Exegetical Outline

➡ **1. Jesus Curses the Fig Tree (11:12 – 14)**
    a. Jesus' hunger while leaving Bethany (11:12)
    b. Finding a barren fig tree (11:13)
    c. Jesus pronounces judgment against the tree (11:14)

2. Jesus Clears the Temple (11:15 – 19)
    a. Driving out the buyers, sellers, and money changers (11:15)
    b. Preventing transport through the temple (11:16)
    c. Pronouncement of judgment from Isa 56:7 and Jer 7:11 (v. 17)
    d. Response of the religious leaders (11:18)
    e. Jesus' departure from the city (11:19)

3. Discovery of the Withered Fig Tree (11:20 – 21)
    a. Discovering the withered tree (11:20)
    b. Peter's response (11:21)

4. Jesus' Teaching on Keys to Spiritual Success (11:22 – 25)
    a. Teaching about faith: casting a mountain into the sea (11:22 – 23)
    b. Teaching about prayer (11:24)
    c. Teaching about forgiveness (11:25)

10. Brown, *John*, 1:118, 123 – 25.

11. Morris, *John*, 167 n. 55, argues for two separate events, pointing out that "there are practically no resemblances between the two narratives, apart from the central act." Some have pointed that if Jesus found the temple in the same sad state as before, he would surely have been compelled to act again. See now E. Randolph Richards, "An Honor/Shame Argument for Two Temple Clearings," *TJ* 29 (Spring 2008): 19 – 43.

Explanation of the Text

11:12 – 13b The next day as they were leaving Bethany, he was hungry. Seeing in the distance a fig tree with leaves, he went to find out if there was anything on it (Καὶ τῇ ἐπαύριον ἐξελθόντων αὐτῶν ἀπὸ Βηθανίας ἐπείνασεν. καὶ ἰδὼν συκῆν ἀπὸ μακρόθεν ἔχουσαν φύλλα ἦλθεν, εἰ ἄρα τι εὑρήσει ἐν αὐτῇ). "The next day" (τῇ ἐπαύριον; only here in Mark) refers to the morning after Jesus' approach to Jerusalem and his short inspection of the temple (11:1 – 11). Only here in Mark's gospel is Jesus described as hungry, though Mark elsewhere reveals more of Jesus' human emotions and limitations than the other gospels (1:41; 3:5; 4:38; 6:34; 10:21; 14:33 – 34). The suggestion that the reference is to spiritual hunger[12] is far-fetched and runs contrary to the narrative setting, where Jesus goes in search of real food from a real tree. From a narrative perspective, Jesus' hunger prepares for the actions related to the fig tree.

The common fig (*ficus carica*) is a deciduous tree that can grow to a height of up to six meters (19 feet). Fig trees generally produce two crops. The first, or *breva*, crop comes in the spring on the previous year's shoots. Leaves sprout in March or April and produce fruit in May or June. These are the "early figs" (*bikkûrâ*; Isa 28:4; Jer 24:2; Hos 9:10; Mic 7:1)[13] or "early fruit" (*paggim*; Song 2:13) referred to in the OT. The main crop of figs (*tĕʾēnîm*), which is better in quantity and quality, develops from the current year's growth and produces in late summer or fall. Since this is Passover, Jesus would likely have been looking for the early fruit. The leaves indicate the potential of fruit.

11:13c – 14 When he came to it, he found nothing but leaves, because it was not the season for figs. In response he said, "May no one ever eat fruit from you again!" And his disciples heard what he said (καὶ ἐλθὼν ἐπ᾽ αὐτὴν οὐδὲν εὗρεν εἰ μὴ φύλλα· ὁ γὰρ καιρὸς οὐκ ἦν σύκων. καὶ ἀποκριθεὶς εἶπεν αὐτῇ· μηκέτι εἰς τὸν αἰῶνα ἐκ σοῦ μηδεὶς καρπὸν φάγοι. καὶ ἤκουον οἱ μαθηταὶ αὐτοῦ). Jesus is disappointed to find only leaves and no fruit. In response he pronounces a curse on the tree. The Greek idiom "answering ... said" (ἀποκριθεὶς ... λέγει) does not necessarily mean to reply to someone (the tree has not spoken!). It can mean any kind of response to a person or situation. Here his response, "May no one ... eat" (μηδεὶς ... φάγοι), is a rare voluntative or "wish" optative (from ἐσθίω) functioning as an imprecation.[14]

Jesus' cursing of the tree and its subsequent withering (v. 21) seem to many readers petty and vindictive and have caused much consternation and debate. Mark's narrative comment, "because it was not the season for figs" (ὁ γὰρ καιρὸς οὐκ ἦν σύκων), makes it even worse, since Jesus should know better than to expect fruit out of season. T. W. Manson's famous verdict sums up the concern of many: "It is a tale of miraculous power wasted in the service of ill temper (for the supernatural energy employed to blast the unfortunate tree might have been more usefully expended in forcing a crop of figs out of season); and as it stands it is simply incredible."[15] Bertrand Russell, in his essay "Why I Am Not a Christian," singled out this passage for criticism: "This is a very curious story,

---

12. L. Goppelt, *TDNT*, 6:20.

13. *HALOT*, 130. Pliny the Elder, *Nat.* 16.49, says that the fig tree is unusual in that it produces fruit before leaves. This probably refers to the buds that appear in the fall and swell into green knobs in the early spring. The leaves follow shortly and the knobs continue to grow into the early fruit. Leaves on

the tree mean the promise of fruit.

14. See J. H. Moulton and N. Turner, *A Grammar of New Testament Greek*; vol. 3: *Syntax* (Edinburgh: T&T Clark, 1963), 122. Cf. Acts 8:20.

15. T. W. Manson, "The Cleansing of the Temple," *BJRL* 33 (1951): 259.

because it was not the right time of year for figs, and you really could not blame the tree. I cannot myself feel that either in the matter of wisdom or in the matter of virtue Christ stands quite as high as some other people known to history."[16]

The strangeness of the story and its negative reflection on Jesus' character have caused many interpreters to treat it as legendary.[17] Some claim that the story arose around a withered fig tree discovered between Bethany and Jerusalem,[18] or on the basis of Jesus' parable of the barren fig tree in Luke 13:6 – 9,[19] or from OT passages like Mic 7:1 ("there is no cluster of grapes to eat, none of the early figs that I crave") or Jer 8:13 (" 'I will take away their harvest,' declares the LORD. 'There will be no grapes on the vine. There will be no figs on the tree and their leaves will wither' ").[20] Manson suggests that the statement was not originally a curse, but a prediction that no one would ever eat from the tree again because of the coming eschatological judgment against Jerusalem.[21]

Yet Jesus' actions are neither petty nor vindictive if he is intentionally acting out a parable symbolizing the unfruitfulness of Israel and the nation's coming judgment.[22] This is not a fit of temper against an innocent tree, but an object lesson for the benefit of the disciples. From this perspective, Jesus was hungry and went to the tree looking for fruit. Finding none, he took the opportunity to teach the disciples an object lesson. This interpretation was taken by Victor of Antioch in the earliest extant commentary on Mark's gospel. He wrote

that Jesus "used the fig tree to set forth the judgment that was about to fall on Jerusalem."[23]

(1) The strongest evidence for this interpretation — at least in Mark's narrative — is the juxtaposition of the fig tree episode and the clearing of the temple. As in Mark's other intercalations, the two actions interpret one another, both signifying God's judgment.

(2) Symbolic actions like this are characteristic of the prophets (1 Kgs 11:29 – 31; Isa 8:1 – 4; 20:1 – 6; Ezek 4:1 – 15; Hos 1:2). Jeremiah especially communicated to his audience with enacted parables (Jer 13:1 – 11; 19:1 – 13; 27:1 – 22).

(3) Figs or fig trees are common symbols in OT judgment oracles related to Israel (Isa 28:4; Jer 8:13; 24:1 – 10; 29:17; Hos 2:12; 9:10, 16 – 17; Mic 7:1) or the nations (Isa 34:4; Nah 3:12).

(4) More specifically, figs and grapes are commonly used to illustrate spiritual unfruitfulness (Hos 9:16 – 17; Mic 7:1). Most famous is the Song of the Vineyard in Isa 5:1 – 7, where God pronounces coming judgment against Israel at the hand of the Assyrians because of the nation's unfaithfulness. In the parable of the wicked tenant farmers just a few paragraphs after this one (12:1 – 12), Jesus will adapt Isaiah's parable to a new context, portraying Israel's leaders as wicked tenant farmers who will be judged because of their rejection of the owner's messengers (God's prophets) and the owner's Son (Jesus himself).

One point of debate is whether the fig tree here represents the nation of Israel or more specifically Jerusalem's leaders. Marcus argues for the lat-

16. Bertrand Russell, *Why I Am Not a Christian and Other Essays* (New York: Touchstone, 1957), 19.

17. For detailed discussions of historicity, see Evans, *Mark 8:27 – 16:20*, 149 – 53; Meier, *Marginal Jew*, 2:884 – 96.

18. Taylor, *Mark*, 459; Lohmeyer, *Markus*, 234.

19. Anderson, *Mark*, 263 – 64; C. F. D. Moule, *The Gospel according to Mark* (CBC; Cambridge: Cambridge University Press, 1965), 90.

20. Telford, *Barren Temple*, 237; J. Ernst, *Das Evangelium nach Markus* (RNT; Regensburg: Pustet, 1981), 325.

21. Manson, "Cleansing," 271 – 82.

22. So most commentators: Cranfield, *Mark*, 356; Hooker, *Mark*, 261 – 62; Telford, *Barren Temple*, passim; France, *Mark*, 439 – 40; Evans, *Mark 8:27 – 16:20*, 153 – 54; Stein, *Mark*, 512; Marcus, *Mark 9 – 16*, 789 – 90. Contra Taylor, *Mark*, 460, who calls it a "miracle of power."

23. Cited by Cranfield, *Mark*, 356.

ter, pointing out that at this point in the story the opposition is coming from the ruling priests and scribes, and the people in general are still responsive to Jesus.[24] Stein, by contrast, writes that "Jesus has rejected Israel. She has been weighed in the balances and found wanting. The kingdom will be given over to the Gentiles."[25]

This question, however, probably does not have a simple either/or answer. The fig tree's withering, juxtaposed beside the clearing of the temple, represents the destruction of the temple and Jerusalem, and so all Israel will suffer the consequences of the leaders' actions. It is certainly true, as Evans points out, that in the parable of the tenant farmers the vineyard is not destroyed (unlike in Isaiah's Song of the Vineyard; Isa 5:1 – 7) but given to "others" (12:9). The vineyard must therefore represent the kingdom, or God's people, whose leadership will be transferred from the Jewish leaders to the apostles.[26] Jesus has not "rejected Israel." Many Jews will respond to the gospel, and the remnant of Israel will become the foundation for the apostolic church. Yet metaphors like this are flexible, and the immediate context suggests the unfruitful fig tree is indeed a symbol of Israel. Under her unrepentant and recalcitrant leadership, the nation as a whole (except its righteous remnant) is unfruitful and will suffer horrific consequences.

All this still leaves unexplained Mark's problematic final comment, "because it was not the season for figs" (ὁ γὰρ καιρὸς οὐκ ἦν σύκων). On the one hand, if Jesus is indeed looking for early fruit, then Mark is wrong, since it *is* the season of (early) figs.

On the other hand, if it were *not* the season of figs, Jesus seems disingenuous in looking for them (setting the tree up for failure). Various explanations have been proposed.

(1) Some commentators claim that the last phrase is a scribal gloss.[27] Jesus' actions might be justified in cursing the unfruitful tree if it were, in fact, the season for figs. This is unlikely, however, since there is no textual evidence to support the phrase's omission and since such explanatory clauses are characteristic of Mark's style (cf. 1:16; 5:42; 7:3 – 4, 19; 13:14; 16:4).

(2) W. J. Cotter seeks to soften Jesus' actions by claiming that this last clause actually modifies the earlier one about Jesus' search for fruit. The first sentence would then read something like, "Seeing in the distance a fig tree with leaves, he went to find out if it had any fruit on it (for it was not the season for figs)."[28] In this case, Jesus would be holding out hope that, because of the leaves, some fruit might have already appeared. When disappointed, he takes the opportunity to teach his disciples an object lesson.

(3) Edwards similarly exonerates Jesus with a distinction between early and late figs. While Jesus is looking for early figs (*paggim*), Mark's editorial comment is about late (mature) figs (Gk: σῦκα; Heb: *tĕ'ēnîm*). Edwards paraphrases the last clause, "It was, of course, not the season for figs, but it was for *paggim*."[29] The problem is that Mark does not actually say this. Why make the comment at all if some (early) figs were in season?

If a solution must be found, we could perhaps

24. Marcus, *Mark 9 – 16*, 790; cf. Evans, *Mark 8:27 – 16:20*, 154.

25. R. H. Stein, "The Cleansing of the Temple in Mark (11:15 – 19): Reformation or Judgment?" in *Gospels and the Tradition: Studies on Redaction Criticism of the Synoptic Gospels* (Grand Rapids: Baker, 1991), 121 – 33; quote from p. 131; idem, *Mark*, 521; cf. Hooker, *Mark*, 261; France, *Mark*, 441.

26. Evans, *Mark 8:27 – 16:20*, 154.

27. Lohmeyer, *Markus*, 234; Anderson, *Mark*, 265.

28. W. J. Cotter, "For It Was Not the Season for Figs," *CBQ* 48 (1986): 62 – 66; cf. Meier, *Marginal Jew*, 2:891 – 92; Evans, *Mark 8:27 – 16:20*, 156 – 57; Gundry, *Mark*, 636.

29. Edwards, *Mark*, 339 – 40; citing G. Dalman, *Arbeit und Sitte in Palästina*, Band 1/2 (Hildesheim: Georg Olms Verlagsbuchhandlung, 1964), 378 – 81.

combine (2) and (3). The Greek in v. 13a does not actually say Jesus was looking for figs, but for "something" (τί) on the tree, perhaps the green knobs, or "early figs."[30] Mark then explains this with the clause "for it was not the season for figs" (ὁ γὰρ καιρὸς οὐκ ἦν σύκων), that is, fully ripe figs of the autumn harvest. Yet to focus too much on finding such logic risks missing Mark's real point, which is that Jesus turned a search for a snack into an object lesson on faith and spiritual unfruitfulness. France concludes, "A tree in full leaf at Passover is making a promise it cannot fulfill; so, too, is Israel. And just as Micah, speaking for God, described his disappointed search ... for the 'first-ripe fig for which I hunger' (Mic 7:1), so Jesus on his initial visit to the temple has found all leaves, but no fruit."[31]

11:15–16 They arrived in Jerusalem. Entering into the temple courts, he began to throw out those selling and buying in the temple courts. He turned over the tables of money changers and the chairs of those selling doves, and would not allow anyone to carry merchandise through the temple courts (Καὶ ἔρχονται εἰς Ἱεροσόλυμα. καὶ εἰσελθὼν εἰς τὸ ἱερὸν ἤρξατο ἐκβάλλειν τοὺς πωλοῦντας καὶ τοὺς ἀγοράζοντας ἐν τῷ ἱερῷ, καὶ τὰς τραπέζας τῶν κολλυβιστῶν καὶ τὰς καθέδρας τῶν πωλούντων τὰς περιστερὰς κατέστρεψεν, καὶ οὐκ ἤφιεν ἵνα τις διενέγκῃ σκεῦος διὰ τοῦ ἱεροῦ).

The temple in Jerusalem was built on a massive raised platform almost five hundred meters north to south and over three hundred meters east to west.[32]

The outer court, the Court of Gentiles, was lined on the south side with a covered portico known as Solomon's Colonnade.[33] This outer court was as far as Gentiles could proceed. Plaques on the gates leading into the inner court warned Gentiles that entrance would result in their immediate death. The inner court, in which the temple proper stood, was made up of the Court of Women, the Court of Israel (only for Jewish men), and the Court of Priests (only for the priests). Jesus' actions must have taken place in the outer Court of the Gentiles, since merchants would not be allowed in the inner courts.

Jesus is described as "throwing out" (ἐκβάλλειν) the sellers and buyers, a strong term used elsewhere of casting out demons. The money changers exchanged various local currencies for the Tyrian shekel (the silver didrachma), the coin used to pay the temple tax (presumably because of its purity and consistent weight). Every Jewish male twenty years or older was required to pay the annual half-shekel temple tax.[34] Mark mentions only sellers of doves or pigeons (περιστεραί), which were sacrificial offerings designated for the poor (Lev 5:7, 11; 12:8; Luke 2:24). John's gospel also refers to sheep and oxen and describes the whip of cords that Jesus used to drive them out (John 2:15).

Rabbinic evidence indicates that shops for selling articles for sacrifices (sheep, doves, meal, oil) were originally located on the Mount of Olives.[35] V. Epstein suggests that their presence in the temple courts was a recent innovation by the high priest Caiaphas.[36] If this is true, it would help to explain

---

30. Gundry, *Mark*, 636; France, *Mark*, 440.

31. France, *Mark*, 441.

32. Detailed descriptions of the temple are provided by Josephus (*Ant.* 15.11.3–7 §§391–425; *J.W.* 5.5.6 §§222–224) and in the Mishnah (*m. Mid.*), though the specifics are open to significant interpretation.

33. Josephus says the colonnade was made up of 162 columns set in four rows. See comments on 13:1.

34. Exod 30:11–16; Neh 10:32–33; Josephus, *Ant.* 18.9.1 §§312–313; *m. Šeqal.* 1:3–7. Cf. Matt 17:24–27. The Mishnah

says that on the first of the month of Adar, announcement is made of the coming shekel tax. Tables are then set up in the provinces on Adar 15 and in the temple on Adar 25, so that the tax can be made by Nisan 1 (*m. Šeqal.* 1:1–3). Passover is Nisan 15.

35. Jeremias, *Jerusalem*, 48.

36. V. Epstein, "The Historicity of the Gospel Account of the Cleansing of the Temple," *ZNW* 55 (1964): 42–58; Lane, *Mark*, 403–4; France, *Mark*, 444.

Jesus' righteous anger. Jesus is not opposing the transactions themselves. The merchants performed a vital service for the temple, providing sacrificial animals and valid currency for pilgrims coming to Jerusalem to worship. It is their location in the temple and the subsequent disruption of worship that is the problem. This is indicated by the fact that Jesus clears not just the sellers, but also the buyers, and then prevents merchandise from passing through the temple courts (only in Mark).[37] Jesus is creating and protecting sacred space. The citation of Isa 56:7 that follows also points in this direction. It is the temple's function as a house of prayer that is being compromised by the commerce.

11:17 He began to teach them with these words,[38] "Is it not written, 'My house will be called a house of prayer for all the nations'? But you have made it 'a den of robbers.'" (καὶ ἐδίδασκεν καὶ ἔλεγεν αὐτοῖς· οὐ γέγραπται ὅτι ὁ οἶκός μου οἶκος προσευχῆς κληθήσεται πᾶσιν τοῖς ἔθνεσιν; ὑμεῖς δὲ πεποιήκατε αὐτὸν σπήλαιον λῃστῶν). Jesus cites two passages to justify his actions. The main quote comes from Isa 56:7, followed by the phrase "den/ cave of robbers" (σπήλαιον λῃστῶν) from Jer 7:11. Jesus seeks to restore the temple as "a house of prayer for all the nations" (Isa 56:7).

Only Mark among the Synoptics includes the last phrase, "for all the nations" (πᾶσιν τοῖς ἔθνεσιν). As predicted in the OT, the temple was meant to be the light of God's glory to the nations. Isaiah 2:3 predicts that in the last days, "Many peoples will come and say, 'Come, let us go up to the mountain of the LORD, to the temple of the God

of Jacob'" (cf. 66:18 – 24). Since the term for "robber" (λῃστής) normally means "highway bandit" or "insurrectionist" rather than extortionist (cf. 14:48; 15:27; BDAG, 594), it is unclear whether it refers here to the sellers, who may or may not be charging exorbitant prices,[39] or to the priestly aristocracy, under whose authority the temple has become a defiled place. The latter seems more likely in light of the context of Jer 7:9, which speaks of Israel's broader sins of theft, murder, adultery, perjury, and idolatry.

Almost all scholars accept as historically reliable the reports that Jesus took some action against the temple during this last week in Jerusalem and that it was this action more than any other that led to his arrest and execution. Yet what was the significance of the event? Few today would accept the claim of S. G. F. Brandon that this was a revolutionary move to seize the temple precincts.[40] This claim not only runs counter to much of Jesus' teaching (cf. 12:17; Matt 5:38 – 45), but such a move would no doubt have elicited a much stronger response from the authorities.

The two most common answers are that Jesus was symbolically "cleansing" the temple (the traditional title given to it), purging and restoring it for authentic worship, or that he was symbolically judging it and predicting its destruction. If the temple clearing is a symbolic act of destruction, this raises further questions. Did Jesus expect this destruction to be followed by its rebuilding and restoration? Or did his actions signify the end of the sacrificial system?

---

37. Using the Temple Mount as a shortcut for travel was forbidden. The Mishnah says a man "may not enter the Temple Mount with his staff or his sandal or his wallet or with the dust upon his feet, nor may he make it a short by-path" (*m. Ber.* 9:5).

38. The dual imperfects, "was teaching and was saying" (ἐδίδασκεν καὶ ἔλεγεν) are probably inceptive, "began to teach and say," with the dual expression stressing the significance of his words.

39. While the Mishnah suggests that the price of temple pigeons was sometimes inflated (*m. Ker.* 1:7), Mark himself does not say this.

40. S. G. F. Brandon, *Jesus and the Zealots: A Study of the Political Factor in Primitive Christianity* (Manchester: Manchester University Press, 1967). Against Brandon see Martin Hengel, *Was Jesus a Revolutionist?* (Facet Books, Biblical Series 28; Philadelphia: Fortress, 1971).

E. P. Sanders claims that Jesus' actions were those of an eschatological prophet, and that he was symbolically predicting that God would destroy the present temple and rebuild another "not made with hands" (14:58).[41] As noted above, symbolic actions like this are characteristic of the OT prophets. Indictments against a corrupt priesthood and temple appear in both the OT and in Judaism.[42]

Evans agrees that Jesus' actions are prophetic, but also sees royal and messianic significance.[43] Following Gundry, he points out that in the OT it was kings, not prophets, who cleansed and restored the temple. Joash and Josiah removed idols from the temple and restored its worship (2 Kgs 12:2 – 17; 23:1 – 37). Judas Maccabeus cleansed and rededicated the temple after the desecration of Antiochus Epiphanes (1 Macc 4:36 – 59). In *Pss. Sol.* 17:30 – 31 the Davidic Messiah is one who will "purge Jerusalem" so that all nations will "come from the ends of the earth" to see God's glory.[44] There are also significant parallels between Solomon's prayer of dedication for the temple (1 Kgs 8:43) and the two passage Jesus cites here (Isa 56:7; Jer 7:11). Following his royal entrance into Jerusalem in fulfillment of Zech 9:9, Jesus' actions must be seen as both prophetic and messianic.

There are also indications that Jesus' actions signify both purification *and* destruction. As noted above, after driving out the money changers and sellers, Jesus prevents merchandise from being carried through the temple courts (v. 16). This indicates protection or restoration of a sacred space for

its proper use. The two OT passages he cites also point in this direction.

Yet Jesus' actions also seem to represent an act of judgment and symbolic destruction. Jesus will shortly predict the destruction of the temple (13:2; cf. Luke 13:34 – 35; 19:41 – 44) and will be accused of threatening to destroy it himself both at his trial (14:58) and during the crucifixion (15:29 par.; cf. Acts 6:14). Even more importantly, the close parallel and intercalation of the temple cleansing with the withered fig tree indicate an act of judgment leading to destruction.[45] Jesus is acting with messianic authority. As God's agent to inaugurate the kingdom, he calls the religious authorities to restore true worship to the temple or face God's judgment and destruction.

A final question is whether Jesus ultimately expected the restoration and replacement of the temple after its destruction or the abolition of the sacrificial system.[46] The gospel writers certainly see the temple's destruction as evidence of its replacement by Jesus and the new community of faith. He is the stone that was rejected, yet became the cornerstone for the new temple of God (12:10).[47] But what about the historical Jesus? Most claim Jesus was surely expecting the temple's restoration, since the sacrificial system was rooted in the commands of God.[48] But if Jesus in fact referred to his death as a ransom for sins (10:45) and if he instituted a new Passover centered on his own imminent death rather than the sacrifice of lambs in the temple

---

41. Sanders, *Jesus and Judaism*, 61 – 76.

42. Mic 6:6 – 8; Mal 3:3 – 4; *Pss. Sol.* 2:3 – 5; 8:11 – 13; 1QHab 8:8 – 13; 12:1 – 10; CD 5:6 – 8; 6:12 – 17.

43. Evans, *Mark 8:27 – 16:20*, 173 – 82; idem, "Jesus' Action in the Temple: Cleansing or Portent of Destruction?" *CBQ* 51 (1989): 237 – 70.

44. Gundry, *Mark*, 642.

45. Some have argued that while Jesus was calling for the restoration of Israel's worship, Mark (and the other Evangelists) saw in this a portent of the end of the temple with its sacrificial

system and its replacement with Christ's sacrificial death on the cross. Hooker, *Mark*, 263, writes, "The whole incident … symbolizes the replacement of Judaism by Christianity."

46. See Sanders, *Jesus and Judaism*, 77 – 90.

47. For a comprehensive defense of the view that Mark sees Jesus and the messianic community as the replacement of the Jewish temple, see Gray, *The Temple in the Gospel of Mark*, passim.

48. Hooker, *Mark*, 263.

(14:22–25), then he likely envisioned the ultimate replacement of the temple and its sacrificial system.

11:18 The ruling priests and the experts in the law heard this and began looking for a way to destroy him, for they feared him because the whole crowd was amazed at his teaching (Καὶ ἤκουσαν οἱ ἀρχιερεῖς καὶ οἱ γραμματεῖς καὶ ἐζήτουν πῶς αὐτὸν ἀπολέσωσιν· ἐφοβοῦντο γὰρ αὐτόν, πᾶς γὰρ ὁ ὄχλος ἐξεπλήσσετο ἐπὶ τῇ διδαχῇ αὐτοῦ). Jesus' actions in the temple provoke a hostile reaction from Jerusalem's religious leaders. Two groups are named. The "ruling priests" (ἀρχιερεῖς; traditionally, "chief priests") were the priestly aristocracy of Jerusalem (see comments on 8:31). The "experts in the law" (γραμματεῖς; traditionally, "scribes") were experts in religious law (see on 1:22).

The statement recalls 3:6, where the Pharisees and the Herodians similarly plotted Jesus' death (cf. 12:13). The ruling priests and scribes have been named in the passion prediction in 10:33 and, together with the "elders," in 8:31. These three constituted the Sanhedrin, the Jewish high council (14:55; 15:1). The omission of the "elders" here may be simple economy of language (representatives from all three challenge Jesus' authority in 11:27). Or here the scribes and ruling priests may respectively represent Israel's two great institutions, Torah and temple, whose authority Jesus is seen as challenging. Throughout his Galilean ministry Jesus clashed repeatedly with the scribes and their allies, the Pharisees (2:6, 16; 3:22; 7:1, 5; 9:14), often over issues of the law (2:16, 18, 24; 3:4; cf. 10:2). Now, by acting against the temple, he is challenging the priests at their center of authority. So they begin to plot against him.[49]

In contrast to the religious leaders, "all the people" (πᾶς γὰρ ὁ ὄχλος) remain favorably disposed to Jesus. Their response to his teaching recalls the similar amazement in the synagogue at Capernaum at the beginning of Jesus' ministry (1:22; same verb: ἐκπλήσσω), "because he was teaching them as one who had authority, and not like the experts in the law." The crowd's amazement thus forms a kind of inclusio. It is this same "authority" (ἐξουσία) in both word and action (cf. 1:27) that the religious leaders will challenge in the following episode (11:28). Their "fear" here is connected to Jesus' influence with the people, a loss of power for the leaders (cf. 11:32; 12:12; 14:1–2).

11:19 When evening came, they went out of the city (Καὶ ὅταν ὀψὲ ἐγένετο, ἐξεπορεύοντο ἔξω τῆς πόλεως). As is their pattern throughout Passion Week, Jesus and his disciples withdraw from the city for the night, presumably to Bethany (11:11–12). Mark does not say whether they stayed outside Jerusalem because of the city's crowded conditions or the offer of hospitality provided in Bethany, or because Jerusalem was not a safe place for Jesus. From a narrative perspective, the departure allows for the discovery of the fig tree the next morning.

11:20–21 Early the next morning as they passed by, they saw the fig tree withered away from the roots. Remembering, Peter said to him, "Rabbi, look! The fig tree you cursed has withered." (Καὶ παραπορευόμενοι πρωῒ εἶδον τὴν συκῆν ἐξηραμμένην ἐκ ῥιζῶν. καὶ ἀναμνησθεὶς ὁ Πέτρος λέγει αὐτῷ· ῥαββί, ἴδε ἡ συκῆ ἣν κατηράσω ἐξήρανται). Mark now finishes the story that began in 11:12–14. It is presumably Tuesday morning of Passion Week (see Literary Context on 11:1–11). By intercalating this episode with the temple clearing, Mark indicates that both are symbolic gestures related to Israel's unfruitfulness and the coming destruction of Jerusalem and the temple.

The fig tree's withering "from the roots" indicates

---

49. The imperfect ἐζήτουν is probably inceptive ("began to look for") rather than iterative (contra Stein, *Mark*, 518), since this is the beginning of the plot *by the priestly authorities* in Jerusalem.

its total destruction. This is a dead tree, not a sickly one that could be nursed back to health. The implication is that the tree represents the temple, where "not even one stone will be left here on another" (13:2). It does not represent Israel per se, since many Jews will be saved and the remnant of the nation will be restored. The temple's destruction results from the nation's unfaithfulness as a whole and more specifically, her corrupt leadership. Peter, as a representative of the disciples, notices and comments on the withered fig tree. As throughout Mark's gospel, amazement (here implied) is the appropriate response to Jesus' messianic authority (1:22, 27; 2:12; 5:15, 20, 42; 6:2, 51; 7:37; 11:18; 12:17). For the address "Rabbi," see comments on 9:5–6; 10:51.

11:22–23 Jesus replied to them, "Have faith in God. Truly I say to you, if anyone says to this mountain, 'Be lifted up and thrown into the sea,' and does not doubt in his heart, but believes that what he says will happen, it will be done for him." (καὶ ἀποκριθεὶς ὁ Ἰησοῦς λέγει αὐτοῖς· ἔχετε πίστιν θεοῦ. ἀμὴν λέγω ὑμῖν ὅτι ὃς ἂν εἴπῃ τῷ ὄρει τούτῳ· ἄρθητι καὶ βλήθητι εἰς τὴν θάλασσαν, καὶ μὴ διακριθῇ ἐν τῇ καρδίᾳ αὐτοῦ ἀλλὰ πιστεύῃ ὅτι ὃ λαλεῖ γίνεται, ἔσται αὐτῷ). Strangely, while Mark's narrative strongly implies the symbolic relationship between the cursing of the fig tree and the coming judgment against the temple, Jesus does not make this connection in the teaching that follows. Instead, he appears to turn the withered fig tree into a lesson on faith and prayer.

Some claim from this that Mark himself did not see symbolic judgment in the fig tree episode. Evidence is that Mark himself appears to have brought these sayings together (vv. 22–25), since they occur in different places in the other gospels (Matt

6:14–15; 17:20; cf. Luke 17:6). Nevertheless, since intercalation is so characteristic of Mark's literary style and always indicates a thematic relationship between two events, it seems likely that he saw a similar relationship here. It is probably best to see Jesus' lessons on faith (Mark 11:22–24) as a secondary application of the fig tree episode.

One possibility is that the original episode, with its allusion to the destruction of the temple, concluded with a call to faith and perseverance in the face of trials ahead (v. 22), something characteristic of apocalyptic discourses (13:9, 13, 18, 23, 33, 35–37). Mark, then, took this opportunity to include other sayings related to faith (vv. 22–23), prayer (v. 24), and forgiveness (v. 25). The sayings appear to be linked to one another by a series of catchwords: "faith/believe" (vv. 22–23; v. 24); "prayer" (v. 24; v. 25); "forgive" (v. 25; v. 26).

On the idiom "answering … he said," see comments on vv. 13–14. "Faith in God" (πίστιν θεοῦ) is an objective genitive, with God as the object of faith. This call for faith (v. 22) is followed in v. 23 by a promise introduced by Jesus' solemn introductory formula, "Truly I say to you" (ἀμὴν λέγω ὑμῖν; see comments on 3:28–30).[50] Similar sayings on the power of faith appear throughout in the gospel tradition. In addition to Matthew's parallel in Matt 21:21, Matt 17:20 speaks of the ability to move mountains with mustard-seed faith (cf. *Gos. Thom.* 48, 106), and in Luke 17:6 mustard-seed faith is sufficient to uproot a mulberry tree. Paul similarly speaks of "faith that can move mountains" (1 Cor 13:2).

Though the mountain is, of course, proverbial, in Mark's narrative context ("*this* mountain"), it likely refers either to the Temple Mount or the Mount of Olives. Both would fit an eschatologi-

---

50. Some manuscripts make v. 22 a conditional clause, "if [εἰ] you have faith in God …" (א D Θ *f*[13] 28 33[c] 565 700 pc it syr[s]). Though this has strong external support, the word is prob-

ably a scribal assimilation to the saying in Luke 17:6 (cf. Matt 21:21), since the ἀμήν formula is never preceded by the protasis of a conditional clause (Metzger, *Textual Commentary*, 92).

cal context. The "mountain of the LORD" (Mount Zion) as the location of the eschatological temple appears in Isa 2:2 – 3 and Mic 4:1, and in Zech 14:4 the Mount of Olives splits in two at the coming of the Lord. In light of Jesus' prediction of the temple's destruction, the former is more likely. Jesus' primary point, however, is not about identifying the mountain, but the power of faith.[51] Moving a mountain is proverbial for something humanly impossible, but possible with God (cf. Zech 4:7).[52] Faith as the prerequisite for miracles is a common theme in Mark (1:40; 2:5; 5:34, 36; 6:5 – 6; 7:29, 32; 9:23 – 24; 10:52). The language of faith that does not doubt or waver appears in Jas 1:6.

11:24 "Therefore I tell you, whatever you pray and ask for, believe that you have received it, and it will be yours." (διὰ τοῦτο λέγω ὑμῖν, πάντα ὅσα προσεύχεσθε καὶ αἰτεῖσθε, πιστεύετε ὅτι ἐλάβετε, καὶ ἔσται ὑμῖν). The efficacious power of faith is now applied specifically to prayer (cf. "therefore"). If you pray with faith, Jesus says, you will receive what you ask for. This is another common theme in Jesus' teaching (Matt 7:7; 18:19; Luke 11:9; John 14:13 – 14; 15:7, 16; 16:23 – 24). On the thorny question of unanswered prayer, see Theology in Application.

11:25 "And whenever you stand praying, if you have anything against anyone, forgive them, so that your Father in heaven will forgive you your sins." (Καὶ ὅταν στήκετε προσευχόμενοι, ἀφίετε εἴ τι ἔχετε κατά τινος, ἵνα καὶ ὁ πατὴρ ὑμῶν ὁ ἐν τοῖς οὐρανοῖς ἀφῇ ὑμῖν τὰ παραπτώματα ὑμῶν). The topic shifts again from faith and prayer to prayer and forgiveness. The verbal link is prayer. To "stand praying" is a common posture for prayer in Judaism (1 Sam 1:26; 1 Kgs 8:22; Matt 6:5; Luke 18:11, 13). Our failure to forgive others is not only detrimental to our relationship with them, but also with God; so Jesus commands his followers to offer forgiveness, just as they have been forgiven.

This command parallels Matt 5:23 – 24, where the context is offering a sacrifice in the temple. Forgiving others as a prerequisite for forgiveness from "your Father in heaven" also appears in the Lord's model prayer (Matt 6:12) and in Jesus' subsequent teaching (6:14 – 15).

Mark 11:26 ("but if you do not forgive, neither will your Father who is in heaven forgive your sins") is absent from the earliest and most reliable manuscripts.[53] While it is possible that it was accidently omitted through homeoteleuton ("like ending"), where the eye of a copyist skipped from "your sins/trespasses" in v. 25 (τὰ παραπτώματα ὑμῶν) to the same phrase at the end of v. 26, it seems more likely that a copyist has introduced it from Matt 6:15, where it serves as the inverse to 6:14.

Theology in Application

Jesus' Authority to Cleanse and to Judge

Jesus' actions in the temple were both a symbolic cleansing and a pronouncement of coming destruction. As with his teaching, miracles, and entering Jerusalem as King (11:1 – 11; cf. Zech 9:9), Jesus is acting with messianic authority. Just as

---

51. Contra Gray, *The Temple in the Gospel of Mark*, 48 – 53, who thinks the *primary* reference is to the Temple Mount and the coming destruction of Jerusalem. Cf. Marshall, *Faith as a Theme,* 168 – 69.

52. For rabbinic references, see Str-B 1:759.

53. The sentence, with some variation, appears in A C D Θ 𝑓[1, 13] 33 𝔐 lat syr [p,h] boh[pt]. It is omitted in ℵ B L W Δ Ψ 565 700 892 2427 syr[s] sah boh[pt].

Solomon dedicated the first Jerusalem temple and other kings of Judah restored the purity of its worship, so Jesus casts out the sellers who are impeding worship and restores the temple as a house of prayer for all nations.

Yet Jesus' actions in judging and purging the temple reveal even greater authority than this. In the OT it is God himself who pronounces judgment on the nation Israel for her sins of idolatry and injustice. In Isaiah's Song of the Vineyard (Isa 5:1 – 7), the owner of the vineyard is God, who breaks down the vineyard's walls so that the nation's enemies (the Assyrians) can overrun and destroy her. Jesus is acting in the role of Yahweh himself, pronouncing judgment against Israel's unfaithfulness. He is "the Lord" who comes suddenly to his temple to purge and to judge (Mal 3:1).[54]

This implicit high Christology appears throughout Mark's gospel. It begins with Jesus as the Lord, whose messenger (John the Baptist) prepares the way before him to lead the righteous remnant of Israel on a new exodus deliverance (Mark 1:2 – 3; cf. Isa 40:3; Mal 3:1). While John baptized with water, Jesus will baptize with the Holy Spirit and with fire (Mark 1:8; Luke 3:16). Since in the OT the Spirit is the very vitality of God, this is an act of God himself (cf. Acts 2:17, 33; 16:6 – 7). It is no wonder that in the next episode the religious leaders will challenge Jesus to tell by what authority he is performing these audacious actions (11:27 – 28).

The Responsibility to Bear Fruit

The fig tree's problem is that it is bearing no fruit, and this is the problem of Israel and her leaders. Jesus' actions against the fig tree and the temple point forward to the parable of the tenant farmers (12:1 – 12), in which the vineyard's caretakers (Israel's leaders) refuse to return the owner's share of the produce, killing the owner's messenger and eventually his son. For this they face judgment, as the owner comes and kills the tenants and gives the vineyard to others (12:9).

This theme also recalls Jesus' parable of the sower, in which the seed of "the word" (= the message of the kingdom of God) fails to bear fruit in many who hear it (4:1 – 12). The religious leaders are like the seed that is snatched by Satan before it even has a chance to sprout (4:4, 15). The people, who at this point in Mark are still amazed and delighted at his teaching (11:18; 12:12, 37), are like the seed on rocky ground, who receive the message with joy but will soon fall away. The question hanging heavy over the narrative is whether the disciples will eventually bear fruit — or will they too fall away?

The responsibility to bear fruit has direct application to the church today. Jesus repeatedly tells parables about good stewardship, the need for his followers to be faithful with the gifts and calling God has given them (Matt 24:43 – 51; 25:1 – 13, 14 – 25; Luke 12:38 – 40, 42 – 46; 16:10 – 12; 19:11 – 27). In John's gospel Jesus speaks

54. On this theme from Malachi, see Gray, *The Temple in the Gospel of Mark*, 22 – 23.

of the need to stay connected to the vine in order to bear fruit (John 15:1 – 8). The fruit that we bear represents the impact we have on others for the kingdom of God. This can refer to bringing others to Christ, the fruit of new birth in Christ, as well as our behavior that has a positive impact on others for the sake of the kingdom — the fruit of the Spirit that Paul refers to in Gal 5:22: "love, joy, peace, forbearance, kindness, goodness, faithfulness, gentleness and self-control."

The Power of Faith and Prayer

Jesus also turns the fig tree episode into a powerful lesson on faith, prayer, and forgiveness. He cites the common refrain through the NT that God answers prayer and that whatever we ask for we will receive (Matt 7:7; 17:20; 18:19; Mark 9:29; Luke 11:9; John 14:13 – 14; 15:7, 16; 16:23 – 24; Jas 1:5 – 8; 1 John 5:14 – 15). This is because behind our requests stands the awesome Creator of the universe, who has infinite resources.

Yet this promise must not be misunderstood as a promise that God will give us anything we want, whatever are our selfish desires. There are a number of qualifications to this promise. Most importantly, we must ask according to God's will (1 John 5:14); we must ask in Jesus' name (John 14:13 – 14; 15:16; 16:23 – 24, 26), that is, in accord with the person and work of Christ; we must ask from a position of obedience (1 John 3:21 – 22) and having forgiven others in the same way God has forgiven us (Mark 11:25).

It is clear throughout the Bible that God is not a magic genie or a cosmic bellhop who immediately jumps to meet our every desire. We are *his slaves*, and since he has redeemed us from Satan, sin, and death, we owe him total allegiance. Our requests must therefore be according to his will and his kingdom purposes (Matt 6:33). Even Jesus, in the garden of Gethsemane, prayed, "Not what I want, but what you want" (Mark 14:36). The Lord's model prayer summarizes well how we should pray: "Your kingdom come, your will be done, on earth as it is in heaven" (Matt 6:10).

45

Mark 11:27 – 33

Literary Context

This passage connects closely to both what precedes and what follows. Jesus has just demonstrated remarkable authority in clearing the temple of money changers and sellers (11:15 – 18). Now he returns to the "scene of the crime" and is confronted by Israel's religious leaders, who challenge him about the authority by which he took this action.

This episode connects with what follows as the beginning of a series of six controversy stories that represent a showdown between Jesus and the leaders. In these controversies he demonstrates superior wisdom and exposes the religious leaders as self-centered, deceitful, hypocritical, and unworthy to lead God's people (cf. 12:38 – 40). This series recalls the controversy stories that occurred during Jesus' early Galilean ministry (2:1 – 3:6). Just as those ended with a plot on Jesus' life (3:6), so these begin with one (11:18).

III. The Suffering Way of the Messiah (8:22 – 15:47)
    A. Revelation of the Messiah's Suffering (8:22 – 10:52)
    B. The Messiah Confronts Jerusalem (11:1 – 13:37)
        1. The Triumphal Entry (11:1 – 11)
        2. Prophetic Action in the Temple and Cursing a Fig Tree (11:12 – 25)
➡   **3. Controversies in the Temple (11:27 – 12:44)**
          a. A Challenge to Jesus' Authority (11:27 – 33)
          b. The Parable of the Tenants (12:1 – 12)

Main Idea

Having demonstrated his messianic authority by clearing the temple, Jesus is questioned by the religious leaders about the source of his authority. Recognizing an attempt to trap him, Jesus counters by asking whether John the Baptist's authority was from God or of human origin. The leaders' unwillingness to answer reveals Jesus' superior wisdom and exposes them as hypocrites and fraudulent leaders.

Translation

Mark 11:27–33

27a	Action/Character entrance	**They came again to Jerusalem,**
b	setting (temporal & spatial)	and … while he was walking in the temple courts,
c	Character entrance	**the ruling priests, the experts in the law, and the elders** came up to him and said to him,
28a	question/ challenge	"By what authority are you doing these things?
b	parallel question/challenge	Or who gave you this authority to do these things?"
29a	Response	**Jesus said to them,**
b	challenge	"I will ask you one question.
c		Answer me and I will tell you by what authority I am doing these things.
30a	question	The baptism of John — was it from heaven or merely human?
b	challenge	Answer me."
31a	Response	**They began discussing it among themselves and said,**
b	condition	"If we say, 'From heaven,'
d	result	he will say,
e		'Then why didn't you believe him?'
32a	condition	But if we say, 'Merely human'…?"
b	Narrative comment	**They feared the crowd,**
c	reason	for they all believed that John was a prophet.
33a	Response to 29–30	So **they answered Jesus,**
b		"We don't know."
c	Response to 33a	**Jesus said,**
d		"Then neither will I tell you by what authority I am doing these things."

Structure

The episode is a controversy story, with a challenge to Jesus by Israel's religious leaders (vv. 27–28), a counterquestion by him (vv. 29–30), a discussion among the religious leaders resulting in a nonresponse to his question (vv. 31–33b), and Jesus' final response exposing their deceit (v. 33c-d). The counterquestion is a common rabbinic style of teaching.[1] It was generally used to establish common ground to lead toward an answer to the original question. Jesus does this in 10:2–7 and 12:14–17, where the answer to his counterquestion is agreed on by both parties and builds to his solution.

---

1. Str-B 1:861; Evans, *Mark 8:27–16:20*, 203; G. S. Shae, "The Question on the Authority of Jesus," *NovT* 16 (1974): 1–29; cf. *b. Sanh.* 65b and *Gen. Rab.* 27.4.

Here, however, the counterquestion creates a conundrum for the questioners, forcing them toward a solution they do not want to accept.[2] In this way it is closer to Jesus' questions (not counterquestions) in 3:23 and 12:37. By (rhetorically) asking, "How can Satan cast out Satan?" (3:23), Jesus refutes the claim that he is casting out demons by Satan's power. By asking, "How can the Messiah be both David's son and David's Lord?" he reveals the Messiah is different from what they were expecting.

The present episode is widely believed to have a historical foundation since it is closely related to the temple incident, which itself has a strong claim to authenticity.[3] It is significant that John's account of the cleansing of the temple, which appears to come from independent tradition (John 2:13 – 17), is also followed by a challenge to Jesus' authority (2:18).

Exegetical Outline

→ 1. Jesus Questioned about the Source of His Authority (11:27 – 28)
   2. Jesus' Counterquestion: The Authority of John the Baptist (11:29 – 30)
   3. The Leaders' Discussion and Response (11:31 – 33b)
   4. Jesus' Conclusion (11:33c-d)

Explanation of the Text

11:27 – 28 They came again to Jerusalem, and while he was walking in the temple courts, the ruling priests, the experts in the law, and the elders came up to him and said to him, "By what authority are you doing these things? Or who gave you this authority to do these things?" (Καὶ ἔρχονται πάλιν εἰς Ἱεροσόλυμα. καὶ ἐν τῷ ἱερῷ περιπατοῦντος αὐτοῦ ἔρχονται πρὸς αὐτὸν οἱ ἀρχιερεῖς καὶ οἱ γραμματεῖς καὶ οἱ πρεσβύτεροι καὶ ἔλεγον αὐτῷ· ἐν ποίᾳ ἐξουσίᾳ ταῦτα ποιεῖς; ἢ τίς σοι ἔδωκεν τὴν ἐξουσίαν ταύτην ἵνα ταῦτα ποιῇς;). The mention of Jerusalem as the destination of Jesus and his disciples reminds the reader that the climax of Jesus' ministry is near (cf. 10:33).

This is reinforced as the three groups named in the first passion prediction (8:31; cf. 10:33) show up to question Jesus. These three groups made up

the Sanhedrin, the seventy-member Jewish ruling council. The "ruling priests" (ἀρχιερεῖς; see on 8:31) and the "experts in the law" (γραμματεῖς; see on 1:22) have appeared just before this in 11:18, plotting Jesus' death. The "elders" (πρεσβύτεροι; see comments on 8:31) were influential lay leaders in the Sanhedrin. The point is that these elite Jewish authorities of Jerusalem come together to challenge the authority of this upstart rabbi. The fact that Jesus is walking around freely in the temple courts is itself evidence of his authority. He shows no fear of retribution. The question of the source of Jesus' authority is not without precedent in Mark's gospel. Back in 3:22 the experts in the law from Jerusalem claimed that he was casting out demons by Beelzebul, the prince of demons.

The leaders ask two parallel questions, the sec-

---

2. Marcus, *Mark 9 – 16*, 799.
3. Taylor, *Mark*, 469; Cranfield, *Mark*, 362; Evans, *Mark*

8:27 – 16:20, 198; Stein, *Mark*, 523 – 24; Marcus, *Mark 9 – 16*, 798.

ond clarifying the first. "By what authority…?" means essentially "Who gave you this authority?" "These things" (ταῦτα) in context refers to Jesus' provocative actions in the temple and perhaps his royal entrance into Jerusalem the day before.[4] The purpose of the question is not to embarrass Jesus, as Stein asserts.[5] The crowds would probably welcome such a claim to authority. Nor are they "complaining that he is acting without their authorization."[6] They are most likely seeking evidence for messianic claims to authority or opposition to the temple. It is these accusations that will be brought against Jesus at his trial and crucifixion (14:58, 61; 15:29, 32). The Romans did not look favorably on would-be insurrectionists, and false prophets could be executed under Jewish law (Deut 13:1 – 5; 18:20).

11:29 – 30 Jesus said to them, "I will ask you one question. Answer me and I will tell you by what authority I am doing these things. The baptism of John — was it from heaven or merely human? Answer me." (ὁ δὲ Ἰησοῦς εἶπεν αὐτοῖς· ἐπερωτήσω ὑμᾶς ἕνα λόγον, καὶ ἀποκρίθητέ μοι καὶ ἐρῶ ὑμῖν ἐν ποίᾳ ἐξουσίᾳ ταῦτα ποιῶ· τὸ βάπτισμα τὸ Ἰωάννου ἐξ οὐρανοῦ ἦν ἢ ἐξ ἀνθρώπων; ἀποκρίθητέ μοι). Jesus turns the tables by asking a counterquestion that presents a conundrum and challenges the sincerity of their question. John the Baptist

was widely regarded as an authentic prophet, a reputation firmly cemented by his martyrdom (6:14 – 29). And Jesus' ministry was closely linked to John's, both because of his baptism by John (1:9) and because John pointed to Jesus as his successor (1:7 – 8).[7] If they accept the divine authority behind John's ministry, they should accept Jesus' as well.

The phrase "baptism of John" is shorthand for John's whole ministry — his call to repent and be baptized for the forgiveness of sins in preparation for the coming of the Lord (1:2 – 8). "Heaven" is a common circumlocution for "God,"[8] so "from heaven" (ἐξ οὐρανοῦ) means divinely ordained and accomplished. "Merely human" (ἐξ ἀνθρώπων; lit., "from people") thus carries a derogatory sense; it means arising from error and destined to fail. Various messianic movements of the first century failed because they were not from God. In Acts 5 Gamaliel uses the same language when comparing the fledgling church with the failed rebellions of Theudas and Judas the Galilean. If the Jesus movement is "from men," he said, it will fail, but if it is "from God," no one will be able to stop it (Acts 5:35 – 39).

The repetition of the imperative, "Answer me" (vv. 29, 30), at the end emphasizes Jesus' authority. With audacity the young prophet and rabbi from Galilee demands an answer from Israel's religious elite![9]

---

4. Boring, *Mark*, 326, says that the plural "these things" refers to Jesus' whole ministry rather than the single temple event; Gundry, *Mark*, 657, claims the present tense "are doing" and the near demonstrative "these" indicates that Jesus is continuing to stop traffic in the temple. Both are overly literal readings of a normal way of referring to the actions (plural!) of the previous day.

5. Stein, *Mark*, 525, 528.

6. Hooker, *Mark*, 271.

7. Though the historicity of this second point is hotly debated, it is deeply embedded in the Jesus tradition (Matt 3:11 – 12; Luke 3:15 – 18; John 1:24 – 28; Acts 1:5; 10:37; 11:16; 13:24 – 25). John's claim that he is unworthy to unlatch the

Coming One's sandals (1:7 par.; John 1:27) indicates he was expecting a human successor, and his doubts about Jesus (Matt 11:2 – 19; Luke 7:18 – 35) — a story unlikely to have been created by the church — confirm that he previously had messianic expectations concerning him.

8. Dan 4:26; 1 Macc 4:10, 24; Luke 15:18, 21. See Matthew's frequent replacement of "kingdom of God" with "kingdom of heaven" (3:2; 4:17; 5:3; etc.); Marcus, *Mark 9 – 16*, 796.

9. Marcus, *Mark 9 – 16*, 799, claims that in biblical dialogue the repetition of a phrase without an intervening response sometimes implies that the interlocutors have been rendered speechless (Gen 16:10 – 11; 20:9 – 10; 41:39 – 41; 42:1 – 2).

11:31 – 32 They began discussing it among themselves and said, "If we say, 'From heaven,' he will say, 'Then why didn't you believe him?' But if we say, 'Merely human' …?" They feared the crowd, for they all believed that John was a prophet (καὶ διελογίζοντο πρὸς ἑαυτοὺς λέγοντες· ἐὰν εἴπωμεν· ἐξ οὐρανοῦ, ἐρεῖ· διὰ τί οὖν οὐκ ἐπιστεύσατε αὐτῷ; ἀλλὰ εἴπωμεν· ἐξ ἀνθρώπων; ἐφοβοῦντο τὸν ὄχλον· ἅπαντες γὰρ εἶχον τὸν Ἰωάννην ὄντως ὅτι προφήτης ἦν). Jesus' question creates a dilemma for the religious leaders, who huddle to discuss it (on διαλογίζομαι, see comments on 8:16; the imperfect is probably inceptive: "began discussing …").

The first conditional clause is a third class condition in the subjunctive, with a protasis and an apodosis ("If we say [ἐὰν εἴπωμεν] … he will say [ἐρεῖ]").[10] The second is unusual in that it omits the word "if" and does not contain an apodosis, reading literally, "But we might say" (ἀλλὰ εἴπωμεν). This may be a deliberative subjunctive, meaning "Dare we say, 'merely human'?" (cf. NLT, ESV, REB).[11] More likely the "if" is elided (dropped for economy of language) and followed by an anacoluthon (an unfinished sentence): "But [if] we say, 'from men' …?" leaving the dreaded consequences unstated (cf. NIV, NET, HCSB, NASB, NKJV). Both Matthew and Luke understood the sentence in this way, smoothing Mark's construction by adding an "if" (ἐάν) and then finishing the apodosis, Luke with "all the people will stone us" (Luke 20:6), and Matthew with "we are afraid of the people" (Matt 21:26). As usual, Mark's rhetoric is the more powerful, suggesting the consequences are too frightening to express.

The leaders' dilemma relates first to John the Baptist and then to Jesus. Whether or not they had actively opposed John's ministry, his arrest and execution meant they no longer had to deal with his call for repentance and baptism. Now, however, Jesus puts them on the spot by asking whether John was indeed sent from God (cf. John 1:6). An affirmative answer would open them up to the charge of rejecting God's messenger: "Then why didn't you believe him?" But a negative answer would place them in opposition to the people, who revered John and believed he was God's prophet.[12] Their hypocrisy is evident in that their deliberations are motivated not by what is true about John, but by the potential backlash from Jesus or the crowds.

The second (implied) dilemma they face is related to Jesus. If they were to accept the legitimacy of John's ministry, then they should also accept the authority of Jesus, since John was the forerunner who pointed to Jesus (1:2 – 8; Matt 3:11 – 12; Luke 3:15 – 18; John 1:15, 24 – 31, 35 – 36; Acts 1:5; 10:37; 11:16; 13:24 – 25).

11:33 So they answered Jesus, "We don't know." Jesus said, "Then neither will I tell you by what authority I am doing these things." (καὶ ἀποκριθέντες τῷ Ἰησοῦ λέγουσιν· οὐκ οἴδαμεν. καὶ ὁ Ἰησοῦς λέγει αὐτοῖς· οὐδὲ ἐγὼ λέγω ὑμῖν ἐν ποίᾳ ἐξουσίᾳ ταῦτα ποιῶ). The only way out of their dilemma is to claim ignorance about John's authority. Yet such agnosticism indicates a humiliating loss for them. Their inability to discern spiritual matters with reference to John invalidates their claim to be leaders over God's people. How can they shepherd God's flock if they cannot discern his will? Furthermore, in a shame/honor culture, to admit ignorance signals humiliation and loss of face. From the perspective of Mark's readers, the leaders' internal dialogue reveals that they are hypocrites, since they obviously know but refuse to

---

10. Wallace, *Greek Grammar*, 697.
11. Marcus, *Mark 9 – 16*, 797.
12. John's impact and reputation as a prophet are deeply embedded in the gospel tradition and are even attested by Josephus (*Ant.* 18.5.2 §§116 – 119). Followers of John appear in the book of Acts, long after his death (19:3 – 4; cf. 18:25).

acknowledge John's status as a prophet. Their pride and self-interest outweighs their submission to the will of God.

If they will not answer Jesus' question, he will not answer theirs. This is more than just a tit for tat. His refusal to answer is essentially saying that if they have no discernment in the ways of God with reference to John, they have no authority or ability to judge the source of his authority. So there is no reason to answer.

Theology in Application

The question of who has authority as God's representative is at the center of this episode. The religious leaders who claim to be God's anointed leaders over the temple and the Torah turn out to be frauds. They are unable or unwilling to identify John's status as a true prophet from God. By contrast, Jesus, who has no official position in the temple hierarchy or as a recognized teacher of the law, speaks and acts with God's authority.

Jesus' Authority as Validation of His Person and Message

Jesus' authority has been a major theme throughout Mark's gospel. At his first synagogue appearance the people marveled at this authority in exorcisms and teaching, which was far superior to the authority of the scribes (1:22, 27). In the chapters that follow, Jesus demonstrated remarkable authority in proclaiming the kingdom of God, healing the sick, casting out demons, forgiving sins, raising the dead, calming the sea, and walking on water.

The source of his authority is implicit throughout. Jesus proclaims the kingdom of God and, like God, forgives sins, commands the sea, and raises the dead. He refutes the claim that he casts out demons by Satan's power (3:23 – 29), which implies his authority is from God. Twice, at the baptism (1:11) and the transfiguration (9:7), the Father's voice from heaven affirms his mission and declares him to be "my beloved Son." These passages have a clear connection to the present one, since in the passage that follows (12:1 – 12) Jesus will portray himself as the Son sent (with authority) from the Father, who will face opposition and rejection. Though Jesus refuses to answer the religious leaders' question, he has already answered it through his words and actions; he will continue to do so in the days ahead. Those with "eyes to see" already know the answer.

The Authority to Give Up His Life

Ironically, the authority of the Son is what leads to his death. The religious leaders feel threatened by him and so take action against him. This is no tragedy, however, but is precisely what he has been sent by the Father to accomplish. It is as the authoritative Son of Man that Jesus has come to give his life as a ransom for many (10:45).

By virtue of his authority he will submit his will to the Father and say, "Not what I want, but what you want" (14:36).

This combination of authority, sacrifice, and vindication appears throughout the NT. In Phil 2:6 – 11, the Son's status of equality with God makes his incarnation and sacrifice for sins efficacious for all, and it results in his exaltation to the highest place. In Col 2:13 – 15 Christ's sacrificial death on the cross disarms all "powers and authorities" and results in his triumph over all. For Mark's readers who are undergoing suffering and persecution, the promise is that after suffering will come vindication for those willing to take up their cross and follow the Son.

Mark 12:1 – 12

Literary Context

The parable of the tenants is the second in a series of six controversy stories (11:27 – 12:44) that take place in the temple during Jesus' last days in Jerusalem. On the role of these stories in the structure of Mark's gospel, see Literary Context on 11:27 – 33.

Jesus' royal approach to Jerusalem (11:1 – 11) and the challenge to his authority by the religious leaders (11:27 – 33) prepare for the tenants' challenge of the owner of the vineyard (God), his messengers (the prophets), and his son (Jesus). The judgment against Israel's leaders, symbolized by the temple clearing (11:15 – 17) and the withered fig tree (11:12 – 14, 20 – 21), plays out in this parable as the tenant farmers reject the owner and his representatives and are judged.

The plot against Jesus by the religious leaders following the temple clearing (11:18) prepares for the further plot after the parable (12:8). The parable may also be seen as an implicit answer to the question about the source of his authority in the previous episode, which Jesus refused to answer (11:33). His authority comes from his Father, who is the vineyard's owner, and he has been sent to claim what is rightfully his.

The parable also forms a kind of thematic inclusio with Jesus' teaching in parables in chapter 4. After Jesus' rejection by the religious leaders in chapter 3, where they accuse him of casting out demons by Satan's power, Jesus pronounces judgment against them by speaking in parables, "so that they may look and look but not perceive, and hear and hear but not understand" (4:12; citing Isa 6:9 – 10). While Jesus' parables *reveal* the kingdom's mysteries to the disciples, they *conceal* them from the religious leaders who have rejected him (4:11 – 12). Now, however, at the climax of Jesus' ministry, he tells a parable *whose message is clear to them*. Their eyes are briefly opened so that they recognize themselves in the parable (12:12), ironically provoking the fulfillment of the parable. They reject the Son and so unwittingly bring Mark's narrative to its climax, fulfilling God's plan to offer Jesus up as a ransom for many (10:45).

Main Idea

The allegorical parable of the tenants draws from Isaiah's Song of the Vineyard (Isa 5:1 – 7) to portray Israel's religious leaders as wicked tenant farmers over God's vineyard, who refuse to give the owner his due and eventually kill his son (Jesus). Judgment against them follows, and the son who was rejected becomes the cornerstone in the new temple that God will build (Ps 118:22 – 23), the people of God in the new age of salvation.

Translation

Mark 12:1 – 12

1a	Introduction	**Then** **he began to speak to them in parables:**	
b	Parable/action	*"A man*	planted a vineyard.
c	action (sequence)	*He*	put a wall around it,
			dug a pit for the winepress, and
			built a watchtower.
d	action	*Then he*	leased it to tenant farmers
		and	went on a journey.
2a	setting (temporal)		At harvest time
b	action: first servant sent	*he*	sent a servant to the tenant farmers
c	purpose		to receive from them his portion of the produce of the vineyard.
3a	response to 1st servant	*But*	seizing him,
b		*they*	beat him and
			sent him away empty-handed.
4a	action: second servant sent	*Then*	again
		he	sent another servant to them,
b	response to second servant	*and* **this one they**	beat on the head and
			treated shamefully.

5a	action: third servant sent	He		sent another,
b	response to third servant	*and* this one they		killed.
c	action: many others sent	*And* many others:		
d	summary response		some they	beat and
			others they	killed.
6a	character description	He had one left,		
b			a beloved son.	
c	cliimactic action: son sent	Finally, he		sent him to them, saying,
d		'They will respect my son.'		
7a	response to son	*But* those tenant farmers said to one another,		
b	action: plotting	'This is the heir.		
c		Come, let's		kill him,
		and the inheritance will be ours.'		
8a	action: killing			Seizing him,
b		they		killed him
		and		threw him out of the vineyard.
9a	rhetorical question	What, then,		will the owner of the vineyard do?
b	answer (sequence)	He		will come
		and		destroy the tenant farmers
c		*and*		will give the vineyard to others.

10a	Scripture quotation	Haven't you read this Scripture,
b		'The stone that the builders rejected, this has become the cornerstone.
11		The Lord has done this, and it is marvelous in our eyes'?" [Ps 118:22 – 23]
12a	Action: Plotting	**They were looking for a way to arrest him,**
b	obstacle to 12a	but **they were afraid of the crowd,**
c	reason for 12a	for **they knew that he had spoken the parable against them.**
d	result of 12	So leaving him,
		they went away.

Structure

This passage contains a parable (12:1 – 9), a supporting OT passage (12:10 – 11), and the plot against Jesus that the parable provokes (v. 12). While most of Jesus' parables are not allegories but make one main theological point (see 4:1 – 34), some do have allegorical features.[1] Of all of Jesus' parables, the parable of the tenants is the most allegorical, with the vineyard and each of the characters having counterparts in the context of Jesus' ministry (see Main Idea, above). Jesus recontextualizes

---

1. On the nature and purpose of Jesus' parables, see "In Depth: The Parables about the Kingdom of God" at 4:2.

Isaiah's Song of the Vineyard to reflect the situation of his ministry (see comments on vv. 1 – 2). While Isaiah's song concerned the unfaithfulness of the nation of Israel, Jesus' parable focuses on the nation's caretakers, who refuse to give God his due.

The parable also appears in Matthew (Matt 21:33 – 46), Luke (Luke 20:9 – 19), and *Gos. Thom.* 65 – 66. Matthew's version is close to Mark's, while Luke drops much of the introduction, obscuring the allusion to Isa 5:2. The gnostic editor of the *Gospel of Thomas* apparently ignored its allegorical elements and linked it together (§§63 – 64) with two other Synoptic parables as part of a gnostic polemic against materialism.[2]

Much debate has centered on the historicity and original form of the parable. While a detailed discussion of tradition-critical questions is beyond the scope of this commentary (which focuses on the Evangelist's message), a few comments are in order because of the importance of this parable for Jesus' self-understanding. Adolf Jülicher, who claimed that all allegorical elements in Jesus' parables were secondary, treated this parable as a creation of the Hellenistic church.[3] C. H. Dodd and J. Jeremias responded that the original parable came from Jesus himself, but the allegorical elements were later additions.[4] Those who reject these allegorical elements often point to the shorter versions in Luke and (esp.) the *Gospel of Thomas* as closer to the original.

More recently, many commentators have defended the essential historicity of the parable, including its allegorical elements.[5]

1. The parable fits well the Galilean setting of Jesus' day, with its large landed estates and tension between absentee landowners and local farmers (see comments on v. 1).

2. The allegorical features of the parable are unlikely to be secondary, since the parable is modeled after Isaiah's Song of the Vineyard (Isa 5:1 – 7), which itself is allegorical.

3. The version of the parable in the *Gospel of Thomas* is likely not original, since it removes the parable's introductory allusions to Isa 5:1 – 7 and reworks the parable's message toward a gnostic interpretation (see comments above). Furthermore, the fact that *Thomas* alludes to Ps 118:22 (despite the author's anti-Jewish stance) without actually citing it suggests this quotation was already part of the source used.

2. Meier, *Marginal Jew*, 1:134; Evans, *Mark 8:27 – 16:20*, 217 – 18, both following J.-M. Sevrin, "Un groupement de trois paraboles contre les richesses dans l'Evangile selon Thomas," in *Les paraboles évangeliques: Perspectives nouvelles* (ed. J. Delorme; Paris: Cerf, 1989), 425 – 39. The owner in this case is not God, but a wealthy lender who loses all because of his obsession with material things.

3. A. Jülicher, *Die Gleichnisreden Jesu* (Tübingen: Mohr [Siebeck], 1889), 2:385 – 406.

4. Dodd, *Parables of the Kingdom*, 124 – 32; Jeremias, *Parables of Jesus*, 70 – 77.

5. See esp. Evans, *Mark 8:27 – 16:20*, 215 – 31; Klyne Snodgrass, *The Parable of the Wicked Tenants: An Inquiry into Parable Interpretation* (Tübingen: Mohr [Siebeck], 1983).

4. The Dead Sea Scrolls interpret Isa 5:1 – 7 allegorically, identifying the vineyard with Jerusalem, the temple, and its corrupt leadership. This illustrates these allegorical possibilities in Second Temple Judaism.[6]

5. There is strong evidence of a Semitic original to the parable,[7] including a likely wordplay between the rejected "son" (*bēn*) of the parable and the rejected "stone" (*'eben*) of Ps 118:22.[8] This suggests that the parable and the OT quotation were already linked before the parable entered a Hellenistic context.

6. The absence of any explicit reference to the resurrection argues against the parable being a creation of the early church.

7. The supposedly "unrealistic" elements of the parable (see comments on vv. 6 – 8) in fact favor its historicity, since hyperbole and unusual behavior are common features in parables, those of both Jesus[9] and the rabbis.[10]

Exegetical Outline

→ **1. The Parable of the Tenant Farmers (12:1 – 9)**
   2. Scriptural Support from Psalm 118:22 – 23 (12:10 – 11)
   3. The Response of the Religious Leaders (12:12)
       a. The plot against Jesus (12:12a)
       b. The reason for the plot (12:12b-c)
       c. Their departure for fear of the crowd (12:12d)

Explanation of the Text

12:1 Then he began to speak to them in parables: "A man planted a vineyard. He put a wall around it, dug a pit for the winepress, and built a watchtower. Then he leased it to tenant farmers and went on a journey." (Καὶ ἤρξατο αὐτοῖς ἐν παραβολαῖς λαλεῖν· ἀμπελῶνα ἄνθρωπος ἐφύτευσεν καὶ περιέθηκεν φραγμὸν καὶ ὤρυξεν ὑπολήνιον καὶ ᾠκοδόμησεν πύργον καὶ ἐξέδετο αὐτὸν γεωργοῖς καὶ ἀπεδήμησεν). Having outwitted the religious leaders on their question about his authority (11:27 – 33), Jesus now goes on the offensive, challenging them in a parable about their authority as caretakers over Israel. The introduction to Jesus' parable has striking parallels to Isaiah's Song of the Vineyard:

---

6. George J. Brooke, "4Q500 1 and the Use of Scripture in the Parable of the Vineyard," *DSD* 2 (1995): 268 – 94; Collins, *Mark*, 543 – 44.

7. Evans, *Mark 8:27 – 16:20*, 224 – 30, points to (1) the presence of Semitisms in the parable; (2) allusions to the MT of Isa 5:1 – 7 and to targumic traditions related to it; and (3) the wordplay between "son" and "stone."

8. M. Black, "The Christological Use of the Old Testament in the New Testament," *NTS* 18 (1971 – 72): 1 – 14, esp. 11 – 14; Snodgrass, *Parable of the Wicked Tenants*, 63 – 65, 113 – 18.

9. Stein, *Mark*, 531, points to the shepherd who leaves ninety-nine sheep to seek the one (Luke 15:4), the commendation of the unrighteous steward (16:8), and the forgiveness of a servant's impossibly massive debt (Matt 18:24, 27).

10. See examples in Evans, *Mark 8:27 – 16:20*, 220 – 21.

ISAIAH 5:1–2	MARK 12:1
I will sing for the one I love a song about his vineyard: My loved one had a vineyard on a fertile hillside. He dug it up and cleared it of stones and planted it with the choicest vines. He built a watchtower in it and cut out a winepress as well. Then he looked for a crop of good grapes, but it yielded only bad fruit.	He then began to speak to them in parables: "A man planted a vineyard. He put a wall around it, dug a pit for the winepress, and built a watchtower. Then he leased it to tenant farmers and went away on a journey."

In Isaiah the vineyard represents Israel and Judah (5:7), which God will judge for their failure to produce good spiritual fruit. Because of the nation's injustice and idolatry, God will "take away its hedge" of protection and allow the Assyrians to overrun it (5:5). Jesus takes this imagery and modifies it, portraying Israel's leaders as wicked tenant farmers over the vineyard, who refuse to give God his share of the produce, first rejecting and abusing his messengers the prophets and then his Son, Jesus. The tenant farmers will be judged and the authority over the vineyard (God's people) will be given to others.[11]

The aorist "began to" (ἤρξατο) with verbs of speaking/teaching/preaching is common in Mark (1:45; 4:1; 5:17, 20; 6:2, 34; 8:11, 31; 10:28, 32; 12:1; 13:5) and carries a force similar to the ingressive aorist. The "them" refers to the religious leaders of 11:27–33. Jesus' teaching "in parables" (ἐν παραβολαῖς) recalls 3:23 and 4:2, and especially the purpose of parables in 4:10–12 (see Literary Context, above). The plural is odd, since only one parable is cited; this expression is likely an adverbial prepositional phrase meaning "parabolically."[12]

The actions of the man in planting the vine-

yard, building a wall and a watchtower (for protection against thieves), and digging out a winepress are probably not themselves allegorical,[13] but intentionally introduced to echo Isa 5:1–2. These features of a vineyard would be recognized by a Mediterranean audience. The vineyard itself is no doubt a reference to Israel. In the OT the nation is often portrayed as a vineyard (Isa 1:8; 5:1–7; 27:2; Ezek 19:10) and her leaders sometimes as failed guardians who exploit and ruin her (Isa 3:14; Jer 12:10).

The practice of leasing a vineyard to others was common in the Galilee, with its large landed estates and absentee landowners, and would be familiar to Jesus' audience.[14] Evans argues that these are not "peasant" farmers, as they are often described, but wealthy commercial farmers managing multiple farms.[15] This is uncertain from the parable itself, but would fit well the analogy to Israel's aristocratic religious leaders.

12:2 At harvest time he sent a servant to the tenant farmers to receive from them his portion of the produce of the vineyard (καὶ ἀπέστειλεν πρὸς τοὺς γεωργοὺς τῷ καιρῷ δοῦλον ἵνα παρὰ τῶν γεωργῶν λάβῃ ἀπὸ τῶν καρπῶν τοῦ ἀμπελῶνος).

---

11. For a response to the views of William Herzog, Luise Schottroff, and others that a parable like this one does not represent God's dealings with Israel but rather the harsh and inequitable realities of Palestinian life and Roman hegemony, see Blomberg, *Interpreting the Parables*, 186–88.

12. France, *Mark*, 458.

13. Contra Brooke, "4Q500 1 and the Use of Scripture," 268–94, who points to evidence in the Targums and at Qumran identifying the temple as the tower and the altar as the winepress.

14. Dodd, *Parables of the Kingdom*, 93–98; Jeremias, *Parables of Jesus*, 175–76; Snodgrass, *Parable of the Wicked Tenants*, 31–40; Craig A. Evans, "Jesus' Parable of the Tenant Farmers in Light of Lease Agreements in Antiquity," *JSP* 14 (1996): 65–83; J. D. Hester, "Socio-Rhetorical Criticism and the Parable of the Tenants," *JSNT* 14 (1992): 34–36.

15. Evans, *Mark 8:27–16:20*, 232–33; idem, "Jesus' Parable," 74–80.

The dative "in time/season" (τῷ καιρῷ) probably means "at harvest time," but could perhaps mean "in due course," meaning the four years or so necessary for a vineyard to produce a crop, or "at the appointed time," meaning the time specified by the lease.[16] The phrase "of the produce" (ἀπὸ τῶν καρπῶν) means that portion of the produce that the contract stipulated. The "produce" or "fruits" (καρποί) may mean the crop itself or the proceeds from its sale.[17]

We have translated δοῦλος as "servant" rather than "slave" not because this individual is not owned by the master (he surely is), but because the point is his role in fulfilling the master's wishes.[18] This also fits better the allegorization of the prophets, who are often referred to as God's servants, ignored and rejected by his people (Jer 7:25 – 26; 25:4; Amos 3:7; Zech 1:6).

12:3 – 5 But seizing him, they beat him and sent him away empty-handed. Then again he sent another servant to them, and this one they beat on the head and treated shamefully. He sent another, and this one they killed. And many others: some they beat and others they killed (καὶ λαβόντες αὐτὸν ἔδειραν καὶ ἀπέστειλαν κενόν. καὶ πάλιν ἀπέστειλεν πρὸς αὐτοὺς ἄλλον δοῦλον· κἀκεῖνον ἐκεφαλίωσαν καὶ ἠτίμασαν. καὶ ἄλλον ἀπέστειλεν· κἀκεῖνον ἀπέκτειναν, καὶ πολλοὺς ἄλλους, οὓς μὲν δέροντες, οὓς δὲ ἀποκτέννοντες). The response to the servant is shocking. Rather than giving the servant the owner's due, they "beat" him and send him packing without the contracted portion due

the owner. The owner sends more servants, with each one treated progressively worse.

The meaning of the verb "beat on the head" (κεφαλιόω) is uncertain, since the Greek word occurs nowhere else. Paired with "shamed" or "dishonored" (ἀτιμάω), it could mean some act of great insult, such as slapping the face (cf. the humiliation in 2 Sam 10:2 – 5). It probably does not mean decapitate,[19] since the shaming follows and the next servant's killing is meant to be a worse fate. The addition of "many others" seems unnecessary and redundant, but in fact emphasizes the outrageous behavior of the tenants and parallels the fact that God sent many more than three prophets to Israel. Some have questioned the historicity of the story because no owner would act so irresponsibly. But the point is that God *did* keep sending prophets to Israel despite the rejection of many (Acts 7:52).[20]

12:6 He had one left, a beloved son. Finally, he sent him to them, saying, "They will respect my son." (ἔτι ἕνα εἶχεν υἱὸν ἀγαπητόν· ἀπέστειλεν αὐτὸν ἔσχατον πρὸς αὐτοὺς λέγων ὅτι ἐντραπήσονται τὸν υἱόν μου). Again the actions have been deemed as "unrealistic." Why would the owner be so naïve as to send his only son after the abuse of his servants? How could he possibly think they would now respect his son? But, again, the allegory is meant to reflect the audacity of the tenants and the realities taking place in Jesus' ministry. As Stein points out, "the 'unrealistic' behavior of the landowner and the tenants in the imagery of the parable corresponds exactly with the 'unrealistic,'

16. France, *Mark*, 459.
17. Evans, *Mark 8:27 – 16:20*, 233, followed by Stein, *Mark*, 535, argues for the latter.
18. Translating δοῦλος creates enormous challenges for English translators today because of the association of the word "slave" with African chattel slavery in America. See J. Albert Harrill, *Slaves in the New Testament: Literary, Social, and Moral Dimensions* (Minneapolis: Fortress, 2006), and the survey of research in John Byron, *Recent Research on Paul and Slavery* (Recent Research in Biblical Studies 3; Sheffield: Sheffield Phoenix, 2008).
19. Crossan, *In Parables*, 87, sees an allusion to the beheading of John the Baptist.
20. On the persecution and murder of the prophets see 2 Chr 24:20 – 22; Jer 26:20 – 30; Matt 5:12; 13:57; 23:29 – 39; Mark 6:4; 11:26 – 33; Luke 4:24; 6:23, 26; 11:47 – 50; 13:33 – 35; 1 Thess 2:15; Heb 11:36 – 38.

but *true* behavior of the God of Israel.... What some criticize as absurd and unrealistic is in reality the inconceivable 'amazing grace' of God!"[21]

The reference to a "beloved son" (υἱὸς ἀγαπητός) echoes the divine voice at Jesus' baptism (1:11) and the transfiguration (9:7) and recalls the description of Isaac in Gen 22:2 as Abraham's "only son, whom you love." The fact that this is the owner's only son heightens the drama and the sense of loss. The word "respect" (ἐντρέπω) can also carry the sense of shame or remorse at past behavior (1 Cor 4:14; 2 Thess 3:14; Titus 2:8).

12:7 – 8 But those tenant farmers said to one another, "This is the heir. Come, let's kill him, and the inheritance will be ours." Seizing him, they killed him and threw him out of the vineyard (ἐκεῖνοι δὲ οἱ γεωργοὶ πρὸς ἑαυτοὺς εἶπαν ὅτι οὗτός ἐστιν ὁ κληρονόμος· δεῦτε ἀποκτείνωμεν αὐτόν, καὶ ἡμῶν ἔσται ἡ κληρονομία. καὶ λαβόντες ἀπέκτειναν αὐτὸν καὶ ἐξέβαλον αὐτὸν ἔξω τοῦ ἀμπελῶνος). Again the story takes a shocking and apparently unrealistic turn. How could the tenants expect to inherit the vineyard? J. D. M. Derrett claimed that under Jewish law the possession of property without the payment of rent for four years could result in a claim to ownership. The tenants may be thinking that if they kill the son, they will be able to possess the land long enough to claim it.[22]

Others have suggested that the tenants thought the owner was dead or was too far away to intervene. Such suggestions miss the point, which is the absurdity and foolishness of the tenants. The religious leaders are acting just like the tenants, viewing the nation of Israel as *theirs* rather than God's. They foolishly refuse to submit to Jesus, God's Son, or to respond to his proclamation of the kingdom of God.

Since the murder of the son reflects the crucifixion of Jesus, one might expect the order to be seizing, throwing out of the vineyard, and then killing, since Jesus was crucified outside the city.[23] Both Matthew (Matt 21:39) and Luke (Luke 20:15) reorder in this way. Yet the point in Mark is that they first kill him, then throw his body outside the vineyard without a proper burial. For a person's body to be exposed publicly as carrion for wild animals rather than receiving an honorable burial was a great humiliation in the ancient world (Gen 40:19; Josh 8:29; 1 Sam 31:10; 1 Kgs 13:22 – 30).

12:9 What, then, will the owner of the vineyard do? He will come and destroy the tenant farmers and will give the vineyard to others (τί οὖν ποιήσει ὁ κύριος τοῦ ἀμπελῶνος; ἐλεύσεται καὶ ἀπολέσει τοὺς γεωργοὺς καὶ δώσει τὸν ἀμπελῶνα ἄλλοις). Jesus raises the natural question and provides the obvious answer (in Matt 21:41 it is the religious leaders who answer). Such despicable behavior will be met with swift and decisive judgment by the owner of the vineyard. The wicked tenants will be destroyed, and the vineyard given to others who will respect the owner's property.

Here again we see a parallel with Isaiah's Song of the Vineyard, which similarly asks the audience to draw an appropriate conclusion: "Now you dwellers in Jerusalem and people of Judah, judge between me and my vineyard. What more could have been done for my vineyard...?" (Isa 5:3 – 4; cf. v. 5). The verb "destroy" (ἀπόλλυμι) instead of "kill" (ἀποκτείνω; vv. 5, 7, 8) may indicate a more comprehensive and devastating judgment. They will get even worse than they gave. It also recalls their schemes against Jesus in 3:6 and 11:18, where the same verb is used. The leaders' plot to destroy Jesus will result in their own destruction.

---

21. Stein, *Mark*, 531 – 32.

22. J. D. M. Derrett, *Law in the New Testament* (Leiden: Brill, 1974), 286 – 312; Witherington, *Mark*, 320. For a response, see Snodgrass, *Stories with Intent*, 38.

23. This is further evidence that the parable was not created by the church after the fact.

Here for the first time the "man" (ἄνθρωπος; 12:1) who owned the vineyard is called the "owner/master/lord of the vineyard" (ὁ κύριος τοῦ ἀμπελῶνος). Although κύριος could mean "owner" or "master," Stein suggests, probably correctly, that the allegory is beginning to become reality as the owner is revealed to be "the Lord" (ὁ κύριος).[24]

Who are the "others" who receive the vineyard? Some say the church;[25] others, the Gentiles;[26] still others, Jesus and the apostles, who assume the leadership over God's people formerly held by these religious leaders.[27] The structure of the story points most naturally to this third, since the vineyard represents God's people, whose leadership passes to others.

12:10 – 11 "Haven't you read this Scripture, 'The stone that the builders rejected, this has become the cornerstone. The Lord has done this, and it is marvelous in our eyes'?" (οὐδὲ τὴν γραφὴν ταύτην ἀνέγνωτε· λίθον ὃν ἀπεδοκίμασαν οἱ οἰκοδομοῦντες, οὗτος ἐγενήθη εἰς κεφαλὴν γωνίας· παρὰ κυρίου ἐγένετο αὕτη καὶ ἔστιν θαυμαστὴ ἐν ὀφθαλμοῖς ἡμῶν;). Jesus concludes the parable with a rhetorical question and a citation of Ps 118:22 – 23 (LXX Ps 117), one of the Hallel psalms recited at Passover. "Haven't you read…?" means "You have surely read, but obviously not understood …" (see 2:25; 12:26 for similar rhetorical questions).

Verses 25 – 26 of Psalm 118 were cited in Mark 11:9 when the pilgrims entered Jerusalem at his triumphal entry ("Hosanna! Blessed is the one who comes in the name of the Lord!"). Now Jesus cites other verses in the psalm that refer to the rejection and vindication of the Messiah.[28] The psalm shifts the emphasis in the parable both in terms of imagery — from agriculture to architecture — and in terms of theme, from the judgment against the tenants to the vindication of the Son. The scenario is that of a stone that is cast aside as inadequate by builders, but eventually becomes the most important stone in the building.[29]

The meaning of "cornerstone" (κεφαλὴ γωνίας; lit., "head of the corner") is debated and could be a foundational "cornerstone," a "capstone" that completes an arch, a "keystone" that unites and holds together a building, or a "capital" that sits atop a column or pinnacle of the building. Most versions go with the first (NIV, NET, NLT, HCSB, ESV). This is because in 1 Cor 3:11 and Eph 2:20 – 22 the stone is foundational and in 1 Pet 2:6 – 8 it can be stumbled over (cf. Isa 8:14). Whichever is correct, it clearly indicates the most important stone in the building or temple. This passage is the clearest evidence that Mark understands Jesus and the messianic community to be the replacement for the Jerusalem temple. As Gray observes,

---

24. Stein, *Mark*, 537.

25. Nineham, *Mark*, 313; Best, *Following Jesus,* 219 – 20; James A. Brooks, *Mark* (NAC; Nashville: Broadman, 1991), 191; France, *Mark*, 462; Stein, *Mark*, 537. Matthew himself understands it this way (21:43).

26. Hooker, *Mark*, 191; Edwards, *Mark*, 359 – 60.

27. Gundry, *Mark*, 688 – 89; Evans, *Mark 8:27 – 16:20*, 237; Donahue and Harrington, *Mark*, 339, 342; Boring, *Mark*, 332. Marcus, *Mark 9 – 16*, 813 – 14, points to this meaning, though he says Christian readers would likely identify it with the church.

28. The original meaning of the psalm is debated, with some claiming the stone has an individual referent, perhaps David (an interpretation taken in the Targum; see Evans, *Mark*

8:27 – 16:20, 228 – 30, 238), or the Davidic king in an annual ritual of thanksgiving. Others claim the stone is a corporate reference to the community of faith, an interpretation taken at Qumran. For details, see J. D. M. Derrett, "The Stone That the Builders Rejected," *SE* 4 (1968): 180 – 86; F. J. Matera, *The Kingship of Jesus: Composition and Theology in Mark 15* (SBLDS 66; Chico, CA: Scholars, 1982), 79 – 84; B. Gärtner, *The Temple and the Community in Qumran and the NT* (SNTSMS 1; Cambridge: Cambridge University Press, 1989), 133 – 36.

29. Some rabbinic literature uses "builders" as a title for scribes or the temple leadership (Boring, *Mark*, 332 n. 24; Marcus, *Way of the Lord*, 124), but it seems unlikely Mark's readers would recognize such imagery.

By quoting Psalm 118 in the temple, therefore, the Markan Jesus is claiming to be the new cornerstone of the eschatological temple. God is doing a new work, leading his people out of exile of sin and death.... Despite his rejection and death, God will raise him to be the cornerstone of the new temple.[30]

Mark continues with Ps 118:23: "The Lord has done this, and it is marvelous in our eyes," which follows the LXX text exactly. The statement picks up the theme of amazement common in Mark's gospel[31] and also the emphasis that the owner is in charge. It is the Lord God who is guiding the events of the passion of the Messiah and will bring about his vindication.

12:12 They were looking for a way to arrest him, but they were afraid of the crowd, for they knew that he had spoken the parable against them. So leaving him, they went away (Καὶ ἐζήτουν αὐτὸν κρατῆσαι, καὶ ἐφοβήθησαν τὸν ὄχλον, ἔγνωσαν γὰρ ὅτι πρὸς αὐτοὺς τὴν παραβολὴν εἶπεν. καὶ ἀφέντες αὐτὸν ἀπῆλθον). The "they" are the ruling priests, the experts in the law, and the elders to whom the parable was told (11:27; 12:1). As noted above (Literary Context), the purpose of parables is here reversed. Whereas prior to this they concealed the truth from those with hard hearts (4:11 – 12), this one reveals the truth and so provokes the climax of the story. The messianic secret is being unveiled and with it, a rising tide of opposition.

This is the third of four statements that reflect plotting against Jesus to kill or arrest him (3:6; 11:18; 14:1 – 2). The imperfect "were looking for" (ἐζήτουν) is likely iterative ("kept looking for"). The crowd as an obstacle and cause of fear also occurred at 11:18 ("They feared him because the whole crowd was amazed at his teaching") and just before this at 11:32 ("They feared the crowd, for they all believed that John was a prophet"). In the passages that follow the religious leaders will seek to undermine Jesus' authority with the crowds (12:13 – 27). When this doesn't work, they will enlist a betrayer and arrest Jesus under cover of darkness (14:10, 43 – 51).

Theology in Application

The parable of the wicked tenant farmers plays out in miniature the narrative of salvation history, climaxing in the coming of Jesus the Son, his death, and his vindication. A number of major biblical themes appear in the parable.

The Grace and Patience of the Father

Isaiah 5:1 – 7, the background to our parable, begins with the care and favor the owner (God) bestows on his vineyard (5:1 – 2), the people of Israel. In v. 4 the owner asks in frustration, "What more could have been done for my vineyard that I have not done for it?" Though God gave Israel everything necessary for her care and pro-

---

30. Gray, *The Temple in the Gospel of Mark*, 76. Psalm 118 became a favorite proof text for the early Christians as a prediction of Jesus' rejection and ultimate vindication (Acts 4:11; 1 Pet 2:7). Two other "stone" prophecies, the stumbling stone of Isa 8:14 (cf. Rom 9:33) and the tested and precious cornerstone of Isa 28:16 (cf. Rom 9:33; 10:11), appear together with it in 1 Pet 2:6 – 8, which suggests the three may have been part of a catena of early Christian messianic prophecies.

31. See 1:22, 27; 2:12; 5:15, 20, 42; 6:2, 51; 7:37; 11:18; 12:17.

tection, the nation failed to produce good fruit. In Jesus' parable too, the sending of multiple servants demonstrates the patience and persistent love of the owner, who keeps reaching out through his prophets despite their rejection by the people.

This theme of God's persistent love is a major one in the OT prophets, especially Hosea, where Hosea's willingness to take back his wife despite her repeated unfaithfulness represents God's persistent love for his people (Hos 2:19; cf. Isa 54:5; 62:5; Jer 3:12 – 14; 4:1; Mal 2:11). Psalm 86:5 reads, "You, Lord, are forgiving and good, abounding in love to all who call to you" (cf. Exod 34:6; Pss 103:8; 145:8 – 9; Joel 2:13).

What is thematic in the OT becomes the central theme of the NT. While we were sinners and in rebellion against God, he sent his Son to save us: "But God demonstrates his own love for us in this: While we were still sinners, Christ died for us" (Rom 5:8; cf. 2:4; 5:6). It was not because of any righteous things we had done, but solely from his kindness, love, and mercy (Titus 3:4 – 5).

The Demand for Fruitfulness

Jesus' parable, like Isaiah's Song of the Vineyard, expresses God's demand for spiritual fruit. This too is a theme that runs throughout the OT and NT alike. In a play on words in Isa 5:7, God looks to his vineyard for "justice" (*mišpāṭ*), but finds only "bloodshed" (*mišpāḥ*); he looks for "righteousness" (*ṣĕdāqâ*), but hears instead "cries of distress" (*ṣĕʿāqâ*). The fruit God demands is not being produced and so judgment will follow. In Mark's gospel the metaphor of fruitfulness appeared in the parable of the sower (4:1 – 12) and more recently in the barren fig tree (11:12 – 14, 20 – 21), which similarly serves as an indictment on Israel and her leaders.

Fruitfulness is here linked to spiritual stewardship. The religious leaders are guardians of the vineyard Israel and so carry a responsibility for her well-being. This has great application for church leaders today. Just as Israel's leaders were unwilling to relinquish their authority, so Christian leaders often get into "turf wars," threatened by others with superior gifts or growing ministries. It is easy to see others as competitors rather than allies. Paul addresses this issue in 1 Corinthians, where the church was becoming partisan around various human leaders. In response, Paul calls the Corinthians to get their eyes off human authorities and focus on their common allegiance to Christ (1 Cor 1:12 – 17). Christian leaders like Paul or Apollos are mere slaves, coworkers in *God's* vineyard (3:5 – 9).

The Vindication of the Son and the Establishment of a New Temple

The parable and the Scripture quotation that follows carry forward the theme of divine necessity introduced already in Mark's passion predictions of the death and resurrection of the Son (8:31; 9:31; 10:33 – 34). Though the parable itself does not speak of the Son's vindication, the quotation from Ps 118:22 – 23 confirms that after suffering comes victory. The rejected stone becomes the cornerstone or capstone in the building, which holds together the whole (Acts 4:11; Rom 9:33; 10:11; 1 Cor 3:11; Eph 2:20 – 22; 1 Pet 2:6 – 8).

In Eph 2:21 – 22 the building for which Jesus is the cornerstone is a new temple, made up of God's people. In light of Jesus' actions just before this, in judging the temple and cursing the fig tree, and his prediction of the temple's destruction in Mark 13:2, we have seeds of the belief that Jesus and his church represent the new temple of God, where God's presence will reside (John 2:19 – 21; 1 Cor 3:16 – 17; 6:19; 2 Cor 6:16; Eph 2:21). Mark's inclusion of Ps 118:23, "the Lord has done this," confirms the divine necessity and sovereign purpose behind Christ's passion.

This theme of suffering followed by vindication echoes the Christ hymn of Phil 2:6 – 11, where after humbling himself and becoming obedient to death, Christ is exalted to highest place and given a name above every name (2:9). Its OT precedents can be seen in Isa 53:10 – 11, where the Suffering Servant "will see his offspring and prolong his days" and "after he has suffered … will see the light of life and be satisfied."[32] For Mark's readers, the vindication of the rejected stone and the subsequent building of the new temple of God confirm that they too will be vindicated after suffering.

The Judgment of Those Who Reject the Son and Their Replacement

Though God demonstrates extraordinary patience and mercy, his patience will not last forever, and persistent rebellion results in judgment. In Isaiah's Song of the Vineyard, the wall of protection is broken down and the Assyrian hordes devastate Israel. In Jesus' parable, it is not the vineyard that is judged, but the tenant farmers, representing Israel's leaders. Their rejection and murder of the Son results in their own destruction and the vineyard passing to the care of others.

This is an important point. Too often this parable and other NT passages have been used to justify anti-Semitism and persecution of the Jews. But the "others" that the vineyard passes to are not the Gentiles alone, but the leadership of the church made up of the restored remnant of Israel and the Gentiles who respond (Luke 2:30 – 32; 22:30; Acts 15:16 – 17; Rom 11:1 – 6, 25). It is not the Jews, but all who reject God's kingdom who face judgment. In Rom 11 Paul warns the Gentiles — as the wild branches grafted into the olive tree — not to become arrogant, since they too could be broken off if they don't persist in faith. All people, Jew and Gentile alike, are saved wholly through God's grace.

---

32. The word "light" is not found in the MT text, but it appears in both the LXX and Great Isaiah Scroll from Qumran (1QIsaᵃ).

Mark 12:13 – 17

Literary Context

This is the third of six controversies in the temple (11:27 – 12:37), all of which revolve around the issue of Jesus' authority, a question raised in 11:28. It is also the first of three questions introduced by different groups of religious and political leaders: Pharisees and Herodians (12:13 – 17), Sadducees (12:18 – 27), and an expert in the law (12:28 – 34). The first two are clearly hostile, while the third is more positive. Ironically, though this expert in the law is portrayed positively, Jesus follows the controversies with a warning against the hypocrisy and oppression of the experts in the law (12:38 – 40). Mark clearly wishes to portray Israel's religious and political establishment as allied together against Jesus.

III. The Suffering Way of the Messiah (8:22 – 15:47)
   A. Revelation of the Messiah's Suffering (8:22 – 10:52)
   B. The Messiah Confronts Jerusalem (11:1 – 13:37)
      3. Controversies in the Temple (11:27 – 12:44)
         b. The Parable of the Tenants (12:1 – 12)
→   **c. A Question about Paying Taxes to Caesar (12:13 – 17)**
         d. A Question about Marriage at the Resurrection (12:18 – 27)

Main Idea

When representatives from two ends of the political spectrum seek to trap Jesus with a question about paying taxes to Caesar, Jesus responds with Solomonic wisdom: "The things that are Caesar's, give back to Caesar, and the things that are God's, to God" (v. 17). By distinguishing legitimate spheres of authority in life, Jesus resolves the dilemma and silences his critics.

Translation

Mark 12:13 – 17

13a	Action/Character entrance	**Then they sent some of the Pharisees and Herodians**
b	purpose	to trap him with a question.
14a	action	Coming to him,
b	Question	**they said,**
c	affirmation	*"Teacher, we know that you are a person of truth*
d		*and do not care what others say,*
e	reason for 14d	*because you show no partiality.*
f	affirmation	*Rather, you teach the way of God truthfully.*
g	question	*Is it right before God to pay taxes to Caesar?*
h	parallel question	*Should we pay or shouldn't we?"*
15a		But knowing their hypocrisy,
b	Response	**he said to them,**
c	rhetorical question	*"Why are you testing me?*
d	command	*Bring me a denarius so that I can look at it."*
16a	Response to 15	**So they brought him one.**
b	Response to 16a	**He said to them,**
c	question	*"Whose image is this and whose inscription?"*
d	Answer to 16b	**They said to him,**
e		*"Caesar's."*
17a	Response/Instruction	**Jesus said to them,**
b	aphorism	*"The things that are Caesar's, give back*
		to Caesar, and
c	aphorism	*the things that are God's,*
		to God."
d	Response to 17a-c	**And they were amazed at him.**

Structure

The passage is a common Markan form that is both a controversy and a pronouncement story (cf. 2:14 – 17, 18 – 22, 23 – 28; 6:1 – 6; 8:10 – 13; 10:13 – 16). After flattering Jesus by affirming his uncompromising integrity, the Pharisees and Herodians ask him a question meant to compromise his status with either the Roman authorities or the people. As in 11:29, he responds with a counterquestion. This one, however, is not meant to silence them with a dilemma, but to place the answer to their question in their own mouths. By acknowledging Caesar's coins, they are participating in Rome's economic system and so come under its authority. Jesus voices this conclusion by pronouncing to the Herodians and the Pharisees to give to Caesar and God what is respectively their own.[1]

Exegetical Outline

→ **1. The Question about Taxes (12:13 – 14)**

    a. A trap set by the Pharisees and Herodians (12:13)

    b. Flattery affirming Jesus' integrity (12:14a-f)

    c. Question about paying taxes to Caesar (12:14g – h)

2. Jesus' Response to the Question (12:15 – 17c)

    a. Awareness of their hypocrisy (12:15a-c)

    b. Request for a denarius (12:15d – 16a)

    c. First Question: "Whose image is this?" (12:16b-c)

    d. Their answer: "Caesar's" (12:16d-e)

    e. Final Pronouncement: rendering what is due (12:17a-c)

3. Their Amazement (12:17d)

Explanation of the Text

12:13 Then they sent some of the Pharisees and Herodians to trap him with a question (Καὶ ἀποστέλλουσιν πρὸς αὐτόν τινας τῶν Φαρισαίων καὶ τῶν Ἡρῳδιανῶν ἵνα αὐτὸν ἀγρεύσωσιν λόγῳ). The "they" points back to 12:12 (cf. 11:27) — the ruling priests, the elders, and the experts in the law, the three groups that constituted the Sanhedrin (see comments on 11:18, 27 – 28). Mark portrays Jerusalem's diverse leaders as allied together, rising one after another to challenge Jesus.

The two groups sent here, "Pharisees and Herodians," appeared together already in the plot described in 3:6 (see comments there). As noted there, they are strange bedfellows, since the Hero-dians were supporters of the Herodian dynasty and so pro-Roman, while the Pharisees were anti-Roman, hoping for the Davidic Messiah to come and destroy their Gentile overlords (*Pss. Sol.* 17:21 – 25). Their common fear is the authority of Jesus, which for the Herodians threatened political stability and for the Pharisees compromised their religious influence over the people.[2]

Their goal is to "trap" (ἀγρεύω) Jesus, a verb commonly used of wild animals tracking their prey (Job 10:16 LXX). The dative "in/with/by a word" (λόγῳ) could refer either to Jesus' words or their own, meaning to be caught "with his own words" (NET; cf. NIV, NLT, NKJV) or to trap him "with

1. The episode is widely regarded as historical, because of both its pithy nature and its appearance in four different sources: the Synoptics, *Egerton Papyrus 2*, *Gospel of Thomas* 100, and Justin, *1 Apol.* 1:17. These latter three, however, are almost certainly dependent on the Synoptics. See details in Evans, *Mark 8:27 – 16:20*, 243 – 44. Collins, *Mark*, 553 – 55, argues for historicity based on the accurate description of coinage.

2. The claim by some that the episode most likely occurred in Galilee, since Herod Antipas ruled there, is not a strong one. The Herodian dynasty always had its sights on Jerusalem and Judea, hoping to regain authority over Judaism's capital once ruled by Herod the Great. (They would regain it for a short time [AD 41 – 44] under Herod Agrippa I.) There were no doubt Herodians — political advocates of the Herodian dynasty — always present as "lobbyists" in Jerusalem.

a question" (REB). Without a possessive pronoun "his" (αὐτοῦ), the latter seems more likely, although the basic sense is the same.

12:14 Coming to him, they said, "Teacher, we know that you are a person of truth and do not care what others say, because you show no partiality. Rather, you teach the way of God truthfully. Is it right before God to pay taxes to Caesar? Should we pay or shouldn't we?" (καὶ ἐλθόντες λέγουσιν αὐτῷ· διδάσκαλε, οἴδαμεν ὅτι ἀληθὴς εἶ καὶ οὐ μέλει σοι περὶ οὐδενός· οὐ γὰρ βλέπεις εἰς πρόσωπον ἀνθρώπων, ἀλλ᾽ ἐπ᾽ ἀληθείας τὴν ὁδὸν τοῦ θεοῦ διδάσκεις· ἔξεστιν δοῦναι κῆνσον Καίσαρι ἢ οὔ; δῶμεν ἢ μὴ δῶμεν;). Seeking to catch Jesus off guard, his questioners begin with flattery, shown to be hypocritical by the narrator's statement about seeking to trap Jesus (v. 13) and by Jesus' claim that they are "testing" him (v. 15).

The phrase "you are true" (ἀληθὴς εἶ) here means a person whose actions are guided by what is true rather than what is expedient. This is defined in the following three clauses: "You do not care what others say" means that Jesus is not swayed by human opinion. "You do not look into (the) face of people" (lit. trans. of οὐ ... βλέπεις εἰς πρόσωπον ἀνθρώπων) is an idiom meaning that he does not show favoritism. That is, he does not teach in deference to the status or position (the "face") of others. Jesus changes his message for no one, but instead teaches the "way of God" (τὴν ὁδὸν τοῦ θεοῦ) "with integrity" or "truthfully."

The statement by Jesus' interlocutors is doubly ironic. First, they praise Jesus for his integrity while they themselves are being hypocritical and insincere. Second, with this "false" flattery they end up making a profoundly true statement about his teaching and character. He is everything they say he is.

Here is their question: "Is it right before God [ἔξεστιν] to pay taxes to Caesar?" The verb ἔξεστιν (lit., "it is lawful") here means in accord with the divine law of God (2:24, 26; 3:4; 6:18; 10:2); that is why our translation reads: "Is it right before God...?" Since Jesus teaches the true way of God, he should know whether paying taxes is in accord with God's will.

The "tax" (κῆνσος) is probably the Roman poll (or head) tax. Instituted in AD 6, this tax sparked a revolt led by Judas the Galilean that was violently put down by the Romans (Josephus, *Ant.* 18.1.1 §§5 – 7; 18.1.6 §23; cf. Acts 5:37). According to Josephus, this Judas claimed that "they were cowards if they would endure to pay a tax to the Romans, and would, after God, submit to mortal men as their lords" (*J.W.* 2.8.1 §118). The ideology behind this was that if Israel was a theocracy, paying taxes to Caesar was treasonous. The later Zealot movement that sparked the Jewish war of AD 66 – 74 looked to Judas and his revolt for their inspiration.

"Caesar" was originally a family name of Julius Caesar, but it came to refer to any emperor. Here it is metonymy for the Roman empire as represented by Emperor Tiberias. The dilemma is that if Jesus answers yes, he will anger the people, who despise Roman oppression and taxes; but if he says no, he will be guilty of sedition and liable to arrest and crucifixion.

12:15 – 16 But knowing their hypocrisy, he said to them, "Why are you testing me? Bring me a denarius so that I can look at it." So they brought him one. He said to them, "Whose image is this and whose inscription?" They said to him, "Caesar's." (ὁ δὲ εἰδὼς αὐτῶν τὴν ὑπόκρισιν εἶπεν αὐτοῖς· τί με πειράζετε; φέρετέ μοι δηνάριον ἵνα ἴδω. οἱ δὲ ἤνεγκαν. καὶ λέγει αὐτοῖς· τίνος ἡ εἰκὼν αὕτη καὶ ἡ ἐπιγραφή; οἱ δὲ εἶπαν αὐτῷ· Καίσαρος). Jesus' awareness of their hypocrisy does not necessarily require supernatural insight (cf. 2:8; 5:30), since any person with reasonable discernment could recognize their question as a trap. The verb "test" (πειράζω) can mean either tempt or test (1:13; 8:11; 10:2), but here clearly means the latter.

"Bring me" is probably little different from "show me" (cf. Matt 22:19: Luke 20:24) and does not mean that they had to leave and find one. The coin was readily available. The denarius (δηνάριον) was a Roman coin worth about a day's wages (Matt 20:2). Jesus' request for this particular coin is almost certainly significant, since it was the coin used to pay the poll tax and it bore the image of the emperor. The coin they produced would likely have borne the image of Tiberius Caesar (ruled AD 14–37), with an inscription reading, TI[BERIUS] CAESAR DIVI AUG[USTI] F[ILIUS] AUGUSTUS ("Tiberius Caesar, son of the divine Augustus, [himself] Augustus").[3] The irony is that while seeking to trap Jesus into saying something either seditious or blasphemous, they are carrying coins with idolatrous images and messages.[4]

Apart from this apparent indictment of their own hypocrisy and idolatry, Jesus' request for a coin is unnecessary for the answer he is about to give. He could simply have said, "Give to Caesar...." Yet from the perspective of Mark's narrative, the delay heightens the drama and builds to the climactic pronouncement.

12:17 Jesus said to them, "The things that are Caesar's, give back to Caesar, and the things that are God's, to God." And they were amazed at him (ὁ δὲ Ἰησοῦς εἶπεν αὐτοῖς· τὰ Καίσαρος ἀπόδοτε Καίσαρι καὶ τὰ τοῦ θεοῦ τῷ θεῷ. καὶ ἐξεθαύμαζον ἐπ'

αὐτῷ). Jesus' answer is at the same time profound and enigmatic. In one sense it is straightforward, pointing out that there are realms of authority for both Caesar and God, and allegiance to one does not necessarily mean disloyalty to the other. By possessing and using a denarius with the image of Caesar on it, the Pharisees are already implicitly acknowledging Caesar's authority over a certain realm of life. As Paul teaches in Rom 13:1–7 and Peter in 1 Pet 2:13–17, submission to human authorities is part of God's will for his people. For more on this, see Theology in Application.

While Jesus' answer on the surface is straightforward, it also carries a measure of ambiguity.[5] For the Herodians (and to a certain extent, the Sadducees) it would be heard as legitimizing and affirming the rule of Caesar and Rome. For the Pharisees and other groups who chafed under Roman rule (Zealots, Essenes, and others), it could be heard as a tacit rejection of Caesar's rule. "The things that are Caesar's, give back to Caesar" raises the fundamental question of what belongs to Caesar. After all, "the earth is the LORD's, and everything in it, the world, and all who live in it" (Ps 24:1; cf. 1 Cor 10:26). If everything belongs to God, then nothing is left for Caesar.[6]

Jesus' remarkable answer results in amazement on the part of those who hear him. Though the amazement of the disciples and the crowd is a common theme throughout Mark,[7] only here do his opponents react in this way.[8]

---

3. See H. St J. Hart, "The Coin of 'Render Unto Caesar' (a Note on Some Aspects of Mark 12:13–17; Matt 22:15–22; Luke 20:20–26," in *Jesus and the Politics of His Day* (ed. E. Bammel and C. F. D. Moule; Cambridge: Cambridge University Press, 1984), 241–48.

4. France, *Mark*, 468, further notes that the opposite side of the coin would have read PONTIF[EX] MAXIM[US], "High Priest," "a further provocation to Jewish sensibilities" (cf. Marcus, *Mark 9–16*, 824).

5. According to Luke, Jesus' answer is distorted at his trial, where he is accused of "subverting our nation. He opposes payment

of taxes to Caesar and claims to be Messiah, a king" (Luke 23:2).

6. See Horsley, *Hearing the Whole Story*, 43, who thinks this is Jesus' primary point.

7. See 1:22, 27; 2:12; 5:15, 20, 42; 6:2, 51; 7:37; 11:18.

8. Mark uses an emphatic form (ἐκθαυμάζω; only here in the NT) of the verb θαυμάζω (5:20; 6:6; 15:5, 44), which may carry the sense of utter amazement (*Let. Aris.* 312; 4 Macc 17:17; Sir 27:23; BDAG, 303). This cannot be pressed, however, since in some contexts it seems little different from θαυμάζω (Sir 27:23). Mark uses a variety of terms for amazement (θαμβέω; ἐκπλήσσω; ἐξίστημι).

Theology in Application

Jesus' Wisdom and Authority

The most important theme of the passage is the wisdom of Jesus as the authoritative Son of God. The Pharisees and Herodians ironically acknowledge that he is indeed a man of integrity, who speaks God's truth. The depth of his wisdom is emphasized in the astonished response after his answer (v. 17). Even his opponents are amazed.

The conceptual background to this wisdom is the portrait of the Messiah in Isa 11, where the messianic "shoot" from Jesse will be endowed with "the Spirit of wisdom and of understanding, the Spirit of counsel and of might, the Spirit of the knowledge and fear of the LORD" (Isa 11:2). In this way the question of Mark 11:28, "By what authority are you doing these things?" is answered not only in the parable of the vineyard (by the authority of the Father who sent him), but also (implicitly) here (by the Spirit of God, who empowers and guides him; cf. 1:10). Such wisdom is confirmation that Jesus is indeed the Messiah and Son of God (1:1; 8:29).

Responsibilities to God and Human Authorities

For Jesus' followers the application of his wisdom relates to the sensitive question of a believer's responsibility to the government. Contrary to those few scholars who claim Jesus was a revolutionary seeking to overthrow the Romans,[9] Jesus here affirms the legitimacy of human government and the principle of taxation. Paul takes a similar stance in Rom 13:1 – 7, where he calls on believers to

> be subject to the governing authorities, for there is no authority except that which God has established.... [Rulers] are God's servants, agents of wrath to bring punishment on the wrongdoer.... Give to everyone what you owe them: If you owe taxes, pay taxes; if revenue, then revenue; if respect, then respect; if honor, then honor. (cf. 1 Pet 2:13 – 17; Titus 3:1)

The Bible consistently affirms God's sovereignty in raising up and bringing down human governments (Dan 2:21; 4:17, 25, 32) and using them as his agents of justice (Rom 13:4; 1 Pet 2:14).

There are exceptions to the principle, of course, when the commands of government run directly contrary to the commands of God. The Bible has a number of such examples, as when the Hebrew midwives "fear God" and so refuse to heed Pharaoh's command to kill newborn boys (Exod 1:17); the refusal of Shadrach, Meshach, and

---

9. See Brandon, *Jesus and the Zealots,* and the response by Hengel, *Was Jesus a Revolutionist?*

Abednego to bow down before Nebuchadnezzar's statue (Dan 3:16 – 18); Daniel's defiance of Darius's decree to pray to no other god (Dan 6:10 – 13); and the apostles' unwillingness to stop preaching the gospel in Acts 4:19; 5:29. Because love for God and obedience to him are the believer's greatest responsibilities (1 Sam 15:22 – 23; Jer 7:22 – 23), "We must obey God rather than human beings" (Acts 5:29).

48

Mark 12:18 – 27

Literary Context

This is the fourth of six controversies in the temple, all of which highlight Jesus' authority as the Messiah, increasing the opposition to him and setting the stage for his arrest and crucifixion. It is also the second of three questions raised by different Jewish groups. While the question about paying taxes to Caesar (12:13 – 17) was raised by Pharisees and Herodians (groups with different views of Rome's authority), this one about the resurrection is raised by Sadducees, who differed from the Pharisees in their view of the resurrection. The third will be raised by an expert in the law (see 12:28 – 34). The controversies then climax with a question by Jesus (12:35 – 37), which puzzles and delights the crowd.

III. The Suffering Way of the Messiah (8:22 – 15:47)
    A. Revelation of the Messiah's Suffering (8:22 – 10:52)
    B. The Messiah Confronts Jerusalem (11:1 – 13:37)
        3. Controversies in the Temple (11:27 – 12:44)
            c. A Question about Paying Taxes to Caesar (12:13 – 17)
→   **d. A Question about Marriage at the Resurrection (12:18 – 27)**
            e. A Question about the Great Commandment (12:28 – 34)

Main Idea

The Sadducees here seek to discredit Jesus' belief in the resurrection and his authority as a teacher with a question about multiple marriages in the resurrection. Jesus responds by rebuking their ignorance of the Scriptures and the power of God. Resurrection life will be a different kind of existence, so that marriage in its present form will not exist. Furthermore, Scripture confirms God's continuing relationship with the patriarchs and so the reality of resurrection life.

Translation

Mark 12:18–27

| 18 | Character entrance/description | Then **the Sadducees, who say there is no resurrection, came to him and ↻ asked him a question,** |

19a address/indirect discourse — "Teacher, Moses wrote for us that

b condition — if someone's brother *dies* and *leaves a wife but no child,*

c result — his brother should *marry the woman* and *raise up offspring for his brother.*

20a story — There were seven brothers.

b first brother — The first one *took a wife*

c — *but,* because he died, left no offspring.

21a second brother — The second *married her*

b — *and* also *died without leaving offspring.*

c third brother — And likewise the third.

22a summary of last four — All seven *left no offspring.*

b woman's death — Last of all, the woman *died.*

23a question — At the resurrection, when they rise,

b — whose wife will she be,

c — since all seven had her as a wife?"

24a Response — **Jesus said to them,**

b rebuke — "Are you not mistaken

c reason for 24b — because you do not know the Scriptures or the power of God?

25a First answer — *For* when they rise from the dead,

b assertion — they neither *marry* nor *are given in marriage;*

c contrast with 25b — *rather,* they *are like the angels in heaven.*

26a Second answer — *Now* about the dead that rise,

b rhetorical question — have you not read in the book of Moses,

c — in the passage about the bush,

d — how God said to him,

e Scripture quotation — *'I am the God of Abraham, the God of Isaac, and the God of Jacob'?* [Exod 3:6]

27a assertion — He is not the God *of the dead,*

b — *but* of the living.

c rebuke — You are badly misled."

Structure

The passage may be classified as a pronouncement story presented as a controversy story,[1] with an elaborate question posed by the Sadducees and a two-part answer by Jesus. The Sadducees question has three parts: (1) a citation of the OT law of levirate marriage (v. 19), (2) a hypothetical story of a woman who married seven brothers (vv. 20 – 22), and (3) a question meant to reduce the doctrine of the resurrection to absurdity (v. 23). Garland proposes a chiastic structure for Jesus' answer:[2]

1 You are in error [πλανάω].
   2 You do not know the Scriptures.
      3 You do not know the power of God.
      3′ [The power of God] raises the dead and they become like angels.
   2′ [Scripture is cited] In the bush passage, the God of Abraham, Isaac, and Jacob is God of the living.
1′ You are badly mistaken [πλανάω].

The answer is framed by two statements about their erroneous thinking, the second made more emphatic with the term "greatly" or "badly" (πολύ). Jesus states their two errors — not knowing Scripture and not knowing the power of God — and answers them in reverse order.

Exegetical Outline

→ **1. The Question by the Sadducees (12:18 – 23)**
    a. The approach by the Sadducees (12:18)
    b. The law of levirate marriage (12:19)
    c. The story of a woman widowed seven times (12:20 – 22)
    d. The question: "Whose wife will she be in the resurrection?" (12:23)

2. Jesus' Response (12:24 – 27)
    a. The Sadducees' ignorance of the Scriptures and the power of God (12:24)
    b. No marriage in the resurrection (12:25)
    c. God is the God of the living, not the dead (12:26 – 27)

---

1. Bultmann, *History*, 26; Evans, *Mark 8:27 – 16:20*, 251.   2. Garland, *Mark*, 470.

Explanation of the Text

12:18 Then the Sadducees, who say there is no resurrection, came to him and asked him a question (Καὶ ἔρχονται Σαδδουκαῖοι πρὸς αὐτόν, οἵτινες λέγουσιν ἀνάστασιν μὴ εἶναι, καὶ ἐπηρώτων αὐτὸν λέγοντες). This is the first and only appearance of the Sadducees in Mark's gospel (see "In Depth: The Sadducees"). Jesus had far more in common theologically with the Pharisees than the Sadducees, especially concerning the authority of Scripture and the reality of the resurrection. It is on this latter issue that the Sadducees seek to discredit him.

The resurrection is not a major doctrine in the OT, but it is clearly set out in Dan 12:1 – 2: "At that time … multitudes who sleep in the dust of the earth will awake: some to everlasting life, others to shame and everlasting contempt." Though this is the most explicit statement, a number of other passages allude to the resurrection in one way or another (Job 19:26; Ps 16:9 – 11; Isa 25:7 – 8; 26:19; Hos 13:14). Second Temple literature, and especially the rise in apocalyptic thought, brought the resurrection to much greater prominence. Most Jews of Jesus' day would have affirmed it.[3]

The Mishnah expresses strong polemic against Sadducean belief by pointing out that those who say "there is no resurrection of the dead prescribed in the Law" have no share in the world to come (*m. Sanh.* 10:1). The phrase "prescribed in the Law" may allude to the Sadducean denial of the resurrection based on its (purported) absence from the Pentateuch, which they viewed as the only authoritative Scripture.

IN DEPTH: The Sadducees

The Sadducees were a politico-religious party within Judaism, the main competitors of the Pharisees.[4] Their origin is uncertain, though they most likely arose from the priestly aristocracy that supported the Hasmonean dynasty following the Maccabean revolt. Their name may have been derived from the priestly line of Zadok, a high priest during the time of David and Solomon (2 Sam 8:17; 1 Kgs 1:8, 45; 2:35). Their chief rivals, both politically and theologically, were the Pharisees. Not much is known about the Sadducees because none of their writings are extant. What we do know comes from their opponents and rivals and is found in the Gospels and Acts, Josephus, and later rabbinic writings.

Josephus identifies them as one of the four main "philosophies" of Judaism (together with the Pharisees, Essenes, and Zealots) and contrasts their beliefs

---

3. See especially Wright, *Resurrection of the Son of God,* 129 – 206.

4. On the Sadducees, see J. Le Moyne, *Les Sadduceens* (Paris: Librarie Lecoffre, 1972); G. G. Porton, "Sadducees," *ABD,* 5:892 – 95; Sanders, *Judaism: Practice and Belief;* Günter Stemberger, *Jewish Contemporaries of Jesus: Pharisees, Sadducees, Essenes* (Minneapolis: Fortress, 1995); A. J. Saldarini, *Pharisees, Scribes and Sadducees in Palestinian Society: A Sociological Approach* (Grand Rapids: Eerdmans, 2001); J. Wellhausen, *The Pharisees and the Sadducees: An Examination of Internal Jewish History* (trans. Mark E. Biddle; Mercer Library of Biblical Studies 4; Macon, GA: Mercer University Press, 2001 [Germ. orig., 1874]).

with those of the Pharisees and the Essenes.[5] While Pharisees believed in the resurrection, the final judgment, and the immortality of the soul, the Sadducees denied these (cf. Acts 23:6 – 10, where Paul divides the Sanhedrin over this issue). While Pharisees accepted the whole of the Hebrew Scriptures as well as the oral "traditions of the fathers," the Sadducees accepted only the Pentateuch (Genesis to Deuteronomy) as inspired Scripture. Luke affirms the Sadducean denial of the resurrection (Acts 4:2; 23:6 – 8) and adds that they did not believe in angels (23:8). This latter is surprising, since angels appear in the Pentateuch. Luke's statement may refer not to angels in general but to the kind of speculation about names and hierarchies of angels that appears in Jewish apocalyptic literature.

In terms of their political influence, Luke associates the Sadducees with the priestly leadership in Jerusalem, the high priest, and the Sanhedrin (Acts 4:1; 5:17; 23:6 – 7). This agrees with Josephus's description that they were upper class and aloof, associated with the priestly aristocracy and the temple leadership. At least two high priests (Acts 5:17; Jos. *Ant.* 20.9.1 §199), and probably others, were Sadducees. In Jesus' day they dominated the Sanhedrin, though the Pharisees also had an influential voice there (Acts 5:17; 23:6 – 8).

It is not surprising that Jesus came into conflict with the Pharisees and experts in the law in Galilee, where they were the most influential, while opposition from the high priest, the Sanhedrin, and the Sadducees intensified when he was in Jerusalem. Like the Herodians and the Jewish aristocracy in general, the Sadducees were conservative politically and pro-Roman, supporting the status quo. As priestly aristocrats, they were not looking for a Messiah who would come and free them from their Roman overlords. Prophecies about the Messiah also occur primarily in the Prophets, which the Sadducees did not regard as authoritative. With the destruction of the temple and the Jewish state in AD 70, their power base was gone and the Sadducees disappeared from history.

12:19 "Teacher, Moses wrote for us that if someone's brother dies and leaves a wife but no child, his brother should marry the woman and raise up offspring for his brother." (διδάσκαλε, Μωϋσῆς ἔγραψεν ἡμῖν ὅτι ἐάν τινος ἀδελφὸς ἀποθάνῃ καὶ καταλίπῃ γυναῖκα καὶ μὴ ἀφῇ τέκνον, ἵνα λάβῃ ὁ ἀδελφὸς αὐτοῦ τὴν γυναῖκα καὶ ἐξαναστήσῃ σπέρμα τῷ ἀδελφῷ αὐτοῦ). The Sadducees address Jesus as

"Teacher" (διδάσκαλε; vocative; cf. 12:14), but this is only because of his popular reputation; they have no desire to learn from him. While the goal of the Pharisees and Herodians was to trap Jesus (12:15), the Sadducees hope to humiliate him and so discredit him among the people by showing that belief in the resurrection is illogical and absurd.

The Sadducees here appeal to the OT law of

5. Josephus, *Life* 2 §10 – 12; *J.W.* 2.8.14 §§162 – 66; *Ant.* 13.5.9 §171 – 72; 13.10.6 §293 – 98; 18.1.4 §§16 – 17.

"levirate" (Latin, *levir* = "brother-in-law") marriage (Deut 25:5 – 10), which required the brother of a deceased man to marry his brother's widow in order to raise up heirs for him. A whole tractate of the Mishnah, *Yebamot* ("Sisters-in-law"), deals with levirate marriage. The law is illustrated in Gen 38:8 – 10, where Onan is judged by God for failing to fulfill his levirate duty.

12:20 – 23 "There were seven brothers. The first one took a wife but, because he died, left no offspring. The second married her and also died without leaving offspring. And likewise the third. All seven left no offspring. Last of all, the woman died. At the resurrection, when they rise, whose wife will she be, since all seven had her as a wife?" (ἑπτὰ ἀδελφοὶ ἦσαν· καὶ ὁ πρῶτος ἔλαβεν γυναῖκα καὶ ἀποθνῄσκων οὐκ ἀφῆκεν σπέρμα· καὶ ὁ δεύτερος ἔλαβεν αὐτὴν καὶ ἀπέθανεν μὴ καταλιπὼν σπέρμα· καὶ ὁ τρίτος ὡσαύτως· καὶ οἱ ἑπτὰ οὐκ ἀφῆκαν σπέρμα. ἔσχατον πάντων καὶ ἡ γυνὴ ἀπέθανεν. ἐν τῇ ἀναστάσει ὅταν ἀναστῶσιν τίνος αὐτῶν ἔσται γυνή; οἱ γὰρ ἑπτὰ ἔσχον αὐτὴν γυναῖκα). The Sadducees propose a hypothetical situation where a woman in turn marries six brothers of her first husband in order to raise up an heir, but each dies before providing children. They conclude by asking whose wife she will be in resurrection.[6] Their point is that resurrection belief is absurd since it leads to ridiculously complex marital situations in the afterlife, including polygamy. "In the resurrection" (ἐν τῇ ἀναστάσει) is shorthand for the end-time resurrection of the dead, the final

judgment, and eternal life with God (Luke 14:14; John 11:25; Acts 17:32; 23:6, 8; 24:15; 26:8).

This story may have been a well-known riddle or joke meant to ridicule the Pharisaic belief in the resurrection.[7] It appears to be based loosely on the story of Sarah in the apocryphal book of Tobit. This distraught woman marries seven husbands one by one, all kinsmen (Tob 7:11), but each is killed by the demon Asmodeus before the marriage is consummated (3:7 – 8; 6:14 – 15). Sarah eventually marries Tobias, son of Tobit (another relative), who survives the wedding night through prayer and by repelling the demon with the help of the angel Raphael (8:1 – 18). The stories are different in terms of purpose, but both include the death of seven husbands in the context of levirate marriage.

Another much less likely parallel sometimes suggested[8] is to seven brothers during the Maccabean period who endured martyrdom at the hands of Antiochus Epiphanes (2 Macc 7:1 – 42). They were able to persevere through gruesome torture and die with dignity because of their hope in the resurrection. But that story has nothing to do with levirate marriage, and the one told by the Sadducees does not concern martyrdom.

12:24 Jesus said to them, "Are you not mistaken because you do not know the Scriptures or the power of God?" (ἔφη αὐτοῖς ὁ Ἰησοῦς· οὐ διὰ τοῦτο πλανᾶσθε μὴ εἰδότες τὰς γραφὰς μηδὲ τὴν δύναμιν τοῦ θεοῦ;). Jesus' answer to the Pharisees and Herodians about paying taxes to Caesar was clever and enigmatic; this one to the Sadducees is explicit and corrective. Jesus accuses the Sadducees of

---

6. The clause ὅταν ἀναστῶσιν ("when they rise") is absent from a number of important early manuscripts (א B C D L W Δ Ψ 33 579 892 2427). Despite this strong external evidence, the internal evidence weighs heavily for its inclusion. A copyist would likely have omitted it because of its redundancy and to harmonize with Matthew and Luke. But no reason can be adduced for its addition. See Metzger, *Textual Commentary*,

110 – 11. Such redundancies are also characteristic of Markan style (Neirynck, *Duality in Mark*, 105).

7. Josephus says that the Sadducees loved to debate the resurrection with their opponents, even though their view was unpopular with the wider Jewish population (*Ant.* 18.1.4 §16).

8. Evans, *Mark 8:27 – 16:20*, 253; Stein, *Mark*, 553.

being "deceived," or better, "mistaken"[9] (πλανάω) in two areas, with reference to the Scriptures and the power of God. He then addresses these two in reverse order (see Structure, above). They are misled concerning the power of God because resurrection life will be more than a continuation of mortal earthly life; it will be a new kind of immortal glorified existence, like that of the angels in heaven (see v. 25). They are misled with reference to the Scriptures because even the Pentateuch — which the Sadducees accepted as authoritative — teaches the continuing existence of God's servants after death (see vv. 26 – 27).

12:25 For when they rise from the dead, they neither marry nor are given in marriage; rather, they are like the angels in heaven (ὅταν γὰρ ἐκ νεκρῶν ἀναστῶσιν οὔτε γαμοῦσιν οὔτε γαμίζονται, ἀλλ' εἰσὶν ὡς ἄγγελοι ἐν τοῖς οὐρανοῖς). Jesus says that marriage is an institution of the present world, not the world to come. Rabbinic Judaism similarly affirmed that "in the world to come there is no … propagation" (*b. Ber.* 17a). The verb "marry" (γαμέω) normally refers to the husband's actions in acquiring a wife, while "given in marriage" (γαμίζω) refers to parents giving their daughter away (see the same pairing in Matt 24:38; Luke 17:27).

Jesus did not say that believers become angels at death, a misconception often promoted in popular culture.[10] In the biblical worldview, human beings and angels were created as different kinds of beings by God, with different functions and destinies (Heb 1:7, 14; 2:5 – 9). Humans, rather, become *like* angels, having similar glory and immortality. The glorification of believers into an angel-like state is taught elsewhere in Second Temple Judaism (Wis 4:13 – 5:5; Tob 12:19; *2 Bar.* 51:5, 9 – 10; *1 En.* 15:7; 51:4; 104:4 – 6; *T. Isaac* 4:43 – 48; 1QSb [= 1Q28b] 4:24 – 28).

Some have claimed that Jesus' reference to angels here is a further challenge to Sadducean belief, since they did not believe in angels (Acts 23:8). Yet angels appear often in the Pentateuch, which the Sadducees viewed as authoritative.[11] Luke's statement in Acts 23:8 may refer to their denial of complex hierarchies of angels, rather than the existence of angels per se (see "In Depth: The Sadducees" at 12:18).

12:26 – 27 "Now about the dead that rise, have you not read in the book of Moses, in the passage about the bush, how God said to him, 'I am the God of Abraham, the God of Isaac, and the God of Jacob'? He is not the God of the dead, but of the living. You are badly misled." (περὶ δὲ τῶν νεκρῶν ὅτι ἐγείρονται οὐκ ἀνέγνωτε ἐν τῇ βίβλῳ Μωϋσέως ἐπὶ τοῦ βάτου πῶς εἶπεν αὐτῷ ὁ θεὸς λέγων· ἐγὼ ὁ θεὸς Ἀβραὰμ καὶ [ὁ][12] θεὸς Ἰσαὰκ καὶ [ὁ] θεὸς Ἰακώβ; οὐκ ἔστιν θεὸς νεκρῶν ἀλλὰ ζώντων· πολὺ πλανᾶσθε). Jesus now turns to his second charge, that the Sadducees do not know the Scriptures. For similar appeals to Scripture using "have you not read" (οὐκ ἀνέγνωτε), see 2:25 (οὐδέποτε ἀνέγνωτε;) and 12:10 (οὐδὲ … ἀνέγνωτε). All three are polemical contexts challenging the discernment of Scripture. Although the Sadducees are Is-

---

9. BDAG, 821, points out the term can mean to "deceive oneself" or "be mistaken in one's judgment" as well as passively "deceived" (cf. 1 Cor 6:9; Gal 6:7; Jas 1:16).

10. Nor does Jesus explicitly assert that angels are sexless beings, though this might be implied. The Jewish apocalyptic work *1 Enoch* develops a midrash around the "sons of God" in Gen 6:1 – 4. Though created as eternal spirit beings with no need to procreate (*1 En.* 15:4 – 7), a number of the angels sinned by taking wives for themselves among human women

("the daughters of man"), producing giants as offspring, and were eventually judged by God (*1 En.* 6 – 10).

11. Gen 16:7; 19:1; 21:17; 22:11; 28:12; Exod 3:2; 14:19; 23:20; 33:2; Num 22:23; etc.

12. The presence or absence of the article (ὁ) before the third and fourth occurrences of "God" (θεός) varies widely among the manuscripts, so that the UBS text includes them in brackets. The question is purely one of style, without exegetical significance.

rael's leaders, they have failed to comprehend God's revelation.

Jesus could have appealed to any number of passages in the Prophets or the Writings, especially Dan 12:1 – 2 (see comments on 12:18). But since the Sadducees only viewed the first five books of Moses as authoritative, he points to a text in the Pentateuch.[13] He identifies it as the passage "about the bush" (ἐπὶ τοῦ βάτου) in the "book of Moses" (Exod 3:1 – 22). Before the introduction of chapters and verses, passages were often identified by their theme or a descriptive characteristic.[14] The "book of Moses" could mean the Pentateuch generally (Genesis to Deuteronomy), as in the expression "Moses and the Prophets" (Luke 16:29, 31; 24:27, 44), or the primary volume about Moses's life, Exodus.

It is sometimes claimed that Jesus makes his argument based on the tense of a verb, a present rather than a past tense: God "is" rather than "was" the God of Abraham, Isaac, and Jacob. But this is not quite right, since neither the Hebrew text of Exod 3:6 (ʾānōkî ʾĕlōhê) nor Mark's Greek quotation, "I [am] the God" (ἐγὼ ὁ θεός) includes the verb, "I am" (εἰμί). In both the verb is implied.[15] Jesus' point is instead based on the reality of a continuing relationship with God by virtue of his covenant with them. He remains their God even after their physical death because of the abiding nature of that covenant.[16]

Jesus concludes by restating his charge of v. 24, but even more emphatically. "You are mistaken" becomes "you are badly [πολύ][17] misled."

Theology in Application

While Jesus often found himself opposed to the Pharisees for their self-righteousness, pride, and hypocrisy, on the question of the resurrection he clearly sided with them against the Sadducees. Resurrection hope is central in the Christian faith (cf. 1 Cor 15:1 – 58). Two theological themes merit special attention in this episode: the authority and wisdom of Jesus and the hope of the resurrection.

The Wisdom and Authority of Jesus

This passage carries forward the theme that is central to the series of controversies from 11:27 – 12:40, which is the authority and wisdom of Jesus as Messiah (see also Theology in Application on 12:13 – 17). In fulfillment of the prophecies of the Messiah in Isa 11:2, Jesus is endowed with "the Spirit of wisdom and of understanding."

---

13. A similar rabbinic example appears in *Midrash Sipre on Numbers* 112, where Rabbi Simeon ben Eleazar says, "On the following basis I proved that the versions of Scripture of the Samaritans are forgeries, for they maintained that the dead do not live. I said to them, 'Lo, Scripture says, " … that person shall be utterly cut off; his iniquity shall be upon him." ' " He uses the phrase "shall be upon him" (Num 15:31) to prove that this person will face a future judgment, and so there must be a resurrection. Cited in Boring et al., eds., *Hellenistic Commentary*, 127 (cf. *Sipre* on Deut 32:2). For more examples see Boring, *Mark*, 339 n. 28.

14. France, *Mark*, 475. Paul does something similar in Rom 11:2, where he refers to 1 Kings 19 as "the passage about Elijah."

15. The LXX does include the verb (ἐγώ εἰμι ὁ θεός), as does Matt 22:32.

16. There is an interesting parallel in 4 Macc 16:25, where it is said of the Maccabean martyrs that "they knew also that those who die for the sake of God live to God, as do Abraham and Isaac and Jacob and all the patriarchs" (NRSV; cf. 7:19).

17. For this adverbial use of πολύς, see Luke 7:47; Acts 18:27; 27:14.

The challenge by the Sadducees fails because they do not understand two things: the Scriptures and the power of God.

While Jesus is referring here to Scripture's teaching about the resurrection (vv. 26 – 27) and the power of God to raise believers to a new kind of existence (v. 25), in a larger sense these two proofs relate to his ministry as a whole; and they apply not only to the Sadducees' rejection of him, but to the rejection by Israel's leaders generally. They have failed to comprehend that Scripture predicted both his coming and his death and resurrection (cf. 12:10). From the beginning of his gospel, Mark has placed Jesus' ministry under the banner of the eschatological salvation promised by Isaiah and the prophets (1:1 – 3). If the Sadducees believed the prophets, they would believe in him. To know the Scripture truly is to have hearts ready to receive God's kingdom and its King, Jesus the Messiah.

The same wider application applies to Jesus' second indictment, that they do not know the power of God. From the beginning of his Galilean ministry, Jesus has been demonstrating the power and authority of the kingdom of God. His proclamation of the kingdom, his authoritative teaching and pronouncements about the law, his healings and exorcisms, his nature miracles, and — most significantly for the present episode — his power to raise the dead (5:22 – 43) have all demonstrated the power of God's kingdom at work in him. The Sadducees (and others who have rejected Jesus) do not know the power of God because they do not know Jesus, who acts in fulfillment of Scripture and demonstrates the authority of God in his words and deeds.

The same is true today. The message of the cross may seem foolish to those who have never experienced its power to transform their lives. I have heard skeptics say, "Show me a miracle and I'll believe." But the greatest miracle of all is a transformed life. As Paul says in 1 Cor 1:18, "For the message of the cross is foolishness to those who are perishing, but to us who are being saved it is the power of God." And then again in Rom 1:16: "I am not ashamed of the gospel, because it is the power of God that brings salvation to everyone who believes: first to the Jew, then to the Gentile." The message of the resurrection was foolishness to the Sadducees because they had not experienced the life-giving message of the kingdom of God.

The Hope of the Resurrection

The second major theme of this passage is the reality and nature of resurrection life. The Sadducees think they have caught Jesus in their trap because they view resurrection life as an eternal continuation of normal human existence, which would play havoc with temporal institutions like marriage. Jesus responds that the resurrection is an entrance into a new and glorified existence that is far beyond anything we can imagine. As Paul says, "What no eye has seen, what no ear has heard, and what no human mind has conceived — the things God has prepared for those who love him" (1 Cor 2:9).

The hope of the resurrection is the believer's greatest hope, providing strength to face life's greatest challenges. Although the Maccabean account of seven brothers who endured martyrdom is unlikely to have been the inspiration behind the Sadducees' story (see comments on 12:20 – 23), like all accounts of Jewish and Christian martyrs through the centuries it reminds us that resurrection hope provides strength to face any crisis, even death itself. Christ's resurrection life means that "neither death nor life … nor anything else in all creation, will be able to separate us from the love of God that is in Christ Jesus our Lord" (Rom 8:38 – 39).

This passage bothers some Christians today, who fear that their deep and meaningful relationships with their spouses, nurtured over many years, will not continue into eternity. But this is to read too much into Jesus' words. Though there is no need for procreation in eternity and so no marriage in its present form, we can assume that all relationships in God's presence will be profoundly deeper than anything we experience in this life. In other words, our relationships with our spouses and families will no doubt be more intimate, not less, in eternity. Some people, influenced by popular cultural depictions, fear heaven will be an endless bore of floating on clouds and playing harps. Yet the Bible teaches that the infinitely creative God of the universe, who has given us a glimpse of his creative genius in this marvelously diverse planet, is preparing something so much greater that our human mind cannot even fathom it. That doesn't sound boring at all.

CHAPTER 49

Mark 12:28 – 34

Literary Context

This is the fifth of six controversy stories that take place in the temple in Jerusalem, set during the last week of Jesus' ministry. This episode differs from the other five in that it is less a controversy story and more a pronouncement, since Jesus finds common ground with the expert in the law who questions him (see Structure, below). At the same time, it shares the theme common to the other five episodes of Jesus' superior wisdom and insight. It is linked to the previous pericope by the introductory sentence, in which the expert in the law has overheard Jesus' discussion with the Sadducees. Impressed by his answers, the man asks him a question of his own (v. 28).

Main Idea

When an expert in the law asks Jesus about the greatest commandment, they both find common ground on the two greatest commands: to love God with your whole being (Deut 6:4 – 5) and to love your neighbor as yourself (Lev 19:17 – 18). In the context of Markan theology, such mutual admiration demonstrates that despite the general opposition to Jesus among the religious leaders, the truly wise among them recognize that Jesus' wisdom and authority come from God.

Translation

Mark 12:28 – 34

28a	Character entrance	**One of the experts in the law approached and heard them debating.**
b		Seeing that he had answered them well,
c	Question	**he asked him,**
d		*"Which is the most important commandment of all?"*
29a	Response	**Jesus answered,**
b	first answer	*"The most important is,*
c	Scripture quotation	*'Hear, Israel, the Lord our God, the Lord is one.*
30a	Scripture quotation	*You shall love the Lord your God with all your heart,*
b		*with all your soul,*
c		*with all your mind, and*
d		*with all your strength.'*
		[Deut 6:4 – 5]
31a	second answer	*The second is this:*
b	Scripture quotation	*'You shall love your neighbor as yourself.'* [Lev. 19:18]
c	conclusion	*There is no other commandment greater than these."*
32a	Response	**The expert in the law said to him,**
b	commendation	*"Well said, Teacher.*
c	affirmation	*You have spoken the truth that he is one and*
d		*that there is no other except him.*
33a		*And to love him with all your heart,*
b		*with all your understanding, and*
c		*with all your strength, and*
d		*to love your neighbor as yourself*
e		*are more important than all burnt ⫰*
		offerings and sacrifices."
34a		Whe*n Jesus saw that he had answered wisely,*
b	Response to 32 – 33	**he said to him,**
c	commendation/conclusion	*"You are not far from the kingdom of God."*
d	Response/Conclusion	**And no one dared to question him any more.**

Structure

In its present literary context surrounded by controversy stories, this episode takes a surprising turn. The approach of one of the experts in the law, who have been almost universally hostile to Jesus throughout Mark's gospel, prepares the reader for a controversy story similar to those in the immediate context (11:27 – 33; 12:1 – 12, 13 – 17, 18 – 27). Instead, the episode becomes a pronouncement story and a narrative of (potential) faith, as the expert in the law commends Jesus for his answer and is in turn commended by him.

The origin and historicity of the story is much debated. Luke omits the episode here but records a similar answer given to the "law expert" (νομικός) who asks, "What must I do to inherit eternal life?" (Luke 10:25 – 28; cf. the rich man of Mark 10:17 – 22 pars.). For Luke, however, that episode introduces the parable of the good Samaritan. One of these stories may have given rise to the other, or more likely, Jesus was approached with similar questions on various occasions. Rabbinic literature testifies to the popularity of questions like this among the experts in the law. In terms of its historicity, Evans points out the unlikelihood that the early church would create a story in which Jesus recites the Shema, the basic affirmation of the Jewish faith, or one in which a scribe is presented is such a favorable light.[1]

Exegetical Outline

→ **1. Approach and Question of an Expert in the Law (12:28)**

2. Jesus' Answer (12:29 – 31)

    a. The greatest command (12:29 – 30)

    b. The second greatest command (12:31)

3. The Man's Response (12:32 – 33)

4. Jesus' Commendation (12:34a-c)

5. Jesus' Opponents are Silenced (12:34d)

Explanation of the Text

12:28 One of the experts in the law approached and heard them debating. Seeing that he had answered them well, he asked him, "Which is the most important commandment of all?" (Καὶ προσελθὼν εἷς τῶν γραμματέων ἀκούσας αὐτῶν συζητούντων, ἰδὼν ὅτι καλῶς ἀπεκρίθη αὐτοῖς ἐπηρώτησεν αὐτόν· ποία ἐστὶν ἐντολὴ πρώτη πάντων;). In light of the variety of religious leaders approaching Jesus (Pharisees and Herodians, 12:13; Sadducees, 12:18), the reader is not surprised to see an expert in the law (γραμματεύς) coming with a question (on this vocation, traditionally called "scribes" [KJV] or "teachers of the law" [NIV], see comments on 1:22). The experts

in the law appear frequently in Mark's gospel, often with the Pharisees and almost always in an adversarial role.[2]

This positive encounter is surprising not only because of the role of the scribes elsewhere in Mark, but also in light of the context where every other question and challenge has had hostile intent, and where Jesus will shortly give a scathing indictment on the experts in the law (12:38 – 40). The passage shows that Mark does not view the Jewish leadership as universally opposed to Jesus.[3] As elsewhere in the NT, Israel is divided between a righteous remnant and an unrepentant majority (cf. Acts 17:4; 28:24 – 25; Rom 9:6; 11:5; see Theol-

1. Evans, *Mark 8:27 – 16:20*, 261.
2. See 1:22; 2:6, 16; 3:22; 7:1, 5; 8:31; 9:11, 14; 10:33; 11:18, 27; 12:35, 38; 14:1, 43, 53; 15:1, 31.

3. Contra Gundry, *Mark*, 709 – 10, who thinks the man is antagonistic toward Jesus.

ogy in Application). In this case, the outcome is open-ended, since the scribe is not yet a disciple; but he is "not far from the kingdom of God" (v. 34).

Hearing Jesus "debating" (συζητούντων)[4] with the Sadducees and impressed by his answer, the expert in the law raises his own question. He is likely impressed, in part, because he agrees with Jesus about the resurrection. Most scribes aligned with the Pharisees in their theology, including their teaching on the resurrection and the authority of Scripture. Matthew's parallel presents the man in a less favorable light. Instead of asking an honest question, he is one of a group of Pharisees taking their shot to "test" (πειράζω) Jesus after the Sadducees have failed (Matt 22:33 – 34; cf. Luke 10:25). Matthew also drops the positive exchange between Jesus and the man at the end — most notably, Jesus' claim that the man is "not far from the kingdom of God" (Mark 12:32 – 34).

The man's question concerns the "first" (πρῶτος) or "most important" of the commandments.[5] Such questions concerning the greatest commandment of all were common in Judaism. Simeon the Just, two centuries before Jesus, is reported to have said, "By three things is the world sustained: by the Law, by the temple-service, and by deeds of lovingkindness" (*m. ʾAbot* 1:2). Similarly, the great rabbi Hillel (c. 40 BC – AD 10) was approached by a Gentile who said, "Make me a proselyte on condition that you teach me the whole law while I stand on one foot" (i.e., "until I lose my balance" = a very short time). Hillel responded with a negative version of the Golden Rule, "Do not do to your neighbor

what is hateful to you: this is the whole Torah, the rest is commentary" (*b. Šabb.* 31a; cf. Tob 4:15).

Rabbi Akiba (c. AD 50 – 135) similarly summed up the law, "but you shall love your neighbor as yourself.... This is the encompassing principle of the Law."[6] In his Sermon on the Mount in Matthew, Jesus had already said something similar: "So in everything, do to others what you would have them do to you, for this sums up the Law and the Prophets" (Matt 7:12).

12:29 – 30 Jesus answered, "The most important is, 'Hear, Israel, the Lord our God, the Lord is one. You shall love the Lord your God with all your heart, with all your soul, with all your mind, and with all your strength.'" (ἀπεκρίθη ὁ Ἰησοῦς ὅτι πρώτη ἐστίν· ἄκουε, Ἰσραήλ, κύριος ὁ θεὸς ἡμῶν κύριος εἷς ἐστιν, καὶ ἀγαπήσεις κύριον τὸν θεόν σου ἐξ ὅλης τῆς καρδίας σου καὶ ἐξ ὅλης τῆς ψυχῆς σου καὶ ἐξ ὅλης τῆς διανοίας σου καὶ ἐξ ὅλης τῆς ἰσχύος σου). Jesus responds by reciting two OT passages, Deut 6:4 – 5 and Lev 19:17 – 18. The former is the first part of the Shema, the fundamental creed of Jewish faith and monotheism cited by pious Jews every morning and evening (*m. Ber.* 2:2; *m. ʾAbot* 2:13). The Shema itself is comprised of Deut 6:4 – 9; 11:13 – 21; Num 13:37 – 41. Its title comes from the opening word of Deut 6:4 in Hebrew, "Hear" (*šĕmaʿ*). Only Mark has Jesus starting with 6:4. In Matthew he quotes only 6:5: "You shall love the Lord your God...."

The "Lord is one" (κύριος εἷς ἐστιν; Heb: *yhwh ʾeḥād*) is Israel's monotheistic creed that set Judaism apart from all the polythestic religions of

---

4. Συζητέω can mean discussing, questioning, debating, or arguing, depending on the context (see 1:27; 8:11; 9:10, 14, 16).

5. The Greek is awkward, since "of all" (πάντων) should presumably be feminine in agreement with "commandment" (ἐντολή). Edwards, *Mark*, 379, thinks the intention is to generalize beyond the OT law, meaning "which commandment supersedes *everything* and is incumbent on all humanity — including Gentiles" (cf. C. I. K. Story, "Marcan Love Com-

mandment: 'The greatest of these is love' (1 Corinthians 13:13)," *Lexington Theological Quarterly* 34/3 (1999): 152. More likely, the expression has become idiomatic, with the neuter form being used regardless of the gender of its antecedent (BDF §164 1. 91; France, *Mark*, 479).

6. *Sipre Lev.* §200 on Lev 19:15 – 20. For other examples, see Str-B 1:900 – 908; France, *Mark*, 477 n. 62.

the Greco-Roman world and became a rallying cry during times of persecution. It was often the last words on a martyr's lips. Paul will play off the Shema in 1 Cor 8:6, affirming monotheism yet including Christ within that category: "Yet for us there is but one God, the Father, from whom came all things and for whom we live, and there is but one Lord, Jesus Christ, through whom came all things and through whom we live" (cf. Rom 3:30; Eph 4:6; 1 Tim 2:5).

The quotation here of Deut 6:5 generally follows the LXX. "You shall love" (ἀγαπήσεις) is an imperatival future,[7] which is why many versions translate as an imperative: "Love the Lord your God ..." (NIV, NET, HCSB, etc.). Mark's text includes four modifiers: "heart" (καρδία), "soul" (ψυχή), "mind" (διάνοια), and "strength" (ἰσχύς). The MT of Deut 6:5 has only three, equivalent to "heart" (lēb), "soul" (nepeš), and "strength" (mĕ'ōd). The LXX similarly does not have "mind" and also differs from Mark's text in using "power" (δύναμις) instead of "strength" (ἰσχύς). Mark's use of the latter may be due to manuscript variations or to different ways of translating the same Hebrew term. This could also explain his introduction of "mind" (διάνοια), which appears in some Greek OT traditions.[8] Curiously, Matt 22:37 includes three terms, like the MT and LXX, but differs from them by omitting "strength" instead of "mind." Luke 10:27 has all four of Mark's terms, but with the last two reversed.

There is significant overlap in meaning between these four terms, and it would be a mistake to distinguish sharply their meanings, as though four

distinct features of personhood are in view. "Heart" (καρδία) commonly means the seat of physical, spiritual, and mental life (BDAG, 508) and so overlaps considerably with both "soul" and "mind." "Soul" can mean the "life principle" or "seat of inner human life" (BDAG, 1098). "Mind" (διάνοια) commonly refers to more cognitive functions, "the faculty of thinking, comprehending, and reasoning,"[9] semantic components that can be present in both "heart" or "soul." "Strength" (ἰσχύς) is perhaps the most distinct of the four, but it can refer to the vitality or life force that motivates them all.

In short, these four do not represent separate components of human life, but function as a kind of hendiatetris[10] meaning "all you are and do." This sense is reinforced by the repetition of the qualifier "with all your ...," or "from your whole ..." (ἐξ ὅλης), with each one.

12:31 **"The second is this: 'You shall love your neighbor as yourself.' There is no other commandment greater than these."** (δευτέρα αὕτη· ἀγαπήσεις τὸν πλησίον σου ὡς σεαυτόν. μείζων τούτων ἄλλη ἐντολὴ οὐκ ἔστιν). While the man asked only about the "first" commandment, Jesus gives the second as well, quoting from Lev 19:18. The two are intimately related and belong together.[11] Those who truly love God will also love those who are created in his image.

Furthermore, those who love God are reckoned as his children and so reflect his divine nature, which is pure love (1 John 3:10; 4:8, 16; cf. John 3:16). The pairing of the two commands, to love God and to love others, finds its precedent in the

---

7. Wallace, *Greek Grammar*, 452, 569, 718–19.

8. Evans, *Mark 8:27–16:20*, 264.

9. BDAG, 234.

10. Latin for "one through four" = four words used to express one idea. The more common *hendiadys* means "one through two."

11. It is not quite right, however, to say that the two commands are identified by Jesus as a single one (contra Wither-

ington, *Mark*, 330–31; Stein, *Mark*, 562). The singular ἐντολή in v. 31 means, rather, that there is no other (single) command (ἐντολή) "greater than these" (μείζων τούτων; note the plural). The singular ἐστιν in v. 33 ("to love [God] ... and to love your neighbor ... is [ἐστιν] more important ...") is singular because neuter plural subjects (note the two neuter infinitives as a compound subject) commonly take singular verbs in Greek.

two tables of the Decalogue (Exod 20:1 – 17; Deut 5:6 – 21), with the first four of the Ten Commandments relating to love for God and the final six to love for fellow human beings (cf. Mark 10:19).[12] The former provides the foundation for the latter.

The command to love your neighbor appears frequently in Second Temple Judaism (*Jub.* 7:20; 36:7 – 8; CD 6:20 – 21; Sir 7:21; 34:15; *T. Benj.* 3:3 – 4). Though much less commonly, the two are paired in such texts as *T. Iss.* 5:2, "Love the Lord and your neighbor; be passionate toward poverty and sickness" (cf. 7:6), and *T. Dan* 5:3, "Throughout all your life love the Lord and one another with a true heart."[13] The Jewish philosopher Philo, while not quoting these OT texts, refers to them conceptually when he speaks of the "two most especially important heads of all the innumerable particular lessons and doctrines." These are (1) "regulating of one's conduct towards God by the rules of piety and holiness," and (2) regulating "one's conduct towards men by the rules of humanity and justice" (*Spec.* II, 15.63).

In these Second Temple contexts, love for one's neighbors relates especially to fellow Israelites. Jesus, of course, extended the definition of a "neighbor" to everyone, even one's enemies (Matt 5:43 – 44; Luke 6:27, 35; 10:25 – 37).[14]

12:32 – 33 The expert in the law said to him, "Well said, Teacher. You have spoken the truth that he is one and that there is no other except him. And to love him with all your heart, with all your under-standing, and with all your strength, and to love your neighbor as yourself are more important than all burnt offerings and sacrifices." (καὶ εἶπεν αὐτῷ ὁ γραμματεύς· καλῶς, διδάσκαλε, ἐπ᾽ ἀληθείας εἶπες ὅτι εἷς ἐστιν καὶ οὐκ ἔστιν ἄλλος πλὴν αὐτοῦ· καὶ τὸ ἀγαπᾶν αὐτὸν ἐξ ὅλης τῆς καρδίας καὶ ἐξ ὅλης τῆς συνέσεως καὶ ἐξ ὅλης τῆς ἰσχύος καὶ τὸ ἀγαπᾶν τὸν πλησίον ὡς ἑαυτὸν περισσότερόν ἐστιν πάντων τῶν ὁλοκαυτωμάτων καὶ θυσιῶν). Mark alone includes this positive response by the expert in the law and Jesus' concluding commendation (v. 34). The man's answer confirms that he does not have insidious motives in questioning Jesus. Mark's theological point is that, when not motivated by pride or hypocrisy, even Israel's leaders recognize that Jesus' wisdom is from God.

The man first acknowledges that Jesus has answered "well" (καλῶς) and that he has spoken the truth (ἐπ᾽ ἀληθείας). The former may mean "cleverly," so the latter emphasizes that what was said was biblically accurate. The truth is that "he [God] is one" (εἷς ἐστιν) — another allusion to Deut 6:4 — and that "there is no other except him" (οὐκ ἔστιν ἄλλος πλὴν αὐτοῦ). The latter phrase is an allusion to Deut 4:35, an expansion on Jesus' words and another strong monotheistic statement (cf. Ps 86:8; Isa 45:6, 21; 46:9; 47:8, 10). When he recites back Deut 6:5, the expert in the law omits "with all your soul [ψυχή]" and replaces "mind" (διάνοια) with "understanding" (συνέσις). The sense is essentially the same, confirming the point made above that

---

12. France, *Mark*, 480.

13. There is debate, however, whether these texts have undergone editing by Christians. See H. C. Kee, "The Testaments of the Twelve Patriarchs," in *OTP*, 776 – 80.

14. The injunction to love one's enemies was unusual, but not unheard of in Judaism or the ancient world in general. Exodus 23:4 – 5 enjoins God's people to give help to an enemy whose ox or donkey has been lost or has stumbled under its load. Proverbs 25:21 says to provide food or water to an enemy who is hungry or thirsty. In the Qumran scrolls we find similar advice: "I shall not repay anyone with an evil reward; with goodness I shall pursue the man. For to God belongs the judgment of every living being" (1QS 10:18 – 19). Such ideas were occasionally expressed in the pagan world. A Babylonian wisdom text reads, "Do not return evil to the man who disputes with you; requite with kindness your evil-doer" (*Counsels of Wisdom,* lines 41 – 45; from the translation by W. G. Lambert, *Babylonian Wisdom Literature* [Oxford: Clarendon, 1960], 101). The philosopher Seneca (c. 4 BC – AD 65) wrote, "If you wish to imitate the gods, do good deeds also to the ungrateful; for the sun also goes up upon the evil" (*Ben.* 4.26.1). These texts, however, represent exceptions rather than the rule.

the phrase as a whole means to love God *with your whole being.*

As the expert in the law expanded and emphasized Deut 6:4, so now he expands on Deut 6:5 and Lev 19:18. To love God and love others "are more important than all burnt offerings and sacrifices." The thought is common in the OT, emphasizing the importance of a relationship of love and obedience over merely external ritual and sacrifice (1 Sam 15:22; Pss 40:6; 51:16 – 17; Isa 1:11; Jer 6:20; 7:21 – 23; Hos 6:6). The term "sacrifice" (θυσία) is a general one for various kinds of sacrifices and offerings. A "burnt offering" or "holocaust" (ὁλοκαύτωμα) was a sacrifice in which the animal was entirely consumed (BDAG, 703) — hence the translation by some versions, "whole burnt offerings" (NKJV, ESV, NRSV).

12:34 When Jesus saw that he had answered wisely, he said to him, "You are not far from the kingdom of God." And no one dared to question him any more (καὶ ὁ Ἰησοῦς ἰδὼν αὐτὸν[15] ὅτι νουνεχῶς ἀπεκρίθη εἶπεν αὐτῷ· οὐ μακρὰν εἶ ἀπὸ τῆς βασιλείας τοῦ θεοῦ. καὶ οὐδεὶς οὐκέτι ἐτόλμα αὐτὸν ἐπερωτῆσαι). Jesus is impressed with the man's discernment and his priorities and commends him. "Wisely" (νουνεχῶς) is a rare word that occurs only here in the NT or the LXX. Its meaning is close to its etymology (νοῦς, "mind" + ἔχω, "have"), and it appears elsewhere in Greek and Jewish literature with the sense of "sensible," "thoughtful," or "prudent" — using the faculties of one's mind (Aristotle; Polybius; *Sib. Or.* 1:7; *T. Job* 36:6 ["if you answer me *sensibly* ..."]).[16]

The kingdom of God has been central to Jesus' teaching in Mark's gospel (see comments on 1:15).

It means, essentially, submission to God's rule, values, and purpose in the world. Though Jesus does not yet identify the expert in the law as part of the kingdom of God, he is close and moving in the right direction. This statement should not be seen as negative, so that we ask, "What is still preventing the scribe from entering?"[17] Rather, we should think of a journey image, with Jesus saying that the man is on the right road and close to his destination. He needs only to cross the line of faith. The scribe thus stands in stark contrast to the rich man in 10:22 – 25, whose riches were a crippling hindrance to entering the kingdom and who turned away on a different road. The reader is left wondering what happened to this man and whether in the end he believed. Perhaps Mark leaves the story open to invite his readers to finish their journeys.

The episode concludes with the narrative comment that no one dared asked Jesus any more questions. The ability to silence your opponent was viewed in Hellenistic rhetoric as one of the marks of a wise man and a skilled orator. Wisdom 8:12 reads, "When I am silent they will wait for me, and when I speak they will give heed; if I speak at greater length, they will put their hands on their mouths" (NRSV).

The statement here seems a little surprising after so positive an exchange with the expert in the law. Matthew apparently thought so, since he moved it after the question of David's son that follows (Matt 22:46). Mark no doubt intended the phrase to refer not to the present account alone, but to the whole series of controversies from 11:27 on. Jesus has decisively answered every challenge and will now respond with a question of his own (12:35 – 37).

---

15. The omission of αὐτόν from many manuscripts (א D L W Δ Θ ƒ[1.13] 28 33 565 579 892 2542) is likely a scribal attempt to smooth out Mark's (typically) redundant language.

16. BDAG, 680.

17. Contra Evans, *Mark 8:27 – 16:20*, 266.

Theology in Application

The Greatest Commandments

As we have seen, the summing up of God's law by its greatest commandments was not unique to Jesus, having precedents in Second Temple Judaism (see comments on 12:28). Yet for Jesus and the early Christians, this epitomizing of the law had special significance. In the Sermon on the Mount in Matthew and its parallel in Luke, Jesus calls for obedience that goes beyond mere external regulations of the OT law to the true heart of God behind it.

These two laws — love God and loving others — are the greatest because they epitomize the nature and character of God from which all other laws of the Torah arise. Obedience to God is not about making sure every "i" is dotted and every "t" is crossed so that we are worthy to enter God's presence. True obedience comes from a heart that has experienced God's amazing grace and been transformed by it. As Paul says, it is Christ's love — not merely a sense of duty — that "compels" him, that drives him forward to obedience (2 Cor 5:14). His great passion is to "know Christ — yes, to know the power of his resurrection and participation in his sufferings, becoming like him in his death" (Phil 3:10).

Loving God with heart, soul, mind, and strength has as its foundation and motivation the transforming love that God has poured out on us. The natural response to this overwhelming gift of love and grace is to love others with the same kind of self-sacrificial love God has shown us. This too epitomizes the whole law: "For the entire law is fulfilled in keeping this one command: 'Love your neighbor as yourself'" (Gal 5:14; cf. Rom 13:8 – 10; Jas 2:8; *Did.* 1:2; 2:7).

The Open Invitation to the Kingdom

Jesus' optimistic conclusion to this episode surprises the reader of Mark's gospel, who has known the experts in the law only as the intractable opponents of Jesus. We are reminded here that not all of Israel's religious authorities rejected Jesus. Leaders such as Joseph of Arimathea and Nicodemus became his followers (15:43; Matt 27:57; John 19:38 – 39), even if sometimes in secret (John 19:38). The book of Acts illustrates this further, as some Pharisees seem positively disposed toward Christians (Acts 5:34; 23:9) and a large number of priests believe (6:7). James reports to Paul that "many thousands" of law-keeping Jews have believed in gospel (21:20). Israel has not completely rejected the gospel but is instead divided. As Paul points out, a "remnant" has been saved even if a majority has turned away (Rom 11:1 – 5). Hope and opportunity remains.

In my ministry I have met a number of people who, like this scribe, are "not far from the kingdom of God." They are seekers with open hearts and minds. The Holy Spirit is clearly at work in their lives. I remember in particular one young man who came to the college group at the church where I was interning. The look in his eyes and attitude of his heart suggested to me that he was not a "non-Christian" but a "pre-Christian," someone who was on a journey that would end in faith. Sure enough, several months later he responded to the gospel and eventually became a leader in the group.

While many Christians can point to a definitive moment in their lives when they experienced salvation, the transforming power of the Spirit making them a new creation in Christ, for others the spiritual journey is just that, a gradual recognition and awareness of the truth of the gospel and the reality of a relationship with Christ. We can certainly speak of salvation as having past, present, and future dimensions. The past is the moment of regeneration, when the Spirit cleanses a person's heart and makes them into a new creation in Christ (2 Cor 5:17). The future is the glorification of our bodies, when our salvation will be consummated and we will know Christ fully as we are fully known (1 Cor 13:12; cf. Rom 8:11, 18 – 25; 1 Cor 15:42 – 58). Yet there is also a present dimension that may best be described as a process or a journey, as we continue to work out our salvation with fear and trembling (Phil 2:12).

Mark 12:35 – 37

Literary Context

This is the sixth in a series of controversies with the religious leaders of Israel in the temple during the last stage of Jesus' ministry. The second of these was the parable of the wicked tenant farmers, in which Jesus indicted the leaders for their failure to give God his due (12:1 – 12). The other four all involved questions from Jesus' opponents. Three had hostile intent (11:27 – 33; 12:13 – 17; 12:18 – 27), while the fourth — the question about the greatest commandment — was more positive and resulted in a favorable response by a particular scribe (12:28 – 34). In all cases, Jesus has either defeated or impressed his opponents with his great wisdom. Now Jesus takes the offensive with a question of his own.

Following the positive encounter with the expert in the law in 12:28 – 34, Mark follows up with two episodes that present these scribes in a much less favorable light. The present one challenges their notions about the Messiah (12:35 – 37) while the next is a scathing denunciation of their character and motives (12:38 – 40). Mark seems to be balancing the previous episode to show that, though there were exceptions, the religious leaders were stubborn and resistant to God's purpose and kingdom.

Main Idea

Having silenced the religious leaders trying to trap him (12:34), Jesus now turns the tables on them with a riddle about the Messiah as the "son of David." The question, which is not answered by Jesus, shows that the Messiah is much more than the traditional Jewish expectations about him.

Translation

Mark 12:35 – 37

35a	setting (social & spatial)	While Jesus was teaching in the temple courts,
b	Question/Riddle	**he asked,**
c	introductory question	*"Why do the experts in the law say that the Messiah is the son of David?*
36a	Scripture quotation	*David himself said by the Holy Spirit,*
b		*'The Lord said to my Lord,*
c		*"Sit at my right hand until I place your enemies under your feet."'*
		[Ps. 110:1]
37a	question/riddle	*David himself calls him 'Lord';*
b		*so how can he be his son?"*
c	Summary	**The great crowd enjoyed listening to him.**

Structure

The present account may be called a controversy story, since Jesus' riddle apparently confounds his opponents. Yet no question from or response by the Jewish leaders is recorded.[1] A more basic description would be simply "teaching," a category that fits the favorable response of the crowds (12:37c; cf. 1:22, 27; 11:18). With its placement after a series of controversies and before Jesus' denunciation of the scribes, Mark treats it as another example of Jesus' divine knowledge and superior wisdom. The religious leaders have no answer for this wisdom from God (12:34c) and so must find other means to eliminate Jesus (11:18; 14:1 – 2).[2]

---

1. Cranfield, *Mark*, 381 – 82, following R. P. Gagg, thinks the story was originally a controversy story, but that the original question from Jesus' opponents has been lost in the course of transmission. The leaders might have asked Jesus about the Davidic descendant of the Messiah in order to elicit a messianic claim from him and so provide evidence for a charge of sedition — similar to the question about paying taxes to Caesar (12:13 – 17). Whether this is the case, it is unlikely that Mark himself removed the question, since an original form starting with a question would have fit nicely with his other controversy stories in this chapter.

2. The authenticity of the episode is debated. Those who view it as a church creation generally claim it arose either in disputes between Jews and Christians over whether Jesus was the Messiah or as an internal Christian debate about Jesus' Davidic descent (Hooker, *Mark*, 290 – 91). In both cases the original purpose would have been to defend Jesus' messiahship despite his apparent lack of Davidic ancestry. Against this

Exegetical Outline

→ **1. Jesus' Question about the Messiah as the Son of David (12:35)**

2. The Conundrum of Psalm 110:1: David's Son or David's Lord? (12:36 – 37b)

3. The Response of the Crowd (12:37c)

Explanation of the Text

12:35 While Jesus was teaching in the temple courts, he asked, "Why do the experts in the law say that the Messiah is the son of David?" (Καὶ ἀποκριθεὶς ὁ Ἰησοῦς ἔλεγεν διδάσκων ἐν τῷ ἱερῷ· πῶς λέγουσιν οἱ γραμματεῖς ὅτι ὁ χριστὸς υἱὸς Δαυίδ ἐστιν;). The episode is linked to the previous ones by the reference to the "temple courts" (ἱερόν; see comments on 11:15 – 16), where Jesus has been since 11:27. The participle "answering" (ἀποκριθεὶς) does not mean Jesus has been asked a question. The verb can indicate a response to any person or situation (see comments on 11:13c – 14). Mark likely means that Jesus is now responding to the previous questions with one of his own.

Jesus is now "teaching" (διδάσκων), something he did daily in the temple (14:49). Though Mark provides less teaching content than the other Synoptics, he often identifies Jesus as a teacher and refers to his authoritative teaching, a key part of his messianic identity as announcer and inaugurator of the kingdom (see comments on 1:15, 21 – 22).[3] In the three previous episodes Jesus has been addressed as "teacher" (διδάσκαλε; 12:14, 19, 32).

Jesus raises a question related to the Davidic ancestry of the Messiah. Expectations that the Messiah would be a "son" (= descendant) of David

arose from the Davidic promise tradition in 2 Sam 7:11b – 16. Through Nathan the prophet, God promised David that from his "offspring" (lit., "seed") God would raise up a king who would reign on his throne forever in justice and righteousness. This hope for a messianic king from David's line was developed further in the OT prophets, where the Messiah is referred to as "a shoot ... from the stump of Jesse" (Isa 11:1; cf. 9:2 – 7), a "righteous Branch" (Jer 23:5; 33:15; cf. Zech 3:8; 6:12), and a new "David" (Jer 30:9; Ezek 34:23 – 24; 37:24; Hos 3:5). Though "son of David" is not a messianic title in the OT, it is conceptually parallel to titles referring to ancestry, like "offspring," "shoot," and "Branch."

"Son of David" first appears as a messianic title in the first-century BC *Psalms of Solomon* (17:21) and became a favorite title for the Messiah in rabbinic Judaism.[4] The shout of Bartimaeus in 10:47 – 48, together with the cry of the crowd at Jesus' entrance into Jerusalem ("Blessed is the coming kingdom of our father David!" 11:10), illustrates that the title was coming into use with reference to the Messiah in Jesus' day.[5]

Jesus' question is "how" (πῶς), meaning "in what sense" or "on what basis," the experts in the

---

claim, there is significant NT evidence for Jesus' Davidic ancestry (Matt 1:1, 6, 17, 20; Luke 1:27, 32, 69; 2:4, 11; 3:31; Rom 1:3 – 4; 2 Tim 2:8; Heb 7:14; Rev 5:5; 22:16; Meier, *Marginal Jew*, 1:216 – 19; 238 n. 49). See also comments on 10:47.

3. Teacher: 4:38; 5:35; 9:17, 38; 10:17, 20, 35; 11:17 – 18;

12:14, 19, 32; 13:1; 14:14. Teaching: 1:21 – 22, 27; 2:13; 4:1 – 2; 6:2, 6, 34; 8:31; 10:1; 12:35, 38; 14:49.

4. See numerous examples in Evans, *Mark 8:27 – 16:20*, 272.

5. See Strauss, *Davidic Messiah*, 40 – 43, 53 – 57.

law say that the Messiah is the son of David. Jesus does not wait for an answer, but instead proposes a riddle or conundrum.

12:36 "David himself[6] said by the Holy Spirit, 'The Lord said to my Lord, "Sit at my right hand until I place your enemies under your feet."'" (αὐτὸς Δαυὶδ εἶπεν ἐν τῷ πνεύματι τῷ ἁγίῳ· εἶπεν κύριος τῷ κυρίῳ μου· κάθου ἐκ δεξιῶν μου, ἕως ἂν θῶ τοὺς ἐχθρούς σου ὑποκάτω τῶν ποδῶν σου). To speak "by the Holy Spirit" (ἐν τῷ πνεύματι τῷ ἁγίῳ) is to speak as a prophet by divine inspiration (2 Tim 3:16; 2 Pet 1:21). In 2 Sam 23:2 David says, "The Spirit of the LORD spoke through me; his word was on my tongue." David is similarly identified as a prophet in Acts 2:29 – 30 and in Josephus (*Ant.* 6.6.2 §166), and he is said to have spoken by the Holy Spirit in Acts 1:16 and 4:25.[7] The NT authors viewed the Holy Spirit's guidance in the production of Scripture as so intimate that OT quotes in the NT are sometimes introduced with phrases like, "The Holy Spirit spoke …" (Acts 28:25; cf. Heb 3:7; 10:15).

Jesus cites Ps 110:1, the most quoted OT passage in the NT. It is frequently used to affirm Jesus' vindication at God's right hand after his suffering.[8] Jesus will allude to this passage again in combination with Dan 7:13 at his trial before the Sanhedrin (Mark 14:62). There is little evidence from the rabbis that Psalm 110 was viewed messianically before the third century AD. While Jesus may have been the first to use it this way, as Gundry suggests,[9] a more likely possibility is that the psalm's earlier messianic interpretations have been suppressed by later Jewish interpreters because of its polemical use by Christian apologists.[10]

IN DEPTH: The Original Context of Psalm 110

The original meaning and setting of Psalm 110 is much disputed.[11] Some scholars view it as a true "messianic" psalm, a prophetic prediction for the coming Messiah. In this case David would be prophesying about the vindication and the future glorification of the Messiah. Others see it as a royal psalm, originally connected historically to the Davidic dynasty, but which can be ultimately linked to the Messiah (cf. Pss 2; 18; 20; 45; 72; 89; 132; etc.). In this case an unnamed court prophet is extolling the Davidic king at his coronation, so that the psalm means, "The LORD God said to my lord [= the new king], 'Sit at my right hand….'" It is a psalm of assurance and confidence that God's protection will continue over the Davidic dynasty. The difficulty with the first view is that Psalm 110 would presumably be the only purely messianic psalm in the Psalter. The

---

6. An adjectival intensive use of αὐτός.

7. David's composition of the psalms "by the Spirit" is affirmed at Qumran (11QPs^a 27:2 – 4, 11) and often in the rabbinic literature (cf. *b. Ber.* 4b; *b. ʿArak.* 15b; *b. Sukkah* 52a).

8. Mark 14:62; Acts 2:34; 5:31; 7:56; Rom 8:34; 1 Cor 15:25; Eph 1:20; Col 3:1; Heb 1:3, 13; 8:1; 10:12 – 13; 1 Pet 3:22; Rev 3:21; cf. Heb 5:6; 7:17, 21.

9. Gundry, *Mark*, 718.

10. For Jewish use of the psalm, see D. Hay, *Glory at the Right Hand: Psalm 110 in Early Christianity* (SBLMS 18; Nashville: Abingdon, 1973), 19 – 33; France, *Jesus and the Old Testament*, 164 – 65; Str-B 4/1.452 – 65.

11. For a good summary, see L. C. Allen, *Psalms 101 – 150* (WBC 21; Waco, TX: Word, 1983), 83 – 86.

difficulty with the second is that it would contradict Jesus' claim that David was the original speaker in the psalm.

One unique solution is that the psalm is both royal and messianic, with David originally speaking of his son Solomon at his coronation.[12] Solomon, the original referent of the Davidic promise (2 Sam 7:13 – 15), typologically represents the Messiah — the "son of David" — who will reign forever on David's throne. Though Solomon failed to live up to the expectations of the Davidic covenant and so passed from the scene, the messianic hope expressed in the psalm carried forward, ultimately realized in Jesus, the Messiah.

Mark's quotation follows the LXX, except that "under" (ὑποκάτω) replaces the LXX's more literal rendering of the Hebrew "footstool" (ὑποπόδιον; Heb: *hĕdōm*).[13] The MT uses two different words for Lord — "The Lᴏʀᴅ [*yhwh*] said to my Lord/Master [*ʾadōnî*]" — both of which are translated "Lord" (κύριος) in the LXX. If Jesus cited the text in Aramaic, as Fitzmyer suggests, the same word (*mārî*) would have been used for both.[14] But Jesus' argument does not depend on the LXX or the Aramaic (as some have claimed). David refers to the Messiah as his "Lord" or "Master" (κύριος/ *ʾadōnî* / *mārî*), not as an acclamation of his deity, but to affirm the Messiah's lordship or superior status.

The "right hand" is the position of highest honor beside the king, as the request by James and John has shown (10:35 – 45). The psalm thus positions the Davidic king as God's vice-regent, ruling at his side. To place someone "under your feet" (ὑποκάτω τῶν ποδῶν σου) is to subdue them. God will vindicate the king by subjugating his enemies.

12:37a-b **"David himself calls him 'Lord'; so how can he be his son?"** (αὐτὸς Δαυὶδ λέγει αὐτὸν κύριον, καὶ πόθεν αὐτοῦ ἐστιν υἱός;). Now Jesus proposes the conundrum: *How can the Messiah be both David's Lord and David's son?* Jesus starts with the recognized assumption that the Messiah would be a "son" or descendant of David. Yet the title "son" suggests a measure of subordination and inferiority. The son of a king is merely the prince until his father dies, when he assumes the status of supreme lord. The saying, "The king is dead … long live the king!" emphasizes not only the perpetuity of the dynasty, but the immediate transformation of the prince to king over the whole realm. The shocking thing about Ps 110:1 – 2 is that David refers to his "son" as his "Lord." This is upside down, unless the son somehow has greater status than the father.

---

12. Herbert W. Bateman IV, "Psalm 110:1 and the New Testament," *BibSac* 149 (1992): 438 – 53. Cf. Gray, *The Temple in the Gospel of Mark*, 82 – 89, who develops this Solomonic reference with reference to Markan theology. He claims that Mark is here attributing both royal and priestly authority to Jesus by virtue of the Melchizedekian priesthood affirmed in Psalm 110. Though an intriguing possibility, this would seem to go beyond anything Mark says in the text.

13. Luke here follows the LXX, though, not surprisingly, the

manuscripts in all three Synoptics are mixed. Many Markan manuscripts read "footstool" (ὑποπόδιον: ℵ A L Θ Ψ 087 *f*[1.13] 33 2427 𝔐 lat syr[p.h]). Since "under" (ὑποκάτω) is the harder reading (different from MT, LXX, and most NT citations of Ps 110) and has relatively strong textual evidence (B D W 28 2542 syr[s] cop), it is to be preferred here. Copyists likely altered Mark to agree with the others.

14. J. A. Fitzmyer, *A Wandering Aramean: Collected Aramaic Essays* (SBLMS 25; Missoula, MT: Scholars, 1979), 90.

Some have claimed that the pericope is a denial of the Messiah's Davidic descent, either by Jesus,[15] the pre-Markan community[16] or the Evangelist himself.[17] As noted above, however, this is unlikely to have been the original meaning, and it certainly was not Mark's. Jesus' Davidic descent is deeply rooted in the tradition and has been positively affirmed in Mark by Bartimaeus's cry (10:47–48) and, by implication, at Jesus' entrance into Jerusalem (11:10). The point must therefore be that the Messiah is more than simply a new David or heir to the Davidic throne, the traditional (scribal) expectations for the Messiah.

Yet Jesus does not answer his own question, and the episode remains enigmatic. Various answers have been proposed. One is that the Messiah is David's Lord because he will one day reign over all the earth, a realm far greater than David's empire. From the perspective of the Hebrew Scriptures, the "LORD of all the earth" is none other than Yahweh himself (Josh 3:11, 13; Ps 97:5; Mic 4:13; Zech 4:14). Others suggest Jesus has in mind the Messiah's role as the exalted Son of Man of Dan 7:13, Jesus' favorite self-designation (cf. esp. Mark 13:26; 14:62).[18]

From the perspective of Mark's theology, however, the most likely answer is that Jesus is the Son of God.[19] "Son of God" has been an important title from the beginning of Mark's gospel (1:1). It is highlighted through the Father's acclamation of Jesus as his beloved Son (1:11; 9:7; cf. 12:6), through the recognition of demons (3:11; 5:7), in the question of the high priest at Jesus' trial (14:61), and, climactically, at the centurion's acclamation at the foot of the cross (15:39).

12:37c The great crowd enjoyed listening to him (καὶ ὁ πολὺς ὄχλος ἤκουεν αὐτοῦ ἡδέως). To "hear gladly" (ἀκούω ἡδέως) is an idiom meaning to delight in or enjoy listening to someone or something. The amazement of the crowds at Jesus' teaching has been a common refrain throughout Mark's gospel (1:22, 27; 6:2; 10:24, 26). Since Jesus' arrival in Jerusalem, the emphasis has been on the fear of the religious leaders because of Jesus' popular teaching (11:18, 32; 12:12, 17; 14:2). This popularity will be fickle, however, and the "crowd" (ὄχλος) will soon be provoked by the priestly leadership to choose Barabbas over Jesus (15:11). The same phrase, "hearing him gladly" (ἡδέως αὐτοῦ ἤκουεν), was used of Herod Antipas's delight in conversing with John the Baptist (6:20). But this did not prevent him from executing him![20]

15. J. Klausner, *Jesus of Nazareth: His Life, Times, and Teaching* (New York/London: George Allen & Unwin, 1925).

16. Bultmann, *History,* 66, 145–46; Burger, *Jesus als Davidssohn,* 57.

17. W. Wrede, "Jesus als Davidssohn," in *Vorträge und Studien* (Tübingen: Mohr, 1907), 147–77, 168, 175; A. Suhl, "Der Davidssohn im Matthäus-Evangelium," *ZNW* 59 (1968): 57–81, 60; idem, *Die Funktion der alttestamentlichen Zitate und Anspielungen im Markusevangelium* (Gütersloh: Gerd Mohn, 1965), 93; Kelber, *The Kingdom in Mark,* 95–96.

18. F. Neugebauer, "Die Davidssohnfrage (Mark xii. 35–7 parr.) und der Menschensohn," *NTS* 21 (1974): 81–108; Lohmeyer, *Markus,* 162–63; Evans, *Mark 8:27–16:20,* 274.

19. Matthew's parallel suggests this answer, with Jesus explicitly raising the question, "Whose son is he?" (Matt 22:42).

20. Garland, *Mark,* 479. There is an interesting parallel in Josephus's famous (and controversial) *Testimonium Flavianum,* where he refers to Jesus as "a teacher of such people who receive the truth with pleasure [ἡδονῇ]" (*Ant.* 18.3.3 §63).

Theology in Application

This episode shares with the previous ones an emphasis on Jesus' superior wisdom and knowledge. Theologically, it is primarily christological. Jesus is indeed the Son of David, the messianic King from David's line who will fulfill the promises of the Hebrew Scriptures (cf. Isa 11:1 – 9). But he is much more than the Son of David: he is the Son of God and Lord of all.

Both the lordship and divine sonship of Jesus have profound implications for Christians. To declare Jesus as Lord in Mark's day would be viewed as sedition, since Caesar alone was "Lord of all." Just as many Jews throughout history died with the Shema on their lips (see on 12:29 – 30), many Christians died with "Jesus is Lord" as their last cry — and their hope of vindication. In Peter's sermon on the day of Pentecost, Jesus' exaltation to the right hand of the Father (Ps 110:1) as "both Lord and Messiah" is confirmation of his resurrection-vindication and assurance that we too will be raised (Acts 2:33 – 36, 38 – 39; cf. 1 Cor 15:20).

While few Christians in the West will likely suffer martyrdom for confessing Jesus as Lord, this is not the case for believers throughout history or around the world. In some places today, to confess Jesus as Lord is to invite persecution and even death. Yet as believers in the persecuted church of Mark's day would remind us, the perseverance that comes from this confession results in eternal life. Those who wish to save their lives will lose them, but whoever gives up their life for Jesus and for the gospel will save it (Mark 8:35).

The divine sonship of Christ — implied in this passage — also has profound implications for believers. Our adoption as children of God is dependent on Jesus' own sonship (Rom 8:29; 1 John 3:1 – 2). Those who have died and risen again "in Christ" share his resurrection life and become part of God's spiritual family. As God's children, we are heirs of God and co-heirs with Christ (Rom 8:17), sharing his spiritual life in the present and inheritance of the kingdom of God in the future.

CHAPTER 51

Mark 12:38 – 44

Literary Context

Jesus' denunciation of the "experts in the law" (or "scribes," γραμματεῖς) concludes the controversies of 11:27 – 12:40. After repeatedly clashing with the religious leaders, Jesus pronounces a final statement of judgment against them. This episode is linked to the previous ones with its reference to the scribes, since Jesus had a positive encounter with one in 12:28 – 34 and then raised a question about their traditions in 12:35 – 37. It is connected to the episode of the poor widow that follows with the reference to the scribes who "devour the widows' homes" (v. 39). We have kept these two episodes together since they form a pair, representing positive and negative examples of religious behavior (see Main Idea).

Jesus' teaching against the scribes is particularly striking so soon after the positive encounter in 12:28 – 34. Mark may be intentionally balancing that episode to show that, although there were exceptions, the scribes in general were hostile to Jesus and stood in opposition to his message and mission.

III. The Suffering Way of the Messiah (8:22 – 15:47)

    A. Revelation of the Messiah's Suffering (8:22 – 10:52)

    B. The Messiah Confronts Jerusalem (11:1 – 13:37)

        3. Controversies in the Temple (11:27 – 12:44)

           f. A Question about David's Son (12:35 – 37)

➡   **g. Warning about the Experts in the Law and the Widow's Offering (12:38 – 44)**

        4. The Olivet Discourse (13:1 – 37)

Main Idea

Jesus' denunciation of the experts in the law (vv. 38 – 40) and his observations related to a poor widow in the temple (vv. 41 – 44) form parallel and contrasting episodes, representing, respectively, positive and negative examples of stewardship and discipleship.

Translation

Mark 12:38 – 44

38a	Instruction/Warning	**In his teaching he was saying,**
b	warning	*"Beware the experts in the law,*
c	character description	*who like to walk around in fine robes and*
d		*to receive honorific greetings in the marketplaces, and*
39a		*the most important seats in the synagogues, and*
b		*the places of honor at banquets.*
40a	character description	*They devour the widows' homes and*
b		*show off with long prayers.*
c	threat of judgment	*These men will receive even more severe punishment."*
41a	setting (spatial & social)	While sitting opposite the offering receptacle,
b	Action/Observation	**he was watching how the crowd put money in the offering receptacle.**
c	Action	**Many rich people were putting in large amounts.**
42a	Action/Contrast	Then **one poor widow,** coming up, **put in two lepta,**
b	explanation	worth a quadrans.
43a	action	Summoning his disciples,
b	Instruction	**he said to them,**
c	veracity statement	*"Truly I say to you,*
d	assertion	*this poor widow put in more than all those who put their offering in the offering ⤶ receptacle.*
44a	explanation	*For all the rest gave from their surplus,*
b	contrast with 44a	*but she, from her poverty, gave everything, all that she had to live on."*

Structure

Both episodes recorded here represent teaching by Jesus. The first is a warning against the behavior of the experts in the law and a judgment oracle. It has OT parallels both in the OT Wisdom literature, especially Proverbs, and in the judgment oracles of the Prophets. As throughout Proverbs, the "wise" are warned against following the foolish behavior of the wicked, who exploit and take advantage of the poor. As in the Prophets, judgment and condemnation is threatened against those who act in opposition to God's people.

The second episode is a pronouncement story. Mark presents a scene in the temple, with various people placing offerings in the treasury; Jesus then makes a pronouncement in the form of a commentary on the widow's actions.

A different perspective on the genre of this latter episode has been proposed in recent years — that it does not represent a pronouncement story commending the widow, but rather illustrates the previous teaching by showing how the religious leaders of Israel "devour the widows' homes." In this view, the scene is not set in contrast to the previous one, but continues the denunciation against the religious leaders begun in v. 40. The temple, which should be "a house of prayer for all the nations," is instead "a den of robbers" (11:17; Isa 56:7; Jer 7:11), with its corrupt priesthood snatching the last copper coins from a poor widow's hand.[1]

Whether or not this was the original intent of the passage, it cannot be Mark's, since Jesus commends the widow, who gives all she had, and contrasts her with the wealthy, who give out of their abundance. Furthermore, she cannot be seen merely as a victim, since she does exactly what Jesus earlier commanded the rich man to do — to give all he had (10:21). She therefore serves as a positive example not only against the greedy religious leaders, but also against the rich man, who could not bring himself to give up all for the kingdom of God. This is the model of Jesus himself, who gives up his life for others (10:45; 14:22, 24) and calls on his disciples to do the same (8:34–35).

Exegetical Outline

→ **1. Warning against the Experts in the Law (12:38–40)**
   a. Warning against their pride (12:38–39)
   b. Warning against their corruption and hypocrisy (12:40a-b)
   c. Pronouncement of their coming judgment (12:40c)

2. The Widow's Offering (12:41–44)
   a. The context: Offerings at the temple treasury (12:41)
   b. The poor widow's offering (12:42)
   c. Jesus' teaching (12:43–44)

Explanation of the Text

12:38–39 In his teaching he was saying, "Beware the experts in the law, who like to walk around in fine robes and to receive honorific greetings in the marketplaces, and the most important seats in the synagogues, and the places of honor at banquets." (Καὶ ἐν τῇ διδαχῇ αὐτοῦ ἔλεγεν· βλέπετε ἀπὸ τῶν γραμματέων τῶν θελόντων ἐν στολαῖς περιπατεῖν καὶ ἀσπασμοὺς ἐν ταῖς ἀγοραῖς καὶ πρωτοκαθεδρίας ἐν ταῖς συναγωγαῖς καὶ πρωτοκλισίας ἐν τοῖς δείπνοις). Jesus earlier warned the disciples against "the leaven of the Pharisees and the leaven of Herod" (8:15) — likely a reference to the stubborn resistance of these people to the kingdom of God. Now he warns against the pride, greed, and corruption of the scribes, or the experts in Jewish law (γραμματεῖς; see comments on 1:22).[2]

Jesus criticizes four examples of their pride or

1. See A. G. Wright, "The Widow's Mites: Praise or Lament — A Matter of Context," CBQ 44 (1982): 256–65; R. S. Sugirtharajah, "The Widow's Mites Revalued," ExpT 103 (1991): 42–43;

Evans, Mark 8:27–16:20, 282; Fitzmyer, Luke, 2:1320–21.
2. Matthew greatly expands these denunciations with a long list of "woes" against the Pharisees (Matt 23:1–36).

ostentation, all related to love of high social status and position. As Marcus points out, the adjectival participle "who like ..." (τῶν θελόντων) is a restrictive modifier, referring not necessarily to all scribes, but to those who exhibit this behavior (cf. 3:22).[3] A "fine robe" (στολή) was a long, flowing robe, like those used for ceremonial or festal occasions (BDAG, 946). In the NT the term is used of angels' garments (16:5), the father's robe as patriarch in the parable of the prodigal son (Luke 15:22), and the robes of glorified saints in heaven (6:11; 7:9, 13 – 14; 22:14). In the LXX it is commonly used of royal (Gen 41:42; 49:11; 2 Chr 15:27; 18:9) and especially priestly garments (Exod 28:3, 4; 29:29). Some interpreters claim that most scribes were in fact priests (so Marcus)[4] or that they were dressing in imitation of the priests as a sign of religious devotion (so Evans).[5] In any case, their flowing robes were meant to show off their status as religious leaders.

"Greetings in the marketplaces" indicated deference and respect, with the lesser person initiating the greeting and using honorific titles like "Master," "Father," or "Rabbi" (cf. Matt 23:7). The Jerusalem Talmud says that "a person must greet one who is greater than he in knowledge of Torah" (*y. Ber.* 2.1). It was a sign of humility that the great Rabbi Yohanan ben Zakkai was the first to greet others in the marketplace, including even Gentiles (*b. Ber.* 17a).

The "most important seats" in the synagogues are likely the bench that faced the congregation in front of the ark containing the sacred scrolls.[6] This spot was reserved for honored guests or the senior elders and teachers.

"Banquets" were rituals of social status in the first century, with the best seats and the best food given to the most honored guests.[7] In Luke 14:7 – 11 Jesus encourages his followers not to seek the greater positions at such banquets, but to humbly take a lower seat.

12:40 "They devour the widows' homes and show off with long prayers. These men will receive even more severe punishment." (οἱ κατεσθίοντες τὰς οἰκίας τῶν χηρῶν καὶ προφάσει μακρὰ προσευχόμενοι· οὗτοι λήμψονται περισσότερον κρίμα). Widows and fatherless children were among the most vulnerable and defenseless members of society.[8] Scripture is full of injunctions to care for them, as well as warnings that God is their defender and will avenge those who exploit them.[9]

It is uncertain what it means that the scribes "devour" (κατεσθίω) widows' homes.[10] It could be that they were exploiting the estate of widows for whom they had been appointed guardians.[11] Or Jesus may be using hyperbole to describe those who abuse

---

3. Marcus, *Mark 9 – 16*, 852.

4. Ibid.; idem, *Mark 1 – 8*, 524.

5. Evans, *Mark 8:27 – 16:20*, 278. Cf. Philo, *Legat.* 296; Josephus, *Ant.* 3.7.1 §§151 – 156; 11.4.2 §80.

6. Lane, *Mark*, 440; Cranfield, *Mark*, 384.

7. Malina and Rohrbaugh, *Social-Science Commentary*, 135 – 36, 191 – 92 (cf. Jos. *Ant.* 15.2.4 §21).

8. Isa 1:7; Jer 7:6; 49:11.

9. Exod 22:22; Deut 10:18; 24:17; 27:19; Pss 68:5; 146:9; Isa 1:23; 10:1 – 4; Jer 7:6; 22:3; 49:11; Ezek 22:7; Zech 7:10; Mal 3:5; Acts 6:1 – 7; 1 Tim 5:16; Jas 1:27; cf. 2 Esd 2:20; Sir 35:17 – 21; Wis 2:10.

10. The grammar is awkward, since the substantival participles οἱ κατεσθίοντες and προσευχόμενοι should be in the genitive to agree with their antecedent, "the scribes" (τῶν γραμματέων) in v. 38. It could be (1) the beginning of a new verbless sentence, a *casus pendens* ("hanging case"), which resumes with the subject restated by οὗτοι: "Those who devour the widows' homes ... these men will receive even more severe judgment" (so Cranfield, *Mark*, 385; cf. REB). (2) More likely, the distance from the genitive has resulted in a *constructio ad sensum* ("construction according to sense"), whereby the nominative is used despite the grammatical irregularity: "Beware the scribes ... who devour ..." (so France, *Mark*, 491, and most versions).

11. *b. Giṭ.* 52a-b. See J. D. M. Derrett, "'Eating Up the Houses of Widows': Jesus' Comment on Lawyers," *NovT* 14 (1972): 1 – 9.

the hospitality and generosity of widows.[12] The *Testament of Moses* (first century AD) says of the priestly aristocracy in Jerusalem that "they consume the goods of the poor, saying their acts are according to justice, while in fact they are simply exterminators" (7:6–7; cf. *Pss. Sol.* 4:1–13).[13]

The dative noun "with pretense" (προφάσει) may go with what precedes, meaning that they cover up their actions against widows with long prayers (NLT: "and then pretend to be pious by making long prayers"), or it could refer to the prayers themselves, which are showy and ostentatious (CEV: "and then pray long prayers just to show off"). The latter seems more likely. Such exploitation, Jesus says, will not go unpunished on judgment day. As leaders entrusted with leadership over God's flock, they will receive greater punishment (cf. Jas 3:1).

12:41 While sitting opposite the offering receptacle, he was watching how the crowd put money in the offering receptacle. Many rich people were putting in large amounts (Καὶ καθίσας κατέναντι τοῦ γαζοφυλακίου ἐθεώρει πῶς ὁ ὄχλος βάλλει χαλκὸν εἰς τὸ γαζοφυλάκιον. καὶ πολλοὶ πλούσιοι ἔβαλλον πολλά). The setting of this episode is the Court of Women, the first inner court of the temple proper, beyond the outer Court of the Gentiles.

The term translated "offering receptacle" (γαζοφυλακίον) could also mean "treasury" (NIV, NASB, ESV, HCSB), referring to one of the treasury storerooms located in the inner courts (cf. Neh 12:44).[14] More likely it refers to one of the chests or receptacles where offerings were placed (NLT: "collection box"; NET, CEV: "offering box").

The Mishnah speaks of thirteen "Shofar-chests" (trumpet-shaped receptacles) located in the temple. These were inscribed with the names of various kinds of offerings, and worshipers would put their offering in the specified receptacle (*m. Šeqal.* 6:1, 5). Since people are "putting" or "throwing" (βάλλω) money in, this latter sense seems most likely.

Jesus finds a place to sit opposite the Shofar-chests and watches the wealthy placing large numbers of coins in. The amount given would be obvious by the rattle of the coins as they were poured into the metal receptacles.

12:42 Then one poor widow, coming up, put in two lepta, worth a quadrans (καὶ ἐλθοῦσα μία χήρα πτωχὴ ἔβαλεν λεπτὰ δύο, ὅ ἐστιν κοδράντης). On the alternate, but unlikely, interpretation of this episode as a condemnation of the greedy temple leadership, see Structure above. On widows as poor and vulnerable members of society — the recipients of God's special care — see comments on v. 40.

This woman puts in two *lepta*. The term *lepton* (λεπτόν; meaning "a tiny thing") was used of a small copper coin, the smallest in circulation in Palestine. Mark explains that two *lepta* are equivalent to a *kordantēs* (κοδράντης), a transliteration of the Latin *quadrans*, worth 1/64 of a denarius (cf. Matt 5:26). This use of a Latin equivalent is one piece of evidence that Mark may be writing to the church in Rome (see Introduction to Mark: Audience). Translations that use minuscule amounts, like "worth less than a penny" (NET) or "which make a penny" (ESV; cf. NRSV, NASB), are not quite accurate, since a *quadrans* would be worth

12. Cranfield, *Mark*, 385. Jeremias, *Jerusalem*, 111–16, points to the Mishnah's prohibition against scribes receiving payment for teaching the law and claims that many scribes were poor, living off subsidies (*m.* ʾAbot 1:13; *m. Bek.* 4:6; cf. *b. Ned.* 37a, 62a). This passage, he says, refers to "the scribes' habit of sponging off the hospitality of people of limited means" (114).

13. Translation from J. Priest, "Testament of Moses," in *OTL*, 1:930.
14. Josephus, *J.W.* 6.5.2 §282; 5.5.2 §200; *Ant.* 19.6.1 §294; 1 Macc 14:49; 2 Macc 3:4–40. In John 8:20 Jesus is said to be teaching "in the treasury" (ἐν τῷ γαζοφυλακίῳ), which probably means "in the temple courts near the place where the offerings were put" (NIV).

about eight minutes worth of work for a day laborer (assuming an eight-hour day to earn a denarius [Matt 20:2]). Even at a very low hourly wage of $3.50 (USD), this would be about 50 cents. We are referring here to "small change," enough to purchase a meager meal.

12:43 – 44 Summoning his disciples, he said to them, "Truly I say to you, this poor widow put in more than all those who put their offering in the offering receptacle. For all the rest gave from their surplus, but she, from her poverty, gave everything, all that she had to live on." (καὶ προσκαλεσάμενος τοὺς μαθητὰς αὐτοῦ εἶπεν αὐτοῖς· ἀμὴν λέγω ὑμῖν ὅτι ἡ χήρα αὕτη ἡ πτωχὴ πλεῖον πάντων ἔβαλεν τῶν βαλλόντων εἰς τὸ γαζοφυλάκιον· πάντες γὰρ ἐκ τοῦ περισσεύοντος αὐτοῖς ἔβαλον, αὕτη δὲ ἐκ τῆς ὑστερήσεως αὐτῆς πάντα ὅσα εἶχεν ἔβαλεν ὅλον τὸν βίον αὐτῆς).

Jesus often summons his disciples in Mark for special instructions or teaching (3:13; 6:7; 8:1; 10:42). The importance of the teaching is marked by his solemn introduction, "Truly I say to you" (ἀμὴν λέγω ὑμῖν), used thirteen times in Mark (see comments on 3:28). Jesus says the woman's small offering exceeded even the largest gifts of the wealthy, since they gave a small percentage of their wealth, while she gave from her poverty — everything she had (cf. 2 Cor 8:2 – 3). She serves as an example of fulfilling the greatest commandment, loving God with one's whole self (12:29 – 32).

A similar thought concerning proportional giving appears in Aristotle, who wrote that "one's generosity is to be evaluated in terms of one's resources.... People who are truly generous give in proportion to what they actually have. It is possible, therefore, that a person who gives but little out of small resources is more generous than another."[15] There is an even closer rabbinic parallel in *Lev. Rab.* 3:5 on Lev 1:17 (4th – 5th cent. AD?), where a priest despises a woman for bringing a mere handful of flour as an offering. In a dream, however, he is told not to despise her since her gift is the equivalent to sacrificing her own life.[16] In both stories a tiny offering is viewed as encompassing "her whole life" (v. 44: ὅλον τὸν βίον αὐτῆς).

Theology in Application

The contrasting portraits of the scribes and the poor widow illustrate for Mark's readers two radically different responses to the kingdom of God. The experts in the law represent those who are in it for themselves, building personal empires rather than God's kingdom. They violate the two greatest commands because they love self rather than God and exploit others for personal gain. The widow, by contrast, is not thinking of herself when she gives self-sacrificially out of her poverty. She lives a life of trust and dependence on God. In these contrasting passages, we see two of the greatest dangers for Christian leaders, pride and abuse of power; and we see two of the most important character traits for godly leadership, self-sacrificial service and total commitment to the kingdom of God.

---

15. Aristotle, *Eth. nic.* 4.1.19; cited by F. Danker, *Jesus and the New Age: A Commentary on St. Luke's Gospel* (2nd ed.; Philadelphia: Fortress, 1988), 328. Cf. Euripides, *Danaë* frag. 319.

16. See Boring et al., eds., *Hellenistic Commentary*, §246, pp. 178 – 79.

The Danger of Pride

"Pride goes before the fall" is proverbial, and it is certainly true in Christian ministry. The greatest sin of human beings is to worship and serve the creature (themselves) rather than the Creator (Rom 1:25). Pride is the self-deception that we have earned position and power for ourselves and deserve to be recognized for it.

One does not need to look far in Christian ministry to see the destructive power of pride. As a seminary professor, over the years I have seen many churches and ministry agencies in crisis. Almost inevitably, these crises are not caused by heresy or false teaching from outside the church. They are caused by pride and self-interest from within, where strong personalities wage war over the right way to do things or over turf wars between church factions. In 1 Cor 1 – 4, Paul deals with many issues of immaturity in the struggling church at Corinth. But the one on which he spends the most time and space is disunity and factions caused by pride in human wisdom. Little has changed in two thousand years. While pride results in destructive divisions, humble service for others results in true unity (Phil 2:1 – 11).

Abuse of Power

Closely related to pride is the exploitation of others that often results from an arrogant heart. Cult leaders are famous for holding such absolute power over their followers that they can force or coerce others to do almost anything. Whether it is extreme cases like Jim Jones of the People's Temple in Guyana or Marshall Applewhite of the Heaven's Gate cult, who led their followers in mass suicide, or more common abuse like demanding control of finances or coercing sexual favors, these leaders abuse others for personal gain.

Yet abuse of power is not limited to cult leaders.[17] Pastors and ministry leaders sometimes wield excessive power without adequate accountability. While the much-publicized televangelist scandals of the 1970s are the most visible examples of this in recent history, it has occurred throughout church history. In the short letter known as 3 John, the apostle John criticizes a certain Diotrephes, "who loves to be first" (prideful), withholding hospitality from traveling teachers, slandering other leaders, and excommunicating believers (3 John 9 – 10). In 2 Corinthians, Paul speaks of "false apostles," who masquerade as apostles of Christ but who exploit and take advantage of believers (2 Cor 11:13, 20).

Such abuse inevitably results when leaders view themselves as indispensable to God's kingdom and unaccountable to others. Some scribes of Jesus' day "devoured" widows' homes because they were more interested in padding their own wallets than in the needs of others, and they had lost sight of their accountability before God.

17. See Ronald M. Enroth, *Churches That Abuse* (Grand Rapids: Zondervan, 1993).

Humble and Self-Sacrificial Service

In stark contrast to the experts in the law stands the poor widow, who humbly gives to God instead of hoarding resources for herself. Her example parallels that of the churches in Macedonia, which Paul says gave out of their extreme poverty to help the struggling churches of Judea (2 Cor 8:1 – 5). Those who give in this way have come to recognize that their resources are not their own but belong to God. We are reminded of the early church in Acts, which self-sacrificially met the needs of others, and individuals like Barnabas, who was willing to sell even his own property to help the poor (2:44 – 45; 4:32 – 37).

Commitment to the Kingdom of God

Behind this kind of self-sacrificial giving lies an even greater value, namely, total commitment to the kingdom of God. To give from poverty means your eyes are not on earthly rewards but on treasures in heaven (Matt 6:20). The writer to the Hebrews describes God's faithful servants who have gone before us, who remained faithful to the end even though they did not see the fulfillment of the promise. Their eyes were on the heavenly city rather than the earthly one (Heb 11:13 – 16).

This theme of self-sacrificial service has been a major one throughout Mark's gospel, as Jesus describes the cost of discipleship. Those who want to be Jesus' disciples must take up their cross and follow him (8:34 – 35). In his parallel to this passage, Luke adds the word "daily" to make it clear that this is not only about martyrdom (Luke 9:23). It means daily placing God's kingdom and God's values above our own. This is the mark of true leadership.

52

Mark 13:1 – 23

Literary Context

Jesus' discourse on the Mount of Olives forms a transition in Mark's narrative between the controversies in the temple (11:12 – 12:44) and the Passion Narrative (chs. 14 – 15). At the beginning of these controversies, Jesus entered the temple (11:27; cf. 11:11, 15). Now he leaves it for the last time in Mark's gospel and crosses eastward to the Mount of Olives. On the way, one of his disciples comments on the magnificence of the temple complex, the pride of Judaism.

With the "Olivet Discourse" (13:5 – 37), Jesus first responds by predicting the temple's destruction and then answers a question about the timing and circumstances of this event. This discourse is also linked conceptually to Jesus' cursing of the fig tree and clearing of the temple (11:12 – 25) — both symbolic of the temple's destruction — and the parable of tenant farmers (12:1 – 12), in which Jesus predicted coming judgment against Israel's corrupt religious leaders and identified himself (implicitly) as the cornerstone of a new and greater temple (12:10 – 11).

III. The Suffering Way of the Messiah (8:22 – 15:47)
  A. Revelation of the Messiah's Suffering (8:22 – 10:52)
  B. The Messiah Confronts Jerusalem (11:1 – 13:37)
➡ **4. The Olivet Discourse (13:1 – 37)**
    a. Introduction and the Coming Destruction of Jerusalem (13:1 – 23)
    b. The Coming of the Son of Man and Parables Related to Watchfulness (13:24 – 37)

Main Idea

In response to a comment from his disciples about the beauty of the temple, Jesus predicts its destruction and delivers an eschatological discourse describing the signs (and nonsigns) leading to the destruction of Jerusalem, the persecution of his followers, the worldwide proclamation of the gospel, the coming of the Son of Man, and the end of the age. The central theme is a call for watchfulness, perseverance, and faithfulness in the face of coming crisis (13:5, 9, 23, 33, 35, 37).

Translation

Mark 13:1 – 23

1a	setting (temporal & spatial)	As he was leaving the temple courts,
b	Comment	**one of his disciples said to him,**
c		*"Teacher, look! What magnificent stones and magnificent buildings!"*
2a	Response to 1b	**Jesus said to him,**
b	rhetorical question	*"Do you see these great buildings?*
c	prophecy	*Not even one stone will be left here on another, which will not be demolished."*
3a	setting (spatial)	While he was sitting on the Mount of Olives ♻
		opposite the temple complex,
b	Character entrance	**Peter, James, John, and Andrews asked him privately,**
4a	question	*"Tell us, when will these things happen,*
b	question	*and what will be the sign that all these things are about to be accomplished?"*
5a	Response	**Jesus began to say to them,**
b	warning of false messiahs	*"Watch out that no one deceives you.*
6a		*Many will come in my name, saying,*
b		*'I am the one!'*
c		*and they will deceive many.*
7a	warning of wars	*When you hear about wars and rumors of wars,*
b		*do not be alarmed.*
c		*These things must happen,*
d		*but the end is not yet.*
8a		*Nation will rise against nation and kingdom against kingdom.*
b	warning of other disasters	*There will be earthquakes in various places;*
c		*there will be famines.*
d	summary	*These are the beginning of birth pains.*
9a	warning of persecution	*As for you, watch out for yourselves.*
b		*They will hand you over to councils and flog you in the synagogues.*
c		*You will stand before governors and kings for my sake, as a witness to them.*
10	gospel proclaimed worldwide	*And the gospel must first be preached to all nations.*
11a	the Holy Spirit's guidance	*When, after handing you over, they bring you to trial,*
b		*don't worry beforehand what you will say.*
c		*But say whatever is given to you in that hour,*
d		*because it is not you speaking, but the Holy Spirit.*
12a	family betrayal	*Brother will hand over brother to death and a father his child.*
b		*Children will rise up against their parents and have them put to death.*
13a		*You will be hated by all because of my name.*
b	promise of salvation	*But the one who endures to the end — this one will be saved.*

Continued on next page.

Continued from previous page.

14a	setting	*But*	*when you see the 'abomination that causes desolation'*
			[Dan 9:27; 11:31; 12:11]
			standing where it should not be
b	Narrative aside		**(let the readers understand),**
c	warning to flee		*then let those in Judea flee to the mountains.*
15			*Let no one on the rooftop come down or go in to take anything out of their house,*
16			*and the one in the field must not return to get their cloak.*
17			*But woe to those who are pregnant and*
			who are nursing babies in those days!
18			*Pray that it will not happen in winter.*
19a	warning of great tribulation	*For*	*those days will bring tribulation*
			of a kind unlike anything that has happened
			since the beginning of creation,
b			*when God ☝*
			made the world,
			until now.
c		*And*	*it will never happen again.*
20a	the shortening of days	*And*	*if the Lord had not cut short those days,*
b			*no life would be saved.*
c		*But*	*for the sake of the chosen ones, whom he has chosen,*
d			*he has shortened the days.*
21a	warning of false messiahs	*Then,*	*if anyone says to you, 'Look, here is the Messiah!' or 'Look, he is there,'*
b			*do not believe them.*
22a		*For*	*false messiahs and false prophets will give signs and wonders*
b			*in order to deceive, if possible, the elect.*
23a	final warning of vv. 1 – 23		*You watch out.*
b			*I have told you all these things ahead of time."*

Structure

The background, structure, and significance of the Olivet Discourse is one of the most difficult issues in Mark's gospel, giving rise to a myriad of source and redaction theories.[1] From a narrative perspective, the primary problem arises from the fact that the disciples ask Jesus about the timing and signs related to the destruction of

---

1. The literature on the discourse is immense. For a history of research (through about 1990), see G. R. Beasley-Murray, *Jesus and the Last Days: The Interpretation of the Olivet Dis-* *course* (Peabody, MA: Hendrickson, 1993), 1 – 349. For research since, see Telford, *Writing on the Gospel of Mark*, 30 – 31, 451 – 53, 456, 513 – 16.

the temple. Jesus (apparently) answers their question about Jerusalem, but he also describes events related to the coming of the Son of Man and the end of the age. So when is Jesus talking about the destruction of Jerusalem and when is he talking about the end of the age? Or are these events one and the same? Did Jesus (and Mark?) get it wrong by connecting these two events?

Some commentators resolve this issue by seeing the entire discourse related to the events surrounding the destruction of Jerusalem in AD 70. The coming of the Son of Man in this case would refer not to the parousia (the second coming of Christ to earth), but to the judgment of God witnessed in the destruction of the temple and/or the vindication of the Son of Man at the right hand of God (Ps 110:1 – 2; Dan 7:13 – 14; see comments on 13:24 – 27).[2] The problem with this view is that certain statements, such as the apocalyptic signs of 13:24 – 25 and the gathering of the elect by the angels in 13:27, seem to relate to the end of the age.

Other interpreters see the entire discourse as related to the eschatological consummation, with no reference to the events of AD 70. This, too, seems unlikely. The whole discourse arises from Jesus' prediction about the destruction of the temple (v. 2) and the disciples' question about the timing and signs related to this event (v. 4). Are we to believe that Jesus completely ignores this question? Furthermore, certain descriptions in the discourse, such as Jesus' warning to flee Judea (vv. 14 – 19) and the reference to "this generation" (v. 30), seem to relate directly to the siege and destruction of Jerusalem.

Most commentators see the discourse as concerning, in some sense, both events. The simplest solution is to see the first half (13:5 – 23) referring to the coming destruction of Jerusalem and the second (13:24 – 37) referring to the return of the Son of Man and the end of the age. The problem with this is that certain events in the first seem to relate to the end of the age (e.g., the worldwide proclamation of the gospel, v. 10; the unequaled days of distress, v. 19) and certain events of the second seem to relate to the destruction of Jerusalem ("when *you* see ...," 13:29; "this generation," 13:30). A possible solution is to propose a back-and-forth (A-B-A-B) pattern between the two events. Edwards suggests the following:[3]

A[1] 13:5 – 13   End of the temple and fall of Jerusalem
  B[1] 13:14 – 27 Tribulation and parousia
A[2] 13:28 – 31   End of the temple and fall of Jerusalem
  B[2] 13:32 – 37 Parousia and watchfulness

One problem with this structure is that the abomination of desolation and the warning to flee (vv. 14 – 18) seem to relate to the destruction of Jerusalem.[4] As a

---

2. See, e.g., Wright, *Jesus and the Victory of God*, 339 – 66; France, *Mark*, 497 – 503; idem, *Jesus and the Old Testament*, 227 – 39. France agrees that the discourse up to 13:31 concerns AD 70, but views 13:32 – 37 as referring to the parousia.

3. Edwards, *Mark*, 386.

4. Edwards (ibid., 399) says the "abomination of desolation" is a mysterious "double referent" that alludes to the destruction of Jerusalem but also looks beyond it to a still-future antichrist (p. 399). Hence, 13:14 – 27 points both to the destruction of Jerusalem and to the end of the age.

result, others shift this central section (vv. 14 – 23) forward so that the abomination of desolation and the warning of false messiahs relate to the destruction of Jerusalem, not to the return of the Son of Man.[5] The following pattern results:

A¹ 13:5 – 23   Destruction of Jerusalem and the temple
  B¹ 13:24 – 27 Parousia and the end of the age
A² 13:28 – 31   Destruction of Jerusalem and the temple (lesson of the fig tree)
  B² 13:32 – 37 Parousia and call to watchfulness

This latter also has the advantage of "framing" the first part of the discourse with commands to "watch out" (vv. 5b, 23) and warnings against false messiahs (vv. 6, 22 – 23), an "elegant inclusion," as Moloney describes it:[6]

A Warning to take heed (βλέπετε) (13:5b)
  B Many will come to deceive (πλανάω) (13:6)
  B′ False prophets and messiahs arise to lead astray (ἀποπλανάω) (13:21 – 22)
A′ Warning to take heed (βλέπετε) (13:23)

In the following outline and discussion, we adopt this general structure. Verses 5 – 23 concern the events leading up to the destruction of Jerusalem in AD 70, and 13:24 – 27 the return of the Son of Man and the end of the age. This is followed by two explanatory "parables," each relating to the timing of one of these events. The parable of the fig tree (13:28 – 31) concerns the destruction of Jerusalem and asserts that it will be preceded by confirmatory signs (13:28 – 29) and will occur within the generation of the disciples (13:30). The parable of the owner's return (13:32 – 37), by contrast, asserts the *unknown time* of the Son of Man's return and the need for constant watchfulness.

This structural analysis has several strengths. First, it provides a ready explanation for Jesus' enigmatic saying in 13:30 that "this generation" will not pass away until these events take place. This makes sense if in 13:26 – 31 Jesus has moved away from discussion of the Son of Man's return and the end of the age (13:24 – 27) and returned to the discussion of Jerusalem's destruction (13:14 – 23). This outline also resolves the apparent contradiction between 13:29 and 13:32. Although the destruction of Jerusalem will be preceded by clear signs and will occur within one generation, the timing of the return of the Son of Man is unknown to all, even to the angels and the Son, and may be pushed into the distant future.[7]

---

5. See, e.g., Stein, *Mark*, 593 – 97; Garland, *Mark*, 491 – 500.

6. Moloney, *Mark*, 249.

7. The biggest problem with this structure remains the close connection apparently made between Jerusalem's destruction and the return of the Son of Man. "In those days" (13:24) seems to connect 13:24 – 27 directly with "those days" of 13:17, 20, identifying the return of the Son of Man closely with the events related to Jerusalem. Furthermore, Jesus says in 13:30 that the present generation will see "all these things" happening, presumably including both the destruction of Jerusalem and the return of the Son of Man. The best explanation is that the passage represents typical prophetic foreshortening, in which details and chronology remain hazy and indeterminate from the prophet's perspective, but become clear as the events unfold. This would be similar to OT prophecies about the first coming of the Messiah and the consummation of his eternal kingdom,

In terms of its genre, the Olivet Discourse in its broadest sense is teaching by Jesus, prompted by a question from the disciples. More specifically, it combines exhortatory, prophetic, and apocalyptic material. Similar to Jewish apocalyptic literature, the discourse includes references to widespread deception and apostasy (vv. 5, 22), catastrophic events such as wars, earthquakes, and famines (vv. 7 – 8), persecution and tribulation for God's people (vv. 9 – 13), cosmic signs in the heavens (vv. 24 – 25), angelic intervention (v. 27), and the ultimate vindication of the righteous (vv. 13, 27). Because of these many parallels, commentators often consider Mark's primary source to have been a Jewish or Jewish-Christian apocalypse that he took up and modified.[8]

Yet as Gundry points out, the discourse has many differences from apocalypses. There are no visions or angelic revelations; no historical surveys, numerical calculations or divisions of history into epochs; no esoteric secrets revealed or symbolic objects or events; no mythical beasts or demonic powers; no final war, destruction of the wicked, final judgment, or reward and glorification of the righteous. In addition, the passage has far more commands and exhortations than is typical of an apocalyptic vision.[9] So while the discourse has apocalyptic elements, it is not an apocalypse per se. The same criticism can be leveled against other genre classifications, such as a farewell discourse[10] or a Greco-Roman peripatetic dialogue.[11] Though there are some similarities to these genres, there are too many differences to treat them as true parallels.[12]

Exegetical Outline

➡ **1. Introduction (13:1 – 4)**

    a. A disciple's comment about the temple (13:1)

    b. Jesus' prophecy of the temple's destruction (13:2)

    c. The disciples' twofold question on the Mount of Olives (13:3 – 4)

 2. The Events Leading to the Destruction of the Temple (13:5 – 23)

    a. Signs that do not signal the end (13:5 – 13)

       i. Warning against deceivers (13:5 – 6)

---

which appear to the prophet to be a single event (cf. Isa 9:1 – 7; 11:1 – 9). Like the prophets before him, Jesus can speak of the certainty of God's future, while viewing its details and timing only dimly (13:32). See further comments on 13:24 – 27.

8. This "Little Apocalypse Theory" was first proposed by T. Colani, *Jésus-Christ et les croyances messianiques de son temps* (2nd ed.; Strasbourg: Treuttel et Würtz, 1864) and was adopted by Bultmann, *History*, 125; Taylor, *Mark*, 498; and many others. For a detailed response, see Beasley-Murray, *Jesus and the Last Days*, passim.

9. Gundry, *Mark*, 751 – 52; cf. Cranfield, *Mark*, 388; Evans, *Mark 8:27 – 16:20*, 289.

10. So Grundmann, *Markus*, 347; Klosterman, *Markusevangelium*, 131; Lane, *Mark*, 144; Moloney, *Mark*, 250 – 51. Examples of farewell discourses in Judaism and Christianity include Deut 33; Josh 23 – 24; 1 Sam 12; 1 Kgs 2:1 – 9; 1 Chr 28 – 29; John 13 – 17; Acts 20:17 – 38; 2 Tim; 2 Peter; Tob 14:3 – 11; 1 Macc 2:49 – 70; and the pseudepigraphic *Testaments* (of Adam, Abraham, the Twelve Patriarchs, Moses, Job, etc.; see Charlesworth, ed., *OTP*, vol. 1).

11. David E. Aune, *Prophecy in Early Christianity and the Ancient Mediterranean World* (Grand Rapids: Eerdmans, 1983), 186 – 87, 399 – 400 n. 93.

12. See the criticism of both in Gundry, *Mark*, 751 – 52.

Explanation of the Text

13:1 As he was leaving the temple courts, one of his disciples said to him, "Teacher, look! What magnificent stones and magnificent buildings!" (Καὶ ἐκπορευομένου αὐτοῦ ἐκ τοῦ ἱεροῦ λέγει αὐτῷ εἷς τῶν μαθητῶν αὐτοῦ· διδάσκαλε, ἴδε ποταποὶ λίθοι καὶ ποταπαὶ οἰκοδομαί). Jesus' departure from the temple courts forms a kind of inclusio with 11:27, when he entered the temple at the beginning of the series of controversies with the religious leaders (11:27 – 12:44). Now he will predict the temple's destruction, a result of the nation's rejection of their Messiah.

Various commentators have pointed to the parallel between this departure and Ezekiel's description of the departure of God's glory from the temple (Ezek 10:18 – 19; 11:22 – 23). There God's glory rises above the temple, departs from the city, and stops "above the mountain east of it" (11:23). In the same manner Jesus departs from the temple courts (probably through the east gate) and crosses the Kidron Valley to this same Mount of Olives, leaving the city to its destruction.[13] Whether this allusion would be too subtle for Mark's audience is difficult to say.

As Jesus is crossing over, an unnamed disciple remarks on the temple's magnificence.[14] The address to Jesus as "Teacher" (διδάσκαλε) has been common throughout this section (12:14, 19, 32) and is probably a translation of the Hebrew *rabbî*. The exclamation by the disciple is not that of an awestruck tourist arriving from the Galilean backwater.[15] The disciples knew the temple complex well, having been there many times during this Jerusalem visit and in previous pilgrimages to the city. This is instead an expression of national pride at the magnificence of Israel's crown jewel. (See "In Depth: The Jerusalem Temple").

---

13. France, *Mark*, 495; Boring, *Mark*, 353.

14. For the use of "what sort of" (ποταπός) in the sense of "how great/magnificent," see BDAG, 856.

15. Stein, *Mark*, 588; contra France, *Mark*, 496; Edwards, *Mark*, 388.

IN DEPTH: The Jerusalem Temple

The massive temple complex, greatly expanded by Herod the Great, was one of the great wonders of the ancient world. It was built on a huge platform over 300 meters wide and 500 meters long, encompassing thirty-five acres. Josephus provides detailed descriptions of its massive buildings and ornamentation,[16] claiming that "the exterior of the building wanted nothing that could astound either mind or eye." In one place he claims some of the stones used in its construction were 45 cubits (67 ft.) long (*J.W.* 5.5.6 §224).[17] These white stones gave the entire complex a brilliant white appearance so that at a distance the temple looked like a snow-covered mountain (*War* 5.5.6 §222).[18]

The southern end of the complex was dominated by Solomon's Colonnade, a covered portico made up of 162 forty-foot-high columns, set in four rows. These columns were so massive that three men with arms extended could join hands around the base of each (*Ant.* 15.11.5 §§413–414). The temple proper rose a hundred cubits high (150 ft) in the center of the temple complex. Its walls were covered in gold plates, which reflected the sun with "so fiery a flash that persons straining to look at it were compelled to avert their eyes as from solar rays" (*J.W.* 5.5.6 §§221–222). Though some of Josephus's dimensions may be exaggerated, there is no doubt that the structure was one of the great architectural wonders of the ancient world. A famous rabbinic proverb said, "He who has not seen the temple of Herod has never seen a beautiful building in his life."[19]

13:2 Jesus said to him, "Do you see these great buildings?[20] Not even one stone will be left here on another, which will not be demolished." (καὶ ὁ Ἰησοῦς εἶπεν αὐτῷ· βλέπεις ταύτας τὰς μεγάλας οἰκοδομάς; οὐ μὴ ἀφεθῇ ὧδε λίθος ἐπὶ λίθον ὃς οὐ μὴ καταλυθῇ). Jesus redirects the disciples from their misplaced national pride. These monumental buildings — built by human hands — will be demolished. This is the first specific prediction of

the destruction of the temple or the city in Mark's gospel (but cf. Luke 19:43–44). However, Jesus' cleansing of the temple (11:15–17), cursing of the fig tree (11:12–14, 20–21), and parable of the tenant farmers all imply coming judgment (12:1–12).

Jesus will be accused at his trial of threatening to destroy the temple and rebuild it in three days (14:58; cf. John 2:19) and then mocked about this at the crucifixion (Mark 15:29). Mark treats these

16. *J.W.* 5.5.1–8 §§184–246; *Ant.* 15.11.1–7 §§380–425; cf. *m. Mid.*

17. Elsewhere he describes them as 25 cubits long (37.5 ft; *Ant.* 15.11.3 §392). One recently discovered stone from the western foundation wall is 42 feet (28 cubits) long. See D. Bahat, "Jerusalem Down Under: Tunneling along Hero's Temple Mount Wall," *BAR* 21/6 (1995): 30–47, 39.

18. For detailed discussion of the temple complex, see Sanders, *Judaism: Practice and Belief*, 51–102; J. Patrich, "Re-

constructing the Magnificent Temple Herod Built," *BRev* 4/5 (1988): 16–29; K. Ritmeyer and L. Ritmeyer, "Reconstructing Herod's Temple Mount in Jerusalem," *BAR* 15/6 (1989): 23–42.

19. *b. B. Bat.* 4a; *b. Sukkah* 41b.

20. This phrase could be a rhetorical question ("Do you see these great buildings?" NET; NIV; etc.), a command for attention ("Look at these great buildings" NLT), or a mild rebuke ("You should not be looking at these buildings with such admiration"). The first seems most likely.

accusations as false testimony (14:57), since Jesus did not threaten to destroy the temple himself; rather, he predicted its destruction. These passages, together with Jesus' enigmatic reference in John 2:19 and his lamenting over Jerusalem in Luke 13:34 – 35; 19:41 – 44 confirm for most scholars that the historical Jesus indeed predicted the destruction of the temple and/or Jerusalem, and that this was one of the key precipitating factors for his crucifixion.[21]

Predictions of the temple's destruction were not new to Judaism. The prophet Micah (eighth century BC) foresaw the destruction of the city and the first (Solomon's) temple: "Therefore because of you, Zion will be plowed like a field, Jerusalem will become a heap of rubble, the temple hill a mound overgrown with thickets" (Mic 3:12). In the years leading up to Nebuchadnezzar's siege in 586 BC, Jeremiah repeatedly predicted the temple's destruction (Jer 7:12 – 15; 12:7; 22:5; 26:6). Jeremiah also reports that King Jehoiakim had the prophet Uriah assassinated for predicting the same (26:20 – 23).

The second temple also had its doomsayers. Josephus describes a certain peasant herdsman named Jesus son of Ananus, who for four years before the Jewish revolt predicted the destruction of "Jerusalem and the holy house" and then wandered the city for three years during the siege, crying "Woe, woe to Jerusalem!" (cf. Jer 7:34). Though whipped repeatedly by the authorities, he continued his tirade until he was killed by a stone from a Roman catapult (*J. W.* 6.5.3 §§300 – 309).[22]

Josephus himself viewed the temple's destruction as a fulfillment of the OT prophets (*J. W.* 6.2.1 §109; 6.5.4 §311) and claimed that he had dreams foreseeing "the future calamities of the Jews" (*J. W.* 3.8.3 §§351 – 352). So too the famous rabbi Yohanan ben Zakkai (c. AD 30 – 90) is said to have responded to the mysterious event of the temple gates opening at night by saying, "O Temple, why do you frighten us? We know that you will end up destroyed. For it has been said, 'Open your doors, O Lebanon, that the fire may devour your cedars' [Zech 11:1]" (*y. Soṭah* 6.3).[23]

The double negation (οὐ μή) with both verbs "be left" (ἀφεθῇ) and "be demolished" (καταλυθῇ) has the sense of "certainly not!" The idiom "stone upon stone" (λίθος ἐπὶ λίθον) recalls Hag 2:15 LXX, a passage referring to the original construction of the Second Temple. The stone reference would also recall for Mark's readers the stone prophecy of Ps 118:22 – 23, which Jesus quoted at the end of the parable of the tenants (12:10 – 11). Jesus himself will become the foundation stone of a new temple, not made with human hands (14:58; cf. John 2:19).

Some see Jesus' claim that "not even one stone will be left here on another" as problematic, since some of the massive stones supporting the temple platform were not torn down by Titus's troops. The so-called "Wailing Wall" that still stands today was part of the western retaining wall of the temple complex. One possible response is that Jesus is referring to the temple proper, not to the entire complex or its foundations. This is possible, but the

---

21. Evans, *Mark 8:27 – 16:20*, 295, points to the lack of detail and precise correspondence as key evidence that the prophecy in 13:2 was not created after the fact (*ex eventu*). First, there is no mention of the great fire that engulfed the temple, which Josephus treats as the most memorable feature of the destruction. Second, Jesus' call to pray that your flight does not occur in winter (13:18) would make no sense after the fact, since the destruction happened in August and September.

22. Josephus describes in dramatic detail the man's fate. As

he went about the city one last time, he cried, "Woe, woe, to the city again, and to the people, and to the holy house!" Just as he added at the last — "Woe, woe, to myself also!" a stone from one of the catapults struck him, killing him instantly (*J. W.* 6.5.3 §309).

23. Lebanon is sometimes metaphorically connected to the temple, probably because its cedars were used in the building of the temple. For other predictions in Second Temple literature and rabbinic sources, see Evans, *Mark 8:27 – 16:20*, 296 – 97.

word for "temple" (ἱερόν) used in 13:1, 3 normally designates the whole complex, not the sanctuary (ναός).

A better answer is that the phrase is a hyperbolic idiom meaning total destruction and should not be read in a wooden, literal manner. The same phrase, "not … one stone on another," is used in Luke 19:44 of the whole city, where it surely means "total destruction." Historically, the temple was certainly demolished and "leveled to the ground." Josephus illustrates this when he says that after the city's fall, Caesar ordered "the entire city and temple to be destroyed" (τήν τε πόλιν ἅπασαν καὶ τὸν νεὼν κατασκάπτειν) so that "there was left nothing to make those that came thither believe it had ever been inhabited" (*J.W.* 7.1.1. §§1 – 3; cf. 6.9.1 §413; 6.9.4 §434; 7.8.7 §§375 – 377). Yet he still describes several towers and walls left intact in order to garrison Roman troops (*J.W.* 7.1.1 §1).

13:3 – 4 While he was sitting on the Mount of Olives opposite the temple complex, Peter, James, John, and Andrew asked him privately, "Tell us, when will these things happen, and what will be the sign that all these things are about to be accomplished?" (Καὶ καθημένου αὐτοῦ εἰς τὸ ὄρος τῶν ἐλαιῶν κατέναντι τοῦ ἱεροῦ ἐπηρώτα αὐτὸν κατ' ἰδίαν Πέτρος καὶ Ἰάκωβος καὶ Ἰωάννης καὶ Ἀνδρέας· εἰπὸν ἡμῖν, πότε ταῦτα ἔσται καὶ τί τὸ σημεῖον ὅταν μέλλῃ ταῦτα συντελεῖσθαι πάντα;). The scene now changes as Jesus crosses to the east and sits down opposite the temple on the Mount of Olives, a position with a commanding view of the temple complex. Sitting is a common position for teaching (4:1; cf. Matt 5:1), though here it might be better seen as the posture of a king or judge — the

Son of Man — pronouncing judgment over the city (cf. 14:62).

The Mount of Olives is an appropriate setting, since the hill plays a prominent role in eschatological expectations in Judaism (cf. 11:1). Zechariah describes the final eschatological battle when the Lord will go out to fight against the nations, his feet touching down on the Mount of Olives, splitting it in two from east to west (Zech 1:1 – 9; cf. Ezek 11:22 – 23; 43:1 – 4; *T. Naph.* 5:1; cf. vv. 5 – 6, below, for the Egyptian insurrectionist who led his followers to the Mount of Olives).

Private instruction for the disciples is common in Mark, particularly after enigmatic statements by Jesus.[24] The presence of Andrew may seem surprising since he is not one of the "inner circle" of disciples: Peter, James, and John (5:37; 9:2; 14:33). Yet here the two sets of brothers apparently approach Jesus on their own initiative, whereas elsewhere Jesus chose the three to accompany him. Andrew's inclusion here is likely the result of historical recollection (Peter's?). For Mark's readers it would recall the original call of the four fishermen brothers (1:16 – 20) and the appointment of the Twelve (3:16 – 19).

The disciples ask two questions, the first concerning the timing of these events, the second about "the sign" that will accompany them. Some commentators understand these two questions to refer to separate events, the destruction of Jerusalem and the end of the age.[25] This is apparently how Matthew took them, since his second question concerns "the sign of your coming and of the end of the age" (Matt 24:3). In Mark, however (as in Luke 21:7), the two seem to focus on two aspects of the same event, the timing and signs associated

---

24. See 4:10, 34; 7:17 – 23; 9:28 – 29, 30, 35; 10:10 – 12, 32 – 34, 42; 12:43 – 44.

25. So Pesch, *Markusevangelium*, 2:275; Beasley-Murray, *Jesus and the Last Days*, 387; A. Y. Collins, "The Apocalyptic Rhetoric of Mark 13 in Historical Context," *BR* 41 (1996):

5 – 36, 13. Boring, *Mark*, 355, claims this is indicated by the change in verb in the second question (from εἰμί ["happen"] to συντελέω ["come to an end; be accomplished"]) and the change from "these things" (ταῦτα) to "all these things" (ταῦτα πάντα). These small changes, however, are more likely stylistic.

with the destruction of Jerusalem.[26] The plural "these things" refers to the whole series of events leading up to the temple's destruction.

13:5 – 6 Jesus began to say to them, "Watch out that no one deceives you. Many will come in my name, saying, 'I am the one!' and they will deceive many." (ὁ δὲ Ἰησοῦς ἤρξατο λέγειν αὐτοῖς· βλέπετε μή τις ὑμᾶς πλανήσῃ· πολλοὶ ἐλεύσονται ἐπὶ τῷ ὀνόματί μου λέγοντες ὅτι ἐγώ εἰμι, καὶ πολλοὺς πλανήσουσιν). Jesus begins with the imperative "watch out" (βλέπετε), repeated three times (vv. 9, 23, 33); it is the main theme of the discourse (see Structure, above). Compare the repeated injunctions to "listen" in the parables chapter (4:3, 9, 12, 23, 24, 33), the only other lengthy discourse in Mark's gospel.[27]

Jesus describes various kinds of events that will characterize the present age but should not be mistaken for harbingers of the destruction of Jerusalem or the end of the ages. These include the appearance of false messiahs (v. 6), catastrophic events (vv. 7 – 8), and severe persecution (vv. 9 – 13). The only real sign of the coming destruction of Jerusalem will be the "abomination of desolation," which will be the indicator to flee Jerusalem (vv. 14 – 18).

This is the first of two warnings to watch out for messianic pretenders, which form an inclusio around the first half of the discourse (vv. 5, 21 – 23). This implies that the greatest danger to the disciples will *not* be persecution, though it will be severe (vv. 9 – 13), but deceivers and false teachers. The later NT letters witness an increase in false teachers in the latter part of the first century.[28] "I am" (ἐγώ εἰμι) is a normal Greek idiom for "I am he" or "I am the one" and is unlikely to allude to God's self-identification as the "I AM" in the OT (Exod 3:14; Isa 41:4; 43:10, 13) or to Jesus' use of this divine title in John's gospel (John 8:58; cf. 8:24, 28). These are messianic pretenders, not people claiming to be God. Matthew understands the statement this way, with Jesus explicitly saying, "I am the Messiah" (ἐγώ εἰμι ὁ χριστός; Matt 24:5).

That this is Mark's intention is clear from v. 22, which refers to "false prophets" and "false messiahs" who seek to deceive. To come "in my name" (ἐπὶ τῷ ὀνόματί μου) could mean (1) claiming to be Jesus himself, (2) claiming the authority of Jesus, or (3) claiming to be a/the messiah. The first is unlikely, since there is no evidence for such imposters in the first century. The second is a common use of the phrase in Acts (Acts 3:6; 9:27; 16:18; 19:13, etc.), but doesn't do justice to the parallel, "I am the one." The third is the most likely, since it fits both the present context (cf. vv. 21 – 23) and the first-century historical context.[29]

A number of messianic figures appeared in the first century, gathering followers and making various messianic claims. In Acts 5, the Pharisee Gamaliel describes a man named Theudas, who "claimed to be somebody" and rallied four hundred men around him who were eventually dispersed and killed.[30] He also speaks of Judas the Galilean, who led a tax revolt against the Romans in AD 6. Judas too was killed and his followers dispersed (Acts 5:36 – 37). In 21:38, Paul is mistaken for an Egyptian who led four thousand Jews into the wilderness in a messianic action of some sort. Josephus refers to this same Egyptian, claiming he had thirty thousand followers. He led them to the Mount of Olives, boasting that the walls would fall down at his command. The governor Felix sent

---

26. So Lane, *Mark*, 455; France, *Mark*, 506 – 7; Donahue and Harrington, *Mark*, 368; Stein, *Mark*, 590.

27. Hooker, *Mark*, 306.

28. Cf. 2 Tim 4:3 – 4; 2 Pet 2; Jude; 1 John 2.

29. Taylor, *Mark*, 504; Hooker, *Mark*, 306 – 7; France,

Mark, 510 – 11; Collins, *Mark*, 604.

30. Josephus also refers to an insurrectionist named Theudas, but the revolt he led was in AD 44 – 46 (*Ant.* 20.5.1 §§97 – 99), too late for Gamaliel's remark. Either Luke is mistaken or this is a different Theudas.

troops from the Jerusalem garrison, who routed the insurrectionists, though the Egyptian himself escaped.[31]

Josephus also refers to Judas the Galilean, who became the inspiration for the later Zealot movement,[32] and a variety of other messianic figures.[33] In one account he relates how a group of "wicked men" deceived the people by claiming divine inspiration and led them into the wilderness to await a sign of God's deliverance. Felix responded by sending troops to kill and disperse them (*J.W.* 2.13.4 – 6 §§258 – 265; cf. *J.W.* 6.5.4 §§312 – 313). Finally, the second Jewish revolt was led by Simon bar-Kosiba in AD 132 – 135. Rabbi Akiba is said to have hailed bar-Kosiba as "king messiah" and applied the "star" prophecy of Num 24:17 to him — hence the nickname, Bar-Kokhba, "son of the star."[34]

13:7 – 8 When you hear about wars and rumors of wars, do not be alarmed. These things must happen, but the end is not yet. Nation will rise against nation and kingdom against kingdom. There will be earthquakes in various places; there will be famines. These are the beginning of birth pains (ὅταν δὲ ἀκούσητε πολέμους καὶ ἀκοὰς πολέμων, μὴ θροεῖσθε· δεῖ γενέσθαι, ἀλλ᾽ οὔπω τὸ τέλος. ἐγερθήσεται γὰρ ἔθνος ἐπ᾽ ἔθνος καὶ βασιλεία ἐπὶ βασιλείαν, ἔσονται σεισμοὶ κατὰ τόπους, ἔσονται λιμοί· ἀρχὴ ὠδίνων ταῦτα). Jesus continues with more general signs of the present age that do *not* indicate the end. Cataclysmic events that produce devastation for lives and nations are often mistaken for evidence that the end

is near. If *my* world is ending, perhaps the whole world is ending.

Wars, earthquakes, plagues, and famine are often associated with divine judgment in Scripture,[35] and the coming day of the Lord is frequently described with earthquakes and other cosmic disturbances.[36] Such images are common in apocalyptic Judaism as heralds of the coming apocalypse. The third vision of 2 Esdras (= 4 Ezra) reads:

> Measure carefully in your mind, and when you see that some of the predicted signs have occurred, then you will know that it is the very time when the Most High is about to visit the world that he has made. So when there shall appear in the world earthquakes, tumult of peoples, intrigues of nations, wavering of leaders, confusion of princes, then you will know that it was of these that the Most High spoke from the days that were of old, from the beginning. (2 Esd 9:1 – 5 NRSV)[37]

By contrast, Jesus says that when you see such things, "do not be alarmed" (μὴ θροεῖσθε), since "the end is not yet" (οὔπω τὸ τέλος). These events do not herald the end of time, but instead are part of the normal course of human history. That such events "must happen" means that God is in sovereign control and is leading history to its proper end. Jesus says these events are merely the beginning of the "birth pains" (ὠδίνες), imagery indicating intense suffering and anxious longing that will give way to the joy of birth (cf. John 16:20 – 22; Rom 8:21 – 23; 1 Thess 5:3). The OT often uses a woman's travail as a metaphor for the suffering of

---

31. *Ant.* 20.8.6 §§167 – 172; *J.W.* 2.13.5 §§261 – 263; cf. Act 21:38.

32. *Ant.* 17.10.5 §§271 – 272.

33. For example, Simon (*Ant.* 17.10.6 §§273 – 277); Anthronges (*Ant.* 17.10.7 §§278 – 281); a Samaritan (*Ant.* 18.4.1 §§85 – 87).

34. *y. Ta'an.* 4.8; (68d, 48 – 51). Rabbi Johanan ben Torta is said to have answered: "Akiba, grass will grow out of thy jaw-bone, and still the son of David will not come." Cf.

van der Woude, *TDNT*, 9:523.

35. Wars: 2 Chr 15:6; Isa 19:2; Jer 4:16 – 20; Dan 11:44; Joel 3:9 – 14; Zech 14:2; cf. Rev 6:4, 8; 11:13. Earthquakes: 1 Sam 14:15; Ps 18:7 – 8; Isa 5:25; 13:13; 29:6; Jer 4:24; Amos 1:1; Hag 2:6, 21. Plagues and famines: Isa 14:30; Jer 14:12; 21:6 – 7; Ezek 14:21; cf. 2 Bar. 27:6; 2 Esd 13:31.

36. Isa 2:19, 21; 13:13; 24:18; 29:5 – 6; Ezek 38:19; Joel 2:10.

37. Cf. 2 Esd 13:31; *2 Bar.* 27:7; 70:2 – 8; Josephus, *J.W.* 6.5.3 §299; cf. Rev 6:12; 8:5; 11:13, 19; 16:18.

nations,[38] imagery that developed in an eschatological direction in the Second Temple period.[39] In later rabbinic literature, the "messianic woes," or "birth pains of the Messiah," became technical terms for the period of tribulation and distress leading up to the coming of the Messiah and the messianic age.[40]

13:9 As for you, watch out for yourselves. They will hand you over to councils and flog you in the synagogues. You will stand before governors and kings for my sake, as a witness to them (Βλέπετε δὲ ὑμεῖς ἑαυτούς· παραδώσουσιν ὑμᾶς εἰς συνέδρια καὶ εἰς συναγωγὰς δαρήσεσθε καὶ ἐπὶ ἡγεμόνων καὶ βασιλέων σταθήσεσθε ἕνεκεν ἐμοῦ εἰς μαρτύριον αὐτοῖς). Jesus has warned of false messiahs (vv. 5 – 6) and cataclysmic events (vv. 7 – 8). This third warning is of coming persecution (vv. 9 – 13). Jesus again calls for watchfulness (βλέπετε; vv. 5, 23, 33), this time emphasizing ("as for you"; ὑμεῖς) and personalizing it for the disciples ("for yourselves"; ἑαυτούς). This is because of the turn from general signs of societal turmoil (vv. 5 – 8) to specific trials and persecution that Jesus' followers will face (vv. 9 – 13).

This section is punctuated by three references to being "handed over" (παραδίδωμι; vv. 9, 11, 12), with the various nuances of arrest, trial, or betrayal.[41] The first refers to being handed over to religious and civil courts (v. 9); the second promises the Holy Spirit's presence when Jesus' followers are delivered up for trial (v. 11); and the third refers to family division, as brother betrays brother to persecution and even death (vv. 12 – 13). Luke includes these sayings in his parallel account (21:12 – 17), with the exception of v. 10, while Matthew introduces them instead in Jesus' earlier mission charge to the Twelve (10:17 – 22).

The plural "councils" (συνέδρια) refers not to the Sanhedrin, the Jewish high court in Jerusalem (συνέδριον; 14:55; 15:1; cf. Acts 4:15; 5:21), but to local Jewish councils in towns and villages that generally met in synagogues. Josephus says that each city had a council of seven elders, a mandate he claims was handed down by Moses.[42] The Mishnah and later rabbinic traditions refer to twenty-three elders per city (*m. Sanh.* 1:6). The latter may be later tradition or could refer to larger cities.

Floggings are first mentioned in Acts 5:40, where the apostles are ordered to be beaten by the Jerusalem Sanhedrin for preaching in Jesus' name. Paul repeatedly felt the wrath of local Jewish councils, and by the time he wrote 2 Corinthians (c. AD 55 – 56) he had five times "received from the Jews the forty lashes minus one" (2 Cor 11:24).[43] In Acts, Paul claims to have been the agent administering such floggings prior to his conversion (Acts 22:19).

In addition to Jewish religious councils, the disciples will appear before secular rulers — governors and kings. "Governor" (ἡγεμών) is a general term for Roman prefects and procurators. Jesus himself will appear before the prefect Pontius Pilate (15:1 – 15), and Paul will later stand before the procurators Felix (Acts 23:24 – 27:27) and Festus (25:1 – 26:32). In Luke 23:7 – 12, Jesus appears

---

38. Isa 13:8; 66:7 – 9; Jer 22:23; Hos 13:13; Mic 4:9 – 10.

39. See 2 Esd 4:40 – 43; 6:24; 9:1 – 12; 13:29 – 31; *1 En.* 90 – 100; *2 Bar.* 27:1 – 15; 48:31 – 41; 70:2 – 8; 1QM; *m. Soṭah* 9:15 ("the footprints of the Messiah"); cf. 1 Cor 7:26.

40. *b. Sanh.* 97a, 98ab; *b. Šabb.* 118a; *b. Ketub.* 111a; *Gen. Rab.* 42:4; G. Bertram, *TDNT*, 9:670ff.; Str-B 1:950; Boring, *Mark*, 363 n. 54; Dale C. Allison Jr., *The End of the Ages Has Come: An Early Interpretation of the Passion and Resurrection of Jesus* (Philadelphia: Fortress, 1985), 8 – 10.

41. This same term was used by Jesus in the passion predictions (9:31; 10:33) and will be repeatedly used for his being "handed over" to betrayal, arrest, trial, and crucifixion (14:10, 11, 18, 21, 41, 42, 44; 15:1, 10, 15).

42. *Ant.* 4.8.14 §214; cf. *J.W.* 2.20.5. §571.

43. The number forty comes from Deut 25:1 – 3 and the "minus one" (*m. Mak.* 3:10 – 12) was perhaps to avoid an accidental violation of the law.

at his trial before the Jewish tetrarch (a title for a minor king), Herod Antipas.

In Acts, Paul too appears before a Jewish king in his hearing before Herod Agrippa I, arranged by Festus (Acts 25:13 – 26:32), and then heads to Rome to appear before Rome's ultimate king, Caesar himself (25:11 – 12; 27:24). Jesus' statement that the disciples will be a "witness to them" (εἰς μαρτύριον αὐτοῖς) could carry a negative sense, meaning "as evidence against them" (see comments on 1:43 – 44; 6:11; cf. Luke 10:12), but more likely is positive, "bearing witness to the gospel" (see 1:44), since the next sentence speaks of the worldwide proclamation of the good news (13:10).

13:10 And the gospel must first be preached to all nations (καὶ εἰς πάντα τὰ ἔθνη πρῶτον δεῖ κηρυχθῆναι τὸ εὐαγγέλιον). This statement interrupts the flow of Jesus' discourse, which otherwise could move smoothly from v. 9 to v. 11. Many commentators consider it to be a Markan insertion (from a redaction-critical perspective) or a narrative aside (from a narrative-critical perspective).[44] If the former, it could be Mark's own interpretation or an independent saying of Jesus inserted at this point (Jesus will say something similar in 14:9).

In either case, it is important for Mark's purpose. As in v. 7, "must" (δεῖ) indicates God's sovereign purpose and plan for human history. In common with Luke's central theme of the book of Acts (Acts 1:8; 5:39; 28:31), for Mark the progress of the gospel is unstoppable because it is the sovereign work

of God. The point is that the persecution described here (vv. 9, 11 – 13) will not stop the worldwide dissemination of the gospel; in fact, it will even promote it (v. 9: "as a witness"; cf. Acts 8:1 – 4; 28:31).

A major question concerns whether "first" (πρῶτον) means that the worldwide proclamation of the gospel will occur before the destruction of Jerusalem or before the eschaton.[45] If the structure we have proposed for the discourse as a whole is correct, it likely means the former. While it is true that the gospel had not yet been proclaimed to every person in the world by AD 70, it had reached the limits of the Roman empire, the "civilized world" (cf. Luke 2:1, πᾶσαν τὴν οἰκουμένην, "the entire Roman world"). Paul, writing in the AD 50s and early 60s, seems to take this perspective, speaking of the gospel's proclamation "throughout the whole world" (Col 1:6), to "every creature under heaven" (Col 1:23), and "all the Gentiles" (Rom 16:26; cf. 1:5; 10:18; 15:19).[46]

Mark's statement thus parallels Luke's narrative purpose in Acts, where Paul's arrival in Rome (28:31; c. AD 60) marks the symbolic fulfillment of the commission to take the gospel from "Jerusalem … to the ends of the earth" (Acts 1:8) — though it is only the beginning of the worldwide dissemination of the gospel. This conclusion also argues against the missiological claim by some that Mark 13:10 places a specific condition on the time of Christ's return, namely, the evangelization of every people group around the globe. While we would strongly affirm the need to "finish the task" of worldwide

---

44. Another possibility, proposed by G. D. Kilpatrick ("The Gentile Mission in Mark and Mark xiii.9 – 11," in *Studies in the Gospels* [ed. Nineham], 145 – 58), is to change the punctuation, taking "and to all nations" (καὶ εἰς πάντα τὰ ἔθνη) with the previous clause, so that it reads, "to bear witness to them and to all nations" (as in some Latin and Syriac mss). This, it is argued, is more in line with the historical Jesus, who would not so clearly have announced the Gentile mission at this point. The next phrase would read simply, "The gospel must first be preached," a reminder to the disciples of their primary task. But see comments on 14:9.

45. Matthew may understand it as the latter, since he ends with, "then the end will come" (Matt 24:14). Yet this could still be the end of Jerusalem rather than the end of history.

46. France, *Mark*, 516 – 17; Stein, *Mark*, 600. Cf. Rainer Reisner, *Paul's Early Period: Chronology, Mission Strategy, Theology* (Grand Rapids: Eerdmans, 1998), 245 – 56, who takes Rom 15:19 to mean that Paul has fulfilled the mission to the Gentile nations as predicted in Isa 66:18 – 21.

evangelism and to obey Christ's commission to take the gospel to every remote nation, tribe, and person (Matt 28:18–20; Acts 1:8), it is unlikely that the present passage sets this specific qualification. Believers are commanded to proclaim the gospel to all people everywhere, yet to live a life of constant readiness for Christ's return.

13:11 When, after handing you over, they bring you to trial, don't worry beforehand what you will say. But say whatever is given to you in that hour, because it is not you speaking, but the Holy Spirit (καὶ ὅταν ἄγωσιν ὑμᾶς παραδιδόντες, μὴ προμεριμνᾶτε τί λαλήσητε, ἀλλ᾽ ὃ ἐὰν δοθῇ ὑμῖν ἐν ἐκείνῃ τῇ ὥρᾳ τοῦτο λαλεῖτε· οὐ γάρ ἐστε ὑμεῖς οἱ λαλοῦντες ἀλλὰ τὸ πνεῦμα τὸ ἅγιον). After the parenthetic remark of v. 10, Jesus resumes his discussion of persecution. When the disciples are "arrested" (or "handed over"; παραδίδωμι; vv. 9, 11, 13) and brought to trial for their faith, they need not be anxious, since the Holy Spirit will give them words to speak.

The OT background for this may be found in the reluctance of Moses and Jeremiah to be God's spokespeople (Exod 4:10–17; Jer 1:6–9) and God's promise to "teach you what to say" (Exod 4:12) and to "put my words in your mouth" (Jer 1:9). The fulfillment of this promise is seen in the early chapters Acts, where the apostles, though "unschooled, ordinary men" (Acts 4:13; cf. 1 Cor 1:26), proclaim the gospel with boldness and eloquence by the Spirit's power (Acts 2:4; 4:8, 31; 6:10). Significantly, the promise here is for the right words to speak, not for physical protection or escape. The apostles are to follow the lead of Jesus, proclaiming the gospel boldly whatever the cost. It is, of course, a misuse of this passage to justify a lack of study in preparation for teaching and preaching. The passage concerns those whose sudden arrest makes formal preparation for their own defense impossible. They are to trust the Holy Spirit for divine guidance.

13:12 Brother will hand over brother to death and a father his child. Children will rise up against their parents and have them put to death (καὶ παραδώσει ἀδελφὸς ἀδελφὸν εἰς θάνατον καὶ πατὴρ τέκνον, καὶ ἐπαναστήσονται τέκνα ἐπὶ γονεῖς καὶ θανατώσουσιν αὐτούς). These severe trials and persecution will even divide families. The verb "hand over" (παραδίδωμι), used now for a third time (cf. vv. 9, 11), here means "betray." The language of familial discord recalls Micah's description of the collapse of societal values: "For a son dishonors his father, a daughter rises up against her mother, a daughter-in-law against her mother-in-law — a man's enemies are the members of his own household" (Mic 7:6; cf. Isa 19:2).

Such strife became a common image in the eschatological expectations of Second Temple Judaism (2 Esd 6:24; *1 En.* 100:1–2; *Jub.* 23:19). Matthew introduces the present saying into his charge to the Twelve (Matt 10:21), where Jesus also alludes to Micah's words to describe the division of households that allegiance to him will produce (Matt 10:34–36; cf. Luke 12:49–53). Betrayal is even worse than division and conflict, and Jesus says it will lead even to execution.

Though such betrayals are not mentioned in the NT, the Roman historian Tacitus (*Ann.* 15.44.4) describes how in the early 60s during the Neronian persecution of Roman Christians, many were convicted and executed on the testimony of others. Somewhat later, in a letter written around AD 112 by Pliny the Younger, governor of Bithynia in Asia Minor, the governor asks Emperor Trajan for advice on how to handle Christians who refused to worship the image of Caesar. He speaks of informers turning in the names of Christians, who were then arrested, questioned, and executed (*Ep.* 10.96.5–6).

13:13 You will be hated by all because of my name. But the one who endures to the end —

this one will be saved (καὶ ἔσεσθε μισούμενοι ὑπὸ πάντων διὰ τὸ ὄνομά μου. ὁ δὲ ὑπομείνας εἰς τέλος οὗτος σωθήσεται). Beyond family conflicts, Jesus' followers "will be hated by all," that is, by society as a whole. This hatred is "because of my name" (διὰ τὸ ὄνομά μου), where "the name" represents the person ("me") and "because of" is shorthand for "because of your allegiance to" (cf. Matt 10:22; John 15:21; 1 Cor 1:10; 1 John 2:12; Rev 2:3). Total allegiance to Jesus as Lord and a corresponding unwillingness to worship the emperor or the gods of Rome will result in hatred from the general population. Various Roman historians and satirists speak of the public's disdain for Christians in the early years of the church. Suetonius refers to Christians as "a race of human beings given to a new and wicked superstition" (*Nero* 16.2), and Tacitus refers to them as a class "hated for their shameful deeds" and followers of a "destructive superstition" (*Ann.* 15.44).

Yet in the midst of this persecution and hatred is the promise of salvation for endurance. Two questions arise here. What is the "end" (τέλος), and is being "saved" spiritual or physical? The "end" could be (1) the destruction of Jerusalem, (2) the end of the age, when the Son of Man will return, or (3) the end of life, having stayed faithful through many trials. The first two would indicate physical deliverance, either escape from the destruction of Jerusalem (see vv. 14 – 19) or preservation till the coming of the Son of Man (13:26 – 27). The third would be spiritual, inheriting eternal life by remaining faithful to the end. This third option seems the most likely, especially since death is mentioned in the immediate context (v. 12; cf. Matt 10:21 – 22).[47] Those who are martyred will be (spiritually) saved.

This also fits best Jesus' teaching in 8:35 that those who lose their lives will gain true life. Promises of salvation for those who endure are common in Scripture. Second Timothy 2:12 says, "If we endure, we will also reign with him" (cf. Rom 8:17; 1 Cor 9:25; 2 Tim 4:8; Heb 10:36; Jas 1:12; 1 Pet 5:4; Rev 2:7, 10, 17, 26 – 28; 3:5, 12, 21; 20:4).

13:14a-b But when you see the "abomination that causes desolation" standing where it should not be (let the readers understand) (Ὅταν δὲ ἴδητε τὸ βδέλυγμα τῆς ἐρημώσεως ἑστηκότα ὅπου οὐ δεῖ, ὁ ἀναγινώσκων νοείτω). General signs that are characteristic of the present age now give way to the one obvious sign that will take place before the destruction of Jerusalem — "the abomination that causes desolation" (τὸ βδέλυγμα τῆς ἐρημώσεως). This represents the answer to the disciples' question in v. 4, "What will be the sign that all these things are about to be accomplished?" The injunctions throughout vv. 5 – 13 are for patient endurance and not to worry or fear. But now the command will be to flee Jerusalem, for her destruction is about to take place (v. 14c).

The mysterious "abomination that causes desolation" has been the subject of endless debate. The phrase comes from the book of Daniel (Dan 9:27; 11:31; 12:11; Heb.: *šiqqûṣ šōmēm*), where it predicts the desecration of the temple by the Seleucid ruler, Antiochus IV Epiphanes, in 167 BC. First Maccabees describes how Anitiochus decreed that the Jews must give up their customs, forbidding burnt offerings and outlawing circumcision, and that "whoever does not obey the command of the king shall die" (1 Macc 1:50).

Now on the fifteenth day of Chislev, in the one hundred forty-fifth year [= 167 BC], they erected

---

47. Oddly, the parallel in Luke speaks of some losing their lives (Luke 21:16) and promises that they will "win life" (21:19), but then makes the apparently physical promise that "not a hair of your head will perish" (21:18). This latter is most likely a proverbial expression referring here to spiritual safety (so I. H. Marshall, *Gospel of Luke* ([NIGTC; Grand Rapids: Eerdmans, 1978]), 769 – 70).

a desolating sacrilege [βδέλυγμα ἐρημώσεως] on the altar of burnt-offering. They also built altars in the surrounding towns of Judah, and offered incense at the doors of the houses and in the streets. The books of the law that they found they tore to pieces and burned with fire. Anyone found possessing the book of the covenant, or anyone who adhered to the law, was condemned to death by decree of the king. They kept using violence against Israel, against those who were found month after month in the towns. On the twenty-fifth day of the month they offered sacrifice on the altar that was on top of the altar of burnt-offering. (1 Macc 1:54 – 59 NRSV)

Josephus similarly says that Antiochus built a pagan altar on God's altar and sacrificed swine on it (*Ant.* 12.5.4 §253).

The term "abomination" (Heb: *šiqqûṣ*; Gk: βδέλυγμα) used in Daniel means something loathsome, detestable, or repugnant to God, and is often used in the context of pagan worship.[48] The Hebrew phrase as a whole means the abomination "that makes desolate" or "makes appalled."[49] The former is the meaning of the LXX translation, since "desolation" (ἐρήμωσις) means something devastated or rendered uninhabitable.[50] The Greek genitive (ἐρημώσεως) is likely a genitive of product,[51] where the sacrilege produces or results in the desolation of the Holy Place.

While the meaning in Daniel and 1 Maccabees is clear enough, Jesus' application of the phrase is much more difficult. Three main possibilities have been proposed.

(1) It relates to some event early in the first century, such as (a) Pontius Pilate's order for his soldiers to enter Jerusalem with Roman standards bearing idolatrous images (c. AD 26; Josephus, *J. W.* 2.9.2 – 3 §§169 – 174; *Ant.* 18.3.1 §§55 – 59), or (b) Caligula's order to erect a statue of himself in the temple (c. AD 39 – 40; Josephus, *Ant.* 18.8.2 – 3 §§261 – 272; Philo, *Legat.*; Tacitus, *Hist.* 5.9). Though these events caused disturbances among the Jews, neither is plausible here. The first occurred before Jesus spoke these words and was resolved without violence.[52] The second was never carried out, since the order was first delayed by the Syrian legate Petronius and then cancelled when Caligula was assassinated.[53] They were both certainly too early for Mark's readers to view as an impending crisis.

(2) The phrase relates in some way to the destruction of Jerusalem in AD 70. There are various possibilities: (a) a general reference to events leading up to and including the destruction of Jerusalem and the temple (cf. Luke 21:20);[54] (b) the entrance of the Roman general Titus into the temple sanctuary at the climax of the destruction (Josephus, *J. W.* 6.4.7 §260); (c) the actions of Roman soldiers, who set their standards up in the temple and offered sacrifices, proclaiming Titus to be emperor (Josephus, *J. W.* 6.6.1 §316);[55] (d) some earlier desecration of the temple by the Zealot de-

---

48. *HALOT*, 1640 (28 times in the Hebrew Bible).

49. J. J. Collins, *Daniel* (Hermeneia; Minneapolis: Fortress, 1993), 357, suggests that the Hebrew in Daniel is a derogatory pun on *ba'al šāmayim*, the Syrian counterpart of Zeus Olympius, mocking Antiochus's renaming of the Jerusalem temple in honor of Olympian Zeus (2 Macc 6:2).

50. BDAG, 392.

51. For this category, see Wallace, *Greek Grammar*, 106, though he does not cite this passage.

52. When Pilate sent troops to surround and kill the Jewish protestors, they fell to the ground and bared their necks, ready to die for their beliefs. Pilate, impressed by this level of commitment, backed down and withdrew the standards.

53. Evans, *Mark 8:27 – 16:20*, 318 – 19. A number of commentators think the Caligula event lay behind the source that Mark used for the discourse. So Ernst, *Markus*, 380; Grundmann, *Markus*, 358; Gnilka, *Markus*, 2:194; N. H. Taylor, "Palestinian Christianity and the Caligula Crisis: Part II: The Markan Eschatological Discourse," *JSNT* 18 (1996): 13 – 41, esp. 20 – 21.

54. Cf. Beasley-Murray, *Jesus and the Last Days*, 411; D. Ford, *The Abomination of Desolation in Biblical Eschatology* (Washington, DC: University Press of America, 1979), 166 – 69; Boring, *Mark*, 367.

55. Pesch, *Markusevangelium*, 2:291; Hooker, *Mark*, 314; Moloney, *Mark*, 259.

fenders themselves (c. AD 67–68; *J.W.* 4.3.6–8 §§147–157; 4.3.9 §160).[56]

(3) The third view is that the phrase relates to the eschatological future, beyond the events of the first century.[57] In this case it would concern a still-future antichrist, likely the same as Paul's "man of lawlessness," who is associated with the coming day of the Lord (2 Thess 2:1–10; cf. the "antichrist" of 1 John 2:18 and the "beast" of Rev 11:7; 13:1–18). Paul's description of this man of lawlessness who "will exalt himself over everything that is called God" and will set "himself up in God's temple, proclaiming himself to be God" (2 Thess 2:4), is conceptually similar to the abomination of desolation, "standing where it should not be" (Mark 13:14). Also significant is the masculine participle "standing" (στηκότα) used in Mark, since one would expect a neuter participle in agreement with the neuter "abomination" (βδέλυγμα). This suggests that Mark envisions a person rather than a thing.[58] Of course, the main evidence for this view is the close connection made throughout the discourse between these events and the return of the Son of Man (vv. 24, 26, 29–30).

The problem with this third view, as we have noted earlier (see Structure, above), is that the following verses about fleeing Jerusalem seem to represent Jesus' answer to the disciples' question about the coming destruction of Jerusalem. Furthermore, Mark's narrative aside ("let the readers understand") suggests the immediate relevance of this event for his readers (see discussion below). The masculine participle "standing" in v. 14 is not decisive for an eschatological interpretation, since this could also refer to one of the persons involved

in the destruction of Jerusalem, such as the Roman general Titus or one of the Zealot leaders, or could even signify an idolatrous image set up in the temple.

The primary reference, then, seems to be to the destruction of Jerusalem. Yet which specific event? The problem with both (2b) and (2c) is that they occurred at the end of the destruction, too late to encourage believers to flee Jerusalem (13:14–19). The time to flee would be at the beginning of the siege, not the end. View (2a) is possible, but seems too general, since the description of the abomination "standing where it should not be" seems to refer to a specific event. This leaves (2d) — some atrocity committed by the Zealots themselves — as the most likely.

Though it is impossible to be specific, Josephus refers to various events that could be viewed as abominations that defiled the temple. In the winter of AD 67/68 the Zealots under John of Gischala took over the temple and made it their headquarters, "entering the Holy Place with defiled feet" (*J.W.* 4.3.6. §150) and appointing their own high priest (*J.W.* 4.3.7–8. §§153–157). The legitimate high priest Ananus said, "Certainly, it had been good for me to die before I had seen the house of God full of so many abominations, or these sacred places that ought not to be trodden upon at random, filled with the feet of these blood-shedding villains" (*J.W.* 4.3.10 §163).[59] Though we must filter these statements through the lens of Josephus's anti-Zealot views, the events noted could certainly qualify as an "abomination" that results in desolation.

Because of the many uncertainties, we cautiously conclude that Jesus' primary reference is to

56. Lane, *Mark*, 469; Marcus, *Mark 1–8*, 454–56; idem, "The Jewish War and the *Sitz im Leben* of Mark," *JBL* 111 (1992): 441–62; esp. 454–55; Witherington, *Mark*, 345–46; France, *Mark*, 525.

57. Taylor, *Mark*, 511; Evans, *Mark 8:27–16:20*, 317, 319–20; Edwards, *Mark*, 398–99.

58. Cf. NIV text note: "Or *he*"; NLT: "… standing where he should not be" (cf. ESV).

59. For further references to the temple's "defilement" by the Zealots, see Josephus, *J.W.* 4.3.10 §§182–183; 4.3.12 §201; 4.6.3 §388; 6.2.1 §95; Lane, *Mark*, 469; Marcus, *Mark 9–16*, 891; France, *Mark*, 525.

some event related to the destruction of Jerusalem, which itself is viewed by Mark as a preview or foreshadowing of the return of the Son of Man and the end of the age. As throughout the discourse, the destruction of Jerusalem and the end of the age are closely linked, with the former foreshadowing and pointing forward to the latter.

What is the significance of the phrase "let the readers understand" (ὁ ἀναγινώσκων νοείτω)? There are three main views. (1) The most widely held is that this is Mark's narrative aside and is intended to alert his readers that this event — the abomination of desolation — is about to take place.[60] If so, it would date Mark's gospel to the late 60s of the first century, just before or after the outbreak of the Jewish war (see Introduction to Mark: Date).

(2) Another view is that the phrase is not a narrative aside but is part of Jesus' discourse. The reader in this case would be the reader of the book of Daniel, and the exhortation is to examine the prophecy in Daniel to discern the significance of the abomination that causes desolation.[61] This view is possible for Matthew, since he identifies the reference as coming from Daniel (Matt 24:15); it is less likely for Mark, who does not identify the reference.

(3) A third possibility is proposed by Ernst Best, who claims that the phrase is an editorial note to the public reader of Mark's gospel, telling that person not to correct the grammatical irregularity noted above — the neuter word "abomination" (βδέλυγμα) followed by a masculine participle "standing" (στηκότα). Best compares the note to the contemporary use of "*sic*," which alerts the reader that what looks like an error is in fact how the text should be read. Mark is saying, "But when you see that thing, the abomination of desolation, standing where he [*sic*] should not be...."[62]

The first view remains the most likely. Mark cryptically tells his readers to keep their eyes on Jerusalem and the events that will take place there. While this may indicate the imminence of the Jewish war, this is not certain. It may simply be Mark's cue to his readers to keep their eyes on Jerusalem, where the eschatological climax will eventually play out. Mark knows that Jesus predicted the destruction of Jerusalem and likely expects this event to happen in his lifetime. For him and his readers, God's judgment against the temple will be both evidence of Jesus' divine foresight and also confirmation that his death and resurrection signaled the end of the sacrificial system and the establishment of a new people of God.

13:14c – 16 Then let those in Judea flee to the mountains. Let no one on the rooftop come down or go in to take anything out of their house, and the one in the field must not return to get their cloak (τότε οἱ ἐν τῇ Ἰουδαίᾳ φευγέτωσαν εἰς τὰ ὄρη, ὁ δὲ ἐπὶ τοῦ δώματος μὴ καταβάτω μηδὲ εἰσελθάτω ἆραί τι ἐκ τῆς οἰκίας αὐτοῦ, καὶ ὁ εἰς τὸν ἀγρὸν μὴ ἐπιστρεψάτω εἰς τὰ ὀπίσω ἆραι τὸ ἱμάτιον αὐτοῦ). The appearance of the desolating sacrilege is the sign for Jesus' followers to flee to the Judean hills. The advice is surprising since normally in times of war one would flee *into* a walled city for protection (Jer 4:6). Jesus' point is that Jerusalem is doomed and will not offer a safe refuge (cf. similar counsel in Jer 6:1; Rev 18:4).

The third person imperatives that follow point to the extreme urgency of the situation. The first

---

60. Collins, *Mark*, 597 – 98, suggests that since the text would normally be read by a single reader to a gathered (mostly illiterate) audience, the note is primarily intended for this reader, who would have read and studied the text in preparation for this oral presentation.

61. Evans, *Mark 8:27 – 16:20*, 320.

62. Ernst Best, "The Gospel of Mark: Who Is the Reader?" *IBS* 11 (1989): 14 – 32; Garland, *Mark*, 496.

two verbs ("let no one … come down or go in") form a hendiadys, meaning "come down for the purpose of entering" (how could they flee if they didn't go down?). Flat rooftops in Palestine were used as living space and were accessible by an outside ladder or staircase. Jesus says, "Don't go into the house to pack; there is no time!" (cf. NLT). The cloak (ἱμάτιον), left at home when working in the field, was the outer garment worn at night to keep warm and thus essential gear for someone on the move, especially in winter. Jesus uses hyperbole to emphasize urgency: there is no time to return for even the most basic necessities.

The early church historian Eusebius describes an oracle received by the Jerusalem church before the siege, telling them to flee to the city of Pella in Perea, across the Jordan. In this way, the church escaped the calamity (*Hist. eccl.* 3.3.3; cf. Epiphanius, *Pan.* 29.7.7–8; 30.2.7). Some scholars reject Eusebius's report as legendary.[63] Most accept its authenticity but debate whether the oracle refers to Jesus' teaching here[64] or to a separate prophetic message received closer to the event.[65] The latter seems most likely, since Pella is not located in the mountains of Judea, but in the Jordan Valley northeast of Jerusalem (in Decapolis).

13:17–18 But woe to those who are pregnant and who are nursing babies in those days! Pray that it will not happen in winter (οὐαὶ δὲ ταῖς ἐν γαστρὶ ἐχούσαις καὶ ταῖς θηλαζούσαις ἐν ἐκείναις ταῖς ἡμέραις. προσεύχεσθε δὲ ἵνα μὴ γένηται χειμῶνος).

From the urgency of the situation, Jesus turns to its extreme hardship. The context (vv. 15–16, 18) suggests the reference is to those who are fleeing, not to those left in Jerusalem (but see v. 19). Jesus pronounces "woes" (οὐαί; cf. 14:21) on those who will suffer the most during this time.

The biblical "woe" is a prediction of coming disaster or calamity. While it often indicates God's judgment — getting what one deserves (Num 21:29; 1 Sam 4:7; Job 10:15; Isa 3:11; 5:8; Matt 11:21; 23:13–29), here it indicates compassion toward those who suffer because of external circumstances (cf. Prov 23:29; Eccl 4:10). Escape over rough terrain would be particularly difficult for pregnant women and those with small children. To travel in the winter would increase the danger because of the colder weather and the rain-swollen wadis. Although "in those days" is sometimes used in eschatological contexts (Jer 31:29; 33:15–16), it is a common enough idiom and here likely refers to the time of escape from Jerusalem (cf. v. 14).

13:19 For those days will bring tribulation of a kind unlike anything that has happened since the beginning of creation, when God made the world,[66] until now. And it will never happen again (ἔσονται γὰρ αἱ ἡμέραι ἐκεῖναι θλῖψις οἵα οὐ γέγονεν τοιαύτη ἀπ᾽ ἀρχῆς κτίσεως ἣν ἔκτισεν ὁ θεὸς ἕως τοῦ νῦν καὶ οὐ μὴ γένηται). The scene now shifts from those escaping Jerusalem (vv. 14c–18) to the siege itself (v. 14a-b), to the terrors faced by those inside the city. Josephus describes these horrors in

63. See S. G. F. Brandon, *The Fall of Jerusalem and the Christian Church* (London: SPCK, 1957), 168–78; G. Lüdemann, "The Successors of Pre-70 Jerusalem Christianity: A Critical Evaluation of the Pella Tradition," in *Jewish and Christian Self-Definition* (ed. E. P. Sanders; 3 vols.; London: SCM, 1980) 1:161–73.

64. So S. Sowers, "The Circumstances and Recollection of the Pella Flight," *TZ* 26 (1970): 305–20; Lane, *Mark*, 468; Pesch, *Markusevangelium*, 2:292, 295. For a thorough defense of authenticity from this perspective, see Vicky Balabanski,

Eschatology in the Making: Mark, Matthew and the Didache (SNTSMS 97; Cambridge: Cambridge University Press, 1997), 101–34.

65. So Beasley-Murray, *Jesus and the Last Days*, 412–13; France, *Mark*, 526; Evans, *Mark 8:27–16:20*, 320; Stein, *Mark*, 604.

66. The phrase "creation, when God made" (κτίσεως ἣν ἔκτισεν ὁ θεός) is a Semitism and typical Markan redundancy, here emphasizing God's sovereign control over human history. Cf. "the chosen … whom he has chosen" in v. 20, below.

great detail (*J.W.*, books 5 – 6). Outside the city the Romans crucified so many Jews that they ran out of wood for crosses. Inside there was extreme infighting, murder, famine, disease, and even cannibalism.[67] Thousands were slaughtered when Romans breached the walls (*J.W.* 6.3.3 §§193 – 195; 6.8.5 §§403 – 406). In all Josephus claims that 1,100,000 died during the siege and 97,000 were taken captive (*J.W.* 6.9.3 §§420 – 421). These numbers must surely be exaggerations, but they well illustrate the horrible sufferings the city experienced.

Here again we have the great challenge of discerning whether the language describes Jerusalem's destruction or the end of the age. The absolute statement ("unlike anything that has happened …") is an allusion to Dan 12:1, which describes the end of days: "There will be a time of distress such as has not happened from the beginning of nations until then. But at that time your people — everyone whose name is found written in the book — will be delivered" (cf. Jer 30:7; Joel 2:2). At the same time, this kind of language can be idiomatic and hyperbolic in Scripture, referring to temporal times of great calamity.[68] Lane points out that Jesus' addition, "and it will never happen again," implies the continuation of history beyond this point, and future (though less severe) tribulations to come.[69] As

elsewhere in the discourse, the images apparently mix the historical with the eschatological, the siege of Jerusalem with the end of the age.

13:20 And if the Lord had not cut short those days, no life would be saved. But for the sake of the chosen ones, whom he has chosen,[70] he has shortened the days (καὶ εἰ μὴ ἐκολόβωσεν κύριος τὰς ἡμέρας, οὐκ ἂν ἐσώθη πᾶσα σάρξ· ἀλλὰ διὰ τοὺς ἐκλεκτοὺς οὓς ἐξελέξατο ἐκολόβωσεν τὰς ἡμέρας). The coming destruction will be so severe that "no life [σάρξ]" would survive "if the Lord had not cut short [κολοβόω] those days." The idea of God "shortening" days or, more commonly, "hastening" the time of the end, appears in some apocalyptic literature, though there is no exact parallel to Mark's language.[71] France points to conceptual parallels in Isa 65:8, where the threatened judgment is held back for the sake of God's servants, and Gen 18:23 – 33, where God would have relented from his judgment against Sodom for the sake of ten righteous people.[72]

In the OT and Judaism, "the chosen ones" commonly refers to God's covenant people,[73] and in the NT to believers in Jesus Christ.[74] The term occurs in Mark only in this discourse (vv. 20, 22, 27). One's interpretation here depends on one's understanding of the discourse as a whole. If this section

67. In one horrific incident, Josephus describes a woman whose only food was stolen by certain marauders. In despair she killed and cooked her own infant. When city defenders arrived and demanded the food they smelled cooking, she offered them half of the child. In horror, they fled. Josephus writes that when this report went throughout the city, "those that were thus distressed by the famine were very desirous to die; and those already dead were esteemed happy, because they had not lived long enough either to hear or to see such miseries" (*J.W.* 6.3.4 §§201 – 213).

68. France, *Mark*, 527, citing Exod 9:18; 11:6; Deut 4:32; Dan 12:1; Joel 2:2; Rev 16:18; 1 Macc 9:27; *T. Moses* 8:1; 1QM 1.11 – 12.

69. Lane, *Mark*, 472.

70. "The chosen ones, whom he has chosen" (ἐκλεκτοὺς οὓς ἐξελέξατο) is another Semitism and typical Markan redun-

dancy (cf. v. 19: "creation, when God made").

71. 4Q385 [= 4QpsEzᵃ] frag. 3; 2 Esd 2:13; *1 En.* 80:2; Sir 36:10; *2 Bar.* 20:1 – 2; 83:1; Beasley-Murray, *Jesus and the Last Days*, 419 n. 124; France, *Mark*, 527; Evans, *Mark 8:27 – 16:20*, 322.

72. France, *Mark*, 527.

73. Deut 7:6; 14:2; 1 Chr 16:13; Pss 33:12; 105:6, 43; 106:5; 135:4; Isa 41:8; 42:1; 43:10, 20; 44:1; 45:4; 65:9 – 11; Wis 3:9; 4:15; Sir 46:1; Tob 8:15; 2 Esd 15:21; 16:73 – 74. Like the present passage, 2 Esd 16:74 speaks of the elect with reference to eschatological deliverance: "Listen, my elect ones, says the Lord; the days of tribulation are at hand, but I will deliver you from them" (NRSV).

74. Rom 8:33; 16:13; Col 3:12; 2 Tim 2:10; Titus 1:1; 1 Pet 1:1; 2:4, 6, 9; 2 John 1, 13; Rev 17:14.

concerns the eschatological future, then "the chosen/elect" refers to all believers suffering through the tribulation period leading up to the return of the Son of Man. If, as we have suggested, it concerns the destruction of Jerusalem, then it probably refers to the few Jewish Christians left in the city during the siege. In what sense were there days "shortened"? This too is unclear. France points out that the siege of Jerusalem, though terrible, lasted only five months, a relatively short time for an event of this kind.[75]

13:21 – 22 Then, if anyone says to you, "Look, here is the Messiah!" or "Look, he is there," do not believe them. For false messiahs and false prophets will give signs and wonders in order to deceive, if possible, the elect (καὶ τότε ἐάν τις ὑμῖν εἴπῃ· ἴδε ὧδε ὁ χριστός, ἴδε ἐκεῖ, μὴ πιστεύετε· ἐγερθήσονται γὰρ ψευδόχριστοι καὶ ψευδοπροφῆται καὶ δώσουσιν σημεῖα καὶ τέρατα πρὸς τὸ ἀποπλανᾶν, εἰ δυνατόν, τοὺς ἐκλεκτούς). This section ends as it began (v. 6), with a warning against deceivers — false messiahs and false prophets (vv. 21 – 22) — and a call to watchfulness (v. 23). While in v. 6 the context seems to be the years leading up to Jerusalem's destruction, here the primary context appears to be the war itself.[76] Josephus speaks of various attempts by insurrectionists during the siege to proclaim themselves king.[77] False prophets also arose in the city, deceiving the doomed inhabitants with promises of God's deliverance (*J. W.* 6.5.2 – 3 §§285 – 300; cf. 2.13.4 – 5 §§258 – 263).

These false messiahs and prophets will deceive through "signs and wonders" (σημεῖα καὶ τέρατα). This phrase is common in biblical literature, referring in the OT especially to God's works of power

against Egypt (Exod 7:3; Deut 4:34; 6:22; 26:8; Neh 9:10; Ps 135:9; etc.) and in the NT to the miracles of the apostles in Acts (Acts 2:22, 43; 4:30; 5:12; 6:8; 14:3; 15:12; cf. Rom 15:19; 2 Cor 12:12). Such miracles can be counterfeited, however, and Deut 13:1 – 3 warns of false prophets who perform "a sign or wonder" (LXX: σημεῖον ἢ τέρας) and then coax Israel to worship false gods.

Josephus echoes this language when he speaks of various messianic imposters in the first century who deceived the masses, pretending to do "wonders and signs" (τέρατα καὶ σημεῖα; *Ant.* 20.8.6 – 7 §§167 – 172). Paul similarly says that the "man of lawlessness," who sets himself up in God's temple as God, will use "all sorts of displays of power through signs and wonders" (ἐν πάσῃ δυνάμει καὶ σημείοις καὶ τέρασιν; 2 Thess 2:9). The impressive nature of these false miracles will be such to deceive, "if possible, [even] the elect." "If possible" (εἰ δυνατόν) could carry the sense, "if it were possible," meaning it is *not*. More likely, it speaks only of their attempt: "They will try, if they can, to deceive even the elect."

13:23 You watch out. I have told you all these things ahead of time (ὑμεῖς δὲ βλέπετε· προείρηκα ὑμῖν πάντα). The point with which the discourse began (v. 5) and its main theme is now reiterated: "Watch out!" (βλέπετε). The "you" (ὑμεῖς) is emphatic. In contrast to those who will be led astray, *you* will be ready. Jesus has warned his followers ahead of time and so equipped them to face any persecution or deception. As noted above, the two warnings against false teachers (vv. 5 – 6, 21 – 22) and exhortations to "watch out" (vv. 5, 23) form an inclusio around this first major section of the discourse (vv. 5 – 23).

---

75. France, *Mark*, 528; Stein, *Mark*, 606 – 7.

76. Contra Hooker, *Mark*, 316 – 17, who claims that the scene now changes to after the war. Contra, also, Edwards, *Mark*, 401, who views this as the end of the age.

77. E.g., Menahem (*J. W.* 2.17.8 – 9 §§433 – 448) and Simon Bar-Giora (4.9.3 – 8 §§503 – 544).

Theology in Application

Like much of the gospel tradition, the application of the Olivet Discourse is complicated since three audiences must be kept in mind: the original hearers of Jesus, the church of Mark's day, and our contemporary world. Jesus is speaking first of all to his disciples, and the warnings to flee Jerusalem apply especially to them. Yet Mark is also addressing the church of his day, which is likely far from its Jerusalem roots (see Introduction to Mark: Audience), though facing the same prospect of persecution and even martyrdom. Finally, we must determine how these truths apply to the church of all time. Common themes that apply to all three audiences are the need for spiritual diligence, warnings against false teachers, the danger of eschatological fervor, and the reality of persecution.

Readiness for the Lord's Return

The repeated refrain throughout this discourse and its central theme is to be aware of the situation, to "watch out," to be prepared. Jesus' disciples are to be aware of deceivers, who will come claiming Jesus' authority; they are to be aware that wars and natural disasters are not necessary harbingers of the end. They must be ready to face persecution, suffering, and even betrayal by friends and family, and be ready to flee Jerusalem when the abomination that causes desolation appears. Most of all, they must watch and pray for the return of the Son of Man.

The overall message is that followers of Jesus must be acutely aware of their place in salvation history, that they are living in the "end times" between the first coming of Christ and the second, when the God-ordained drama of redemption is nearing its consummation. By discerning our place as God's actors on this salvation-historical stage, we will be able to "improvise" well when confronted with frightening twists and turns in the script.[78]

Warning against False Messiahs

Readiness means especially the ability to discern truth from error. The importance of this theme is evident in that Mark frames this section of the discourse (vv. 5 – 23) in warnings against false teachers (vv. 6, 21 – 22). There were certainly false prophets leading up to the destruction of Jerusalem, as Josephus attests (see comments on vv. 5 – 6, 21 – 22). But Jesus' warning looks beyond that event to the reality of false teachers and prophets throughout history.

---

78. On history as a divine drama, see Kevin Vanhoozer, *The Drama of Doctrine: A Canonical Linguistic Approach to Christian Theology* (Louisville: Westminster John Knox, 2005); on the concept of "improvisation," see Samuel Wells, *Improvisation: The Drama of Christian Ethics* (Grand Rapids: Brazos, 2004).

One obvious sign of such deceivers is the claim to be "the one," that is, the one to replace the authority of Jesus with their own. This can be as explicit as a cult leader like David Koresh, who claimed messianic authority over his followers, or as subtle as a ministry leader whose followers are encouraged to devote unquestioned allegiance to his teachings. Paul addresses the danger of such human allegiances in 1 Cor 1, where the church in Corinth was dividing into factions around leaders such as Peter, Apollos, and Paul himself. Paul is appalled at such partisan strife and vehemently responds, "Is Christ divided? Was Paul crucified for you?" (1 Cor 1:12 – 13). The focus and center of our faith must be Christ himself, not any human leader.

The Danger of End-Time Speculation

It is significant that Jesus takes time to warn against the "nonsigns" that do not signal the end, including false messiahs, wars, earthquakes, famines, and persecution (13:6 – 11). The natural tendency of human beings is to believe that catastrophic events threatening our own lives are also signs of the end of the world. There is a huge industry of books and videos touting the "keys" to Bible prophecy and promoting end-time speculation. Self-proclaimed "prophecy experts" point to contemporary events as sure signs that the end of the world is near. The sad fact is that throughout history all such prognosticators have been proven false, resulting in disappointment, confusion, and even loss of confidence in biblical authority.

One of the most famous examples in history is the "Millerites," followers of William Miller (1782 – 1849), a Baptist preacher of Bible prophecy, who claimed with a series of calculations based on Dan 8 – 9 that Christ would return on October 22, 1844. His followers waited anxiously, some even selling their possessions, only to experience disillusionment at what came to be known as the "Great Disappointment."[79] While most prophetic speculators today avoid such specific date setting,[80] there is still an unfortunate tendency to read the Bible through the lens of today's headlines.

Yet we should all know better. Even in a passage full of eschatological images like this one, the message is not to calculate the end, but always to be alert and ready, living a life of spiritual preparation. Similarly, in Acts 1, when Jesus was asked by his disciples after his resurrection whether he would "at this time" restore the kingdom to Israel, he responded, "It is not for you to know the times or dates the Father has set by his own authority." Instead, they were to be his *witnesses* from Jerusalem to the ends of the earth (Acts 1:6 – 8). The church's role is to proclaim the gospel, not to speculate about the end.

---

79. See George R. Knight, *Millennial Fever and the End of the World* (Boise, ID: Pacific, 1993).

80. One well-publicized exception was Harold Camping's prediction (and billboard campaign) that Christ would return on May 21, 2011.

The Certainty of Persecution

The realities of the present age include not only catastrophic events like wars, earthquakes, and famines, but also the persecution of God's people. Earlier in Mark, Jesus called on his followers to take up their cross and follow him (8:34). Now he warns of the specifics of that persecution, including floggings in the synagogues, trials before governors and kings, and even betrayal by friends and family (13:9 – 13). The book of Acts testifies to the persecution of the first-century church, from the early days in Jerusalem (4:3; 5:40 – 41; 7:57 – 60; 12:1 – 2) to the many beatings and imprisonments experienced by Paul (14:19; 16:22; 21:30 – 32; 2 Cor 11:23 – 29). The NT as a whole portrays a church that is suffering (1 Thess 2:14; Heb 10:32 – 35; 1 Pet 1:6; 4:12 – 19; Rev 1:9; 2:10, 13) so that Paul can affirm to Timothy that "everyone who wants to live a godly life in Christ Jesus will be persecuted" (2 Tim 3:12).

In the Western church, where physical persecution is seldom experienced, we can easily forget this reality. For Mark's readers, however, the growing hostility against Christians meant that proclaiming Jesus as Lord often resulted in arrest, beatings, imprisonment, and even death. Yet faithfulness to Jesus was worth it, since "whoever loses their life for me and for the gospel will save it" (8:35), and "the one who endures to the end — this one will be saved" (13:13).

Mark 13:24 – 37

Literary Context

The literary context of the Olivet Discourse has been discussed in detail in the previous chapter. Jesus leaves the temple after a series of controversies with the religious leaders and crosses to the Mount of Olives. There he predicts the temple's destruction, linking this event closely (thematically if not chronologically) to the final act of God's drama of redemption, which will culminate in the return of the Son of Man and the gathering of the elect.

Main Idea

The second half of the Olivet Discourse concerns events surrounding the destruction of Jerusalem, the eschatological climax of the return of the Son of Man, and the vindication of his people. The central theme is the need for watchfulness, faithfulness, and perseverance.

Translation

(See next page.)

Mark 13:24–37

24a	setting (temporal)	"*But* in those days after that tribulation,
b	Scriptural quotation	'*The sun will be darkened,*
c		and *the moon will not give its light,*
25a		and *the stars will be falling from the sky,*
b		and *the powers in the heavens will be shaken.*' [Isa 13:10; 34:4]
26	prophecy	*Then* they will see the Son of Man coming in the clouds with great power and glory.
27a	action	*Then* he will send his angels
b	action/setting	*and* he will gather his chosen ones from the four winds,
	setting	from the end of the earth to the end of heaven.

28a	command/analogy	Learn this lesson from the fig tree:
b	condition of 28c	When its branch becomes tender and it puts out leaves,
c	result of 28b	you know the summer is near.
29a	application of 28	*So* also you,
b	condition of 29c	when you see these things happening,
c	result of 29b	know that it is near, at the door.
30a	veracity statement	Truly I say to you,
b	prophecy/result of 30c	this generation will certainly not pass away
c	condition of 30b	until all these things take place.

| 31a | analogy | The heavens and the earth will pass away, |
| b | contrast | *but* my words will certainly not pass away. |

32a	assertion	*But* concerning that day or hour,
		no one knows,
b		neither the angels in heaven,
		nor the Son, but
		only the Father.
33a	command	Watch! Be vigilant!

b	reason for 33a	*For* you do not know
		when the time will come.
34a	analogy	It is like a man journeying,
b		leaving his home and
c		giving each of his servants authority
d		to do the work assigned to them;
e		he commanded the doorkeeper to be alert.
35a	command	*Therefore,* be alert!
b	reason for 35a	*For* you do not know when the lord of the house is coming, whether
c		in the evening, or
		at midnight, or
		when the rooster crows, or
		at dawn.

36a	condition of 36b	If he comes suddenly,
b	result of 36a	he might find you sleeping.
37a	command	What I say to you, I say to all,
b		'Be alert!'"

Structure

In part 1 (13:1 – 23) we argued that Jesus' discourse on the Mount of Olives is made up of three main parts: (1) the events leading to the destruction of Jerusalem (13:5 – 23), including both signs and nonsigns, (2) the return of the Son of Man and the gathering of the elect (13:24 – 27), and (3) two "parables" that relate, respectively, to these two events: (a) the parable of the fig tree, relating to the destruction of Jerusalem (vv. 28 – 31), and (b) a parabolic call for watchfulness, relating to the Lord's return and the end of the age (vv. 32 – 37). Here we cover (2) and (3).

Exegetical Outline

See the previous chapter (13:1 – 23) for a full exegetical outline of Mark 13 (pp. 567 – 68).

Explanation of the Text

13:24 – 25 But in those days after that tribulation, "The sun will be darkened, and the moon will not give its light, and the stars will be falling from the sky, and the powers in the heavens will be shaken." (Ἀλλὰ ἐν ἐκείναις ταῖς ἡμέραις μετὰ τὴν θλῖψιν ἐκείνην ὁ ἥλιος σκοτισθήσεται, καὶ ἡ σελήνη οὐ δώσει τὸ φέγγος αὐτῆς, καὶ οἱ ἀστέρες ἔσονται ἐκ τοῦ οὐρανοῦ πίπτοντες, καὶ αἱ δυνάμεις αἱ ἐν τοῖς οὐρανοῖς σαλευθήσονται). Now we come to the most difficult question of the discourse, since Jesus seems to directly connect ("in those days") the coming of the Son of Man (v. 26) with the events associated with the destruction of Jerusalem (13:14 – 23).

As we noted in the previous chapter, one way to avoid this difficulty is to identify all the events of 13:14 – 23 with the eschatological future rather than the destruction of Jerusalem.[1] Another way is to see the whole discourse, including the coming of the Son of Man, as concerned with the destruction of Jerusalem.[2] Yet both of these are problematic. The former does not do justice to the close relationship between Jesus' prediction of the temple's destruction (13:2) and the warning to flee Jerusalem (13:14 – 15). The latter cannot explain the finality implied in the coming of the Son of Man and the gathering of the elect (vv. 26 – 27; cf. vv. 32 – 36).

A third option is to see a clear chronological transition and gap between the events surrounding the destruction of Jerusalem (13:14 – 23) and the parousia and the end of the age (vv. 24 – 27). Lane, for example, argues for a greater disjunction at v. 24 than is immediately apparent. The strong adversative "but" (ἀλλά) sets vv. 24 – 27 off from earlier parts of the discourse and marks the transition to a new subject.[3] "In those days" (ἐν ἐκείναις

---

1. Evans, *Mark 8:27 – 16:20*, 329: "The eschatological tenor of vv 14 – 23 looks to events beyond the catastrophe of 70 C.E. to the appearance of an antichrist figure who will stand in the temple of God, who will be accompanied by false prophets, and who will inaugurate a period of tribulation unprecedented in human history."

2. Wright, *Jesus and the Victory of God*, 354 – 65; France, *Mark*, 530 – 34; idem, *Jesus and the Old Testament*, 227 – 39.

3. Gnilka, *Markus*, 2:200; Pesch, *Markusevangelium*, 2:302. Cf. Lane, *Mark*, 473 n. 87.

ταῖς ἡμέραις) often carries eschatological connotations (Jer 3:16, 18; 31:29; 33:15–16; Joel 3:1; Zech 8:23); yet it has no precise temporal value: "In verse 24 this phrase designates a period subsequent to the days of tribulation described in verses 19–20, but the matter of chronological sequence is left imprecise." The events described in 13:5–23 are necessary *precursors* to the coming of the Son of Man, "yet they do not determine the time of that event."[4] In this case, "after that tribulation" (μετὰ τὴν θλῖψιν ἐκείνην) does not necessarily point back to the specific tribulation of 13:14–17, but to the general tribulation of 13:9–11, which is characteristic of the present age.[5]

Yet this too is problematic. The adversative "but" (ἀλλά) is not so much chronological as thematic, contrasting the preliminary events of 13:14–23 with the climactic events of 13:24–27.[6] "In those days after that tribulation" (ἐν ἐκείναις ταῖς ἡμέραις μετὰ τὴν θλῖψιν ἐκείνην) points most naturally to the events immediately preceding, that is, those surrounding the destruction of Jerusalem. It seems best to conclude that Mark sees the events as part of the same eschatological complex. Stein concludes:

> For Mark, the events of 13:14–23 and 24–27 are intimately associated, and it is unlikely that he saw a great gap of time between them. They are intimately associated in that they are part of the same great divine act of history. This includes Jesus's coming, ministry, death, and resurrection, which bring the kingdom of God; the divine judgment on Jerusalem in AD 70; and the parousia of the

Son of Man, which brings history to its conclusion and goal.[7]

As often in prophetic literature, events that may be centuries or even millennia apart are identified together because of their unique eschatological and soteriological relationship. This "foreshortened" or two-dimensional prophetic vision is sometimes compared to mountains that from a great distance appear to be side by side, but in fact are many miles apart.[8] From Mark's perspective, the destruction of Jerusalem is direct vindication of God's saving work through the life, death, and resurrection of Jesus the Messiah and also the precursor and preview of the consummation of the kingdom of God at the parousia. From his limited vantage point, these two latter events appear together. A hint to this chronological haziness will appear again in v. 32, where Jesus says that even the Son does not know the time of his return. In the same breath that he affirms the absolute certainty *that* these events will take (v. 31), he expresses ignorance concerning *when* they will occur (v. 32).

The apocalyptic language that follows in vv. 24b–25 echoes various OT texts, especially Isa 13:10b ("the rising sun will be darkened and the moon will not give its light") and 34:4 ("all the starry host will fall ... like shriveled figs from the fig tree").[9] As Beasley-Murray points out, these are not preparatory signs that herald the coming of the Son of Man. They are rather the language of theophany, representing the radical upheaval of creation that accompanies his appearance. "The elements of creation go into confusion and fear *be-*

---

4. Lane, *Mark*, 474.
5. D. A. Carson argues similarly for Matthew's version of the discourse, despite the fact that Matthew seems to connect the destruction of Jerusalem *even more closely* to the coming of the Son of God by saying that the cosmic events of Matt 24:29 will occur "immediately" after the tribulation of those days. This "tribulation" (θλῖψις), he claims, is not the "great tribulation" of 13:15–21, but "the tribulation of those days," mean-

ing the tribulation "of the entire interadvent period" (Carson, "Matthew," in *EBC*², 9:567).
6. France, *Mark*, 531–32.
7. Stein, *Mark*, 612.
8. Garland, *Mark*, 501 n. 38.
9. Cf. Isa 24:23; Ezek 32:7–8; Joel 2:10, 30–31; 3:4, 15, 20; Amos 8:9.

cause he appears, not as a sign that he is about to do so (see, e.g., Judg 5:4 – 5; Amos 1:2; Hab 3:3 – 6, 10 – 11; Pss 77:14 – 16; 114:1 – 8)."[10]

Some argue that the cosmic nature of this language confirms that the passage is describing the end of the age, not the historical destruction of Jerusalem. It is certainly true that the end of the age is often described in terms of cosmic upheavals such as this (Joel 3:15; 2 Pet 3:10; Rev 6:12 – 13; 8:10). Yet the context of many of these OT passages is God's judgment of the nations within history (e.g., Babylon, Egypt, Edom, Israel, Judah, etc.), rather than the final judgment at the end of the age. As N. T. Wright points out, the language is not necessarily describing "the collapse or end of the space-time universe," but rather "typical Jewish imagery for events within the present order that are felt and perceived as 'cosmic' or, as we should say, 'earth-shattering.'"[11] Whether Mark is thinking of the parousia or the destruction of Jerusalem must be decided on broader contextual grounds.

13:26 Then they will see the Son of Man coming in the clouds with great power and glory (καὶ τότε ὄψονται τὸν υἱὸν τοῦ ἀνθρώπου ἐρχόμενον ἐν νεφέλαις μετὰ δυνάμεως πολλῆς καὶ δόξης). "Son of Man" has been Jesus' favorite self-designation throughout Mark's gospel (14x; see comments on 2:10 – 11; 8:31, 38). Key background for the title is Dan 7:13 – 14, where "one like a son of man" (i.e., a human being) comes on the clouds of heaven, approaches the Ancient of Days (God himself), and is given "authority, glory and sovereign power." Jesus' use of the title up to this point in Mark has mostly concerned the Son of Man's authority on earth (2:10, 28) and his coming suffering (8:31; 9:9, 12, 31;

10:33, 45; cf. 14:21, 41). Yet Jesus has already alluded to the "coming" of the Son of Man "in his Father's glory with the holy angels" (8:38). He will allude again to this passage in Daniel at his trial (14:62), when he will combine Ps 110:1 with Dan 7:13.

The emphasis here is on revelation and vindication. The glorious Son of Man, whose identity has been veiled through his public ministry (9:9 – 10), will be revealed for all to see ("they will see"). The one who came humbly "to serve, and to give his life as a ransom for many" (10:45) will return to judge and save "with great power and glory" (μετὰ δυνάμεως πολλῆς καὶ δόξης).

Those who interpret these verses with reference to the destruction of Jerusalem point out that Dan 7:13 – 14 in its original context does not refer to the Son of Man *coming* to earth, but rather *going* to heaven, where he receives eternal dominion and authority. The "coming" (ἐρχόμενον) referred to here is about "the vindication and enthronement of the Son of Man at the right hand of God, to receive and exercise supreme authority." What is being described is "a change of government: the temple and all that it stood for is out, and the Son of Man is in."[12] This interpretation has three important points to commend it: (1) the original context of Daniel, which concerns the Son of Man's vindication before God; (2) the strong narrative connection in v. 24 between the destruction of Jerusalem and the coming Son of Man; and (3) the reference in v. 30 to "this generation," which will see all these things happen.

Nevertheless, the evidence against this interpretation seems overwhelming. First, the verb "they will see" fits well the parousia but seems out of place with reference to the heavenly exaltation,

---

10. Beasley-Murray, *Jesus and the Last Days*, 375.

11. Wright, *Jesus and the Victory of God*, 362. Cf. T. R. Hatina, "The Focus of Mark 13:24 – 27: The Parousia, or the Destruction of the Temple?" *BBR* 6 (1996): 43 – 66; France, *Mark*, 532 – 33.

12. France, *Mark*, 501; cf. 534 – 35; France, *Jesus and the Old Testament*, 235 – 36; Wright, *Jesus and the Victory of God*, 360 – 65; C. S. Mann, *Mark* (AB 27; Garden City, NY: Doubleday, 1986), 528.

which was observed by no human being.[13] Second, throughout the NT the "coming" of the Son of Man is closely associated with the end of the age, the sending of his angels to gather the elect, the resurrection of the dead, and the final judgment. Note Matt 13:40–41, where the Son of Man comes "at the end of the age" and sends his angels to weed out everything that causes sin. In Matt 16:27 the Son of Man comes "in his Father's glory with his angels, and then he will reward each person according to what they have done." In Matt 25:31 the Son of Man comes in his glory and all the angels with him, and he will determine the final destiny of all people — the sheep and the goats.

Throughout the NT letters the "coming" of the Lord is associated with the return of Christ and the end of the age, not his exaltation to the right hand of God (1 Cor 11:26; 15:23, 52; 16:22; 1 Thess 2:19; 3:13; 4:14–17; 5:23; 2 Thess 1:7; 2:1, 8; James 5:7–8; 2 Pet 1:16; 3:4, 10–12; 1 John 2:28; cf. Rev 1:7).[14] In light of this body of evidence, it seems inconceivable that Mark's readers would take Jesus' saying as a reference to Jesus' exaltation rather than the parousia.

13:27 Then he will send his[15] angels and he will gather his chosen ones from the four winds, from the end of the earth to the end of heaven (καὶ τότε ἀποστελεῖ τοὺς ἀγγέλους καὶ ἐπισυνάξει τοὺς ἐκλεκτοὺς αὐτοῦ ἐκ τῶν τεσσάρων ἀνέμων ἀπ'

ἄκρου γῆς ἕως ἄκρου οὐρανοῦ). The purpose of the Son of Man's return is to save and vindicate "his chosen ones." On the people of God as the "chosen ones" or the "elect" (ἐκλεκτοί) in Judaism and early Christianity, see comments on 13:20.

The eschatological regathering of God's people is a common theme in the OT and Judaism. Isaiah 11:11 speaks of "that day" when "the Lord will reach out his hand a second time to reclaim the surviving remnant of his people from Assyria, from Lower Egypt, from Upper Egypt, from Cush, from Elam, from Babylonia, from Hamath and from the islands of the Mediterranean." Similarly, Jer 23:3 promises, "I myself will gather the remnant of my flock out of all the countries where I have driven them and will bring them back to their pasture, where they will be fruitful and increase in number."[16] The scope of the regathering is "from the four winds" (ἐκ τῶν τεσσάρων ἀνέμων) and "from the end of the earth to the end of heaven" (ἀπ' ἄκρου γῆς ἕως ἄκρου οὐρανοῦ; cf. Deut 30:4). The two phrases are synonymous parallelism, meaning "the whole earth." They recall, respectively, Deut 30:4 and Zech 2:6 (LXX 2:10), both of which concern the regathering of God's people.

Here God's elect are Jesus' followers, those who have remained faithful to the Son of Man. All the emphasis is on their vindication and deliverance. No detailed eschatological schema is set forth with reference to events often associated with the end,

---

13. France, *Mark*, 535, challenges this, pointing out that other allusions to Dan 7:13–14 in Mark involve "seeing." In 8:38–9:1, after referring to the coming Son of Man, Jesus says some of the disciples will not taste death before they "see" the kingdom of God come with power. And in 14:62 seeing is explicitly identified with the exaltation, when Jesus says the high priest will "see" the Son of Man seated at the right hand of God and coming on the clouds of heaven. France suggests that what is seen may be the destruction of Jerusalem or the gathering of the elect through the evangelization of the world. This, however, seems a stretch, since Jesus says they will see the Son of Man himself.

14. Carson, "Matthew," in *EBC*[2], 9:554. Carson points out

that it would take "overwhelmingly convincing reasons to overturn this set of associations."

15. Some manuscripts include the pronoun "his" (αὐτοῦ) after "angels" (א A C Θ Ψ *f*[1.13] 𝔐 lat syr), which may be a harmonization to Matt 24:31. The definite article alone, however, may itself indicate possession and so be translated "his" (Wallace, *Greek Grammar*, 215). The same two points apply to "the elect" (τοὺς ἐκλεκτούς), where the evidence for the pronoun is slightly stronger, so that the UBS text includes the word in brackets (א A B C Θ 083 *f*[13] 2427 𝔐 lat syr).

16. Cf. Deut 30:4; Neh 1:9; Isa 27:12–13; 43:5–6; 49:12; 60:1–9; Pss 107:2–3; 147:2; Jer 31:10; 32:37; Ezek 11:16–17; 34:12–13; 36:24; 39:27; Zech 2:6–13.

such as the resurrection of the dead, the judgment of the wicked, and the consummation of kingdom.[17] This is likely because the discourse has focused primarily on the disciples and their coming trials and vindication.

Those who relate these verses to the destruction of Jerusalem rather than to the end of the age identify the gathering of the elect with the missionary expansion of the gospel in the first century. The "angels" (ἄγγελοι) then would be either human "messengers" of the gospel[18] or angels viewed as supporting missionaries in the task of world evangelism (cf. Heb 1:14).[19]

13:28–29　Learn this lesson from the fig tree: When its branch becomes tender and it puts out leaves, you know the summer is near. So also you, when you see these things happening, know that it is near, at the door (Ἀπὸ δὲ τῆς συκῆς μάθετε τὴν παραβολήν· ὅταν ἤδη ὁ κλάδος αὐτῆς ἁπαλὸς γένηται καὶ ἐκφύῃ τὰ φύλλα, γινώσκετε ὅτι ἐγγὺς τὸ θέρος ἐστίν· οὕτως καὶ ὑμεῖς, ὅταν ἴδητε ταῦτα γινόμενα, γινώσκετε ὅτι ἐγγύς ἐστιν ἐπὶ θύραις). We have argued above that Jesus, after describing the eschatological climax (13:14–27), concludes his discourse with two parabolic clarifications. The first, the parable of the fig tree (vv. 28–30), relates to the destruction of Jerusalem and confirms that it will be preceded by signs to be recognized and will occur within the generation of the disciples. The second, the parable of the owner's return (vv. 31–37), relates to the uncertain time of the return of the Son of Man and the end of the age. Both continue the main theme of the discourse, which is preparation and watchfulness in light of

the danger and uncertainty of the times (13:5, 9, 23, 33–35, 37).

The term "parable" (παραβολή; translated "lesson" here), has a much wider range of meanings in Greek than in English (see comments on 3:23–26). Mark has used the term for a variety of figures of speech, from analogies (3:23; 4:30–34) to proverbs (7:17) to true parables (4:2, 10–13; 12:1, 12). Here the term is used in the sense of a lesson, analogy, or illustration. The fig tree is one of the few deciduous trees in Palestine, losing its leaves in the fall and putting forth new ones in March or April (cf. 11:12–13a). The general point of the analogy is clear enough. Just as the budding and leafing of the fig tree confirms to the observer that summer is near, so also when you see "these things" taking place, know that "he/it is near" (ἐγγύς ἐστιν).

It is the specific referents, however, that are debated: (1) Is the fig tree merely an agricultural analogy, or is it being used allegorically for Israel, the temple, or something else? (2) What are "these things" that the disciples will witness: the return of the Son of Man, the abomination of desolation, the destruction of Jerusalem, or something else? (3) What is the person or event that is "near": the events surrounding the destruction of Jerusalem ("it") or the coming of the Son of Man ("he")?

(1) We have noted earlier that Jesus' cursing of the fig tree and its withering (11:12–14, 20–21) symbolically represent God's judgment against the Jerusalem leadership and the temple hierarchy. Could Jesus be continuing this analogy here, with the budding of the fig tree representing the restoration of God's people and a new community that springs from the old?[20] While this is possible, it

---

17. Boring, *Mark*, 373.

18. Wright, *Jesus and the Victory of God*, 362–63; France, *Jesus and the Old Testament*, 238.

19. So France, *Mark*, 536–37, who acknowledges a change in opinion from his earlier work.

20. Cf. Hooker, *Mark*, 320; T. J. Geddert, *Watchwords: Mark 13 in Markan Eschatology* (JSNTSup; Sheffield: Sheffield Aca-

demic, 1989), 251–52. Some popular prophecy writers have gone so far as to claim that the establishment of Israel as a nation in 1948 was the fulfillment of this prophecy, marking a one-generation countdown to the eschaton. See, e.g., Hal Lindsey, *The Late Great Planet Earth* (Grand Rapids: Zondervan, 1970), 53–54; idem, *The 1980's: Countdown to Armageddon* (King of Prussia, PA: Westgate, 1981).

seems unlikely. Fig trees were endemic to Palestine, and the mere mention of one would not necessarily invoke an allegory in the mind of Mark's readers. The point in chapter 11 is the fig tree's barrenness. Here there is no mention of fruit, only of leaves.

(2) This brings up the question of the referent of "these things," which the disciples "will see." While the nearest antecedents are the apocalyptic signs of vv. 24–25 or the coming of the Son of Man and the gathering of the elect (vv. 26–27), we have argued above that a reference to the destruction of Jerusalem fits better the overall structure of the discourse.[21] In this case, "these things" of v. 29 would be the same as "all these things" of v. 30, and both correspond with the same expressions in 13:4a and 13:4b, which clearly refer to the destruction of the temple. Furthermore, the phrase "when you see" (ὅταν ἴδητε) of v. 29 would parallel "when you see" (ὅταν ... ἴδητε) of 13:14, which refers to the abomination of desolation and the destruction of the temple.

(3) In light of these conclusions, the phrase "he/it is near" (ἐγγύς ἐστιν) is better translated "it is near" (NIV; cf. TEV, CEV) than "he is near" (NRSV, NET, HCSB, ESV; cf. NLT), referring not to the coming of the Son of Man but to the abomination of desolation and/or the events related to the destruction of Jerusalem. Just as the leafing of the fig tree previews the coming of summer, so the signs Jesus has described in 13:5–23 will herald the destruction of Jerusalem and the temple. Some commentators claim that the appositional phrase "at the door" demands a personal rather than an impersonal referent.[22] This is not the case, however, since the phrase is a fixed idiom for something about to happen. Events as well as people can be "on the threshold."[23]

13:30 Truly I say to you, this generation will certainly not pass away until all these things take place (ἀμὴν λέγω ὑμῖν ὅτι οὐ μὴ παρέλθη ἡ γενεὰ αὕτη μέχρις οὗ ταῦτα πάντα γένηται). The importance of this saying is evident from both Jesus' solemn introduction, "Truly I say to you" (ἀμὴν λέγω ὑμῖν; 13x in Mark; see comments at 3:28), and the emphatic negation (οὐ μή), "certainly not." The most natural interpretation of "this generation" (ἡ γενεὰ αὕτη) is the present generation, that is, the generation of Jesus and his contemporaries. This is the meaning of the phrase elsewhere in Mark (8:12, 38; 9:19). This interpretation makes good sense if, as we have argued above, "all these things" (ταῦτα πάντα) corresponds to "these things" (ταῦτα) of v. 29 (cf. 13:4), and both have as their referent the events surrounding the destruction of Jerusalem (13:2, 4, 14–23) rather than the return of the Son of Man.

A biblical generation was about forty years, which was "not coincidentally the length of time between Jesus' prediction and the destruction of Jerusalem."[24] Those who claim that "these things" refers to the whole discourse (13:5–27), including the coming of the Son of Man and the end of the age (13:24–27), must conclude (1) that Jesus was mistaken, (2) that the Son of Man's return coincided with the destruction of Jerusalem (so France and Wright), or (3) that "generation" here carries a different meaning. Various proposals have been made, including the church, the Jewish race, humanity as a whole, or the last generation before the end.[25] None of these is convincing.

13:31 The heavens and the earth will pass away, but my words will certainly not pass away (ὁ οὐρανὸς καὶ ἡ γῆ παρελεύσονται, οἱ δὲ λόγοι μου οὐ

21. Cf. Cranfield, *Mark*, 502; Lane, *Mark*, 478–80; France, *Mark*, 538–40; Garland, *Mark*, 502; Witherington, *Mark*, 348–49; Stein, *Mark*, 618.
22. Gundry, *Mark*, 788.
23. France, *Mark*, 538.
24. Witherington, *Mark*, 349.
25. For various views see Cranfield, *Mark*, 409; Beasley-Murray, *Jesus and the Last Days*, 443.

μὴ παρελεύσονται). It is somewhat ironic, in light of the immense difficulties in interpreting v. 30, that Jesus here makes a statement of the absolute certainty of his words. The best explanation is that Jesus' vision of the coming destruction of Jerusalem was crystal clear, even if his knowledge of the time of the Son of Man's return was hazy (see v. 32).

The OT speaks of the temporal nature of the present universe in contrast to the eternality of God (Ps 102:25 – 27) and his word (Isa 40:6 – 8; cf. 51:6), and there are Jewish parallels to the eternality of Torah (Bar 4:1; Philo, *Mos.* 2.14; *Deut. Rab.* 8.6; 10:1; Wis 18:4). Second Esdras 9:36 – 37 reads, "For we who have received the law and sinned will perish ... the law, however, does not perish but survives in its glory." In the Q saying of Matt 5:18//Luke 16:17 Jesus speaks in similar terms of the perpetuity of the law "until heaven and earth disappear."[26] That Jesus here identifies his words, like God's, as eternal bears witness to a high implicit Christology.

13:32 But concerning that day or hour, no one knows, neither the angels in heaven, nor the Son, but only the Father (Περὶ δὲ τῆς ἡμέρας ἐκείνης ἢ τῆς ὥρας οὐδεὶς οἶδεν, οὐδὲ οἱ ἄγγελοι ἐν οὐρανῷ οὐδὲ ὁ υἱός, εἰ μὴ ὁ πατήρ). If our analysis of the discourse as a whole is correct, Jesus now shifts from the certainty of Jerusalem's destruction within a generation (vv. 28 – 30) to the unknown time of the Son of Man's coming (vv. 32 – 37). The opening phrase, "but concerning" (περὶ δέ), signals this transition and a change of subject.[27] Though Jesus' statements are absolutely certain and trustworthy, the timing of their fulfillment has not

been revealed and so should not provoke undue speculation. The repeated theme of the paragraph (vv. 32 – 37) is watchfulness in light of the uncertainty of the Lord's return: "Watch!" (βλέπετε; v. 33), "Be vigilant!" (ἀγρυπνεῖτε; v. 33), "Be alert!" (γρηγορεῖτε; vv. 35, 37; cf. v. 34).

"That day" often has eschatological significance, referring to judgment day — the eschatological "day of the LORD" (Joel 3:18; Amos 8:3, 9, 13; 9:11; Obad 1:8; Mic 4:6; Zeph 1:9 – 10; 3:11, 16; Zech 9:16; Matt 7:22; Luke 10:12; 1 Cor 3:13; 2 Tim 1:12, 18; 4:8). This meaning is likely here in light of the close parallel between the parable of the return of the owner of the house that follows (vv. 34 – 36) and the return of the Son of Man (vv. 26 – 27). "That day" is the parousia, the day of Christ's return.

This is the only use of the absolute "the Son" (ὁ υἱός) by Jesus in Mark (but cf. 12:6). Though common in John's gospel, this kind of language occurs elsewhere in the Synoptics only in the "Q" text Matt 11:27//Luke 10:22, the so-called "meteorite from the Johannine sky,"[28] where Jesus expresses a relationship of unique intimacy with the Father. Its use here has caused some to question the authenticity of the saying.[29] Yet most commentators recognize that the church is unlikely to have created a saying in which Jesus expresses ignorance concerning the time of the end.[30] The criterion of embarrassment argues in its favor.[31]

Jesus implies the same thing in Acts 1:7, where he says, "It is not for you to know the times or dates the Father has set by his own authority." The

---

26. Both the OT and NT also affirm that the present heavens and earth are temporal and will one day give way to a new heaven and new earth (Job 14:12; Isa 65:17; 66:17; 2 Pet 3:10, 13; Rev 20:11; 21:1).

27. See Paul's use of this transition in 1 Cor 7:1, 25; 8:1; 12:1; 16:1, 12; 1 Thess 4:9; 5:1 (France, *Mark*, 541).

28. This designation comes from K. A. von Hase, *Geschichte Jesu* (2nd ed.; Leipzig: Breitkopf & Härtel, 1891), 422.

29. See, e.g., Bultmann, *History*, 123.

30. See, e.g., Taylor, *Mark*, 522; Cranfield, *Mark*, 410; Gundry, *Mark*, 793; Evans, *Mark 8:27 – 16:20*, 336.

31. Luke omits the sentence altogether, and some manuscripts of Matthew omit the phrase οὐδὲ ὁ υἱός (ℵ B D È *f*[13]). The omission is no doubt the result of embarrassment, either by Matthew himself (if the omission is his) or by later scribes.

Father, not the Son, has set the timetable for the future. Even with this reference to the Son's lack of knowledge, the passage points to a high implicit Christology. The threefold reference to the Father, Son, and angels indicates a heavenly hierarchy (and preexistence?), in which the Son is higher than the angels. This goes beyond a merely adoptionistic or messianic sonship to God. The passage also fits well the doctrine of the incarnation, which holds that the Son "empties" himself of the independent exercise of certain attributes (Phil 2:6 – 8), including omniscience.

13:33 Watch! Be vigilant! For you do not know when the time will come (βλέπετε, ἀγρυπνεῖτε· οὐκ οἴδατε γὰρ πότε ὁ καιρός ἐστιν). Mark picks up again the main theme of the discourse (13:5, 9, 23), which will be repeated again and again in the statements that follow (vv. 33, 34, 35, 37). "Watch" (βλέπω) and "be vigilant/keep awake" (ἀγρυπνέω) are basically synonymous here, the dual expression adding emphasis. The need for vigilance arises because of the uncertainty regarding the Son of Man's return. "Time" (καιρός) often carries the sense of a time or season appointed by God (Act 1:7; 17:26; Rom 3:26; 11:5; 13:11; Eph 1:10; 1 Tim 6:15; Titus 1:3; 1 Pet 1:3, 11; 4:17; Rev 1:3; 11:18; 22:10).

13:34 It is like a man journeying, leaving his home and giving each of his servants authority to do the work assigned to them; he commanded the doorkeeper to be alert (Ὡς ἄνθρωπος ἀπόδημος ἀφεὶς τὴν οἰκίαν αὐτοῦ καὶ δοὺς τοῖς δούλοις αὐτοῦ τὴν ἐξουσίαν ἑκάστῳ τὸ ἔργον αὐτοῦ καὶ τῷ θυρωρῷ ἐνετείλατο ἵνα γρηγορῇ). As the first "parable" or "lesson" (παραβολή) of the fig tree called for close observation for the *signs* of the destruction of Jerusalem (v. 28), so this second one calls for constant

vigilance in light of the *uncertainty* of the return of the Son of Man and the end of the age. In Mark's narrative the meaning of the analogy is clear. "The lord of the house" (v. 35) represents Jesus, the Son of Man, and both the servants and the doorkeeper represent his followers, who must remain faithful and vigilant.

The sentence is grammatically incomplete with the verb elided: "[It is] like a man journeying ..." (ὡς ἄνθρωπος ἀπόδημος). Two subordinate aorist participles ("leaving [ἀφεὶς] ... giving [δοὺς]") describe the man's actions with reference to his servants/slaves (δοῦλοι). He leaves and gives each a "charge" or "authority" (ἐξουσία), defined appositionally: "to each his task" (ἑκάστῳ τὸ ἔργον αὐτοῦ). This part of the scene recalls various stewardship parables: the parable of the talents (Matt 25:14 – 30), the minas (Luke 19:11 – 27), the ten virgins (Matt 25:1 – 13), and the good and wicked servants (Matt 24:45 – 51; Luke 12:42 – 48).

The main verb and the emphasis, however, lies with the doorkeeper (θυρωρός), who is "commanded" to stay alert. This is closest to Luke 12:35 – 48, where the master returns from a wedding feast to find his servants either awake or asleep. Doors were generally locked from the inside, so the doorkeeper of a wealthy household played a critical role in keeping out undesirable or dangerous visitors and letting in those who were welcome (John 10:3; Luke 12:36).[32]

13:35 – 36 Therefore, be alert! For you do not know when the lord of the house is coming, whether in the evening, or at midnight, or when the rooster crows, or at dawn. If he comes suddenly, he might find you sleeping (γρηγορεῖτε οὖν· οὐκ οἴδατε γὰρ πότε ὁ κύριος τῆς οἰκίας ἔρχεται, ἢ ὀψὲ ἢ μεσονύκτιον ἢ ἀλεκτοροφωνίας ἢ πρωΐ, μὴ

---

32. The LXX of 2 Sam 4:5 – 7 (cf. NLT) describes how Rekab and Baanah slipped by a sleeping doorkeeper (θυρωρός) to assassinate Ish-Bosheth and Mephibosheth (cf. Esth 2:21). See

also E. Lövestam, *Spiritual Wakefulness in the New Testament* (Lund: Gleerup, 1963), 80 – 82; Marcus, *Mark 9 – 16*, 919.

ἐλθὼν ἐξαίφνης εὕρῃ ὑμᾶς καθεύδοντας). The emphasis on the watchfulness of the doorkeeper becomes clear as Jesus repeats the verb and applies it to the disciples: "Therefore, be alert!" (γρηγορεῖτε οὖν). The reason for vigilance is the uncertainty concerning the time of the return of the master/lord (ὁ κύριος).

In a striking way, the disciples are now drawn into the parable ("be alert ... for *you* do not know"). They become the watchman awaiting the master's return.[33] Travel at night was unusual (but cf. Luke 11:5 – 6) because of the danger from bandits (cf. Matt 24:43; 1 Thess 5:2), reinforcing the point that the Son of Man will return at a most unexpected time. The fourfold description of time represents the Roman division of the night into four "watches" of three hours each (ὀψέ ["in the evening," 6 – 9 p.m.]; μεσονύκτιον ["midnight," 9 – 12 p.m.]; ἀλεκτοροφωνίας ["cockcrow/before dawn";

12 – 3 a.m.]; πρωΐ ["in the morning," 3 – 6 a.m.).[34] In typical Markan style, the emphatic repetition adds drama and color. Alertness is required so that the master will not "find you sleeping." Sleep is a metaphor for spiritual dullness elsewhere in the NT (Eph 5:14; 1 Thess 5:6 – 7). Ironically, the disciples will be caught sleeping shortly (14:32 – 39), despite Jesus' repeated exhortation to watchfulness (14:34, 37 – 38, 41).[35]

13:37 "What I say to you, I say to all, 'Be alert!'" (ὃ δὲ ὑμῖν λέγω πᾶσιν λέγω, γρηγορεῖτε). The final call for watchfulness intentionally widens the application beyond the four disciples (13:3) to "all" of Jesus' followers (cf. Luke 12:41). This agrees with our interpretation of the discourse as a whole, where the parable of the fig tree concerns the disciples and the destruction of Jerusalem, while the parable of the absent owner is for all future generations.

Theology in Application

The second part of Jesus' Olivet Discourse continues two important themes introduced in the first part, the danger of eschatological speculation and the call for watchfulness.

The Danger of Eschatological Speculation

Just as the disciples must not fall into the error of assuming that catastrophic events like wars, famines, and earthquakes are sure signs of the destruction of Jerusalem or the end of the age (13:7 – 8), so they must not seek to calculate the time of the end, since only the Father knows this (13:32). Instead, they must remain constantly faithful and vigilant, living lives of holiness.

33. France, *Mark*, 545, notes that R. J. Bauckham refers to this literary technique as "deparabolization" ("Synoptic Parousia Parables and the Apocalypse," *NTS* 23 [1976 – 1977]: 162 – 76, 167 – 69).

34. Taylor, *Mark*, 524.

35. Evans, *Mark 8:27 – 16:20*, 341. Some scholars have run with this parallel, claiming that the parable with its four watches previews the whole Passion Narrative that follows,

from the Last Supper to Gethsemane, to the trial before the Sanhedrin. See R. H. Lightfoot, "The Connection of Chapter Thirteen with the Passion Narrative," in *The Gospel Message of St. Mark* (Oxford: Oxford University Press, 1962), 48 – 59; Geddert, *Watchwords*, 89 – 103; A. Stock, *The Method and Message of Mark* (Wilmington, DE: Glazier, 1989), 346 – 47. For a critique of this view, see France, *Mark*, 546 n. 48.

The Call for Watchfulness

The themes of vigilance and spiritual preparation (cf. 14:34–38) are common throughout the NT. In addition to various stewardship parables in the Gospels (see comment on 13:34), Paul reminds the Thessalonians that as "children of the light" and "children of the day" they must not be spiritually asleep like others, but must be awake and "sober, putting on faith and love as a breastplate, and the hope of salvation as a helmet" (1 Thess 5:5–8). Vigilance is here linked to the practice of Christian virtues, such as faith, hope, and love.

Similarly, Paul encourages the Corinthians to "be alert" (γρηγορεῖτε), which is defined as standing firm in the faith, being strong and courageous, and doing everything in love (1 Cor 16:13–14). Preparation for Christ's return is not about calculating the date of Armageddon or linking world events to the fulfillment of biblical prophecies. It is about letting our spiritual lights shine by bearing the fruit of the Spirit (Matt 5:16; Gal 5:22).

The Triumphant Return of the Son of Man and the Vindication of His People

A third theological theme important to this passage is the return of the Son of Man "coming in the clouds with great power and glory" (13:26) and the gathering of "his chosen ones" (13:27). As noted above, this theme has its background in Dan 7:13–14, where one like "a son of man" (*bar ʾĕnāš* = a human being) approaches the Ancient of Days and receives all glory and sovereignty and an eternal kingdom. Though some identify Mark's reference with Jesus' ascension and exaltation to the right hand of God (see comments on 13:26), we have argued that for Mark this is the second coming of Christ, the consummation of the kingdom of God. The kingdom that was announced by Jesus (1:15), explained in parables (4:11, 26, 30), and offered in the present (10:14, 15, 23–25; 12:34), and will be consummated in the future (9:1, 47; 11:10; 14:25; 15:43), will arrive in its fullness when the Son of Man returns.

Throughout the NT, the second coming of Christ is identified with the closing act of human history. It is most commonly called his "coming" or "presence" (παρουσία; 1 Thess 2:19; 3:13; 4:13; 5:23; 2 Thess 2:1, 8; Jas 5:7–8; 2 Pet 3:4), but also his "revelation" (ἀποκάλυψις; 1 Cor 1:7; 2 Thess 1:6–7; 1 Pet 4:13) and "manifestation" (ἐπιφανεία; 1 Tim 6:14; 2 Tim 4:8; Titus 2:13–14; cf. Col 3:4; 1 John 2:28). Though its time is unknown (Matt 25:13; Mark 13:32; 1 Thess 5:2), Christ's return will be bodily and visible, the same in nature as his departure (Acts 1:11; cf. Matt 24:26–27; Luke 17:24; 1 Thess 4:16; Rev 1:7). It will deliver his people from suffering (2 Thess 1:6–7; 1 Pet 4:13) and will rescue them from wrath (1 Thess 1:10), bringing reward to those who have persevered (Matt 16:27; 2 Tim 4:8; Heb 9:28). It will be accompanied by the resurrection of those who have died "in Christ" (1 Cor 15:22–23;

1 Thess 4:16) into glorified, imperishable bodies (1 Cor 15:42 – 44, 51 – 54; Col 3:4) and will initiate the permanent dwelling of Christ with this people (John 14:2 – 3; 1 Thess 4:17; 2 Thess 2:1).

In the book of Revelation the return of Christ is marked by a series of events bringing the present age to its end: the triumphant return of Christ (Rev 19:11), the judgment of the wicked (19:15 – 20:15; cf. Matt 13:40 – 41; 25:31 – 46), the vindication of the righteous (Rev 20:4 – 6), the resurrection of the dead (20:4 – 6, 12 – 13), a thousand-year reign of Christ (20:4 – 7), and a new heaven and new earth (Rev 21 – 22). Mark's concern in the present passage, however, is not with these details, but with the certainty of the coming revelation of the Son of Man (13:26) and the vindication of his faithful followers (13:27).

Sadly, the second coming of Christ has been the source of endless debate among Christians, concerning its nature, timing, and sequence. Will it be a single event or divided into two stages (pre-, mid-, or post-tribulational)? Will it be followed by a literal millennium of a thousand years, or by the immediate establishment of the new heavens and earth? While such questions are not without merit and are worth investigating, they should not be allowed to hinder Christian fellowship. These were not the concerns of the biblical authors, who viewed the return of Christ as the great and glorious hope for all believers. As Paul so eloquently affirms, the promise of Christ's return reminds us that all of life's difficulties will one day be over, when we receive imperishable, glorified bodies and reunite with those "in Christ" we have lost along the way (1 Cor 15:51 – 54; 1 Thess 4:13 – 17). His conclusion: "Therefore encourage one another with these words" (1 Thess 4:18).

54

Mark 14:1 – 11

Introduction to the Passion Narrative

The plot to arrest Jesus and the anointing at Bethany mark the beginning of the passion and resurrection narratives, which comprise the remainder of Mark's gospel. This large section may be divided into three parts: the events leading to Jesus' arrest (14:1 – 42); his arrest, trial, crucifixion, and burial (14:53 – 15:47); and the announcement of the resurrection (16:1 – 8). The first contains the anointing of Jesus at Bethany (14:3 – 9) "sandwiched" between the plot against Jesus and Judas's agreed-upon betrayal (14:1 – 2, 10 – 11), the Last Supper narrative (14:12 – 26), the prediction of Peter's denial (14:27 – 31), and Jesus' prayer in Gethsemane (14:32 – 42). The second includes the betrayal and arrest (14:43 – 52), Jesus' trial before the Sanhedrin (14:53 – 65), Peter's denial (14:66 – 72), Jesus' trial before Pilate (15:1 – 15), the mocking of Jesus (15:16 – 20), Jesus' crucifixion (15:21 – 32), death (15:33 – 41), and burial (15:42 – 47). The last part includes the women's visit to the tomb and the announcement of the resurrection (16:1 – 8), which brings Mark's gospel to its conclusion.

The Passion Narrative is unique. Unlike the rest of the gospel, which form and redaction critics view as Mark's compilation of many short, semi-independent traditions (pericopes) more or less loosely connected to their narrative context, the Passion Narrative is generally viewed as having been a continuous narrative from the beginning.[1] As central to the proclamation of the gospel (the *kerygma*; 1 Cor 15:1 – 4), the Passion Narrative was likely the earliest part of the Jesus story put into writing.[2]

If one theme holds the narrative together, it is the sovereign purpose of God, who is accomplishing his saving work through his servant, Jesus the Messiah. Though Jesus is rejected, betrayed, abandoned, condemned, and crucified, he remains in control, faithfully following God's purpose. He will be vindicated in the end.

This theme runs throughout the Passion Narrative. Jesus predicts that one of his disciples will betray him (14:18), but then affirms that this is God's scripturally

---

1. Evans, *Mark 8:27 – 16:20*, 352, notes that "form critics have long recognized the cohesion of this material" (citing Dibelius, *From Tradition to Gospel*, 178 – 217; Bultmann, *History*, 262 – 84; Taylor, *Formation*, 44 – 62; and others).

2. For bibliography and a brief summary of diverse views, see Evans, *Mark 8:27 – 16:20*, 347 – 53.

ordained plan (14:21, 49) to inaugurate the new covenant in his blood (14:22–24). Though Scripture predicted that the shepherd would be struck and the sheep scattered (14:27; Zech 13:7), Jesus affirms with confidence that he will rise again and go before his disciples into Galilee (Mark 14:28; 16:7). When Judas arrives with a mob to arrest him, Jesus rebukes them for their duplicity but then affirms that in all this, "the Scriptures must be fulfilled" (14:48–49). Though facing his coming death with dread and agony, Jesus faithfully asserts, "Not what I want, but what you want" (14:36), and willingly goes to the cross.

At his trial before the Sanhedrin, false charges are brought against him (14:55–59), but Jesus confidently asserts that he is the Messiah and Son of God (14:61–62) and that they will see the Son of Man vindicated at the right hand of God and coming on the clouds of heaven (14:62). Though Jesus dies in agony and despair, the torn curtain of the temple and the cry of the centurion remind the reader, "Truly this man was the Son of God!" (15:39). The ultimate vindication comes with the angelic announcement that the tomb could not hold him: "He has risen! He is not here" (16:6). Despite all appearances, the dreadful events about to unfold in Jerusalem represent the sovereign purposes of God, the good news of salvation, and the inauguration of the kingdom of God.

Literary Context

The account of the plot to kill Jesus (14:1–2, 10–11) contains the first specific chronological reference since Jesus entered Jerusalem (11:1). We are now "two days away" from the Passover and Feast of Unleavened Bread. The present episode is connected to the previous narrative as a continuation of the plots against Jesus, which began already in 3:6 but intensified after Jesus' arrival in Jerusalem and his clearing of the temple (11:18; 12:12). The anointing narrative that follows (14:3–9) is geographically linked to the previous narrative with its reference to Bethany (11:2, 11–12).

III. The Suffering Way of the Messiah (8:22 – 15:47)
   A. Revelation of the Messiah's Suffering (8:22 – 10:52)
   B. The Messiah Confronts Jerusalem (11:1 – 13:37)
➡   **C. The Passion of the Messiah in Jerusalem (14:1 – 15:47)**
     1. The Plot to Arrest Jesus (14:1 – 2)
     2. The Anointing at Bethany (14:3 – 9)
     3. The Betrayal by Judas (14:10 – 11)
     4. The Last Supper (14:12 – 26)

Main Idea

In one of Mark's famous intercalations (see Structure), the anointing of Jesus by an unnamed woman is framed on either side by a renewed plot to destroy Jesus. The reverential love and honor offered to Jesus by the woman stands in stark contrast to the evil plotting of Israel's religious leadership to destroy him.

Translation

Mark 14:1 – 11

1a	Setting (temporal)	Now **the Passover and the Festival of Unleavened Bread were two days away**,
b	Action/Plot	and **the ruling priests and experts in the law were seeking some treacherous ↵ way to arrest him and kill him.**
2a	Condition of 1b	For **they were saying,**
b		*"Not during the Festival, or there might be a riot by the people."*
3a	Setting (spatial)	**He was in Bethany at the home of Simon the Leper.**
b	setting (temporal & social)	While he was dining,
c	Action	**a woman came with an alabaster flask of expensive perfume made of pure nard.**
d	action	Breaking open the alabaster flask,
e	Action	**she poured it on his head.**
4a	Response to 3c-e	But **some of those present were saying indignantly to each another,**
b	rhetorical question/rebuke	*"Why this waste of expensive perfume?*
5a	assertion/rebuke	*This perfume could have been sold for more than three hundred denarii and*
b		*given to the poor."*
c	Rebuke/Response to 3c-e	And **they rebuked her sternly.**
6a	Response to 4 – 5	But **Jesus said,**
b	command	*"Leave her alone.*
c	rhetorical question	*Why are you bothering her?*
d	affirmation	*She has done a beautiful thing for me.*
7a	assertion	*For you always have the poor with you,* [Deut 15:11]
b	setting of 7c	*and whenever you wish*
c	assertion	*you can do good to them.*
d	contrast with 7a-c	*But me you will not always have.*
8a	affirmation	*She did what she could.*
b	explanation	*She has anointed my body in preparation for burial.*
9a	veracity statement	*Truly I say to you,*
b	setting of 9c	*whenever the gospel is preached in all the world,*
c	prophecy	*what she has done will be told,*
		in memory of her."
10a	Character entrance	Then **Judas Iscariot,**
b	character description	one of the Twelve,
c	Action	**went to the ruling priests to betray him to them.**

11a	setting (temporal)	When they heard this,
b	Response to 10	**they were glad and promised to give him money.**
c	Response to 11b	So **he began looking for an opportunity to betray him.**

Structure

These two episodes represent one of Mark's "sandwiches," or intercalations, where one episode is framed by another and the two mutually interpret one another (cf. 3:20 – 35; 5:21 – 43; 6:7 – 30; 11:12 – 25; see Introduction to Mark: Literary Features). The plot to arrest Jesus (14:1 – 2, 10 – 11) is interrupted by the anointing account (14:3 – 9), which stands in thematic contrast to it (see Main Idea, above). The plot to kill Jesus moves from general to specific, with the general plan to arrest Jesus (v. 2) coming to fruition in the betrayal by Judas (v. 10). The anointing account plays out in four stages: the setting in the home of Simon (v. 3a), the woman's shocking actions (v. 3b-e), the indignant response of those present (vv. 4 – 5), and Jesus' response and commendation of the woman (vv. 6 – 9).

Similar anointings appear in all the Gospels, and scholars puzzle over their relationship. The accounts in Matthew and Mark clearly represent the same event, appearing at the same point in the narrative and with nearly identical descriptions. It is their relationship to the accounts of Luke and John that is debated. Consider the following comparison:

GOSPEL ACCOUNTS OF ANOINTING

MATTHEW 26:6 – 13; MARK 14:3 – 9	JOHN 12:18	LUKE 7:36 – 50
Presumably two days before Passover, though this may refer to the plot against Jesus (Matt 26:2; Mark 14:1)	Six days before Passover	Not specified
Occurs in Bethany	Occurs in Bethany	Presumably Galilee
At the home of Simon the Leper	No home ownership named; though Lazarus is present and Martha his sister serves	At the home of Simon, a Pharisee
An unnamed woman	Mary, sister of Martha and Lazarus	A unnamed sinful woman
An alabaster flask of expensive perfume (Mark adds, "of pure nard")	A pound of expensive perfume of pure nard	An alabaster flask of perfume
She pours it on Jesus' head.	She anoints Jesus' feet and wipes his feet with her hair.	She wets Jesus' feet with her tears, wipes them with her hair, kisses them, and anoints his feet with perfume.
The disciples object (Matthew); "some" of those present object (Mark).	Judas objects.	The Pharisee objects.

Continued on next page.

MATTHEW 26:6 – 13; MARK 14:3 – 9	JOHN 12:18	LUKE 7:36 – 50
The objection is that the perfume could have been sold for a large sum (Mark: 300 denarii) and given to the poor.	The objection is that the perfume could have been sold and given to the poor.	The objection is that if this man were a prophet, he would know the kind of woman who is touching him.
Jesus responds: (1) let her be; (2) she has done something beautiful; (3) you always have the poor, but you will not always have me; (4) she has anointed my body for burial; (5) wherever the gospel is proclaimed, she will be memorialized.	Jesus responds: (1) let her be; (2) let her keep it for the day of my burial; (3) you always have the poor, but you will not always have me.	Jesus responds with (1) the parable of the two debtors; (2) a contrast between the woman's actions and Simon's lack of hospitality; (3) a pronouncement of forgiveness; (4) a pronouncement of saving faith .
No response by others is recorded.	No response by others is recorded.	The people respond, "Who is this who even forgives sins?"

Close study of the chart suggests that the accounts of Matthew//Mark and John are likely the same event. Both occur during Passion Week and both are followed by basically the same objection by the same people (disciples) and essentially the same response by Jesus. The discrepancy in chronology may be due to the fact that Mark's "two days" refers to the plot against Jesus rather than the anointing itself. Mark (followed by Matthew) moves the episode forward to juxtapose (intercalate) it with the plot against Jesus. It is not surprising that John names the three siblings in light of his prior interest in the family (John 11). The home could be Simon's (a leper healed by Jesus?), with Lazarus as a dinner guest and his sisters helping to serve. Others have suggested that Simon could be the father of the three.

While these Mark/Matthew/John harmonizations are plausible, Luke's account is very different. It occurs in an entirely different setting in the gospel (in Galilee early in Jesus' ministry), concerns a notorious sinner (surely not Mary of Bethany), and is followed by a different objection and a different response by Jesus. The incidental agreement in the name Simon is not surprising, since this was a common Jewish name. Two separate anointings should not surprise us, since this was a common cultural sign of honor and hospitality. It is even possible that the story of the Galilean anointing was the impetus for Mary's actions.

Exegetical Outline

➡ **1. The Plot to Arrest Jesus (14:1 – 2)**

2. The Anointing at Bethany (14:3 – 9)

   a. The context: the home of Simon (14:3a)

   b. The woman's actions (14:3b)

   c. The response of those present (14:4 – 5)

   d. Jesus' answer (14:6 – 9)

      i. Command to leave her alone (14:6)

      ii. Saying about the poor (14:7)

iii. Anointing for burial (14:8)

iv. The woman's actions to be remembered (14:9)

3. The Betrayal by Judas (14:10 – 11)

a. Judas approaches the ruling priests (14:10)

b. The agreement and plot against Jesus (14:11)

Explanation of the Text

14:1 – 2 Now the Passover and the Festival of Unleavened Bread were two days away, and the ruling priests and experts in the law were seeking some treacherous way to arrest him and kill him. For they were saying, "Not during the Festival, or there might be a riot by the people." (Ἦν δὲ τὸ πάσχα καὶ τὰ ἄζυμα μετὰ δύο ἡμέρας. καὶ ἐζήτουν οἱ ἀρχιερεῖς καὶ οἱ γραμματεῖς πῶς αὐτὸν ἐν δόλῳ κρατήσαντες ἀποκτείνωσιν· ἔλεγον γάρ· μὴ ἐν τῇ ἑορτῇ, μήποτε ἔσται θόρυβος τοῦ λαοῦ). This is the first reference in Mark to a specific time of year or date on the Jewish calendar (unlike in John, whose narrative is structured around Jesus' visits to Jerusalem for the festivals).

There is only one Passover in Mark, the one where Jesus offers himself "as a ransom for many" (10:45). The Jewish Passover (Gk. τὸ πάσχα; Heb. *pesaḥ*) commemorated the exodus from Egypt, and more specifically the tenth plague, in which the angel of death killed the firstborn sons of the Egyptians but "passed over" (*pāsaḥ*) the homes of the Hebrews on which the blood of the Passover lamb had been smeared (Exod 12:1 – 13, 23, 27). The (Festival of) Unleavened Bread (Heb. *maṣṣôt*; Gk. ἄζυμα) began with Passover and continued for seven days, Nisan 15 – 21. Its name comes from the fact that Israel was commanded to remove leaven from their homes and eat only unleavened bread during the festival (Exod 12:15 – 20; 23:15;

34:18; Num 28:17; Deut 16:1 – 8). The prohibition on leaven is associated in Exod 12:39 with the urgency with which the Israelites left Egypt. Leaven also came to signify the permeating power of sin, and so its removal was an act of purification (see comments on 8:15).

Passover occurred on the fifteenth day of the Jewish month of Nisan (April/May). Since the Jewish day began in the evening, Passover lambs were sacrificed on Nisan 14 and the Passover began that evening, at sundown. In Mark's narrative, the Last Supper is likely a Passover meal and occurred on Thursday night. Mark here says that Passover and Unleavened Bread were coming "after two days" (μετὰ δύο ἡμέρας), an ambiguous expression that could mean either "on the second day"[3] (= the next day) or "after two days" (i.e., on the third day). This event would therefore have occurred on Tuesday or Wednesday of Passion Week (for various possible chronologies, see "In Depth: The Chronology and Significance of the Last Supper," pp. 617 – 18).

Plots against Jesus by the religious and secular leaders began during his Galilean ministry (3:6; Pharisees and Herodians) but have intensified since his arrival in Jerusalem. His clearing of the temple provoked a plot on his life (11:18), and the parable of the tenant farmers resulted in plans to arrest him (12:12). His opponents are the three groups that made up the Sanhedrin: the "ruling

---

3. This would be on the analogy of "after three days" (8:31; 9:31; 10:34), which with reference to the resurrection means "on the third day" (Friday evening through Sunday morning).

priests" (ἀρχιερεῖς; see comments on 8:31), the "scribes" or "experts in the law" (γραμματεῖς; 1:22) and the "elders" (πρεσβύτεροι; see comments on 8:31), the aristocratic lay leaders of Jerusalem. Now this opposition is renewed by the ruling priests and experts in the law. Though wishing to kill Jesus, they know they must arrest him "treacherously" or "secretly" (ἐν δόλῳ; "with deceit") because of his popularity with the people (cf. 11:18; 12:12, 37).

Passover was one of the three great pilgrim festivals of Judaism (together with Tabernacles and Pentecost), and the city's population doubled or tripled during these times as visitors streamed to the city from throughout the Mediterranean world.[4] The Passover theme of redemption and emancipation provoked strong nationalist feelings, making the Roman authorities nervous. As Roman governor, Pilate would travel to Jerusalem from Caesarea during this time to keep a wary eye on the crowds. Various popular revolts had in the past started during the festival, and the religious leaders fear that any action against Jesus could provoke a "riot" (θόρυβος), bringing in the Roman legions and threatening their own authority.[5] They resolve not to act until after the festival, when the crowds have gone home. Their plans will change, however, when Judas offers them an opportunity too good to pass up (14:10 – 11).

14:3 He was in Bethany at the home of Simon the Leper. While he was dining, a woman came with an alabaster flask of expensive perfume made of pure nard. Breaking open the alabaster flask, she poured it on his head (Καὶ ὄντος αὐτοῦ ἐν Βηθανίᾳ ἐν τῇ οἰκίᾳ Σίμωνος τοῦ λεπροῦ, κατακειμένου αὐτοῦ ἦλθεν γυνὴ ἔχουσα ἀλάβαστρον μύρου νάρδου πιστικῆς πολυτελοῦς, συντρίψασα τὴν ἀλάβαστρον κατέχεεν αὐτοῦ τῆς κεφαλῆς). Mark interrupts the account of the plot against Jesus to describe a remarkable act of devotion (see Structure, above).

Jesus is in Bethany, the village where he has presumably been returning each evening while visiting Jerusalem (11:11 – 12). It was located on the eastern slope of the Mount of Olives about two miles from Jerusalem. Jesus is "reclining" (κατάκειμαι), a verb commonly used for dining at a banquet or dinner party (cf. 2:15; Luke 7:37).[6] His host is Simon "the Leper" (ὁ λεπρός; on leprosy see comments on 1:40). Simon is probably a *former* leper, since his illness would have rendered him unclean and unable to host such a party. Perhaps he had been healed by Jesus. As noted above (see Structure), Mark's account is probably unrelated to the anointing in Luke 7:36 – 50, so this Simon should be distinguished from the Pharisee with that name. Simon was a common name in first-century Palestine.

The woman is not identified by Mark. If this is the same episode as that recorded in John 12:1 – 8 (as suggested above), she is Mary of Bethany, and her siblings Lazarus and Martha are present at the dinner. But Mark is not interested in this information, and to introduce it would be alien to his narrative purpose. What is important for him is the woman's devotion and sacrifice.

An "alabaster flask" was made of a soft calcite stone and was commonly used for the finest

4. Just how many people lived in Jerusalem in the first century is a matter of significant debate. Jeremias, *Jerusalem*, 84, posited a mere 20,000 in the city and 5,000 – 10,000 in the surrounding region. Others claim between 60,000 and 120,000, swelling to between 85,000 and 300,000 during festival times. See Wolfgang Reinhardt, "The Population Size of Jerusalem and the Numerical Growth of the Jerusalem Church," in *The Book of Acts in Its First Century Setting*; vol. 4: *Palestinian Setting* (ed. R. Bauckham; Grand Rapids: Eerdmans, 1995), 237 – 65. Josephus's numbers are almost certainly wildly exaggerated, since he claims three million visitors during Passover (*J.W.* 2.14.3 §280; 6.9.3 §§423 – 427).

5. For an example, see Josephus, *Ant.* 17.9.3 §§213 – 223.

6. κατακειμένου αὐτοῦ is a genitive absolute ("while he was dining"), used by Mark because the main subject of the sentence is the woman, not Jesus.

perfumes and ointments.[7] "Perfume" (μύρον) is a general term for perfume or ointment, and Mark clarifies that this perfume is made of pure "nard" and "very expensive." Nard is a perennial herb of the Valerian family, native to India (cf. Song 1:12; 4:13).[8] Just how expensive we are told in v. 5, where those present claim it is worth more than three hundred denarii, about a year's wages for a day laborer. Breaking the jar may have been the only way to reach the content[9] or, more likely, is intended as a dramatic gesture to show the complete outpouring of the costly perfume.[10] Nothing is held back.

Pouring oil on someone's head could be done for various purposes, including the consecration or installment of a priest or king (Exod 29:7; Lev 8:12; 21:10; 1 Sam 10:1; 2 Kgs 9:3, 6) or as a sign of devotion and/or hospitality (Pss 23:5; 133:2; 141:5; Luke 7:46).[11] Some have suggested that the woman here performs a messianic anointing,[12] but this is unlikely. (1) One would expect the verb "anoint" (χρίω), as in the Lord's "Anointed" or Messiah (χριστός). Mark, however, uses two different verbs, one meaning "poured" (καταχέω; v. 3) and the other "to anoint with myrrh/perfume" (μυρίζω; v. 8). (2) The woman uses perfume, not olive oil, which was typical for a royal or priestly anointing. (3) Royal or priestly anointing was performed by an authorized individual of recognized authority, not a commoner. (4) Jesus' reception of the Spirit at his baptism is identified by Luke as his messianic anointing (Luke 3:21 – 22; 4:1, 14, 18). This is likely Mark's understanding as well. (5) Jesus himself

identifies this as an anointing for his burial (v. 8), not as a messianic installation.

14:4 – 5 But some of those present were saying indignantly to each another, "Why this waste of expensive perfume? This perfume could have been sold for more than three hundred denarii and given to the poor." And they rebuked her sternly (ἦσαν δέ τινες ἀγανακτοῦντες πρὸς ἑαυτούς· εἰς τί ἡ ἀπώλεια αὕτη τοῦ μύρου γέγονεν; ἠδύνατο γὰρ τοῦτο τὸ μύρον πραθῆναι ἐπάνω δηναρίων τριακοσίων καὶ δοθῆναι τοῖς πτωχοῖς· καὶ ἐνεβριμῶντο αὐτῇ). The woman's actions are over-the-top extravagant, resulting in criticism from those present. Matthew 26:8 identifies these as "the disciples," and John 12:4 – 6 says it was Judas Iscariot (adding that Judas's real interest was not in the poor, but in pilfering from the money bag, which is why he was the treasurer). Mark, however, refers generally to "some" (τινες) of those present.

The language used is strong. They "are indignant" (ἀγανακτέω) and "rebuke" (ἐμβριμάομαι) her sternly. This verb of indignation is used of Jesus when the disciples prevent children from coming to him (10:14), and when the ten disciples grumble at James and John for seeking to usurp the chief seats in the kingdom (10:41). The imperfect tense "were rebuking" (ἐνεβριμῶντο) suggests an ongoing or repeated action. They berate her.

The reason for the rebuke is the "waste"[13] (ἀπώλεια) of the perfume, since it could have been sold for more than three hundred denarii and the money given to the poor. Since a denarius was

---

7. Pliny the Elder wrote that "unguents keep best in containers of alabaster" (*Nat.* 13.3.19); BDAG, 40.

8. BDAG, 666.

9. BDAG, 40.

10. So Gundry, *Mark*, 802, 813, who claims that the container could have been resealed, but that "breaking the flask makes it henceforth unusable and therefore dramatizes the completeness of the outpouring: not a drop is held back" (802).

11. Collins, *Mark*, 642, suggests that the woman's gesture

represents the custom of anointing the head in preparation for a joyous feast (Amos 6:6 LXX; Ps 23:5; Josephus, *Ant.* 19.4.1 §239).

12. So Cranfield, *Mark*, 415; J. K. Elliott, "The Anointing of Jesus," *ExpTim* 85 (1974): 105 – 7; Hooker, *Mark*, 328, 330; Garland, *Mark*, 516; Evans, *Mark 8:27 – 16:20*, 360.

13. "Waste" is a better translation of ἀπώλεια than the more common "destruction," since the perfume is not destroyed, but lost to other uses (Stein, *Mark*, 633).

worth roughly a day's wages for a laborer, the NIV renders "more than a year's wages" (cf. NLT). The reference to gifts for the poor may be significant in this context, not only because almsgiving was an important sign of piety in Judaism,[14] but because it was a custom to give gifts to the poor on the evening of Passover.[15]

14:6 But Jesus said, "Leave her alone. Why are you bothering her? She has done a beautiful thing for me." (ὁ δὲ Ἰησοῦς εἶπεν· ἄφετε αὐτήν· τί αὐτῇ κόπους παρέχετε; καλὸν ἔργον ἠργάσατο ἐν ἐμοί). Jesus returns the rebuke, calling on the woman's accusers to stop criticizing her. She has done something "beautiful," "good," or "noble" (καλός) for him.

Following the lead of F. W. Danker, Lane claims that the anointing has as its background Psalm 41, and that Jesus is being portrayed as a poor sufferer who, though betrayed by his closest friend, is confident that God will vindicate him. The woman recognizes his poverty and reaches out to meet the needs of this poor sufferer.[16] This interpretation, however, seems unlikely. In the following line, Jesus will set her actions in contrast to helping the poor.[17] Jesus has a greater vision in mind.

14:7 For you always have the poor with you, and whenever you wish you can do good to them. But me you will not always have (πάντοτε γὰρ τοὺς πτωχοὺς ἔχετε μεθ᾽ ἑαυτῶν καὶ ὅταν θέλητε δύνασθε αὐτοῖς εὖ ποιῆσαι, ἐμὲ δὲ οὐ πάντοτε ἔχετε). This statement is surprising — even shocking — in light of Jesus' strong concern for the poor elsewhere in the gospel tradition (Matt 5:3; 6:2–4; 19:21; Luke 6:20, 36–38; 19:8, 19–31; 21:1–4; John 13:29). This is clearly not a denial of the daily obligation of God's people to help the poor. Indeed, the phrase,

"You always have the poor with you" echoes Deut 15:11, which is a call for generosity toward the poor and needy among the Israelites. Jesus' point is, "You can (and should) help the poor anytime at all ... *but something more important is at work here.*"

This is a striking reminder of the uniqueness and significance of Jesus' coming, marking the arrival of eschatological salvation. Jesus has not come simply to heal the sick and feed the poor. He is here to defeat sin, Satan, and death, to inaugurate the kingdom of God. Poverty is a symptom of a much greater problem — the fallenness of humanity and all creation. Jesus' statement recalls 2:18–20, where he is asked why his disciples don't fast. His answer is that no one can fast during a wedding banquet, when the bridegroom is present. His coming, representing the inauguration of God's final salvation, should be a time of extravagant joy and celebration, not solemn mourning. Lavish acts like the pouring out of this expensive perfume signify the extravagance of God's grace at the dawn of eschatological salvation.

14:8 She did what she could. She has anointed my body in preparation for burial (ὃ ἔσχεν ἐποίησεν· προέλαβεν μυρίσαι τὸ σῶμά μου εἰς τὸν ἐνταφιασμόν). Jesus now defines the woman's action. "She did what she could" (ὃ ἔσχεν ἐποίησεν; lit., "what she had she did") does not mean her actions were small (i.e., "this is the most she could do"). Rather, it indicates the extraordinary nature of her sacrifice. She gave everything she had — a momentous sacrifice. The passage parallels the widow of 12:41–44, who gave out of her poverty, "all that she had to live on." Both women are models of generosity and self-sacrificial service and stand in stark contrast, respectively, to the greedy and

14. See Jeremias, *Jerusalem*, 126–34; Tob 12:8.

15. John 13:29; *m. Pesaḥ* 9:11–10:1; Jeremias, *Eucharistic Words*, 54; Lane, *Mark*, 493; Gundry, *Mark*, 811.

16. Lane, *Mark*, 493–94; F. W. Danker, "The Literary Unity of Mark 14,1–25," *JBL* 85 (1966): 467–72.

17. Evans, *Mark 8:27–16:20*, 361.

exploitative scribes (12:38–40) and the scheming religious leaders (14:1–2, 10–11).[18]

Jesus interprets her actions as an anointing for burial (not a messianic anointing; see comments on v. 3). Jews did not embalm; they anointed bodies with perfume and spices as a sign of love and honor and to cover the stench of decay (see comments on 16:1; *m. Šabb.* 23:5). It is unlikely that the woman did this intentionally or was aware of Jesus' impending death. Hers is an act of love and devotion. But Jesus' mind is on his coming fate, and he sees in the woman's actions an expression of reverence in preparation for his burial.[19] We have here another (implicit) passion prediction (8:31; 9:31; 10:33–34; cf. 10:45; 12:7–8; 14:8, 18–21, 24).

14:9 "Truly I say to you, whenever the gospel is preached in all the world, what she has done will be told, in memory of her." (ἀμὴν δὲ λέγω ὑμῖν, ὅπου ἐὰν κηρυχθῇ τὸ εὐαγγέλιον εἰς ὅλον τὸν κόσμον, καὶ ὃ ἐποίησεν αὕτη λαληθήσεται εἰς μνημόσυνον αὐτῆς). The importance of Jesus' final pronouncement is reinforced by his solemn introductory formula, "Truly I say to you" (13x in Mark).[20] As in 13:10, Jesus envisions the worldwide proclamation of the gospel, which, according to this passage, will include the stories of Jesus now contained in our Gospels (cf. John 14:26).[21]

Significantly, it is not the woman's name that will be remembered (Mark does not give it!), but her act of devotion. As with the nature of the actions themselves, all the glory goes to God.

14:10–11 Then Judas Iscariot, one of the Twelve, went to the ruling priests to betray him to them. When they heard this, they were glad and promised to give him money. So he began looking for an opportunity to betray him (Καὶ Ἰούδας Ἰσκαριὼθ ὁ εἷς τῶν δώδεκα ἀπῆλθεν πρὸς τοὺς ἀρχιερεῖς ἵνα αὐτὸν παραδοῖ αὐτοῖς. οἱ δὲ ἀκούσαντες ἐχάρησαν καὶ ἐπηγγείλαντο αὐτῷ ἀργύριον δοῦναι. καὶ ἐζήτει πῶς αὐτὸν εὐκαίρως παραδοῖ). Mark now returns to the plot introduced in vv. 1–2, concluding the Markan "sandwich." Though the religious leaders intended to wait until after the Passover to move against Jesus, an opportunity now arises that they cannot pass up. The identification of Judas Iscariot (see comments on 3:18–19) as "one of the Twelve" (cf. 14:20) shows that the betrayal comes from Jesus' closest followers, magnifying the crime. It is he who initiates the actions, going to the priestly leadership with the goal of betraying or "handing over" (παραδίδωμι) Jesus to them.

Why did Judas betray Jesus? This has been the subject of endless speculation. Mark does not say, but the other Gospels suggest greed (Matt 26:15;

18. Gray, *The Temple in the Gospel of Mark*, 8–10, 100–101, suggests an even more significant structural relationship between these two accounts. His thesis is that the temple dominates Mark's narrative from chs. 11–15 and Jesus is presented by Mark as the temple's replacement. Chs. 11–12 speak of the end of the temple while chs. 14–15 speak of the end of Jesus, with ch. 13 standing in between as a narrative link. The account of the widow's gift for the temple (12:41–44) prepares for its destruction in the same way that the woman's anointing of Jesus (14:3–9) prepares for his destruction. The two also form a kind of intercalation around the Olivet Discourse and its focus on the destruction of Jerusalem. In the same way, the preparation for Jesus' entrance to Jerusalem (11:1–7) has striking parallels with the preparation to the Passover (14:12–16), each introducing the two halves of Mark 11–15.

19. Taylor, *Mark*, 533; France, *Mark*, 550, 554–56; Stein, *Mark*, 635; Boring, *Mark*, 384.

20. See 3:28; 8:12; 9:1, 41; 10:15, 29; 11:23; 12:43; 13:30; 14:9, 18, 25, 30; see comments on 3:28–30.

21. Many commentators question the authenticity of a saying that so explicitly refers to the church's worldwide missionary outreach, since (they say) Jesus expected the kingdom in the near future (Bultmann, *History*, 36–37; Hooker, *Mark*, 330). J. Jeremias, "Markus 14.9," *ZNW* 44 (1952–53): 103–7, avoids this conclusion by claiming Jesus' original words referred to her vindication at the final judgment. But, as Cranfield, *Mark*, 400, points out, the idea of a universal mission to the Gentiles is part of OT eschatology (Ps 46; Isa 42:6; 49:6, 12) and so should not be surprising on Jesus' lips.

John 12:6) and/or satanic inspiration (Luke 22:3; John 13:2, 27). Some modern scholars have postulated that Judas had Zealot tendencies and expected Jesus to overthrow the Roman overlords and establish an Israelite theocracy. When Jesus failed to act and even suggested the legitimacy of Roman taxation (Mark 12:13 – 17), Judas became disillusioned, turning Jesus over to the authorities. While possible, this motivation is speculative, with little evidence from the narrative itself.

Even less likely is the motivation suggested by the recently discovered Gnostic *Gospel of Judas* (c. mid-second century AD).[22] The text presents Judas as a protagonist who is acting on Jesus' orders. He alone among the disciples understands that Jesus will achieve true release by escaping from the physical shell of his mortal body and returning to the realm of pure spirit. This dualistic explanation surely arose from the imagination of second-century Gnostics rather than from the historical record.

What did Judas provide to the religious leaders? The narrative that follows suggests that he revealed the time and place where Jesus could be seized away from the crowds (14:11, 48 – 49; cf. Luke 22:6; John 18:2). Judas seeks "how" (πῶς) to deliver Jesus "opportunely" (εὐκαίρως; 14:11). Some have proposed that the betrayal also included evidence that Jesus claimed to be the Messiah and perhaps that he threatened the temple, since these are accusations made against Jesus at his trial (14:57 – 61).[23] Hooker thinks this is unlikely, since Judas plays no role in the trial scene.[24] In his remorse, however, Judas may have refused to participate in the trial, or he may have already committed suicide.[25]

Mark does not say why Judas betrayed Jesus or what information he passed on to the leaders. What is important to him is that while one of Jesus' closest followers — "one of the Twelve" (cf. 14:20) — betrayed Jesus, this was all along part of God's purpose and plan (8:31; 9:31; 10:32 – 34; 14:18 – 21, 49). While Matthew says the price of betrayal was thirty pieces of silver (Matt 26:15; 27:3, 9; cf. Zech 11:12 – 13), Mark refers simply to an undisclosed amount of "money" (lit., "silver"; ἀργύριον).

Theology in Application

Two Responses to Jesus

The gospel represents a call to decision, and Mark's "sandwich" structure highlights the contrast between the scheming of Judas and the religious leaders and the love and devotion of the woman.[26] While she acts out of sacrificial love for him, the religious leaders act out of self-interest, seeking to destroy the one they view as a threat to their authority. She acts with humility; they demonstrate pride. She has the mind-set of the kingdom; they are building their own personal empires. As elsewhere in Mark, an "outsider" — in this case, a woman of no social standing — comprehends

---

22. Rodolphe Kasser et al., *The Gospel of Judas* (Washington, DC: National Geographic, 2008); Simon Gathercole, *The Gospel of Judas: Rewriting Early Christianity* (Oxford: Oxford University Press, 2007); Nicholas Perrin, *The Judas Gospel* (Downers Grove, IL: InterVarsity Press, 2006).

23. Sanders, *Jesus and Judaism*, 309; Evans, *Mark 8:27 – 16:20*, 365; France, *Mark*, 557.

24. Hooker, *Mark*, 331; cf. Stein, *Mark*, 637.

25. Unlike Matthew (Matt 27:3 – 5) and Luke (Acts 1:18 – 19), Mark provides no information about Judas's fate.

26. E. S. Malbon, "Narrative Criticism," in *Mark and Method* (ed. Anderson and Moore), 35, points out that while the woman gives up money for Jesus, Judas gives up Jesus for money.

Jesus' status and so receives commendation, while Israel's religious "insiders" plot to destroy the Lord's Anointed, and so will suffer loss (cf. 4:11–12).

In the episode itself, those who rebuke the woman are themselves rebuked by Jesus. Though the disciples are clearly on Jesus' side, as throughout Mark they fail to comprehend the nature and significance of Jesus' mission. They consider the perfume a wasteful extravagance, while Jesus affirms that the honor given to the Son of God is appropriate for the momentous events about to unfold in the gospel. As he prepares to give his life as a ransom for many, she reverently anoints his body for burial. It is easy in the church to focus on the mundane and lose focus on our true kingdom purpose. We become so concerned with daily tasks, programs, events, and budgets that we lose sight of our mission to call people to respond to Jesus' fundamental message: "the kingdom of God is close at hand; repent and believe in the good news" (1:15).

Allegiance to Jesus Trumps All Other Passions and Purposes

Who is right, the woman or those who criticize her? Judging from the gospel tradition as a whole, our initial answer might be the latter. Is it better to frivolously throw away a year's worth of wages on expensive perfume or to help those in desperate poverty? Jesus makes the shocking assertion that, in this case, the former is better! This is not because the poor are unimportant. The entire biblical tradition demands that God's people care for the poor and strongly warns of judgment against those who don't (cf. Matt 25:31–46; Jas 2:15–16; 1 John 3:12). Yet the one thing that trumps this is commitment to God and his kingdom. Jesus says, "Seek first [God's] kingdom" (Matt 6:33) and warns that our love for others—even our own family—should look like hate in contrast to our commitment to God (Luke 14:26).

Some churches focus so much on "winning souls" that they do nothing to help the poor and the exploited in their community. Others are so focused on social concerns that they never call for sinners to repent or to submit to God's righteous standards. While both are essential tasks for the church, this passage reminds us that our ultimate purpose in life is to worship God and give him the glory. In the end, all sin, all poverty, all war, all exploitation are symptoms of the greater problem of humanity's fallenness, which alienates us from a right relationship with our creator God. Jesus came for a purpose far greater than feeding the poor, healing the sick, and raising the dead. He came to bring reconciliation between God and his creation.

The Death of Christ

Jesus commends the woman's actions as "good" or "beautiful" (καλός) because she has symbolically anointed his body for burial. This is the ultimate purpose of his coming. It is fitting that this passage marks the beginning of the Passion Narrative and that so much of Mark's gospel is focused on the last week of Jesus' life. Though his central message is the kingdom of God, this kingdom is inaugurated not through physical conquest, but through his atoning death on the cross.

For the church today, this has profound application. First, like the church in Mark's day, we must recognize that suffering is a part of our Christian life, and to follow Jesus means to suffer like he did (Mark 8:34; Rom 5:3; Phil 1:29; Col 1:24; 2 Thess 1:5; 2 Tim 1:8; 1 Pet 2:21). It also means that our ministry and message must center not just on social concerns and injustices of this world (though these are critically important!), but on the fundamental *kerygma* that "Christ died for our sins according to the Scriptures" (1 Cor 15:3) and that "the Son of Man [came] ... to give his life as a ransom for many" (Mark 10:45).

Mark 14:12 – 31

Literary Context

After the anointing at Bethany (14:1 – 11), three episodes lead up to Jesus' arrest and trials: the Last Supper (14:12 – 26), the prediction of Peter's denial (14:27 – 31), and the agony of Gethsemane (14:32 – 42). These lead, in turn, to the passion proper: the arrest (14:43 – 52), trials (14:53 – 12:1), and crucifixion of Jesus (15:16 – 32), followed by the burial and resurrection narratives (15:42 – 16:8). As noted in the previous section, unlike much of Mark's gospel the passion account represents a continuous narrative, with each episode leading directly to the next. It represents the narrative version of the *kerygma* that "Christ died for our sins" (1 Cor 15:3 – 4).

The Last Supper is linked to the previous episode in two of its themes: (1) the prediction of betrayal (14:18 – 21), which picks up the betrayal plot (14:10 – 11), and (2) Jesus' eucharistic words predicting his sacrificial death (14:22 – 25), which correspond to the woman's sacrificial anointing as preparation for his burial (14:8).

Main Idea

At the Last Supper Jesus establishes a new Passover, for which his blood "poured out for many" (v. 24) represents the blood of the Passover lamb, inaugurating a new covenant with the new people of God. The prediction of Judas's betrayal and the disciples' abandonment stand in stark contrast to Jesus' faithfulness to God's purpose and plan.

Translation

Mark 14:12 – 31

12a	setting (temporal)	On the first day of Unleavened Bread,
b	setting (temporal & social)	when they sacrifice the Passover lamb,
c	Question	**his disciples said to him,**
d		*"Where do you want us to go to prepare for you to eat the Passover?"*
13a	Response to 12c-d	**He sent two of his disciples and told them,**
b	command/instruction	*"Go into the city,*
c	prophecy	*and a man carrying a jar of water will meet you.*
d	command/instruction	*Follow him, and*
e	setting of 14a	*wherever he enters,*
14a	command/instruction	*say to the owner of the house,*
b		*'The teacher says,*
c		*"Where is my guest room, where I may eat the Passover with my disciples?"'*
15a	prophecy/response to 14	*He will show you a large room upstairs,*
b		*furnished and ready.*
c	command/instruction	*Make preparations for us there."*
16a	Response to 13 – 15	**The disciples left and went into the city and found it just as he said,**
b		*and* **they prepared the Passover.**
17a	setting (temporal)	When evening came,
b	Action	**he arrived with the Twelve.**
18a	setting (temporal & social)	While they were reclining and eating,
b	Action/Prophecy	**Jesus said,**
c	veracity statement prophecy	*"Truly I say to you,* *one of you will betray me — one who eats with me."*
19a	Response to 18	**They began to be distressed and said to him one by one,**
b	question	*"Surely not I?"*
20a	Response to 19	**He said to them,**
b	prophecy	*"It is one of the Twelve, one who dips with me into the bowl.*
21a	prophecy	*The Son of Man will go just as it has been written concerning him.*
b	woe statement	*But woe to that man though whom the Son of Man is betrayed!*
c	woe statement	*It would be better for him*
d		*if that man had never been born."*
22a	setting (social)	While they were eating,
b	action	after taking bread and
c	action	offering a blessing,

d	Action	**he broke it, gave it to them, and said,**
e	command	*"Take, this is my body."*
23a	action	Then after taking the cup and giving thanks,
b	Action	**he gave it to them,**
c	Action	**and they all drank from it.**
24a	Assertion/Analogy	**He said to them,**
b		*"This is my blood of the covenant,*
c		*which is poured out for many.*
25a	veracity statement	*Truly I say to you,*
b	prophecy	*I will certainly not drink again from the fruit of the vine*
c	condition of 25b	*until that day when I drink it new in the kingdom of God."*
26a	setting (temporal & social)	When they had sung a hymn,
b	Action	**they went out to the Mount of Olives.**
27a	Prophecy	**Jesus said to them,**
b	prophecy	*"You will all fall away, for it is written,*
c	Scripture quotation	*'I will strike the shepherd, and the sheep will be scattered.'* [Zech 13:7]
28a	setting of 28b (temporal)	But *after I am raised,*
b	prophecy/contrast with 27	*I will go before you into Galilee."*
29a	Response to 27	**Peter said to him,**
b		*"Even if all fall away,*
		I will not!"
30a	Response to 29	**Jesus said to him,**
b	veracity statement	*"Truly I say to you,*
c	setting to 30d (temporal)	*today, this very night, before the rooster crows twice,*
d	prophecy	*you will deny me three times."*
31a	Response to 30	But **he kept saying emphatically,**
b	condition of 31c	*"If I must die with you,*
c	assertion	*I will certainly not deny you."*
d	Response to 27, 30	**All the others were saying the same thing.**

Structure

This section is made up of four episodes or scenes: (1) the setting of the Passover/Last Supper, in which Jesus instructs his disciples to prepare the meal (14:12–16); (2) the Last Supper itself, made up of two scenes, (a) Jesus' prediction of betrayal (14:17–21) and (b) the Lord's Supper, or the eucharistic words (14:22–26a); and (3) the departure to the Mount of Olives, and (4) Jesus' prediction of the disciples' abandonment and Peter's denial (14:26–31). This last serves as a transition to Jesus' agony in the garden of Gethsemane and the arrest scene that follows.

This section is sometimes treated as another example of Mark's sandwich structures, or intercalations, with the institution of the Lord's Supper (14:22 – 26a) sandwiched between the prediction of Judas's betrayal (vv. 17 – 21) and the prediction of Peter's denial (vv. 26 – 31).[1] The failure and unfaithfulness of the disciples is set in contrast to the faithfulness of Jesus to complete his messianic task. While this parallelism may be intentional on Mark's part, it is more of an *inclusio* ("framing") than an intercalation, since the predictions of betrayal (vv. 17 – 21) and abandonment (vv. 26 – 31) are thematically similar events, rather than a continuous story into which another episode has been inserted (intercalated).

Exegetical Outline

➡ **1. The Last Supper (14:12 – 26a)**

　　a. Preparation for the meal (14:12 – 16)

　　　i. Setting (14:12)

　　　ii. Jesus' instructions (14:13 – 15)

　　　iii. The disciples' preparation (14:16)

　　b. Announcement of the betrayer (14:17 – 21)

　　　i. Setting (14:17)

　　　ii. Announcement of betrayal (14:18)

　　　iii. Response of the disciples (14:19)

　　　iv. Clarification by Jesus (14:20 – 21)

　　c. Institution of the Lord's Supper (14:22 – 26a)

　　　i. The bread (14:22)

　　　ii. The cup (14:23 – 25)

　　　iii. Singing of hymn (14:26a)

2. Prediction of Peter's Denial on the Way to Gethsemane (14:26b – 31)

　　a. Jesus' prediction of scattering and reconciliation in Galilee (14:26b – 28)

　　b. Peter's declaration of loyalty (14:29)

　　c. Jesus' prediction of Peter's denial (14:30)

　　d. Peter's and the disciples' objection and affirmation of allegiance (14:31)

---

1. Stein, *Mark*, 640.

IN DEPTH: The Chronology and Significance of the Last Supper

One of the most difficult chronological questions in the Gospels relates to the time of the Last Supper and its relationship to the Jewish Passover. The Synoptics identify the meal as a Passover celebration (Mark 14:12, 14, 16; cf. Matt 26:17–19; Luke 22:7–8, 11–12), where Jesus inaugurates a new Passover in remembrance of his sacrificial death on the cross. By contrast, John apparently treats it as an ordinary meal prior to the Passover celebration (John 13:2; 18:28). In John 18:28 the religious leaders have not yet eaten the Passover when they bring Jesus to Pilate (Friday morning). Jesus is crucified on the eve of Passover (Friday afternoon), "the day of Preparation of the Passover" (παρασκευὴ τοῦ πάσχα; John 19:14, 31, 42), when the Passover lambs were sacrificed (Nisan 14). In this way Jesus dies as the new Passover Lamb.

A variety of proposals have sought to harmonize the Synoptics and John.[2] These can be divided into three main categories:

(1) *The Last Supper was not the Jewish Passover, but a "new Passover" that Jesus inaugurated and celebrated early with the disciples.*[3] This view claims that the Jewish Passover (Nisan 15) began on Friday evening, as John's gospel indicates, and continued through Saturday afternoon. What the Synoptics refer to as "Passover" is in fact an ordinary meal during Passover week that Jesus has turned into a new Passover celebration. Knowing that he would be arrested before he could celebrate the Passover at the normal time, Jesus instituted the meal on Nisan 14 (which began Thursday evening and ran through Friday afternoon), the evening before the lambs were slaughtered. This would explain why no Passover lamb is mentioned at the meal.[4]

(2) *The Last Supper was the Jewish Passover.*[5] In this proposal, Jesus celebrated Passover with his disciples on Thursday evening (Nisan 15), as the Synoptics

2. For good surveys of the issues and evidence, see I. H. Marshall, *Last Supper and Lord's Supper* (Grand Rapids: Eerdmans, 1980), 57–75; R. T. France, "Chronological Aspects of 'Gospel Harmony,'" *VE* 16 (1986): 33–59, 43–54; Raymond E. Brown, *The Death of the Messiah: From Gethsemane to the Grave* (2 vols.; New York: Doubleday, 1994), 2:1361–69; Andreas Köstenberger, "Was the Last Supper a Passover Meal?" in *The Lord's Supper. Remembering and Proclaiming Christ until He Comes* (ed. T. R. Schreiner and M. R. Crawford; Nashville: Broadman & Holman, 2010), 6–30.

3. This view is ably defended by France, *Mark*, 560–65, and McKnight, *Jesus and His Death*, 264–73. Many others hold to the Johannine chronology but don't seek to harmonize it with the Synoptics. See Brown, *Death of the Messiah*, 2:1369–73; G.

Ogg, "The Chronology of the Last Supper," in *Historicity and Chronology in the New Testament* (ed. D. E. Nineham et al.; London: SPCK, 1965), 75–96.

4. McKnight, *Jesus and His Death*, 270, views this as decisive for support of John's chronology: "had lamb been eaten, why did not Jesus suggest that 'this *lamb* is my body'? Such is a virtual soteriological necessity for the one who is seeking to communicate to his followers that what is being consumed is analogous to the very offering of himself." For a contrary view, see Köstenberger, "Was the Last Supper a Passover Meal?" 10–11.

5. Cranfield, *Mark*, 420–22; Jeremias, *Eucharistic Words*, 41–62; B. D. Smith, "The Chronology of the Last Supper," *WTJ* 53 (1991): 29–45; idem, *Jesus' Last Passover Meal* (Lewiston, NY: Mellen, 1993).

suggest, and was crucified the next morning (still Nisan 15, which ran Thursday evening through Friday afternoon). John's reference to "the preparation of the Passover" (παρασκευὴ τοῦ πάσχα; John 19:14; cf. 19:31, 42) does not mean preparation day for Passover, the day the lambs were killed, but preparation day *for the Sabbath* of Passover week (i.e., Friday before sundown).[6] This meaning of "preparation" is a common one and appears in Mark 15:42: "It was Preparation day, that is, the day before the Sabbath" (ἦν παρασκευὴ ὅ ἐστιν προσάββατον). To "eat the Passover" (John 18:28) could carry the general sense of "celebrate the Feast [of Unleavened Bread]."[7]

(3) *The Jewish Passover was celebrated at two different times.*[8] A variety of views consider both chronologies to be correct, but posit two different Passover celebrations, either because of calendar differences (with Nisan 15 falling on different days for different groups) or because the Passover was spread out over two days (perhaps because of the large number of lambs to be slaughtered). Some propose different Passovers celebrated by (a) Sadducees and Pharisees, (b) Galileans and Judeans, or (c) visiting pilgrims and local residents. Another popular view is that Jesus and his disciples were following the solar calendar used at Qumran and in the *Book of Jubilees,* where Nisan 15 began on Tuesday evening, while the religious leaders were following the traditional lunar calendar, where Nisan 15 began on Friday evening.[9]

A decision here is difficult, and there are strengths and weaknesses with each view. The Johannine chronology (view 1) has perhaps the most scholarly support in recent years. Its greatest difficulty is the repeated assertion in the Synoptics that the Last Supper was indeed a Passover meal (Mark 14:12, 14, 16) and that the preparations for Passover took place on the day when the Passover lambs were being sacrificed (v. 12; see comments below). View 2 risks losing the Johannine connection between Jesus and the Passover lamb and also apparently contradicts the explicit statement that the religious leaders were anticipating eating the Passover during Jesus' trial (John 18:28). The various proposals in view 3 are plausible but mostly speculative, though the suggestion of solar versus lunar calendars has some support in the literature. In the commentary below we will take into account the two main possibilities: that Jesus and the disciples are eating a traditional Passover meal or that Jesus celebrates the meal early in anticipation of his coming arrest.

6. Lane, *Mark*, 498, followed by many others.

7. Köstenberger, "Was the Last Supper a Passover Meal?" 20–21.

8. For the many views and their adherents, see Brown, *Death of the Messiah,* 2:1362–64; Marshall, *Last Supper and Lord's Supper,* 71–75.

9. See esp. A. Jaubert, *The Date of the Last Supper* (trans. I. Rafferty; Staten Island, NY: Alba House, 1965); E. Ruckstuhl, *Chronology of the Last Supper* (New York: Desclée, 1965), and the summary and helpful chart in Brown, *Death of the Messiah,* 2:1366–69.

Explanation of the Text

14:12 On the first day of Unleavened Bread, when they sacrifice the Passover lamb, his disciples said to him, "Where do you want us to go to prepare for you to eat the Passover?" (Καὶ τῇ πρώτῃ ἡμέρᾳ τῶν ἀζύμων, ὅτε τὸ πάσχα ἔθυον, λέγουσιν αὐτῷ οἱ μαθηταὶ αὐτοῦ· ποῦ θέλεις ἀπελθόντες ἑτοιμάσωμεν ἵνα φάγῃς τὸ πάσχα;). For the Festivals of Passover and Unleavened Bread, see comments on 14:1–2. The two festivals were often identified together as "Passover."[10] Passover itself was celebrated on Nisan 15, which began at dusk on the evening of Nisan 14 (Lev 23:5–6; Num 28:16–17). This explains Mark's comment that this was the day "when they sacrifice the Passover lamb."

The lambs were sacrificed on preparation day (Nisan 14), and that evening Passover began (Nisan 15). There is also first-century evidence that preparation day (Nisan 14) was treated as the first day of the festival. Josephus refers to Nisan 14 as the first day of Unleavened Bread (*J.W.* 5.3.1 §§98–99; cf. Lev 23:5; Num 28:16–17) and speaks of the sacrifices that took place then as part of the festival (*J.W.* 2.1.3 §10; *Ant.* 17.9.3 §213).

If the Johannine chronology for the Jewish Passover is correct (see "In Depth: The Chronology and Significance of the Last Supper," view 1) and the lambs were not sacrificed until Friday afternoon of Passion Week (at the time of the crucifixion), Mark may mean that the events described here occurred just after sundown on Thursday evening, the beginning of Nisan 14. The sacrifice of Passover lambs would then refer to those held the following morning and afternoon (still Nisan 14, by Jewish reckoning).[11] The meal Jesus ate Thursday night would not have been the traditional Passover meal, but the "new Passover" he was initiating a day earlier.

If, however, the Synoptics record a Passover meal (view 2) or there was more than one Passover celebrated in Jerusalem at the time (view 3), then the events described here could have taken place anytime between Wednesday evening and Thursday afternoon (Nisan 14), and Passover began that Thursday evening (Nisan 15).

The verb in the clause "when they sacrifice [ἔθυον] the Passover lamb" is an impersonal and customary imperfect, referring to the priests in the temple rather than Jesus and his disciples.[12] The noun "Passover" (τὸ πάσχα) can mean "the Passover lamb" (as here), the Passover festival (14:1), or the Passover meal (14:12b, 14, 16), depending on the context. Jesus is presumably still in Bethany (14:3). Since the Passover had to be celebrated inside the city of Jerusalem,[13] his disciples ask Jesus where he wants to eat the meal.

14:13–15 He sent two of his disciples and told them, "Go into the city, and a man carrying a jar of water will meet you. Follow him, and wherever he enters, say to the owner of the house, 'The teacher says, "Where is my guest room, where I may eat the Passover with my disciples?"' He will show you a large room upstairs, furnished and ready. Make preparations for us there." (καὶ ἀποστέλλει δύο τῶν μαθητῶν αὐτοῦ καὶ λέγει αὐτοῖς· ὑπάγετε εἰς τὴν πόλιν, καὶ ἀπαντήσει

---

10. Cf. Luke 22:1: "Now the Festival of Unleavened Bread, called the Passover"; cf. Josephus, *Ant.* 14.2.1 §21; 17.9.3 §213; 18.2.2 §29; 20.5.3 §106.

11. See France, *Mark*, 561.

12. Taylor, *Mark*, 537; Gundry, *Mark*, 820; Boring, *Mark*, 386; contra Evans, *Mark 8:27–16:20*, 373; Casey, *Aramaic Sources*, 223.

13. See *t. Pesaḥ* 8:2; *Sipre Num.* §69; cf. Deut 16:2; *m. Pesaḥ* 7:9.

ὑμῖν ἄνθρωπος κεράμιον ὕδατος βαστάζων·
ἀκολουθήσατε αὐτῷ καὶ ὅπου ἐὰν εἰσέλθῃ εἴπατε
τῷ οἰκοδεσπότῃ ὅτι ὁ διδάσκαλος λέγει· ποῦ ἐστιν
τὸ κατάλυμά μου ὅπου τὸ πάσχα μετὰ τῶν μαθητῶν
μου φάγω; καὶ αὐτὸς ὑμῖν δείξει ἀνάγαιον μέγα
ἐστρωμένον ἕτοιμον· καὶ ἐκεῖ ἑτοιμάσατε ἡμῖν).

Jesus sends two disciples (identified as Peter
and John in Luke 22:8) with instructions similar to
those given in preparation for his triumphal entry
(11:1–6). As in that case, his detailed knowledge
may come from divine insight or prior arrangement. The latter seems more likely since Jesus says
the man "will meet you," and since a guest room
has already been prepared ("Where is *my* guest
room?"). In either case, Jesus is clearly orchestrat-
ing events. A man carrying a water jar would stand
out, since women normally performed this task.
The large upstairs room will be "furnished and
ready" (ἐστρωμένον ἕτοιμον), meaning equipped
with low tables and couches suitable for dining.[14]

**14:16 The disciples left and went into the city
and found it just as he said, and they prepared
the Passover** (καὶ ἐξῆλθον οἱ μαθηταὶ καὶ ἦλθον
εἰς τὴν πόλιν καὶ εὖρον καθὼς εἶπεν αὐτοῖς καὶ
ἡτοίμασαν τὸ πάσχα). The disciples fulfill Jesus'
command and find things exactly as he said.
Whether Jesus has prearranged this or not, he is
clearly in control of events. Their preparations for
the meal would include acquiring the lamb, having
it sacrificed at the temple, and procuring the food:
unleavened bread, wine, bitter herbs, and *haroseth*
(fruit) sauce for dipping. Whether a lamb was ob-
tained and roasted depends on whether this is a
true Passover meal or whether Jesus is instituting
his new Passover a day early.

**14:17–18 When evening came, he arrived with
the Twelve. While they were reclining and eating, Jesus said, "Truly I say to you, one of you
will betray me — one who eats with me."** (Καὶ
ὀψίας γενομένης ἔρχεται μετὰ τῶν δώδεκα. καὶ
ἀνακειμένων αὐτῶν καὶ ἐσθιόντων ὁ Ἰησοῦς εἶπεν·
ἀμὴν λέγω ὑμῖν ὅτι εἷς ἐξ ὑμῶν παραδώσει με ὁ
ἐσθίων μετ' ἐμοῦ). The Last Supper has two scenes,
the prediction of betrayal (vv. 18–21) and the institution of the Lord's Supper (vv. 22–26a). If the
two disciples who prepared the room were Peter
and John, as Luke 22:8 says, then "the Twelve"
(οἱ δώδεκα) must designate the group as a whole,
whether all are present or not. Or perhaps the two
returned to Bethany to accompany the others.[15]

The group "reclines" (ἀνάκειμαι) for the meal,
the posture of a formal dinner or banquet (6:26;
cf. John 13:23). Although the original exodus was
eaten in haste, "with your cloak tucked into your
belt, your sandals on your feet and your staff in
your hand" (Exod 12:11), by the first century the
meal had became a celebratory banquet commem-
orating the exodus and freedom from slavery. The
Mishnah says that even the poorest of Israelites
must recline at Passover and be given four cups of
wine to drink (*m. Pesaḥ.* 10:1). This was to be a
party for all, whatever their social status.

Jesus introduces the prediction of betrayal with
his solemn formula, "Truly I say to you" (ἀμὴν
λέγω ὑμῖν; 13x in Mark; see 3:28). While the reader
has known about Judas's betrayal since the naming of the Twelve (3:19; cf. 14:10–11) and Jesus
has repeatedly warned his disciples that he would
be delivered into the hands of the religious leaders (8:31; 9:31; 10:33), now for the first time he
reveals to them that the betrayer will be one of

---

14. The traditional site of the Last Supper is the *Cenacle* (a
Latin word meaning "dining room"), a Crusades-era building
on Mount Zion in Jerusalem. The building has been destroyed
and rebuilt several times, but the site itself has a tradition going
back to the fourth century AD.

15. Edwards, *Mark*, 422, suggests that there was likely a
larger group than the Twelve present (including other followers
and perhaps the women), but the parallel between "one of *you*
will betray me" (v. 18) and "one of the Twelve" (v. 20) suggests
that Mark envisions only the Twelve.

their own. The description of the betrayer as "one who eats with me" recalls Ps 41:9 ("Even my close friend, someone I trusted, one who shared my bread, has turned against me"), a passage quoted in John 13:18.[16] Meals were rituals of social status in the Mediterranean world, and to share a meal indicated trust and friendship. The point here is that this is the worst kind of betrayal, coming from a close friend and confidant (cf. Mark 14:20; also Ps 55:12–13).

14:19–20 They began to be distressed and said to him one by one, "Surely not I?" He said to them, "It is one of the Twelve, one who dips with me into the bowl." (ἤρξαντο λυπεῖσθαι καὶ λέγειν αὐτῷ εἷς κατὰ εἷς· μήτι ἐγώ; ὁ δὲ εἶπεν αὐτοῖς· εἷς τῶν δώδεκα, ὁ ἐμβαπτόμενος μετ' ἐμοῦ εἰς τὸ τρύβλιον). The disciples are justifiably "distressed" or "grieved" (λυπέω) that the betrayer is one of their own. The question they ask, "Surely not I?" (μήτι ἐγώ;) expects a negative answer.[17] Jesus drives the point home by specifying, "It is one of the Twelve."

The phrase "one who dips with me into the bowl" (ὁ ἐμβαπτόμενος μετ' ἐμοῦ εἰς τὸ τρύβλιον) is not meant to be a signal identifying the betrayer, but repeats in a different way the statement of v. 18, this time applying it to the Passover ritual of dipping bread into the *haroseth* sauce. The betrayer is one who shares closest fellowship with Jesus. In Matt 26:25 Judas himself asks, "Surely you don't mean me, Rabbi," and Jesus responds, "You have said so," and John 13:21–30 records both Jesus' giving of the morsel to Judas and Judas's departure into the night. Mark does not mention Judas's presence at the meal nor his departure into the night. For the

disciples (though not for the reader) the identity of the betrayer remains a mystery.

14:21 "The Son of Man will go[18] just as it has been written concerning him. But woe to that man though whom the Son of Man is betrayed! It would be better for him if that man had never been born." (ὅτι ὁ μὲν υἱὸς τοῦ ἀνθρώπου ὑπάγει καθὼς γέγραπται περὶ αὐτοῦ, οὐαὶ δὲ τῷ ἀνθρώπῳ ἐκείνῳ δι' οὗ ὁ υἱὸς τοῦ ἀνθρώπου παραδίδοται· καλὸν αὐτῷ εἰ οὐκ ἐγεννήθη ὁ ἄνθρωπος ἐκεῖνος). Jesus has repeatedly spoken of the necessity of the Son of Man's suffering (8:31; 9:31; 10:33–34, 45), and in 9:12 identified this as the fulfillment of Scripture. Now he speaks of the scriptural necessity of the betrayal. Jesus will make a similar comment at his arrest in Gethsemane: "But the Scriptures must be fulfilled" (14:49).

Mark does not say which Scripture. One possibility is Ps 41:9 ("one who shared my bread, has turned against me"), to which Jesus has just alluded (v. 18). Another is Zech 13:7 ("[I will] strike the shepherd, and the sheep will be scattered"), which Jesus will cite in the following passage (Mark 14:27). A third is Isa 53:11 and the Suffering Servant, which may be alluded to in Mark 14:24 ("poured out for many"), as it was in 10:45.[19] While any or all of these could be in Mark's mind, more important than a specific reference is the general point that what is happening to Jesus is not a tragedy, but is part of God's purpose and plan.

Jesus pronounces severe condemnation — a "woe" formula[20] — against the betrayer for his actions. Although the death of the Messiah is in fulfillment of Scripture and part of God's plan, this

---

16. Cf. 1QH 13:22–25, which similarly quotes Ps 41:9.

17. Gundry, *Mark*, 836.

18. The verb "goes" (ὑπάγει) is a futuristic present. For this euphemistic terminology for death, see Marcus, *Mark 9–16*, 951.

19. Other possibilities include Dan 7:13–14, since in context the "one like a son of man" represents God's suffering

people (Dan 7:21, 25), or 9:26, where an "anointed prince" is "cut off" (Evans, *Mark 8:27–16:20*, 377). Yet all of Jesus' passion predictions have referred to the Son of Man, so that passage does not stand out here.

20. A "woe" can indicate calamity in general (cf. 13:7) or (as here) disaster resulting from the judgment of God (cf. Num 21:29; 1 Sam 4:7; Job 10:15; Isa 3:11; 5:8; Matt 11:21; 23:13–29).

does not remove human responsibility. The convergence of divine sovereignty and human responsibility is especially striking if, as Marcus suggests, the translation should read "*through* whom [δι' οὗ] the Son of Man is betrayed" instead of "*by* whom …" (NET, ESV, NASB, etc.) — with God as the ultimate agent of the "handing over" (cf. divine passives in 9:31; 10:33 – 34).[21]

14:22   While they were eating, after taking bread and offering a blessing, he broke it, gave it to them, and said, "Take, this is my body." (Καὶ ἐσθιόντων αὐτῶν λαβὼν ἄρτον εὐλογήσας ἔκλασεν καὶ ἔδωκεν αὐτοῖς καὶ εἶπεν· λάβετε, τοῦτό ἐστιν τὸ σῶμά μου). The third part of this narrative, after the preparation for the meal (vv. 12 – 16) and the announcement of betrayal (vv. 17 – 21), is the meal itself — the "Lord's Supper," or the eucharistic words of Jesus (vv. 22 – 25). The relationship between the Lord's Supper and the Jewish Passover is a question of considerable debate. As we have seen, it is also a multifaceted question: Did the Last Supper occur on the Jewish Passover? (see "In Depth: The Chronology and Significance of the Last Sup-

per"). Did Jesus interpret the meal as a "new Passover"? Did Mark understand it this way?

Whether or not the meal took place on Passover or a day earlier, the answer to the latter two questions is surely "yes." Mark repeatedly refers to the meal as Passover (vv. 12, 14, 16), and, as Jeremias and others have shown, many contextual features point in this direction.[22] (1) The location is Jerusalem, not Bethany; Passover had to be eaten in the city (*m. Pesaḥ.* 7:9). (2) Like Passover, the meal is at night rather than in the afternoon; on nonfestival days, Jews normally ate two meals a day, in the morning and afternoon. (3) The meal is eaten reclining, the position for a banquet and for Passover (*m. Pesaḥ.* 10:1). Normal meals were eaten sitting. (4) The use of wine was generally reserved for festivals and was characteristic of Passover (*m. Pesaḥ.* 10:1). (5) The interpretation of the elements fits the pattern at Passover (*m. Pesaḥ.* 10:5). (6) The phrase "fruit of the vine" (v. 25) is the traditional one used for the wine in the Passover liturgy (*m. Ber.* 6:1). (7) The hymn sung at the end (v. 26) recalls the Hallel Psalms (Pss 113 – 118) sung at Passover (*m. Pesaḥ.* 10:6).

IN DEPTH: The Jewish Passover

It is unclear how firmly established the Passover liturgy was in Jesus' day, but the Mishnah (c. AD 200) and later sources describe the meal as structured around four cups of wine.[23] After initial blessings over the day and over the wine, the first cup of wine is drunk (*m. Pesaḥ.* 10:2). This is followed by vegetable appetizers and the mixing of the second cup of wine (*m. Pesaḥ.* 10:3). The youngest son then asks the patriarch of the family, "Why is this night different from

---

21. Marcus, *Mark 9 – 16*, 952. Marcus also notes Origen's suggestion of Satan as the ultimate agent (cf. Luke 22:3; John 6:70 – 71; 13:2, 27).

22. Jeremias, *Eucharistic Words*, 41 – 84; Lane, *Mark*, 497; Stein, *Mark*, 642 – 43, 649; Köstenberger, "Was the Last Supper a Passover Meal?" 6 – 30.

23. The details and order are debated. See G. J. Bahr, "The Seder of Passover and the Eucharistic Words," *NovT* 12 (1970): 181 – 202. Bahr cites and interprets five main texts that describe the order of the Seder: *t. Ber.* 4:8; *y. Ber.* 10d; *b. Ber.* 43a; *m. Pesaḥ* 10:1 – 9; *t. Pesaḥ* 10:1 – 14.

other nights?" The patriarch recounts the exodus story, explaining three key components: "the Passover, because God passed over the houses of our father in Egypt; unleavened bread, because our fathers were redeemed from Egypt; and bitter herbs, because the Egyptians embittered the lives of our fathers in Egypt." The patriarch is to put himself in the story: "And thou shalt tell thy son in that day saying, 'It is because of that which the Lord did for me that I came forth out of Egypt'" (*m. Pesaḥ.* 10:4 – 5).

This is followed by the singing of the first part of the Hallel psalms (Pss 113 – 115). The patriarch pronounces a blessing over the bread, breaks it, and distributes it to the participants. The main Passover meal is then eaten, including unleavened bread, bitter herbs, *haroseth* (fruit) sauce, and the lamb. This is followed by the third cup of wine and the singing of the rest of the Hallel (Pss 116 – 118). A fourth cup concludes the meal (*m. Pesaḥ.* 10:7).

Parallels to the Last Supper are significant, if not decisive, and include the blessing (14:22a-c), the breaking and distribution of the bread (v. 22d), the description of the meal's significance (vv. 22e), a cup of wine (v. 23), and the singing of a hymn (v. 26a).

The words of institution appear in all three Synoptics and in 1 Cor 11:23 – 25 (see chart). Mark and Matthew have almost identical wording, while Luke and 1 Corinthians appear to be following a different tradition. All four include the blessing or thanksgiving, the breaking of the bread, the saying "This is my body," and the passing of the cup. Only Paul and the longer reading in Luke (22:19b – 20) include that Jesus' body is "[given] for you" and to do this "in remembrance of me."

THE EUCHARISTIC WORDS

	MARK 14:22 – 25 (CF. MATT 26:26 – 29)	LUKE 22:15 – 20	1 COR 11:23 – 25
Introduction	While they were eating, (v. 22a) (see v. 25 below)	And he said to them, "I have eagerly desired to eat this Passover with you before I suffer. For I tell you, I will not eat it again until it finds fulfillment in the kingdom of God." (vv. 15 – 16)	For I received from the Lord what I also passed on to you: The Lord Jesus, on the night he was betrayed,
First Cup (Luke only)		After taking the cup, he gave thanks and said, "Take this and divide it among you. For I tell you I will not drink again from the fruit of the vine until the kingdom of God comes." (vv. 17 – 18)	

Continued on next page.

	MARK 14:22 – 25 (CF. MATT 26:26 – 29)	LUKE 22:15 – 20	1 COR 11:23 – 25
Bread	… taking bread and offering a blessing, he broke it, gave it to them, and said, "Take; this is my body." (v. 22b-e)	And he took bread, and gave thank and broke it, and gave it to them, saying, "This is my body *[given for you; do this in remembrance of me.]" (v. 19)	… took bread, and when he had given thanks, he broke it and said, "This is my body, which is for you; do this in remembrance of me." (vv. 23 – 24)
Cup (2nd cup in Luke)	Then after taking a cup, and giving thanks, he gave it to them, and they all drank from it. He said to them, "This is my blood of the [new] covenant, which is poured out for many." (vv. 23 – 24)	[In the same way, after the supper, he took a cup, saying, "This cup is the new covenant in my blood, which is poured out for you]." (v. 20)	In the same way, after the supper, he took a cup, saying, "This cup is the new covenant in my blood; do this, whenever you drink it, in remembrance of me." (v. 25)
Conclusion	"Truly I say to you, I will certainly not drink again from the fruit of the vine until that day when I drink it new in the kingdom of God." (v. 25)	[see v. 15 above]	

*[textually debated material in brackets]

In line with the Passover liturgy, Jesus, as host of the meal, takes the unleavened bread, pronounces a blessing, breaks it, and distributes it. "To bless" (εὐλογέω) in this sense is equivalent to praise or thanksgiving. It is not clear from the Greek syntax whether the blessing was for the bread or for God. The latter is more likely, considering the Jewish precedents and in light of the parallel to "giving thanks" (εὐχαριστέω) in v. 23. Taylor and others suggest the blessing was likely the typical Jewish prayer of thanksgiving: "Blessed are you, O Lord our God, king of the universe, who brings forth bread from the earth" (cf. m. Ber. 6:1).[24]

Jesus now radically reinterprets the unleavened bread as a symbol for his "body" (τὸ σῶμά). The accounts in Luke and Paul include, "which is [given] for you." Lane claims the bread and the cup say-

ings were originally separated in the Passover meal and should be expounded separately. Jesus' blood means his sacrificial death, but his body means Jesus himself and a promise of his abiding presence with the disciples.[25] More likely, the two sayings are closely related (as Mark has them), and Jesus' body, like his blood, represents his sacrificial death on the cross — his body "which is [given] for you" (1 Cor 11:24).[26] The text does not say that Jesus' *body* was "broken for you." The word "broken" (κλώμενον) that appears in some manuscripts at 1 Cor 11:24 is a later scribal addition.[27] The breaking of the bread was part of the Passover ritual, a necessity for its distribution. John emphatically says that no bone in Jesus' body was broken (John 19:35 – 36).

14:23 – 24 Then after taking the cup and giving thanks, he gave it to them, and they all drank

24. Taylor, Mark, 544; Gundry, Mark, 830; Evans, Mark 8:27 – 16:20, 389.

25. "Jesus was not referring to his physical body as such, but to himself" (Lane, Mark, 506).

26. It is surprising that Jesus does not identify his body with the Passover lamb, which would draw a closer analogy to his

sacrificial death. As noted above, this has fueled speculation that no lamb was present and that the meal took place a day before Passover (McKnight, Jesus and His Death, 270).

27. Its weak manuscript evidence includes ℵ² C³ D² F G Ψ 1739^{mg} 1881 𝔐 syr.

from it. He said to them, "This is my blood of the covenant, which is poured out for many." (καὶ λαβὼν ποτήριον εὐχαριστήσας ἔδωκεν αὐτοῖς, καὶ ἔπιον ἐξ αὐτοῦ πάντες. καὶ εἶπεν αὐτοῖς· τοῦτό ἐστιν τὸ αἷμά μου τῆς διαθήκης τὸ ἐκχυννόμενον ὑπὲρ πολλῶν). If the cup here is part of the Passover liturgy, it was likely the second or third Passover cup, the one before or after the main meal (see "In Depth: The Jewish Passover," above). Though Mark uses a different verb here than in v. 22 — "thank" (εὐχαριστέω) instead of "bless" (εὐλογέω) — the sense is the same and the same Hebrew term probably lies behind them (bārak). Luke uses "thank" (εὐχαριστέω) for both the bread and the cup (22:17, 19). From this term we get the word "Eucharist."

According to the Mishnah, the Passover benediction over the wine would be, "Blessed are you, O Lord our God, king of the universe, creator of the fruit of the vine."[28] Mark says, "they all drank from it" (ἔπιον ἐξ αὐτοῦ πάντες), suggesting a single shared cup. It is debated whether the Passover liturgy of Jesus' day used a separate cup for each person or a single cup, but the former seems most likely. Jesus may be intentionally breaking tradition to make a theological point about unity.[29] The celebration of the Eucharist is meant to be a unifying event, a point Paul strongly stresses to the Corinthians (1 Cor 11:18).

As Jesus identified the bread with "my body," so the wine is identified with "my blood of the covenant" (τὸ αἷμά … τῆς διαθήκης). The phrase echoes Exod 24:8 LXX and the ratification of the Mosaic covenant: "Behold the blood of the covenant [τὸ αἷμα τῆς διαθήκης] that the Lord has made with you" (cf. Zech 9:11). Just as a blood sacrifice sealed the first covenant, so Christ's death seals or ratifies the new covenant. Though the adjective "new"

(καινῆς) in some manuscripts is likely a scribal assimilation to 1 Cor 11:25 (cf. Luke 22:10),[30] Mark surely has in mind the new covenant of Jer 31:31 – 34 (cf. Heb 8:7 – 13).

The blood being "poured out" (ἐκχυννόμενον) is the language of sacrificial atonement (cf. Exod 24:6), and "for many" (ὑπὲρ πολλῶν) recalls Mark 10:45, which has as its background the Suffering Servant of Isa 53:11 – 12. As noted there, "for many" is not to be understood exclusively (for many but not all), but rather inclusively (the one dies for the many). Jesus' one sacrifice will provide atonement for all.

Jesus simply states "this is my body" and "this is my blood" without clarifying the nature of the image. Since Jesus is bodily present, his disciples would not have thought that he was saying the bread had literally become his body. In the same way, since Judaism forbade the drinking of blood (Lev 3:17; 7:26 – 27; 17:14), the disciples would not have thought the blood was literal.[31] In John's gospel, Jesus often uses metaphors to refer to himself (the bread of life, the light of the world, the gate, the vine, the way, etc.; John 6:35; 8:12; 9:5; 10:7, 9; 11:25; 14:6; 15:5), and there is no reason to suppose he is speaking literally here. The bread and the cup signify, or represent, his body and blood.

14:25 "Truly I say to you, I will certainly not drink again from the fruit of the vine until that day when I drink it new in the kingdom of God." (ἀμὴν λέγω ὑμῖν ὅτι οὐκέτι οὐ μὴ πίω ἐκ τοῦ γενήματος τῆς ἀμπέλου ἕως τῆς ἡμέρας ἐκείνης ὅταν αὐτὸ πίνω καινὸν ἐν τῇ βασιλείᾳ τοῦ θεοῦ). Jesus concludes the meal with another solemn affirmation, "Truly I say to you" (ἀμὴν λέγω ὑμῖν; cf. v. 18, and comments on 3:28). Jesus knows his death is near and affirms that this is the last time

---

28. *m. Ber.* 6:1; Bahr, "Seder of Passover," 192.
29. See Marshall, *Last Supper and Lord's Supper*, 63.

30. A *f*[1.13] 𝔐 lat syr.
31. Stein, *Mark*, 650 – 51.

he will celebrate the Passover with his disciples.[32] The "fruit of the vine" is the traditional Passover language used for the Jewish benediction over the wine (see comments on 14:22).

"When I drink it new in the kingdom of God" recalls OT imagery related to the "messianic banquet," God's eschatological salvation portrayed as a great end-time feast, with "the best of meats and the finest of wines" (Isa 25:6 – 8; cf. Isa 65:13; Matt 8:11; Luke 13:29; 14:15; 22:29 – 30; Rev 19:9; *1 En.* 62:14; *2 Bar.* 29:5 – 8; 1QSa 2:11 – 22). The adjective "new" (καινός) could refer to "new wine" (meaning banquet or festival wine),[33] "in a renewed state" (= a glorified body),[34] or "in a redeemed world."[35] Most likely, however, the adjective is functioning adverbially in the sense of "drink it *again*."[36] Jesus does not mean that he will not eat or drink at all before the consummation of the kingdom. He is seen eating (and presumably drinking) after the resurrection (Luke 24:30, 41 – 43; John 21:9 – 13; though wine is not mentioned). Rather, Jesus means what he says explicitly in Luke, that he will not celebrate the Passover again (Luke 22:16) until it is fulfilled at the consummation of the kingdom.[37]

14:26 When they had sung a hymn, they went out to the Mount of Olives (Καὶ ὑμνήσαντες ἐξῆλθον εἰς τὸ ὄρος τῶν ἐλαιῶν) This final scene (vv. 26 – 31) of the larger Last Supper narrative (vv. 12 – 31) serves as a transition from the Passover meal (vv. 17 – 25) to the events that follow: the agony in Gethsemane (14:32 – 42) and Jesus' arrest (14:43 – 50). Verse 26 is transitional, concluding the Last Supper narrative with a hymn and commencing the journey to Gethsemane. The hymn was likely one of the Hallel Psalms (Pss 113 – 118) that concluded the Passover celebration. It would be some time before midnight, since the Passover had to end by then (*m. Pesaḥ.* 10:9). Jesus and the disciples head east out of Jerusalem to the western slopes of the Mount of Olives, the location of the garden of Gethsemane.

14:27 Jesus said to them, "You will all fall away, for it is written, 'I will strike the shepherd, and the sheep will be scattered.'" (καὶ λέγει αὐτοῖς ὁ Ἰησοῦς ὅτι πάντες σκανδαλισθήσεσθε, ὅτι γέγραπται· πατάξω τὸν ποιμένα, καὶ τὰ πρόβατα διασκορπισθήσονται). The context of Jesus' words appears to be on the way from the upper room in Jerusalem to the Mount of Olives. Having earlier predicted the betrayer (vv. 17 – 21), Jesus now warns that all his disciples will abandon him.

The verb translated "fall away" (σκανδαλίζω) can have a variety of senses, including "cause to fall/stumble," "cause to sin," "cause to apostasize," "offend," "anger," "shock."[38] It is used in the active voice in 9:42, 43, 45 of something or someone who provokes or causes someone to sin. It is used in the passive in 6:3 of the people of Nazareth who are angered or offended by Jesus' words. In the parable of the sower (4:17), the passive carries the sense of apostasy or falling away from the faith. Here the passive is best defined by Jesus' quotation of Zech 13:7, where the shepherd is struck down and the sheep "will be scattered." Under the pressure

---

32. Luke's fuller version of the saying (22:15 – 18) refers both to the Passover generally (22:15 – 16) and to the cup specifically (22:17 – 18).

33. France, *Mark*, 571 – 72; Casey, *Aramaic Sources*, 220 – 21, 242 – 43.

34. So Taylor, *Mark*, 547; Evans, *Mark 8:27 – 16:20*, 395 (referring to Jesus' original words, which may have been mistranslated from the Aramaic).

35. Lane, *Mark*, 508.

36. Gundry, *Mark*, 834.

37. Another possibility is that Jesus is not referring to the consummation of the kingdom, but its inauguration following his death and resurrection (cf. 9:1, 9). This seems unlikely here, however, since banquet imagery is elsewhere used of the eschaton (cf. Matt 8:11; Luke 13:29, and the "messianic banquet" references above).

38. BDAG, 926.

of the circumstances, the disciples will "be made to stumble" (NKJV) or "caused to abandon" Jesus and his cause.

In the Hebrew (and LXX) text of Zech 13:7, "strike" the shepherd is an imperative, a command by God to the sword to strike his shepherd, God's associate, and as a result the sheep (the people of God) "will be scattered." The point is that God will strike down his appointed leader and scatter his people as judgment for their sin. Mark's text has essentially the same sense, but puts the verb in the first person ("I will strike the shepherd"), again driving home the point that God is the ultimate agent of these events and all that is happening is part of his will and design. In light of the many allusions to Zech 9–14 in the Last Supper narrative, Marcus concludes that Mark portrays Jesus' last night before his crucifixion as the time of eschatological testing predicted by Zechariah.[39]

14:28 "But after I am raised, I will go ahead of you into Galilee." (ἀλλὰ μετὰ τὸ ἐγερθῆναί με προάξω ὑμᾶς εἰς τὴν Γαλιλαίαν). Along with Jesus' prediction of scattering is one of reunion and restoration. Jesus will "go ahead of" or "go before" the disciples into Galilee, where he will meet them. This reunion is reaffirmed when the resurrection is announced in 16:7. This resurrection appearance in Galilee is narrated in Matt 28:16–20 (cf. John 21:1–23), and some scholars think Mark's gospel originally ended with this resurrection appearance.[40] (For discussion of the various endings of Mark, see comments on 16:8 and the appendix, "The Endings of Mark").

This promise of restoration refutes the claim by some that one of Mark's purposes is to discredit the Twelve in favor of others in the early church.[41] "Go before" could mean that Jesus will lead them there as a shepherd leads the flock, continuing the imagery of Zechariah 13.[42] Yet in the Markan narrative it must mean "precede" or "go there first," since Mark 16:7 says, "You will see him there."[43] For the view of Lohmeyer, Marxsen, and others that this Galilean appearance originally referred to the promise of the parousia, see comments on 16:7.

14:29–31 Peter said to him, "Even if all fall away, I will not!" Jesus said to him, "Truly I say to you, today, this very night, before the rooster crows twice, you will deny me three times." But he kept saying emphatically, "If I must die with you, I will certainly not deny you." All the others were saying the same thing (ὁ δὲ Πέτρος ἔφη αὐτῷ· εἰ καὶ πάντες σκανδαλισθήσονται, ἀλλ᾽ οὐκ ἐγώ. καὶ λέγει αὐτῷ ὁ Ἰησοῦς· ἀμὴν λέγω σοι ὅτι σὺ σήμερον ταύτῃ τῇ νυκτὶ πρὶν ἢ δὶς ἀλέκτορα φωνῆσαι τρίς με ἀπαρνήσῃ. ὁ δὲ ἐκπερισσῶς ἐλάλει· ἐὰν δέῃ με συναποθανεῖν σοι, οὐ μή σε ἀπαρνήσομαι. ὡσαύτως δὲ καὶ πάντες ἔλεγον). Although elsewhere Peter serves as spokesperson for the others (1:36–37; 8:29; 9:5; 10:28; 11:21), here he speaks for himself. "Even if all fall away, I will not!"

Again Jesus responds with his solemn *amen* formula (see v. 18). Peter not only will abandon him like the rest, but this very night he will deny Jesus three times. Those who claim to be first will end up last, failing worse even than the others (9:35; 10:44). The statement is made emphatic not only by the *amen* statement, but by the threefold reference to the time, "today, this very night, before

---

39. Marcus, *Way of the Lord*, 157–59; idem, *Mark 9–16*, 969; cf. Garland, *Mark*, 530; France, *Mark*, 575–76. Marcus notes the following parallels: v. 24, "my blood of the covenant" (Zech 9:11); v. 25, "that day," dominion of God (Zech 14:4, 9); v. 26, Mount of Olives (Zech 14:4); v. 27, strike the shepherd, scatter the sheep (Zech 13:7); v. 28, restoration of scattered sheep (Zech 13:8–9).

40. So Gundry, *Mark*, 1021.

41. So Weeden, *Mark — Traditions in Conflict*.

42. So C. F. Evans, "I Will Go before You into Galilee," *JTS* n.s. 5 (1954): 3–18; Hooker, *Mark*, 345; Evans, *Mark 8:27–16:20*, 401–2.

43. Gundry, *Mark*, 845; France, *Mark*, 577; Stein, *Mark*, 655; Boring, *Mark*, 394.

the rooster crows twice," and by the triple denial ("three times"; τρίς). The reference to the rooster crowing is not to establish a particular hour (roosters are notoriously unpredictable), but to make it clear that all this will occur in the near future, before dawn the next morning.

Some have claimed that the rooster crowing is not a literal rooster, but the Roman bugle call marking the end of the third watch of the night, called *gallicinium* in Latin and "cockcrow" in Greek (ἀλεκτοραφωνία; cf. 13:35).[44] This is unlikely. Mark does not use this technical language, instead speaking of the actions of a rooster (ἀλέκτωρ; cf. 14:72).[45] Why does Jesus say the rooster will crow "twice" (δίς)? In the account of the denial that follows, Mark records only one cockcrow, but it is identified as the "second" (ἐκ δευτέρου; 14:72). While some

see symbolism or rhetorical effect at play, France is probably right that the best explanation is that this is Peter's personal recollection of the way things actually happened.[46]

Peter now responds even more "emphatically" (ἐκπερισσῶς; v. 31). He is willing even to die for Jesus. Like James and John in 10:39, who were willing to drink the cup that Jesus would drink, Peter is almost certainly thinking of the potential of messianic war rather than Jesus' death as a sacrifice of atonement (10:45). He is willing to stand beside Jesus no matter what the cost, even to the point of death. The other disciples join in, enthusiastically affirming their loyalty to Jesus. The reader knows that such pride and self-confidence will be short-lived.

Theology in Application

God's Sovereign Purpose

The strongest theme of this section is God's sovereign purpose in the unfolding events of the narrative. This is seen in Jesus' prescience every step of the way: (1) his instructions to the disciples concerning preparation for the Passover/Last Supper (vv. 13 – 16); (2) his prediction of the betrayal of Judas (vv. 17 – 21); (3) his expectation of the eschatological banquet (v. 25); (4) his awareness that all will fall away and that Peter will deny him three times (vv. 27 – 30); and (5) yet that he will rise from the dead and be restored to the disciples in Galilee (v. 28). It is significant that while two of these are expectations of eschatological salvation, two are tragedies provoked by evil human decisions (Judas's betrayal) or human weakness (the disciples' abandonment).

The point is that God is sovereignly at work, even through those who oppose or fail him. This theme recalls Mark's parable of the tenants (12:1 – 12), where the tenant farmers (representing the religious leaders) reject and murder the owner's son. Yet the stone the builders rejected becomes the cornerstone (12:10; citing Ps 118:22 – 23). God's purpose is accomplished despite and even through the evil intention of sin-

44. C. H. Mayo, "St. Peter's Token of the Cock Crow," *JTS* 22 (1921): 367 – 70.

45. See D. Brady, "The Alarm to Peter in Mark's Gospel," *JSNT* 2 (1979): 44 – 46; Brown, *Death of the Messiah*, 1:606.

46. France, *Mark*, 579.

ners: "The Lord has done this, and it is marvelous in our eyes" (Mark 12:11; cf. Ps 118:23). In the broader context of Scripture, this calls to mind Pharaoh's opposition to God's command to let his people go. God repeatedly "hardens" Pharaoh's already hard heart in order to display his own glory and power to save.

The Sacrificial Death of Christ

This is one of only two passages in Mark that emphasize the vicarious and atoning nature of Jesus' death. The other is the ransom saying of 10:45, where the Son of Man gives himself as a sacrifice of atonement to pay for the sins of "the many." Here Jesus defines his coming death with a combination of covenant ratification and Passover language. Jesus' death represents the "blood of the covenant" (v. 24; Exod 24:8), the blood sacrifice that inaugurates and ratifies the new covenant (Jer 31:31). Though Jer 31 is not explicitly cited, conceptually it lies behind Jesus' words and is highlighted by both Luke (Luke 22:20 — assuming the longer reading) and Paul (1 Cor 11:25) in their versions of the eucharistic words.

The new covenant, in turn, promises the law written on the heart, authentic knowledge of God, and true forgiveness of sins (Jer 31:31 – 34). Here we have the heart of the Christian message, that "Christ died for our sins according to Scripture" (1 Cor 15:3), and that "God was reconciling the world to himself in Christ" (2 Cor 5:19).

Celebrating the Eucharist

Whether called the Lord's Supper, the Eucharist, or Communion, the ritual Jesus inaugurated at his last Passover is the most significant worship experience for the church today. As Christians gather around the table, we look back at Christ's sacrificial and self-giving love for us through his death on the cross; we look forward to our hope in his future return to consummate our salvation and bring us into his presence; and we look to the present, where sharing the bread and the cup unites us as one body — the people of God.

Here are a few communion services that have been significant for me. A bride and groom publicly announce their lifelong commitment to the Lord and to one another by sharing communion before family and friends. After trekking all night to a high mountain peak, a group of backpackers celebrate the Eucharist at sunrise with saltine crackers and Gatorade, praising God for his awesome creation and the joy of experiencing it together. A group of Holy Land pilgrims, who have spent several weeks "walking where Jesus walked" and reading Scripture at the sites where these events took place, share the Lord's Supper in the tranquility of the garden tomb, celebrating the death and resurrection of the Lord, who gives them life. This is what communion means to me.

56

Mark 14:32 – 42

Literary Context

The Passion Narrative (14:1 – 15:47) continues as Jesus leaves the upper room in Jerusalem, the site of the Last Supper, and proceeds eastward to the garden of Gethsemane on the Mount of Olives. Jesus has just announced his betrayal (14:17 – 21) and abandonment (14:27 – 31) by his close friends, and he has inaugurated a new Passover celebration symbolizing the sacrifice of his body and blood to establish a new covenant — the one dying for "the many" (14:22 – 25; cf. 10:45). Now Jesus suffers deep distress and agony over the challenge of fulfilling this commitment and drinking the "cup" of suffering (14:23, 36). The episode ends with the announcement of the arrival of the betrayer (v. 42), the fulfillment of Jesus' prediction. The passage also has thematic links to the Olivet Discourse (ch. 13), as Jesus repeatedly calls the disciples to "watch" and pray in preparation for the eschatological events unfolding before them.

III. The Suffering Way of the Messiah (8:22 – 15:47)
   C. The Passion of the Messiah in Jerusalem (14:1 – 15:47)
      4. The Last Supper (14:12 – 26)
      5. The Prediction of Peter's Denial (14:27 – 31)
   ➡ **6. The Agony of Gethsemane (14:32 – 42)**
      7. The Betrayal and Arrest (14:43 – 52)

Main Idea

Jesus' experience in the garden of Gethsemane reveals his true humanity and faithfulness to the Father's will and stands in stark contrast to the spiritual and physical dullness of the disciples.

Translation

Mark 14:32 – 42

32a	Action/Setting (spatial)	**They went to a place called Gethsemane,**
b	Command	and **he said to his disciples,**
c		*"Sit here while I pray."*
33a	Action	**He took Peter and James and John with him,**
b	Response to situation	and **he began to be deeply distressed and troubled.**
34a	Response to situation	**He said to them,**
b	assertion	*"My soul is grieving intensely to the point of death.*
	command	*Stay here and keep watch."*
35a	setting of 35b	Going a little further,.
b	Action/first prayer	**he fell to the ground and prayed**
	Indirect discourse	**that, if possible, the hour would pass from him.**
36a	Prayer	**He was saying,**
b	affirmation	*"Abba, Father, everything is possible for you.*
c	entreaty	*Take this cup from me;*
d	condition of 36c	*yet not what I want,*
e	contrast with 36d	*but what you want."*
37a	Action/first return	Then **he came and found them sleeping and said to Peter,**
b	rhetorical question	*"Simon, are you sleeping?*
c	rhetorical question	*Couldn't you watch one hour?*
38a	command	*Watch and pray,*
b	purpose of 38a	*so that you do not give in to temptation.*
c	aphorism	*The spirit is willing, but the flesh is weak."*
39a	setting of 39b	Again after leaving,
b	Action/second prayer	**he prayed,**
c	manner of 39b	saying the same thing.
40a	setting of 40b	Then, coming back again,
b	Action/second return	**he found them sleeping,**
c	reason for 40b	for **their eyes were heavy.**
d	Response	**They did not know what to say to him.**
41a	Action/ third prayer & return	**He came the third time and said to them,**
b	rhetorical question	*"Are you still sleeping and resting?*
c	rhetorical question	*Is it far off?*
d	announcement/warning	*The hour has come!*
e	announcement/warning	*Look, the Son of Man is delivered into the hands of sinners.*
42a	command	*Arise! Let's go!*
b	announcement/warning	*Look, the one who betrays me draws near!"*

Structure

The passage is structured to highlight the isolation of Jesus and the failure of the disciples: he will tread this path alone. Jesus arrives with all the disciples (except Judas; v. 32), withdraws with the three (v. 33), and then withdraws further alone (v. 35). Mark's fondness for threes is evident as three times Jesus returns to find the disciples sleeping (i.e., failing to stay faithful to him), and three times he rebukes them. As in the three boat scenes (4:35 – 41; 6:45 – 52; 8:14 – 21), the three cycles of events associated with the Passion predictions (see Literary Context on 8:34 – 9:1), and Peter's threefold denial (14:66 – 72), the repetition highlights their failure and Jesus' success. He faithfully fulfills God's commission as they waver through physical and spiritual weakness.

Exegetical Outline

→ **1. Setting and Withdrawal with the Three (14:32 – 34)**
    a. Arrival at Gethsemane and call for prayer (14:32)
    b. Withdrawal with three disciples (14:33a)
    c. Jesus' distress and call for watchfulness (14:33b – 34)
2. First Prayer and Return (14:35 – 38)
    a. Departure and prayer (14:35 – 36
    b. Return and rebuke of the disciples (14:37 – 38)
3. Second Prayer and Return (14:39 – 40)
4. Third Prayer and Return (14:41 – 42)
    a. Return and rebuke (14:41)
    b. Announcement of the betrayer (14:42)

Explanation of the Text

14:32 They went to a place called Gethsemane, and he said to his disciples, "Sit here while I pray." (Καὶ ἔρχονται εἰς χωρίον οὗ τὸ ὄνομα Γεθσημανὶ καὶ λέγει τοῖς μαθηταῖς αὐτοῦ· καθίσατε ὧδε ἕως προσεύξωμαι). Jesus and his disciples leave Jerusalem and cross the Kidron Valley (John 18:1) to the western slopes of the Mount of Olives (Luke 22:39). Mark calls the place "Gethsemane," a Hebrew or Aramaic name meaning "olive press." John identifies it as a "garden" (κῆπος), which probably means an olive grove with a mill for pressing the olives.

Luke 22:39 says Jesus went regularly to this place (κατὰ τὸ ἔθος: "as usual"), and John says Judas knew where to come because Jesus met there often with his disciples (John 18:2).

14:33 – 34 He took Peter and James and John with him, and he began to be deeply distressed and troubled. He said to them, "My soul is grieving intensely to the point of death. Stay here and keep watch." (καὶ παραλαμβάνει τὸν Πέτρον καὶ τὸν Ἰάκωβον καὶ τὸν Ἰωάννην μετ' αὐτοῦ καὶ ἤρξατο ἐκθαμβεῖσθαι καὶ ἀδημονεῖν καὶ λέγει αὐτοῖς· περίλυπός ἐστιν ἡ ψυχή μου ἕως θανάτου· μείνατε ὧδε καὶ γρηγορεῖτε). Jesus leaves the larger group of disciples and takes his "inner circle" — Peter, James, and John — as he has done on several other occasions (5:37; 9:2; cf. 13:3). Mark does not say why only these three; perhaps it was because they had so strongly expressed their willingness to suffer for him (10:38 – 39; 14:31).

The narrator emphasizes Jesus' acute emotional distress with the words that Jesus "began to be deeply distressed and troubled" (v. 33) and with Jesus' own statement that he is grieved to the point of death (v. 34). The strong verb "be deeply distressed" (ἐκθαμβέω; an intensive form of θαμβέω) occurs in the NT only in Mark and always in the passive, where it indicates being moved to an intense emotional state (see also 9:15; 16:5, 6).[1] Here, in combination with "be troubled/distressed/anxious" (ἀδημονέω) the sense is dread and fear rather than surprise or shock. Jesus knows what is coming, but he is deeply distressed by it.

The clause "my soul is grieved" (περίλυπός ἐστιν ἡ ψυχή μου) recalls the repeated refrain of the righteous sufferer in Pss 42:5, 6, 11 (LXX: 41:6, 7, 12) and 43:5 (LXX: 42:5): "Why are you grieved, my soul [LXX: ἵνα τί περίλυπος εἶ, ψυχή]? Why so disturbed within me?" Jesus turns to the psalms of lament to express his anxiety before God (see Ps 22:1 in Mark 15:34). "My soul" is a Semitic and poetic way to refer to oneself. Grief "to the point of death" (ἕως θανάτου) probably means sorrow so deep that it feels as if he is dying.[2] The command "keep watch" (γρηγορεῖτε; vv. 34, 37, 38; cf.

13:34, 35, 37) may mean (1) to stay spiritually alert in prayer, or (2) to watch for the betrayer. In light of Jesus' parallel command to prayer in v. 38, the former is most likely here.

14:35 – 36 Going a little further, he fell to the ground and prayed that, if possible, the hour would pass from him. He was saying, "Abba, Father, everything is possible for you. Take this cup from me; yet not what I want, but what you want." (καὶ προελθὼν μικρὸν ἔπιπτεν ἐπὶ τῆς γῆς καὶ προσηύχετο ἵνα εἰ δυνατόν ἐστιν παρέλθῃ ἀπ᾽ αὐτοῦ ἡ ὥρα, καὶ ἔλεγεν· αββα ὁ πατήρ, πάντα δυνατά σοι· παρένεγκε τὸ ποτήριον τοῦτο ἀπ᾽ ἐμοῦ· ἀλλ᾽ οὐ τί ἐγὼ θέλω ἀλλὰ τί σύ). Leaving the three behind, Jesus now moves "a little further" (μικρός)[3] into Gethsemane to seek solitude with the Father. Falling to the ground could be a sign of reverent submission or a result of Jesus' overwhelming sorrow.[4] Both fit well in context.

Mark describes the content of Jesus' prayer in indirect discourse, "that, if possible, the hour would pass from him." Then he puts the prayer itself in direct discourse: "Abba, Father …" This is the only prayer of Jesus recorded in Mark except for the cry from the cross (15:34), though Jesus is said to be praying at 1:35 and 6:46.[5]

Mark records both a transliteration of Jesus' Aramaic address, "Abba" (αββα), and also its Greek translation, "Father" (πατήρ). Much scholarly discussion has centered on Jesus' use of this term. In various works, J. Jeremias argued that Jesus' address with the Aramaic vocative 'abbā' was unique in Judaism, expressing an unprecedented level of

---

1. BDAG, 303. In Sir 30:9 the verb is used in the active voice of a spoiled child terrorizing its parents: "Pamper a child, and he will terrorize [ἐκθαμβήσει] you" (NRSV).

2. On the possible use of hyperbole by Jesus here, see martin M. Culy, "Would Jesus Exaggerate? Rethinking Matthew 26.28//Mark 14.34," *BT* 57 (2006): 105 – 9.

3. Luke 22:41 identifies the distance as a "stone's throw" (λίθου βολή).

4. The use of the imperfect ("was falling") with ἔπιπτεν is unusual. One would expect the aorist ("fell"). It may be viewed as a single action together with the imperfect προσηύχετο: "was bowing in prayer."

5. Cf. teaching about prayer in 9:29; 11:24 – 25; 13:18. Luke places great stress on Jesus' prayer life (3:21; 5:16; 6:12; 9:18, 28; 11:1; 22:32; 23:34; 23:46).

intimacy with God. While Jews occasionally referred to God as "the Father," they did not address him with the vocative as "Father" or "my Father."[6]

While Jeremias's claims are significant, they have sometimes been overstated and require some qualification.[7] God is occasionally addressed as Father and "our Father" in the OT (Deut 32:6; Isa 63:16; etc.), and there are several examples from Hellenistic Jewish sources (Sir 23:1, 4; 3 Macc 6:3; Wis 14:3) and the Dead Sea Scrolls (4Q372 1:16; 4Q460 5:6) where God is addressed with a vocative as "Father" or "my Father." Nor does *'abbā'* necessarily mean "Daddy," as many preachers have claimed. The term was used by adult children as well as younger ones and also by disciples for their teachers. Without necessary childlike connotations, the sense is closer to "Father" than "Daddy."[8]

While Jesus' use of this language may not be unique, it was unprecedented in terms of its scope and significance.[9] As far as we can tell, no one before had spoken of their relationship to God in such intimate terms or used "Father" as the standard way of addressing God in prayer. Jesus not only consistently called God "Father," but he also invited his followers to do the same as mediated through his own unique relationship with God. That this terminology made a deep impact on the early church is clear from Paul's use of the Aramaic term in Rom 8:15 and Gal 4:6.

Jesus' true humanity is evident in his request that God would take away this "cup" (ποτήριον).

Jesus has used the cup as a metaphor for his approaching death already in 10:38 – 39. As noted there, the image is a common one in the OT for suffering, and especially for divine judgment.[10] While Jesus' human desire is to avoid the coming agony, he willingly submits to the Father's will: "Not what I want, but what you want."

The prayer represents a model for believers in that Jesus brings his needs and desires to God, but emphasizes most of all his submission to God's will. Prayer should not be focused primarily on getting what we want, but on aligning our will with God's. There are important parallels here to the Lord's Prayer (Matt 6:9 – 13; cf. Luke 11:1 – 4), including the address to God as "Father," the prayer for God's will to be done, and the prayer for deliverance from testing/temptation (v. 38).[11]

14:37 – 38 Then he came and found them sleeping and said to Peter, "Simon, are you sleeping? Couldn't you watch one hour? Watch and pray, so that you do not give in to temptation. The spirit is willing, but the flesh is weak." (καὶ ἔρχεται καὶ εὑρίσκει αὐτοὺς καθεύδοντας, καὶ λέγει τῷ Πέτρῳ· Σίμων, καθεύδεις; οὐκ ἴσχυσας μίαν ὥραν γρηγορῆσαι; γρηγορεῖτε καὶ προσεύχεσθε, ἵνα μὴ ἔλθητε εἰς πειρασμόν· τὸ μὲν πνεῦμα πρόθυμον ἡ δὲ σὰρξ ἀσθενής). Jesus will return three times, a characteristic Markan pattern that highlights the disciples' failure (see Structure, above).

The statement in v. 37 is addressed to Peter in the singular, while v. 38 ("Watch and pray") is

6. J. Jeremias, *The Central Message of the New Testament* (London: SCM, 1965), 9 – 30; idem, *The Prayers of Jesus*, 11 – 65; cf. J. A. Fitzmyer, "Abba and Jesus' Relation to God," in *À cause de l'Évangile* (FS J. Dupont; Paris: Cerf, 1985), 1:15 – 38.

7. See Brown, *Death of the Messiah*, 1:172; Evans, *Mark 8:27 – 16:20*, 412 – 13; Mary Rose D'Angelo, "'Abba' and 'Father': Imperial Theology and the Jesus Traditions," *JBL* 111 (1992): 611 – 30; idem, "Theology in Mark and Q: *Abba* and 'Father' in Context," *HTR* 85 (1992): 149 – 74.

8. See James Barr, "Abba Isn't 'Daddy,'" *JTS* 39 (1988): 28 – 47.

9. So most commentators. With reference to *'abbā'*, Fitzmyer concludes that "there is no evidence in the literature of pre-Christian or first-century Palestinian Judaism that *'abbā'* was used in any sense as a personal address for God by an individual" ("Abba," 28). Brown, *Death of the Messiah*, 1:173, says that this usage is "highly unusual"; Boring, *Mark*, 399, says it was "a shockingly unusual address to God."

10. Pss 11:6; 60:3; 75:8; Isa 51:17 – 23; Jer 25:15 – 29; 49:12; 51:57; Lam 4:21; Ezek 23:31 – 34; Hab 2:16; Zech 12:2; *Pss. Sol.* 8:14; Rev 14:10; 16:19.

11. Boring, *Mark*, 399.

plural and addressed to all three. Peter is probably singled out because of his bold statement of support in vv. 29, 31: "You — who claimed you would stay faithful to the end — could not watch for even one hour!" Some have claimed Jesus' address to Peter as "Simon" is intended as a rebuke, a reversion to Peter's pre-call name (1:16, 29, 36; 3:16). He is not being the "rock" (πέτρος) that he should be.[12] This seems unlikely, however. "Peter" is used elsewhere in contexts critical of Peter (8:32 – 33; 9:5 – 6; 14:29, 31) — most significantly in the denial that follows (14:54, 66, 67).[13] In any case, the sample size is too small, since this is the only place in Mark where Jesus addresses Peter/Simon with a vocative. If we bring in the other gospels, Jesus commends "Simon" in Matt 16:17 ("Blessed are you, Simon …") and rebukes "Peter" in Luke 22:34 (the only vocative with Πέτρος in the Gospels). Other examples of the vocative with "Simon" are more neutral (Matt 17:25; Luke 22:31; John 21:15, 16, 17).

"Watch and pray" points to both human responsibility ("stay alert") and divine enablement ("depend on God").[14] The noun "temptation" (πειρασμός) and its cognate verb (πειράζω) can mean "testing" (cf. 1:13; Matt 4:1; etc.), and this sense is probably present here. "That you may not enter into temptation/testing" (ἵνα μὴ ἔλθητε εἰς πειρασμόν) does not mean merely to experience it, but to succumb to it or to fail the test. The test is to remain vigilant and faithful to Jesus (cf. Matt 6:13: "Lead us not into temptation [testing]").

Jesus adds a proverb: "the spirit is willing, but the flesh is weak." The "spirit" (πνεῦμα) here re-

fers to the human spirit, a person's desire or will.[15] "Flesh" (σάρξ) probably means the weakness and frailty of the human body (cf. Isa 31:3; Jer 17:5) rather than the Pauline sense of sinful nature or the realm of fallen humanity. In their physical and emotional exhaustion, the disciples find it difficult to stay awake.

14:39 – 40 Again after leaving, he prayed, saying the same thing. Then, coming back again, he found them sleeping, for their eyes were heavy. They did not know what to say to him (καὶ πάλιν ἀπελθὼν προσηύξατο τὸν αὐτὸν λόγον εἰπών. καὶ πάλιν ἐλθὼν εὗρεν αὐτοὺς καθεύδοντας, ἦσαν γὰρ αὐτῶν οἱ ὀφθαλμοὶ καταβαρυνόμενοι, καὶ οὐκ ᾔδεισαν τί ἀποκριθῶσιν αὐτῷ). Mark emphasizes the repetition with a double use of "again": "again going … again coming" (πάλιν ἀπελθὼν … πάλιν ἐλθών). Rather than restating the prayer, Mark simply adds, "saying the same thing."[16] The third time (v. 41) he will abbreviate even further, not mentioning Jesus' departure or prayer, only his return (contrast Matt 26:42, 44).

The reason for their sleep is "their eyes were heavy" (οἱ ὀφθαλμοὶ καταβαρυνόμενοι). The verb (καταβαρύνω) commonly means to be weighed down, burdened, or oppressed; with "eyes" the idiom points to exhaustion resulting from the lateness of the hour and the stress of the circumstances. Yet this does not excuse them. Mark adds that "they did not know what to say to him," evidence of their shame and embarrassment. They can make no excuses. While the similar narrator

---

12. Hooker, *Mark*, 349; Edwards, *Mark*, 435; Garland, *Mark*, 542.

13. Brown, *Death of the Messiah*, 1:195; Stein, *Mark*, 663.

14. The punctuation here is disputed, with the clause about temptation either indicating the content of the prayer ("Watch! And pray that you don't give in to temptation") or both verbs indicating the means by which temptation is avoided ("Watch and pray, so that you don't give in to temptation"). The latter seems most likely in context.

15. Contra Witherington, *Mark*, 380, who thinks this is the Holy Spirit.

16. Matthew is more expansive (surprisingly, since he is usually more concise), narrating the prayer a second time (Matt 26:42) and then noting Jesus' departure and prayer on the third time (26:44). Luke does not mention Jesus' second or third prayers.

comment in 9:6 points to Peter's misdirected zeal, this one points more seriously to spiritual insensitivity and unfaithfulness.

14:41–42 He came the third time and said to them, "Are you still sleeping and resting? Is it far off? The hour has come! Look, the Son of Man is delivered into the hands of sinners. Arise! Let's go! Look, the one who betrays me draws near!" (καὶ ἔρχεται τὸ τρίτον καὶ λέγει αὐτοῖς· καθεύδετε τὸ λοιπὸν καὶ ἀναπαύεσθε· ἀπέχει;[17] ἦλθεν ἡ ὥρα, ἰδοὺ παραδίδοται ὁ υἱὸς τοῦ ἀνθρώπου εἰς τὰς χεῖρας τῶν ἁμαρτωλῶν. ἐγείρεσθε ἄγωμεν· ἰδοὺ ὁ παραδιδούς με ἤγγικεν). The compound sentence, "Are you still sleeping and resting?" could be a question, as translated above (NIV, NET, HCSB, NLT[1], NRSV, ESV, NASB), or could be ironic, "Go ahead and sleep. Have your rest." (NLT, GW: "You might as well sleep now"; cf. NJB).[18] The former seems more likely in light of the parallel in v. 37 (cf. 7:18).

Even more difficult is the verb we have translated, "Is it far off?" (ἀπέχει), more commonly translated "Enough!" (NIV). The verb (ἀπέχω) has a wide range of possible senses: "to suffice/be enough," "to be paid in full," "to be distant," "to abstain from."[19] (1) "Enough!" in the sense of "enough sleeping" seems the most natural meaning in context[20] and is followed by most versions (NIV;

cf. HCSB, GNT, NRSV, NET, NAB; the Vulgate has *sufficit*).[21] The problem is this sense is otherwise unattested in Greek literature.[22]

(2) The common financial sense, "paid in full," could refer to (a) Judas, who has been "paid in full" for the betrayal.[23] This seems unlikely, however, since Judas has not yet appeared in the episode.[24] (b) Another possibility is "paid in full" in a metaphorical sense, meaning "the account is closed" or "the end has come" (GW: "It's all over"; cf. NJB).

(3) Another common meaning of the verb, "to be distant," could indicate (a) an ironic question, "Is it far off?" (i.e., "Is the end so distant that you can still sleep?");[25] (b) a statement referring to Judas, "He is far off," with the follow-up, "He has arrived," in v. 42;[26] or (c) a *question* referring to Judas, "Is he far off?" with the answer following, "No, he has arrived!"[27]

A decision here is difficult. If meaning (1) is lexically too far-fetched, the next best solution is (3a), since it balances lexical probability and contextual factors. The ironic question, "Is it so far off?" follows naturally from the previous one, "Are you still sleeping?" and is answered by what follows, "No! The hour has come!"

As elsewhere, the verb "deliver/hand over" in v. 41e (παραδίδωμι) could refer to Judas as the betrayer, or it could be a divine passive referring to God's ultimate actions (see comments on

17. We have introduced a Greek question mark here (USB[4] has a semi-colon), in light of our conclusion on the meaning of the verb.

18. This latter makes better sense of τὸ λοιπόν, which more naturally means "the rest (of the time)." In our translation it must carry the more unusual sense of "still" or "continually."

19. BDAG, 102.

20. Garland, *Mark*, 544.

21. A related possibility is that the phrase refers to Jesus' frustrated attempts to keep the disciples awake: "I have tried enough." So Collins, *Mark*, 682. Cf. ESV, NASB, NAB: "it is enough."

22. BDAG nevertheless accepts this sense as a colloquialism that emerges in a dramatic statement.

23. J. de Zwaan, "The Text and Exegesis of Mark xiv.41 and the Papyri," *Expositor* 6.12 (1905), 452–72; Stein, *Mark*, 665.

24. France, *Mark*, 589; Garland, *Mark*, 543–44.

25. J. T. Hudson, "Irony in Gethsemane? (Mark xiv. 41)," *ExpTim* 46 (1934–35): 382; Taylor, *Mark*, 557; Evans, *Mark 8:27–16:20*, 416–17. Several Western manuscripts (D W *f*) and a few later ones include the Greek τό τέλος ("the end"), suggesting that some early copyists understood the phrase to mean, "Is the end far away?"

26. Gundry, *Mark*, 857, 874–75.

27. Hooker, *Mark*, 350.

9:30c–31). Since immediately after this (v. 42b) Judas is called "the betrayer" (ὁ παραδιδούς; substantival participle), the former sense is most likely here. This, of course, does not negate that this is God's doing, and the whole passage is permeated with the theme of God's sovereign control of events (vv. 21, 27, 30, 35, 41).

The description of the religious leaders as "sinners" is surprising and may be an ironic reversal by Jesus. Those who view themselves as better than sinners and tax collectors (2:16) have now committed the greatest sin of all, rejecting the Lord's Anointed.[28] Ironic too is that Jesus is delivered over by Judas to sinners, but also by God *for* sinners (Rom 4:25).

"Arise! Let's go!" in a different context could indicate an attempt to flee, but here it clearly means to rise up to meet the approaching mob. Jesus willingly accepts God's purpose for him. No response is recorded by the disciples, but in a short time (after one act of misguided valor, 14:47) they will all abandon Jesus and flee (v. 50). They are not yet willing to take up their crosses and follow him (8:34).

Theology in Application

Jesus' Agony and the Significance of the Cross

Jesus' sorrow and deep distress is understandable, considering his coming betrayal, abandonment, excruciating suffering, and death. Yet in another sense it is surprising — even scandalous. Martyrs are supposed to face death with courage and confidence, expressing steadfast faith in God and hope for the resurrection. Consider the example of aged Eleazar, whose noble martyrdom in the days of the Maccabees at the hands of Antiochus Epiphanes is described as "an example of nobility and a memorial of courage, not only to the young but to the great body of his nation" (2 Macc 6:31 NRSV). Or consider seven brothers and their mother, who praise God and mock the arrogance of Antiochus the king even as they are one by one gruesomely tortured and executed. After six have died, the youngest refuses to recant and even taunts the king:

> But you, unholy wretch, you most defiled of all mortals, do not be elated in vain and puffed up by uncertain hopes, when you raise your hand against the children of heaven. You have not yet escaped the judgment of the almighty, all-seeing God. For our brothers after enduring a brief suffering have drunk of ever-flowing life, under God's covenant; but you, by the judgment of God, will receive just punishment for your arrogance. (2 Macc 7:34–36 NRSV)

While not always so defiant, martyrs throughout history have been praised for showing serene courage in the face of imminent death. The writer to the Hebrews speaks of those who remained faithful despite suffering and martyrdom (Heb

---

28. "Sinners" could perhaps refer to the Romans (cf. 10:33b), but the immediate context of the conspiracy of Judas with the religious leaders (14:10–11) and their naming in the passion predictions (8:31; 10:33a) suggest *they* are the referents.

11:32–38), and Stephen faces martyrdom with peace and confidence (Acts 7:54–60; cf. Phil 2:20–21; 2 Tim 4:6–8, 16–18).

Some have seen in Jesus' distress and sorrow in Gethsemane a less noble approach to martyrdom. Celsus, the second-century philosopher and opponent of Christianity, used the Gethsemane account to attack Jesus' character and his divinity.[29] How do we respond? First, it must be noted that for Mark, Jesus' death is far more than the death of a martyr. It is a ransom payment for the sins of the world (10:45), inaugurating the kingdom of God and a new covenant sealed through his sacrificial death on the cross (14:24). Jesus' cry of dereliction from the cross, "My God, my God, why have you forsaken me?" (15:34; cf. Ps 22:1), reflects Jesus' experience of abandonment by the Father as the punishment of the sins of the world is placed on him.

Here we may dip into the deep well of Pauline theology, since Mark's thinking is surely not far from Paul's. The death of Jesus was a sacrifice of atonement, offered for the sins of the world (Rom 3:25). Though Jesus had no sin, he became sin for us (2 Cor 5:21), taking the curse of the law on himself (Gal 3:13; cf. Deut 21:23). This profound cosmic and eschatological significance of the cross helps to explain Jesus' deep and profound distress experienced at Gethsemane. So too does Jesus' true humanity.

Jesus' True Humanity

Perhaps more than in any other event in Jesus' ministry, Gethsemane reveals his true humanity. The Markan Jesus feels the same pain and emotions that we feel. He experienced fatigue (4:38) and hunger (11:12), anger and indignation (1:41; 3:5; 10:14), frustration (8:17, 21), and overwhelming sorrow and distress (14:33–34). He felt the emotional weight of betrayal and abandonment by his closest friends (14:18–21, 27–31). The author of Hebrews develops this theological theme of Jesus' humanity more than any other NT writer. Jesus was made like us "in every respect, so that he could become a merciful and faithful high priest in things relating to God, to make atonement for the sins of the people" (Heb 2:17–18 NET). Alluding to Gethsemane, the author writes:

> During the days of Jesus' life on earth, he offered up prayers and petitions with fervent cries and tears to the one who could save him from death, and he was heard because of his reverent submission. Son though he was, he learned obedience from what he suffered and, once made perfect, he became the source of eternal salvation for all who obey him. (Heb 5:7–9 NIV)

That Jesus "learned obedience from what he suffered" is as scandalous to some as the Gethsemane event. Yet Jesus had to be fully human so that he could be our

---

29. Origen, *Cels.* 2:24.

substitute, the "pioneer of our salvation" who was made "perfect through what he suffered" (Heb 2:10). Jesus' substitutionary and vicarious death broke the curse of the law, paid the penalty for our sins, and through his resurrection established a new and perfected humanity, a status we can now have through identification with Christ. While the deity of Christ is a doctrine that is well defended in evangelical circles, his humanity is often a neglected one. Yet it is because of this humanity that Jesus could be *our* substitute and *our* Savior.

True Discipleship

A third key theme in the present episode is the nature of true discipleship. As so often in Mark, the disciples serve as a negative foil, and Jesus acts as the true disciple. They fall asleep, a symbol of spiritual insensitivity (Rom 13:11; 1 Thess 5:5 – 6), while he remains alert. He is in constant prayer (Eph 6:18; 1 Thess 5:17), living a life of dependence on God. They cannot even watch and pray for one hour. He experiences the same temptation to turn and run, praying earnestly that God would remove this "cup" of suffering and find another way to accomplish his purpose. Yet he stays faithful and obedient, praying, "Not what I want, but what you want."

God wants us to come to him with our needs. He wants us to express our desires and to pour out our concerns and anxieties before him. Yet he calls on us to trust him, recognizing that he has sovereign control over every situation and will bring us safely home. Like Jesus, we need to pray, "Not what I want, but what you want." Or, as it is so clearly expressed in the Lord's Prayer, "Your kingdom come, your will be done, on earth as it is in heaven" (Matt 6:10).

57

Mark 14:43 – 52

Literary Context

The Passion Narrative continues with the arrival of the betrayer (14:43), an event Jesus has just announced (14:42). As we have seen, this narrative, unlike the pericope style of the rest of the gospel, represents a continuous story. Linking the present episode to the previous ones are Judas's betrayal agreement (14:10 – 11), Jesus' prediction of his betrayal at the Last Supper (14:18 – 21), and the various passion predictions, where Jesus earlier said he would be rejected by (8:31) or handed over to (10:33 – 34; cf. 9:31) the religious leaders.

Main Idea

Even at his betrayal and arrest, when Jesus is "delivered into human hands" (9:31; cf. 8:31; 10:33; 14:18), he is in charge, continuing to follow God's script by acknowledging that these events are in fulfillment of Scripture. In contrast to Jesus' faithfulness, the disciples abandon him and flee at the first sign of trouble.

Translation

Mark 14:43 – 52

43a	setting (temporal)	Immediately, while he was speaking,
b	Character entrance	**Judas, one of the Twelve, arrived,** and
		with him
c	character description	
		a crowd
		with swords and clubs,
d		sent from the ruling priests and
e		the experts in the law and
f		the elders.
44a	Action/Flashback	**The one who betrayed him had given them a signal, saying,**
b	instruction	*"Whomever I kiss is the one. Arrest him and lead him away under guard."*
45a	action	Stepping forward and going immediately to him,
b	Greeting/Betrayal	**he said,**
c	address	*"Rabbi,"*
d	Action	and **kissed him.**
46	Action	And **they laid their hands on him and arrested him.**
47a	Action/Response to 46	But **a certain one of those standing there,** drawing his sword,
b		**struck the servant of the high priest**
c		and **cut off his ear.**
48a	Response to 46	Responding, **Jesus said to them,**
b		*"Why are you coming out here with swords and clubs to seize me like an outlaw?*
49a		*Every day I was with you in the temple courts teaching,*
b		*and you did not arrest me.*
c		*But the Scriptures must be fulfilled."*
50a		Deserting him,
b	Action/Response	**they all fled.**
51a	Character entrance	**A certain young man was following him,**
b	character description	with a linen garment wrapped around his naked body.
52a	Action	**They seized him,**
b	Response	but **he fled naked,**
c	character description	leaving his linen garment behind.

Structure

This brief episode contains five events or scene parts: the arrival of Judas with a crowd (v. 43), the arrest of Jesus (vv. 44 – 46), the violent response by an unnamed bystander (v. 47), Jesus' rebuke of his opponents for their duplicity (vv. 48 – 49), and the abandonment and flight of all, including an unidentified youth (vv. 50 – 52).

Exegetical Outline

→ **1. The Arrival of the Crowd (14:43)**

2. The Arrest of Jesus (14:44–46)

    a. The plan (14:44)

    b. Judas's action (14:45)

    c. The arrest (14:46)

3. A Bystander Strikes Back (14:47)

4. Jesus Rebukes His Opponents (14:48–49)

5. The Flight of the Disciples (14:50–52)

    a. All abandon Jesus and run (14:50)

    b. A young man's escape (14:51–52)

Explanation of the Text

14:43 Immediately, while he was speaking, Judas, one of the Twelve, arrived, and with him a crowd with swords and clubs, sent from the ruling priests and the experts in the law and the elders (Καὶ εὐθὺς ἔτι αὐτοῦ λαλοῦντος[1] παραγίνεται Ἰούδας εἷς τῶν δώδεκα καὶ μετ᾿ αὐτοῦ ὄχλος μετὰ μαχαιρῶν καὶ ξύλων παρὰ τῶν ἀρχιερέων καὶ τῶν γραμματέων καὶ τῶν πρεσβυτέρων). Mark's characteristic "immediately" (εὐθύς; see 1:10) here means just that — at that very moment. "One of the Twelve" would seem to be redundant after the identification of Judas in 14:10 (cf. 3:19; 14:18, 20).[2] Mark's purpose is likely to emphasize again the shocking point that one of Jesus' own betrayed him (cf. 14:18, 20). Since Mark did not mention Judas's departure from the group during the Last Supper, his sudden appearance here is surprising (contrast John 13:27–30). This could simply be Mark's abbreviated style, but it also emphasizes Judas's deception. Though presumed to be with the group, he suddenly shows up as the betrayer.

The nature of the arresting party is debated. Mark describes them as a "crowd" (ὄχλος) sent by the ruling priests, the experts in the law, and the elders — the three groups that made up the Sanhedrin (see comments on 8:31). This would likely include a contingent of temple police, Jewish soldiers who kept order within the large temple complex. Luke 22:47, 52 explicitly refers to a crowd that included "officers of the temple [police]" (στρατηγοί τοῦ ἱεροῦ), ruling priests, and elders.

Were Roman soldiers present? John's gospel speaks of two groups: Jewish officers/police (οἱ ὑπηρέται τῶν Ἰουδαίων) representing the ruling priests and Pharisees, and a cohort (σπεῖρα) with a "tribune" or "chiliarch" (ὁ χιλίαρχος = "ruler of a thousand") leading them (John 18:3, 12) — terms commonly used for Roman military.[3] A Roman cohort was a tenth of a legion (6,000 men), numbering about 600 to 1,000 soldiers and led by a tribune. At Paul's Jerusalem arrest in Acts, Lysias is "tribune of the cohort" (ὁ χιλίαρχος τῆς σπείρης)

---

1. The genitive absolute is used here because the subject of the participial phrase ("Jesus") is different from the subject of the main clause ("Judas").

2. Some commentators propose that the redundancy results from Mark's use of a source, which introduced Judas for the first time here. While this is possible, the explanation above is just as likely.

3. Brown, *John*, 2:807–8.

of Roman soldiers stationed at the Fortress of Antonia, overlooking the temple complex (Acts 21:31; 24:22). These soldiers were normally garrisoned in Caesarea, but they moved to Jerusalem to keep the peace during a festival.

Since the Roman soldiers are not mentioned in the Synoptics, some commentators reject their historicity, especially in such large numbers. Yet the Romans were obsessed with keeping the peace, especially during the nationalistic Passover feast and concerning potential "messianic" movements (like this one). It is not surprising that Pilate would have been kept informed of the high priest's actions and sent soldiers, perhaps a smaller "detachment" (NIV) or "squad" (NET) from the larger temple cohort.[4] The reference to a crowd armed with swords and "clubs"[5] has suggested to some that this is an unruly mob. But the word can refer to police batons or war clubs, part of the equipment of soldiers.[6]

14:44 The one who betrayed him had given them a signal, saying, "Whomever I kiss is the one. Arrest him and lead him away under guard." (δεδώκει δὲ ὁ παραδιδοὺς αὐτὸν σύσσημον αὐτοῖς λέγων· ὃν ἂν φιλήσω αὐτός ἐστιν, κρατήσατε αὐτὸν καὶ ἀπάγετε ἀσφαλῶς). In a brief flashback, Mark relates the plan to arrest Jesus. The participial phrase (ὁ παραδιδοὺς αὐτόν) means "the one betraying him," but because of its awkward English style, it is rendered "the betrayer." The adverb "under guard" or "securely" (ἀσφαλῶς) can also mean "safely" and could relate to a guarantee made to Judas not to harm Jesus. This is unlikely, however, since in Mark's narrative Judas is painted in wholly negative terms.

The kiss is a "signal" (σύσσημον) necessary to identify Jesus in the darkness of Gethsemane. Only Judas could get close enough to the group without arousing suspicion and allowing the prey to escape. A kiss in the ancient Near East (as today) was a sign of hospitality and friendship (2 Sam 20:9; Luke 7:45), especially indicating family affection (Gen 27:26; 33:4; 45:15; Luke 15:20). Peter and Paul both encourage believers to greet one another with a kiss, evidence that they are brothers and sisters in Christ (Rom 16:16; 1 Cor 16:20; 2 Cor 13:12; 1 Thess 5:26; 1 Pet 5:14). The claim that rabbis typically greeted their disciples this way comes from later rabbinic tradition (nowhere else seen in the Gospels), but is likely true in light of common social convention.[7] The kiss was normally given on the cheek or hand.

14:45 – 46 Stepping forward and going immediately to him, he said, "Rabbi," and kissed him. And they laid their hands on him and arrested him (καὶ ἐλθὼν εὐθὺς προσελθὼν αὐτῷ λέγει· ῥαββί, καὶ κατεφίλησεν αὐτόν· οἱ δὲ ἐπέβαλον τὰς χεῖρας αὐτῷ καὶ ἐκράτησαν αὐτόν). Judas approaches Jesus and addresses him as "Rabbi" ("my master/ teacher"), the common address used by the disciples for Jesus (9:5; 11:21; cf. 10:51). For Judas this is another signal of identification for the crowd. For the reader it is further evidence of Judas's duplicity. The verb for "kiss" used in v. 45 (καταφιλέω) is a cognate of the one used in v. 44 (φιλέω) and may be an intensive form indicating a dramatic or prolonged kiss to ensure identification.[8] Yet the verbs can be used synonymously in Greek, with no particular drama in the former, so this may be merely

---

4. D. A. Carson, *The Gospel according to John* (Grand Rapids: Eerdmans, 1991), 577, points out that "cohort" (σπεῖρα) could be used of a "maniple" of 200 men or even less.

5. ξύλον means "wood" or objects made of wood, hence "clubs" or "cudgels" (BDAG, 685).

6. Polybius, *Hist.* 6.37.3; Herodotus, *Hist.* 2.63; Josephus, *J.W.* 2.9.4 §176; *Life* 45 §233.

7. Much more speculative is the claim that only the rabbi was supposed to initiate the kiss (cf. Mann, *Mark*, 596), so that Judas's actions are a "calculated insult."

8. See Luke 7:45, where the kiss of greeting (φίλημα) not offered by Simon the Pharisee is contrasted with the woman's kisses of true devotion (καταφιλέω) (cf. the father's emotional kisses in Luke 15:20, also καταφιλέω).

stylistic variation.[9] The hypocrisy of Judas's action recalls Prov 27:6: "Wounds from a friend can be trusted, but an enemy multiplies kisses" (cf. 2 Sam 20:9; Sir 29:5).

14:47 But a certain one of those standing there, drawing his sword, struck the servant of the high priest and cut off his ear (εἷς δέ τις τῶν παρεστηκότων σπασάμενος τὴν μάχαιραν ἔπαισεν τὸν δοῦλον τοῦ ἀρχιερέως καὶ ἀφεῖλεν αὐτοῦ τὸ ὠτάριον). This event, which occurs in all four Gospels, is most abbreviated in Mark. He mentions only that some individual struck with a sword, cutting off the ear of the high priest's servant. John identifies the attacker as Peter and says the servant's name was Malchus (John 18:10). In Luke, the disciples first ask, "Should we strike with our swords?" (Luke 22:49). Both Luke and John identify it as the "right ear" (Luke 22:50; John 18:10). Nor does Mark mention any response by Jesus to the man (Jesus only rebukes his opponents; see vv. 48 – 49). In the other three gospels, Jesus calls for a halt to opposition, adding in Matthew the proverb that "all who draw the sword will die by the sword" and that if he wished, he could call twelve legions of angels to his defense (Matt 26:52 – 53). In Luke alone Jesus heals the man's ear (Luke 22:51).

Some have claimed Mark's "one standing there" (εἷς ... τῶν παρεστηκότων) is not a disciple at all, but either one of the arresting party who changed his mind about Jesus, or, more likely, part of a third group of bystanders.[10] Yet no other bystanders are mentioned, and, as Evans points out, both Matthew

and Luke understood Mark to be referring to a disciple (Matt 26:52 – 53; Luke 22:49).[11] Some interpreters explain Mark's lack of identification as an attempt to protect the identity of the man, whether it was Peter[12] or another unnamed disciple.[13]

14:48 – 49 Responding, Jesus said to them, "Why are you coming out here with swords and clubs to seize me like an outlaw? Every day I was with you in the temple courts teaching, and you did not arrest me. But the Scriptures must be fulfilled." (Καὶ ἀποκριθεὶς ὁ Ἰησοῦς εἶπεν αὐτοῖς· ὡς ἐπὶ λῃστὴν ἐξήλθατε μετὰ μαχαιρῶν καὶ ξύλων συλλαβεῖν με; καθ᾽ ἡμέραν ἤμην πρὸς ὑμᾶς ἐν τῷ ἱερῷ διδάσκων καὶ οὐκ ἐκρατήσατέ με· ἀλλ᾽ ἵνα πληρωθῶσιν αἱ γραφαί). The idiom "responding ... said" (ἀποκριθεὶς ... εἶπεν) represents a single response ("he said") rather than two and does not necessarily indicate an "answer." It can be a verbal response to any situation (see comments on 11:13c – 14), in this case the approach of the arresting party.

Jesus challenges both the justification and the manner of their actions. They have come out after him with weapons as though he were a violent criminal. And they have chosen the secret of darkness, no doubt because they feared his influence with the people (cf. 11:18, 32; 12:12; 14:1 – 2). The noun translated "outlaw" (λῃστής) originally meant a "robber," "bandit," or "highwayman," but was used by the Romans and their supporters of revolutionaries and insurrectionists, whom they considered common thugs and criminals.[14] Some

9. See the references cited in BDAG, 529 (καταφιλέω) and 1056 (φιλέω), where no distinction is evident.

10. So Hooker, *Mark*, 351; Gundry, *Mark*, 860; Brown, *Death of the Messiah*, 1:266 – 67; van Iersel, *Reading Mark*, 438 – 39; Boring, *Mark*, 402; cf. Marcus, *Mark 9 – 16*, 993.

11. Evans, *Mark 8:27 – 16:20*, 424. The claim that "those standing by" does not refer to the disciples elsewhere in the Passion Narrative (14:69, 70; 15:35, 39; so Brown, *Death of the Messiah*, 1:266) is not a strong one. This is not a technical term,

and the verb is too general to identify who is or is not included.

12. Lagrange, *Marc*, 394.

13. Theissen, *Gospels in Context*, 184 – 89. Theissen does not think it was Peter, but sees both this episode and the one that follows (14:51 – 52) as attempts to protect still-living followers of Jesus — evidence of the early date of Mark's Passion Narrative (cf. Marcus, *Mark 9 – 16*, 993).

14. R. A. Horsley, "Popular Messianic Movements around the Time of Jesus," *CBQ* 46 (1981): 409 – 32; idem, "Popular

versions use the more literal "robber" (ESV, NASB, NKJV, REB) or "bandit" (NRSV, NJB), but this is not quite right, since Jesus was not accused of stealing things. More accurate is "revolutionary" (NLT) or "leading a rebellion" (NIV), or the more general "renegade," "outlaw" (NET), or "criminal" (HCSB; Message). The so-called "thieves" (λῃσταί) crucified with Jesus were almost certainly insurrectionists like Barabbas,[15] who is said to have committed murder in the "uprising" or "rebellion" (ἡ στάσις; 15:7).

Since arriving in Jerusalem, Jesus had taught "daily" and openly in the temple courts (12:1 – 37). His ministry was one of transparency and integrity (12:14). Yet these people have come at night to seize him. Despite their duplicity, Jesus again acknowledges that all that is happening is in fulfillment of Scripture (cf. 14:21, 27).[16] He does not quote any text, and Mark does not indicate which one he had in mind. The most likely candidate is Zech 13:7 ("Strike the shepherd, and the sheep will be scattered"), which Jesus quoted in Mark 14:27 (see comments) and which relates directly to his arrest and the abandonment by the disciples (v. 50). As in 14:21, however, the main point is not the particular reference but the fact that God is guiding these events.

14:50 Deserting him, they all fled (καὶ ἀφέντες αὐτὸν ἔφυγον πάντες). Just as Jesus predicted (v. 27; Zech 13:7), his disciples all flee, abandoning him to face this crisis alone. Apart from Peter's denial (14:66 – 72), this is the last we hear of the disciples until the resurrection announcement (16:7).

14:51 – 52 A certain young man was following him, with a linen garment wrapped around his naked body. They seized him, but he fled naked, leaving his linen garment behind (καὶ νεανίσκος τις συνηκολούθει αὐτῷ περιβεβλημένος σινδόνα ἐπὶ γυμνοῦ, καὶ κρατοῦσιν αὐτόν· ὁ δὲ καταλιπὼν τὴν σινδόνα γυμνὸς ἔφυγεν). This is one of the strangest incidents, not only in Mark, but in the whole of the gospel tradition. Who was this young man, and why did Mark include this odd episode in his gospel? A bewildering array of suggestions have been made.[17] We may divide them between gospel characters and symbolic interpretations.

Proposals for characters include: (1) John Mark, the author of the gospel; (2) John the apostle (identified as the "beloved disciple" of the Fourth Gospel); (3) Lazarus (also when identified as the beloved disciple); (4) James, the half brother of Jesus; (5) the rich "young" ruler of Mark 10:17 – 31; (6) a young disciple Jesus raised from the dead known from the *Secret Gospel of Mark* (see "In Depth: The *Secret Gospel of Mark*"); (7) the "young man" (νεανίσκος) who appeared at the tomb of Jesus (16:5); (8) a local youth who came out to investigate and was inadvertently seized by the crowd; (9) an unknown follower of Jesus outside the circle of the Twelve. Symbolic interpretations include: (10) a midrash based on the image of a warrior fleeing naked in Amos 2:16 or the escape of Joseph without his cloak from Potiphar's wife (Gen 39:12); (11) a symbol of the risen Christ; (12) a symbol of baptismal candidates shedding their garments of baptism; (13) a symbolic representation of the abandonment by the disciples.

Prophetic Movements at the Time of Jesus: Their Principal Features and Social Origins," *JSNT* 8 (1986): 3 – 27; cf. Evans, *Mark 8:27 – 16:20,* 425 – 26.

15. John 18:40 refers to Barabbas as a λῃστής.

16. There is an ellipsis in the Greek with a verb that must be supplied, "but [this happened] so that the Scriptures would be fulfilled" (ἀλλ᾿ ἵνα πληρωθῶσιν αἱ γραφαί). Matthew 26:56
fills in Mark's ellipsis with, "this has all taken place ..." (τοῦτο δὲ ὅλον γέγονεν) and by adding "of the prophets ..." (τῶν προφητῶν) after "the Scriptures/writings" (αἱ γραφαί).

17. For summaries of various views and advocates, see Brown, *Death of the Messiah,* 1:294 – 304; Evans, *Mark 8:27 – 16:20,* 427 – 29; Marcus, *Mark 9 – 16,* 1124 – 25.

None of the symbolic views work well. The disciples have already fled (against view 13), and fleeing naked is a sign of shame, hardly applicable to Christ himself (view 11) or baptismal candidates (view 12). Amos 2:16 and Gen 39:12 have little in common with Mark's account (view 10). Neither John (view 2) nor Lazarus (view 3) works, since the beloved disciple was at the Last Supper (John 13:23–25) and so would have been properly clothed. James the brother of Jesus (view 4) seems unlikely, since he was so well-known in the early church. The rich man of Mark 10:17–31 (view 5) is not called "young" by Mark, losing any connection to this passage. The young man of the *Secret Gospel of Mark* (view 6) is likely a literary fiction based on this passage, created long after Mark wrote (see below). The "young man" dressed in white sitting inside the tomb in 16:5 (view 7) is surely an angel,[18] and so could not be a frightened, fleeing youth. Mark's statement that the boy was "following" Jesus seems to rule out a local boy who has merely stumbled onto the scene (view 8).

The best guess — and they are little more than that — is either the default answer that this is an unknown follower of Jesus (view 9), perhaps known to Mark's readers, or that it is John Mark himself (view 1). A circumstantial case has been made for view 1, since it explains why Mark would include such an unusual account in his gospel.[19] Mark's mother Mary was apparently well off, with a home in Jerusalem large enough for the church to gather (Acts 12:12). If Jesus and his disciples spent the Last Supper there (another hypothesis), perhaps young Mark grabbed a linen sheet and followed the disciples out of the city. This would explain why he is wearing only a "linen garment" (σινδών) against his body, rather than the traditional tunic or undergarment (χιτών). Linen is the material of the wealthy, another circumstantial connection to Mark's family. Against this interpretation is Papias's claim (c. AD 130) that Mark "neither heard the Lord nor followed him,"[20] which implies Mark was not present during Jesus' ministry. Papias, of course, could be mistaken or may mean only that Mark was not a disciple of Jesus. Since Mark lived in Jerusalem rather than Galilee, his contacts with Jesus would have been limited.

Although the identity of the young man remains a mystery, Mark's purpose in the passage seems a bit clearer: to show the chaos that surrounded Jesus' arrest and the total abandonment of his followers.

IN DEPTH: The *Secret Gospel of Mark*

The *Secret Gospel of Mark* is a putative early Christian source, a few passages of which were allegedly recorded in a letter written by Clement of Alexandria. In two books published in 1973, Morton Smith of Columbia University claimed that in 1958 he discovered a previously unknown letter of Clement at the monastery of Mar Saba on the West Bank.[21] The letter was hand copied (in eighteenth-century style handwriting) by an unknown copyist into the blank end

---

18. See evidence in Brown, *Death of the Messiah*, 1:300.

19. Cranfield, *Mark*, 439; Lane, *Mark*, 526; Evans, *Mark 8:27–16:20*, 428.

20. Eusebius, *Hist. eccl.* 3.39.15.

21. M. Smith, *Clement of Alexandria and a Secret Gospel of Mark* (Cambridge, MA: Harvard University Press, 1973); idem, *The Secret Gospel: The Discovery and Interpretation of the Secret Gospel according to Mark* (New York: Harper & Row, 1973); cf. idem, "Clement of Alexandria and Secret Mark: The Score at the End of the First Decade," *HTR* 75 (1982): 449–61.

pages of a printed edition of the works of Ignatius of Antioch by Isaac Voss (published in 1646). In the letter, which was presumably written by Clement to a man named Theodore around AD 200, Clement makes reference to this *Secret Gospel of Mark*. According to Clement, after Peter's martyrdom in Rome, Mark went to Alexandria, where he expanded his original gospel into a more "spiritual" one. Clement quotes two passages from this expanded gospel. The longer and more important passage appears after Mark 10:34 and recounts how Jesus raised a young man from the dead in Bethany. The story has similarities to John's account of the raising of Lazarus. At one point after he is raised, the young man comes to Jesus "clothed with a linen garment over his nakedness" (similar to the phrase used in 14:51).

Some scholars doubt Smith's claim entirely, believing Clement's letter to be a forgery.[22] The pages from Voss's book containing the manuscript have since been lost and scholars must rely on photographs and copies made by Smith and others. Other scholars accept the authenticity of the letter, but doubt Clement's assertions that the gospel is from Mark's hand, believing it to be a later Gnostic expansion dependent on the four canonical Gospels.[23] Still others accept both Smith's and Clement's claims that the excerpts are from an authentic revision of Mark's gospel.[24] Although the jury is still out, the scholarly consensus appears to be leaning toward viewing the work as a forgery, either by Smith himself or from an earlier period.[25]

Theology in Application

The theme of God's sovereign purpose continues in this episode as Jesus again points out that all that is happening — even his betrayal — is the fulfillment of Scripture and part of God's saving purpose (v. 49). God will accomplish his plan despite and even through the evil actions of sinful human beings.

The various actions taken by those present also provide us with examples of inappropriate responses to Jesus:

22. See Quentin Quesnell, "The Mar Saba Clementine: A Question of Evidence," *CBQ* 37 (1975): 48 – 67; Craig A. Evans and Emanuel Tov, *Exploring the Origins of the Bible: Canon Formation in Historical, Literary, and Theological Perspectives* (Grand Rapids: Baker, 2008), 270 – 72; Stephen C. Carlson, *The Gospel Hoax: Morton Smith's Invention of* Secret Mark (Waco, TX: Baylor University Press, 2005); Peter G. Jeffery, *The Secret Gospel of Mark Unveiled: Imagined Rituals of Sex, Death and Madness in a Biblical Forgery* (New Haven, CT/London: Yale University Press, 2007).

23. See, e.g., Raymond E. Brown, "The Relation of 'The Secret Gospel of Mark' to the Fourth Gospel," *CBQ* 36 (1974): 466 – 85; Gundry, *Mark*, 603 – 23.

24. S. G. Brown, *Mark's Other Gospel: Rethinking Morton Smith's Controversial Discovery* (Waterloo, ON: Wilfrid Laurier University Press, 2005).

25. See the excursus in Collins, *Mark*, 486 – 93, for a good summary of the debate.

1. *Outright rejection.* Judas, the religious leaders, and the crowd represent complete rejection of Jesus and his claims related to the kingdom of God (vv. 43 – 46). While pretending to be on the side of right (by greeting Jesus as "Rabbi" and with a kiss), Judas is actually opposing God's kingdom purposes. Many people and movements in this world stand defiantly against God: those who oppress the poor, violate human rights, or exploit women and children; those who persecute Christians in the name of communism, nationalism, or other religions; those who attack the authority and historicity of God's Word and the claims of Christ.

2. *Abandonment.* Another inappropriate response to Jesus is seen in the disciples, who, though vehemently proclaiming their allegiance (14:31), flee the scene at the first sign of trouble (14:50 – 52). Many people are attracted to Christianity or come to church for social reasons or business opportunities. Others hope Chrsitianity will meet their emotional needs or make their problems go away. Yet when temptations, difficulties, or hardships come, they decide it is not worth it and move on to other self-help fads. They are like the seed that falls on rocky ground in Jesus' parable, who receive the Word with joy but then fall away when trouble or persecution comes (4:16 – 17).

3. *Inappropriate action.* The disciple who draws his sword to strike has good intentions — to advance Jesus' cause — but uses inappropriate means to do so. Many people in this world seek to promote the Christian faith, but do so in inappropriate ways or with the wrong motives. Consider what is sometimes called "Jesus junk": toys, trinkets, souvenirs, or bumper stickers that promote Jesus or Christianity. While some of these these may be positive tools for sharing the gospel, others distort the message or promote an inaccurate picture of Christianity. In the same way, health-care products, weight-loss plans, self-help groups, child-raising techniques, and business models are often claimed to be "biblical," "God's way," or "Christ-centered." Yet they often apply biblical texts out of context or promote their own faddish theories. Following Jesus is not about using his name to promote our own agendas. It is about taking up our cross to follow *him,* adopting the self-giving message and mind-set of the kingdom of God.

Mark 14:53 – 65

Literary Context

The closely connected episodes of Mark's Passion Narrative continue as Jesus is led from Gethsemane to the high priest's residence. Mark's notice that Peter followed and got as far as the high priest's courtyard (v. 54) prepares for his denial in the next episode (14:66 – 72). This is the first of two trial scenes in Mark, a Jewish one before the Sanhedrin (14:53 – 65) and a Roman one before Pontius Pilate, the Roman governor (15:1 – 15).

The purpose of the Jewish hearing is apparently to marshall evidence to be used against Jesus to gain a capital sentence from the Roman governor (see comments on vv. 63 – 64). Matthew follows Mark's basic structure while John and Luke mention additional trial phases. In John the Jewish trial comes in two stages, with hearings before Annas, the father-in-law of the high priest (John 18:12 – 14, 19 – 23), and Caiaphas (18:24). Luke includes an additional phase in the Roman trial, as Pilate sends Jesus to Herod Antipas, who is in Jerusalem for the Passover festival. Herod interrogates Jesus and returns him to Pilate (Luke 23:7 – 12).

Main Idea

At Jesus' trial before the Sanhedrin, false charges against him fail, but when questioned by the high priest Jesus acknowledges that he is the Messiah and Son of God, who will be vindicated as the exalted and returning Son of Man. This is enough to provoke a charge of blasphemy by the high priest and condemnation by the Sanhedrin. Though seemingly a disaster for Jesus, God's plan of redemption moves forward toward his death as a ransom for sins.

Translation

Mark 14:53–65

53a	Action/Setting (spatial)	**They took Jesus to the high priest.**
b	Action/Character entrance	**All the ruling priests and the elders and the experts in the law gathered together.**
54a	Action/Character entrance	**Peter followed him at a distance,**
b		going as far as the courtyard of the high priest.
c	Setting/Character description	**There he was sitting with the guards** and
d		**warming himself by the fire.**
55a	Action/Interrogation	**The high priest and the whole Sanhedrin were looking for evidence against Jesus**
b	purpose of 55a	to put him to death,
c	Result of 55a	but **they could not find any.**
56a	Reason for 55c	For **many falsely testified against him,**
b	Contrast with 56a	but **their testimonies did not agree.**
57	Testimony	**Some, standing up, were falsely testifying against him, saying,**
58a	report of speech	"We heard him saying,
b	prediction	'I will destroy this temple made with hands
c	prediction	and in three days I will build another not made with hands.'"
59	Result of 58	**Yet even their testimony about this did not agree.**
60a	character description	Standing up in their midst,
b	Questions/Demand	**the high priest asked Jesus,**
c		"Are you not going to answer?
d		What are these charges they are making against you?"
61a	Response to 60	But **he remained silent and answered nothing.**
b	Question	**Again the high priest asked him,**
c		"Are you the Messiah, the Son of the Blessed One?"
62a	Response to 61c	**Jesus said,**
b	affirmation	"I am,
c	prophecy	and you will see the Son of Man sitting at the right hand of Power
d	prophecy	and coming with the clouds of heaven."
63a	character description	Tearing his garments,
b	Accusation/Request for Verdict	**the high priest said,**
c	rhetorical question	"Why do we need any more testimony?
64a	assertion	You have heard the blasphemy.
b	question	What do you think?"
c	Response to 64b/Verdict	**They all condemned him as worthy of death.**

65a	Actions/Response to 64	**Some began** **to spit on him,**
b		**to blindfold him,**
c		**to strike him with fists,** and
d		**to say to him,**
e	mockery	*"Prophesy."*
f	Action	Then **the guards took him away and beat him.**

Structure

This episode is made up of five scenes: an introduction (vv. 53 – 54), false testimony against Jesus (vv. 55 – 59), the dialogue between the high priest and Jesus (vv. 60 – 62), accusation of blasphemy and condemnation by the Sanhedrin (vv. 63 – 64), and the abusive treatment of Jesus (v. 65). It also represents another of Mark's sandwiches, or intercalations (see Introduction to Mark: Literary Features). The account of the arrest and trial (14:53 – 15:2) is interrupted twice, first by the statement about Peter following at a distance and entering the courtyard (v. 54) and then by Peter's denial (14:66 – 72). The account concludes with the Sanhedrin's plan to take Jesus to Pilate (15:1 – 2). The relationship of the two scenes is one of contrast. While Jesus faithfully testifies that he is the Messiah, suffering condemnation and beating, Peter denies that he even knows Jesus, escaping punishment but suffering shame and humiliation. Jesus represents the model disciple who will ultimately gain true life by losing his physical life, while Peter risks losing his soul while protecting his physical life (cf. 8:35). As Jesus has taught, those who are ashamed of him will suffer shame and loss (8:38).

The historicity of the trial scene has been challenged by some on the basis that it violates regulations set down in the Mishnah.[1] According to the Mishnaic tract *Sanhedrin*, capital cases could not be tried at night. While a verdict of acquittal could be reached on the day of the trial, a conviction must wait until the next day (*m. Sanh.* 4:1). No trials could be held on the eve of the Sabbath or during festivals (ibid.). A second hearing was necessary for a death sentence (ibid., 5:5). Witnesses were to be strongly admonished to speak the truth (ibid., 4:5) and contradictory evidence must be discounted (ibid., 5:2). A charge of blasphemy could be made only if the defendant had pronounced the divine name (ibid., 7.5). Trials were to be held in one of three courts in Jerusalem (the residence of the high priest was not one of them; ibid., 11:2).

Jesus' trial in Mark clearly violates these regulations. He is tried at night and during the festival. A verdict is announced immediately without waiting for a second

---

1. See especially Paul Winter, *On the Trial of Jesus* (2nd ed.; Berlin: deGruyter, 1974), passim. Cf. Brown, *Death of the Messiah*, 1:357 – 63; France, *Mark*, 601 – 3.

hearing or the next day. The witnesses are encouraged to testify falsely and their testimony is self-contradictory. A charge of blasphemy is made for claiming to be the Messiah, not for uttering the divine name.

Despite these apparent violations, there is little reason to doubt the historicity of Mark's account. (1) The Mishnah was codified at the end of the second century (c. AD 200), long after the gospel accounts, and it is not certain that its regulations go back to Jesus' day. (2) The regulations likely arose in the context of past abuses, such as those found in Jesus' trial. (3) In any case, Mark does not portray this as a formal trial, but more as a hearing to prepare a case against Jesus before the governor. (4) The Mishnah represents Pharisaic traditions, while the Sanhedrin of Jesus' day was dominated by the Sadducees. (5) Bock and others have found good evidence that charges of blasphemy could be brought for a variety of reasons, including idolatry, disrespect for God, or insulting God's anointed leaders.[2] (6) Finally, Mark presents the trial as a travesty of justice by those intent on killing Jesus. Regulations are more likely to have been overlooked in such a volatile environment. (On the question of responsibility for Jesus' death, see Theology in Application on 15:1 – 15.)

Exegetical Outline

→ **1. Introduction and Setting (14:53 – 54)**
    a. Taking Jesus to the high priest (14:53)
    b. Peter's entrance into the courtyard (14:54)
2. False Testimony against Jesus (14:55 – 59)
3. The High Priest's Question and Jesus' Answer (14:60 – 62)
4. The Accusation of Blasphemy and Condemnation by the Sanhedrin (14:63 – 64)
5. Abuse by the Sanhedrin and by the Guards (14:65)

Explanation of the Text

14:53 They took Jesus to the high priest. All the ruling priests and the elders and the experts in the law gathered together (Καὶ ἀπήγαγον τὸν Ἰησοῦν πρὸς τὸν ἀρχιερέα, καὶ συνέρχονται πάντες οἱ ἀρχιερεῖς καὶ οἱ πρεσβύτεροι καὶ οἱ γραμματεῖς). The crowd, likely made up of Jewish and Roman authorities (see comments on 14:43), now leads Jesus to the residence of the high priest (cf. Matt 26:3).[3] Mark never names the high priest, though the other gospels identify him as Caiaphas (Matt 26:57; cf. 26:3; Luke 3:2; John 11:49; Acts 4:6). Caiaphas held the office from AD 18 – 36. He was the son-in-law of Annas, the former high priest, who had been deposed by the Romans in AD 15.[4]

2. Bock, *Blasphemy and Exaltation*, 30 – 112. See comments on 14:63 – 64, below.

3. Mark simply says, "to the high priest," but the reference to the courtyard and upper room suggest we are to think of his

palace rather than the official courtrooms located in and around the temple (*m. Sanh.* 11:2).

4. Annas still exercised considerable power, as evidenced by the fact that Luke refers to him as "high priest" beside Caiaphas

Gathered at Caiaphas's residence are representatives from the ruling priests, elders, and experts of the law, the three groups that made up the Sanhedrin (cf. 8:31; 11:27; 14:43). When Mark says "all" (πάντες) were present, he means "the whole Sanhedrin" (ὅλον τὸ συνέδριον; v. 55), not every scribe or elder in Jerusalem. According to the Mishnah, the Sanhedrin was made up of seventy members, plus the high priest (*m. Sanh.* 1:6). The whole Sanhedrin does not necessarily mean every member, but a sufficient number to represent a quorum. Jesus is taken to an upstairs room of Caiaphas's palace, since Peter is described as "in the courtyard below" (14:66).

14:54 Peter followed him at a distance, going as far as the courtyard of the high priest. There he was sitting with the guards and warming himself by the fire (καὶ ὁ Πέτρος ἀπὸ μακρόθεν ἠκολούθησεν αὐτῷ ἕως ἔσω εἰς τὴν αὐλὴν τοῦ ἀρχιερέως καὶ ἦν συγκαθήμενος μετὰ τῶν ὑπηρετῶν καὶ θερμαινόμενος πρὸς τὸ φῶς). Mark inserts this comment to prepare for the account of the denial that follows (14:66 – 72). Although all the disciples abandoned Jesus in Gethsemane, Peter — true to his professed loyalty (14:29, 31) — doubled back and followed the large crowd "at a distance" (ἀπὸ μακρόθεν). In line with his character as portrayed elsewhere in the Gospels, Peter is at the same time brave and brash, yet wavering.

Peter gets as far as the "courtyard" of the high priest. This word can also mean "estate" or "palace" and could refer to the residence in general.[5] But 14:66 suggests we are to think of an open-air courtyard around which the large residence is built. According to John, Peter was able to enter the gate

to this courtyard with the help of another disciple (the beloved disciple?) who was known by the high priest (John 18:16). Peter sits by the fire[6] with the "guards" (ὑπηρέται). The word can mean servants or assistants of various kinds and could refer to the high priest's servants. Yet John has used it for the temple police who arrested Jesus (John 18:12), and in v. 65 Mark uses it of the "guards" who take charge of Jesus after the hearing.[7] It seems some guards stayed below in the courtyard while others accompanied Jesus to the upper room.

14:55 – 56 The high priest and the whole Sanhedrin were looking for evidence against Jesus to put him to death, but they could not find any. For many falsely testified against him, but their testimonies did not agree (Οἱ δὲ ἀρχιερεῖς καὶ ὅλον τὸ συνέδριον ἐζήτουν κατὰ τοῦ Ἰησοῦ μαρτυρίαν εἰς τὸ θανατῶσαι αὐτόν, καὶ οὐχ ηὕρισκον· πολλοὶ γὰρ ἐψευδομαρτύρουν κατ᾽ αὐτοῦ, καὶ ἴσαι αἱ μαρτυρίαι οὐκ ἦσαν). As Mark had referred to "all" (πάντες) the ruling priests, elders, and experts in the law (v. 53), now he refers to the "whole" (ὅλος) Sanhedrin. This is hardly a legitimate trial, since the goal is simply to find sufficient evidence to put Jesus to death. The Pharisees and Herodians had plotted to kill Jesus since early in his Galilean ministry (3:6), yet it was Jesus' arrival in Jerusalem and the clearing of the temple that had provoked this more recent plot (11:18; 14:1, 10 – 11).

Even though it is the middle of the night, false witnesses are on hand, showing that careful plans have been made. Yet the many charges brought against Jesus result only in contradictory testimony. France suggests that the contradictions arose from cross-examination in line with the Mishnaic

---

(Luke 3:2) and by John's account of Jesus' initial hearing before him (John 18:13 – 24, 28). Five of Annas's sons and his son-in-law served as high priests (Josephus, *Ant.* 20.9.1 §197).

5. BDAG, 150.

6. Mark speaks of "the light" (τὸ φῶς), which clearly means a fire since Peter "warmed himself" there. Luke speaks of a "fire" (πῦρ) and John of a "charcoal fire" (ἀνθρακιά).

7. John 18:18 speaks of both "servants" (δοῦλοι) and "officials" (ὑπηρέται) around the fire.

guidelines (*m. Sanh.* 4:5–5:4), and that the religious leaders were intent on showing that justice had been done. They are seeking to adhere to the Decalogue's command against false testimony (Exod 20:16; Deut 5:20) and the need for at least two witnesses in capital cases (Num 35:30; Deut 17:6; 19:15).[8] While this is possible, Mark does not say so. His whole focus is on the fraudulence of the case and the duplicity of those involved, twice emphasizing that these testified falsely (vv. 56, 57) and "did not agree" (vv. 56, 59).

14:57–59 Some, standing up, were falsely testifying against him, saying, "We heard him saying, 'I will destroy this temple made with hands and in three days I will build another not made with hands.'" Yet even their testimony about this did not agree (καί τινες ἀναστάντες ἐψευδομαρτύρουν κατ᾽ αὐτοῦ λέγοντες ὅτι ἡμεῖς ἠκούσαμεν αὐτοῦ λέγοντος ὅτι ἐγὼ καταλύσω τὸν ναὸν τοῦτον τὸν χειροποίητον καὶ διὰ τριῶν ἡμερῶν ἄλλον ἀχειροποίητον οἰκοδομήσω. καὶ οὐδὲ οὕτως ἴση ἦν ἡ μαρτυρία αὐτῶν). Mark reports only one specific charge against Jesus: threatening to destroy and rebuild the temple. The same charge will be leveled by those mocking him on the cross (15:29).

Although Jesus implicitly threatened the temple by clearing its merchants (11:15–17) and then predicted its destruction in the Olivet Discourse (13:2), nowhere in the gospel tradition does he claim that *he* will destroy it. The closest parallel to the testimony here is John 2:19, where Jesus says,

"Destroy this temple, and I will raise it again in three days." There the narrator adds that Jesus "had spoken of his body" when he referred to the temple (2:21). From Mark's perspective, the witnesses "bear false testimony" (ψευδομαρτυρέω) since Jesus did not personally threaten the temple, instead predicting its destruction.[9]

Yet there is more to this charge than a prediction of the temple's demise. The word "temple" (ναός) here means the sanctuary itself, including the Holy Place and the Most Holy Place, rather than the larger temple compound (ἱερόν). The adjective "made with [human] hands" (χειροποίητος) is denigrating here, meaning "merely a human construction,"[10] and "not made with hands" (ἀχειροποίητος) means built by God himself. In Acts, Stephen uses the same adjective with reference to Solomon's temple to show that the Most High does not live in houses "made by human hands" (χειροποίητος), since heaven is his throne and the earth his footstool (Acts 7:48; citing Isa 66:1, 2; cf. Acts 17:24). Similarly, in Hebrews the heavenly tabernacle in which Jesus made his once-for-all sacrifice for sins is one "not made with human hands" (οὐ χειροποιήτου; Heb 9:11, cf. 9:24; 2 Cor 5:1).

The idea of a new and greater eschatological temple appears already in Ezek 40–48 and shows up elsewhere in Judaism.[11] In some traditions God himself will build this temple;[12] in others, based especially on 2 Sam 7:13 and Zech 6:12, the Messiah will build it.[13] Mark's readers would

---

8. France, *Mark*, 604–5.

9. Geddert, *Watchwords*, 131; Gray, *The Temple in the Gospel of Mark*, 173.

10. In the OT and Judaism this word is associated with idols that have no real life (Ps 115:4; Isa 46:6; Wisd 13:10; Garland, *Mark*, 560 n. 5).

11. *1 En.* 90:28–29 ("a new house, greater and loftier than the first one"); 91:13; *Jub.* 1:17, 27; 4QFlor [4Q174] 1:1–7. For details, see D. Juel, *Messiah and Temple: The Trial of Jesus in the Gospel of Mark* (SBLDS 31; Missoula, MT: Scholars, 1977), 172–96; Brown, *Death of the Messiah*, 1:441–43; Bock, *Blas-*

phemy and Exaltation, 213 n. 69; Evans, *Mark 8:27–16:20*, 445–46; France, *Mark*, 607 ns. 24, 25.

12. 11QTemple [= 11Q19] 29:7–10: "I shall sanctify my temple with my glory … until the day of creation, when I shall create my temple" (Martínez and Tigchelaar, *Dead Sea Scrolls*, 2:1251).

13. *Tg. Zech* 6:12: "Behold, the man whose name is Messiah will be revealed, and he shall be raised up, and shall build the Temple of the Lord" (cf. *Tg. Isa* 53:5). Contra Brown, *Death of the Messiah*, 1:442, who says no pre-NT text supports this idea.

no doubt think here of Jesus' own resurrection, since the phrase "after three days" has appeared repeatedly in the passion predictions (8:31; 9:31; 10:34; cf. John 2:19). It seems likely that Jesus' own words, distorted here but found also in John 2:19, together with the Jewish traditions of an eschatological temple, became the foundation for the early Christian identification of Jesus as the new temple and the early Christians as his "body" — the new and greater eschatological temple (cf. Matt 12:6; Mark 12:10 – 11; 1 Cor 3:16 – 17; 6:19; 1 Pet 2:4 – 5). While the Qumran sect viewed their own community as the new temple, the early Christians went beyond this to identify their community with Jesus himself, the eschatological temple of God.

14:60 Standing up in their midst, the high priest asked Jesus, "Are you not going to answer? What are these charges they are making against you?" (καὶ ἀναστὰς ὁ ἀρχιερεὺς εἰς μέσον ἐπηρώτησεν τὸν Ἰησοῦν λέγων· οὐκ ἀποκρίνη οὐδέν; τί οὗτοί σου καταμαρτυροῦσιν;). The high priest recognizes that the testimony against Jesus is going nowhere and so intervenes, seeking direct self-incrimination. Rising and standing "in the middle" (εἰς μέσον) indicates a dramatic climax to the hearing. The high priest's statement could be understood either as two questions (as translated above) or as a single question with "what" (τι) functioning as a relative pronoun: "Don't you have any answer to what these men testify against you?" (GW; cf. REB, HCSB, UBS[4]). The former seems more likely and is followed by most versions (NIV, NET, NLT, ESV, NRSV, etc.)

14:61 But he remained silent and answered nothing. Again the high priest asked him, "Are you the Messiah, the Son of the Blessed One?"

(ὁ δὲ ἐσιώπα καὶ οὐκ ἀπεκρίνατο οὐδέν. πάλιν ὁ ἀρχιερεὺς ἐπηρώτα αὐτὸν καὶ λέγει αὐτῷ· σὺ εἶ ὁ χριστὸς ὁ υἱὸς τοῦ εὐλογητοῦ;). Jesus at first refuses to answer. Though Mark does not cite or directly allude to it, the alert reader would recall the Suffering Servant's silence in Isa 53:7: "as a sheep before its shearers is silent, so he did not open his mouth."

The high priest then follows with a direct question of identity, "Are you the Messiah, the Son of the Blessed One?" From the perspective of Mark's narrative, the question is surprising. After all, Jesus has been extremely reserved with reference to his messianic identity, silencing demons who recognize him (1:25, 34; 3:11 – 12), and the disciples after Peter's confession (8:30; cf. 9:9). Only by implicitly acknowledging Peter's confession (8:30 – 31) and in the (surprising) self-designation of 9:41 has Jesus accepted the title "Messiah/Christ" (χριστός).

Similarly, his divine sonship has been acknowledged by demons (3:11; 5:7) and by the Father at the baptism and the transfiguration (1:11; 9:7), but explicitly by Jesus only at 13:32 and opaquely in the parable of the tenants (12:6). Yet many of Jesus' actions have had "messianic" implications, especially his approach to Jerusalem on a donkey and his actions against the temple. There was surely speculation among the general population that Jesus was the Messiah (cf. Matt 11:2 – 3; Luke 3:15; John 1:19 – 20, 41; 4:29; 7:26 – 27, 41 – 42).

Some have argued that the high priest's question is historically unlikely, since there was no single messianic idea in Judaism. While it is true that the first century evidenced a diversity of messianic hopes, the conception of an eschatological king from the line of David was the most important one,[14] and "Messiah" (χριστός) was becoming a technical term for this figure.[15] "Son of the Blessed

---

14. See 2 Sam 7:11 – 16; Isa 9:1 – 5; 11:1 – 10; Jer 23:5 – 6; Ezek 34:23 – 24; 37:24 – 25; Pss 2; 89; 110; *Pss. Sol.* 17:21 – 25; 1QS 9:11. See comments on 1:1 and "In Depth: Jewish Expec-

tations for the 'Messiah' " at 8:29.
15. *Pss Sol.* 17:30; cf. Matt 2:4; Mark 12:35; Luke 2:11, 26; 3:15; John 1:20; 7:41 – 42. See Strauss, *Davidic Messiah*, 35 – 57.

One" (ὁ υἱὸς τοῦ εὐλογητοῦ) stands in apposition to "Messiah," with "Blessed One" (ὁ εὐλογητός) serving as a reverential circumlocution to avoid speaking the divine name.

The identification of the Messiah as God's Son arose from various OT texts in which the coming Davidic king is identified as having a special father-son relationship with God (2 Sam 7:14: "I will be his father, and he will be my son"; cf. Pss 2:7; 89:26). While some have doubted that the title "Son of God" was used of the Messiah in the first century, evidence from the Qumran scrolls has tipped the scales in favor of this usage.[16] The two titles are basically synonymous here. The high priest is not asking whether Jesus is claiming divinity, but whether he is claiming to be the Messiah, with the special father-son relationship with God that was predicted in Scripture.[17] Mark's readers, of course, would see deeper significance in the Son of God title, which in many NT contexts carries divine connotations.

14:62 Jesus said, "I am, and you will see the Son of Man sitting at the right hand of Power and coming with the clouds of heaven." (ὁ δὲ Ἰησοῦς εἶπεν· ἐγώ εἰμι, καὶ ὄψεσθε τὸν υἱὸν τοῦ ἀνθρώπου ἐκ δεξιῶν καθήμενον τῆς δυνάμεως καὶ ἐρχόμενον μετὰ τῶν νεφελῶν τοῦ οὐρανοῦ). Jesus' response in Mark is a straightforward "I am" (ἐγώ εἰμι), the clearest self-identification yet in this gospel.[18] In Matthew (and Luke)[19] Jesus responds with the indirect, "You have said so" (σὺ εἶπας; Matt 26:64), an answer similar to what Jesus gives to Pilate in Mark 15:2 (σὺ λέγεις).[20] The indirect answer in Matthew and Luke is probably an affirmation, but a qualified one, meaning something like, "Yes, but your understanding is different from mine." In Mark, however, there is no such reluctance. The messianic secret is over and Jesus is moving inexorably toward the cross.

If Jesus' first answer is simple and direct, his following one is defiant. Bringing together allusions to Ps 110:1 and Dan 7:13, Jesus asserts that he will be vindicated by God at his right hand and will come in judgment with the clouds of heaven. Jesus has already cited Ps 110:1 ("The LORD says to my lord: 'Sit at my right hand until I make your enemies a footstool for your feet'") in 12:36 to show that the Messiah must be more than the son of David, since he is David's Lord. It is the most frequently cited OT text in the NT, a favorite of the early church with reference to the vindication and exaltation of

---

16. 4QFlor [4Q174] 1:10 – 14; 1QSa [1Q28a] 2:11 – 12; 4QpsDan Aᵃ [4Q246]; cf. Hengel, *Son of God*, 43 – 45; I. H. Marshall, *The Origins of New Testament Christology* (Downers Grove, IL: InterVarsity Press, 1976), 113; J. A. Fitzmyer, "4Q246: The 'Son of God' Document from Qumran," *Bib* 74 (1993): 153 – 74.

17. This is more likely than Marcus's claim that this is a case of a restrictive apposition, where the second term qualifies the first, contrasting the Son-of-David Messiah with a quasi-divine Son-of-God one (Joel Marcus, "Mark 14:61: 'Are You the Messiah-Son-of-God?" *NovT* 31 [1989]: 125 – 41; idem, *Mark 9 – 16*, 1004 – 5). The high priest is not asking what kind of Messiah Jesus is; he is asking whether Jesus is claiming authority to rule as the Lord's Anointed.

18. The suggestion that Jesus is here echoing the "I AM" language of Isa 43:10, 13; Exod 3:14 (cf. John 8:58) and so claiming equality with God is unlikely and would not serve to answer the high priest's question. Jesus' "I am" (ἐγώ εἰμι) is a normal Greek idiom of affirmation.

19. Luke 22:67 – 70 has two questions and two answers. To the question, "Are you the Messiah?" Jesus answers that they will not believe him if he tells them and then refers to his role as the Son of Man. To the follow-up question, "Are you then the Son of God?" he replies, "You say that I am" (ὑμεῖς λέγετε ὅτι ἐγώ εἰμι).

20. Some Caesarean manuscripts read, "You said that I am" (σὺ εἶπας ὅτι ἐγώ εἰμι; Θ ƒ¹³ 565 700 Origen), a reading supported by those who think it fits better Jesus' circumspect messianic self-disclosure in Mark (so Taylor, *Mark*, 568). Yet the external evidence is weak, and it seems better to regard it as an assimilation to Matthew and Luke. See the discussion in R. Kempthorne, "The Markan Text of Jesus' Answer to the High Priest (Mark xiv.62)," *NovT* 19 (1977): 197 – 208.

the Messiah after his suffering.[21] The term "power" (δύναμις) in the phrase "right hand of Power" is a circumlocution for God, like the high priest's use of the word "Blessed One" for God in v. 61. The right hand was the position of greatest influence and prestige beside the king and is used to indicate Jesus' position of supreme authority following his ascension (cf. Acts 2:33 – 36).

Both "Son of Man" and "coming with the clouds of heaven" come from Dan 7:13 – 14, where "one like a son of man" (= in human form) comes on the clouds of heaven before the Ancient of Days (God himself) and is given glory, dominion, and an everlasting kingdom (cf. Mark 8:38; 13:26). While this text too points to Jesus' vindication, it is debated whether it refers to the exaltation[22] or to the parousia.[23] In favor of the former is the context of Dan 7, which refers to a heavenly vindication before the Ancient of Days. Yet as we have have argued earlier, Mark uses the same text in 13:26 – 27 with reference to the parousia (see discussion there), and this seems to be his intention here as well (cf. Rev 1:7). Jesus' immediate vindication will come when he ascends to the right hand of God. His ultimate vindication will occur when he comes in glory to judge and to save. At that time, those who are presently standing in judgment over the Son of Man will be judged by him.

In what sense will these religious leaders "see" the Son of Man vindicated ("you will see" [ὄψεσθε] is plural)? Brown is no doubt right that here we have a representative role for the Sanhedrin.[24] All who oppose (or affirm) Jesus will one day see

his vindication. Revelation 1:7, which combines Dan 7:13 and Zech 12:10, sums it up: "Look, he is coming with the clouds, and every eye will see him, even those who pierced him; and all peoples on earth will mourn because of him" (cf. Phil 2:10 – 11).[25]

14:63 – 64 Tearing his garments, the high priest said, "Why do we need any more testimony? You have heard the blasphemy. What do you think?" They all condemned him as worthy of death (ὁ δὲ ἀρχιερεὺς διαρρήξας τοὺς χιτῶνας αὐτοῦ λέγει· τί ἔτι χρείαν ἔχομεν μαρτύρων; ἠκούσατε τῆς βλασφημίας· τί ὑμῖν φαίνεται; οἱ δὲ πάντες κατέκριναν αὐτὸν ἔνοχον εἶναι θανάτου). The high priest is outraged by Jesus' statement and calls for a verdict. There is no need for further witnesses since Jesus' own words have condemned him. Tearing one's garments can indicate sorrow, anguish, or dismay (Gen 37:29, 34; Num 14:6; Josh 7:6; 2 Sam 1:11; 19:1; 2 Kgs 18:37; 19:1; Job 1:20; Isa 36:22; 37:1; Jdt 14:19; 2 Macc 4:38). Here it is clearly outrage, but may also be a formal judicial act. The Mishnah says that in the case of blasphemy, "the judges stand up on their feet and rend their garments" (*m. Sanh.* 7:5).

In what sense had Jesus committed blasphemy? As noted above, the Mishnah says a charge of blasphemy could be made only if the defendant had pronounced the divine name (*m. Sanh.* 7.5). Yet it is unlikely that this limitation was widely held or strictly enforced (if in force at all in Jesus' day), and there is good evidence that the term "blasphemy" was used more generally with reference to "a whole

---

21. Matt 22:44; 26:64; Mark 12:36; 14:62; Luke 20:42 – 43; 22:69; Acts 2:34; 5:31; 7:56; Rom 8:34; 1 Cor 15:25; Eph 1:20; Col 3:1; Heb 1:3, 13; 8:1; 10:12 – 13; 1 Pet 3:22; Rev 3:21; cf. Heb 5:6; 7:17, 21.

22. Taylor, *Mark*, 568; France, *Mark*, 612 – 13; Hooker, *Mark*, 362.

23. Cranfield, *Mark*, 444 – 45; Lane, *Mark*, 537; Brown, *Death of the Messiah*, 1:497 – 98; Evans, *Mark 8:27 – 16:20*,

451 – 52; Gundry, *Mark*, 886 – 87; Boring, *Mark*, 414; Marcus, *Mark 9 – 16*, 1008, 1017.

24. Brown, *Death of the Messiah*, 1:498 – 99.

25. For a similar statement in apocalyptic Judaism with reference to the exalted Son of Man, see *1 En.* 62:3 – 5. It is debated, however, whether the Similitudes of *1 Enoch* (chs. 37 – 71) are pre- or post-Christian. See comments on 1:10 – 11 and notes there.

range of actions offensive to God," especially "idolatry, a show of arrogant disrespect toward God, or
the insulting of his chosen leaders."[26] Jesus' words
about his authority as the Son of Man who will be
exalted to God's heavenly throne and will return
to judge these religious leaders would certainly
qualify as blasphemy in the eyes of the high priest.

The Sanhedrin responds by condemning Jesus
as "worthy of death" (ἔνοχον ... θανάτου). The penalty for blasphemy was stoning (Lev 24:10 – 16; *m.
Sanh.* 7:4 – 5), but at this time the Sanhedrin did
not have the right to capital punishment (John
18:31).[27] Their goal was to gather sufficient evidence to bring a charge of sedition against Jesus
before Pilate (15:1). Some have argued that the
stoning of Stephen (Acts 7:58 – 60) and the later
stoning of James the Just (Josephus, *Ant.* 20.9.1
§200) show that Jews *did* have the right to execute
at this time.[28] But these were probably illegal mob
actions rather than legitimate trials. Josephus
points out that the latter took place in the interim
between the governorship of Festus and Albinus
and that the high priest Ananus was deposed because of it.[29]

The "all" here may be hyperbolic, meaning the
consensus rather than every member, since Mark
will later identify Joseph of Arimathea as a member of the council (15:43; cf. Nicodemus in John
7:50 – 52; 19:38 – 40).[30]

**14:65 Some began to spit on him, to blindfold
him, to strike him with fists, and to say to him,
"Prophesy." Then the guards took him away and
beat him.** (Καὶ ἤρξαντό τινες ἐμπτύειν αὐτῷ καὶ
περικαλύπτειν αὐτοῦ τὸ πρόσωπον καὶ κολαφίζειν
αὐτὸν καὶ λέγειν αὐτῷ· προφήτευσον, καὶ οἱ
ὑπηρέται ῥαπίσμασιν αὐτὸν ἔλαβον). The decision of the council results in abuse of the prisoner.
"Some" (τινες) likely means "some members of the
council" (as in Matt 26:67 – 68), since the guards
(ὑπηρέται) will take charge of him afterward
(v. 65b).[31] Spitting was a derisive action meant to
shame and demean (Num 12:14; Deut 25:9; Job
30:10). Isaiah's Suffering Servant is said to be insulted and spit upon (Isa 50:6). These actions recall
the third passion prediction, where Jesus predicted
the Son of Man would be handed over to the religious leaders, condemned, mocked, spit upon, and
beaten (10:33 – 34).

There is irony here: those who blindfold Jesus
(lit., "cover his face") and mock him to "prophesy"
are unaware that he has indeed prophesied this very
scene.[32] The blindfolded questioning may be meant
to mock his messianic claims, since Isa 11:3 says
that by virtue of his endowment with God's Spirit,
the Messiah "will not judge by what he sees with
his eyes, or decide by what he hears with his ears."[33]

Mark concludes with the temple police taking
Jesus into custody and continuing the abuse ini-

---

26. Bock, *Blasphemy and Exaltation*, 111. Cf. the excursus in Evans, *Mark 8:27 – 16:20*, 453 – 58; A. Y. Collins,
"The Charge of Blasphemy in Mark 14.64," *JSNT* 26 (2004):
379 – 401; Brown, *Death of the Messiah*, 1:534 – 47. Brown lists
a variety of claims and actions of Jesus that could have been
viewed as blasphemous.

27. The exception was execution of Gentiles who entered
the inner court of the temple (Josephus, *J.W.* 6.2.4 §126; Acts
21:28, 36; 24:6).

28. See Winter, *On the Trial of Jesus*, 110 – 30.

29. A. N. Sherwin-White, *Roman Society and Roman Law
in the New Testament* [Oxford: Oxford University Press, 1963),
32 – 47; France, *Mark*, 602 n. 5; Brown, *Death of the Messiah*,
1:363 – 72.

30. Stein, *Mark*, 686 n. 15.

31. Cf. Matt 26:67 – 68, where the antecedent to "they" is
the Sandhedrin. By contrast Luke 22:63 attributes this action
to "the men who were guarding Jesus."

32. The relationship between the blindfold, the beating,
and the call to prophesy is clearest in Luke, where Jesus' assail-
ants ask, "Who hit you?" (22:64; cf. Matt 26:67 – 68, though no
blindfold is mentioned there). Some later manuscripts of Mark
add, "Messiah, who hit you?" (Χριστε τις εστιν ο παισας σε; N
W X Θ *f*[13] 33 565 579 700 892 1424 vg^ms syr^h sah^mss).

33. Later rabbinic tradition, drawing on Isa 11:1 – 4, held
that the Messiah would be able to identify people by smell (*b.
Sanh.* 93b; Lane, *Mark*, 540 n. 148).

tiated by their superiors. The dative plural noun "with blows/slaps" (ῥαπίσμασιν) could mean either blows with an object like a club or whip or slaps in the face.[34] This could be another allusion to the Suffering Servant of Isa 50:6 LXX, where the same noun is used.

Theology in Application

This passage brings to a head the key themes of Jewish opposition to Jesus and Jesus' messianic self-understanding.

Jesus, the Messiah and Son of God

Jesus' messianic self-disclosure reaches a key climax here. From the beginning of the gospel, the reader has known that Jesus is the Messiah, the Son of God (1:1). Yet this truth has been revealed only gradually to the characters in the drama. At Jesus' baptism and the transfiguration the Father acknowledges that he is the Son of God (1:11; 9:7), and demons recognize this truth throughout the Galilean ministry (1:24, 34; 3:11; 5:7). Yet Jesus repeatedly silences demons and tells the disciples and those healed not to disclose his identity or his miracles. Finally, at Peter's confession a human character explicitly proclaims Jesus as "the Messiah" (8:29). But even here, Jesus silences the disciples and radically redefines his messiahship as one of suffering and sacrifice (8:30 – 31). The passion predictions that follow only mystify and confuse the disciples (8:32; 9:32).

At Jesus' entrance into Jerusalem, however, the messianic secret begins to be fully disclosed. Jesus' entrance into Jerusalem riding a colt, his clearing of the temple, and his parable of the tenant farmers all have messianic implications, accelerating the plots of the religious leaders against him. Now, at this trial, Jesus takes the decisive step to acknowledge that he is indeed the Messiah and Son of God.

Why would Jesus, who has been so reserved throughout his ministry, now openly admit to this? The answer is that, as always in Mark's narrative, Jesus is in control. He is guiding events toward their God-ordained conclusion. Jesus forces the hand of the high priest and the Sanhedrin by admitting he is the Messiah and affirming his vindication at the right hand of God and his return to judge his oppressors. This audacious claim guarantees his execution. Jesus' parable of the tenant farmers plays out before our eyes, as "the Son" of the owner is destroyed by the wicked caretakers of God's vineyard (12:1 – 12). Yet the rejection of the cornerstone is no disaster: "The Lord has done this, and it is marvelous in our eyes" (12:11; cf. Ps 118:23).

Jesus' messianic purpose is not to conquer the Romans, but to suffer and die as a ransom for sins (10:45). This initial christological climax will be followed by an even greater one at his crucifixion, as the Gentile centurion at the foot of the cross recognizes in Jesus' death his true identity as the Son of God (15:39). It is through suffering and sacrifice that Jesus fulfills the messianic task (8:34).

Truth from False Witnesses

There is much irony in the present scene. The "false witnesses" against Jesus in fact speak a great deal of truth. Though their accusation that Jesus threatened to destroy the temple is a distortion of his words (cf. 13:2; John 2:18 – 20), in fact, as God's representative, he will be responsible for the temple's destruction in AD 70 as judgment for the nation's rejection of him. The Jerusalem temple is soon to be replaced "after three days" by the temple of his body and by the community of faith that will arise in allegiance to him.

The high priest's words are also ironic. While accusing Jesus of blasphemy he implicates himself of the same charge, blaspheming the Son of God. Garland rightly says, "Either the high priest is correct that Jesus is a deluded blasphemer, or Jesus is correct that the high priest is the deluded blasphemer."[35] The reader knows the truth. Jesus, the Messiah and Son of God, will one day stand in judgment as the exalted Son of Man over the high priest, the Sanhedrin, and the whole world.

The application for us today is evident. All evil, deception, false testimony, and oppression will one day be brought into the light and will be judged for what it is. All will "see" the Son of Man coming on the clouds of heaven in judgment, and every knee will bow and every tongue will confess "that Jesus Christ [the Messiah] is Lord, to the glory of God the Father" (Phil 2:10 – 11). As Peter says in another eschatological context, if the day of Lord is coming in this manner, "what kind of people ought you to be? You ought to live holy and godly lives as you look forward to that day of God and speed its coming" (2 Pet 3:11 – 12).

---

35. Garland, *Mark*, 563.

Mark 14:66–72

Literary Context

The Markan intercalation, or sandwich structure, continues (see Structure on 14:53–65) as Mark returns to the account of Peter that began in 14:54. The present participial phrase in v. 66a, "While Peter was in the courtyard below," functions as a flashback to what was happening during Jesus' hearing before the Sanhedrin (14:55–65). Peter's denial is linked thematically to the earlier prediction of his denial by Jesus and Peter's grandiose claim that he would never disown Jesus, even on pain of death (14:30–31). The Sanhedrin trial will conclude in 15:1, when they take Jesus to Pilate to obtain a sentence of death.

Main Idea

While Jesus faithfully confesses his identity as Messiah and Son of God before the powerful and potentially lethal Sanhedrin, Peter cowardly denies before a simple servant girl that he even knows Jesus. The two accounts together serve as positive and negative models of faithful discipleship.

Translation

Mark 14:66 – 72

66a	setting (temporal & spatial)	While Peter was in the courtyard below,
b	Action	**one of the high priest's servant girls came by.**
67a	action/setting (social)	Seeing Peter warming himself and
b	action	looking closely at him,
c	Response to 67a-b	**she said,**
d	accusation	*"You were also with the Nazarene, Jesus."*
68a	Response to 67c-d	But **he denied it,** saying,
b	first denial	*"I have no idea what you're talking about."*
c	Action	And **he went outside into the entryway.**
d	Action	[Then **the rooster crowed.**]
69a	action/setting (social)	When the servant girl saw him,
b	Response to 69a	**she again began to say to those standing around,**
c	accusation	*"This is one of them."*
70a	Response to 69/second denial	**Again he kept denying it.**
b	setting (temporal)	After a little while,
c	Response to 69	**those standing around began saying to Peter,**
d	accusation	*"Surely you are one of them,*
e	reason for 70d	*because you are a Galilean."*
71a	Response to 70b-e	**He began to call down curses and to swear an oath,**
b	third denial	*"I do not know this man you're talking about!"*
72a	Action	**Immediately a rooster crowed a second time.**
b	Response to 72a	Then **Peter remembered what Jesus had said to him:**
c	prophecy	*"Before the rooster crows twice, you will disown me three times."*
d	manner of 72e	And breaking down,
e	Response to 72b-c	**he began to weep.**

Structure

The episode is made up of three scenes. After the initial setting (v. 66a), there is the threefold denial by Peter (vv. 66b – 71), followed by his recognition of and remorse for what he has done (v. 72). The account's historicity is assured by its multiple attestation in the Gospels and by the unlikelihood that the church would create a story in which one of its great heroes fails so miserably. If the tradition is accurate that Mark's gospel comes from Peter's own testimony (see Introduction to Mark: Authorship), this account would likely have been passed down by Peter himself.

Exegetical Outline

→ **1. Setting (14:66a)**

  2. Three Accusations and Three Denials (14:66b – 71)

    a. First accusation by the servant girl (14:66b – 67)

    b. Peter's first denial (14:68)

    c. Second accusation by the servant girl (14:69)

    d. Peter's second denial (14:70a)

    e. Third accusation by others (14:70b-e)

    f. Peter's third denial with curses and oaths (14:71)

  3. Conclusion (14:72)

    a. The rooster crows (14:72a)

    b. Peter's recognition and remorse (14:72b-e)

Explanation of the Text

14:66 – 67 While Peter was in the courtyard below, one of the high priest's servant girls came by. Seeing Peter warming himself and looking closely at him, she said, "You were also with the Nazarene, Jesus." (Καὶ ὄντος τοῦ Πέτρου[1] κάτω ἐν τῇ αὐλῇ ἔρχεται μία τῶν παιδισκῶν τοῦ ἀρχιερέως καὶ ἰδοῦσα τὸν Πέτρον θερμαινόμενον ἐμβλέψασα αὐτῷ λέγει· καὶ σὺ μετὰ τοῦ Ναζαρηνοῦ ἦσθα τοῦ Ἰησοῦ). We learn for the first time that Jesus is in an upstairs room at the high priest's residence, since Peter is "below" (κάτω) in the courtyard.

The events described here occur concurrently with Jesus' Sanhedrin trial. The female servant is probably not taking a break by the fire[2] but rather passing through on her duties, since Mark says she "came by" (ἔρχεται; historical present). The term "servant girl" (παιδίσκη) is a diminutive and could refer to a youth; but the force of the diminutive had decreased in the Koine period,[3] and the word commonly refers to any female slave. John refers to her as a doorkeeper (John 18:16 – 17).

First "looking" (ἰδοῦσα), then "staring" (ἐμβλέψασα),[4] the girl recognizes Peter as being one of Jesus' disciples. Where she had seen him with Jesus is not stated, though the most likely location would have been during his earlier teaching in the temple (11:15 – 12:44). On "Nazarene," see comments on 10:47. The word order may indicate a slightly derogatory sense ("that Nazarene, Jesus"), since Judean Jews often looked down on their northern cousins in Galilee.[5]

14:68 But he denied it, saying, "I have no idea what you're talking about." And he went outside into the entryway. [Then the rooster crowed.] (ὁ δὲ ἠρνήσατο λέγων· οὔτε οἶδα οὔτε ἐπίσταμαι σὺ τί λέγεις. καὶ ἐξῆλθεν ἔξω εἰς τὸ προαύλιον [καὶ ἀλέκτωρ ἐφώνησεν]). Peter's expression, (lit.) "I neither know nor understand what you are saying,"

---

1. The genitive absolute is used because the subject of the participial phrase ("Peter") is different from the subject of the main clause ("the servant girl").

2. Contra France, *Mark*, 620; Stein, *Mark*, 690.

3. Cf. 6:9; 14:47, where "sandals" and "ear" are diminutive.

4. ἐμβλέπω can be synonymous with βλέπω, but following ἰδοῦσα here probably carries an intensive sense.

5. Mann, *Mark*, 630; Stein, *Mark*, 691.

is idiomatic and a typical Markan redundancy. Knowing and understanding are not two different ideas, but a single emphatic denial (translated: "I have no idea …"). Peter now knows he is vulnerable to recognition, so moves to the "forecourt" (τὸ προαύλιον), which probably means the entryway or vestibule just inside the gate. He wants to be closer to the exit if escape is necessary.

The reference to the first rooster crow is a difficult textual issue.[6] The phrase may have been introduced by a later scribe (1) to show the fulfillment of Jesus' prophecy in 14:30 and (2) to explain why v. 72 refers to a *second* crowing. Or it may have been omitted to harmonize with the other gospels, where there is only one crowing. The former seems more likely in light of the (slightly) better manuscript evidence. If a copyist were seeking to harmonize with the other gospels, why omit the phrase in v. 68 but retain the "second" crowing in v. 72?[7]

14:69–70a When the servant girl saw him, she again began to say to those standing around, "This is one of them." Again he kept denying it (καὶ ἡ παιδίσκη ἰδοῦσα αὐτὸν ἤρξατο πάλιν λέγειν τοῖς παρεστῶσιν ὅτι οὗτος ἐξ αὐτῶν ἐστιν. ὁ δὲ πάλιν ἠρνεῖτο). Peter's actions in moving away from the fire make him look even more suspicious. "Seeing him" probably means seeing that he was moving away from the light and toward the relative safety of the entryway. Instead of speaking to Peter in the second person as in v. 67, she now solicits the support of the bystanders. "Those standing around" presumably includes the guards involved in the arrest, who had been warming themselves

with Peter by the fire (14:54). "This is one of them" identifies Peter as one of the followers of Jesus.

Peter again denies the accusation, though this time Mark does not record his words. The switch to the imperfect (ἠρνεῖτο) instead of the aorist of Peter's first denial (ἠρνήσατο; v. 68) is likely iterative, indicating a repeated and more emphatic action ("kept denying").

14:70b–71 After a little while, those standing around began saying to Peter, "Surely you are one of them, because you are a Galilean." He began to call down curses and to swear an oath, "I do not know this man you're talking about!" (καὶ μετὰ μικρὸν πάλιν οἱ παρεστῶτες ἔλεγον τῷ Πέτρῳ· ἀληθῶς ἐξ αὐτῶν εἶ, καὶ γὰρ Γαλιλαῖος εἶ. ὁ δὲ ἤρξατο ἀναθεματίζειν καὶ ὀμνύναι ὅτι οὐκ οἶδα τὸν ἄνθρωπον τοῦτον ὃν λέγετε). The third accusation occurs "after a short time" and comes from the bystanders who have been alerted by the servant girl (v. 69). The implication may be that they have conferred and agreed that Peter is one of Jesus' disciples.

Their accusation is that "surely" or "truly" (ἀληθῶς) he is one of them, since he is a Galilean. It is not stated how they know, but the most obvious answer is his accent. Matthew's account makes this explicit, with the bystanders saying, "Your speech/accent [ἡ λαλιά σου] gives you away" (Matt 26:73).

Peter responds to this third accusation by pronouncing curses and oaths. The translation, "He began to curse and swear" (NASB, KJV, NKJV, NAB) misses the point, since this is not profanity. To "swear" (ὀμνύω) means to "swear with an oath" (so NET, REB, HCSB, GW), and "to curse"

---

6. The phrase is omitted in ℵ B L W Ψ* 579 892 2427 syr[s] sah[mss] boh, but included in A C D Θ Ψ[c] 067 *f*[1,13] 33 𝔐 lat syr[p,h] Eusebius. See Metzger, *Textual Commentary*, 97; France, *Mark*, 573 n. 68, 618.

7. For a different solution see John W. Wenham, "How Many Cock-Crowings? The Problem of Harmonistic Text-

Variants," *NTS* 25 (1978–79): 523–25, who claims that Mark originally had references to only one crowing in vv. 30, 68, and 72, but that the accidental interpolation of καὶ ἀλέκτωρ ἐφώνησεν ("and the rooster crowed") by a slip of the eye in v. 68 set in motion scribal activity resulting in the other references to a second crowing.

(ἀναθεματίζειν) means to "pronounce a curse." NIV captures the latter well: "He began to call down curses, and he swore to them. . . ."

But who or what is Peter cursing? Some versions follow BDAG (63) and take it as a intransitive verb, meaning Peter pronounces a curse on himself (ESV, NLT, NIV 1984). It would therefore mean something like, "May I be cursed if I am lying" (cf. 1 Sam 14:44; 1 Kgs 20:10; Acts 23:12, 14, 21).[8] In this case the two verbs, "curse" (ἀναθεματίζω) and "swear" (ὀμνύω), are roughly synonymous, both indicating solemn oaths. This would be typical Markan redundancy. The problem with this view is that the verb "curse" (ἀναθεματίζω) is commonly transitive, meaning to call down curses on someone or something, not on oneself. When the verb is used reflexively, as in Acts 23:12, 14, 21, the reflexive pronoun (ἑαυτούς) follows.

Many recent commentators therefore think that Peter is cursing Jesus.[9] Yet while this is possible, it seems unlikely, especially in light of 1 Cor 12:3. First, no language or repudiation of Jesus this severe is attributed to the disciples elsewhere in the gospel tradition. Second, Jesus predicted that Peter would *deny* him, not that he would curse him to hell (and Jesus' predictions always come true in Mark's gospel). Finally, Matthew's failure to soften Mark's language (he uses the equally strong cognate καταθεματίζω) suggests that he does *not* view Mark's language as particularly offensive. This is especially significant in light of Matthew's generally more positive presentation of Peter (cf. Matt 16:17 – 20). The best solution is that Peter is calling down curses on his interlocutors, so that we could translate, "He began to curse *them*. . . ." He is

essentially saying, "Go to hell for making such accusations against me! I swear to you I do not know the man."

14:72 Immediately a rooster crowed a second time. Then Peter remembered what Jesus had said to him: "Before the rooster crows twice, you will disown me three times." And breaking down, he began to weep (καὶ εὐθὺς ἐκ δευτέρου ἀλέκτωρ ἐφώνησεν. καὶ ἀνεμνήσθη ὁ Πέτρος τὸ ῥῆμα ὡς εἶπεν αὐτῷ ὁ Ἰησοῦς ὅτι πρὶν ἀλέκτορα φωνῆσαι δὶς τρίς με ἀπαρνήσῃ· καὶ ἐπιβαλὼν ἔκλαιεν). Jesus' prophecy is fulfilled as the rooster crows (14:30). Mark's characteristic "immediately" here means "at that very moment" (see comments on 14:43). Some have argued that the rooster crow here is a technical term for the Roman bugle call marking the end of the third watch of the night ("cockcrow"; ἀλέκτοραφωνία; cf. 13:35) rather than a literal rooster, citing rabbinic evidence that raising fowl was forbidden in Jerusalem (*m. B. Qam.* 7.7). This is unlikely. As at 14:29 – 31 (see comments there), Mark does not use the technical term but instead says "a rooster crowed" (ἀλέκτωρ ἐφώνησεν) and cites this as the second time (the bugle would not be blown twice). The ban on fowl in the Mishnah (c. AD 200) only shows that their presence was a problem in earlier days, and other rabbinic passages do mention roosters in Jerusalem (*m. ʿEd.* 6:1; *y. ʿErub.* 10.1).

Garland points to the irony that a rooster, known for its foolish pride and "cocky" strutting, reminds Peter of his own foolish boast (14:29).[10] Hearing the rooster and suddenly remembering Jesus' earlier words, Peter breaks down and weeps. The imperfect "was weeping" (ἔκλαιεν) is likely ingressive,

---

8. Hooker, *Mark*, 287; Boring, *Mark*, 416.

9. H. Merkel, "Peter's Curse," in *The Trial of Jesus: Cambridge Studies in Honour of C. F. D. Moule* (ed. E. Bammel; Naperville, IL: Allenson, 1970), 66 – 71; Brown, *Death of the Messiah*, 1:604 – 5; Gundry, *Mark*, 890; France, *Mark*, 622; Stein, *Mark*, 692; Marcus, *Mark 9 – 16*, 1019 – 20. Suggested

as a possibility by Garland, *Mark*, 567; Boring, *Mark*, 416 n. 416. On cursing Jesus as a repudiation, see Pliny the Younger, *Ep.* 10.96.3 – 5; cf. *Mart. Pol.* 9 – 10; Justin Martyr, *1 Apol.* 31.6; 1 Cor 12:3.

10. Garland, *Mark*, 567 – 68.

meaning "he began to weep."[11] The meaning of its modifying aorist participle (ἐπιβαλών) is a mystery. The verb (ἐπιβάλλω) has a wide ranges of senses ("put on," "throw over," "set to," "beat upon," "belong to," "undertake"),[12] none of which work well here.[13] Most versions have either "he broke down" (NIV; cf. NLT, NRSV, NET, ESV, GNT) or "he began to weep/started crying" (cf. NASB, CEV, REB). KJV has "and when he thought thereon …" (cf. NKJV, HCSB).

Peter, the rock, here reaches rock bottom. His denial is particularly ominous in light of Jesus' words in 8:38 that at his return the Son of Man will be ashamed of those who are ashamed of him. Yet, unlike Judas, Peter feels immediate remorse and Mark's readers know that he will be restored and assume a position of leadership in the early church. In Mark's narrative, he will not be mentioned again until 16:7, the angel's promise of a reunion with Jesus in Galilee (cf. 14:28).

Theology in Application

The Fulfillment of Prophecy

Mark's statement in v. 72b that Peter "remembered what Jesus had said to him" picks up the theme that has permeated the Passion Narrative: the divine necessity of the events of the passion. This has been brought out by Jesus' own predictions as well as his identification of events as the fulfillment of Scripture. In addition to the three passion predictions (8:31; 9:31; 10:33 – 34), note that Jesus' parable of the tenant farmers (12:1 – 12) and his predictions of his betrayal (14:18, 20 – 21), desertion (14:27), and denial (14:30) at the Last Supper all confirm both Jesus' own divine insight as the Son of God and the scriptural necessity of the events that are closing in around him. The apparent tragedy unfolding in Mark's gospel is all part of God's plan of salvation.

For Mark's original readers, this would bring assurance that their suffering and persecution is not in vain. It is part of the greater purpose of God. Paul says something similar in Col 1:24, where he tells the Colossian church: "I rejoice in what I am suffering for you, and I fill up in my flesh what is still lacking in regard to Christ's afflictions, for the sake of his body, which is the church." Peter similarly points out that a Christian's suffering, when endured for doing good and not evil (see 1 Pet 2:19 – 20; 3:17 – 18), brings glory to God and advances the gospel (2:12).

The Demands of Discipleship

Peter's denial reminds the reader of the demands of discipleship. As noted in the Literary Context, above, this episode is one of Mark's intercalations or sandwiches.

---

11. Wallace, *Greek Grammar*, 544 – 45.

12. All from BDAG, 367.

13. Brown, *Death of the Messiah*, 1:609 – 10, mentions nine possibilities, including "having broken down," "having fallen [to the ground]," "having rushed outside," "having begun [to weep]," "having remembered [Jesus' prediction]," "having cast [his eyes on Jesus]," "having answered back," "having covered [his face with his robe]," and "having beat [his chest]."

In fact, it is a double intercalation. Peter's actions in the courtyard are introduced in 14:54, interrupted by the trial of Jesus before the Sanhedrin (14:55 – 65), and then completed by his threefold denial (vv. 66 – 72). Or seen another way, Jesus' trial before the Sanhedrin (14:55 – 65) is interrupted by Peter's denial (vv. 55 – 65) and then completed in Jesus' transfer to Pilate (15:1). In either case, Jesus' resolve in the face of suffering is clearly set in contrast to Peter's cowardly collapse under pressure. Jesus represents the model disciple who refuses to deny his calling despite persecution and even death.

The example of Jesus would have established a growing imperative for Mark's readers. Under increasing opposition from the Roman authorities and the general population, the easy way out was to deny Christ and to repudiate the church. In a famous letter written a few decades after Mark's gospel, around AD 112, Pliny the Younger, governor of Bithynia, wrote to the emperor Trajan for advice on how to deal with the "depraved superstition" that was Christianity. He tells Trajan that those arrested and accused were asked three times if they were Christians. If they admitted it, they were executed. If they denied it, they were required to prove it by worshiping images of Caesar and cursing Christ, "a thing, which, it is said, genuine Christians cannot be induced to do" (Pliny, *Ep.* 10.96.1 – 9).

Similarly, in the story of the martyrdom of Polycarp, bishop of Smyrna, the proconsul in charge of the trial calls on Polycarp to "swear the oath, and I will release you; revile Christ." Polycarp replied, "For eighty-six years I have been his servant, and he has done me no wrong, and how can I blaspheme my King who saved me?" (*Mart. Pol.* 9.3).[14] Will Mark's readers be willing to take up their own cross and follow Jesus, even to death? Or will they shrink back and deny him, saving their life but losing their souls?

The Hope of Restoration

Though the episode is a tragic one for Peter, it is not without hope. God is a God of second chances. Though the passage itself says nothing about Peter's restoration, the reader knows that Peter did not continue his denial, but he was restored and became a leader in the apostolic church. This has been indicated already when Jesus predicts the abandonment of the disciples but promises, "After I am raised, I will go before you into Galilee" (14:28). It is affirmed in 16:7, where the angel at the empty tomb tells the women to report to "his disciples *and Peter*" that he "is going ahead of you into Galilee. You will see him there, just as he told you." While Judas's betrayal was permanent, Peter's denial is temporary. The requirement of restoration is repentance and faith. Peter's remorse when the rooster crowed (14:72) indicates the repentance that will eventually result in restoration.

---

14. *Apostolic Fathers* (Holmes, ed.), 317.

The book of Acts provides the evidence for Peter's restoration and transformation after the resurrection. Peter is no longer a cowering disciple running from a servant girl's accusation. He is now the Spirit-filled apostle of Jesus Christ, facing down the most powerful religious leaders in the country. When ordered not to teach in Jesus' name, Peter and John reply, "Which is right in God's eyes: to listen to you, or to him?" (Acts 4:19). When the religious leaders arrest the apostles a second time and threaten them, Peter and the other apostles assert, "We must obey God rather than human beings!" (5:29), and they boldly accuse the Sanhedrin of murdering their own Messiah (5:30). These are the words of one who is now acting like the "rock" he was meant to be. Church tradition tells us that Peter was crucified in Rome during the persecutions of the emperor Nero (AD 64).[15] In the end, he did indeed "take up his cross" and follow Jesus.

All of us have experienced failure at various times in our Christian lives, whether by falling into sin, allowing our relationship with God to grow cold, or keeping silent about our faith at times of doubt. Peter's story reminds us that God loves us despite our failings, and like the loving father in the parable of the prodigal son, he is always waiting with open arms to welcome us back into full fellowship with him.

---

15. *First Clem.* 5. The apocryphal *Acts of Peter* 37 says Peter was crucified upside down, at his own request, and attributes the execution to the prefect Agrippa.

Mark 15:1 – 15

Literary Context

After the interlude of Peter's denial (14:66 – 72), Mark picks up where he left off at the conclusion of Jesus' Jewish hearing (14:55 – 65). The council reaches a decision to take Jesus to Pilate to seek a capital sentence. Since the Romans denied the Jewish leadership the right to capital punishment (see comments on 14:63 – 64; 15:1), the Jewish "trial" was more of a hearing to confirm Jesus' guilt and to prepare a case against him before the governor.

Luke replaces the late night Jewish hearing recounted in Mark (and Matthew) with an early morning one (Luke 22:54 – 71). The two accounts are sometimes harmonized by claiming that Mark's phrase "after holding a council" (συμβούλιον ποιήσαντες) in 15:1 refers to a second (early morning) meeting with the whole Sanhedrin to gain a formal validation of the verdict reached the night before (14:63 – 64). While this is possible, most likely the phrase either summarizes the previous trial proceedings as a whole ("after holding their council") or refers to the decision to take Jesus to Pilate ("after making their plans"). See further on v. 1, below.

Main Idea

At Jesus' Roman trial before Pontius Pilate, Jesus again acknowledges — albeit indirectly — that he is indeed the Messiah, the king of the Jews. Ironically, the guilty insurrectionist Barabbas is released by Pilate in the Passover clemency, while the righteous and innocent Son of God is delivered over to crucifixion. Yet this is all part of God's purpose and plan to accomplish his promised salvation.

Translation

Mark 15:1 – 15

1a	setting (temporal)		Early in the morning,
b	action/setting (social)		after making their plans,
c	Character entrance/ description	**the ruling priests,**	
			together with the elders and experts in the law and the whole Sanhedrin,
	Actions		bound Jesus,
d		**led him away, and**	
e		**handed him over to Pilate.**	
2a	Question	**Pilate asked him,**	
b		*"Are you the king of the Jews?"*	
c	Response to 2a-b	**He answered him,**	
d	affirmation	*"You have said so."*	
3	Response/accusation	Then **the ruling priests began accusing him of many things.**	
4a	Response	**Again Pilate asked him,**	
b	question	*"Are you not going to answer?*	
c	assertion	*Look at all the charges they are bringing against you."*	
5a	Response to 4	But **Jesus said nothing more,**	
b	result of 5a	so that Pilate was amazed.	
6a	Narrator explanation	Now **at the festival Pilate normally released one of the prisoners**	
b		whom the people requested.	
7a	Character introduction	**A man called Barabbas was in prison with the rebels**	
b	character description	who had committed murder in ↵ the insurrection.	
8a	action	Going up,	
b	Request	**the crowd began to ask Pilate to do as he normally did for them.**	
9a	Response to 8	**Pilate responded to them,**	
b	question	*"Do you want me to release the king of the Jews to you?"*	
10	reason for 9	because he knew that the ruling priests had handed Jesus over because of envy.	
11	Response to 9/Contrast	But **the ruling priests stirred up the crowd to have Barabbas released instead.**	
12a	Question	**Again Pilate asked them,**	
b		*"What, then, shall I do with the one you call king of the Jews?"*	
13a	Response to 12	**They shouted back,**	
b		*"Crucify him!"*	
14a	Response to 13	**Pilate kept asking them,**	
b		*"Why? What evil has he done?"*	
c	Response to 14a-b	But **they shouted even more,**	
d		*"Crucify him!"*	
15a	Action	So **Pilate … released Barabbas to them.**	
b	reason for 15a	… wanting to satisfy the crowd …	
c	action/setting (temporal)	After having Jesus flogged,	
d	Action	**he delivered him over to be crucified.**	

Structure

This episode has four scenes: (1) the transfer to Pilate (v. 1), (2) Pilate's questioning of Jesus (vv. 2 – 5), (3) the release of Barabbas in the Passover clemency (vv. 6 – 11), and (4) the decision to crucify Jesus (vv. 12 – 15). Among the Gospels, Mark has the briefest version of these events. Matthew adds the account of Pilate's wife sending a message to him to have nothing to do "with that innocent [or 'righteous'] man" (Matt 27:19). Only Luke records that Pilate sent Jesus to Herod Antipas for a hearing (Luke 23:6 – 12) before eventually sentencing him to death. John records a lengthy dialogue between Pilate and Jesus, where Jesus acknowledges he is "king of the Jews" but denies that his kingdom is "of this world" (18:28 – 19:16).

The historicity of the Roman trial is closely linked to the question of responsibility for Jesus' death (see "In Depth: Who Was Responsible for Jesus' Death?" in Theology in Application, below). The two main arguments against the details of the present account are the lack of evidence for a Passover release of prisoners and the unlikely portrayal of a vacillating Pilate caving to the will of the religious leaders. In fact, both are historically plausible. All four Gospels describe the release of Barabbas as part of a Passover clemency, showing its firm place in the tradition. Although there is no direct evidence for this practice in Roman Judea, such clemencies were not uncommon in the Roman world (see comments on 15:6), and this one fits well the Passover theme of emancipation from slavery in Egypt. It is also difficult to explain how the name Barabbas entered the tradition if not from some historical recollection of the exchange.

The actions of Pilate described by Mark are also in line with what we know of the governor's character from other sources. An unscrupulous ruler, Pilate was contemptuous of his Jewish subjects and willing to violently suppress opposition (see comments on 15:1). Yet his position as prefect in Judea was tenuous, since he served at the whim of the emperor, who could be swayed by the complaints of his Jewish subjects. Although Pilate must have seen little in Jesus that constituted a threat, he would also have had few qualms about executing one innocent man to placate the influential Jerusalem leaders.

A third important piece of evidence in support of the episode is the repeated use of the title "king of the Jews" in Pilate's questions (15:2, 9, 12; cf. vv. 18, 32) and then on the *titulus* on the cross (15:26). The title, which was not used of Jesus by the early church and so is unlikely to have been created by Christians, provides good evidence that Jesus was crucified under the charge of sedition, that is, claiming to be a king in opposition to Caesar.

Exegetical Outline

→ **1. The Conclusion of the Jewish Trial and Transfer to Pilate (15:1)**

2. The Hearing before Pilate (15:2 – 5)

   a. Pilate's question (15:2a)

   b. Jesus' initial answer (15:2b)

   c. The accusations of the ruling priests (15:3)

   d. Pilate's continuing questions (15:4)

   e. Jesus' silence and Pilate's amazement (15:5)

3. The Passover Clemency (15:6 – 11)

   a. The custom (15:6)

   b. The crowd's request (15:7 – 8)

   c. Pilate's attempt to release Jesus (15:9 – 10)

   d. The crowd demands Barabbas at the prompting of the ruling priests (15:11)

4. The Handing over of Jesus for Scourging and Crucifixion (15:12 – 15)

   a. Pilate's question about Jesus (15:12)

   b. The crowd's insistence: "Crucify him!" (15:13 – 14)

   c. Pilate's acquiescence: flogging and crucifixion (15:15)

Explanation of the Text

15:1 Early in the morning, after making their plans, the ruling priests, together with the elders and experts in the law and the whole Sanhedrin, bound Jesus, led him away, and handed him over to Pilate (Καὶ εὐθὺς πρωῒ συμβούλιον ποιήσαντες οἱ ἀρχιερεῖς μετὰ τῶν πρεσβυτέρων καὶ γραμματέων καὶ ὅλον τὸ συνέδριον, δήσαντες τὸν Ἰησοῦν ἀπήνεγκαν καὶ παρέδωκαν Πιλάτῳ). The Sanhedrin did not have authority to execute criminals (see comments on 14:63 – 64), so they take Jesus to the Roman governor to gain a capital sentence.

The phrase "after making plans" (συμβούλιον ποιήσαντες) is a difficult one. It could mean: (1)

"after calling a council," referring to a second hearing before the whole Sanhedrin in the early morning (see Literary Context, above, and Luke 22:54 – 71; cf. HCSB: "had a meeting with …"); (2) "having held their council," a summary of the trial of the night before;[1] or (3) "after making their plans," referring to their decision made in the morning to take Jesus to Pilate (cf. REB; NIV: "made their plans"; NLT: "met to discuss their next step"). The first seems unlikely, since Mark has already said the "whole Sanhedrin" was present the night before (14:55). Most commentators go with the second, though the third seems equally viable.[2]

---

1. So Josef Blinzler, *The Trial of Jesus: The Jewish and Roman Proceedings against Jesus Christ Described and Assessed from the Oldest Accounts* (trans. I. McHugh and F. McHugh; Westminster, MD: Newman, 1959), 145 – 48; Brown, *Death of the Messiah*, 1:629 – 32; Evans, *Mark 8:27 – 16:20*, 475; France, *Mark*, 626; Stein, *Mark*, 697.

2. With other verbs the noun "plan" or "council" (συμβούλιον) often has the sense of devising a plan or plotting an action (with δίδωμι, Mark 3:6; with λαμβάνω, Matt 12:14; 22:15; 27:1, 7; 28:12). Matthew's parallel here has συμβούλιον ἔλαβον (Matt 27:7). The textual variant ετοιμασαντες ("after preparing"; ℵ C L 892) also suggests some copyists understood the sentence this way and sought to smooth out Mark's awkward grammar.

Mark's characteristic "immediately" (εὐθὺς; see comments on 1:10) does not mean "just then." It functions as a transition word indicating the next narrative event ("after this …") and so is already well captured by the temporal participle, "after making plans …" (cf. NIV, NASB, NET, etc.). It is now early Friday morning, following Jesus' Passover celebration, Gethsemane agony, and arrest the night before. There is some evidence that Roman trials began at dawn,[3] which may be the reason they transfer Jesus at this time. The mention of the "whole Sanhedrin" together with its constituting groups — ruling priests, elders, and experts in the law — suggests a formal transfer to the Roman authorities.

Here the ruling priests take the lead; the elders and scribes are "with" them. This is because the high priest and his associates are viewed by the Romans as the official leadership of the Jewish nation. The statement that they "delivered [him] to Pilate" (παρέδωκαν Πιλάτῳ) recalls Jesus' passion prediction that the Son of Man would be "handed over" (παραδοθήσεται) to Gentiles (10:33; cf. 9:31). On the possible use of this verb as a divine passive, see 1:14; 9:31; 10:33; 14:21, 41.

Pontius Pilate was governor of Judea from AD 26 to 36. Judea was at this time an imperial province, which means it was under the direct control of the Roman emperor (Tiberius Caesar) and administered by governors appointed by him. Though sometimes identified anachronistically as a "procurator," Pilate's official title was "prefect," a fact confirmed by an inscription discovered in Caesarea Maritima in 1961. The two-by-three-foot stone is in Latin, with the fragmentary inscription, [CAESARIEN]S TIBERIEVM [PON]TIVS PILATVS [PRAEF]ECTVS IVDA[EA]E DEDIT. The translation is debated, but likely means, "Pontius Pilate, Prefect of Judea, has presented the Tiberieum to the Caesareans." The Tiberieum was likely a building or monument dedicated to Tiberius Caesar.

This inscription is not only the first direct *archaeological* evidence for the existence of Pilate (there was already much literary evidence), but it also confirms that Pilate's official title was "prefect."[4] The title "procurator" came to be used of the Roman governors of Judea after the reign of Agrippa I (AD 41 – 44). The Gospels use the general term "governor" (ἡγεμών; Matt 27:2, 11, 14, 15; Luke 20:20), though Mark simply refers to him as "Pilate." He is called "Pontius Pilate" in Luke 3:1; Acts 4:27; and 1 Tim 6:13. "Pontius" was his *nomen* (tribal name) and "Pilatus" his *cognomen* (family name). His *praenomen* (personal name) is nowhere preserved.[5]

The governor's residence and the seat of Roman government in Judea was in Caesarea Maritima on the Mediterranean coast. Yet Pilate would take up residence in Jerusalem during the major Jewish festivals, when nationalistic ambitions were high, in order to keep a wary eye on the crowds and respond quickly to any sign of trouble. The traditional site of Jesus' Roman trial shown to visitors to Jerusalem today is the ancient pavement of the Fortress of Antonia, where Roman troops were garrisoned, overlooking the northwest corner of the Temple Mount. Yet it is unlikely that Pilate would have stayed in these spartan barracks. More likely, he took up residence in Herod's palace, in the southwestern part of the city, and Jesus' trial took place there.[6] Mark refers to this palace as the "Praetorium" (πραιτώριον), meaning the governor's residence, in 15:16.

3. According to Seneca, *Ira* 2.7.3.
4. J. Vardaman, "A New Inscription Which Mentions Pilate as 'Prefect,'" *JBL* 81 (1962): 70 – 71. For extensive bibliography, see Evans, *Mark 8:27 – 16:20*, 470 – 71.
5. Brown, *Death of the Messiah*, 1:694.
6. Josephus writes that Gessius Florus, one of the later Roman procurators, resided in Herod's palace and had his tribunal set up in the square in front of it (*J.W.* 2.14.8 §301).

IN DEPTH: Pontius Pilate in Mark and in History

Some have argued that the portrait of Pilate here in Mark, and in the Gospels generally, is unrealistic and unhistorical, since he is portrayed as weak and vacillating, affirming the innocence of Jesus yet caving in to the demands of the religious leaders. Yet the description here fits well what we know of the man. Pilate could act with insensitivity and ruthless oppression against his Jewish subjects. Josephus describes an incident when demonstrations broke out because Pilate used money from the temple treasury to build an aqueduct for Jerusalem. Pilate sent soldiers to secretly mingle with the protestors and then suddenly attack, killing many and scattering the crowd (*J.W.* 2.9.4 §§175 – 177; *Ant.* 18.3.2 §§60 – 62). Luke 13:1 refers to a similar episode near the Temple Mount where Pilate massacred some Galileans, "mixing their blood with their sacrifices."

Yet Pilate was also pragmatic and opportunistic, knowing when to back down for his own good. Josephus writes that when Pilate first arrived in Palestine in AD 26, he provoked protests by secretly bringing army standards bearing the images of Roman emperors — idols in Jewish eyes — into Jerusalem. When a large group of Jews from Caesarea protested, passively declaring their willingness to be slaughtered, Pilate withdrew the standards (*J.W.* 2.9.2 – 3 §§169 – 174; *Ant.* 18.3.1 §§55 – 59).

The Jewish philosopher Philo similarly writes about an incident when the Jews protested Pilate's actions in placing idolatrous golden shields in Herod's palace in Jerusalem. Here too Pilate eventually removed the shields, fearing that if the Jews sent an embassy to Rome, "they would also expose the rest of his conduct as governor by stating in full the briberies, the insults, the robberies, the outrages and wanton injustices, the executions without trial constantly repeated, the ceaseless and supremely grievous cruelty" (Philo, *Legat.* 299 – 305). Philo is likely exaggerating Pilate's offenses because of his disdain for the man.[7] Yet here again we see a combination of pragmatism and ruthlessness. Pilate was eventually recalled to Rome in AD 36 after taking military action against a group of Samaritans who took up arms in support of a particular prophet (Josephus, *Ant.* 18.4.1 – 2 §§85 – 89).

The account of Pilate in Mark (and the other gospels) fits well this portrait of a pragmatic ruler interested in self-preservation. Pilate recognizes that Jesus is likely innocent and not a threat to the Roman authorities (15:14). He also recognizes that the religious leaders are acting out of envy and self-interest (15:10). In the interest of justice, he halfheartedly, yet repeatedly, seeks to set Jesus free. Yet in the end it is easier to turn him over for crucifixion rather than

---

7. See Blinzler, *Trial of Jesus*, 182 – 83.

to risk a riot or an embassy sent to Rome, which might threaten his position before Caesar. One would-be Jewish prophet can easily be sacrificed for the greater (and Pilate's own!) good.

15:2 Pilate asked him, "Are you the king of the Jews?" He answered him, "You have said so." (Καὶ ἐπηρώτησεν αὐτὸν ὁ Πιλᾶτος· σὺ εἶ ὁ βασιλεὺς τῶν Ἰουδαίων; ὁ δὲ ἀποκριθεὶς αὐτῷ λέγει· σὺ λέγεις). Though no specific charge is stated, Pilate's question implies that the religious leaders have accused Jesus of claiming royal authority. The religious charges of blasphemy and messianic pretention (14:62–64) would have been of little concern to Pilate, so the religious leaders modify these to political charges of sedition and claiming to be a king.[8]

The title "king of the Jews" (ὁ βασιλεὺς τῶν Ἰουδαίων), which appears here for the first time in Mark's gospel, will become the repeated refrain of the Roman trial and crucifixion (15:2, 9, 12, 18, 26).[9] It is likely meant as a Gentile interpretation of the Jewish titles "Messiah" and "king of Israel" (15:32), which are used mockingly by the Jewish religious leaders when Jesus is on the cross. Though the titles are meant to mock and deride Jesus, ironically they are true, since Jesus is the messianic King who will enter into his royal glory through suffering and death.

Jesus' response to Pilate, "You have said so" (σὺ λέγεις), is the same given in the other Synoptics (Matt 27:11; Luke 23:3; cf. John 18:37: "You say that I am a king"). It was also the answer given to the high priest in Matt 26:64 (cf. Luke 22:70: "You say that I am" [ὑμεῖς λέγετε ὅτι ἐγώ εἰμι]), where Mark has the explicit "I am" (ἐγώ εἰμι; 14:62). Scholars

debate its meaning. Gundry views it as a denial because of the contrast with the emphatic "I am" in 14:62 and because Pilate says to the crowd that *they* call him king of the Jews, not that Jesus himself claims such.[10] Yet the parallel in Matt 26:64 and the fact that Pilate will crucify Jesus under this charge indicates some kind of affirmation.[11] Its meaning is likely a qualified "yes," something like, "This is true, but your idea of kingship is different from my own" (cf. John 18:36). Catchpole calls it "affirmative in content, and reluctant or cucumlocutory in formulation."[12]

15:3–5 Then the ruling priests began accusing him of many things. Again Pilate asked him, "Are you not going to answer? Look at all the charges they are bringing against you." But Jesus said nothing more, so that Pilate was amazed (καὶ κατηγόρουν αὐτοῦ οἱ ἀρχιερεῖς πολλά. ὁ δὲ Πιλᾶτος πάλιν ἐπηρώτα αὐτὸν λέγων· οὐκ ἀποκρίνῃ οὐδέν; ἴδε πόσα σου κατηγοροῦσιν. ὁ δὲ Ἰησοῦς οὐκέτι οὐδὲν ἀπεκρίθη, ὥστε θαυμάζειν τὸν Πιλᾶτον). The imperfect tense here is likely ingressive, meaning "they began accusing" (κατηγόρουν) him.

Mark does not say what accusations are leveled against Jesus, but Luke identifies three, "subverting our nation," "oppos[ing] payment of taxes to Caesar," and "claim[ing] to be Messiah, a king" (Luke 23:2). In the larger context of Mark's gospel, we can think of other possible charges: violating the law of Moses (3:2, 6) and encouraging others to do

---

8. Josephus uses the title "king of the Jews" with reference to the Hasmonean king Alexander Jannaeus (*Ant.* 14.3.1 §311) as well as Herod the Great (*Ant.* 16.10.2 §311). It would clearly carry political implications.

9. See Matera, *Kingship of Jesus,* passim.

10. Gundry, *Mark,* 932; cf. van Iersel, *Mark,* 459.

11. So most commentators.

12. D. R. Catchpole, "The Answer of Jesus to Caiaphas (Matthew xxvi.64)," *NTS* 17 (1970–1971): 213–26 (quote from p. 226).

so (2:24), disrupting and defiling temple worship (11:18, 28), threatening the temple's destruction (13:2; 15:38), and undermining religious authority (12:1 – 12). "Many things" (πολλά) could be functioning either adverbially (accusing him "much" of claiming to be king) or as a plural direct object (accusing him of "many things"). The latter is more likely since Pilate refers in v. 4 to "all the charges" (πόσα) against Jesus.

Jesus' silence parallels his initial silence before the Sanhedrin (14:61) and would likely recall for Mark's readers Isaiah's Suffering Servant, who was "oppressed and afflicted, yet he did not open his mouth" (Isa 53:7).[13] Although amazement is a common response to Jesus' teaching and miracles throughout Mark's gospel (1:22, 27; 2:12; 5:15, 20, 42; 6:2, 51; 7:37; 11:18; 12:17, 37), Pilate's response is surprising. What amazed him? Some scholars draw a connection to Isa 52:15, where the Servant is the object of amazement by the nations,[14] but this seems a bit obscure. There is also a Greco-Roman tradition of admiration for stoic silence in the face of persecution and suffering.[15] Perhaps Pilate is impressed with Jesus' perseverance. In the present context, however, Pilate seems baffled that Jesus would refuse to defend himself, despite his apparent innocence. Like the disciples, Pilate is oblivious that Jesus has chosen this path for himself and that

it is God's purpose in "deliver him over" to suffering and death as a ransom for sins (9:31; 10:33, 45).

15:6 Now at the festival Pilate normally released one of the prisoners whom the people requested (Κατὰ δὲ ἑορτὴν ἀπέλυεν αὐτοῖς ἕνα δέσμιον ὃν παρῃτοῦντο). The phrase "at [κατά] the festival" could mean that this was a custom at all the festivals or more specifically at Passover. In either case, the custom is unattested outside the Gospels, causing some to deny its historicity.[16]

Yet emancipation of prisoners to gain political advantage was common in the ancient world.[17] Deissmann cites a papyrus from around AD 85 where a prisoner is released because of the petition of the people. G. Septimius Vegetus, the governor, says to Phibion, the accused: "You are worthy of scourging, but I will give you to the people."[18] According to Josephus, after the death of Herod the Great, his son Archelaus reduced taxes and released many prisoners in order to gain the favor of his father's subjects (*Ant.* 17.8.4 §§204 – 205).

Similarly, decades later when the procurator Albinus (AD 62 – 64) was preparing to leave office, he executed all prisoners he deemed worthy of death, but took bribes for the release of all other prisoners. Josephus adds, "by this means the prisons were indeed emptied, but the country was filled with

---

13. The textual variant in v. 3, αυτος δε ουδεν απεκρινατο ("but he answered nothing"; N W Δ Θ Ψ *f*¹³ 33 565 579 1424), likely arose because the οὐκέτι ("yet" or "still") in v. 5 was interpreted by copyists as indicating a prior silence.

14. Hooker, *Mark*, 368; Marcus, *Way of the Lord*, 187 – 88; Evans, *Mark 8:27 – 16:20*, 479.

15. Evans, *Mark 8:27 – 16:20*, 479, points to references in Plutarch (*Mor.* 498 D – E) and Plato (*Resp.* 2.5 §361e)

16. See, e.g., Winter, *On the Trial of Jesus*, 131 – 43, who concludes, "The *privilegium paschale* is nothing but a figment of the imagination. No such custom existed" (p. 134). Marcus, *Mark 8 – 16*, 1028, doubts the custom, arguing that the Romans are unlikely to have agreed to such a release, but then acknowledges that the Jews may have regularly requested and sometimes received from the Romans such an amnesty at Passover

(in John 18:39 it is described as a *Jewish* custom), especially in light of the Passover theme of liberation. This distinction seems to be unnecessary quibbling. Mark's language allows for the practice to have become the governor's "custom" even if it occurred each year as a Jewish request.

17. For these and other examples, including Assyrian, Babylonian, Greek, and Roman ones, see R. L. Merritt, "Jesus Barabbas and the Paschal Pardon," *JBL* 104 (1985): 57 – 68; Blinzler, *Trial of Jesus*, 205 – 8; Evans, *Mark 8:27 – 16:20*, 479 – 80. Merritt actually argues that Mark's story is unhistorical but is based on these common traditions.

18. Papyrus Florentinus 61.59 – 64; Deissmann, *Light from the Ancient East*, 269 – 70; Taylor, *Mark*, 580; Evans, *Mark 8:27 – 16:20*, 480.

robbers" (*Ant.* 20.9.5 §215). The Mishnah, though later in date, gives hints of a possible Passover release. It is said that a paschal lamb may be slaughtered for those unable to do it for themselves, such as those who are unclean or "for one who has been promised release from prison" (*m. Pesaḥ* 8:6a).[19]

In support of the custom is its independent attestation in the Synoptics and in John (18:39). If the practice did not exist, where did the idea come from? Evans points to the implausibility that the Evangelists would assert such a custom if it did not exist, since the claim would be easily refuted, causing embarrassment to the church.[20] As noted earlier, the Passover theme of liberation from bondage makes such a release theologically appropriate and would give the Romans a means of placating the restless Passover crowds.

15:7 A man called Barabbas was in prison with the rebels who had committed murder in the insurrection (ἦν δὲ ὁ λεγόμενος Βαραββᾶς μετὰ τῶν στασιαστῶν δεδεμένος οἵτινες ἐν τῇ στάσει φόνον πεποιήκεισαν). Barabbas is an Aramaic name (*bar ʾabbāʾ*), a patronymic (a name identifying a person's father) meaning "son of Abba" (a common personal name) or "son of the father," perhaps referring to a revered teacher or rabbi.

Matthew's parallel (Matt 27:16 – 17) has a variant reading identifying his full name as "Jesus Barabbas" (Ἰησοῦν [τὸν] Βαραββᾶν = Jesus, the son of Abba, a reading followed by GNT, NET, REB, NIV). Although the external evidence is weak, mostly coming from Caesarean manuscripts, the internal transcriptional evidence is almost overwhelming. Jesus/Joshua/Yeshua was a common name in Israel in the first century. Yet for such a criminal to bear the Lord's name would be offensive to Christian scribes. It is easy to explain why the name would have been deleted by a copyist, but almost inexplicable why it would have been added.

The third-century church father Origen shows awareness of this variant but rejects it on the basis that "in the whole range of the scriptures we know that no one who is a sinner [is called] Jesus."[21] Origen thinks it may have been added by heretics.[22] Some scholars have suggested the name originally appeared not only in Matthew, but also here in Mark.[23] The present text (lit., "the one called Barabbas") is awkward and may have originally read, "Jesus, the one called Barabbas" (Ἰησοῦς ὁ λεγόμενος Βαραββᾶς). Yet there is no textual evidence for this reading in Mark and so it remains purely speculative.

Barabbas is said to be "bound [δεδεμένος, trans. here 'in prison'] with the rebels who had committed murder in the insurrection [ἡ στάσις]." Mark seems to assume this rebellion was a well-known incident, though we cannot identify it more specifically.[24] There were many opposition movements and violent demonstrations against the Romans in first-century Palestine. These included both insurrectionist movements — those seeking to violently overthrow the government — and social banditry — disenfranchised peasants who turned to robbery out of poverty and exploitation by the upper classes.[25] Like first-century Robin Hoods, these bandits tended to be popular with the common

---

19. See B. Chavel, "The Releasing of a Prisoner on the Eve of Passover in Ancient Jerusalem," *JBL* 60 (1941): 273 – 78; Blinzler, *Trial of Jesus,* 218 – 21.

20. Evans, *Mark 8:27 – 16:20,* 480.

21. Metzger, *Textual Commentary,* 56.

22. Brown, *Death of the Messiah,* 1:798. Origen actually treats it as the majority reading of his time, saying that he is aware of some manuscripts that *do not* have "Jesus" here.

23. Taylor, *Mark,* 581; Cranfield, *Mark,* 450; Nineham, *Mark,* 416.

24. For various possibilities, see Evans, *Mark 8:27 – 16:20,* 2:1029 – 30.

25. See R. A. Horsley and J. S. Hanson, *Bandits, Prophets, and Messiahs* (New York: Winston, 1985); R. A. Horsley, *Jesus and the Spiral of Violence: Popular Jewish Resistance in Roman Palestine* (San Francisco: Harper & Row, 1987).

people, who despised the Roman rulers and their wealthy countrymen who profited from their rule.

Whether rebel or robber (or both), Barabbas was likely part of the broad movement(s) of opposition to the Roman authorities. The two "robbers" or "bandits" (λῃσταί) crucified with Jesus were probably part of this same rebellion and had been arrested with him (see comments on 15:27). Whether Barabbas himself had committed murder is not clear (he is in prison *with* the murderers). Luke 23:19 says he was in prison for insurrection and murder.

15:8 Going up, the crowd began to ask Pilate to do as he normally did for them (καὶ ἀναβὰς ὁ ὄχλος ἤρξατο αἰτεῖσθαι καθὼς ἐποίει αὐτοῖς). On the Passover clemency see comments on v. 6 above. It is perhaps significant that the people approach Pilate. This is not a Roman custom per se, but an annual Jewish request to the Romans at Passover. The imperfect ἐποίει is a habitual or customary imperfect[26] and so is well translated "as he normally did." "Going up" (ἀναβάς; aorist participle) may indicate that the location was indeed Herod's palace (see v. 1), since the palace was located on a hill in the southwest part of the city. Or the verb could simply indicate their approach to Pilate's judicial platform.

The "crowd" (ὁ ὄχλος) is not specifically identified. Some think these were the high priest's henchmen; others that they were a group of Barabbas's supporters who had gathered in anticipation of the prisoner release.[27] Yet Mark says that the ruling priest had to stir up the crowd to call for Barabbas's release (v. 11), which would not seem necessary in either case.[28] Whoever they were historically, as a *character* in Mark's narrative the crowds represent the Jewish people who have marveled at Jesus' authority and teaching but are eventually swayed to turn against him by their corrupt leadership.

15:9–10 Pilate responded to them, "Do you want me to release the king of the Jews to you?" because he knew that the ruling priests had handed Jesus over because of envy (ὁ δὲ Πιλᾶτος ἀπεκρίθη αὐτοῖς λέγων· θέλετε ἀπολύσω ὑμῖν τὸν βασιλέα τῶν Ἰουδαίων; ἐγίνωσκεν γὰρ ὅτι διὰ φθόνον παραδεδώκεισαν αὐτὸν οἱ ἀρχιερεῖς). This is Pilate's first of three questions (vv. 9, 12, 14), following the common pattern of triads in Mark's gospel (see Introduction to Mark: Literary Features).[29] Why did Pilate propose Jesus for the Passover release? Some have suggested that he misheard the crowds asking for Jesus Barabbas (see comments on v. 7) as a request for Jesus of Nazareth. The text, however, implies Pilate sees this as an opportunity to release a prisoner whom he considers to be innocent and generally harmless.

Knowing the ruling priests have brought Jesus to him out of "envy," Pilate supposes the crowd will side with this popular teacher and miracle worker. "Envy" summarizes well the confrontation between Jesus and the religious leaders, since his popularity threatened their authority and influence among the people (11:18; 12:12, 37; 14:1–2). The theme of Jesus' popularity has been a major one throughout Mark's gospel (1:33–34, 37; 2:2, 4, 13; 3:7–9, 20; 4:1, 36; 5:21, 24, 30–32; 6:14–15, 31–34; 7:24; 8:1–3; 9:14–15, 30; 10:1, 13).

15:11 But the ruling priests stirred up the crowd to have Barabbas released instead (οἱ δὲ ἀρχιερεῖς ἀνέσεισαν τὸν ὄχλον ἵνα μᾶλλον τὸν Βαραββᾶν ἀπολύσῃ αὐτοῖς). On the identity of the crowd, see comments v. 8. It seems surprising that the priestly aristocracy would favor the release of Barabbas,

---

26. Wallace, *Greek Grammar*, 521–22.

27. Cranfield, *Mark*, 450; Evans, *Mark 8:27–16:20*, 481; France, *Mark*, 631.

28. Stein, *Mark*, 701.

29. Ibid., 702.

since insurrectionists and social bandits posed a threat to their own authority as well as that of the Romans. But they obviously consider Jesus a greater immediate threat because of his influence with the people. Barabbas is the natural alternative for release, since as a "freedom fighter," he would be popular with the people.

15:12 – 14 Again Pilate asked them, "What, then, shall I do with the one you call king of the Jews?" They shouted back, "Crucify him!" Pilate kept asking them, "Why? What evil has he done?" But they shouted even more, "Crucify him!" (ὁ δὲ Πιλᾶτος πάλιν ἀποκριθεὶς ἔλεγεν αὐτοῖς· τί οὖν [θέλετε]³⁰ ποιήσω [ὃν λέγετε]³¹ τὸν βασιλέα τῶν Ἰουδαίων; οἱ δὲ πάλιν ἔκραξαν· σταύρωσον αὐτόν. ὁ δὲ Πιλᾶτος ἔλεγεν αὐτοῖς· τί γὰρ ἐποίησεν κακόν; οἱ δὲ περισσῶς ἔκραξαν· σταύρωσον αὐτόν). Pilate had not counted on the influence of the priestly leadership with the crowds and finds himself in a quandary. If Barabbas is to be released, what to do with the apparently innocent Jesus?

The response is shocking: "They shouted back, 'Crucify him!'" It is not clear in the Greek who the "they" are, the ruling priests or the crowd. The latter seems most likely, though there is little difference, since the priests are urging them on (v. 11). The word "again" in v. 12 does not mean "a second time" (this is the first call for crucifixion), but rather "in response," and so is translated, "They shouted *back*." This is the first reference to crucifixion in Mark's gospel, except for Jesus' call in 8:34 for disciples to take up their cross and follow him. For more on crucifixion, see comments on 15:24.

Pilate's third question turns from what to do with Jesus to the injustice of crucifying an innocent man: "Why? What evil has he done?" The verb ἔλεγεν is likely an iterative imperfect, meaning that Pilate "kept asking." The question goes unanswered. The crowd is uninterested in debate and shouts all the louder for Jesus' death.

15:15 So Pilate, wanting to satisfy the crowd, released Barabbas to them. After having Jesus flogged, he delivered him over to be crucified (Ὁ δὲ Πιλᾶτος βουλόμενος τῷ ὄχλῳ τὸ ἱκανὸν ποιῆσαι ἀπέλυσεν αὐτοῖς τὸν Βαραββᾶν, καὶ παρέδωκεν τὸν Ἰησοῦν φραγελλώσας ἵνα σταυρωθῇ). Pilate's actions are not those of a weak and vacillating ruler, cowering before the powerful Jewish leaders. Nor is he the seeker of justice, who repeatedly tries to release Jesus but is eventually overwhelmed by circumstances. Rather, true to form he is a ruthless pragmatist, who sees the direction of the tide and rides along.

Pilate's goal is to "satisfy the crowd" (τῷ ὄχλῳ τὸ ἱκανὸν ποιῆσαι), which means to come out politically ahead. The death of one Jewish eccentric is better than provoking the ire of the religious establishment and perhaps a riot at his doorstep. It is politically a double win, to release Barabbas for the people and to crucify Jesus for the religious leaders.

The text does not say to whom Pilate "delivered over" (παρέδωκεν) Jesus to be crucified, but it is clear from 15:16 that the Roman soldiers were in charge of the execution. Flogging was often done in preparation for crucifixion,³² and this seems to be the case here. Such scourging was incredibly severe

---

30. θέλετε may have been either omitted by copyists because of its awkwardness or added to harmonize with the same verb in v. 9. The latter seems more likely in light of the strong external evidence (א B C W Δ Ψ *f*¹ ¹³ 33 892 2427).

31. The relative clause "whom you call ..." (ὃν λέγετε) is textually disputed. If original (א C Ψ 0250 33 𝔐), it confirms that the accusation in vv. 1 – 2 came from the religious leaders and has Pilate shifting the responsibility on them. Copyists

may have omitted it to harmonize with Pilate's statement in v. 9. If it were originally absent (A D W Θ *f*¹,¹³ 565 700 2542), copyists may have added it to emphasize that the charge came from the religious leaders.

32. Hengel, *Crucifixion,* 28 – 29; Josephus, *J. W.* 2.14.9 §306. The Romans distinguished between three kinds of beatings: *fustes, flagella,* and *verbera.* The first was the lightest and used as a warning against further infractions. The third was the most

and often resulted in death. The victim would be stripped and their hands tied above their head. A whip of leather cords with pieces of bone, lead, or glass imbedded in them would be used. The Jews limited scourges to forty lashes, but the Romans had no such limitations.[33] The whipping would cause severe lacerations not only to the skin but also to muscle tissue and bone. Josephus speaks of Jesus son of Ananus being "whipped with scourges to the bones" (Josephus, *J. W.* 6.5.3 §304).

Theology in Application

Christology: Jesus, the King of the Jews

Jesus' messianic status is on center stage here. Having affirmed before the Sanhedrin that he is indeed Israel's Messiah and the Son of God, Jesus is now brought before Pilate on a political version of that charge: "king of the Jews" (15:2). Though guarded and cryptic, Jesus' response to Pilate's question is certainly a positive one: "You have said so," or "That is your way of saying it." Though not the kind of king Pilate envisages (cf. John 18:33 – 37), Jesus affirms he is Israel's Messiah, the Savior of the world. The repeated use of the title by Pilate (15:9, 12), the mocking soldiers (15:18), the *titulus* on the cross (15:26), and the taunting religious leaders (15:32; "king of Israel") all provide ironic affirmation of Jesus' kingship, and with it his messianic identity. Pilate's identification of Jesus as "king of the Jews" is ironic confirmation of Jesus' messianic identity.

In today's world most of the few remaining monarchies are symbolic and traditional. The queen of England holds little real power. Yet in the ancient world kings held absolute authority over their people. In the NT Christians are often identified as "slaves" of Jesus Christ, a designation that sounds jarring to our ears today. Yet this is exactly what it means to acknowledge Jesus as our king. It means to place ourselves in absolute submission to his will, to turn our lives over to his service, and to make him Lord of our lives.

The Innocence of Jesus: The Suffering Servant of the Lord

Just as the Christology of this passage comes primarily from Pilate's lips, so also does this second theme — Jesus' innocence, or righteousness. Both explicitly and implicitly, Pilate affirms Jesus' innocence/righteousness. In v. 4 Pilate asks Jesus why he is not answering these obviously trumped-up charges against him. In v. 9 he tries to release Jesus in the Passover clemency because he views the charge of sedition as ludicrous. In v. 12 he apparently expects the crowd to ask for Jesus to be released in

severe and was usually a prelude to execution (Sherwin-White, *Roman Society and Roman Law*, 27). In Luke 23:16, Pilate says he will "punish" (παιδεύω) Jesus and release him, likely a reference to *fustigatio.* Similarly, in John's gospel Pilate has Jesus flogged and then again tries to persuade the crowd to release him (John 19:1 – 7). What Mark (and Matthew) describe is no doubt *verberatio,* a prelude to crucifixion.

33. Blinzler, *Trial of Jesus,* 222.

addition to Barabbas. Finally, in v. 14 he explicitly asks, "Why [crucify him]? What evil has he done?"

This Markan theme is even more pronounced in Luke's gospel, where Jesus' innocence is repeatedly asserted by Pilate (Luke 23:4, 14, 22), Herod (23:15), the repentant criminal (23:41), and even the centurion at the foot of the cross (23:47). Whereas in Mark the centurion cries out, "This man was the Son of God!" (15:39), in Luke he says, "Surely this was an innocent/righteous [δίκαιος] man." This theme continues in Acts, where Jesus is called by the messianic title "the Righteous One" (ὁ δίκαιος; Acts 3:14; 7:52). The title recalls Isaiah's Servant Songs, where the Messiah is "my righteous servant [who] will justify the many" (Isa 53:11).

Here we have a remarkable paradox. Pilate mockingly acknowledges that Jesus is the king of the Jews and so crucifies him under that accusation. Yet at the same time he repeatedly asserts his innocence. How can one who claims royal authority that belongs to Caesar alone be innocent of the charge of rebellion? While Pilate obviously thinks the latter charge is a sham, the reader knows better. Jesus is indeed Israel's King, the Messiah who will establish an eternal throne and crush all human kingdoms under his feet (Ps 2:1 – 9; Isa 11:4 – 5; Dan 2:44 – 46). Yet to accomplish this he must suffer and die as the righteous and innocent servant of the Lord, who provides atonement for sins (Isa 53:11).

In this passage and on the lips of a pagan governor, the two great themes of Mark's Christology are revealed: victorious King and Suffering Servant. Jesus is both "the Lion of the tribe of Judah" and the sacrificial "Lamb" of God (Rev 5:5 – 6). As we have seen, the Christology of Mark's gospel has been structured around this theme. Mark 1 – 8:30 focuses on Jesus' authority as the mighty Messiah and Son of God, while Mark 8:31 – 15:47 emphasizes his suffering role as Servant of the Lord.

For Mark's readers this dual theme would be of immense comfort. In their suffering, trials, and persecution, there is hope. Those who persevere will be rewarded, since the Lamb who was slain is worthy "to receive power and wealth and wisdom and strength and honor and glory and praise!" (Rev 5:12). All who faithfully follow him will be vindicated in the end: "For the Lamb at the center of the throne will be their shepherd; he will lead them to springs of living water. And God will wipe away every tear from their eyes" (Rev 7:17).

IN DEPTH: Who Was Responsible for Jesus' Death?

One critically important issue that arises from this passage and throughout the trial and crucifixion narrative is the question of responsibility for Jesus' death. Pilate's repeated insistence on Jesus' innocence contrasted with the religious leaders' and the Jewish crowd's vehement cries for his death have caused many historians to claim an anti-Semitic bias in Mark and in the Gospels generally (especially Matthew and John). This debate is particularly volatile in light of the history of anti-Semitism culminating in the Holocaust and the frequent misuse of these texts to blame Jews for Jesus' death.

In response to this, scholars in recent years have tended to shift blame back to the Romans, arguing that Mark and the other gospel writers have distorted the facts by blaming the Jews.[34] This distortion (it is argued) resulted from two main factors: (1) the need for the early Christian communities to avoid offending the Roman authorities, who were increasingly viewing Christianity as a dangerous and divisive religious sect, and (2) increasing hostility between Jewish communities and the fledgling church, both claiming to be the true people of God and heirs of the promises to Israel. In this climate, the tendency of the Evangelists was to paint the Roman governor Pilate as an impartial advocate of justice who was reluctantly coerced by the evil Jewish authorities.

So who was responsible for Jesus' death? Most scholars today recognize that there must have been *both* Roman and Jewish involvement. First, Jesus was *crucified,* which was a Roman rather than a Jewish punishment (Jews generally stoned).[35] It must have been the Roman governor who ordered the execution and Roman soldiers who carried it out. Yet there was little in Jesus' message or actions that would provoke a Roman military response. Jesus preached love for enemies and encouraged paying taxes to Caesar. The temple incident — the closest thing to a violent outburst by Jesus — appears to have been a relatively minor affair, and order in the temple was quickly restored. The fact that his followers were not arrested and executed after his death confirms that Jesus was not viewed as a violent insurrectionist leading a revolt.

The Jewish religious leaders, however, and especially the priestly hierarchy, had much to fear in Jesus. He had acted against the temple (their power base), repeatedly challenged their authority, and accused them of hypocrisy, and his popularity threatened their influence among the people. This scenario fits well the gospel tradition. The religious leaders likely instigated the actions against Jesus, but the Romans were quick to assent, since any movement with messianic implications threatened the *Pax Romana*. After some initial reluctance, Pilate determined that crucifixion was the best way to prevent further trouble and to placate the powerful religious establishment.

In the end we must say it was neither the Jews nor the Romans who were responsible for Jesus' death. It was rather *his enemies* who were responsible, a

34. See especially Winter, *On the Trial of Jesus*, passim.

35. The crucifixion of 800 Pharisees by the Hasmonean king Alexander Jannaeus (Josephus, *J.W.* 1.4.6 §§97 – 98; *Ant.* 13.14.1 §380) was an exception that proved the rule. This is the only account in Josephus of a Jewish ruler practicing crucifixion. See D. W. Chapman, *Ancient Jewish and Christian Perceptions of Crucifixion* (Grand Rapids: Baker, 2008), 52 – 57.

small subgroup within these two groups. As often throughout human history, those whose power and influence are threatened lash back at those perceived to be the threat. For both the priestly leadership and the Roman authorities Jesus was a problem to be eliminated to protect their own power and turf.

Of course, from a theological perspective, the question of who killed Jesus has a more profound answer. We are all ultimately responsible for Jesus' death, since he died as a sacrifice for *our* sins. Yet as Mark repeatedly asserts, this was no accident of history. Ultimately, it was *God himself* who was responsible for Jesus' death. It was he who "delivered over" Jesus to his suffering and death, "who did not spare his own Son, but gave him up for us all" (Rom 8:32). And it was the Son himself who voluntarily "humbled himself by becoming obedient to death — even death on a cross!" (Phil 2:8). The response to Jesus' death should not be to seek someone to blame, but to offer praise and thanks to God for his indescribable gift (2 Cor 9:15).

Mark 15:16 – 32

Literary Context

These two episodes are part of the continuous narrative that makes up Mark's Passion Narrative (14:1 – 15:47). Having been declared guilty of blasphemy by the religious leaders of his own nation (14:53 – 65), disowned by his leading disciple (14:66 – 72), and unjustly condemned by the Roman governor because of political expediency (15:1 – 15), Jesus will now suffer the most humiliating and excruciating death imaginable — crucifixion (15:16 – 41).

III. The Suffering Way of the Messiah (8:22 – 15:47)
    C. The Passion of the Messiah in Jerusalem (14:1 – 15:47)
        9. Peter's Denial of Jesus (14:66 – 72)
        10. The Trial before Pilate (15:1 – 15)
➡   **11. The Mocking of Jesus (15:16 – 20)**
        12. The Crucifixion (15:21 – 32)
        13. The Death of Jesus (15:33 – 41)

Main Idea

Having been condemned by Pilate to be crucified, Jesus is mocked and humiliated as "king of the Jews" by the cohort of soldiers and then taken to Golgotha to be crucified. Mark's description of the crucifixion emphasizes both the extreme humiliation of the Son of God and also the irony that the mocking of Jesus as "king of the Jews" in fact affirms his true identity.

Translation

(See next page.)

Mark 15:16 – 32

16a	Action/Setting (spatial)	**The soldiers** **led him into** **the palace courtyard**
		(that is, the Praetorium)
b	Action/Mocking	and **called together the whole cohort.**
17a	Action	**They** **put a purple cloak on him,**
b	Action	and twisting together a crown of thorns,
c	Action	**they put it on him.**
18a	Mocking	And **they began to address him,**
b		*"Hail, king of the Jews!"*
19a	Action/Abuse	**They kept** **striking him on the head** with a reed
b		and **spitting on him.**
c	manner of 19d	Falling on their knees,
d	Action/Mocking	**they were paying homage to him.**
20a	setting (temporal)	When they had mocked him,
b	Action	**they** **stripped him of the purple cloak**
c	Action	and **put his own clothes back on him.**
d	Action	Then **they led him away to crucify him.**
21a	Action/Conscription	**They forced** **a certain man who was passing by,**
b	character description	Simon of Cyrene
c	character description	(the father of Alexander and Rufus),
d	character description	who was coming in from the country, **to carry his cross.**
22a	Action	**They brought him to a place called Golgotha,**
b	interpretation	which is translated, "Place of the Skull."
23a	Action	**They tried to give him wine mixed with myrrh,**
b	Contrast with 23a	but **he did not take it.**
24a	Action	**They** **crucified him** and
b	Action	divided his garments,
c	manner of 24b	casting lots for them to see who would get what. [Ps 22:18]
25	Setting (temporal)	**It was the third hour when they crucified him.**
26a	Narrative comment	**The inscription of the charge against him read,**
b		*"The king of the Jews."*
27a	Character introduction	**They crucified** **two outlaws with him,**
b	character description	one on his right and one on his left.
29a	Action/Mocking	**Those who passed by were blaspheming him, shaking their heads and saying,**
b	mocking	*"Ha! The one who would destroy the temple and build it in three days!*
30	challenge	*Save yourself by coming down from the cross!"*
31a	Action/Mocking	**In the same way the ruling priests** together with the experts in the law ↻
		mocked him and
b		**were saying to one another,**
c	assertion	*"He saved others,*
d	contrast with 31c	*but he is not able to save himself.*
32a	challenge	*Let the Messiah, the king of Israel, come down now from the cross so we can see ↻*
		and believe."
b	Action/Mocking	**Even those who were crucified with him insulted him.**

Structure

These two episodes are rightly treated together since they share the common themes of the repeated humiliation of Jesus and the mocking declaration that he is "king of the Jews." Each episode is made up of a series of scenes. The first (vv. 16 – 20) has the soldiers leading Jesus into the palace courtyard for a mock coronation, where they place on him a royal robe and a crown of thorns and pay homage to him. The second (vv. 21 – 32) narrates the crucifixion itself, where Jesus is subsequently mocked and abused by those who witness the event.

Mark's simple and unadorned narrative is marked by striking irony. Jesus is mocked repeatedly as "king of the Jews" and on the cross is told to save himself, since he claimed to save others. Yet, ironically, Jesus is indeed the King of the Jews, who is now saving his people not by coming down from the cross, but by staying on it, giving his life as a ransom for sins (10:45).

Exegetical Outline

➡ **1. The Mocking of Jesus by the Soldiers (15:16 – 20)**

    a. Leading Jesus into the Praetorium (15: 6)

    b. Mocking and abusing Jesus as "King" (15: 17 – 19)

    c. Departure for crucifixion (15: 20)

2. The Crucifixion (15:21 – 32)

    a. Events leading to the crucifixion (15:21 – 23)

        i. The conscription of Simon (15: 21)

        ii. The location of the crucifixion at Golgotha (15:22)

        iii. The offer and refusal of drugged wine (15:23)

    b. The crucifixion (15:24 – 27)

        i. The soldiers divide Jesus' garments (15:24)

        ii. The time of the crucifixion (15:25)

        iii. The notice of the charge: King of the Jews (15:26)

        iv. Crucified with two outlaws (15:27)

    c. The mocking of Jesus on the cross (15:29 – 32)

        i. By passersby (15:29 – 30)

        ii. By the religious leaders (15:31 – 32a)

        iii. By the crucified outlaws (15:32b)

Explanation of the Text

15:16 The soldiers led him into the palace courtyard (that is, the Praetorium) and called together the whole cohort (Οἱ δὲ στρατιῶται ἀπήγαγον αὐτὸν ἔσω τῆς αὐλῆς, ὅ ἐστιν πραιτώριον, καὶ συγκαλοῦσιν ὅλην τὴν σπεῖραν). The Roman soldiers who have just flogged Jesus (15:15) now mock and abuse him. Unlike the temple guard, who were Jewish soldiers, these were likely Gentile auxiliaries, drawn perhaps from the Syro-Palestinian region.[1] "Palace courtyard" (αὐλή) can refer to a courtyard surrounded by a complex of buildings or to the whole complex (i.e., "the palace/residence"). Mark clarifies, "that is, the Praetorium" (ὅ ἐστιν πραιτώριον), to show he means the courtyard of Pilate's headquarters. (See comments on 15:1 for the likelihood that this was Herod's palace in Jerusalem rather than the fortress of Antonia.)

"Praetorium" (πραιτώριον) is a Latin loan word that originally referred to the praetor's (commander's) tent in an military encampment, but it came to designate the governor's official residence (HCSB, "headquarters"; NRSV: "governor's headquarters").[2] Mark says they called together the "whole cohort." A "cohort" (σπεῖρα; Latin: *cohors*) was a tenth of a legion, and so approximately six hundred soldiers. The Greek term, however, could be used of a smaller "maniple" of two hundred soldiers or even less.[3] Mark is likely using the term loosely to refer to the portion of the garrison on duty at the time.

15:17 – 19 They put a purple cloak on him, and twisting together a crown of thorns, they put it on him. And they began to address him, "Hail, king of the Jews!" They kept striking him on the head with a reed and spitting on him. Falling on their knees, they were paying homage to him (καὶ ἐνδιδύσκουσιν αὐτὸν πορφύραν καὶ περιτιθέασιν αὐτῷ πλέξαντες ἀκάνθινον στέφανον· καὶ ἤρξαντο ἀσπάζεσθαι αὐτόν· χαῖρε, βασιλεῦ τῶν Ἰουδαίων· καὶ ἔτυπτον αὐτοῦ τὴν κεφαλὴν καλάμῳ καὶ ἐνέπτυον αὐτῷ καὶ τιθέντες τὰ γόνατα προσεκύνουν αὐτῷ). The charge "king of the Jews" elicits derision from the soldiers since Jesus looks nothing like a king, so they take the opportunity to mock him.

The "purple" (πορφύραν) cloth or cloak thrown on Jesus was likely a faded scarlet military cloak, as Matt 27:28 suggests ("a scarlet robe"), which looked purple enough to mimic royalty.[4] The "crown" (στέφανος) the soldiers weaved together from thorns mimicked the laurel wreath used to celebrate conquering heroes, victorious athletes, and honored citizens. The adjective "thorny" (ἀκάνθινος) is a general one and could refer to any of various Palestinian plants with thorns or barbs. Matthew adds that they put a "reed" or "staff" in his right hand, no doubt a parody of a royal scepter. The mocking cry, "Hail, king of the Jews (v. 18), parodies the Latin greeting to the emperor, *Ave, Caesar, imperator* ("Hail, Caesar, Emperor!").[5] The scene as a whole resembles the Roman triumph, where Caesar would be hailed as emperor wearing a purple robe and laurel wreath and holding a scepter.[6]

In addition to the mocking, the physical abuse

1. Brown, *Death of the Messiah*, 1:701 n. 64; Marcus, *Mark 9 – 16*, 1039; Josephus, *Ant.* 14.10.6 §204; 19.9.2 §365.

2. BDAG, 859.

3. See comments on 14:43 (cf. John 18:3, 12, where a "detachment of soldiers" arrests Jesus in Gethsemane).

4. On purple as the color of royalty see Judg 8:26; Esth 8:15; 1 Macc 8:14; 10:20; Josephus, *Ant.* 17.8.3 §197; Horace, *Odes* 1.35.12; Plutarch, *Ti. C. Gracch.* 14.2; Strabo, *Geog.* 14.1.3; Marcus, *Mark 9 – 16*, 1040 – 41.

5. See, e.g., Suetonius, *Claud.* 21.6; Evans, *Mark 8:27 – 16:20*, 390.

6. For references, see T. E. Schmidt, "Mark 15.16 – 32: The Crucifixion Narrative and the Roman Triumphal Procession," *NTS* 41 (1995): 1 – 18; Evans, *Mark 8:27 – 16:20*, 488 – 89.

continues as the soldiers repeatedly beat Jesus' head with a reed or staff (κάλαμος) — probably the mock scepter reported by Matthew — and spit on him. The two imperfects (ἔτυπτον … ἐνέπτυον) are likely iterative,[7] meaning they did it again and again ("kept striking … and spitting"). For spitting as an act of humiliation and derision, see comments on 14:65. The attentive reader would remember the third passion prediction (10:33 – 34) and allusions to Isaiah's Suffering Servant, who is insulted and spit on (Isa 50:6 – 7). The parody continues as the soldiers fall to their knees and "pay homage" (προσκυνέω) to him. Although this verb can mean "to worship," the royal context suggests that reverent homage is intended. They are bowing before their "king."

The Jewish philosopher and statesman Philo relates a similar mocking episode from Alexandria, Egypt, around AD 38, when Herod Agrippa I was visiting the city. With the consent of the governor Flaccus Avillius, who despised Herod, a pagan crowd mocked the Jewish king by seizing a mentally-disturbed Jewish vagrant named Carabas and bringing him into the gymnasium. There they raised him on a platform, placed an old rug on him as a royal robe, crowned him with a folded sheet of papyrus, and put a papyrus stalk in his hand as a scepter. Two young men with staffs stood on either side as his "bodyguards" and people came forward, paying homage, asking for favors, and crying *Mari* (Aramaic for "My lord!"). Philo severely criticizes the governor for not putting a stop to this mockery.[8]

15:20 When they had mocked him, they stripped him of the purple cloak and put his own clothes back on him. Then they led him away to crucify him (καὶ ὅτε ἐνέπαιξαν αὐτῷ, ἐξέδυσαν αὐτὸν τὴν πορφύραν καὶ ἐνέδυσαν αὐτὸν τὰ ἱμάτια αὐτοῦ. καὶ ἐξάγουσιν αὐτὸν ἵνα σταυρώσωσιν αὐτόν). It is surprising that the soldiers would put Jesus' clothes back on. Roman sources suggest victims were led to their execution naked,[9] and Jesus' clothes will be removed again before his crucifixion (v. 24). Some commentators think that the reclothing was a concession to Jewish sensibilities related to nudity.[10]

15:21 They forced a certain man who was passing by, Simon of Cyrene (the father of Alexander and Rufus), who was coming in from the country, to carry his cross (καὶ ἀγγαρεύουσιν παράγοντά τινα Σίμωνα Κυρηναῖον ἐρχόμενον ἀπ᾽ ἀγροῦ, τὸν πατέρα Ἀλεξάνδρου καὶ Ῥούφου, ἵνα ἄρῃ τὸν σταυρὸν αὐτοῦ). Crucifixion victims were commonly required to carry their own cross to the crucifixion site.[11] This was normally the wooden crosspiece (Latin, *patibulum*), which was then affixed to the upright stake (*palus*) that remained at the execution site. The Greek term "cross" (σταυρός) originally referred to a stake sunk in the ground for capital punishment,[12] but Mark's "cross" here likely refers to the *patibulum*.

According to John 19:17, Jesus carried his own cross. All three Synoptics say Simon of Cyrene was compelled to carry it (Matt 27:32; Luke 23:26). The simple harmonization is that Jesus began carrying it but collapsed in his weakened condition, and the soldiers "forced" or "conscripted" (ἀγγαρεύουσιν)

---

7. See Wallace, *Greek Grammar*, 546 – 47.

8. Philo, *Flacc.* 6 §§36 – 40. For other examples of mockery, see Brown, *Death of the Messiah*, 1:874 – 75.

9. So Dionysius of Halicarnassus, *Ant. rom.* 7.69.2; Valerius Maximus, *Facta* 1.7.4; Josephus, *Ant.* 19.4.5 §270. Cited by Blinzler, *Trial of Jesus*, 244 n. 17; Brown, *Death of the Messiah*, 1:870; Marcus, *Mark 9 – 16*, 1040.

10. So Brown, *Death of the Messiah*, 1:870; 2:953; France,

Mark, 639; Stein, *Mark*, 708; Marcus, *Mark 9 – 16*, 1040. For the shame of nakedness in Judaism, see *Jub.* 3:30 – 31; 7:20; *m. Sanh.* 6.3; Midrash *Sipre* 320.

11. Plutarch, *Sera* §9, says, "every wrongdoer who goes to execution carries his own cross"; cf. Plautus, *Carbonaria* frag. 1; *Mil. Glor.* 2.4.6 – 7 §§359 – 360; all cited by Evans, *Mark 8:27 – 16:20*, 499.

12. BDAG, 941.

Simon to take it. Conscription was a common practice in the Roman military, whereby civilians could be enlisted for menial tasks (see comments on 11:1c – 2; cf. Matt 5:41; Josephus, *Ant.* 13.2.3 §52).

Cyrene in North Africa had a large Jewish population, and Simon is likely a Jew. It is not clear whether he was a resident of Jerusalem formerly from Cyrene (Acts 6:9; cf. 11:20; 13:1), or whether he was visiting the city for the Passover (Acts 2:10). "Coming in from the country" could mean arriving at the city for the festival or coming in for the day from the countryside. The mention of Alexander and Rufus suggests that Simon's sons were known to the church or churches to which Mark is writing. If this is the same Rufus mentioned by Paul in Rom 16:13, this would be one more piece of evidence that Mark is writing to a Roman audience (see Introduction to Mark: Audience).

15:22 They brought him to a place called Golgotha, which is translated, "Place of the Skull."
(Καὶ φέρουσιν αὐτὸν ἐπὶ τὸν Γολγοθᾶν τόπον, ὅ ἐστιν μεθερμηνευόμενον Κρανίου Τόπος). The name Golgotha is a slightly modified version of the Aramaic word for "skull" (*gulgultā'*). Mark paraphrases it as "Place of the Skull." The word "Calvary" comes from the Latin Vulgate, where the Greek was translated *calvariae locus*, "place of the skull."[13] The reason for the name is unknown. It may have been because the place was associated with capital punishment and death, with "skull"

functioning as metonymy for "death." Those who favor Gordon's Calvary as the site of the crucifixion (see below) suggest the place was a hill above a rock formation resembling a large skull.

Executions were normally performed outside the city walls, and this was the case with Jesus (Lev 24:14; John 19:17, 20; cf. Heb 13:12). The Romans tended to crucify near major roads, since the act was intended to be a public spectacle and a warning to others.[14] Quintilian wrote, "Whenever we crucify the guilty, the most crowded roads are chosen where the most people can see and be moved by this fear. For penalties relate not so much to retribution as to their exemplary effect."[15]

The location of Golgotha is uncertain, though the evidence favors the traditional site within the Church of the Holy Sepulchre.[16] This location has been rejected by some because it is within the present walls of the city, but archaeologists have determined that in Jesus' day it was outside Jerusalem's walls.[17] Herod Agrippa I (AD 40 – 44) expanded the walls of Jerusalem, encompassing the present site. Its identification as a pilgrim site dates back to the fourth century. By contrast, the skull-like outcrop known as Gordon's Calvary and the adjacent Garden Tomb, though popular devotional sites, have little corroborating evidence and were first identified as possible sites in the nineteenth century.[18]

15:23 They tried to give him wine mixed with myrrh, but he did not take it (καὶ ἐδίδουν αὐτῷ

---

13. V. C. Corbo, "Golgotha," *ABD*, 2:1071 – 72.

14. Justinian, *Dialogue* 48.19.28.15: "That the sight may deter others from such crimes and be a comfort to the relatives and neighbours of those whom they have killed"; cited by Hengel, *Crucifixion*, 50.

15. Quintilian, *Decl.* 274; cited in Hengel, *Crucifixion*, 50 n. 14. The authorship of this work is in question; he is often identified as pseudo-Quintilian (perhaps a student of Quintilian).

16. For a good summary of the archaeology, see Corbo, "Golgotha," *ABD*, 2:1072.

17. D. Bahat, "Does the Holy Sepulchre Church Mark the Burial of Jesus?" *BAR* 12/3 (1986): 26 – 45; P. Benoit, "Les remparts de Jérusalem," in *Exégèse et Théologie* (Paris: Cerf, 1982) 4:292 – 310; Brown, *Death of the Messiah*, 2:938 – 40.

18. For details, see G. Barkay, "The Garden Tomb — Was Jesus Buried There?" *BAR* 12/2 (1986): 40 – 57. The tomb itself dates to the seventh or eighth century BC, long before Jesus' time, and the supposed groove for the rolling stone is actually a Crusades-era water trough.

ἐσμυρνισμένον οἶνον· ὃς δὲ οὐκ ἔλαβεν). The imperfect ἐδίδουν is a conative imperfect (cf. 10:13), meaning "they tried to give" him the wine.[19] Wine was sometimes given as an act of mercy to condemned prisoners, to dull their pain. Proverbs 31:6 reads: "Give strong drink to the one who is perishing, and wine to those who are bitterly distressed" (NET). This passage is cited in b. Sanh. 43a with reference to the practice of the women of Jerusalem giving wine spiked with frankincense as an act of mercy to numb the pain of the condemned.

There is little evidence, however, that myrrh had narcotic properties; it was rather used as a flavoring for fine wines.[20] Since the wine here appears to be offered by the soldiers, not Jesus' supporters, Evans is probably correct that it was part of the mockery of Jesus, providing the "king" with the finest of wines (cf. Luke 23:36–37, where the soldiers mock Jesus as king of the Jews and offer him sour wine).[21] Jesus' refusal to take the wine has been attributed to (1) his (Nazirite?) vow to abstain from wine until he drinks it anew in the kingdom of God (14:25),[22] (2) his refusal to participate in the mockery,[23] (3) his desire to drink only the "cup" the Father had given him (10:38–39; 14:36), or (4) his desire to face his messianic task with full awareness.[24] These are not mutually exclusive, and several could be factors. The most likely is that Jesus refuses to play their games, facing his death with dignity and courage.

15:24 They crucified him and divided his garments, casting lots for them to see who would get what (Καὶ σταυροῦσιν αὐτὸν καὶ διαμερίζονται τὰ ἱμάτια αὐτοῦ, βάλλοντες κλῆρον ἐπ᾽ αὐτὰ τίς τί ἄρῃ). All four Gospels describe the crucifixion with remarkable brevity and restraint. Mark uses only three words in Greek (καὶ σταυροῦσιν αὐτόν; a historical present). Though crucifixion was not invented by the Romans, having been practiced by Persians, Greeks, and others before them, it became their favorite means of execution. It served not only as a means of capital punishment, but also as a weapon of terror, a warning to the populace of the catastrophic consequences of challenging Roman authority.[25] "The Romans used crucifixion to bring mutinous troops under control, to break the will of conquered peoples, and to wear down rebellious cities under siege."[26]

Dangerous criminals and rebellious slaves were often crucified. The practice was viewed with horror by writers of the day, too cruel and severe a punishment to be inflicted on Roman citizens. Cicero calls it "the cruelest and most hideous punishment possible."[27] Josephus refers to it as "the most miserable of deaths."[28]

The Romans practiced various forms of crucifixion. Sometimes victims were impaled on a stake. More often, a crossbeam (*patibulum*) was used, either on top of the *palus* like a T (*crux commissa*) or in the traditional cross shape (†; *crux immissa*).[29] Various methods of crucifixion were used for

19. Wallace, *Greek Grammar*, 534.
20. Pliny the Elder, *Nat.* 14.15 §92, wrote, "The finest wine in early days was that spiced with the scent of myrrh"; cf. 14.19 §107; Brown, *Death of the Messiah*, 2:942; Evans, *Mark 8:27–16:20*, 501; Stein, *Mark*, 710.
21. Evans, *Mark 8:27–16:20*, 501.
22. See Marcus, *Mark 9–16*, 1049.
23. Evans, *Mark 8:27–16:20*, 501. Marcus, *Mark 9–16*, 1049, calls Jesus' refusal to take the wine "an act of resistance."
24. Tertullian, *Jejun.* 12.3, relates the story of a certain "Christian" martyr named Pristinius, who was so intoxicated

on drugged wine by his friends that he could not confess Jesus as Lord when questioned by the examining officer. Put on the rack because of his silence, he could "utter nothing but hiccoughs and belchings," and "died in the very act of apostasy."
25. Gerald G. Collins, "Crucifixion," *ABD*, 1:1207–11.
26. Ibid., 1:1208.
27. Cicero, *Verr.* 5.64.165. See Hengel, *Crucifixion*, 29–32, for the general Roman revulsion towards crucifixion.
28. Josephus, *J.W.* 7.6.4 §203.
29. Collins, "Crucifixion," *ABD*, 1:1208.

maximum torture and humiliation. Seneca wrote that "some hang their victims with head toward the ground, some impale their private parts, others stretch out their arms on a fork-shaped gibbet."[30]

Josephus records that Titus crucified thousands of Jews during the siege and destruction of Jerusalem: "So the soldiers, out of the rage and hatred they bore the prisoners, nailed those they caught, in different postures, to the crosses, by way of jest; and their number was so great that there was not enough room for the crosses, and not enough crosses for the bodies."[31] Victims would be fastened with ropes or with nails. Jesus was apparently nailed, since John 20:25 refers to the nail marks in his hands (cf. Luke 24:39: "Look at my hands and my feet").

Death by crucifixion resulted from bleeding, exposure, exhaustion, and asphyxiation. Sometimes a small seat (*sedile*) was attached to the cross and/or footrests to allow the victim to push themselves up to breathe, thus lengthening the time of torture. Victims could linger for days on the cross, gradually becoming prey for birds and wild dogs. Seneca, in arguing for suicide as a means of quick and merciful death, contrasts it with the agony of the cross:

> Can anyone be found who would prefer wasting away in pain dying limb by limb, or letting out his life drop by drop, rather than expiring once for all? Can any man be found willing to be fastened to the accursed tree, long sickly, already deformed, swelling with ugly weals on shoulders and chest, and drawing the breath of life amid long-drawn-out agony?[32]

Mark relates that the soldiers "divided his garments," casting lots to see who would get what. It was not uncommon for executioners to divide the meager possessions of their victim, a custom related to the practice of dividing plunder after a battle.[33] Although all four Gospels describe the division of Jesus' clothing in language echoing Ps 22:18, only John explicitly cites the psalm in a fulfillment formula and explains that the soldiers gambled for Jesus' "tunic" (χιτών) because it was a seamless garment that they did not want to tear (John 19:24). While the language of the psalm has clearly shaped Mark's description of the event, there is no reason to doubt its historical veracity, since the division of possessions was common practice. "Casting lots" may have been a game of dice, or perhaps a version of the ancient Italian game of *morra,* played by guessing the number of fingers held behind one's back.[34] Psalm 22 will be alluded to several more times in the crucifixion narrative (see vv. 29, 34).

The Romans normally crucified victims naked, and this may have been the case with Jesus. Yet since he is described as being reclothed for the trip to Golgotha (15:20; see comments there) — probably as a concession to Jewish sensibilities — the Romans soldiers may have left a loincloth on him.[35]

15:25 It was the third hour when they crucified him (ἦν δὲ ὥρα τρίτη καὶ ἐσταύρωσαν αὐτόν). The third hour is 9:00 a.m. Though elsewhere Mark rarely gives precise chronological references, he carefully charts the time of the crucifixion. Jesus is

30. Seneca, *Marc.* 20.3.

31. Josephus, *J.W.* 5.11.1 §451.

32. Seneca, *Ira* 2.2; cited by Hengel, *Crucifixion,* 30 – 31.

33. Evans, *Mark 8:27 – 16:20,* 502; Brown, *Death of the Messiah,* 2:953 – 58; Sherwin-White, *Roman Society and Roman Law,* 46. The fact that Hadrian outlawed the confiscation of prisoners' possessions in the second century (Justinian, *Digest* 48.20.6) is the exception that proves the rule.

34. Suggested by A. de Waal, "Das Mora-Spiel auf den Darstellungen der Verlogung des Kleides Christi," *Römische Quartalschrift für christliche Altertumskunde und Kirchengeschichte* 8 (1894): 145 – 46; cited by Brown, *Death of the Messiah,* 2:955. De Waal thought it unlikely that the Roman soldiers would carry dice to a crucifixion, but it seems no more unusual than modern soldiers carrying playing cards or other games to relieve the boredom.

35. See Brown, *Death of the Messiah,* 2:953, and comments on 15:20.

crucified in the third hour; the darkness comes on the land until the sixth hour (noon; 15:33); Jesus cries out and dies at the ninth hour (3:00 p.m.; 15:34). Joseph of Arimathea then approaches Pilate about the body "when evening approached" (ὀψίας γενομένης; v. 42; approx. 6:00 p.m.?).

Mark's chronology makes good sense with reference to an early morning Roman trial, but appears to contradict the Fourth Gospel, where Jesus' Roman trial concludes around the sixth hour (noon; John 19:14), and Jesus is crucified sometime after this (19:18). Various harmonizations have been suggested.[36] (1) Some have claimed John is counting time from midnight, as in our modern system, so that the sixth hour is 6:00 a.m.[37] This is unlikely, however, since there is no Latin or Greek attestation of this reckoning of hours.[38]

(2) Others suggest the differences resulted from a textual error. There are many possibilities. Some say Mark 15:25 as a whole was added by a later scribe (neither Matthew nor Luke includes it), so that Mark's first chronological reference, like John's, is to the sixth hour (15:33).[39] But there is no textual support for this omission. Another possibility is that an early copyist misread a Greek Ϝ (digamma), standing for "6," as a Γ (gamma), standing for "3," and that the latter was later changed to the word "third" (τρίτη). While there is some weak textual support for the reading "sixth" in v. 25 (Θ syr^hmg), this would contradict the subsequent references to the sixth and ninth hours in 15:33 – 34. It is clearly a harmonization to John 19:14. Another possibility is that the textual error is in John 19:14, which originally read "third" instead of "sixth," a variant that also occurs in a few manuscripts.[40] Yet the evidence for this reading is weak, and it too seems to be a harmonizing attempt to bring John in line with Mark.

(3) Many other commentators attribute the differences in time to different theological purposes. The most common view is that John has altered the time reference to place Jesus' death near the noon time sacrifice of the Passover lambs.[41]

(4) Other attempts at harmonizations appeal to the imprecision of timekeeping in the ancient world. Both writers could be speaking in generalities or referring to blocks of time, where any time between nine and noon could be called the third or the sixth hour.[42] If a choice must be made, this last is perhaps the least unsatisfactory.

15:26 The inscription of the charge against him read, "The king of the Jews." (καὶ ἦν ἡ ἐπιγραφὴ τῆς αἰτίας αὐτοῦ ἐπιγεγραμμένη· ὁ βασιλεὺς τῶν Ἰουδαίων). All four Gospels describe a written notice, or "inscription" (ἐπιγραφή), identifying the charge against Jesus. John 19:19 uses the Greek version of the Latin loanward *titulus* (τίτλος). Mark does not say where it was located, but Matthew says it was "above his head" (Matt 27:37; cf. Luke 23:38, "above him"), and John says it was fastened "to the cross" (ἐπὶ τοῦ σταυροῦ, John 19:19). It was common to force condemned criminals to wear placards identifying their crime. Dio Cassius describes a slave about to be crucified being forced to carry a notice around the Forum identifying his offense.[43]

Jesus' inscription differs slightly in the various Gospel accounts:

---

36. See the list and discussion in Brown, *Death of the Messiah*, 2:959; France, *Mark*, 644 – 45.

37. B. F. Westcott, *The Gospel acording to St. John* (London: John Murray, 1896), 282.

38. Brown, *Death of the Messiah*, 1:846 n. 45; 2:959 n. 61; J. V. Miller, "The Time of the Crucifixion," *JETS* 26 (1983): 157 – 66.

39. Lane, *Mark*, 566 – 67; Blinzler, *Trial of Jesus*, 268 – 69.

40. ℵ² Dˢ L Δ Ψ 844.

41. Cranfield, *Mark*, 455 – 56; Gundry, *Mark*, 957; Evans, *Mark 8:27 – 16:20*, 503.

42. See Stein, *Mark*, 713; Miller, "The Time of the Crucifixion," 157 – 66.

43. Dio Cassius 54.3.6 – 7; cf. Eusebius, *Hist. eccl.* 5:1.44; Suetonius, *Cal.* 32.2; *Dom.* 10.1; BDAG, 291; Evans, *Mark 8:27 – 16:20*, 504.

MATTHEW	"This is Jesus, the King of the Jews" (οὗτός ἐστιν Ἰησοῦς ὁ βασιλεὺς τῶν Ἰουδαίων)
MARK	"The King of the Jews" (ὁ βασιλεὺς τῶν Ἰουδαίων)
LUKE	"This is the King of the Jews" (ὁ βασιλεὺς τῶν Ἰουδαίων οὗτος)
JOHN	"Jesus of Nazareth, the King of the Jews" (Ἰησοῦς ὁ Ναζωραῖος ὁ βασιλεὺς τῶν Ἰουδαίων)

John adds that it was written in three languages, Hebrew (or Aramaic), Latin, and Greek, and that Pilate posted it against the protestations of the Jewish leaders (John 19:20 – 21). Whatever its exact wording, the inscription is widely accepted as historical by scholars. As noted previously, "king of the Jews" (rather than "king of *Israel*") is a Roman, not a Jewish formulation (see 15:2) and was not a confession used by the early Christians of Jesus. The inscription provides good evidence that Jesus was crucified as a royal pretender — indirect evidence that during his trial he claimed to be the Messiah.[44]

15:27 They crucified two outlaws with him, one on his right and one on his left (Καὶ σὺν αὐτῷ σταυροῦσιν δύο λῃστάς, ἕνα ἐκ δεξιῶν καὶ ἕνα ἐξ εὐωνύμων αὐτοῦ). Whether the two "outlaws" (λῃστάς) crucified with Jesus were robbers or insurrectionists is not clear, but the latter seems most likely. The Romans often referred to political rebels as thieves or common criminals,[45] while the Jewish masses viewed them as freedom fighters. These two were likely companions of Barabbas, arrested for the same acts of rebellion and murder (15:7) — but not so fortunate as to be released in the Passover clemency. The phrase "one on his right and one on his left" recalls Jesus' words to James and John in

10:37, 40, and some see an intentional echo here on Mark's part.[46] If so, this could be a reminder that Jesus receives his "glory" (10:37) not through conquest but through suffering and sacrifice.

Mark 15:28, which cites Isa 53:12 in a fulfillment formula,[47] is a later addition to Mark's text and so is omitted in modern versions. It was likely a scribal addition based on Luke 22:37. The evidence against it is overwhelming: (1) It does not appear in the earliest and most reliable Greek manuscripts;[48] (2) its inclusion is easily explained as an assimilation to Luke 22:37; (3) it does not fit well Markan style, since the author seldom uses fulfillment formulas. The verse made its way into the KJV via the Byzantine manuscripts used by Erasmus for his Greek NT. Verse references are, of course, later additions to the text and have no bearing on its original form.[49]

15:29 – 30 Those who passed by were blaspheming him, shaking their heads and saying, "Ha! The one who would destroy the temple and build it in three days! Save yourself by coming down from the cross!" (Καὶ οἱ παραπορευόμενοι ἐβλασφήμουν αὐτὸν κινοῦντες τὰς κεφαλὰς αὐτῶν καὶ λέγοντες· οὐὰ ὁ καταλύων τὸν ναὸν καὶ οἰκοδομῶν ἐν τρισὶν ἡμέραις, σῶσον σεαυτὸν καταβὰς ἀπὸ τοῦ σταυροῦ). Three groups are described as mocking

---

44. See especially Nils Alstrup Dahl, *Jesus the Christ: The Historical Origins of Christological Doctrine* (ed. Donald H. Juel; Minneapolis: Fortress, 1991), 34, 36 – 37.

45. See Josephus, *Ant.* 14.9.2 §159; 20.8.5 §160; 20.8.6 §167.

46. Hooker, *Mark*, 373; France, *Mark*, 646; Matera, *Kingship of Jesus*, 62. Contra Stein, *Mark*, 714; Brown, *Death of the Messiah*, 2:969 n. 84.

47. "And the Scripture was fulfilled that says, 'And he was

numbered with the lawbreakers'" (και επληρωθη η γραφη η λεγουσα· και μετα ανομων ελογισθη).

48. The "verse" is omitted in ℵ A B C D Ψ 2427 k syrˢ sah bohᵖᵗ and included in L Θ 083 0250 *f*¹·¹³ 33 𝔐 lat syrᵖ·ʰ Eusebius

49. The verse divisions used in today's versions were introduced by Robert Estienne in his Greek-Latin New Testament of 1551. The first English Bible to use them was the Geneva Bible of 1557.

Jesus: passersby (vv. 29 – 30), the religious leaders (vv. 31 – 32a), and even those crucified with Jesus (v. 32b). The first group shows that the crucifixion is taking place on a public thoroughfare, magnifying the shame and humiliation (see comments on 15:22).

The presence of this group also shows that the Jerusalem public has now turned against Jesus, reiterating the cries of 15:13 – 14. Those who acclaimed him as "the one who comes in the name of the Lord" (11:9) and who delighted in his debates with the religious leaders (12:37) have now rejected him. The verb "blaspheme" (βλασφημέω) can mean "verbally abuse," without implications of sacrilege, and this fits the context here. Yet for Mark and his readers, such abuse would indeed be blasphemy, and so we have retained the word in the translation. Ironically, the one accused of blasphemy (14:64) is now being blasphemed.[50] "Shaking their heads" is a sign of derision and contempt. This is another allusion to Ps 22:7, where the enemies of the righteous sufferer "hurl insults, shaking their heads" (cf. Ps 109:25; Jer 18:16; Lam 2:15).

The charge of threatening to destroy the temple, brought against Jesus at his trial (see comments on 14:57 – 59), is now used to mock Jesus' weakness. Anyone who could destroy the temple and rebuild it in three days could surely save himself from such a fate. Again the irony is thick. By staying on the cross, Jesus is bringing an end to the sacrificial system and so "destroying" the purpose and function of the temple.

15:31 – 32 In the same way the ruling priests together with the experts in the law mocked him and were saying to one another, "He saved others, but he is not able to save himself. Let the Messiah, the king of Israel, come down now from the cross so we can see and believe." Even

those who were crucified with him insulted him (ὁμοίως καὶ οἱ ἀρχιερεῖς ἐμπαίζοντες πρὸς ἀλλήλους μετὰ τῶν γραμματέων ἔλεγον· ἄλλους ἔσωσεν, ἑαυτὸν οὐ δύναται σῶσαι· ὁ χριστὸς ὁ βασιλεὺς Ἰσραὴλ καταβάτω νῦν ἀπὸ τοῦ σταυροῦ, ἵνα ἴδωμεν καὶ πιστεύσωμεν. καὶ οἱ συνεσταυρωμένοι σὺν αὐτῷ ὠνείδιζον αὐτόν).

The second group to mock Jesus is the ruling priests and the law experts, who led the way in his arrest and trial (11:18; 14:1). Unlike the crowds, who spoke directly to Jesus, these speak to "one another." The sense Mark gives is that they are congratulating themselves on their long-sought goal of destroying Jesus (3:6; 11:18; 12:12; 14:1 – 2, 10 – 11, 64; 15:1, 3, 11).[51]

The statement "he saved others" (ἄλλους ἔσωσεν) must refer especially to Jesus' healing ministry, for which the verb "save/heal" (σῴζω) has been frequently used (5:23, 28, 34; 6:56; 10:52). Yet the context immediately following suggests a wider application, since Jesus is mocked as "the Messiah, the king of Israel," that is, as the one who came to bring salvation to Israel. Here we see the close Markan connection between Jesus' messianic identity, his announcement of the kingdom of God, healings, exorcisms, and forgiveness of sins. As Messiah, Jesus' role is to bring ultimate salvation, which includes not just physical healings, but national restoration and renewal. The religious leaders view Jesus as a failure because he is unable to save himself from Roman crucifixion. The irony of the Markan drama is that by staying on the cross, Jesus is fulfilling the role of the Messiah, bringing salvation to Israel by offering his life as a ransom for sins (10:45).

By claiming they will believe if they see Jesus come down from the cross, the religious leaders are again demanding a sign. Yet as Jesus responded to the request in 8:11 – 12, no sign will be given. Their hearts are hardened (3:5; 7:6; 10:5) and their eyes

---

50. Hooker, *Mark*, 373.

51. Lane, *Mark*, 569.

are blind (4:12) to God's purpose. The irony is that by enacting their plans against Jesus, they have become unwitting pawns in the salvation they are now demanding from Jesus. They are the wicked tenant farmers whose rejection and murder of the Son results in the establishment of the cornerstone of a new temple for God (12:1 – 11).

The third group to mock Jesus is the two outlaws crucified with him (only Luke relates the story of the repentant criminal; Luke 23:40 – 43). The impression is one of "the ultimate in shaming humiliation."[52] Even those suffering the same fate as Jesus have nothing but derision for him and his apparently deluded messianic claims.

Theology in Application

The Rejection of Jesus by All and the Depravity of Humanity

Mark's crucifixion scene is one of despair and humiliation. Though the crucifixion itself is stated in a simple and unadorned manner, "They crucified him" (v. 24), the author dwells on the mocking and taunting of all those around Jesus. We are not surprised when the cruel Roman soldiers mock and abuse Jesus, since they are the historical enemies of Israel. Yet when Jewish passersby do the same, our author indicates that the people of Israel have rejected their Messiah. The one who announced the kingdom, offered hope, expelled demons, fed the multitudes, healed the sick, and raised the dead has himself come to nothing.

We tend to despise the most those who disappoint us the most, and the people who once eagerly flocked to Jesus in hope now despise him in his weakness. The derision by the religious leaders is not surprising to the readers of Mark, who have witnessed entrenched opposition to Jesus from the beginning. The taunting by the crucified criminals is perhaps the most surprising and audacious. They are in the same position as Jesus, yet in their own depravity all they can do is lash out at one more humiliated than themselves. Mark's portrait is one of total rejection by a depraved humanity.

Yet those with eyes of faith recognize that while humanity has turned against God, God has not rejected them. The death of Jesus is an act of reconciliation, God's sacrificial gift to the world, an atoning sacrifice for our sins. In our world today we see and hear of unspeakable acts of evil. Corrupt leaders exploit their people and take bribes to pad their own wallets. Respected coaches, priests, and Boy Scout leaders who oversee children turn out to be pedophiles who prey on the innocent and wreak havoc on young lives. An American soldier somehow snaps and goes on a shooting spree into an Afghan village, massacring women and children. A renegade army in the Congo terrorizes the local population with rape and murder. We wonder, "Where is God?" The answer we see here is that he is on the cross, experiencing and absorbing the hatred and evil of humanity — refusing to lash back and instead offering

52. Witherington, *Mark*, 397.

God's forgiveness. By refusing to save himself, Jesus is saving others, giving himself as a ransom for sins.

The Fulfillment of Scripture

The theme of fulfillment has permeated Mark's Passion Narrative and is equally present in the crucifixion scene. Especially prominent are the allusions to Psalm 22. The division of Jesus' garments (v. 24) recalls Ps 22:18; the insults of the passersby (v. 29) brings to mind Ps 22:7; the taunts to save himself (vv. 30–31) echo Ps 22:8; the reviling of those crucified with him parallels Ps 22:6. Finally, Jesus will cite the first verse of the psalm in his cry from the cross (15:34), "My God, my God, why have you forsaken me?"

While scholars debate the theological significance of these final words (see comments on 15:34), beyond dispute is Mark's assertion that all that is happening is part of the God-ordained plan of salvation. Jesus' own predictions of his betrayal, arrest, abandonment, trial, mocking, crucifixion, and resurrection (8:31; 9:31; 10:33–34; 14:18–21, 27–31, 49) and his emphatic assertion that Scripture *must* be fulfilled (14:21, 49) confirm the same thing. None of these events is an accident or outside of God's sovereign purpose. The resurrection, also repeatedly predicted by Jesus (8:31; 9:9, 31; 10:34; 14:28), will provide the ultimate vindication of Jesus' messiahship and God's sovereign plan.

For Mark's readers, facing suffering, persecution, and even death, this truth would provide hope and encouragement. No challenges we face in life are outside of God's control or sovereign will. After suffering comes vindication for those who trust in him.

IN DEPTH: The Irony of the Cross

Paradox and irony occur throughout Mark's gospel,[53] but are especially prominent in the trial and crucifixion narratives. Lamar Williamson points out that while John portrays the cross as glory and Luke highlights Jesus' solidarity with the oppressed, Mark "presents the crucifixion of Jesus as the paradoxical enthronement and coronation of the suffering King of the Jews."[54] (1) Jesus is accused of blasphemy at his trial because he claims to be the Messiah and Son of Man, who will sit at the right hand of God and come on the clouds of heaven (14:62). Ironically, it is those who reject him and his authority who are committing the real blasphemy (15:29).

53. See J. Camery-Hoggat, *Irony in Mark's Gospel: Text and Subtext* (SNTSMS 72; Cambridge: Cambridge University Press, 1992), passim.

54. Williamson, *Mark*, 278.

(2) Jesus is repeatedly mocked as the "king of the Jews" (15:2, 9, 12, 18, 26) and the "king of Israel" (15:32). From the perspective of Pilate, the soldiers, and the religious leaders, Jesus' humiliation renders his claim to kingship ludicrous. Yet, ironically, Jesus is fulfilling the true suffering role of the Messiah predicted in Scripture (8:29 – 31).

(3) Jesus is falsely accused at his trial of threatening to destroy the Jerusalem temple (14:58) and then mocked for this on the cross (15:29). Yet, ironically, the Jerusalem temple and its sacrificial system will be rendered obsolete *by his death and resurrection* and then will be destroyed by these same Romans. It will be replaced by a new temple, Jesus' own body sacrificed for sins and providing access to God's presence (John 2:21; Heb 10:20 – 22). The new temple is also the community of believers — itself the "body" of Christ (1 Cor 6:19) — that will rise up to mediate God's presence to the world.

(4) The passersby mock Jesus because he saved others yet cannot save himself. If he is truly the Messiah, he should come down from the cross. Yet it is precisely by *staying on the cross* that Jesus is accomplishing salvation, giving his life as a ransom for sins.

Mark's ironic paradox of the cross recalls similar paradoxes throughout the NT. The Christian life turns the world system and values on their head. For example: (1) The *foolish* message of the cross is the true *wisdom* of God (1 Cor 1:18 – 25); (2) by *dying* with Christ to our old selves, we *live* through him (Rom 6:1 – 10); (3) true *freedom* from sin and death comes by becoming a *slave* of God and of righteousness (Rom 6:15 – 7:6); (4) whoever wants to *save their life will lose it,* but whoever loses their life for Christ and for the gospel will save it (Mark 8:35); (5) there is *strength* through *weakness* for those who learn to depend on God, because "when we I am weak, then I am strong" (2 Cor 12:1 – 10); (6) those who want to be *first* must become *last*; and those who want to *lead* must *serve* (Mark 10:35 – 45). These upside-down values of the kingdom of God are subversively bringing transformation and renewal to a fallen world.

Mark 15:33 – 47

Literary Context

The closely connected series of events that make up Mark's Passion Narrative (14:1 – 15:47) come to their climax in Jesus' death and burial. Having described the cruelty and mockery experienced by Jesus on the cross (15:21 – 32), Mark now concludes with his climactic words and the accompanying signs confirming his identity as the Son of God and the significance of his atoning death. This is followed by an account of the burial of Jesus. All that remains after this is the announcement of the resurrection.

Main Idea

Jesus' death is accompanied by four key events that have theological significance for Mark: (1) the darkness, symbolizing eschatological judgment; (2) Jesus' cry of dereliction from Ps 22:1, indicating his despair in experiencing God's cup of wrath; (3) the tearing of the temple curtain, representing judgment against the nation and the coming cessation of the sacrificial system; and (4) the cry of the centurion, confirming the identity of Jesus and foreshadowing the gospel's acceptance by the Gentiles. The burial scene testifies to the piety of Joseph and the faithfulness of the women, setting the stage for the resurrection announcement.

Translation

(See next two pages.)

Mark 15:33 – 47

33a	setting (temporal)	At the sixth hour
b	Epiphany	**darkness came upon the whole land**
c	setting (temporal)	until the ninth hour.
34a	Setting (temporal)/Action	Then **at the ninth hour Jesus cried out with a loud voice,**
b	Scripture quotation	*"Eloi, Eloi, lema sabachthani,"* [Ps 22:1]
c	interpretation	which means, *"My God, my God, why have you forsaken me?"*

35a		When some of those standing nearby heard this,
b	Response to 34	**they said,**
c		*"Look, he is calling Elijah."*

36a		Running,
b	Response to 35/Action	**someone** filled a sponge with sour wine,
c	sequence	put it on a reed, and
d		**gave it to him to drink,** saying,
e	command	*"Leave him alone.*
f	mocking	*Let's see if Elijah will come to take him down!"*
37a	Action/Death of Jesus	But **Jesus … expired.**
b	setting (temporal)/action	… after letting out a loud cry…

38	Response to 37/Epiphany	And **the curtain of the temple was torn in two from top to bottom**.

39a	setting (temporal and social)	When the centurion who stood in front of him saw how he died,
b	Response to 37	**he said,**
c	acclamation	*"Truly this man was the Son of God!"*

40a	Character introduction	**There were also women watching from a distance,**
b	character identification	among whom were Mary Magdalene and
c	character identification	Mary the mother of James the 🕊 younger and Joseph, and
d	character identification	Salome.
41a	setting (temporal & spatial)	When he was in Galilee,
b	Character description	**these women were following him**
c		and **ministering to him.**
d	Character introduction	**There were also many other women**
e	character description	who had come up with him to Jerusalem.

42a	Setting (temporal)	Evening was already approaching,
b	explanation of 42a	because it was Preparation Day, that is,
c	explanation of 42b	the day before the Sabbath.
43a	Character entrance/action	So **Joseph of Arimathea …**
b	character description	a respected member of the Council
c	character description	who was himself waiting for the kingdom of God,
d	Action	… **boldly went to Pilate** and **requested the body of Jesus.**

Continued on next page.

Continued from previous page.

44a	Response to 43	**Pilate was surprised that Jesus would have died already.**
b	manner of 44c	Summoning the centurion,
c	Question	**he asked him if he had already died.**
45a	reason for 45b	Confirming this with the centurion,
b	Response to 43/ Result of 45a	**he granted the corpse to Joseph.**
46a	setting (temporal)/action	After buying a linen cloth and
b	setting (temporal)/action	taking the body down,
c	Action (sequence)	he **wrapped it in the linen cloth**
d	Action	and **placed him in a tomb that had been carved out of rock.**
e	Action	Then
		he **rolled a stone across the entrance of the tomb.**
47	Character introduction/ action	**Mary Magdalene and Mary the mother of Joseph were watching where he ↵ was laid.**

Structure

The structure of the first episode is related directly to the previous one. The first half of the crucifixion scene describes what is done to Jesus by others: the scourging, the crucifixion, the dividing of garments, and the mockery (15:16 – 32). The second half describes events related to the significance of the crucifixion: Jesus' shout from Ps 22:1, the darkness on the land, the tearing of the temple curtain, Jesus' final shout, and the climactic words of the centurion (15:17 – 41).[1] This is followed by the second episode, an account of the burial of Jesus.

Exegetical Outline

➡ **1. The Death of Jesus (15:33 – 41)**

    a. The darkness from the sixth to ninth hours (15:33)

    b. Jesus' cry from Psalm 22:1 (15:34)

    c. Statements about Elijah and an offer of wine vinegar (15:35 – 36)

    d. Jesus' last cry and death (15:37)

    e. The tearing of the temple curtain (15:38)

    f. The cry of the centurion (15:39)

---

1. K. E. Brower ("Elijah in the Markan Passion Narrative," *JSNT* 5 [1983]: 85 – 101) suggests a chiastic structure here with two acts of God (vv. 33, 38) framing two cries of Jesus (vv. 34, 37) framing two references to Elijah (vv. 35c, 36f), with the offer of a drink at the center point (v. 36a-e). One problem with this structure is that the climactic cry of the centurion becomes an add-on at the end (summing up the whole, according to Brower). Also, the center point of a chiasm is normally its climax, which hardly seems appropriate for the offer of a drink. Cf. France, *Mark*, 651 n. 39.

g. The women watching the crucifixion from afar (15:40 – 41)

2. The Burial of Jesus (15:42 – 47)

   a. Setting: Preparation Day (15:42)

   b. Joseph's request for the body (15:43)

   c. Pilate's release of the body (15:44 – 45)

   d. Burial by Joseph (15:46)

   e. Observation by the women (15:47)

Explanation of the Text

15:33 At the sixth hour darkness came upon the whole land until the ninth hour (Καὶ γενομένης ὥρας ἕκτης σκότος ἐγένετο ἐφ᾽ ὅλην τὴν γῆν ἕως ὥρας ἐνάτης). The sixth hour is noon, so the darkness continued from noon to 3:00 p.m. This is part of Mark's careful chronology of the crucifixion, which began at about 9:00 a.m. (the third hour; 15:25). Darkness is often associated with the judgments of God in Scripture. The ninth plague against Egypt in the exodus account was darkness covering "all Egypt for three days" (Exod 10:21 – 23). The judgments of the day of the Lord bring darkness (Isa 13:9 – 13; Joel 2:10; 3:14 – 15; Amos 5:18, 20). Amos 8:9 reads, " 'In that day,' declares the Sovereign LORD, 'I will make the sun go down at noon and darken the earth in broad daylight.' "

Darkness is also associated with the deaths of great men in both Greco-Roman and Jewish traditions. The sun is said to have hidden its face at the death of Caesar,[2] and darkness is reported with reference to the deaths of Alexander the Great, Aeschylus, and others .[3] While in these cases the point seems to be that creation mourns their passing, in the case of Jesus the darkness more likely indicates God's displeasure and a preview of coming judgment.

Mark does not try to explain the cause of the darkness. It could not have been a solar eclipse, since Passover took place during the full moon. Other suggestions include dark clouds obscuring the sun or a desert sandstorm ("sirocco"). Whatever its immediate cause, for Mark and the other Synoptics it is clearly a supernatural event.

The darkness is said to have come "upon the whole land/earth" (ἐφ᾽ ὅλην τὴν γῆν). Since "land" (γῆ) can also mean "earth," this could refer either to the land of Judea or the whole earth.[4] The former seems more likely in context.[5] The tearing of the curtain and the coming judgment of God against the temple (13:2) concern Israel in particular (although they have soteriological implications for all people). This more limited sense is also suggested by the parallel to the Egyptian plague of darkness (see above).

15:34 Then at the ninth hour Jesus cried out with a loud voice, *"Eloi, Eloi, lema sabachthani,"* which means, "My God, my God, why have you forsaken me?" (καὶ τῇ ἐνάτῃ ὥρᾳ ἐβόησεν ὁ Ἰησοῦς φωνῇ μεγάλῃ· ελωι ελωι λεμα σαβαχθανι; ὅ ἐστιν μεθερμηνευόμενον· ὁ θεός μου ὁ θεός μου, εἰς τί ἐγκατέλιπές με;). This third and last chronological

---

2. Virgil, *Georg.* 1.463 – 68.

3. BDAG, 932; H. Conzelmann, *TDNT*, 7:439. For rabbinic parallels, see Str-B 1:1040 – 41.

4. Edwards, *Mark*, 475, favors the latter, since "the whole earth … is implicated in Jesus' death, not just the Jews."

5. So France, *Mark*, 651; Stein, *Mark*, 715; Pesch, *Markusevangelium*, 2:493. This is also the interpretation found in the apocryphal *Gospel of Peter* 5:15, which says the darkness "covered all Judea."

reference by Mark (cf. 15:25, 33) has Jesus' shouting out at the ninth hour, about 3:00 p.m. Jesus has
now been on the cross six hours and will expire
shortly (v. 37). Jesus' loud cry is surprising and
dramatic, since he has been silent since the words
spoken to Pilate in 15:2. The language is doubly
emphatic, combining the verb "cry/shout out"
(βοάω; cf. 1:2) with the dative of manner ("with a
great voice"; φωνῇ μεγάλῃ), together expressing the
depth of Jesus' emotion.

Jesus' words are from Ps 22:1 and Mark provides both the Aramaic words (transliterated into
Greek), "Elōi Elōi lema sabachthani," and a Greek
translation, "My God, my God, why have you forsaken me?"[6] Matthew's version (27:46) begins with
the Hebrew, Ēli, Ēli (ηλι ηλι), and then finishes
with the Aramaic, lema sabachthani.[7] Although it
is possible Jesus recited the psalm in Hebrew (as
in Matthew) and the Aramaic-speaking church
translated it into Aramaic, more likely he originally spoke in Aramaic, his common vernacular,
and Matthew adapted it to the Hebrew text. Mark
elsewhere records Jesus' Aramaic words at climactic and dramatic points in the narrative: the raising
of Jairus' daughter (5:41; Talitha koum), the healing of a deaf/mute (7:34; Ephphatha), and in the
garden of Gethsemane (14:36; Abba).

These words of despair are Jesus' only words
from the cross recorded by Mark (but see also the

cry in v. 37).[8] There is no call for forgiveness of
others (Luke 23:34), no concern expressed for his
mother (John 19:26 – 27), no offer of salvation to
the repentant criminal (Luke 23:43), no final words
of assurance that he will soon be in God's presence
(Luke 23:46), and no triumphant cry of achievement, "It is finished" (John 19:30). Instead, there
is only the single cry of dereliction from Ps 22:1.
Mark's entire focus is on the gloomy darkness of
the scene, the agonizing suffering and aloneness of
the Son of God.

The significance of Jesus' words, however, is debated by scholars. Some have argued that in citing
Ps 22:1, Jesus has the whole of the lament psalm
in view, which ends with the righteous sufferer's
vindication and restoration (Ps 22:22 – 31).[9] The
Lord is to be praised, since he "has not hidden
his face from him but has listened to his cry for
help" (22:24). This is not, then, a cry of despair, but
rather an assurance of victory. While it is certainly
true that the context of the broader psalm must be
kept in mind, Jesus' actual words must be given
their full weight. Mark records only Jesus' words of
despair from Ps 22:1, not the latter words of assurance. This suggests that he is indeed experiencing
what the psalmist expresses, the agony of suffering
and the pain of forsakenness.

At the same time it cannot be true that Jesus
has lost his hope or faith in God (he still addresses

---

6. There is considerable debate concerning whether Mark's
words are Hebrew or Aramaic, but the majority of scholars
favor Aramaic. For details, see Brown, Death of the Messiah,
2:1051 – 53, and Douglas J. Moo, The Old Testament in the Gospel Passion Narratives (Sheffield: Almond, 1983), 264 – 68. The
issue is further complicated by a variety of textual variants in
both Matthew and Mark. For details and defense of the present text, see Metzger, Textual Commentary, 97 – 98; France,
Mark, 649.

7. Curiously, the Targum of Ps 22:1 does not begin with
Eloi, but with Eli. This suggests Jesus is not citing the Targum
directly, but his own Aramaic rendering of the Hebrew text.

8. The four Gospels altogether record seven sayings from
the cross, the famous "seven last words." These are (in likely

chronological order): (1) "Father, forgive them, for they do not
know what they are doing" (Luke 23:34); (2) "Woman, here is
your son" (to his mother), and "Here is your mother" (to the
beloved disciple; John 19:26 – 27); (3) to the repentant criminal:
"Truly I tell you, today you will be with me in paradise" (Luke
23:43); (4) "I am thirsty!" (John 19:28); (5) "My God, my God,
why have you forsaken me?" (Mark 15:34; see Matt 27:46); (6)
"Father, into your hands I commit my spirit" (Luke 23:46); (7)
"It is finished" (John 19:30).

9. See esp. Marcus, Way of the Lord, 180 – 82, who develops
the theme that the Passion Narrative as a whole draws exten-
sively from Psalm 22. Cf. Jeremias, New Testament Theology,
189; Matera, Kingship of Jesus, 132 – 37.

him as "*my* God"). Throughout Mark's gospel Jesus is aware of his coming crucifixion and assurance of his vindication in resurrection (8:31; 9:31; 10:33 – 34; 12:10 – 11; 14:28). In Gethsemane he is similarly in agony, but he continues to submit to the will of God (14:36). The same must be true here. Jesus' anguish and feelings of despair are real, but he nevertheless remains faithful to his calling. By refusing to save himself, he will save others.

Mark does not provide a theological interpretation of Jesus' words, and we should be cautious about imposing a developed theory of the atonement on them. Still, from the perspective of Markan theology, the best explanation of "why have you forsaken me?" is that Jesus is experiencing the full weight of God's "cup" of judgment (14:36). He is suffering as a ransom payment for the sins of the world (10:45) and pouring out his blood to inaugurate the new covenant (14:24). These ideas of sacrifice, judgment, and ransom are not far from Paul's assertion that "Christ redeemed us from the curse of the law by becoming a curse for us" (Gal 3:13) and that "God made him who had no sin to be sin for us" (2 Cor 5:21).

The historicity of these words seems beyond dispute, since the early church is unlikely to have invented a saying in which Jesus expressed such despair.[10]

15:35 – 36 When some of those standing nearby heard this, they said, "Look, he is calling Elijah." Running, someone filled a sponge with sour wine, put it on a reed, and gave it to him to drink, saying, "Leave him alone. Let's see if Elijah will come to take him down!" (καί τινες τῶν παρεστηκότων ἀκούσαντες ἔλεγον· ἴδε Ἡλίαν φωνεῖ. δραμὼν δέ τις καὶ γεμίσας σπόγγον ὄξους περιθεὶς καλάμῳ ἐπότιζεν αὐτόν λέγων· ἄφετε ἴδωμεν εἰ ἔρχεται Ἡλίας καθελεῖν αὐτόν). Jesus' cry *Elōi* (or *Ēli*) sounds similar to the Hebrew for Elijah (*'ēlîā* or *'ēliāhû*), and some of those present think Jesus is crying out to the prophet.[11] As seen already in Mark's gospel (6:15; 8:28; 9:11 – 13), there was widespread eschatological expectation that Elijah would return before the day of the Lord, based both on his dramatic departure to heaven (2 Kgs 2:11) and the prophecies of Mal 3:1; 4:5. There were also Jewish traditions that Elijah would come (or had come at times) to rescue the righteous and aid those in distress.[12]

The person who runs to get sour wine is not identified, but the fact that he speaks about Elijah (v. 36) suggests that he is one of the Jewish bystanders rather than a Roman soldier. The fact that he places the sponge on a reed (κάλαμος; identified as *hyssop* in John 19:29) indicates that Jesus' cross is high, certainly above ground level.[13]

John 19:29 says that the wine vinegar "was there," which may indicate that it was intended for the soldiers (and taken by a bystander?). Such sour wine (ὄξος), according to BDAG, "relieved thirst

---

10. Some Western manuscripts read, "Why have you reproached me?" (εις τι ωνειδισας με;) instead of "Why have you abandoned me?" (εἰς τί ἐγκατέλιπές με;), probably to soften the harshness of the saying. Ehrman, however, thinks scribes made the change to "reproached" to avoid the Gnostic idea that the divine Christ abandoned the man Jesus on the cross (B. Ehrman, *The Orthodox Corruption of Scripture* [New York/Oxford: Oxford University Press, 1993], 143 – 45).

11. Some think Jesus must have originally said *Ēli Ēli* instead of *Elōi, Elōi,* since the former sounds more like the name Elijah. But the anguished cry of a dying man would likely be distorted, and either cry could have been mistaken for Elijah.

12. Sir 48:9 – 10; 4Q558 (4QVision); *b. Ta'an.* 21a; *Pesiq. Rab Kah.* 18.5; *Gen. Rab.* 33.3 [on Gen 8:1]). Cf. Matt 11:14; 17:10 – 12; John 1:21, 25; J. Jeremias, *TDNT,* 2.930; Str-B 4/2.769 – 79. France, *Mark,* 654 n. 50, points to Jewish traditions like *b. 'Abod. Zar.* 17b, which describes the deliverance of a certain Rabbi Eleazar from a Roman trial when Elijah, dressed as a Roman official, intercepted the imperial messenger who was sent to bring evidence against him.

13. France, *Mark,* 655; Stein, *Mark,* 716; Blinzler, *Trial of Jesus,* 249 – 50. The repeated references to "coming down" from the cross (15:30, 32, 36) suggest the same thing.

more effectively than water and, being cheaper than regular wine, was a favorite beverage of the lower ranks of society and of those in moderate circumstances ... especially of soldiers."[14] It is not clear whether the offer is meant as an act of mercy or further mocking. The latter is preferred if this is an allusion to Ps 69:21, where a righteous sufferer remarks that his tormenters "put gall in my food and gave me vinegar for my thirst."

Luke 23:36 has the soldiers offering Jesus sour wine and mocking him as king of the Jews. The purpose of the drink would then be to prolong Jesus' life so that the game can continue. Just as they mocked Jesus to come down from the cross (15:30, 32), so now they mock him to get help from Elijah.[15] Mark does not state whether Jesus actually drank the wine or whether he refused, as when offered wine with myrrh by the soldiers (v. 23).[16] Only John records that Jesus himself cried out "I am thirsty" and then "received the drink" (John 19:28, 30).

15:37 But Jesus, after letting out a loud cry, expired (ὁ δὲ Ἰησοῦς ἀφεὶς φωνὴν μεγάλην ἐξέπνευσεν). The "loud cry" (φωνὴν μεγάλην; cf. v. 34) is again surprising, since crucifixion victims near death would not normally have the strength to speak. The implication is that Jesus dies voluntarily, still in control of his senses. Mark does not say what Jesus said, whether he simply cried out or used audible words. Luke 23:46 introduces Jesus' last words with language similar to Mark — Jesus crying out with a loud voice (φωνῇ μεγάλῃ) and then

expiring (ἐξέπνευσεν) — and provides the content as, "Father, into your hands I commit my spirit." John gives Jesus' last words as the triumphant, "It is finished" (John 19:30). In light of Jesus' only other words from the cross (v. 34) we might expect this to be a cry of despair. Yet the response of the centurion in v. 39 suggests something more positive.

15:38 And the curtain of the temple was torn in two from top to bottom (Καὶ τὸ καταπέτασμα τοῦ ναοῦ ἐσχίσθη εἰς δύο ἀπ' ἄνωθεν ἕως κάτω). The first supernatural event associated with the crucifixion was the darkness (v. 33). The second is the tearing of the temple curtain. "From top to bottom" indicates that this is a direct act of God, coming down from above. This is more likely than the view of Gundry and others that the tearing results from a gust of wind/spirit produced by Jesus' expiration.[17]

All three Synoptics record the curtain tearing (Matt 27:51; Luke 23:45). It is not clear from the language, however, whether this is the curtain separating the temple from the inner courtyard or the curtain between the Holy Place and the Most Holy Place (Exod 26:31 – 37; 27:16).[18] Josephus describes the outer one as "a Babylonian curtain, embroidered with blue, and fine linen, and scarlet, and purple, and of a contexture that was truly wonderful." Its design symbolically represented the universe.[19] In favor of the outer curtain is that this would have been a more public event, seen by many people (though in either case, it could not have been seen by the centurion from so far away;

---

14. BDAG, 715.

15. The imperative "leave/permit" (ἄφετε; from ἀφίημι) could mean "leave him alone" (NIV, NET) or "wait" (NLT, NRSV), meaning let's wait to see if Elijah will come. Or it could introduce the deliberative subjunctive ἴδωμεν so that together ἄφετε ἴδωμεν (lit., "let [so that] we might see") idiomatically means "Let's see" (so HCSB, NASB; see Gundry, *Mark*, 969; Mark 7:4).

16. The imperfect ἐπότιζεν is likely conative, meaning they "tried to give him a drink."

17. Gundry, *Mark*, 948 – 50; cf. Evans, *Mark 8:27 – 16:20*, 509; H. M. Jackson, "The Death of Jesus in Mark and the Miracle from the Cross," *NTS* 33 (1987): 16 – 37; cf. T. E. Schmidt, "Cry of Dereliction or Cry of Judgment? Mark 15:34 in Context," *BBR* 4 (1994): 145 – 53, esp 151 – 52.

18. For detailed discussion and advocates, see Brown, *Death of the Messiah*, 2:1109 – 13. Both curtains are called τὸ καταπέτασμα in the LXX, though the outer one is more commonly referred to as τὸ κάλυμμα (Evans, *Mark 8:27 – 16:20*, 510).

19. Josephus, *J.W.* 5.5.4 §§212 – 213; cf. *Ant.* 3.7.7 §§181 – 183.

see v. 39). In favor of the inner curtain is that this fits better the theological significance of the tearing as opening up the way into the presence of God.

This raises the question of the symbolism of the curtain tearing. Two main interpretations have been proposed. (1) The tearing is a symbol of the temple's destruction, judgment against the Jewish leadership and the nation as a whole.[20] Like Jesus' cursing of the fig tree (11:12 – 14, 20 – 21) and clearing of the temple (11:15 – 17), this act points forward to the coming destruction of the temple predicted by Jesus in 13:2 (cf. 14:58; 15:29).[21]

(2) The second view is that the tearing of the curtain confirms the cessation of temple sacrifices and a new way open for all into the presence of God. This is how the writer to the Hebrews interprets it, identifying the true curtain as Jesus' body, through which "a new and living way" is opened up into the Most Holy Place, that is, the presence of God (Heb 10:19 – 20; cf. 9:3, 24 – 25). Support for this view is in the apparent inclusio at the beginning and end of Mark's gospel. In Mark 1:10 – 11, the same verb is used when heaven is "split open" (σχίζω) and the voice of God declares Jesus to be the Son of God. Now, at the end of the gospel, the temple curtain is torn open and the centurion declares Jesus to be the Son of God (v. 39). This suggests that the tearing is more than an act of judgment. It is also a revelation of Jesus' identity

and the significance of his death. These two views are not, of course, mutually exclusive, and both are likely to have been part of Mark's understanding.[22]

15:39 When the centurion who stood in front of him saw how he died, he said, "Truly this man was the Son of God!" (Ἰδὼν δὲ ὁ κεντυρίων ὁ παρεστηκὼς ἐξ ἐναντίας αὐτοῦ ὅτι οὕτως ἐξέπνευσεν εἶπεν· ἀληθῶς οὗτος ὁ ἄνθρωπος υἱὸς θεοῦ ἦν). A centurion was a captain of a "century" (i.e., approximately a hundred men). This one was likely in charge of the Roman detachment carrying out the crucifixion. Mark does not identify specifically what impressed the man about Jesus, but only that his statement arose from seeing "how he died" (ὅτι οὕτως ἐξέπνευσεν; lit., "that thusly he expired"). This could refer to his final shout,[23] or more broadly to the events surrounding the crucifixion, including the darkness, Jesus' response to the mocking, and even his comportment during the Roman trial.

The significance of the man's acclamation is also a difficult issue. Rulers and semidivine figures were sometimes referred to as sons of god(s) in the pagan world.[24] Since the Greek has no articles here, the "son of God" (υἱὸς θεοῦ) could mean "a son of a god." Yet the lack of the article does not necessarily indicate indefiniteness in Greek, and Colwell's rule confirms that *definite* predicate nouns preceding a

---

20. Josephus reports various omens of the destruction of the temple (see *J.W.* 6.5.3 §289, 297 – 290; cf. *Sib. Or.* 3.795 – 807; Tacitus, *Hist.* 5.13;). One was the mysterious opening of the massive eastern gate of the temple on midnight of a certain Passover, a gate that normally took twenty men to open. On this night it mysteriously opened on its own and was closed only with great difficulty. According to Josephus, some fools considered this to be a positive sign — God's opening the door of happiness to the nation, while other more sober individuals recognized it as an omen of destruction — the opening of the gates to the enemy (*J.W.* 6.5.3 §§293 – 296).

21. So France, *Mark*, 657 – 58; Brown, *Death of the Messiah*, 2:1099 – 109.

22. So Hooker, *Mark*, 378; Evans, *Mark 8:27 – 16:20*, 509; Stein, *Mark*, 718; H. L. Chronis, "The Torn Veil: Cultus and Christology in Mark 15:37 – 39," *JBL* 101 (1982): 97 – 114; Gray, *The Temple in the Gospel of Mark*, 185 – 94. Gray claims that since the design on the temple curtain symbolized the cosmos (Josephus, *J.W.* 5.5.4 §§212 – 213), its tearing indicates the eschatological end of the old age and the dawning of the new.

23. Some manuscripts add "how he cried out and died" (ὅτι οὕτως κράξας ἐξέπνευσεν; A C W Θ *f*[1.13] 33 2427 𝔐 lat syr), but the participle κράξας is likely an interpolation from Matt 27:50. See Metzger, *Textual Commentary*, 100 – 101.

24. On the beliefs of Roman soldiers, see E. S. Johnson, "Is Mark 15:39 the Key to Mark's Christology?" *JSNT* 10 (1987): 3 – 22, esp. 12 – 13.

copulative verb normally do *not* have an article (as here).[25] In other words, this is the normal way in Greek to say, "Surely this man was *the Son of God*."

Though it is impossible to confirm historically what the centurion meant by these words, there is little doubt how Mark intended the phrase to be understood by his readers. "Son of God" has been a critically important title from the beginning of this gospel, indicating not only messiahship, but also a unique relationship of intimacy with the Father. Jesus' divine sonship has been announced in the title of the gospel (1:1; if authentic), acclaimed by the Father at his baptism (1:11) and transfiguration (9:7), recognized by demons (3:11; 5:7), and implicitly affirmed in parable (12:6) and riddle (12:37) and at Jesus' trial (14:61). Now, at the climax of the crucifixion, a pagan centurion acknowledges it.

The importance of this confession should not be missed. Although Peter (and by implication, the other disciples) recognized Jesus' messianic identity (8:29), the disciples have been consistently spiritually blind to his teaching concerning the suffering of the Messiah (8:32; 9:32; 10:37 – 38; cf. 4:13; 6:52; 8:17 – 18, 21). Shockingly, it is this Gentile centurion who first recognizes that Jesus' divine sonship and messianic identity are confirmed *not through conquest, but through suffering.*

As noted above (see on v. 38), two acclamations of Jesus' divine sonship serve as "bookends" to Mark's gospel. The first is when heaven is "split open" (σχίζω, 1:10) and the Father's voice confirms and validates that Jesus is indeed the Son of God, his agent of messianic salvation. Now, at the climax of the gospel, it is not Israel's religious elite, nor even Jesus' disciples, who recognize his true identity, but a pagan Gentile. Mark hints here that the salvation accomplished by Jesus is indeed "good news" (1:1, 14 – 15) not only for Israel, but for the whole world. Gentiles will welcome and receive it (cf. 13:10).

15:40 – 41 There were also women watching from a distance, among whom were Mary Magdalene and Mary the mother of James the younger and Joseph, and Salome. When he was in Galilee, these women were following him and ministering to him. There were also many other women who had come up with him to Jerusalem ('Ἦσαν δὲ καὶ γυναῖκες ἀπὸ μακρόθεν θεωροῦσαι, ἐν αἷς καὶ Μαρία ἡ Μαγδαληνὴ καὶ Μαρία ἡ Ἰακώβου τοῦ μικροῦ καὶ Ἰωσῆτος μήτηρ καὶ Σαλώμη, αἳ ὅτε ἦν ἐν τῇ Γαλιλαίᾳ ἠκολούθουν αὐτῷ καὶ διηκόνουν αὐτῷ, καὶ ἄλλαι πολλαὶ αἱ συναναβᾶσαι αὐτῷ εἰς Ἱεροσόλυμα). Jesus' male disciples had all deserted him at his arrest (14:50), and although Peter had followed the arresting party to Caiaphas's house, he had denied Jesus and then fled (14:66 – 72). It is only the women disciples who remained faithful and now "were observing" (ἦσαν ... θεωροῦσαι; a periphrastic construction) the crucifixion "from afar." (Only the Fourth Gospel records that the "beloved disciple" was also an observer of the crucifixion; John 19:26 – 27.)

This is Mark's first reference to the women who "were following him and ministering to him" (ἠκολούθουν αὐτῷ καὶ διηκόνουν αὐτῷ). "Follow" (ἀκολουθέω) is the language of discipleship, something that is surprising and even shocking in its first-century Jewish context. Unlike other rabbis of his day, Jesus elevated women to the position of disciples (cf. Luke 10:39). "Ministering/serving" (διακονέω) probably means meeting needs such as food and clothing and assisting with those who came to Jesus for teaching and healing.

Luke introduces these women earlier in his gospel and indicates that they were patrons who sup-

---

25. See Wallace, *Greek Grammar,* 256 – 69; Johnson, "Mark 15:39," 3 – 7; P. B. Harner, "Qualitative Anarthrous Predicate Nouns: Mark 15:39 and John 1:1," *JBL* 92 (1973): 75 – 87; Brown, *Death of the Messiah,* 2:1146 – 52.

ported Jesus and disciples "out of their own means" (ἐκ τῶν ὑπαρχόντων αὐταῖς; Luke 8:2 – 3). In that context Luke names three, Mary Magdalene, Joanna the wife of Chuza, and Susanna; here he simply refers to them as "the women who had followed him from Galilee" (Luke 23:49, 55). Mark names three as well: Mary Magdalene, Mary the mother of Joses [or Joseph] and James, and Salome.

This is Mark's first reference to Mary "the Magdalene" (ἡ Μαγδαληνή), which probably means "from Magdala," a fishing village on the western shore of Galilee. Mark tells us nothing else about her, but Luke says that she had seven demons cast out of her, presumably by Jesus (Luke 8:2). Contrary to popular opinion, there is no evidence that she was a prostitute. This myth arose from a conflation of various women: Mary Magdalene, Mary of Bethany (who anointed Jesus' feet, John 12:1 – 8; cf. Luke 10:38 – 41, John 11:1 – 44), another woman with a sinful reputation who anointed Jesus (Luke 7:36 – 50), and the unnamed woman caught in adultery (John 7:53 – 8:11). Mary is the most prominent of Jesus' female disciples and is almost always named first. According to John's gospel, she had the privilege of being the first person to see Jesus alive after his resurrection (John 20:1 – 2, 10 – 18). There is, of course, no credible evidence, ancient or modern, that Mary was Jesus' sexual companion or his wife, as claimed in popular books like *The Da Vinci Code*.[26]

The second woman mentioned is "Mary the mother of James the younger and Joseph" (Μαρία ἡ Ἰακώβου τοῦ μικροῦ καὶ Ἰωσῆτος μήτηρ). Curiously,

she is subsequently called "Mary the [mother] of Joseph" (Μαρία ἡ Ἰωσῆτος) in v. 47 and then "Mary, the [mother] of James" (Μαρία ἡ Ἰακώβου) in 16:1. This is probably a result of Mark's abbreviated style.[27] "The younger" (τοῦ μικροῦ) could instead mean "the shorter" (a nickname), "the less known," or even "the less prominent." Nothing else is known about this Mary or her sons. She could perhaps be the mother of James the son of Alphaeus (3:18) or Mary, the wife of Clopas, who is mentioned at the cross with other women in John 19:25. Although Jesus had brothers named James and Joseph (and Simon and Jude; Mark 6:3), she is unlikely to be Jesus' mother, since this would be a strange way to identify her (why not, "his mother," as in John 19:25?).

The third woman is Salome, who in the parallel in Matt 27:56 appears to be identified as the mother of James and John, the wife of Zebedee.[28] If so, she also appears in Matt 20:20, approaching Jesus on behalf of her sons to request chief seats in the kingdom.[29] According to Mark, these three are just representative, and "many" others had come up with Jesus from Galilee and were present at the crucifixion.

The women will be important witnesses not only of Jesus' death, but also of his burial (v. 47), the empty tomb, and the resurrection announcement (16:1 – 8). Indeed in Mark's gospel only the women receive the announcement of the resurrection, confirming their critical roles as eyewitnesses (see comments on 16:1 – 8).

---

26. For details, see Mark L. Strauss, *Truth and Error in "The Da Vinci Code": The Facts about Jesus and Christian Origins* (San Diego: Alethinos, 2006), 61 – 70.

27. See Brown, *Death of the Messiah*, 2:1154 n. 34, for various interpretations. Some speculate that two different women are actually named here, the mother (or wife) of James and the mother of Joseph. Pesch, *Markusevangelium*, 2:504 – 7, for example, follows the reading of manuscript B, which has an article (ἡ) before Ἰωσῆτος, so that the text reads, "Mary, the [mother or wife] of James the younger, and the mother of Joseph" (ἡ Ἰακώβου τοῦ μικροῦ καὶ ἡ Ἰωσῆτος μήτηρ). The textual

support for this reading is very weak (B Ψ 13), however, and in the present text ἡ ... μήτηρ governs both names. The references in vv. 40, 47 probably result from Mark's abbreviated style (and desire for variation).

28. For more on Salome, including later traditions, see Richard J. Bauckham, "Salome the Sister of Jesus, Salome the Disciple of Jesus, and the Secret Gospel of Mark," *NovT* 33 (1991): 245 – 75.

29. Some have identified Salome further with Jesus' "mother's sister" in John 19:25, which might make James and John Jesus' cousins. All this is speculation.

15:42 – 43 Evening was already approaching, because it was Preparation Day, that is, the day before the Sabbath. So Joseph of Arimathea, a respected member of the Council who was himself waiting for the kingdom of God, boldly went to Pilate and requested the body of Jesus (Καὶ ἤδη ὀψίας γενομένης, ἐπεὶ ἦν παρασκευὴ ὅ ἐστιν προσάββατον, ἐλθὼν Ἰωσὴφ ὁ ἀπὸ Ἀριμαθαίας εὐσχήμων βουλευτής, ὃς καὶ αὐτὸς ἦν προσδεχόμενος τὴν βασιλείαν τοῦ θεοῦ, τολμήσας εἰσῆλθεν πρὸς τὸν Πιλᾶτον καὶ ἠτήσατο τὸ σῶμα τοῦ Ἰησοῦ). Mark's grammar is awkward ("already evening having come"; ἤδη ὀψίας γενομένης; a genitive absolute), but his meaning is clear. Jesus had died about 3:00 p.m. (the ninth hour; vv. 34 – 37), and evening was now approaching.

Deuteronomy 21:22 – 23 commands that bodies of executed victims must be buried before nightfall, and this would especially be the case on the eve of the Sabbath. "Preparation Day" here refers to the weekly preparation before the Sabbath, as Mark clarifies, not preparation day for the Passover festival.[30] Since no work could be done on the Sabbath, all preparations for burial must be finished before sundown.

Joseph of Arimathea is identified as a "respected" or "prominent" (εὐσχήμων) "councilor" (βουλευτής), that is, a member of the Sanhedrin. The location of Arimathea is debated, but the name likely refers to Ramathaim-zophim (1 Sam 1:1; Josephus, *Ant.* 13.4.9 §127), the birthplace of Samuel, also known as Ramah (1 Sam 1:19; 2:11) and Rathamin (1 Macc 11:34). It is located in the hill country of Ephraim twenty miles northwest of Jerusalem and east of Joppa.

Joseph's actions are evidence that not all the Jewish leaders were allied against Jesus (cf. Nicodemus; John 7:50 – 51; 19:39). Mark describes him as one who "was himself waiting for the kingdom of God." This unusual statement indicates that he was at least sympathetic with Jesus' message (cf. 1:15), if not an open follower. Luke adds that he was a good and righteous man who had not consented to the Sanhedrin's decision (Luke 23:51).

Whether Joseph of Arimathea was present for the trial of Jesus is not known. Both Matthew and John assert that Joseph was already a disciple (Matt 27:57; John 19:38), though John adds "secretly," for fear of the Jewish authorities. Matthew also refers to him as "rich" (Matt 27:57), which explains his ownership of a new, rock-hewn family tomb. Mark describes Joseph as coming "boldly" or "courageously" (τολμήσας; aorist participle) to Pilate. To identify so positively with a victim accused of both blasphemy and sedition could put him in jeopardy with his own Jewish associates as well as the Roman authorities.

J. D. Crossan denies the existence of Joseph of Arimathea, claiming that Mark invented him to explain the events of Jesus' burial and the empty tomb.[31] This is part of Crossan's assertion that Jesus' body was not buried but thrown to the dogs, the common fate of crucified victims. Yet Crossan's claims cannot be sustained. There is little evidence, for example, that Jewish victims of crucifixion were left unburied.[32] The examples we do have occurred during times of war, such as during the Roman siege of Jerusalem in AD 66 – 70, when thousands of Jews were crucified outside the city walls.[33] This

---

30. Cf. Josephus, *Ant.* 16.6.2 §163, for this usage; see "In Depth: The Chronology and Significance of the Last Supper" at 14:12 – 31.

31. Crossan, *The Historical Jesus*, 391 – 94; idem, *Who Killed Jesus? Exposing the Roots of Anti-Semitism in the Gospel Story of the Death of Jesus* (San Francisco: HarperSanFrancisco, 1995), 172 – 73.

32. See Evans, *Mark 8:27 – 16:20*, 516 – 17.

33. Josephus, *J. W.* 5.11.1 §450. See also the actions of Varus, the Roman legate of Syria, who crucified two thousand Jews after the uprisings following the death of Herod the Great (Josephus, *Ant.* 17.10.10 §295).

was exceptional, however, and both Philo and Josephus criticize those who would refuse burial to those crucified, treating such cases as impious and outrageous.[34] Archaeological evidence for this came in 1968, when the bones of a crucified man named Jehohanan were discovered in an ossuary northeast of the Old City of Jerusalem in the Kidron Valley — proof that at least some victims of crucifixion were given a proper burial.[35]

Even apart from this question, the evidence for the historicity of Joseph of Arimathea is overwhelming. He appears independently in the Synoptics and John (Matt 27:57; Mark 15:43; Luke 23:51; John 19:38), and his hometown has no symbolic significance (and so was unlikely to have been created). Furthermore, if Mark had created such a character, he is unlikely to have made him a member of the Sanhedrin, the group that condemned Jesus![36]

15:44 – 45 Pilate was surprised that Jesus would have died already. Summoning the centurion, he asked him if he had already died. Confirming this with the centurion, he granted the corpse to Joseph (ὁ δὲ Πιλᾶτος ἐθαύμασεν εἰ ἤδη τέθνηκεν καὶ προσκαλεσάμενος τὸν κεντυρίωνα ἐπηρώτησεν αὐτὸν εἰ πάλαι ἀπέθανεν· καὶ γνοὺς ἀπὸ τοῦ κεντυρίωνος ἐδωρήσατο τὸ πτῶμα τῷ Ἰωσήφ). Joseph's request for the body of Jesus takes Pilate by surprise, since victims of crucifixion normally languished for days.[37] Jesus' death took only a few hours. Pilate summoned the one he could trust most to confirm the death, the centurion in charge of the crucifixion.

Mark's use of the term "already" (πάλαι) is unusual. It carries the sense of "long before" or "in times past" and so emphasizes that Jesus had expired at some time previous.[38] Mark may use this term for stylistic variation, since he has just used the more common "already" (ἤδη) in the previous sentence. The same may be true for the use of "corpse" (τὸ πτῶμα) in v. 45, since "body" (τὸ σῶμα) was used in v. 43. As in English, the Greek "body" (τὸ σῶμα) can mean either a live or dead body, while "corpse" (τὸ πτῶμα) is limited to the dead (cf. 6:29). English versions commonly translate both as "body" for stylistic reasons (NIV, NET, NASB, NRSV, NAB, REB, NLT, CEV; "corpse" is used in ESV, HCSB, GW),[39] since English "corpse" is generally used in forensic contexts rather than in everyday discourse.

The official verdict by the centurion confirms

---

34. Philo criticizes Flaccus, the Roman governor of Egypt, for failing to properly take down before a Jewish holiday those who had died on the cross (*Flacc.* 10 §83). Josephus similarly speaks of a group of impious rebels who failed to give proper burial to two high priests they murdered, contrasting them with proper Jews, who are careful to bury crucifixion victims before sunset (*J. W.* 4.5.2 §317).

35. Part of a nail remained in the ankle bone, confirming that his feet had been nailed to the cross (though his arms may have been tied). The remains have been dated to the early decades of the first century. For details, see V. Tzaferis, "Jewish Tombs at and near Giv'at ha-Mivtar," *IEJ* 20 (1970): 18 – 32; J. Zias and E. Sekeles, "The Crucified Man from Giv'at ha-Mivtar: A Reappraisal," *IEJ* 35 (1985): 22 – 27; J. Zias and J. H. Charlesworth, "Crucifixion: Archaeology, Jesus, and the Dead Sea Scrolls," in *Jesus and the Dead Sea Scrolls* (ed. Charlesworth), 273 – 89.

36. See G. G. O'Collins and D. Kendall, "Did Joseph of Arimathea Exist?" *Bib* 75 (1994): 235 – 41.

37. Isidore of Seville, *Etymologia* 5.27.34, wrote that "hanging is a lesser penalty than the cross. For the gallows kill the victim immediately, whereas the cross tortures for a long time those who are fixed to it." Seneca, *Dial.* 3.2.2, speaks of a "wasting away in pain" and a "long-drawn-out agony" (Hengel, *Crucifixion*, 29 – 31). Cf. comments on 15:24 above.

38. The oddness of the expression "long ago" accounts for the variant "already" (ἤδη) in some manuscripts (B D W Θ 2427 lat). Copyists likely sought to smooth over Mark's awkward expression.

39. Some manuscripts read "body" (σῶμα) instead of "corpse" (πτῶμα) in v. 45 (so A C W Ψ 083 *f*[1,13] 33 𝔐 lat syr[p.h] cop). Whether this scribal change was prompted by stylistic or theological (eucharistic?) concerns is uncertain.

Jesus' death, and Pilate releases the body to Joseph.[40] This permission by Pilate is taken by some as evidence that the governor viewed Jesus as innocent, since he is unlikely to have so quickly released the body of a dangerous insurrectionist or criminal.[41]

Could Jesus have survived the cross and then faked his own resurrection? Evans points to a few cases where victims were taken down from the cross alive. One is a fictional satire by Petronius, where the family of a crucified man releases him while the sentry is away (*Satyricon* 111). The other is related by Josephus, who found three of his friends being crucified by the Romans in the village of Thecoa and begged Titus for their release. Titus granted the favor, but only one of the three survived (*Life* 75 §421).[42] None of these, of course, are cases of "misdiagnosis" of death by a Roman soldier. The claim by some that Jesus somehow survived the cross and then announced his victory over death is ludicrous.

15:46 After buying a linen cloth and taking the body down, he wrapped it in the linen cloth and placed him in a tomb that had been carved out of rock. Then he rolled a stone across the entrance of the tomb (καὶ ἀγοράσας σινδόνα καθελὼν αὐτὸν ἐνείλησεν τῇ σινδόνι καὶ ἔθηκεν αὐτὸν ἐν μνημείῳ ὃ ἦν λελατομημένον ἐκ πέτρας καὶ προσεκύλισεν λίθον ἐπὶ τὴν θύραν τοῦ μνημείου). Joseph's actions follow traditional Jewish burial procedures of that day. The body would be washed and wrapped in linen cloth, with spices to cover the stench of decomposition (cf. 14:8; *m. Šabb.* 23:5). It would be laid on a stone bench, or "niche," in a rock-hewn tomb and then sealed with a large square or disc-shaped stone. Hundreds of these *kokhim*, or

"niche," tombs have been discovered around Jerusalem. When the flesh had decomposed, the stone would be rolled back and the bones placed in an ossuary, or "bone box." In this way family tombs would be used for multiple burials.

Joseph likely had help in the burial process. Since he was rich, as Matthew asserts (Matt 27:57), his servants likely did the work. Mark does not mention the washing of the body, although this was surely done, since it was an essential part of the burial procedure. Washing and anointing a dead body is allowed even on the Sabbath (*m. Šabb.* 23:5). Nor does Mark mention the use of spices in the initial burial, and the women subsequently purchase them to anoint the body on Sunday morning (Mark 16:1–2).

In John's gospel Nicodemus aids Joseph in the burial, providing a large quantity of spices (myrrh and aloes; John 19:38–42).[43] The other gospels provide other details about the tomb. Matthew mentions it was new (Matt 27:60), and Luke says that no one had yet been laid in it (Luke 23:53). This helps to explain why Joseph was willing to relinquish what was meant to be his family tomb — it was not yet occupied. John mentions both of these points (that it was new and unoccupied) and adds that the tomb was near the place of the crucifixion (John 19:42).

15:47 Mary Magdalene and Mary the mother of Joseph were watching where he was laid (ἡ δὲ Μαρία ἡ Μαγδαληνὴ καὶ Μαρία ἡ Ἰωσῆτος ἐθεώρουν ποῦ τέθειται). On these women, see comments on v. 40. Salome is not mentioned here but will be named again in 16:1. The observation of the burial site is important, since the women will return on

---

40. Edwards, *Mark*, 489, claims that the terminology used for release represents the "stylized diction of Roman orders" and so likely reflects Pilate's actual directive: "summoning" (προσκαλέω) in v. 44, the Latinized word for "centurion" (κεντυρίων rather than the normal Gk. ἑκατοντάρχης), and especially "bestowed

[δωρέομαι rather than δίδωμι] the corpse" in v. 45.

41. France, *Mark*, 667; Edwards, *Mark*, 489.

42. Evans, *Mark 8:27–16:20*, 520.

43. See comments on 16:1 for a possible harmonization of the two accounts.

the third day to anoint the body. The role of the women as witnesses to the crucifixion, the burial, and the empty tomb is important to the resurrection narratives. Since women were not viewed in Judaism as reliable witnesses and could not testify in court,[44] the early church would never have invented stories in which women were the main eyewitnesses. This is strong evidence for the histo-

ricity of the accounts of the burial of Jesus and the discovery of the empty tomb. The imperfect verb "were watching" (ἐθεώρουν) suggests they stood for a time observing the burial process.

Mark does not report the appointment of a Roman (or Jewish?) guard at the tomb, a detail provided only in Matthew's gospel (Matt 27:62 – 66; 28:4, 11 – 13).

Theology in Application

The Judgment of God and the Problem of Evil

As discussed above (see on v. 33), the darkness that covers the land during Jesus' crucifixion likely symbolizes God's displeasure and judgment. This theme has been an important one in Mark's gospel. Jesus symbolically judges Israel and its leaders with the cursing of the fig tree (11:14), the clearing of the temple (11:15 – 17), and the parable of the tenants (12:1 – 12). He warns the people against the scribes, who will receive "more severe punishment" because of their pride, hypocrisy, and exploitation of the poor (12:38 – 40). Israel's leaders have been given great responsibility and so will be held accountable for their actions. The future destruction of Jerusalem and the temple in AD 70 will provide the capstone to this theme, serving as God's judgment against the nation for rejecting the Messiah and the offer of the kingdom of God.

This theme of God's judgment permeates Scripture from beginning to end. God is not only a God of love and grace; he is also a God of justice. His perfect righteousness demands that sin be punished. From the fall of Adam and Eve onward, humanity's inclination is to reject God's authority. In his righteous judgment God expelled the first couple from the garden, cursed the ground, and produced pain in childbirth (Gen 3). The flood narrative shows that God cannot tolerate sin forever and judgment will eventually come (Gen 6 – 9).

The history of Israel throughout the OT represents cycles of sin, judgment, repentance, and restoration, as Israel repeatedly chose to go her own way in defiance of God. The discontent and disobedience of the wilderness generation resulted in death by the sword (Exod 32:28), fire from heaven (Num 11:1), the earth swallowing whole clans (Num 16), plagues of snakes (21:6), and other judgments. The pattern continued in the period of the judges and the kings, when prophets pronounced oracles of judgment against Israel, and God used pagan nations as tools to discipline his

---

44. Josephus, *Ant.* 4.219: "But let not the testimony of women be admitted, on account of the levity and boldness of their sex." Cf. *m. Roš Haš* 1:8; *m. Šebu.* 4:1; *Sipre* on Deut 19:15.

wayward people. Yet not only was Israel the object of God's wrath; the prophets are full of oracles against the nations for their defiance of God and cruelty to his people.

In the end, however, the theme of judgment is a theme of hope. God's justice is the ultimate answer to the problem of evil: *How can a good and all-powerful God allow evil to continue in the world?* It will not continue forever, and every sin and injustice will be paid for. From a human perspective, tyrants and evildoers seem to escape justice. But God's righteousness means that every cruel emperor (Nero in Mark's day), every Adolf Hitler, Pol Pot, Idi Amin, Saddam Hussein, or Osama bin Laden, will eventually receive just punishment for their sins — if not in this life, then in the life to come. The darkness that comes over the land is a symbol of *eschatological judgment*, the final accounting of the day of the Lord.

A Ransom for Sins

The theme of justice reminds us that everyone is in jeopardy, since "all have sinned and fall short of the glory of God" (Rom 3:23). So beside this theme of judgment stands a theme of atonement and salvation from sins. In context, God's judgment in the darkness of the cross is directed not against sinful humanity, but against his own Son. While Jesus' quotation of Ps 22:1 can be interpreted in a variety of ways, we have suggested above that it ought to be understood in light of Mark's theology of 10:45 (a ransom for sins), 14:22 – 24 (his body given for them), and 14:36 (the cup of God's wrath that awaits him). Jesus goes to the cross knowing that the crucifixion is not the worst he will suffer. He will become a ransom for sins, paying the price for the transgression of his people (Isa 53:4 – 6).

The cry of dereliction is best understood as the moment when Jesus experienced God's wrath and the sense of forsakenness that came with it. The one who had no sin *became sin* for us (2 Cor 5:21). This moment, then, is the climax of salvation history, the point to which the whole of the biblical testimony has been pointing. Through Jesus, God is claiming back his creation, inaugurating the kingdom of God (Mark 1:13), and reconciling the world to himself (2 Cor 5:19).

Salvation for the Nations

This restoration includes not just the people of Israel, but the nations of the world. The death of Jesus in Mark elicits an unexpected confession from the Roman centurion in charge of the crucifixion: "Truly this man was the Son of God" (v. 39). Astonishingly, it is a Gentile who first recognizes that Jesus' divine sonship is not repudiated by his death, but is confirmed by it. It is as the suffering Messiah and Son of God that Jesus fulfills his purpose and calling.

The theme of the salvation of the Gentiles is not as prominent in Mark as it is in Luke (his gospel and Acts). Yet it has been hinted at throughout Mark's gospel. This is true in the healing of the Syrophoenician woman's daughter (7:24 – 30), other healings in the Decapolis (7:31 – 37), the feeding of the four thousand (8:1 – 9), Jesus' predictions that the "vineyard" will be given to "others" (12:9), and the declaration that the gospel will be preached to all nations (13:10). This theme should not have been surprising to the Jewish nation, since the OT repeatedly predicted that God's salvation would one day go forth to all people everywhere.[45] In that day, "the earth will be filled with the knowledge of the LORD as the waters cover the sea" (Isa 11:9). For Mark's readers this is a present reality, as the gospel is being proclaimed to the ends of the earth.

A Faithful Remnant

While Mark emphatically stated that at his arrest all of Jesus' disciples deserted him, the women at the crucifixion remind us that devotion to Jesus is still alive. If not fully identifying with Jesus by taking up their own cross, at least they watch "from afar" and will witness the burial and the empty tomb. Joseph of Arimathea too represents the seed of faith. While Mark does not identify him as a full believer — he is "waiting for the kingdom of God" — he *is* a sympathetic observer who wants to do what is right for the body of Jesus. This kind of sympathetic hearer will be open to the gospel as the church takes the message of salvation to the ends of the earth.

---

45. Gen 12:3, 5; 22:18; 49:10; Deut 32:21; Pss 2:8; 22:27 – 31; 65:5; 72:1 – 20; 86:9; 102:15, 18 – 22; 145:10, 11; Isa 2:2 – 5; 9:1 – 7; 11:1 – 10; 35:1 – 10; 40:4 – 11; 42:1 – 12; 45:6, 8, 22 – 24; 49:1, 5 – 6, 18 – 23; 54:1 – 3; 55:5; 60:1 – 14; 66:7 – 23; Jer 3:17; 4:2; 16:19 – 21; Ezek 47:3 – 5; Dan 2:35, 44 – 45; 7:13, 14; Hos 2:23; Joel 2:28 – 32; Amos 9:11 – 12; Mic 4:3, 4; Hag 2:7; Zech 2:10 – 11; 6:15; 8:1 – 23; 9:1, 9 – 17; 14:8 – 21; Mal 1:11.

63

Mark 16:1 – 8

Literary Context

Mark's detailed Passion Narrative — focusing at length on Jesus' suffering and rejection by all (14:1 – 15:47) — now gives way to a remarkably short and puzzling account of the resurrection (16:1 – 8). Conclusions concerning the literary context, main idea, and structure of this passage necessarily relate to the question of Mark's original ending. Virtually all scholars agree that the longer ending that appears in most manuscripts (16:9 – 20) is not original. Its style and content are non-Markan, and it does not appear in the most important early manuscripts. It represents a compendium of resurrection appearances from other gospels and was likely composed by a second-century copyist disturbed by the abrupt ending of Mark. In addition to this "longer ending," there is another "intermediate ending," also spurious, that appears in a few manuscripts between verses 8 and 9. For details on these various endings, see the appendix, "The Endings of Mark," at the end of the chapter.

If 16:9 – 20 is not original, the question becomes whether (1) the original ending has been lost (or possibly never finished), or (2) Mark intended to end his gospel at verse 8. Scholars are well divided on this issue, with the tide of opinion shifting back and forth through the years.[1] Both perspectives come with their own set of problems and additional questions. If the original ending was lost, how could this have happened so early in the transmission process? Why have no traces of it remained? If it once existed, what did it contain? Resurrection appearances? The Great Commission? An account of the ascension?

If, however, Mark intended to end at v. 8, why so puzzling and abrupt an ending, with the women's fear and silence and no resurrection appearances? In the discussion below we will (tentatively!) conclude that v. 8 is indeed the intended ending of Mark's gospel and that his purpose is to call his readers to greater faith in the resurrected Son of God and perseverance in the face of doubt, suffering, and persecution.

---

1. For a discussion of the dramatic shifts in consensus on this issue, see N. Clayton Croy, *The Mutilation of Mark's Gospel* (Nashville: Abingdon, 2003), 18 – 32.

Main Idea

In its present form, Mark's gospel comes to its resolution with the discovery of the empty tomb and the announcement of the resurrection by an angel. Whichever view is taken on the ending, Mark leaves no doubt about the historical reality of the resurrection of Jesus the Messiah and the appropriate response of those who have faith in him: to persevere through suffering and to boldly proclaim the resurrection and the kingdom of God.

Translation

Mark 16:1 – 8

1a	setting (temporal)	When the Sabbath was over,
b	Characters entrance/Action	**Mary Magdalene,**
c		**Mary the mother of James,** and
d	Action	**Salome bought spices so that they could go and anoint him.**
2a	setting (temporal)	Very early on the first day of the week,
b	setting (temporal)	at sunrise,
c	Action	**they went to the tomb.**
3a	Action/Question	And **they were saying to each other,**
b		*"Who will roll the stone away from the door of the tomb for us?"*
4a	action/setting (temporal)	But looking up,
b	Action/Observation	**they saw that the stone had been rolled back**
c	narrative aside	(for it was very large).
5a	action/setting (temporal)	Entering the tomb,
b	Action/Observation	**they saw a young man sitting on the right side,**
c	character description	dressed in a white robe,
d	Response to 5b	and **they were alarmed.**
6a	Response to 5d	But **he said to them,**
b	encouragement	*"Don't be alarmed.*
c	statement of fact	*You are seeking Jesus the Nazarene, who was crucified.*
d	affirmation	*He has risen!*
e	affirmation	*He is not here.*
f	evidence	*See the place where they laid him.*

Continued on next page.

Continued from previous page.

7a	Command	*But go, tell his disciples and Peter,*
b	action	*'He is going ahead of you into Galilee.*
c	prophecy	*You will see him there, just as he told you.'"*
8a	manner of 8b	Leaving,
b	Action	**they fled from the tomb,**
c	reason for 8b	because trembling and amazement seized them,
d	Response/Result of 8e	and **they said nothing to anyone,**
e	reason for 8d	for they were afraid.

Structure

The passage as it presently stands contains five brief scenes: the purchase of spices (v. 1), the journey to the tomb (vv. 2 – 3), the discovery of the empty tomb (v. 4), the angelic announcement of the resurrection (vv. 5 – 7), and the confused and fearful departure of the women (v. 8).

For those who hold that the original ending has been lost, the question of its original structure must be raised. While here we must speculate, in light of the command to report the resurrection to the disciples (v. 7a) and the promise that Jesus would go ahead of them to Galilee (16:7b-c), Gundry plausibly suggests a reconstruction including a resurrection appearance to the women (cf. Matt 28:9 – 10), a report by the women to the disciples and perhaps a visit by Peter to the tomb (cf. Luke 24:9b – 12), and a resurrection appearance to the Eleven in Galilee (cf. Matt 28:16 – 20).[2]

Exegetical Outline

→ **1. Setting and Purchase of Spices (16:1)**

2. Journey to the Tomb (16:2 – 3)

3. Discovery of the Empty Tomb (16:4)

4. Announcement of the Resurrection (16:5 – 7)

    a. The young man dressed in white (16:5)

    b. Resurrection announced (16:6)

    c. Command to tell the disciples (16:7)

5. The Fearful Response of the Women (16:8)

    a. Their fear and departure (v. 8a-c)

    b. Their silence because of fear (v. 8d-e)

2. Gundry, *Mark*, 1021.

Explanation of the Text

16:1 When the Sabbath was over, Mary Magdalene, Mary the mother of James, and Salome bought spices so that they could go and anoint him (Καὶ διαγενομένου τοῦ σαββάτου Μαρία ἡ Μαγδαληνὴ καὶ Μαρία ἡ τοῦ Ἰακώβου καὶ Σαλώμη ἠγόρασαν ἀρώματα ἵνα ἐλθοῦσαι ἀλείψωσιν αὐτόν). The Sabbath ended at sunset (about 6:00 p.m.) on Saturday evening.[3] At that time shops that were closed for the Sabbath would reopen, so the women could buy spices to anoint Jesus' body.[4] Since it was too dark to visit the tomb on Saturday evening or night, the women plan to go early the next morning. The spices were not meant to preserve the body (Jews, unlike the Egyptians, did not embalm), but to cover the stench of decay, after which the bones would be placed in an ossuary, or bone box (see comments on 14:8; 15:46; cf. *m. Šabb.* 23:5).

Although, unlike John 19:38 – 42, Mark does not mention the use of spices (or the presence of Nicodemus) in Jesus' burial by Joseph of Arimathea, it is supposing too much to say that spices were omitted out of haste or that the women were now rectifying "what was omitted by Joseph."[5] Nothing in 15:46 suggests the first burial was deficient. If Joseph had time to purchase linen cloth (15:46), he surely could have purchased spices. The accounts of John and Mark can be easily harmonized if the women are coming to pay their own respects and provide additional honor to the body of Jesus.

The women are those named in 15:40 and again (without Salome) in 15:47. Some claim the repetition of names so soon after 15:47 indicates Mark's use of a different source.[6] This is possible, but the clarification of those present is important in its own right, to identify specifically the witnesses to the empty tomb. The second Mary is now called "the [mother] of James" instead of "the mother of James … and Joseph" (15:40) or "the [mother] of Joseph" (15:47). For this variation, see comments on 15:40 – 42 and 15:47.[7]

As noted earlier (comment on 15:47), the discovery of the empty tomb by women — reported in all four Gospels — constitutes important evidence for the veracity of this account. Since in first-century Judaism the testimony of women was not considered reliable, the early church would never have created stories in which women were the primary witnesses. It seems beyond dispute that a group of women discovered the empty tomb on the third day after Jesus' crucifixion.

16:2 Very early on the first day of the week, at sunrise, they went to the tomb (καὶ λίαν πρωῒ τῇ μιᾷ τῶν σαββάτων ἔρχονται ἐπὶ τὸ μνημεῖον ἀνατείλαντος τοῦ ἡλίου). In typical fashion, Mark uses a dual temporal expression, "very early … at sunrise" (cf. 1:35; 2:20; 4:35; 10:30; 13:24; 14:12, 43; 15:42).[8] This one is seen as problematic by some commentators, since "very early" (λίαν πρωῒ) suggests the time before dawn, but the sun apparently has already risen (ἀνατείλαντος τοῦ ἡλίου).[9] John

---

3. "When the Sabbath ended" (διαγενομένου τοῦ σαββάτου) is a genitive absolute, used because the subject of the participial phrase (the Sabbath) is different from the subject of the main clause (the women).

4. Luke 23:56, by contrast, says the women went home *before* the Sabbath "and prepared spices and perfumes." This may be an abbreviated way of saying the same thing ("they prepared to bring spices"), or perhaps they had some spices but purchased others after the Sabbath.

5. So Stein, *Mark*, 729, and many commentators.

6. See Bultmann, *History*, 284 – 87; Hooker, *Mark*, 383; Evans, *Mark 8:27 – 16:20*, 530; Stein, *Mark*, 720.

7. Hooker, *Mark*, 383, sees in the diversity of evidence that Mark is faithfully reproducing the traditions that came to him.

8. Neirynck, *Duality in Mark*, 96.

9. Mann, *Mark*, 664 – 65. The difficulty scribes had with the expression is evident in some Western manuscripts (D it[c n q]), which have the present aorist participle, "while the sun was rising" (ἀνατέλλοντος τοῦ ἡλίου) instead of the aorist, "when the sun had risen."

20:1 explicitly says Mary Magdalene went to the tomb "while it was still dark." But this problem is more imagined than real. Mark's expression clearly means an early hour, yet light enough for the women to see. Whether the sun has yet crept over the horizon is moot.

The "first day of the week" (τῇ μιᾷ τῶν σαββάτων) is Sunday and is the expression used in all four Gospels for the time of discovery of the empty tomb (Matt 28:1; Luke 24:1; John 20:1, 19). For a discussion of how a Friday crucifixion and a Sunday resurrection can be "after three days" (8:31; 9:31; 10:33 – 34), see comments on 8:31.

16:3 – 4 And they were saying to each other, "Who will roll the stone away from the door of the tomb for us?" But looking up, they saw that the stone had been rolled back (for it was very large) (καὶ ἔλεγον πρὸς ἑαυτάς· τίς ἀποκυλίσει ἡμῖν τὸν λίθον ἐκ τῆς θύρας τοῦ μνημείου; καὶ ἀναβλέψασαι θεωροῦσιν ὅτι ἀποκεκύλισται ὁ λίθος· ἦν γὰρ μέγας σφόδρα). Why had the women not considered the stone before heading for the tomb, especially since they were present at the burial (15:46 – 47)? From the perspective of Mark's story, their question is meant to set up the dramatic discovery of the empty tomb. They are not expecting a resurrection.

The participle "looking up" (ἀναβλέψασαι) heightens the drama.[10] This is the moment of revelation as they come upon the scene and discover, to their shock and surprise, that the stone has been rolled back! Mark's narrative aside, "For it was very large" (ἦν γὰρ μέγας σφόδρα), seems out of place at the end of the sentence and would have been expected after the question, "Who will roll the stone

away...?" Its placement at the end provides an exclamation point to the scene before them: " — and so large a stone!"

The passive "had been rolled back" (ἀποκεκύλισται) may be a divine passive, meaning God had rolled back the tomb. But there is no indication here or in the other canonical gospels that removal of the stone was necessary to allow the resurrection.[11] The purpose is to reveal the empty tomb. Even in Matthew, where an earthquake occurs and an angel rolls back the stone (Matt 28:3), the tomb is already empty (cf. 28:6: "He is not here"). This agrees with resurrection accounts in Luke and John, where the resurrected Jesus passes through walls and can appear and disappear at will (cf. Luke 24:31, 36; John 20:19).

16:5 Entering the tomb, they saw a young man sitting on the right side, dressed in a white robe, and they were alarmed (καὶ εἰσελθοῦσαι εἰς τὸ μνημεῖον εἶδον νεανίσκον καθήμενον ἐν τοῖς δεξιοῖς περιβεβλημένον στολὴν λευκήν, καὶ ἐξεθαμβήθησαν). Though Mark does not explicitly identify the "young man" as an angel, the context and the white robes confirm this identification (cf. Matt 28:3; John 20:12; Acts 1:10; Rev 4:4; 19:14).[12] Matthew explicitly identifies him as an "angel" (ἄγγελος), flashing "like lightning" and in garments "white as snow" (Matt 28:2 – 3). Luke 24:4 speaks of two men "in clothes that gleamed like lightning." It is unlikely that Mark intends any connection between this young man and the one who fled at Jesus' arrest (see comments on 14:51 – 52).

The response of the women is typical of those who encounter angelic messengers — shock and fear (Judg 6:22 – 23; 13:6, 22; Dan 8:16 – 17;

---

10. Though Boring, *Mark*, 444, probably reads too much into the verb by suggesting it means to "have their sight restored" (cf. 8:24).

11. Contrast Mark's understated narrative with the dramatic scene in the *Gospel of Peter* 9 – 10 (37 – 40), where the stone rolls back on its own and Jesus emerges triumphant, ac-

companied by two angels (whose heads reach to the heavens, but Jesus' head is beyond the heavens) and with the cross following behind.

12. For angels identified as "young men," see 2 Macc 3:26, 33; 5:2 (νεανίαι); Josephus, *Ant.* 5.8.2 §522 (νεανίας).

10:10 – 11; Tob 12:16; Luke 1:12 – 13; 2:9). The verb translated "alarmed" (ἐκθαμβέω) occurs only in Mark in the NT (4x) and indicates an "intense emotional state because of something causing great surprise or perplexity."[13] It is used of Jesus' distress in the garden of Gethsemane (14:33) and of the shock of the people when Jesus returns from the transfiguration (9:15).

16:6 But he said to them, "Don't be alarmed. You are seeking Jesus the Nazarene, who was crucified. He has risen! He is not here. See the place where they laid him." (ὁ δὲ λέγει αὐταῖς· μὴ ἐκθαμβεῖσθε· Ἰησοῦν ζητεῖτε τὸν Ναζαρηνὸν τὸν ἐσταυρωμένον· ἠγέρθη, οὐκ ἔστιν ὧδε· ἴδε ὁ τόπος ὅπου ἔθηκαν αὐτόν). Alarm at the sight of an angel is often followed by words of encouragement not to fear (Gen 21:17; Judg 6:23; Dan 10:12; Matt 1:20; Luke 1:13, 30; 2:10). Some have argued that "you are seeking ..." is meant as a rebuke, since "seek" (ζητέω) is elsewhere always used pejoratively in Mark.[14] This is unlikely. The verb is too common in Greek collocations to be limited to this one sense, and there is nothing in the context to suggest a rebuke.[15] The intention of the women is to honor the body of Jesus, and the angel provides reassuring, not threatening, words. For Jesus "the Nazarene," see comments on 10:47.

With the words "He has risen!" the angel functions as a divine interpreter for the scene in front of them. The empty tomb alone is not proof of the resurrection. It only invites the question, "What happened to the body of Jesus?" Through the cen-turies skeptics have answered in a variety of ways: the disciples stole the body; the Jewish or Roman authorities took possession of it; the women went to the wrong tomb; Jesus somehow survived and escaped the tomb. These claims are all answered decisively by God's own explanation delivered through his messenger: "He has risen!"

Two verbs are used in the NT for the resurrection (ἐγείρω; ἀνίστημι), both meaning "to rise" with no apparent difference in meaning. Elsewhere in the passion predictions, Mark uses ἀνίστημι, either in the active (8:31; 9:9) or middle voice (9:31; 10:34), both apparently carrying the active meaning, "he will rise." Here in 16:6 and in 14:28, he uses the aorist passive of ἐγείρω (ἠγέρθη), "he is risen," which can carry either a passive sense, "he has been raised" (by God), or an active sense, "he has risen" (by his power). Both ideas are affirmed elsewhere in the NT.

In many passages God is said to have raised Jesus from the dead (Acts 2:24; 3:15; 4:10; 5:30; 10:40; 13:30; Rom 4:24; 6:4; 8:11; 10:9; 1 Cor 6:14; 15:15; 2 Cor 4:14; Gal 1:1; 1 Pet 1:21). Yet in other passages an active sense may be intended (Mark 8:31; 9:9 – 10, 31; 10:34; Luke 18:33; 24:7, 46; John 20:9; Acts 17:3; 1 Thess 4:14).[16] In John 10:17 – 18 Jesus says that he has the power to lay down his life and to take it up again. A decision here is difficult and it is not certain that Mark would even distinguish between these two senses. Yet since elsewhere Mark more commonly uses the passive of ἐγείρω with an active meaning (2:12; 4:27; 13:8, 22),[17] it seems likely that is his intention here.

---

13. BDAG, 303.

14. Lightfoot, *Gospel Message of St Mark*, 23 – 24 (see 1:37; 3:32; 8:11 – 12; 11:18; 12:12; 14:1, 11, 55); cf. Lane, *Mark*, 588. Edwards, *Mark*, 494, writes: "The women, intent on their funereal errand, are preoccupied with death."

15. France, *Mark*, 680; Stein, *Mark*, 731.

16. These passages are difficult to interpret, since "to rise" from the dead could still carry a passive sense, that the Father caused the Son to rise.

17. So Stein, *Mark*, 731. Contra Lohmeyer, *Markus*, 355, 357 – 58; Cranfield, *Mark*, 466; Hooker, *Mark*, 385; Moloney, *Mark*, 346 n. 30. The only exceptions are in 12:26 (the dead "are raised") and possibly 6:16, where it is unclear whether Herod fears John the Baptist "has risen" or "has been raised" from the dead.

16:7 "But go, tell his disciples and Peter, 'He is going ahead of you into Galilee. You will see him there, just as he told you.'" (ἀλλὰ ὑπάγετε εἴπατε τοῖς μαθηταῖς αὐτοῦ καὶ τῷ Πέτρῳ ὅτι προάγει ὑμᾶς εἰς τὴν Γαλιλαίαν· ἐκεῖ αὐτὸν ὄψεσθε, καθὼς εἶπεν ὑμῖν). The message given to the women is not for them alone, but for all Jesus' followers. Peter is likely singled out not only because of his key leadership role among the disciples (3:16; 5:37; 8:29; 9:2; 10:28; 14:29, 33; 37, 54), but especially in light of his need for restoration after denying Jesus (14:66 – 72). Both Luke (Luke 24:34) and Paul (1 Cor 15:5) report unique resurrection appearances to Peter apart from the other disciples, probably for this purpose (cf. John 21:15 – 19).

The angel's words "just as he told you" (καθὼς εἶπεν ὑμῖν) refer to Jesus' words in 14:28. In the Last Supper narrative Jesus had predicted not only that the disciples would fall away and be scattered (14:27) and that Peter would deny him (14:30 – 31), but also that he would "go ahead of you into Galilee" (14:28). Why Galilee? And what does it mean to "go ahead" of them? As the place of their original calling and appointment and Jesus' home turf, where the majority of his ministry took place, Galilee is an appropriate place for this reunion and preparation for the next steps of their discipleship. Some have suggested that "go ahead" originally meant that Jesus would lead them there like a shepherd leads his flock, imagery taken from Zech 13 (cf. Mark 14:28).[18] Yet this cannot be Mark's meaning, since the angel says that "you will see him there" (rather than along the way).

A number of scholars of the previous generation argued that Jesus' words in 14:28 and 16:7 referred not to resurrection appearances, but to the promise of the parousia. Jesus' disciples were commanded to go to Galilee and wait for his second coming.[19] From this perspective, there were no resurrection appearances predicted in Mark, but only the continued hope and expectation for Christ's return. This view has been generally rejected in recent years.[20]

Stein summarizes well the evidence against it.[21] (1) Since Peter had likely died by the time Mark's gospel was written, it would make no sense to Mark's readers to portray him awaiting the parousia in Galilee (16:7). (2) In light of the well-attested tradition that Peter received a personal resurrection appearance (Luke 24:34; 1 Cor 15:5), readers would surely connect 16:7 with this tradition rather than with the parousia. (3) The present tense in 16:7 (compare the future tense in 14:28) shows that the resurrection appearance will happen shortly, something that was not true of the parousia. (4) The parousia is never elsewhere portrayed as Jesus' awaiting his disciples in Galilee. We could add to this that Matthew's gospel will end with this resurrection appearance in Galilee (Matt 28:16 – 20; cf. John 21:1 – 23), which confirms that this is how he understood the angel's words in Mark.

16:8 Leaving, they fled from the tomb, because trembling and amazement seized them, and they said nothing to anyone, for they were afraid (Καὶ ἐξελθοῦσαι ἔφυγον ἀπὸ τοῦ μνημείου, εἶχεν γὰρ αὐτὰς τρόμος καὶ ἔκστασις· καὶ οὐδενὶ οὐδὲν εἶπαν·

18. Evans, "I Will Go before You into Galilee," 3 – 18; Hooker, *Mark*, 345; Evans, *Mark 8:27 – 16:20*, 401 – 2.

19. Lohmeyer, *Markus*, 355 – 58; Marxsen, *Mark the Evangelist*, 75 – 92; Nineham, *Mark*, 446; Weeden, *Mark — Traditions in Conflict*, 111 – 16; Kelber, *The Kingdom in Mark*, 129 – 47; J. D. Crossan, "Empty Tomb and Absent Lord (Mark 16:1 – 8)," in *The Passion in Mark* (ed. W. H. Kelber; Philadelphia: Fortress, 1976), 135 – 52; Nicholas Perrin, *The Resurrection Narratives: A*

New Approach (London: SPCK, 1977), 17 – 40.

20. See esp. Robert H. Stein, "A Short Note on Mark XIV.28 and XVI.7," *NTS* 20 (1973): 445 – 52; Ernst Best, *Mark: The Gospel as Story* (Edinburgh: T&T Clark, 1983), 72 – 78; Kingsbury, *Christology of Mark's Gospel*, 25 – 45; Marcus, *Mark 1 – 8*, 73 – 79; A. T. Lincoln, "The Promise and the Failure: Mark 16:7, 8," *JBL* 108 (1989): 283 – 300.

21. Stein, *Mark*, 732.

ἐφοβοῦντο γάρ). Mark's gospel ends on a puzzling note. Though awe and astonishment are common responses to supernatural works in Mark's gospel (1:27; 2:12; 5:15, 20, 42; 6:2, 51; 7:37), the women's flight from the tomb and their continued silence, "because they were afraid," leaves the reader with a negative perception of what should have been a joyful and triumphant announcement. Many questions are left unanswered. Did the women get over their fear? Did they announce the resurrection? Did they see Jesus alive? Did Peter and the other disciples see Jesus alive?

As noted above (Literary Context), the longer ending of Mark (16:9–20) is almost universally rejected as the work of later copyists (see appendix, below). The question remains whether Mark intended to end his gospel at v. 8 or whether the original ending was either lost or never finished. In the discussion below, we provide arguments for both views, but give a slight edge to the view that Mark intended to end at v. 8.

Arguments for a lost ending. Among those who think 16:8 was not Mark's intended ending, a few have suggested that the gospel was never finished, perhaps due to illness, persecution, arrest, death, or other such circumstances.[22] Most, however, assume that the ending was somehow lost before it was first copied.[23] The following are arguments for this view:

(1) The present ending (16:8) is grammatically odd and jarring. It is unusual to end a Greek sentence with a "for" (γάρ) and almost without precedence to end a book this way.[24]

(2) The presence of the shorter and longer endings confirm that early copyists considered the gospel in its present form to be incomplete. These early readers were in a better position than we are to detect that something was amiss.

(3) In Mark's gospel Jesus repeatedly predicts his resurrection (8:31; 9:9; 9:31; 10:33–34) and specifically that he would see the disciples in Galilee (14:28; 16:7). Since his other predictions concerning his betrayal, arrest, abandonment, trial, denial by Peter, and death were so specifically fulfilled (8:31; 9:9; 9:31; 10:33–34; 14:18–21, 27, 29–30), one would expect this one to be as well.[25]

(4) The explanation of the present ending as an implicit call to response (see discussion below) is too subtle, modern, and existential to have occurred to Mark's first-century readers.[26] As Edwards points out, "ancient texts ... with very few exceptions show a dogged proclivity to state conclusions, not suggest them."[27]

(5) It is unlikely that a gospel that begins with the resounding, "The beginning of the good news about Jesus the Messiah" (1:1), and climaxes with the announcement by the centurion, "Truly this man was the Son of God!" (15:39), would end on such a depressing note of fear, shock, and silence.[28]

(6) There is no doubt that accounts of resurrection appearances were circulating long before Mark's time and that these were available to him (14:28; 16:7). Since the resurrection was the foundation of the apostolic gospel (1 Cor 15:3–8) and essential to Mark's theology (8:31; 9:9, 31; 10:34; 14:28; 16:7), it seems inexplicable that he would not narrate such appearances.

22. So Cranfield, *Mark*, 471.

23. Recent supporters include Gundry, *Mark*, 1009–12; Evans, *Mark 8:27–16:20*, 539; Witherington, *Mark*, 42–49; Edwards, *Markus*, 500–504; France, *Mark*, 671–76; Wright, *Resurrection of the Son of God*, 617–24; Stein, *Mark*, 734–37; idem, "The Ending of Mark," *BBR* 18 (2008): 79–98. For a fuller list through the history of scholarship, see appendix A in Croy, *Mutilation of Mark's Gospel*, 174–77.

24. See the evidence presented in P. L. Danove, *The End of Mark's Story: A Methodological Study* (Leiden: Brill, 1993), 128–29.

25. France, *Mark*, 672; Stein, *Mark*, 734.
26. France, *Mark*, 671–72.
27. Edwards, *Mark*, 501.
28. Ibid.; Stein, *Mark*, 735–36.

These arguments, though strong, are not decisive. Ending the book with γάρ is indeed awkward (argument 1), but it is not unprecedented, and parallels have been found in ancient literature of sentences, paragraphs, and even books ending with this conjunction (γάρ).[29] It should also be noted that Mark has a number of explanatory comments with γάρ that follow the statement they are explaining or elaborating.[30] This suggests that no continuation of the narrative is necessary after Mark's final clause.

Although there is no doubt that later copyists were uncomfortable with the shorter ending of Mark (argument 2), this does not prove it was not Mark's intention. We can point to dozens of examples where Matthew and Luke "correct" Mark's (apparent) grammatical or theological difficulties.[31] The fact that others are uncomfortable with Mark's ending is hardly an argument against it, since Mark so often surprises. Marcus reminds us that this is the gospel where a young man shows up out of nowhere and then flees naked (14:51–52); Jesus gets angry at someone who asks to be healed (1:41–43) and is sometimes unable to heal or is initially unsuccessful (6:5; 8:23–24); he speaks in parables so that people cannot understand (4:10–12) and curses a fig tree for not producing fruit (11:12–14). "If Mark can create such cryptic

and even shocking scenes, can we be sure that he did not choose to end his work in an abrupt but suggestive manner."[32] (This also relates to arguments 4 and 5.) Mark's proclivity to surprise and his generous use of irony, paradox, and mystery should caution against assuming too quickly that he would provide a straightforward and unambiguous ending.

In response to the arguments related to the necessity of resurrection appearances — either because of Jesus' prophetic predictions (argument 3) or by virtue of the resurrection's centrality in the apostolic gospel (argument 6) — it must be remembered that even in 16:1–8 the resurrection *has* taken place. The angel announces the resurrection and the disciples are assured that they *will* see Jesus in Galilee. The shorter ending does not deny or omit the resurrection; it simply does not narrate resurrection appearances.

Arguments that Mark intended to end at 16:8. While the claim of a lost ending has garnered significant support, the majority of commentators still conclude that Mark intended to end his gospel at 16:8.[33] Among these, some see the ending as wholly negative, a repudiation of the original Jewish disciples and an affirmation of Mark's Gentile church.[34] Others see it as wholly positive, with the women

---

29. Examples of books ending this way include Plotinus, *Enn.* 5.5; Musonius Rufus, *Tractatus XII;* Plato, *Prot.* 328c. See R. H. Lightfoot, *Locality and Doctrine in the Gospels* (New York: Harper, 1938), 11–15; idem, *Gospel Message of Mark,* 80–97; Lincoln, "The Promise," 284; P. W. van der Horst, "Can a Book End with a ΓΑΡ? A Note on Mark XVI.8," *JTS* 23 (1972): 121–24; T. E. Boomershine and G. L. Bartholomew, "The Narrative Technique of Mark 16:8," *JBL* 100 (1981): 213–23, 213 n. 4; S. L. Cox, *A History and Critique of Scholarship concerning the Markan Endings* (Lewiston, NY: Mellen, 1993), 223–27.

30. Collins, *Mark,* 799, citing Olof Linton, "Der vermisste Markusschluss," *Theologishe Blätter* 8 (1929): 229–34. Note esp. 9:6, "for they became terrified" (ἔκφοβοι γὰρ ἐγένοντο) and 11:18, "for they feared him" (ἐφοβοῦντο γὰρ αὐτόν). The final phrase of 16:8 is little different from these, except that it contains two words instead of three, so that the postpositive γάρ must take the final position.

31. Consider, e.g., the Matthean and Lukan redaction of Mark 1:12, 32, 43; 3:4–5, 9; 4:10; 6:5; 10:14.

32. Marcus, *Mark 9–16,* 1093.

33. Supporters of this view include Lightfoot, *Locality and Doctrine in the Gospels;* idem, *Gospel Message of Mark,* 80–97; Lane, *Mark,* 591–92; Hooker, *Mark,* 391–94; Garland, *Mark,* 617–18; Tolbert, *Sowing the Gospel,* 295–96; Best, *Mark: The Gospel as Story,* 132; Danove, *The End of Mark's Story,* 221–22; Marcus, *Mark 9–16,* 1088–96; Moloney, *Mark,* 348–53; Boring, *Mark,* 448–53; Collins, *Mark,* 799–801; idem, "The Empty Tomb in the Gospel according to Mark," in *Hermes and Athena* (ed. E. Stump and T. P. Flint; Notre Dame, IN: University of Notre Dame Press, 1993), 107–40; and many others. For a detailed defense from a literary perspective, see J. L. Magness, *Sense and Absence: Structure and Suspension in the Ending of Mark's Gospel* (Atlanta: Scholars, 1986).

34. Weeden, *Mark — Traditions in Conflict,* 50–51: "Mark

responding not with fear, but with amazement and faith, and their silence as only temporary.[35] Most, however, see Mark's purpose as somewhere in between. The failure of the women, like the failure of the disciples earlier, serves as a positive challenge to the readers to respond with faith — an implicit call to discipleship.[36]

(1) The present ending fits well the overall tenor of mystery and awe that surrounds Jesus' person in Mark's gospel. Characters repeatedly ask, "Who is this?" and the narrative leaves the reader to answer. This same sense of awe and mystery surrounds the closing narrative. The announcement of the resurrection leaves the women awestruck and confused. Mark is implicitly asking his readers, "How will *you* respond to the announcement of the resurrection?"[37]

(2) Similarly, the ending is in line with Mark's characterization, in which all those around Jesus abandon him, except the reader. Boring writes:

> The narrator has permitted the reader to be "with Jesus" the whole time, from beginning to end.... When family rejected him, the reader persisted. When religious leaders, crowds, and disciples misunderstood and abandoned Jesus, the reader stood by him.... Now, the readers stand at the brink of the incomplete narrative in which all have failed, and with terrible restraint, the narrator breaks off the story and leaves the readers ... with a decision to make.[38]

Hooker similarly writes, "This is the end of Mark's story, because it is the beginning of discipleship."[39]

(3) It is almost inconceivable that a final page from the gospel would be lost so early in the transmission process, without a hint of its existence anywhere in the manuscript tradition. This is especially so if, as most scholars assert, Mark was originally written on a scroll rather than a codex.[40]

(4) Even more surprising is that the text would be cut off (or left unfinished) at such a convenient spot of closure.[41] The pericope that began in 16:1 with the women's journey to the tomb ends naturally in 16:8 with their departure from it. If the last page of the original manuscript were lost, we might expect the text to end in the middle of a pericope.

(5) The lack of resurrection appearances is less strange than it might at first sight appear, since the reader already knows these stories well. It is common in ancient literature to allude to well-known events without narrating them.[42]

With such an impressive array of scholars and arguments on both sides, our conclusions must be cautious and tentative. Yet based on the above arguments, we give a small edge to the view that Mark intended to end his gospel on this surprising note. Mark's enigmatic story of Jesus leaves the women (and the disciples) in the same position as Mark's readers — with the resurrection announcement and a call to faith and perseverance. *How will they respond?*

---

is assiduously involved in a vendetta against the disciples. He is intent on totally discrediting them" (in favor of his Gentile church); cf. W. R. Telford, *Mark* (NTG; Sheffield: Sheffield Academic, 1997), 149.

35. See, e.g., Dwyer, *Motif of Wonder,* 185 – 93; E. Schüssler Fiorenza, *In Memory of Her: A Feminist Theological Reconstruction of Christian Origins* (New York: Crossroad, 1983), 316 – 23.

36. For various interpretations, see J. F. Williams, "Literary Approaches to the End of Mark's Gospel," *JETS* 42 (1999): 26 – 35; cf. Stein, "Ending of Mark," 86 – 88.

37. Hooker, *Mark*, 392; Garland, *Mark*, 616.

38. Boring, *Mark*, 449; cf. Moloney, *Mark*, 351 – 52; Lincoln, "The Promise," 283 – 300.

39. Hooker, *Mark*, 394.

40. Moloney, *Mark*, 341. Though the early Christians were likely the first to use the codex, this innovation seems to have arisen in the late first or early second century. See Bruce M. Metzger, *The Text of the New Testament: Its Transmission, Corruption, and Restoration* (2nd ed.; Oxford: Clarendon, 1968), 5 – 8.

41. Marcus, *Mark 9 – 16*, 1091.

42. Garland, *Mark*, 616; Magness, *Sense and Absence*, 30 – 31.

Theology in Application

The Vindication of the Suffering Messiah

It is easy to get bogged down in the complex questions related to the ending of Mark and miss the historical and theological assertion that is crystal clear: *Jesus of Nazareth has risen from the dead!* The Messiah has been vindicated by God, confirming that he is indeed the Son of God, God's agent of redemption whose death paid the ransom price for sins. Whether or not the gospel originally ended at v. 8, the resurrection is an assured fact for Mark and his readers.

This is clear from the nature of Mark's story. As Mark's hero and protagonist, Jesus is an absolutely reliable character, who represents the evaluative point of view of God and the kingdom of God. His predictions concerning his betrayal, arrest, desertion, denial, trial, and crucifixion have precisely come true (8:31; 9:31; 10:33 – 34; 14:18 – 21, 27 – 31). His predictions that he would rise from the dead (8:31; 9:9, 31; 10:34) and that his disciples would see him in Galilee (14:28; 16:7) must also be true — an accomplished fact. We can add to this the testimony of the angel (16:7), also an indisputably reliable character in Mark's story.

By the time Mark wrote, the church had been proclaiming the resurrection for decades as the center point of the apostolic gospel (1 Cor 15:1 – 8). Despite the perplexing ending, Mark leaves his readers with no doubt that Jesus rose from the dead and subsequently appeared to his followers in Galilee. Whether he ended abruptly to provoke his readers to greater faith, or he originally narrated resurrection appearance(s) that were subsequently lost, there can be no doubt that he is calling his readers to faith and action in light of the certain victory of God.

A Call to Faith and Perseverance

Though the christological theme of the vindication of the Messiah is central for Mark, he is also calling his readers to faith and perseverance. The confusion, fear, and silence that the women disciples exhibit at the end is the same response that Jesus' disciples have shown throughout the second half of Mark's gospel. Amazed by Jesus' power to heal the sick, cast out demons, feed the multitudes, calm the sea, and walk on water, they are nevertheless confused by his teaching, plagued by pride and self-interest, and bewildered by his predictions of his coming death. Peter confesses that Jesus' mighty works confirm he is the Messiah, but he cannot accept that the Messiah will suffer and die (8:27 – 33). Many of Mark's readers are likely also confused and uncertain. Yes, they believe that Jesus is the Messiah and Son of God, who paid the penalty for their sins. But why is the church not experiencing more victory in the world? Why are the persecutions and ostracism growing more severe? Why are some abandoning the faith?

In the face of such challenges, Mark calls his readers to keep their eyes on Jesus and on the finish line. When agonizing in the garden, Jesus affirmed to the Father, "Not what I want, but what you want" (14:36). When abandoned by his disciples (14:50) and accused of blasphemy before the Sanhedrin, he remained faithful, confessing his messiahship and confidence in God's vindication (14:60 – 64). As the writer to the Hebrews says, "Let us run with perseverance the race marked out for us, fixing our eyes on Jesus, the pioneer and perfecter of faith" (Heb 12:1). Indeed, Mark's readers are not so different from the recipients of Hebrews, and Mark's gospel is a narrative call to the same goal: persevere and stay faithful, and God will vindicate you in the end. This is also the message of Mark for readers today.

The Endings of Mark's Gospel

Though discussions of the ending of Mark relate primarily to the authenticity of 16:9 – 20 and whether Mark intended to end at 16: 8, there are actually four endings in the manuscript tradition. These are:

(1) The short ending, which concludes the gospel at 16:8.

(2) The long ending, which includes 16:9 – 20 (see discussion below).

(3) An intermediate ending[1] that reads, "They quickly reported all these instructions to those around Peter. And after this Jesus himself also sent out through them from east to west the sacred and imperishable proclamation of eternal salvation. Amen."[2] This variant appears with minor differences in four uncial manuscripts from the seventh, eighth, and ninth centuries (L [020], Ψ [044], 099, 0112), the Old Latin manuscript k (it[k]), the margin of the Harclean Syriac (syr[hmg]), several Sahidic (sah[mss]) and Bohairic (boh[mss]) manuscripts, and a number of Ethiopian (eth[mss]) manuscripts. All of these continue with 16:9 – 20, with the exception of it[k], where the shorter ending stands alone after 16:8. Both the external and internal evidence are overwhelmingly against this reading. Its textual evidence is weak and it contains non-Markan words and style.[3]

(4) The so-called Freer Logion, which occurs after v. 14 in only one extant manuscript, Codex Washingtonianus (W or 032), was also attested by the early church father Jerome (*Pelag.* 2.15). It reads:

> And they excused themselves, saying, "This age of lawlessness and unbelief is under Satan, who does not allow the truth and power of God to prevail over the unclean things of the spirits. Therefore, reveal thy righteousness now" — thus they spoke to Christ. And Christ replied to them, "The term of years of Satan's power has been fulfilled, but other terrible things draw near. And for those who have sinned I was delivered over to death, that they may return to the truth and sin no more, in order

---

1. See Daniel B. Wallace, "Mark 16:8 as the Conclusion to the Second Gospel," in *Perspectives on the Ending of Mark: 4 Views* (ed. D. A. Black; Nashville: Broadman & Holman, 2008), 1 – 39, esp. 24 – 25.

2. Πάντα δὲ τὰ παρηγγελμένα τοῖς περὶ τὸν Πέτρον συντόμως ἐξήγγειλαν. Μετὰ δὲ ταῦτα καὶ αὐτὸς ὁ Ἰησοῦς ἀπὸ ἀνατολῆς καὶ ἄχρι δύσεως ἐξαπέστειλεν δι' αὐτῶν τὸ ἱερὸν καὶ ἄφθαρτον κήρυγμα τῆς αἰωνίου σωτηρίας. ἀμήν.

3. Edwards, *Mark*, 498, points out that 9 of the 34 words don't appear elsewhere in Mark.

that they may inherit the spiritual and incorruptible glory of righteousness which is in heaven."[4]

Appearing in only one manuscript, the reading is clearly secondary. Metzger suggests that it is the work of a second- or third-century scribe who wished to soften the severe condemnation of the Eleven in 16:14.[5]

Of these readings, the Long Ending (vv. 9 – 20) is the only viable alternative to the short ending.[6] Although its external evidence is impressive, the internal evidence is overwhelmingly against it.

External Evidence

The long ending appears in the great majority of manuscripts (over 95 percent) and a diversity of families, including A C D E H K X W Δ Θ P Ψ 099 0112 f^{13} 28 33. Irenaeus and Tatian's *Diatessaron* (both second century) are the earliest patristic witnesses of its existence, indicating that it was in circulation by the middle of the second century. Yet the two oldest uncials, ℵ and B, do not contain these verses. It is also absent from the Old Latin codex Bobiensis (it[k]), the Sinaitic Syrian (syr[s]), about one hundred Armenian manuscripts, and the two oldest Georgian manuscripts (AD 897 and AD 913). Neither Clement of Alexandria nor Origen shows any knowledge of it. Most of the manuscripts known to Eusebius and Jerome did not contain these verses, and a number of manuscripts contain scribal notes saying that they are absent from earlier Greek copies. The original form of the Eusebian sections makes no provision for numbering sections beyond 16:8.[7]

Internal Transcriptional Evidence

While the external evidence is divided, the internal evidence is overwhelmingly against the long ending. We must ask why a copyist would have intentionally dropped the ending, resulting in such an odd and abrupt conclusion. By contrast, it is easy to explain why a copyist would try to "fix" the abrupt ending by summarizing resurrection appearances and including Jesus' final commission. The longer ending appears to be a compilation of postresurrection events from the other gospels. Verses 9 – 10, for example, recount the appearance to Mary Magdalene found in John 20:11 – 18, and the reference to her healing from demonization comes from Luke 8:2; vv. 12 – 13 summarize Luke's account of the Emmaus disciples (Luke 24:13 – 35); Jesus' commission, ascension, and the worldwide proclamation by the apostles (vv. 15 – 20) summarize themes from Luke 24 and Acts.

---

4. Cited from Metzger, *Textual Commentary*, 104.

5. Ibid.

6. The most important scholarly defense of the long ending is W. R. Farmer, *The Last Twelve Verses of Mark* (Cambridge: Cambridge University Press, 1974).

7. Metzger, *Textual Commentary*, 102 – 6.

The intermediate ending (see above) itself provides indirect evidence against the longer reading, since it attests to the latter's absence in the early tradition. As Metzger writes, "No one who had available as the conclusion of the Second Gospel the twelve verses 9 – 20, so rich in interesting material, would have deliberately replaced them with a few lines of a colorless and generalized summary."[8]

Internal Intrinsic Evidence

Most telling against the longer ending is its disjuncture with the rest of Mark's narrative. The vocabulary and style is distinctly non-Markan, with fifteen words that do not appear elsewhere in Mark and a number of others used with a different sense than typical Markan usage.[9] The connection with what precedes is awkward. Verse 9 begins with a masculine participle referring to Jesus, but the previous verse has as its subject the women. Mary Magdalene is introduced as if she were a new character ("from whom he had cast out seven demons"), even though she has been present in the previous three episodes (15:40, 47; 16:1). The other women who were commissioned by the angel to tell the disciples in 16:7 now disappear from the scene, and only Mary sees Jesus and reports to the disciples (as in John 20). Finally, while the angel spoke about appearances in Galilee (v. 7), the longer ending relates only appearances in and around Jerusalem.

The theology of the section is also different from Mark's. Speaking in tongues (v. 17) and confirmation of the gospel through signs (vv. 17 – 20) are more characteristic of Acts than Mark (Acts 2:3 – 4; 4:30; 5:12; 10:46; 19:6). Picking up snakes with their hands and drinking poison without harm (v. 18) are certainly non-Markan ideas.

A translation and brief commentary on these verses follows.

Explanation of the Text

16:9 After arising early on the first day of the week, he appeared first to Mary Magdalene, from whom he had cast out seven demons (Ἀναστὰς δὲ πρωῒ πρώτῃ σαββάτου ἐφάνη πρῶτον Μαρίᾳ τῇ Μαγδαληνῇ, παρ' ἧς ἐκβεβλήκει ἑπτὰ δαιμόνια). As noted above, the transition is awkward, since Jesus is not specifically named and there is no clear antecedent to the masculine nominative participle "arising" in 16:9. Also odd is the description of Mary Magdalene, as though she had not been introduced to the readers, but she has been a character in the previous three episodes (15:40; 15:47; 16:1). Although "early" (πρωῒ) is a Markan word (1:35; 11:20; 13:35; 15:1; 16:2), a different word for "first [day]" (πρώτῃ) of the week is used than in 16:2 (μία). The description of Mary Magdalene

---

8. Ibid., 105.

9. See J. K. Elliot, "The Text and Language of the Endings of Mark's Gospel," *TZ* 27 (1971), 258 – 62; Metzger, *Textual Commentary*, 104; Bratcher and Nida, *Handbook on Mark*, 519ff.;

Edwards, *Mark*, 498 n. 4. For a recent evaluation of the longer ending using a stylistic analysis, see Travis B. Williams, "Bringing Method to the Madness: Examining the Style of the Longer Ending of Mark," *BBR* 20 (2010): 397 – 418.

comes from Luke 8:2, though there the demons are the subject of the verb and no agent is named: "from whom seven demons had come out."

16:10 Going, she reported this to those who had been with him, while they were mourning and weeping (ἐκείνη πορευθεῖσα ἀπήγγειλεν τοῖς μετ᾽ αὐτοῦ γενομένοις πενθοῦσι καὶ κλαίουσιν). "Those who had been with them" refers to the disciples. The scene recalls John 20:18, where Mary announces to the disciples that she has seen Jesus. The reference to the disciples "mourning and weeping" is unique to the resurrection narratives, though Peter is seen weeping after denying Jesus a third time (Mark 14:72).

16:11 When they heard that he was alive and had been seen by her, they did not believe it (κἀκεῖνοι ἀκούσαντες ὅτι ζῇ καὶ ἐθεάθη ὑπ᾽ αὐτῆς ἠπίστησαν). The disbelief of the women's report by the disciples recalls Luke 24:11, where the women's report of the resurrection "seemed to them like nonsense." The verb "see" (θεάομαι) is common in John, but appears nowhere else in Mark.[10]

16:12 – 13 After these things, he appeared in a different form to two of them while they were walking in the country. After returning, they reported to the rest; but they did not believe them either (Μετὰ δὲ ταῦτα δυσὶν ἐξ αὐτῶν περιπατοῦσιν ἐφανερώθη ἐν ἑτέρᾳ μορφῇ πορευομένοις εἰς ἀγρόν. κἀκεῖνοι ἀπελθόντες ἀπήγγειλαν τοῖς λοιποῖς· οὐδὲ ἐκείνοις ἐπίστευσαν). Verses 12 – 13 are clearly a summary of the account of the Emmaus disciples in Luke 24:13 – 35, who were traveling in the countryside between Jerusalem and Emmaus when Jesus encountered them. "In another form" alludes to the fact that in Luke 24:16 the two disciples "were kept from recognizing him." Luke similarly

records that they returned to Jerusalem and told the disciples what they had seen (24:33 – 35). The response of disbelief is taken from 24:41.

16:14 Later he appeared to the Eleven as they reclined at a meal and rebuked their unbelief and hardheartedness because they did not believe those who had seen him after he had risen (Ὕστερον δὲ ἀνακειμένοις αὐτοῖς τοῖς ἕνδεκα ἐφανερώθη καὶ ὠνείδισεν τὴν ἀπιστίαν αὐτῶν καὶ σκληροκαρδίαν ὅτι τοῖς θεασαμένοις αὐτὸν ἐγηγερμένον οὐκ ἐπίστευσαν). This "later" appearance to the Eleven as they "reclined at a meal" (ἀνακειμένοις) apparently continues from Luke's account, where the meal is implied by Jesus' request for food (Luke 24:41). The "rebuke" described here probably reflects Jesus' words in Luke 24:38 not to be troubled or to let doubts rise in their minds. Rebuke for unbelief also appears in John 20:19, 26. The so-called Freer Logion (see discussion above) appears at this point in Codex W.

16:15 He said to them, "When you go into all the world preach the gospel to every creature." (καὶ εἶπεν αὐτοῖς· πορευθέντες εἰς τὸν κόσμον ἅπαντα κηρύξατε τὸ εὐαγγέλιον πάσῃ τῇ κτίσει). The call to preach the gospel to every creature recalls Matthew's Great Commission to make disciples of all nations (28:18 – 20) as well as the command in Acts 1:8 to be Jesus' witnesses to the ends of the earth.

16:16 Whoever believes and is baptized will be saved, but whoever does not believe will be condemned (ὁ πιστεύσας καὶ βαπτισθεὶς σωθήσεται, ὁ δὲ ἀπιστήσας κατακριθήσεται). For a close connection between faith and baptism, see Acts 2:38. For condemnation resulting from failure to believe, see John 3:17 – 18, 36.

---

10. Taylor, *Mark*, 611.

16:17 And these signs will accompany those who believe: in my name they will cast out demons; they will speak in new tongues (σημεῖα δὲ τοῖς πιστεύσασιν ταῦτα παρακολουθήσει· ἐν τῷ ὀνόματί μου δαιμόνια ἐκβαλοῦσιν, γλώσσαις λαλήσουσιν καιναῖς). The Johannine language found in v. 16 continues here with the promise of confirmatory signs (John 14:12). Confirmatory signs also appear throughout Acts (see esp. Acts 5:12). In Acts the apostles cast out demons (16:18) and speak in tongues (2:4; 10:46; 19:6).

16:18 "They will pick up snakes with their hands; and if anyone drinks deadly poison, it will not hurt them; they will place their hands on sick people, and they will get well." (καὶ ἐν ταῖς χερσὶν ὄφεις ἀροῦσιν κἂν θανάσιμόν τι πίωσιν οὐ μὴ αὐτοὺς βλάψῃ, ἐπὶ ἀρρώστους χεῖρας ἐπιθήσουσιν καὶ καλῶς ἕξουσιν). Jesus' assurance related to snakes recalls Jesus' promise of protection in Luke 10:19: "I have given you authority to trample on snakes and scorpions." The promise is fulfilled in Acts 28:3–6 on Malta during Paul's voyage to Rome, where he is bitten by a poisonous snake but not harmed. Healing by laying on of hands is found in 9:12, 17; 28:8. It hardly needs to be stated that the promises of protection here and in Luke 10:19 were never intended to justify the kind of snake-handling "worship" services practiced by some sects (often with injurious and even fatal consequences).

16:19 Then, after the Lord Jesus had spoken to them, he was taken up into heaven and sat at the right hand of God (Ὁ μὲν οὖν κύριος Ἰησοῦς μετὰ τὸ λαλῆσαι αὐτοῖς ἀνελήμφθη εἰς τὸν οὐρανὸν καὶ ἐκάθισεν ἐκ δεξιῶν τοῦ θεοῦ). The title "Lord Jesus" is found in Acts 1:21; 4:33; 7:59 and in Paul (Rom 14:14; 1 Cor 5:4, 5; 11:23), but nowhere else in Mark or the other gospels.[11] Jesus' ascension is elsewhere described at the end of Luke's gospel (Luke 24:51) and the beginning of Acts (Acts 1:2–11; cf. 1 Tim 3:16). Allusions to Psalm 110:1 ("Sit at my right hand") appear throughout the NT (Matt 22:44; 26:64; Mark 12:36; 14:62; Luke 20:42; 22:69; Acts 2:33, 34; 5:31; 7:55; Rom 8:34; Eph 1:20; Col 3:1; Heb 1:3, 13; 8:1; 10:12; 12:2; 1 Pet 3:22).

16:20 Then the disciples went out and preached everywhere, and the Lord worked with them and confirmed his word by the signs that accompanied it (ἐκεῖνοι δὲ ἐξελθόντες ἐκήρυξαν πανταχοῦ, τοῦ κυρίου συνεργοῦντος καὶ τὸν λόγον βεβαιοῦντος διὰ τῶν ἐπακολουθούντων σημείων). Here we have a general summary of the book of Acts, though the language of the first clause recalls the mission of the Twelve in Luke 9:6, who "set out and went from village to village, proclaiming the good news and healing people everywhere." For confirmatory signs, see comments on v. 17, above.

---

11. Evans, *Mark 8:27–16:20*, 549.

The Theology of Mark

The Identity of Jesus

There is little doubt that Christology is central to Mark's theological purpose. The opening line makes this clear: "The beginning of the good news about *Jesus the Messiah*" (1:1). In addition to this heading, the gospel is framed on either side with acclamations of Jesus' identity — from God's announcement that Jesus is "my beloved Son" at his baptism (1:11) to the cry of the centurion at the foot of the cross (15:39). The identity of Jesus is on center stage throughout the gospel. The question, "Who is this?" hangs in the air, expressed both explicitly or implicitly:

1. The people of Capernaum are astonished at Jesus' teaching and power to cast out demons, wondering, "What is this? A new teaching with authority!" (1:27).

2. The religious leaders are appalled at Jesus' claim to forgive sins and ask skeptically, "Who can forgive sins except God?" (2:7).

3. The disciples stand awestruck when Jesus calms the sea, asking, "Who, then, is this, that the wind and the sea obey him!" (4:41).

4. The people of Jesus' hometown marvel at his wisdom and miracles and wonder, "Isn't this the carpenter, the son of Mary?" (6:3).

5. Herod Antipas hears about Jesus and speculates about his identity, whether he might be John the Baptist risen from the dead (6:16).

6. The initial climax of the gospel comes when Jesus asks his disciples who *the people* think he is and who *they* believe he is (8:27 – 29).

7. In the end, Jesus is crucified when he answers affirmatively to the high priest's question, "Are you the Messiah, the Son of the Blessed One?" (14:61).

Mark's Christological Purpose

Mark christological purpose is to show that Jesus is indeed the mighty Messiah predicted in Scripture, but that his surprising role is to suffer and die as a sacrifice for sin. The so-called "messianic secret" in Mark[1] is really no secret at all, but serves to emphasize the importance of knowing Jesus' identity and mission and to dramatize its progressive revelation. Jesus silences demons "because they knew who he was" (1:34; cf. 1:25; 3:11 – 12; 5:7) and later warns his disciples not (yet) to disclose his identity as the Messiah (8:30; cf. 9:9).

There is a gradual revelation of his identity as the narrative progresses. While the reader is informed from the beginning that Jesus is the Messiah (1:1), at first only characters from the supernatural realm know who he is. God calls him "my beloved Son" (1:11; cf. 9:7), and demons repeatedly cry out that they know (and fear) him (1:24, 34; 3:11 – 12; 5:7). Not until Peter's confession in 8:30 does the first human character finally acknowledge that Jesus is "the Messiah" (8:29). Even then, Peter's knowledge is incomplete, and he cannot comprehend the Messiah's suffering role (8:32 – 33).

It is ultimately a Gentile centurion who recognizes that *in his passion* Jesus' identity is ultimately revealed: "Truly this man was the Son of God!" (15:39). Mark's primary christological purpose is to confirm that all along it was part of God's purpose and plan that his Messiah would suffer and die as a ransom for sins (10:45).

A "Low" Christology?

It is sometimes said that Mark has a "low" Christology when compared to the other gospels. This is not quite right. It would be better to describe Mark's Christology as enigmatic and paradoxical. To be sure, Mark presents the most human and down-to-earth portrait of Jesus. Jesus expresses a range of human emotions, including indignation (1:41; 10:14), exasperation (8:12; 9:19), anger and grief (3:5), sorrow (3:5), amazement (6:6), love (10:21), and overwhelming anxiety and distress (14:33 – 34; 15:34). His knowledge is limited — only the Father, not the Son, knows the day and hour of the end times (13:32). At times Jesus seems limited in his miraculous powers. He is unable to do many miracles in his hometown because of their lack of faith (6:5) and must heal a blind man in two stages (8:22 – 26).

At the same time, the narrative exhibits an extraordinarily high Christology. Jesus knows the thoughts and hearts of his opponents (2:8; 3:5). He forgives sins, a prerogative of God alone (2:9), and raises the dead (5:41 – 42). Though God himself established Israel's law, Jesus claims authority over it. He is Lord of the Sabbath (2:28) and apparently reverses the dietary laws of the OT (7:14 – 18). Just as Yahweh called Israel into being as a nation, so Jesus appoints the Twelve, representing a new Israel. It is significant that Jesus does not identify himself as one of the Twelve, but sets himself above them as their Lord, just as Yahweh is Israel's Creator and Lord.

---

1. See the Introduction to Mark, Mark's Gospel in Historical Perspective; also the comments on 1:25.

Other actions and attributes recall the actions and attributes of God. The feeding miracles (6:32 – 44; 8:1 – 9) recall God's ability to send manna from heaven (Exod 16) and to bring forth food from the earth (Ps 104:14). Calming the storm (Mark 4:35 – 41) reminds the reader of Yahweh's mastery over the sea's primeval chaos: "You rule over the surging sea; when its waves mount up, you still them" (Ps 89:9; cf. 65:5 – 7; 107:23 – 29). Walking on water (Mark 6:45 – 51) is a divine act, since God alone "treads on the waves of the sea" (Job 9:8; cf. Ps 77:19; Isa 43:16; 51:10; Sir 24:5 – 6). In this latter event, Jesus' intention to "pass by" the disciples is probably theophanic language, since the God of the OT reveals himself by "passing before" his people (cf. Exod 33:18 – 23; 1 Kgs 19:10 – 12).

The Christological Titles: Messiah, Son of God, Son of Man

The identity of Jesus is revealed in the narrative in a variety of ways: by Jesus' actions, by the response of others to him, and by the titles used of him. Three titles are particularly important for Mark: Messiah, Son of God, and Son of Man.

(1) Mark introduces Jesus as the "Messiah" or "Christ" (ὁ χριστός) in his opening line, making this the foundational category for Mark's Christology. The title represents the Greek translation of the Hebrew *māšîaḥ*, originally meaning "anointed one." Though various leaders in Israel — prophets, priests, and kings — were set apart for God's service by being anointed with oil, by the first century the title "Anointed One," or "Messiah," was coming into use as a title for the eschatological king from the line of David (see 2 Sam 7; Pss 2; 89; 110; Isa 9; 11; Jer 23:5 – 6; Ezek 34:23 – 24; see comments on 1:1). With David, Israel's greatest king, as the model and prototype, this figure was generally viewed as a warrior king who would purge Israel of her unrighteous rulers, defeat Israel's enemies, and reign over a gloriously restored Israel in righteousness and justice as God's vice-regent (see *Pss. Sol.* 17 – 18).[2]

Unlike Matthew and Luke, who introduce their gospels with birth narratives identifying Jesus as the heir to the Davidic throne and with genealogies tracing his Davidic ancestry, Mark does not explicitly identify Jesus as the Davidic Messiah. Yet this identification is confirmed from the account of the healing of blind Bartimaeus, who twice cries out to Jesus as "Son of David" (10:47, 48) — a messianic title (cf. *Pss. Sol.* 17:21) — just before Jesus' royal entrance into Jerusalem. Mark's juxtaposition of this cry with the shout of the crowds as Jesus approaches the city ("Blessed is the coming kingdom of our father David!" 11:10) and with Jesus' implicit fulfillment of the royal Davidic prophecy of Zech 9:9 ("See, your king comes ... lowly and riding on a donkey") confirms that Mark views Jesus as the eschatological Savior and King from David's line.[3]

---

2. See Strauss, *Davidic Messiah*, 35 – 74.

3. Robbins, "The Healing of Blind Bartimaeus," 224 – 43; Kingsbury, *Christology of Mark's Gospel*, 102 – 8; Strauss, *Davidic Messiah*, 68 – 69.

Yet Mark also sees Jesus as more than the traditional Messiah. During his debates with the religious leaders in Jerusalem, Jesus poses the riddle of how the experts in the law can say that the Messiah is David's son, since David himself calls him "Lord" in Ps 110:1 – 2 (Mark 12:35 – 37). Though the riddle goes unanswered in Mark's narrative, the implication is that Jesus is *more* than the traditional Jewish expectations concerning the Messiah.

The inadequacies of traditional messianism become clearer in Mark's crucial central section (8:22 – 10:52). After Peter correctly identifies Jesus as the Messiah (ὁ χριστός), Jesus begins to teach that he must suffer and die (8:27 – 30). When Peter rebukes him — no doubt because Jesus is challenging traditional messianic expectations — Jesus rebukes Peter back, accusing him of pursuing Satan's agenda, not God's. The Messiah's mission is to suffer and die, and his disciples must be willing to follow him on this suffering path (8:33 – 38). This theme is repeated twice more in the context of the next two passion predictions (9:20 – 37; 10:32 – 45). Jesus radically redefines the role of the Davidic Messiah as one of suffering and sacrifice.

(2) If "Messiah" is a true but inadequate description of Jesus' identify, "Son of God" captures more clearly the essence of Mark's Christology.[4] Whether or not this title was originally part of the opening line (see comments on 1:1), acclamations of Jesus' divine sonship still frame the whole gospel. At Jesus' baptism the Father announces, "You are my beloved Son" (1:11), and at the climax the centurion cries out, "Truly this man was the Son of God!" (15:39). The title often carries a messianic sense, nearly synonymous with "Christ/Messiah."

This usage comes from the Davidic promise tradition, where David was promised that his "seed" (= descendant) would reign forever on his throne and would have a unique father-son relationship with God (2 Sam 7:14; cf. Pss 2:7; 89:26). At Jesus' trial before the Sanhedrin in Mark 14:61, the high priest links divine sonship with Jesus' messianic identity: "Are you the Messiah, the Son of the Blessed One?" (σὺ εἶ ὁ χριστὸς ὁ υἱὸς τοῦ εὐλογητοῦ;). Similarly, demonic acknowledgment that Jesus is "God's Holy One" (= the Messiah; 1:24) parallels recognition that he is the "Son of God" (3:11) and "Son of the Most High God" (5:7).

Yet for Mark "Son of God" goes beyond merely messianic (royal) categories. When Peter confesses that Jesus is the Messiah (ὁ χριστός), the title must be sharply qualified by Jesus' definition of the Messiah's suffering role (8:31 – 33). Similarly, Jesus' question about the Messiah as David's son (12:35 – 37) indicates that traditional messianic categories are inadequate to describe the One who is *both* David's son and David's Lord. By contrast, Jesus' divine sonship more comprehensively sums

---

4. The title is widely acknowledged as Mark's most important one. See especially Kingsbury, *Christology of Mark's Gospel*, who writes: "because Mark binds the secret of Jesus' identity more narrowly to the truth of his divine sonship, and because 'Son of God' is the sole title that constitutes the 'evaluative point of view' concerning Jesus' identity of supernatural beings and human characters alike, Mark may be said to describe Jesus more singularly as the royal Son of God" (173). Many others have followed Kingsbury in this assessment.

up Jesus' identity. "My beloved Son" is the title God himself uses to address Jesus at both the baptism (1:11) and the transfiguration (9:7). The demons, who are privy to supernatural realities, acknowledge that this One with absolute authority over them is God's own Son (3:11; 5:7).

Though the parable of the tenant farmers is allegorical (12:1 – 12), the description of the owner's final representative as a unique and "beloved son" (υἱὸν ἀγαπητόν; 12:6) echoes the divine voice from heaven at the baptism and transfiguration (1:11; 9:7), revealing Jesus' fundamental identity. Finally, the title's appearance in the centurion's climactic cry at the cross (15:39) serves as Mark's final answer to the question "Who is this person?" Though it would be going too far to say that "Son of God" carries the full Trinitarian sense of the later creeds, the title certainly points beyond traditional messianism to the One who has a unique relationship of intimacy with the Father and speaks and acts with God's authority: forgiving sins, exercising authority over the Sabbath, commanding the sea, walking on water, and raising the dead.

(3) If the title "Christ" identifies Jesus as the fulfillment of Israel's promised salvation and "Son of God" confirms a relationship of unique intimacy with the Father, "Son of Man" serves as an important bridge between Jesus' messianic identity, his suffering role, and his glorious vindication. This title is Jesus' favorite self-designation, appearing fourteen times in Mark's gospel, always on the lips of Jesus.[5] The phrase is an unusual one in Greek (ὁ υἱὸς τοῦ ἀνθρώπου), a literal rendering of the Hebrew (*ben-ʾādām*) and/or Aramaic (*bar-ʾenāš*), both of which mean "human being." The expression can simply mean "a person" or "mankind," but is often used with reference to the lowliness of humanity in contrast to the majesty of God. Psalm 8:4 reads, "What is man [*ʾenôš*] that you are mindful of him, the son of man (*ben-ʾādām*) that you care for him?" (NIV 1984). In Ezekiel the phrase is used ninety-three times in God's address to the prophet (NRSV, "O mortal").

It has long been recognized that there are three types of Son of Man sayings in Mark (and the Synoptics generally): those related to the earthly authority of the Son of Man (2:10, 28), those concerning his suffering, death, and resurrection (8:31; 9:9, 12, 31; 10:33, 45; 14:21 [2x], 41), and those related to his coming in glory and power (8:38; 13:26; 14:62). This last category alludes to Dan 7:13 – 14, where a glorified messianic figure — "one like a son of man [= a human being]" — comes with the clouds of heaven and appears before the Ancient of Days (God himself). He is given universal power, glory, and an eternal kingdom. There may also be a link in Daniel to the suffering role of the Son of Man. In the larger context of Dan 7, this exalted figure is identified with the corporate people of God, who are persecuted and oppressed but ultimately vindicated, inheriting "the sovereignty, power and greatness of all the kingdoms under heaven" (Dan 7:27; cf. 7:21 – 22, 26 – 27).

---

5. With the possible exception of 2:10, 28, where it may be the narrator's comment; see commentary there.

Mark appears to use Son of Man as a title qualifying and clarifying Jesus' messianic role. At two key points in Mark's narrative Jesus' identity as the Messiah (ὁ χριστός) is affirmed, but then sharply qualified with a Son of Man saying. First, after Peter's confession ("You are the Messiah"; 8:29), Jesus predicts the Son of Man will suffer and die (8:31), returning again and again to this theme (9:12, 31; 10:33, 45; 14:21). Second, after being questioned before the high priest whether he is "the Messiah, the Son of the Blessed One," Jesus affirms that he is, but then describes his vindication, "And you will see the Son of Man sitting at the right hand of Power and coming with the clouds of heaven" (14:61 – 62; citing Ps 110:1; Dan 7:13). By adopting Son of Man as his primary self-designation, the Markan Jesus not only avoids the traditional political connotations of messianic titles like "Messiah" and "Son of David," but also redefines his role with reference to the Danielic Son of Man, whose suffering role will be followed by his heavenly vindication.

In summary, Jesus likely adopted the Son of Man title (a) to identify with humanity, and especially the oppressed and suffering people of God; (b) to declare his messiahship in a veiled manner, without the political connotations of other messianic titles and in a manner that he himself could define; and (c) to identify himself as the Danielic Son of Man, who after suffering would be vindicated and exalted to a position of glory, honor, and power.

The Message and Mission of Jesus

How does Jesus' identity relate to his message and mission? As the Messiah, Jesus' primary role is to accomplish God's salvation and to establish his kingdom.

Proclaiming and Inaugurating the Kingdom of God

Jesus' central message in Mark's gospel is the kingdom of God (1:14 – 15; 4:11, 26, 30; 9:1, 47; 10:14, 15, 23 – 25; 12:34; 14:25; 15:43). At the beginning of his public ministry, Jesus comes into Galilee proclaiming the good news of God: "The time is fulfilled, the kingdom of God is close at hand; repent and believe in the good news" (Mark 1:15). But what is the kingdom of God? Though the specific phrase is absent from the OT and rare in Judaism, the concept of God's reign or rule is pervasive. God is the sovereign Lord of the universe and reigns as King over all things. Exodus 15:18 says, "The LORD reigns for ever and ever" (cf. Pss 29:10; 47:7; 97:1; 99:1; 103:19; Isa 43:15).

Yet this universal reign is not yet acknowledged by all, and the present world stands in rebellion against God. The reign of God is therefore both a present reality and a future hope. Isaiah 24:23 predicts that one day "the LORD Almighty will reign on Mount Zion and in Jerusalem, and before its elders — with great glory" (cf. 33:22; 52:7; Zeph 3:15; Zech 14:9 – 21). The apocalyptic Judaism of Jesus' day emphasized this future aspect of the kingdom. Facing oppression and hardship, Israel longed for the day when God would return to save his people, judge the wicked, and establish his eternal kingdom (cf. *1 En.* 1:3 – 9). Though expectations differed among various groups within Judaism, this hope commonly centered on the messianic King from the line of David, who would reign as God's vice-regent in peace, justice, and righteousness (cf. Isa 9:6 – 7; Jer 23:5 – 6; *Pss. Sol.* 17 – 18).

What does Mark mean by the "kingdom of God"? In some respects, Jesus' teaching in Mark recalls apocalyptic Judaism, with its emphasis on future kingdom and coming judgment. Jesus says that some of his disciples "will certainly not taste death until they see the kingdom of God come in power" (9:1). Joseph of Arimathea is portrayed as "waiting for the kingdom of God" (15:43), and at the Last Supper Jesus says he will not drink the fruit of the vine with his disciples again until the coming of the kingdom (14:25). These apocalyptic elements are enhanced when seen in the light of Jesus' teaching concerning the future coming of the Son of Man "with great power and glory … [to] gather his chosen ones" (13:26 – 32; cf. 8:38; 13:33 – 34; 14:62).

Yet there are also present spiritual dimensions to the kingdom. Jesus teaches that the prerequisite for entrance into the kingdom is to "receive" the kingdom like a child in the present (10:15), and he tells a scribe that he is not far from the kingdom of God (12:34). The kingdom is in some ways mysterious and unseen. In his "parables of the kingdom," Jesus compares the kingdom to seed that grows secretly and mysteriously, yet persistently until harvest day (4:26 – 29). It is like a mustard seed that expands from something tiny to something vast (4:31 – 32). The "secret" or "mystery" of the kingdom of God is intentionally hidden from those who oppose Jesus but has been revealed to his disciples (4:11). The kingdom is difficult to enter for those who are rich and must be received like a little child, presumably meaning in faith and dependence (10:14 – 15, 23 – 25). To enter the kingdom of God means to "inherit eternal life" (10:17, 25), to "enter into [true] life," and to avoid the fires of Gehenna (9:43 – 48). The kingdom is clearly both "already" and "not yet." It comes to individuals in the present by faith and will be consummated in heaven and on earth in the eschaton.

To comprehend more fully the nature of the kingdom in Mark, we must move beyond passages that speak explicitly about the kingdom, since Mark places the whole ministry of Jesus under the banner of the kingdom of God (1:14 – 15). Five key themes help to define the nature of the kingdom in Mark.

(1) Jesus' ministry represents the fulfillment of Scripture. From his first line, Mark places Jesus' life and ministry under the banner of the fulfillment of Scripture, and more specifically, as part of Isaiah's prediction of eschatological salvation (1:2; Isa 40:3; Mal 3:1). "The beginning of the good news about Jesus the Messiah" came to pass "just as it is written in Isaiah the prophet" (Mark 1:1 – 2). Jesus repeatedly stresses that all that is happening to him is in fulfillment of Scripture (9:12 – 13; 11:17; 12:10; 14:21, 27, 49). Yet, unlike Matthew, where statements of Scripture fulfillment are scattered throughout his gospel, in Mark these statements occur almost

exclusively with reference to Jesus' passion. The implication is that the coming of the kingdom announced by Jesus is not only the culmination of God's purpose and plan set forth in the Hebrew Scriptures, but results from Jesus' sacrificial death on the cross.

(2) The kingdom involves the restoration of Israel. Jesus' appointment of the Twelve (3:13 – 19) and his focus on their training throughout Mark's gospel implies that Jesus' ministry is in some sense a reconstitution or restoration of Israel. This point is reinforced by Jesus' constant conflicts with the religious leaders, both in Galilee (2:1 – 3:6; 8:11 – 13) and Jerusalem (11:12 – 12:40). The present leadership of Israel is apostate and will be replaced by the restored remnant of the people of God. Jesus' prediction of the temple's destruction (13:2; cf. 14:57 – 58) also confirms that Israel's leadership stands under God's judgment and will be replaced.

(3) From the beginning Mark presents Jesus' ministry as one of spiritual and cosmic significance on a supernatural plane. Jesus' first conflicts in the gospel are with the spiritual forces of evil: Satan in the wilderness (1:13) and a demon in the Capernaum synagogue (1:23 – 26). More demonic encounters follow (1:13, 23 – 26, 34; 3:11 – 12; 5:7; 6:7; 9:14 – 28). Jesus' exorcisms are portrayed as the invasion of Satan's realm and the victory of the kingdom of God over the kingdom of Satan. When accused by the religious leaders of acting in league with Satan, Jesus refutes the claim by identifying his exorcisms as the plundering of Satan's house and kingdom (3:22 – 27). The arrival of the kingdom of God means the emancipation of those formerly held by Satan. Since Satan was the original adversary who incited Adam and Eve to sin, to defeat him and his evil forces is to reverse the effects of humanity's fall, to bring in the time of eschatological renewal.

(4) Jesus' healings represent the Isaianic signs of eschatological salvation. Although Mark, unlike Matthew and Luke, does not explicitly link Jesus' healings to Isaiah's prophecies (Matt 11:5//Luke 7:22; cf. Matt 12:18 – 21), there is little doubt that Jesus' miracles represent the fulfillment of Isaiah's prophecies concerning the renewal of creation. At that time, Isaiah says, "the eyes of the blind [will] be opened and the ears of the deaf unstopped. Then will the lame leap like a deer, and the mute tongue shout for joy" (Isa 35:5 – 6; cf. 29:18 – 19; 61:1). The raising of Jairus's daughter (Mark 5:21 – 24, 35 – 43) similarly recalls the eschatological promise that one day "[the] dead will live … their bodies will rise" (Isa 26:19; cf. Dan 12:2, 13), and the Lord will "destroy the shroud that enfolds all peoples … he will swallow up death forever" (Isa 25:7 – 8). Particularly significant is the healing of a paralyzed man, where Jesus connects spiritual healing — the forgiveness of sins — with physical healing (Mark 2:1 – 12). The inbreaking power of the kingdom means Jesus is at war not only with the spiritual forces of evil, but with the devastating effects of humanity's fall: sin, suffering, and death.

(5) The so-called "nature miracles" also point to the eschatological restoration of creation. Calming the sea (4:35 – 41) and walking on water (6:45 – 51) indi-

cate the exercise of God's authority over the forces of chaos. The feeding miracles (6:32 – 44; 8:1 – 10) point back to the wilderness feedings and forward to the messianic banquet — God's eschatological salvation portrayed as a great end-time feast (Isa 25:6 – 8). The arrival of the bridegroom means that the new wine of the kingdom is now being poured out (Mark 2:18 – 22).

All of these features confirm that Jesus' proclamation of the "kingdom of God" is a shorthand way of referring to God's eschatological salvation, his intervention in human history to reverse the results of humanity's fall and to bring creation back into a right relationship with its Maker. The coming of the kingdom represents the transition from the present evil age to the age of salvation. What is surprising, however, is the means by which that salvation is achieved. If Jesus' *message* is the inauguration of the kingdom of God, his *mission* is to suffer and die as a ransom for sins.

Suffering as a Ransom of Sins

As we have noted, the key christological turning point in Mark's gospel is 8:27 – 33, Peter's confession and the first passion prediction. Peter's confession represents the climax of the narrative up to this point. Jesus' remarkable authority in teaching, healing, and exorcism have confirmed for Peter that Jesus is indeed the Messiah, the eschatological Savior. Yet, shockingly, Jesus now begins to teach that the Son of Man must suffer and die to fulfill his messianic mission.

The rest of the gospel may be seen as the way to the cross. Jesus three times predicts his death. Each time, the disciples fail to understand, and Jesus must teach them about humility and servant leadership (8:31 – 38; 9:30 – 50; 10:33 – 45). The third time represents the climax. After James and John ask for the chief seats in the kingdom and the other disciples respond with indignation, Jesus teaches them again about the need for servant leadership. The model for this is the role of the Son of Man: "For even the Son of Man did not come to be served, but to serve, and to give his life as a ransom for many" (10:45). Jesus defines the Messiah's role not as conquest, but as suffering as a ransom for sins.

We have discussed above the link between the Son of Man and the suffering people of God. The "son of man" of Dan 7 is portrayed not only as a glorified figure who receives all authority, glory, and sovereign power (7:13 – 14); he is also identified with the "saints of the Most High," who are persecuted by a great king (the "horn") but then vindicated by the Most High God (7:21 – 22, 26 – 27). This association with the suffering people of God may therefore be part of the background to the ransom saying in Mark 10:45.

Yet an even more important parallel to Mark 10:45 is the Suffering Servant of Isaiah, who dies vicariously for the sins of others. Despite some claims to the contrary,[6]

---

6. See "In Depth: The Ransom Saying of Mark 10:45" at 10:45.

Jesus' statement here has strong conceptual links to Isaiah's fourth Servant Song (Isa 52:13 – 53:12).[7] Just as the Son of Man came "not to be served, but to serve" (Mark 10:45), so this messianic figure in Isaiah comes as a "servant" (Isa 52:13; 53:11) on behalf of others. Both passages reflect the language of vicarious sacrifice. The Son of Man gave his life as a ransom for many (Mark 10:45). In the same way the Servant "took up our pain and bore our suffering" (Isa 53:4); he was "pierced for our transgressions" and "crushed for our iniquities" (53:5a); "the punishment that brought us peace was on him, and by his wounds we are healed" (53:5b). Finally, both passages reflect the image of *one* suffering for the *many*. The Servant will "justify many" and "bore the sin of many" (Isa 53:11, 12) in the same way that the Son of Man gave his life as a ransom for "many" (cf. Mark 14:24). "Many" here does not mean "some but not all," but rather contrasts the *one* who died with the *many* who are saved (cf. John 11:49 – 52; 18:14).

The link to Isaiah's Servant is strengthened by events in Mark's Passion Narrative. In Isaiah's third Servant Song (Isa 50:4 – 9), the servant offers his back to those who beat him and endures mocking and spitting. In the same way, Jesus is spit on and beaten by the soldiers following his Jewish trial (Mark 14:65) and endures repeated mocking and abuse before and during his crucifixion (15:17 – 20, 29 – 32). In Isaiah, the Servant "was oppressed and afflicted, yet did not open his mouth … and as a sheep before its shearers is silent, so he did not open his mouth" (Isa 53:7). In the same way Jesus remains silent before the high priest (Mark 14:60 – 61) and before Pilate (15:3 – 5).

Both Jesus and the Servant suffer innocently. Isaiah's "righteous" Servant "had done no violence, nor was any deceit in his mouth" (Isa 53:9). Similarly, none of the evidence brought against Jesus before the Sanhedrin is valid, and even those who testify falsely against him cannot agree (Mark 14:55). Pilate recognizes that the religious leaders are acting out of envy rather than substance (15:10) and concludes that Jesus has committed no crime worthy of death (15:14). When we add to this the fact that at the beginning of Jesus' ministry the Father addresses him with allusions to Isa 42:1, the first of the Servant Songs (see Mark 1:11), it seems appropriate to conclude that Mark sees Jesus' role as that of the Isaianic Servant.

There is one other important text that brings out the vicarious and sacrificial nature of Jesus' death. At the Last Supper, Jesus establishes a new Passover liturgy centered on his death as the inauguration of the new covenant (14:22 – 25). The bread of the Passover meal represents Jesus' body, given for others, and the wine represents the blood establishing the new covenant. The phrase "this is my blood of the covenant" (14:24b) recalls "the blood of the covenant" that inaugurated the

---

7. The four "Servant Songs" (first identified as such by B. Duhm), include Isa 42:1 – 4; 49:1 – 6; 50:4 – 9; 52:13 – 53:12. See R. T. France, "Servant of Yahweh," in *DJG*, 744 – 47.

Mosaic covenant (Exod 24:8) as well as the new covenant promised in Jer 31:31 – 34. The phrase "which is poured out for many" (Mark 14:24c) again emphasizes vicarious atonement, linking the passage to 10:45 and the allusion of the Servant's vicarious sacrifice found there (cf. Isa 53:11 – 12). Jesus, the one, has died for "the many."

In summary, though Mark does not provide a detailed soteriology in the course of his narrative, Jesus' death is clearly presented as a vicarious and atoning sacrifice for sins. People receive this gift of salvation by responding in simple, childlike faith to Jesus' proclamation of the kingdom of God. The result is forgiveness of sins, the inheritance of eternal life, and entrance into the kingdom of God.

While salvation comes through childlike faith and dependence on God, such dependence means total allegiance, a willingness to forsake one's own life and follow Jesus the Messiah even to the point of death. We turn finally to Mark's theology of discipleship, the response to Jesus' kingdom proclamation.

Discipleship: Responding to Jesus' Call

Just as Mark does not develop a detailed soteriology, so also ecclesiology does not play a prominent role in his gospel. Unlike Matthew, Mark does not explicitly refer to the church (Matt 16:18; 18:17) or include teaching on church life and practice (18:15 – 20). Unlike Luke, Mark has no second volume like Acts narrating the mission and patterns of the early church. Yet faith and discipleship play a prominent role in Mark's narrative, and his ecclesiology may be summed up in Jesus' call to authentic discipleship.

Jesus' Teaching on Discipleship

Jesus' ministry begins with his announcement of the kingdom of God (1:15), followed immediately by his calling of disciples (1:17, 20; 2:14). The implication is that to respond positively to the coming of the kingdom means to "follow" Jesus. Following him means absolute commitment, a willingness to leave possessions (1:18), family (1:20), and occupation (2:14). A rich man unwilling to forsake his riches falls short of the kingdom of God (10:21 – 22). Yet those, like Peter and the Twelve, who "have left everything and followed you" (10:28), receive not only treasures in heaven (10:21), but also "a hundred times as much in the present age: homes and brothers and sisters and mothers and children and fields — together with persecutions — and in the age to come, eternal life" (10:30).

Here, then, is Mark's ecclesiology. The church is a new family, a community whose possessions are meant for the good of all and for the advancement of the kingdom. Family relations in the new community of faith are based not on physical relationships, but on spiritual ones. When Jesus' family comes to take charge of him, he responds, "Whoever does God's will is my brother and sister and mother" (3:35).

Identification with this community means entrance in the kingdom of God. Membership comes not through merit, position, wealth, or power, but by simple faith and dependence on God. In the parable of the sower, it is those "who hear the message and accept it" who produce a good crop for God (4:20). Jesus welcomes children — viewed as irrelevant in first-century society — because "the kingdom of God belongs to ones like this" (10:15a). Indeed, "whoever does not receive the kingdom of God like a child will certainly not enter it" (10:15c-d).

It is those with simple yet persistent faith who receive God's blessings. Jesus offers forgiveness and healing to a paralyzed man when he sees the faith of his friends (2:5). The woman with a bleeding disorder is restored because "your faith has saved/ healed you" (5:34). Jairus is told, "Don't be afraid; just believe" (5:36), and as a result he sees his daughter raised from the dead. The Syrophoenician woman's persistent faith results in the exorcism of her daughter (7:29). A demon-possessed boy finds release when his father cries out, "I believe! Help my unbelief!" (9:24). Blind Bartimaeus receives his sight because he refuses to be silenced by the crowd, calling out for healing from the Son of David (10:47 – 48). "Your faith," Jesus says, "has saved/ healed you" (10:52).

The opposite is also true. Lack of faith results in loss of blessings. The religious leaders commit blasphemy against the Holy Spirit when they defiantly attribute the Spirit's work to Satan's power (3:20 – 30). In his own hometown, Jesus "could not do any miracles there" because of their lack of faith (6:5 – 6).

Though salvation and healing are received by simple faith, the cost of discipleship is high. To be Jesus' disciple means to deny oneself, take up one's cross, and follow him. To save one's own life by denying Christ will result in losing true life — eternal life (8:35 – 37; 10:17, 23). Discipleship means putting others first. To be first you have to be the very last (9:35). To be great, you must learn to serve others (10:43 – 44). Following Jesus means welcoming the lowliest and least significant members of society (9:36) and offering a cup of water to the thirsty in Jesus' name (9:40). The essence of discipleship is service, because "even the Son of Man did not come to be served, but to serve" (10:45).

The Positive Model of the Disciples

In certain respects the disciples are positive models of discipleship. At the outset of Jesus' ministry, Peter and Andrew respond to Jesus' call, immediately leaving their nets and following him (1:18). James and John, too, follow immediately, "leaving their father Zebedee in the boat with the hired men" (1:20). Levi leaves his lucrative tax-collecting business to follow Jesus (2:14). These are people willing to give up all for Jesus and the kingdom.

While the religious leaders reject Jesus' authority and become "outsiders" for whom the parables conceal the message of the kingdom, the disciples are the "insiders" who have been given "the secret of the kingdom of God" (4:11). They faithfully stand by Jesus' side as he teaches, heals, and casts out demons. When he sends them out in pairs throughout Galilee, they successfully reproduce his ministry — teaching, healing, and casting out demons (6:7 – 11, 30). At the climax of Jesus' Galilean ministry, Peter recognizes and acknowledges that Jesus is the Messiah (8:29). At the Last Supper he emphatically asserts his willingness to die for Jesus, and the others join in with a chorus of support (14:13).

The Negative Model of the Disciples

Yet these positive snapshots of loyal discipleship are offset by the disciples' many failures. Mark's critique of the disciples shows up especially in two triads of events, the first centered on three boat trips and the second on three passion predictions. When Jesus calms a storm at sea, he marvels at the disciples' lack of faith: "Why are you so afraid? Do you not yet have faith?" (4:40). A few chapters later, in a second boat scene, Jesus comes to the disciples, walking on water. They are completely astonished and the narrator gives the reason: "because they had not understood about the loaves [at the feeding miracle]; their hearts were hardened" (6:52). Hard hearts is a serious charge, formerly attributed to the religious leaders who actively oppose Jesus (3:3). Finally, in a third and climactic boat scene, Jesus warns the disciples against the leaven of Herod and of the Pharisees. When they misunderstand, thinking he is referring to their failure to bring bread, Jesus responds, "Do you not yet comprehend or understand? Are your hearts hardened? Do you have eyes but cannot see and ears but do not hear?" (8:17 – 18). This warning, drawn from Jer 5:21 and Ezek 12:2, sounds frighteningly close to Jesus' earlier indictment against the religious leaders, who are taught in enigmatic parables, "so that they may look and look but not perceive, and hear and hear but not understand" (4:11; citing Isa 6:9). The disciples seem in danger of going the way of the religious leaders.

The negative portrait continues through three cycles of passion predictions in Mark's central section (8:22 – 10:52). In each cycle, Jesus predicts his death, the disciples show some act of pride or self-interest, and Jesus teaches on the need for humility and cross-bearing discipleship. The first cycle follows Peter's confession (8:27 – 29). When Jesus predicts his death, Peter responds by rebuking him. Jesus rebukes him back and accuses him of following Satan's agenda, thinking only of human interests rather than God's. He then follows with teaching on the need for all disciples to take up their cross and follow him (8:31 – 38).

The second passion prediction is also followed by an act of pride as the disciples argue about who is the greatest. Jesus responds by teaching that those who want to be first must be last (9:30 – 37).

Finally and climactically, Jesus' third passion prediction is followed by the attempt of James and John to claim the best seats in the kingdom. This third cycle

(10:32 – 45) climaxes with another call to servanthood (10:42 – 44) and what many have identified as the theme verse of the whole gospel: "For even the Son of Man did not come to be served, but to serve, and to give his life as a ransom for many" (10:45).

The Positive Model of Jesus

These cycles reveal Mark's primary purpose in portraying the disciples in such a negative light. They serve as a negative foil for Jesus, who is the model disciple. While the disciples demonstrate spiritual dullness, pride, and self-centeredness, Jesus remains faithful to God and gives up his life for others. When the disciples fail repeatedly to exorcise a demon-possessed boy, Jesus steps in and heals with a word (9:14 – 28). While they cannot stay awake in the garden of Gethsemane, he submits to the Father's plan, accepting his coming fate by saying, "Not what I want, but what you want" (14:36). When all abandon him and flee before the arresting party, Jesus gives himself up and affirms that Scripture must be fulfilled (14:43 – 50). While Peter is denying him three times (14:66 – 72), Jesus is testifying boldly before the Sanhedrin and asserting his confidence in God's ultimate vindication (14:72). In Mark's gospel only one person denies himself and takes up the cross (8:34). He is the true model for all true disciples to follow.

To be sure, there are a number of positive examples of faith in Mark's gospel, including the woman with the bleeding disorder, Jairus the synagogue ruler, the Syrophoenician woman, the father of the demon-possessed boy, the woman who anointed Jesus, and blind Bartimaeus. Yet each receives God's blessings in the same way: they respond in faith to Jesus. Salvation comes by *following the Messiah* through suffering to glory.

Summary: The Good News according to Mark

Mark's gospel is a gospel of paradox. At the beginning the narrator announces the good news that the promised Messiah has arrived. Jesus comes on the scene announcing that the kingdom of God — God's final salvation — is at hand. He demonstrates the signs of eschatological salvation: casting out demons, healing the sick, raising the dead. Yet as the story develops, the king does not assume his throne in Jerusalem. He does not defeat Israel's enemies. He rather suffers and dies a horrendous and humiliating death. This is a shocking reversal. Where is the kingdom of God? Where is the promised salvation?

Mark's answer is that the kingdom is present for those with eyes of faith. Although in this world tyrants still rule and evil often seems to have the upper hand, yet through Jesus the Messiah the kingdom of God has broken into human history. Jesus' death has accomplished far more than physical conquest. All along, God's purpose through Christ's first coming was not to defeat the Roman legions or to establish a physical kingdom in Jerusalem. It was rather to achieve true spiritual victory over Satan, sin, and death through Christ's sacrificial death on the cross.

Mark's gospel is almost certainly written to a suffering church or churches, facing the same paradox we confront in the gospel story. Although people in Mark's gospel follow the Messiah, they experience suffering instead of salvation and persecution instead of glory. In the face of such hardships, Mark calls his readers to submit to God's kingdom, to have faith in the One who healed the sick, cast out demons, and raised the dead, and to be willing to take up their cross and follow him. Those who do so will receive forgiveness of sins, a new family of faith, entrance into the kingdom of God, and ultimate vindication when the Son of Man comes in the clouds with great power and glory to gather his elect (13:26 – 27).

Scripture Index

16 385
16:1 – 8 605
17:6 . . . . .250, 654
17:12 173
18:15 . . . . 360, 384, 386
18:20 505
19:15 . . . . .250, 654
21:3 479
21:22 – 23 708
21:23 638
22:12 292
23:21 – 23 302
23:25 144
24:1 – 4 . . . . 420, 422, 423, 424
24:17 557
25:1 – 3 574
25:5 – 10 . . . . .263, 533
25:9 658
26:8 583
27:15 170
27:19 557
28:1 – 14 443
28:12 414
28:27 121
28:49 332
29:22 332
30:4 592
30:15 – 16 441
32:2 535
32:5 . . . . .339, 397
32:6 634
32:20 . . . . 312, 339, 397
32:39 286
33 567
34:1 383
34:5 – 6 384

Joshua

1:11 331
3:11 552
3:13 552
5 467
7:6 657
8:29 516
9:6 332
9:13 140
11:2 291
13:27 83
15:8 413
18:1 145
18:16 413
19:35 291
23 – 24 567

Judges

3:6 116
3:24 414
5:4 – 5 591
6:22 – 23 718
6:23 719
6:36 – 40 338
7 203
8:26 687
10:4 479
10:6 168
11:12 92
13:6, 22 718
14:17 139
18:6 232
19:1 71

Ruth

3:7 414

1 Samuel

1:1 708
1:9 145
1:17 232
1:19 708
1:26 499
2:11 708
4:2 – 4 145
4:7 . . . . .581, 621
6:7 479
8:16 479
10:1 607
12 567
14:15 573
14:44 665
15:22 – 23 527
15:22 . . . . .149, 544
16 – 17 203
16:1 – 13 145
16:6 361
16:14 – 23 91
16:14 – 16 95
17:16 74
17:43 312
20:42 232
21 – 22 146
21:1 – 6 145
22:20 – 23 146
22:20 145
24:6 361
28 384
30:12 331
31:10 516

2 Samuel

1:11 657
4:5 – 7 596
7 . . . . .203, 735
7:11 – 16 . . . . 60, 61, 361, 469, 655
7:13 – 15 551
7:13 654
7:14 – 16 482
7:14 . . . . 61, 155, 170, 375,
390, 656, 736
7:16 . . . . .169, 408
8:17 . . . . .145, 531
10:2 – 5 515
12:13 121
16:10 92
19:1 657
19:22 92
20:9 . . . . .643, 644
21 149
23:2 550

1 Kings

1:8 531
1:32 – 48 481
1:45 531
2:1 – 9 567
2:35 531
3:14 340
8:10 – 13 385
8:22 499
8:39 170
8:41 332
8:43 496
9:4 274
11:29 – 31 492
12 169
13:1 – 5 489
13:4 . . . . .243, 389
13:8 266
13:22 – 30 516
14:11 312
15:5 489
16:29 – 19:3 259
17:17 – 24 261
17:18 92
17:19 – 22 . . . . .234, 236
18:4 245
18:13 . . . . 243, 245, 389
18:20 383
18:28 414
19:1 – 3 389
19:2 . . . . 243, 245, 265, 389
19:8 74

Romans

1 Corinthians

Subject Index

Author Index